A NEW HISTORY OF IRELAND

UNDER THE AUSPICES OF THE ROYAL IRISH ACADEMY
PLANNED AND ESTABLISHED BY THE LATE T. W. MOODY

BOARD OF EDITORS

F. X. MARTIN   F. J. BYRNE

W. E. VAUGHAN   ART COSGROVE

J. R. HILL

II

MEDIEVAL IRELAND
1169-1534

A NEW HISTORY OF IRELAND

UNDER THE AUSPICES OF THE ROYAL IRISH ACADEMY
PLANNED AND ESTABLISHED BY THE LATE T. W. MOODY

*Already published

A NEW HISTORY OF
IRELAND

II

MEDIEVAL IRELAND
1169–1534

EDITED BY

ART COSGROVE

CLARENDON PRESS · OXFORD
1987

Oxford University Press, Walton Street, Oxford OX2 6 DP

Oxford New York Toronto
Delhi Bombay Calcutta Madras Karachi
Petaling Jaya Singapore Hong Kong Tokyo
Nairobi Dar es Salaam Cape Town
Melbourne Auckland
and associated companies in
Beirut Berlin Ibadan Nicosia

Oxford is a trade mark of Oxford University Press

Published in the United States
by Oxford University Press, New York

British Library Cataloguing in Publication Data
A New History of Ireland.
2: Medieval Ireland, 1169—1534
1. Ireland—History
I. Cosgrove, Art
941.5   DA910
ISBN 0—19—821741—2

Library of Congress Cataloging-in-Publication Data
(Revised for vol. 2)
A New History of Ireland.
Vol. 2 edited by Art Cosgrove.
Includes bibliographies and indexes.
Contents: —v. 2. Medieval Ireland, 1169—1534—
v. 3. Early modern Ireland, 1534—1691—[etc.]—v. 9.
Maps, genealogies, lists.
1. Ireland—History—Collected works.   I. Moody, T. W.
(Theodore William), 1907— .   II. Martin, F. X.
(Francis X.)   III. Byrne, F. J. (Francis John),
1934— .
DA912.N48   941.5   76—376168
ISBN 0—19—821741—2

Typeset by Joshua Associates Limited, Oxford
Printed in Great Britain
at the University Press, Oxford
by David Stanford
Printer to the University

PREFACE

FOR reasons already noted in volume IV, there has been an unforeseen delay in the publication of this volume. Most of the contributions were completed by 1973, but all authors were given the opportunity to revise their material during 1982–3.

It was originally intended to include a chapter by Dr Brian Scott on Latin literature *c*.1169–*c*.1500, but this has now been transferred to volume I.

In deciding on forms of names we have followed the guidelines in volume VIII (pp 4–5). A Middle Irish standard has been adopted for the period up to 1333, but classical Modern Irish forms have been used thereafter, e.g. Áed Ó Conchobair (d. 1233) but Aodh Ó Conchobhair (d. 1363). Irish plurals or collectives have been avoided in favour of anglicised plurals such as 'the O'Neills' and 'the O'Briens' or circumlocutions such as 'the Mac Fir Bhisigh family'. Place-names have been given in their current English form (as used by the Ordnance Survey) except where obscure or unidentifiable.

Once again we thank Dr John A. Mulcahy, of New York, and the directors of the American Irish Foundation, for the generous financial help that enabled us to carry out much-needed research in the early stages of work on this volume.

We record with sorrow the deaths of three contributors: Françoise Henry, on 10 February 1982; Michael Dolley, on 29 March 1983; and Alan Bliss, on 24 November 1985. All had made unique contributions to their fields of study, and we are grateful that their work appears in this volume.

We also record with deep regret the death, on 11 October 1985, of C. S. Andrews, one of the outstanding public servants of his time. At the meeting of the Irish Historical Society on 4 December 1962, when T. W. Moody first publicly advocated the production of 'a new history of Ireland', Dr Andrews was foremost in urging that specific action should be taken; and his cordial and vigorous support was indispensable in making it possible to set the project in motion.

F. X. MARTIN
F. J. BYRNE
W. E. VAUGHAN
ART COSGROVE
J. R. HILL

Royal Irish Academy
24 April 1986

CONTENTS

XVII ENGLAND AND IRELAND, 1399–1447
by Art Cosgrove

XVIII THE EMERGENCE OF THE PALE, 1399–1447
by Art Cosgrove

XIX ANGLO-IRELAND AND THE YORKIST CAUSE, 1447–60
by Art Cosgrove

XXII 'IRISH' IRELAND AND 'ENGLISH' IRELAND
by D. B. Quinn

XXIII THE HEGEMONY OF THE EARLS OF KILDARE,
1494–1520   by D. B. Quinn

XXIV THE REEMERGENCE OF ENGLISH POLICY AS A MAJOR FACTOR IN IRISH AFFAIRS, 1520–34
by D. B. Quinn

XXVII ARCHITECTURE AND SCULPTURE, 1169–1603
by Edwin C. Rae

XXIX COINAGE, TO 1534: THE SIGN OF THE TIMES
by Michael Dolley

CONTRIBUTORS

Peter William Anthony Asplin	M.A. (Dubl.), Dip. Lib. (Strathclyde); senior assistant librarian, University of Glasgow
Alan Joseph Bliss	B.A. (Lond.), M.A., B. Litt. (Oxon.); M.R.I.A.; professor of Old and Middle English, University College, Dublin (died 24 Nov. 1985)
Francis John Byrne	M.A. (N.U.I.); M.R.I.A.; professor of early and medieval Irish history, University College, Dublin
James Patrick Carney	B.A. (N.U.I.); M.R.I.A.; senior professor, School of Celtic Studies, Dublin Institute for Advanced Studies
Wendy Rosemary Childs	M.A., Ph.D. (Cantab.); lecturer in medieval history, University of Leeds
Art Cosgrove	B.A., Ph.D. (Q.U.B.); F.R.Hist.Soc.; statutory lecturer in medieval history, University College, Dublin
Michael Dolley	B.A. (Lond.), D. Litt. (Hon. N.U.I.); F.S.A.; F.R. Hist. Soc.; M.R.I.A. (died 29 Mar. 1983)
Kevin Down	B.A. (Birm.); lecturer in medieval history, department of extramural studies, University of Birmingham
Robin Edgar Glasscock	B.A., Ph.D. (Lond.), M.A. (Cantab.); F.R.G.S., F.S.A.; university lecturer in geography and fellow of St John's College, Cambridge
Françoise Henry	D. ès L., D. Litt. (Hon. N.U.I.), Lttt. D. (Hon. Dubl.); F.R.I.A.I. (Hon.), F.R.S.A.I. (Hon.), F.S.A.; M.R.I.A.; formerly director of department of history of European painting, University College, Dublin (died 10 Feb. 1982)
Joseph Long	M.A., Dr de l'Université (Strasbourg); statutory lecturer in French, University College, Dublin
James Francis Michael Lydon	M.A. (Dubl., N.U.I.), Ph.D. (Lond.); M.R.I.A.; Lecky professor of history, Trinity College, Dublin
Francis Xavier Martin	L.Ph., B.D., M.A., Ph.D. (Cantab.); M.R.I.A.; professor of medieval history, University College, Dublin
Geneviève Louise Marsh-Micheli	D. ès L.
Kenneth William Nicholls	Lecturer in Irish history, University College, Cork

Timothy O'Neill

M.A. (N.U.I.); teacher of history, St Benildus College, Dublin

David Beers Quinn

M.A., D. Lit. (Q.U.B.), Ph.D. (Lond.), D. Litt. (Hon. N.U.I., Nfld, and N.U.U.); D.H.L. (Hon. St Mary's, Md); LL.D. (Hon. N.C.); F.R. Hist. Soc.; M.R.I.A.; Andrew Geddes and John Rankin professor emeritus of modern history, University of Liverpool

Edwin Carter Rae

Ph.D. (Harvard); Légion d'honneur; emeritus professor of the history of art, University of Illinois

John Anthony Watt

B.A. (Leeds), Ph.D. (Cantab.); professor of medieval history, University of Newcastle upon Tyne

The maps have been drawn by Mary Davies, B.A., cartographical adviser to this history, and by Valerie Keegan, B.Sc., from material supplied by contributors and (in the case of maps 1, 3–6, 8, 9, 13, and 14) from material used in the reference maps in volume IX.

The index is the work of Helen Litton.

MAPS

PLAN

ILLUSTRATIONS

PLATE

The originals of these illustrations were made available through the courtesy of the following, and are published by their permission: Professor E. C. Rae, plates 1, 2c, 3a, 3d, 4b, 4c, 6a, 7b, 8c, 9, 10a, 11b, 11c, 12a, 13a, 13b, 14b, 14d, 18a, 18d, 19b, 20a, 20c, 20d, 21, 22, 23, 24; the Commissioners of Public Works, Ireland, plates 2a, 2d, 2e, 2f, 3b, 4d, 5b, 7a, 8a, 8b, 8d, 10b, 11d, 12b, 13c, 14a, 15, 17b, 17c, 18c, 20b; Dr Roger Stalley, plate 2b; the Green Studio, Dublin, plates 3c, 4a; the Royal Society of Antiquaries of Ireland, plate 5a; Mr Tom Brett, plate 6b; Bord Fáilte Éireann, the Irish Tourist Board, plates 10c, 11a, 16a, 16b, 18b; the National Museum of Ireland, plates 10d, 19a; the Bodleian Library, Oxford, plates 25, 26c, 27, 28b, 29b, 32a; the Royal Irish Academy, plates 26a, 26b, 28a, 29c, 30; the Trustees of the National Library of Ireland, plate 29a; the Library of the King's Inns, Dublin, plates 31a, 31b; the Trustees of the National Library of Scotland, plate 31c; the Board of Trinity College, Dublin, plate 32b; Mrs Ada K. Leask, the plan of the Irish Cistercian abbey.

Plates 26a and 26b are photographed from the reproductions in *Facsimiles of the national manuscripts of Ireland*, ed. J. T. Gilbert (4 vols, Dublin, 1874-84).

Thanks are due to Monsignor Charles Burns of the Vatican Archives for permission to publish the jacket illustration. Information on the fresco was supplied by Monsignor Burns and Dr Fabrizio Mancinelli, Inspector of Medieval and Modern Art, Pontifical Museums, Vatican.

The assistance of Mrs Siobhán de hÓir and Mr William O'Sullivan is gratefully acknowledged.

ABBREVIATIONS AND CONVENTIONS

Abbreviations and conventions used in this volume are listed below. They consist of (a) the relevant items from the list in *Irish Historical Studies*, supplement I (Jan. 1968) and (b) abbreviations, on the same model, not included in the *Irish Historical Studies* list.

A.F.M.	*Annala rioghachta Eireann: Annals of the kingdom of Ireland by the Four Masters from the earliest period to the year 1616*, ed. and trans. John O'Donovan (7 vols, Dublin, 1851; reprint, New York, 1966)
A.H.R.	*American Historical Review* (New York, 1895–)
A.L.C.	*The Annals of Loch Cé: a chronicle of Irish affairs, 1014–1590*, ed. W. M. Hennessy (2 vols, London, 1871; reflex facsimile, I.M.C., Dublin, 1939)
A.U.	*Annála Uladh, Annals of Ulster; otherwise Annála Senait, Annals of Senat: a chronicle of Irish affairs, 431–1131, 1155–1541*, ed. W. M. Hennessy and B. MacCarthy (4 vols, Dublin, 1887–1901)
Account roll of Holy Trinity, Dublin	*Account roll of the priory of the Holy Trinity, Dublin, 1337–1346*, ed. James Mills (Dublin, 1891)
Acts of Colton	*Acts of Archbishop Colton in his metropolitan visitation of the diocese of Derry*, ed. William Reeves (Ir. Arch. Soc., Dublin, 1850)
Adam of Usk, *Chronicon*	Adam of Usk, *Chronicon*, ed. E. M. Thompson (London, 1904)
Alen's reg.	*Calendar of Archbishop Alen's register, c.1172–1534; prepared and edited from the original in the registry of the united dioceses of Dublin and Glendalough and Kildare*, ed. Charles MacNeill; index by Liam Price (R.S.A.I., Dublin, 1950)
Amer. Jn. Legal Hist.	*American Journal of Legal History* (Philadelphia, 1957–)
Anal. Bolland	*Analecta Bollandiana* (Paris and Brussels, 1882–)
Anal. Hib.	*Analecta Hibernica, including the reports of the Irish Manuscripts Commission* (Dublin, 1930–)
Anc. rec. Dublin	*Calendar of ancient records of Dublin in the possession of the municipal corporation*, ed. Sir J. T. Gilbert and Lady Gilbert (19 vols, Dublin, 1889–1944)
Anglia	*Anglia* (London, 1962–)
Annala Dhamhliag	*Annala Dhamhliag: the annals of Duleek. The yearbook of Duleek Historical Society* (n.p., 1971–)

Ann. Clon.	*The Annals of Clonmacnoise, being annals of Ireland from the earliest period to A.D. 1408, translated into English, A.D. 1627, by Connell Mageoghagan*, ed. Denis Murphy (R.S.A.I., Dublin, 1896)
Ann. Conn.	*Annála Connacht, . . . (A.D. 1224—1544)*, ed. A. Martin Freeman (Dublin Institute for Advanced Studies, 1944)
Ann. Inisf.	*The Annals of Inisfallen (MS Rawlinson B 503)*, ed. and trans. Seán Mac Airt (Dublin Institute for Advanced Studies, 1951)
Ann. Tig.	'The annals of Tigernach', ed. Whitley Stokes, in *Rev. Celt.*, xvi–xviii (1895–7)
Archaeologia	*Archaeologia; or, miscellaneous tracts relating to antiquity* (London, 1804–)
Archiv. Hib.	*Archivium Hibernicum: or Irish historical records* (Catholic Record Society of Ireland, Maynooth, 1912–)
B.L.	British Library
B.L., Add. MSS	—, Additional MSS
B.L., Cott. MSS	—, Cottonian MSS
B.L., Eg. MSS	—, Egerton MSS
B.L., Harl. MSS	—, Harleian MSS
B.L., Lansd. MSS	—, Lansdowne MSS
B.M. cat. Ir. MSS	*Catalogue of Irish manuscripts in the British Museum*, vol. i, by S. H. O'Grady; vols ii and iii, by Robin Flower (London, 1926, 1953)
Baldwin, *King's council*	J. F. Baldwin, *The king's council in England during the middle ages* (Oxford, 1913)
Barrow, *Robert Bruce*	G. W. S. Barrow, *Robert Bruce and the community of the realm of Scotland* (2nd ed., Edinburgh, 1976)
Béaloideas	*Béaloideas: the journal of the Folklore of Ireland Society* (Dublin, 1927–)
Belfast Natur. Hist. Soc. Proc.	*Proceedings and Reports of the Belfast Natural History and Philosophical Society* (Belfast, 1873–)
Bernard, *Navires & gens de mer*	Jacques Bernard, *Navires et gens de mer à Bordeaux vers 1400—vers 1500* (3 vols, Paris, 1968)
Beresford & Hurst, *Deserted med. villages*	Maurice Beresford and J. G. Hurst (ed.), *Deserted medieval villages* (London, 1971)
Betham, *Dignities*	Sir William Betham, *Dignities feudal and parliamentary and the constitutional legislature of the United Kingdom* (Dublin, 1830)
Bibl. Nat.	Bibliothèque Nationale, Paris
Binchy, *Celtic and Anglo-Saxon kingship*	D. A. Binchy, *Celtic and Anglo-Saxon kingship* (Oxford, 1970)

Bk Ballymote	*The Book of Ballymote . . . from the original manuscript in the library of the Royal Irish Academy*, ed. Robert Atkinson (Dublin, 1887)
Bk Lec.	*The Book of Lecan; Leabhar Mór Mhic Fhir Bhisigh Leacain*, with foreword by Eoin MacNeill and introduction by Kathleen Mulchrone (facsimile, I.M.C., Dublin, 1937)
Bk Leinster	*The Book of Leinster, formerly Lebar na Núachongbála*, ed. R. I. Best, Osborn Bergin, M. A. O'Brien, and Anne O'Sullivan (6 vols, Dublin Institute for Advanced Studies, 1954–83)
Bk Uí Maine	*The Book of Uí Maine, otherwise called 'The Book of the O'Kellys'*, with introduction by R. A. S. Macalister (collotype facsimile, I.M.C., Dublin, 1942)
Blake family records	*Blake family records, series i: 1300—1600*, ed. M. J. Blake (London, 1902)
Bodl.	Bodleian Library, Oxford
Brand, 'Ireland and the early common law'	Paul Brand, 'Ireland and the literature of the early common law' in *Ir. Jurist*, i (1966), pp 84–91
Breifne	*Breifne: journal of Cumann Seanchais Bhreifne (Breifne Historical Society)* (Cavan, 1958–)
Bristol town duties	*Bristol town duties*, ed. Henry Bush (Bristol, 1828)
Brit. Acad. Proc.	*Proceedings of the British Academy* (London, 1903–)
Brit. Numis. Jn.	*The British Numismatic Journal and Proceedings of the British Numismatic Society* (London, 1903–)
Bryan, *Great earl of Kildare*	Donough Bryan, *Gerald FitzGerald, the great earl of Kildare* (Dublin and Cork, 1933)
Butler Soc. Jn.	*Journal of the Butler Society* ([Kilkenny], 1968–)
Byrne, *Ir. kings*	F. J. Byrne, *Irish kings and high-kings* (London, 1973)
Byrne, *1000 years of Ir. script*	[F. J. Byrne], *1000 years of Irish script: an exhibition of manuscripts at the Bodleian Library* (Oxford, 1979)
c.	*circa* (about)
Caithr. Thoirdh.	Sean [MacRuaidhrí] Mac Craith, *Caithréim Thoirdhealbhaigh*, ed. S. H. O'Grady (Ir. Texts Soc., 2 vols, London, 1929)
Cal. Carew MSS, 1515—74 [etc.]	*Calendar of the Carew manuscripts preserved in the archiepiscopal library at Lambeth, 1515—74* [etc.] (6 vols, London, 1867–73)
Cal. chart. rolls, 1226—57 [etc.]	*Calendar of the charter rolls, 1226—57* [etc.] (6 vols, London, 1903–27)
Cal. close rolls, 1272—9 [etc.]	*Calendar of the close rolls, 1272—9* [etc.] (London, 1900–)
Cal. doc. Ire., 1171—1251 [etc.]	*Calendar of documents relating to Ireland, 1171—1251* [etc.] (5 vols, London, 1875–86)

Cal. inq. post. mort.	*Calendar of inquisitions post mortem and other analogous documents . . . Henry III—[15 Richard II]* (16 vols, London, 1904–74)
Cal. justic. rolls Ire., 1295—1303 [etc.]	*Calendar of the justiciary rolls, or proceedings in the court of the justiciar of Ireland . . . [1295—1303]* [etc.], ed. James Mills (2 vols, Dublin, 1905, 1914)
Cal. mem. rolls	*Calendar of memoranda rolls (exchequer) . . . 1326—1327* (London, 1968)
Cal. misc. inq.	*Calendar of inquisitions miscellaneous (chancery) [1219—1422]* (7 vols, London, 1916–69)
Cal. papal letters, 1198—1304 [etc.]	*Calendar of entries in the papal registers relating to Great Britain and Ireland: papal letters, 1198—1304* [etc.] (London, 1893–)
Cal. pat. rolls, 1232—47 [etc.]	*Calendar of the patent rolls, 1232—47* [etc.] (London, 1906–)
Cal. pat. rolls Ire., Hen. VIII—Eliz.	*Calendar of patent and close rolls of chancery in Ireland, Henry VIII to 18th Elizabeth*, ed. James Morrin (Dublin, 1861)
Cal. pat. rolls Ire., Jas I	*Irish patent rolls of James I: facsimile of the Irish record commissioners' calendar prepared prior to 1830*, with foreword by M. C. Griffith (I.M.C., Dublin, 1966)
Cal. S.P. Ire., 1509—73 [etc.]	*Calendar of the state papers relating to Ireland, 1509—1573* [etc.] (24 vols, London, 1860–1911)
Camb. med. hist.	*Cambridge medieval history* (8 vols + maps, Cambridge, 1911–36)
Campion, *Hist. Ire.*, ed. Vossen	Edmund Campion, *Two bokes of the histories of Ireland*, . . . ed. A. F. Vossen (Assen, Netherlands, 1963)
Carus-Wilson, *Merchant venturers*	E. M. Carus-Wilson, *Medieval merchant venturers* (London, 1954; reprint, 1967)
Carus-Wilson, *Overseas trade of Bristol*	E. M. Carus-Wilson, *The overseas trade of Bristol in the later middle ages* (Bristol, 1937)
Carus-Wilson, 'Overseas trade of Bristol'	E. M. Carus-Wilson, 'The overseas trade of Bristol' in Eileen Power and M. M. Postan (ed.), *Studies in English trade in the fifteenth century* (London, 1933)
Celtic Soc. misc.	*Miscellany of the Celtic Society*, ed. John O'Donovan (Dublin, 1849)
Celtica	*Celtica* (Dublin, 1946–)
Chartul. St. Mary's, Dublin	*Chartularies of St Mary's Abbey, Dublin . . . and annals of Ireland, 1162—1370*, ed. J. T. Gilbert (2 vols, 1884–6)
Chron. Scot.	*Chronicum Scotorum: a chronicle of Irish affairs . . . to 1135, and supplement . . . 1141—1150*, ed. W. M. Hennessy (London, 1866)
Civil Survey	*The Civil Survey, A.D. 1654—56*, ed. R. C. Simington (I.M.C., 10 vols, Dublin, 1931–61)
Clogher Rec.	*Clogher Record* ([Monaghan], 1953–)

Clonmel Hist. Soc. Jn.	*Clonmel Historical and Archaeological Society: journal of the proceedings* (Clonmel, 1952–)
Close rolls, 1227–31 [etc.]	*Close rolls of the reign of Henry III, 1227–31* [etc.] (14 vols, London, 1902–38)
Clyn, *Annals*	*The annals of Ireland by Friar John Clyn and Thady Dowling, together with the Annals of Ross*, ed. Richard Butler (Dublin, 1849)
Collect. Hib.	*Collectanea Hibernica: sources for Irish history* (Dublin, 1958–)
Conway, *Henry VII, Scot. & Ire.*	Agnes Conway, *Henry VII's relations with Scotland and Ireland* (Cambridge, 1932)
Conway, *Mellifont*	Colmcille [Conway], *The story of Mellifont* (Dublin, 1958)
Corish, *Ir. catholicism*	Patrick J. Corish (ed.), *A history of Irish catholicism* (16 fascs, Dublin and Melbourne, 1967–72)
Cork Hist. Soc. Jn.	*Journal of the Cork Historical and Archaeological Society* (Cork, 1892–)
Cosgrove, *Late med. Ire.*	Art Cosgrove, *Late medieval Ireland, 1370–1541* (Dublin, 1981)
Curtis, *Rich. II in Ire.*	Edmund Curtis, *Richard II in Ireland, 1394–5, and submissions of the Irish chiefs* (Oxford, 1927)
Curtis, *Med. Ire.*	Edmund Curtis, *A history of medieval Ireland* (London, 1923; 2nd ed., 1938; reprint, 1968)
Curtis & McDowell, *Ir. hist. docs.*	Edmund Curtis and R. B. McDowell (ed.), *Irish historical documents, 1172–1922* (London, 1943; reprint, 1968)
Cymmrod. Soc. Trans.	*Transactions of the Honourable Society of Cymmrodorion* (London, 1892–)
d.	died
D.N.B.	*Dictionary of national biography*, ed. Sir Leslie Stephen and Sir Sidney Lee (66 vols, London, 1885–1901; reprinted with corrections, 22 vols, London, 1908–9)
Dal gCais	*Dal gCais: the magazine of Clare, its people and culture* (Miltown Malbay, [1972]–)
Davies, *Discovery*	Sir John Davies, *A discovery of the true causes why Ireland was never entirely subdued ... until ... his majesty's happy reign* (London, 1612; facsimile reprint, with introduction by J. G. Barry, Shannon, 1969)
Decies	*Old Waterford Society: Decies* ([Waterford], 1976–)
Dept. Agric. Jn.	*Éire, Department of Agriculture Journal* (Dublin, 1938)
Dinnseanchas	*Dinnseanchas: journal of An Cumann Logainmneacha* (Dublin, 1964–)

Dolley, *Anglo-Norman Ire.*   Michael Dolley, *Anglo-Norman Ireland, c.1110–1318* (Dublin, 1972)

Donegal Annual   *Journal of the County Donegal Historical Society; iris Cumann Seanchais Dún na nGall* (vol. i, Derry, 1947–50); continued as *The Donegal Annual, incorporating the journal of the County Donegal Historical Society* (Derry, [1951]–)

Dowdall deeds   *Dowdall deeds*, ed. Charles McNeill and A. J. Otway-Ruthven (I.M.C., Dublin, 1960)

Dowling, *Annals*   *The annals of Ireland by Friar John Clyn and Thady Dowling, together with the Annals of Ross*, ed. Richard Butler (Dublin, 1849)

Dublin Hist. Rec.   *Dublin Historical Record* (Dublin, 1938–)

ed.   edited by, edition, editor(s)

E.H.R.   *English Historical Review* (London, 1886–)

Econ. Hist. Rev.   *Economic History Review* (London, 1927–)

Edwards, *Ire. in the age of the Tudors*   R. Dudley Edwards, *Ireland in the age of the Tudors* (London, 1977)

Éigse   *Éigse: a journal of Irish studies* (Dublin, 1939–)

Éire-Ireland   *Éire-Ireland: a journal of Irish studies* (Irish American Cultural Institute, St Paul, Minn., 1965–)

Encycl. Brit.   *Encyclopaedia Britannica* (date of edition cited)

Ériu   *Ériu: founded as the journal of the School of Irish Learning* (Dublin, 1904–)

Études Celt.   *Études Celtiques* (Paris, 1936–)

Evans, *Ir. folkways*   E. Estyn Evans, *Irish folkways* (2nd ed., London, 1957)

Evans, *Personality of Ire.*   E. Estyn Evans, *The personality of Ireland: habitat, heritage, and history* (Cambridge, 1973)

Extents Ir. mon. possessions   *Extents of Irish monastic possessions, 1540–1541, from manuscripts in the Public Record Office, London*, ed. Newport B. White (I.M.C., Dublin, 1943)

Facs nat. MSS Ire.   *Facsimiles of the national manuscripts of Ireland*, ed. J. T. Gilbert (4 vols, Dublin, 1874–84)

Falkiner, *Illustrations*   C. Litton Falkiner, *Illustrations of Irish history and topography, mainly of the seventeenth century* (London, 1904)

Farrell, *Ir. parliamentary tradition*   Brian Farrell (ed.), *The Irish parliamentary tradition* (Dublin, 1973)

Féil-sgríbhinn Eóin Mhic Néill   *Féil-sgríbhinn Eóin Mhic Néill: Essays and studies presented to Professor Eóin MacNeill on the occasion of his seventieth birthday*, ed. John Ryan (Dublin, 1940)

Fiants Ire., Eliz.   'Calendar of fiants of reign of Queen Elizabeth', in *P.R.I. rep. D.K. 11–22* (Dublin, 1879–90)

Fitzmaurice & Little, *Franciscan province Ire.*

E. B. Fitzmaurice and A. G. Little, *Materials for the history of the Franciscan province of Ireland* (Manchester, 1920)

Flower, *Ir. tradition*

Robin Flower, *The Irish tradition* (Oxford, 1947)

Folk Life

Folk Life: the journal of the Society for Folk Life Studies (Cardiff, 1963–)

Folk-liv

Folk-liv (Stockholm, 1937–)

Frame, *Colonial Ire.*

R. F. Frame, *Colonial Ireland* (Dublin, 1981)

Frame, *Eng. lordship*

R. F. Frame, *English lordship in Ireland, 1318–1361* (Oxford, 1982)

Frame, 'Murder of the MacMurroughs'

R. F. Frame, 'The justiciar and the murder of the MacMurroughs in 1282' in *I.H.S.*, xviii, no. 70 (Sept. 1972), pp 223–30.

Frame, 'Justiciarship of Ralph Ufford'

R. F. Frame, 'The justiciarship of Ralph Ufford: warfare and politics in fourteenth-century Ireland' in *Studia Hib.*, xiii (1973), pp 7–47.

Froissart, *Chronicles*

Froissart's chronicles, ed. and trans. John Joliffe (London, 1967)

G.E.C., *Peerage*

G. E. C[okayne], *The complete peerage of England, Scotland, Ireland, Great Britain and the United Kingdom* ... (8 vols, Exeter, 1887–98; ed. Vicary Gibbs and others, 13 vols, London, 1910–59)

Galvia

Galvia: irisleabhar Chumann Seandáluíochta is Staire na Gaillimhe ([Galway], [1954]–)

Galway Arch. Soc. Jn.

Journal of the Galway Archaeological and Historical Society (Galway, 1900–)

Geneal. tracts

Genealogical tracts, ed. Toirdhealbhach Ó Raithbheartaigh (I.M.C., Dublin, 1932)

Gervase of Canterbury, *Historical works*

Gervase of Canterbury, *Historical works*, ed. William Stubbs (2 vols, London, 1879–80)

Gilbert, *Viceroys*

J. T. Gilbert, *History of the viceroys of Ireland* (Dublin, 1865)

Giraldus, *Expugnatio*

Giraldus Cambrensis, *Expugnatio Hibernica: the conquest of Ireland*, ed. A. B. Scott and F. X. Martin (Dublin, 1978)

Giraldus, *Topographia*

Giraldus Cambrensis, *The history and topography of Ireland*, ed. J. J. O'Meara (Mountrath and Harmondsworth, 1982)

Gir. Camb. op.

Giraldi Cambrensis opera, ed. J. S. Brewer, J. F. Dimock, and G. F. Warner (8 vols, London, 1861–91)

Gormanston reg.

Calendar of the Gormanston register, ed. James Mills and M. J. McEnery (R.S.A.I., Dublin, 1916)

Griffiths, *Reign of Henry VI*

Ralph A. Griffiths, *The reign of Henry VI: the exercise of royal authority, 1422–61* (London, 1981)

Gwynn, *Med. province Armagh*	Aubrey Gwynn, *The medieval province of Armagh, 1470—1545* (Dundalk, 1946)
Gwynn & Gleeson, *Killaloe*	Aubrey Gwynn and D. F. Gleeson, *A history of the diocese of Killaloe* (Dublin, 1962)
Gwynn & Hadcock, *Med. relig. houses*	Aubrey Gwynn and R. Neville Hadcock, *Medieval religious houses: Ireland* (London, 1970)
H.B.C.	F. M. Powicke and E. B. Fryde (ed.), *Handbook of British chronology* (R. Hist. Soc., 2nd ed., London, 1961)
H.M.C.	Historical Manuscripts Commission
H.M.C. rep. 1 [etc.]	*Historical Manuscripts Commission, first* [etc.] *report* (London, 1870–)
H.M.C. rep. 9 [etc.]	*Historical Manuscripts Commission, ninth* [etc.] *report*, appendix, part I [etc.] (London, 1884–)
Hand, *Eng. law in Ire.*	G. J. Hand, *English law in Ireland, 1290—1324* (Cambridge, 1967)
Hand, 'English law in Ireland'	G. J. Hand, 'English law in Ireland, 1172–1351' in *N.I. Legal Quart.* xxiii (1972), pp 393–422
Hayes, *MS sources*	R. J. Hayes (ed.), *Manuscript sources for the history of Irish civilisation* (11 vols, Boston, Mass., 1966)
Hermathena	*Hermathena: a series of papers . . . by members of Trinity College, Dublin* (Dublin, 1874–)
Heuser, *Kildare-Gedichte*	Wilhelm Heuser (ed.), *Die Kildare-Gedichte* (Bonn, 1904)
Hist. Jn.	*The Historical Journal* (Cambridge, 1958–)
Hist. & mun. doc. Ire.	*Historic and municipal documents of Ireland, 1172—1320*, ed. J. T. Gilbert (London, 1870)
Hist. Studies	*Historical Studies: papers read before the Irish Conference of Historians* (vols i–vii, London, 1958–69; viii, Dublin, 1971; ix, Belfast, 1974; x, Indreabhan (Co. na Gaillimhe), 1976; xi, Belfast, 1978; xii, London, 1978; xiii, Belfast, 1981; xiv, Belfast, 1983; xv, Belfast, 1985; in progress)
History	*History: the quarterly journal of the Historical Association* (London, 1916–)
Holinshed, *Chronicles* (1577 ed. [etc.])	Raphael Holinshed, *The . . . chronicles of England, Scotlande and Irelande* (London, 1577; ed. John Hooker and others, 3 vols, 1587; ed. Henry Ellis, 6 vols, 1807–8)
Hollingsworth, *Hist. demography*	T. H. Hollingsworth, *Historical demography* (London, 1969)
Hore, *Wexford town*	P. H. Hore, *History of the town and county of Wexford* (6 vols, London, 1900–11)
Hore & Graves, *Southern & eastern counties*	H. F. Hore and James Graves (ed.), *The social state of the southern and eastern counties of Ireland in the*

sixteenth century ... (Annuary of the Royal Historical and Archaeological Association of Ireland for 1868–9)

Hughes, *Ch. in early Ir. soc.*   Kathleen Hughes, *The church in early Irish society* (London, 1966)

Hunt, *Figure sculpture*   John Hunt, *Irish medieval figure sculpture, 1200–1600* (2 vols, Dublin and London, 1974)

Hy Fiachrach   John O'Donovan (ed.), *The genealogies, tribes, and customs of Hy Fiachrach, commonly called O'Dowda's country* (Ir. Arch. Soc., Dublin, 1844)

Hy Many   John O'Donovan (ed.), *The tribes and customs of Hy Many, commonly called O'Kelly's country* (Ir. Arch. Soc., Dublin, 1843)

I.B.L.   *The Irish Book Lover* (Dublin, 1909–57, 32 vols)

I.C.H.S.   Irish Committee of Historical Sciences, Dublin

I.C.H.S. Bull.   *Bulletin of the Irish Committee of Historical Sciences* (typescript, [Dublin], 1939–)

I.E.R.   *Irish Ecclesiastical Record* (171 vols, Dublin, 1864–1968)

I.H.R. Bull.   *Bulletin of the Institute of Historical Research* (London, 1923–)

I.H.S.   *Irish Historical Studies: the joint journal of the Irish Historical Society and the Ulster Society for Irish Historical Studies* (Dublin, 1938–)

I.M.C.   Irish Manuscripts Commission, Dublin

Inq. cancell. Hib. repert.   *Inquisitionum in officio rotulorum cancellariae Hiberniae ... repertorium* (2 vols, Dublin, 1826–9)

Ir. Arch. Soc.   Irish Archaeological Society

Ir. Arch. Soc. misc.   *The miscellany of the Irish Archaeological Society*, i (Dublin, 1846; no subsequent volumes)

Ir. Booklore   *Irish Booklore* (Belfast, 1971–)

Ir. Cath. Hist. Comm. Proc.   *Proceedings of the Irish Catholic Historical Committee* (Dublin, 1955–68; continued in *Archiv. Hib.*, 1973–)

Ir. cartul. Llanthony   *The Irish cartularies of Llanthony Prima & Secunda*, ed. Eric St John Brooks (I.M.C., Dublin, 1953)

Ir. Econ. & Soc. Hist.   *Irish Economic and Social History: the journal of the Economic and Social History Society of Ireland* [(Dublin and Belfast], 1974–)

Ir. Geneal.   *The Irish Genealogist: official organ of the Irish Genealogical Research Society* (London, 1937–)

Ir. Geography   *Irish Geography (bulletin of the Geographical Society of Ireland)* (vols i–iv, Dublin, 1944–63); continued as *The Geographical Society of Ireland, Irish Geography* (vol. v– , Dublin, 1964–)

Ir. Jurist	*The Irish Jurist, new series* (Dublin, 1966–)
Ir. Mem. Assoc. Jn.	*Journal of the Irish Memorials Association, formerly the Association for the Preservation of the Memorials of the Dead in Ireland, and now incorporating the Dublin Parish Register Society* (Dublin, 1921–)
Ir. mon. deeds, 1200—1600	*Irish monastic and episcopal deeds, A.D. 1200—1600, transcribed from the originals preserved at Kilkenny Castle, with an appendix of documents of the sixteenth and seventeenth centuries relating to monastic property after the dissolution*, ed. N. B. White (I.M.C., Dublin, 1936)
Ir. Monthly	*Irish Monthly Magazine* [later entitled *Irish Monthly*] (London and Dublin, 1873–1954)
Ir. Sword	*The Irish Sword: the journal of the Military History Society of Ireland* (Dublin, [1949]–)
Ir. Texts Soc.	Irish Texts Society
Ir. texts	*Irish texts*, ed. J. Fraser, P. Grosjean, and J. G. O'Keefe (fasc. 1–5, London, 1931–4)
Ir. Theol. Quart.	*Irish Theological Quarterly* (17 vols, Dublin, 1906–22; Maynooth, 1951–)
Irisleabhar Muighe Nuadhat	*Irisleabhar Muighe Nuadhat: the Columban Record* (Maynooth, 1907– ; title *Irisleabhar Mhá Nuad* from 1967)
Ivernian Soc. Jn.	*Journal of the Ivernian Society* (8 vols, Cork, 1908–15)
James, *Wine trade*	M. K. James, *Studies in the medieval wine trade*, ed. E. M. Veale (Oxford, 1971)
Jn. Celtic Studies	*Journal of Celtic Studies* (Philadelphia, 1949–)
Jn. Ecc. Hist.	*Journal of Ecclesiastical History* (London, 1950–)
Jn. Relig. Hist.	*Journal of Religious History* (Sydney, N.S.W., 1960–)
Jeanroy & Vignaux, *Voyage au purgatoire*	Alfred Jeanroy and Alphonse Vignaux, *Voyage au purgatoire de St Patrice: visions de Tondal et de St Paul: textes languedociens du quinzième siècle* (Toulouse, 1903)
John Rylands Lib. Bull.	*Bulletin of John Rylands Library* (Manchester, 1903–)
Johnston, 'Richard II and the submissions of Gaelic Ireland'	Dorothy Johnston, 'Richard II and the submissions of Gaelic Ireland' in *I.H.S.*, xxii, no. 85 (Mar. 1980), pp 1–20.
Kaeuper, *Bankers*	Richard W. Kaeuper, *Bankers to the crown: the Riccardi of Lucca and Edward I* (Princeton, 1973)
Kerry Arch. Soc. Jn.	*Journal of the Kerry Archaeological and Historical Society* ([Tralee], 1968–)
Kildare Arch. Soc. Jn.	*Journal of the County Kildare Archaeological Society* (Dublin, 1891–)
King's Inns cat. Ir. MSS	Pádraig de Brún, *Catalogue of Irish manuscripts in King's Inns Library, Dublin* (Dublin Institute for Advanced Studies, 1972)

L. & P. Rich. III & Hen. VII	*Letters and papers illustrative of the reigns of Richard III and Henry VII*, ed. James Gairdner (2 vols, London, 1861–3)
L. & P. Hen. VIII, 1509—13 [etc.]	*Letters and papers, foreign and domestic, Henry VIII* (21 vols, London, 1862–1932)
Law Quart. Rev.	*Law Quarterly Review* (London, 1885–)
Leask, *Castles*	H. G. Leask, *Irish castles and castellated houses* (Dundalk, 1941; 2nd ed., 1944)
Leask, *Churches*	H. G. Leask, *Irish churches and monastic buildings* (3 vols, Dundalk, 1955–60)
Le Bouvier, *Description des pays*	Giles le Bouvier, dit Berry, *Le livre de la description des pays*, ed. E. T. Hamy (Paris, 1908)
Lee, *Ir. histor., 1970—79*	Joseph Lee (ed.), *Irish historiography, 1970—79* (Cork, 1981)
Libelle	*The libelle of Englysche polycye*, ed. George Warner (Oxford, 1926)
Liber primus Kilkenn.	*Kilkenny city records; Liber primus Kilkenniensis*, ed. Charles McNeill (I.M.C., Dublin, 1931)
Lisronagh rental	Edmund Curtis (ed.), 'Rental of the manor of Lisronagh, 1333, and notes on "betagh" tenure in medieval Ireland' in *R.I.A. Proc.*, xliii (1935–7), sect. C, pp 41–76
Longfield, *Anglo-Irish trade*	A. K. Longfield, *Anglo-Irish trade in the sixteenth century* (London, 1929)
Louth Arch. Soc. Jn.	*Journal of the County Louth Archaeological Society* (Dundalk, 1904–)
Lr Cl. Aodha Buidhe	*Leabhar Cloinne Aodha Buidhe*, ed. Tadhg Ó Donnchadha (I.M.C., Dublin, 1931)
Lydon, *Ire. in later middle ages*	J. F. Lydon, *Ireland in the later middle ages* (Dublin and London, 1973)
Lydon, *Eng. & Ire.*	J. F. Lydon (ed.), *England and Ireland in the later middle ages* (Dublin, 1981)
Lydon, *Lordship*	J. F. Lydon, *The lordship of Ireland in the middle ages* (Dublin and London, 1972)
Lydon, 'Ireland's participation'	J. F. Lydon, 'Ireland's participation in the military activities of English kings in the thirteenth and early fourteenth century' (Ph.D. thesis, University of London, 1955)
Lydon, *English in med. Ire.*	J. F. Lydon (ed.), *The English in medieval Ireland* (Dublin, 1984)
Mac Con Midhe, *Poems*	*The poems of Giolla Brighde Mac Con Midhe*, ed. N. J. A. Williams ([London], 1980)
McCracken, *Ir. woods*	Eileen McCracken, *The Irish woods since Tudor times* (Newton Abbot, 1971)
McNeill, *Anglo-Norman Ulster*	T. E. McNeill, *Anglo-Norman Ulster* (Edinburgh, 1980)

MacNeill, *Phases* — Eoin MacNeill, *Phases of Irish history* (Dublin, 1919; reprint, 1968)

Mac Niocaill, *Na búirgéisí* — Gearóid Mac Niocaill, *Na búirgéisí, xii—xv aois* (2 vols, Dublin, 1964)

Marlborough, *Chronicle* — Henry of Marlborough (Marleburrough), 'Chronicle of Ireland' in *Historie of Ireland*, ed. James Ware (Dublin, 1633), iii, 207–23; reprint in *Ancient Irish histories*, ed. James Ware (Dublin, 1809), ii, 1–32

Med. studies presented to A. Gwynn — *Medieval studies presented to Aubrey Gwynn, S.J.*, ed. J. A. Watt, J. B. Morrall, and F. X. Martin (Dublin, 1961)

Medieval Archaeology — *Medieval Archaeology* (London, 1957–)

Medium Aevum — *Medium Aevum* (Oxford, 1932–)

Misc. Ir. Annals — *Miscellaneous Irish annals (A.D. 1114–1437)*, ed. Séamus Ó hInnse (Dublin Institute for Advanced Studies, 1947)

Mollat, *Commerce maritime normand* — Michael Mollat, *Le commerce maritime normand à la fin du moyen âge* (Paris, 1952)

Moody, *Ir. histor., 1936—70* — T. W. Moody (ed.), *Irish historiography, 1936—70* (Dublin, 1971)

Moody & Martin, *Ir. hist.* — T. W. Moody and F. X. Martin (ed.), *The course of Irish history* (Cork, 1967; revised ed., Cork, 1984)

N.H.I. — *A new history of Ireland* (Oxford, 1976–)

N.I. Legal Quart. — *Northern Ireland Legal Quarterly: [the journal of the Incorporated Law Society of Northern Ireland]* (Belfast, 1936–)

N.L.I. — National Library of Ireland

N.L.I. cat. Ir. MSS — Nessa Ní Shéaghda, *Catalogue of Irish manuscripts in the National Library of Ireland* (2 fasc., Dublin Institute for Advanced Studies, 1961–7)

N. Munster Antiq. Jn. — *North Munster Antiquarian Journal* (Limerick, 1936–)

N. & Q. — *Notes and Queries* (London, 1849–)

N.U.I. — National University of Ireland

Nat. Mus. Ire. — National Museum of Ireland

Nicholls, *Gaelic Ire.* — K. W. Nicholls, *Gaelic and gaelicised Ireland in the middle ages* (Dublin and London, 1972)

Nicholls, *Land, law and society* — K. W. Nicholls, *Land, law and society in sixteenth-century Ireland* ([Cork], 1976; O'Donnell Lectures XX)

Nicholls, *O Doyne MS* — K. W. Nicholls (ed.), *The O Doyne (Ó Duinn) manuscript* (I.M.C., Dublin, 1983)

Numismatic Chronicle — *Numismatic Chronicle and Journal of the Royal Numismatic Society* (London, 1837–)

O.S. memoir, Londonderry	Ordnance survey of the county of Londonderry: memoir of the city and north-western liberties of Londonderry (Dublin, 1837)
Ó Cuív, Seven centuries	Brian Ó Cuív (ed.), Seven centuries of Irish learning, 1000—1700 ([Dublin], 1961; reprint, 1971)
O'Curry, MS materials	Eugene O'Curry, Lectures on the manuscript materials of ancient Irish history (Dublin, 1861)
O'Dwyer, Conspiracy of Mellifont	B. W. O'Dwyer, The conspiracy of Mellifont (Dublin, 1970)
O'Flaherty, West Connaught	Roderick O'Flaherty, A chorographical description of West or h-Iar Connaught, written A.D. 1684, ed. James Hardiman (Ir. Arch. Soc., Dublin, 1846)
Ó Huiginn, Poems	The bardic poems [1550—91] of Tadhg Dall Ó Huiginn, ed. Eleanor Knott (Ir. Texts Soc., 2 pts, Dublin, 1922, 1926)
Old Athlone Soc. Jn.	Old Athlone Society Journal (Athlone, 1969–)
Old Drogheda Soc. Jn.	Old Drogheda Society Journal (Drogheda, 1976–)
Old Kilkenny Rev.	Old Kilkenny Review (Kilkenny, 1948–)
Old Wexford Soc. Jn.	Old Wexford Society Journal (1968– ; no. 9 (1983–4) entitled Wexford Historical Society Journal)
Ormond deeds, 1172—1350 [etc.]	Calendar of Ormond deeds, 1172—1350 [etc.], ed. Edmund Curtis (I.M.C., 6 vols, Dublin, 1932–43)
Orpen, Normans	G. H. Orpen, Ireland under the Normans, 1169—1333 (4 vols, Oxford, 1911–20; reprint, 4 vols, Oxford, 1968)
Ossory Arch. Soc. Trans.	Transactions of the Ossory Archaeological Society (Kilkenny, 1874–83, 3 vols)
O'Sullivan, Econ. hist. Cork city	William O'Sullivan, The economic history of Cork city, from the earliest times to the act of union (Cork, 1937)
O'Sullivan, Italian bankers	M. D. O'Sullivan, Italian merchant bankers in Ireland in the thirteenth century (Dublin, 1962)
O'Sullivan, Old Galway	M. D. O'Sullivan, Old Galway: the history of a Norman colony in Ireland (Cambridge, 1942; reprint, with introduction by W. J. Hogan, Galway, 1983)
Otway-Ruthven, Med. Ire.	A. J. Otway-Ruthven, A history of medieval Ireland (London, 1968; 2nd ed., 1980)
P.R.I. rep. D.K. 1 [etc.]	First [etc.] report of the deputy keeper of the public records in Ireland (Dublin, 1869–)
P.R.O.	Public Record Office of England
P.R.O.I.	Public Record Office of Ireland
P.R.O.N.I.	Public Record Office of Northern Ireland
Past	The Past: the organ of the Uí Ceinnsealaigh Historical Society (Wexford, 1920–)
Past & Present	Past and Present: a journal of scientific history (London, 1952–)

Pat. rolls, 1216—25 [etc.]	*Patent rolls of the reign of Henry II, 1216—25* [etc.] (2 vols, London, 1901—3)
Peritia	*Peritia: journal of the Medieval Academy of Ireland* ([Cork], 1982—)
Phillips, 'Documents'	J. R. S. Phillips, 'Documents on the early stages of the Bruce invasion of Ireland, 1315—16' in *R.I.A. Proc.*, lxxix (1979), sect. C, pp 247—70.
Pipe roll Ire., 1211—12	'The Irish pipe roll of 14 John, 1211—12', ed. Oliver Davies and David B. Quinn, in *U.J.A.*, 3rd ser., iv, supp. (July 1941)
Postan, *Med. econ.*	M. M. Postan, *The medieval economy and society* (London, 1972)
Proc. king's council, Ire., 1392—3	*A roll of the proceedings of the king's council in Ireland for a portion of the sixteenth year of the reign of Richard II, 1392—93*, ed. James Graves (London, 1877)
Quinn, *Elizabethans & Irish*	D. B. Quinn, *The Elizabethans and the Irish* (Ithaca, New York, 1966)
Quinn, 'Guide finan. rec.'	D. B. Quinn, 'Guide to English financial records for Irish history, 1461—1558 with illustrative extracts, 1401—1509' in *Anal. Hib.*, no. 10 (1941), pp 1—69
R. Hist. Soc. Trans.	*Transactions of the Royal Historical Society* (London, 1872—)
R.I.A.	Royal Irish Academy
R.I.A. cat. Ir. MSS	T. F. O'Rahilly and others, *Catalogue of Irish manuscripts in the Royal Irish Academy* (fascs 1—27 and indexes, Dublin, 1926—58; fasc. 28, Dublin, 1970)
R.I.A. Proc.	*Proceedings of the Royal Irish Academy* (Dublin, 1836—)
R.I.A. Trans.	*Transactions of the Royal Irish Academy* (33 vols, Dublin, 1786—1907)
R.S.A.I.	Royal Society of Antiquaries of Ireland
R.S.A.I. Jn.	*Journal of the Royal Society of Antiquaries of Ireland* (Dublin, 1892—)
Rec. Comm.	Record Commission
Rec. comm. Ire. rep., 1811—15 [etc.]	*Reports of the commissioners appointed by his majesty to execute the measures recommended in an address of the house of commons respecting the public records of Ireland; with supplement and appendixes* (3 vols, [London, 1815—25]: i, rep. 1—5, 1811—15; ii, rep. 6—10, 1816—20; iii, rep. 11—15, 1821—5)
Red Bk Kildare	*The Red Book of the earls of Kildare*, ed. Gearóid Mac Niocaill (I.M.C., Dublin, 1964)
Red Bk Ormond	*The Red Book of Ormond*, ed. N. B. White (I.M.C., Dublin, 1932)

Reg. Octavian	Register of Ottaviano Spinnelli (Octavianus de Palatio, Octavian), archbishop of Armagh (1478–1513), in P.R.O.N.I., DIO 4; copy in Armagh Public Library (transcript in T.C.D., MS 557)
Reg. Prene	Register of John Prene, archbishop of Armagh (1439–43), in P.R.O.N.I., DIO 4; copy in Armagh Public Library (transcript in T.C.D., MS 557)
Reg. Swayne	The register of John Swayne, ed. D. A. Chart (Belfast, 1935)
Registrum Johannis Mey	Registrum Johannis Mey: the register of John Mey, archbishop of Armagh, 1443–1456, ed. W. G. H. Quigley and E. F. D. Roberts (Belfast, 1972)
Reg. St John, Dublin	Register of the hospital of S. John the Baptist without the Newgate, Dublin, ed. Eric St John Brooks (I.M.C., Dublin, 1936)
Register of wills, ed. Berry	Register of wills and inventories of the diocese of Dublin, in the time of . . . Archbishops Tregury and Walton, ed. H. F. Berry (Dublin, 1898)
Reportorium Novum	Reportorium Novum: Dublin Diocesan Historical Record (Dublin, 1955–71)
Rev. Celt.	Revue Celtique (Paris and London, 1870–1924, 41 vols)
Richardson & Sayles, Admin. Ire.	H. G. Richardson and G. O. Sayles, The administration of Ireland, 1172–1377 (I.M.C., Dublin, 1963)
Richardson & Sayles, Ir. parl. in middle ages	H. G. Richardson and G. O. Sayles, The Irish parliament in the middle ages (Philadelphia, 1952; reprint, 1964)
Richardson & Sayles, Parl. & councils med. Ire., i	H. G. Richardson and G. O. Sayles, Parliaments and councils of medieval Ireland, vol. i (I.M.C., Dublin, 1947)
Richardson & Sayles, Rot. parl. hact.	H. G. Richardson and G. O. Sayles, Rotuli parliamentorum Anglie hactenus inediti (R. Hist. Soc. London, 1935)
Ríocht na Midhe	Ríocht na Midhe: records of the Meath Archaeological and Historical Society (Drogheda, [1955]–)
Roger de Wendover, Flor. hist.	Rogeri de Wendover liber qui dicitur Flores Historiarum . . ., ed. Henry G. Hewlett (3 vols, London, 1886–9)
Rot. chart.	Rotuli chartarum in Turri Londinensi asservati, 1199–1216 (London, 1837)
Rot. litt. claus., 1204–24 [etc.]	Rotuli litterarum clausarum in Turri Londonensi asservati, 1202–24 [etc.] (2 vols, London, 1833, 1834)
Rot. oblatis	Rotuli de oblatis et finibus in Turri Londinensi asservati, tempore Regis Johannis (London, 1835)
Rot. pat. Hib.	Rotulorum patentium et clausorum cancellariae Hiberniae calendarium, ed. Edward Tresham (Dublin, 1828)

Rot. parl. *Rotuli parliamentorum* [*1278–1503*] (7 vols, London, 1783–1832)

Rot. pip. Clon. *Rotulus pipae Clonensis*, ed. Richard Caulfield (Cork, 1859)

Rot. Scotiae *Rotuli Scotiae in Turri Londinensi...*, ed. David Macpherson, John Caley, and William Illingworth (2 vols, London, 1814–19)

Rymer, *Foedera* Thomas Rymer (ed.), *Foedera, conventiones, litterae et cujuscunque generis acta publica* [edition cited]

S.P. Hen. VIII *State papers, Henry VIII* (11 vols, London, 1830–52)

Sayles, *Affairs of Ire.* G. O. Sayles, *Documents on the affairs of Ireland before the king's council* (I.M.C., Dublin, 1979)

Sayles, 'Legal proceedings' G. O. Sayles, 'The legal proceedings against the first earl of Desmond' in *Anal. Hib.*, no. 23 (1966), pp 1–47.

Scot. Hist. Rev. *Scottish Historical Review* (Glasgow, 1903–28, 25 vols; 1947–)

Seanchas Ardmhacha *Seanchas Ardmhacha: journal of the Armagh Diocesan Historical Society* ([Armagh], 1954–)

Seymour, *Anglo-Irish literature* St John D. Seymour, *Anglo-Irish literature 1200–1582* (Cambridge, 1929)

Sheehy, *Pontificia Hib.* M. P. Sheehy (ed.), *Pontificia Hibernica: medieval papal chancery documents concerning Ireland, 640–1261* (2 vols, Dublin, 1962, 1965)

Shirley, *Royal letters* *Royal and other historical letters illustrative of the reign of Henry III*, ed. W. W. Shirley (2 vols, London, 1862–6)

Simms, 'Dysert O'Dea' Katharine Simms, 'The battle of Dysert O'Dea and the Gaelic resurgence in Thomond' in *Dal gCais*, v (1979), pp 59–66.

Simms, 'Medieval kingdom of Lough Erne' Katharine Simms, 'The medieval kingdom of Lough Erne', in *Clogher Rec.*, ix (1977), pp 126–41.

Song of Dermot *The song of Dermot and the earl*, ed. G. H. Orpen (Oxford, 1892)

Speculum *Speculum: a journal of medieval studies* (Cambridge, Mass., 1926–)

Stalley, *Architecture* R. A. Stalley, *Architecture and sculpture in Ireland, 1150–1350* (Dublin, 1971)

Stat. Ire., John–Hen. V *Statutes and ordinances, and acts of the parliament of Ireland, King John to Henry V*, ed. H. F. Berry (Dublin, 1907)

Stat. Ire., Hen. VI *Statute rolls of the parliament of Ireland, reign of King Henry VI*, ed. H. F. Berry (Dublin, 1910)

Stat. Ire., 1–12 Edw. IV *Statute rolls of the parliament of Ireland, 1st to 12th years of the reign of King Edward IV*, ed. H. F. Berry (Dublin, 1914)

Stat. Ire., 12—22 Edw. IV	*Statute rolls of the parliament of Ireland, 12th and 13th to the 21st and 22nd years of the reign of King Edward IV*, ed. James F. Morrissey (Dublin, 1939)
Stat. Ire., Hen. VII & VIII	'The bills and statutes of the Irish parliaments of Henry VII and Henry VIII', ed. D. B. Quinn, in *Anal. Hib.*, no. 10 (1941), pp 71–169
Stat. of realm	*The statutes of the realm* . . . [of England and Great Britain], to 1713 (9 vols in 10 + 2 index vols, Rec. Comm., London, 1810–18)
Stephens & Glasscock, *Ir. geog. studies*	Nicholas Stephens and R. E. Glasscock (ed.), *Irish geographical studies in honour of E. Estyn Evans* (Belfast, 1970)
Studd, 'Edward and Henry III'	J. R. Studd, 'The Lord Edward and King Henry III' in *I.H.R. Bull.*, l (1977), pp 4–19.
Studia Celt.	*Studia Celtica* (Cardiff, 1966–)
Studia Hib.	*Studia Hibernica* (Dublin, 1961–)
Studies	*Studies: an Irish quarterly review* (Dublin, 1912–)
Studies in Ir. law	*Studies in early Irish law*, by Rudolf Thurneysen and others, with a preface by D. A. Binchy (R.I.A., Dublin, 1936)
T.B.C. (Stowe)	*The Stowe version of Táin Bó Cuailnge*, ed. Cecile O'Rahilly (Dublin Institute for Advanced Studies, 1961)
T.C.D.	Trinity College, Dublin
T.C.D. cat. Ir. MSS	T. K. Abbott and E. J. Gwynn, *Catalogue of the Irish manuscripts in the library of Trinity College, Dublin* (Dublin, 1921)
Theiner, *Vetera mon.*	Augustinus Theiner, *Vetera monumenta Hibernorum et Scotorum* (Rome, 1864; reprint, Osnabrück, 1969)
Titow, *Eng. rural society*	J. Z. Titow, *English rural society, 1200—1350* (London and New York, 1969)
Tools and Tillage	*Tools and Tillage: journal of the history of the implements of cultivation and other agricultural processes* (Copenhagen, 1968)
Touchard, *Commerce maritime breton*	Henri Touchard, *Le commerce maritime breton à la fin du moyen âge* (Paris, 1967)
trans.	translated by
U.C.C.	University College, Cork
U.C.D.	University College, Dublin
U.C.G.	University College, Galway
U.J.A.	*Ulster Journal of Archaeology* (Belfast, 3 series: 1853–62, 9 vols; 1895–1911, 17 vols; 1938–)
Ulster Folklife	*Ulster Folklife* (Belfast, 1955–)

Ulster maps c.1600	*Ulster and other Irish maps c.1600*, ed. G. A. Hayes-McCoy (I.M.C., Dublin, 1964)
Walsh, *Richard FitzRalph*	Katherine Walsh, *A fourteenth-century scholar and primate: Richard FitzRalph in Oxford, Avignon and Armagh* (Oxford, 1981)
Walsh, *Ir. men of learning*	Paul Walsh, *Irish men of learning*, ed. Colm Ó Lochlainn (Dublin, 1947)
Warren, *Henry II*	W. L. Warren, *Henry II* (London, 1973)
Warren, *King John*	W. L. Warren, *King John* (London, 1961; 2nd ed., 1966)
Watt, *Ch. & two nations*	J. A. Watt, *The church and the two nations in medieval Ireland* (Cambridge, 1970)
Watt, *Ch. in med. Ire.*	J. A. Watt, *The church in medieval Ireland* (Dublin and London, 1972)
Welsh hist. rev.	*Welsh Historical Review; Cylchgrawn Hanes Cymru* (Cardiff, 1960–)
Z.C.P.	*Zeitschrift für celtische Philologie* (Halle, 1896–1943, 23 vols; Tubingen, 1953–)

The en rule (–), solidus (/), and saltire (×) are used in dates, as in the following examples.

1184–6   denotes a process extending from the first to the second date.

1184/6   denotes alternative dates for a specific event.

1184×1186   denotes the period within which a specific event, which cannot be more precisely dated, occurred.

INTRODUCTION

Medieval Ireland

F. X. MARTIN

THE period covered by this volume opens with the coming of the Anglo-
Normans to Ireland and the enunciation by the English crown of a claim to
lordship over the whole island; it ends with a rebellion in 1534 which in itself
demonstrated the fragility of England's grip upon the country and the erosion
of English authority in the preceding centuries. For the establishment of an
English administration and the influx of a large, if indeterminate, number of
settlers to form an English colony did not lead to a conquest of the country.
The settlers and their descendants were never able to dominate the whole
island. On the other hand, they were never fully assimilated into the Gaelic
Irish population. The result was a country divided into two cultures and two
'nations', and the interaction between them forms a central if complex feature
of Irish medieval history. In the thirteenth century it seemed more probable
that English language and culture would triumph in the wake of settler expansion. By the early sixteenth century fears were being expressed within the
diminished area of English settlement that the resurgent Gaelic tide would
ultimately engulf the whole island. But though the balance shifted it was never
overturned, and at the end of the period English authority, culture, language,
and institutions intermingled with Gaelic Irish counterparts.

It might be supposed that the events of this period are sufficiently far
removed to be free from the partisan controversies which have raged about
later centuries. Yet some Irish nationalists still speak of 'eight hundred years of
English oppression' or misrule, and it is significant that the eighth centenary of
the Anglo-Norman advent in Ireland in 1969 passed with little official recognition. Indeed, a stone tablet erected at Baginbun to commemorate the Anglo-
Norman landing at the beach eight centuries earlier was destroyed shortly
afterwards.[1] And, paradoxically, condemnation of the coming of the Anglo-
Normans will be heard even from those whose surnames indicate that they are
descended from these 'new arrivals' of the twelfth and thirteenth centuries.
The explanation for such attitudes lies in the much later controversies over
whether the link between England (or Britain) and Ireland should be retained

[1] F. X. Martin, *No hero in the house: Diarmait Mac Murchada and the coming of the Normans to Ireland*
(Dublin, 1975; O'Donnell Lecture, XIX), p. 5.

or severed. Thus a nationalist or unionist conviction could colour the view
taken of the events of 1169–71, which were seen as beginning the conquest of
the country.

For centuries historians and political writers, English and Irish, nationalist
and unionist, were content to speak of the 'English conquest' of Ireland. In the
last century it became fashionable to refer instead to the 'Norman invasion' or
'Norman conquest', by analogy with the Norman conquest of England a hundred and three years earlier. This endowed a political event with racial overtones, in keeping with the concept of the Normans as a *Herrenvolk* (an idea that
the Normans themselves assiduously propagated).[1] The debate as to whether
the conquest was 'a good thing' has been carried on in Ireland on much the
same lines as that in England between the advocates of Anglo-Saxon vernacular culture and those of Norman feudalism. Much more recently some Irish
historians have raised the question which had already been aired by their English colleagues: did a form of 'feudalism' exist in the native polity before the
Normans came?[2] But in Ireland the debate was more than a matter of scholarship: it had serious relevance to the politics of this century.

For, while it is true that the advent of the Anglo-Normans in 1169 was not in
fact an invasion (the contemporary notice in the Annals of Tigernach passes it
over in a single sentence: 'A strong force of knights [*ritiri*] came to Mac
Murchada'), and certainly did not result in a conquest of the whole country,[3]
the arrival of Henry II in 1171, given formal papal blessing the following year,
did inaugurate English sovereignty over Ireland. It might not have done so had
Prince John not inherited the English throne in 1199. But in the event that fateful involvement began whose consequences are with us to this day. In 1155 or
1156 Pope Adrian IV had granted the lordship of Ireland—to be held as a papal
fief—to the young Henry, some of whose advisers, motivated probably by the
thwarted metropolitan ambitions of Canterbury, had urged the conquest of the
country. But the bull *Laudabiliter* was left to moulder in the royal archives, and
when Henry did come it was not as a conqueror: the majority of Irish kings submitted readily to him, the titular high-king completing the formalities by the
treaty of Windsor in 1175. The validity of the papal grant was never challenged
by the Irish: the famous remonstrance of Domnall Ó Néill in *c*.1317 addressed
to Pope John XXII argued merely that the English kings had broken its terms.
Henry VIII's breach with Rome in 1534 led logically to his proclamation as king
(rather than lord) of Ireland in 1541. The period covered by the present volume
has therefore a constitutional unity.

Yet it can be argued that the lordship of the king of England over Ireland was
not the most important feature of this period. Such could after all have been

[1] For a corrective see R. H. C. Davis, *The Normans and their myth* (London, 1976).

[2] See, for example, Donnchadh Ó Corráin, 'Nationality and kingship in pre-Norman Ireland' in
Hist. Studies, xi (1978), pp 1–35.

[3] But John de Courcy's invasion of Ulster in 1177 (unauthorised by Henry II, to whom the king
of Ulster had submitted in 1171) *was* an invasion and *did* result in a conquest.

exercised over a native population, just as Henry II ruled Anjou, Brittany, and Aquitaine. And in the later middle ages the area over which royal authority could be effectively exercised shrank dramatically. The Gaelic lords rarely denied that authority, but they largely ignored it. Their hostility (when not directed against each other) was reserved for the Anglo-Irish. It was the establishment of an English colony in Ireland, the introduction of the English language, of English law and administration, of English institutions (most notably the parliament that grew up in the second half of the thirteenth century) that have proved the most long-lasting results of the landing of the little group of 'Flemings' at Bannow Bay.

The Four Masters refer to the knights as Flemings since the bulk of the first arrivals came from Pembroke, 'Little England beyond Wales', where the Normans had planted many Flemings at the beginning of the twelfth century. Among those who took part in the Irish adventure were Maurice Prendergast and the first of all (in 1167), Richard fitz Godebert. It was these Anglo-Flemings who imparted to Bargy and Forth in south Wexford the peculiar character that was to survive into the nineteenth century.

Nomenclature presents serious problems. We have referred to the use of the word Normans.[1] Irish sources before 1169, like the Welsh annals, refer to the Normans as 'French' or 'Franks' (*Frainc*). (Eastern writers call the crusaders Franks, regardless of their national origins: to them it was a cultural rather than a racial term.) But after 1169 the Irish often call the Anglo-Normans 'English' (*Saxain*) or simply the 'men from overseas' (*Allmuraig*). Finally they settled on 'Foreigners' (*Gaill*) which had already been in use for some centuries to denote the vikings and Hiberno-Norse; perhaps it may more accurately be translated as 'Irish residents of non-Gaelic origin'. In the late twelfth century the Anglo-Normans are sometimes called *Gaill glassa*, 'grey foreigners', to distinguish them from the long-settled Hiberno-Norse—the Norman mercenaries hired by Ua Ruairc are referred to as his *glasfhian*, 'grey warrior-band'.[2] It has usually been assumed that the adjective *glass* describes the distinctive mail armour of the Norman knights. But it may denote overseas origin, as the word *cú glass*, 'grey hound or wolf', was a technical term in ancient Irish law for an alien resident in Ireland. In the later middle ages the *Gaill*, the Anglo-Irish, are distinguished from the *Saxain*, the English of England. Interestingly the word *Éirennach*, 'Irishman', is applied to both Gael and Gall alike.[3]

Giraldus Cambrensis distinguishes between the English, of whom he had a low opinion, and the Normans, but he makes a separate breed of his own family, the Geraldines. These and their immediate associates from Wales many modern historians dub 'Cambro-Normans', and we have used this term where

[1] As used for instance by G. H. Orpen, *Ireland under the Normans* (4 vols, Oxford, 1911–20; reprint, 1968).
[2] *A.L.C.*, 1204.
[3] *Ann. Conn.*, 1419; see also a poem written in 1350 by Gofraidh Fionn Ó Dálaigh for Uilliam Buidhe Ó Ceallaigh, edited and translated by Eleanor Knott in *Ériu*, v (1911), pp 64–5.

it is appropriate. Since these had Welsh blood, and moreover brought over with them large numbers of Welsh archers and others (the name Walsh, or Breathnach, is still the commonest non-Gaelic surname in Ireland), and since Bretons formed one of the largest contingents in William the Conqueror's invasion of England, and the family of le Poer who settled in County Waterford were Breton, we might be tempted to refine terms yet further and so celebrate 1169 as the second arrival of the Celts in Ireland. The Byzantine historian Anna Comnena does indeed call the Norman crusaders 'Celts', barbarian warriors from the west—as a classicist she disliked using words not to be found in the vocabulary of the ancient historians.[1] The author of the 'Song of Dermot and the earl', itself written in Norman French, blandly terms his heroes *Engleis*.[2] More recently some have favoured the terms 'Anglo-French'[3] or 'Anglo-Continental'.[4] We have preferred the term 'Anglo-Norman'.[5]

These varied descriptions are themselves a reflection of the fact that 'between 1066 and 1200 there were real doubts and some confusion' about what made an Englishman,[6] and none is entirely satisfactory. And in our use of 'Anglo-Norman' we should note, for example, the reservation that 'the colonial nobility of medieval Ireland whom we describe as Anglo-Norman in fact came from a variety of sources, which included England and Normandy, but with substantial contributions from Wales, from areas of France other than Normandy, and also, on a small but significant scale, from Scotland'.[7]

A further problem arises in considering the descendants of the settlers, natives of Ireland in the sense of being born in the country. How should they be described? Sources from the thirteenth and fourteenth centuries refer to them simply as 'the English',[8] 'the English nation',[9] 'the English born in Ireland',[10] or 'the English inhabiting our land'.[11] Such usages are either confusing or cumbersome, and we have therefore chosen to use the term 'Anglo-Irish', though this is not found in contemporary sources before the late fourteenth century.[12]

[1] Anna Comnena, *The Alexiad*, trans. E. R. A. Sewter (Harmondsworth, 1969; reprint, 1982), p. 9; index, p. 549, under 'Kelts'.

[2] *The song of Dermot and the earl*, ed. G. H. Orpen (Oxford, 1892), *passim*.

[3] So K. W. Nicholls, 'Anglo-French Ireland and after' in *Peritia*, i (1982), p. 371, n. 2; see J. A. Watt, *The church and the two nations in medieval Ireland* (Cambridge, 1970), p. xi.

[4] Used to describe the settlers in Scotland by G. W. S. Barrow, *The Anglo-Norman era in Scottish history* (Oxford, 1980), pp 155–6.

[5] Cf. Robin Frame, *Colonial Ireland, 1169–1369* (Dublin, 1981), p. vii, for the argument in favour of 'Anglo-Norman'.

[6] Barrow, *Anglo-Norman era*, p. 6.

[7] J. R. S. Phillips, 'The Anglo-Norman nobility' in James Lydon (ed.), *The English in medieval Ireland* (Dublin, 1984), p. 88.

[8] *Stat. Ire., John–Hen. V*, p. 210.   [9] *Rot. parl.*, iv, 102.

[10] *Chartul. St Mary's, Dublin*, ii, 383; *Stat. Ire. John–Hen. V*, pp 417, 436–7.

[11] So termed by Domnall Ó Néill in the remonstrance of *c.* 1317 (Johannis de Fordun, *Scotichronicon*, ed. Thomas Hearne (5 vols, Oxford, 1722), iii, 916).

[12] Cf. *Ypodigma Neustriae a Thoma Walshingham*, ed. H. T. Riley (London, 1876), p. 367. For reservations about the use of 'Anglo-Irish', see Phillips, 'Anglo-Norman nobility', p. 88; Robin Frame, 'Power and society in the lordship of Ireland, 1272–1377' in *Past & Present*, no. 76 (1977), p. 4, n. 5.

There remains the question: at what point does Anglo-Norman become Anglo-Irish? The answer to this would vary according to the individual, the institution, or the part of the country being described. By and large, however, we have tended to use the term Anglo-Norman for the period before 1216, and Anglo-Irish thereafter.

THE coming of the Anglo-Normans to Ireland was part of a vast migratory movement of peoples seeking outlets beyond the immediate boundaries of settled feudal Europe.[1] It was a complex and uncoordinated movement of independent units. In northern Europe it was the Germanic *Drang nach Osten* into territories now known as Prussia, Poland, and Russia, while eastwards it pressed into Transylvania as far as the Carpathian mountains. In the south of Europe the migratory movement found its clearest expression in the crusades, with expansion into the eastern Mediterranean, having the Holy Land as its special focus of attention. Expansion to the west was limited by the Atlantic Ocean, but outlets were found in Wales, Scotland, and Ireland. The international character of the migratory movement is well illustrated by a curious item of information linking Ireland, the *Drang nach Osten*, and Russia (Kievland). Some time shortly after 1179 the Irish Benedictine monks at the Vienna *Schottenkloster* undertook control of a German monastery at Kiev, until recently the capital town of the Russian principality.[2]

The form which settlement, colonisation, or full occupation assumed in these very different areas was conditioned to a major degree by existing regional conditions, economic, social, and political. Obviously there was not going to be a uniform pattern of settlement in territories as diverse as Prussia, Transylvania, Syria, and Ireland. The Norman lord in his apparently impregnable fortress at Krak in Syria had a very different view, literally and politically, from his cousin in the apparently equally impregnable castle at Carrickfergus

[1] There is no comprehensive survey of this migratory movement, though there are many relevant comments and useful comparisons about the *Völkerwanderung* scattered throughout the ten volumes of Arnold Toynbee, *A study of history* (2nd ed., Oxford, 1935–6; two additional volumes, 1969–71). For the northern crusades see Eric Christiansen, *The northern crusades: the Baltic and the catholic frontier, 1100–1525* (London, 1980). For expansion into the Ukraine see Nicholas L. Chirovsky, *An introduction to Ukranian history*, i (New York, 1981). For activity eastwards into Transylvania see Heinz Stoob, 'Die mittelalterliche Städtebildung im Karpatenbogen' in *Die mittelalterliche Städtebildung in südöstlichen Europa*, ed. Heinz Stoob (Cologne and Vienna, 1977), pp 184–225. The only comparison, brief but valuable, made between the Norman colonisation in Ireland and German colonisation is by Anngret Simms, 'Irland: Überformung eines keltischen Siedlungsraumes am Rande Europas durch externe Kolonisationsbewegungen' in *Gefügemuster der Erdoberfläche* (Göttingen, 1979), pp 280, 287–8. The standard work in English on the crusades in the middle east is Steven Runciman, *History of the crusades* (3 vols, Cambridge, 1951–4), while the most important work in recent years is H. E. Mayer, *The crusades*, trans. John Gillingham (Oxford, 1971).

[2] Ludwig Hammermeyer, 'Die irischen Benediktiner "Schottenklöster" in Deutschland und ihr institutioneller Zusammenschluss vom 12. bis 16. Jahrhundert' in *Studien und mitteilungen zur Geschichte des Benedictiner-Ordens und seiner Zweige*, Band 87, Heft iii–iv (1976), pp 259–60.

in Ulster. Still more did these views differ from those of the Teutonic knights at Königsberg and of the German settlers in the *Siebenbürgen* of Transylvania.

It is over thirty years since the Belgian scholar Charles Verlinden expounded a provocative thesis about the continuity of ideas and methods stretching from medieval Europe to the sixteenth-century European colonies overseas in the Atlantic islands, Africa, Asia, and America.[1] In the same year (1950) as Verlinden first caught international attention with his views on continuity, two American scholars, Jensen and Reynolds, published an article which reached the same conclusion about continuity, stressing the financial and business impulses behind these colonial ventures.[2] All three scholars were agreed that Ireland was of particular relevance because it figured both in the twelfth and sixteenth centuries as a scene of colonial efforts directed from England. They saw continuity in the clash between settlers and natives, as well as in the relation of both to the government in England. They called for in-depth studies of what they believed was a most promising subject in comparative history. There was little or no response to their appeal, except for a valuable suggestion by D. B. Quinn in 1955 that the Normans in Ireland be reviewed against the wider background of Norman activity in Scotland and Wales.[3] In the years following the questions raised by Verlinden, Jensen, Reynolds, and Quinn, several highly important studies were published on the Anglo-Normans in Ireland, but they were mostly concerned with administrative and parliamentary history, thus inevitably viewing Irish affairs through the eyes of royal officials in England or in Dublin castle.[4] A wider perspective was, however, maintained by Aubrey Gwynn, in an enlightening series of minor studies, in which he drew attention to the European dimension of church affairs in Ireland, as did J. F. O'Doherty.[5] Their contributions were limited in their effect until the late 1960s.

Within the last twenty years the picture has been brought back into a more accurate focus, due to the contributions from two different quarters. W. L.

[1] Charles Verlinden, 'Les influences médiévales dans la colonisation de l'Amérique' in *Revista de Historia de America* (1950), pp 440–50; 'La problème de la continuité en histoire coloniale' in *Revista de Indias*, xii (1951), pp 219–30; 'Sentido de la historia colonial americana' in *Etudios Americanos*, iv (1952), pp 551–64; *Précédents médiévaux de la colonie en Amérique* (Mexico City, 1950).

[2] M. Jensen and R. L. Reynolds, 'European colonial experience. A plea for comparative studies' in *Studi in onore di Gino Luzzato*, ed. A. Giuffré, iv (Milan, 1949–50), pp 75–90.

[3] D. B. Quinn, 'Ireland and sixteenth-century expansion' in *Hist. Studies*, i (1958), pp 3–15.

[4] The major works in these fields during this period were by H. G. Richardson, G. O. Sayles, and A. J. Otway-Ruthven, and are listed by P. W. A. Asplin, *Medieval Ireland, c.1170–1495: a bibliography of secondary works* (Dublin, 1971). See the brief commentary on primary and secondary source publications by A. J. Otway-Ruthven, 'Medieval Ireland, 1169–1485' in T. W. Moody (ed.), *Irish historiography, 1936–70* (Dublin, 1971), pp 16–22.

[5] The most prolific writer on Irish ecclesiastical affairs during the twelfth and early thirteenth centuries was Aubrey Gwynn; see F. X. Martin, 'The historical writings of Reverend Professor Aubrey Gwynn, S.J.' in *Medieval studies presented to Aubrey Gwynn*, ed. J. A. Watt, J. B. Morrall, and F. X. Martin (Dublin, 1961), pp 502–9. Professor Gwynn continued to publish on the subject up to the late 1970s.

Warren of the Queen's University, Belfast, in a series of publications beginning in the year 1969 and dealing with Ireland in the reigns of Henry II and John, has restored a sense of perspective by placing Ireland during the years 1169–1216 within the context of the 'Angevin empire', thus allowing a comparison with contemporary Norman development in Wales and Scotland.[1] This still left the predominantly large but obscure area of Gaelic Ireland in the shade. Fortunately a flood of light was thrown on that shaded area when the revolution in Irish historical studies, which began in the 1930s, finally began to produce its fruits among medieval scholars in the 1970s, with the publications of G. J. Hand, J. F. Lydon, J. A. Watt, Gearóid Mac Niocaill, Michael Dolley, F. J. Byrne, Donnchadh Ó Corráin, Michael Richter, A. P. Smyth, and K. W. Nicholls.[2] They have been followed by an encouraging participation of younger scholars in this area, who are now beginning to produce the fruits of their research in the 1980s. We are thus in a position to take a more objective picture of Ireland during this period than has hitherto been possible. Much remains to be done in pursuing the conclusions of these scholars in order to reconstruct an accurate picture of Ireland, in which the incoming lords and lesser settlers still retained their interests in France, England, and Wales, but were themselves part of a greater world extending to Rome, Sicily, and the Holy Land. Nevertheless, while it is essential that the Angevin and the wider European backgrounds be borne in mind, the basic fact remains that settlement in Ireland was conditioned by that apparently indestructible element, the Irish inhabitants of the island.

A surprising feature of the Anglo-Norman advance was how much was accomplished by peaceful penetration, without warfare. It owed its success not so much to military campaigns as to political alliances, to the proliferation of mottes and baileys, castles, settlements, markets, vills, and towns, to intermarriage with the Irish at every level of society from baron to serving soldier, to trade and commerce, to the introduction and practice of English common law, to the extension of church organisation through the diocesan and parochial systems, backed by the spread throughout Ireland of the new religious orders from England, Scotland, Wales, and the Continent. There is no doubt that the combination of these elements represented a revolution in Irish affairs, but it was a highly qualified revolution which maintained a noticeable continuity with the past, as had the twelfth-century church reformers in establishing as an innovation the diocesan system but founding it territorially on existing kingdoms. It was likewise in civil affairs. Strongbow married Aífe, daughter of Diarmait Mac Murchada, and succeeded him in effect as king of Uí Chennselaig and king of Leinster. Hugh de Lacy took over (with the blessing of Henry II) the Ua Máel Sechnaill kingdom of Mide, transforming it into the feudal lordship of Meath

[1] For Professor W. L. Warren's writings on Irish history see below, pp 884, 886.
[2] See the commentary and bibliography by Art Cosgrove, 'Medieval Ireland, 1169–1534' in Joseph Lee (ed.), *Irish historiography, 1970–79* (Cork, 1981), pp 13–33.

but maintaining the borders of the twelfth-century Irish kingdom. To clinch his position he married a daughter of the Irish high-king Ruaidrí Ua Conchobair. These were notable but not isolated cases. Nevertheless those first decades of friendly relations between Irish and Anglo-Normans have been generally ignored.

Out of that relationship could have come a fusion of the two races, the emergence of a new breed, as happened in several countries where the Normans settled, notably in England, Wales, and Sicily. This is not fantasy in the Irish context. There are two pieces of notable contemporary literary evidence to support it, 'The song of Dermot and the earl', and 'Durmart le Gallois'. The first, published in 1892, with critical edition and translation by Orpen, is well known. The second is, in effect, unknown, though published in a scholarly edition in the United States in 1965–6.[1] 'The song of Dermot and the earl' concerns Diarmait Mac Murchada and Strongbow. It is sympathetic to both, and draws with assurance on Irish sources of information. 'Durmart le Gallois' is in something of a different category. It is more obviously in the literary tradition of a *chanson de geste* but it obviously draws on Irish sources of information, with the daughter of the king of Limerick, Ua Briain, as a central figure. The two works share a triple feature. They are written in French; are based on Irish sources; furthermore, they were written apparently some time between the years 1190–1220, that period of transition when the pattern of relations between Irish and Anglo-Norman in Ireland was being determined. They are evidence, valuable not only as polite literature but as history, of a most promising development cut short by single-minded Anglo-Norman officials, William Marshal, Geoffrey de Marisco, and Henry of London.[2]

Instead of fusion, there came division. A recent authority has observed that 'the uncompleted and faltering nature of the conquest impeded the acceptance of an ethos of assimilation and perpetuated an outlook of confrontation. The English settlers in Ireland retained their links with England and paraded and exploited their Englishness as a badge of their uncertain superiority.'[3] The 'faithful English' opposed the 'Irish enemies'; the 'land of peace' was contrasted with the 'land of war'.[4] By the beginning of the fourteenth century there were 'innumerable local balances of peace' in 'a land of numerous frontiers'.[5]

Within the colonial area the pattern and intensity of settlement varied. Clearly Leinster and Munster were more heavily settled than the north and west, while in some regions the newcomers failed to make any permanent impact.

A recent study of Celtic Leinster argues convincingly that the attempted Anglo-Norman occupation of Ireland failed because these hardy adventurers

---

[1] *Durmart le Gallois*, ed. J. J. Gildea (2 vols, Villanova, 1965–6).
[2] See below, pp 149–54.
[3] R. R. Davies, 'Lordship or colony?' in Lydon, *English in med. Ire.*, p. 154.
[4] See below, p. 240.
[5] Robin Frame, *English lordship in Ireland, 1318–1361* (Oxford, 1982), pp 2, 328.

did not succeed in controlling, either by military conquest or by cultural influences, the heartland of the whole island, what is aptly described as the 'bogland
zone' in the midlands, that area lying between the Shannon and the Liffey
plain.[1] Bogland, so often regarded in modern times as a symbol of what is inferior, is here presented in a new historical and cultural light. The Bog of Allen,
the central land mass of the area, is described as 'the cradle land of Gaelic
civilisation',[2] and it is stated with good reason that the literary contribution of
the bogland zone cannot be overstated, that the heart of Irish learning was
located there.[3] The artistic activity in this zone has been put beyond dispute in
recent years by the discovery of the Derrynavlan hoard in 1980.[4]

The bogland zone was given character by the Great Esker, which made it the
midland corridor between the provinces of Ireland, the highway of communication for marauding armies, footloose scholars, dynamic religious
reformers. While it is true that there could be no full conquest of the country as
long as that central mass of bogland remained intact in Gaelic hands, it would
be a mistake to believe that the Anglo-Normans simply disregarded the area.
They made incursions into the territory, established castles at places such as
Birr and Ballyroan, and placed great value on the fortress which they built on
the massive rock at Dunamase in Leix.[5] One of the prizes which John took to
himself out of the hands of William Marshal in 1210 was Dunamase, and in
1214 the Anglo-Normans established castles at Roscrea, Clonmacnoise, and
Durrow, but these were outposts in territory which they could not fully occupy.
There were not sufficient settlers to cope with the advances which were also
being attempted simultaneously in Ulster and Connacht. Occupation of the
bogland zone was not dismissed as unprofitable or unimportant, but at that
time it came low in the list of priorities, and was postponed.

Some of the younger generation of medieval historians and archaeologists
who have taken a fresh look at the settled areas tend, if anything, to exaggerate
the continuity from early medieval Ireland, through the Anglo-Norman period,
on to the fourteenth century. Their stand appears to be backed up by the parallel findings of European scholars who have recently been studying somewhat
similar circumstances of countries such as East Germany, Poland, and Norway, where the irresistible German expansion eastwards was formerly thought
to have been responsible for the foundation of so many trading centres and
towns.[6] Now, however, it is realised, as a result of archaeological excavations

---

[1] A. P. Smyth, *Celtic Leinster: towards a historical geography of early Irish civilization, A.D. 500—1600*
(Dublin, 1982), pp 10–11, 92–5, 102.

[2] Ibid., p. 116.   [3] Ibid., pp 92–5.

[4] 'Derrynavlan': three articles, by Hilary Richardson, F. J. Byrne, and Próinséas Ní Chatháin, in
R.S.A.I. Jn., cx (1980) [1982], pp 92–126; Michael Ryan (ed.), *The Derrynaflan hoard: a preliminary
account* (Dublin, 1983).

[5] Smyth, *Celtic Leinster*, pp 101–3.

[6] H. B. Clarke and Anngret Simms (ed.), *The comparative history of urban origins in non-Roman
Europe: Ireland, Wales, Denmark, Germany, Poland, and Russia from the ninth to the thirteenth century*
(Oxford, 1985), pp 669–703.

and various interdisciplinary investigations since 1945, that the places where
German traders, merchants, and settlers established themselves were already
recognised regional meeting points for markets and fairs before they arrived
there, as well as having groups of permanent residents. Such meeting points are
now described as proto-towns, since they formed the basis for the later fully
fledged towns of the German traders and settlers.

It is now being widely accepted that settlements which developed east of the
river Elbe did not owe their existence solely to German pioneers but were built,
in many cases literally, on existing Slav trading centres. The same holds true
for Bergen, the Norwegian seaport,[1] and may well be proved true for other
Scandinavian towns when the archaeologists and other specialists in settlement history have had opportunity to investigate and assess the evidence. In
such cases one must first identify the proto-town, which supplied a definite
site, usually on a river or in an estuary, and with permanent foundations for a
trading centre. The next stage was the gradual evolution of an independent
urban unit, ringed with a wall, secure with guards and gates, authorised by a
charter from some authority such as king, prince, or bishop, and thereafter
issuing its own municipal regulations formulated by the town council. To what
extent does such a pattern apply to Ireland?

The continuity from viking seaports to the fully established Norman towns is
self-evident. While there is little or no documentary evidence for the formation
and early centuries of the viking seaports, the hitherto almost blank picture has
been transformed by archaeological excavations, mainly at High Street and
Wood Quay, Dublin, which have made available abundant evidence about the
daily lives and interests of the inhabitants of the Hiberno-Norse towns.[2] For
the Gaelic market centres we have to depend mainly on scattered references in
literary and historical records.[3] The real problem, which is close to generating
a controversy, concerns the Gaelic monastic settlements. Since these pre-
Norman monasteries, some dating back to the sixth century, were the only Irish
equivalent to urban centres, it is not surprising that they witnessed both a concentration of religious, monks and nuns, and also the presence of lay people in
considerable numbers, auxiliaries in the economic and cultural activities of the
monasteries. In the Irish annals such settlements are on occasions described as
'towns',[4] and while it is doubtful if the annalists had an accurate concept of
what constituted a town, a recent authority considers such monastic settlement
to have been 'semi-urban'.[5]

Apart from the initial considerable military effort of occupying the Hiberno-

---

[1] Asbjørn E. Herteig, 'The continent of Scandinavia' in Asbjørn E. Herteig, *Archaeological contributions to the early history of urban communities in Norway* (Oslo, 1975), pp 9–22.

[2] See below, p. 53.

[3] Charles Doherty, 'Exchange and trade in early medieval Ireland' in *R.S.A.I. Jn.*, cx (1980),
pp 67–89.

[4] *A.F.M.*, 1046 and 1170, for the monastic settlement ('city') at Clonard.

[5] Smyth, *Celtic Leinster*, pp 4, 71.

Norse seaports the Anglo-Normans faced no great challenge when they took control of what were in all five cases thriving trading centres at Dublin, Wexford, Waterford, Cork, and Limerick. The remarkable Anglo-Norman achievement in Ireland was the visible extension of their influence throughout much of the country by a network of new rural and urban settlements with all its consequences in the economic, social, religious, and cultural spheres. Settlement was, however, determined by natural features of the countryside, the rivers, mountains, bogs, and woods, but the Anglo-Normans in Ireland, as in all other countries they entered, were nothing if not adaptable to local conditions. The newcomers, like the Irish kings in previous centuries, settled in the most productive agricultural lands.[1] Just as the monasteries in pre-Norman Ireland were almost all located well below the 500-foot contour line, so the Anglo-Normans initially settled in the plains and the river basins. This draws attention to an important question which is now gaining notice from scholars, namely that the Irish economy was not, as previously supposed, almost exclusively pastoral, but had agriculture as a prominent feature, particularly in the production of oats.[2] Enclosures and the field systems were not unknown in pre-Norman Ireland, but the endemic warfare of Gaelic Ireland ensured that agriculture was more vulnerable than the pastoral system. Corn could be burned by an invader, whereas cattle and pigs could be driven to safety by those attacked. Other factors enticed the Anglo-Normans to extend their advance still further. Ireland, in relation to its land mass, was underpopulated.[3] Secondly, apart from the available, and therefore tempting, land already productive under agriculture and pastoral care, there were vast stretches of woods which could be put to fruitful uses.

Undoubtedly at first glance the most impressive feature of Anglo-Norman Ireland was the urbanisation of its extensive territories with a network of seaports, towns, and manorial villages, but this was not a totally new element since the vikings had already established five main seaports and a number of minor seacoast settlements as at Arklow, Wicklow, Larne, and Donegal. The real change introduced by the Anglo-Normans was in the rural areas, where the introduction of the feudal system consolidated the power of the barons and lords on their estates, as well as ensuring that the nearby seaports and towns could expand with the certainty of food, market produce, and raw materials for trades, crafts, and town industries.[4] This commercial activity was not possible without extensive use of coined money, visits by foreign merchants, and the arrival of the first bankers in Ireland, most likely from Italy. Ireland, living its civil life for so long in a splendid and warlike isolation, was becoming part of a forceful and highly organised international community.

The links with the Scandinavian world were severed; for the Anglo-Normans

---

[1] Ibid., pp 22, 107–8.   [2] Ibid., pp 30, 109.
[3] For some qualification of this view see below, pp 35–6.
[4] Orpen, *Normans*, iv, 263–70, 273–9.

turned the country away from northern Europe so that thereafter it looked to the Norman lands and the Mediterranean. The closer church ties developing with Rome also strengthened this change.

The newly arrived barons and knights proved to be liberal benefactors of the religious orders, apart from promoting the organisation of parochial life. The foundation of religious houses by the Gaelic Irish continued, but at a slower pace, since a substantial number had been founded in the fifty years before the coming of the Anglo-Normans. By the year 1230 the number of religious houses for men in Ireland was in the region of 200: 120 had been founded by the Irish, 80 by the Anglo-Normans.[1] Thereafter the great increase of religious houses for men in the thirteenth century was due to the advent of the mendicant friars, Dominicans in 1224, Franciscans in 1234, and Carmelites and Augustinians in the second half of the century. Their rapid success was largely due to the fact that they came to serve the urgent spiritual needs of the people living in the towns and urban centres. All four orders were sponsored by the Anglo-Normans, and their continued success up to the end of the century is a fair gauge of the progress made by the Anglo-Normans.[2]

By that stage expansion was coming to an end. Whether or not one accepts the notion of a Gaelic rally or resurgence in the thirteenth century,[3] it is clear that even before 1300 the limits of the colonial settlement had been reached. The Gaelic polity had been shaken but not shattered. The authority of the English king, the lord of Ireland, exercised through his administration at Dublin, never extended over the whole island. It is true that the newcomers may have had a negative effect outside the areas which had been fully colonised 'by smashing the power of the Irish provincial kings without being in a position to impose a stable alternative government'.[4] And certainly divisions between and within Gaelic Irish dynasties did much to aid the initial Anglo-Norman advance. Yet it is worth noting that the majority of Gaelic Irish families who were prominent in the twelfth century were still prominent in the sixteenth. Despite, or perhaps because of, a less defined and potentially more factious succession system, they outlasted families of Anglo-Norman origin which petered out through failure to produce the male heirs essential to primogeniture.

In the fourteenth century the Bruce invasion, famine, and plague produced in the colonial area conditions that mirrored those in other parts of Europe: a shrinkage in settlement, a dearth of people, and, ultimately, deserted villages. The colonists believed, and continued to believe into the sixteenth century,[5] that the plague had a much more destructive effect among them than among the Gaelic Irish, and that the disproportionate impact had enabled the Gaelic

[1] Watt, *Ch. in med. Ire.*, pp 118–21.   [2] See map below, pp 400–01.
[3] Eoin MacNeill, *Phases of Irish history* (Dublin, 1919; reprint 1968), pp 323–56.
[4] Katharine Simms, 'The O'Hanlons, the O'Neills and the Anglo-Normans in thirteenth-century Armagh' in *Seanchas Ardmhacha*, ix (1978), p. 92.
[5] *S.P. Hen. VIII*, ii, 11.

Irish to recover much of their former territories and power. Pleas for aid from England, accompanied by predictions of disaster if aid were not forthcoming, now became a regular feature in the relations between the Irish administration and its English counterpart. Doubtless these pleas exaggerated the plight of the colonists in an attempt to gain the attention of English kings preoccupied else-where. But while there was little likelihood that the 'Irish enemies' would over-run the colonial settlement, fears of being overwhelmed culturally were real and culminated in the 1366 statute of Kilkenny. The attempt to cordon off the colonial area in order to prevent the further spread of Gaelic language and cus-toms was unrealistic. But it reflects an anxiety that the erosion of English culture would breed political disaffection.

The statute also pointed to another division, between the 'English by birth' and the 'English by blood', in the terminology of the annalists, between the *Saxain* and the *Gaill*, between English and Anglo-Irish. It is not surprising that the colonial population, in the different environment and circumstances of Ire-land, should develop an identity which was distinctively Anglo-Irish. This is not to accept the older nationalist view that they became 'more Irish than the Irish themselves',[1] even though there were some of English descent who ful-filled the worst fears of the administration by rejecting both their cultural and political allegiances and becoming 'English rebels'. Rather did they occupy the position of a 'middle nation' who were 'neither wholly English, nor yet Irish, but something in between'.[2] And they continued to look to England for solu-tions to the problems facing them.

The missions of Richard II to Ireland can be seen as a response to Anglo-Irish demands that the English king should come in person to rescue his lord-ship from the perils which threatened it. But Richard achieved little, and none of his successors during this period followed his example and visited Ireland. The reopening of the French war inevitably reinforced Ireland's low ranking in the list of English priorities, and there it remained, despite the isolated plea of the author of the 'Libelle of Englyshe polycye'.

The emergence of the Pale in the mid-fifteenth century underlined both the contraction and fragmentation of the colonial area. Ireland was not so much a lordship as a collection of lordships, Gaelic and Anglo-Irish, and regional rather than national considerations dictated political outlooks. A man's 'country' or *patria* was not Ireland, but his own locality. A recent writer has observed that 'the political fragmentation of the country . . . made the average man a foreigner thirty miles from his own doorstep',[3] and it has been pointed out that by the year 1500 the political map of Ireland had in a remarkable fashion reverted to somewhat the same fragmentation as had existed a thousand years earlier.[4] The authority of

[1] See Art Cosgrove, 'Hiberniores ipsis Hibernis' in Art Cosgrove and Donal McCartney (ed.), *Studies in Irish history presented to R. Dudley Edwards* (Dublin, 1979), pp 1–14.

[2] Lydon, *English in med. Ire.*, p. 15.

[3] Katharine Simms, 'Guesting and feasting in Gaelic Ireland' in *R.S.A.I. Jn.*, cviii (1978), p. 75.

[4] Michael Richter, *Irland im Mittelalter: Kultur und Geschichte* (Stuttgart, 1983), p. 163.

the lord of Ireland faced many rivals in the complex power-struggles of the later medieval period, and its exercise came increasingly to depend on its effective delegation to a local Anglo-Irish magnate.

The earls of Kildare proved themselves capable of filling that role, and their near-monopoly of the office of chief governor made them the most powerful family within the country. Yet, ultimately, the extent of their power depended not only on their own resources within Ireland but also on the weakness or strength of the English kings with whom they had to deal. An increasingly strong and self-confident Tudor monarchy was not prepared to accept the freedom of action formerly conceded to its representatives in Ireland. How far it would have gone in its desire to curb local autonomy is debatable. But the events of 1534 forced the hand of the English government and set it upon a path which was to lead ultimately to the assertion of English authority over the whole island.

CHAPTER I

The trembling sod: Ireland in 1169

F. J. BYRNE

Coccadh mór isin mbliadhainsi co mboí Ere ina fód crithaigh, 'great war in this year, so that Ireland was a trembling sod'—such is the memorable phrase with which the seventeenth-century annalists known to us as the Four Masters sum up the events of 1145. But modern historians, perusing their record and that of the earlier, contemporary annals on which they drew, have found it hard to avoid the conclusion that there is barely a year in the history of twelfth-century Ireland before the advent of the Anglo-Normans in 1169 that would not qualify for the same description.

So gloomy a view of the native Irish polity is only partly due to the nature of our principal sources, the annals, which, like modern newspaper headlines, concentrate on violence and disaster. It is undoubtedly true that warfare and assassination were prevalent in the Ireland of the time, as they were throughout Europe. England was perhaps more peaceful than most of its neighbours, or at least English historians, following a tradition established by Bede, have agreed to make it appear so. Certainly it had more stable institutions and a potentially powerful centralised monarchy that predated the Norman conquest, and for which it would be hard to find a parallel near at hand, except possibly in Scotland. But in 1145 England itself was in the throes of civil war, and the lament of the Peterborough monk, writing at the end of the nineteen years of Stephen's troubled reign (1135–54), is, as Plummer remarked, 'more often quoted than any passage in the Chronicle'.[1]

In this king's time there was nothing but disturbance and wickedness and robbery, for forthwith the powerful men who were traitors rose against him . . . for every powerful man built his castles and held them against him and they filled the country full of castles. They oppressed the wretched people of the country severely with castle-building. When the castles were built, they filled them with devils and wicked men. . . .

I have neither the ability nor the power to tell all the horrors nor all the torments they inflicted upon wretched people in this country; and that lasted the nineteen years while Stephen was king, and it was always going from bad to worse. They levied taxes on the

[1] Charles Plummer, *Two of the Saxon chronicles parallel* (2 vols, Oxford, 1899), ii, 309.

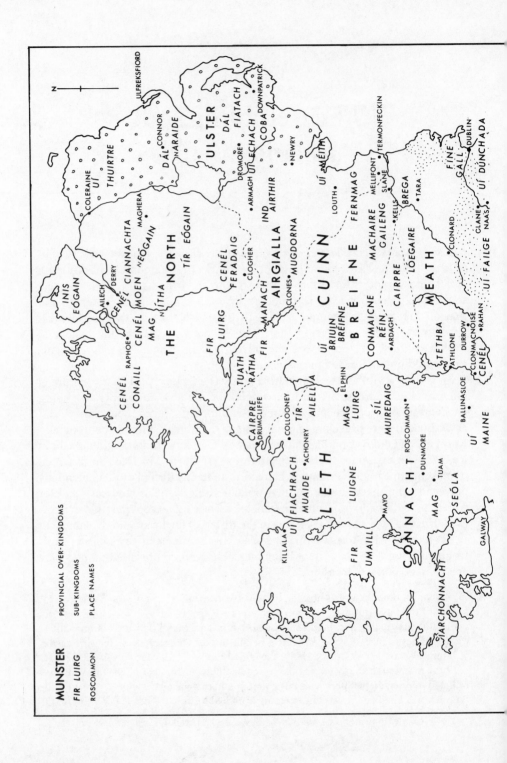

MUNSTER — PROVINCIAL OVER-KINGDOMS
FIR LUIRG — SUB-KINGDOMS
ROSCOMMON — PLACE NAMES

N

ULFREKSFIORD

ULSTER

UÍ THUIRTRE
COLERAINE
MAGHERA
DÁL NARAIDE
CONNOR
DÁL FIATACH
DROMORE
ARMAGH
UÍ ECHACH COBA
DOWNPATRICK
IND AIRTHIR
NEWRY

CENÉL CIANNACHTA
CENÉL MOEN
NEÓGAIN
MAG NÍTHA
TÍR EÓGAIN
CENÉL FERADAIG
CLOGHER
CLONES
FIR MANACH
MUGDORNA
AIRGIALLA

THE NORTH

AILECH
DERRY
INIS EÓGAIN
CENÉL CONAILL
RAPHOE

UÍ MÉITH
LOUTH
MELLIFONT
TERMONFECKIN
SLANE
KELLS
TARA

FERNMAG
MACHAIRE GAILENG
BREGA
CAIRPRE
LOEGAIRE
MEATH
CLONARD
DURROW
RAHAN
CLONMACNOISE
CENÉL

FÍNE GALL
DUBLIN
UÍ DÚNCHADA
UÍ FAILGE
CLANE
NAAS

FIR LUIRG
TUATH RÁTHA
FIR RÁTHA

CAIRPRE
DRUMCLIFFE
COLLOONEY
TÍR AILELLA
ACHONRY
MAG LUIRG
ELPHIN
SÍL MUIREDAIG
ROSCOMMON
DUNMORE

UÍ BRIUIN BRÉIFNE
BRÉIFNE
CUINN
CONMAICNE RÉIN
ARDAGH
TETHBA
ATHLONE
BALLINASLOE
UÍ MAINE

LETH

KILLALA
UÍ FIACHRACH MUAIDE
LUIGNE
FIR UMAILL
MAYO
MAG SEÓLA
TUAM
GALWAY
CONNACHT
CÍARCHONNACHT

Map 1 POLITICAL DIVISIONS, *c.*1169, by F. J. Byrne

villages every so often, and called it 'protection money'. When the wretched people had no more to give, they robbed and burned all the villages, so that you could easily go a whole day's journey and never find anyone occupying a village, nor land tilled. . . .

There had never been till then greater misery in the country, nor had heathens ever done worse than they did. . . . Neither did they respect bishops' land nor abbots' nor priests', but robbed monks and clerics, and everybody robbed somebody else if he had the greater power. If two or three men came riding to a village, all the villagers fled, because they expected they would be robbers . . . and they said openly that Christ and his saints were asleep.[1]

The modern English translation is perhaps too bland and flowing for the staccato horror of the Anglo-Saxon, which has for us the additional pathos of representing the dying gasp of a great vernacular.

Very rarely do the Irish annalists indulge in the personal tone or the extended narratives of the Anglo-Saxon Chronicle, and herein lies another difficulty facing the modern historian. It is frustrating to read a catalogue of seemingly aimless acts of violence, from which no obvious pattern seems to emerge. Only too easily do we condone pillage and slaughter in past ages if they can be seen as part of an historical process towards some great achievement, whether it be the establishment of a monarchy or its overthrow by bourgeois or proletarian revolution. But the aim that spurred on Irish provincial kings to march and countermarch across the trembling sod, the high-kingship of all Ireland, remained unrealised, and their activities can all too readily be dismissed as the senseless tribal anarchy of Celtic clans.

Such was the view of Orpen, the greatest historian of the Normans in Ireland. He further endowed the sons and nephews of the castle-building barons of Stephen's reign with an altruistic sense of mission to spread the benefits of English rule, and attributed to them the successful establishment of a *pax Normannica*. MacNeill's protests against such anachronisms did not make much impact on subsequent historians of medieval Ireland (most of whom were unable to read, still less to interpret, the native sources), perhaps because he was not entirely free of anachronism himself in his view of the nature of the twelfth-century Irish 'state'.[2] If he did not resort to *suppressio veri*, Orpen skilfully employed *suggestio falsi* to minimise or condone the infighting, greed, disloyalty, and sheer opportunism of the Anglo-Normans. Perusal of Otway-Ruthven's *History of medieval Ireland* will rapidly disabuse the reader of any delusions about a *pax Normannica*, though in view of the Anglo-Norman achievements in Ireland it would be unfair to comment with Tacitus *ubi*

---

[1] David Douglas and G. W. Greenaway, *English historical documents*, vol. ii: *1042–1189* (London, 1953), pp 199–200.

[2] Binchy has aptly remarked: 'It has always seemed to me that these two eminent scholars, despite their violent collision, started out from precisely the same suppressed premise: that law and order were impossible in any society where the state had not substantially the same functions as in the late Victorian era in which they both grew up' (D. A. Binchy, 'Secular institutions' in Myles Dillon (ed.), *Early Irish society* (Dublin, 1954), p. 62).

solitudinem faciunt pacem appellant. A cynic would be tempted to say merely that feudal anarchy had replaced tribal.

But was the undoubted anarchy of twelfth-century Ireland tribal in the first place? Nearly a hundred years ago Standish Hayes O'Grady propounded a truer thesis in an article that has been totally ignored ever since Round dismissed it out of hand.[1] In characteristically colourful language he painted a brilliantly impressionistic sketch of Irish politics in the twelfth century, the basic truth of which has only recently been demonstrated.[2]

The history of Ireland in the eleventh and twelfth centuries is the history of a race evolving its monarchy, and is therefore likely to prove a valuable contribution to general European history. For the process which in most other countries is sunk in oblivion lies all revealed in Ireland; so generous have been our monkobardic historians. . . . There is no trace of tribal warfare in the history of these centuries. All the wars are of dynastic kings warring upon kings to assert domination or retain independence—a most salutary warfare, inevitable, indispensable, enjoined by nature itself. Tribes and nations have ceased to count; of each generation the history is that of some half-dozen strong men striving for the mastery. . . . The genius of the age more and more imperatively demanded a new type of kings . . . who would interfere strongly in dynastic quarrels and make their power felt and their persons feared.[3]

This fact was recognised by the author of the 'Song of Dermot and the earl', when he remarked that

> En yrland erent reis plusur
> Cum alures erent les cunturs

(that kings in Ireland were as plentiful as counts elsewhere) but that the six kings of Meath, Leinster, Desmond, Munster, Connacht, and Ulster were the chief *reis de yrlande*.[4] The ancient *tuath* or tribal kingdom had long been obsolete as a political entity, and by the twelfth century was merely a district under a *toísech* (a term originally meaning 'leader of a war-band'). The *rí* or 'king' ruled over a *trícha cét* ('thirty hundreds'), an area which the Cambro-Normans equated with the cantred of their native Wales (*cantref*, 'hundred homesteads'), and which they found a convenient unit on which to base their baronies in the subinfeudation of Leinster and Meath.[5]

But the archaic retention of the word *rí* gives a false impression of the power

[1] 'The last high-kings of Ireland' in *E.H.R.*, iv (1889), pp 286–303; see J. H. Round, 'The conquest of Ireland' in *The commune of London, and other studies* (Westminster, 1899), pp 137–70.

[2] Adumbrated by F. J. Byrne, *Irish kings and high-kings* (London, 1973), pp 269–74, and now fully exemplified by Donnchadh Ó Corráin, 'Nationality and kingship in pre-Norman Ireland' in *Hist. Studies*, xi (1978), pp 1–35; each author, at the time of writing, was unaware of the existence of O'Grady's article.

[3] *E.H.R.*, iv (1889), pp 287, 291, 294; O'Grady here uses 'nations' in the Elizabethan sense, as in 'captain of his nation', referring to the Gaelic Irish lords.

[4] *Song of Dermot*, p. 16, lines 2191–8.

[5] James Hogan, 'The Tricha Cét and related land-measures' in *R.I.A. Proc.*, xxxviii (1929), sect. C, pp 148–235; F. J. Byrne, 'Tribes and tribalism in early Ireland' in *Eriu*, xxiii (1971), especially pp 158–60.

of such a lord, who in the Latin documents of the period, such as the charters and the hagiography, is sometimes styled *comes* or *dux*. In the annals too we find such kings acting no longer as tribal rulers but as officers of the provincial king: thus Ua Máille of Fir Umaill, Ua Dubda of Uí Fiachrach Muaide, Ua hAinglide of Uí Briúin Sinna are Ua Conchobair's admirals on sea and Shannon, while Ua Conchobair Ciarraige seems to perform a similar function for Ua Briain, and Ua hAinbéith of Uí Méith is the marshal of Mac Lochlainn's cavalry. More important, influential, and potentially dangerous to their overlords were the overkings (sometimes called *ardríg*, corresponding to the *ruirig* of the ancient laws), such as those of Osraige, Airgialla, or Bréifne. Such men were not yet prestigious enough to aim at the high-kingship, but they could be king-makers. It was the revolt of Donnchad Ua Cerbaill of Airgialla that brought down Muirchertach Mac Lochlainn in 1166, while in 1170 Tigernán Ua Ruairc swore that Ruaidrí Ua Conchobair would not remain king of Ireland unless he killed the hostages of Diarmait Mac Murchada.[1]

The presence of such overmighty vassals would not have surprised a twelfth-century European observer. Their territories formed the normal basis for the new diocesan system, although occasionally smaller units such as Corco Mruad (Kilfenora) and Corco Loígde (Ross) achieved diocesan status.

Provincial kings (Ua Briain of Munster, Ua Conchobair of Connacht, and Mac Lochlainn of the North) did succeed in winning recognition for themselves as high-kings of all Ireland for brief periods in the twelfth century, but their rivalry necessitated almost yearly campaigning. While it may be anachronistic to speak of nationalism in twelfth-century Ireland, it is salutary to remind ourselves that the official biography of Brian Bóruma, written for his great-grandson Muirchertach Ua Briain in the early years of the century, is entitled 'Cocad Gáedel re Gallaib' ('The war of the Irish against the Foreigners'), and by cleverly manipulating the historical evidence presents its hero as motivated by the purest patriotism.[2] So skilful was its propaganda that it continues to deceive historians of the viking era down to the present day. Another work from the same court circle is the Book of Rights, which presents an idealised and somewhat archaistic polity of Ireland, clearly related to the O'Brien-inspired ecclesiastical polity worked out at the synod of Ráith Bressail in 1111, though it is realistic enough to recognise that other provincial kings may on occasion be entitled to claim the high-kingship.[3] But the literary traditions of Ulster and Leinster, persisting from the sixth to the twelfth century, reveal the strength of provincial patriotism among the age-old enemies of Uí Néill pretensions to the high-kingship of Tara.

Nevertheless all our sources are in agreement as to the existence of the high-

[1] *Ann. Tig.*, 1170: 'uair tuc Ua Ruairc a chubais na budh rí Erenn Ruaidri muna marbad íat'.

[2] J. H. Todd (ed.), *Cogadh Gaedhel re Gallaibh: the war of the Gaedhil with the Gaill* (London, 1867); see John Ryan, 'The battle of Clontarf' in *R.S.A.I. Jn.*, lxviii (1938), pp 1–50.

[3] Myles Dillon (ed.), *Lebor na cert: the book of rights* (London, 1962; Ir. Texts Soc., xlvi); see F. J. Byrne in *Studia Hib.*, v (1965), pp 155–8.

kingship. The only disagreement was as to who should hold it. The cultural unity of Ireland, as reflected in the standard literary language, was maintained by the men of learning, lay and ecclesiastical, who, whatever their provincial loyalties, established an agreed history and pseudo-history of Ireland, the *senchas coitchenn*. Ulster saga material was composed by Munster poets and preserved in manuscripts written at Clonmacnoise and in Leinster. The 'Cocad Gáedel re Gallaib' was copied into the Book of Leinster shortly after Diarmait Mac Murchada had inflicted a crushing defeat on Ua Briain at Móin Mór in 1151.

It was particularly during the period of interregnum between 1022 and 1072, when there was no obvious candidate for the high-kingship, that the men of learning, whom Eoin MacNeill dubbed the 'synthetic historians', elaborated the pseudo-historical theory of an immemorial high-kingship of Tara, which since the fifth century had allegedly been held by the Uí Néill dynasties of the North and the midlands until their monopoly had been broken by Brian Bóruma from Munster.[1] Prominent among the Uí Néill propagandists was Flann Mainistrech (d. 1056), *fer léigind* or lector of Monasterboice, and it is essentially his version of the official king-list that is reproduced in the Munster Annals of Inisfallen, written probably at Emly before 1092.[2]

Such learned theorising served to fuel the ambitions of the twelfth-century kings, who learned both that the high-kingship was an ancient institution and that now it was open to all suitable candidates from any province. Leinster advocates claimed that their own king, Diarmait Mac Máel na mBó (ruled 1042–72), great-grandfather of Diarmait Mac Murchada, had been 'king of Ireland with opposition' (*rí Érenn co fressabra*) because he had controlled all of Leth Moga (the southern half of the country, Leinster and Munster) together with areas in the northern half, Leth Cuinn, namely Meath, Connacht, Ulster, and Airgialla.[3] It was a somewhat exaggerated claim, for while Diarmait had acted as king-maker in Munster, helping to depose Donnchad mac Briain and to install his own protégé Toirrdelbach ua Briain, was in alliance with Niall mac Eochada (king of Ulster from 1016 to 1063), had imposed his own son Murchad on the Norse of Dublin and Man, and had been killed in an attempt to conquer Meath, he had hardly controlled all those regions in any real sense. Yet the claim shows that his great-grandson entertained similar ambitions.

The most obvious claimants to the high-kingship of Ireland were the Uí Néill, north and south, who had in the course of the ninth and tenth centuries

---

[1] Eoin MacNeill, *Celtic Ireland* (Dublin, 1921; 2nd ed., with new notes by Donnchadh Ó Corráin, Dublin, 1981), pp 25–42.

[2] Flann Mainistrech, 'Ríg Themra tóebaige iar tain' in *Bk Leinster*, iii, 509–15, written between 1014 and 1022; *Ann. Inisf.*, pp 42–4 (but at p. 104 there is a note on five Munster kings who allegedly had ruled Ireland); see below, ix, 189–94.

[3] *Bk Leinster*, i, 98, lines 3158–66: 'Rapa rí Herend co fressabra Diarmait mac Mael na mBó. . . . Rabo rí Herend amlaidsin mac Mael na mBó uair ra boí Leth Moga uile 7 Connachta 7 Fir Mide 7 Ulaid 7 Airgialla. ace. Is leis ro cured mac Briain dar muir.' The same scribe says of Diarmait Mac Murchada 'ba rí Lethi Moga uili eside 7 Mide eside' (ibid., p. 184, lines 5501–27).

succeeded in establishing a certain hegemony over the whole island.[1] The kingship of Tara had alternated fairly peacefully between the Cenél nEógain of the North and the Clann Cholmáin of Mide. But by the end of the tenth century certain factors had disrupted their dynastic unity and sense of common purpose. The northern high-king Domnall ua Néill (956–80) had begun to build garrisoned fortresses (perhaps inspired by the burghs of Anglo-Saxon England) and tried to make his claim to be king of all Ireland more practicable by basing himself firmly in Mide and Brega, the heart of the island, leaving his home kingdom of Ailech in the far north to be ruled by a kinsman. But he ran into strong local opposition in 970, and was driven from the midlands, to be succeeded in 980 by the Clann Cholmáin king of Mide, Máel Sechnaill mac Domnaill.

Máel Sechnaill was an effective high-king, and on no less than three occasions captured Dublin, not in order to expel the Norse, but rather to exploit their resources. He had the misfortune to be the contemporary of an even abler man, the upstart Brian Bóruma, who wrested the high-kingship from him in 1002. Máel Sechnaill received no help from his disaffected northern kinsmen. Furthermore a geographical wedge was being driven between the Northern and Southern Uí Néill by the rapid growth of the Connacht kingdom of Bréifne, spreading from Leitrim into Cavan. Brian himself found difficulty in gaining even reluctant submission from the north by dint of annual forays, and when he fell at Clontarf in 1014 it was in battle against the rebel king of Leinster and his Norse allies of Dublin, Man, and the Orkneys, and his own forces consisted merely of Munstermen (including the Norse of Limerick and Waterford) together with a few allies from south Connacht. The rest of Ireland stood aloof.

Although Máel Sechnaill reassumed the high-kingship, after his death in 1022 no one took over the reins of power. Flann Mainistrech had expected that Flaithbertach Ua Néill would have resumed the northern alternation, but he failed to do so: henceforth the north showed an increasing isolation from the affairs of the rest of Ireland—an attitude that was to be confirmed during the years of the Anglo-Norman intervention. Donnchad mac Briain had considerable difficulty in establishing himself as king of Munster against both domestic rivalries and the hostility of the Eóganacht dynasties displaced by his father, and it was only by about 1050 that he was able even to pretend to the title 'king of Ireland'. By 1063 he had been deposed by his more successful nephew Toirrdelbach, supported, as we have seen, by Diarmait, king of Leinster, as well as by Áed Ua Conchobair, king of Connacht.

The most remarkable feature of this period is what did not happen: namely, the failure of the Ua Máel Sechlainn family of Meath to build on the achievements of their ancestors and to take advantage of the central geographical position and potential control of both the richest land in Ireland and the richest urban centre, Dublin. The last able king of this dynasty was Conchobar Ua

[1] Byrne, *Ir. kings*, pp 254–74.

Máel Sechlainn, who killed the ambitious king of Leinster, Diarmait, in 1072, but was himself assassinated the following year, to the indecent delight of Toirrdelbach ua Briain, who thereupon proclaimed himself king of Ireland and shortly afterwards installed his son Muirchertach as king of Dublin.

The unexpected collapse of Meath can most plausibly be explained by the extraordinary number of wealthy monasteries concentrated in the province. The monastic map[1] will show how thickly they were clustered, but we have only the vaguest information as to the extent of the lands (often, we know, far removed from the actual church site) that they controlled. In the ninth and tenth centuries church and dynasty offered each other mutual support, beautifully exemplified in the iconography of the Cross of the Scriptures at Clonmacnoise, erected by the high-king Flann Sinna and the abbot of Clonard and Clonmacnoise, Colmán mac Ailella, in 909. But by the second half of the eleventh century the stirrings of reform had reached the Irish churches, and both reformed and unreformed clergy found agreement on one principle: the immunity of church lands from all secular exactions: from the levying of tax, from the duty of providing men for royal hostings, from the billeting of troops. Of course, not all churches succeeded in gaining these liberties easily, immediately, or all at the same time, and some were themselves in the hands of royal dynasties who had imposed their own relatives in hereditary abbatial office. But the fact that by the twelfth century the Ua Máel Sechlainn kings seem to have been practically confined to Durrow and Clonard, and that Clonmacnoise had now become a Connacht fifth column in their land, tends to confirm the impression that they were bankrupt of men and resources. (Murchad Ua Máel Sechlainn, abbot of Clonard and 'king of Mide for three nights', was killed by the local Gailenga when he tried to usurp the abbacy of Kells in 1076.)[2]

The resulting power vacuum in the centre of Ireland was disastrous. It also goes far to explain the extraordinary confusion of Irish political history, as greedy neighbours and ambitious pretenders to high-kingship ate into the territories of the ancient province and carved it up between themselves, their current favourites, or hapless Ua Máel Sechlainn puppets. This policy of partition had been inaugurated by Muirchertach Ua Briain in 1094, and was repeated with depressing frequency by him and all his successors in the high-kingship. Meath thus became the vortex of a whirlpool of conflicting interests. Tigernán Ua Ruairc of Bréifne installed himself at Kells and Slane, and was styled, not altogether incorrectly, as 'king of the Meathmen' by Giraldus Cambrensis.[3] His enemy and uterine brother, Donnchad Ua Cerbaill of

[1] Below, ix, map 23.

[2] *Ann. Tig.*, 1076. These annals at 1055 describe Murchad as abbot of Clonard and Kells, and he is accordingly included in the relevant list below, ix, 244. However, the Annals of Ulster, 1055, call him 'Mac Loingsig', which implies that Muirchertach Mac Lochlainn was the abbot in question.

[3] Giraldus Cambrensis, *Expugnatio Hibernica: the conquest of Ireland*, ed. A. B. Scott and F. X. Martin (Dublin, 1978), p. 24: 'Ororicio . . . Medensium rege.'

Airgialla, engaged him in a race to the Boyne and took over the ancient Brega kingdom of Fir Arda Ciannachta (Ferrard, County Louth). And his deadliest foe, Diarmait Mac Murchada, building on earlier conquests of the Dublin Norse and of his own great-grandfather, extended the borders of Leinster well into southern Brega. Ua Ruairc and Mac Murchada faced each other directly across the Boyne, and the abduction of Derbforgaill in 1152, at the instigation of her Ua Máel Sechlainn brother, was a politically motivated insult. Surprisingly, her father, Murchad, survived all the vicissitudes of a much interrupted 'reign' of fifty years to die peacefully in his bed at Durrow the following year.

Similar partitions were imposed by Toirrdelbach Ua Conchobair on Munster in 1121 and subsequently, by Domnall and Muirchertach Mac Lochlainn, on Ulster in 1113, 1148, and 1165, while as early as 1095 Muirchertach Ua Briain had attempted a bold (but ultimately unsuccessful) rearrangement of the constituent kingdoms of the province of Connacht.[1] Even more drastic was the imposition of a member of the overlord's own family on a subject kingdom. The O'Briens and the Uí Chennselaig kings of Leinster successfully controlled Dublin in this manner for many years, but Toirrdelbach Ua Conchobair failed to maintain his son Conchobar as king of Dublin and Leinster in 1127, and when he installed him as king of Meath in 1143 the intruder was promptly slain by Ua Dublaích of Fir Thulach as a *rí echtar-cheneóil*, 'a stranger in sovereignty'.[2] Such an event illustrates how the innovations of the twelfth century met resistance from atavistic forces of conservatism and local loyalty. Much of the violence, seemingly aimless, of this period was not due to tribal anarchy but represented the birth-pangs of a new feudalism, rendered all the more painful in a country where, for all the effects of viking wars and Norse settlements, no foreign power had ever achieved a conquest or abolished the age-old native polity.

The endemic nature of twelfth-century warfare is itself an indication of how greatly Irish society had changed since the viking era. The Norse had introduced the concept of total warfare with no respect for sanctuary, and had built permanent military and naval encampments. It is notable how the term *cocad*, 'war', now tends in the annals to replace the *cath* or one-day ritual battle of the Old Irish period. The Norse campaigns too had the long-term effect of transforming the political geography of Ireland. The Norse made the Leinster coast, hitherto a political backwater, strategically important, and embarked on long-distance raids by river and on horseback. The rise to power of Osraige in the ninth century and of Dál Cais in the tenth was due to their defence of the rivers Barrow, Nore, and Suir, and of the Shannon respectively. By the middle of the tenth century Domnall ua Néill was bringing fleets up the Bann and Erne and building fortresses in every *tuath* in Meath, a strategy soon to be imitated by Brian Bóruma in Munster. Such fortresses were governed by royal officials

---

[1] Ó Corráin, 'Nationality and kingship', pp 25–6.
[2] *A.F.M.*, 1144.

called *rechtairi*. These royal officers and others—the *máer* or steward who collected local revenues (the great monasteries had similar functionaries), and the *muire*, a sheriff responsible for law and order in the district controlled by a major aristocratic family within a kingdom—now in the eleventh and twelfth centuries figure as personages of importance in the annals (though we know from the law tracts of the seventh and eighth centuries that they had always existed).

The Normans had introduced castle-building into Wales in the first decade of the twelfth century; by the second decade the Welsh were imitating them, and by the third Toirrdelbach Ua Conchobair was encastellating Connacht. He may even have employed foreign or foreign-trained architects: such were certainly necessary for the new romanesque architecture of this generation. Kings were now able to keep large armies, including cavalry, in the field for months at a time: Toirrdelbach Ua Conchobair, for instance, encamped in the hostile territory of Ormond for six months between August 1126 and February 1127. They also had fleets at sea and on the rivers, both Hiberno-Norse and native. This implies the existence of a military caste, men who had specialist skills, who owned horses and could maintain them, who could afford to leave their farms to be tilled by serfs or slaves. It is not possible to demonstrate that these nobles held their land by formal military tenure; and perhaps it is an academic point, since they would hardly have been able to retain their lands had they refused such service. But it is worthy of note that the word *óclach*, 'young man; warrior', in the twelfth century acquires the new connotation of 'vassal', while the abstract *óclachas* comes to mean 'submission; military service'.[1] An account of Ua hEitirsceóil's territory of Corco Loígde describes the major land-holding families as *óclaig dúthaig*, 'native vassals' (contrast the more familiar term *gallóclaig*, 'foreign vassals', those Hebrideans who were given Irish land in the thirteenth and later centuries in return for military service).[2]

At the other end of the social scale the freeman of the ancient law tracts, bound only by certain limited services and renders to his lord, had almost certainly long been reduced to the servile status of *biatach* or *fuidir*—the 'betagh' of Anglo-Norman documents.[3] Such degradation was undoubtedly furthered by the rapid growth of the slave trade that formed the basis of the wealth of the Hiberno-Norse ports of Dublin and Waterford. The professional war-fleets of these cities were in constant demand in England, Scotland, and Wales, and their services were paid for in booty and prisoners of war. Before 1066 the English had been notorious for their readiness to sell their own people into

[1] Cf. *Misc. Ir. Annals*, 1164. 1 (p. 42).

[2] John O'Donovan, 'The genealogy of the Corca Laidhe' in *Miscellany of the Celtic Society* (Dublin, 1849). See further Gearóid Mac Niocaill, 'À propos du vocabulaire social irlandais du bas moyen âge' in *Études Celt.*, xii (1970–71), pp 512–46.

[3] Gearóid Mac Niocaill, 'The origins of the betach' in *Ir. Jurist*, i (1966), pp 292–8, but cf. K. W. Nicholls, 'Ango-French Ireland and after' in *Peritia*, i (1982), p. 378.

captivity. The extensive use of servile labour to work the land serves to explain the contempt in which the twelfth-century Irish reputedly held agricultural activity, an attitude far removed from that of the seventh-century lawyers.

Further evidence of the feudalisation of Irish society is seen in the fact that the over-kings were now acting as *domini terrae*. As early as about 1086 Donnchad mac Domnaill Remair, king of Leinster, granted the lands of Clonkeen in south County Dublin to Christ Church cathedral.[1] These were at the far end of the province from his own demesne lands in Uí Chennselaig. Similarly Diarmait Mac Murchada in 1162 granted Baldoyle in north County Dublin, together with its Mac Fáelacáin tenants, to the Augustinian priory of All Hallows. About the same time he confirmed a grant of land at Killenny, County Kilkenny, to the Cistercians of Ossory, made by his sub-king Diarmait Ua Riain of Uí Dróna (allegedly made with Mac Murchada's permission—*per nostram licentiam*—although the land apparently lay within Ua Riain's own kingdom). In this charter, and in the contemporary grant to the Augustinian canons of Ferns, Diarmait styles himself *nutu Dei rex Laginensium*, and both are attested by Florentius, with the titles of royal notary or chancellor.

Similar charters, albeit dated within a decade or more after the arrival of the Anglo-Normans, are extant from Diarmait Ua Dímmusaig, king of Uí Failge, Diarmait Mac Carthaig, king of Desmond, and Domnall Mór Ua Briain, king of Thomond, with pretensions to be king of all Munster. The earliest surviving such charter is that of 1157 from Muirchertach Mac Lochlainn, *rex totius Hiberniae*, to the Cistercians of Newry, which lay in the territory of Uí Echach Coba, within the province of Ulster (not Mac Lochlainn's own province of the North), and on the borders of Airgialla. Here, however, the high-king is careful to state that the grant is made with the consent of all the magnates of Ulster, Uí Echach, and Airgialla.[2] That such overriding grants could be resented locally is suggested by the contumelious expulsion of the Augustinian canons from Saul by Magnus Mac Duinn Sléibe, king of Ulster, in 1170. In 1165, as part of the reconciliation arranged by Donnchad Ua Cerbaill between Muirchertach Mac Lochlainn and Magnus's brother and predecessor Eochaid, the former had made a grant of a *baile* or townland to Saul *tria rath rígi*, 'through his royal grace'.[3]

While it is certainly true that we may suspect that it was the Cistercians or

---

[1] A. J. Otway-Ruthven, 'The medieval church lands of County Dublin' in *Med. studies presented to A. Gwynn*, p. 60, quoting from Archbishop Alen's register ('Donough son of Donald Grossus').

[2] '... unanimi voluntate et communi concessione magnatum Ultoniae et Ergalliae et de Oneach, scilicet Donnchad O Cearbail regis totius Ergalliae et Murcad ejus filii regis Ometh et Tricaced Erther et Conla regis Ultoniae, Donaldi O Heda regis Oneac ...' (i.e., Donnchad Ua Cerbaill, king of all Airgialla, his son Murchad, king of Uí Méith and of the *trícha cét* of Airthir in County Armagh, Cú Ulad Mac Duinn Sléibe, king of Ulster, and Domnall Ua hÁeda, king of Uí Echach). All the above-mentioned charters have been edited by Dr Marie-Thérèse Flanagan, 'Monastic charters from Irish kings of the twelfth and thirteenth centuries' (M.A. thesis, N.U.I. (U.C.D.), 1972).

[3] *A.U.*, 1165, 1170.

Augustinians who dictated the form of these charters, and may have given the Irish kings notions foreign to their hereditary traditions, it must be remembered that all known abbots and priors of these new 'foreign' orders were native Irishmen, as were the bulk, if not all, of their congregations. A few French monks certainly came to help in the foundation of Mellifont in 1142, but they soon fled, victims of an early culture shock. The idea popular among some nationalist historians that the Cistercians were in some way a Norman fifth column in Ireland is entirely mistaken. The majority of Cistercian foundations in Ireland, even after the advent of the Anglo-Normans, were of Gaelic origin, and the Irish soon learnt to use them as bulwarks against colonial expansion.

It will be evident by now that the twelfth century had seen great changes in Irish political geography, and thus it is not easy to present an accurate survey of the country in the year 1169; the scene was constantly moving. This phenomenon may well explain the comparative ease with which the Anglo-Normans conquered and settled some areas: in Ormond and in east Meath they were moving into lands whose inhabitants had little cause for loyalty to the rival warlords who had been carving up their territory, while in Ulster de Courcy could even be seen, after initial resistance, as a prince who might restore the ancient glories of the province.

The traditional 'five fifths' of Ireland (Ulster, Munster, Leinster, Connacht, and Meath) may have been more a cosmological scheme than a political reality, and had at any rate been rudely disrupted by the Uí Néill at the dawn of Irish history, most notably by their conquest of the North and establishment of hegemony over the Airgialla, which left Ulster proper reduced to a rump east of the Bann. Tradition claimed that Leinster too had lost the midlands to the new dynasty. Twelfth-century antiquarians indulged in various theories as to the proper division of the country. One popular version was sixfold, counting Munster as the equivalent of two provinces—up to the ninth century west Munster had been a distinct entity, only loosely dependent on Cashel, while the twelfth century saw a very real division between north and south, Thomond and Desmond. This was the scheme adopted by the author of the 'Song of Dermot and the earl', and also at times by Giraldus, but it was wildly anachronistic as far as the north was concerned. Later the 'Song' correctly distinguishes between Ua Néill of Cenél nEógain, Mac Duinn Sléibe of Ulster, and Ua Cerbaill of Airgialla:

> E macdunleue de huluestere
> a clontarf ficha sa banere. . . .
> Mes pus lur suruint okaruel
> ki reis esteit de yriel,
> e macdonleue le felun
> de uluestere la regiun. . . .
> de kinelogin onel li reis

od se menad trei mile yrreis.
Assemblez erent les norreis,
e de lethchoin trestut les reis.[1]

But Giraldus gets into serious trouble (and has misled most later historians) when he confuses Ulster with the North.[2]

For as long as the Ulaid retained their separate identity, the northern Uí Néill high-king of Ailech could never be called an Ulsterman. In fact, as late as 1084 the king of Ulster, Donn Sléibe mac Eochada, taking advantage of a period of dynastic strife in Cenél nEógain, made a daring attempt to revive the extent of the ancient province by enlisting the support of Donnchad Ua Ruairc, whose expanding kingdom of Bréifne marched with its former southern border. The adventure was doomed to failure, but Donn Sléibe's programme is spelled out in a poem attached to the Book of Rights.[3]

The Book of Rights proper, in accordance with Ua Briain policy, asserted a heptarchy, led by Munster ('two provinces in one house'), and including Connacht, the North (Ailech), Airgialla, Ulster, Meath (Tara), and Leinster. This scheme was followed by the Armagh scribe Máel Brigte in his gospel book written in 1138. But other regnal lists and synchronisms of the eleventh and twelfth centuries exclude Airgialla, while some raise Osraige to provincial status. In the mid eleventh century Flann Mainistrech listed as the chief kings of his time those of Ailech, Connacht, Leinster, Munster, Ulster, and Meath, adding as a matter of common courtesy the name of his local lord Ua Cathassaig of Brega.[4]

THE over-kingdom of the North (In Fochla or In Tuaiscert), also styled of Ailech after the stone fort at the base of the Inishowen peninsula, had for centuries been dominated by the Cenél nEógain, led now by the family of Mac Lochlainn whose home base was at Derry. Their former dynastic rivals, the Cenél Conaill, were confined to Tír Conaill, the diocese of Raphoe; by the end of the century their royal families of Ua Máel Doraid and Ua Cannannáin had so exhausted each other in internecine feuding that they were replaced first by Ua Taircheirt and then by Ua Dochartaig, until in the thirteenth century Ua Domnaill of Cenél Lugdach at Kilmacrenan obtained that monopoly over the lordship which his descendants were to maintain until the passing of the old order in 1603. In the course of time Ua Dochartaig was to take over Inishowen and Ua Domnaill was to drive the Cenél nEógain family Ua Gairmledaig of

[1] *Song of Dermot*, lines 1756–7, 3184–7, 3258–61.
[2] *Expugnatio*, pp 94, 174–9, 312; 'Giraldus Cambrensis in Topographia Hibernie: text of the first recension', ed. J. J. O'Meara, in *R.I.A. Proc.*, lii (1949), sect. C, pp 121–2, 159–60.
[3] James Hogan, 'The Ua Briain kingship in Telach Óc' in *Féilsgríbhinn Eoin Mhic Néill*, pp 434–6; Byrne, *Ir. kings*, p. 107; *Lebor na cert*, pp 122–47.
[4] *Lebor na cert*, pp 2–115; and cf. p. 22; see review by F. J. Byrne in *Studia Hib.*, v (1965), p. 156.

Cenél Moen from the fertile plain of Mag nÍtha into lands east of the Foyle: both territories were to remain a bone of contention between the O'Neills and O'Donnells into the sixteenth century.

The O'Neills themselves do not emerge into the light of history until 1160, and then from a very murky background.[1] Their centre was at Tullaghogue in Tyrone. In 1167, after the killing of Muirchertach Mac Lochlainn, the new high-king, Ruaidrí Ua Conchobair, marched to Armagh and divided Tír Eógain between Niall Mac Lochlainn 'north of the mountains' (Slieve Gallion) and Áed Ua Néill to the south. The two families contested the kingship for over seventy years until in 1241 the O'Neills wiped out their rivals at the battle of Caiméirge.

Meanwhile other families of the Cenél nEógain had proliferated in bewildering profusion and established their local lordship over older subject peoples. Thus Ua Catháin had conquered the Ciannachta (barony of Keenaght, County Londonderry) and now extended his sway to the banks of the Bann. Mac Cathmaíl of Cenél Feradaig was in Clogher, the ancient capital of the western Airgialla, while his collaterals, the Ua Brolcháin family, were prominent ecclesiastics in Derry and Armagh, and Mac Cana of Cenél nÓengussa infiltrated into the north of County Armagh.

South of Mag nÍtha, on the banks of the rivers Derg and Mourne, lay the kingdom of Uí Fiachrach Arda Sratha, still ruled by the Airgiallan family of Ua Crícháin, whose Ua Farannáin cousins controlled the church of Ardstraw, but they were now directly subject to the over-kingdom of Ailech. Ardstraw had been proposed as a diocesan see for Cenél nEógain at the synod of Ráith Bressail in 1111, and in the thirteenth century the bishops of Clogher were claiming that the deanery of that name had been filched from them by the diocese of Derry.[2] The Book of Rights places the Uí Néill kingdom of Cairpre Dromma Cliab (barony of Carbury, County Sligo), together with the adjoining districts of Tuath Rátha and Fir Luirg on either bank of Lower Lough Erne, in the over-kingdom of Ailech. In the twelfth century Fir Luirg was under the king of Uí Fiachrach Arda Sratha, but Cairpre had been conquered by Tigernán Ua Ruairc of Bréifne, who was also attacking Tuath Rátha, and later both Tuath Rátha and Fir Luirg formed part of the Maguire lordship of Fir Manach, the former having as its lord Ua Flannacáin of the old Cairpre dynasty (Fir Luirg was under Ua hÉicnig of Fir Manach as early as 1201).[3]

Thus the area once occupied by the independent Airgialla had been greatly reduced by the twelfth century. But the diocese of Armagh retained its northern borders as they had existed in the eighth. The lands that had since been taken over by the Cenél nEógain became known as Tír Eógain (Tyrone). Donnchad Ua Cerbaill of the Fernmag (Farney) dynasty, who claimed the title

---

[1] James Hogan, 'The Irish law of kingship' in *R.I.A. Proc.*, xl (1930), sect. C, pp 186–254; Séamus Ó Ceallaigh, *Gleanings from Ulster history* (Cork, 1951), pp 73–87.

[2] Sheehy, *Pontificia Hib.*, ii, 284, no. 457.   [3] *Misc. Ir. Annals*, 1201. 4 (p. 80).

of high-king of all Airgialla, had however made considerable gains to the south. The Ulster buffer state of Conaille Muirtheimne in north Louth had succumbed to him before 1130, and by 1142 Ua Cerbaill had won the whole of the modern county, gaining the blessing of the church for his conquests by his grant of land to the first Irish Cistercian house at Mellifont, situated typically in a border zone. In return for his powerful support St Malachy had ceded all of Louth from the diocese of Armagh to that of Clogher, ruled by his brother Gilla Críst, and subsequently by his own nominee, Áed Ua Cáellaide, confessor to Diarmait Mac Murchada. The see was transferred to Ua Cerbaill's residence at Louth, for Clogher, as we have seen, was now in the hands of Mac Cathmaíl of Cenél nEógain. After the Anglo-Norman settlement of 'English Uriel', Louth was reclaimed by Armagh, but the dispute with Clogher lasted well into the middle of the thirteenth century.

In 1165 Ua Cerbaill won another slice of Ulster when Eochaid Mac Duinn Sléibe ceded Bairrche to him as the price of the short-lived reconciliation he had effected between Eochaid and the high-king Muirchertach Mac Lochlainn; in the course of the next century the Mugdorna of Cremorne in Monaghan moved into this region, to which they gave their name, Mourne. Similarly, another Monaghan group, the Uí Méith, had already settled in the Cooley peninsula (whence Omeath). The Newry charter shows that Donnchad had installed his son Murchad as king of Uí Méith and of Airthir (Orior) in County Armagh.

Murchad succeeded his father in 1168, and it was probably with his connivance that de Courcy made his spectacularly successful invasion of Ulster in 1177. Both de Lacy in Meath and de Courcy in Ulster seem to have welcomed the existence of a friendly Gaelic neighbour in Airgialla, and it was not until after Murchad's death in 1184 that Prince John, lord of Ireland, granted Airgialla (Oriel) to de Verdon and Pipard, and that Ua Cerbaill power collapsed. The successor as leader of Gaelic Airgialla was Mac Mathgamna, who by the fourteenth century re-established an independent lordship in Monaghan and unconvincingly claimed lineal descent from Donnchad Ua Cerbaill. Such a link with twelfth-century kings was a propaganda ploy frequently invoked by leaders of the Gaelic resurgence—the pedigrees of the Maguires of Fermanagh, of Mac Eochacáin of Cenél Fiachach in Westmeath, and of the O'Byrnes and O'Tooles of fourteenth-century Leinster are more than suspect.

But it is to be doubted whether Donnchad Ua Cerbaill at the height of his power exercised lordship over all the lands of Airgialla. The chief rivals to his dynasty had been the Airthir, 'the Easterners' of County Armagh, led by Ua Ruadacháin, and they certainly resented his dominance. But they had been weakened both by the ecclesiastical power of Armagh—though until St Malachy's reforms this had been in the hands of their own kinsmen, the Uí Sínaig—and by the encroachments of the Cenél nEógain. In the later middle ages the O'Neills planted a branch in the Fews, and the only Airthir family to maintain a lordship was Ua hAnluain of Uí Nialláin. Meanwhile in the north-west what was effectively an independent kingdom was being formed in the course of the eleventh and twelfth centuries by the Fir Manach, ruled by Ua hÉicnig, Ua Máel Ruanaid, and others. Although they were Airgialla, in the middle ages the name Oirghialla (Oriel) is in general usage confined to the Mac Mathgamna lordship in Monaghan. It was not until the middle of the thir-teenth century that Mac Uidir emerged as king of Fir Manach.

It is remarkable that the same period was to see the rise to power of the three greatest Gaelic lordships of the north: those of Ua Domnaill, Ua Néill, and Mac Uidir. The phenomena are evidently interconnected. The Mac Uidir pedigree shows some curious resemblances to that of Ua Domnaill, who prob-ably assisted his career, and who was also an ally of Ua Néill against Mac Lochlainn. Ua Néill too owed something to the support of the de Burgh earls of Ulster, who had maintained de Courcy's acquisitions along the northern coast as far as Derry and Inishowen; but in the main these developments seem to have been native and local in a region that remained curiously aloof from the momentous events in Ireland of 1169 and after. The northern kings, with the exception of Ua Cerbaill of Airgialla and Mac Duinn Sléibe of Ulster, ignored the visit of Henry II in 1171.

To conclude our survey of the northern kingdoms we turn to Ulster proper (Ulaid, latinised as Ulidia and Ultonia).[1] Its independence of Mac Lochlainn of the North was maintained with increasing desperation by Mac Duinn Sléibe of Dál Fiatach. His own territory comprised the diocese (as distinct from the county) of Down; Downpatrick was regarded as the capital of Ulster. Its southern portion, Leth Cathail (Lecale) was ruled by his collaterals, Ua Flaithrí and Mac Gilla Muire. In the far north-east the glens of Dál Riata, homeland of the Scots, had been overrun by Dál nAraide in the eighth century. Dál nAraide itself (the diocese of Connor) was ruled by kings of non-Ulidian stock—they were Cruthin, akin to the Picts of Scotland—and many had in previous centuries shared with Dál Fiatach in the high-kingship of the province (the annalists frequently refer to the reduced Ulster as In Cóiced, 'the Province' par excellence). But by the beginning of the twelfth century north Antrim had been acquired by Ua Flainn of Uí Thuirtre, a total outsider from Airgialla who had infiltrated by a long process of military and marital alliance directed against his nominal overlords of Cenél nEógain, but who still retained a foothold in his native Loughinsholin west of Lough Neagh and who styled himself king of Dál nAraide, Dál Riata, and Fir Lí. The legitimate Ua Loingsig kings of Dál nAraide held on to a smaller territory around Mag Line near Antrim town and eastwards. In the south-west another Cruthin kingdom, Uí Echach Coba (Iveagh) was ruled by Ua hAitéid and Mac Óengussa, with

[1] The distinction suggested by Roderick O'Flaherty (Ogygia (London, 1685), iii, p. lxxviii) between Ultonia, the ancient 'fifth' and modern province, and Ulidia, the early medieval kingdom, has no basis in contemporary records.

a sub-kingdom of Cenél Fagartaig under Mac Artáin, and by the end of the century was given its own diocese of Dromore.

After some fierce opposition to the Anglo-Normans, Mac Duinn Sléibe and the other Ulster kings acquiesced in de Courcy's overlordship and aided him against their traditional enemies of Cenél nEógain, retaining their regal status over the local Gaelic Irish. By the second half of the thirteenth century, however, Mac Duinn Sléibe had migrated to Tír Conaill, to be succeeded briefly as *rex Hibernicorum Ulidiae* by Mac Gilla Muire; but with the collapse of the earldom of Ulster after 1333 the chief beneficiaries were not the native dynasties but strangers such as Mac Uidhilín of the Route and Mac Domhnaill of the Isles, and particularly the Clann Aodha Buidhe, a branch of the O'Neills. The stage was now set for the Great O'Neill, Niall Mór, to proclaim himself king of Ulster at Eamhain Macha in 1387 and revive the ancient province within an approximation of its traditional extent from Assaroe to the Boyne.[1] Of all the indigenous families of Ulster only Mág Aonghusa of Iveagh and Mac Artáin of Kinelarty held on to their lordships unscathed into the seventeenth century, while the Whites and Savages protected the forlorn remnants of the Anglo-Irish earldom in Lecale and the Ards.

Before leaving the north it is well to remember the Irish Sea and the Hebrides. Here had been established for over a century a powerful Norse-Gaelic kingdom of Man and the Isles, theoretically subject to Norway and ecclesiastically to Trondheim, but in effect independent, though the kings of Dublin had once exercised suzerainty over Man at least and the archbishops of that see were to claim jurisdiction over *episcopatus Insularum*.[2]

The writing of national history as a genre has had the unfortunate result of obscuring entities once important in their own right that have not survived as nation states or even as geographical units. The kingdom of Man had been weakened in 1156 by the secession of Somarlaide of Argyll, who founded a lordship over the Southern Isles: he was an ally of Muirchertach Mac Lochlainn, and fell in battle against the king of Scots in 1164. But Godred, king of Man and the Northern Isles, remained a power to be reckoned with. Shortly before Diarmait Mac Murchada caught up with Henry II in Aquitaine in 1166 that king had received another visitor: the bishop of the Isles, who came as a delegate of Godred. Robert de Torigny tells us that the latter claimed affinity with Henry, but regrettably does not reveal the purpose of the mission.[3] Both John de Courcy (who married Godred's daughter Affreca) and later King John were to recognise the strategic importance of Man to secure their hold on Ulster.

---

[1] Katharine Simms, 'Propaganda use of the *Táin* in the later middle ages' in *Celtica*, xv (1983), pp 142–9.

[2] Sheehy, *Pontificia Hib.*, i, 35, no. 11 (understood by the editor to refer to Glendalough); see A. O. Anderson, *Early sources of Scottish history, A.D. 500 to 1286* (2 vols, Edinburgh and London, 1922), ii, 381–2, 427. See below, map 2, p. 133.

[3] *Chronicles of the reign of Stephen, Henry II, and Richard I* (4 vols, London, 1884–9), iv: *The chronicle of Robert of Torigni*, ed. Richard Howlett, pp 228–9.

Godred was himself married to a daughter of Niall Mac Lochlainn, and his son
Ragnall was granted lands at Carlingford by John, as well as being the recipient
of a bardic praise-poem which invited him to assume the high-kingship of
Ireland.[1]

Also keenly interested in the Anglo-Norman conquest of Ulster were the
lord of Galloway, Alan fitz Roland, his brother Thomas, earl of Atholl, and
their cousin Duncan fitz Gilbert, earl of Carrick, who were granted extensive
fiefs in Derry and Antrim, some of which were to pass into the inheritance of
Robert Bruce. The grandsons of Somarlaide of Argyll participated in these
adventures, and much later their descendants, the MacDonnells, were to settle
in the Glens of Antrim. By the end of the thirteenth century the *gallóclaig*, fighting men from Innse Gall, 'the islands of the Foreigners', were being endowed
with lands in Ireland by Gaelic lords and given genealogical legitimisation with
pedigrees derived from the Airgialla, or even, in the case of the MacSweeneys,
Ua Domnaill's most trusted vassals, with Uí Néill ancestry.[2]

MEATH suffered more dilapidation than any other province in the twelfth
century. Originally the overlordship of the Southern Uí Néill 'from the
Shannon to the sea' was composed of three regions: Mide itself ('the middle')
in Westmeath and north-west Offaly, the patrimony of Clann Cholmáin,
ancestors of Ua Máel Sechlainn, and of the Cenél Fiachach; Tethba in Longford with two Uí Néill kingdoms of Cairpre at Granard and of Maine at
Ardagh; and Brega ('the heights') covering all modern County Meath together
with the barony of Ferrard in Louth and the north of County Dublin—its kings
were the Síl nÁeda Sláine of Knowth and Lagore. In the west of Brega around
Trim and Tullyard was another Uí Néill kingdom that survived into the twelfth
century under its king Ua Caíndelbáin—that of Lóegaire. But the power of
Brega had been destroyed by the high-king Máel Sechnaill mac Domnaill at
the end of the tenth century, and the Knowth families of Ua Cellaig and Ua
Congalaig hung on to a title that was little more than a shadow. Even that was
sometimes snatched from them, as we find on occasion the style 'king of Brega'
usurped by Ua Cathassaig, representative of the subject Saithne in County
Dublin and a puppet of the Norse who had carved Fine Gall out of his lands.
With the assertion of Ua Máel Sechlainn overlordship the name Mide was
extended to the whole province, including Brega, and the original territory is
sometimes referred to as Iarthar Mide (west Meath).

But in the twelfth century Donnchad Ua Cerbaill had absorbed Fir Arda and
reached the Boyne, while the expansion of Bréifne had had disastrous consequences. Ua Ruairc had moved out of Leitrim into Cavan (which before this
seems to have been sparsely populated) and then took over Machaire Gaileng,

[1] Brian Ó Cuív, 'A poem in praise of Raghnall, king of Man' in *Éigse*, viii (1957), pp 283–301.
[2] Eoin MacNeill, 'Chapters of Hebridean history' in *Scottish Review*, xxxix (summer 1916),
pp 254–76; Paul Walsh (ed.), *Leabhar Chlainne Suibhne* (Dublin, 1920).

the plain of the subject Gailenga north of the Blackwater, where he installed his kinsman Ua Ragallaig as viceroy (*airrí*). Subject to Ua Ruairc were the Conmaicne Réin from Leitrim, who under his aegis moved into Tethba, where they set up new lordships: Muintir Eólais under Mac Ragnaill and Angaile under Ua Fergail. Tigernán Ua Ruairc was styled 'king of Bréifne and Conmaicne from Drumcliffe to Drochat Átha [Oldbridge on the Boyne]'.[1] Bréifne, 'the rough third of Connacht' (*garbthrian Connacht*), with its drumlins and difficult terrain, had always been a natural barrier between the north and the rest of Ireland, but it had now become a formidable political power that rendered it well-nigh impossible for any ruler from north or south to unify the country. Only Ua Conchobair from Connacht, of which Bréifne was technically an extension, could hope to do so, and Ua Ruairc would only support him on his own terms. In 1152 Bréifne (Tír Briúin) was given its own diocese with a see at Kells in Meath, the famous Columban church that Tigernán's father had mercilessly devastated in 1117, but to which Tigernán gave charters that were transcribed on to the pages of the great gospel book. The vassal Conmaicne were provided with a separate see at Ardagh.

Meanwhile the numerous Uí Néill dynasts of Tethba were being crowded southwards into western Mide. Ua Ciarda of Cairpre Gabra (Granard) seems to have remained as an unwilling vassal of Ua Ruairc, but ended up being planted in Leinster, in the barony of Carbury in north-west Kildare (or else found refuge there under the patronage of Diarmait Mac Murchada). But those of the line of Maine transferred the name Tethba to their new territories—thus causing much confusion to later historians. They took over the lands of older *fortuatha* (subject peoples): most prominent were Mac Cargamna of Cuircne (barony of Kilkenny West), Mac Amalgada of Calraige, Ua Bráin of Bregmaine (Brawney), and In Sinnach 'the Fox' Ua Catharnaig of Muintir Thadgáin (Kilcoursey in Offaly). Some must have intruded into the demesne lands of Ua Máel Sechlainn. The latter's hospitality seems to have been ill rewarded. These refugee elements were particularly turbulent and no doubt contributed to the bankruptcy of their overlord. For in the Irish polity, while every sub-king received gifts from the provincial high-king by the acceptance of which he acknowledged his dependence, only the kings of the subject *fortuatha* were burdened with the payment of tribute; those who claimed kinship with the overlord dynasty were exempt. (That the word for gift, *rath*, 'grace', was replaced in the eleventh century by the term *tuarastal*, 'stipend' or 'wages' in return for military service, is another indication of the changing social and political climate).[2]

A few *fortuatha* survived: the Gailenga around Kells (their northern lands

---

[1] Cf. Gearóid Mac Niocaill, *Notitiae as Leabhar Cheanannais* (Dublin, 1961), p. 24: 'ardri Airthir Connacht et na Telcha archena o Thracht Eothaile co Mag Tlachtga et o Shinaind co Drochat Atha'; Charles Plummer, *Bethada náem nÉrenn* (2 vols, Oxford, 1922), i, 202: 'o Druim Cliab go Cenannus'.

[2] See Charles Doherty, 'Exchange and trade in early medieval Ireland' in *R.S.A.I. Jn.*, cx (1980), p. 74.

expropriated by Ua Ragallaig), and their close congeners the Luigne in Lune; the Delbna under Ua Findalláin in Delvin and Fore; the Delbna Ethra under Mac Cochláin beside Clonmacnoise, and the Fir Thulach under Ua Dublaíg in Fartullagh. None of these can have contributed much to Ua Máel Sechlainn's revenues. The Delbna and the Fir Thulach were continually raiding Clonmacnoise, and the remaining Uí Néill king in the south-west, Ua Máel Muaid of Fir Chell and Cenél Fiachach, was harrying Rahan. The truth is that the long-established churches in this boggy land were infinitely richer than their hungry royal neighbours. Only Durrow and Clonard enjoyed relative immunity as the residences of Ua Máel Sechlainn, who also retained his ancestral home at Cró-Inis on Lough Ennel. Clonmacnoise incurred positive hostility since it had fallen victim to the lavish patronage of Ua Conchobair of Connacht, and several attempts were made in the course of the century to prevent this great church from establishing itself as the episcopal see for western Mide.

LEINSTER, on the other hand, while never free from violence, presents a picture of relative stability. For centuries the victim of Uí Néill aggression, the province had not only preserved its frontiers intact, but (apart from the late intrusion of Ua Ciarda of Cairpre into a corner of the north-west) had even extended them. Its cultural self-confidence is expressed in a remarkable series of poems preserved in the two great codices Rawlinson B 502, written c.1130, and the so-called Book of Leinster. The tone of these pieces shows that a patriotic Leinsterman such as one of the compilers, Áed Mac Crimthainn, abbot of Terryglass (a monastery of Leinster origin situated in Munster and rescued from Ua Briain control after the battle of Móin Mór in 1151) would not have regarded Diarmait Mac Murchada's ambitions as anything but admirable or his invitation to the Anglo-Normans as in any way reprehensible. The foundations for the province's new fortunes were laid by Diarmait mac Máel na mBó (1042–72), who restored the high-kingship to the southern dynasty of Uí Chennselaig. The northern Uí Dúnlainge of the plains of Kildare, dominant for three centuries, had been weakened by the dual attacks of the Uí Néill and of the Dublin Norse. By contrast, the Norse town of Wexford was peaceful and always under the control of the Uí Chennselaig (we hear of no Norse kings ruling there). It was probably its trade with Bristol that gave that dynasty the economic power to win hegemony over all Leinster from an unfavourable geographic location, for they were effectively cut off from the rest of the province by the barrier of the Blackstairs mountains.

Diarmait mac Máel na mBó had contacts across the Irish Sea. He was praised by the Welsh annalists and may have entertained Bishop Sulien of St David's.[1]

[1] *Brut y Tywysogyon*, trans. Thomas Jones (Cardiff, 1955), p. 16, s.a. 1070 (=1072): 'And Diarmaid, son of Mael-na-mbo, the most praiseworthy and bravest king of the Irish—terrible towards his foes and kind towards the poor and gentle towards pilgrims—was slain in an unforeseen and unexpected battle.'

He received the sons of Earl Godwin of Wessex on their exile in 1051, and the sons of Harold Godwinson after 1066. A reference in a fragment of bardic verse suggests that he may have been the first Irish king to employ Norman mercenaries:

> Cuirn maicc Donnchada
> dlegait buidechas
> buide benngela;
> Francaig fognama
> fine chuindgeda
> sanntaig senmeda.

(The yellow bright-peaked drinking horns of Donnchad's son deserve thanks: Franks in service, an importunate race, greedy for old mead.)[1]

The *cuirn Cualann*, 'drinking-horns of Cuala', were the royal insignia of the kings of Leinster. The title 'Donnchad's son' could apply equally well to Diarmait Mac Murchada, and the verse might then have celebrated the arrival of his Norman allies, but Thurneysen has given good reasons to believe that the text in question, a metrical tract, was composed not much later than 1060.[2] Edward the Confessor's Norman friends were expelled from England by Earl Godwin in 1052, and we know that some took service with Macbeth in Scotland. Later, in 1102, Arnulf of Montgomery briefly sought refuge with his father-in-law Muirchertach Ua Briain, and references in twelfth-century Irish sagas show that *Franc-amuis*, 'Frankish mercenaries', and *ritiri*, 'knights', were not unfamiliar at the courts of Irish kings.[3] So the arrival of the little band of Flemings at Wexford in 1167 occasioned no particular surprise.

In 1052 Diarmait Mac Máel na mBó intruded his son Murchad as king of Dublin, thereby inaugurating a policy that was to be successfully imitated by the O'Briens. Murchad, eponym of the Mac Murchada family, predeceased his father in 1070; his daughter Gormlaith became abbess of Kildare in 1072. Kildare was the effective capital of Leinster, and control of its ecclesiastical offices was an essential prerequisite for any aspirant to the provincial kingship.

This circumstance explains, if it does not excuse, Diarmait Mac Murchada's first recorded exploit, what might be termed his *crech ríg*:[4] his violation of Mór, abbess of Kildare, in 1132 and the installation of his own kinswoman Sadb. In fact, Mór had been intruded equally violently by Ua Conchobair Failge in 1127 at the expense of Diarmait's own sister-in-law, the daughter of Cerball Mac Fáeláin, who himself was killed in the centre of Kildare. Diarmait was to make

---

[1] Rudolf Thurneysen, 'Mittelirische Verslehren' in Whitley Stokes and Ernst Windisch, *Irische Texte* (3rd ser., 2 vols, Leipzig, 1891), i, 91, no. 128; Kuno Meyer, *Bruchstücke der älteren Lyrik Irlands* (Berlin, 1919), p. 18, no. 36.

[2] *Zu irischen Handschriften und Litteraturdenkmälern* (Berlin, 1912), p. 89.

[3] R. I. Best and Osborn Bergin, *Lebor na hUidre: Book of the Dun Cow* (Dublin, 1929), p. 233, lines 7612–24; *Bk Leinster*, ii, 416, line 12955.

[4] The raid with which an Irish king traditionally inaugurated his reign; cf. Pádraig Ó Riain, 'The "crech ríg" or "royal prey" ' in *Éigse*, xv (1973), pp 24–30.

some reparation by his foundation of at least three houses of Arroasian canonesses.

He was a friend of St Malachy, who had family connections with the Leinster dynasty of Ua Gormáin of Uí Bairrche (though these were to be expelled by Diarmait in 1141), and he skilfully combined support for church reforms with his own political ambitions. He issued charters to the new Augustinian canons at his local residence at Ferns (where he built a stone castle), and to those of All Hallows at Dublin, as well as to the Cistercians at Killenny, strategically placed on the hostile border with Osraige. And in 1148 he founded the Cistercian house at Baltinglass, granting it half of Uí Máil, thereby shrewdly driving a wedge between the demesne lands of Ua Tuathail in Uí Muiredaig and their newly acquired lordship of Uí Máil centred at Glendalough. For this generosity towards the 'poor of Christ' Diarmait was rewarded with a certificate of confraternity by no less a figure than St Bernard of Clairvaux.

It was probably in 1153, shortly after his affair with Ua Ruairc's wife Derbforgaill, that Diarmait was reconciled with Muirchertach Ua Tuathail, took his daughter Mór as his third or fourth wife, and acquiesced in the election of her half-brother Lorcán (St Laurence O'Toole), whom he had mistreated as a hostage in his boyhood, to the abbacy of Glendalough. In 1162 he presided with Archbishop Gilla Meic Liac at the synod of Clane, where the primacy of Armagh was reaffirmed, and where in all probability Lorcán Ua Tuathail was elected to succeed the dying Gréne as archbishop of Dublin. In that year the Annals of Ulster affirm that he forcibly plundered the Dublin Norse and acquired 'great sway over them, such as was not obtained before his time'. This being so, it must have been with his authority that the Dublin fleet went to aid Somarlaide at the disastrous battle of Renfrew in 1164, and, yet again replenished (such was the economic strength of the Dubliners), campaigned unsuccessfully for six months on the Welsh coast in the service of Henry II. Diarmait had rendered the Angevin king a favour for which he was to ask a return the following year.

In spite of power changes the political geography of Leinster had remained surprisingly stable over the centuries. Although some dynasties fell from power, the territorial units, albeit under new masters, retained their identity. The encroachments of Dublin into Brega had been increased by the campaigns of Diarmait mac Máel na mBó, and his great-grandson sought to extend them farther: in 1161 he had even shared briefly in one of the fatal partitions of Meath.

The accession of the large over-kingdom of Osraige to the province was less welcome. It was not a result of Leinster strength but rather of Munster weakness: it had been in progress since the second half of the ninth century, when Cerball mac Dúnlainge shook off the authority of Cashel and turned his attention to the Barrow. While defending the valley against the vikings, his descendants took over the Uí Chennselaig kingdom of Uí Dega (barony of Ida, south Kilkenny) and absorbed a portion of Uí Bairrche to the north; both acquisitions were disguised by the official genealogies, which unconvincingly asserted that the Osraige were as entitled to the name Laigin as the Leinstermen themselves.[1] On the collapse of the Uí Dúnlainge in the mid-eleventh century Donnchad Mac Gilla Pátraic succeeded in proclaiming himself king of Leinster in 1033. His descendants were to be the bitterest and most dangerous of Mac Murchada's many enemies. The change in the centre of Mac Gilla Pátraic's interests is indicated by the choice of Kilkenny rather than the ancient mother church of St Cainnech, Aghaboe, as the diocesan see of Ossory in 1111.

To the north-west of the province lay the extensive kingdom of Uí Failge, ruled by Ua Conchobair Failge from his fortress at Rathangan in Kildare. This dynasty claimed seniority among the Laigin, and in the 1070s attempted to win the over-kingship. Sub-kingdoms were Uí Riacáin in the west under Ua Duinn, and Clann Máel Ugra (in County Leix) under Ua Dímmussaig. For twenty years or so after the Anglo-Norman settlement of Leinster the kingship of Uí Failge was actually held by Diarmait Ua Dímmussaig, who, in a move typical of the chess-game of the period, founded the Cistercian house of Monasterevin on the northern bank of the Barrow.

To the east lay the lands of the three branches of Uí Dúnlainge, who had held the over-kingship in the past. The Uí Dúnchada, having lost ecclesiastical office at Kildare in the late tenth century, turned their attention eastward and took over the kingdom of Cuala in south Dublin and the adjoining Wicklow coast from the Uí Máil dynasties of Uí Chellaig Cualann and Uí Théig, but held on to their ancestral fort at Liamain (Castlelyons) in Kildare. Under Mac Gilla Mo Cholmóc they achieved a remarkable coexistence with the Dublin Norse: Mac Gilla Mo Cholmóc had property in Dublin and was a benefactor of St Mary's abbey, while the Dubliners had lands in Cuala and in a strip that extended down the coast to the outposts of Wicklow and Arklow.[2] But a fifteenth-century genealogical tract makes extravagant claims for the success of Mac Gilla Mo Cholmóc in freeing the local Irish from Norse exactions.[3] Perhaps it was these experiences that enabled the family to adapt so well to the Anglo-Norman settlement.

Around Naas lay the lands of Mac Fáeláin of Uí Fáeláin, while further south at Mullaghmast and Castledermot were those of Ua Tuathail of Uí Muiredaig. Ua Tuathail had also acquired the southern portion of Uí Máil in Wicklow and even displaced the Uí Máil abbots at Glendalough; Lorcán Ua Tuathail's grandfather Gilla Comgaill, king of Uí Muiredaig and abbot of Glendalough, had been murdered in 1127 by the Fortuatha Laigen, the subject peoples of

---

[1] M. A. O'Brien, *Corpus genealogiarum Hiberniae* (Dublin, 1962), i, 101.
[2] Charles Haliday, *The Scandinavian kingdom of Dublin* (Dublin, 1881; reprint Shannon, 1969), pp 138–40.
[3] J. T. Gilbert, *A history of the city of Dublin* (3 vols, Dublin, 1854–9; reprint Shannon, 1972), i, 407–8.

central Wicklow, and Lorcán himself had to face violent opposition to his own tenure of the abbacy.

Along the coast lay the lesser kingdoms of Uí Garrchon under Ua Fergaile and Uí Enechglaiss around Arklow under Ua Fiachrach, dynastic groups long excluded from the high-kingship of the province. Inland, on the middle Barrow about Carlow, were the Uí Bairrche, once powerful but now much reduced. Their lord was Ua Gormáin and their churches Sletty and Killeshin. All these, with the exception of the *fortuatha*, were Laigin, the free peoples entitled to the name of Leinstermen.

The two most important non-Laginian peoples were the Fothairt and the Loíges, each traditionally divided into seven groups scattered throughout the province. But by the twelfth century only two of these retained their status as kingdoms under their own dynasties—Fothairt Fea (the barony of Forth in Carlow) under Ua Nualláin, and Ua Mórda's territory of Loíges, which formed only a small portion of the present County Leix; Ua Duib of Uí Chremthannáin held the Rock of Dunamase, while to the south the petty state of Uí Buide was ruled by Diarmait's protégé Ua Cáellaide. The other territory of Fothairt in Chairn in Wexford and its neighbouring Uí Bairrche (Forth and Bargy) were ruled, not by their native kings, but by Ua Lorcáin from Uí Muiredaig.

All the south of Leinster was divided into the 'ten cantreds of Uí Chennselaig'[1]—the nine baronies of County Wexford plus the barony of Shillelagh in Wicklow. The last-named (Síl nÉladaig) was under Ua Gaíthín and Ua Néill of Mag dá Chonn. In north-east Wexford, Uí Dega was ruled by Ua hÁeda while Ua Murchada ruled Uí Felmeda to the south. Benntraige to the far south-west was also ruled by a branch of the Uí Felmeda, the Clann Choscraig. All these formed the diocese of Ferns, Mac Murchada's home base. But outside these bounds, in the diocese of Leighlin, lay two further Uí Chennselaig kingdoms—another Uí Felmeda under Ua Gairbíth at Tullow and Rathvilly, and Uí Dróna along the banks of the Barrow, ruled by Ua Riáin.

Across the Barrow, beckoning tantalisingly, lay Waterford, after Dublin (or perhaps Limerick) the largest Hiberno-Norse town and port; like Dublin an autonomous city-state, and more successful than Dublin in retaining its native dynasty. It was an obvious prize for Mac Murchada: its possession would round off his province and seal his south-western approaches. But technically it lay across the border in Munster and showed no desire to change its status. The Ua Briain kings had allowed it much freedom, and with the division of Munster between Ua Briain and Mac Carthaig in 1121 its independence increased. As early as 1137 Diarmait summoned the Dublin and Wexford fleets and entered into alliance with Conchobar Ua Briain to lay siege to the city, and Ua Briain submitted to Diarmait in hope of receiving the Mac Carthaig kingdom of Desmond (he shared the rule of Thomond with his brother Toirrdelbach). The

[1] *A.F.M.*, 1167.

attempt was a failure, but the city was to be Strongbow's first target in 1170 and the scene of his marriage with Aífe.

Dublin was a cosmopolitan city: Gréne, its first archbishop, was said to be skilled in many tongues.[1] The foundation of the Savigniac (later Cistercian) house of St Mary's in 1139 may well have been due to the presence of an English merchant community. Such a mixed population, more intent on wealth than war (except in so far as the latter, conducted on a mercenary basis abroad, was a valuable supplier of slaves), may actually have welcomed direct rule by strong kings from Munster or Leinster, and showed little resentment at the expulsion of the dynasty of Sitric Silkbeard. Nevertheless, the Dubliners did kill Diarmait's father Donnchad in 1115, and successfully resisted the intrusion of Conchobar Ua Conchobair in 1127. The origins and background of those Norse kings who do figure in the twelfth-century annals of the city are extremely obscure, and some are said to have been outsiders of Hebridean origin. That rival factions with conflicting interests existed in the city is shown by the events of 1121, when one party welcomed the intervention of the primate, Cellach of Armagh, while another successfully resisted him and sent their bishop-elect, Gréne, to Canterbury for consecration.

Since 1052 candidates for the elusive high-kingship of Ireland recognised that Dublin rather than Tara was the goal they must seek. Muirchertach Ua Briain served his apprenticeship as king of Dublin during his father Toirrdelbach's reign as high-king, and pursued the same policy by putting in his own son Domnall there when he in turn assumed the high-kingship. Domnall unsuccessfully attempted to gain control of Man, but in 1111 his cousin Domnall mac Taidg was invited by the Manxmen to act as regent for the infant Olaf Godredsson, and ruled there until the collapse of O'Brien power in 1114. Toirrdelbach Ua Conchobair supported the rule of Diarmait's brother and predecessor Énna in Dublin, but on his death replaced him with his own son Conchobar; the failure of this experiment seems to have resulted in disenchantment, and Toirrdelbach lost interest in the city—hence his failure, despite his military strength, to maintain his high-kingship. His son Ruaidrí learnt the lesson, and in 1166 had himself inaugurated as high-king of all Ireland at Dublin, rewarding the citizens with a massive *tuarastal* of 4,000 cows. Even Conchobar Ua Briain seized the kingship of Dublin briefly before his death in 1142.

Historians are generally agreed that Giraldus is overly hostile in his characterisation of Diarmait, which stands in stark contrast to the depiction in the 'Song' of *li gentil reis* who 'loved the generous and hated the mean'.[2] But recent research has shown that Giraldus was probably more accurate than he realised when he called him *nobilium oppressor, humilium erector*.[3] His ruthlessness had been demonstrated by the violation of the abbess of Kildare in 1132, and even

---

[1] *A.F.M.*, 1162.   [2] *Song of Dermot*, p. 3, line 15.
[3] *Expugnatio*, p. 40.

more spectacularly by his killing and blinding of seventeen of the Leinster
royalty (mainly of the Uí Dúnlainge and Uí Bairrche) in 1141. This was an
event unprecedented in Irish history, and illustrates not merely his ferocity but
his absolute power, for it was not the result of any victory in battle.

In 'bringing to prominence men of humble rank' he was following a plan laid
down by his father and grandfather before him. His own mother's family was Ua
Bráenáin, of lowly origin, the Fothairt Airthir Life, whose territory of Uí Máel
Ruba (the *terra de Omolrov* that puzzled Orpen)[1] stretched from Laraghbryan and
Maynooth to the Dublin mountains, where the romanesque ruins of Kilteel
probably mark their stronghold, whose strategic position was later appreciated
by the Knights Templar. They thus formed a barrier between Mac Gilla Mo
Cholmóc of Cuala and his cousins of Uí Fáeláin in Kildare, and their pedigree
was updated, first to represent them as a branch of the Déise Temra (with whose
lands in Meath they marched), and then to give them an Uí Néill descent from
Lóegaire of Trim.[2] Ua Bráenáin remained faithful to Mac Murchada in the dark
days of 1166, when he killed the rebel Mac Gilla Mo Cholmóc.

Diarmait had been fostered by Ua Cáellaide, of uncertain origin, but possibly a refugee from the Eóganacht Caisil into Osraige. This family was
installed as kings of Uí Buide in County Leix, and also into Osraige itself: in Uí
Berrchon in the south and at Aghaboe in the north. Some were supported by
Mac Murchada as joint-kings of Osraige in opposition to Mac Gilla Pátraic,
while Diarmait's confessor, Áed Ua Cáellaide, was St Malachy's nominee to
succeed his brother Gilla Críst as bishop of Clogher-Louth in 1138: it was for
his benefit that Diarmait granted Baldoyle to the Augustinians of All Hallows
in Dublin.

Ua Mórda of Loíges had for centuries been an ally of Mac Murchada's
enemy Mac Gilla Pátraic of Osraige, and to counter his influence Diarmait
encouraged the dynasty of Uí Chremthannáin in County Leix; a faithful propagandist was Áed Mac Crimthainn of that family, abbot of Terryglass and
compiler of the Book of Leinster.

Within Diarmait's immediate family circle was Ua Domnaill, whom his bastard son Domnall Cáemánach drove out of Wexford in 1161. But a scion of that
family, Mac Dalbaig (the 'Mactalwey' of Anglo-Norman sources), was reconciled by being granted the kingdom of Uí Felmeda in County Carlow.[3] Since
Amlaíb Ua Gairbíth of Uí Felmeda stayed loyal to both Diarmait and Strongbow, it seems likely that he had been compensated by the territory of Uí
Bairrche to the west. Ua Gormáin of Uí Bairrche disappears from Leinster
history after the massacre of 1141, to reappear later in the retinue of Domnall
Mór Ua Briain of Thomond.

[1] *Song of Dermot*, p. 305; Orpen, *Normans*, i, 380.
[2] O'Brien, *Corpus geneal. Hib.*, pp 83, 161, 168 (= Rawlinson B 502, 126 a 12 (+ Lec.), 144 c 10, 145
b 39).
[3] Marie-Thérèse Flanagan, 'Mac Dalbaig, a Leinster chieftain' in *R.S.A.I. Jn.*, cxi (1981), pp
5–13.

Diarmait also showed himself willing, when it suited his purposes, to give comfort to dynasts who had fallen on evil days. Thus he installed Ua Lorcáin, who had been displaced from the kingship of Uí Muiredaig by his collateral Ua Tuathail, in the lordship of Fothairt in Chairn in the south of County Wexford. Murchad Ua Brain and his son Dalbach were similarly representatives of a discard segment of Uí Fáeláin, the lordship of which was now exercised by Mac Fáeláin. Diarmait placed Murchad to guard the strategically important pass of Fid Dorcha in the gap of the Blackstairs mountains leading into the heart of Uí Chennselaig. Gratitude was not forthcoming, for in 1166, when Diarmait appeared before Murchad's castle in the disguise of an Austin canon, the latter not only refused him aid but even counsel—the minimum duty of any feudal vassal in the twelfth century. The ill-feeling thus engendered was expressed by Strongbow as Diarmait's heir, when he had both Murchad and Dalbach executed and their bodies thrown to the dogs.

The cavalier treatment which Diarmait had meted out to the ancient dynasties of Leinster foreshadowed the subinfeudation of the territory by Strongbow. His disregard of ancestral custom was emphasised by his grant of the whole kingdom of Leinster to Strongbow as the dower of his daughter Aífe. Kingdoms had never before passed by marriage in Ireland, although this had happened in Wales since at least the ninth century, albeit in contravention of legal theory. Yet it is certain that Diarmait did not intend to disinherit his sons. Domnall Cáemánach indeed was allegedly illegitimate, and his mother is not mentioned in the genealogical tracts, but this was no necessary disability in Irish law, if he were a recognised son. In fact he was staunchly loyal both to his father and to Strongbow. But in 1166 Diarmait had two living legitimate sons, Énna and Conchobar, both later to fall victim as hostages to Mac Gilla Pátraic of Osraige and the high-king Ruaidrí Ua Conchobair respectively.

It is clear that Diarmait intended to make himself high-king of all Ireland with the help of his Anglo-Norman allies, and was willing both to acknowledge the overlordship of Henry II—'fitz Empress' as the Irish called him (and they had always recognised in theory the supremacy of the emperor as 'king of the world')—and to cede Leinster itself to Strongbow as his son-in-law and vassal. The kings of the Scots had after all strengthened their authority by bringing in Normans to modernise and feudalise their land. It was Diarmait's unexpected death in May 1170 that brought about a dramatic change in the scenario.

MUNSTER in 1169 presented a sorry contrast to its prosperous state at the beginning of the century, when at the height of Ua Briain power it had been not merely the largest, but also the most powerful province in Ireland. Both Toirrdelbach ua Briain and his son Muirchertach had between 1072 and 1114 bidden fair to achieving a true high-kingship of all Ireland, and, being open to foreign influence, had encouraged ecclesiastical reform. Finally in 1111 Muirchertach presided over the synod that set up territorial dioceses for the

whole island. They had established their capital at Limerick and kept firm
control of Dublin. Mathgamain mac Cennétig and his brother Brian had captured Limerick as early as 967, and while they had expelled the Norse kings, the
bulk of the Ostman (Hiberno-Norse) population remained, and was to provide
the see with several bishops in the twelfth century. Limerick had trading connections with Rouen, the capital of the duchy of Normandy and the largest
Jewish centre in western Europe: thence most probably arrived the delegation
of Jewish merchants that visited Toirrdelbach ua Briain in 1079. Nearly thirty
years later Limerick's first bishop, Gilla Espuic, was to remind St Anselm of
Canterbury of their meetings in that city.

At the other end of the province Waterford retained its Norse kings of the
house of Ivar, cousins of the former kings of Dublin, and was the first city outside Dublin to be provided with a regularly consecrated bishop and territorial
see, at the instigation of Muirchertach himself in 1096. Just as Dublin controlled Fine Gall, so Waterford had a small territory known as *Gall-tír*
(Gaultiere). The third Norse base in Munster, that at Cork, had never
amounted to much and seems to have posed no real threat to the powerful
church there, which commanded its own monastic army. Muirchertach Ua
Briain had concluded marriage alliances in 1102 with Magnus Bareleg, the king
of Norway who was asserting his suzerainty over the Irish Sea, and with the
Norman baron Arnulf of Montgomery in Wales; the latter's envoy on this
occasion was Gerald of Windsor, castellan of Pembroke and ancestor of the
FitzGeralds.

The MacCarthys too had important foreign connections through their
cousin Christian, abbot of Regensburg and head of the rapidly growing community of *Schottenklöster*, the Irish Benedictine monasteries that enjoyed the
special favour of the German emperor. Both O'Briens and MacCarthys
lavished patronage on the great monastery of Lismore, ruled by members of the
Ciarraige Luachra of north Kerry, and a church that had remained through the
centuries a centre of ecclesiastical renewal and reform: it controlled a port of
international reputation. Later in the century the O'Briens were to employ the
services of a professional hagiographer, an Irishman who had studied medicine
and law on the Continent and was a supporter of the emperor Frederick Bar-
barossa; an earlier Life of St Flannán of Killaloe seems to have been written by
an Anglo-Norman cleric attached to the church of Killaloe some time before
1162.[1]

But such awareness of the affairs of the greater world proved of little help in
the long run. The O'Briens' ambitions to the monarchy of Ireland, although
politely recognised by their foreign friends, had to face the harsh realities of

[1] Donnchadh Ó Corráin, 'Foreign connections and domestic politics: Killaloe and the Uí
Briain in twelfth-century hagiography' in Dorothy Whitelock, Rosamund McKitterick, and David
Dumville, *Ireland in early medieval Europe: studies in memory of Kathleen Hughes* (Cambridge, 1982),
pp 213–31.

Irish life and the intransigence of the North. Domnall Mac Lochlainn of Ailech remained from 1083 to 1121 a rival claimant to the high-kingship. Culturally more backward, he was militarily powerful, while the barrier interposed by Ua Ruairc's kingdom of Bréifne made any southern conquest of the North very difficult. Muirchertach Ua Briain made a circuit of the North in 1101, but obtained no lasting submission. The only practical hope lay in an alliance with Ulster, but this (in conjunction with a secret agreement with Magnus Bareleg) collapsed at the battle of Mag Coba in Iveagh in 1103. When Muirchertach was felled by illness in 1114 he was deposed by his brother Diarmait. Although briefly restored, he had lost both power and prestige, and when he died at Lismore in 1119 it was the sons of his brother who succeeded him. It was Diarmait's descendants who ruled Thomond thereafter: those of Muirchertach, through his son Mathgamain, took the surname of Mac Mathgamna and later occupied the territory of Corco Baiscinn in west Clare.

But Mac Lochlainn's hopes of restoring the high-kingship to the Northern Uí Néill were shipwrecked by the unexpected volte-face of his young ally Toirrdelbach Ua Conchobair of Connacht, who first made a secret peace with Ua Briain and then in 1118 partitioned Munster between the sons of Diarmait Ua Briain and Tadg Mac Carthaig, a settlement that he forcibly reimposed in 1121 after proclaiming himself high-king of Ireland. From now onwards Munster ceased to be 'two provinces in one house' and was effectively divided between the Ua Briain kingdom of Thomond (*Tuadmuma*, 'North Munster') at Limerick and the Mac Carthaig kingdom of Desmond (*Desmuma*, 'South Munster') at Cork. There was a brief reunion in 1127 when Toirrdelbach and Conchobar Ua Briain brought Cormac Mac Carthaig out of exile in Lismore and gave him the kingship of all Munster. It was in this period of alliance that Cormac's Chapel at Cashel was built and consecrated in 1134—the first example of romanesque architecture in Ireland. Here also was written the 'Caithréim Chellacháin Chaisil', a pseudo-historical narrative of Mac Carthaig's tenth-century ancestor, which has been described as putting forward an ideal polity for twelfth-century Munster from the Mac Carthaig point of view, while showing due deference to Ua Briain claims.[1] The alliance broke down in 1135, and in 1138 Cormac was assassinated by Toirrdelbach's vassal Ua Conchobair Ciarraige.

Mac Carthaig was the leading family of the old Eóganacht Caisil, who, together with all the other branches of that dynasty throughout Munster, had been deprived of the provincial overkingship by the Dál Cais of Thomond since the days of Brian Bóruma. But even before their partial restoration to power in 1118 they seem to have moved from their ancestral lands in Tipperary towards the south and west. It is clear, though the details remain extremely obscure, that the twelfth century saw great movements of peoples and of

[1] Donnchadh Ó Corráin, 'Caithréim Chellacháin Chaisil: history or propaganda?' in *Ériu*, xxv (1974), pp 1–69.

dynastic families in Munster, culminating in the events recorded in an extraordinary entry for 1177 in the Annals of Inisfallen:

Great warfare this year between Tuadmumu and Desmumu, and from Luimnech to Corcach and from Clár Doire Mór to Cnoc Brénainn was laid waste, both church and lay property. And the Uí Meic Caille and the Uí Liatháin came into the west of Ireland, and the Eóganacht Locha Léin came as far as Férdruim in Uí Echach, the Ciarraige Luachra into Tuadmumu, and the Uí Chonaill and Uí Chairpri as far as Eóganacht Locha Léin.[1]

Certainly this process was accelerated after the arrival of the Anglo-Normans, but equally certainly it did not begin then. By the middle of the century Ua Donnchada of Cenél Lóegaire in west Cork had taken the kingship of Eóganacht Locha Léin from Ua Muirchertaig of that dynasty and tried to promote Aghadoe as a rival see to Ardfert, which lay in the territory of the hostile Ua Conchobair Ciarraige, loyal to Ua Briain.[2] Ua Caím of Eóganacht Glenndamna (Glanworth, County Cork) had occupied the lands of the subject Fir Maige Féine around Fermoy. Ua Faílbe of Corco Duibne in the Dingle and Ivereagh peninsulas of west Kerry had been expelled from his kingdom as early as the beginning of the century, but we do not know if Ua Súillebáin of the Eóganacht Caisil, a close congener of Mac Carthaig, had moved west as early as that date. Ua Donnubáin of Uí Chairpre in west Limerick ended up in the barony of Carbery in west Cork, while the king of Uí Echach Muman in 1151, Donnchadh Ua Mathgamna, was to be known as 'the wanderer around'.[3]

Catastrophic for Thomond was the battle of Móin Mór in 1151, where their forces were annihilated, with a loss of at least three thousand men, by the combined armies of Toirrdelbach Ua Conchobair and Diarmait Mac Murchada, who had come to the aid of Mac Carthaig and his vassals Ua Mathgamna, Ua Donnchada, Ua Caím, and Ua Muirchertaig.[4] Toirrdelbach Ua Briain had to flee Munster, and although he was later restored through the influence of Muirchertach Mac Lochlainn, Ua Briain power remained weak until the accession of his son Domnall Mór in 1169. Domnall Mór, a son-in-law of Diarmait Mac Murchada, rebuilt Thomond during the first generation of Anglo-Norman settlement in Munster. He used the newcomers to his own advantage, but proved able to repel their more unwelcome attentions and retained possession of his capital city of Limerick until his death in 1194. Meanwhile he had staked out claims to Greater Thomond by his charters to the Cistercians, at

[1] Luimnech = Limerick; Corcach = Cork; Clár Doire Mór, the area around Kilcooly on the Tipperary–Kilkenny border; Cnoc Brénainn = Mount Brandon in Kerry; Férdruim is unidentified, but Uí Echach was in west Cork. Uí Meic Caille was a branch of Uí Liatháin (both in east Cork), Eóganacht Locha Léin around Killarney, Ciarraige Luachra in north Kerry, and Uí Chonaill and Uí Chairpri in west Limerick.

[2] Misc. Ir. Annals, 1158. 6 (p. 40).

[3] Ó Corráin, 'Caithréim Chellacháin Chaisil', p. 67.

[4] Misc. Ir. Annals, 1151. 3 (p. 32); A.F.M. states that 7,000 Munstermen were lost, while Ann. Tig. is content with the more poetical estimate that the slain were as many as the sands of the sea and the stars of the sky.

Holy Cross in the centre of Eóganacht Caisil, at Kilcooley in Clár Doire Móir on the border with Osraige, south on the Suir at Inislounaght, and north on the border with the petty state of Corco Mruad, ruled by Ua Lochlainn and Ua Conchobair, which had obtained ecclesiastical independence from his own diocese of Killaloe in 1152.

The effects of the O'Brien defeat at Móin Mór were seen in the diocesan arrangements made at the synod of Kells-Mellifont in the following year. The ancient kingdom of Éile in north Tipperary and southern Offaly raised its own see at Roscrea, but was unable to uphold it for long when O'Brien strength restored the area to Killaloe: the Ua Cennétig family, cousins of the O'Briens, had long since established themselves east of Lough Derg in the old lands of Múscraige Tíre around Nenagh. Similarly, another ancient people, the Déise Muman, established a see at Ardmore, church of their patron St Declan, at the expense of Lismore, whose abbots in previous centuries had always been drawn from the faraway Ciarraige Luachra, and which the Déise felt to be a stronghold of the rival imperial ambitions of both Ua Briain and Mac Carthaig (the latter had a residence in the city). We do not know the proposed extent of the new diocese, but it did not survive the opening years of the thirteenth century.

More successful were the Corco Loígde, the small kingdom of the seafaring Ua hEitirsceóil and Ua Cobthaig: they obtained the diocese of Ross. The reasoning behind the establishment of Cloyne, comprising the territories of Uí Liatháin, Fir Maige Féine, and others, and formed at the expense of Lismore, Emly, and Cork is more obscure: perhaps it was to provide the Mac Carthaig province of Desmond with two dioceses (Cork and Cloyne) totally under the control of the dynasty and its most loyal vassals—for the metropolitan see of Cashel, although in Mac Carthaig homelands (the site had been shrewdly alienated to the church by Muirchertach Ua Briain in 1101) remained under heavy Dál Cais influence, and Emly was insignificant, a mere sop to Eóganacht sensibilities. Ua Briain had his home diocese of Killaloe together with a vassal diocese of Limerick, just as Mac Murchada had his diocese of Ferns flanked by Leighlin, a conglomeration of minor kingdoms under Uí Chennselaig sway, and Ua Conchobair had the metropolitan see at Tuam backed by the diocese of Roscommon–Elphin controlled by his Síl Muiredaig clergy under Ua Dubthaig.[1] Hostility to Ua Briain thus led to attacks on the status of Limerick: an attempt to establish a see at Mungret (in whose interests it is not clear) came to nothing, but Inis Cathaig (Scattery Island) on the Shannon estuary enjoyed a brief existence as a joint diocese for the Uí Fidgente of west Limerick and Ua Domnaill of Corco Baiscinn in west Clare.

A prominent feature both in the annalistic record and in the 'Caithréim Chellacháin Chaisil' is naval warfare conducted by the maritime vassals of both Ua Briain and Mac Carthaig. These were native fleets, unlike those of the

[1] I owe these observations to Breandán Ó Ciobháin of the Ordnance Survey Office, Dublin.

Waterford and Cork Norse—the Norse of Limerick, strangely enough, do not appear to have been active in this regard. The forces of Corco Mruad, Corco Baiscinn, Ua Ségda and Ua Faílbe of Corco Duibne, and the Corco Loígde all appear in the muster rolls, and most important was Ua Conchobair Ciarraige, who in 1151 performed the remarkable feat of bringing 'seven ships on wheels from Eas Duibhe [near Ballylongford] to Loch Léin'.[1] Toirrdelbach Ua Conchobair too made extensive use of fleets from Connacht in his numerous Munster campaigns.

Despite the confusing migrations of the Eóganacht dynasties of Desmond in these years, two large sub-kingdoms in Munster remained surprisingly stable within the bounds that they had occupied since the dawn of Irish history. These were the above-mentioned Déise under Ua Bric and Ua Fáeláin, whose lands covered all of County Waterford together with an extension northward into Tipperary (Uí Fothaid), and the Éile under Ua Cerbaill in the north and Ua Fócarta in the south. A smaller group, the Arada Cliach, who claimed Leinster ancestry, also kept their hold on the borders of Limerick and Tipperary under the families of Ua Máel Riain and Ua Duibir. The Éile retained their lordships into the sixteenth century, like the neighbouring Dál Cais dynasty Ua Cennétig of Ormond under the sometimes nominal control of the earls of Ormond, but much of Déise passed into the hands of the Breton family of le Poer. Ua Conchobair Ciarraige was confined to a very much reduced territory under the earls of Desmond.

All the others, including the Eóganacht families of Ua Cellacháin, Ua Súillebáin, Ua Mathgamna, and Ua Donnchada, were consolidated in the south-west under the strong and relatively stable overlordship of Mac Carthaig Mór. Retrenched into a smaller Thomond the O'Briens were true to their family tradition and proved themselves resilient and at times innovative. They kept their grip on a strong kingdom with the help of vassals such as the distantly related Dál Cais family of Mac Con Mara in central Clare, and their cousins Mac Mathgamna, who had displaced Ua Domnaill of Corco Baiscinn; they extended their overlordship over Corco Mruad in the north-west and exercised control over the Aran Islands for the benefit of the citizens of Galway, protecting them against the incursions of Ua Flaithbertaig and other marauders from Connemara.

CONNACHT too had seen great changes, but they were constructive rather than chaotic. They were the result of a deliberate policy of Toirrdelbach Ua Conchobair, whose failure to retain an effectual high-kingship of all Ireland has blinded historians to his real achievements.[2] During his fifty-year reign from 1106 to 1156 he transformed the face of Connacht. He carved out a central

[1] *Misc. Ir. Annals*, 1151. 3 (p. 35).
[2] For his career see John Ryan, *Toirdelbach Ó Conchubair (1088—1156)* (Dublin, 1966; O'Donnell Lectures X).

territory divorced from ancient tribal boundaries, and moved his dynasty and that of his ecclesiastical allies, the Ua Dubthaig family of Roscommon, from their ancestral lands of Síl Muiredaig into the plains of Mag Seóla, from which the rival dynasty of Ua Flaithbertaig had been expelled into Iarchonnacht west of Lough Corrib. He set up his capital at Dunmore with an archiepiscopal see at Tuam. Metropolitan status was finally accorded to Tuam in 1152 in recognition of Ua Conchobair's high-kingship, but it may have been claimed as early as 1123, when he commissioned the processional Cross of Cong, and it seems that the pretensions of Tuam occasioned unpleasantness at the consecration of Cormac's Chapel at Cashel in 1134.[1]

Ua Conchobair's new kingdom was encircled with castles at Dunmore, at the strategic gap of Collooney in Sligo, at Galway, at Athlone, and at Ballinasloe. Thus he displayed innovating tendencies that have too long been ignored. He also strengthened his borders by the building of bridges across the Shannon and by engineering works diverting the course of the river Suck—probably against the potentially hostile Ua Cellaig of Uí Maine.

In the previous two generations the tight monopoly that the Ua Conchobair family had established over the provincial high-kingship had been challenged by other dynasts of Uí Briúin: Ua Flaithbertaig and Ua Ruairc. In 1093 Muirchertach Ua Briain had actually expropriated the Síl Muiredaig and given their patrimony to Ua hEidin, the petty king of Uí Fiachrach Aidne (diocese of Kilmacduagh); he represented a Connacht dynasty long excluded from the over-kingship of the province, but a friend of Dál Cais interests in southern Connacht. Two years later Muirchertach again expelled the Síl Muiredaig into the badlands of Bréifne, and gave the kingship to the more powerful Domnall Ua Ruairc, who proved too strong to remain a puppet of Munster. By the twelfth century Ua Flaithbertaig had resigned himself to acting as one of Ua Conchobair's admirals on the Atlantic coast, while Ua Ruairc had consoled himself for his losses in Connacht proper by expansion into Tethba and Meath. This extension of the province was to prove ambiguous, as Ua Ruairc became an overmighty vassal potentially as dangerous to his overlord as to his enemies.

Ua Máille of Fir Umaill, in west Mayo, and Ua hAinglide of Cenél nDobtha, on the Roscommon banks of the Shannon, acted as admirals on the ocean and inland; they had been accorded affiliations, most unconvincingly, to the Uí Briúin, but such genealogical promotion was an accepted record of political alliance. More distantly related to the Uí Briúin were the Uí Fiachrach in two branches, north and south, the latter ruled by Ua hEidin and Ua Sechnussaig around Kilmacduagh, and the former, the Uí Fiachrach Muaide under Ua Dubda, also an admiral, ruling an extensive territory represented by the diocese of Killala; after the establishment of the lordship of MacWilliam Burke, Ua Dubda retained lordship of Tireragh east of the Moy estuary.

[1] *Ann. Tig.*, 1134, 1135.

The Uí Briúin Aí of Mag nAí around the ancient capital of Cruachu in Roscommon had established their hegemony over all Connacht in the eighth century, and had since then proliferated into many septs and families, chief among which were the Síl Muiredaig from whom sprang Ua Conchobair himself.[1] Among his relations and allies were Ua Fínnachta of Clann Chonnmaig, across the Suck from Mag nAí in Galway, Ua Fallomain of Clann Uatach in the barony of Athlone, Ua Raduib (later surnamed Mac Airechtaig) of Clann Tommaltaig near Cruachu itself, Ua Flannacáin of Clann Chathail in Elphin, Ua Flainn of Síl Máel Ruain in west Roscommon, and Ua Taidg *in teglaig*, 'of the household', chief marshal to Ua Conchobair. Most prominent of all these was Ua Máel Ruanaid (Mac Diarmata as he was later known), king of Mag Luirg in the plains of Boyle. In the later middle ages this lord was to become the effective king-maker in the rivalries between the Ua Conchobair princes. By the fourteenth century a junior branch, taking the name Mac Donnchada, had set up an independent lordship of Tír Ailella (Tirerill) in south Sligo.

Ancient tribal kings unrelated to the major dynasties survived in outlying areas, such as Ua Cadla and Ua Cadain of Conmaicne Mara in Connemara. The most tenacious were the Gailenga and Luigne of the Sligo–Mayo border, who claimed kinship with the like-named groups in Meath: they were ruled by Ua hEgra and Ua Gadra, and were accorded their own diocese of Achonry.

Also unrelated to the Connachta proper, but maintaining throughout the centuries a powerful overkingdom extending over the whole south-east, were the Uí Maine. Their kingship had since the end of the tenth century been held by Ua Cellaig, while a sub-kingdom of Síl nAnmchada to the south was ruled by Ua Matudáin.[2] By the twelfth century Ua Conchobair had confined them within the bounds of the diocese then assigned to them—that of Clonfert; but in the fourteenth, although they had lost western territory to Burke of Clanricard, they regained ancestral lands in southern Roscommon and they prospered into the Elizabethan era.

The rise of Connacht to be a major national power in the twelfth century under Toirrdelbach Ua Conchobair was one of the greatest surprises in Irish history: hitherto the province had been something of a backwater in Irish politics, but the event had been foreshadowed by the expansion of Bréifne since the late tenth century. Both phenomena can hardly be accounted for except on the supposition that Ireland did indeed share in the population explosion that affected all western Europe in the eleventh century, of which the Norman expansion was itself a result. The view commonly held[3] that Ireland was underpopulated before the arrival of the Anglo-Normans does not seem to be well-founded, and the subject demands much more serious investigation than it has hitherto received. Apart from the numerous and varied population groups, the

---

[1] Byrne, *Ir. kings*, pp 248–53.
[2] J. V. Kelleher, 'Uí Maine in the annals and genealogies to 1225', in *Celtica*, ix (1971), pp 61–112.
[3] See Smyth, *Celtic Leinster*, pp 4–5, 56–8.

size of the armies that the provincial kings were able to put into the field and maintain for many months, and the resources that they drew upon for their other military and building operations, we must also take into consideration the population of the urban and proto-urban centres, both Hiberno-Norse and native monastic. We know from the annals that major sites such as Armagh, Derry, Clonmacnoise, and Duleek contained a hundred houses or more, and it has been estimated that as early as the tenth century Kells was as large as contemporary Rouen.[1]

The foundations of power laid by Toirrdelbach Ua Conchobair were to prove effective until 1224. His youngest son, Cathal Crobderg, had difficulty in obtaining the kingship against his great-nephew Cathal Carrach; both sought and found help from Anglo-Norman allies, official and unofficial, but Crobderg was able through his own military ability, combined with shrewd diplomatic deals with the English royal authorities as well as with the papacy, to preserve the integrity of his kingdom until his death. He patronised ecclesiastical architecture in the new Anglo-French transitional style throughout Connacht, which was differentiated from the Anglo-Welsh style characteristic of the colonial areas of southern and eastern Ireland.[2]

Two impressive bardic poems hailed Cathal Crobderg as the hero-king of prophecy and as the restorer of the high-kingship of Ireland now that the Uí Néill 'salmon' had been displaced from the pool of sovereignty by the invasion of foreign 'coarse fish'.[3] But after the de Burgh conquest of Connacht the O'Connors were increasingly reduced to their Síl Muiredaig homelands in Roscommon. Here, confined like rats in a cage, they exhausted their resources in fierce internecine feuds over their increasingly unreal claim to the kingship of Connacht. One branch, the Clann Muirchertaig, were expelled into Bréifne, where they contended with the O'Rourkes, only eventually to disappear from history. Another, more fortunate, were to establish themselves in the ancient Uí Néill kingdom of Cairpre in north Sligo and claimed overlordship over all Lower Connacht.

The O'Rourke kingship over Uí Briúin Bréifne and Conmaicne collapsed after the killing of Tigernán at the hands of de Lacy's men in 1173. His conquests in Meath were lost, and his see at Kells extinguished, absorbed into the Anglo-Norman diocese of Meath (Tír Briúin was to remain without a see until the establishment of Kilmore in 1453). Ua Ragallaig asserted his independence in east Bréifne, as did Mac Ragnaill of Muintir Eólais and Ua Fergail of Angaile in Longford, while between the rival lordships of Ua Ruairc and Ua Ragallaig were interposed in County Cavan the minor Bréifne territories of Tellach nEchach (Tullyhaw) under Mac Samradáin and of Tellach

[1] Françoise Henry, *Irish art during the viking invasions* (London, 1967), p. 43.

[2] Cf. below, p. 744.

[3] 'Táinig an Croibhdhearg go Cruachain', ed. and trans. E. C. Quiggin in *Miscellany presented to Kuno Meyer* (Halle, 1912), pp 167–77; 'Tairnic in selsa ac Síl Néill', ed. and trans. Brian Ó Cuív in *Ériu*, xxxiv (1983), pp 157–74 (see below, p. 689).

nDúnchada (Tullyhunco) under Mac Tigernáin. In a desperate attempt to save his far northern territory of Cairpre from the encroachments of Cenél Conaill, Áed Ua Ruairc had in 1187 invited Anglo-Normans from Meath to pillage Drumcliffe, but to no avail. Even earlier, in 1185, his enemy Flaithbertach Ua Máel Doraid of Cenél Conaill was himself campaigning on Lower Lough Erne with 'English' mercenaries.[1] For Norman, or perhaps more correctly Fleming and Brabantine, mercenaries, brought over by Prince John and left unpaid, proved only too ready to fight for Irish masters.[2] The annals for the last two decades of the twelfth century have many references to such *seirsennaig* (sergeants, *servientes*) on active service in Connacht and elsewhere.[3]

STRESS has been laid in this chapter on the changes that characterised the politics of the period. But it must be admitted that atavistic tribal feeling was strong enough to hinder the modernisation of Irish society and to render the transition period peculiarly violent. Tendencies to filiogeniture in succession to kingship never overcame the claims of other members of the royal kin. While these claims ensured the succession of the most able representative of a dynasty and thus held certain attractions against the feudal system, which could entrust a lordship to an imbecile or minor, or lead to partible inheritance among heiresses and their often absentee husbands, they remained the bane of the native Irish polity to the end of the sixteenth century. The high-kingship of Ireland was open to all comers, and can more fittingly be compared to the German imperial succession than to the monarchies of England and France, though it must be remembered that even in those countries primogeniture had not yet been established as a *de jure* principle.

Within Ireland itself there were marked regional differences. Beside the ancient provinces there was recognised a division between north and south—Leth Cuinn and Leth Moga—roughly marked by a line from Dublin to Galway Bay. With some reservations we can see the distinction as still holding good in the twelfth century. It is remarkable that no Hiberno-Norse towns grew up north of Dublin on the east coast or of Limerick on the west.

Sizeable Norse bases had existed in the northern half in the ninth and tenth centuries—at Annagassan in Louth, at Carlingford, at Strangford Lough, and on Lough Neagh. With the exception of Ulfreksfjord at Larne, which was a significant port, these all disappeared—destroyed by the combined efforts of the otherwise mutually hostile Northern Uí Néill and Ulaid, or merged into the native population: vikings on Loughs Swilly and Foyle had married into the Cenél nEógain. Paradoxically the military success of the northerners was later

---

[1] *Misc. Ir. Annals*, 1185. 3 (p. 72).

[2] *Gesta Regis Henrici secundi Benedicti Abbatis: the chronicle . . . of Benedict of Peterborough*, ed. William Stubbs (2 vols, London, 1867), i, 339; Roger de Hoveden, *Chronica Magistri Rogeri de Houedene*, ed. William Stubbs (4 vols, London, 1868–71), ii, 304–5; Giraldus, *Expugnatio*, p. 356, n. 492.

[3] e.g. *Ann. Inisf.*, 1196; *A.L.C.*, 1187, 1199, 1200, 1201, 1204, 1208.

to deprive them of the economic benefits that accrued to Leth Moga from the presence of prosperous towns that no longer posed a political threat.

The O'Briens in their heyday, controlling all of these directly or indirectly, were the great modernisers of their time. They threw their whole weight behind the Gregorian reforms in return for international recognition of their high-kingship. The north was able to prevent the realisation of their ambitions, but, though powerful, remained archaic. Even in military matters it was conservative. The Ulaid had once commanded an impressive fleet, which defeated the Dubliners in 1022, but we hear no more of it after 1045, while in 1154 Muirchertach Mac Lochlainn had to hire a Hebridean naval force in an unsuccessful attempt to defend Inishowen against the Connacht ships of Ua Conchobair led by Ua Dubda.

The north was also slow to accept ecclesiastical innovation: there is little sign that the diocesan scheme proposed for that region at the synod of Ráith Bressail in 1111 was ever implemented, and the difficulties that St Malachy encountered in obtaining possession of the primatial see are well known. There were of course individual exceptions—St Malachy himself, his mentor Archbishop Cellach, and his tutor Ímar Ua hÁedacáin, founder of the first Irish Augustinian house in 1126. In the 1150s and 1160s Flaithbertach Ua Brolcháin of Derry led a remarkable attempt to reform the native Columban churches in line with, or in opposition to, the organisation of the new orders imported from abroad. The first Savigniac monastery in Ireland was founded in Ulster in 1127 when Malachy was bishop of Down and Connor, but that very year saw an invasion of the province by Conchobar Mac Lochlainn that forced Malachy to flee south to Lismore, where he gained the friendship of Cormac Mac Carthaig and of the Ua Briain brothers, which eventually won him election to Armagh. The only northern king to lend whole-hearted support to the reformers was the most southerly of them, Donnchad Ua Cerbaill of Airgialla. The high-king, Toirrdelbach Ua Conchobair, took very little interest in the whole affair of the Armagh succession between 1129 and 1136—a lack of concern that is reflected in his court chronicle, the so-called Annals of Tigernach.

Ua Conchobair fittingly enough occupies a half-way house between the tendencies of north and south. We have seen the innovations that he introduced into the politics and military affairs of Connacht, but we have also noted his failure to appreciate the crucial importance of Dublin and of the other Hiberno-Norse towns. In ecclesiastical affairs his lavish gifts to Clonmacnoise and his generous endowments of Roscommon and Tuam seem motivated more by a desire for political prestige and the display of imperial munificence than by any appreciation of religious feeling. With the exception of the saintly Áed Ua hOissín of Tuam, the Síl Muiredaig clergy apparently regarded the adoption of episcopal organisation as a means of strengthening their own hereditary position. The see of Mayo (abolished by the Ulsterman Felix Ua Ruanada when he became archbishop of Tuam in 1202) had probably been created to ensure a permanent Ua Dubthaig succession to Tuam. Not of course that the O'Briens had been innocent of political intent, but they were more subtle, and their Dál Cais clergy included men who had a genuine understanding of the implications of church reform.

That so many modern historians have been misled into seeing twelfth-century Irish society as archaic and tribal is all the more understandable since that is the very picture assiduously presented to us by the bulk of Middle Irish sources. The privileged 'men of art' (*áes dána*) had a vested interest in archaism; the brehons preserved (and were to do so into the sixteenth century) law texts detailing customs and rituals that had been obsolete for centuries; and Irish literature was obsessed by 'the backward look'.

Yet even here the growth in popularity of sagas and ballads about the warrior-hunter Fianna can be seen as illustrating a nostalgia for a way of life long vanished, while the appearance of ballad narrative was an innovation which reflects the growth of a similar phenomenon throughout Europe. Even the most apparently archaising of Irish texts, the 'Lebor Gabála', the pseudo-history of ancient Ireland, which was elaborated in the eleventh and twelfth centuries from eighth-century prototypes, has its parallel in the legend of Charlemagne on the Continent and in the Arthurian romances, in the history of the kings of Britain by Geoffrey of Monmouth, which legitimised the Norman conquest as a re-establishment of the ancient British (and Breton) monarchy against the Anglo-Saxon invaders from Germany, as well as in the prophecies of Merlin that so intrigued Giraldus Cambrensis.

A new literary genre also appeared which showed awareness of the social changes of the time; this was the poem of prophecy, forecasting doom and lamenting the ills of society: 'bad brotherhood within the *túath*, iniquitous law and great arrogance in kings; ... the needy transitory king will subdue the miserable husbandman; ... many judges without justice, sovranty destroyed by base kindreds'.[1] And at least one of the twelfth-century litterati, Gilla in Choimded Ua Cormaic, in a poem preserved in the Book of Leinster quite frankly describes the official genealogical tradition:

> Six ways there are of special note that confound the tree of genealogy:
> intrusion of base stocks usurping the place of free stocks by name;
> migration of serfs, a way of shame; and decay of lords;
> withering of the free races, dreadful horror; with overgrowth of the vassal folks;
> miswriting, in the guise of learning, by the unlearned of evil intent,
> or the learned themselves, no whit better, who falsify the record for lucre.[2]

In contrast to the overwhelming bulk of material contained in the great Middle Irish codices ('Lebor na hUidre', Rawlinson B 502, and the Book of

---

[1] Eleanor Knott, 'A poem of prophecies' in *Ériu*, xviii (1958), pp 55–84; see Donncha[dh] Ó Corráin, *Ireland before the Normans* (Dublin and London, 1972), p. 172.

[2] Eoin MacNeill, 'Early Irish population-groups' in *R.I.A. Proc.*, xxix (1911), sect. C, p. 93.

Leinster) stand some pieces of evidence to show that the new learning of the continental schools was also being taught in Ireland.

Lismore, as has been noted, had always been a centre of ecclesiastical renewal, and here we have clear examples of scholastic disputation. Here in 1121 were being written the Annals of Inisfallen, and an entry for that year in the language of the schools displays acquaintance with theological hair-splitting: Toirrdelbach Ua Conchobair had plundered Lismore this year, but the men of Desmond had 'at the instigation of the Lord and for the honour of its saints' slain two leaders of the Connacht host, Ua Flaithbertaig and Ua hEidin. The difficulty was that this had preceded the actual attack on the church. 'But if any objector should be found to say "Never has God punished a sin before it was committed," it shall be replied to him that it were not extraordinary if God, to whom all time is present, should avenge a wrong done to his Church before it was committed.'[1] At Lismore too St Malachy had between 1140 and 1148 encountered a cleric who disputed with considerable learning on behalf of the heresy of Berengar of Tours concerning the eucharist. Perhaps to this same cleric was addressed a lengthy poem in Middle Irish by Échtgus Ua Cuanáin setting forth the orthodox doctrine. The author may have been the bishop of Roscrea who died in 1161.[2]

From Glendalough there survive fragments of a schoolbook written in 1106 containing the 'De abaco' of Gerbert of Aurillac, which first introduced arabic numerals to the west.[3] A twelfth-century manuscript of Gregory the Great's 'Moralia in Iob' written at Armagh has arabic signatures to its quires.[4] Also possibly from Glendalough comes a copy of Chalcidius' translation of Plato's 'Timaeus', a favourite text in the early twelfth-century schools; it has been extensively corrected by a later scribe from a better exemplar. Bound together with this is an epitome of the 'Periphyseon' of Johannes Eriugena.[5] A twelfth-century Irish copy of Boethius' 'De consolatione philosophiae' also exists.[6] It was most probably at Glendalough that Bishop Sulien of St David's had studied, and at the turn of the eleventh and twelfth centuries a respectable school of Latin poetry flourished under his sons at Llanbadarn Fawr.[7] Here too was studied and glossed a text of Macrobius, whose name was adopted by a later bishop of Glendalough.[8]

[1] *Ann. Inisf.*, p. 280: 'Sed si quis abstinator inuentus fuisset et dicat, "Nunquam Deus uindicauit peccatum antequam factum fuisset," respondebitur ei quod nec mirum sit, si Deus cui omne tempus praesens sit, iniuriam Aeclesiae suae antequam facta fuisset uindicaret.'
[2] Gerard Murphy, 'Eleventh or twelfth century Irish doctrine concerning the real presence' in *Med. studies presented to A. Gwynn*, pp 10–28.
[3] B.L., Eg. MS 3323, ff 16, 18.   [4] Bodl., Laud MS Misc. 460.
[5] Bodl., Auct. MS F.3.15; possibly from Newry or Saul.
[6] Florence, Biblioteca Laurenziana, MS Plut. 78 19.
[7] Michael Lapidge, 'The Welsh-Latin poetry of Sulien's family' in *Studia Celt.*, viii–ix (1973–4), pp 68–106.
[8] Alison Peden, 'Science and philosophy in Wales at the time of the Norman conquest: a Macrobius manuscript from Llanbadarn' in *Cambridge Medieval Celtic Studies*, no. 2 (winter 1981), pp 21–45.

Even the growth of an embryonic university at Armagh is suggested by the decree of the synod of Clane in 1162 that no one but an alumnus of Armagh should hold the office of lector (*fer léigind*) in any church in Ireland, followed as it was by the endowment by the high-king Ruaidrí Ua Conchobair in 1169 of ten cows yearly to the lector of Armagh for teaching students from Ireland and Scotland.[1] The lector in question was Flann or Florinnt Ua Gormáin, who died in 1174 after twenty years 'directing the schools of Ireland' and who had spent twenty-one years studying in France and England.[2] He was most probably a relative of St Malachy (whose father had held the same office), as were Máel Cóemgin Ua Gormáin, abbot of the Augustinian house at Termonfeckin (d. 1164), Máel Muire Ua Gormáin, Augustinian abbot of Knock beside Louth, author of a metrical martyrology (d. 1181), and Bishop Finn of Kildare, who died in 1160 and had been first Cistercian abbot of Newry. The latter was perhaps not the Bishop Finn who collaborated with Áed Mac Crimthainn in the compilation of the Book of Leinster; this antiquarian literary dilletante is more probably to be identified with his predecessor in the see, Finn Ua Cianáin. In the fourteenth century the tradition of the twelfth-century codices was picked up again by Ádhamh Ó Cianáin in Connacht.

But in one major respect twelfth-century Irish society remained archaic, and in the eyes of foreign ecclesiastics barbarous—that of marriage customs. Irish dynasts married early and often, and concepts of illegitimacy were vague. Four marriages in a lifetime were the norm, for divorce was easy for both parties, and marriage alliances were part of the political game. This problem (from the point of view of the canon lawyers) was to be intractable until the end of the Gaelic polity in the early seventeenth century. When Lanfranc, archbishop of Canterbury, wrote to Toirrdelbach ua Briain in 1074 it was on sexual laxity that he fixed as the most characteristic shortcoming of the Irish, and when Muirchertach Ua Briain held the first synod of Cashel in 1101 it was laid down that no man should marry his niece, half-sister, stepmother, or any so near akin. Lanfranc had complained that the Irish were said to put away their wives lightly and even to barter them in the open market. As the tide of reform swept through western Europe and canon law was more strictly applied to clergy and laity alike, Irish conservatism met with little tolerance. Phrases such as 'bestiality', 'abominable filthiness', 'barbarous and uncultivated ignorance of the divine law', 'Christians in name, in reality pagans', became commonplace in ecclesiastical censures, and were often justified by attestation from leading Irish churchmen. When Pope Alexander III wrote to Henry II in 1172 giving formal approval to his claim to the lordship of Ireland, he cited the letters of the Irish hierarchy to the effect that men were not ashamed to marry and beget sons

[1] *A.U.*, 1162: 'na badh ferleighind i cill i n-Erinn nech acht dalta Aird-Macha'. *A.U.*, 1169: 'dorat Ruaidhri hUa Concobair, rí Erenn, deich m-bú cecha bliadhna uad féin 7 o cach righ i n-a dhegaidh co brath do ferleiginn Aird-Macha, i n-onoir Patraic, ar leighinn do dhenamh do macaibh leighinn Erenn & Alban'.

[2] *A.U.*, 1174: 'fiche bliadhain ic follamhnughadh scol n-Erenn'.

on their stepmothers, that a man would cohabit with his sister-in-law in his brother's lifetime, that one man would keep two sisters as concubines, and that many, abandoning the mothers, would take their daughters. A notorious example that would certainly have come to the pope's notice was provided by the killing in 1171 of Magnus Mac Duinn Sléibe, king of Ulster (the same who had the previous year expelled the canons of Saul), by his brother Donn Sléibe: Magnus, says the annalist, had abandoned his own married wife, abducted the wife of his foster-father, Cú Maige Ua Flainn of Uí Thuirtre (she had previously been married to his late brother, Áed), and had raped the wife of his other brother and immediate predecessor, Eochaid.[1] It is clear, however, that such conduct was not approved of even by the lax public opinion of the day.

It may appear odd that the monarch who was given the papal mission to reform the 'barbarous enormities' of the Irish in these and other matters should have been Henry II of England, himself under the cloud of international disapproval for the murder of Archbishop Thomas Becket, and married to Eleanor of Aquitaine, the divorced wife of Louis VII of France. And it has seemed disgraceful to generations of patriotic Irishmen that the clergy should with such equanimity have concurred in the denigration of their country and have accepted so unlikely a reformer. Suffice it to say that their concern for the welfare of the Irish people and of the Irish church (only recently accorded papal recognition as a national institution at the synod of Kells–Mellifont in 1152) did not necessarily make them enamoured of the current state of Irish society and politics; that Alexander III was an experienced statesman and a realist who did not expect kings to be perfect; and that the arrival of Henry II was not unwelcome to many of the Irish kings themselves. He would, they hoped, curb the excesses of the first Cambro-Norman adventurers, and as FitzEmpress, *mac na Peirise*, he was accorded the deference which the Irish had for long theoretically regarded as the due of the emperor as *rí in domain*—king of the world.[2]

---

[1] *A.U.*, 1171.

[2] Cf. *A.U.*, 1023 (*recte* 1024) recording the death of the emperor Henry II and the accession of Conrad: 'Oenreicc, ri in domain do ecaibh in pace. Tara eisi ro gabh Cuana righe in domain.'

CHAPTER II

Diarmait Mac Murchada and the coming of the Anglo-Normans

F. X. MARTIN

FEW events in Irish history have been so consistently misrepresented as the coming of the Anglo-Normans to the country. Irish nationalist and British historians, with rare unanimity, agree in describing the event as 'the Norman invasion of Ireland'. In fact, the Anglo-Normans came not as invaders but by invitation.

The misrepresentation is due to two very different arguments. The Irish nationalist historian sees the Anglo-Normans as the second wave of invaders who have, over the centuries, attempted to subdue the country by force and without any legitimate title to be in Ireland. The vikings are regarded as the first real body of invaders, but are dismissed as peripheral to the development of the country, as a negative, even a destructive, force, and as making no lasting contribution to the cultural, social, and political Gaelic world into which they had so brutally intruded. This is a nationalist myth which conveniently overlooks the previous massive invasion by the Celts and disregards the positive stimulus which the vikings and their Hiberno-Norse descendants made to almost every aspect of Irish society. As we shall see later, the Norsemen were paradoxically one of the few formidable forces which threatened the initial success of the Anglo-Normans in Ireland.

The Irish nationalist theory about the Anglo-Normans recounts a harrowing story of Irish tribulations, beginning with the vikings in the ninth century, continuing with the Anglo-Normans in the eleventh and twelfth centuries, followed by a steady stream of grasping English officials in late medieval times, by waves of adventurers during the reigns of Henry VIII, Mary, Elizabeth, James I, and Charles I, culminating in the Cromwellian and Williamite confiscations, and finalised in the eighteenth century with the rule of the Anglo-Irish 'protestant nation'. Within that comprehensive interpretation of seven hundred years of Irish history, the Anglo-Normans are given a key role and are granted the dubious credit of having introduced in the twelfth century that pervasive system of control, styled 'feudalism', the downfall of which was finally achieved only in the early twentieth century with the re-emergence of the true Irish nation, Gaelic, catholic, and democratic.[1]

The other argument supporting the concept of a 'Norman invasion of Ireland' is based on a false analogy with the Norman invasion of England in 1066.[2] The invasion of England was planned and executed on a grand, almost grandiose, scale. The preparations were public knowledge. Apart from summoning his own feudal host, Duke William of Normandy openly recruited mercenaries from other parts of France, Germany, and elsewhere in Europe. Though his claim to the throne of England was difficult to sustain, when his ships sailed confidently across the Channel they had behind them the almighty wind of papal approval as expressed by Alexander II. With his army on English soil, William's victories were quick, decisive, and initially followed by a rule of some magnanimity. Then the revolts of the northern earls, Edwin and Morcar, in 1069, supported by a two-pronged thrust from an overseas force of vikings and from Welsh allies who surged across Offa's dyke, afforded William the opportunity to show his true form. The 'harrying of the north' followed, and there was a final end to the Danelaw. The barons' rebellion of 1075 gave him his ultimate justification for eliminating all opposition. Domesday Book is the most eloquent commentary on how complete was his success. Thereafter, the Norman conquest was ruthless, systematic, and thorough.

It was quite otherwise in Ireland. There was no intrusion or intervention on such a scale, or of such a nature, as to merit it being described as 'invasion'. Nor was there a conquest. That was not achieved by England until 1603. The first Anglo-Normans who went to Ireland in 1169 were mainly small family groups. They were not mere freebooters, as had been their Norman cousins in Italy and Sicily in the previous century. They arrived in Ireland as allies of a deposed king, Diarmait Mac Murchada, and were shortly to become allies of another more powerful ruler, Domnall Mór Ua Briain of Thomond. Even with the arrival of Strongbow and his men in 1170, the Normans in Ireland could still be described as an auxiliary force, to restore a displaced local king. But in Mac Murchada's overall plan there was, by Irish standards, a startling innova-

[1] It is significant that Michael Davitt dedicated his major work, *The fall of feudalism in Ireland: the story of the land league revolution* (London and New York, 1904), to 'the Celtic peasantry of Ireland and their kinsfolk beyond the seas'.

[2] Owing to a mistaken analogy with William the Conqueror's invasion of England in 1066, historians of late twelfth-century Ireland (e.g. Orpen, MacNeill, Curtis, Gwynn, Otway-Ruthven, Richard Roche, Lydon, and Michael Dolley) have accepted 'invasion' as the description for the coming of the Anglo-Normans to Ireland. I did so myself at one time, e.g. 'The Anglo-Norman invasion, 1169–c.1300' in T. W. Moody and F. X. Martin (ed.), *The course of Irish history* (Cork, 1967), pp 123–43, and 'Gerald of Wales, Norman reporter on Ireland' in *Studies*, lviii (1969), pp 279–92; but in 'The first Normans in Munster' in *Cork Hist. Soc. Jn.*, lxxvi (1971), pp 54–5, I began to question the accuracy of describing the first Anglo-Normans as invaders, and developed the argument in *No hero in the house* (see above, p. xlix, n. 1). In a revised and enlarged edition of *The course of Irish history* (Cork, 1984) I have modified my treatment of the subject, altering the title of my chapter to 'Diarmait Mac Murchada and the coming of the Normans'.

tion with his decision that Strongbow should succeed him as king of Leinster and should have his daughter Aífe in marriage. Another essential part of that plan was the decision to grant large strategic areas to the incoming knights, who were to settle permanently in the country as committed allies guaranteeing Mac Murchada's rule and Strongbow's succession. Nor should the advent of Henry II and his intimidating army in 1171 be regarded as a 'Norman invasion'. His main purpose, as we shall see later, was to curb his overmighty Anglo-Norman subjects in Ireland, as he had done in his other dominions. He was, if anything, an ally of the native Irish rulers. They were quick to see this fact and take advantage of it.

The pioneer Anglo-Normans in Ireland, while determined to fulfil their promises to assist Mac Murchada, were well aware that a favourable turn of the wheel of fortune could lift them to a controlling position. Historians have not taken due note of a passage, written by Gerald of Wales (Giraldus Cambrensis), which he puts into the mouth of Robert fitz Stephen, leader of the first contingent of Anglo-Normans. Fitz Stephen is exhorting his troops, who after taking Wexford town in August 1169 have joined forces with Diarmait Mac Murchada, but are facing an exuberant army of Gaelic Irish as well as Dublin Norsemen. In the course of his speech, fitz Stephen declares:

It is not, then, greed for monetary rewards or the 'blind craving for gold' that has brought us to these parts, but a gift of lands and cities in perpetuity to us and to our children. So we do not come here as pirates or robbers. We are restoring the fortunes of this honourable man [Diarmait Mac Murchada], our excellent and generous benefactor, who has been cheated by the treachery of his own people. . . . This man loves our race, he is encouraging our race to come here, and has decided to settle them in this island and give them permanent roots here. Perhaps the outcome of this present action will be that the five divisions of the island will be reduced to one, and sovereignty over the whole kingdom will devolve upon our race for the future.[1]

Gerald of Wales was undoubtedly idealising the motives of his brothers and cousins, but was also presenting an accurate record of how the first Anglo-Normans in Ireland looked on their prospects in the country.

The views of Irish and English historians have inevitably been conditioned and coloured by the revolution that took place during this period in the record of Irish events. For the first time since Bede, in the eighth century, chronicles written in England, nearly all of them in Latin, give substantial entries and comments about affairs in Ireland. More important still, the first books on Ireland by a foreigner are now written, in Latin, by Gerald of Wales. One of these two books, entitled 'The conquest of Ireland', gives an inside report on the arrival of the Anglo-Normans and on the first two decades of their activity in the country.

The works of Gerald do not stand alone. There is another account in Norman French, missing its original title but now known as 'The song of

[1] Giraldus, *Expugnatio*, p. 49.

Dermot and the earl', which is the complement to Gerald's commentary and not just a supplement to it. Nevertheless, the influence of Gerald of Wales on subsequent historians has been incalculable. He did not begin the denigration of the Gaelic Irish—this had been effectively (though unintentionally) initiated by Bernard of Clairvaux forty years previously with his 'Life of Malachy of Armagh'—but Gerald's commanding position, by reason both of the virtuosity of his style and the amount of colourful information he supplied, ensured that he would be drawn on continually by historians as a main, perhaps *the* main, source about the first Anglo-Normans in Ireland. Even Gaelic annals, such as 'Mac Carthaigh's Book', had to depend on him, in default of any solid native record. He supplied a justification to the English officials of the late medieval and Tudor periods for the repression of the Gaelic Irish and their culture. This, in its turn, produced a pro-Irish reaction during the counter-reformation of the seventeenth century, when both Old English and Gaelic Irish found a common cause in the rallying cry of 'faith and fatherland'. Furthermore, since Gerald presented his story as objective history, quoting oral statements verbatim, citing in several instances what he asserted were the full texts of documents, and even referring to what he had discovered in archives, he has inevitably won a sympathetic hearing from modern critical historians.

In contrast with Gerald is 'The song of Dermot and the earl'. The very style of this composition, written as a *chanson de geste*, meant that it could be dismissed (as it was by J. F. O'Doherty) as mainly literary creation.[1] In fact, it embodies a treasure of detailed accurate information. A close scrutiny reveals how much of it comes from a knowledgeable source, most probably Maurice O'Regan, secretary to Diarmait Mac Murchada. Yet in the heel of the historical hunt Gerald of Wales still stands as an unavoidable primary source. The problem, in his case, is to winnow the tares, as well as the chaff, from the wheat. Whereas Gerald is expressly and consistently anti-Irish, the 'Song' gives pride of place to Mac Murchada, who is pilloried by Gerald. It is to Gerald that we owe the oft-repeated impression of Mac Murchada:

From his earliest youth and his first taking on the kingship he oppressed his nobles, and raged against the chief men of his kingdom with a tyranny grievous and impossible to bear.... Diarmait was tall and well-built, a brave and warlike man among his people, whose voice was hoarse as a result of constantly having been in the din of battle. He preferred to be feared by all rather than loved. He treated his nobles harshly and brought to prominence men of humble rank. He was inimical towards his own people and hated by others. 'All men's hands were against him, and he was hostile to all men'.[2]

Gerald's further comments and stories about Diarmait were repeated, without question, over the centuries. This served to perpetuate the picture of the native Irish as barbarians and of the need to reduce them to Anglo-Norman civility.

[1] J. F. O'Doherty, 'Historical criticism of the song of Dermot and the earl' in *I.H.S.*, i, no. 1 (Mar. 1938), pp 4–20. See also below, pp 715–18.

[2] Giraldus, *Expugnatio*, pp 41–2.

The combative English historian, J. Horace Round, drawing for his information on Gerald of Wales, confidently stated in 1899:

I see no reason to doubt the tale of King Dermot gloating over the heads that his followers brought and piled before him, and leaping for joy as with a loud voice he rendered thanks to his creator on detecting among them the face of a specially hated foe. It may have been the thought of his own son, blinded by his kingly rival, that made him, we read, clutch the head and gnaw the features with his teeth.[1]

Others, who lived closer to Mac Murchada, saw him in a totally different light. The 'Song' did not hesitate to announce:

> In Ireland, at this day,
> There was no more worthy king:
> Very rich and powerful he was;
> He loved the generous, he hated the mean.[2]

The Book of Leinster had an anguished comment on the flight of Mac Murchada from Ireland in 1166:

O King of Heaven, dreadful is the deed that has been perpetrated in Ireland today [the kalends of August] namely, Diarmait, son of Donnchad Mac Murchada, king of Leinster and the Foreigners [i.e. Norsemen of Dublin], has been banished over sea by the men of Ireland. Alas, alas, O Lord what shall I do?[3]

The most disappointing among the sources of this period are the native Irish records. None of them conveys a sense of the momentous events that were gathering irresistible force on the fringe of the Irish scene and were soon to transform the country out of all recognition. A frightening, fascinating change was rapidly taking place. Yet, what did the Gaelic records make of it? The Annals of Ulster simply disregard the arrival of the Anglo-Normans. The Annals of Tigernach laconically state, 'A large body of knights came overseas to Mac Murchada.' Over four hundred years later the Annals of the Four Masters, reflecting faithfully on the one hand the native Irish reaction in 1169, mention that 'the fleet of the Flemings came from England in the army of Mac Murchada, that is Diarmait, to contest the kingdom of Leinster for him; they were seventy heroes, dressed in coats of mail', but adds, on the other hand, with the hindsight of history and the burgeoning of Irish nationalism in the early seventeenth century, the memorable understatement that the Irish 'set nothing by the Flemings'.

It is understandable that the Irish annalists in the late twelfth century did not realise the fundamental changes evolving inexorably throughout Europe. Their interest, as the annalistic entries show, was in the local and the dynastic. Not surprisingly, their attitude has greatly influenced modern historians who, in assessing Irish affairs, draw on the obvious available source in print, namely the annals. The true picture has to be pieced together with considerable difficulty from a variety of sources, such as genealogies, topographical poems,

---

[1] J. H. Round, *The commune of London and other studies* (London, 1899), p. 158.
[2] *Song of Dermot*, p. 3.   [3] *Bk Leinster*, i, p. xvii.

monastic charters, bardic poetry, papal records, archaeological remains, coins, inscriptions, art items.

The vast majority of the Irish in the twelfth century did not grasp what was taking place under their eyes. Nor have historians, up to the present day, shown any real appreciation of the role of Diarmait Mac Murchada and what he signified in the Ireland of his day. He has had the worst of two worlds, the British and the Irish. At one extreme, he is regarded by British historians (in the tradition of Gerald of Wales) as a savage Irish war-lord engaged in tribal dynastic activities; at the other extreme he is relegated by Irish nationalist historians to that ultimate circle of hell in the *Inferno* reserved for traitors and informers. Savage and ruthless he was, but no more so than his Irish and Anglo-Norman contemporaries, though he was more effective than most of them. What distinguished him in his own day, though this was of no significance for most of his fellow-Irishmen, were the dual interacting principles of his activity that impelled him on the one hand to look beyond the shores of Ireland with international eyes, and simultaneously to act at home as a ruler with a sense of the need to update political and social structures.

One profound effect of Duke William's decision to become the successor of Edward the Confessor was to change, as it were, the direction in which England was turned towards Europe. It no longer pointed northwards to Scandinavia. It changed direction and was turned southwards towards the classical world—France, Rome, the Mediterranean, Byzantium, and the Middle East. The same process began in Ireland shortly afterwards, many decades before the Anglo-Norman knights arrived in the country, and Diarmait Mac Murchada was to be the final and crucial catalyst in the change. He was not unique among Irish rulers in his outgoing attitude—the O'Briens of Munster were of a like mind. But he was the man who made the difference. He plunged Ireland into the European melting-pot.

The decision that he took in 1166, to sail overseas for help, was not a panic reaction to military defeat, no mere leap into the unknown. He was no barbaric native chieftain, crazed by defeat and blindly seeking a patron abroad among the superpowers. Two decades before he set out from Ireland he had already been associated with Henry II, to whom he had supplied ships for campaigns in Wales. Nor did Mac Murchada pick Bristol by chance as his first port of call. He had close connections with the leading baron there, Robert fitz Harding, and with the Augustinian canons at Bristol who counted fitz Harding as the founder of their monastery. Mac Murchada was not unknown on the Continent. Bernard of Clairvaux, the greatest religious figure of the twelfth century, had written enthusiastically to him some time about the year 1148, addressing him, with pardonable inaccuracy, as 'glorious king of Ireland', and granting him confraternity with the Cistercian monks.[1] Mac Murchada's position in the

---

[1] Edited in Jean Leclerq, *Recueil d'études sur Saint Bernard et ses écrits* (3 vols, Rome, 1962–9), ii, 313–18; see Martin, *No hero in the house*, pp 19–20, 26.

religious sphere was no bubble reputation, built on pious exaggerated reports abroad. He was a generous patron of monks and nuns, a fact that has been largely overlooked. Instead, he is remembered as the ruler whose soldiers not only raided the renowned and influential nuns' abbey at Kildare but carried off the abbess, one of the Uí Failge, and had her raped. In reality, the violation of the abbess was primarily a political act, which made it possible for Sadb, one of the Mac Murchada family, to succeed her as abbess. To be abbess it was necessary to be a virgin. Much more indicative of Mac Murchada's attitude to nuns was the fact that he founded the great abbey of St Mary de Hogges at Dublin about 1146, and established two further convents of the same Arroasian nuns in 1151, at Aghade and Kilculliheen. He founded an abbey for Augustinian canons of Arrouaise at his own capital, Ferns, about 1160. More significant is his foundation of the Arroasian priory of All Hallows, established for canons at Dublin before 1166.

Mention has already been made of Mac Murchada's association with Bernard of Clairvaux. This was not confined to letters. Mac Murchada was founder in *c.* 1148 of the Cistercian abbey of Baltinglass, County Wicklow, whose first monks came from Mellifont, which community in its turn had its founder members selected by Malachy and trained by Bernard. Mac Murchada's active cooperation with two of the dynamic religious movements of the twelfth century, namely the reform of Arrouaise and the reform of Clairvaux, is a measure of how abreast he was of certain European trends.

In Ireland itself, Mac Murchada did not limit his religious activity to the province of Leinster. He presided over a national synod held at Clane in 1162, with the archbishop of Armagh, a papal legate, and twenty-six bishops present, as well as many abbots. He was brother-in-law of Archbishop Lorcán Ua Tuathail of Dublin, and closely bound to Bishop Áed Ua Cáellaide of Louth, who was described in the charter of All Hallows as Mac Murchada's spiritual father and confessor. The Mac Murchada who figures in these scenes bears little resemblance to the 'Diarmait na nGall' of the nineteenth-century nationalist writers, any more than he fits the portrait drawn with such savage strokes by Gerald of Wales.

Any assessment of the events which led to the introduction of the Anglo-Normans into Ireland demands that comment be made on what is, perhaps, the most famous single incident of Mac Murchada's career, namely his abduction of Derbforgaill, wife of Tigernán Ua Ruairc, prince of Bréifne. Was it of great, or of little, consequence?

That the incident took place is beyond doubt, but it is not usually realised that it occurred in the year 1152, fourteen years before Mac Murchada was driven abroad by a combination of Diarmait Ua Máel Sechlainn of Meath, Tigernán Ua Ruairc, the Norsemen of Dublin, and a number of Leinster princes. The abduction was, therefore, not the immediate cause of Mac Murchada's expulsion from the country; there was a variety of other events between

1152 and 1166 in which Mac Murchada and Ua Ruairc changed allies and part-
ners with no apparent consistency or high policy. Still less was the abduction a
main cause of the events of 1166–9. Gerald of Wales, a well-informed contemporary observer, mentions the turbulent political struggles in which Mac
Murchada was a prominent figure before the coming of the Anglo-Normans,
then refers to the abduction, with a degree of detachment, merely as 'another
unfortunate factor'.

Most of the sources agree that Derbforgaill was a willing accomplice in the
abduction, and Gerald of Wales states that she, herself, arranged that she
become the kidnapper's prize. The Annals of Clonmacnoise blame her
brother, Donnchad Ua Máel Sechlainn, for persuading her to flee with Mac
Murchada in retaliation for the harsh treatment she was receiving from her
husband. The incident is assuredly not one of the great love stories of history.
Whatever Derbforgaill's passion or personal motives may have been, there is
little doubt that Mac Murchada acted in cold blood. The abduction was as cal-
culated a political act as had been the rape of the abbess of Kildare in 1132 by
Mac Murchada's soldiers. In 1152 he was determined to level old scores with
Ua Ruairc and was able to insult him publicly by the abduction when he raided
Bréifne. He aggravated the insult by making no effort to prevent Toirrdelbach
Ua Conchobair from bringing her back to Ua Ruairc the following year.

The incident should not be dismissed as material for the novelist rather than
for the historian. Tigernán's honour as a husband had been impugned. The
galling experience remained over the years with Ua Ruairc, not just a scar but a
festering irritant. The Annals of Tigernach relate that in 1166, when Ua Ruairc,
Diarmait Ua Máel Sechlainn, and the Norsemen of Dublin invaded Uí
Chennselaig and drove Mac Murchada overseas, they did so 'in order to take
vengeance on him for Ua Ruairc's wife'. A year later, when Mac Murchada
returned to Ireland and was initially defeated by Ruaidrí Ua Conchobair and
his allies, he submitted to the high king and also, as the annals relate, 'paid Ua
Ruairc five score ounces of gold for peace and in compensation for his wife'.

There were far bigger issues at stake than Ua Ruairc's male pride and traditional rivalries between him and Mac Murchada, bigger even than the
struggles between provincial leaders, Ua Briain, Ua Conchobair, and Mac
Lochlainn. A new view of Irish affairs on the eve, and at the time, of the coming
of the Anglo-Normans is a necessity if the sequence of events is to be intelligible. Their coming to Ireland must be seen in the context of three interacting
dimensions: the international church-reform movement; the politics of the
'Irish Sea'; local power-struggles in Ireland. The church reform movement in
Europe had a marked effect on Ireland and drew the attention of religious
leaders such as Pope Adrian IV and Bernard of Clairvaux to Ireland, though
their interest was not always well informed. The relevance of affairs outside
Ireland, but in the 'Irish Sea', has received little or no attention from Irish historians of this period, yet that concept involves a common political and cultural

background embracing western Scotland, the Isle of Man, Cumbria, Northumbria, Wales, Ulster, and Leinster. While the Irish local power-struggles
have hitherto gained most attention, they thus appeared in isolation as little
more than parts of a confusing and tiresome sequence of unpredictable dynastic changes, fratricidal strife, cattle-raids, battles, and blindings.

Church affairs had an obvious importance in any European country during
the medieval centuries, but the policy and behaviour of the church when
faced with the extension of Anglo-Norman influence and power to Ireland
are easily misunderstood, particularly when interpreted by Irish nationalists
or nineteenth-century British historians. It is important to note that Anglo-
Norman clerical influence—in the better sense of the word—was already
present in Ireland, notably in Munster, a full century before the mailed
knights stepped ashore at Bannow Bay in 1169. One of the strongest statements of that fact is from the year 1072, when William the Conqueror was still
in the process of ruthlessly establishing his grip on the English realm.
Lanfranc, his selected archbishop of Canterbury, when writing to Pope
Alexander II in 1072, assured him that the archbishops of Canterbury had
always exercised a primatial right not only over the whole island of Britain,
but also over Ireland.[1] Though this was undoubtedly wishful thinking about
the past, the claim was given substance when the second bishop of Dublin,
Gilla Pátraic (Patricius), presented himself at Canterbury for episcopal consecration in 1074 and swore an oath of obedience to Lanfranc.[2] Gilla Pátraic's
three successors, Donngus (1085–95), Samuel Ua hAingliu (1095–1121), and
Gréne (1121–61), likewise made full profession of submission to the archbishops of Canterbury. Nor was Dublin alone in this procedure. Máel Ísu Ua
hAinmere, when elected to Waterford in 1096, and Patricius to Limerick in
1140, likewise made their formal submissions to Canterbury.

The inevitable charge, that these were bishops of Norse kingdoms, and not
representative of the country as a whole, is only half the truth and is wide of the
mark. Dublin, Limerick, and Waterford should not be regarded as foreign
enclaves in the country, as modern Irish nationalists would have it, but as
Hiberno-Norse city kingdoms of three hundred years' standing, and by the
twelfth century a permanent and essential part of the Irish political and social
world. It is true that Dublin was a special case and that its inhabitants saw
themselves as distinct from the rest of Ireland when they wrote to Archbishop
Ralph d'Escures of Canterbury in 1122,[3] but the ties binding the townspeople

[1] Lanfranc to Pope Alexander II, in 1072, declared that a meeting of English dignitaries
recorded to everyone's satisfaction that 'antecessores meos super Eboracensem ecclesiam
totamque insulam, quam Britanniam vocant, necnon et Hiberniam, primatum gessisse' in *Opera
Lanfranci*, ed. J. A. Giles (2 vols, Oxford, 1844), ii, 24.

[2] Text in *Canterbury professions*, ed. Michael Richter (Canterbury and York Society, Torquay,
1974), p. 29.

[3] Burgesses and clergy of city of Dublin to Archbishop Ralph d'Escures of Canterbury, *Eadmeri
historia novorum in Anglia*, ed. Martin Rule (London, 1884), p. 297; trans. Aubrey Gwynn in *Reportorium Novum*, i (1955–6), pp 20–21.

of Waterford and Limerick to Canterbury owed little or nothing to any Norse connections. It was due primarily to the O'Briens, kings of Munster, that Waterford looked to Canterbury, and the O'Briens were motivated largely, though not exclusively, by religious considerations. Canterbury, as the primatial see of England, was a guiding impulse for religious reform in that kingdom, notably under Archbishops Lanfranc (1070–89) and Anselm (1093–1109). The O'Briens, looking for inspiration and support in their policy of religious reform, turned to Canterbury. It was merely coincidental that reform in England was at that time identified with the Anglo-Norman rulers, but it meant that, when a full-hearted spirit of cooperation developed between the O'Briens and Canterbury, an Anglo-Norman presence was established at the right hand of the most powerful ruling family in Ireland.

Nor was Dublin, for all its separatist stance and its explicit suspicion of Armagh, outside the range of the O'Brien and Anglo-Norman influence. When Gilla Pátraic was elected second bishop of Dublin in 1074 he was sent to Canterbury by Toirrdelbach Ua Briain the high-king, for consecration by Lanfranc, who gladly acknowledged the fact in a letter to Ua Briain.[1] At that time Dublin was ruled by a Hiberno-Norse king, Gofraid, who had submitted to Toirrdelbach Ua Briain in 1072, but three years later Toirrdelbach expelled Gofraid and thereafter the O'Briens ruled Dublin directly for a quarter of a century. The influence of the Anglo-Normans in Munster and at Dublin was therefore assured, at least among the higher clerics, and their position was extremely important. Munster, politically and religiously, was the most progressive part of Ireland during these decades.

Inevitably, in the integrated society of the medieval world, the Anglo-Norman influence passed from the clerical to the secular. The most powerful Anglo-Norman family in Wales, the Montgomerys, allied themselves with the O'Briens. Arnulf, lord of Pembroke, married Lafracoth, daughter of Muirchertach Ua Briain, who as high-king presided at the memorable synod of Cashel in 1101. Arnulf, when driven into exile by an indignant King Henry I in 1102, took refuge in Ireland with his father-in-law, Muirchertach Ua Briain.[2] It was the same Ua Briain high-king who presided at the landmark synod of Ráith Bressail in 1111, where the influence of the Anglo-Norman religious reformers was clearly evident.

It would be a mistake to suppose that Norman influence in Ireland before 1169 arrived only with religious reform, the O'Briens, and the clerics. That view, considered enlightened before the 1960s, is now outdated by incontro-

---

[1] Lanfranc to Toirrdelbach Ua Briain, 1074 (letter 38, in J. P. Migne (ed.), *Patrologia Latina*, cl (Paris, 1854), cols 536–7, 614; trans. Aubrey Gwynn in *I.E.R.*, 5th ser., lviii (1941), pp 11–13).

[2] Edmund Curtis, 'Muirchertach O'Brien, high-king of Ireland, and his Norman son-in-law, Arnulf de Montgomery, *circa* 1100' in *R.S.A.I.Jn.*, lvi (1921), pp 116–24. Curtis is supplemented and corrected by J. F. A. Mason, 'Roger de Montgomery and his sons, 1067–1102' in *R. Hist. Soc. Trans.*, 5th ser., xiii (1963), p. 129. See F. X. Martin, 'The first Normans in Munster' in *Cork Hist. Soc. Jn.*, lxxvi (1971), pp 50–51.

vertible evidence which came to light during excavations by the National Museum of Ireland in the medieval inner city area of Dublin during 1962–76 and 1977–81. The story of viking and Norse Dublin, which hitherto was almost a closed chapter in medieval history, has been revealed to a significant extent at High Street and Wood Quay.[1] It will take decades to assess fully the wealth of material unearthed at Dublin, and to publish the conclusions. Nevertheless, medieval archaeologists, geographers, and historians are agreed that what has been uncovered at Dublin, particularly at Wood Quay during 1977–81, enables Dublin to share with Novgorod in Russia the claim to be the prime viking site outside Scandinavia.

We now know that a century before Diarmait Mac Murchada's allies set foot in Wexford territory there was substantial trade between Dublin and the Normans in Wales, England, and France. The new evidence must cause a reassessment of the established view. What is true of Dublin may well have been equally true of Wexford, Waterford, Cork, Limerick, and other areas, the viking maritime settlements.[2] Not for the first time, traders and commercial agents blazed a trail followed by missionaries and churchmen. No firm conclusion about these areas outside Dublin can be reached until they have been the subject of excavations similar to those at High Street and Wood Quay. Patrick Wallace, who supervised the excavations at Wood Quay in 1977–81, concludes that the 'normanisation' of Dublin began probably shortly after the battle of Hastings, almost a century before the Anglo-Normans, led by fitz Stephen and Strongbow, arrived in Ireland.[3]

This sweeping glance at the background to the events of 1169 indicates how strong was Norman influence before the ships put in at Bannow Bay. It also explains why the Anglo-Normans who came to succour Diarmait Mac Murchada were readily invited by the O'Brien kings into Munster.

But it was not merely in Uí Chennselaig and Munster that the Anglo-Normans found a welcome. Because of their association with religious reform in England and on the Continent they found many of the church leaders throughout Ireland well-disposed to receive them. Since the church was the only organisation that embraced the whole country and had a unified policy, the settlers who began to come in substantial numbers from 1169 onwards had

---

[1] Breandán Ó Riordáin, 'Excavations at High Street and Winetavern Street, Dublin' in *Medieval Archaeology*, xv (1971), pp 72–85; P. F. Wallace, 'The archaeological significance of Wood Quay, Dublin' in *An Cosantóir*, xxxix, no. 5 (May 1979), pp 141–7; P. F. Wallace, 'Wood Quay, Dublin' in *Popular Archaeology*, ii, no. 9 (Mar. 1981), pp 24–7; P. F. Wallace, 'Anglo-Norman Dublin: continuity and change' in Donnchadh Ó Corráin (ed.), *Irish antiquity: essays and studies presented to Professor M. J. O'Kelly* (Cork, 1981), pp 147–67; P. F. Wallace, 'The archaeology of Anglo-Norman Dublin' in H. B. Clarke and Anngret Simms (ed.), *The comparative history of urban origins in non-Roman Europe: Ireland, Wales, Denmark, Germany, Poland, and Russia from the ninth to the thirteenth century* (Oxford, 1985), pp 379–410; and P. F. Wallace's forthcoming *Viking and Norman Dublin: the Wood Quay excavations*.

[2] P. F. Wallace, 'Wexford' in *Excavations 1974*, ed. T. G. Delaney (Belfast, 1975), p. 28.

[3] P. F. Wallace, 'Wood Quay, Dublin' in *Popular Archaeology*, ii, no. 9 (Mar. 1981), p. 27.

every likelihood of a friendly welcome. It was not that church leaders supported an alien culture or wished for a conquest. There was no obvious threat to Ireland's identity in 1169, but with Anglo-Norman assistance there did seem to be a heaven-sent opportunity to accelerate religious reform and to add or complete those forms of ecclesiastical organisation, such as parishes, which were still lacking in Ireland. That assurance was a factor which must have strengthened the resolve of the papal authorities to bless a church in Ireland dominated by the Anglo-Normans. In addition there was no doubt that Diarmait Mac Murchada was a patron of the church and of reform; it was a justifiable reason why he and his supporters were able to turn to churchmen with confidence in 1169 and again during 1169–71.

It would be a grave injustice to the Gaelic Irish to suppose that religious reform was a benefit introduced into Ireland first through Anglo-Norman influence and then with Anglo-Norman arms. Beginning in the eleventh century, and independently of Norman influence, there was a vigorous movement for reform among the Irish. Reference has already been made to the leading role of the O'Briens of Munster in that sphere, and though this royal family turned to the Anglo-Normans, and to Canterbury in particular, for assistance and inspiration, it was only to confirm what was already a fixed policy of the O'Briens by the time Duke William of Normandy landed in England.[1]

On the eve of the coming of the Anglo-Normans to Ireland there was a twofold upsurge of reform activity emanating from the north. The more renowned impetus appeared unexpectedly in Armagh and was personified in Malachy (1094–1148).[2] The initial impetus and training he received came from dedicated clerics such as Ímar and Cellach of Armagh. Though in his hours of spiritual need he turned to the religious reformers outside Ireland, the Cistercians at Clairvaux and the Augustinian canons at Arrouaise in France and at Guisborough in Yorkshire, there was no turning to Canterbury and no political dependence on the Normans in England or France. Malachy was a product of the old Celtic monastic system but allied himself with the new movement of Cistercians and canons regular of St Augustine. In addition he supported the peaceful revolution in Irish church affairs—the establishment of the full diocesan and parochial systems as operated generally in Europe.

The second impetus in the north to religious reform was the remarkable revival of traditional Irish monasticism radiating from Derry. It found an

---

[1] See articles by Aubrey Gwynn on the Irish church and the reform in the eleventh and twelfth centuries, listed by F. X. Martin in *Med. studies presented to A. Gwynn*, pp 503–4, excellently summarised in Watt, *Ch. & two nations*, pp 1–34; also Aubrey Gwynn, 'The first synod of Cashel' in *I.E.R.*, 5th ser., lxvi (1945), pp 81–92, lxvii (1946), pp 109–22; 'St Malachy of Armagh', ibid., lxx (1948), pp 961–78, lxxi (1949), pp 134–48, 317–31; 'The centenary of the synod of Kells', ibid., lxxvii (1952), pp 161–76, 150–64; *The twelfth-century reform* in Corish, *Ir. catholicism*, ii, fasc. 1.

[2] See Aubrey Gwynn, 'St Malachy of Armagh' in *I.E.R.*, 5th ser., lxx (1948), pp 961–78, lxxi (1949), pp 134–48, 317–31; Brian Scott, *Malachy* (Dublin, 1976).

energetic leader in Abbot Flaithbertach Ua Brolcháin, head of the Columban monks. He was given national recognition in 1158, at the synod of Brí mac Taidg (Breemount, near Laracor, County Meath), where an assembly of twenty-five bishops, presided over by the papal legate, Gilla Críst Ua Connairche, himself a Cistercian, declared Ua Brolcháin to have the status of a mitred abbot and to have jurisdiction over all Columban churches. Three years later an assembly of clerics and laymen at Áth na Dairbrige, on the Meath–Cavan border, gave the high-king, Muirchertach Mac Lochlainn, the opportunity to confirm the jurisdiction of Ua Brolcháin over Columban churches in Meath and Leinster. The political undertones of Mac Lochlainn's sponsorship were indicated in 1164 when he and the archbishop of Armagh, Gilla Meic Liac, forbade Ua Brolcháin to accept the invitation of Somarlaide, king of Argyll and the Isles, to become abbot of Iona. In that same year Mac Lochlainn was the patron who assisted Ua Brolcháin to complete churches in Derry territory.

Perhaps the most striking evidence of the integration of Irish and continental reform movements was in the choice of Lorcán Ua Tuathail as archbishop of Dublin. He was a member of a princely family, brother-in-law of Diarmait Mac Murchada, and had been trained in the seclusion of the monastic settlement at Glendalough, one of the hallowed centres of Irish religious life. He was elected abbot in 1153, and made a brave (and probably locally unpopular) decision when he introduced the Augustinian canons to Glendalough, by founding in 1162 the priory of St Saviour, about half a mile south-east of the cathedral.[1] He is reputed to have lived at the priory for some short time before his election as archbishop of Dublin in that same year. One of his first official acts in Dublin was to transform the character of Christ Church cathedral chapter from secular clergy into Augustinian canons of Arrouaise. It thus became a form of monastic cathedral and remained so until the reformation.

This religious activity was not dominated by any one province, group or person. The very nature of Irish society ensured that there would be religious diversification. It embraced a revived Celtic monasticism in Derry; a new and confident movement in the Hiberno-Norse towns to integrate with the native Irish church; throughout the country an influx of the new religious orders from the Continent, notably the Cistercians and the canons regular of St Augustine; an acceptance of the normal diocesan structure in every province; and a national religious unity exemplified by recognition of the primacy of Armagh.

The dynamism within the Irish church was not confined to Ireland. The expansion of the Irish Benedictine congregation, the *Schottenklöster*, in the German lands was extraordinary.[2] Their monastery at Regensburg was consecrated

---

[1] The only authoritative discussion, though brief, on the adoption by Lorcán Ua Tuathail of the Arroasian reform is by P. J. Dunning, 'The Arroasian order in medieval Ireland' in *I.H.S.*, iv, no. 16 (Sept. 1945), pp 308–9. For the general context of the Arroasian reform in Ireland see Aubrey Gwynn and R. Neville Hadcock, *Medieval religious houses: Ireland* (London, 1970), pp 146–52.

[2] D. A. Binchy, 'The Irish Benedictine congregation in medieval Germany' in *Studies*, xviii (1929), pp 194–210; Aubrey Gwynn, 'Some notes on the history of the Irish and Scottish

in 1111, and found an adventuresome leader in their third abbot, Christian Mac Carthaig, a near relation of the Mac Carthaig king of Desmond. Two small priories founded in Ireland, at Cashel, and at Rosscarbery in west Cork, forged permanent links with the home country, but the real vitality manifested itself in Greater Germany. Within five decades *Schottenklöster* had been founded at Würzburg, Erfurt, Nuremberg, Constance, Vienna, and Eichstätt. During 1167–8, when Diarmait Mac Murchada was desperately striving to regain, and then retain, his kingdom of Uí Chennselaig, as he waited impatiently for the arrival of his allies, another *Schottenkloster* was founded, at Memmingen, in Bavaria. During 1177–80 Irish monks from the monastery at Vienna made the imaginative decision to take over a monastery at Kiev, 'the mother of Russian towns', and capital of Kievan Russia.

Pausing therefore briefly to assess the spirit and activity of the church in Ireland at the time of the arrival of the Anglo-Normans in Ireland, we find cogent evidence of a vigorous religious life among laity and clerics, of a cohesive movement of secular and clerical leaders to update the external structures of the church. Nevertheless, this was not how Canterbury and Rome saw it.

The first positive moves for political (and therefore military) intervention in Ireland date from a meeting of the royal council at Winchester in September 1155. The young monarch, Henry II, a mere twenty-two years old and crowned only in December 1154, raised with his advisers the proposal that Ireland be acquired and placed under the jurisdiction of his brother, William. Eventually the idea was discarded, Henry declaring that his mother, the formidable Empress Matilda, was opposed to the project. However unsure we may be about Henry's motives in raising and then dropping the proposition, the significant fact is the record that those who were promoting the notion of an invasion were the bishops and clergy at the council (*episcopi et religiosi viri*).[1] That evidence must be seen in the context of what had taken place at the synod of Kells, three years previously, when Pope Eugenius III had deliberately set aside

Benedictine monasteries in Germany' in *Innes Review*, v (1954), pp 5–27; Ludwig Hammermayer, 'Die irischen Benediktiner' (see above, p. liii, n. 2), pp 249–337; Pádraig A. Breatnach, *Die Regensburger Schottenlegende: Libellus de fundacione ecclesie Consecrati Petri*, Untersuchung und Textausgabe (Münchener Beiträge zur Mediävistik und Renaissance-Forschung), 27 (1977), Munich; 'The origins of the Irish monastic tradition at Ratisbon' in *Celtica*, xiii (1980), pp 58–77.

[1] This important fact was first mentioned in modern times by J. F. O'Doherty, 'Rome and the Anglo-Norman invasion of Ireland' in *I.E.R.*, xlii (1933), p. 140, citing his source, vaguely and incorrectly, as *Continuatio Anselmi*. O'Doherty's citation was repeated by M. P. Sheehy, 'The bull *Laudabiliter*: a problem in medieval diplomatique and history' in *Galway Arch. Soc. Jn.*, xxix (1960–61), p. 57, and in his *When the Normans came to Ireland* (Cork and Dublin, 1975), p. 7. The correct reference was located by Dr Michael Richter, and separately by Dr Ian Robinson, in an obscure twelfth-century Lotharingian chronicle, 'Auctarium Aquicinense', one of the many continuations of Sigebert of Gambloux's chronicle, in *Monumenta Germaniae Historica: Scriptores*, vi (1844), p. 403. The source and the incident are put in context by Denis Bethell, 'English monks and Irish reform in the eleventh and twelfth centuries' in *Hist. Studies*, viii (1971), p. 135, n. 136.

The whole question of Canterbury's part in these negotiations needs to be reassessed in the light of Michael Richter's 'The first century of Anglo-Irish relations' in *History*, lix (1974), pp 195–210.

the claims of Canterbury over the Irish church, not in any spirit of hostility to Canterbury but in the knowledge that the Irish church was capable of managing its own affairs. The decision at Kells obviously galled the Anglo-Norman clergy, especially the establishment at Canterbury.

Even though the ambitious Anglo-Norman clergy with designs on Ireland were thwarted at Winchester they were to win at another level, in Rome. The archbishop of Canterbury was Theobald of Bec, a Norman and churchman to the core. He was capable, pious, and decisive. His chief adviser was John of Salisbury, who had an international reputation as a philosopher at the University of Paris and as a figure in the literary renaissance. Before returning to England he spent some years in the papal service, and was to end his days as bishop of Chartres (1176–80). In England he became chief minister successively to Archbishops Theobald and Thomas Becket. During his time in Rome he had been friendly with the highly respected English cardinal, Nicholas Breakspear, who was elected pope in 1154, taking the name Adrian IV. It was about a year later that John, during a visit to Rome, made an extraordinary intervention at the papal curia on behalf of Anglo-Norman imperialism in Ireland. He makes no bones about his own role in the affair, nor does he attempt to cloak his proposal in the guise of religious zeal. Unexpectedly, near the end of his philosophical work, 'Metalogicon', he introduces the question of Ireland and Henry II.

In response to my petition the pope granted and donated Ireland to the illustrious king of England, Henry, to be held by him and his successors, as his letters, still extant, testify. He did this in virtue of the long-established right, reputed to derive from the donation of Constantine, whereby all islands are considered to belong to the Roman church. Moreover, through me the pope sent the king a gold ring, set with a magnificent emerald, as a sign that he had invested the king with the right to rule Ireland; it was later directed by the king that this ring be kept in the public treasury.[1]

John does not cite the papal documents donating Ireland to Henry II, but the text (or a version of it), the much controverted *Laudabiliter*, is supplied by Gerald of Wales, who also mentions the ring sent by the pope and the fact that it was deposited in the royal treasury at Winchester with the document. Some twenty years later Gerald solemnly reaffirmed his statement about such a document and its being deposited in the archives at Winchester.[2] There can hardly

[1] 'Metalogicus' in *Opera omnia*, ed. J. A. Giles (5 vols, Oxford, 1848), v, pp 1–207; reprinted in *Patrologia Latina*, cxcix (1855), p. 945; *Metalogicon*, ed. C. C. J. Webb (Oxford, 1929), pp 217–18; *The Metalogicon of John of Salisbury*, trans. Daniel D. McGarry (Berkeley and Los Angeles, 1962), pp 274–5.

[2] Dedicatory letter of second edition of *Expugnatio*, addressed to King John in Giraldus, *Expugnatio*, p. 263.

A great deal has been published on *Laudabiliter*. It is sufficient here to draw attention to three studies. Kate Norgate, 'The bull *Laudabiliter*' in *E.H.R.*, viii (1893), pp 18–52, is a landmark and indispensable. O'Doherty, 'Rome and the Anglo-Norman invasion of Ireland', pp 131–41; and Sheehy, 'The bull *Laudabiliter*', are excellent but now dated. For a succinct analysis see Watt, *Ch. & two nations*, pp 36–40.

An important, hitherto overlooked copy of *Laudabiliter* was recently located by Marie-Thérèse Flanagan. Her discovery, in conjunction with another relevant copy of the bull, is briefly

be room for doubt that there was some such document, and there is undeniable evidence that after the visit of Henry II to Ireland the papacy commanded the Irish to be subject to him.[1] This latter evidence, the letters of Pope Alexander III in September 1172, gives the need for religious reform of the Irish as the compelling reason why they should bow to the Angevin king.

How could Rome, without seeming to have tongue in cheek, adopt such a policy when it was dealing on the one hand with a monarch implicated in the murder of Archbishop Becket and on the other hand with an Irish church which had given, over a period of sixty years, substantial proof of its determination to reform and of its unqualified loyalty to the papacy? The exceptional quality of native Irish religious leaders was later solemnly recognised by Rome when it canonised Malachy of Armagh (1094–1148) in 1199 and Lorcán Ua Tuathail (1128–80) in 1226. Such men were not content merely to sigh for reform and to look to it as an unattainable ideal. Long before the Anglo-Norman knights set foot in Ireland, the Irish church leaders, bishops and abbots, had legislated for reform, notably at the national synods of Cashel (1101), Ráith Bressail (1111), and Kells-Mellifont (1152). The reform was not confined to legislation, but was initiated in fact by the revolutionary introduction of dioceses and provinces, with the bishops in control.

The greater problem was disciplinary reform among the people, and it was an almost insurmountable obstacle since it would demand the abandonment of features of Gaelic society going back to pre-Christian times and of practices which had been accepted for centuries by the church in Ireland, the so-called 'Celtic church'. These were social and practical realities which found expression in attitudes towards marriage, celibacy of the clergy, baptism and the sacramental system, control of church lands. Complaints on these scores had come not just from Bernard of Clairvaux, Gerald of Wales, and Anglo-Normans such as John of Salisbury, but from Irish church leaders, such as Malachy of Armagh and the bishops at the synod of Kells-Mellifont, before the Anglo-Normans arrived in Ireland.[2]

It was apparently the realisation by the Irish church leaders of the incompatibility of the Gregorian reform with the Gaelic social system which induced the bishops, abbots, and other prelates at the synod of Cashel, 1171–2, to accept Henry II as their temporal overlord.[3] It would be foolhardy to suggest that the church leaders were guilty of political perfidy (they were giving priority to their spiritual allegiance as Christian pastors) but it is not unreasonable to doubt the wisdom of their joint decision. Yet the subsequent history of Gaelic Ireland appears to confirm the accuracy of their judgement. The absence of a 'Norman

evaluated by Michael Richter, 'Giraldiana' in *I.H.S.*, xxi, no. 84 (Sept. 1979), pp 422–37, at pp 430–31. His conclusion is unqualified: 'It is no longer permissible to doubt the authenticity of *Laudabiliter*.'

[1] See three papal letters of Sept. 1172, in Sheehy, *Pontificia Hib.*, i, 19–23.
[2] See above, p. 54, n. 1.
[3] Giraldus, *Expugnatio*, pp 97–101.

conquest' meant that the Gaelic system survived with its anomalies in church affairs up to the reformation and into the seventeenth century.[1] Missionaries who came to Ireland during the counter-reformation, in the second quarter of the seventeenth century, asserted that many people in the rural areas were ignorant of fundamentals of Christian belief.[2] This was not something peculiar to Ireland. Delumeau concludes from his investigation of whole areas of France, Germany, and Italy during this same period, that the people were pagan rather than Christian.[3] All this may seem a long cry back to Ireland of the twelfth century, but continuity has been a striking feature of Gaelic Ireland throughout the centuries. The Irish church leaders were in full agreement with the authorities in Rome about the urgent need for disciplinary reform of the Irish people.

WHILE the story of the coming of the Anglo-Normans to Ireland must be seen in the wider context of social, religious, and political forces with international dimensions, the role of the individual should not be discounted. Two men, John of Salisbury and Diarmait Mac Murchada, helped to change the course of Irish history.

John of Salisbury was on familiar terms with the men who had their hands on the levers of power—Bernard of Clairvaux, Pope Adrian IV, Henry II, Archbishop Theobald of Canterbury, and Thomas Becket. His intervention at Rome resulted in the issue of a papal blessing on Henry's political intervention in Ireland. The argument by modern historians that *Laudabiliter* (or its equivalent) was of no real importance, since it was not translated into reality at the time of its publication in 1155–6, is a short-sighted assessment when taken in the context of Roman curial procedure. What was adopted as papal policy in 1155–6 would be continued as papal policy in 1172—as was done by Alexander III—unless there were compelling reasons to the contrary. Papal policy is awesome in its continuity, its disregard of dynastic and governmental changes. Practical arguments and apparently reputable witnesses served only to confirm in 1172 the questionable papal policy first expressed in 1155–6.

It was a quirk of fate that an enthusiastic benefactor of Ireland, Bernard of Clairvaux, had unintentionally prepared the ground at Rome and throughout Europe for the acceptance of John of Salisbury's views of the Irish. One of the most moving stories of the twelfth century is of the friendship between those two men of God, Bernard of Clairvaux from Burgundy and Malachy from Ulster, and the final unforgettable scene on the night of 1–2 November 1148, with Malachy dying in the arms of Bernard. Within a year Bernard had written

---

[1] Canice Mooney, *The church in Gaelic Ireland, thirteenth to fifteenth centuries*, in Corish, *Ir. catholicism*, ii, fasc. 5.

[2] Such were the conclusions of Capuchin missionaries in Ireland in these reports, unpublished, now in Archives of Propaganda Fide, Rome.

[3] Jean Delumeau, *Catholicism between Luther and Voltaire: a new view of the counter-reformation* (Philadelphia, 1977), pp 154–79, 224–31.

his 'Life of Malachy', in which he presented his account of a dedicated Christian who became a model abbot and exemplary bishop. A main object of the 'Life' was to show Malachy as the reforming bishop. Bernard was not a historian, and this particular work is a classic of hagiography, an extended panegyric, written in Bernard's splendid rhetorical style. To exaggerate was a virtue, and Malachy was presented as a lamb among wolves, a light in the darkness. A high point is the description of the circumstances Malachy found as bishop of Connor:

When he began to administer his office, the man of God understood that he had been sent not to men but to beasts. Never before had he known the like, in whatever depth of barbarism; never had he found men so shameless in regard of morals, so dead in regard of rites, so stubborn in regard of discipline, so unclean in regard of life. They were Christians in name, in fact pagans.[1]

That passage conveys the tone of the whole book, and highlights a main message of Bernard's exposition, namely the barbaric and semi-pagan state of the people. All over Europe that story about Ireland, and not the truth about the widespread reform of its clergy, became established. Apart from turning a blind eye on the exciting religious regeneration taking place at this time in Ireland, with which he was partly acquainted, Bernard showed a total disregard for the unbroken high literary and artistic creativity of centuries. Ireland had retained its own culture and had remained outside the Latin secular world. It was therefore, in Bernard's eyes, 'barbaric'. Ireland had for long been regarded in Europe as the *Ultima Thule*, the land of mist and mystery, of wonders and miracles. Now with Bernard in 1149, and his hypnotic gift of publicising his views, it becomes a land of dark shadows and savage inhabitants.

John of Salisbury therefore found a well-attuned audience when he spoke at Rome about the barbaric and impious people of Ireland. He established an anti-Irish tradition at Rome which found official expression first in *Laudabiliter* in 1156 and later in three letters of Pope Alexander III in 1172. That tradition was given a permanent and literary basis when Gerald of Wales wrote about Ireland. He produced two books on the subject—the 'Topography of Ireland', completed probably in 1188, and the 'Conquest of Ireland', finished probably in 1189. His lively comments on the Irish outdid even the rhetorical phrases of Bernard. Gerald declared that the Irish 'are a wild and inhospitable people. They live on beasts only, and live like beasts'; 'they think that the greatest pleasure is not to work, and the greatest wealth is to enjoy liberty'; 'moreover above all other peoples they always practise treachery'; 'this is a filthy people, wallowing in vice; of all peoples it is the least instructed in the rudiments of the

[1] *St Bernard of Clairvaux's life of St Malachy of Armagh*, trans. and ed. H. J. Lawlor (London, 1920), p. 37. For the original text see 'Vita S. Malachiae', ed. Aubrey Gwynn, in *Sancti Bernardi opera*, ed. Jean Leclercq and H. M. Rochais, iii (Rome, 1963), pp 295–387. Of particular relevance for our purpose is B. W. O'Dwyer, 'St Bernard as a historian: the "Life of St Malachy of Armagh" ' in *Journal of Religious History*, x (1978–9), pp 128–41.

faith'; '[their bishops] neither preach the word of God to the people, nor tell them of their sins, nor extirpate vice from the flock committed to them, nor instil virtue'.[1]

Bernard of Clairvaux was the first foreigner to write a book about an Irishman, and it was as anti-Irish as it was favourable to Malachy of Armagh. Gerald of Wales was the first foreigner to write a book about Ireland, and his comments added rare spice to what Bernard of Clairvaux had expressed so vividly and what John of Salisbury's inspiration had incorporated in *Laudabiliter*. Thus, with the Anglo-Normans, but not entirely due to them, there was established an anti-Irish literature as a political factor.

A great responsibility rests on John of Salisbury for inducing the papacy to commit itself to blessing Anglo-Norman military intervention in Ireland. It became part of papal policy under Alexander III and continued thereafter as an important element in medieval Irish history. However, while it is difficult to assess precisely the effects of such papal policy on practical politics in Ireland, and therefore to weigh the extent of John of Salisbury's responsibility, there is no doubt about the part played by Diarmait Mac Murchada and the effect of his decision to call in the Anglo-Normans. While he cannot be given the credit or discredit for events which occurred after his death, and which he could not have foreseen, he was in fact the man who by a conscious decision released and attracted forces that radically altered the course of Irish history and continue to have effects even in our own day.

It has been a common mistake of historians to see Diarmait Mac Murchada simply as ruler of a petty kingdom, battling ruthlessly, and usually effectively, with other Irish war-lords. This misconception is the result of depending mainly on the Irish annals for information. Understandably, the annalists rarely looked beyond the shores of Ireland. Mac Murchada had a much wider vision and range of activity.[2] He was fortunate to make the right political choice among the contenders for the English crown in the 1140s. When Henry I, son of William the Conqueror, died in December 1135, the throne was rapidly occupied by his nephew, Stephen, and though Stephen was duly acclaimed at London, and crowned king, his position was challenged by the Empress Matilda, on behalf of her son, Henry. Stephen was captured by supporters of Matilda in February 1141 and spent most of that year in captivity, significantly at Bristol. He was released in November 1141, recrowned in December, and continued to rule a disorderly kingdom until his death in October 1154.

[1] *The first version of the Topography of Ireland*, trans. J. J. O'Meara (Dundalk, 1951), pp 85, 86, 90, 97; issued in a revised edition as *The history and topography of Ireland* (hardback, Mountrath 1982; paperback (Penguin Classics), Harmondsworth, 1982). For the original text see 'Giraldus Cambrensis in Topographia Hibernie: text of the first recension', ed. J. J. O'Meara, in *R.I.A. Proc.*, lii, sect. C (1949), pp 113–78. See further Robert Bartlett, *Gerald of Wales, 1146–1223* (Oxford, 1982).
[2] I am greatly indebted to the late Denis Bethell for his notes on the 'Irish Sea' dimension in the time of Diarmait Mac Murchada, which he placed at my disposal, and for several discussions on the subject.

Mac Murchada was in effect the ally of Henry from at least 1144, possibly earlier. His opportunity for a choice had come in 1141 with the capture of Stephen. After that he became a firm ally of Henry and of King David I of Scotland. Like them, and probably influenced by their example, he became a patron of Cistercian monks and Augustinian canons. The fruits of Mac Murchada's friendship with Henry came in the 1150s. The death of David of Scotland in May 1153 gave Henry an opportunity to reconsider the situation north of the border, once he himself had acceded to the English throne in December 1154. He showed little enthusiasm for the new king of Scotland, Malcolm 'the Maiden', and was quite prepared to use Somarlaide (lord of Argyll, 1158–64) with Muirchertach Mac Lochlainn (king of Cenél nEógain, 1145–66; also highking, 1148–66) in order to keep pressure on King Malcolm. It was during this formative period of new alliances, with the young Henry attempting to strengthen his power in the frontier lands of the Celtic peoples, that there also occurred the unsuccessful attempts by some Anglo-Norman clerics to promote an invasion of Ireland at the council of Winchester in September 1155. By 1160 Somarlaide and Mac Lochlainn were riding on the crest of the wave, and Mac Murchada prospered also. Malcolm had been forced in 1157 to cede Northumberland, Lancaster, and Cumberland to Henry II, and in 1160 to make peace with Somarlaide, his former subject. In 1161 Mac Murchada was given the eastern half of Meath by Mac Lochlainn, after the high-king had invaded Bréifne; and Mac Lochlainn also forced Ruaidrí Ua Conchobair of Connacht to submit.

The year 1162 was probably the high point of Mac Murchada's career. He presided at the synod of Clane with the archbishop of Armagh, Gilla Meic Liac, when the primacy of Armagh was reaffirmed. This unity of the Irish church, and the political alliance between Mac Lochlainn and Mac Murchada, were further reflected in the consecration of Lorcán Ua Tuathail, brother-in-law of Mac Murchada, as archbishop of Dublin by Gilla Meic Liac later in the year. It was also in 1162 that the Dublin Norsemen recognised Mac Murchada as full overlord of their city state. He showed confidence in his position there by founding the priory of All Hallows, for Augustinian canons of Arrouaise, a short distance outside the city walls.

His fortunes were tied in with those of Mac Lochlainn and Somarlaide. The reverses which they were to suffer also put his power into decline, and set him in his desperation on a course of action that brought the Anglo-Normans to Ireland. The first serious blow came in 1164 when Somarlaide, in a bold attempt to defeat Malcolm, sailed up the Clyde, backed by a fleet from Dublin. Walter fitz Alan, steward of Scotland, counter-attacked at Renfrew, defeating and killing Somarlaide, thus weakening Mac Lochlainn's position in the northern half of the Irish Sea. The defeat at Renfrew did not shatter the Dublin fleet, which for six months, in 1165, formed part of Henry II's attempt to subdue north Wales. Though this alliance with Dublin strengthened Mac Murchada's

ties with the Angevin king, the failure of Henry's expedition brought no prestige to Mac Murchada in Ireland. It was however the defeat of Mac Lochlainn,
in the following year, which finally exposed Mac Murchada's flank to his
enemies. The high-king fell at the hands of Donnchad Ua Cerbaill and Tigernán Ua Ruairc. Independently of the turmoil in the north, Ruaidrí Ua Conchobair of Connacht, now the contender for the high-kingship, invaded Meath
and secured the submission of Airgialla, Meath, and Leinster. Mac Murchada
was thus in isolation, his back to the sea. His old enemy, Tigernán Ua Ruairc,
in company with Diarmait Ua Máel Sechlainn of Meath and the Norsemen of
Dublin, marched on Uí Chennselaig, drove Mac Murchada from Ferns, and
burnt his castle there.

The crisis put Mac Murchada on his mettle. He made a last attempt to
organise local resistance and sought help from one of his underlords, Murchad
Ua Brain, of the Duffry (*Dubhthír*, 'dark country'), a thickly wooded district
between the river Slaney and the mountains, protected by steep hills, mountain
streams, bogs, and marshes. Ua Brain continued to avoid him until Mac
Murchada adopted a subterfuge that indicated his desperation. From the
Augustinians at Ferns he got the robes of a canon regular, and in this disguise
was allowed into Ua Brain's presence, who, discovering his real identity, repudiated him with insults. It is not without point that Mac Murchada had gone in
the guise of one of the continental religious orders which he had sponsored in
Ireland. Most other chieftains in his circumstances would now have parleyed
with the enemy for submission or taken refuge in the woods, hoping that the
wheel of fortune would take a favourable turn. A warrior of Mac Murchada's
own stature, such as Tigernán Ua Ruairc, would have attempted a reckless
military coup and probably gone down in a blaze of glory. That was the old-
style Irish chieftain, the man of unbounded courage and limited vision. Not so
Mac Murchada. What Ireland would not give, his friends abroad could supply.
He took ship for Bristol, to seek assistance. It was a fateful decision, one of the
most momentous ever taken by an individual in the history of the country. After
that all was changed, changed utterly.

It was not blind chance or mere geographical convenience that caused him
to set sail for Bristol. He had a trusted friend there, Robert fitz Harding, the
provost or reeve of Bristol, and ruler of the area.[1] Not enough attention has
been given to this man's key role in the transformation of Irish history. He was
not of Norman stock, and that fact had a message for Mac Murchada. Robert's
grandfather, Eadnoth, was 'staller' (master of the horse, principal military
officer of the Anglo-Saxon kings), successively to Edward the Confessor and
King Harold. Robert himself was a merchant of great wealth and influence who

---

[1] Nothing substantial has been published on fitz Harding, but see the notice by William Hunt in
D.N.B.; G.E.C., *Peerage*, ii, 124–5. An informative source, often overlooked, is Samuel Seyer,
Memoirs, historical and topographical, of Bristol and its neighbourhood, i (Bristol, 1821), pp 289–315, 364–
443, 462–81.

had resolutely upheld the cause of the Empress Matilda in the bleak circumstances of the 1140s. Her son, the young Prince Henry, lived at Bristol for four years and received much-needed support from Robert, most probably in hard cash which was then urgently required. The reward came in 1153–4 when Henry, shortly before his accession, conferred on Robert the castle and territory of adjoining Berkeley. Mac Murchada was not merely the nearest Irish ruler to Bristol. His control of Dublin meant that he had a major say in the disposal of its goods and ships. Fitz Harding and Mac Murchada had a common religious interest—they were eager to promote religious reform as exemplified in the Augustinian canons of Arrouaise. Fitz Harding founded an abbey for the canons on his own estate in 1141, endowed it liberally, and ended his days as a member of the community. Indeed, it would seem that he was already an Augustinian canon when Mac Murchada arrived there in 1166. We have previously noted that Mac Murchada founded three houses for Augustinian nuns in Ireland, as well as an abbey for the canons at Ferns and a priory for them at Dublin.

Mac Murchada brought a modest shipload of followers with him to Bristol in August 1166, including his wife, Mór, and daughter, Aífe. They were housed in fitz Harding's home, near to St Augustine's abbey. Mac Murchada had come to seek help, not refuge, and was determined to recruit the best soldiers. After consultation with fitz Harding he set out to find Henry II, that restless, energetic monarch, and followed in his tracks, first to Normandy, then south to Aquitaine, and then in an unnamed 'city he found him, of which he is called lord'. Henry received him with sympathy, Mac Murchada explained his predicament, asked for help, and promised solemnly that in return he would swear loyalty to Henry as his lord. He did not, it would seem, offer homage—an important feudal distinction.

Henry had little interest in Ireland at this stage, and was beset by a variety of problems, some inherited, some of his own making. His heavy-handed treatment of the bishops at Clarendon had brought about a confrontation with the papacy; Becket had fled abroad and was under the protection of King Louis VII of France. The papacy might well have taken a hard line against Henry but for the danger of an alliance between him and the Emperor Frederick already with an antipope, Paschal III, in his train; besides, a German army was in Italy by the summer of 1166, and Pope Alexander III was at a double disadvantage after the death of his generous ally, King William I of Sicily, early in 1166. However, not all was well with Henry. Brittany had been subdued by him in the summer of 1166 but was stirring to action once again behind Eudo, viscount of Porhoët; within Aquitaine itself the counts of Angoulême and La Marche had formed a confederation to resist Henry, and were threatening to transfer their allegiance to King Louis. The new king of Scotland, William I, made no secret of his hostility to Henry; the Welsh were steadily and successfully besieging the royal castles into which Henry's forces had retreated after the disastrous campaign of 1165.

All in all it was no time for Henry to commit himself to a new venture and in an uncertain area, Ireland. Yet Mac Murchada's offer held certain advantages. Mac Murchada, if restored in Leinster, would surely regain Dublin with its valuable fleet, and that would be a bonus for Anglo-Norman campaigns against Welsh and Scots. For Henry to encourage such of his subjects as were bellicose and restless to take service with Mac Murchada could siphon off dissident groups within his scattered territories. Mac Murchada was therefore given a free hand to recruit within the lands of the 'Angevin empire': England, Wales, Normandy, Anjou, Aquitaine, and Brittany.[1] It was up to himself to realise the permission, and Henry showed that it was more than fair words when he sent instructions to fitz Harding, both by letter and by messenger, that all facilities should be extended to Mac Murchada and his entourage. This was an encouraging start on the journey back to Ireland, but little more, as Mac Murchada quickly found out.

Mac Murchada returned to Bristol, through Henry's French possessions and on through England, but he made no attempt to recruit until he arrived in Wales; even then there was little response to his appeal. His offers of lands and money were not taken seriously until one outstanding figure, Richard fitz Gilbert, lord of Strigoil, put him to the test.[2] Fitz Gilbert, better known in Irish history as Strongbow, went to see Mac Murchada and agreed to lead an expedition to Ireland, but on conditions. Aífe, Mac Murchada's eldest daughter, should be given in marriage to Strongbow, who also was to succeed Mac Murchada as king of Leinster. Strongbow was gambling, but cautiously, on an Irish venture, and Mac Murchada accepted his terms, though the kingship he promised Strongbow was not his to give.

Mac Murchada, continuing on through south Wales, looking for recruits, had a further stroke of good luck at St David's. He caught the interest of David fitz Gerald, bishop of St David's, and Rhys ap Gruffydd, 'the Lord Rhys of Deheubarth'. They shared with Strongbow a total lack of enthusiasm for Henry II and his policy for Wales, but each manifested it in a different way. They also shared suspicions of one another. Strongbow was a member of the de Clare family, powerful in England as in Wales, but personally was in Henry's bad books because of the support he had given to King Stephen against the Empress Matilda. Nevertheless, he was a tenant-in-chief of the king of England and professed full loyalty and homage to him. David fitz Gerald was of mixed Welsh and Norman stock, son of a Welsh princess and a high-ranking

---

[1] Text in Giraldus, *Expugnatio*, pp 26–7. See discussion on its authenticity and genuineness, ibid., pp 289–90.

[2] There is no near-adequate published account of Richard fitz Gilbert ('Strongbow'), but see Michael Altschul, *A baronial family in medieval England: the Clares, 1217–1314* (Baltimore, 1965), ch. I; T. A. Archer, 'Clare, Richard de' in *D.N.B.*; G.E.C., *Peerage*, x, 352–7; Giraldus, *Expugnatio*, index, under 'fitz Gilbert (Richard de Clare)', pp 369–70. With reference to Ireland, there is much of value in Marie-Thérèse Flanagan, 'Strongbow, Henry II, and Anglo-Norman intervention in Ireland' in John C. Holt and John Gillingham (ed.), *War and government in the middle ages: essays in honour of J. O. Prestwich* (Woodbridge, N.Y., 1984), pp 62–77.

Anglo-Norman official, and had equally mixed political sympathies, but in practice was a trimmer. Rhys ap Gruffydd, formerly king of north Wales, had submitted to Henry II in 1158, but joined the great Welsh uprising of 1164–5, and though now in arms against Henry was on amicable terms with Bishop David fitz Gerald and his brother, Maurice. He shared with them a common problem, their half-brother, Robert fitz Stephen, who at this stage had been a prisoner of Rhys for three years. Robert, a dashing soldier and a man of honour, was captured by treachery while commanding the royal castle at Aberteifi (Cardigan) and handed over to his cousin, Rhys, who offered him liberty if he would take up arms against Henry II. To his credit Robert refused the offer, and remained in chains. Bishop David and Maurice fitz Gerald then arranged with Rhys that Robert be temporarily released in order to meet Diarmait Mac Murchada in their company. The upshot was a bargain. Robert would be given full freedom, so that he and Maurice could lead the advance troops to Ireland. The Anglo-Normans would help to restore Mac Murchada to his inheritance, and in return Robert and Maurice would receive the town of Wexford and two neighbouring cantreds. Mac Murchada had no legal right to grant away Wexford town and the adjoining acres, but in the context of the power struggle in Leinster he aimed by one ruthless stroke to subjugate the Norsemen of Wexford and to establish permanent allies in their place. Might was right.

Mac Murchada was impatient to be back in his native Uí Chennselaig, and he needed to re-establish himself there in order to prepare the way for the arrival of his foreign allies. With him in August 1167 came one knight, Richard fitz Godebert from Pembrokeshire, a small number of archers and sergeants, and at least one Welsh warrior, the son of Rhys ap Gruffydd. Mac Murchada resumed power smoothly in Uí Chennselaig, his reception gladly assured by the Augustinian canons at Ferns, with whom he made his headquarters. His old enemies, Ruaidrí Ua Conchobair and Tigernán Ua Ruairc, disturbed by the news of his return, set out with limited forces to attack him. Mac Murchada did not wait for the assault but confronted them at Killistown, in Ossory. There was no pitched battle, just two minor skirmishes, and in one of them the son of Rhys ap Gruffydd was killed by Ua Ruairc's men. Mac Murchada's obvious political isolation and the sight of so few foreign allies with him gave Ua Conchobair and Ua Ruairc a false sense of security. They allowed him to come to terms. He gave seven hostages to Ua Conchobair and a hundred ounces of gold to Ua Ruairc as the honour price for the abduction of Derbforgaill fifteen years beforehand. Fitz Godebert returned to Wales and Mac Murchada retired to Ferns to bide his time. It was a long wait, almost two years. He might well have suffered further intrusions, particularly from Ua Ruairc, had it not been for the fact that Ua Conchobair and Ua Ruairc, still acting in concert, were busy during this time, first with their invasion and division of Munster in 1168, then with a similar treatment of Meath in 1169.

CHAPTER III

Allies and an overlord, 1169–72

F. X. MARTIN

THE year 1168 came and went, but no Anglo-Normans arrived in Uí Chenn-selaig to allow Mac Murchada to take the initiative against his enemies. The following spring wore on, and with no allies in sight his impatience grew. Time was running out on him, as were the circumstances that were keeping his in-veterate opponents, Ua Conchobair and Ua Ruairc, occupied in Meath and Munster. Diarmait's insecurity was made evident early in 1169 when the high-king Ruaidrí Ua Conchobair, made a hosting into Meath and Leinster. He visited Dublin as its overlord, then proceeded to Uí Chennselaig, and, having secured Conchobar Mac Murchada, Diarmait's son, as a hostage, returned satisfied to Connacht. A more immediate danger, on Mac Murchada's very border, was the implacable Mac Gilla Pátraic of Ossory.

The writing appeared to be on the wall for Diarmait, who was now isolated and beleaguered. Only decisive action could undo the adverse circumstances in which he found himself. He despatched his latimer (interpreter), Maurice O'Regan, to Wales to notify all interested parties, as a matter of urgency, that now was the time to move, that Mac Murchada's money awaited them, that lands in Ireland were for the taking. Fitz Stephen, whose unenviable choice was between an indefinite stay in a dungeon at Cardigan and the hazards of a military expedition to a strange land overseas, was the pioneer who led the first force of Anglo-Normans westward.

They sailed in three ships from Milford Haven, tightly packed contingents which altogether amounted to about 300 fighting men. It might be more precise to describe them as Cambro-Normans, the lively mixed breed of Normans and Welsh, accompanied by many of the Flemings who had been settled in Pem-broke since the beginning of the century. The spearhead of this advance force was a family group of thirty knights, relatives of fitz Stephen and their depen-dants. Later they were joined by other blood-relations. Gerald of Wales, who knew them all personally, gilded their origins by describing them as 'Geral-dines', descendants of Gerald of Windsor, his own grandfather. More accur-ately they should be described as 'Nestines', descendants of the extraordinary

Nesta, their common physical link, wife of Gerald of Windsor. This amorous lady, daughter of Rhys ap Tewdwr, prince of south Wales, had children by Stephen, constable of Cardigan (father of Robert fitz Stephen), King Henry I of England (grandfather of Meiler fitz Henry), and at least one other man. But she was married to Gerald of Windsor, and therefore her descendants all proudly claimed to be 'Geraldines'.

With that first group of Anglo-Normans at Bannow came Hervey de Montmorency, whom Gerald of Wales introduces on the scene with hostile comment as 'another fugitive from fortune, unarmed and destitute, a spy sent in the interest of Earl Richard, whose uncle he was, rather than a would-be conqueror of Ireland'.[1] At a later stage in his narrative Gerald, in a typical demonstration of style and spite, presents his estimate of Hervey. The description of Hervey's physical appearance was laudatory, but Gerald then adds what is nothing short of character assassination.[2] This denunciation of Hervey indicates an important fact that Gerald obscures and even misrepresents, namely the wholehearted involvement of Strongbow in the project. Most modern historians have accepted Gerald's presentation of Strongbow's role. Since Gerald wished to highlight the part played by the descendants of Nesta in establishing the Anglo-Normans in Ireland, he presents Strongbow as reluctant to commit himself to Mac Murchada's invitation and finally as pushed to active participation by messages from Mac Murchada. The facts, on the contrary, show that by the time O'Regan arrived in Wales, Strongbow already had his mind set on Ireland. This was understood by Mac Murchada. Strongbow sent Hervey de Montmorency ahead as a convincing pledge of his intentions and as a trusted observer to monitor the crucial early stages of the venture.

The evidence indicates that Strongbow was the guiding spirit in Wales behind the expedition, even if it was the Geraldines who formed the van in Ireland and captured the first glory. Gerald of Wales took good care to stress that latter aspect. Modern propagandists could profitably study how a myth was fashioned by Gerald. In contrast with the supposedly vacillating Strongbow the Geraldines appear as a race of heroes, men of decision. They are presented as emboldened with a messianic belief in their own high destiny, the conviction that they were a chosen race with a doubly noble descent, from the unconquerable Trojan exiles who had reputedly settled in Wales in the seventh century B.C., and from the adventurous Normans who invaded Wales in the eleventh century and married those who claimed to be descendants of the Trojan exiles. It would be hard to overrate the psychological advantage of this conviction, no matter how historically unreliable was the belief in descent from heroic Trojans.

The incoming ships from Wales were almost certainly guided by a Wexford navigator, or at least had precise directions from Mac Murchada as to where they should land. On 1 May the Anglo-Normans beached their ships on

[1] Giraldus, *Expugnatio*, pp 31, 33.   [2] Ibid., pp 159, 161.

Bannow Island, which in those days was still separated from the mainland on both sides by narrow channels, and on the eastern side had a sandy beach suitable for ships with a low draught. It was one of the few safe anchorages on the southern stretch of the Wexford coast. It had natural defences—the channels on both sides, with the bay to the north and the sea to the south, completing the security. It was sufficiently distant from both Wexford and Waterford to be free from immediate attack by the Norsemen, yet it was conveniently situated for the Anglo-Normans to ferry their troops easily across the channels for an attack on either town. This they did in due time.

The newcomers camped on the seashore and sent word of their arrival to Ferns. Mac Murchada responded promptly with an advance group of followers headed by his natural son, the hardy Domnall Cáemánach. On 2 May a second contingent of Anglo-Normans arrived in two ships, some 200 men, ten knights with accompanying archers, led by Maurice de Prendergast. Shortly afterwards Mac Murchada drew rein at Bannow strand, with a force of 500 men. On the following day the combined Irish and Anglo-Norman force began its assault on Wexford town. After two days' resistance the townsmen decided to negotiate for peace. Within a short time a bargain had been struck. No retribution would be exacted from the Wexfordmen for their resistance, but they agreed to acknowledge Mac Murchada as their sovereign lord, and, in proof of their good faith, to hand over possession of the town, with four principal burgesses as hostages. Mac Murchada, for his part, proved his good faith to the Anglo-Normans by making over the town and its immediate possessions to fitz Stephen and Maurice fitz Gerald. Significantly he granted the two strategic cantreds of territory between Wexford and Waterford to Strongbow's uncle, Hervey de Montmorency. Strongbow's controlling figure was there in the background.

What had been achieved was a memorable victory for Mac Murchada. He had secured for his allies an essential condition for ultimate victory—a secure sea-base. Furthermore, there was now no danger that when a larger force landed, with Waterford as the prize to be seized, it would be attacked from the rear.

The most obvious danger was from Mac Gilla Pátraic of Osraige. It was inevitable that any effort by Mac Murchada to expand, even to survive, would be opposed by his neighbouring ruler, Mac Gilla Pátraic. Osraige was a strategic kingdom, considered by reason of its geographical position sometimes as part of Leinster, sometimes as part of Munster, but at all times playing a role in both provinces. Since there was a long-standing enmity between Diarmait Mac Murchada and Mac Gilla Pátraic, it was no surprise that when Diarmait was banished overseas in 1166 his kingdom had been divided between Mac Gilla Pátraic and Diarmait's own brother, Murchad Mac Murchada. To add to Diarmait's miseries his heir-apparent, Énna, was taken prisoner in that year by the men of Osraige, and two years later, in 1168, after Diarmait returned but before the arrival of the Anglo-Normans, the captive son was blinded by Donnchad Mac Gilla Pátraic. The following year Diarmait had to hand over his remaining legitimate son, Conchobar, as a hostage to Ruaidrí Ua Conchobair, thus leaving him with his natural son, Domnall Cáemánach, as his only mainstay.

Now in 1169 Diarmait decided that with the advantage of Anglo-Norman and Wexford allies it was high time to take the initiative against Osraige. However, experience had taught him the dangers of trying to fight Mac Gilla Pátraic in his native woods and thickets. Instead Diarmait and his allies feigned an attack on the border of Osraige, and retreated under a vigorous counter-attack. Mac Gilla Pátraic's men were thus drawn out to an open space where they were immediately attacked and crushed by a wave of mounted knights. The Irish and Wexfordmen completed the rout with their dreaded axes.

Mac Gilla Pátraic was undeterred by the reverses he had suffered, and gave no sign that he was willing to submit to Mac Murchada, who claimed to be his overlord. Yet there could be no security for Mac Murchada as long as there was a strong and hostile kingdom of Osraige on his flank. Besides, there were the restless lords of north Leinster, notably Mac Fáeláin of Uí Fáeláin and Ua Tuathail of Uí Muiredaig, who, like Mac Gilla Pátraic, resented Mac Murchada's claim to be their overlord. A bold stroke was his answer. He and his allies marched northwards to Kildare, raiding and pillaging the territories of Uí Fáeláin and Uí Muiredaig. He then turned south, and rounded on Mac Gilla Pátraic at a strategic point, the pass of Achad Úr (Freshford, County Kilkenny). The defeat did not become another rout of the men of Osraige: Mac Gilla Pátraic was able to withdraw to the security of the woods in his own territory.

Mac Murchada and his allies returned to Ferns with their plunder, but the victory turned sour when Prendergast announced, inexplicably, that he was withdrawing from Ireland with his 200 men. Since these formed two-fifths of Mac Murchada's foreign allies in the field it was a severe military setback, apart from loss of face. Prendergast intended to sail from Wexford, but Mac Murchada sent word to the town that no ships were to be put at the disposal of Prendergast and his defecting Flemings. Prendergast turned the tables on Mac Murchada by offering himself and his men to Mac Gilla Pátraic, who replied promptly, accepting them into his service and arranging to meet them at St Mullins. There were now foreign allies on both sides in the struggle. Prendergast was a mercenary, and saw nothing dishonest in changing sides.

To the unenlightened observer there seemed to be a stalemate in Leinster, with Mac Murchada undoubtedly stronger now that he had the Norsemen of Wexford under control, had subdued Uí Fáeláin and Uí Muiredaig, and defeated Mac Gilla Pátraic. Yet Mac Gilla Pátraic was still defiant, retained his territory, and had foreign allies in his service. Was Mac Murchada any better off with fitz Stephen, fitz Henry, and Montmorency, than he had been in 1167 with fitz Godebert? In fact there was an essential difference, but only those in

Mac Fernsada's confidence would have known of his agreement with Strong-bow and of the assurance that reinforcements would be coming shortly.

Fortunately for Mac Murchada he appeared to his enemies to be check-mated by Mac Gilla Pátraic at the very time when Ruaidrí Ua Conchobair came hosting into Leinster, attended by Tigernán Ua Ruairc of Bréifne, Diarmait Ua Máel Sechlainn of Meath, and the Norsemen of Dublin. The wonder is that Mac Gilla Pátraic did not join Ruaidrí in order to overwhelm Mac Murchada, but he had his own interests to safeguard against the high-king. Mac Murchada had everything to gain by avoiding a pitched battle against such superior numbers, but even more important were his private expectations of help from Wales. Deciding that it was better to live and fight another day, he withdrew to an almost impenetrable place of defence near Ferns apparently the Duffry. Ruaidrí first attempted, but without success, to set Mac Murchada and his foreign allies against one another. The opposing armies then went through all the motions of manoeuvring for a direct clash of arms, but the soldiers never came to blows.

Ruaidrí, who saw no profit in expending his forces on a stubborn and inven-tive enemy, already isolated in the woods and hills near Ferns and apparently without further friends or resources, allowed 'men of good will' (presumably clerics, who so constantly favoured Mac Murchada) to negotiate a settlement. Ruaidrí was to be accepted as high-king and Mac Murchada as king of Leinster; Conchobar, Mac Murchada's son, was to be given as a hostage to Ruaidrí, and the high-king in his turn promised a daughter in marriage to Con-chobar, as soon as permanent peace was established. According to Gerald of Wales there was also a private agreement between Ruaidrí and Mac Murchada that no more foreign soldiers would be introduced to the country and that those already with Mac Murchada would be sent back to Wales, as soon as Leinster was pacified. Both sides were playing for time, and Mac Murchada's unfortu-nate son, Conchobar, was an expendable pawn in the game.

Fortune turned a timely eye on Mac Murchada, even if it also turned a blind eye on his son Conchobar. Ruaidrí and his allies departed, only to be replaced shortly afterwards, to Mac Murchada's great satisfaction, by a further contingent of Anglo-Normans, who arrived in two ships at the now friendly port of Wexford. It was a limited but powerful force of 10 knights, 30 mounted archers, and 100 foot archers, all led by a formidable warrior, Maurice fitz Gerald. This third contingent was quickly put to use. Mac Gilla Pátraic, supported by Prendergast, led an expedition into Loíges (Leix) against Ua Mórda, a subject of Mac Murchada. Ua Mórda, overwhelmed for the moment, agreed to submit to Mac Gilla Pátraic in order to gain time while he appealed for help to his overlord, Mac Murchada, who moved rapidly to Loíges, with a force of Anglo-Normans led by fitz Stephen and fitz Gerald. Prendergast, doubtless for mixed motives of honour and military prudence, refused to join battle with his former companions-in-arms, and managed to withdraw unscathed to Waterford and take ship with his men back to Wales.

Mac Murchada took full advantage of the favourable turn of events. He and fitz Gerald marched north to the neighbourhood of Dublin town and laid waste the hinterland with its crops and cattle. The citizens understood the message and did not put him to the test of storming their walls. Instead they hastily submitted to him as overlord, as they had already done in 1162, and thus did not allow him a justification to dispose of the town to one of his lieutenants, as he had already done with Wexford after it had initially resisted him, when the first Anglo-Normans landed with fitz Stephen. For the moment Mac Murchada was content to bide his time with Dublin. He now had Leinster, with Dublin, under his control, and Mac Gilla Pátraic was subdued, at least temporarily.

Mac Murchada's ambition to be high-king, and an opportunity to settle his score with a long-standing rival, Ruaidrí Ua Conchobair, king of Connacht and *ard-rí*, coincided with an appeal for help from Domnall Mór Ua Briain, king of Thomond and son-in-law of Mac Murchada. Ruaidrí, in order to keep the O'Briens weak, had divided Munster between Domnall Ua Briain and Diarmait Mac Carthaig, king of Desmond, but Domnall now appealed to Mac Murchada for support. With Leinster in submission, Mac Murchada was free to send a force of Anglo-Normans, led by fitz Stephen and fitz Henry, to Limerick. The foreign allies made all the difference to Domnall, who was able to worst Ruaidrí and force him to retire across the Shannon. Ruaidrí retaliated by returning with a great fleet, apparently down the Shannon, and then counter-attacked across the river into Thomond and Ormond, destroying the plank bridge at Killaloe in the process. Yet as long as the small but expert band of Anglo-Normans remained with Domnall the best that Ruaidrí could accomplish was to attack, not to defeat or conquer. When it was clear to Domnall that the immediate danger from Connacht was over, fitz Stephen and his men withdrew to rejoin Mac Murchada in Uí Chennselaig and to await the arrival of Strongbow. Brief as had been the intervention in Munster it had revealed one all-important fact: how comparatively easy it was for a small military force of Anglo-Normans to play a decisive part there between the contending principalities and to thwart the high-king with his army and fleet.

The portent of what the Anglo-Normans could achieve in Irish affairs, even in adverse circumstances, was starkly indicated with the arrival of Raymond fitz Gerald, better known as Raymond 'le Gros' ('the Fat'). He and his uncle, Maurice fitz Gerald, are the two heroes of the epic presented by Gerald of Wales in his 'Conquest of Ireland'. Raymond with his followers, ten knights and seventy archers, arrived in two ships, probably in early May 1170. They put in at the creek of Dún Domnaill, eight miles to the east of Waterford town. The creek, later known as Baginbun, apparently because of the two ships named *La Bague* and *La Bonne*, has been immortalised in the rhyme:

> At the creek of Baginbun
> Ireland was lost and won.

The landing place had been carefully selected, and was as strategic an entry point as had been Bannow Bay, the scene of the first landing a year previously. Just as Bannow Bay gave easy access to Wexford but had natural defences, so it was with Baginbun which was selected as the springboard for the taking of Waterford. Rising steeply above the creek of Baginbun is a high rocky headland, which has an ample flat area of about two acres, narrowing to an easily defensible neck, where it joins the mainland. Furthermore, a substantial earthwork, apparently of Celtic origin, runs across the neck of land and makes the headland into a fort.

As soon as word reached Wexford that Raymond had landed he was joined by Hervey de Montmorency, with three knights and their followers. It was the only welcoming party to greet Raymond until his first battle was over. The significance of Hervey's prompt arrival has not been appreciated by historians, and Gerald of Wales assiduously avoids more than mere mention of Hervey at this point. Raymond, though a Geraldine, a nephew of Stephen and Maurice fitz Gerald, was a member of Strongbow's retinue, and came expressly as the advance guard for him and his army. Strongbow was obviously directing the whole project and was not the reluctant supporter of the expedition to Ireland, as Gerald would have us believe.

One of Raymond's first actions was practical and limited, but it was to have important military consequences. To ensure that he would have victuals for his men, and perhaps also to provide stores in advance for Strongbow's army, he plundered the surrounding countryside and drove a herd of cattle back to the camp on Dún Domnaill headland. To raid cattle was to strike at the basic economy of the Gaelic system, and would guarantee an automatic reprisal. Besides, it was becoming evident to the Norsemen of Waterford town that Mac Murchada might well have ambitions, backed by the Anglo-Normans from overseas, which would engulf them all. After the Norse of Waterford had rapidly taken counsel with Máel Sechnaill Ua Fáeláin, prince of the Déise (Decies), and with Ua Riain of Uí Dróna, a tripartite force converged on Dún Domnaill. There were about 100 Anglo-Normans in the camp, and against them, according to both Gerald of Wales and 'The song of Dermot and the earl', was advancing a combined force of some 3,000 Norse and Gaelic Irish. This latter figure is, almost certainly, much exaggerated. There were, perhaps, 1,000 Norse and Irish against the Anglo-Normans. Even that was, for the Anglo-Normans, an adverse ratio of 10:1.

The battle began with what may have seemed to be a false move by the Anglo-Normans. Raymond and his followers, knights, sergeants, and archers, sallied forth to confront the attackers, who surged forward through the neck of land towards the fort on the headland. The Anglo-Normans, either because of a prearranged plan or genuinely overcome by the onslaught, rapidly withdrew back into the fort, leaving Raymond as sentinel at the gate. He lunged with his sword, transfixing the first of the attackers attempting to enter the fort, and at that point, as if by a signal, the herd of cattle inside the fort rushed through the gate straight into the massed ranks of the Irish and Norsemen. The cattle, crazed with noise and excitement, charged to right and left, creating havoc among the soldiers on the headland. The Anglo-Normans emerged once again from the fort, but this time had the comparatively easy task of routing a confused mob of armed men. At least 500 attackers were left dead on the field, and 70 of the Waterford Norse were taken prisoner.

According to Gerald of Wales the prisoners became the subject of a dispute among the leaders, Raymond arguing that they be used as hostages to secure ransom from Waterford, while Hervey de Montmorency declared that they should be executed as an example to all who might be wavering in their support for Diarmait and the Anglo-Normans. Hervey's argument carried the day, and an orgy of executions took place. The prisoners had their limbs broken and were then beheaded by Alice of Abergavenny, a camp-follower who had come with the Anglo-Normans. She used the axe without pity, to avenge the death of her lover, one of those who had fallen in battle. The bodies were then thrown over the cliffs, to complete the lesson in terrorism. The massacre was a grim curtain-raiser for the siege of Waterford, but only served to strengthen the resolve of the townsfolk.

Waterford did not have long to wait. On the other side of the Irish Sea Strongbow had already assembled 200 knights and a supporting force of some 1,000 soldiers of other ranks. They marched through south Wales, along the coastal road, with St David's as the assembly point. On the way Strongbow succeeded in persuading Maurice de Prendergast and his men to join him. There was one unnerving last-minute hitch. Strongbow, with his troops assembled, got word that Henry II had forbidden the expedition to leave Wales. Would he defy his king and feudal lord? This was the acid test for a medieval man. Strongbow felt no personal loyalty to his monarch, having long been in the political wilderness. He was out of royal favour, having supported King Stephen against the Empress Matilda and her son, Henry. Already a loser in popular estimation, he would now totally lose face and political credibility if he withdrew at the eleventh hour. Strongbow decided to brazen it out, and had a reasonable argument to justify his decision. He had previously sought permission to lead the expedition to Ireland, and Henry had given it orally, in a casual, almost jocose, manner. It was a cunning method which would later allow the king to benefit, no matter what the outcome. If Strongbow succeeded it would be apparently with the initial blessing of his king. If he failed Henry could wash his hands of the affair, claiming that he spoke merely in jest. The king was to use the same form of ambiguous reply when John de Courcy was contemplating the invasion of Ulster.

The expedition sailed from Milford Haven on 23 August 1170, and put in without incident at Passage, a well-chosen anchorage a few miles from Waterford, below the junction of the sister rivers, the Suir and the Barrow. Raymond's victory at Dún Domnaill had seen to it that there would be no hostile intervention by Irish or Norsemen, during those crucial hours when the army was disembarking. The following day, Raymond arrived at the camp with forty knights, a timely appearance, demonstrating that the Anglo-Normans, other than those who fought at Dún Domnaill, had been expecting their leader. Nevertheless, events now began to move so fast that the main group of Strongbow's allies and supporters, already in the country, led by Diarmait Mac Murchada and fitz Stephen, were late for the earl's first decisive victory, the taking of Waterford.

There was no attempt to negotiate the surrender of the town, as at Wexford, nor was the assault carefully planned. On 25 August, the day after Raymond and his followers arrived at Passage, Strongbow moved against Waterford, obviously expecting to take it by surprise. This was a miscalculation. The town covered a triangular area of about fifteen acres, secured on one side by the Suir, defended by strong walls, fortified by towers, notably Reginald's tower. The shock of the events at Dún Domnaill had stiffened the traditional independence of the townsfolk, and with them they had Máel Sechnaill Ua Fáeláin and the Gaelic Irish who had survived the disaster on the headland. Twice the Anglo-Normans swept up to the walls, but failed to overrun them. In the crucial minutes of uncertainty which followed these failures Raymond le Gros showed that quality, improvisation, essential to a successful leader in battle. He was the commander in the field, while Strongbow directed from a distance. Raymond's gimlet eye noticed a small building jutting out from the wall, supported on the outside by a wooden beam. He urged the Anglo-Normans to assault simultaneously the two walls available for attack by land, but he also instructed a separate group to cut down the beam. The troops launched themselves at the walls, and, as soon as the beam was cut through, the building collapsed outwards, dragging with it a substantial section of the wall. Through that gap rushed troops who had been standing by for the opportunity. Thus fell the Norse city kingdom of Waterford.

Even with the Anglo-Normans battling within the walls of Waterford the Norse did not readily submit. There was savage fighting in the streets, and 700 defenders are reputed to have perished. Two Norse commanders, both named Sitric, and taken in Reginald's tower, were executed on the spot, probably cut down in the heat of battle. Two other leaders, Ragnall, a Norseman, and Máel Sechnaill, prince of the Déise, captured in the same place, were spared for the moment. As soon as Waterford had been taken, Strongbow sent word to Mac Murchada, who came post-haste with fitz Stephen, Maurice fitz Gerald, and their troops. Surprisingly it was Mac Murchada, normally pictured by Gerald of Wales as a savage and bloodthirsty character, who, on arrival in Waterford, intervened to save the lives of Ragnall and Máel Sechnaill. That act of magnanimity was a prelude to the hour of triumph when, with the benediction of the church, and in the presence of the Anglo-Normans and their Irish allies, Mac Murchada handed over his daughter, Aífe, in marriage to Strongbow.

The importance of the capture of Waterford has not been properly assessed. It has always had a dramatic place in the story of Ireland because of the marriage of Strongbow and Aífe. At a different level historians have looked with little emotion but keen perception on a new phenomenon, a marriage alliance between Gaelic and Anglo-Norman ways of life. That had already been initiated, though without much political fruit, when the Cambro-Norman, Arnulf of Montgomery, married Lafracoth, daughter of Muirchertach Ua Briain, king of Munster, in 1102. For the Anglo-Normans attempting to establish themselves in Ireland the taking of Waterford was more important militarily than the capture of Wexford or any other town except Dublin. Had Strongbow fallen short at that stage there would have been no need for Henry II to intervene in Ireland. The Anglo-Normans already in Ireland, in the persons of the Geraldines, would have remained powerful military allies and mercenaries for various Irish kings, but like the Norsemen before them they would have remained on the periphery of Irish affairs. The taking of Waterford made Strongbow a major power in the land, and it rendered possible the capture of Dublin. It brought Henry II to Ireland and with him the Anglo-Norman way of life and institutions on a national scale.

Mac Murchada and Strongbow held a council of war at Waterford, with Maurice fitz Gerald, fitz Stephen, Raymond le Gros, Maurice de Prendergast, fitz Henry, and other knights present. The Anglo-Norman leaders were of one mind: Dublin should be taken, and as soon as possible. Mac Murchada readily assented to this view since he realised that he would never have security as king of Leinster unless he effectively controlled Dublin. It was not merely of great strategic importance because of its geographical position vis-à-vis Ulster, Man, Wales, and England. It was an internationally famous trading centre, and had developed as a wealthy Hiberno-Norse settlement with its own character, remaining aloof even when it had to submit to successive overlords from the other provinces of Ireland. It was also of increasing ecclesiastical importance as a metropolitan see, competing with the traditional centres at Armagh and Cashel. Besides, Mac Murchada had a personal score to settle with the Norse of Dublin. Not content to defeat and kill his father Donnchad in 1115, they had then buried the body, with a dog, in front of the speaker's platform in the courtyard of their assembly hall. It was a calculated insult added to injury.

Mac Murchada returned to Ferns with the pioneer Anglo-Normans, leaving Strongbow and his men to consolidate their position at Waterford. Mac Murchada gathered together as many men as possible from his Irish allies and led them to Waterford. Now he was on the offensive, determined to subdue Dublin. Strongbow, as intent as Mac Murchada on capturing Dublin, left no more than a skeleton force to hold Waterford in his absence. The news of Mac Murchada's intentions travelled and was not taken lightly in Dublin by its Norse ruler, Askulv, son of Ragnall, who had already heard of what had befallen his Norse cousins at Wexford and Waterford. He had no experience of the Anglo-Normans as opponents in battle but knew what to expect from Mac Murchada, whose rule he had accepted, even if reluctantly, in 1162, and rejected in 1169 when he allied himself with Ua Conchobair and Ua Ruairc.

Askulv's urgent appeal to the high-king, Ruaidrí Ua Conchobair, brought a powerful response. Limited as were Ruaidrí's horizons he realised that more was at stake than a dispute between Mac Murchada and the Dublin Norse, that his own role as high-king would next be in question. On the other hand there is no convincing evidence that Ruaidrí saw the Anglo-Normans as the real danger, as introducing a way of life which might well supplant or absorb the traditional Irish pattern.[1] It was enough to know that Mac Murchada and his foreign allies were altering the balance of power in the country. Ruaidrí promptly led a large army to Dublin and was supported by separate forces under Tigernán Ua Ruairc of Bréifne, Máel Sechlainn Ua Máel Sechlainn of Meath, and Murchad Ua Cerbaill of Airgialla. It was a formidable combination, but far from 'all the pride of Ireland', or 'almost all the inhabitants of Ireland' as two main contemporary sources of information would have us believe.[2] Ruaidrí, arguing probably from the case of Waterford, was aware that the Anglo-Normans, unlike the Irish, were well-versed in storming towns and cities, and wisely made it his main object to prevent Mac Murchada and the Anglo-Normans getting within assault distance of the walls of Dublin. With that in mind he set his army down on the plain at Clondalkin, five miles south-west of Dublin, confidently awaiting them.

Mac Murchada recommended that an unexpected approach should be made to Dublin, over the Wicklow–Dublin mountains. The plan worked, with startling results. The army at Clondalkin and its associated groups, suddenly finding Mac Murchada and his allies between themselves and Dublin, folded up their tents and stole away. It was a bloodless victory, but only a preliminary to Mac Murchada's main object, the capture of Dublin. Askulv and the citizens of Dublin were now on their own but they had the security of their city walls and the tradition of reckless viking courage. Neither was to prove adequate in the circumstances.

Mac Murchada, for all his personal bravery, saw no point in expending his own men and his allies in an assault that might not be successful. He sent his trusted secretary, Maurice O'Regan, to negotiate the surrender of Dublin with Askulv and the citizens. His demands were not excessive. He wanted to be

---

[1] Ruaidrí's alleged speech, as reported by Giraldus, *Expugnatio*, pp 43, 45, is a remarkable appeal 'in defence of our fatherland and our freedom', but was a concoction by Gerald of what he rightly saw as a clash between two cultures; see ibid., p. 297, n. 50.

[2] Giraldus, *Expugnatio*, p. 51; *Song of Dermot*, p. 117.

recognised once again as overlord, and, for security, to have thirty citizens as hostages. Askulv agreed to the condition, and the citizens accepted it in principle but showed an understandable reluctance as individuals to volunteer to be hostages. A hostage suffered death or blinding if the lord he represented betrayed his trust. The fate of two of Mac Murchada's sons, Énna and Conchobar, proved that. It was often easier to trust the man who held you hostage than the lord whom you represented. The archbishop of Dublin, Lorcán Ua Tuathail, anxious to prevent bloodshed, agreed to act with O'Regan as negotiator. The fact that the archbishop was a brother-in-law of Mac Murchada, though admittedly no ally of his, gave solid ground for a peaceful solution, but the citizens continued to argue among themselves about the dubious honour of being nominated, or volunteering, as hostages. They were further demoralised by what they assumed to be divine displeasure when, in the course of a storm, lightning struck Dublin and burned part of the town.

While the negotiations and wrangling dragged on for three days patience was wearing thin among the younger Anglo-Norman knights, particularly de Cogan and Raymond le Gros. They decided, without consulting Mac Murchada or Strongbow, to attack, and de Cogan had the advantage of being encamped with his men near to the city walls. Even Mac Murchada must have been startled by the battle-cry 'Barons! Knights! A Cogan! A Cogan!' as de Cogan and his men, followed by Raymond le Gros, streamed towards the town walls. It was all over quickly. The attack was launched with ferocity and bloody success. Little of the traditional viking courage was displayed by Askulv and his followers, who took to their heels, seizing whatever precious movable possessions were within reach, then escaping in their ships overseas to the Isle of Man and the northern isles. They declared their intention to return and fight another day, and to their credit they did so, as we shall see. De Cogan's attack was little short of treachery, as peace negotiations were well in progress at the time. Furthermore, it left Archbishop Lorcán Ua Tuathail in a dubious role in the eyes of his Dublin flock, since they might well assume that his peace negotiations were a blind, and that he was privy to the deception. The victors had no qualms of conscience. Mac Murchada and Strongbow gladly accepted the *fait accompli*, and were even more satisfied when they found Dublin rich in valuables and victuals—two items essential to freebooting expeditions in the Norman tradition.

Significantly, it was not to Mac Murchada but to Strongbow that de Cogan gave the control of the town, even though it was Mac Murchada who had been negotiating for its surrender. This was a sharp indication of the real issues at stake. The prevalent Irish system of individual war-lords campaigning for particular prizes was ending. A new era was beginning, based on the Anglo-Norman way of life. Allies were becoming overlords. The change did not prevent Mac Murchada from pursuing his own aims, even though all of his gains were being amassed to the credit of his son-in-law, Strongbow. Predictably Mac Murchada first set out to cripple the unrelenting Tigernán Ua Ruairc, whose kingdom now extended diagonally across Ireland from the mouth of the Erne to the mouth of the Boyne. Mac Murchada had a powerful Irish ally in his new campaign, Domnall Bregach Ua Máel Sechlainn, who in the previous year had murdered an uncle, Diarmait, king of Meath, but had then been expelled by Ruaidrí Ua Conchobair. The high-king had taken the opportunity to carve up the kingdom of Meath, retaining much of the western part for himself, giving most of east Meath to Tigernán Ua Ruairc, and the remaining portion of the kingdom to a cooperative member of the family, Máel Sechlainn Ua Máel Sechlainn. This arrangement was now in danger, with Ruaidrí and Tigernán withdrawn to the west, and Dublin in the hands of the Anglo-Normans.

Mac Murchada and Strongbow went on a devastating campaign through Meath and up into Ua Ruairc territory in Bréifne. In the process they burned Clonard, Kells, and several other monastic settlements. To complete the campaign they restored Domnall Bregach as ruler of the Ua Máel Sechlainn territory. When Tigernán reacted, by demanding of Ruaidrí that he exact the price of Mac Murchada's attack, three hostages held by Ruaidrí were put to death: Mac Murchada's own son, Conchobar; his grandson, son of Domnall Cáemánach; and Murchad Ua Cáellaide, son of Diarmait's foster-brother. Though Mac Murchada was victorious in Leinster it was thus at great personal loss. He returned with his army to Ferns for the last time, spent the winter there, and died unexpectedly about May 1171.

Diarmait had been a turbulent figure on the Irish scene for almost half a century. He was a capable, ruthless, and imaginative leader, who (it can be argued) was not only ahead of the Ireland of his own day but has not yet been properly assessed by Irish historians in the twentieth century. The stark contrast of opinion about him is evident in the record of his death in two contemporary Irish annals. The Armagh Annals of Ulster state that he 'died in Ferns without unction, without body of Christ, without penance, without a will, in reparation to Columcille and Finnian and to the saints besides, whose churches he destroyed'. The annalist was outraged by Diarmait's ravaging of Meath, not by his introduction of the Anglo-Normans. But Diarmait's friend Áed Mac Crimthainn, abbot of Terryglass, wrote in the Book of Leinster that he died 'at Ferns, after the victory of [extreme] unction and penance, in the sixty-first year of his age'.

Though considerable power now passed to Strongbow he found himself beset both with troubles in Ireland and with the threat from his lord overseas. The satisfaction of knowing that Ruaidrí Ua Conchobair had retired to his native Connacht was offset by an alarming change in Munster. The MacCarthys of Desmond, currently allies of Ruaidrí, attacked the town of Waterford, held by a small garrison of Anglo-Normans in the absence of Strongbow with his main army based in Dublin. It was a crucial hour for the Anglo-Normans. Had

Ruaidrí, with the army which he had withdrawn intact from the unsuccessful challenge to Mac Murchada and the Anglo-Normans at Dublin, marched in support of his allies, the MacCarthys, at Waterford, he might well have imperilled the whole Anglo-Norman venture in Ireland. Ruaidrí was, however, checkmated by the O'Briens who, as the Annals of Tigernach expressed it, 'rebelled against him', and thus barred his route to Waterford.

This was the breathing-space which Strongbow desperately needed in view of the ominous message from his Angevin master. It had been convenient for Henry II to accept Diarmait Mac Murchada as his ally and to impart a general blessing to the Anglo-Normans willing to try their luck in Ireland. He was doubtless relieved to be rid of Strongbow, with his restless Cambro-Norman cousins and supporters, from the marcher lands in south Wales. One of his problems would be solved if Ireland now treated Strongbow as north Wales had dealt with Henry himself in 1157. Instead Henry was served with the news that Strongbow had become a favoured son of fortune in Ireland, and had married a daughter of the king of Leinster, with the right of succession to his territories. Henry might accept that, with Mac Murchada dead, Strongbow would become lord of the towns of Wexford and Waterford, but the affair was no longer of merely local or provincial importance when Strongbow took Dublin directly under his rule. An established lord of Dublin would have a fleet with which he could control the Irish Sea and intervene in Welsh and English affairs. Furthermore, an ambitious king of Leinster, with a loyal Dublin at his back, could reasonably aim to be high-king of Ireland. Altogether it was a far from reassuring prospect for the vigilant Henry II, who was conscious that Strongbow was not only a member of the powerful de Clare family with lands in England, Wales, and France but was also connected by his first marriage with William the Conqueror and was a direct descendant of Richard I, count of Normandy (942–96). What was to prevent Strongbow, lord of Strigoil, from attempting in Ireland what Duke William of Normandy had achieved in England?

Henry II was in his element in this dangerous game of guess and chance. The dice were loaded in his favour as feudal lord of the Anglo-Normans already in Ireland. He issued a decree forbidding any ship to sail from his dominions to Ireland. More importantly, he also ordered that all of his subjects who had gone to Ireland be given an option: to return to his territory before Easter, or to forfeit all their possessions and be excluded from the realm. Under those conditions Strongbow could not remain unresponsive, and he made his first move to neutralise Henry by sending his trusted lieutenant, Raymond le Gros, to the king, who was then in distant Aquitaine. The message brought by Raymond was a studied piece of diplomatic tact.[1] By way of intro-

---

[1] The text of the letter is given in Giraldus, *Expugnatio*, p. 71. Mention of the two other emissaries, Maurice fitz Gerald and Hervey de Montmorency, sent separately from Raymond, is made, ibid., pp 81, 89.

duction it gently reminded Henry that Strongbow had gone to Ireland, with the king's permission, in order to restore Mac Murchada to his lawful inheritance. Strongbow hastened to add that whatever had come into his hands in Ireland was there by grace and favour of Henry, and was at his disposal. This was welcome, even if not alluring, music to Henry, but he affected to turn a deaf ear to it.

With Raymond, or shortly after him, had gone Maurice fitz Gerald, another trusted ally of Strongbow. He appeared to be as unsuccessful as Raymond, but it is noticeable that Henry did not slam, or even close, the door against further negotiations. There was always the danger that excessive demands on loyalty would push Strongbow and his companions too far. Had not the Montgomery settlers in Wales claimed that they were goaded into rebellion by Henry I in 1102? If it had been difficult for Henry I to subdue rebellious subjects in Wales, would it not be doubly more difficult for Henry II to control them in Ireland? Henry II was in the dark as to what probabilities Ireland held for Strongbow, who undoubtedly appeared to have established himself as a power in that incomprehensible land. All these reasons added up to convince Henry II that he should inspect the Irish scene with his own eyes, and with his armed forces.

Predictably, the next move was made by Strongbow. As a further spokesman to the king he sent his uncle, Hervey de Montmorency, one of his most trusted agents and a senior figure, who had been with the advance contingent of troops which landed at Bannow Bay in May 1169. Hervey made, or was allowed to think that he had made, a favourable impression on Henry. He was given to believe that the problem might well be resolved if Strongbow would show his true loyal colours by appearing in person before the king. The suggestion hardly left any choice since it also became known that Henry intended to visit Ireland, and with an army. However, it would be a mistake to see the situation merely in an Irish context. A crisis, with international ramifications, had developed over the murder of Archbishop Thomas Becket on 29 December 1170. One consequence was Henry's decision to distance himself as far as possible from the papal legates, Cardinals Albert and Theodinus, who had travelled to France to demand an explanation, and if necessary an admission of guilt and submission for absolution, for the shocking deed in Canterbury cathedral. Where better for Henry to isolate himself from the two legates than in Ireland, the *Ultima Thule*?

Besides, the political situation in Ireland, as it developed after the death of Diarmait Mac Murchada in 1171, was a genuine pressing reason for visiting the country with a show of arms. Strongbow and his followers had become during 1170–71 the most powerful military force in Ireland, but only after an excruciating ordeal when everything had been balanced on a knife-edge, with Dublin besieged by a massive convergence of armies from three provinces of Ireland. Henry would have wept no tears on that occasion if Strongbow and his companions had been defeated, rather than victorious and independent. As a preliminary to that ordeal there had been a nerve-racking crisis at Dublin, months earlier, when Strongbow was absent from the town, apparently on a visit to Ferns shortly after Mac Murchada's death in 1171. Miles de Cogan, governor of Dublin, suddenly found the mouth of the Liffey filled with ships bristling with hostile soldiers. Askulv, defeated king of Dublin, had returned to exact vengeance from the Anglo-Normans who had driven him ignominiously into exile. He brought a formidable fleet of sixty or more ships, loaded with warriors from the Isle of Man and the Orkneys.

They erupted on to the shore, led by 'John the Furious', a Norseman in the authentic berserker style. Gerald of Wales supplies a vivid description of the Norse attackers:

They were warlike figures, clad in mail in every part of their body after the Danish manner. Some wore long coats of mail, others iron plates skilfully knitted together, and they had round, red shields protected by iron round the edge. These men, whose iron will matched their armour, drew up their ranks and made an attack on the walls at the eastern gate.[1]

The attack was repulsed by Miles de Cogan, the fleeing Norsemen were slaughtered by Mac Gilla Mo Cholmóc, lord of Cuala (south Dublin), who had prudently held aloof from the actual battle, and Askulv himself was captured. It was intended that he be used for ransom, presumably at the expense of the Norse of Dublin and their cousins in the Isle of Man and the Orkneys. However, when he was marched into court before Miles and his council, to discuss terms of the ransom, he displayed a defiance due either to presumption or to courage based on shame at his conduct in the face of the Anglo-Norman attacks on his town. He hotly informed his captors that if he survived they could expect larger expeditions against Dublin and a very different result. He signed his own death-warrant. No foreign power occupying Dublin could afford such a public challenge to go unanswered, with a majority of the citizens still undoubtedly hostile to the Anglo-Normans. Miles did not hesitate. Askulv was beheaded, promptly, and in public. Dubliners must know who were the masters.

Whatever relief Strongbow may have experienced on returning from Ferns in the early summer of 1171, to a Dublin firmly controlled by Miles de Cogan, was quickly dissipated on finding that Ruaidrí Ua Conchobair and his allies were moving in to crush him. For a beginning there was a revolt within Leinster itself, led by Murchad Mac Murchada, brother of the recently deceased King Diarmait. Murchad understandably resented the intrusion of an Anglo-Norman into the already complicated Mac Murchada family succession line,

---

[1] Giraldus, *Expugnatio*, p. 77. An equally important account of the battle is in *Song of Dermot*, pp 165–81. Gerald of Wales and the author of the 'Song' differ about the time of the attack by Askulv, whether before or after the siege of Dublin by Ruaidrí and his allies; see the notes by Scott and Martin in Giraldus, *Expugnatio*, pp 304–5, n. 105. Historians differ on the question, e.g. Orpen and J. F. O'Doherty.

and had armed support from other Leinster princes: Mac Fáeláin, Mac Dalbaig, Ua Tuathail, Ua Cathasaig, and the opportunist Mac Gilla Mo Cholmóc.[1] The more impressive names and numbers ranged against Strongbow were of kings from the other provinces: the high-king Ua Conchobair, Tigernán Ua Ruairc of Bréifne, Ua Máel Sechlainn of Meath, Murchad Ua Cerbaill of Airgialla, Mac Duinn Sléibe of Ulster, and Domnall Ua Briain of Thomond. Their armies took up positions to seal off Dublin from any possible Anglo-Norman reinforcements: Ua Conchobair with the main force at Castleknock, Mac Duinn Sléibe at Clontarf, Ua Briain at Kilmainham, and Murchad Mac Murchada at Dalkey.

This combination of troops could be, and has been, interpreted as a national hosting against the foreigner, but such a temporary alliance of the armies had little or nothing of a national ideal or organisation. It was hardly more than another variation of frequent dynastic power-struggles in medieval Ireland, except that in this case there was an added edge of rivalry because another dangerous competitor, the Anglo-Norman, had appeared in the arena. There is no evidence for the suggestion, first made by Gerald of Wales and since repeated even by J. F. O'Doherty, that Archbishop Lorcán Ua Tuathail was part, if not the inspiration, of the combination against the Anglo-Normans at Dublin.[2] To complete the isolation of the Anglo-Normans at Dublin a fleet of thirty ships, sent by King Godred of Man and the Norse of the northern isles, arrived to form a blockade at the mouth of the Liffey.

At this point the only Irish lords to side with the Anglo-Normans were Domnall Cáemánach (son of Diarmait), Ua Ragallaig of Uí Briúin Bréifne (who had long feuded with Tigernán Ua Ruairc), and Ua Gairbíth of Uí Felmeda (Co. Carlow). No help could be expected at Dublin from the only other Anglo-Norman bases in Ireland, Waterford and Wexford. There was a mere skeleton garrison at Waterford and it had just managed to survive the recent attack on the town by the MacCarthys of Desmond. The Anglo-Norman situation had worsened at Wexford when the intrepid commander, fitz Stephen, generously but unwisely sent thirty-six of his best troops to strengthen his beleaguered companions in Dublin. His depleted garrison was then attacked from within the town by the resentful Norsemen and besieged from without by a large force of disaffected followers of Murchad Mac Murchada of Uí Chennselaig. Fitz Stephen suffered heavy casualties but managed to withdraw to the comparative safety of a military encampment at Carrick, some two miles outside the town. This too was besieged in its turn.

---

[1] For a list of the different forces besieging Dublin see Scott and Martin in Giraldus, *Expugnatio*, p. 306, n. 115. The Mac Gilla Mo Cholmóc family, of south Dublin, later adopted the name Fitz-Dermot. The mysterious 'Machtalewi' family, as given by Giraldus, *Expugnatio*, p. 94, was first identified by Eric St John Brooks as 'Mac Dalwi' in *R.S.A.I. Jn.*, lxxi (1941), pp 53–5, but a more precise identification was recently established by Marie-Thérèse Flanagan, 'Mac Dalbaig, a Leinster chieftain' in *R.S.A.I. Jn.*, cxi (1981), pp 5–13.

[2] See notes by Scott and Martin in Giraldus, *Expugnatio*, p. 306, n. 116.

The investment of Dublin dragged on for two months in an uneventful fashion. The Irish, unused to storming castles and walled towns, were content to starve out the Anglo-Normans, who for their part were not prepared to risk their limited numbers in a pitched battle against the combined forces of their enemies. In other circumstances Strongbow could have relied on his Cambro-Norman cousins to send a fleet and armed men to his relief, but that prospect was ruled out when two of his envoys to Henry II, Raymond le Gros and Maurice fitz Gerald, returned from Aquitaine with the deflating report that the king had forbidden any ship from any of his many lands to travel to Ireland. Furthermore, all of Henry's subjects in Ireland were to return to England and Wales before the following Easter or suffer exile and disinheritance. The predicament for the Anglo-Normans at Dublin came to crisis point when a small band of Irish allies, led by Domnall Cáemánach Mac Murchada, arrived from Wexford with the news that fitz Stephen and his garrison at Carrick were under severe siege and would have to surrender unless they received help in a matter of days.

A decision had to be taken by Strongbow, but even in those grim circumstances he thought a compromise was possible. He summoned a council of his barons and knights, some twenty of them, and proposed that he negotiate with Ruaidrí Ua Conchobair, rather than gamble everything on a battle. He explained that he had in mind to send two delegates, Archbishop Lorcán Ua Tuathail and Maurice de Prendergast, with the message that he, Strongbow, would accept Ruaidrí as his lord and would hold Leinster from him. It was a radical proposal which would prevent bloodshed, and could save face on both sides. It wisely took no account of the brooding presence of Henry II in the background. The council gave full support to the proposal.[1]

The choice of delegates was astute. The chief delegate, the archbishop, highly respected by all parties, was of the Irish but fully acceptable even to the Norse of Dublin. Maurice de Prendergast was a leader of Anglo-Norman troops, but had changed sides in 1169 to serve with Mac Gilla Pátraic of Osraige, and in complimentary recognition of that fact had received the sobriquet 'Maurice of Osraige'.

Ruaidrí, believing that he had the whip hand, gave little change to the delegates. His response was blunt and immediate: the Anglo-Normans could retain Dublin, Wexford, and Waterford (at the expense of the Norsemen) but not a whit more. Unless they agreed immediately they would be attacked on the morrow. The archbishop and Maurice returned promptly to Dublin and relayed the answer, which was in effect an ultimatum. The council of barons and knights did not accept it meekly, and Maurice fitz Gerald gave vent to their feelings when he proposed that they reject the ultimatum and instead mount a vigorous attack as soon as possible. His speech included the memorable line

[1] The information about this unexpected proposal of Strongbow is available only in the *Song of Dermot*, pp 133–9.

(which might well be regarded as the motto of the later Anglo-Irish): 'just as we are English as far as the Irish are concerned, likewise to the English we are Irish, and the inhabitants of this island and the other assail us with an equal degree of hatred'.[1] He declared that if the Anglo-Normans took an instant and decisive initiative they would rout their ill-organised foes. Strongbow, sensing the mood of the meeting, spoke up, rousing his lieutenants to action, and appointed his most trusted lieutenant, Miles de Cogan, to lead the van.

Unknown to Ruaidrí and his complacent allies the Anglo-Norman force slipped out of the town, forded the Liffey, and, no doubt guided by their Irish companions, headed north towards Finglas, then changed course to the south-west in order to arrive unexpectedly beside Ruaidrí's camp at Castleknock. The sortie had been carefully timed, leaving Dublin at 4 p.m., arriving at Castleknock in the quiet of the evening as the Irish troops were relaxing before their main meal. Over 100 of them, including Ruaidrí, were bathing in the nearby river. The Irish were overwhelmed. Those bathing were butchered, though Ruaidrí escaped ingloriously. Altogether about 1,500 Irish were slain, while the only Anglo-Norman casualty was one wounded foot-soldier. Apart from the resounding military success there was the wealth of victuals, 'corn, meal, and bacon', which provided the Anglo-Normans and their horses with a year's supply of foodstuffs. This made a continuation of the siege pointless, and the Irish forces dispersed to their provinces. Strongbow returned to Dublin, confident that the citizens would cause him no trouble, and that he had a position of some strength in dealing with Henry II. But there was no time to relax, with fitz Stephen in dire need.

Strongbow, leaving Dublin once again in the resourceful hands of Miles de Cogan, set off with the intention of rescuing fitz Stephen. After a clash with Ua Riain of Uí Dróna (Idrone), who was killed, Strongbow received the news that fitz Stephen and his followers at Carrick had been captured.

Fitz Stephen had not surrendered, nor was he overpowered. He had been tricked by a false report that Dublin had fallen to the Irish, that Strongbow, Maurice fitz Gerald, Raymond le Gros and their followers were dead, that the Irish armies from Connacht and Leinster were heading towards Wexford.[2] The Wexfordmen professed to be intervening out of high regard for fitz Stephen, in order to allow him and his men to escape to Wales before the arrival of their enemies. As soon as fitz Stephen surrendered, he and his five knights were seized and put into chains, while some of his other soldiers were slaughtered. At that point news arrived that Strongbow was approaching with his troops, whereupon the Norsemen set fire to their own town, then ferried their most valuable movable possessions and the prisoners to Beggerin Island near the mouth of Wexford harbour. To storm the island would have been no great challenge for the Anglo-Normans, but Strongbow was stopped in his tracks when an emissary from the Norsemen assured him that in such an event the

[1] Giraldus, *Expugnatio*, p. 81.   [2] Ibid., p. 85.

captives would be executed and their heads sent to the attacking Anglo-Normans. Strongbow, convinced that this was not an empty threat, diverted his troops to Waterford where they were warmly welcomed by the garrison.

It was now that Strongbow showed his considerable ability to make the best of difficult circumstances.[1] At Waterford he found his uncle Hervey de Montmorency, newly returned from his visit to Henry II at Argentan with the message that Strongbow would do well to appear in person before the king, rather than wait for Henry to arrive in Ireland. It was in effect a royal command, but Strongbow had first to secure his position in Ireland before he travelled overseas. The most pressing need was to neutralise, and if possible defeat, Mac Gilla Pátraic of Osraige, who remained, as he had with Diarmait Mac Murchada, a constant threat on the borders of Uí Chennselaig and to the stability of peace in Leinster. With this in mind Strongbow called on the assistance of Domnall Mór Ua Briain, king of Thomond, whose wife was a sister of Aífe, Strongbow's new wife. Mac Gilla Pátraic was pacified—for the moment.

It was even more important to ensure stability within the Uí Chennselaig territory, which Strongbow had inherited in 1171 from his father-in-law, Diarmait Mac Murchada, with Ferns as the seat of power. Domnall Cáemánach, Diarmait's only surviving active son, was willing to accept Strongbow as his overlord, but not so Murchad, Diarmait's brother, who on Diarmait's death in 1171 had claimed the right to be king of Uí Chennselaig, according to Irish law. Murchad was succeeded in that same year by his son, Muirchertach. Murchad, and presumably Muirchertach, had been among the many Irish leaders who had joined with Ruaidrí Ua Conchobair in besieging Strongbow at Dublin some months earlier, but the memory of those two desperate months did not deflect Strongbow from a Solomon-like solution to the Uí Chennselaig problem. He recognised Muirchertach as king of Uí Chennselaig, allowing him substantial lands with the title. Domnall Cáemánach, who had never wavered in his loyalty to Diarmait and later to Strongbow, was also given the title of king, with jurisdiction on behalf of Strongbow over his Irish subjects in the other parts of Leinster, and with substantial lands in Uí Chennselaig territory.[2] It is enlightening to note that Muirchertach remained faithful to the Anglo-Normans until his death in 1193, as did Domnall Cáemánach until his violent death in 1175.

Strongbow, setting sail from Waterford, was facing one of the greatest tests, perhaps the greatest test, of his public life. He had to deal with an artful, masterly, and unscrupulous monarch, but he himself was not without considerable talents and advantages. Undoubtedly he had never been in favour with Henry II, but as a member of the powerful de Clare family, with its lands and satellite supporters in Normandy and England, Wales, and now Ireland, he

---

[1] The 'Song', favourably inclined to Strongbow, has substantial information on these events, not mentioned in Giraldus, *Expugnatio*.

[2] For this novel decision see the interpretation by Orpen, *Normans*, i, 238–9.

could not be lightly dismissed or suppressed. He was brave in battle, but shrewd and no hot-head. Furthermore, no matter how casually Henry wished to interpret the permission he had given Strongbow to go to Ireland there was the inescapable fact that by feudal standards Strongbow had acquired sword-land, territory gained by force of arms. It was an accepted tradition among the Normans, the foundation of their conquests in England, Wales, Sicily, and the Holy Land.

Henry was not going to haggle about rights and traditions. He already knew from Strongbow's emissaries, Maurice fitz Gerald, Raymond le Gros, and particularly from Hervey de Montmorency, that Strongbow had no intention of setting up an independent kingdom in Ireland. He saw the Irish scene as an opportunity to solve several of his other pressing problems, notably Wales and, more immediately, the papal legates who were on his trail.

Historians have misunderstood what took place between Henry and Strongbow. They met at Pembroke, while the feudal host destined for Ireland was assembling on the muster-ground at Newnham in Gloucestershire.[1] Gerald of Wales dramatically pictures a confrontation between the two men, with the king's anger gradually subsiding until an amicable agreement was reached. The Norman chronicler, Robert of Torigny, states that when Hervey visited Henry at Argentan in July 1171, with Strongbow's disarming offer to hand over all that he had won in Ireland, the king responded in equally generous fashion, confirming Strongbow in his lands in England, Wales, and Normandy, granting him (with obvious reservations) the territories he had acquired in Leinster, and even honouring him with the post of royal constable in Ireland.[2] This, in contrast with Gerald of Wales's version, is confirmed by 'The song of Dermot and the earl', which recounts that the subsequent meeting between Henry and Strongbow at Pembroke was friendly, that the king 'made no show of anger'.[3]

All was set for departure, with the army assembled and the fleet of 400 ships riding at anchor in nearby Milford Haven. It was an impressive, and by Irish standards intimidating, force of some 4,000 expert soldiers: 500 knights with their immediate followers, backed by a large body of archers. Most of them were feudal tenants, but they also included 163 mercenaries. While it was a substantial force it was not on a grand scale, and was certainly not intended for a conquest of the country. A main purpose of Henry's expedition was shown when several *castella lignea* were shipped abroad. These wooden towers, ready-made in sections, were not for use against the Gaelic Irish, who had neither walled towns nor castles. They were intended to be employed, if necessary, for the assault of towns such as Waterford and Dublin, already held by the Anglo-Normans, and of other towns, still outside the Norman areas, such as Cork

[1] The *Song of Dermot*, p. 163, rather than Giraldus, *Expugnatio*, p. 89, appears to be correct about the meeting-place of Henry and Strongbow.
[2] *Chronicles of the reigns of Stephen, Henry II, and Richard I* (4 vols, London, 1884–9), iv: *The chronicle of Robert of Torigni*, ed. Richard Howlett, p. 252.
[3] *Song of Dermot*, p. 165.

and Limerick. There were, as yet, no castles worthy of the name in Ireland. The assault towers were therefore for the demonstration rather than for the exercise of military power. The real method of conquest which the king had in mind was indicated by the consignment of 1,000 lbs of wax, most of it obviously to supply lighting during the long winter nights, but a share of it certainly to seal charters and other documents. The rule of feudal law, under a centralised monarch, in its sophisticated Angevin form, was about to make its entry into Ireland.

Unfavourable winds held the fleet at Milford Haven for seventeen days, but it finally sailed on 16 October 1171, making a successful and uncontested landing on 17 October at Crook, five miles from Waterford. On the following day Henry led his troops into Waterford, which was formally surrendered to him by Strongbow, as was Leinster, which was returned to the earl in fee. At this crucial point the king established the royal demesne in Ireland: Dublin with its hinterland, and its littoral south to Arklow, and the towns of Wexford and Waterford, with their lands. The rest of Leinster was to be held of the king for the service of 100 knights. But Henry had other designs for the kingdom of Meath.

An immediate problem, but not the most important, was how to deal with the captive fitz Stephen. The Wexford Norse, anxious to curry favour with Henry, brought fitz Stephen in chains before the king. Henry upbraided and threatened fitz Stephen, had him chained to another prisoner, and consigned both under guard to Reginald's tower. While the author of the 'Song' and Gerald of Wales agree that this was a ruse to take fitz Stephen out of the hands of the vengeful Wexfordmen, they seem to have been unaware that the king was under a debt of personal gratitude to the prisoner. When Henry led his first expedition into North Wales, against Owain of Gwynedd in 1157, and found himself in mortal danger, it was fitz Stephen who came to his rescue with a fleet and was badly wounded during the fighting inland. Now at Waterford Henry cancelled the debt, had fitz Stephen released in due time from Reginald's tower, and later made good use of him in the royal service.

The Gaelic Irish were not slow to put themselves in Henry's favour. Indeed, there seems to have been competition as to which Irish chieftains would be first to offer loyalty. The leader from Cork was ahead of the others. Diarmait Mac Carthaig, king of Desmond, arrived at Waterford, swore an oath of fealty to the king, handed over hostages (including one of his sons), and paid tribute as evidence of his submission. Mac Carthaig was thus quick to outmanoeuvre his traditional enemy Domnall Mór Ua Briain, who had already allied himself with the first Anglo-Normans in the country. While Henry was at Waterford, and as he moved through Munster and up towards Dublin, a succession of Irish kings and princes came to make submission and swear fealty. They seem to have had no hesitation about bowing to a foreign king, and nationalism played no part in their thinking. The Irish had always recognised the Roman emperor as 'king of the world', and it is significant that Henry II was known to them as 'fitz Empress' (his mother's first marriage had been to the Emperor Henry V). It is not clear from the evidence if they did homage, as well as swearing fealty, but the balance seems to be in favour of fealty only.[1] In any case, the very important feudal distinction between homage and fealty would have meant little to the Irish, and it is doubtful if Henry, with his dearly-bought experience and knowledge of Wales, would have insisted on homage at this stage.

Henry was well-informed about Ireland, and in the absence of any central civil power in the country saw the advantage of using the church, the only effective national institution. He led his army to Lismore, where his object was not the hallowed monastery but the bishop, Gilla Críst Ua Connairche, who was also papal legate. The fact that Henry was in extremely hot water with the reigning pope, Alexander III, because of the murder of Archbishop Becket, did not deter the king from securing agreement for a national church council. Military realities were never far from Henry's mind, and he also utilised the two-day stay at Lismore to select the site for a castle. He passed on to Cashel, which he had in mind as the venue for the proposed church council, but which required the permission of the local archbishop, Domnall Ua hUallacháin. Once this was secured Henry pursued his object with tenacity, deputing the organising of the event to two clerics in his entourage, his chaplain, Nicholas, and Ralph, the archdeacon of Llandaff (Wales).

It has often been assumed that the widespread submission of Irish kings and princes to Henry II was due to, or at least strongly influenced by, the papal bull, *Laudabiliter*, and the support which the bishops at the council of Cashel gave to the Angevin king. The assumption lacks foundation. There is no evidence that Henry II made use of *Laudabiliter*, and the Irish leaders submitted to him weeks before the bishops assembled at Cashel.

The day after Henry arrived at Cashel he was greeted on the banks of the river Suir by Domnall Mór Ua Briain, king of Thomond, who made his submission, as did his companion, Donnchad Ua Mathgamna, prince of Uí Echach in Cork,[2] who was there almost certainly as an ally of Ua Briain against his rival, Diarmait Mac Carthaig, king of Desmond. Henry, well advised on which submissions were strategically important, promptly sent his constables and officers to occupy Cork and Limerick, the chief towns respectively of Desmond and Thomond. As Henry's army continued on its way towards Dublin there were two further important submissions, Máel Sechnaill Ua Fáeláin of Déise, and Domnall Mac Gilla Pátraic of Osraige. Their example was followed shortly afterwards, or when Henry reached Dublin, by the principal princes in Leinster. Those mentioned by name are Ua Tuathail of Uí Muiredaig (south Kildare), Máel Sechlainn Mac Fáeláin of Uí Fáeláin (north Kildare), Mac Dalbaig (south Carlow), Mac Gilla Mo Cholmóc (south

---

[1] Warren, *Henry II*, pp 201–2.
[2] 'Mac Carthaigh's Book' in *Misc. Ir. Annals*, p. 57.

Dublin), and Ua Cathasaig (north Dublin). Of greater weight were three from outside Leinster who submitted: the irrepressible Tigernán Ua Ruairc of Bréifne, Murchad Ua Cerbaill of Airgialla, and Donn Sléibe Mac Duinn Sléibe of Ulster.

There is confusion as to whether Ruaidrí Ua Conchobair, the high king, submitted in 1171. The English chroniclers, Gervase of Canterbury and Roger of Howden, state that Ruaidrí flatly refused to deal with Henry, whereas the Irish annals are puzzlingly silent on the subject. On the other hand Gerald of Wales gives a detailed statement, relating that Ruaidrí would not come to Henry but instead met two royal emissaries, Hugh de Lacy and William fitz Audelin, at the river Shannon, where Connacht borders on Meath, and there made his submission.[1] The circumstances are a striking parallel with the practice of the kings of England, who as dukes of Normandy would meet their feudal lord (the king of France), or his representatives, on the borders of Normandy and France, but not on French soil. However, Gerald is almost certainly wrong (as he was probably wrong also on this point in the cases of Diarmait Mac Carthaig and Domnall Mór Ua Briain) in adding that Ruaidrí gave homage as well as fealty. All the weight of the limited evidence is in favour of fealty only. Henry knew, in dealing with Celtic leaders, that enough was enough. The only major rulers who kept aloof from him in Ireland were the Cenél nEógain and the Cenél Conaill, remote in their northern kingdoms. Nor did Henry approach them. Isolated by distance and geographic barriers they had little interest in what was happening elsewhere in Ireland. Henry, for his part, had not to take them into account.

Gerald of Wales sums up the effect of Henry's first two months in the country: 'There was almost no one of any repute or influence in the whole island who did not present himself before the king's majesty or pay him the respect due to an overlord.'[2] He adds, almost sententiously, 'So, the whole island remained quiet under the watchful eye of the king, and enjoyed peace and tranquillity.' Though the late autumn and winter weather may have had much to do with the lack of warfare, the comment can still stand as accurate. Henry wanted to appear as the powerful and generous ruler. He did not, as was common with triumphant kings, build a massive fortress to manifest his victory and ensure his rule. We are indebted to English chronicles for the information that at Dublin, outside the city walls, he erected a magnificent temporary palace, on the advice of Irish leaders, in the Hiberno-Norse style of wattle construction. Here during Christmas, the Irish leaders were sumptuously entertained, as guests of honour. Henry had learned in Wales the importance for Celtic peoples of the open door and prodigal entertainment.

It is easy to account for Henry's bloodless victory. Each ruler or group in the

---

[1] Giraldus, *Expugnatio*, p. 95. For the conflicting evidence about Ruaidrí's submission, see ibid., p. 312, n. 157.
[2] Ibid., p. 97.

country, contending for power, saw him as a solution to immediate problems. He came at an opportune moment, when there was a power vacuum in the country with no one obvious Irish leader to seize control, now that Diarmait Mac Murchada was dead. Ruaidrí Ua Conchobair, a weak ruler, was high-king in name, unchallenged largely in default of a strong opponent. Domnall Ua Briain of Thomond was unreliable, and Diarmait Mac Carthaig was also a weak ruler. The one-eyed, battle-scarred Tigernán Ua Ruairc had the spirit and energy to take the lead, but he lacked the status and the manpower. An obvious alternative was Strongbow, who had brought apparently invincible Anglo-Norman military arms in his train, and on whom had fallen the mantle of Mac Murchada. The Anglo-Normans, though divided between the pioneer settlers, the Geraldines, and the equally ambitious followers of Strongbow, accepted Strongbow as their leader, but all of them now bowed in feudal awe to the authority of their anointed monarch, Henry. In short, Henry had queered the pitch for Strongbow.

It was otherwise with the bishops. Henry rightly attributed the greatest importance to the support he might receive officially from the church. Kings would die, dynasties be overthrown, political alliances change, but a policy formally adopted by the church would not be lightly reversed. Hence the importance he placed in the decrees of the council of Cashel, which met, probably, early in 1172. It was conducted with full solemnity, presided over by the papal legate, Gilla Críst Ua Connairche, bishop of Lismore. The arch-bishop of Armagh, Gilla Meic Liac, aged eighty-five, was unable to be present owing to physical infirmities, but he later gave his consent to the conciliar decrees. All the other bishops were there with their suffragans, as well as 'abbots, archdeacons, priors and deans, and many other prelates of the Irish church'. Henry had three representatives, Ralph, abbot of Buildwas (Shrop-shire), Ralph, archdeacon of Llandaff, and Nicholas, his chaplain.

It is fortunate that Gerald of Wales supplies a copy of the decrees, but it is unfortunate that his is the only copy available.[1] Though Gerald asserts that he gives the exact wording of the decrees, as they were issued, it is obvious that some of them are summarised in his own words. Furthermore, the accuracy of some of his statements, introducing the decrees, is open to question, and in the concluding part of the document it is uncertain whether one all-important statement comes from the council or is a commentary by Gerald.

It is difficult to decide precisely what Henry's role and authority were in this council. The English chronicles and Gerald agree that he was responsible for having the council summoned, but they underplay the fact that the final responsibility for authorising the meeting would have lain with the papal legate. Gerald also states that it was Henry who issued the decrees, but this is ambiguous. Most of the decrees were disciplinary, concerning marriage ceremonies and church attendance. Others dealt with tithes, murder, and

[1] Giraldus, *Expugnatio*, pp 98, 100.

disposal of property. Taken together they could have been issued by the king, but only in the sense that he agreed with, and even approved them, not that he formulated them. However, the most important, and what is now likely to be the most controversial, part of the document as given by Gerald is what follows the seventh statute: 'thus in all parts of the Irish church all matters relating to religion are to be conducted hereafter on the pattern of Holy Church, and in line with the observances of the English church'.[1] Commentators on the council have assumed that this sentence was part of canon 7, or a separate canon 8, or at least a genuine declaration of the council. Recently this has been challenged, and it now appears that the sentence, which has led so many historians to one apparently obvious (but mistaken) conclusion, was in fact a commentary by Gerald and not a declaration by the council.[2]

There can be no doubt, however, that the hierarchy, assembled in council, approved of Henry II as overlord in Ireland. This we know from three formal letters of Pope Alexander III, all dated 20 September 1172 from Tusculum, in response to reports from the council of Cashel.[3] The first letter is appropriately to the papal legate in Ireland, Gilla Críst Ua Connairche, and the bishops; the second to King Henry; the third to the Irish kings and leaders. The pope's message to all three parties was plain and consistent. Ireland was to accept Henry as its 'king and lord', in accordance with the oaths of fealty sworn by its kings and rulers; any one who broke his oath incurred ecclesiastical censure. The reason for this papal approval was that Henry, 'stirred by divine inspiration and with his united forces' had entered the country as a religious reformer, to rescue it from barbarism and religious degradation. The pope had been informed about the lamentable level of religious practice in the country by letters of the papal legate and his episcopal colleagues. Historians have overlooked the highly significant fact, mentioned by Alexander, that his information about religious conditions in Ireland was also derived from Ralph, archdeacon of Llandaff, who had gone to visit the pope in person to give an eye-witness account of what he had himself seen in Ireland.[4] It may safely be assumed that it was Ralph who brought the letters of the papal legate and bishops to Alexander, as well as the decrees of the council of Cashel.

---

[1] Giraldus, *Expugnatio*, p. 100.

[2] See ibid., p. 315, n. 178. The classic misrepresentation is by the authoritative Irish medieval historian, Edmund Curtis, in his edition and translation of the decrees of the council of Cashel, in Edmund Curtis and R. B. McDowell, *Irish historical documents, 1172—1922* (London, 1943; repr., 1968), p. 19, where he includes that sentence as the final decree, and to clinch his case mistranslates the introductory word *itaque* as 'finally'. Watt accepts this statement as the will of the council and of Henry II on the basis of further passages from Giraldus and the independent evidence of Ralph de Diceto: *Ch. & two nations*, p. 41, and *Ch. in med. Ire.*, pp 35, 89, 105, 122, 172.

[3] In Sheehy, *Pontificia Hib.*, i, 19–23. They are available in translation in Curtis & McDowell, *Ir. hist. docs*, pp 19–22.

[4] Curtis, like most other historians, by a simple but unfortunate error of transcription and translation, recorded that Archdeacon Ralph's report was transmitted *viva vobis* ('made known to you in person'). Sheehy edits it correctly as *viva nobis*, in *Pontificia Hib.*, i, 21, which Watt correctly translates as 'revealed to us orally' (*Ch. in med. Ire.*, p. 38).

Modern Irish nationalists have found it difficult to swallow the fact that the entire Irish hierarchy gave their support to Henry II.[1] This is to misunderstand the bishops' motive, and is a false projection of a modern ideology back to a medieval scene. It was not merely the bishops, but also the lay rulers in Ireland who submitted to Henry, as the pope tactfully pointed out when he reminded the Irish leaders that 'you have of your own free will submitted to so powerful and magnificent a king'.[2] The bishops had a single-minded dedication to the religious regeneration of the people, which they believed would be achieved only if Ireland adopted the full Gregorian reform and came into conformity, in organisation, doctrine, and worship, with the rest of western Christianity. They knew that while a miracle of transformation had taken place in organisation between the synod of Ráith Bressail in 1111 and the synod of Kells in 1152, another miracle was required to update the centuries-old life-style and social pattern of the people. They also knew that the Anglo-Normans, and Canterbury in particular, had set the new standards to be followed. Despite the Psalmist's warning against putting their trust in princes, they decided to trust Henry II.

Nevertheless, neither the Irish bishops nor the authorities at Rome were displaying only the simplicity of the dove. English chroniclers of the time state that the Irish prelates swore fealty to Henry as king and lord, pledged themselves to conform in all things to the example of the church of England, and in each case testified to their loyalty by signing a document with a seal attached, confirming to him and his heirs the kingdom of Ireland. When Pope Alexander wrote to the bishops in 1172, exhorting them to support Henry for the purpose of religious reform in Ireland, he mentioned the oaths of fealty sworn by the lay rulers, but omitted any reference to similar oaths by the bishops.[3] He confined himself to a spiritual message and to a statement that the king 'is said to have obeyed our wishes in pious and generous fashion in restoring to you the tithes and other ecclesiastical rights and all things which belong to the liberties of the church'.[4] His letter to Henry ended on the note that his majesty should 'carefully seek to preserve the rights of the see of Saint Peter for us in the aforesaid land'.[5]

One of the most perceptive studies within recent decades of Hiberno-papal relations in the late twelfth century declares that 'Alexander III conceded nothing to Henry II as far as the rights of the church and the papacy were concerned. . . . The pope never contemplated the ecclesiastical subjection of the Irish church to the English church or actively fostered its anglicisation.'[6] This

---

[1] E.g., Colmcille [Conway], *The story of Mellifont* (Dublin, 1958), p. 40, sees the papal legate Gilla Críst Ua Connairche, bishop of Lismore, as leader of the Irish bishops in favour of Henry II, and Archbishop Lorcán Ua Tuathail, of Dublin, as leader of the pro-Irish party.

[2] In Sheehy, *Pontificia Hib.*, i, 23; trans. in Curtis & McDowell, *Ir. hist. docs*, p. 22.

[3] Sheehy, *Pontificia Hib.*, i, 19–20; Curtis & McDowell, *Ir. hist. docs*, pp 19–20.

[4] Sheehy, *Pontificia Hib.*, i, 20; Curtis & McDowell, *Ir. hist. docs*, p. 20.

[5] Sheehy, *Pontificia Hib.*, i, 22; Curtis & McDowell, *Ir. hist. docs*, p. 22.

[6] Marie-Thérèse Flanagan, 'Hiberno-papal relations in the late twelfth century' in *Archiv. Hib.*, xxxiv (1976–7), pp 58, 67.

judgement is supported by the impressive evidence of papal policy in appointing separate legates to Ireland and England, even after the advent of Henry II
to Ireland. The first papal legate for Ireland was Máel Muire Ua Dúnáin,
bishop of Meath, appointed in 1101, and a succession of legates, specifically
nominated for Ireland, bears witness to a fixed papal determination which was
not abandoned even when Rome accepted, and indeed welcomed, Henry II as
the new political master of the country. The papal authorities were understandably alarmed by the reports they had received from the council of Cashel
about widespread disregard of the marriage bond, non-payment of tithes, and
lay interference with church property, as well as the absence of established
catholic ceremonies for baptism and funeral services. It was not explained to
those in Rome that many of these 'aberrations' were survivals of brehon law
and the ancient Gaelic social code; that parishes, and the tithe system that went
with them, were characteristics of the continental ecclesiastical system based
on Roman urban civilisation and as yet had no basis in Ireland outside the
Hiberno-Norse towns. The attempt to introduce and enforce the Gregorian
reform was based on high ideals, but it presupposed a social system alien to
Ireland. There was, therefore, inherent in the attempt to introduce the full
Gregorian reform a tension, if not an actual clash, between two different cultures. Even the leading Irish reformers, men such as Malachy of Armagh and
Lorcán Ua Tuathail, did not face the radical consequences of the vision that
inspired them.

There was ambiguity and even make-believe on the parts of both Henry II
and Alexander III. The king wanted the support of the papacy to ensure that all
the bishops would accept him as their temporal lord, and with the consequences which this would have in the ecclesiastical areas of property and jurisdiction, areas which had however been the subject of bitter dispute in England.
The pope was anxious for the full implementation of the Gregorian reform in
Ireland, and though this would require royal sanction and support he wanted to
limit Henry's right to intervene in church affairs, both local and national.

How many official documents Henry authorised before leaving Dublin in
late February 1172 is unknown, but the original of one of the most important is
still to be seen, in which he tells all his faithful subjects that he has 'given and
granted and by the present charter confirmed to my men of Bristol my city of
Dublin for [them] to inhabit'.[1] From the archaeological evidence which was
unearthed at High Street and Wood Quay between 1962 and 1981, we know that
there were trading links between Dublin and Bristol during the eleventh and
early twelfth centuries, and we may assume that there were individual Bristol
men settled in the town, but Henry now swept the board and made Dublin
available as a colony for his loyal subjects from Bristol. The Hiberno-Norse
inhabitants were forced to settle on the north side of the city, across the Liffey

---

[1] Orpen, *Normans*, i, 284–5. See Aubrey Gwynn, 'Medieval Bristol and Dublin' in *I.H.S.*, v, no.
20 (Sept. 1947),pp 279–80.

in a suburb of St Mary's abbey, later known as *Villa Ostmannorum* (the modern Oxmantown).

Gerald of Wales states that Henry had intended to stay on for many more months, into the summer of 1172, establishing law and order throughout the country, and guaranteeing peace by founding a series of castles.[1] This is borne out by the king's own statement when he first met the papal legates in Normandy in May 1172 and told them, with a show of impatience (probably as part of his diplomatic game), 'I am returning to Ireland, where I have to deal with many affairs'.[2] Whatever his intentions had been when he was in full command of events at Dublin at Christmas 1171 he was soon frustrated by an exceptionally harsh winter and by dysentery of epidemic proportions among his troops. A Welsh chronicle records under 1172 that 'there was great mortality upon the host that was with the king in Ireland, because of the novelty of the unaccustomed foods and because of the stress of famine, for the ships with merchandise could not sail to them in winter through the tempestuous rage of the Irish sea'.[3] The Annals of Tigernach under the same year tell of 'very bad weather this year, which killed the greater part of the cattle of Ireland', and the English chronicler, Ralph de Diceto, records that dysentery gripped the king's soldiers in Ireland.[4]

During those unpleasant winter and spring months it was not the situation in Ireland, but in the other parts of his realm that worried Henry. The weather was in league with conspirators in England, Normandy, and Aquitaine. Gerald of Wales relates that continuous stormy seas allowed hardly a single ship to cross from Wales to Ireland, 'and no one could get any news whatsoever from other lands'.[5] Henry knew that when messengers could come they would take the shortest possible route across the Irish Sea; with this in view he moved to Wexford. Finally, early in March, the winds blew favourably and brought ships with news which was ominous and bitter. From Normandy came word that papal legates were there, irked by the king's absence which they suspected was an escape tactic, and were threatening to lay an interdict on all his territories, not just England, unless he made himself available to have his case heard. That message was merely ominous and he felt that he could cope with the problem. The bitter tidings were about his eldest son, Henry, 'the young king' already crowned, and his brothers Richard and Geoffrey, who were fomenting a conspiracy against him with barons in England and France. They had the support of their mother, the unhappy Eleanor of Aquitaine, and were

[1] *Expugnatio*, p. 105.

[2] An anonymous report, commenting on the meeting of the king and the papal legates, stated that 'rex ab eis cum indignatione discessit in haec verba: "Redeo", inquit, "in Hiberniam, ubi multa mihi incumbiunt" '; in J. C. Robertson and J. B. Sheppard (ed.), *Materials for the history of Thomas Becket, archbishop of Canterbury* (7 vols, London, 1875–85), vii, 514.

[3] *Brut y Tywysogion* (Red Book of Hergest version), ed. Thomas Jones (Cardiff, 1955), p. 159.

[4] Ralph de Diceto, 'Ymagines historiarum' in *Radulfi de Diceto decani Lundonensis opera historica: the historical works of Master Ralph de Diceto*, ed. William Stubbs (2 vols, London, 1876), i, 350.

[5] *Expugnatio*, p. 103.

intriguing with King Louis VII of France. England itself was stirring uneasily under his rule, excited as it was by the many reported visions and miracles in favour of Archbishop Thomas. Henry owed much of his authority to his personality, agility, intelligence, and will-power, but a king out of sight was a king half out of power. He had now to regain control both of his kingdom and of his scattered dominions. Ireland could be used to advantage, instead of being a danger at his back. It could be a source of strength for his immediate campaigns and a redoubt to which he could retreat if all went against him in England and on the Continent.

Henry wanted to leave an Ireland that was strong, as far as the Anglo-Norman settlement was concerned, but loyal to himself. Gerald of Wales, who bore no love for Strongbow, states that Henry set out to weaken Strongbow's position by detaching from him some of his leading knights, such as Raymond le Gros, Miles de Cogan, and William Maskerell.[1] This is to misinterpret the king's attitude to the earl. Henry had no real evidence that Strongbow was disaffected, received him into his favour when they met at Pembroke in September 1171, called upon his support during the crises of 1173–4, and eventually rewarded him for his proven loyalty. Nevertheless, Henry realised that Strongbow was the single strongest baron in Ireland, and with royal aspirations because of his marriage to Aífe, daughter of Diarmait Mac Murchada. He therefore sought to counterbalance, rather than to weaken him, and with this in view called on the services of Hugh de Lacy, who in his turn a few years later was to become an object of suspicion as an overmighty subject. Shrewd political sense made Henry strike a balance of power between Strongbow and de Lacy.

The obvious signs that de Lacy was being established as Henry's *alter ego* were his appointments as 'custos' (the first of the viceroys) and as constable (governor) of Dublin. These gave him authority and the means to enforce it, but any such nominee could fall from favour overnight and be dismissed by the stroke of a royal pen. The basis of immediate and permanent power in the medieval world was land, and this was the importance of Henry's decision while at Wexford to grant de Lacy 'the land of Meath'. Strongbow, as heir to Diarmait Mac Murchada's rights and claims, may have seen himself in 1171 as both king of Leinster and overlord of Meath, but that latter title had been acquired by the sword only shortly before Mac Murchada died. Henry conveniently disregarded those recent events, and in 1172 before leaving Wexford conferred the lordship of Meath on de Lacy, for the service of fifty knights, to be held as Murchad Ua Máel Sechlainn, the king of Meath who died in 1153, had held it.[2]

Even though Strongbow was not appointed as the king's chief governor in Ireland he and his supporters were not entirely out of royal favour. Hugh de

---

[1] *Expugnatio*, p. 103.
[2] Charter of Henry II, in Orpen, *Normans*, i, 285–6, at p. 285.

Lacy at Dublin was given a garrison of twenty knights, and his lieutenants included Strongbow's supporters, Robert fitz Stephen, Maurice fitz Gerald, Meiler fitz Henry, and Milo fitz David. The practical problems of communication by sea always made Henry place more store on Wexford and Waterford than on Dublin, and it is significant that he appointed his *familiares* to these ports: fitz Audelin, de Hastings, and de Braose to Wexford with thirty knights, fitz Bernard, de Bohun, and de Gundeville to Waterford with forty knights. Strongbow's party was complimented, but also weakened, when Henry took Miles de Cogan, the most inventive of Strongbow's lieutenants, with him to Wales. Apparently he also took Raymond le Gros, who was regarded as the ideal military commander by most of the pioneers in Ireland. The crises with which Henry had now to contend in England and on the Continent were to test beyond doubt the loyalty of Strongbow and his followers to the monarch. He left Wexford on Easter Monday, 17 April 1172, landed near St David's in Wales, and a month later was with the papal legates at Savigny in Normandy.

CHAPTER IV

Overlord becomes feudal lord, 1172–85

F. X. MARTIN

BY the end of 1172 Henry appeared to have reestablished harmony in both church and political affairs within his dominions, Ireland included. Negotiations with the papal legates at Savigny in May 1172 had begun on a highly strained note. A consummate actor and hard bargainer, he had, as we have seen, stormed out of the first session of talks, declaring angrily that he would return to Ireland where he had much to occupy his attention. It was a shrewd thrust, reminding Cardinals Albert and Theodinus that, if proof were needed of his good faith and efficacy, he had gone to Ireland to reform the church there and had held a national synod for that purpose.

The two legates were seasoned and flexible papal agents, who judged their man correctly. The negotiations were resumed and concluded three days later, followed by a public ceremony of reconciliation in the cathedral of Avranches on 21 May. In the negotiations he had lost nothing except, by intent, his temper. He did not abandon his interest in Ireland, but he never again visited the country. It remained a marginal pawn on his extensive political chessboard. The important pieces, kings, queens, knights, and bishops, were more strategically positioned, in Scotland, Wales, England, and France.

Henry had induced stability in Ireland during his visit there, though it could be argued that the lack of warfare during those months was due less to his role as an angel of peace than to the fact that he was there during winter and spring. War was a way of life and a seasonal occupation in Gaelic Ireland. The test would come with the finer weather after Easter. Nevertheless, Henry must be given credit for so steadying the political situation that the temptation to go to war was considerably reduced. His object was not peace for its own sake but a system of checks and counter-checks to prevent any one man, particularly an Anglo-Norman baron, becoming dominant. For this reason he set up Hugh de Lacy to counterbalance Strongbow. The native Irish did not cause Henry equal concern. They had readily submitted to his distant jurisdiction, believing that, as they were now his allies, he in return would act as a curb on unprovoked Anglo-Norman expansion into their lands.

De Lacy's advance into Meath inevitably brought him into conflict with Tigernán Ua Ruairc of Bréifne, and a clash of arms seemed unavoidable. The parties met, the two leaders dismounted and withdrew apart for discussion, while their aides reined their horses nearby. A gesture by Tigernán was interpreted by the Anglo-Normans as a treacherous signal to his aides, and de Lacy's men sprang to the attack. Tigernán was killed and his head spiked over the gate of the fortress at Dublin. Thus perished the one-eyed warrior whom the Annals of Tigernach described as 'deedful leopard of the Gael, Leth Cuinn's man of battle and lasting defence, Erin's raider and invader, surpasser of the Gael in might and abundance'.

Strongbow's attempt to enforce his rule in Leinster also provoked opposition. He led an expedition into the midlands, to exact by force the tribute which the Uí Failge were not prepared to give. There was no initial resistance to the Anglo-Normans, who plundered the territory, principally of cattle, and set out on the return journey, but an ambush on the rearguard was launched by Diarmait Ua Dímmusaig, king of Uí Failge. Robert de Quency, constable of Leinster, and recently married to Strongbow's daughter, was killed in command of the rearguard, and his death created a crisis for Strongbow. Raymond le Gros, the most popular and the most capable of the Anglo-Norman military commanders, asked that he be appointed constable of Leinster and be allowed to marry Basilia, sister of Strongbow. Surprisingly, the earl refused. It was not that the lady objected; her heart was set on Raymond. Nor could Strongbow query Raymond's loyalty or service, both of which had been amply demonstrated ever since the earl decided to commit himself to the adventure in Ireland. All in all Raymond had every reason to expect preferential treatment, and when his requests were refused he, 'very suddenly in evil humour', returned to his father's castle at Carew, in Wales. His place in Ireland was taken by Strongbow's uncle, Hervey de Montmorency, who became constable for Leinster.

It had not been an easy decision for the earl to refuse the faithful lieutenant on whom he greatly relied, but he had to safeguard his own hard-won insecure position. Raymond was a fitz Gerald and, though he personally gave no sign of disloyalty, his many cousins and relatives in Ireland (the first Anglo-Normans to establish themselves in the country) felt that they had not been duly rewarded and had even been displaced. Strongbow had as yet no heir and had to protect himself and the line he was founding against an overmighty subject. It is likely he would have agreed to appoint Raymond constable of Leinster, but not to combine it with marriage to Basilia. The fact that Henry II thought highly of Raymond was useful to Strongbow, but it was also a danger since the king was a master of the 'divide and rule' policy.

The danger of friction between Strongbow and de Lacy, or of further Anglo-Norman involvement in Gaelic family feuds and provincial wars, was resolved by the need for the colonists in Ireland to play a part in the greater events which were convulsing the world of Henry II. The king had hardly begun to breathe freely after making his peace with the papal legates when a sea of troubles was loosed upon him by his three older sons, Henry, Geoffrey, and Richard. They organised an armed revolt and were supported by many nobles in Normandy, Brittany, and Gascony. The revolt spread to England, and William the Lion, king of Scotland, attacked from the north. The French king, Louis VII, did not miss the opportunity to attack Henry's possessions in Normandy. In his desperate plight Henry appealed to his barons in Ireland, and they rallied to his cause. Strongbow and Hugh de Lacy were among those who joined him in Normandy early in 1173. The earl brought a number of knights, and Henry gladly named him governor of the sturdy frontier fortress of Gisors, built by Henry I of England, less than 50 miles north-west of Paris. Strongbow gave a good account of himself, and was summoned by Henry in August to join him with an army, paradoxically to relieve his main rival in Ireland, Hugh de Lacy, who had been conducting a gallant defence of Verneuil but was now at the end of his resources. King Louis, knowing that Henry was on the way with an army to raise the siege, agreed to a truce. While negotiations were in progress the French treacherously attacked, and, though unable to capture the fortress defended by de Lacy, burned 'the great burgh' of Verneuil, then retreated rapidly across the frontier, leaving a pall of smoke to greet Henry when he reached the town on 9 August.

Both Strongbow and de Lacy had acquitted themselves with much credit so far in the war, and though Henry was loath to part with either of them he thought it best to retain de Lacy with him under arms and to allow Strongbow back to Ireland. It was not only that de Lacy was younger and had more flair as a military commander, but Henry had urgent need for more soldiers. Strongbow, by reason of his status and seniority, was likely to have more influence than de Lacy in rousing the knights and barons in Ireland to rally to the king's standard. To strengthen the earl's authority Henry appointed him his representative in place of fitz Audelin, and named him constable of two key towns, Dublin and Waterford. As public proof that Strongbow was fully restored to royal favour, Henry made over to him the town of Wexford and the castle at Wicklow. Even with all these assets Strongbow was hardly able to exercise control within the limited area where the Anglo-Normans had settled.

The earl's first task was to put soldiers in the field on behalf of their beleaguered monarch. Fitz Bernard, fitz Stephen, Maurice de Prendergast, and their peers did not hesitate. Fortunately for Henry they did not sail directly to Normandy, but travelled across the Irish Sea to Druidston Chins, in St Bride's Bay, south Wales, and were on their way to London when they heard of the imminent threat to Henry's rule in England.[1] Robert ès Blanchemains, third

---

[1] The intervention by the barons from Ireland is of some importance for Anglo-Norman history, and is an important unwritten chapter in the story of Henry's relations with his Anglo-Norman subjects in Ireland. For the battle of Fornham see Warren, *Henry II*, pp 128–31; cf. Orpen,

earl of Leicester, was one of the disaffected barons who had joined King Louis of France in 1173 in the campaign that focused on the attempt to take Verneuil, defended by Hugh de Lacy. When that failed the resourceful Earl Robert recruited a force of Fleming mercenaries and shipped them across the English Channel to East Anglia, where he joined forces with another rebellious lord, Hugh Bigod, earl of Norfolk. The two earls, with their followers and mercenaries, set out for the midlands to relieve Earl Robert's castle at Leicester, then in grave danger of succumbing to the siege by royal troops. It was at this point that the barons from Ireland arrived on the English scene. Instead of continuing on to Normandy they headed to East Anglia, to join the royal army. The battle took place in August at Fornham, in the marshes near Bury St Edmunds, and though the odds were said by Ralph of Diceto to have been four to one in favour of the rebels, it was the king's men who won a resounding victory, taking Earl Robert captive in the process. The part played by the troops from Ireland was almost entirely ignored by Anglo-Norman chronicles, but the 'Song of Dermot' proudly recorded that the rebels were routed

> by the aid of Leinster,
> And by the might of the Irish
> The field remained with the English.[1]

The 'Song' also asserts that the barons from Ireland stayed on to restrain the northern rebels under Roger de Mowbray and to hold the line against King William the Lion of Scotland, who invaded England shortly after Easter 1174. It is claimed that they had a part 'in this brawl', when on 13 July, in the mist of an early morning, the unwary royal lion was surprised and captured in a meadow before Alnwick castle.[2] That unexpected stroke of luck solved a major problem for Henry II, who had come back to England in desperaion but now found that the rebels and the king of the Scots were willing to submit. Henry returned to France, where the troops from Ireland were with him in the victorious campaign against King Louis, which concluded with peace at Montlouis on 30 September 1174.

Strongbow had not inherited an easy position as the king's representative in Ireland. Most of the barons and many of their followers had left, at his exhortation, to succour Henry in England and France. This greatly weakened Anglo-Norman strength in Ireland, and did not go unnoticed by the Gaelic leaders.

Normans, i, 327, n. 1. For sources on the battle see *The historical works of Gervase of Canterbury*, ed. William Stubbs (2 vols, London, 1879–80), i, 146; *Radulfi de Diceto decani Lundoniensis opera historica: the historical works of Master Ralph de Diceto*, ed. William Stubbs (2 vols, London, 1876), i, 377–8; *Gesta Regis Henrici Secundi Benedicti Abbatis: the chronicle . . . of Benedict of Peterborough*, ed. William Stubbs (2 vols, London, 1867), i, 58, 60–62; *Chronica Magistri Rogeri de Houedene*, ed. William Stubbs (4 vols, London, 1868–71), ii, 54–5; J. C. Robertson and J. B. Radcliffe, *Materials for the history of Thomas Becket* (7 vols, London, 1875–85), i, 246; *Chronicles of the reigns of Stephen, Henry II, and Richard I*, ed. Richard Howlett (4 vols, London, 1884–9), i: *The Historia rerum Anglicorum of William of Newburgh*, p. 179.

[1] *Song of Dermot*, lines 2968–71.   [2] Ibid., lines 2972–9; cf. Warren, *Henry II*, pp 132–5.

Discontent among his soldiers led them to present Strongbow with a series of unenviable alternatives. Either he should restore Raymond le Gros (in whom they had total confidence), or they would desert, and then return to England, or (in the tradition of Maurice de Prendergast) take service with the native Irish.[1] It was near mutiny.

At this stage, in 1173, with Henry II harassed on all sides by enemies in England and France, there was no likelihood of his sending more money to his deputy in Ireland. Strongbow had no alternative but to negotiate with Raymond, still in Wales, to whom he sent an intermediary, asking him to return to Ireland as commander of the troops, assuring him that he would also have Basilia, Strongbow's sister, in marriage. Raymond gathered together a company of his followers, probably about 200 soldiers, and they sailed to Wexford in three ships. The two leaders met on Little Island in the Suir, below Waterford, Raymond with his full company, while Strongbow came with a select group of followers and his sister, Basilia, as the tempting pledge of good faith. Raymond became commander of the garrison troops and constable of Leinster, with a wide jurisdiction that extended over even the Duffry, territory which had belonged briefly to Robert de Quency and was to be ruled in trust until de Quency's baby daughter came of age. Marriage with Basilia was to take place as soon as conveniently possible, and the valuable territory of Forth in Wexford was to go to Raymond as a gift from the earl.

The immediate problem was to pacify the restless Anglo-Norman soldiers. Raymond led them in a plundering raid into the territory of the Déise in Waterford.[2] The raid was highly successful, yielding not only booty but also much-needed horses and war equipment. There is no known justification for a raid on the Déise any more than a legitimate reason for the raid which followed, on Lismore in County Waterford. Both Máel Sechlainn Ua Fáeláin, king of the Déise, and Diarmait Mac Carthaig, king of Desmond, had submitted to Henry II, and their territories should have been exempt from attack. It may be that plunder for restless soldiers was the sole brutal reason; there are no known extenuating circumstances.[3] A successful raid on the rich ecclesiastical town of Lismore was interrupted by a Hiberno-Norse fleet from Cork. After one of the few recorded naval engagements in medieval

---

[1] For discrepancies between the 'Song' and 'Expugnatio' on these events see editorial notes, *Expugnatio*, p. 321, n. 223; p. 322, n. 225; cf. Orpen, *Normans*, i, 334–5.

[2] Orpen, *Normans*, i, 329, interpreted Gerald of Wales (see *Expugnatio*, p. 136, lines 15–16) to mean that the expedition was into Uí Fáeláin in the north-east of Kildare; this had been the supposition of Dimock in his edition of *Expugnatio*, p. 308, no. 2, as also of Otway-Ruthven, *Med. Ire.*, p. 54, and likewise my interpretation in the modern edition of *Expugnatio*, p. 321, n. 218. Professor F. J. Byrne recently pointed out to me that the phrase used by Gerald is 'in Ophelanos', meaning 'against the O'Phelans' (of the Déise in Waterford), not the Uí Fáeláin territory in Kildare.

[3] There is no evidence to support the suggestion in Otway-Ruthven, *Med. Ire.*, p. 54, that the attack 'if it was not quite unprovoked, as it may have been, must have been caused by some hostile action on the part of either Melaghlin O'Phelan, king of the Decies, the area immediately attacked, or Dermot MacCarthy, king of Desmond'.

Irish history, the victorious Anglo-Normans returned to Waterford with their plunder.

The food and plunder restored the morale of the troops, but those successful forays into Munster were to be the last hours of glory for many a month. Raymond, because of the death of his father, William fitz Gerald, returned to Wales, and Hervey de Montmorency resumed the office of constable. It was Hervey's ill-fortune to be again in charge of the troops when the position in Ireland became imperilled owing to a widespread movement against the settlers by the Irish. It is at first perplexing to find that at this stage the leading role on the Irish side was taken by Domnall Mór Ua Briain, king of Thomond, who first invited the Anglo-Normans to Munster in 1170, was later an ally of Strongbow, and submitted to Henry II during 1171–2. Two Irish medievalists have suggested that Domnall was moved to change sides in face of the attack on Diarmait Mac Carthaig, and because of the similar danger to himself he foresaw from Strongbow. This theory does not fit the facts or Domnall's character, who 'was constant only in his inconstancy'.[1] Domnall was ever ready to best the MacCarthys, and, whenever possible, with the aid of the Anglo-Normans. Furthermore, the danger from Strongbow was less in 1173 than it had been at any time since his arrival in 1170, if we except the occasion in 1171 when the earl was besieged in Dublin. The Anglo-Norman settlers were depleted and discouraged in 1173; this was the most probable reason why Domnall chose to strike at them. He was an incurable opportunist and an unreliable ally, but a not unshrewd judge of events.

Late in 1173, supported by a contingent of Connachtmen under Conchobar Máenmaige Ua Conchobair, son of King Ruaidrí, he led an army against Strongbow's motte-and-bailey stronghold at Kilkenny. The fortress of wood on a high earthen mound was not nearly as defensible as the later stone castle, and the garrison wisely evacuated it. They retreated to Waterford, leaving Domnall to destroy the stronghold and plunder the surrounding countryside. However, the Anglo-Normans regrouped their forces, and early in 1174 an expedition led by Hervey de Montmorency (and with Strongbow present) set out from Dublin with the purpose of coming to grips with Domnall Ua Briain. Hervey and Strongbow did not reach Limerick. While en route they received the alarming news that Ruaidrí Ua Conchobair was mustering his forces across the Shannon to attack them. An appeal to Dublin for reinforcements brought a contingent of Norsemen marching south under the command of Anglo-Norman knights. The main army of Anglo-Normans was halted at Cashel, awaiting the reinforcements which got as far as Thurles and camped there overnight.[2] Domnall decided it was now or never. In the grey dawn he

[1] For his political somersaults see editorial notes, *Expugnatio*, pp 328–9, n. 278. Orpen, *Normans*, i, 331, and Otway-Ruthven, *Med. Ire.*, p. 54, try to give Domnall Ua Briain more credit than he deserves.

[2] The most substantial account of this episode is in *Ann. Tig.* Giraldus, *Expugnatio*, p. 139, glosses over the disaster.

surprised the camp at Thurles and attacked with resolution, slaying four hundred of the Dublin Norse and their four Anglo-Norman commanders.

The immediate result was that Strongbow abandoned his march to Limerick and retreated to Waterford. In the military circumstances it was probably the prudent decision, but politically speaking his withdrawal had almost disastrous results. Anglo-Norman power in Ireland seemed to be disintegrating, and in the words of Gerald of Wales, 'the entire population of Ireland took the opportunity of this disorder to rise with one consent against the English'.[1] The Norse at Waterford revolted and killed the Anglo-Norman garrison of two hundred soldiers, as well as the governor, Fretellus. Strongbow had to take refuge as a man under siege on Little Island in the Suir, below Waterford. The Norse at Wexford were not to be outdone by their cousins at Waterford, and it became evident that they were preparing to expel or massacre their Norman garrison. News from Connacht presaged disaster. Ruaidrí Ua Conchobair, hostile to the Anglo-Normans but chary of crossing Domnall Ua Briain's path, led an impressive hosting of troops into Meath to undo the Anglo-Norman settlement, now that de Lacy was overseas. Most of the princes of Leth Cuinn were in the high-king's train—the Irish leaders from Meath, Bréifne, Airgialla, Ulster, and (a rare phenomenon in Meath and Leinster) from the Cenél nEógain and the Cenél Conaill. The army penetrated beyond Meath to the very confines of Dublin.

In his desperate plight Strongbow sent another urgent message to Raymond le Gros in Wales. Raymond, as resourceful as ever, rapidly gathered kinsmen and some thirty knights, as well as 100 mounted soldiers and 300 archers.[2] These he transported in fifteen ships to Wexford, arriving just in time to quell a revolt by the Norse inhabitants. Thence he marched to Waterford and brought the earl with his men back safely to Wexford. At that point he held Strongbow to the previous bargain, and the marriage with Basilia followed, but while the marriage celebrations were still in full spate he heard that Ruaidrí had led his troops within sight of Dublin town. Straight away, relinquishing food, wine, and new-found wife, and, in the words of Gerald of Wales, 'not in the least slowed down by the effects of either wine or love',[3] he rode rapidly north to Dublin, where his very approach caused Ruaidrí to retreat across the Shannon. When Raymond restored the Anglo-Normans to their castles and outposts in Meath an uneasy peace returned to the country. The crisis was over, at least for the present.

On the face of it, Anglo-Norman power had been in utmost jeopardy, and the crisis was largely concentrated in Munster. Had Domnall Ua Briain and Conchobar Máenmaige Ua Conchobair followed up their victory at Thurles they might well have routed Strongbow and, in conjunction with the uprisings

---

[1] Giraldus, *Expugnatio*, p. 139.
[2] Ibid., pp 139–41; cf. *Song of Dermot*, lines 2994–3035.
[3] Giraldus, *Expugnatio*, p. 141.

elsewhere, crushed the Anglo-Norman strongholds in Ireland. The Irish princes missed their opportunity, but to expect a united effort by them, with or without the Norse of the towns, is to misunderstand Ireland of the twelfth century. It was still every man for himself, except for temporary alliances such as Ruaidrí Ua Conchobair with his hosting of Connacht and northern troops into Meath and Leinster.

It would be easy to misrepresent the facts and to interpret the events of 1173–4 as an almost national uprising against the Anglo-Normans. It should be understood that, when Raymond led his troops into Munster, there were no question of a 'Norman conquest' or even an extension of control. The mailed knights who descended on Lismore and engaged Diarmait Mac Carthaig were, in the tradition of their viking ancestors, on a freebooting expedition. The uproar and fighting that filled Munster and Leinster during 1173–4 were no different from what Ireland had been experiencing before the coming of the Anglo-Normans, when the country was, in the words of the annalists, 'a trembling sod'.[1] Whether it was an Ua Conchobair or a Strongbow invading Munster made no difference. Nor was it a surprise to find Domnall Ua Briain abandoning the pursuit of the Anglo-Norman army, or Ruaidrí Ua Conchobair withdrawing across the Shannon with his fair-weather allies. There would always be another year, a reversal or interchange of alliances, more campaigns, greater cattle-raids. As yet there was no indication of a 'Norman conquest' of Ireland. That did not even begin to take shape until 1177.

Anglo-Norman retaliation for the defeat and setbacks of 1173–4 came within a year. It began with reprisals in Meath, the hanging of Magnus Ua Máel Sechlainn at Trim, and the reoccupation and refortification of Trim and Duleek in the de Lacy lordship. Later in 1175 Raymond le Gros led an expedition against Domnall Ua Briain of Thomond, setting out with a force drawn from Dublin and Waterford of 120 knights, 300 other mounted soldiers, and 400 archers on foot. Now comes the surprise. Not only did Ruaidrí Ua Conchobair not oppose the campaign in Meath, but he became an ally of the Anglo-Normans against Domnall Ua Briain. As yet there was no national principle involved, no cultural opposition between Gael and Anglo-Norman. Indeed, the Annals of Tigernach would have it that the expedition into Munster was undertaken at the invitation of Ruaidrí Ua Conchobair, just as, paradoxically, the first Anglo-Norman expedition into Munster, in 1170, had been at the request of Domnall Ua Briain to counteract an invasion by Ruaidrí Ua Conchobair across the Shannon. Connachtmen played an active part in these events during 1175, for it was they, again according to the Annals of Tigernach, who burned the greater part of Thomond. As a further surprise we find that Raymond was guided across the country by Irish scouts under Domnall Mac Gilla Pátraic of Osraige, the inveterate enemy of Diarmait Mac Murchada.

Limerick town was taken, but not without difficulty. The troops on arriving

[1] *A.F.M.*, 1145 and 1171.

at the bank of the Shannon found themselves facing a daunting series of obstacles—a fortified hostile town, a stone wall, a dyke, and, most formidable of
all, a deep, fast-flowing river.[1] A bloody battle ensued. The town was taken with ·
rich spoil of gold and other booty, which Raymond divided up among his soldiers. He chose a number of them to remain as a garrison under his cousin,
Milo fitz David, and then set out back to Leinster.

With Limerick captured and the surrounding territory overrun, Ruaidrí Ua
Conchobair saw to it that Domnall Ua Briain was deposed and his son,
Muirchertach, placed in his stead. Gerald of Wales states that the reason for
Raymond's campaign was because Domnall 'went back on the oath of loyalty
which he had taken to the king',[2] but it is much nearer the mark to see it as a
punitive expedition because of Domnall's military campaign against the
Anglo-Normans during the previous year. No high national motive can be
attributed to Ruaidrí Ua Conchobair for his intervention on the side of the
Anglo-Normans. Nevertheless, he was unconsciously playing his part in the
process by which Ireland was beginning to move into the feudal system and the
European polity. Though he was still wholeheartedly playing the old game of
dynastic warfare, he was simultaneously sponsoring negotiations which were to
establish for the first time a constitutional relationship between Anglo-
Norman and Gaelic rulers in Ireland.

During that same month of October 1175, when Raymond was leading the
Anglo-Normans to storm Limerick town and, with the aid of Ruaidrí, subdue
Thomond, three of the high-king's agents, Archbishop Cadla Ua Dubthaig of
Tuam, Abbot 'Canthordis' of Clonfert, and Ruaidrí's chancellor, Laurence,
were negotiating a treaty with Henry II. So far there has been no study of the
circumstances in which the treaty was initiated and concluded, but for our purposes it will suffice to identify the main problem and suggest an explanation.

What motivated Ruaidrí in this instance, and what, or who, prompted him to
act at this particular moment? It has been assumed that the Anglo-Norman
march on Limerick followed the signing of the treaty; with Ruaidrí, conscious
from his several unfortunate encounters with the Anglo-Normans that the
mailed might of the newcomers was almost irresistible, now utilising them as
allies.[3] In that interpretation of the treaty Ruaidrí aimed to place an effective

---

[1] Described in vivid detail by Giraldus, *Expugnatio*, pp 149–53, and in shorter form in *Song of
Dermot*, lines 3412–59, which ends abruptly at this point. Both accounts need to be supplemented
from other sources; see editorial notes in *Expugnatio*, pp 323–4, n. 241.

[2] *Expugnatio*, p. 149.

[3] For the text of the treaty see Thomas Rymer, *Foedera, conventiones, litterae, et . . . acta publica*, ed.
Adam Clarke and Frederick Holbrooke, i (London, 1816), pp 31–2; English translation in Curtis &
McDowell, *Ir. hist. docs*, pp 22–4, but with two of the sources given inaccurately. The only extended
commentary on the treaty is by J. F. O'Doherty, 'St Laurence O'Toole and the Anglo-Norman
invasion' in *I.E.R.*, l (1937), pp 620–25, where he assigns (though without hard evidence) the chief
responsibility for the treaty to Ua Tuathail. O'Doherty shows a nationalist bias. For the treaty in its
Angevin context see the comments of Warren, *Henry II*, pp 201–4, particularly the observations on
p. 201, n. 1.

restraint on the land-hungry, marauding Anglo-Normans by signing a formal agreement with their feudal lord, Henry II, and thus coming under his protection. The Angevin overlord should consequently see to it that his Anglo-Norman and Gaelic subjects keep the peace among themselves. Ruaidrí thus emerges unexpectedly as a man of sophisticated judgement and diplomatic foresight, qualities notably absent hitherto in his career. That interpretation is attractive and appears to be logical, but it fits neither the chronology nor Ruaidrí's character.

Gerald of Wales rarely dates the events he narrates, but he mentions that the assault on Limerick town was about 1 October.[1] The signing of the treaty took place five days later at Windsor, and it was therefore not due to any treaty obligations that the Anglo-Normans campaigned on the side of Ruaidrí against Domnall Ua Briain. The campaign was a convenient military alliance between Ruaidrí and the Anglo-Normans, a demonstration (perhaps with an eye to a treaty) that the two could work together harmoniously and with mutual profit. We must look to see who, or what forces, could have induced Ruaidrí to undertake the negotiations at Windsor, independently of a military expedition to Limerick. There is no obvious answer, but certain events of the previous years in Ireland, as well as the Irish representatives at Windsor, suggest that the guiding influence in promoting the treaty came from Irish church leaders, and that their objects were not political but were church reform and peace, a continuation of the policy they had adopted with the first settlers and later with Henry II.

The signatories of the treaty on behalf of Ruaidrí were his chancellor Laurence, with Archbishop Ua Dubthaig and Abbot 'Canthordis'. It is almost certain that the chancellor, 'Master Laurence', was a cleric, as were certainly the archbishop and the abbot. The archbishop, and probably the abbot, had been present at the synod of Cashel during 1171–2, when the assembled bishops, abbots, and prelates accepted Henry II as their temporal overlord. Their decision was confirmed and blessed by Pope Alexander III in the letters which he sent in September 1172 to the Irish kings, princes, and bishops, and which were reinforced by the additional exhortation that the pope sent at Henry's request, and which was read out, with the approval of the bishops, at an episcopal synod summoned at Waterford in 1173 by William fitz Audelin, as Henry's representative in Ireland.[2] The national synod of Cashel was followed in 1172 by a provincial synod of laity and clerics held at Tuam, presided over by King Ruaidrí and Archbishop Ua Dubthaig.[3] Though its deliberations have not been recorded it may safely be assumed that the political message from the synod of Cashel was taken by Ruaidrí; it certainly would not have been lost on Archbishop Ua Dubthaig. That Rome continued to keep a vigilant pastoral eye

---

[1] *Expugnatio*, p. 151.
[2] Ibid., p. 143; Orpen, *Normans*, i, 293–307.
[3] *Ann. Tig.*, 1172.

on Ireland may be deduced from the Annals of Ulster, which record in 1175 the death (at Chambéry, in Savoy) of Conchobar mac Meic Con Chaille, archbishop of Armagh, on his way back to Ireland after conferring with the pope.

A more tangible sign of papal interest in the negotiations at Windsor was the presence of Lorcán Ua Tuathail, archbishop of Dublin. Though he is sometimes described, without evidence, as having been present at Windsor in the capacity of ambassador for Ruaidrí Ua Conchobair,[1] he was there as an official witness to the treaty, the only Irishman among the nine witnesses.[2] He was the ideal observer on behalf of church interests, at a meeting fraught with political complications. Regarded as an exemplary cleric and devoted pastor, he was trusted by Gaelic Irish, Hiberno-Norse, and Anglo-Normans, during the bloody upheavals of the years 1170–71, which included at Dublin two sieges, a long blockade, and several battles. He had the confidence of Ruaidrí, and in 1175 had not yet incurred the displeasure of Henry II.

The fact that the Irish church leaders apparently promoted the treaty of Windsor did not mean that Ruaidrí was a pliant instrument in their hands. It well suited his plans to do a deal with the Angevin king. It should curb the Anglo-Norman adventurers, and guarantee their invaluable military support when he had to cope with aggressors or rebellious subjects. The arrangement also suited Henry. He had more than enough on his hands, with his sons and rebellious barons, to involve himself personally in Irish affairs. The high-king, who had not previously made his submission, at least personally, to Henry during 1171–2 as had most of the other Irish rulers,[3] was now willing to become his liegeman and to pay him an annual tribute in hides. Ruaidrí was required to accept Henry's direct jurisdiction over Meath, Leinster, and those other areas extending between Dublin, Wicklow, Wexford, and Waterford, which were held in the king's name by his vassals. Outside Henry's direct jurisdiction Ruaidrí was recognised as high-king, as were his traditional rights such as the taking of hostages, but he in turn was to give hostages to Henry.

However, the plan succumbed to a double failure. Henry, a strong ruler, was able to suppress his rebellious children and fractious barons in his English and continental territories, but was unable to check the expansion of his subjects in Ireland. Ruaidrí, a weak ruler, had, like Henry, rebellious children and unruly underlords, but unlike him he could not subdue them, even within his immediate jurisdiction in Connacht. The net result over the next two years was that the treaty of Windsor came apart. It was not in itself an impractical scheme. A similar arrangement made by Henry II eighteen months later at the council of Oxford with the two leading Welsh leaders, Dafydd of Gwynedd in

---

[1] E.g. J. F. Lydon, *The lordship of Ireland in the middle ages* (Dublin and London, 1972), p. 47; M. T. Flanagan, 'Hiberno-papal relations in the late twelfth century' in *Archiv. Hib.*, xx (1976–7), pp 55–70, at p. 60. See also O'Doherty, 'St Laurence O'Toole', op. cit., pp 620–25.

[2] Rymer, *Foedera*, i, 31, lists the witnesses.

[3] *Expugnatio*, pp 94–7. For the conflicting stories about Ruaidrí's supposed submission, see editorial notes, ibid., p. 312, n. 157, and above, p. 90.

the north, and Rhys of Deheubarth in the south, was to prove remarkably successful.

The fallacy in the treaty of Windsor was the supposition that Ruaidrí would prove to be an effective *ard-rí*. It was obvious that the northern princes would not accept his claims over them as high-king, and there was no question of Ua Briain of Thomond voluntarily submitting to his rule. Indeed, Ruaidrí could not obtain cooperation even from his own sons, one of whom he blinded. The realities of the situation became apparent early in 1176, when the Anglo-Norman garrison at Limerick found itself strongly besieged by an army under Domnall Ua Briain, who had now regained control of Thomond, having displaced his son, the usurper, who had been thrust on the throne by Ruaidrí Ua Conchobair. Responding to an appeal from the garrison, Raymond le Gros led a force south and raised the siege.

Since for the Irish kings there was no conscious cultural bond or national principle at stake, it is not surprising to find Domnall Ua Briain quickly coming to terms with Raymond and Ruaidrí Ua Conchobair, and all three agreeing on their loyalty to King Henry of England. The outcome of this triangular negotiation was quite satisfactory, as far as appearances went. Both Ruaidrí and Domnall swore fealty to Henry, and gave hostages to Raymond as the king's representative. Domnall also gave hostages to Ruaidrí, whose dual role as *ard-rí* and overlord for the king of England was recognised by Domnall Ua Briain, at least for the time being. The oaths of fealty and the hostages were all in conformity with the treaty of Windsor, which appeared, thanks to Raymond le Gros's intervention, to be an effective working arrangement.

The treaty was put to another test before Raymond had time to return to Leinster. Diarmait Mac Carthaig, king of Desmond, who had recently been overthrown and imprisoned by his son, Cormac Liathánach, appealed for help, as Henry's liegeman and loyal subject, to Raymond. The Anglo-Norman troops did not hesitate, and led by the indefatigable Raymond were once again on the march. They not only restored Diarmait but, in the process, seized cattle and other provisions, which were sent to the needy garrison at Limerick. It seemed to be further proof that the treaty of Windsor could work and that Henry would do well to rely on Strongbow and Raymond le Gros to implement it.

While Raymond was still fully engaged in Desmond a messenger arrived with a fateful sealed letter. When the messenger was dismissed, the letter was broken open and read privately in the presence of Raymond, presumably illiterate, by a trusted cleric in his retinue. The letter was from Basilia, wife of Raymond and sister of Strongbow; the message, though cryptic, was plain to Raymond. 'That large molar tooth, which caused me so much pain, has now fallen out. So I beg of you, if you have any thought for your own future safety or mine, return quickly and without delay.' It could mean only that Strongbow had died. He had been seriously ill even before Raymond left Dublin at the end of March, and the death took place apparently about the end of May 1176.[1]

Raymond returned without delay to Limerick and confided the news to a few of his lieutenants. It was agreed that while the future was uncertain at Dublin it was in these circumstances still more uncertain at Limerick. Accordingly it was decided to put a brave face on the situation at Limerick and to withdraw the troops to Dublin with banners flying. Custody of Limerick was handed over to Domnall Ua Briain, who as liege vassal of Henry II cheerfully renewed his oath of allegiance, handed over more hostages as surety, and assured Raymond that the town would be held in trust for the king. Raymond and his men had only just reached the other side of the river, on the first stage of their homeward journey, when the bridge behind them was demolished and they saw the town they had strongly fortified and stocked with provisions going up in flames at four different points. Domnall Ua Briain had not waited even for an excuse to renege on his oath of allegiance; once more he was sole master of Thomond. The Anglo-Normans were not to set foot in Limerick town again for another twenty years. There was the ring of realism in Henry II's comment: 'The assault on Limerick was a bold enterprise, the relief of the city even more so, but only in abandoning the place did they show any wisdom.'[2]

It was becoming clear to Henry that the treaty of Windsor was a failure. Ruaidrí Ua Conchobair, without the assistance of the Anglo-Normans, had no effective answer to Domnall Ua Briain, who now successfully defied the Irish high-king and repudiated his Angevin overlord. It was not the only example of Ruaidrí's inability to keep the Irish provincial kings in order. Máel Sechlainn Mac Lochlainn of Cénél nEógain came ravaging south into Meath in 1176, destroyed the fort at Slane, and made the settlers abandon Galtrim, Kells, and Derrypatrick. Nor were the Irish alone at fault. While Geraldines such as Raymond le Gros, who had attacked without justification Ua Fáeláin of the Déise and Mac Carthaig of Desmond in 1173, were now temporarily restrained by the treaty of Windsor, a new example of Anglo-Norman rapacity was the invasion of Ulster by John de Courcy in February 1177, with his spectacular success in capturing Downpatrick and establishing himself there. A raid into the Déise for plunder was a disturbing but a temporary affair; permanent expansion northwards into Ulster represented a threat that could not be disregarded. De Courcy's piratical campaign was a blow both to the native Irish and to Anglo-Norman royal authority. It had an ominous significance since de Courcy was not one of the restless pioneering Geraldines, but was from the second wave of adventurers, and he was only a year in the country. In these circumstances, what did the future hold for Ireland but a sea of troubles? So Henry saw it.

He decided on a major change of policy for Ireland and had it promulgated

---

[1] Giraldus, *Expugnatio*, p. 165, gives the date as 'about the kalends of June'. See the various dates cited in G.E.C., *Peerage*, x, 356, note c.
[2] Giraldus, *Expugnatio*, p. 167.

at the council of Oxford in May 1177. It is only very recently that the apparently arbitrary changes of policy for Ireland by Henry have been explained convincingly in terms of a constructive attempt to fit this latest Anglo-Norman acquisition into the complicated dynastic and political developments of the conglomerate entity known as the 'Angevin empire'.[1] Against such a background one can understand Henry's several shifts of policy towards Ireland over the years 1167–77.

By the year 1177 he was head of a commonwealth of seven separate dominions, linked to him personally by dynastic ties and solemn oaths of fealty or homage. The basis of his power was the inherited territories of England, Normandy, and Anjou; then as separate units came Aquitaine, Brittany, Ireland, Wales, Scotland, and Toulouse, over each of which he claimed authority, and exercised it in varying degrees. As he saw it, in 1177, he fortunately had four sons to whom he would consign the four units most deserving of direct royal attention. Henry, the eldest, would as of right inherit England, Normandy, and Anjou; Aquitaine would be ruled by Richard, Brittany by Geoffrey, and Ireland by John; Welsh Wales would be controlled through its native princes of Gwynedd and Deheubarth, who had agreed to become his vassals; Scotland would be governed by its native king, William, likewise a vassal of Henry since the treaty of Falaise in 1174; and Toulouse would be under its hereditary count, who accepted Henry as his overlord.[2]

Henry originally had no wish to include Ireland among his dominions. When the Irish question reappeared at the royal court in 1167, in the person of Diarmait Mac Murchada, Henry showed no enthusiasm for embarking on a campaign in Ireland; he handled the situation deftly, by publishing a letter addressed to his subjects 'English, Norman, Welsh, and Scots, and all peoples subject to his rule', encouraging them to join Mac Murchada in the attempt to regain his kingdom. Henry was quite willing to allow Mac Murchada the same support from Anglo-Norman knights that had helped to consolidate the Scottish kings, Malcolm Canmore (1058–93) and David I (1124–53), on their thrones but had also ensured an Anglo-Norman presence north of the Tweed.

That convenient arrangement for Ireland worked as long as Mac Murchada lived, but when he was succeeded in 1171 by Strongbow, a senior Anglo-Norman baron married to Mac Murchada's daughter, Henry decided that his own direct intervention was necessary. Henry's visit to Ireland in 1171–2 convinced him that with most of the country still under a variety of native

---

[1] For the Council of Oxford decrees concerning Ireland see Orpen, *Normans*, ii, 30–38; Curtis, *Med. Ire.* (2nd ed.), pp 81–2; Otway Ruthven, *Med. Ire.*, pp 60–63; Lydon, *Lordship*, pp 49–50. Note in particular the comments of Warren, *Henry II*, pp 202–4.

[2] Credit for this fresh and enlightening interpretation must go principally to Professor W. L. Warren. He presented it in outline as 'The interpretation of twelfth-century Irish history', read as a paper at the eighth Irish Conference of Historians at Belfast in 1967 and published in *Hist. Studies*, vii (1969), pp 1–19. Professor Warren developed his interpretation in a number of subsequent studies, the most recent being 'King John and Ireland' in Lydon, *Eng. & Ire.*, pp 26–42.

rulers he could not expect a neat arrangement. His compromise solution was the treaty of Windsor in 1175. When that proved delusive, his final solution, announced at the council of Oxford in May 1177, was to establish Ireland, by intention the whole of the country, as a separate kingdom under his youngest son, John, then aged ten. Viewed therefore in the context of the 'Angevin empire' Henry's positive policy for Ireland began in 1167, after Mac Murchada's visit to him in Aquitaine, when he sought to apply what had worked in Scotland. That system of indirect control faded with Strongbow's success. It decided Henry to think in terms of Wales, with direct control over the Anglo-Norman lords, who were to be counterbalanced by the Gaelic Irish allies of Henry. Finally, when that scheme became a manifest failure he turned to the example of Brittany. Like Ireland it had been torn by internal feuds until Henry intervened, subdued it during 1166 and 1173–4, installed his son, Geoffrey, as governor, and gave him the beginnings of an administration worthy of a duke.

The final solution for Ireland was imaginative, but was it realistic? Could John gain control of a situation containing so many volatile elements? For a beginning John had literally to grow up, so that it would be at least ten years before he would be of age to participate actively in Irish affairs. Secondly, this presupposed an administrative structure which would either be set up in advance of his going to Ireland or would have to be formed immediately after his arrival in the country. Thirdly, it was assumed that the Irish would be submissive to his rule, and fourthly and more importantly, that the settlers would be obedient and cooperative.

Waiting for John to grow up meant that some strong royal representative had, in the interim, to control affairs in Ireland. Fitz Audelin, who had taken over from Raymond le Gros in April 1176, was replaced after the council of Oxford by Hugh de Lacy, with the title of 'procurator'. Leinster was divided into three 'custodies' under de Lacy at Dublin, fitz Audelin at Wexford, and Robert le Poer at Waterford. The grant of Meath to de Lacy was confirmed. These appointments merely steadied control over territories already occupied by the Anglo-Normans. More was required for a future king of Ireland. To ensure that John would have a group of barons whose loyalty would be assured (unlike that of Irish leaders such as Domnall Ua Briain of Thomond and of independent-minded Anglo-Norman pioneers such as Maurice de Prendergast) Henry made a number of sweeping land-grants and gave powerful offices to a selected number of ambitious settlers. This represented the second stage of Anglo-Norman colonisation in Ireland. The most notable beneficiaries were Hugh de Lacy, Robert fitz Stephen, Miles de Cogan, Philip de Braose, and Robert le Poer. Each person to whom grants were made at the council had to do homage and take an oath of fealty to John, as well as to Henry himself.

The kingdom of Desmond was granted to Robert fitz Stephen and Miles de Cogan; the kingdom of Thomond to Philip de Braose; and the custody of Waterford to Robert le Poer. There was no difficulty about Waterford: it was already firmly in Anglo-Norman hands, and le Poer assumed command there. There was, in feudal terms, a clear justification for the confiscation of Thomond, since Domnall Ua Briain had welshed on his oath of fealty to Henry II. There was no such apparent reason for the seizure of Mac Carthaig territory in Desmond, but in the ultimate analysis a ruthless Angevin monarch and his restless subjects in the frontier lands needed neither justification nor excuse; they wanted only an opportunity. Ruaidrí Ua Conchobair, the high-king, was distracted by his own family feuds, and could not control his underlords, such as Ua Briain of Thomond and Mac Carthaig of Desmond. Each of these in turn was distracted by family disputes. It meant that the treaty of Windsor was not worth the parchment on which it was inscribed. There was no authority among the native Irish to keep the peace. That is where a Diarmait Mac Murchada could have made all the difference, yet even some such strong ruler was no permanent solution. A fortuitous turn of the Irish political wheel or a sudden death would put everything back into the melting pot. What was needed essentially on the Irish side of the treaty of Windsor was not so much a strong man as a predictable system, but by the twelfth century (and long before it) there was built into the Irish polity and tradition a fatal double weakness. There were savage succession disputes within the main ruling families, fostered by the prevailing Irish system of succession. Secondly, there were the shifting alliances of groups of minor families who refused to accept for very long the hegemony of any one ruling family. It would have suited Henry II had he been able to leave the *status quo* operating in Ireland under Ruaidrí Ua Conchobair, but in the unstable political circumstances he chose to give official rein to the freebooting instincts of his barons and to direct their energies into Munster.

The kingdoms of Thomond and Desmond were the objects of conquest, but, ironically, while Desmond succumbed, Domnall Ua Briain of Thomond, who had broken his oath of fealty to Henry II, thwarted the Anglo-Norman advance. After the grants were announced at the council of Oxford in May 1177, the three favoured barons, de Braose (for Thomond), de Cogan and fitz Stephen (for Desmond), agreed to act in unison. They crossed over to Ireland together in November 1177, each bringing his own body of armed followers. They travelled from Waterford through Lismore to Cork, where they were received with honour by the Anglo-Norman governor, Richard de Londres. Diarmait Mac Carthaig seems to have made no more than a token resistance. He and his underlords in Desmond agreed to submit on terms. Two highly significant facts about the invasion of Munster are known from Irish annals, not from Anglo-Norman sources, namely that Muirchertach Mac Carthaig, son of the king of Desmond, 'took Miles de Cogan and fitz Stephen to Cork',[1] and that during the campaign 'the churches of the plain of Munster were burnt by Domnall Ua Briain and by Miles de Cogan, Philip Cnam, Henry, and fitz Stephen'.[2] In what

[1] 'Mac Carthaig's Book' in *Misc. Ir. Annals*, p. 63.
[2] *Ann. Tig.*, 1177, where variant forms of the names are used.

was an hour of crisis for Munster the internal family feuds, as well as the traditional armed hostility between the two leading families in the province, continued unabated.

Diarmait Mac Carthaig agreed to let the Anglo-Normans have seven
cantreds of the territory around Cork town, the three eastern going to fitz
Stephen, the four western to de Cogan. Fitz Stephen and de Cogan were to
have joint charge of Cork town, though it also retained its royal governor. With
the installation of the two barons in Desmond, south-west Munster theoretically passed into Anglo-Norman hands. Whether they could control it
remained to be seen.

The attempt to take Thomond began with like determination, but fizzled
out. The help which the O'Briens had given in conquering the kingdom of
Desmond did not dissuade the Anglo-Normans from their ambitions in
Thomond, since they were well aware that the O'Briens had acted primarily
with the purpose of defeating a rival ruling family in the province. The three
barons set off together from Cork for Limerick. When they arrived on the bank
of the Shannon opposite Limerick the citizens signalled their arrival by setting
the town on fire, obviously expecting that the Anglo-Normans would, as
before, successfully storm the walls. Eventually, without any attempt to storm
the town or occupy the lands in Thomond, the Anglo-Normans set off back to
Cork. The failure of the expedition to occupy Thomond was due as much to
the resolution of the citizens of Limerick as to the pusillanimity of de Braose.

The year 1177 was all-important in the history of the Anglo-Norman
presence in Ireland. In Leinster it witnessed the arrival and activity of Hugh de
Lacy, after Strongbow the most important of the Anglo-Norman leaders and
the man who was to establish the colonists so successfully in Meath. In Munster it saw the subjugation of the kingdom of Desmond and the consolidation of
Anglo-Norman power in Waterford. Connacht in this same year experienced
for the first time the might of the mailed knights when Murchad Ua Conchobair, son of King Ruaidrí, invited the Anglo-Normans 'to destroy Connacht
for evil towards his father'.[1] Miles de Cogan, then constable of the troops at
Dublin, seized the opportunity to march across the country with a band of 540
soldiers and, guided by Murchad Ua Conchobair, advanced into Roscommon.
The Anglo-Normans suffered the loss of only three archers, then thankfully
withdrew across the Shannon, leaving Murchad Ua Conchobair at the mercy of
his father, who blinded him for his perfidy.

It was in 1177 also that the most remarkable of the Anglo-Norman expeditions in Ireland took place when John de Courcy, an energetic young warrior
from Somerset, set out to conquer the kingdom of Ulster (the modern counties
of Down and Antrim). There are several misconceptions, even in standard historical works, about this campaign. It is usually presented as a gloriously

---

[1] 'Do milleadh Connacht ar ulca fri Ruaidhrí' (*A.F.M.*, 1177). *Ann. Tig.* has a substantial account
of the Anglo-Norman expedition into Connacht. See also Giraldus, *Expugnatio*, p. 183.

impulsive decision, starred with good luck, and crowned with rapid success. The evidence on close examination indicates that it was a carefully planned operation, guided by advice from Irish sources, and that on several occasions during the first three years it led to the brink of disaster.[1] Nevertheless, it was an outstanding achievement, due largely to de Courcy's foresight, sense of timing, unorthodox methods, and leonine courage.

It was out of the war season when he began, early in February, heading north from Dublin with some of its garrison, presumably with the tacit consent of de Lacy, royal governor both of Dublin and of Anglo-Norman Ireland. He almost certainly needed the connivance of de Lacy to pass through the lordship of Meath, and he was not opposed by Ua Cerbaill of Airgialla. With him he had twenty-two knights, three hundred other Anglo-Norman soldiers, and some Irish allies. If the later 'Book of Howth'[2] is correct in stating that he had seven hundred under his command at the battle of Downpatrick in June 1177, almost half of his army were Irish, some of whom he must have collected en route or in Airgialla or further north. De Courcy almost certainly had the connivance of Ua Cerbaill. De Courcy and his followers barely succeeded in defeating the Mac Duinn Sléibe army at Downpatrick, but it was here that the de Courcy legend was established. Gerald of Wales narrates his feats in battle, ferocious in his onslaught on the enemy, as he 'lopped off now a head from someone's shoulders, or again arms or hands from their body'.[3]

Thus began the de Courcy saga, and he himself later carefully fostered it. He was pictured, probably truthfully, as tall, lean, and with bright blond hair, riding a white charger into battle, flourishing a shield emblazoned with his coat of arms of eagles. He had been a dapifer (a traditional royal official) in the court of Henry II and later a royal seneschal in Normandy, but in Ireland he appeared as the hero figure for the young Anglo-Norman adventurers. Even his sceptical contemporary, Gerald of Wales, was fascinated by his deeds. Gerald described one raid into Fir Lí in north Antrim when de Courcy's force was ambushed, severely defeated, and unhorsed, and he and the eleven surviving knights, weighed down with armour, fought their way back on foot to his castle, thirty miles away, with nothing to eat for two days and nights.[4]

Ruaidrí Mac Duinn Sléibe was back to the attack in June 1177, when the second battle of Downpatrick took place, de Courcy's small but compact force facing a formidable hosting of Ruaidrí with his men of Ulster backed by an army of the Cenél nEógain under Máel Sechlainn Mac Lochlainn. In order to boost the morale of his troops Ruaidrí was accompanied by the archbishop of Armagh, the bishop of Down, a flock of clergy, and a collection of rare relics. The religious props were of no avail, and the Irish were routed, but de Courcy

---

[1] The best single account of de Courcy's activities in Ulster is still Orpen, *Normans*, ii, 5–23, but see also Curtis, *Med. Ire.* (2nd ed.), pp 77–9; Otway-Ruthven, *Med. Ire.*, pp 58–9; Lydon, *Lordship Ire.*, pp 55–8; Robin Frame, *Colonial Ireland, 1169–1369* (Dublin, 1981), pp 26–9; T. E. McNeill, *Anglo-Norman Ulster* (Edinburgh, 1980), pp 3–14.

[2] *Cal. Carew MSS*, v, 81.   [3] *Expugnatio*, p. 177.   [4] Ibid., p. 179.

showed himself magnanimous and far-sighted in victory. The prelates were set free, including the primate, and the more important relics were restored to Armagh. We shall see later that while de Courcy was steadily extending his power northwards into Antrim, he was also promoting the cult of St Patrick, and finally showed his political hand in 1180 by an alliance with the rulers of Man. De Courcy's personal bravery and his conquest of Ulster became proverbial, but his victories were hard-won. His contemporary, Gerald of Wales, realistically summed up de Courcy's military progress during those first few years. 'So he was victorious in three of these battles, while in two he experienced the vicissitudes of war and the uncertainty of fortune. Yet although he suffered in the fighting, he inflicted far heavier losses on the enemy than he suffered himself.'[1] In fact, it would seem that it was only by 1181 that de Courcy was secure in Ulster. By then, he had not only concluded the strategic marriage alliance with Man, but had won over Ruaidrí Mac Duinn Sléibe and Cú Mide Ua Flainn, king of Uí Thuirtre and Fir Lí in County Antrim, who subsequently served loyally as his sub-kings. It is not unlikely that Ruaidrí added to his ambitions by suggesting the restoration of the ancient Ulster, extending over the whole north from Armagh to Derry, lost to the Ulaid since the fifth century. Hence (if he needed any prompting) his raid on Armagh in 1189 and his campaigns in Derry and Inishowen in 1197.

Victory of a different kind was gained for the Anglo-Normans in the same year, 1177. By a coincidence a papal legate, Cardinal Vivian, was at Downpatrick and witnessed one of de Courcy's victories, probably the second battle of Downpatrick. Vivian had just come from Scotland via the Isle of Man, and was captured by de Courcy's troops. Released shortly afterwards, he made his way to Dublin where he summoned a synod of bishops and abbots. The main purpose of the meeting was to repeat papal approval for Henry II's lordship of Ireland, and the legate left no room for doubt. Though he charged both clergy and people, under threat of excommunication, to observe their allegiance to the king, abstaining from all acts of rebellion, it is difficult to judge how effective was the command. The evidence suggests that then, as centuries later, the Irish adopted the principle 'religion from Rome, but politics from home'. Undoubtedly the prelates present, including Archbishop Lorcán Ua Tuathail, accepted the papal directive, but the Irish leaders in the different provinces went their own political ways, as we shall see shortly.

On almost every score 1177 was an *annus mirabilis* for the Anglo-Normans in Ireland. A series of disconnected expeditions assumed the character of country-wide penetration, though it could not yet be accurately described as either invasion or conquest. De Courcy managed independently to establish himself in Ulster, but his survival there remained in the balance. The more serious advance, backed by royal authority, was in Munster, spearheaded by fitz Stephen, de Cogan, and de Braose. Yet this was the time when the king of

[1] *Expugnatio*, p. 179.

Thomond, Domnall Mór Ua Briain, decided to spring a large-scale attack on two minor family groups, the O'Donovans (Uí Dondubáin) and the O'Collinses (Uí Chuiléin), traditional opponents of the O'Briens. So successful was his campaign that he drove them from Limerick down to west Cork as his ancestors had done decades earlier with the MacCarthys (Meic Carthaig) and the O'Sullivans (Uí Shúillebáin). The expulsion of these four family groups created a vacuum that the Anglo-Normans were to fill when they set about a systematic conquest of the Ua Briain territory at the very end of the twelfth century. These short-sighted family interests pinpoint an essential weakness of the Gaelic polity. It was the Achilles' heel of the entire Gaelic political system.

Henry's problem was to ensure that John, at some stage, would rule the country effectively. How could the gap of at least ten years be safely bridged until the stripling of ten years would be of age to rule his lordship? It would require interim government by royal representatives, preferably by one strong man, loyal and prudent. It had to be somebody of standing, and with a power base in the country. It could not be one of the Geraldines, who had successfully blazed the Anglo-Norman trail in Ireland, but were too firmly entrenched to be trusted. A royal nominee, without roots in the country, would carry no weight, and would leave a weak foundation on which the Lord John would have to build. Henry's solution was to appoint a series of royal deputies, changing them as often as they incurred his suspicion or displeasure. This explains why Hugh de Lacy was first appointed, in 1177, replaced by two joint deputies, John de Lacy and Richard of the Peak, in 1181, succeeded by Hugh de Lacy who was reinstated in the same year, who in his turn was superseded by Philip of Worcester in September 1184 as the preparation for the arrival of the Lord John himself in Ireland in April 1185.

De Lacy not only gave reassurance to the colonists; he set out to conciliate the Irish. It was sound economic and political strategy. He invited back the Irish who had fled from their lands during the raids and counter-raids of Anglo-Norman and Irish since 1170, reestablished them with cattle and farms, guaranteed them protection, and while rewarding his followers kept their ambitions within bounds.[1] To complete his identity with the land of his adoption, in which he now had the unofficial status of a provincial king, he married a daughter of Ruaidrí Ua Conchobair, in 1180, without seeking the permission of Henry II. De Lacy's alliance was for Henry a repetition of the threat which Strongbow had raised by marrying Aífe, daughter of Diarmait Mac Murchada, and resurrected the spectre of a kingdom ruled not by an Angevin but by one of his overmighty subjects. There were those in Ireland and England who took it on themselves to stir the dark pot of royal suspicions. De Lacy was summoned back to England in summer 1181, and in his place was appointed not one but two royal agents, John de Lacy and Richard of the Peak.

[1] Ibid., p. 195; editorial notes, pp 339-40, nn 361-6.

Hugh de Lacy, for all his bravery in battle, was not one to rush hastily to arms. Having soldiered for several years with Henry II he was confident he could convince him of the true state of affairs in Ireland. It no doubt added to his credibility in Henry's estimation that instead of resenting his own dismissal he went out of his way to cooperate with John de Lacy and Richard of the Peak in establishing a series of castles at strategic points in Leinster before he left for England. These were built at Forth (Carlow), Knocktopher (Osraige), Castledermot (Kildare), Leighlin Bridge, and Tullow (Carlow). Once back in Henry's company, Hugh de Lacy's resolute and unpretentious personality worked the trick. Within a matter of months he returned to Ireland as royal deputy, but he had to tolerate the presence of a royal watchdog, Robert of Shrewsbury, who was constantly at his heels to report back to Henry. On his return to Ireland de Lacy intensified his activity as a builder of castles in Meath and Leinster, so that by 1186 the Annals of Loch Cé recorded that the land 'from the Shannon to the sea was full of castles and of foreigners'. In the process of thus extending Anglo-Norman influence and royal authority he inevitably came to be regarded by the Irish as a power in his own right, and this gave his Anglo-Norman critics in Ireland and at court in England the opportunity to revive the accusation that he was aiming at independence of his lord and master, Henry II. It was a risk the king could not afford to let go unchallenged, and he decided to implement, possibly to accelerate, the plans for his son John and for Ireland. In September 1184 de Lacy was once again superseded, and in his place was sent Philip of Worcester, a brave soldier and generous character by all accounts, but first and foremost a king's man.[1] In fact, the preparations for the lordship of Ireland had already been activated owing to an unforeseen and (for Henry) not unwelcome event, the death of Lorcán Ua Tuathail, archbishop of Dublin.

Commentators, ranging from Gerald of Wales in the twelfth century to J. F. O'Doherty in our own day, have found it difficult to decide whether the archbishop was pro-Irish or pro-Anglo-Norman.[2] Their mistake has been to try to fit him into either category. He was that rare phenomenon, a religious leader without political affiliations, a pastor whose care was equal for all members of a flock composed of Hiberno-Norse, Irish, and newly arrived Anglo-Normans. Though of the belligerently independent princely Ua Tuathail family of Uí Muiredaig, and trained in traditional Celtic monasticism in the monastery at Glendalough, he had been readily chosen as archbishop by the Hiberno-Norse in 1162. He cooperated in religious affairs with Diarmait Mac Murchada during the next four years, though their family interests clashed, just as he accepted the Anglo-Norman occupation of Dublin as a fact of political life.

---

[1] *Expugnatio*, p. 199.
[2] See editorial notes, ibid., pp 306, n. 116, 314, n. 107. A recent and satisfactory study of Lorcán Ua Tuathail is Maurice F. Roche, 'The Latin lives of St Laurence of Dublin' (Ph.D. thesis, N.U.I. (U.C.D.), 1981).

Undoubtedly the strong papal directives in 1172, that Henry be acknowledged as secular ruler of the country, made submission to the Angevin king easier. While it is significant that the archbishop was a witness to the treaty of Windsor in October 1175, it is equally significant that Henry commissioned Lorcán to convey Augustine, bishop-elect of Waterford, back to Ireland for his canonical examination and consecration by the archbishop of Cashel. Augustine was the first Irish bishop whose selection and consecration were supervised by Henry II.[1] Normally bishops in Henry's dominions were, according to feudal practice, regarded as tenants-in-chief, and Waterford was of great strategic importance on the military map.

The archbishop of Dublin stood well with Henry, and he was one of six Irish prelates who were at Windsor in January 1179 on their way to the third Lateran council at Rome. They were required to swear solemnly before they left Windsor that while at the council they would not participate in any activity harmful to the king's interests. The reassurance which Henry gained from their oaths was badly shaken, several months later, when he discovered after the closure of the council in March 1179 that the archbishop had arranged with Pope Alexander III for the dioceses of Dublin and Glendalough, with all their possessions, rights, and privileges, to be taken under papal protection.[2] To make matters worse, in Henry's eyes, Lorcán Ua Tuathail had secured double protection, since he was also appointed papal legate in Ireland.[3] To try to intimidate an archbishop was not without precedent, as had been all too evident in the case of Thomas Becket, but to molest a papal legate would be to affront the pope himself. Henry fumed at what he assumed was Lorcán's duplicity and his betrayal of the oath he had sworn at Windsor, but he did not understand the archbishop's mentality. Lorcán was willing to render to Caesar the things that were Caesar's, and to adapt to a succession of political masters (Diarmait Mac Murchada, the Hiberno-Norse of Dublin, the Anglo-Norman adventurers, and Henry II), but he was also, and as a priority, going to try to ensure that the dioceses under his care were not shackled by the feudal system. Nor would he tolerate abuses surviving from the Celtic church, as he quickly demonstrated when he returned to Ireland, later in 1179, and convened a synod at Clonfert for the province of Tuam.[4] Nobody was spared in its reforming decrees—bishops, simple clerics, or laity. Lorcán had the support, or at least the tacit consent, of Ruaidrí Ua Conchobair, high-king and ally of Henry II, for the reforms. This

---

[1] Watt, *Ch. & two nations*, pp 43–4.

[2] See documents of 20 Apr. 1179 and 13 May 1179 in Sheehy, *Pontificia Hib.*, i, 26–9, 29–31.

[3] Aubrey Gwynn, 'St Lawrence O'Toole as legate in Ireland' in *Anal. Bolland.*, lxviii (1950), pp 226–8. Cf. O'Doherty, 'St Laurence O'Toole', pp 141–2; Flanagan, 'Hiberno-papal relations', pp 60–61.

[4] *Ann. Clon.*, p. 213. This important entry, for the year 1179, has been misplaced in the MS after the entries for 1170; see Gwynn, 'St Lawrence O'Toole', p. 228, n. 2. The Annals of Clonmacnoise survive only in a curious English translation made in 1627 by Conall Mac Geoghegan. See the comments on the surviving texts of the annals by Aubrey Gwynn, 'Tomaltach Ua Conchobair, coarb of Patrick (1181–1201)' in *Seanchas Ardmhacha*, viii (1977), pp 238–9.

helps to explain the extraordinary decision by which Tommaltach Ua Conchobair, nephew of Ruaidrí, was appointed archbishop of Armagh and primate of
Ireland.[1] It was a revolution in Irish ecclesiastical affairs: a man from Connacht
placed in the see of Patrick. Only the determination, integrity, and authority of
a Lorcán Ua Tuathail could have achieved it.[2] Furthermore, Henry II had no
option but to support the appointment. According to the treaty of Windsor,
which was theoretically still in force, Ruaidrí was recognised as the supreme
authority in Gaelic Ireland, and any appointment that strengthened that
authority should have Henry's support. This argument had the logic and
strength of simplicity, but to the Angevin king it seemed to have much of the
cunning of the serpent. How do you deal with a cleric such as Lorcán Ua
Tuathail, a genuine religious reformer, of personal sanctity, exasperating simplicity, and high intelligence, who also had the status of a papal legate? Here
was Thomas Becket in more insidious guise.

Henry got the opportunity to show his displeasure when the archbishop
arrived at court in Oxford about the first week of February 1180.[3] He came
ingenuously, not on his own behalf, but representing Ruaidrí, who had also
incurred royal displeasure by failing to pay the tribute agreed to at the treaty of
Windsor in 1175. Lorcán brought with him Ruaidrí's nephew as a hostage from
the *ard-rí*. Henry's reply was to leave for France, and he was followed by the
archbishop, who had been forbidden to return to Ireland. After some weeks of
pointless delay a cleric named David went on ahead to the court and handed
over the boy hostage, thus helping to pacify the irascible monarch. David
returned with the good news to Lorcán, who died at Eu a few days later, before
midnight on 14 November 1180, thereby resolving problems for himself and the
king. It was a golden opportunity for Henry, who was determined that in future
a cooperative subject should rule the see of Dublin. John Cumin was elected
archbishop of Dublin in September 1181, the first Englishman to occupy the
see. The way was cleared, at a very important clerical level, for the Lord John to
come to Ireland.

Irish historical studies will be forever indebted to Gerald of Wales. It was a
singular stroke of good fortune which brought this gifted writer and acute
observer to Ireland with the first generation of Anglo-Normans. Admittedly he
was not in permanent residence, but he made four visits to the country, and his
two books on Ireland are an imperishable part of the national literature.[4] Yet

---

[1] Gwynn, 'Tomaltach Ua Conchobair', pp 245–52; Gwynn, 'St Lawrence O'Toole', pp 236–7.

[2] Tommaltach was mysteriously replaced by Máel Ísu Ua Cerbaill, bishop of Clogher-Louth (d.
1186/7) in 1184, probably as a result of the invasion of Armagh by de Lacy and Murchad Ua Cerbaill. Philip of Worcester's occupation of the city in Lent 1185 may have resulted in the restoration
of Tommaltach.

[3] Gwynn, 'St Lawrence O'Toole', pp 237–8.

[4] There is an extensive literature on Gerald: see Eileen Williams, 'A bibliography of Giraldus
Cambrensis, *c.* 1147–*c.* 1223' in *National Library of Wales Jn.*, xii (1961–2), pp 97–140. The most comprehensive single survey of his life and works is by J. Conway Davies, 'Giraldus Cambrensis, 1146–
1946' in *Archaeologia Cambrensis*, xcix (1946), pp 85–108, 256–80. These two surveys are brought up

his account of John's expedition to Ireland in 1185 represents a golden opportunity missed. Even worse, he has muddied, and even poisoned, the wells of
information in that account.

While Gerald is an invaluable source of information on the coming of the
Anglo-Normans to Ireland and their history up to 1185, he is both incomplete
and unreliable on John and the Irish scene after that date. Just as we suffer the
loss of a major source of information when the 'Song of Dermot and the earl'
ceases abruptly with the taking of Limerick in 1175, so Gerald of Wales, the
other main source for the early history of the Anglo-Normans in Ireland, dries
up at 1185. The Irish annals of these decades omit to mention even major
events, and at best supply meagre information. However, we are not left in the
dark at this crucial stage of Anglo-Norman involvement in Ireland. It is almost
as if a *genius loci* for Irish history is carefully arranging that a new source takes
over when another fails or dries up. In this instance we witness what can be
regarded as a revolution in Irish historical source-material, with the appearance of official Anglo-Norman administrative records. It is a landmark, which
may be accepted as important as, and more immediately instructive than, the
compilation of the Gaelic annals.[1]

Credit for this achievement cannot be given to the John of 1185. He was, as
yet, a callow youth, though admittedly precocious. The overall plan for his
appearance and activities on the Irish scene bore the hallmark of his father's
practical genius, but the architect who supervised the administrative details
was almost certainly Ranulf de Glanville, the sage and experienced jurist who
was at King Henry's elbow from 1178 onwards. His influence on John, on the

to 1976 by the editors of *Expugnatio*, A. B. Scott, 'The writer and his work', pp xii–xxxiii, and F. X.
Martin, 'Giraldus as historian', pp 267–84. For separate treatment of his works on Ireland, see
F. X. Martin, 'Gerald of Wales, Norman reporter on Ireland' in *Studies*, lviii (1969), pp 279–92. See
Michael Richter, 'Giraldiana' in *I.H.S.*, xxi, no. 84 (Sept. 1979), pp 422–37, for authoritative com-
ments on the most recent publications concerning Gerald of Wales and for a reassessment of his
importance.

[1] There is no in-depth study, nor even a comprehensive survey, of medieval Anglo-Irish
records; nothing similar to J. F. Kenney, *The sources for the early history of Ireland*, vol. i, *ecclesiastical*
(New York, 1929). It is a wry consolation to note that an invaluable parallel source, the Irish annals,
with so much material published during the last century and a half, did not receive a comprehensive, even if brief, survey until the publication of Gearóid Mac Niocaill, *The medieval Irish annals*
(Dublin, 1975).

Some estimate of the official Anglo-Irish material available may be gleaned from Margaret C.
Griffith, 'The Irish record commission, 1810–30' in *I.H.S.*, vii, no. 25 (Mar. 1950), pp 17–38; Hayes,
MS sources; Eric St John Brooks, 'The sources for medieval Anglo-Irish history' in *Hist. Studies*, i
(1958), 86–92; Aubrey Gwynn, 'Bibliographical note on medieval Anglo-Irish history', ibid.,
pp 93–9. Topics and offices have been dealt with in individual studies, in particular by H. G.
Richardson and G. O. Sayles, and A. J. Otway-Ruthven; see the bibliography below, pp 886–91.

For the high-class quality of what still remains, but unpublished, see A. J. Otway-Ruthven in
T. W. Moody (ed.), *Irish historiography, 1936–70* (Dublin, 1971), p. 17, and the comment of the exceptionally well informed G. O. Sayles in *Med. studies presented to A. Gwynn*, p. 203, 'Certainly if the historian of medieval Scotland had at his service a thousandth part of what lies in English archives to
illumine medieval Ireland, he would count himself blessed.' A guide to medieval Irish sources,
1100–1534, is being prepared under the editorship of James Lydon, for publication by the I.M.C.

1185 expedition, and on this formative decade of Irish history has not been properly appreciated. John had spent the previous three years, 1182–5, in the de Glanville household, whose children therefore became by Irish standards, as the annals were to record, his foster-brothers. Hardly less important was the fact that the same household also contained two of Ranulf's nephews, the brothers Theobald and Hubert Walter. Theobald was to be part of the 1185 expedition and has a permanent place in Irish history as founder of the Butler family. Hubert remained in England, becoming in due time justiciar (1180–89, 1193–8), chancellor (1199–1205), and archbishop of Canterbury (1193–1205), thus holding a series of commanding posts which were crucial for John in England and for the development of Anglo-Norman settlement in Ireland.

Henry, advised by Ranulf, saw to it that John was surrounded in Ireland by a valuable range of talent, promising young men and experienced agents of the crown. They fall into three categories. First, the king's *familiares*, the equivalent of the later privy councillors, men of modest families, such as John Cumin, Gilbert Pipard, and Bertram de Verdon, whose abilities and loyalties were already tested by services to Henry himself. Secondly, the younger hand-picked men, of John's own generation, such as Theobald and Hubert Walter, of intelligence and energy, but as yet without wide experience. Thirdly, the indispensable military lieutenants, such as Philip of Worcester, who often also showed administrative qualities. One characteristic common to all these men was that they were neither from the ranks of the pioneer Geraldines securely established in the country nor from the later arrivals, such as the de Lacys or de Courcy, who by grant or conquest had become great lords by 1185. Henry intended that these latest arrivals in Ireland with John should form a new class, *familiares*, administrators, soldiers, and clerics, surrounding and supporting Lord John. They were to be members of a modest royal court, and with this in mind Henry sent a messenger to Rome requesting a crown and recognition of John as king of Ireland. The English records show that he was given officers of royal state, including chancellor, seneschal, steward, dapifer, and chamberlain, as well as the facilities for a great lord to enjoy life and to entertain, with chamber and huntsmen, kitchen and bakehouse. But a basic factor had to be a demonstration of military might, and with this in view he was accompanied by an army of some 300 knights, supported by a force of archers, mounted and on foot. Altogether there was an imposing assembly of about 3,000 professional soldiers, many of them mercenaries, hired for the occasion. Though it was intended that they impress the Gaelic Irish, the main object was to ensure that John was accepted by the settlers as their ruler. The festering suspicions about de Lacy's ambitions, and the disturbing example of what de Courcy had so rapidly achieved within recent years without any authority from Henry II or his representatives in Ireland, gave an added urgency to John's commission in leading the expedition. He was knighted at Windsor by his father on 31 March 1185, and left shortly afterwards for Pembroke to join the army assembling at

Milford Haven. Significantly, he was escorted as far as his ship by Ranulf de Glanville. The fleet arrived without incident at Waterford on 25 April.

If we are to believe Gerald of Wales, who was aboard one of the royal vessels, the expedition was ill-starred from the evening it left Milford Haven, because in its hurried departure it bypassed St David's, a pious but inconvenient pilgrimage place in south Wales.[1] Gerald then sketches a picture which has been gladly adopted by modern Irish nationalist writers as a backcloth to delineate sharply the contrast between hospitable Irish hosts and insensitive visiting foreigners. The most famous scene depicts a number of the Irish chieftains, visiting the court of Lord John at Waterford, anxious to demonstrate their loyalty and goodwill, but having their long beards tugged in derision by John's high-spirited young companions.[2] The Irish chieftains, in Gerald's account, suppressed their burning indignation until they had left Waterford, then betook themselves to Mac Carthaig of Desmond, Domnall Mór Ua Briain of Limerick, and Ruaidrí Ua Conchobair of Connacht, to express their resentment at the churlish treatment they had received from John's companions. As a result these native leaders formed a league to resist John, and this counted as a main reason (or so Gerald would have us believe) why the Irish withheld their cooperation from John, thus ensuring the failure of his expedition and a weakening of the whole Anglo-Norman position in Ireland.

It is probably true that with the wine flowing freely at the feasts of welcome in Waterford in April 1185 there was an amount of horseplay, including the tugging of beards, but this rough humour is likely to have been mutual between Anglo-Norman visitors and Irish guests. Gerald, who was present, doubtless resented the camaraderie between members of the royal entourage and the Irish guests, who belonged to a people whom he consistently described as barbaric and inferior to the Anglo-Normans. He was certainly not in the confidence of the Irish, and cannot have known with any certainty what these guests discussed among themselves once they left Waterford, nor does he give us their names. He is also conveniently vague about their supposed indignation sessions, shortly afterwards, with Mac Carthaig, Ua Briain, and Ua Conchobair. On the other hand there are hard facts which indicate that the league of Irish leaders did not exist, except in Gerald's imagination. Two of the main families in question, the MacCarthys of Desmond and the O'Connors of Connacht, were riven at this time by succession disputes. There is no evidence of any such league in practice nor of its putting soldiers in the field against the Anglo-Normans. In reality John's army suffered a decline because it was unemployed, whereas military campaigns would have given the soldiers plunder and occupation. There were some skirmishes, and garrison troops were involved in local armed clashes, but there was no military movement of any importance. Money for payment of the mercenaries became scarce, and some of them deserted to

[1] Giraldus, *Expugnatio*, p. 227.
[2] Ibid., p. 237.

take service with the Irish kings, who were glad to have professional soldiers for their family disputes and inter-provincial campaigns.

John followed not merely his father's plan but literally in his footsteps when he visited Tibberaghny, Ardfinnan, and Lismore, ensuring that castles were established in all three places.[1] Tibberaghny on the borders of Osraige, with both Ardfinnan (Tipperary) and Lismore (Waterford) on the borders of the Déise, thus formed a bastion frontage which gave access both to the frontier lands of Leinster and to the kingdom of Desmond. The next stage of the plan was to have the frontier lands, north of this line, under the control of new Anglo-Norman lords, loyal to the crown. Hence the extensive grants, in what is now County Tipperary, to Philip of Worcester, William de Burgh, Theobald Walter, and Ranulf de Glanville. This extended the frontier bastion so that it fanned out to touch the territory of the O'Briens to the north-west, the river Shannon (and Connacht by implication) to the north and north-east, and the fluid frontier lands between the Anglo-Norman settlers of Leinster and the Irish lords of the midlands to the north-east. These frontier lands were always bones of contention, and the Anglo-Norman adventurers found control of these 'swordlands' no easier than had the Irish when contending among themselves. Domnall Ua Briain resented what he considered was an intrusion into his area by the garrison of Ardfinnan and bested them in a fierce contest at a nearby wood on 24 June 1185, killing among other Anglo-Normans a prominent knight, apparently one of Ranulf de Glanville's sons who had come to witness his father's right to broad acres in Tipperary. There were several other such bloody incidents in these frontier areas.[2] Sometimes the Anglo-Normans took heavy punishment: nineteen knights perished in another contest at Ardfinnan; Gerald of Wales's nephew, Robert de Barry, was killed at Lismore, as were Raymond fitz Hugh in Desmond, and Raymond de Kantitun in Osraige. Neither did the Irish go unscathed: a second contest at Ardfinnan on that same day, 24 June 1185, saw the Irish heavily defeated with the loss among others of Ruaidrí Ua Gráda, one of Domnall Ua Briain's lieutenants. Still heavier was the loss for the Irish when the Ostmen of Cork and a force under Theobald Walter killed Diarmait Mac Carthaig, prince of Desmond, and many of his followers, near Cork in 1185. Yet all of these contests were merely incidents in the marchlands, and did not represent any campaign by John's army as a whole. There was no grand rally of the Irish against John. They had not the unity to do so, and he had no overall quarrel with them, nor did he consider them an inferior race, as did Gerald of Wales. If his army was being held in reserve it was with an eye to possible treason, or rebellion, by the settlers. That never came. They outfoxed him, particularly in the person of Hugh de Lacy.

John cut short his stay in Ireland, travelling back to England in mid-December, a very unseasonable time to travel across the Irish Sea. According

[1] Giraldus, *Expugnatio*, pp 233–5.
[2] For these incidents, including the killing of Ranulf de Glanville's son, ibid., pp 235, 352, n. 475.

to the Irish annals he explained to his disgruntled father that he could not fulfil his role as lord of Ireland, due to the intrigues of Hugh de Lacy, 'who had prevented the Irish kings from sending him either tribute or hostages'.[1] The Annals of Loch Cé made no bones about the situation: 'for it was Hugh de Lacy who was king of Ireland when the son of the king of the Saxons came'; and this is corroborated in more sober terms by Gerald of Wales with his comment that de Lacy had already reduced the country to a peaceful condition: 'winning the support of the Irish by generous treatment and flattering them with his friend-ship, he made the more important of them his allies'.[2] It had been an unequal game of political chess between John and de Lacy, where diplomacy, manoeuvre, and personal influence were decisive factors, but with no overt sign of hostility or rebellion on de Lacy's part. John was an inexperienced and volatile stripling, whereas de Lacy was a veteran of wars in the field and intrigues in the council chamber, much of this experience gained under the eye and direction of a calculating Henry II. It is therefore hardly fair to see John, as have almost all historians of the period, as a feckless young man, unable to master the situation in Ireland, scurrying back to his father with a querulous explanation at de Lacy's expense to disguise his own failure. De Lacy was in control of affairs in Ireland, and was the first Anglo-Norman leader who had gained widespread confidence from both Irish and settlers. Yet he could not be faulted on the score of loyalty to the crown, and had accorded John all the necessary courtesies. He had achieved precisely what Henry wished John to accomplish, but this outcome did not suit Henry's plans for Ireland and for his youngest son. The king was released from his dilemma by an unforeseen event, the murder of de Lacy at Durrow in 1186.

The killing of de Lacy did not even have the redeeming characteristic of taking place in heroic circumstances, as befitted a warrior such as de Lacy, nor as part of a great national movement to halt the advance of Anglo-Norman settlement. It was apparently a plot by a Meath chieftain, In Sinnach ('the Fox') Ua Catharnaig, to avenge the death of his son, Muirchertach, in battle against the Anglo-Normans eight years earlier when de Lacy was Henry II's represen-tative in Ireland. The individual who struck de Lacy down with an axe, in the course of an apparently amicable conversation, was foster-son of In Sinnach. Anglo-Norman chroniclers of the time note the death as an event of impor-tance, and William of Newburgh comments that Henry welcomed the news that an overmighty subject had disappeared from the Irish scene.[3] The king, always alert to an opportune moment, ordered John to take ship for Ireland, and he was actually waiting for a favourable wind to take him across the Irish Sea when a messenger from France brought still more momentous news which caused Henry to cancel John's departure and thus set Irish history on

---

[1] *A.F.M.*, 1185.
[2] Giraldus, *Expugnatio*, p. 191.
[3] William of Newburgh, *Historia rerum Anglicorum*, i, 240.

a different course. John's elder brother, Duke Geoffrey of Brittany, was fatally wounded during a tournament at Paris, and, with the eldest brother, Henry the Younger, already dead, this meant that John was an invaluable counter in Henry's hand as a check on the other remaining brother, Richard, duke of Aquitaine, who was now in the direct line of succession to the English throne. These events had occurred in rapid succession. De Lacy was killed in late July 1186, and Geoffrey died at Paris on 19 August. What Henry had in mind for Ireland up to the news of Geoffrey's death only became fully apparent five months later, in January 1187, when legates from Rome arrived in England with permission from Pope Urban III for a separate Irish kingdom and with a crown of peacock feathers for its monarch designate, John.[1] Henry had applied to the previous pope, Lucius III, for these concessions in 1185, but they were not granted until Urban succeeded Lucius, and they were then too late to be accepted.

The prospect of what Henry had in mind raises a provocative thought, and one that was close to actuality: Ireland, a separate realm under its own King John, within the Angevin 'empire' of federated statelets, Normandy, Anjou, Aquitaine, Brittany, in association with Scotland and the Welsh territories, all in a family consortium under a patriarchal Angevin king of England. It was not just a fantasy, nor is it simply one of the great *ifs* of medieval Irish history. The plan survived the demise of Henry the Younger in 1183, but the death of Geoffrey in 1186 inevitably changed the whole structure of Henry II's ambitious design for the sprawling inheritance that had now to be divided between two sons, Richard and John. Nevertheless, John remained lord of Ireland, as declared in 1177 at the council of Oxford. The significance of John's expedition in 1185, as part of the plan to make him king of Ireland, will be appreciated only if we continue to see Ireland in the context of the Angevin 'empire'. Likewise, it is only in that same context that we can make sense of the activities and ambitions of Norman lords who held lands in France, England, Wales, and Ireland, particularly great barons such as Strongbow, de Lacy, and shortly afterwards de Braose and William Marshal.

---

[1] Benedict of Peterborough, *Gesta Regis Henri Secundi*, ii, 4.

CHAPTER V

John, lord of Ireland, 1185–1216

F. X. MARTIN

ALMOST all historians who treat of Irish events between 1185 and 1216 see it as a period without any sharp or consistent features. The one acknowledged exception is the decisive intervention of King John in 1210, and this is seen as a flash in the pan, though it is conceded that there had been during the same period a slow but largely untraceable growth of Anglo-Norman institutions which were given a firm grounding and direction by John during his nine weeks descent on Ireland in 1210. Recently, however, Professor Warren has presented an assessment of John and Ireland so novel that it is likely to arouse scepticism.[1]

The evidence is marshalled to show how the policy of Henry II and John developed in four stages. First, with the advent of John in Ireland in 1185 there was a consolidation of the royal base at Waterford, while the 'new men', such as Philip of Worcester, William de Burgh, and Theobald Walter, were installed along the border between Munster and Leinster. Secondly, a new base was established during the 1190s at Drogheda, so that its royal power could extend up into the territory of Uriel (Airgialla), for which John had made speculative grants to Bertram de Verdon and Roger Pipard, thus strategically separating the lordship of Meath (under the problematic de Lacys) from the lordship of Ulster (under the still more problematic de Courcy). Thirdly, when John became king of England in 1199 a further royal base already established at Athlone, the centre of Ireland, was developed both as an additional point of control of Meath and of entry across the Shannon into Connacht. Fourthly, John's energetic campaign with his army in Ireland during 1210 facilitated the placing of a fortress at Clones, a convenient point of departure into north Connacht and Cenél nEógain. John by the end of his reign thus had royal fortresses to influence, even if not as yet to control, all the provinces of Ireland. There would be no repetition in any part of the country of a freebooter's expedition by Anglo-Norman settlers, such as de Courcy had initiated in Ulster in 1177. John had become the custodian of

---

[1] W. L. Warren, 'King John and Ireland' in Lydon, *Eng. & Ire.*, pp 26–42.

peace, the one central authority accepted (admittedly to varying degrees) by both Anglo-Normans and Irish.

An overall survey of events in Ireland for the years 1185–1216 does reveal a consistency in royal policy begun by Henry II and pursued by John, first as lord of Ireland, then as king of England. It would be naïve to believe that from the time of Henry there was a detailed blueprint in the royal archives at Winchester, describing the method and stages for an Anglo-Norman conquest of Ireland. The facts show, however, that there was a broad royal policy which adapted itself to changing circumstances. It was based on accurate local knowledge, obviously acquired from royal agents in the country or from Irish allies. This was shown, for example, in the judicious selection of strategic fortress sites, such as Tibberaghny, Ardfinnan, Lismore, Drogheda, Athlone, and Clones. Contrary to later, particularly nineteenth-century, nationalist belief, neither Henry nor John intended a conquest of the country in the sense proposed by Gerald of Wales in the last two chapters of his persuasive account of the first adventurers in Ireland. Paradoxically these nationalists were willing, for their own purposes, to accept his interpretation. For Henry and John the lordship of Ireland was intended to be a separate entity, embracing settlers and Gaelic Irish. Its stability was threatened more by restless Anglo-Norman barons than by Irish lords.

The most important advances made by John were in north Munster. The development began with his expedition in 1185, when his only known military activity in the country was to establish castles at Tibberaghny, Ardfinnan, and Lismore. Their immediate purpose was to safeguard the royal enclave stretching from Waterford to Dungarvan and westward to the Blackwater. Waterford was the royal *caput*, the port of call, and the lifeline to south Wales. The political significance of the enclave was that on the north-east it flanked the marchlands of Leinster, as it did the kingdom of Desmond on the west. Furthermore, it was positioned to intervene in the affairs of the O'Briens of Thomond, to aim at the strategic town of Limerick, and beyond it to Connacht and the affairs of the O'Connors. It was to ensure the northern frontage of the enclave that grants were made by John while in Ireland to reliable royal agents: Philip of Worcester, William de Burgh, and Theobald Walter jointly with his uncle, Ranulf de Glanville. With these grants royal influence forestalled the efforts of Anglo-Norman freebooters by assuming control, at least in theory, of what was later County Tipperary. It meant that the 'land of peace' would separate the O'Briens and MacCarthys, the perpetually warring families of Thomond and Desmond. Limerick town, though a Norse settlement, was dominated by the O'Briens, and as long as the astute and unscrupulous Domnall Mór Ua Briain ruled as king of Thomond it would be unwise for the grantees to press their claims too far or too hastily. Equal care had to be taken with Domnall Mór Mac Carthaig, king of Desmond, who, 'of all the contemporary kings of Ireland, was most feared by the foreigners and by the Gaedil', according to the Annals of

Inisfallen, which also made the exaggerated and grisly claim that 'by him nine justiciars were slain and twenty-one battles fought in Mumu [Munster]'.[1] In 1189 Domnall launched an onslaught on a wide range of Norman settlements in the Déise, Osraige, and Desmond. With the aid of the Uí Chuiléin and Uí Faeláin he razed a series of castles, including Tibberaghny and Lismore. The Anglo-Normans reacted by leading an expedition the following year to Thurles, where Mac Carthaig 'caught up with them and routed them'.[2] It was on one of these expeditions 'by this Domnall that Geoffrey de Cogan was killed, and he was flayed, together with his speckled kerns, to avenge his father'.[3]

The reverses suffered by the Anglo-Normans gave sour satisfaction to Domnall Mór Ua Briain. He wanted to see the foreigners checked, but had no desire to allow an increase of the MacCarthy power.

It was probably the show of strength by the Anglo-Normans in 1192 that decided him to ally once again with them. In that year they marched through north Tipperary into east Limerick, and even crossed the Shannon into Killaloe, the very heartland of the Ua Briain country. Domnall Ua Briain could not be seen to submit to mere military might, but he consented to the marriage of one of his daughters to William de Burgh, who had been granted extensive territory in south Tipperary and east Limerick by the Lord John in 1185. A main purpose of the marriage alliance showed itself in 1193 when Domnall agreed to the building of a castle on Breckinish Island, in the Shannon estuary, 'with the consent of Ua Briain, if the general report be true, as a check on Domnall, son of Mac Carthaig'.[4]

The need for the O'Briens to have support from the Normans against the MacCarthys was accentuated by the death of Domnall Ua Briain in 1194. This left Domnall Mór Mac Carthaig of Desmond as the dominant figure among the Irish leaders in Munster. The kingdom of Thomond became weakened by competition between the three sons of Domnall Ua Briain, who agreed to let the Anglo-Normans take possession of Limerick town rather than to see any one of them gain control of it. The Anglo-Norman advance in Munster, until the second quarter of the thirteenth century, was achieved mainly without violence, by marriage alliances, political compromise, and economic development. It indicates how inaccurate is the term 'conquest' when applied without qualification to Anglo-Norman progress in Ireland during this period. Domnall Mac Carthaig was quicker than the rest of the Irish leaders in Munster to appreciate the strategic position of the Anglo-Normans in Limerick town. In 1196, before they had time to establish themselves securely

[1] *Ann. Inisf.*, 1206, p. 337 (7).

[2] Ibid., 1190, p. 317 (2).

[3] 'Mac Carthaig's Book' in *Misc. Ir. Annals*, 1206, p. 85 (1). The significance of 'speckled' is uncertain.

[4] Ibid., 1193, p. 75 (1); cf. *Ann. Inisf.*, 1193, p. 319 (2). Cf. Aubrey Gwynn and D. F. Gleeson, *A history of the diocese of Killaloe* (Dublin, 1962), p. 177, n. 3.

behind the walls he drew them into a battle, which he won, drove them from the town, pursued them, and in two further clashes with their harassed troops confirmed his victory.[1] Nevertheless, he had made no more than a successful expedition into hostile territory. When he returned to Desmond the Anglo-Normans reestablished themselves in Limerick, and their presence there was given solemn approval by the Lord John in 1197 when he conferred on the town a charter with all the privileges of Dublin.

There is evidence now and later of amicable relations at Limerick between the descendants of the original Norse settlers, the Irish who joined them, and the newly arrived Anglo-Normans. The first mayor of the freshly chartered town was one of the Norse, Syward. William de Burgh, closely allied with the O'Briens by his marriage to a daughter of Domnall Mór, granted part of his fief of Esclon (Aes Cluana) to Bishop Donnchad Ua Briain of Limerick. John, when king, took the bishop specifically under his protection, commending him for fidelity and activity on behalf of royal business.[2] The bond between John and the house of Ua Briain was solemnly ratified at Waterford in 1210 when Donnchad Cairprech Ua Briain, king of Thomond (1210–42), submitted in person to John, was knighted, and given the lordship of Carrigogunnel on the Shannon for an annual rent.[3] Limerick town, assured of support from the settlers in north Munster, as well as the goodwill of the O'Briens under the long-reigning Donnchad Cairprech, had become part of the Anglo-Norman system, and this with remarkably little use of the sword. The frontier had now been advanced from Waterford and the Déise up to Limerick and Thomond.

Limerick, like Athlone, was an obvious springboard from which to launch an expedition into Connacht. Both were on the Shannon, but the river was wider and deeper at Limerick, thus greatly increasing its defensive capabilities. At this point Limerick had the added advantage for William de Burgh of having friendly Irish neighbours, whereas Athlone lay in the path of invading armies from Connacht and Meath, with bitter disputes between members of the ruling Ua Conchobair family of Connacht creating greater uncertainty in the province. It was these very disputes that gave de Burgh the opportunity to intervene in Connacht. With the O'Connors it was not an affair of cousin against cousin, but incredibly of a father, two sons, grandson, and brother of the father, pitted one against the other. In 1185 the veteran high-king, Ruaidrí, had emerged from his retirement in the monastery of Cong to contest the kingship of Connacht with his sons, Conchobar Máenmaige and Conchobar Ua nDiarmata, as well as with Cathal Carrach, son of Conchobar Máenmaige, and with Cathal Crobderg, Ruaidrí's younger brother.[4] It is a classic example of the inherent defect in the Irish system of royal succession.

[1] *A.F.M.*, 1196.
[2] *The Black Book of Limerick*, ed. James MacCaffrey (Dublin, 1907), no. cxxxv, pp 110–11; no. xxxix, p. 38.
[3] 'Mac Carthaig's Book' in *Misc. Ir. Annals*, 1210, p. 87 (1). Cf. Orpen, *Normans*, ii, 168, n. 2, 244; *A.F.M.*, 1209, p. 163 n.   [4] *A.L.C., A.U.*, and *A.F.M.*, 1185–6.

Some time early in the 1190s the Lord John granted Connacht to de Burgh, but in 1195 John de Courcy met Cathal Crobderg at Athlone and granted him some form of recognition as king of Connacht. The death of Ruaidrí Ua Conchobair in 1198 helped to simplify the situation, and in the spring of 1200 de Burgh, supported by an Ua Briain army, campaigned in Connacht on behalf of Cathal Carrach, drove Cathal Crobderg from the province, and installed Cathal Carrach in his place. Cathal Crobderg had retreated to Ulster, and in 1201 made two vain attempts to recapture Connacht, supported in his first expedition by Ua Néill of Cenél nEógain and Ua hÉicnig of Fir Manach who were badly routed by Cathal Carrach and de Burgh, and in his second effort had the armed assistance of John de Courcy and Hugh de Lacy, but they likewise were decisively defeated. These two barons had no royal authority for their intervention, but seem to have been fishing for their own purposes in the troubled waters of Connacht. John, who had become king of England in 1199, decided to support Cathal Crobderg. Thus de Burgh was given no option, and successfully restored Cathal Crobderg in 1202.

The happy alliance did not last long. De Burgh's soldiers, many of them mercenaries, were billeted in the Ua Conchobair territory, waiting for payment. A rumour spread like wildfire that de Burgh was dead and, as if by a prearranged signal, the Irish in every part of Connacht where his soldiers were billeted rose and killed them, up to the tune of 700 or more. Cong was an exception, where de Burgh had his personal forces, but he could do no more than fume, gather his men, and return warily to Limerick. It is unknown to what extent Cathal Crobderg was privy to the massacre. Early in 1203 de Burgh set out for Connacht, with his own followers, accompanied by a force of Irish led by brothers of Cathal Carrach Ua Conchobair. De Burgh had a score to settle and a concession to claim: the grant of Connacht to him by John in the early 1190s. Cathal Crobderg was unwilling to challenge de Burgh on the field, but was saved by the intervention of the justiciar, Meiler fitz Henry, and Walter de Lacy.

John was at his best in manoeuvring the pieces on the Connacht chessboard. Cathal Crobderg was already aware that a question mark hung over his ability to continue ruling Connacht, and that he was there by favour of King John, who took the opportunity in December 1205 to conclude a shrewd deal with him. In 1203 Cathal had offered to surrender all Connacht to the king, on condition that he be allowed to retain one-third of it as his vassal. Now, in December 1205, John agreed to a modified form of Cathal's offer. Two cantreds of Connacht were to be set aside, to be dealt with at the king's discretion. Of the remainder, one-third would be held by Cathal in fee, making him a feudal tenant-in-chief; the remaining two-thirds would be held by Cathal as a client-king in Irish style, on payment of a tribute of 300 marks to John as his high-king. The arrangement was in many ways a remarkable echo of the treaty of Windsor in 1175, but with vitally important differences which improved the bargain for both parties. Cathal, as vassal, could call on the help of his lord, John, against invading Irish war-lords and Anglo-Norman freebooters, but he also had security of succession in that fief for his eldest son, Áed, instead of it being the object of the inevitable family disputes that characterised the Irish dynastic system. In fact he remained king of Connacht until his death in 1224. As well as negotiating with the English court shortly before his death to ensure the succession of his son Áed, Cathal had taken the additional precaution in 1220 or 1221 of obtaining papal protection for himself, his son, and his kingdom.[1]

John, for his part, did well out of the bargain. He tied Cathal into the feudal system by a personal obligation, and had at his disposal a ruler who, according to the Irish dynastic system, was a legitimate king of Connacht, and who could be held responsible for maintaining order in the province. Besides, it would now be an offence for Anglo-Norman adventurers to invade Cathal's territory, as had de Courcy and de Lacy in 1201. The two cantreds which John had earmarked for separate attention became strategic pawns when they were exchanged for two cantreds near Athlone, which had been granted to Geoffrey de Costentin in November 1200. By establishing the royal presence at Athlone John staked his claim to control the all-important passage across the Shannon between Meath and Connacht. He could now depend at the Connacht end on Cathal Crobderg, but he had yet to deal with the de Lacys in Meath. That showdown with the two brothers did not take place until 1210, when he confronted and subdued them, taking the occasion of his victory to establish a castle at Athlone. It remained thereafter throughout the centuries a royal military post of the greatest importance.

John's activities during his expedition to Ireland in 1210 were so dramatic in character that they may obscure the systematic attention he had already given to the country over the previous six years. His policy for Ireland during those years, and for the rest of his reign, will not be appreciated unless it is seen in the wider context of the complexity of political, military, and economic problems with which he was grappling in England and on the Continent. Several of the problems were of his own making, others were thrust upon him, and some he inherited from his hapless brother, Richard I. John was not only capricious, mean, and vindictive. He was ill-starred. With the dice twice loaded against him, it was ironic that in Ireland alone, the most unpromising of all his jurisdictions, he demonstrated qualities of foresight and constructive leadership. John, so often described as the worst of the kings of England, was, paradoxically, the best for Ireland. Of the successive crises that marked his reign, two in particular, the loss of Normandy in 1204 and continuous inflation, had marked repercussions in Ireland. It was more than a coincidence that in 1204–5 he both lost Normandy and imposed stability on Connacht. Just as diminishing Anglo-Norman participation in the crusades during the twelfth century had helped to turn barons such as Strongbow westward to Ireland, so now the loss of

[1] Sheehy, *Pontificia Hib.*, i, 233–4, no. 147.

Map 2 ANGLO-NORMAN IRELAND AND ITS NEIGHBOURS,
c. 1210, by F. J. Byrne

Based on maps in A. A. M. Duncan, *Scotland: the making of the kingdom* (Edinburgh, 1975), p. 619,
and William Rees, *An historical atlas of Wales from early to modern times* (2nd ed., London, 1972),
plate 38.

The king of Man and the earls of Galloway, Carrick, and Atholl were all enfeoffed by King John
with lands in Ulster. It is uncertain whether North and South Uist were controlled by Man and
the Isles or formed part of Argyll and the Western Isles. One-third of Connacht was held by Ua
Conchobair of the king as a feudal barony, the rest as a tributary kingdom.

Normandy caused several of the other barons, such as William de Braose and William Marshal, to involve themselves deeply in Irish affairs. Though these two men were of great consequence in England, Wales, and Ireland, and were close associates of the king up to the loss of Normandy, he managed to alienate them both. Marshal was abused, and excluded from the English court for over five years, until John had urgent need of him in 1213. De Braose rebelled, his wife and eldest son disappeared into a royal prison, while he himself escaped into exile and died at Corbeil, France, in 1211. The two barons were key figures in the crises of John's last years. It was most likely the callous treatment of de Braose and his family that finally convinced the baronial rebels in 1215 that John must be deposed. On the other hand it was the transcendent loyalty of Marshal that rallied sufficient support to save the king in his hour of need. Rarely has the Irish scene been of such importance for England; this was indicated by John's expedition to the country in 1210. Then, as in the time of Henry II, it was the Anglo-Norman barons, not the Irish, who were the danger for the king of England.

Having lost out in Normandy in 1204 John was determined to recoup his losses by consolidating his position in Ireland. It was during the summer of this same year that an order was issued to build a castle at Dublin, not only as a fortress and the seat of justice, but to house the treasury. Finance has always been the nerve centre of political administration, and Dublin Castle was to become both the centre and the symbol of English authority in Ireland. The evidence of authority was the enforcement of a legal system, and in November 1204 John extended to Ireland five of the most needed original writs, covering in particular succession rights to land and property.[1] In the same month he established in Ireland the system of criminal procedure. As far back as 1200, when John confirmed Meiler fitz Henry as justiciar, he reserved to himself all pleas from Ireland concerning the crown, the mint, and exchange. He applied these directives to everyday financial transactions by authorising in 1207 the first Irish national coinage, marked with the symbol of the harp.

Even before John became king of England he had encouraged, by the granting of charters, the development of towns in his lordship of Ireland, and this he continued after 1199. Dublin, Waterford, Limerick, Cork, Dungarvan, and Drogheda were granted charters or had existing charters confirmed or improved. All these decisions, affecting the legal system, finance, property, urban development and trade, augured well for continuity and prosperity, but they presupposed a stability of institutions and government that would only be achieved if there were harmony between John, as lord of Ireland, and the great barons in the country. John's mistrust of his agents, and especially of his barons, was a fatal flaw.

In 1204 he had it within his power to make a success of his lordship of Ireland. At that stage the only fly in the ointment was John de Courcy in Ulster,

[1] G. J. Hand, *English law in Ireland, 1290—1324* (Cambridge, 1967), pp 1–2.

who had assumed the rule and belligerent independence of an autonomous Irish king. Above all, de Courcy's raids on Irish kingdoms in Ulster and Connacht aroused the jealousy of the de Lacy brothers, who stood to benefit from his downfall. They had little difficulty in convincing an already suspicious King John that de Courcy was unreliable because of his brother-in-law, Reginald, king of Man, and his supposed dealings with William the Lion, king of the Scots.

John de Courcy was a remarkable person, even when it is known that he consciously created a legend around himself during his lifetime, and that it was largely accepted by historians from the time of Gerald of Wales down to our own time.[1] His daring expedition into Ulster in 1177 gained him within five years a lordship at the expense of four minor principalities in the area, Uí Echach Coba, Dál Fiatach, Uí Thuirtre, and Fir Lí. He soon gave himself the trappings of a monarch—court officials and feudal officers, such as marshal, constable, seneschal, and chamberlain; he created barons, distributed lands, authorised coinage, and allowed himself to be described as *princeps Ulidiae*. He was a patron of religious orders, and gave provincial piety a boost by promoting the cults of Saints Patrick, Brigid, and Colum Cille, particularly that of Patrick. About the year 1180 he married Affreca, daughter of Godred, king of Man, and this gave him a double advantage. The Manx fleet was likely to support him in an hour of crisis, and this protected his whole right flank with its coastline. Godred was married to Finnguala, daughter of Niall Mac Lochlainn, king of Cenél nEógain (1170–76), and this created for de Courcy bonds of common interest with the most powerful family group on his left flank. Henry II thought it worth the risk to appoint him justiciar in 1185, and he continued to hold the post for several years into the reign of Richard I. It was during his time as justiciar that he developed a fatal taste for interference in Connacht.

It is not clear what had put him in King John's bad books, but his fall from favour would suit the de Lacys. On the evidence available it does not appear to have been de Courcy's powerful and almost independent status that aroused John's antipathy, nor even the troubles he was stirring up in Connacht and Ulster. It may well be that the king's inbuilt suspicion of his barons was triggered off in this case, as tradition related, by the report that de Courcy was outspoken in his belief that John had been less than fair to his nephew, Prince Arthur, son of Geoffrey, whom he had displaced from succession to the throne, on the death of Richard I. The report may have been no more than a malicious rumour, but it would have been galling news to John, who was then trying to

[1] The creation of the de Courcy hero image began with the *Expugnatio* of Gerald of Wales, barely twelve years after the invasion of Ulster; see op. cit., bk II, chaps 18 and 19. The de Courcy legend is enshrined in the Book of Howth, which Curtis (*Med. Ire.* (2nd ed.), p. 77, n. 1) described as 'the earliest specimen on a large scale of literary English in Ireland'. For the Book of Howth see *Cal. Carew MSS*, v, 80–94, 105–8, 111–15. For information on de Courcy's first twelve years in Ulster, the creation of the de Courcy legend and of the 'de Courcy prophecies', see editorial notes by F. X. Martin in *Expugnatio*, pp 331–5, nn 295–321.

survive the continuing intrigues between Arthur and Philip Augustus of France. Hugh de Lacy had failed to deliver de Courcy into John's hands in 1201, but in July 1201 the king wrote to de Courcy, now back safely in Ulster, offering him a safe-conduct to and from the court in order to arrive at a peaceful solution to their differences. De Courcy would have none of it, and Hugh de Lacy, who was sent after him, defeated him in battle at Down-patrick, but de Courcy fled out of reach. Over the next five years there were raids, battles, and negotiations, with de Courcy in September 1204 a prisoner in de Lacy's custody, but a free man shortly afterwards among Irish allies in Tír Eógain. He won allies in the Isles, but they failed to reestablish him in Ulster. The tempestuous affair ended peacefully but ingloriously for de Courcy in November 1207, when the king gave him permission to visit England and stay with friends. By that time de Courcy was a man of no property and therefore no danger to John. Over two years previously, in May 1205, the king by one decree had stripped de Courcy of his lands and created Hugh de Lacy earl of Ulster, conferring on him all the land of Ulster that de Courcy held when he was captured in battle by de Lacy in September 1204. De Courcy was not without consolation in his later years. He not only lived to enter the king's service, but he outlived him. Better still, he had been in John's entourage when the king came to Ireland in 1210, determined to break the power of William de Braose and the de Lacy brothers. King John received full cooperation from de Courcy in this exercise.

The downfall of de Courcy was regarded by the barons in England, Wales, and Ireland as salutary, and did not occasion the shock produced by the crushing of de Braose. De Courcy was a self-made man, a mere knight from Somerset who had made himself into a great lord, but remained a maverick and not part of the baronial network, whose members had wealth and power through inheritance, marriage, and royal favour. De Courcy's power and interests were limited to Ulster, with an occasional overspill of his energies into other provinces of Ireland. It was otherwise with de Braose, the de Lacy brothers, and William Marshal. Like their master, John, they still thought in terms of Normandy, where Marshal continued to have substantial estates. Much of their power and status in the Anglo-Norman world came not from their considerable possessions in Ireland, but from their vast estates in Wales where custom and circumstances allowed them to manage their own affairs almost independently of the king. Yet for the first five years of his reign John was willing to grant de Braose and Marshal further possessions and to rank them among the *familiares* of his court. De Braose became the most powerful baron in south Wales, and about January 1201 was granted the extensive lands in Thomond that had originally been conferred on his uncle, Philip de Braose, in 1177, minus the town of Limerick. William, who had already earned the reputation of being the terror of the Welsh marches, quickly crossed over to Ireland to make visible his personal authority in Thomond. As he was needed by King John in France in 1201 he confidently left the care of the Thomond lands to his son-in-law, Walter de Lacy, and by way of compensation and security he guaranteed to keep a fraternal eye on Walter's lands in Wales, where they bordered on his own.

It is not known precisely at what point and for what reason the king turned against de Braose, as he did also against the powerful and favoured William Marshal. It is likely that in both cases it was the Normandy factor which made the difference. Marshal saved his estates in Normandy by doing homage to King Philip Augustus, and however correct this may have been according to feudal procedure it was taken as treachery by John, who had just been ousted from the duchy by the king of France. (It doubtless counted in Marshal's favour that when Richard I restored him to favour, while penalising John, Marshal refused to do homage to the king for his Irish lands, which he held from the prince as lord of Ireland.) Marshal compounded his betrayal, in John's eyes, by his reasonable opposition to the king's wildcat preparations early in 1205 for an armada to retake Normandy. Marshal managed to make his way unscathed to the safety of his principality in Ireland, where he had inherited the lordship of Leinster by marriage to Isabel, daughter of Strongbow. Here he remained for the next six years, keeping a low profile as far as John was concerned, concentrating to a highly successful degree, as we shall see later, on developing the agricultural, commercial, and urban potentialities of the territories he ruled almost as a palatine lord.

It says much for the patience of Marshal and Walter de Lacy that unlike de Braose they did not resort to rebellion despite a policy of harassment by John from 1206 onward. The king encouraged his justiciar in Ireland, Meiler fitz Henry, to attack the lands of de Braose and Marshal, and this involved Walter de Lacy, since he was acting as guardian for de Braose, his father-in-law. In Ireland the forces of William Marshal and Hugh de Lacy carried on open war against fitz Henry, but did so against him as a fellow baron, not in his capacity as justiciar. An irony of the feudal system was that Meiler could be regarded by Marshal as a rebellious vassal of his own! King John also indulged in a similar game of make-believe, pretending ignorance of what was happening in Ireland, but as the situation worsened for fitz Henry the king felt obliged in October 1207 to summon both Marshal and fitz Henry to court. Fitz Henry failed to crush the opposition and his forces were routed at Thurles in 1208 by Geoffrey de Marisco, one of the barons in Munster allied with de Braose and the de Lacys. King John, while still feigning ignorance of events in Ireland, decided it was time to cut his losses, at the expense of fitz Henry. On 20 March 1208 a royal commission was established to examine the administration of fitz Henry as justiciar. A week later a new charter for Leinster was granted to Marshal, and within a futher month there was a new grant of Meath to Walter de Lacy. The new charters reduced somewhat the privileges in the original charters of Henry II, and the confirmatory charter of the Lord John to Walter de Lacy in 1194, but it was a profitable and face-saving operation for the king.

The more important decision was the appointment in June 1208 of John de Grey, bishop of Norwich, to succeed fitz Henry as justiciar. Here, from the king's point of view, was the ideal type of royal servant. De Grey was a cleric, therefore without political affiliations through marriage; a tested servant of the crown who had been the king's secretary, therefore loyal; a son of the lesser nobility, therefore free of personal involvement with the great barons in Ireland, Marshal, de Braose, and de Lacys. Besides, he had already proved himself to be decisive and efficient in the king's service. The justiciar was constricted by practical circumstances in dealing with these barons. Dublin, the centre of his power, was hemmed in by Walter de Lacy's lordship of Meath and by Marshal's lordship of Leinster. Hugh de Lacy was a distant power in Ulster, as was de Braose at the other end of the island, and it was de Braose who was to prove to be the most recalcitrant of the barons. He was less of an opportunist than Marshal, and much less intelligent. Many of his troubles with the king he drew on himself, though one cannot but admire his courage. It is even less clear than in the case of Marshal why John turned against him. It may well be that like Marshal, and in conjunction with him, he expressed to the king his scepticism about the reality of the preparations to recover Normandy, but it is only from about 1207 onward that de Braose began to feel the chill. The last royal favour was bestowed when he was appointed sheriff of Hereford for 1206–7, and shortly afterwards the custody of Glamorgan castle, which he had received in October 1202, was taken from him.

It was de Braose's Irish possessions that brought ill-feeling to crisis point. When the honour of Limerick had been given to him in January 1201 he agreed to pay 500 marks per annum in fee. By 1207 he had paid no more than a total of 700 marks (according to John), and de Braose was not a poor man. John's legitimate demand for arrears of payment was followed by a further demand that de Braose deliver up his sons as hostages. Security by way of hostages was not unusual in medieval times, and John resorted to it frequently, but according to the chronicler, Roger of Wendover, the king met his match in Matilda de Saint-Valérie, the high-spirited wife of de Braose.[1] She commented that she did not want her sons to end like John's nephew, Arthur, murdered. Supposedly it was her sharp comment which spurred the king to move against the de Braoses, but perhaps too much weight has been given to the story. The basic fact was John's need, urgent need, for money, and that de Braose had not paid his dues and showed no inclination to do so. John gave orders that the whole de Braose family was to be imprisoned, but William took to arms, and when this failed he fled, with wife and children, to Ireland, probably in the winter of 1208–9. They found refuge first with William Marshal, who refused to hand

---

[1] *Rogeri de Wendover liber qui dicitur Flores Historiarum ...; the Flowers of History, by Roger de Wendover*, ed. Henry G. Hewlett (3 vols, London, 1886–9), ii, 48–9; cf. Warren, *King John*, p. 205.

them over to John de Grey, the new justiciar. Marshal argued adroitly that by reason of the feudal bond he could not in conscience hand over his lord, de Braose, to another authority. Apparently Marshal held some lands in Wales from de Braose. While this argument was being played out, the de Braoses moved on to the protection of Walter de Lacy, lord of Meath and son-in-law of de Braose. The king, already deeply embroiled in disputes with his barons in England and Wales, with the papacy, and with the untiring Philip Augustus of France, could not dismiss the situation in Ireland as peripheral or of minor moment. It had become a serious challenge to his authority, and he decided he would have to deal with it by personal intervention, with an army.

He did not act on impulse in deciding to visit Ireland. While it was imperative for John that the barons there be reduced to full submission or, if rebellious, that they be driven into outer darkness, he was fully aware that once he left the shores of England his kingdom could be disrupted by rebellion from within or attacked from outside by William of Scotland and Philip Augustus of France. He had also to budget for possible troubles in Wales from either Welsh or rebellious Anglo-Normans. Though it says much for the importance he attached to his Irish lordship that he was still willing to go ahead with the expedition to that country, he took certain precautions before leaving. He was convinced, not without some evidence, that there was a conspiracy afoot for a simultaneous invasion of his kingdom by the Scots and the French, linked with a rebellion in Ireland by the de Lacys and de Braose, allied with their subjects and relatives in the marcher lands of Wales. A show of force was necessary, and in August 1209 John marshalled an intimidating army on the right bank of the Tweed, beside his border fortress of Norham, and demanded evidence of loyalty from William of Scotland in specific form, namely two of William's daughters as hostages, three Scottish castles near the border, and the payment of 15,000 marks within two years. The Scottish lion may have growled privately, but publicly he submitted. With this bloodless victory to his credit John was free to pressurise the Welsh leaders, and in October 1209 most of the prominent Welsh chieftains, led by Llywelyn ap Iorwerth, who was married to John's illegitimate daughter, Joan, came to him at Woodstock and did homage, which 'had never been heard of in times past'.[1] In fact the Welsh were to prove unreliable in their loyalty, as John discovered when he was in Ireland, but this was not at all apparent in the autumn of 1209.

The king's assurance about the fidelity of his English subjects was confirmed in this same year when he arranged that all his free tenants did him homage, so that, in the words of Gervase of Canterbury, 'there was not a man in the land who could resist his will in anything'.[2] This comment applied equally to the church, the only powerful self-organised body in the country which now had good reason to resist him. Owing to John's refusal to accept Stephen Langton,

[1] Roger de Wendover, *Flor. hist.*, ii, 50–51.
[2] Gervase of Canterbury, *Historical works*, ii, 100.

the papal nominee, as archbishop of Canterbury, the country was under interdict since March 1208, and the king was excommunicated in November 1209.
The effect on the bishops, as Roger of Wendover sadly recorded, was that
'when they saw the wolf coming they quitted the sheep and fled'.[1] Seven of the
bishops joined Langton in exile, but this presented John with an ideal opportunity to impound their property and that of the religious orders, which was
then administered by the remaining clergy on his behalf. They were obliged to
pay for this privilege, and had also to grant him part of their annual revenues.
Since the interdict and the excommunication did not apply to John as lord of
Ireland, John de Grey, bishop of Norwich and the king's nominee for the see of
Canterbury, was free to come to Ireland with a clear clerical conscience when
he was appointed justiciar in June 1208, in succession to Meiler fitz Henry.
This meant that the bishops and clergy in Ireland had no grounds of conscience on which to repudiate de Grey's authority as justiciar, and he was there
to prepare the way for the coming of the king.[2]

John did not treat his expedition to Ireland with a meagre hand. Despite his
chronic shortage of money he planned and prepared on a major scale.[3] Ships,
sailors, galleymen, and mariners, were hired, and most of them instructed to
assemble at the port of departure, Cross below Pembroke. The feudal army
assembled, earls, barons, knights, and the common soldiers, mounted and on
foot, supported by a substantial force of Flemish mercenaries. The army had its
normal auxiliary forces, such as carpenters, but more significantly it had
quarrymen, ditchers, and miners: Anglo-Norman fortresses in Ireland might
have to be stormed. The king's court was provided for, as was the administrative organisation, with bailiffs and the like. Perhaps the most significant payment was for 53 dozen skins of parchment, reminiscent of a similar provision by
Henry II in 1171. The Anglo-Norman presence in Ireland was to be ensured by
law and order, not just by military might.

The fleet of 700 ships set sail and put in at Crook, five miles from Waterford,
on 20 June 1210. Henry II had disembarked at the same place in October 1171.
The exact number of fighting men brought by John is not stated, but since
Henry's army of 4,000 men travelled in a fleet of 400 ships it would seem that
John had mustered almost twice that force for his expedition. We lack colourful
details about this visit by John. Gerald of Wales does not bring his account of
Irish affairs up to 1210, and the Anglo-Norman chroniclers, all of them un-
sympathetic to John, record much less information about his expedition com-
pared to that of his father. Nevertheless, the official royal accounts supply hard
facts, placenames, personal names, and sums of money, which allow us to plot
John's itinerary and progress throughout the country.

[1] Roger de Wendover, *Flor. hist.*, ii, 48. Ironically, Echdonn Mac Gilla Uidir, the Irish archbishop of Armagh, whose candidature John had strongly opposed between 1202 and 1206, was
happy to serve as suffragan in Exeter and Worcester.   [2] *A.F.M.*, 1208.
[3] Details of payments made for soldiers, sailors, stores, and equipment are available in the
prestita, liberate, and pipe rolls of 12 John and 13 John; cf. *Cal. doc. Ire., 1171—1251*, pp 59—67.

John's objects in this descent on Ireland were threefold. He wanted visible proof of the personal submission of his feudal subjects, particularly of the magnates led by Marshal, the de Lacys, and de Braose. He had to ensure that the Irish leaders also accepted him as lord. He was determined to implement the main institutions of his government with an administrative system geared to receipt of regular revenue. The odds, represented by the formidable armada that sailed from Pembroke, were in favour of submission by his Anglo-Norman subjects, but the outcome was by no means a foregone conclusion. If Marshal, the de Lacys, and de Braose had acted in unison, had activated their subjects in England and Wales, and had timed their armed activity in conjunction with substantial intervention by an only too willing king of France, they might well have overthrown John.

De Braose's nerve failed him on hearing of the preparations for John's armada, and fleeing before the wrath to come he crossed the Irish Sea to the greater security of his estates in Wales, leaving his wife and children in the care of Hugh de Lacy in Ulster. De Braose then travelled to the neighbourhood of Pembroke, where John was with his army, and through intermediaries offered to make his peace with the king for 40,000 marks. John, deeply committed to his expedition to Ireland, and still smarting from Matilda de Saint-Valérie's accusation that he had murdered his nephew, Arthur, replied that since de Braose's real power lay with his wife in Ireland it would be better for him to cross over with the armada and settle his differences with the king there.[1] To travel in John's company was a risk de Braose was not prepared to take, but Marshal, back in royal favour though with a question mark against his name, had been summoned to join his lord at Pembroke and thought it prudent to obey. That had been the testing time for Marshal, for the expedition to Ireland, and for John's security on the throne. With de Braose a fugitive in Wales, and Marshal a public ally of the king, there was no future in Ireland for Anglo-Norman resistance to their feudal monarch.

The details of his military campaign need not detain us.[2] He went by New Ross, Kilkenny, and Naas to Dublin, where he arrived on 28 June. Here he was met by a deputation of barons from Meath, pleading on behalf of their lord, Walter de Lacy, trying to dissociate him from his more obviously rebellious brother, Hugh, earl of Ulster. John would have none of it. Taking over the lordships of Meath and Ulster was to be part recompense for the financial outlay of the expedition to Ireland. John moved into Meath and occupied Walter de Lacy's principal fortress, at Trim. A little later, at Ardbraccan, he received the submission of Cathal Crobderg Ua Conchobair, king of Connacht, whose soldiers also joined John's army. Its progress thus far was little

[1] See King John's memorandum on de Braose in Rymer, *Foedera*, pp 52–3; *Cal. doc. Ire., 1171–1251*, pp 65–6, no. 48. Rymer dates the document to 1212, but late 1210 is more likely from internal evidence.
[2] For details see Orpen, *Normans*, ii, 242–68.

short of a triumphal march. With Walter de Lacy in flight, and the feudal nobility of Meath instinctively submissive to the king, the lordship of Meath was
John's for the taking; but it was otherwise with the lordship of Ulster.

Hugh de Lacy wisely made no attempt to confront the royal army at the outposts of his earldom. He abandoned the baronies of upper and lower Dundalk,
burning the castles there, and withdrew his forces behind the security of Carlingford Lough and the Mourne mountains. His main base was to the north
with the formidable castles at Carlingford, Dundrum, Ardglass, Downpatrick,
Ballymaghan, and Dundonald, most of them on the sea-coast, and with the
castle at Antrim overlooking Lough Neagh as an ultimate redoubt to sustain
the supposedly impregnable castle at Carrickfergus. John took all before him.
He was at Carlingford by 9 July, seized the castle without difficulty, landed near
Ardglass and overran its fortress by 12 July. De Lacy's garrison at Dundrum
were so dismayed by the unexpected arrival of the royal army that they
retreated without a fight, and John was in occupation by 14 July. De Lacy fled
first to Scotland, thence to France, leaving his men to defend Carrickfergus,
but when John's ships and army invested the castle the garrison surrendered
without a fight. During his return journey to Dublin John met and intimidated
Cathal Crobderg, king of Connacht, from whom he exacted hostages. At
Dublin, where he arrived on 18 August, he did likewise with William Marshal,
now the most prominent baron to have survived John's wrath. Within the next
eight days he dealt briskly with Irish chieftains and Anglo-Norman barons and
officials. By 26 August he was across the Irish Sea.

By any normal standards John's success in Ireland was remarkable. Within
the space of nine weeks he had rid the country of the de Braose family, had
expelled the powerful de Lacys and confiscated the earldom of Ulster, had
seized the principal castles in the lordship of Meath, exacted full submission
from William Marshal with his lordship of Leinster, and taken from him the
powerful fortress of Dunamase in the midlands. He had thus achieved his
primary purpose in coming to Ireland, by reducing the barons there to submission. To ensure success he used intimidation, blackmail (by taking hostages),
but more often he depended on ironclad force or a show of it. His opponents
themselves did not suffer from scruples about such methods.

His success was not limited to the settlers in Ireland. He was conscious of
the fact that he was *dominus Hiberniae* and, like his father, Henry II, he treated
the Irish rulers as potentates with sovereign rights though within his jurisdiction. He had induced Donnchad Cairprech Ua Briain, king of Thomond, his
brother Muirchertach, king of Limerick, Cathal Crobderg, king of Connacht,
and Áed Ua Néill, king of Tír Eógain, to lead their followers with his army
against de Lacy. According to Roger of Wendover more than twenty Irish
chieftains came to Dublin to make submission to John, as lord of Ireland.[1] Only
some few Irish rulers, in isolated parts of the north, remained outside his

[1] Roger de Wendover, *Flor. Hist.*, ii, 56.

control, direct or indirect. In a very real sense John was *dominus Hiberniae*, both
of the Anglo-Normans and of the Irish. Professor Warren, with a dash of
puckish humnour, has described John as the most successful high-king Ireland
had ever seen.[1] John's title might be refined even further, by describing him as
high-king 'without opposition' (*cen fressabra*).

John's success in Ireland might well have been a flash in the pan if it had
rested only on his army, castles, and ships. His special claim to permanent
fame in the country is that he established, or at least developed, the structures
of a centralised administration for the whole land, although it could not be
effective throughout the country until his officers or his jurisdiction in a real
form were accepted by all. The symbol of this centralised administration was
the 'strong castle' which in 1204 he commanded his justiciar, Meiler fitz Henry,
to erect at Dublin.[2] John's mandate stated that the fortress was to be for the
custody of the royal treasury in Ireland, as well as for the government and
defence of Dublin. It is significant that until the end of the thirteenth century
the treasurer took precedence in the Irish council over both chancellor and
escheator. Dublin castle was to become over seven centuries a symbol and a
reality of foreign domination, but this was not so in the time of King John. It is
probably accurate to say that he had a personal regard for Ireland, ever since he
was declared to be *dominus Hiberniae* in 1177, and was to have been crowned its
king in 1187. He was thus being given the status he so eagerly desired but which
he normally, as the youngest of four sons, could not expect. Not even he could
have foreseen that by 1199 his three brothers would be dead and he would be
ruler of the whole 'Angevin empire', a powerful but unwieldy inheritance. He
did not then, as might have been expected, reduce Ireland to the status of a
province with an administration geared to that level. Just as the papacy continued its policy of regarding Ireland as separate from England, in the ecclesiastical sphere, so John established a separate Irish administration.

We are fortunate in having in the one surviving Irish pipe roll of 1211–12
clear evidence of his administration in the country.[3] Even before John's reign
there was already an efficient exchequer, drawing revenue not only from the
royal demesne and the towns but also from the great franchises. Of these franchises Meath, Ulster, and Uriel were now in John's hands, and though William
Marshal had been confirmed as lord of Leinster, the king's writs ran in his
lands and it was Marshal's duty to collect the royal revenues there. As yet there
were only three sheriffs: at Dublin, Waterford (which also covered Cork), and
Munster (which embraced Limerick, Thomond, and Tipperary). The sheriff of
Dublin collected the revenue from places in the modern counties of Leix,
Louth, and Meath (including Drogheda). The stewards for Meath and Ulster,

[1] Warren, 'King John and Ireland', p. 39.

[2] *Rot. litt. claus., 1202–24*, p. 66; *Hist. & mun. doc. Ire.*, p. 61.

[3] Oliver Davies and D. B. Quinn (ed.), 'The Irish pipe roll of 14 John, 1211–1212' in *U.J.A.*, 3rd
series, iv (1941). For an estimate of its value see H. G. Richardson, 'Norman Ireland in 1212' in
I.H.S., iii, no. 10 (Sept. 1942), pp 144–58.

who were also responsible for Uriel, enjoyed much the same position as sheriffs. It can be seen that John's direct power, as witnessed by his ability to collect revenue, the touchstone of effective government, extended over a great part of the country. The pipe roll does not manifest the indirect power that John also exercised through his agreements with the twenty and more Irish rulers in Thomond, Limerick, Connacht, Tír Eógain, and elsewhere. Truly, he was hardly less than a high-king.

The structure of central government in Ireland was as yet quite simple, even rudimentary by later standards. The justiciar's personal household, like that of the king in England, was an essential and dominant element in government, but at this point the entire royal administration in Ireland was based on the exchequer. Money was the power necessary to sustain the machinery of administration. As yet there is no trace of a separate judiciary; it was only emerging in England, and never existed in Normandy. Even the Irish exchequer had as yet a simple character, with the official in charge working under the justiciar. The first Irish treasurer we know by name is John of St John, who did not arrive in the country until late 1212, and the title of treasurer of Ireland was formally recognised before July 1215. Nevertheless, the functions of an exchequer were already being fulfilled even before John's accession as king in 1199. There is evidence of a sheriff of Dublin in the 1190s, of early pipe rolls, of an exchequer at Dublin in 1200, and the transfer of large sums from Ireland to King John early in his reign. All of this suggests an established organisation, dating back perhaps to 1185. Before 1212 the justiciar had no chancellor or treasurer. The justiciar dealt with these matters but he had very limited powers for the issuing of writs, since John reserved to himself many of the powers that in England were essential for the administration of the country. The royal chancery, attached to the king's person, was the chief source of writs, and apparently as early as November 1210 the whole range of writs normally issued by the chancery in England was available in Ireland.[1]

Hardly less important than the exchequer was the creation of a judiciary system, with the introduction of the common law to Ireland.[2] Its effects were to be more permanent and far-reaching than any immediate revenue or any military victory. The justiciar brought a court with him on his many journeys, but this professional assistance was from administrators rather than from those with legal experience. Common law, as it operated in the local seignorial courts, must have come to Ireland with the Anglo-Normans, but it is noticeable that it

---

[1] The basic work is Richardson & Sayles, *Admin. Ire.*; cf. the painstaking survey 'The government of the Norman-Irish state' in Otway-Ruthven, *Med. Ire.*, pp 144–90.

[2] The growing awareness of the importance of this subject can be seen in F. W. Maitland, 'The introduction of English law into Ireland' in *E.H.R.*, iv (1889), pp 516–17 (reprinted in his *Collected papers*, ed. H. A. L. Fisher (Cambridge, 1911), ii, 81–3); W. J. Johnston, 'The first adventure of the common law' in *Law Quart. Rev.*, xxxvi (1920), pp 9–30; G. J. Hand, 'English law in Ireland, 1172–1351' in *N.I. Legal Quart.*, xxiii (1972), pp 393–422; Paul Brand, 'Ireland and the literature of the early common law' in *Ir. Jurist*, xvi (1981), pp 95–113.

is in 1199, the year of John's accession to the throne, that we first read of 'the king's court in Ireland'.[1] The dominant figure in the court was the king's other self, the chief governor, who normally bore the significant title 'justiciar'. Meiler fitz Henry, as justiciar (?1198–1200, 1200–08), was authorised by John in 1204 to issue five of the original writs most in demand, and in 1207 he was given powers to hold pleas of the crown. Up to this time he seems to have been the only royal official engaged in judicial work in Ireland; other royal 'justices' were apparently confined to the levying of royal taxation. Certainly there were 'justices itinerant' in Ireland, other than the justiciar, by 1218, but their appearance was apparently due to the visit of John in 1210 and more precisely after the despatch of an 'Irish' register of writs to Ireland in November 1210.

When John visited Ireland in 1210 he issued a charter concerning the observance of the common law of England in the lordship of Ireland.[2] John issued the charter with the goodwill of the magnates in Ireland, spiritual and temporal, some Irish as well as Anglo-Norman, and had their promise, under oath, that they would abide by its terms.[3] It was to apply to 'all the men of Ireland'.

The charter did not introduce the common law to Ireland. Several of its procedures were already there, such as trial by a jury of twelve men, the assizes of *novel disseisin* and *mort d'ancestor*, and the writ of right. Nevertheless, it appears that the charter was the first authoritative declaration that the law in the courts of the lordship of Ireland was to be identical with the common law of England in all respects. Thereafter the settlers in Ireland were not free to pick and choose from the common law to their own advantage. This was intended as a manifest assertion of even-handed justice for all the king's subjects in the lordship of Ireland. Nor did John let the charter stand as a mere ideal to be respected. Without much delay, on his return to England John issued, apparently in November 1210, a register of writs for despatch to Ireland to ensure that the full range of English writs would be available in the lordship. If the November 1210 date is correct, as a recent study convincingly argues,[4] we have in the register the only one of its kind from the reign of John and a document of exceptional value for the history of the transmission of English common law to Ireland. Furthermore, the charter of 1210, and the 'Irish' register of writs as it has come to be called, are only part of the evidence demonstrating that from its very early history the common law developed as an Anglo-Irish legal system, common both to England and the lordship of Ireland.[5] Paradoxically, the need to state clearly that the common law applied in Ireland probably helped to create a single, fixed rule in England. The charter of 1210 represents the first attempt to produce an official *summa* of the English common law, and it was

[1] *Rot. oblatis*, p. 36.
[2] Brand, 'Ireland and the literature of the early common law', pp 95–6.
[3] Ibid., p. 97, for the legists in the royal circle.
[4] Ibid., pp 100–06.
[5] Ibid., p. 112, and see below, pp 173–5, 377–8.

a precursor of the statute of Wales in 1284 to be applied to the territories in Wales under Anglo-Norman rule.

When John returned to England in August 1210 he had reason to be well satisfied with his expedition to Ireland. In the light of his success, his decision to visit his Irish lordship can be seen as a brilliant stroke. For John de Grey, bishop of Norwich and justiciar of Ireland (1208–12), the problem of ruling the country was now simplified. The barons and settlers were to be kept on a tight rein of feudal obedience, while the Irish chieftains were to be firmly drawn on a leading rein to accept John as their overlord. De Grey was associated particularly with the building of castles at Athlone, Cáeluisce (near Beleek), and Clones. The significance of Athlone need hardly be stated; it was the gate giving access from Connacht to Meath, Leinster, and the midlands, but in reverse it was the Anglo-Norman entrance from Meath to the whole province of Connacht, and through Connacht to the north-west by Cáeluisce to Cenél Conaill, as well as to the north-east by Clones to Airgialla and Cenél nEógain. For the first time since the coming of the Anglo-Normans to Ireland it was possible to come to grips, or terms, with the independent lords of the far north. De Grey began successfully, building a stone castle at Athlone on a great artificial platform of earth which rose twenty-five feet above the Shannon and was held in position by strong retaining walls, bearing on top a massive decagonal donjon tower. While the castle and a wooden bridge across the river were being built in 1210 de Grey sent a military force into Connacht to ensure that Cathal Crobderg would continue to prove cooperative, now that King John was back in England. Cathal Crobderg quickly came to terms with de Grey, and an agreement was sealed by the peace of Athlone. Cathal gave hostages, including his son, Toirrdelbach, and agreed to pay rent; in return he was guaranteed protection by the English crown. The agreement was confirmed in more solemn form five years later by the charter of Connacht in 1215.[1]

De Grey had less success with the Irish of the north, though initially he seemed to be assuming control. He intended to establish his master's presence, not necessarily by war but by three-pronged pressure through Cáeluisce, Clones, and Inishowen. In 1211 a force under Gilbert de Angulo established a castle at Cáeluisce, while de Grey led an expedition to Clones and built a motte there as a base for action. The following year, and almost certainly with the connivance of de Grey, Thomas fitz Roland ('Mac Uchtraig'), earl of Atholl, and the sons of Mac Sumarlaide of the Isles, 'came to Derry with a fleet of seventy-six ships, and plundered and destroyed the town. They passed thence into Inishowen, and ravaged the entire island'.[2] Early in that same year de Grey

---

[1] *Rot. chart.*, p. 219a; *Cal. doc. Ire., 1171–1251*, pp 100–01, no. 654. It was typical of John's method that on the same day, 13 September, he also granted Connacht to Richard de Burgh; see *Rot. chart.*, p. 218b; *Cal. doc. Ire., 1171–1251*, p. 100, no. 653. Earlier in the year, on 1 February, John had taken Cathal and his men under royal protection, cf. *Rot. pat. Hib.*, p. 122a; *Cal. doc. Ire., 1172–1251*, p. 84, no. 530.

[2] *A.F.M.*, 1211. Cf. *A.U.*, 1212; *A.L.C.*, 1211. The entries in *A.F.M.* during this period are mistakenly antedated by a year. For this entry the same mistake is made by *A.L.C.*, dating it to 1211.

was at Carrickfergus arranging, with King John's permission, for the fitz Rolands to settle along the north-east coast of Ulster, from the River Foyle to the Glens of Antrim. This was the beginning of a permanent Scottish settlement in Ulster. It was followed in 1214 by the building of a castle at Coleraine for the fitz Rolands, and a confirmation in June 1215 of their rights there by King John.[1]

De Grey's plans were admirable in theory and on a military map, but there were not sufficient manpower and resources to hold the castles against the onslaughts of the Irish in the province. Áed Ua Neill, king of Tír Eógain, had been happy to join King John in 1210, in order to eliminate Hugh de Lacy from Carrickfergus, but a year later he, with the chiefs of the Cenél Conaill and Airgialla, defeated the Anglo-Normans at Cáeluisce, repulsed de Grey from Tír Eógain in 1212, and destroyed Clones castle the following year, while Ua hÉicnig took the opportunity to burn the fortress at Cáeluisce. The castle at Coleraine survived these years of troubles, because of the surrounding protective settlement of Scots from Galloway, but even Coleraine castle was to be taken in 1224 by Áed Ua Néill and the de Lacys.

It was not that de Grey was without his successes. He was a highly efficient administrator at Dublin, and the castle under construction there, and nearing completion, was evidence of a royal centre that could give unity, justice, and peace to the whole country. The convincing proof of his efficiency was the considerable sums of money he was able to send John for his wars in Wales and France, as well as the fact that he remodelled the coinage in Ireland. He is also credited with assimilating Irish local government to the system prevailing in England, but he was understandably constrained by the extent to which John's authority, as lord of Ireland, could be directly extended throughout the country. De Grey made no more than a start, a frustrated start, with the north, but had undoubted though limited success with Connacht, where his peace of Athlone in 1210 led directly to the charter of Connacht in 1215 and to the stability which that produced in the western province until the death of Cathal Crobderg in 1224.

Between the end of 1212 and the death of John in October 1216 there is a new alignment of Anglo-Norman forces in Ireland, with new masters (William Marshal, Geoffrey de Marisco, and Henry of London) emerging.[2] These men began a policy, tolerated but not favoured by John, of setting the settlers against the Gaelic Irish inhabitants. It was a policy described by modern Irish nationalists as *apartheid*, but this is misrepresentation of a situation in which the decisive forces were economic and cultural, not racial in the modern precise sense of the word.[3]

[1] *Rot. chart.*, p. 210a; *Cal. doc. Ire.*, *1171–1251*, pp 87–8, nos 564–5.
[2] W. L. Warren, 'The historian as "private eye" ' in *Hist. Studies*, ix (1974), pp 1–18, after an elaborate introduction (pp 1–12) introduces an original interpretation, which he develops further in his 'King John and Ireland', pp 35–9.
[3] This Irish nationalist interpretation is expounded by the Franciscan historian, Cainneach Ó Maonaigh (Canice Mooney), 'Ciníochas agus náisiúnachas san eaglais in Éirinn, 1169–1534' ('Racialism and nationalism in the Irish church, 1169–1534') in *Galvia*, x (1964–5), pp 4–17.

The new development begins with John in October 1212 when he sent letters to Marshal and the justiciar, de Grey, indicating that he would be glad of a declaration of support in his clash with the papacy. The reply was all that he could have hoped for, and was issued by Marshal and twenty-six of the barons in Ireland, on behalf of the rest of the magnates.[1] It declared, on a note of high feeling, that they were moved 'with grief and astonishment' on hearing of the pope's threat to absolve the king's subjects from their fealty, that his majesty was merely defending the established rights of the crown, and they ended with a rousing proclamation that for the king they 'were prepared to live or die, adhering to him faithfully and inseparably unto the end'.

The barons in Ireland lived up to their word. John decided to demonstrate the loyalty of his subjects, and with the threat of a French invasion assuming real shape on the other side of the Channel called for a muster at Dover as Easter 1213 ended. Marshal is credited with having advised John to hold the muster. The royal magic still worked, and it was calculated that some 60,000 men assembled and were reviewed at Barham Down near Canterbury. Among those present was an impressive contingent from Ireland, asserted by Roger of Wendover to consist of 500 knights and many mounted sergeants, headed by the justiciar, de Grey, and Marshal.[2] Though Roger of Wendover exaggerated the number of knights from Ireland, the salient fact emerges that all, or most, of the feudal levy could absent themselves from the country without fear of rebellion by the settlers or major attacks by the Irish. The lordship of Ireland was in good shape.

John pressed ahead with initiatives to win over Pope Innocent III and to cripple the French armada assembled on the Flemish coast. On both scores he was eminently successful. He was at Dover in May 1213 to meet the papal legate, Pandulph, who had been prepared for protracted negotiations but not for John's disarming offer that England and Ireland become fiefs of the apostolic see, and therefore come under papal protection. John sealed the formal charter of agreement on 15 May, by which 'the whole kingdom of England and the whole kingdom of Ireland' became feudal vassals of the Roman church. It is worthy of note that the thirteen witnesses to the charter included de Grey, the Irish justiciar, Henry of London, the new archbishop of Dublin, and Marshal. Before the month of May was out John's navy had descended on the unprepared French armada at Damme in Flanders, and wrecked it beyond recovery. For the moment John had pulled the chestnuts out of the fire in England. Had he then stuck to his kingdom, and not embarked on the expedition to France in 1214, all might have gone well for him. This is not the place to trace the road to Runnymede, except in so far as it bears on the history of Ireland in those years.

---

[1] *Cal. doc. Ire.*, *1171—1251*, p. 73, no. 448, from the Red Book of the Exchequer, and dated by Orpen (*Normans*, ii, 309–10) to about Oct. 1212. John's response to Marshal is in *Rot. litt. claus.*, *1204—24*, p. 132b; *Cal. doc. Ire.*, *1171—1251*, pp 72–3, no. 444.

[2] Roger de Wendover, *Flor. hist.*, ii, 67.

After 1213 John did not have to worry about Ireland, but there was a price to be paid for the assured support he had for the rest of his reign from the barons and officials of his lordship. They wanted to run the country efficiently, for their personal benefit and for the royal coffers. This meant that there was no place for indirect rule through Irish kings and chieftains, though this was the system which both Henry II and John had found acceptable. The first official sign of change was the appointment, albeit temporary, of de Marisco as *custos* or deputy governor in April 1213, followed in July by the appointment of Henry of London as justiciar. Marshal was undoubtedly privy to the appointments.

De Marisco and Henry were able royal servants but appear as somewhat sinister characters, as far as the Irish were concerned. De Marisco was a member of a well established landed Somerset family and a nephew of John Cumin (archbishop of Dublin, 1181–1212). He was highly favoured by King John and established himself within the Butler lordship of Ormond. He was impatient with the compromise by which the Butlers were adapting themselves to the Irish world of north-east Munster, extending their influence steadily, but usually without warfare, by means of marriage alliances and legal agreements. He had to be pardoned by King John for his attacks on Meiler fitz Henry (justiciar, 1199–1208) and he campaigned vigorously in 1210 against the Irish in Connacht, as he did later against Áed Ua Néill. He stood firmly with Marshal on King John's side against Pope Innocent III in 1212, and received his reward in July 1215 when appointed justiciar, though John, with a typical gesture, simultaneously retained two of de Marisco's sons as hostages. De Marisco was an active and powerful justiciar (1215–21). His belief in extending Anglo-Norman power across the Shannon was shown by the castle he had established at Killaloe by 1216, and for the same reason, though with a personal bias, he intruded his nephew, Robert Travers, an English clerk, into the bishopric of Killaloe in 1216 without canonical election or papal provision.

De Marisco's belief in extending Anglo-Norman power in Ireland at every level was shared by Henry of London, but the archbishop was careful to operate within the law.[1] He was a Londoner, son of an alderman, and as archdeacon of Stafford served John loyally, and apparently without a qualm of conscience, during the interdict (1208–13) and the excommunication (1209–13). He would defy the pope, not the king. The death of Archbishop Cumin late in 1212 gave John a welcome opportunity to install in the see of Dublin a man in whom he could have full trust. Henry was with him at Dover as archbishop-elect when the king made submission to the papal legate, Pandulph, in May 1213, as he was to stand beside him on the field of Runnymede in June 1215. From first to last Henry was a king's man. Why Geoffrey de Marisco was appointed justiciar of Ireland on 6 July 1215, in place of Henry, is not clear, but it did not represent

---

[1] The best single account of the archbishop is Aubrey Gwynn, 'Henry of London, archbishop of Dublin: a study of Anglo-Norman statecraft' in *Studies*, xxxviii (1949), pp 295–306, 389–402, but it needs to be updated in the light of subsequent research.

disapproval of Henry or of his policy, since he and de Marisco were at one in their policy for the lordship. The reason may well be that Henry was due to attend the fourth Lateran council in Rome, and this would involve his absence from Ireland for at least a year. Henry's policy, as archbishop and as justiciar, is permanently expressed in two fine monuments of stone, St Patrick's cathedral and Dublin castle. Though Henry is given credit for both buildings he did not initiate the projects, but he did complete them. Since he could not fully control the existing cathedral, Christ Church, which was staffed by Augustinian Arroasian canons, he took the extraordinary step of creating a second cathedral in the city so that he could staff it with secular canons, under his direct control. There is no need to indicate the significance of Dublin castle as the administrative nerve-centre of the lordship.

Archbishop Henry was to become the key figure in Ireland, as Marshal did in England, but Henry had to depend on Marshal's approval. Neither of them took a sympathetic view of the Irish, and though they were in agreement on the need to extend Anglo-Norman power in Ireland, and were dedicated to the king's service, they were driven by different motives. Marshal's were those of a great feudal baron and were heavily economic. Archbishop Henry's were those of a totally committed royal official, and while primarily political they had a special cultural dimension that placed the Irish in the shade, if not in outer darkness. The end result of Marshal's and Archbishop Henry's policies was the same for the Irish, but this did not become officially apparent until after the death of John in 1216. Though John had to rely to a significant extent on the support of the barons in Ireland for the security of his throne in England, he was a brake on the narrower policies of his officials in Ireland. He was quite agreeable to the native Irish lords continuing their centuries-old inherited pattern of social and political life, as long as they accepted him as their overlord, their *ard-rí*. This they were prepared to do. Several of John's advisers differed from their master about the policy for Ireland. They believed in imposing the Anglo-Norman tenurial system on the country, but John with greater commonsense realised that this could only be achieved by a military conquest at least as total as that of William the Conqueror after 1075 in England. In Ireland it would have meant even more since it would have required the elimination of the entire sociopolitical fabric of Gaelic society. Besides, John had inherited from his father, Henry II, the concept of an 'Angevin empire' as a federation of principalities with diverse traditions, not as a monolithic structure with a uniform system in all its territories. He would allow Irish lordships, but not baronial kingdoms as in Wales, or those attempted in Ireland by de Braose, de Courcy, and de Lacy.

The clue to the change of Anglo-Norman policy for Ireland is the loss of Normandy in 1204, and the decisive figure in the change is William Marshal.[1]

[1] For Marshal's role in this crucial change of Anglo-Norman policy in Ireland, see Warren, 'The historian as "private eye" ' and 'King John and Ireland'.

Though he tried to retain a foothold in Normandy by feudal submission to King Philip Augustus of France, he thereby incurred the displeasure of King John of England and was forced into exile in Ireland in 1206. It was a blessing in disguise for him. He was now in control of the lordship of Leinster, because of his marriage to Isabel de Clare, heiress to Strongbow, but the vast acres were not profitable by European standards. He had a keen business sense, and quickly realised that though it was underdeveloped it was potentially highly suitable for grain production. At that time it was precisely grain that was in great demand from the industrial and commercial areas of the Low Countries and Germany, and Marshal was already sharply aware of this fact because of his association with London merchants such as the Cornhills, and with ships carrying corn from his English estates to France.[1] The Gaelic Irish economy depended mainly on cattle-grazing, but by reason of climate and soil Ireland was an ideal choice for the new techniques of the European agricultural revolution: spring and winter sowing, and a three-field crop rotation producing wheat, oats, beans, and peas. It could compensate for the loss of Normandy. Marshal had the instincts and ruthlessness of his contemporary Italian entrepreneurs. He was responsible for a deep-water port at New Ross on the river Barrow (thereby bypassing the royal port of Waterford), and he removed Mac Gilla Pátraic from his traditional home in central Osraige. The existing Irish population were obviously unsuitable for implementing the new techniques, and were an obstruction to progress, in colonists' terms. It was necessary therefore, as Marshal and his colleagues saw it, to be rid of the Gaelic Irish on their estates and to import peasants from England and Wales.[2] This they did, acting not on racial or political but on economic grounds. And it paid rich dividends to Marshal and his successors in the lordship of Leinster.

Marshal's achievement was symbolised by the creation of New Ross not merely as a new town, but as the port of south Leinster. It quickly overshadowed Wexford as a trade centre, and it even outpaced Waterford despite the many concessions granted to that town by John and his successors. The strength of New Ross lay in its hinterland and the transformation that had been effected by Marshal. Large numbers of settlers were introduced, English and Welsh free tenants, to farm the land. With them came the agricultural revolution. Inevitably and rapidly a series of satellite towns sprang up in Kildare, Kilkenny, Carlow, and Wexford, looking to Kilkenny as the capital and New Ross as the port. With this urbanisation came a thriving commercial life,

[1] Warren, 'King John and Ireland', p. 35, where he acknowledges his debt on this point to a former pupil, Dr Brian Feeney.

[2] This was a radical change from the policy of Henry II, King John, and the early settlers, all of whom tried to ensure that the two Irish classes who cultivated the soil (the free class in Irish law, and the serf class, the betaghs), but who had been displaced by warfare, would return to their lands. The treaty of Windsor (1175) not merely encouraged the displaced Irish to return to their lands but stipulated that they could be forced to return; see text of the treaty in Curtis & McDowell, *Ir. hist. docs*, pp 22–4, at p. 23. Tribute is paid to Hugh de Lacy by Gerald of Wales for bringing back the native cultivators of the soil in Meath, in *Expugnatio*, p. 191.

which meant income for Marshal and revenue for the crown. The lordship of Leinster was not unique in a transformation that was a many-sided but integrated process embracing settlement, agriculture, urbanisation, and trade. Meath was undergoing a similar process, and whole areas of Munster, notably in Limerick, Tipperary, and Cork, were developing on similar lines, though in varying degrees due to local conditions.[1] The immediate beneficiaries of the change were the Anglo-Norman barons, and John was in no position to resist fully their policy since he needed their support if he were to survive in England. He knew he could rely on them, even though they officially sided with their peers when he was forced to agree to Magna Carta in June 1215. William Marshal was by his side on that occasion, as was Archbishop Henry of London. Marshal remained as John's chief counsellor during the remaining sixteen months of his reign.

John died on 18/19 October 1216, and Marshal became regent of England on 29 October. A series of events that followed shortly afterwards indicate the change of policy for Ireland. Magna Carta was issued for Ireland on 12 November, and was transmitted to Dublin in February 1217. Thus the rights of the magnates in Ireland were rendered secure. Not so the rights of the Irish. On 14 January 1217 Marshal sent an order in the king's name from Oxford to de Marisco, directing the justiciar to see that no Irishman was to be elected or promoted to any cathedral church in Ireland, since 'our land of Ireland' could be disturbed by such appointments.[2] The directive was repeated in more formal terms on 17 January, enjoining de Marisco by his oath of fealty to the king not to permit any Irishman to be elected or promoted to any Irish see.[3] There was a significant addition to this second directive. The justiciar was to consult with the archbishop of Dublin, Henry of London, and was to use every means in his power to ensure the election and promotion of the king's clerks and of other worthy English clerks when each vacancy arose, as measures necessary for the welfare of the king and his realm. The mention of Archbishop Henry is a telling pointer to the figure who was to represent a rigid policy of placing loyal servants of the crown at every level of civil and ecclesiastical administration in Ireland. He was in Rome, attending the fourth Lateran Council, at the time of the king's death, but this was no disadvantage since he was literally close to the new pope, Honorius III, elected on 18 July 1216, and could be sure of support from Marshal, now regent of England, and Guala, the papal legate in England. It should be remembered that the pope was feudal overlord of England since

---

[1] For a general survey see A. J. Otway-Ruthven, 'The character of Norman settlement in Ireland' in *Hist. Studies*, v (1965), pp 75–84. For Meath see Orpen, *Normans*, ii, 75–90. There is much information about the early settlements in Ormond in Gwynn & Gleeson, *Killaloe*, pp 174–95, but further detailed research is needed for each local area.

[2] *Cal. doc. Ire., 1171—1251*, p. 112, no. 736; *Pat. rolls, 1216—25*, p. 22.

[3] *Cal. doc. Ire., 1171—1251*, p. 113, no. 739; *Pat. rolls, 1216—25*, p. 23. Curtis (*Med. Ire.*, pp 108, 124) twice slips into a major error by ascribing to King John the directives of 14 and 17 Jan. 1217 sent to de Marisco by Marshal.

May 1213, committed to its interests and therefore to its policy for Ireland. Henry was apparently still in Rome when Honorius issued a brief on 6 October 1216 confirming the union of the see of Glendalough with Dublin, a project much desired by Henry. Glendalough was far greater in extent than Dublin, stretching from Maynooth to Athy, comprising south Kildare as well as Wicklow: its best lands were in the hands of the settlers, but Glendalough itself, the centre of the diocese, was an impregnable Gaelic redoubt.

There is no doubt that Marshal, de Marisco, and Archbishop Henry were acting in unison with their policy for Ireland, and with the full cooperation of Honorius III and Guala. On 16 April 1217 Marshal wrote to de Marisco and to all the king's barons and loyal subjects in Ireland, informing them of the archbishop's return to Ireland, ordering them to obey the archbishop and the justiciar in all matters concerning the king. In that same month, April 1217, Henry of London was appointed papal legate in Ireland. The bull of appointment identified the interests of the Almighty and those of England, stating that Henry was nominated as legate so 'that you may make those decisions which you judge expedient in the Lord, both for the restoration of peace and for the support of the king'.[1] Even before his appointment as legate he had secured a directive from the pope in January 1217 empowering him to ensure fealty among the people 'in the kingdom of Ireland' (this included both Gaelic Irish and settlers) to the boy-king Henry III.[2] Fortified by that directive the archbishop of Dublin made effective use of his position as papal legate to forward the interests of the crown. He succeeded in placing Anglo-Normans as bishops in the provinces of Dublin, Cashel, and Armagh, and it was only the personal intervention of Archbishop Donnchad Ó Lonngargáin of Cashel by a trip to Italy in 1220 that brought home to Honorius III how Henry of London was abusing the office of papal legate for secular purposes.[3] The pope acted decisively. He informed Henry, in a letter of 6 July 1220, that his term as legate was terminated, and on 31 July announced that a new legate, Master James, a papal chaplain, was being sent to Ireland.[4] Honorius followed that public announcement with a strong, almost indignant, letter to Master James, which ran:

It has come to our knowledge that certain Englishmen have, with unheard-of audacity, decreed that no Irish cleric, no matter how educated or reputable, is to be admitted to any ecclesiastical dignity. We are not prepared to allow so temerarious and wicked an abuse to pass in silence, and we command you by authority of this letter to denounce the decree as null and void, forbidding the said Englishmen from enforcing it or attempting anything of the kind in future. You are to make known that Irish clerics, whose merits are attested by their lives and learning, are to be freely admitted to ecclesiastical dignities, provided they have been canonically elected to these posts.[5]

[1] Sheehy, *Pontificia Hib.*, i, 193–4. [2] Ibid., i, 191–2.
[3] Gwynn, 'Henry of London', pp 390–92.
[4] Sheehy, *Pontificia Hib.*, i, 221–3, nos 135–6.
[5] Ibid., i, 225, no. 140.

It is not within the scope of this chapter to follow the career of Henry of London and the struggle within the Irish church that continued throughout the thirteenth century. However, there is one aspect that needs attention, since it first becomes apparent during the reign of John. The evidence for an ideological clash between Irish and Anglo-Normans appears in substantial form before 1216. Such a clash was not part of the outlook of Henry II or King John. It is facile to describe it as racial. In its initial stage it was a medley of economic, political, and cultural factors, but as these merged and hardened throughout the thirteenth century they did produce a racial confrontation.

The clash found vivid expression in the 'conspiracy of Mellifont' (1216–31).[1] The chief Irish monastery of a highly disciplined international order of contemplative monks, the Cistercians, was, on the face of it, a most unlikely setting for a bitter and unchristian struggle. The Cistercians came to Ireland in the most favourable religious conditions, under the dual patronage of Bernard of Clairvaux and Malachy of Armagh. With their joint blessing, Mellifont, the first Cistercian abbey in Ireland, was founded in 1141, and by the end of the twelfth century there were twenty-seven such monasteries in the country. Twenty-three were daughter houses of Mellifont, the others were outside its orbit, under Anglo-Norman patronage. Tension between Irish and outsiders did not have to wait for the coming of the Anglo-Norman knights to Ireland in 1169. Of the thirteen monks who founded the monastery at Mellifont in 1141 three-quarters were French, and most, if not all of them, returned to France within a short time, dismayed by primitive conditions in Ireland and by the cultural shock of a totally different environment. Cistercian asceticism had its limits. Peace was restored between Clairvaux and Mellifont, but already by 1192 there were rumblings of discontent about the Irish brethren, at the general chapter, the international annual gathering of the monks at Clairvaux. Complaints about Mellifont multiplied during the successive general chapters at Clairvaux, and came to a head at the general chapter in 1216, with mention of the 'many enormities' (by Cistercian standards) flourishing at Mellifont and other Cistercian houses in Ireland. The abbots of Mellifont and Jerpoint were deposed, and special agents, entitled 'visitators', were sent to Ireland to see conditions and to report back to the next general chapter. The welcome at Mellifont consisted of a band of hostile armed monks, and similar reception groups awaited the visitators at the monasteries of Jerpoint, Baltinglass, Killeny, Kilbegan, and Bective. Obviously, though this probably escaped the monastic visitators, there was a deep-seated division that was social and cultural, not just a matter of monastic uniformity and discipline.

The 'conspiracy of Mellifont' must be seen in the context of the Irish scene,

[1] There are two special studies of this turbulent subject, B. W. O'Dwyer, *The conspiracy of Mellifont, 1216—1231* (Dublin, 1970), and J. A. Watt, 'The crisis of the Cistercian order in Ireland', chap. 4 of his *Ch. & two nations*. O'Dwyer interprets the 'conspiracy' within a context where inherited Irish social and religious traditions clashed with an aggressive Anglo-Norman conviction of cultural and moral superiority.

political, economic, and cultural. It was more than a coincidence that in the same year the Cistercian visitors came to Ireland William Marshal issued the royal mandate excluding Irishmen from promotion to cathedral benefices. In this he was undoubtedly inspired by Henry of London, who with Geoffrey de Marisco believed that the only permanent solution for the lordship of Ireland was direct political supervision by trusted royal agents controlling the land, the towns, the civil administration, and the church, in all parts of Ireland. Marshal, as we have seen, had been initially motivated by the economic factor, governing his wide estates in Leinster. This meant the introduction of large numbers of settlers from England and Wales, forcing the Irish to the poorer lands and hilly areas. Subsequently, as regent, he fell in with the political policy advocated by Henry of London and de Marisco. A new dimension, a cultural exclusiveness, was added, or at least clearly expressed, by the Cistercian visitors to Mellifont and the other Irish monasteries of the order. Their immediate purpose was to ensure religious uniformity, but they believed that it would be achieved only in a French form and in an Anglo-Norman environment. It may be argued that their attitude had already been forcibly expressed by Gerald of Wales a generation earlier, in his two books on Ireland, where he frankly expounded a racialist view about the inferiority of the Irish.[1] Gerald was, however, not representative of his own peers, who were willing to intermarry with their Irish equals. The fact that Gerald was himself of mixed Norman and Welsh stock may largely explain why with snobbish zeal he trumpeted the virtues of the Anglo-Normans and with equal fluency denounced the Welsh, as inferior almost as the Irish.

The conviction about the moral and cultural superiority of the Anglo-Normans was starkly expressed by Stephen of Lexington, one of the Cistercian visitors in Ireland, with a rhetorical question: 'How can you love the cloister and learning, if you know only Irish?'[2] Stephen displayed a blithe ignorance of the history of Irish monasticism and its massive contribution to sacred and profane literature. His question had already been answered over eighty years previously by the Irish at Bangor, protesting against Malachy's architectural innovations, when they crisply commented 'We are Gaels, not Gauls'.[3] That first memorable written expression of racialism in Ireland came from the Irish, not from the Anglo-Normans.

---

[1] F. X. Martin, 'Gerald of Wales: Norman reporter on Ireland' in *Studies*, lviii (1969), pp 279–92, at pp 286–90.

[2] Stephen of Lexington to the abbot of Clairvaux, in 'Registrum epistolarum Stephani de Lexington', ed. Bruno Griesser, in *Analecta Sacri Ordinis Cisterciensis*, ii (1946), pp 45–8, at p. 47. B. W. O'Dwyer, continuing his study of the 'conspiracy', has published a translation of the letters of Stephen of Lexington, *Letters from Ireland, 1228–1229* (Kalamazoo, 1982), and points out in the introduction, p. 3, that the sequence of the letters in the original manuscript, and in Griesser's edition, is erroneous. O'Dwyer dates this letter to the abbot of Clairvaux to early August 1228.

[3] 'Scoti sumis, non Galli', cited by Bernard of Clairvaux ('Vita S. Malachiae', ed. Aubrey Gwynn, in *Sancti Bernardi opera*, ed. Jean Leclerq and H. M. Rochais, iii (Rome, 1963), p. 365.

CHAPTER VI

The expansion and consolidation of the colony, 1215–54

JAMES LYDON

On 11 November 1216, only two weeks after the hurried coronation of the boy king Henry III, the English council met at Bristol. Among the leading personalities present there were two, both executors of the late king's will, with important Irish connections: William Marshal, lord of Leinster, and Walter de Lacy, lord of Meath. As regent the elderly Marshal had an unenviable job, for much of England was controlled by the French and the English rebels. As a last resort, Ireland might provide asylum for the king: there is some evidence that the Irish government had already pressed to have the queen mother and the king's younger brother sent to Dublin. Personal interest, then, and a possible need of Ireland dictated a cautious approach to Irish affairs.

This is reflected in the first official communication of the new English government with Ireland. A long letter was sent from the council to the justiciar, Geoffrey de Marisco, conveying a formal announcement of the death of King John and the coronation of his son. Then followed a remarkable statement, in which we can detect the hand of Marshal, of the king's will 'to abolish and forget the anger which had once arisen between our lord father and the nobles of our kingdom, whether with or without cause we know not'; and to remove evil customs and renew liberties, thus restoring the 'days of our noble ancestors'. This note of apology was also, as we shall see, sounded in a letter to the exiled lord of Ulster, Hugh de Lacy. Clearly the Bristol council, on the advice of Marshal and Walter de Lacy, had decided to adopt a conciliatory attitude towards Ireland and take no chances with the baronage there. The same letter, in admonishing the justiciar to be more faithful than ever to the new king ('for in this our tender youth we most need it') and to take fealty from each magnate, finished by saying that the king willed that his subjects of Ireland should enjoy the same liberties as had been granted to the king's subjects of England.[1] This clear reference to the great charter was fulfilled when it was extended to Ireland in February 1217.[2]

[1] The full text is in Rymer, *Foedera*, i, 145. A calendared version is in *Cal. doc. Ire., 1171–1251*, no. 723.
[2] *Pat. rolls, 1216–25*, p. 31. See H. G. Richardson, 'Magna Carta Hiberniae' in *I.H.S.*, iii, no. 9 (Mar. 1942), pp 31–3.

Ireland had played no part in the civil war, and the baronage in Ireland made no attempt to take advantage of the upheaval caused by the war and by the minority which followed the death of King John. The lordship remained quiet; so much so, as we saw, that the Dublin government offered refuge to some members of the royal family. The magnates, having been won over to the king's side by Marshal in the later years of John's reign, were now too preoccupied with the creation of feudal lordships to worry much about what was happening in an England which was becoming increasingly remote to most of them. It would never have entered their minds to use the difficulties of the king in England to rebel against him and strike out on their own in Ireland. What would this gain them? They were content to look after their own affairs in Ireland and to let England take care of itself.

Ireland was now beginning to show a return on the heavy investment made by the first generation of settlers. Prosperity was evident. Early in 1217 the Irish justiciar was ordered to forward no fewer than 1000 hogs to England, as well as three shiploads of grain. Later in the year 2000 marks of a royal debt to bankers of St Omer was paid off by the sale of 100 sacks of wool and 100 lasts of hides from Ireland.[1] A tallage was imposed and an aid sought in Ireland, to help pay off the war indemnity to Louis of France, all the more important because of the devastated condition of much of England. Within six months money was on its way to the English exchequer.[2] The lordship was now producing a surplus, the result of the high level of production achieved on the manors. Material gain was far more important to the baronage than any ideal of feudal rights. Besides, with Marshal as head of a regency government in England, they must have felt secure. He had previously shown himself able to lead the baronage of Ireland when the need arose. The declaration of loyalty to King John in 1213 is the most notable, though not the only, example.[3] Now as regent he was able to maintain a conciliatory attitude towards the great men of Ireland, and incidentally to look after the interests of himself and his friends there. It is hardly surprising, for example, that Marshal procured a restoration to himself in Leinster of certain services owed by Meiler fitz Henry (and, incidentally, procured the glowing testimonial that he deserved the best because 'in time of necessity he proved himself like gold in a furnace').[4] But it is more characteristic of his determination to exploit his office that he appropriated lands which properly belonged to the bishop of Ferns. He held on to these grimly until his death in 1219, despite papal threats of excommunication, and his sons after him defied ecclesiastical censure for many years. No wonder that the St Albans chronicler,

[1] A mark was two-thirds of a pound sterling. A sack of wool was generally 364 lb. (165.5 kg), and a last consisted of 100 hides (R. E. Zupko, *A dictionary of English weights and measures* (Madison and London, 1968).

[2] *Rot. litt. claus., 1204—24*, pp 325, 375; *Pat. rolls, 1216—25*, pp 114, 125, 160; *Cal. doc. Ire., 1171—1251*, nos 799, 810, 843.

[3] For text and dating see Richardson & Sayles, *Ir. parl. in middle ages*, pp 285–7.

[4] *Pat. rolls, 1216—25*, pp 9–10.

Matthew Paris, recorded the extinction of the Marshal family in the male line as the result of the curse of the bishop. It is worthy of note, too, that it was Marshal who inaugurated the new, invidious policy of racial discrimination in ecclesiastical preferment in Ireland, with the orders of 4 and 17 January 1217 that 'no Irishman in our land of Ireland is to be elected or promoted to any cathedral'. The excuse was that such elections very frequently disturbed the peace.[1]

Walter de Lacy was another to use his powerful influence in England, to procure a restoration of his lordship of Meath. Reginald de Braose, son of that William who had been mercilessly hounded by King John, was given his lands in Munster, and Nicholas de Verdon was similarly restored to lands in Louth.[2] But the most remarkable sign of the new government's wish to restore the displaced feudatories in Ireland is the wooing of Hugh de Lacy. It is clear that the decision to do so was taken at the Bristol council meeting of 11 November 1216, though there had been some negotiations in progress before King John died.[3] A week later, from Bristol, a letter was sent to him promising him safe conduct in coming to a discussion with the regent. The letter went on to say that 'we wish you to know that if you will come to us we will fully restore to you your rights and your liberties . . . for if John our father of good memory truly did wrong you in any way, we should be free of that wrong, nor should your wrong in any way be attributed to us'.[4] Some contact must have been established, for in late February 1217 Hugh was given safe conduct in coming to the king, probably from France where he was taking part in the Albigensian crusade. But he remained crusading until 1219 and subsequent protracted negotiations proved useless. Possibly the death of William Marshal in May 1219 and the rise to power in England of Hubert de Burgh brought about a change in the attitude of the government. Certainly by the end of 1222 the deposed earl was only being offered the restoration of his wife's estates and a parcel of land that he had received from his brother Walter. Apparently this was the final offer and it was spurned.[5]

The following summer the Irish justiciar was informed of the government's failure to persuade the earls of Chester, Salisbury, and Gloucester, together with Walter de Lacy, to accept custody of the confiscated lands in Ulster. More sinister was the report that Hugh de Lacy was now plotting to reconquer his lands by force, so that the Irish government was instructed to fortify the royal castles against him. Nothing was left to chance. The pope had been persuaded to issue letters of excommunication against those participating in an invasion and these, too, were sent to Ireland to be used 'at the proper time'. The key fortress of Carrickfergus was placed in the charge of men sent especially from England.[6]

[1] *Pat. rolls, 1216—25*, p. 106. For comment see Watt, *Ch. in med. Ire.*, pp 100–02, and above, pp 152–3.
[2] For these restorations see Orpen, *Normans*, iii, 19–21; Otway-Ruthven, *Med. Ire.*, p. 86.
[3] *Cal. doc. Ire., 1171—1251*, no. 550.   [4] *Pat. rolls 1216—25*, p. 4.
[5] Ibid., p. 34; *Cal. doc. Ire., 1171—1251*, nos 1073–4, 1110.
[6] For all this see *Cal. doc. Ire., 1171—1251*, no. 1110.

Soon after this de Lacy began his raids and early in 1224 a full-scale war had broken out in Ireland.

Despite the forewarnings, the Irish government was not well prepared.[1] The justiciar had garrisoned the castles of Ulster and tried to protect its coasts against Hugh. But a shortage of money made it difficult to raise an army and he had, he said in a letter to the king, to borrow 'a great sum' from Dublin and other towns before he could get magnates to serve.[2] A loan of £366 had to be procured from Dublin; £200 was seized from the monks of St Mary's abbey; and 600 cows and 40 marks from Mellifont, to help wage the war.[3] It is clear, too, that many tenants in Ulster and Meath rose in support of Hugh. In Meath his half-brother William had seized the lordship, and the English government forced Walter de Lacy to return to Ireland to help put down the rebellion. As the situation in Ireland worsened, some more positive intervention by England was required: it came on 2 May 1224, with the appointment of William Marshal II as justiciar.

To some extent Marshal was already involved. His lands in Wales had been attacked by Llywelyn, whose daughter was married to William de Lacy. This family connection had been used by Hugh de Lacy to win the Welshman as an ally. He had looked elsewhere, too, for allies. At the time of his invasion of Ireland, Henry III received a letter from his sister Joan, queen of Scotland, which told him that her husband was preventing military aid from going to de Lacy; but she added the alarming rumour that the king of Norway was to join Hugh in Ireland in the summer.[4] There is no other evidence of foreign intervention. But it is characteristic of Hugh de Lacy's determination to win in Ireland that he should attempt to involve powerful foreigners in his enterprise. The spirit that animated the leaders of the Anglo-Norman invasion of the twelfth century was far from dead.

By the time Marshal landed at Waterford on 10 June 1224, the war had engulfed Meath and Ulster. Hugh de Lacy, his half-brother William, and their allies had gained the upper hand. They do not seem to have secured any worthwhile Gaelic support. Cathal Ó Conchobair of Connacht wrote to the king protesting his loyalty and complaining of those who 'shamefully fail against the enemy'.[5] After his death, his son Áed, who succeeded him, joined a great confederation against de Lacy: 'Áed Mac Cathail Chrobdeirg king of Connacht, Donnchad Cairbrech Ó Briain king of Thomond, Diarmait Cluasach Mac Carthaig king of Desmond, and the leading men of Ireland generally, except

---

[1] The inadequate state of preparation of the castles of Dublin, Athlone, and Limerick is illustrated by the inventories in ibid., no. 1227.

[2] See the letter from P.R.O., S.C. 1/60/120, quoted in Otway-Ruthven, *Med. Ire.*, p. 91.

[3] *Cal. doc. Ire., 1171–1251*, nos. 1245, 1266. St Mary's was still waiting for restitution in 1232 (ibid., no. 1984).

[4] Ibid., no. 1179. The full text is in *Royal and other historical letters illustrative of the reign of Henry III*, ed. W. W. Shirley (Rolls Series, 2 vols, London, 1862–6), i, no. 195.

[5] *Cal. doc. Ire., 1171–1251*, no. 1174.

the Cenél Eógain and Cenél Conaill'.[1] This army proved too strong for the rebels. Marshal sent a long report to the king, describing his successful seven-week siege of Trim castle, the important relief of Carrickfergus castle, and the taking of the O'Reilly crannog (where the daughter of Llywelyn, and a daughter of Ó Conchobair, wife of the first Hugh de Lacy and mother of William de Lacy, were taken prisoner).[2] It was these successes, and apparently the intervention of Ó Conchobair's daughter, which decided the king of Connacht to join forces with the government. One may suppose, too, that de Lacy's new alliance with Ó Néill forced his hand. It certainly worried the government and caused Marshal to hurry north. The annals suggest[3] that de Lacy and Ó Néill occupied the key mountain passes and that this forced the government to offer terms which de Lacy accepted. Certainly he surrendered, was sent to the king, and within the next two years he was fully restored in Ulster.[4] He soon won back the trust of the king, so much so that in 1234 he was one of four important magnates summoned to advise Henry on 'steps regarding Ireland'; and was summoned again, with three others, in 1237.[5]

It is impossible to discover the real motive behind this remarkable restoration of a rebel twice over, whose invasion of Ireland 'produced assaults of war and dispersion among the Galls of Ireland',[6] and nearly brought the government to its knees. His alliance with Ó Néill showed how far he was prepared to go, and it is likely that it was this more than anything else which forced his restoration. The failure, in the summer of 1223, to find responsible custodians of de Lacy's Ulster lands and castles must have alarmed the regency government in England. In the event it meant bringing back Hugh, however bitter a pill that was to swallow. As the future was to show, this paid a handsome dividend in the end, helping the expansion of feudal Ireland in the second quarter of the century. Hugh joined de Burgh in the conquest of Connacht, helped the government in its attack on Richard Marshal, and was responsible for advances made in the western parts of Ulster. So strong a stabilising force was he in the north that Stephen of Lexington, whose visitation in 1228 caused a furore in Cistercian Ireland, was able to contrast the peace of the area governed by Hugh (together with Meath and Leinster) with rebellious Munster, where the king held dominion.[7]

The story of Hugh de Lacy is useful as a reminder of the continuing need of strong men in Ireland during this era of expansion and consolidation. Even more than in England, the government depended on the magnates and could not afford to rule without them. The twelfth-century conquests had been achieved by great men, such as Strongbow, the first Hugh de Lacy, or John de

---

[1] *Ann. Conn.*, p. 7.
[2] Shirley, *Royal letters*, i, 500–03; *Cal. doc. Ire., 1171—1251*, nos 1203–5.
[3] See, for example, *Ann. Conn.*, p. 7.
[4] See especially *Cal. doc. Ire., 1171—1251*, nos 1371–4, 1385–6, 1498–9.
[5] Ibid., nos 2112–4, 2383.   [6] *Ann. Conn.*, p. 7.
[7] An tAthair Colmcille [Conway], *Comcheilg na Mainistreach Moíre* (Dublin, 1968), p. 185.

Courcy. Great personalities still dominated the Irish scene and pushed forward the frontiers of the feudal area. Their power made them dangerous and their family quarrels could threaten the rule of law; but without them the frontiers of feudal Ireland would not have been so dramatically extended. Such a man was Richard de Burgh. Through ruthless opportunism and the adroit exploitation of political influence in England he succeeded in winning a vast new lordship for his family in Ireland and in ousting the O'Connors from an inheritance they had frantically tried to save. At one swoop the so-called 'conquest of Connacht' enormously increased the area of feudal Ireland.

CATHAL Crobderg Ó Conchobair, king of Connacht, had never made any secret of his ambitions. According to a proposal he put before King John in 1205, he demanded 'to hold in fee of the king a third part of Connacht as a barony and at 100 marks a year' and promised to pay a rent of 300 marks annually for the other two-thirds.[1] He succeeded in making his point and in September 1215 was granted 'all the land of Connacht to hold of the king in fee during good service'.[2] He was thus breaking with Gaelic convention, in order to secure the inheritance of his son Áed. His whole policy in relation to the absent lord of Ireland was determined by this overriding consideration. Not unnaturally the de Burgh pretensions in Connacht aroused his anxiety, and he lost no opportunity of protesting his fidelity to the king. In 1224 he made one final effort to secure a charter of Connacht for his son and heir Áed, reminding the king of his faithful service to himself and King John. In particular he asked for a grant of Bréifne and Conmaicne which William de Lacy (then in open rebellion) held, in return for the 'fideli homagio' that Áed would render.[3] The reply of the king, on 14 June, was an order to the justiciar to give Áed seisin of these particular lands. But no mention was made of Connacht.[4] Áed, obviously, would have to take his chance when King Cathal died.

It is important that the Connacht king was willing to render homage and not simply fealty to Henry. This would make him a tenant-in-chief of the crown, and his land of Connacht a fee that he could pass on intact to his son. There seems little doubt that the original arrangements made by Henry II with the Gaelic kings involved simple fealty and no homage, so that Gaelic custom could be accommodated. Cathal's insistence on holding in fee marks a notable advance of feudal practice in Ireland. One would never suspect this from reading the Gaelic sources. The long and extraordinary panegyric that marks Cathal's death in the Annals of Connacht depicts him as a great king in the heroic Gaelic tradition, including the remarkable survival of the old pagan belief in the good king's being responsible for making the earth fruitful. No physical blemish could be tolerated in such a king. Cathal was the best in everything, even, be it noted, in killing, blinding, and mutilating his enemies.

[1] *Cal. doc. Ire., 1171—1251*, no. 279.   [2] Ibid., no. 654.
[3] Shirley, *Royal letters*, i, 223.   [4] *Rot. litt. claus., 1204—24*, ii, 604.

But this formal eulogy, composed by someone steeped in the Gaelic tradition, is as unreal as James Clarence Mangan's portrait of 'Cathal Mór of the wine-red hand' in his great poem 'A vision of Connacht in the thirteenth century'. The fact is that by now the O'Connors of Connacht were willing to embrace English custom in return for security of tenure. The two sons of Cathal, Áed (d. 1228) and Fedlimid (d. 1265) both showed the same anxiety to establish a secure tenurial relationship with the lord of Ireland. It was this, combined with the disastrous challenges of their O'Connor cousins (the sons of Ruaidrí Ó Conchobair), which produced the circumstances which allowed Richard de Burgh to assert successfully old claims to Connacht.

The origins of de Burgh interest in Connacht go back to the previous reign. So, too, does the family connection with the O'Briens, which was to be a prominent feature of the family history in the thirteenth century. And the marriage of Richard de Burgh to Egidia, daughter of Walter de Lacy, not only brought with it rich lands, but the support of the most powerful Anglo-Irish[1] family in Ireland. The advent of his uncle, Hubert de Burgh, to power in England naturally helped to promote family interests in Ireland; and when these began to fasten on Connacht, the position of Áed Ó Conchobair became precarious.

At first the Irish government favoured Áed's claim to kingship. When Toirrdelbach Ó Conchobair, aided by Ó Néill and other Gaelic lords, made himself king in 1225, Áed was able to get official help.[2] At the same time Richard de Burgh, with Ó Briain as ally, intervened on Áed's side, possibly asserting family interest. A confusion of campaigns followed, so that when a measure of peace was finally restored, it was greeted in the annals as 'a much-needed rest, for there was not a church or lay property in Connacht which had escaped destruction'. To add to the horror, 'a severe attack of sickness came upon the countryside, a kind of fever, which emptied towns of every living soul'.[3] But further devastation was in store. Áed, despite victory, was seemingly unacceptable to the government now. The reason for the change in attitude is a matter of opinion; but de Burgh influence must have been the paramount consideration. Richard hoped to see Connacht confiscated and then granted to himself. The main obstacle was the attitude of some magnates, and in particular William Marshal the justiciar. There seems to be no doubt of Anglo-Irish opposition to confiscation and support for Áed's claims to Connacht. Marshal was removed from office and replaced on 22 June 1226 by the notorious Geoffrey de Marisco, who was ordered to summon Áed to 'surrender the land of Connacht, which he ought no longer to hold, on account of his father's and his own forfeiture'. If the forfeiture

[1] For the use of the term 'Anglo-Irish' see above, pp lii–liii.

[2] The best account of the wars in Connacht is Orpen, *Normans*, iii, 158–89. For a detailed examination of English involvement in Connacht during these years see Helen Walton, 'The English in Connacht' (Ph.D. thesis, University of Dublin, 1980), ch. I.

[3] *Ann. Conn.*, pp 19–21.

were proved, the land was to be confiscated and then granted to Richard de
Burgh (apart from five cantreds along the Shannon, which were to be reserved
for the king) at an annual rent.[1]

There is not much doubt that the letter of the law was being strictly
observed. Ironically, the success of King Cathal in procuring a charter from
Henry III was to prove the undoing of his son. It was easy to establish forfeiture: rent was in arrears for years, and some of Áed's acts could now easily be
construed as contraventions of the good behaviour demanded by the charter.
De Burgh interests could thus legally be upheld. But the whole business was so
treacherous that it alienated not only Gaelic Ireland, but Anglo-Irish sympathies as well. William Marshal certainly made no secret of his support of Áed
and may even have warned him. An official communication from Ireland
reported that Marshal's officials were refusing to hand over castles that had
been in his care as justiciar and, more ominously, that 'all the castles of Ireland
are fortified against the king, save the castle of Limerick in the custody of
Richard de Burgh, who always assists the justiciar in the king's affairs'.[2] But
Marshal could be got at through his Welsh lands and so he was neutralised.
Before long he was forced to go to Ireland, to supervise the handing over of the
royal castles to the new government. The way was now clear for the confrontation with Áed Ó Conchobair.

Áed, naturally, refused to go to Dublin and so a meeting was arranged at
Athlone. According to the account of the meeting preserved in the Annals of
Loch Cé, 'remembering the treachery and deception practised against him in
Dublin', Áed attacked the official party and then took and burned Athlone.
Foolishly he had given the government the perfect excuse for confiscation, and
soon the inevitable grant of Connacht (with five cantreds and the crosses
reserved for the king) was made to Richard de Burgh, at an annual rent and the
service of ten knights. Among the witnesses to the grant was William Marshal.[3]
To assist de Burgh to make good this grant, the feudal host was summoned.[4]
Connacht was easily overrun by this royal army, aided inevitably by the sons of
Ruaidrí Ó Conchobair, and Áed was forced to flee for his life. The following
year he returned, and during negotiations with the justiciar he was killed. Connacht was now open to full exploitation by de Burgh. Yet another O'Connor
war, this time between the sons of Ruaidrí themselves, made exploitation all
the easier. De Burgh's hand was greatly strengthened by his appointment as
justiciar in February 1228 and he quickly asserted his rights by playing the part
of kingmaker in Connacht. His choice, Áed son of Ruaidrí, was inaugurated
and the first grants of land were made in the province.

In 1230, however, there was renewed war in Connacht, when King Áed took

[1] *Cal. doc. Ire., 1171–1251*, nos 1402–3.
[2] Ibid., no. 1443. The full text is in Shirley, *Royal letters*, i, 290.
[3] *Cal. doc. Ire., 1171–1251*, no. 1518.
[4] See ibid., no. 1581, for scutage exacted for this campaign.

up arms. Once again de Burgh invaded and this time he favoured the rival branch of the O'Connors, making Fedlimid son of Cathal the new king. But for some inexplicable reason de Burgh changed his mind once more, and in 1231 he threw Fedlimid into prison, was reconciled with Áed, and for the second time had him made king. One can only conclude that de Burgh was trying to establish rights that both O'Connors found difficult to accept, very likely the same kind of rights exercised subsequently in Ulster, when Áed Ó Néill, for example, admitted formally in 1268 that his kingship was held from de Burgh ('from whom I ought to hold it') and that the earl could depose him and give or sell that kingship to another of his own choice, if Áed broke the agreement between them.[1]

At any rate, Richard de Burgh was clearly hard to please. He had already begun to occupy Connacht and had commenced the building of a castle in Galway. But now events in England took a hand. When Hubert de Burgh was dismissed as justiciar at the end of July 1232, his nephew in Ireland naturally lost favour. A curt letter ordered the release of Fedlimid Ó Conchobair, treated 'grievously and shamefully' by de Burgh,[2] who was stripped of all office. The consequences were disastrous for his hopes in Connacht. Fedlimid went on the rampage, destroyed the de Burgh castles, undermined the power of his O'Connor rivals, and swept aside all obstacles to his kingship. All of de Burgh's work was undone.

For the second time in two years English politics played a fatal part in Irish affairs. The leader of the mounting opposition to the unpopular influence of Peter de Rievaulx in England was Richard Marshal, now earl of Pembroke in succession to his brother. Passions ran high and the outcome was a vicious conspiracy against Marshal by the king, as a result of which Marshal was finally brought to his death in Ireland. Richard de Burgh had astutely taken the king's side in this sordid affair and thus regained his favour. On 27 September 1234, for a fine of 3,000 marks, subsequently reduced, Connacht was restored to him, though the service required was now substantially increased to twenty knights. In a letter, the king specifically reported that 'on account of his faithful service in the war with Richard Marshal, late earl of Pembroke', he was forgiving de Burgh 'the ire conceived against him by reason of Hubert, earl of Kent'.[3] The conquest of Connacht could now be undertaken in earnest.

In the summer of 1235 a great army, led by the justiciar Maurice fitz Gerald, invaded Connacht. They swept northwards as far as Boyle, and then turned aside to invade Thomond: the previous year Ó Briain, for the first time, had allied himself with Ó Conchobair and now had to be punished for his defection. Eventually, after a campaign involving several spectacular naval engage-

---

[1] *H.M.C. rep. 3*, p. 231.
[2] *Cal. doc. Ire., 1171—1251*, no. 1975.
[3] Ibid., no. 2217.

ments, the most interesting being the taking of the MacDermot island fortress on Lough Key, the royal army forced Fedlimid into submission. He was given the five king's cantreds at a rent of £400 (later reduced to £300) a year. Fedlimid subsequently tried to maintain good relations with the king and was for a time fairly consistent in paying his rent; but by 1284 arrears had reached the enormous sum of nearly £17,000 and were never paid subsequently.[1]

Richard de Burgh now began the subinfeudation of Connacht.[2] In 1236 he commenced the construction of a castle at Loughrea in County Galway, which was to be his principal manor in Connacht. He had other manors and castles; but the greatest part of the land he had acquired was granted away, much of it to those men who had come with the invading army of 1235. Hugh de Lacy, for example, was given five cantreds in Sligo; but he in turn made over most of these to others, including Maurice fitz Gerald. In this way the manor of Sligo was formed. Elsewhere in Counties Galway and Mayo, Maurice got lands from de Burgh: the manors of Ardrahan and Kilcolgan were set up in Galway, and that of Lough Mask in Mayo. The Geraldines thus began that expansion in Connacht that was subsequently to produce a major confrontation with the de Burghs, causing much destruction before it was settled.

Many other grants, too, were made to lords who already had extensive lordships elsewhere, and they naturally tended to make further grants in their turn. This had the effect of producing a very uneven pattern of settlement. Some parts of Galway, Mayo, Sligo, and even Roscommon (largely held by Ó Conchobair) were densely settled, with manors and boroughs springing up all over. Naturally these tended to be in the eastern part of Connacht, where the best land lay. But many out-of-the-way areas were also settled. As early as 1238 a castle was begun at Headfort in Galway, for example. Most astonishing were the settlements in Erris and Tirawley in Mayo, where the Barretts in particular proliferated and were involved in fierce faction fights with Cusacks and Flemings later in the century, a time of violence and unrest in Connacht.

At the same time it is clear that large parts of the confiscated province were never adequately settled and remained wholly gaelicised. This produced the kind of tension that could easily erupt into war. And for the remainder of the thirteenth century war in some shape or other was part of the pattern of life in Connacht, either because of Gaelic reaction to further Anglo-Irish expansion, or because of internal feuds between Gaelic lords or among the Anglo-Irish families. Nevertheless a massive expansion of feudal Ireland had taken place and it did produce an era of prosperity in some parts of the province, which is in marked contrast with what had gone before. The fortunes of the new town of Galway were built upon this increasing prosperity, and new boroughs, like that of the de Berminghams at Athenry, show clear evidence of the economic

[1] Pipe roll 15 Edw. I in *P.R.I. rep. D.K. 37*, p. 24.
[2] There is a full account in Orpen, *Normans*, iii, 190–224, and in Walton, 'English in Connacht', ch. II.

advance resulting from new settlement. In the 1333 de Burgh inquisitions the manor of Sligo was valued remarkably highly at £333 6s. 8d., while Ballintober in Roscommon was valued at £84 yearly, had 300 acres (or 750 statute acres) ploughed and another 12 (30) in meadow.[1] Toolooban in Galway had 570 acres (1505) of demesne land ploughed, as well as 32 (80) in pasture, while at Meelick there were 480 acres (1200) ploughed and 12 (30) in meadow.[2] Earlier, when the manor of Loughrea was in the king's hands during the minority of Richard de Burgh, the escheator accounted for over £2,200 in about eight years.[3]

MEANWHILE, the great lordship of Leinster was being transformed under the Marshal family and their tenants. Although they were naturally preoccupied with their vast estates on the other side of the Irish Sea, and were frequently involved in the high politics of the day, the Marshals never neglected Leinster and never played the part of absentee lords. William Marshal II, who succeeded when his father died in 1219, was in Ireland on at least three occasions before his death in 1231, altogether for more than four years. He acted as justiciar for part of this time; but he was able to devote attention to Leinster. A remarkable stability was maintained, a model of what might have happened in other parts of Ireland had there been settlement in depth and had the local lords employed greater tact in pushing forward the boundaries of what was later called the *terra pacis* ('land of peace'). At least in Leinster the term was apt. Great advances were made in the settlement: new towns, manors, castles, churches, and religious houses were founded. Markets and fairs were established. The many secular and religious foundations of the first two generations of settlers were confirmed and supported. The great castle of Carlow, with its revolutionary concept of combining the best features of the square and the round keep in the one building, was almost certainly begun by this second William Marshal. A similar design was employed at Ferns, another Marshal manor. It was this Earl William, too, who first brought the Dominican friars to Kilkenny, when the Black Abbey was founded in 1225. All of the Marshals, in fact, were great benefactors of the church, despite their stormy relationship with the bishop of Ferns. The great cathedral of St Canice in Kilkenny was begun under their auspices. The town of Kilkenny itself, founded by the first lord of Leinster, was well supported by the Marshals as their principal seat in Ireland.

More interesting is the port of New Ross, the *Pons Novus, villa Willelmi Marescalli* (the New Bridge, the vill of William Marshal), which was to become one of the greatest ports in thirteenth-century Ireland, holding first place for a time in the wool trade. Founded by the first William Marshal, it was in

[1] H. T. Knox, 'Occupation of Connaught by the Anglo-Normans after 1237' in *R.S.A.I. Jn.*, xxxiii (1903), pp 61, 59. As early as 1289 the town of Sligo contained 180 burgages (*Red Bk Kildare*, p. 113).

[2] Knox, 'Occupation of Connaught' in *R.S.A.I. Jn.*, xxxii (1902), pp 133, 393.

[3] Pipe roll 10 Edw. I in *P.R.I. rep. D.K. 36*, p. 63.

a commanding position on both the Nore and the Barrow, and from it traders could follow the rivers deep into the heart of feudal Leinster, certainly as far north as Athy. It soon outstripped its great rival Waterford, which needed the active support of Henry III to compete at all with Ross. A single statistic will illustrate the superiority. Figures for the custom on wool exports from 1275 to 1279 show a total of £2,079 through Ross, £1,421 through Waterford, and only £17 through the old viking port of Wexford.[1] Nothing could illustrate better the superior position of New Ross and the astonishing economic progress made in Leinster, which was able to sustain the export of such enormous quantities of wool and hides. The figures quoted would represent a total of 1,871,207, 1,280,411, and 14,750 fleeces respectively (or 623,402, 426,840, and 4,916 hides).

Typically, New Ross was well endowed with religious foundations, though only two can be directly associated with the Marshals: the beautiful church of St Mary (sister of the priory of St John in Kilkenny, the so-called 'lantern of Ireland') and the priory of the Crutched Friars. It is possible that the Franciscans had arrived before the death of the last Marshal; but the Dominicans had no foundation there until much later in the century, and the Augustinians none until the early fourteenth century. These are signs of the growing size and prosperity of the town. By the middle of the thirteenth century security demanded that it be enclosed, and some time around 1265 a beginning was made, an event which was commemorated in a contemporary poem in Norman French.[2] It describes how the burgesses, impatient at the slow progress of the masons they employed, decided to draft the inhabitants to work. The list of crafts represented on the different days (the vintners, mercers, drapers on Monday; the tailors, fullers, dyers, saddlers, and mantle-makers on Tuesday; and so on) is impressive testimony to the diversity of trades followed in the town. At the end, with justifiable civic pride, the poet boasts of the strength of the armed force which New Ross could muster: 363 crossbowmen, 1,200 archers, 3,000 lancers, 104 fully armed horsemen. The figures must be an exaggeration, though the proportions of the different categories is probably accurate enough. Equally interesting are the details of the arms and armour which were available in the town: different kinds of coats of mail and quilted tunics, crossbows, maces, and shields. All of this prosperity was firmly based on the port, which in turn was supported by the economic development of the lordship under the aegis of the Marshals.

But the Marshal family was doomed to extinction. Not one of the five sons of the first Marshal produced an heir. The second William Marshal was twice

---

[1] The sums are to the nearest pound. They represent a mixture of fleeces and hides which unfortunately cannot be differentiated. They can most conveniently be found in Gearóid Mac Niocaill, *Na búirgéisí XII–XV aois* (2 vols, Dublin, 1964), ii, 527–8.

[2] A racy, if slightly fanciful translation, will be found in St John D. Seymour, *Anglo-Irish literature 1200–1582* (Cambridge, 1929), pp 23–8. There is a modern edition, with translation, in Hugh Shields, 'The walling of New Ross: a thirteenth-century poem in French' in *Long Room*, xii–xiii (1975–6), pp 24–44. See also below, pp 718–19.

married; but when he died suddenly in 1231 he was still childless. His succes-
sor Richard was the victim of the king's spleen. There can be no doubt of
Henry III's complicity in the treacherous attack which led to the fatal wounding of Marshal on the Curragh of Kildare on 1 April 1234. He wrote a letter to
Richard de Burgh, thanking him for his 'strenuous resistance to Richard
Marshal' and promising 'to bestow an adequate reward'. The killing horrified
Ireland. The annals refer to it bluntly as 'one of the worst deeds done in that
age'.[1] The local Kilkenny tradition, reflected in the chronicle of Friar Clyn, was
that Richard was murdered 'by the Geraldines, holding the place and taking
the part of the king'.[2] The passions aroused among the Anglo-Irish are seen in
the murder in London of Henry Clement, who foolishly boasted of the part he
had played in the attack on Marshal. Clement was a clerk of Maurice fitz
Gerald, the justiciar; and his murderer was William de Marisco, son of Geoffrey de Marisco, a recent justiciar. De Marisco and his associates fled after the
murder, finding refuge on Lundy island, in the Bristol Channel, from where he
pursued a colourful career as a pirate, until he was captured and hanged in
1242.[3] Popular memory, too, kept the incident alive: the anniversary was noted
in Kilkenny in 1294 by Clyn.[4]

Richard was succeeded by his brother Gilbert, who was reconciled with the
king. But it was not long before good relations broke down and Gilbert found
himself involved in new quarrels with the king: his sudden death in 1241 left his
brother Walter to inherit Leinster, though not before he too had incurred the
malice of Henry III. He does not seem to have come to Ireland before he died
in November 1245. On 3 December the king wrote to the earl's seneschal in
Leinster and ordered him to deliver all his castles and lands to the justiciar
until Anselm, the last remaining brother and heir of Gilbert, 'shall come to the
king and do his duty'.[5] But hardly was the letter sealed when Anselm died,
within a month of his brother. He, too, left no children behind to inherit his
estates.

This extraordinary extinction of the Marshal family meant that the great
lordship of Leinster now had to be partitioned among the five daughters of the
first William Marshal. Of these only one, Matilda, was still alive. Further partitions followed: Sibyl Marshal left seven daughters, so that her fifth of Leinster
had to be further divided into sevenths. Eva Marshal left three daughters,
which meant a further subdivision into thirds. The great partition, completed
on 3 May 1247, was carried out as fairly and as accurately as possible.[6] Leinster
was valued at something over £1,700 annually, so each parcel was carefully calculated so as to produce £343 5s. 6½d. annually. No one could complain of

[1] *Ann. Conn.*, p. 49.

[2] *The Annals of Ireland by Friar John Clyn . . .* , ed. Richard Butler (Dublin, 1849), p. 7.

[3] The whole story is brilliantly told by Sir Maurice Powicke, *King Henry III and the Lord Edward*
(2 vols, Oxford, 1947), ii, 740–59.

[4] Clyn, *Annals*, p. 10.   [5] *Cal. doc. Ire., 1171—1251*, no. 2798.

[6] The partition is fully described by Orpen, *Normans*, iii, 79–110.

unfair treatment. Each one's interest was protected. Some of the most important families in England were involved: Bigod, earl of Norfolk; de Valence, half brother of the king; de Clare, earl of Gloucester; Mortimer, lord of Wigmore (whose family, as lords of Trim, were later to be intimately connected with Ireland); Bohun, earl of Hereford. But fair as it was, the partition did irreparable damage to the lordship, and a future growth of marchlands in many parts of Leinster, with all the military and economic problems the marches posed, must be attributed in large part to the long-term effects of this partition. For the division of great lordships, which had been conceived as strong units, inevitably led to weakness. The case of Leinster can be paralleled all over Ireland. The weakness was exacerbated by the associated problem of absenteeism, for naturally none of the people who shared in the partition was going to reside in Ireland.

But in the meantime feudal Ireland was still expanding in other directions. In Kerry John fitz Thomas, from whom the later earls of Desmond were descended, received extensive lands, and a new settlement began. The MacCarthys seem to have accepted the inevitable, for the whole forward movement was reasonably peaceful. The occupation of Limerick was continued and in Thomond renewed attempts were made to settle lands that had first been granted with the cooperation of the O'Briens, the Anglo-Irish adroitly exploiting dynastic rivalries. Effective settlement seems to have been achieved, however, only in a few places and it was not until the grant of Tradry (between the Fergus and Limerick) in 1248 to Robert de Muscegros that an important advance was made north of the Shannon, centred around the new castles and boroughs of Bunratty and Clare. The need of fairs and markets in both places is a good indication of the growing prosperity of the area, derived mainly from the agricultural exploitation of the settled lands. It is a measure, too, of the success of this new expansion that it soon led to Gaelic resistance with the revolt of the O'Briens in 1237. This can easily be seen as part of a wider pattern of Gaelic resistance in those areas that were under continuous pressure from the ever expanding feudal lordship. In that expansion the Geraldines played a leading role. We have seen their advance in Kerry and Sligo. In Thomond, too, John fitz Thomas received land near Killaloe and to the north around Corcomroe.

THIS great expansion of the area which was now effectively subject to the Dublin government naturally meant that an increasing burden of administration had to be carried. In order to cope, the administrative system was expanded and made more efficient. So far as the lordship as a whole was concerned there were really two problems. First of all there was the matter of relations with England, between the king and his chief governor in Ireland, between the English administration and its counterpart in Dublin. The other was a domestic problem, of how Dublin could best retain control over the outlying parts of the lordship, safeguarding the king's rights and upholding the

rule of law. In both cases the difficulties of communication raised acute problems. The Irish Sea was often treacherous, so that at all times travel in the tiny,
primitive ships of the day was a problem, and sometimes was impossible. An
unknown correspondent with the chancellor of England in the mid-thirteenth
century apologised for not being able to send as messenger from Ireland someone more fitting: 'so many perils have this winter occurred on the Irish sea that
few will risk the passage'.[1] The famous archbishop of Armagh, Richard Fitz-
Ralph, once commented on the difficulties of the crossing. He remarked that
he had known men who had to wait four months for a favourable crossing, and
that there even had been people trapped in an English port from the feast of St
John the Baptist until Christmas, a period of six months, while waiting for
favourable weather. It was impossible, therefore, to retain complete control
over the Irish administration, and the best that could be achieved was to make
the justiciar and the treasurer, the two most important officials in the thirteenth
century, regularly accountable before the king or his officers in England.

Internally, too, the same problem of communication made efficiency difficult. It was not conducive to the making of rapid decisions when at least forty
days had to be allowed for the summoning of any parliament. This had the
effect of making the chief governor rely very heavily on those royal officials
who were regularly available for consultation, or on such local magnates as
might be conveniently at hand when a policy decision had to be taken
rapidly. It made the justiciar an extremely powerful figure. The only real
control which could be placed on him was to make him act during pleasure,
always with the advice of the council, and according to the laws and customs
of Ireland. Sometimes, particularly in the first half of the thirteenth century,
particular individuals were nominated to act as advisers. The justiciar had his
own household, his own retinue of twenty men at arms (including himself),
and a salary of £500 a year. Over and above that he was paid such sums as
were necessary for the governance of the lordship. His powers, for the most
part, were left deliberately vague, never being precisely defined in the patent
of appointment.[2] But they necessarily included such powers as were essential:
the right to summon parliaments, proclaim royal service, issue writs in the
king's name, and, generally, exercise many of the prerogatives which were
reserved to the king. He presided over the supreme court in the lordship and
was the commander-in-chief of the feudal host or royal army during all campaigns. The office was therefore an exacting one, demanding the skills of a
soldier, judge, administrator, and diplomat. Small wonder that few people
were able to fill it entirely satisfactorily. With very few exceptions, those
appointed as justiciars in the reign of Henry III were not careerists but local
magnates. It was all the more essential, therefore, that backing them should

[1] *Cal. doc. Ire., 1171—1251*, no. 1485.
[2] For the office of justiciar see A. J. Otway-Ruthven, 'The chief governors of medieval Ireland'
in *R.S.A.I. Jn.*, xcv (1965), pp 227—36; Richardson & Sayles, *Admin. Ire.*, pp 8–13.

be a hard core of professionals and that the administration should be diversified to allow specialised skills to be employed.

By the time King John died an Irish exchequer was well established.[1] The office of treasurer had emerged, though the first to survive by name in the records, John of St John, dates from as late as 1217. There was a chamberlain, who held joint responsibility with the treasurer for the issues of the exchequer. The barons presided over the audit and exchequer court in the upper house, and lesser officials looked after the receipt in the lower house, where tallies were cut and clerks kept the records which recounted the day-to-day passage of money in and out of the exchequer. There was a pipe roll (or record of audited accounts) and a memoranda roll (a record of important business, such as proffers by sheriffs, views of accounts, writs from England—anything that might have a bearing on the process of audit or the deliberations of the barons in the exchequer court) compiled on an annual basis; and some record must have been kept of receipts and issues.

The need to check the corrupt activities of the justiciar Geoffrey de Marisco, in the early part of the new reign, produced one important result in 1220, when it was ordained that the clerks appointed for the purpose were to keep a counter-roll of all receipts and issues. This was designed to keep a check on the justiciar in future; but it was also the beginning of that system of checks and counter-checks that was to curtail the freedom of the justiciar and the treasurer in controlling the revenues of Ireland. It was the revolution that followed the fall of Hubert de Burgh in England in 1232, with the concentration of office in the hands of Peter de Rievaulx, which produced the most important advance. A chancery was now created separate from the exchequer, with its own staff and records.[2] The new chancellor was furthermore to have his own clerk at the exchequer, who would keep a roll of his own as a check on the treasurer's roll. By 1232 the system of counter-checks employed at the Irish exchequer was almost complete. The chamberlain compiled his own issue and receipt rolls as counter-rolls to those compiled by the treasurer; the chancellor's clerk compiled the chancellor's roll as a check on the pipe roll. When towards the end of the century a second chamberlain, with his own counter-rolls, was added to the staff of the exchequer, and the Irish treasurer was compelled to submit his rolls of account to the English exchequer for regular audit, the system of check and counter-check was complete.

One technical reform of great importance was also introduced into Ireland at this time. Hitherto debts owing to the king were accounted for individually at the exchequer, and therefore each had its own entry on the pipe roll. As the number of crown debtors increased, so did the number of entries on the roll;

---

[1] On the exchequer see Richardson & Sayles, *Admin. Ire.*, pp 21–6, 42–64; J. F. Lydon, 'Three exchequer documents from the reign of Henry III' in *R.I.A. Proc.*, lxv (1966), sect. C, pp 5–14, and 'The county of Uriel account, 1281–83' in *Louth Arch. Soc. Jn.*, xix (1979), pp 197–9.

[2] For the chancery see A. J. Otway-Ruthven, 'The medieval Irish chancery' in *Album Helen Maud Cam*, ii (1961), pp 119–38; Richardson & Sayles, *Admin. Ire.*, pp 14–21.

and since many of these were bad debts, they appeared time and time again, so that the rolls became greatly inflated with entries of bad debts. Now, however, the sheriff or other responsible official began to account for these collectively; one tally (a *tallia dividenda*) was issued to cover the lot, and only one entry was made on the receipt roll and subsequently on the pipe roll. The particulars of these 'debts of divers' were enrolled on special rolls separately. It was far easier in future to find particular entries on the pipe rolls and the work of administrators was made more efficient.

The appointment of Geoffrey de Tourville as treasurer in August 1234 marked further developments. An annual salary of £20 was fixed. More important, a system was established whereby an annual audit was conducted, after which a view was made of receipts and issues, and a balance struck which was then certified to the king in the form of an indenture. In this way the king was to be kept informed of what treasure was available to him in Dublin. It was not until 1285 that this practice was modified, when the audit was removed to Westminster and the view was enrolled on the memoranda rolls of the English exchequer. But it was the development of the system of certifying out of Ireland by indenture that enabled Henry III and his son Edward to withdraw large (in the Irish context) sums of money from Dublin. One further change that was possibly associated with Geoffrey's tenure of office was the development of the receipt roll. Formerly the roll consisted of a collection of entries arranged under county headings, with writs of liberate enrolled on the dorse. But some time in mid-century the format changed to that which became permanent: a chronological list of receipts, day by day, for each term, with the writs of liberate removed to the close rolls. The receipt roll thus became a register of tallies as they were struck, with the relevant county or other heading noted in the margin for use of reference. This, too, made for greater efficiency.

A major administrative development in this period was undoubtedly the setting up of an independent Irish chancery. This resulted from the fall of Hubert de Burgh in England. When the English chancellor, the bishop of Chichester, was made chancellor of Ireland in 1232, he had to act through a deputy. This was the same Geoffrey de Tourville who later became treasurer. An Irish great seal was provided, the enrolment of records began (probably patent and close rolls), and some clerks were transferred to the new office. But the chancery was slow to develop and the chancellor did not succeed in establishing precedence over other ministers until the end of the century. The chancery itself never seemed able to attract adequate staff, so that its clerks were regularly found to be deficient.

There was one other office of real importance to emerge during this period, that of escheator. There is a degree of confusion about the early history of the office, so that it is not until 1250 that the regular appointment of escheators can be said to begin. Because of the importance of escheats and wardships in the make-up of Irish revenues, and because of the peculiar position which obtained after Edward was granted Ireland in 1254, when the king reserved ecclesiastical rights to himself, the escheator assumed a special status. He was a senior minister, with a place on the council, in control of large funds derived from temporalities during vacancies in bishoprics.

The judiciary, too, was organised and brought into line with that of England.[1] The justiciar itinerated frequently as the chief justice, and a small group of itinerant justices also administered the common law in the localities. It was not until the end of the century that the justiciar's court acquired its own distinct corps of professional officers. But some time around the middle of the century a common bench emerged in Dublin, where it became sedentary. From time to time individual justices still itinerated, and at first the bench might occasionally sit at Limerick, Waterford, or some other provincial centre. But before long it became fixed at Dublin.

Behind these lay the county court and the sheriff's tourn. The shiring of Ireland was a gradual process, beginning with Dublin in the late twelfth century.[2] It is an index of new settlement: Cork and Waterford by 1208; Munster three years later; Louth and Kerry before 1233; Limerick and Tipperary shortly afterwards; Connacht before 1247. Roscommon, Kildare, Meath, and Carlow were added later in the century. A good part of the lordship was organised into liberties for much of the century. So much so, indeed, that outside Ireland contemporaries commented on the importance of Irish liberties. But it is well to remember that these, too, formed part of the pattern of local government, the lord or his seneschal discharging the duties which were elsewhere performed by the shire organisation. And all of them, except Meath, had their franchises restricted, since the four pleas (arson, rape, forestalling, and treasure trove) were reserved to the king.

By the middle of the thirteenth century, then, the Irish judiciary was organised into the system which was to persevere. The justiciar was supreme; a sedentary bench of common pleas was sitting in Dublin; general eyres were still occasionally taking place; the shires and liberties provided justice in the localities. The law administered in all of these courts was, of course, the common law of England (though some variations to suit Irish conditions, or to take account of the custom of Ireland, did occur). The steps by which this law was transmitted to Ireland are complex. But the most important step was the sending of a register of original writs for use in the Irish courts, which probably happened after King John's expedition of 1210.[3] Subsequently the application of English statutes to Ireland became of major importance.

---

[1] See Hand, *Eng. law in Ire.*, and the important essay by Paul Brand, 'Ireland and the literature of the early common law' in *Ir. Jurist*, xvi (1981), pp 95–113.

[2] A. J. Otway-Ruthven, 'Anglo-Irish shire government in the thirteenth century' in *I.H.S.*, v, no. 17 (Mar. 1946), pp 1–28.

[3] Brand, 'Ireland and the early common law', p. 113.

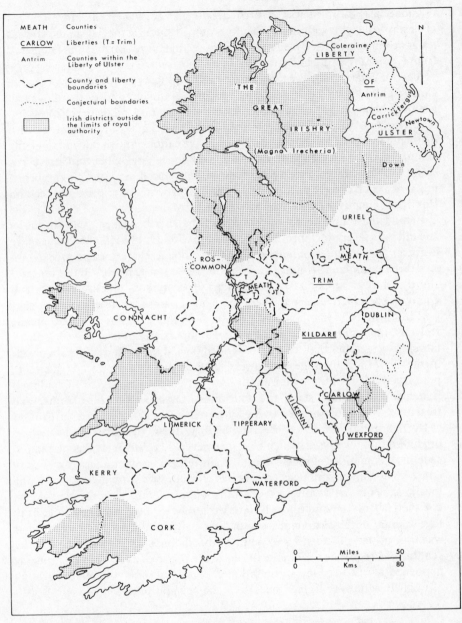

N

Coleraine

LIBERTY

OF

Antrim

Carrickfergus

Newtown

ULSTER

THE

GREAT

IRISHRY

(Magna Irecheria)

Down

URIEL

T

T
MEATH

ROS-
COMMON

T
MEATH

TRIM

T

CONNACHT

DUBLIN

KILDARE

KILKENNY

CARLOW

LIMERICK

TIPPERARY

WEXFORD

KERRY

WATERFORD

CORK

0   Miles   50
0   Kms   80

Map 3 COUNTIES AND LIBERTIES, 1297, by K. W. Nicholls

See below, ix, map 43, and note, p. 107.

IF in Ireland the highest court of appeal was that of the justiciar, there was always recourse outside the lordship to the king himself, either in parliament or, more frequently, to the king's bench. Towards the end of the thirteenth century the volume of such appeals increased rapidly and must have helped to preserve a degree of uniformity in the law in both countries. It was also one channel of communication between the king and his lordship, even if a not very important one. The king, naturally, had to be kept informed of what was going on in Ireland, and royal messengers were frequent travellers across the Irish Sea. Some of these came on important missions, to survey the state of Ireland, to help raise a financial aid for the king, to supervise a particular justiciar. They might even take their place on the council, side by side with the chief ministers of Ireland. But mostly they came on routine business, carrying letters to and fro. Messengers were sent, too, by the Irish government, and frequently the justiciar or leading ministers travelled to England to report in person to the king and confer with him. The impression we get is that the king was kept fully informed of what was going on and he frequently took the initiative himself in policy decisions.

Despite the growth of an efficient civil service and the creation of an administrative system that could function in the absence of the king, the monarchy was still a very personal institution. Perhaps the greatest flaw in relations between England and Ireland was the continuing absence of the king. Contemporaries were aware of this and on more than one occasion plans were made for a royal visitation. Not long after he assumed personal control in England, Henry III made elaborate preparations for an expedition to Ireland. In July and August 1233 the feudal host was summoned to Gloucester for 15 August and extensive arrangements were made to provide adequate shipping at Milford Haven. But within a few weeks, probably because of the quarrel with Marshal, the king changed his mind and the expedition was cancelled.[1] On a number of occasions subsequently royal expeditions were announced, but they never materialised. In April 1243, Henry actually gave precise instructions regarding the construction of a great hall in Dublin castle, which he hoped would be completed in time for him to use: it was to be 120 feet long and 80 feet broad, 'in the style of the hall of Canterbury', with glazed windows and a huge rose window, 30 feet in diameter, in the gable behind the dais. On the same gable the king and queen with their baronage were to be depicted. And a great portal was to be built at the entrance to the hall.[2]

This failure of the king to visit Ireland was certainly a weakening factor in relations between the two countries. Like Gascony, Ireland was in need of a strong hand and a royal presence would have helped to maintain control over a too independent baronage and increasingly disillusioned Gaelic lords. But while the English government seemed to be constantly aware of the danger in Gascony, it was all too complacent about Ireland which was near at hand. This

[1] *Close rolls, 1231–4*, pp 256, 316, 319, 322.   [2] *Close rolls, 1242–7*, p. 23.

attitude worsened later, after Edward was given Ireland in 1254, and it was to lead to disastrous neglect. But it began with the government of Henry III, much earlier in the thirteenth century. This is not to say that the English government had no interest in Ireland. Far from it; for if for no other reason, the king's interest was kept alive because of his ability to exploit the resources of the lordship, and especially the revenue, in time of war.

From the time of King John Irish revenues had been diverted to England at the king's command. We have seen that in the thirteenth century the English government required to be certified annually of the balance of treasure remaining in Dublin. The king never hesitated to avail of this when he needed money. Orders seeking it were sent regularly to Dublin. For example, in 1230 while in Portsmouth on his way to campaign in Poitou, Henry instructed the justiciar that he and the treasurer 'should send to England, with the first favourable wind, all the treasure which at present they have'.[1] In January 1231 he asked the treasurer to keep £500 then in hand 'and all the issues of Ireland which he can obtain' until they were requested.[2]

The Irish exchequer was able to meet the king's demands, since a surplus of revenue seems regularly to have been available, and considerable sums of money were forwarded to England.[3] There was no question of overexploitation, or of excessive demands. Henry III was moderate. He made good use, too, of Irish resources to supply his armies with essential foodstuffs and even war materials. When he was engaged in military operations in north Wales in August 1245, he wrote to the mayor and citizens of Dublin, telling them of the great need of provisions and ordering them to send 'all classes of victuals which can be withdrawn from your vill and its vicinity', together with provision merchants. Waterford, Drogheda, Limerick, Cork, and Carrickfergus received similar letters. The justiciar, too, was ordered to purchase 500 marks worth of corn and to ship it 'both as flour and as grain as fast as possible' to Wales. He was also to cause merchants 'with wines and all other kinds of victuals . . . and masons and other workmen necessary for building operations' to come to the army as well.[4] The great St Albans chronicler, Matthew Paris, has fortunately preserved a letter written by a knight at the camp at Degannwy on 24 September, some two months after the English had arrived. It gives a very vivid picture of the starving condition of the army. There was a chronic shortage of food and the excessive cold added to their sufferings. Irish ships had brought some relief and the letter goes on to describe the arrival of one of these at a time when the army was really starving. Unfortunately, because of faulty steering, the boat ran aground on the side of the estuary opposite the English, where it fell an easy prey to the Welsh. On board were sixty casks of wine, 'besides other much

---

[1] *Close rolls, 1227—31*, p. 342.   [2] Ibid., p. 466.
[3] For a list see J. F. Lydon, 'Edward II and the revenues of Ireland' in *I.H.S.*, xiv, no. 53 (Mar. 1964), p. 54.
[4] *Hist. & mun. doc. Ire.*, pp 103—4.

desired and seasonable provisions of which we were at that time destitute'. The Welsh carried off most of these and then set fire to the ship. By a great effort the English managed to salvage seven precious casks of wine before the vessel was destroyed.[1]

It was on this occasion, too, that Fedlimid Ó Conchobair, king of Connacht, arrived with a large force of men to aid the king against the Welsh. The previous year (1244) Henry III had tried to enlist the Gaelic lords for his proposed campaign in Scotland. At the beginning of July he wrote to the king of Tír Conaill and twenty other Gaelic lords, many of them from the north, and asked them to join in the forthcoming expedition to Scotland.[2] There is a suggestion here that the king was trying to regard these men as being in some sense vassals who might be expected to render military service. It is worth noting, too, that of the Ulster lords listed all but one owed military service to the earl of Ulster. The confused position of the Gaelic lords in relation to the king is obvious. One strange omission from the list of those summoned was Fedlimid Ó Conchobair of Connacht. Possibly Henry knew that Fedlimid went on a hosting into Bréifne in that year and therefore made no attempt to contact him. But the following year, he was enticed into service in Wales. According to the annals, Fedlimid was amongst those who received 'letters from the king of England . . . bidding them to go to meet the king of England in Wales, in order that he might take the kingship of Wales by consent or force, and Feidhlimidh was offered lordship by the Galls of Ireland in return'.[3] It is not clear what this 'lordship' was, but it may have involved the kind of security of tenure which Fedlimid had long sought. Whatever it was, it proved a strong enough bait to bring him to Wales. He brought a huge number of foot with him, 3,000 in all, and on his way to the king at Degannwy castle he and his men ravaged the island of Anglesey, depriving the Welsh of a valuable source of corn. According to the annals Fedlimid 'exacted no pledge or hostage from the Welsh at that time'; but they emphasise that he 'was held in honour by the king then and was well pleased when he returned westwards'.[4] This can hardly be true, since Henry was so incensed by the long delay before the Irish reached him that he paid the soldiers their wages of 2d. a day for only ten days, the actual length of time they were with him at the castle, instead of from the start of their long journey from Connacht, which would have been customary.[5]

This kind of treatment was not calculated to make a Gaelic king more amenable to government from Dublin. But Henry III may well have wished to leave the precise nature of his relations with the Gaelic lords as vague as possible, sometimes choosing to regard them as being in the position of tenants-in-chief, and on other occasions keeping them firmly in the lower position of having

---

[1] Matthew Paris, *Chronica majora*, ed. H. R. Luard (Rolls Series, 7 vols, London, 1872–83), iv, 481–4.

[2] *Close rolls, 1242–7*, pp 254–5.

[3] *Misc. Ir. Annals*, p. 125.

[4] *Ann. Conn.*, p. 85.

[5] *Cal. pat. rolls, 1232–47*, p. 461.

mesne lords between them and him. When it suited he sought military service, aids, and subsidies as he did from the other tenants in chief. But for the most part he backed the claims of the settlers, like the de Burghs, to have superior lordship over the Irish. It is clear that this was resented in Gaelic Ireland and was one of the main irritants which in the course of time was to cause many of them to deny the lordship of the English king in Ireland. It was stated as a grievance in the Irish appeal to Pope John XXII in *c.* 1317 that the settlers had craftily caused dissensions between the Gaelic lords and the kings of England, so that they could not of their own free will hold their lands directly from them.[1] There is plenty of evidence to show that many of them did wish to become tenants in chief, but were not given the chance. It suited the settlers; but in the long run it was to be fatal for the king's interests in Ireland. This never worried Henry III. His interests were elsewhere and Ireland can only very rarely have caught his attention. It did not trouble him too much when in 1254 he decided to free himself from most of his responsibilities there and hand them over to his son, the Lord Edward.

[1] Curtis & McDowell, *Ir. hist. docs.*, p. 44.

CHAPTER VII

The years of crisis, 1254–1315

JAMES LYDON

ON 14 February 1254 Henry III granted Ireland to his son and heir Edward, as part of an extensive package which included Chester, Bristol, the Channel Islands, Gascony, and lands and castles in Wales and England.[1] The creation of such an appanage was intended to provide Edward with a suitable income of 15,000 marks annually, and Ireland was to supply only a portion of that sum. Furthermore, the king reserved to himself the towns and counties of Dublin, Limerick, and Athlone, and 'all the crosses and custodies of vacant churches' (in effect, royal rights over the church), which greatly diminished the value of the grant. Even though the king subsequently, on 20 July, granted Dublin, Limerick, and Athlone to Edward, he still reserved his ecclesiastical regalian rights.[2] There was one other, and an important, reservation mentioned in the July charter: 'provided that the land of Ireland shall never be separated from the crown of England, and no one but Edward and his heirs, kings of England, shall ever claim or have any right in that land'.[3] This public statement of inalienability is a landmark in the history of Anglo-Irish relations: the lordship of Ireland was now inseparable from the English crown and the king of England was *ipso facto* always the lord of Ireland. There was no question, then, of Henry divesting himself of his lordship or of Edward formally assuming it. The king, in all his charters, continued to style himself *dominus Hibernie*, the Lord Edward using the simple style of *illustris regis Anglie primogenitus*.[4] So, on 21 July 1254, the king exercised his rights, established in Magna Carta, of levying an aid on Ireland for making his eldest son a knight; and shortly afterwards imposed another aid for marrying his eldest daughter.[5] He also continued to

---

[1] Rymer, *Foedera*, I, i, 270. See the comments of J. R. Studd, 'The Lord Edward and King Henry III' in *I.H.R. Bull.*, l (1977), pp 4–19.

[2] *Cal. doc. Ire., 1252–84*, no. 371.

[3] This was echoing the words of the February charter which created the appanage: 'so however that all the aforesaid lands and castles shall never be separated from the crown; neither shall it be possible for the aforesaid Edward, either by gift or sale, to alienate any of the above mentioned lands and castles, but they shall remain an integral part of the kingdom of England forever'.

[4] Studd, 'Edward and Henry III', pp 6–7, 14–15.

[5] *Cal. doc. Ire., 1254–84*, nos 373 and 377.

exercise his rights over the church. It was he who assented to the election of Geoffrey of St John as bishop of Ferns in March 1254, and who ordered the justiciar to restore the temporalities to him when the election was confirmed by the archbishop of Dublin and the new bishop had sworn fealty.[1] The revenues from vacant major benefices continued to be received by the king, through the escheator, who thus acquired a higher status.

At the same time Edward had to be allowed to enjoy all the rights which belonged to any lord over lands which he possessed. Wardship, marriage, and escheats produced a considerable revenue which the escheator collected on his behalf. He had his own seneschal in Ireland, Richard de la Rochelle, who looked after his interests. His rights over land were unambiguously recognised by the king in March 1254, when arrangements were made to provide the king's brother with 500 librates of land. These had already been promised by Henry before the February grant to Edward, whose consent was now required before the arrangement could be completed.[2] And Edward lost no time in ordering revenues to be delivered to the treasurer of his exchequer at Bristol.[3] By 13 August 1254, 555 marks of his Irish revenues had already reached his wardrobe at Bordeaux.[4] These revenues were collected by his receiver in Ireland, acting under the supervision of his seneschal, who of necessity had to use facilities provided by the royal administration in the lordship.

In practice, therefore, Edward began to assume rights of lordship. On 7 July 1255 he sent his own seal into Ireland and ordered the chancellor to use it in future, even though the king did not withdraw his seal until the following 16 May.[5] His seneschal, Richard de la Rochelle, was already acting as deputy to the justiciar, John fitz Geoffrey, whom he succeeded in May 1256.[6] Thereafter, apart from exceptional occasions (such as the change in government during the barons' war in England), the justiciars seem to have been appointed by Edward as if he were in fact lord of Ireland.

But the situation was untidy. The king still reserved his rights and even as late as 1272, when Maurice fitz Maurice was appointed justiciar, the appointment was confirmed both by the king and those acting for Edward, who was away on crusade.[7] On 28 October 1272 the king wrote that 'we have discovered for certain' that Edward intended to appoint a justiciar 'not consulting us', and ordered that no one should be intendant to any justiciar appointed 'without our letters patent by our assent and counsel'.[8] After the justiciar William of Dene died in October 1261, it was to the king that the treasurer, the bishop of Meath,

---

[1] *Cal. doc. Ire., 1254–84*, nos 337 and 340.

[2] Ibid., no. 343.   [3] Ibid., no. 359.

[4] Ibid., no. 381; full text in Richardson & Sayles, *Admin. Ire.*, p. 225. In late July the king received 2,300 marks from Ireland in his wardrobe in Gascony (*Cal. doc. Ire., 1252–84*, no. 382).

[5] Ibid., nos 453, 500. Edward had already addressed the treasurer and barons of the Dublin exchequer as his officials (ibid., no. 419).

[6] Richardson & Sayles, *Admin. Ire.*, p. 78.   [7] Ibid., p. 228.

[8] Rymer, *Foedera*, I, i, 373. The fear of 'danger to his inheritance' expressed in the letter may have been the immediate cause for interference, so that no alienation might take place.

wrote, asking him to appoint a new justiciar, as well as a new chancellor.[1] Furthermore, it was to the king that appeals could be carried out of Edward's courts in Ireland, well illustrated in a case which was heard in the famous Oxford parliament of 1258. The abbot of Mellifont claimed in the common bench in Dublin that 'without the lord king he could not reply there' and the defendant was therefore summoned to the king's court in England.[2] The king was still the superior lord. When Edward, probably late in 1254, levied a subsidy on land in aid of the war in Ulster, the lords of Leinster protested to the king on the ground that neither they nor their seneschals had consented. Henry ordered the levy to be postponed.[3]

It is clear, then, that even if Edward began to usurp the rights of lordship in Ireland, his father still retained and occasionally exercised the powers that legally belonged to the true lord. Responsibility was thus divided under what has been described as 'something of a condominium'.[4] This was hardly a satisfactory situation. Coupled with Edward's lack of real interest in Ireland it made good government difficult. From 1254 until the accession of Edward as king in 1272, there were no fewer than eleven different men at the head of the Irish government.[5] The contrast with the earlier period, one of much greater stability, is startling. From 1232, when Henry III assumed personal responsibility for Ireland, until 1254, only two justiciars were appointed. This frequent changing of chief governors under the Lord Edward naturally produced great instability and only encouraged the dissident elements in the lordship.

At no time did the young Edward display any sustained interest in Ireland. When his needs required it, he exploited his Irish resources. He used the revenues to pay his debts, to supply him with cash in Gascony, or to buy food in Ireland for his troops overseas. In June 1255, for example, he ordered his Irish officials to ship a large quantity of wheat to Gascony. At the same time he was looking for more money, and Edward's instructions were that payment for the wheat was to be postponed as long as possible, as all available cash was to be sent on to him.[6]

Edward's responsibilities in Wales soon involved him in war there. According to the English chronicler, Matthew Paris, he threatened to unleash Irishmen, whom he had already summoned, against the Welsh, with such effect that Llywelyn ap Gruffydd actually gathered a fleet to hold them off by sea. Irish records lend some support to this. Payments to about thirty ships, carrying six

[1] G. O. Sayles, *Documents on the affairs of Ireland before the king's council* (I.M.C., Dublin, 1979), no. 6.

[2] H. G. Richardson and G. O. Sayles, 'The Irish parliaments of Edward I' in *R.I.A. Proc.*, xxxviii (1929), sect. C, p. 134.

[3] *Cal. doc. Ire., 1282–4*, no. 428.

[4] Richardson & Sayles, *Admin. Ire.*, p. 10.

[5] This includes Geoffrey de Geneville, who acted on behalf of Richard de la Rochelle from Richard's capture in Dec. 1264 till his release in Apr. 1265.

[6] *Cal. doc. Ire., 1252–84*, no. 446.

hundred horses, are recorded, which suggests that a force of Irish cavalry did participate in the fighting in Wales. That was in the autumn of 1256. The following year two troops of Irish foot-soldiers fought in Wales, one in the north and the other in the south. In addition, some crossbowmen, smiths, carpenters, and the surprisingly high number of eighty ditchers (who were presumably employed in digging defensive earthworks) joined Edward. Brattices, which had been constructed in Dublin, Drogheda, and Dungarvan, were shipped in a prefabricated state. Timber, lime, and a large supply of cloth (for the troops at Cardigan) were sent over. Cargoes of wheat, oats, salted meat, a great quantity of fish, and much wine were despatched from Dublin and other ports. Finally, more than £2,000 of Irish treasure was brought to Chester, which was the place of muster for the troops.[1]

The Irish records for the period of Edward's lordship are almost wholly lacking, so that it is impossible to follow the course of events in this crucial period in any detail. But all the evidence points to the lack of any real interest on the part of either Edward or his father. The shared responsibility was disastrous. Attention turned to Ireland only when acute financial need demanded that every possible source of revenue should be exploited to the full. Even during the barons' war, neither side seemed to think it worth while involving Ireland. There is one peculiar bit of evidence, however, which suggests that King Henry at least had considered the possibility of using Ireland in a way that would infringe the rights of his son there. On 8 September 1261, at a time when the king was busy gathering all his resources because of the insurgent barons, he ordered the Irish treasurer (nominally an official of the Lord Edward) to collect all the money 'of the issues of Ireland' and to store it in Dublin until he was otherwise instructed. No expenses were to be paid out of this fund unless the land was in such danger (*maximo in periculo*) that it would be necessary to apply the money to its defence.[2] The plan came to nothing in the end. But the king continued to exploit his financial rights in Ireland right up to the end of his reign.

THE English civil war seems to have had little effect on Ireland, even though many of the great absentee lords of Irish estates were so heavily involved: men like the earl of Norfolk (lord of Carlow), William de Valence (lord of Wexford), and the earl of Gloucester (lord of Kilkenny). One might expect their divided allegiances to be reflected in Ireland, but there is no evidence to support this. As we shall see, there were serious disturbances in Ireland at this time; but domestic circumstances are sufficient to explain these. The only occasion on which the constitutional crisis in England had certain repercussions in Ireland was in the summer of 1265, at a time when Simon de Montfort was in the

---

[1] J. F. Lydon, 'Three exchequer records' in *R.I.A. Proc.*, lxv (1966), sect. C, pp 14–15; Gilbert, *Viceroys*, p. 518.

[2] *Close rolls, 1259—61*, p. 434.

ascendancy in England and made an attempt to deprive the Lord Edward of his rights in Ireland. On 10 June letters were sent to Ireland announcing that Edward had forfeited his rights and should no longer be obeyed. By this time Edward had joined those marcher lords who had continued to hold out against de Montfort and the new English government.[1] It was feared that he would go overseas,[2] and it is likely that de Montfort was trying to insure that no help would be forthcoming in Ireland. In the event Ireland did not matter. The battle of Evesham in August, the death of de Montfort, and the ultimate defeat of his party in England saw the full restoration of Henry III and the ascendancy of Edward. Though noted in the Anglo-Irish chronicles, none of this had political repercussions in Ireland.

These same letters also referred to the 'discords' between Maurice fitz Gerald and Walter de Burgh. The king said that he had heard that this had been 'appeased' and he urged de Burgh 'to cherish mutual charity between them, abstaining from those things which may cause the sparks of discord to come forth'.[3] Earlier letters in March referred to the 'great dissensions' between 'certain nobles and magnates of Ireland'.[4] The disturbances referred to arose out of a notorious incident on the feast of St Nicholas, 6 December 1264, when the justiciar (Richard de la Rochelle), Theobald Butler, and John de Cogan were seized at Castledermot by the Geraldines under Maurice fitz Maurice and Maurice fitz Gerald. The magnates seem to have been assembled for a council and there is no ready explanation for the unprecedented capture of the justiciar. But the reaction in Connacht suggests that the real cause was rivalry between de Burgh and Geraldine interests.[5] While the Geraldines held their prisoners in Lea and Dunamase castles, Walter de Burgh attacked and seized Geraldine castles and manors in Connacht. But more than Connacht was involved. Widespread disturbances followed, tantamount to a civil war. The annals record that 'a great part of Ireland was ruined between them', which is indicative of an unusual degree of destruction. So serious was the situation that Geoffrey de Geneville, who assumed control of the government in the absence of de la Rochelle, prepared Dublin castle to withstand a siege.[6] In the south the citizens of New Ross, alarmed by the war, hurriedly decided to enclose their town.[7] The alarm of the English government is exposed in letters of 16 February 1265, which asked the archbishop of Dublin to take over the government, because of the disturbance caused by the 'discord between the

---

[1] There is one odd feature of these letters, which suggests that de Montfort may not have been responsible for them. The great de Montfort victory of the previous year is referred to as 'that detestable battle of Lewes' (*Cal. pat. rolls, 1258–66*, p. 432).

[2] Ibid., p. 429.   [3] Ibid., p. 432.   [4]*Close rolls, 1264–8*, p. 107.

[5] *Ann. Conn.*, p. 143. In Clyn's annals it is 'the war between the Geraldines and Walter de Burgo, earl of Ulster' that is first noted, followed by the Castledermot incident (p. 8), and in the annals of Connacht the 'great war' in Connacht between them is equally given prominence.

[6] *P.R.I. rep. D.K. 35*, p. 47. A total of over £342 was spent. The royal castle at Arklow was similarly provisioned (P.R.O.I., RC 11/2).

[7] Shields, 'Walling of New Ross', p. 28.

nobles and magnates of that land, whereby great danger may ensue to the king and Edward his son and the whole land of Ireland'. He was also commanded to take castles into the king's hands and to munition them.[1] The archbishop quickly sent a report on the 'great dissensions . . . between the nobles and magnates of that country', so that by the late spring of 1265 civil war was raging in Ireland.[2]

Geoffrey de Geneville mounted an expedition against the Geraldines, though we cannot tell with what success. But in mid-April he was able to persuade the dissidents to come to Dublin and make peace. An assembly of magnates met and agreed to a series of ordinances embodying peace terms. Of these, only one is known: that all persons 'disseised and expelled from their lands and tenements during the aforesaid disturbances shall recover their lands and tenements without writ or plea'.[3] The magnates present swore to abide by these provisions, and subsequently they were given the force of conciliar ordinances by Edward and his English courts. By the early summer Richard de la Rochelle was once more at the head of the government and peace had been restored.

The scale of this disturbance was unique at this time. But it does reflect the lack of control which existed at the centre and the lack of real direction coming from England. Others were to take advantage of such propitious circumstances to pursue their interests at local level, thus causing hardship and distress and often, too, contributing to the growing menace of Gaelic lords threatening the land of peace. A well documented example is the quarrel between Henry de Mandeville and William fitz Warin in Ulster during the minority of the young earl, when the earldom was in the hands of Edward. De Mandeville had for long been bailiff of Twescard (Tuaiscert, north County Antrim), and he was bitterly resentful when fitz Warin was appointed seneschal of Ulster. A fierce struggle followed which lasted for years. An inquisition by fitz Warin purported to reveal the former extortions of de Mandeville, his support of Irish traitors, and collusion in the murder of loyal English. A letter from 'the whole commonalty of Ulster, as well of English as of Irish' to the lord Edward's regents in England vigorously supported fitz Warin, who had 'fully restored peace between English and Irish, and by the security of good hostages had settled the whole land of Ulster to the advantage of the lord Edward and the profit of the community'. It blamed de Mandeville for 'the state of ruin' in which the land had previously stood and said that if de Mandeville were restored in Twescard 'the commonalty will rise against him', because they 'are unwilling to subject to war and turbulence the land of Ulster now settled in peace'.[4] That this was

---

[1] *Cal. pat. rolls, 1258—66*, pp 406–7. [2] *Close rolls, 1264—8*, p. 107.
[3] Richardson & Sayles, *Ir. parl. in middle ages*, p. 59, n. 15; Sayles, *Affairs of Ire.*, nos 9–10. De Geneville wrote that the 'land was commonly moved to war' and that 'there was common war in those parts'. See also *Cal. doc. Ire., 1252—84*, pp 204–5, which also refers to this period as 'the time of the disturbance'.
[4] *Cal. doc. Ire., 1252—84*, no. 929.

instigated by fitz Warin need not be doubted. But neither is there any doubt of the violent opposition to de Mandeville in some parts. The mayor and community of Carrickfergus complained that it was at the instigation of the former bailiff that Ó Néill and others had raised war and that de Mandeville's supporters had burned five vills and three mills, with 2,000 crannocks of wheat, and proposed 'to destroy and lay waste the land' until they 'were driven to confusion' by fitz Warin and his supporters.[1] Subsequently de Mandeville was killed and his sons then brought the quarrel into the king's court, where they prosecuted fitz Warin. The new earl of Ulster restored the de Mandevilles to office and the end of the story is lost in the obscurity of proceedings in the liberty court of Ulster.

The earldom as a whole was hardly disturbed by this faction fight. Certainly the accounts of the seneschal show an income of nearly £1,400 for less than two years ending in January 1276, which is well up to normal and suggests a continuous prosperity.[2] This is a tribute to the firm foundations laid by Hugh de Lacy and Walter de Burgh. But in Twescard itself the damage was severe. Naturally it was the lands of those involved which suffered most. Fitz Warin was later allowed £105 'for decrease of certain lands and rents from which he could receive nothing owing to the war which arose on the death of Walter de Burgh'.[3]

Private wars of this kind demanded that the magnates have at their disposal bands of armed retainers, the raw material of what some modern historians call 'bastard feudalism'. Conditions in Ireland from the time of the invasion made private armies a normal feature of frontier life. Alliances with cooperative Gaelic lords also provided many a feudatory with armed men. But a more ominous development in the second half of the thirteenth century was the growth of the indenture system, by which men entered the service of a lord, accepted his fee and wore his livery, and promised to follow him into battle when the demand came. The earliest Irish military indenture of this type to survive comes from 1289. It involved John fitz Thomas of Offaly, who at that time was building up his military strength. On 26 April he and Peter de Bermingham mutually sealed an indenture by which Peter became a member of John's household, received his robes, and promised him service against all men, 'saving his fealty to the king'.[4] De Bermingham was an important midland magnate in his own right, liable to be summoned to parliament, for example; his allegiance to fitz Thomas is a remarkable example of the way in which the greatest of the magnates were to group together in self-interest. The factions thus formed were to be a permanent threat to the peace.[5]

---

[1] Ibid., no. 952.   [2] Orpen, *Normans*, iii, 137.

[3] *Cal. doc. Ire., 1252–84*, no. 2130.

[4] *Red Bk Kildare*, no. 11. There are three more indentures from 1290 and 1291, fortunate survivals in the chartulary, which suggest that fitz Thomas was bringing together a formidable array of local magnates in his service; ibid., nos 12, 14, 15.

[5] The many extended families, or lineages, which dominated Anglo-Ireland no less than Gaelic Ireland were a further complication. See the important paper by Robin Frame, 'Power and society in the lordship of Ireland, 1271–1377' in *Past & Present*, no. 76 (1977), pp 3–33, and his *English lordship in Ireland, 1318–1361* (Oxford, 1982), pp 27–51.

The purpose behind this particular indenture is not immediately clear, though it seems to have resulted from fitz Thomas's responsibilities in guarding the marchlands of Offaly. Nevertheless the armed retainers acquired in this way were to prove indispensable in the bitter faction fights in which the lord of Offaly was involved, such as his clash with William de Vesci, lord of Kildare. The quarrel seems to have begun on an official level, after de Vesci became justiciar, over franchisal rights claimed by fitz Thomas and challenged by the government. But there was also a personal clash of rival local interests.[1] As lord of Kildare de Vesci seems to have resented fitz Thomas's growing powerful influence in the area and his relations with potentially dangerous Irishmen. In Connacht, too, there was a confrontation. The government had 'made' another king there after the death of Magnus Ó Conchobair in 1293. This was Áed Ó Conchobair, who shortly after was taken prisoner by fitz Thomas. According to the annals a large number of Áed's followers were killed and his cattle were seized.[2] Áed was eventually restored and it is no surprise to find him taking revenge by attacking and destroying the Geraldine castle of Sligo, thus provoking a new war against him by fitz Thomas, who was accompanied, significantly, by Peter de Bermingham.[3] By then the earl of Ulster, who had a vested interest in the Ó Conchobair kingship, had necessarily become involved and before long he, too, was to be a victim of Geraldine spleen. Old enmities died hard.

Meanwhile de Vesci had tried to turn the tables on fitz Thomas in Offaly. He summoned the royal service to Kildare, ostensibly to make war on Irish rebels, but in reality to march against fitz Thomas.[4] Fitz Thomas had certainly allied himself with the Irish. Anglo-Irish annals record the capture of de Vesci's castle of Kildare in 1294, when the justiciar was absent in England, and add that 'Kildare and the country round about was despoiled by the English and the Irish. Calvagh [Ó Conchobair] burned the rolls and tallies of the county.'[5] Later, during the eyre of Kildare in 1297, it was revealed that fitz Thomas was responsible for 'the robbery of the town and castle of Kildare', with various named O'Connors.[6] And closely associated with fitz Thomas in these felonious acts was the same Peter de Bermingham who had accepted his livery in 1289. Fortunately, before a full-scale civil war broke out, the service was cancelled by the king who wrote that 'it tends to the injury of the king and of the people of Ireland'.[7] Late in 1293 the English parliament received a series of petitions, including some from fitz Thomas, complaining of de Vesci.[8] The justiciar was naturally incensed. In April 1294 he caused fitz Thomas to be summoned

[1] H. G. Richardson and G. O. Sayles, *Rotuli parliamentorum Anglie hactenus inediti* (R.H.S., London, 1935), pp 33–5, 43–5.
[2] *Ann. Conn.*, p. 189.   [3] Ibid., p. 193.
[4] *Cal. close rolls, 1288—96*, p. 291.
[5] *Chartul. St Mary's, Dublin*, ii, 323.
[6] *Cal. justic. rolls Ire., 1295—1303*, p. 190.
[7] *Cal. doc. Ire., 1293—1301*, no. 62.
[8] Ibid., no. 106; full text in Richardson & Sayles, *Rot. parl. hact.*, pp 30—45.

before the council in Dublin to answer a charge of defamation. When fitz Thomas appeared he answered the charge with a sensational accusation. He swore that de Vesci had said to him

that the people of Ireland were the most miserable he knew, for they would be, if they willed anything, great lords and would well maintain the lands and franchises of Ireland, notwithstanding the king. If they knew as much of the king as he knew they would value the king very little, for he is the most perverse and dastardly knight of his kingdom.

Here was treason. But there was more: 'things', said fitz Thomas, 'which were against the king and his state, and I warn the men of the council of this matter to save my fealty'.[1] The outraged de Vesci naturally denied all of this and offered to defend his innocence. Two days later the council met again and fitz Thomas repeated his accusations under oath. The parties concerned were then summoned before the king at Westminster. De Vesci arrived in full armour to fight a judicial duel, but his rival did not appear. The king rejected his demand for judgement by default and soon had the whole thing quashed on a technicality.[2]

Later in the same year, 1294, fitz Thomas was responsible for throwing the whole lordship into confusion, when he seized the earl of Ulster and held him in his castle of Lea. The annals state starkly: 'This led to confusion throughout Ireland.'[3] There is confirmation of the widespread disturbance in the inability of the collectors of the subsidy then current to make any collection because of the confusion. The bald entry on the receipt roll for Hilary term 1295 reads: 'Nothing in this term on account of the war and the capture of the earl of Ulster.'[4] The chancellor later petitioned the king for compensation for his 'great costs' in guarding the land after the capture.[5] The castle of Ferns, which might be thought to be far removed from the conflict, was put in a state of defence 'for fear of the disturbance had in Ireland on account of the taking of the earl of Ulster'.[6] No wonder that the record of the eyre of Kildare in 1297 represents jurors in Kildare and Offaly recalling this period as 'the time of disturbance', or even more starkly as 'the disturbance'.[7] This eyre revealed a terrible, indeed frightening, situation in the midlands, where lawlessness was rampant and all control seemed to be gone. Fitz Thomas and his followers went on the rampage, terrified the people, and virtually held the country to ransom. Crime of every kind increased enormously.[8]

---

[1] *Cal. doc. Ire., 1293–1301*, no. 147; full text in *Rot. parl.*, i, 127–8. De Vesci was also supposed to have accused Edward of cowardice before the battle of Kenilworth during the barons' war.

[2] *Rot. parl.*, i, 132–4.   [3] *Ann. Conn.*, p. 193.

[4] *Cal. doc. Ire., 1293–1301*, no. 191. Twenty-five years later the collectors in Meath were petitioning in parliament to be allowed arrears in their account which 'could not be levied because of the capture of Richard de Burgh, earl of Ulster, by John fitz Thomas and after disturbances elsewhere in Ireland' (*Rot. pat. Hib.*, pp 27–8).

[5] Sayles, *Affairs of Ire.*, p. 40.

[6] *Cal. justic. rolls Ire., 1295–1303*, p. 148.

[7] Ibid., p. 176.   [8] Ibid., pp 167–208.

ELSEWHERE, too, there was widespread disturbance. The treasurer had allowance for payments to various members of the council 'in going to various parts of Ireland with an armed force to establish the king's peace which had been disturbed by the capture of Richard de Burgh, earl of Ulster'.[1] Naturally Gaelic Ireland took advantage of this. The Irish of the mountains, who had been at peace for many years, wasted Leinster, according to a chronicler, and burned Newcastle and other vills.[2] A quick settlement of the quarrel, leading to the release of de Burgh, was an urgent necessity if a complete breakdown was to be avoided. A parliament in Kilkenny managed to free the earl though not until 12 March 1295, nearly three months after his capture, and subsequently fitz Thomas and his men received a pardon from the justiciar.[3] But the king was not satisfied that the danger had been averted. In August 1295 he summoned fitz Thomas to England to answer for his crimes.[4] But there were further outbreaks and in October the king wrote to the chief protagonists and insisted that because 'disturbances may easily arise in Ireland unless a remedy be applied', they were to cease under pain of forfeiture 'inflicting damage on one another'.[5] At the same time John Wogan was appointed justiciar. Not only did he succeed in getting de Burgh and fitz Thomas to agree to a truce, but he brought both of them, with large contingents of men, to serve together in Scotland in the campaign of 1296. By 1298 Wogan at last had persuaded the two to settle their differences. It was then made clear that the real source of their quarrel lay in Connacht, where Geraldine aggrandisement threatened de Burgh ascendancy. Fitz Thomas first of all agreed to surrender a large area of land as compensation for the injury to de Burgh and then agreed to pull out of Connacht altogether. His lands there and in Ulster were given to the earl in exchange for de Burgh lands in Leinster and Munster. Thus both men had in effect agreed on their respective areas of influence for the future. In typical medieval fashion they also agreed to bind the new relationship through a marriage of fitz Thomas's son to one of the earl's daughters.[6] The great quarrel was over, but not forgotten. Too much had happened and opposite sides were likely to be taken in the future, as during the O'Brien civil war in Thomond.

Fitz Thomas clearly emerged as a ruthless man, determined to augment his power and influence at almost any cost. He certainly was largely responsible for 'the time of disturbance' in the midlands and encouraged many Irish to attack English settlements in order to hurt his enemy de Vesci. This was conducive to disorder at a time when the stability of the lordship was being undermined. The gradual increase in lawlessness, which is a marked feature of the second half of the thirteenth century, is an index of the failure of the Irish administration to cope with the problems of the lordship. As we have seen,

[1] *Cal. doc. Ire., 1293—1301*, p. 123.   [2] *Chartul. St Mary, Dublin*, ii, 324.
[3] Ibid., p. 232; *Cal. justic. rolls Ire., 1295—1303*, p. 191.
[4] *Cal. doc. Ire., 1293—1301*, no. 246.   [5] Ibid., no. 268.
[6] *Cal. justic. rolls Ire., 1295—1303*, pp 234–6.

Edward's neglect of his Irish responsibilities, and the rapid turnover in chief governors before he became king, resulted in unstable government. The system that had been so carefully constructed under Henry III was no longer functioning efficiently. Perhaps the most significant illustration of this is the way in which the revenues declined. When the account of the treasurer, Geoffrey de Tourville, was audited in 1253 it showed a receipt of £5,052 from 14 May 1250 to 29 September 1251.¹ The next extant treasurer's account is that of the bishop of Meath, from Michaelmas 1270 to Michaelmas 1272, recording a receipt of £2,085 and £2,593 respectively for each of the two years; so that during the period after 1254 revenues seem to have declined by about half.² By the early years of Edward's reign many accounts were outstanding.³ This reflected the disturbed state of much of Ireland, particularly Connacht and Ulster, in the king's hand because the heir was a minor, and the south where Ó Briain in particular was causing trouble.⁴

After he became king in 1272 Edward seems to have taken a serious look at Ireland and in 1273, while still away on crusade, he appointed his friend Geoffrey de Geneville as justiciar in an attempt to stem the growing disorder in the lordship.⁵ Geoffrey was with him in the Holy Land and the Anglo-Irish annals suggest that he came straight from there to Ireland.⁶ He was to be given every help in carrying out his commission. All the issues of escheats and wardships were assigned to him, including the valuable issues of vacant bishoprics.⁷ This would have included the revenues from the vacant archbishopric of Dublin, a valuable asset that between July 1271 and September 1277 brought in a revenue of over £8,000, of which more than £1,200 came into the treasury.⁸ De Geneville, in fact, does not seem to have been short of money: he received £3,373 in his first year, £2,314 in his second, and £2,227 in his third.⁹ But his expenses left him with a small deficit each year and it is a salutary reminder of the problems that royal officials encountered in trying to recover debts owing to them that as late as 1305 Geoffrey was still trying to get his money. He was also claiming expenses incurred by himself and his son 'in guarding the marches by order of the council of the king in Ireland'.¹⁰

Geoffrey was also given wide powers, such as the right to appoint and

---

¹ Lydon, 'Three exchequer records', p. 19.

² P.R.O., E. 101/230/2, m. 3. The total in *Cal. doc. Ire., 1252–84*, p. 14, is wrong. It is significant that of the total account well over two-thirds (i.e. £3,300) was paid to the justiciar 'for the pacification of Ireland'.

³ *Cal. close rolls, 1272–9*, p. 108.   ⁴ Otway-Ruthven, *Med. Ire.*, p. 200.

⁵ No patent of appointment survives. But his enrolled account as justiciar began 19 Aug. 1273, which must be the date on which he assumed office in Ireland (*P.R.I. rep. D.K. 36*, p. 40).

⁶ *Chartul. St Mary's, Dublin*, ii, 317.

⁷ *Cal. pat. rolls, 1272–81*, p. 29; *Cal. doc. Ire., 1252–84*, no. 977.

⁸ Pipe roll 5 Edw. I in *P.R.I. rep. D.K. 36*, p. 36.

⁹ Ibid., pp 40–41. Compare with the receipt of his successor, Robert d'Ufford: 24 December 1276–29 September 1277, £2,080; 29 September 1277–16 January 1278, £1,383 (ibid., p. 35; *Cal. doc. Ire., 1252–84*, no. 1412).

¹⁰ *Cal. justic. rolls Ire., 1305–7*, pp 72–3.

remove sheriffs, and was given special authority in the earldom of Ulster, then in the king's hand, where fitz Warin and de Mandeville were at open war.[1] De Geneville personally inspected the earldom and seems to have restored some semblance of order.[2] But his main task was clearly elsewhere: to improve the quality of central and local government and to see to the pacification of those areas which had become openly hostile in recent times. In neither was he very successful.

These were years of disturbance in Ireland. In 1275 the justiciar was given permission 'to receive money and other necessaries at his discretion in passing through manors and other places in that land, the king now reflecting that the perturbation of those parts is of long standing and not yet settled'.[3] The normal routine of payments into the exchequer was thus to be disturbed, indicating a breakdown in the regular flow of cash to Dublin. War was now widespread, vividly reflected in the escheator's accounts for 1272–6. His allowance on pipe roll 4 Edward I include payments to the army of Connacht on an expedition to Glenmalure in 1275; to the army going 'in the first advance made by the justiciar against the king's enemies' of Glenmalure in 1274; to William Cadel 'to succour Odymsy against hostile attacks'; to wards at Baltinglass, Ballymore, Saggart; rebuilding the castle of Roscommon; for horses lost 'in the pass of Slydale . . . with the army going against the king's enemies of Slefblam'; and so on.[4] As we shall see, de Geneville led a series of expeditions against the Irish of the Leinster mountains, trying to penetrate their mountain fastness of Glenmalure. But he failed miserably. Surprisingly for one who had such experience in Europe and on crusade, he showed no real capacity as a soldier.

Nor had he much success in his attempts to improve the quality of the administration. A series of royal writs in September 1274 enlarged his powers and set him to correct 'divers injuries and transgressions committed against the king and others in that country'.[5] Part of the intended reform was the appointment of a new treasurer, Stephen de Fulbourn, the bishop of Waterford, who ironically enough was later accused of malpractice on a massive scale. The third man closely associated with the attempted reform was the escheator, John de Sandford, later archbishop of Dublin and a remarkable chief governor for a brief period.

There is some evidence that the new administration was vigorous in attempts to cope with pressing problems. But the real test of its success lies in its ability to increase ordinary revenues derived from escheats, rents, farms, profits of justice, and other traditional sources. By this test it was a failure. The index is supplied by extant figures for receipts at the Irish exchequer, which show no substantial improvement: Michaelmas 1274–Michaelmas 1275, £2,295;

---

[1] *Cal. doc. Ire., 1252—84*, nos 1021, 1024–5, 1032.
[2] Ibid., no. 1088; *P.R.I. rep. D.K. 36*, p. 33.
[3] *Cal. pat. rolls, 1272—91*, pp 103–4.
[4] *P.R.I. rep. D.K. 36*, p. 33.
[5] *Cal. doc. Ire., 1252—84*, no. 1020. See also nos 1021–7 and 1032.

1275/6, £2,726.[1] It is only after de Geneville had been replaced, at his own urgent request, by Robert d'Ufford, that there is a marked improvement.[2]

1276/7	£3,371
1277/8	£6,114
1278/9	£6,249

Thereafter the receipts fluctuate between five and six thousand pounds, except for brief periods when they were inflated by the receipt of extraordinary taxation.[3]

There can be no doubt that this recovery must be attributed to the new treasurer, Stephen de Fulbourn, a remarkable figure who dominated the Irish administration for some years. Treasurer in 1274, he acted as deputy justiciar from 1280 until he was appointed justiciar in 1281. He still retained the office of treasurer. His brother Walter and nephew Adam between them controlled the chancery from 1283 to 1286, and another nephew, John, was also active in the civil service. This de Fulbourn control was nowhere better illustrated than in the exchequer, where the treasurer assumed responsibility for much of the expenditure which hitherto had been at the discretion of the justiciar.

But if there was an improvement in receipts, there seems to have been a continuing failure to improve standards in both houses of the exchequer. The lack of expertise there is well demonstrated by the surviving original rolls. For example, the issue rolls are primitive in their make-up, with no ordered classification of entries to make reference easy or to enable an audit to proceed smoothly.[4] Some of the entries are too abbreviated to be readily acceptable. Worse, entries are cancelled, altered, and even erased. When de Fulbourn had his accounts audited, the auditors were appalled at the state of his records and refused to allow many items of expenditure which he claimed as treasurer. He was found to owe huge sums to the king. For example, at one stage he was charged with debts amounting to over £13,000.[5] Out of the audit, too, there eventually came a long report on the state of Ireland, which was damning in its exposure of the malpractices of de Fulbourn and other royal officials.[6] For example, among the many serious charges laid against the justiciar were that 'no person can be in any office, whether as sheriff or as constable, unless by his gift' and that 'by reason of the Welsh war he now buys granges of rectors,

---

[1] *Cal. doc. Ire., 1252–84*, nos 1038, 1294.

[2] Ibid., nos 1389, 1496. The figure for 1278–9 is taken from de Fulbourn's enrolled account (P.R.O., E. 372/136 (pipe roll 19 Edw. I), m. 9). *Cal. doc. Ire., 1252–84*, no. 2284, is taken from the view of the account in P.R.O., E. 101/230/10, which is less reliable.

[3] H. G. Richardson and G. O. Sayles, 'Irish revenue, 1278–1384' in *R.I.A. Proc.*, lxii (1962), sect. C, p. 99.

[4] The rolls are conveniently listed in Richardson & Sayles, *Admin. Ire.*, p. 199.

[5] *Cal. doc. Ire., 1285–92*, no. 59. The record said that when he appeared to render his account 'it appeared to the barons that his account was so insufficient and suspicious that it was not by any means to be admitted'. It was nevertheless made, according to which he owed over £33,000! Against this was allowed a number of payments (even though all of them were described by the auditors as 'not testified' or 'not credible') which left a final debt of £13,235. 2s. 10½d.

[6] Ibid., pp 1–15.

abbots and others at a low price'. He was supposed to have become enormously rich by misusing the powers of his office, and detailed evidence was produced to condemn him.

Up to a point, medieval governments tolerated a certain amount of peculation. It was taken for granted, for example, that officials would be bribed in return for favours. The petitions of Adam de la Roche, steward to the countess of Pembroke in Waterford, provide good evidence for this in 1303. For granting a delay in accounting at the exchequer, the treasurer and his clerks received 40s. and 10s. respectively; two barons of the exchequer received 26s. 8d. and the ushers 3s. for a respite in the payment of the service of Dundalk; a justice of the bench received a carcass of beef (cost 3s. 7d.) so that he would be lenient in court.[1] But when peculation reached the stage where it bred inefficiency and impeded the satisfactory working of the administration, it had to be stopped. This seems to have been the case in 1285 when the report on Ireland was made. It condemned the rampant corruption and associated inefficiency in the chancery, the mints of Dublin and Waterford, and above all in the exchequer. For example, it was outraged at the farming of the wool custom to Florentine merchants at a loss, which 'is not to be tolerated'. Altogether it is a fierce indictment of the contemporary administration of Ireland and it seriously alarmed the king.

To be fair to de Fulbourn, the report seems to be very biased against him. Some of the charges are demonstrably untrue. Nor is there any doubt that many of the large sums which he claimed to have spent for the king and which were disallowed by his auditors (one of whom, Nicholas de Clere, was his principal accuser and successor in office as treasurer), were in fact paid by him into the king's wardrobe, where they were recorded. Nor did Stephen lose the trust of the king, who retained him as justiciar until he died in 1288. But too much of the undoubted inefficiency and peculation had been exposed and as treasurer the responsibility was his. So Nicholas de Clere became the new treasurer.

A worse problem than the lack of expertise among the officials of the central government was the unscrupulous profiteering of many local government officials and the general inefficiency of the administration at local level.[2] John de Sandford, who worked closely with de Fulbourn for years, blamed officials in Connacht for 'thwarting' the justiciar.[3] De Fulbourn himself bitterly complained to the king in 1281. He named certain sheriffs who had defaulted: 'they are injurious to the king and more to the people, because they receive the king's money and then go away, having nothing to be distrained by'. These were sheriffs appointed from England and they clearly made it their business to

[1] Richardson & Sayles, *Admin. Ire.*, p. 233.

[2] A. J. Otway-Ruthven, 'Anglo-Irish shire government in the thirteenth century' in *I.H.S.*, v, no. 17 (Mar. 1946), pp 1–28.

[3] *Cal. doc. Ire., 1285—94*, p. 265.

amass as much money as possible before decamping. De Fulbourn wrote rather forlornly: 'How to bring them and Alan Lumbard to judgement is a question.'[1] Lumbard, apparently, had 'received moneys at the exchequer without giving tallies to poor persons', thus depriving them of proof of payment, and at the same time leaving no evidence of receipt against himself. He could thus pocket the lot with impunity. There was some confirmation for de Fulbourn's complaint in a set of ordinance sent to Ireland in 1293, in which the king agreed that sheriffs should be appointed by the Irish treasurer, and not under the great seal of England, 'on which account they have been less obedient to the exchequer of Ireland'.[2] But this problem of delinquent officials in England remained insoluble, and for many years the English government was able to bring few such defaulters to justice.[3]

To a certain extent, too, the problem arose from the obsolete way in which Ireland was shired. The county of Dublin, for example, covered an enormous area that was impossible to administer efficiently. The 1297 parliament expressed the problem well:

The county of Dublin is too much scattered and the parts thereof too far removed from each other and dispersed, as well Ulster and Meath, and then Leinster and the vale of Dublin etc., whereby it less obeys the lord the king in his precepts and those of his courts and also his people is less adequately ruled or governed.[4]

A new county was formed in Ulster, another in Meath, and a third in Kildare. But even this drastic reorganisation did not work out, and the ramshackle structure of the Irish shires was not improved until the early modern period.

With a weak and corrupt central government, it was all too easy for local officials to use their offices in their own interest. There is evidence in abundance concerning those who were caught out and ended in court, or in complaints against others which reached the king. But not all the evidence of malpractice by local officials came out into the open. For example, when Stephen de Fulbourn died, about fifty inquisitions into the conduct of ministers, together with 'secret documents . . . touching conspiracies between English and Irish to wage wars', disappeared in mysterious circumstances from supposedly safe custody in the royal castle of Athlone.[5] Some of the complaints that did reach the king were probably the result of inquiries conducted by John de Sandford when he was acting as chief governor in succession to de Fulbourn. A man of enormous experience in the service of the king, long familiar with the deficiencies of local government through his experience as escheator, he was also as archbishop of

---

[1] *Cal. doc. Ire., 1252–84*, no. 1181. This calendared version is faulty. De Fulbourn complained that sheriffs who returned to England vilified him and out of malice turned friends against him (P.R.O., S.C. 1/17/190). I am grateful to Dr Philomena Connolly who checked the original for me in London.

[2] *Stat. Ire., John–Hen. V*, p. 191.

[3] Richardson & Sayles, *Admin. Ire.*, pp 232–3, 243–5.

[4] *Stat. Ire., John–Hen. V*, p. 197.

[5] *Cal. doc. Ire., 1285–92*, p. 255.

Dublin a powerful figure in Irish politics. It is extraordinary, too, that for most of the period when he was acting as chief governor (7 July 1288 to 10 November 1290) he held the office of chancellor, to which he was appointed on 8 April 1289. This naturally gave him an overriding control over the administration. The vigour with which he attacked the problems of the Gaelic revival in many parts of the lordship is well attested. His ceaseless journeys on diplomatic or military missions took him all over Ireland.[1] Having satisfied himself that

the state of Ireland had been regulated and orders thereupon given to the king's ministers according to the Irish council, the keeper prepared himself to survey the land and the deeds of the ministers aforesaid, so that justice might be done to all and the king's dignity everywhere maintained. Throughout this eyre he caused it to be commanded that all complaining of the king's ministers or others in Ireland should be before him on certain days to receive justice in all things.

So he journeyed through June, July, and August 1290, from Dublin to Drogheda, on to Kells, Mullingar, into Connacht through Roscommon, and via Dunmore, Tuam, and Athenry to Loughrea (where he was entertained by the earl of Ulster). From there he went to Athassell via Terryglass, Nenagh, Thurles, and Cashel and then to Limerick, Kilmallock, Cork, Youghal, Bewley in Waterford, Stradbally, Waterford, and New Ross, and finished at Ferns on 17 August.[2] We do not know what the results of these inquiries were, but they must have formed part of the pattern of evidence that was building up in England and causing the government there to worry in particular over the financial administration of Ireland.

Nicholas de Clere, the treasurer, was now the target of a whole series of charges in the Westminster parliament of 1290 and of complaints before the king and council.[3] As a result, there was a full audit of his accounts in 1292 at Westminster. This revealed what one of the barons of the English exchequer called 'great offences in the exchequer of Dublin' and Nicholas de Clere was dismissed from office. For these offences and because of the debt of £717 which he was found to owe the king, he was committed to the tower of London. When last we hear of him, in April 1300, de Clere is still a prisoner, though now in Dublin castle.[4]

De Clere's successor in office, William de Estdene, had been present during the long audit at Westminster. Before he set out for Dublin William consulted with the treasurer and barons of the English exchequer about the state of the exchequer in Dublin and as a result of their deliberations the ordinance of 1292 was produced, setting out the hierarchy of officers and their respective fees.[5] It brought the Irish exchequer more into line with the English one and also estab-

---

[1] *Cal. doc. Ire., 1285—92*, pp 265—77, for his 'expenses of journies to divers parts of Ireland'.
[2] Ibid., pp 274—6.
[3] Ibid., pp 318—20, nos 591, 593, 595, 598, 997—9.
[4] Ibid., nos 964, 1098; *1293—1301*, no. 743.
[5] *The Red Book of the exchequer*, ed. Hubert Hall (3 vols, London, 1896), iii, 974—6.

lished an additional counter-roll of receipt and issues as a check on the treasurer. There were other reforms of a minor nature, but not the kind of revolutionary changes that might have been expected after the scandals of the de Fulbourn and de Clere regimes. One important result was to make the compilation of the main exchequer rolls more sophisticated and easier to use for reference. The issue roll, for example, was now divided into major sections for ease of reference: fees and necessary expenses; foreign expenses; the war in Scotland; the war against the Irish, and so on. The receipt rolls now had daily, weekly, and monthly totals enrolled and the receipts themselves were divided into ordinary and foreign receipts. But the major change which resulted was the practice of an annual audit of the Irish treasurer's accounts at Westminster.[1] In theory this would have prevented the kind of corruption that had been revealed in the audits. But it never happened in practice, since audits were held irregularly and often years after the account had closed.[2] And the corruption continued unabated in the Dublin exchequer, with repeated scandals involving the treasurer and other leading officials.[3]

ONE of the reasons why King Edward was so anxious about the financial administration of Ireland was his determination to exploit to the full his resources there. As we saw, the grant of 1254 was intended to contribute to his annual income and from then on he began to draw on the revenues of the lordship to help him meet various commitments, especially in time of war. Once he became king he made even greater use of Ireland, so much so that during the last ten years or so of his reign the Irish administration was hard pressed to meet a constant stream of demands from England. [4]

During the period of the Welsh wars Irish supplies were regularly used. Indeed one of the things which first drew royal attention to Stephen de Fulbourn was his failure to meet the king's demands adequately. Yet the accounts of the keeper of the king's wardrobe show well enough that the Irish administration was able to supply the king with what in the context of Irish revenues were enormous amounts of money. For example, William de Luda in his account for November 1282–November 1283 recorded the receipt of £666 from loans raised in Ireland for the war; over £7,000 from the issues of Ireland; 1,000 marks from de Fulbourn; £400 from the wool custom; and £233 from the issues of the vacant archbishopric of Dublin, altogether a total of nearly £9,000.[5] De Fulbourn himself, in a letter of 8 June 1282, told the king that he

[1] *Rot. parl.*, i, 98, no. 11.

[2] The list of enrolled treasurers' accounts in Richardson & Sayles, *Admin. Ire.*, p. 217, shows the gaps between audits.

[3] Ibid., pp 47–8.

[4] In general see J. F. Lydon, 'Ireland's participation in the military activities of English kings in the thirteenth and early fourteenth century' (Ph.D. thesis, University of London, 1955); and Michael Prestwich, *War, politics and finance under Edward I* (London, 1972).

[5] P.R.O., E. 372/130 (pipe roll 13 Edw. I), m. 5.

was having great difficulty in getting adequate supplies of food and wine, because when the rumour of a war in Wales reached Ireland, speculators bought up the available supplies and there was a steep rise in prices.[1] Nevertheless, particularly during the last Welsh war, Ireland had a role to play in keeping the Welsh castles supplied by sea. For example, two Bristol ships were plying between Dublin and Conway with supplies throughout the critical winter days. Some small troops served in the army, too, though they were of little importance.[2] Where the Irish contribution was of most importance was in the building of the great Welsh castles which Edward I used to encircle the mountains and to keep the Welsh in check. The huge cost had been estimated at £80,000, and of this nearly £30,000 came from Ireland. It was, of course, spread over many years; but the bulk of it came in great waves in the 1280s, the very period when the English government was worried over the critical state of the financial administration of Ireland.[3]

Such money could not be found easily in Ireland and it undoubtedly put a strain on an already inefficient administration. Borrowing, too, had to be resorted to and this meant putting future income in pawn, or farming out regular sources of revenue like the valuable wool custom. Finally, taxation, clerical as well as lay, was used to inflate the normal revenues and to provide the king with ready cash. This had important constitutional repercussions in Ireland and helped to develop the idea of the parliamentary subsidy. In 1292, for example, a royal agent negotiated a grant of a fifteenth at an assembly in Dublin, though not before many magnates and representatives of the local communities had demanded concessions.[4] And in 1300, when the king sought an aid for the war in Scotland, the justiciar was forced to negotiate individually with the local communities and then bargain with a widely representative parliament.[5] It was not until the fourteenth century that the parliamentary subsidy became firmly established in Ireland; but the practice was established in the last decades of the thirteenth century, based firmly on the principle of consent and the accepted obligation of every freeman to help the king in his necessity, with elected representatives having full power to bind their communities to whatever was agreed on in parliament.

By the summer of 1294 King Edward had involved himself in war with France and was preparing to invade Gascony. The sudden Welsh revolt disrupted his plans. Soon, too, the successful negotiations by the French of a treaty with the Scots precipitated an Anglo-Scottish war. Edward was now in extreme difficulties, with military commitments on many fronts. What Sir Maurice Powicke aptly called 'the years of emergency' had begun.[6] These last

---

[1] P.R.O., S.C. 1/17, no. 186.
[2] John E. Morris, *The Welsh wars of Edward I* (Oxford, 1901), p. 259.
[3] Lydon, 'Ireland's participation', pp 179–84.
[4] Richardson & Sayles, *Parl. & councils med. Ire.*, pp 193–9.
[5] *Stat. Ire., John–Hen. V*, pp 229–37.
[6] Sir Maurice Powicke, *The thirteenth century, 1216–1307* (Oxford, 1953), p. 644.

ten years of Edward's reign saw an intolerable strain placed on the resources of his kingdom, and it was natural that the lordship of Ireland should be exploited to the full to help relieve the burden. The king's decision to open yet another front in Flanders only made matters worse. The constitutional crisis that developed, which caused a political upheaval in England, further frustrated the war effort and made the king more desperate than ever. Because of Ireland's heavy involvement in the last Welsh war, and the Scottish campaign of 1296, it was not until early 1297 that Irish supplies began to reach Gascony. Large quantities were shipped from many ports and the royal purveyors were active over a wide area. For example, the Dublin purveyors seized corn all over Dublin, Kildare, Carlow, Tipperary, Kilkenny, Waterford, Cork, and Limerick.[1] Altogether nearly 15,000 quarters of wheat and over 4,000 of oats went to Gascony.[2] The widespread purveyance naturally produced a reaction and there were many instances of the purveyors being obstructed. Speculators, as always, were quick to cash in on the king's need, and fantastic profits were made on the sale of Irish corn to the royal army in Gascony. One Irish merchant, for instance, who bought wheat for 5s. a crannock in Ireland sold it for 22s. a crannock in Gascony.[3]

The cost of the war was enormous and could only be met by heavy borrowing. The citizens of Bayonne lent nearly £45,000 and after the war Edward assigned to them the wool custom of England and Ireland. By 1298, when their debt was finally satisfied, they had received over £3,270 from the Irish custom, a heavy loss to the needy Irish exchequer.[4] Apart from this there is no evidence that the Dublin government made any financial contribution to the war, which is hardly surprising considering what was spent on Wales and Scotland. But the lordship did supply one military expedition. Six of the most important Irish tenants in chief, including the earl of Ulster, received military summonses in the summer of 1294, ordering them to join the king in London to go on campaign in Gascony.[5] The time could hardly have been more inappropriate, with the great feud between de Vesci and fitz Thomas reaching its climax. Even when that was temporarily healed, it was to Scotland that an Irish expeditionary force went. Not until the autumn of 1297 did an Irish army reach Flanders. Elaborate negotiations had taken place between the king and the leading Irish magnates. Despite his anxiety to have them with him, evidenced in the extraordinarily favourable terms of service which he offered, Edward was aware that their absence from Ireland at this critical time might have unfortunate effects. In a letter to the justiciar, John Wogan, in May 1297 he said Wogan himself should remain in Ireland after the expedition sailed, and added that he was seeking a small number of men on this occasion 'in order that those

[1] *P.R.I. rep. D.K. 38*, p. 44.
[2] Lydon, 'Ireland's participation', p. 196.
[3] *Cal. justic. rolls, 1305–7*, p. 158.
[4] *Cal. doc. Ire., 1293–1301*, no. 631.
[5] Ibid., no. 153.

who come to him shall be well attired and well mounted, and that the land after their departure shall remain well guarded'.[1] Such caution was well justified by the state of Ireland. But it was thrown to the winds in the years following by a king who was desperate and therefore unmindful of the repercussions of his wars on Ireland.

It is evident that there was hard bargaining about the terms under which the magnates were willing to serve overseas. Fitz Thomas, for example, received £40 to fortify his castle of Lea before he left Ireland.[2] In the end the terms demanded were too hard and in October the king wrote to Wogan and instructed him 'to withdraw from the covenants in as courteous a manner as possible so that none shall rightly think themselves ill-content'.[3] But so far as fitz Thomas was concerned the king's decision came too late. He was already in the king's pay since 22 September and he served with a small troop of 3 knights, 56 squires, and 151 foot in Flanders until the end of November. There was another small Irish troop under David Caunton.[4]

It was for the war in Scotland that the Irish lordship was most extensively used by the king. When John Wogan was appointed justiciar on 18 October 1295 he was ordered to raise 10,000 foot and cavalry at his own discretion for service overseas.[5] Wogan, like Wentworth in the seventeenth century, was being sent to Ireland to enrol the lordship in the king's great enterprise. He did not fail Edward, and in the years to come the Irish administration was fully engaged in answering a never-ending stream of demands from the king for money, soldiers, and supplies of war. In the very first campaign, that of 1296 against Balliol, an Irish army took part.[6] The earl of Ulster and twenty-seven other magnates had been summoned on 1 January to muster with the royal army. The fortunate survival of a report from the messenger carrying the summonses enable us to see how the magnates reacted to this royal appeal.[7] They were evasive and indefinite and refused to give a positive answer when asked when they would come to Scotland. They hedged for time in an effort to get the best possible terms of service, and in this they were successful. The earl of Ulster got the highest rate of pay ever paid to an earl in these wars. They got pardon of huge debts and the privilege of payment on a fortnightly basis, as well as pardons for all sorts of offences.

The army that eventually sailed to Scotland numbered 3,157 men in all, and the clerk of the wages accounted for nearly £7,500 in disbursements. The bulk of this force was infantry, though there were well over 300 men-at-arms. But the most interesting contingent was the troop of 261 hobelars, or light

---

[1] *Cal. close rolls, 1296—1302*, pp 105–6.
[2] *P.R.I. rep. D.K. 38*, p. 87.   [3] *Cal. close rolls, 1296—1302*, p. 69.
[4] B.L., Add. MS 7965 (wardrobe book, 25 Edw. I), ff 68ᵛ, 86ᵛ.
[5] Francis Palgrave (ed.), *The parliamentary writs and writs of military summons* (London, 1827), i, 269.
[6] J. F. Lydon, 'An Irish army in Scotland, 1296' in *Ir. Sword*, xx (1962), pp 184–90.
[7] Joseph Stevenson, *Documents illustrative of the history of Scotland* (2 vols, Edinburgh, 1870), ii, 124–5.

cavalry, who now appeared outside Ireland for the first time.[1] They were highly suitable for skirmishing in rough country and made an immediate impression on the king. From now on he always asked for hobelars in Ireland and soon they appeared in England too. They were to help to revolutionise the art of war when archers with longbows were mounted on the same light horses or hobbies and devastated the old-style French armies.

Despite the success of his campaign against Balliol, Edward soon found that Scotland was impossible to conquer. It devoured his resources. In particular it demanded elaborate commissariat arrangements, which were impossible to maintain adequately because of the long distances involved. Many an English army faced starvation as a result. From the ports on the east coast of Ireland, Scotland was easily accessible by sea. Naturally this accessibility was exploited by Edward and in large measure the Dublin government was made responsible for feeding the armies which were based on Carlisle and fought in the west of Scotland. The need was always great. In a letter of 15 April 1298 the king said that as much as possible should be sent to Carlisle—he would not specify any particular quantity, so great was his need.[2] In the summer and autumn of that year the treasurer paid out more than £4,000 to the royal purveyors and huge quantities of grain, wine, and meat were shipped to Carlisle. As the total receipt recorded at the exchequer in 1298 was just £5,671, the strain on the administration must have been enormous.[3] But there was to be no respite. In December 1298, when making early preparations for a campaign the following summer, the king ordered the following from Ireland: 8,000 qrs of wheat, 10,000 qrs of oats, 2,000 qrs of crushed malt, 1,000 tuns of wine, 500 carcasses of beef, 1,000 fat pigs, and 20,000 dried fish.[4] In due course the purveyors spent £4,248 on supplies.[5] And so it went on. Each year the demands came and the exchequer was expected to find impossible sums of money to pay for supplies.

On top of that the hard-pressed administration was expected to raise and pay for Irish armies in Scotland. After 1296 Irish troops served regularly, though with two exceptions never in very large numbers. In 1298, for example, Hugh Bisset of Antrim was employed 'to harass the king's Scotch enemies by sea' and was active along the west coast of Scotland.[6] He had with him four ships, each manned by a crew of forty so that they must have been capable of carrying large numbers of men. In 1300 a small contingent of Irish, numbering about 360, were present at the siege of Caerlaverock and joined the king in his aimless marching through Galloway. But the following year a much larger force of Irish arrived in Scotland after the usual prolonged bargaining.[7] The pardon of all

[1] For the hobelar see J. F. Lydon, 'The hobelar: an Irish contribution to medieval warfare' in *Ir. Sword*, v (1954), pp 12–16.

[2] *Cal. doc. Ire., 1293–1301*, no. 516.

[3] P.R.O., E. 372/144 (pipe roll 27 Edw. I), m. 25.

[4] *Cal. doc. Ire., 1293–1301*, no. 570.   [5] *P.R.I. rep. D.K. 38*, pp 50–51.

[6] *Cal. doc. Ire., 1293–1301*, no. 555.

[7] J. F. Lydon, 'Irish levies in the Scottish wars, 1296–1302' in *Ir. Sword*, xxi (1962), pp 207–17.

their debts at the Dublin exchequer was the chief bait held out by the king. Edward was particularly anxious to have the earl of Ulster with him and sent him word that he 'relies on him more than any other man in the land for many reasons', urging him to set a good example to the other magnates and to offer his service 'without bargain or covenant more quickly and willingly than any others in that country'.[1] Similar messages of flattery failed to move the earl and in the end he refused to serve. This naturally reduced considerably the size of the force that eventually sailed, just over 2,200 in all (though it is interesting that the number of hobelars who served was substantially increased). The cost was high. More than £3,600 was spent on the expedition, mainly on wages; huge sums were pardoned at the exchequer; and the Irish exchequer was left with the huge debt of £3,200 in wages still owing to the leaders of contingents after they returned home. In a desperate attempt to find cash to pay this debt the justiciar seized the money of foreign merchants in Ireland, notably the Spini of Florence, a measure that yielded only £585.

In 1303 another large army served in Scotland.[2] This time the king sought to engage ridiculous numbers in Ireland: 500 men at arms, 1,000 hobelars, and 10,000 foot. But it is a measure of how anxious he was, as are the letters which he sent to no less than 183 Irish vassals (compared with 184 in England). Once again there was hard bargaining, involving pardon of debts, general pardons, and preferential rates of pay. The earl of Ulster demanded the pardon of all his debts up to the present and an examination at the exchequer revealed that these amounted to more than £11,600, besides the money due for Ulster and Connacht, which was 'understood to be great'.[3] That the king should ultimately agree to this and other 'dear bargains' is remarkable, though it was the Irish administration that suffered in the end. A fleet of 173 ships was required to transport the army and Peter de Paris was appointed admiral, the first Irish admiral recorded. Assembling this fleet cost nearly £1,000, of which £500 had to be borrowed from a Kilkenny merchant and his wife. And of the 183 magnates who had received letters from the king, no less than fifty-three were on board when the fleet sailed. Altogether over 3,400 went to Scotland, with the number of hobelars once more showing a substantial increase.

The acute shortage of money meant that wages remained unpaid. In August the keeper of the wardrobe, John of Drokensford, was sent to negotiate a loan from Italian merchants in London, 'of which the king has great need by reason of his long stay with his army in Scotland and by reason of the great number of Irishmen who have come to those parts to his aid'.[4] But nothing was done. The Irish troops were soon in a perilous state, facing starvation because they lacked money to buy food. Some deserted, 'for want of pay', we are told;[5] most of the

---

[1] *Cal. doc. Ire., 1293—1301*, p. 388.
[2] J. F. Lydon, 'Edward I, Ireland and the war in Scotland, 1303–4' in Lydon, *Eng. & Ire.*, pp 43–61.
[3] *Cal. doc. Ire., 1302–7*, no. 151.
[4] *Cal. pat. rolls, 1302–7*, p. 153.
[5] *Cal. justic. rolls Ire., 1303–5*, p. 33.

others left for home the minute their hundred days' service was complete. When he left Scotland the earl of Ulster was owed nearly £6,000 and other leaders were owed sums in proportion to the retinues they brought with them. Even as late as June 1306, when the king desperately needed money in Ireland to forward supplies to Scotland, payment of these debts was once again indefinitely postponed.

It is not surprising then, that this was the last major expedition from Ireland to Scotland, though small troops served later and large quantities of supplies continued to be shipped. More than anything, now, the king needed money, and on 30 July 1305 the English receipt roll recorded the enormous sum of £11,267 from Ireland. This in fact represents various sums received in the wardrobe during the previous year and a half.[1] How the Irish exchequer managed to raise it remains a mystery. But it is indicative of the enormous demands that were being made by Edward during the last years of his reign and the irresponsible way in which he was exploiting the resources of Ireland to the detriment of good government there. For this draining away of money, the constant borrowing and pawning of future income, and the diversion of official attention away from its proper function in Ireland was a very important contributory factor in the growing lawlessness and disorder which is such a marked feature of the time. The government was deprived of the money it needed to do its business properly. The absence of magnates on campaign left their lordships open to attack and an inadequate defence for the land of peace. In this way the Gaelic revival was helped and the feudal settlement weakened.

That the Irish government lost too much revenue in helping the king in his wars is very evident. We have already seen plenty of evidence to support this. One final example will suffice. The recorded expenditure on the issue roll that runs from Michaelmas 1298 to the end of Trinity term 1299 is £5,706, and of this no less than £4,841 went on the war in Scotland.[2] The repayment of debts incurred by the king was a constant drain. For example Nicholas de Clere in his account was allowed £8,400 repaid to the Guidiccione of Lucca; William de Estdene £13,323 to Ricardi merchants (out of a total receipt of just over £18,000).[3] And even allowing for the difficulty the exchequer always experienced in collecting debts, the pardon of debts for service in Scotland must have cost the Irish administration dear. Inevitably the government had to borrow and try to meet as many of its commitments as it could by assignment, a sure sign of financial trouble.

The best exposition of the dangers of this exploitation of the revenues of Ireland is a remarkable letter that Edward II sent to the Irish sheriffs and

---

[1] P.R.O., E. 401/160 (receipt roll 33 Edw. I), 30 July 1305; E. 101/365/6, ff 19ᵛ, 32ᵛ.

[2] Cal. doc. Ire., 1293–1301, nos 548, 589, 614, 634.

[3] P.R.O., E. 372/139, m. 9–9d. De Clere's total receipts came to nearly £32,000 and of this, besides what went to the Italians, over £14,500 was sent to Wales.

seneschals in 1311. The king made it clear that he considered that a wrong use had been made of the issues of Ireland which, to use his own words,

for the most part we have caused to be converted and expended in promoting our affairs in England and Scotland, as well in divers victuals bought in Ireland for the promotion of our Scottish wars and transmitted to us in Scotland, as in sums of money sent to us to advance and execute our other business, so that the residue of our money of the issues of our land of Ireland remaining for a long time past is not sufficient for keeping the peace there (*ad conservacionem pacis ibidem*).

He then enlarges on this failure to maintain peace.

Because of this divers Irish of our land of Ireland, our felons and rebels, both because of this same lack of money (*pecunie defectum*) and their customary pugnacity . . . [are] day by day perpetrating burnings, homicides, robberies, and other innumerable and intolerable transgressions.

From now on, therefore, all the revenues of Ireland are to be spent there, 'both in maintaining the peace of the same land and in expediting our other arduous business there'.[1] It is probable that it was the ordainers who forced this change on the king as part of a wider attempt to control revenues. Certainly the change was stillborn and Edward II continued the fatal policy of exploitation right down to the end of his reign.

The administration of the frequent purveyances was also a contributory factor in the growth of lawlessness in late thirteenth-century Ireland.[2] Unlike other national levies such as taxes on movable property, purveyance did not require consent but could be levied at the king's will. What caused trouble in Ireland was the frequency of these purveyances, especially at a time when so many local communities already had to carry the burden of purveyance for local wars; the failure of the government's agents to recompense the unfortunates whose goods were seized; and the corrupt way in which they were administered. Many people reacted violently and obstructed the purveyors. Even public officials, like a mayor of Dublin, helped to forcibly restrain purveyors in their work. When William de Wythington, a royal agent sent from England to supervise purveyance in Ireland, 'wished to exercise his office on a certain market day in Dublin, certain persons greatly disturbed the market; they forestalled the corn found in the city and corn coming towards the city and hid it in houses so that it should not come to market and victual could not be provided for the king's use'.[3] There is plenty of evidence to show that resistance to purveyance and to the racketeering associated with it led many to take the law into their own hands. This helped to foster that casual attitude towards the law which made it so difficult for the government to maintain public order in the localities.

[1] J. F. Lydon, 'Edward II and the revenues of Ireland' in *I.H.S.*, xiv, no. 53 (Mar. 1964), pp 52–3.
[2] For a general view of the impact of purveyance in England see J. R. Maddicott, *The English peasantry and its demands of the crown, 1294–1341* (*Past & Present*, supplement I, 1975).
[3] *Hist. & mun. doc. Ire.*, pp 504–5.

The withdrawal of troops was also a contributory factor in the breakdown of order. We have already seen that in 1298, before he left for Flanders, John fitz Thomas was given £40 to fortify his castle of Lea. His apprehensions were well justified. After his return to Ireland he sent a petition to the king complaining that in his absence Rathangan had been burned by the Irish, who had committed 'homicides and depredations' in the neighbouring lands, and he looked for a grant of royal service to take his revenge.[1] Fitz Thomas's experience could be matched in many quarters, where not only the Gaelic Irish but Anglo-Irish criminals as well took advantage of the absence of the local lord.

Yet another way in which lawlessness was encouraged was through the grant of pardons for service overseas. Large numbers of these were distributed as an inducement to service and subsequently they could be produced in court and procure an acquittal. Again it was Edward II who drew attention to the danger of this practice when in 1317 and again in 1323 he had to curtail the grant of such pardons because, he said, 'others had been encouraged to commit crime on account of the facility of obtaining such pardons'.[2]

Troop movements gave rise to disturbances too. This was not surprising since armies at this time were highly undisciplined and difficult to control. Troops from Ireland were involved in serious disturbances in Scotland in 1296 and in Ghent in 1297. Soldiers on the move through the Irish countryside often did terrible damage. Towns suffered too from their unruly behaviour and sometimes the townsmen retaliated. In 1303, for example, de Bermingham's men were trapped by the citizens of Drogheda on the bridge leading into the town and three of them were killed. Maurice Carew lodged his men in the Coombe in Dublin, where they were attacked by some Dubliners who killed some men and made off with goods worth £100. In New Ross there was constant trouble between sailors and the town.[3] So bad did relations become between magnates and the citizens of Dublin as a result of these frequent disturbances that in 1317 Edward II had to relocate a parliament which had been summoned to Dublin because he was afraid 'that damage may be done if the magnates of Ireland enter that city, on account of the dispute between them and the community of the city'; and he insisted that the magnates should not be allowed to house 'their men within the city against the will of the community, nor to cause victuals within the city to be taken without their consent'.[4]

On many counts, therefore, the continued exploitation of Ireland by the king contributed to the increasing lawlessness and disorder and to the government's failure to cope adequately. In particular lack of money made the problem of defence an impossible one. Castles were not properly maintained, the king's highways were allowed to deteriorate, bridges fell into disrepair. Gaelic

---

[1] *Cal. justic. rolls, 1295—1301*, pp 230, 362.
[2] *Cal. close rolls, 1313—18*, p. 405; *Cal. pat. rolls, 1321—4*, pp 324-5.
[3] *Cal. justic. rolls, 1305—7*, pp 31-2, 106, 198.
[4] *Cal. close rolls, 1313—18*, p. 476.

Ireland, too, responded to the government's failure. The absence of the magnates on overseas service was also exploited by local Gaelic lords. There can be no doubt that the great Gaelic revival that occurred in the second half of the thirteenth century was greatly assisted by the weakness of the government. Once this revival gained a momentum of its own it made of Ireland a land of war and thereby further increased the problems faced by the Dublin government.

CHAPTER VIII

Land and people, *c.* 1300

R. E. GLASSCOCK

WHILE, like all outsiders to Ireland, Giraldus was easily taken in by the good story, and however suspect his historical interpretations, his observations on the physical characteristics of the country have the ring of truth about them and convey a real feeling for the medieval landscape.

Ireland is a country of uneven surface and rather mountainous. The soil is soft and watery, and there are many woods and marshes. Even at the tops of high and steep mountains you will find pools and swamps.

This is the most temperate of all countries. . . . You will seldom see snow here, and then it lasts only for a short time. . . . There is, however, such a plentiful supply of rain, such an ever-present overhanging of clouds and fog, that you will scarcely see even in the summer three consecutive days of really fine weather.[1]

To those who know the country these remarks leave no doubt that Giraldus had experienced the Irish climate at first hand and that the day-to-day weather in the middle ages was much the same as it is today. Facing the moisture-laden south-westerlies blowing from the Atlantic, Ireland has a more maritime climate than the rest of the British Isles. Over four-fifths of the country receives an annual rainfall of between 30 and 50 inches (750–1300 mm) and amounts exceed this in the uplands. Only a small area near the east coast has less than 30 inches (750 mm). Owing to cloud cover there are more rainy days than in most parts of Britain; even in the drier areas rain falls on an average of 175 days in the year and this increases to up to 250 days in the wetter west. With these maritime conditions there is a smaller range in mean annual temperature; winters are mild, especially in the west where mean monthly winter temperatures are 44°–45°F (6°–7°C) and summers are cool and cloudy with mean monthly temperatures in the range 57°–61°F (14°–16°C). By comparison with Britain, Ireland's climate is mild and wet. The differences, although slight, are enough to influence the optimum use of land; while cereals may be grown in any part of Ireland, physiographic and climatic factors combine to make pastoral farming more attractive, especially in the more rugged areas.

[1] Quotations from Giraldus Cambrensis's 'Topographia Hiberniae' are taken from John J. O'Meara's translation; see above, p. 61, n. 1.

The climate of Ireland around 1300 must have been very similar to that of today, and until there is more scientific study of this country's medieval climate we shall have to continue to pin our faith on Giraldus's random observations. As there are no records of medieval weather conditions from year to year they can only be deduced from collating stray references to harvests, prices, and natural hazards such as floods. As yet there is only a little information from pollen analysis, which, for the most part, has been concerned with the changing vegetation of the prehistoric and early historic periods. Dendrochronology, another possible source of information, is still at a relatively early stage.

The paucity of knowledge of the history of Irish climate is reflected in the lack of references to medieval Ireland in E. Le Roy Ladurie's synopsis of the history of European climate over the last millennium,[1] a work which, by drawing together the evidence from various sources, shows that despite significant climatic cycles over the last thousand years, the range of mean annual temperature in western Europe over the period is only in the order of 1°–1.2°C. Following an optimum period between c. 750 and A.D. 1230 when the climate was as mild as, if not milder than, at present, a cooler and wetter phase set in about 1250, a trend which is certainly confirmed for Ireland from the evidence of peat stratigraphy.[2] The climate of Ireland in 1300 was probably marginally cooler than at present but it is questionable whether this slight difference had any significant effect upon either population or agriculture. While slight rises and falls of annual temperature make for very real differences in cold-climate countries such as Greenland and Iceland, in a temperate country such as Ireland they are likely to have only marginal effects, varying the amounts of tree growth, and changing by a few days the onset of the seasons.

Variations in rainfall from year to year had much more serious effects upon the life of western Europe in the middle ages than did changes in temperature. On the Winchester manors in southern England, for example, the period 1270–1312 was, on the whole, a dry phase. This was followed, as apparently in most of western Europe, by a number of exceptionally wet years when annual rainfall increased by as much as 10 per cent.[3] Between 1312 and 1320, and especially in 1315–17, not only did heavy autumn and spring rains make ploughing and sowing difficult but summer rains beat down crops, prevented ripening, and ruined harvests. Low yields of grain led to a price spiral, to panic, and ultimately to the so-called 'great European famine'. With very little evidence available it is difficult to say how Ireland fared throughout these critical years. We cannot presume that Ireland had similar wet conditions; seasonal weather in England and Ireland can be very different, as was seen for example in 1969, when England had a wet summer and Ireland had one of its driest summers for

---

[1] E. Le Roy Ladurie, *Times of feast, times of famine: a history of climate since the year 1000*, trans. Barbara Bray (London, 1972).

[2] Harry Godwin, *The history of the British flora* (Cambridge, 1956), p. 56.

[3] H. H. Lamb, 'The early medieval warm epoch and its sequel' in *Palaeogeography, Palaeoclimatology, Palaeoecology*, 1 (Mar. 1965), pp 13–37.

years. Exceptional harvests were recorded in Ireland in 1298 and 1299 and these were probably 'good' years in terms of crop yield; the demand for harvest labour increased, thereby accelerating the commutation of labour services, which in turn forced up wages. But these years were probably exceptional, for the scattered evidence for succeeding years suggests considerable change in the early fourteenth century. Analysis of pollen in stratified peat deposits at Littleton Bog, County Tipperary, showed an apparent change in the vegetation at or about 1300 when cereal pollens decline and grass and weed pollens increase.[1] Whether this could have been a response to climatic change in addition to local agrarian conditions is not known. Documentary evidence certainly suggests that the summer weather in Ireland worsened after 1300, especially in the years 1314–18 when, as elsewhere in western Europe, there were bad harvests and consequent famine and pestilence.[2] The annals for the period record torrential rains, storms, crop failures, famine, disease, and death. While it is likely that heavier rains had a more serious effect on the more extensive grain-growing areas of England and France, flood and murrain took their toll of cattle and sheep and leave little doubt that even in the more pastoral areas of Scotland and Ireland there were serious problems in those years. These unsettled agrarian conditions and the consequent economic dislocation probably contributed to the decline of the English lordship in Ireland every bit as much as the Bruce wars of the same years.

With climatic conditions similar to those of today, natural processes were as much at work changing the face of Ireland then as they are now, and, if there was a slightly higher rainfall, then rates of erosion may have been marginally faster than those observed today. Rainfall is an important agent in the weathering of limestone, the destructive and constructive work of rivers, the frequency of mudflow and rockfall activity on slopes, and in the formation of peat. By extrapolation from current rates of change most landforms must have had slightly higher surfaces in the medieval period. For example, recent observations for selected areas suggest that the present solution rate on carboniferous limestone is about 0.051 mm a year, equivalent to a loss over the last seven centuries of perhaps 36 mm (1.4 inches).[3]

The coast, especially where it is composed of unconsolidated glacial deposits, is particularly vulnerable to change, and in places the coastline in 1300 must have been considerably different from that of today. There has probably been only slight change on the rockier west coast except where glacial deposits have been eroded by Atlantic wave action, as, for example, on the Mullet, in Clew Bay, and in Donegal Bay. The east coast, however, has been

[1] G. F. Mitchell, 'Littleton Bog, Tipperary: an Irish agricultural record' in *R.S.A.I. Jn.*, xcv (1965), p. 130.
[2] H. S. Lucas, 'The great European famine of 1315, 1316 and 1317' in *Speculum*, v (1930), pp 346–7, 351, 356–7.
[3] P. W. Williams, 'Limestone morphology in Ireland' in Nicholas Stephens and R. E. Glasscock (ed.), *Irish geographical studies in honour of E. Estyn Evans* (Belfast, 1970), p. 110.

more mobile; the glacial drift of the eastern lowlands has been more easily
eroded by the Irish Sea, which, although a less powerful agent than the
Atlantic, was, in the words of Giraldus, 'surging with currents that rush
together, is nearly always tempestuous, so that even in the summer it scarcely
shows itself calm even for a few days to them that sail'. On the east coast, cliff
recession and constant encroachment of the sea on the land may be seen
wherever glacial drift is exposed to the force of the waves.[1] Recent observations suggest that in some areas cliff recession has been at the rate of 100 feet
or more (30 m plus) over the last century or so, for example, at Blackwater on
the east coast of County Wexford; at Greystones, County Wicklow; at
Killiney, County Dublin; Benhead, County Meath; and between Rathcor and
Templeton, County Louth. Assuming a fairly constant rate of erosion, this
means that many parts of the east coast were probably about 700 feet
(c. 220 m) further seaward in 1300, and that considerable amounts of land have
since been lost to the sea. On the south coast the loss may have been even
greater; cliffs composed of glacial drift are currently being eroded at rates of
between 200 and 700 feet (60–220 m) per century (for example, at Ballycotton
Bay, County Cork, and Ballyhealy, County Wexford) and the medieval coastline may have been as much as half a mile forward of its present position.
While there is clear evidence of loss of land around the coast, exact amounts
are difficult to determine; local people speak of 'a field or two' disappearing
within living memory, and in some places this has obviously been a continual
process since the medieval period.

On the other hand, much of the eroded material has been redeposited, and
some coastal depositional features must have become more prominent since
1300; for example, the tidal flats of the Shannon estuary and the sand complex
off Bloody Foreland, County Donegal. On the east coast, studies of the shingle
and dune complex at Dundrum, County Down, have shown that there has been
a periodic build-up of material since the medieval period, when the coastline
may have been about 200 m inland from its present position. Similar accumula-
tions of both shingle and sand have taken place elsewhere; at Bannow, County
Wexford, all that remains of an Anglo-Norman town (where there were about
160 burgages in 1307) is a ruined church; the rest was slowly overwhelmed by
drifting sand and was finally abandoned by the end of the seventeenth century.
The nearby port of Clonmines was also a victim of coastal deposition, through
the silting up of an estuary.

While changes resulting from physical processes are most easily seen around
the coastline, there have been significant but less perceptible changes in other
landforms, particularly mountain slopes and valley sides. It is only through the
controlled measurement of slope processes that the continuity and rapidity of

[1] Information on rates of recession have kindly been supplied by Professor Nicholas Stephens,
Department of Geography, University of Swansea. For a general account of the geomorphology of
Ireland see G. L. Herries Davies and Nicholas Stephens, *Ireland* (London, 1978).

change on steep slopes have been realised.[1] Landslides, rockfalls, and mud-flows, often triggered off by sudden rains, are constantly changing the faces of steep slopes; the profiles and detail of many cliffs, mountains, and valley sides must have been very different in medieval times. In addition, the removal of the tree cover is likely to have accelerated soil movement and erosion on many slopes.

If, as is claimed, about twelve per cent of Ireland was still wooded in 1600,[2] then we may safely assume that when Giraldus was writing in the 1180s the per-centage was greater, perhaps as high as twenty per cent. Even this percentage would certainly have been enough to give him the impression that the country was well wooded ('Still there are, here and there, some fine plains, but in com-parison to the woods they are indeed small'). Allowing for the clearance of much woodland in the thirteenth century we may postulate that perhaps fifteen per cent of the country was tree-covered about 1300. If a traveller in the eastern lowlands was not passing through woodland he was never far from it; trees must have filled every lowland horizon. In the midlands and west, however, parts of the country were probably as open then as they are today: for example, the Burren of County Clare, north Mayo, and the peat expanses of the Shannon lowlands. By contrast some areas were probably still covered with dense wood-land; for example, the Erne basin, the Lagan valley, and the Lough Neagh low-lands, south Wicklow, and some of the river valleys of Leinster and Munster.

To picture the woodland of medieval Ireland we must, as it were, close our minds to many of the species with which we are familiar today and which were introduced to this country only in the recent past: beech, lime, sycamore, poplar, the chestnuts, and almost all the conifers. The medieval woodland con-sisted of native deciduous trees, dominated by oak and hazel, both far more common than they are today.[3] Birch was also common and ash grew well, especially on strongly calcareous soils. Alder was a dominant species in low-lying, wetter areas. By 1300 there seems to have been very little elm, a species which, although dominant in the late prehistoric period, seems to have dis-appeared almost entirely by the middle ages, perhaps because of disease. Yew (not to be confused with the later Irish yew) was common, and, as Giraldus observed, was associated then, as now, with churches and with other holy places. Other evergreens included holly and juniper; their wood probably had special uses and like other small native trees, including the whitethorn, they had magical associations, powers conspicuously absent from introduced species of later times.

In 1300, as in any other medieval year, the tree cover was depleted a little

---

[1] For example, D. B. Prior, Nicholas Stephens, and G. R. Douglas, 'Some examples of mudflow and rockfall activity in north-east Ireland' in *Slopes: form and process*, Institute of British Geo-graphers, Special Publication no. 3 (1971), pp 129–40.

[2] McCracken, *Ir. woods*, p. 15.

[3] For a general survey of the vegetational history of the medieval period see Frank Mitchell, *The Irish landscape* (London, 1976), pp 176–92.

more as wood was cut for all everyday needs—as fuel for cooking and heating, for furniture and implements, for framing and roofing houses, for boats, slides, and carts. It was also used for fencing, for bridges and mills, as scaffolding for stone buildings, and for charcoal. By 1300 the rate of clearance of woodland for cultivation had probably slowed up and in places cleared land may have been reverting to waste; even then, fire and grazing prevented the regeneration of tree cover.

There has been a continuous but irregular growth of peat in Ireland since the prehistoric period. From a deep boring at Littleton Bog, County Tipperary, the pollen in the various layers of the peat provided a fairly continuous record of the vegetation in that vicinity from the post-glacial period to the beginning of the eighteenth century when beech (*Fagus*) makes its first appearance in the local pollen record. At Littleton peat was accumulating throughout the medieval period. Pollen analysis indicates that in the late twelfth and thirteenth centuries there was an increase in cereal pollens and a corresponding drop in the pollens of ash, birch, and hazel; Mitchell attributes this new activity to a probable expansion of grain-growing by local lay and ecclesiastical landowners and, in particular, to the agricultural activity of the nearby Cistercian abbey of Kilcooly. After about 1300 oak, alder, and hazel pollens continued to decrease, presumably because of further clearance, and grass and plantain pollens increased, perhaps indicative of a local change from grain-growing to pasture, a trend that would certainly fit with the historical evidence for the gradual decline of tillage in the fourteenth century and its gradual replacement by stock-rearing and grazing. At Littleton the pollen record seems to accord, in very general terms, with the historical record of the Butler lordship at this period.

While the pollen record of every site varies with local conditions, there seems to be little doubt, both from other studies of peat stratigraphy and from the number of medieval artifacts found in the bogs, that peat was accumulating in Ireland throughout the medieval period. While in most places there was still a local supply of wood, peat (turf) was important as a fuel for cooking and heating. By the early fourteenth century the cutting, saving, and transport of turf were sometimes specified as duty labours of manorial tenants, and there are references to its use for fuel at all levels of society in the towns, monasteries, and manors. As Lucas has pointed out,[1] the physical labour of providing a year's supply of turf was considerably less than that involved in getting a year's supply of wood. The turf was easily cut (requiring only some form of spade) and comparatively easy to carry both in back-baskets and in the panniers of pack-horses; moreover, as it did not give off sparks it was a safer fuel for use in houses with timber and thatch. As local woodland was depleted so turf was used more widely; according to Petty in the seventeenth century it was the preferred fuel even in places where wood was still plentiful.

[1] A. T. Lucas, 'Notes on the history of turf as a fuel in Ireland to 1700 A.D.' in *Ulster Folklife*, xv–xvi (1970), pp 172–202.

Cleared land must have appeared much less orderly than it does today. The planted hedgerow was unknown. Piecemeal clearance since prehistoric times had left a landscape of natural boundaries along streams and the crests of hills, by contrast to the straight lines of later enclosure. Cultivation stopped where natural obstacles such as rock outcrops and marshy ground either impeded progress or made reclamation uneconomic. On the good land, however, Jäger's view is that agricultural practice seems to have been comparable in intensity to that on the continent.[1]

In both Gaelic and Anglo-Irish areas land was worked under common field systems. In the east the Anglo-Normans had introduced an open-field system similar to, but never as rigid as, that of the English midlands.[2] Many parishes (usually synonymous with manors) must have had large stretches of arable land, open except for access ways, dividing banks and temporary hurdles for stock. Almost all such open-field land was enclosed by the seventeenth century, and only in a few villages, mainly near Dublin, did vestiges of medieval fields survive after 1700. By 1300 some free tenants already had compact holdings, achieved either as a result of agreed consolidation of strips or, maybe, through individual efforts at reclamation of woodland and waste. Demesne labour on the manors was done in the main by betaghs (*betagii*), the unfree Irish tenants of equivalent status to English villeins.[3] Otway-Ruthven has suggested that the betaghs invariably settled and cultivated particular townlands within manors (almost certainly the poorest land), and while little is known of their agricultural methods it is likely that they held land in common and worked it on an infield–outfield arrangement similar to that of the later rundale system. By 1300 basic contrasts in agrarian landscapes could therefore be seen not only between the Gaelic and Anglo-Irish parts of the country but on the micro-scale of single manors where each cultural group used its own traditional methods for winning food from the land.[4]

Infield–outfield systems were almost certainly used in the Gaelic areas where, although the emphasis was on stock, the better land would have been cultivated, especially for oats and to a lesser extent, wheat. Patches of other land (outfield) would have been periodically taken in for cultivation. Livestock were probably kept off the areas of growing crops either by tethering or by being closely watched or herded, a tradition that may still be seen on unenclosed land in parts of the west today.[5]

[1] Helmut Jäger, 'Land use in medieval Ireland: a review of the documentary evidence' in *Ir. Econ. & Soc. Hist.*, x (1983), p. 64.

[2] A. J. Otway-Ruthven, 'The organisation of Anglo-Irish agriculture in the middle ages' in *R.S.A.I. Jn.*, lxxi (1951), pp 1–13; and see below, pp 439–91.

[3] Gearóid Mac Niocaill, 'The origins of the betagh' in *Ir. Jurist*, new series, i (1966), pp 292–8.

[4] For a summary of field systems, see R. H. Buchanan, 'Field systems of Ireland' in A. R. H. Baker and R. A. Butlin (ed.), *Studies of field systems in the British Isles* (Cambridge, 1973), pp 580–618.

[5] See also below, pp 410–16.

IRELAND, with its varied medieval landscape of bog and hill country, wood-land, pasture, and tilled land, may have had a population of about a million in 1300. As there are no detailed records upon which to base reasoned calcula-tions, estimates have tended to vary, and range between Russell's estimate of 675,000 and almost 1½ million.[1] The population of England around 1300 is now estimated at 4–4½ million. Assuming a similar population density, Ireland (approximately three-fifths the size of England) might have had a population of about 2½ million, but it seems most unlikely that, except in a few areas, medieval Ireland was ever as densely populated as the more fertile lowlands of England. An estimate of about half, say a million, seems more realistic; this is still high relative to Russell's estimate, to which Hollingsworth gives general support, and to Smyth's recent estimate of a population of about 250,000 in the dark ages.[2] All would agree, however, that the population was overwhelmingly rural; its distribution was probably a fairly faithful reflection of the fertility and livestock-carrying capacity of the land. Almost certainly there were more people on the better soils of the lowland east than there were on the stonier and wetter areas of the west. Probably less than five per cent lived in towns—although even this small number represented a great increase by comparison with two centuries earlier.

In Ireland, as elsewhere in western Europe, the twelfth and thirteenth cen-turies were centuries of population increase, of the reclamation of land for agri-culture, of new settlements, and of expanding production and trade. These trends had been given added impetus by the arrival of the Anglo-Normans, and by their attempts to bring in new settlers, and to increase contact with Britain and the Continent. The evidence, such as it is, suggests that up to about 1250 there was a steady increase in population despite periodic checks by famine and disease, both of which took their toll of peasants living near subsistence level. But there were probably sharp regional differences in rates of increase. In the more remote areas of the west and north there may have been a slight natural increase, but it is not known whether numbers were further increased by migration of displaced Irish from further east. In the south and east natural increase was augmented after the 1170s by a steady trickle of newcomers from England and Wales, and, while it is impossible to give a reasoned estimate of the numbers involved, it is clear from surviving manorial records that in parts of the lordship settlers of English and Welsh origin formed an important element of the population by 1300.[3] Pressure of population on land in early thirteenth-century England may have been one of the reasons why settlers were prepared to move to a new and relatively unknown country, especially if, by so doing, they were rewarded by an improvement in their social status, maybe

[1] J. C. Russell, 'Late thirteenth-century Ireland as a region' in *Demography*, iii (1966), p. 502; cf. below, pp 408–10, 445–8.

[2] T. H. Hollingsworth, *Historical demography* (London, 1969), p. 269; Smyth, *Celtic Leinster*, p. 5.

[3] Otway-Ruthven, 'Norman settlement', pp 75–84; see also discussion of this question in Robin Frame, *Colonial Ireland* (Dublin, 1981), pp 78–82, and below, pp 443–4.

from a villein to a farmer or a burgess. While this new colonial element may have been locally important it cannot have been very large numerically in the context of Ireland as a whole. Indeed, it was probably because of their relatively small numbers that the Anglo-Normans and their descendants only ever achieved a tenuous hold on the country, and why, after 1250, with the gradual reemergence of Gaelic Irish power, so many of the new settlements, especially in the west, stagnated and were gradually reabsorbed into the indigenous framework.

Despite their relatively small numbers the newcomers had, by 1300, imprinted their culture on the life and landscape of Ireland. Anglo-Norman institutions and many of their settlements were to outlive the Anglo-Normans themselves. The changes that their settlement and agriculture brought to the landscape can be understood only against the background of their social organisation and technology. In the first place, the imposition of feudalism, and with it both manorial and parochial organisation, brought about the reorganisation of land into new territorial units and its allocation to individuals who were held responsible for its effective subjugation, its settlement, and economic development.[1] The result was the creation of an artificial framework for organised settlement which often conflicted with geographical and economic realities. Secondly, within this framework (which, in part, was grafted on to earlier Irish territorial organisation) new settlers, being aliens in a hostile country, had to band together for security; this meant that their settlements, almost without exception, were nucleated and included a military element. The scale of nucleation ranged from that of manor houses with outbuildings and a few retainers' dwellings, through nucleated villages of English-lowland type, to walled towns. Thirdly, the newcomers were largely dependent for their manpower, for supplies, and for trade on their source areas in England and Wales; in settlement terms this led both to the accelerated growth of the ports of the east and south-east coasts, and to the establishment of a network of inland markets for the distribution of essential goods. Fourthly, by bringing in their own systems of settlement and agriculture the Anglo-Normans brought considerable changes to those areas which they occupied. Where they outnumbered or displaced the local population their changes lasted; where they themselves were absorbed or overrun their changes were short-lived and they were reabsorbed, but not altogether lost, in the continuity of Irish culture. By 1300 clear differences had emerged between the cultural landscapes of the Anglo-Irish lordships and of the Gaelic areas. These differences intensified the development of distinct cultural regions which were as characteristic of Ireland in the medieval period as they have been since.[2]

[1] For the effects of manorialisation on a particular area see C. A. Empey, 'Medieval Knocktopher: a study in manorial settlement' in *Old Kilkenny Rev.*, new series, ii, no. 4 (1982), pp 329–42.
[2] One theme of a paper by Robin Frame, 'Power and society in the lordship of Ireland, 1272–1377' in *Past & Present*, no. 76 (1977), pp 3–33.

ALTHOUGH nucleated settlements of various types undoubtedly existed before
1170, the Anglo-Normans reinforced the concept of settlements in which, as in
the English lowlands, dwellings were clustered around a central focus, be it
castle, church, or main street, a settlement form that in England they themselves had probably inherited from the Anglo-Saxons. In the wake of their
territorial conquest and the parcelling-out of land, settlements of this type were
founded in the late twelfth and early thirteenth centuries. Although these new
settlements had mixed fortunes, especially after about 1250, depending upon
both their location and numerous socio-economic factors, it is clear that by
1300, when documents reveal something of the nature and extent of settlement
over the previous century, some parts of the colony, but by no means all, had a
large number of manorial settlements modelled on village lines.[1]

The first step in the primary subinfeudation of land had frequently been the
building of an earthen ringwork, usually a motte,[2] sometimes shaped from a
natural feature, sometimes a modification and heightening of a prehistoric
cairn or ring-fort, and sometimes a newly built mound.[3] This traditional form
of fortification was a carry-over from the conquest of England; by the 1170s,
when mottes began to appear in Ireland, they were going out of fashion in
England and Wales and were giving way to stone castles. By 1300 they were a
conspicuous feature of territory occupied by the Anglo-Irish. Even today, and
allowing for the fact that many have disappeared with subsequent castle-
building and later destruction, their distribution is a fair indicator of the extent
of territorial conquest by the newcomers in Ireland.[4] Except in Ulster there has
not, to date, been an exhaustive survey of mottes; the known distribution in
some counties may reflect the current state of knowledge rather than the
number of actual examples. Even less is known of ringworks, a type of fortification which is only now attracting attention.[5] By 1300 some mottes, especially in
frontier areas, had almost certainly been built by the Gaelic Irish in imitation of
Anglo-Irish military tactics. It is not inconceivable that the Irish knew of
mottes and built them before 1169, but there is, as yet, no archaeological

---

[1] See, for example, B. J. Graham, 'Anglo-Norman setlement in County Meath' in *R.I.A. Proc.*,
lxxv (1975), sect. C, pp 223–48 and map.

[2] See, for example, B. J. Graham's discussion of this process in Meath, 'The mottes of the
Norman liberty of Meath' in Harman Murtagh (ed.), *Irish midland studies: essays in commemoration of
N. W. English* (Athlone, 1980), pp 39–55.

[3] For an excavated example of a motte built upon an earlier ring-fort, see C. J. Lynn, 'The
excavation of Rathmullan, a raised rath and motte in County Down' in *U.J.A.*, 3rd series, xliv–xlv
(1981–2), pp 65–171.

[4] A tentative list of mottes, based ultimately on Orpen's pioneer work of 1906, is included in
R. E. Glasscock, 'Mottes in Ireland' in *Chateau Gaillard*, vii (1975), pp 95–110. Since 1975 new sites
have been added for some counties: see, for example, those for Kilkenny, Wexford, and Tipperary
in T. B. Barry, *The medieval moated sites of south-eastern Ireland* (Oxford, 1977), pp 148–9. For a more
detailed list of mottes in Ulster see T. E. McNeill, 'Ulster mottes: a checklist' in *U.J.A.*, 3rd series,
xxxviii (1975), pp 49–56.

[5] D. C. Twohig, 'Norman ringwork castles' in *Bulletin of the Group for the Study of Irish Historic
Settlement*, v (1978), pp 7–9.

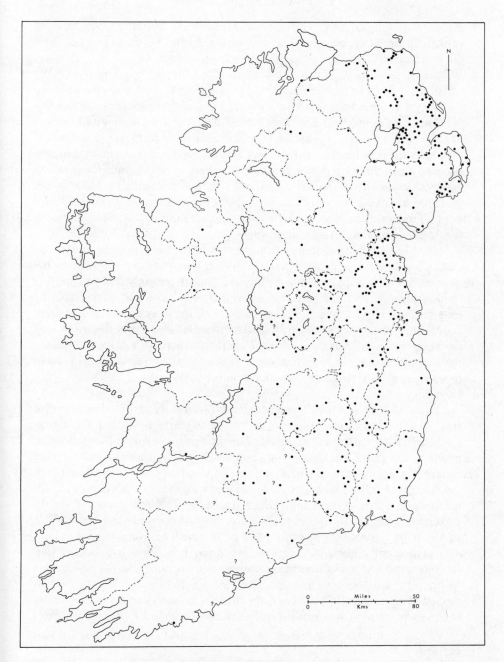

Map 4 MOTTES, by R. E. Glasscock

See below, ix, map 35, and note, p. 104.

evidence to support this possibility; that they were building other types of earthen fortification before the arrival of the Anglo-Normans there is little doubt.[1]

By 1300 the function of mottes, many with adjacent buildings, probably varied from place to place. In relatively peaceful areas such as the heart of the Pale they may already have gone out of use. Their timber palisades and wooden buildings may either have been maintained in case of need or they may by then have been taken down and the timber reused for other purposes. A motte was especially likely to have gone out of use when it had been replaced by a nearby stone castle in the thirteenth century. In other areas, for example the frontiers between Anglo-Irish and Gaelic Irish in Ulster and in Meath, the mottes were probably still in use in 1300, either for military purposes or, in the case of larger ones, as the dwelling places of local lords. In overall terms their importance to the Anglo-Irish was certainly declining.

Not only had the functions of the mottes been taken over by new stone castles but in some parts of the country another type of defended structure, the moated house, was making its appearance. Almost certainly this was another fashion brought in from England, where between 3,000 and 4,000 surviving examples are known, many of them dated both historically and archaeologically to the period 1250–1300. In Ireland there are nowhere near this number; it has been suggested from map evidence alone that there were at most about 750 rectangular earthworks of various types surviving in 1840; detailed field survey in south-eastern Ireland suggests that around 50 per cent of these have since been destroyed.[2]

The detail of these sites differs considerably. A few are of the heavily fortified type, described in County Wexford as 'ramparted forts' by the late Dr George Hadden, who saw them as belonging to the first phase of Anglo-Norman occupation before 1200.[3] The majority of examples, however, are much smaller; they consist of a square or rectangular platform (in Wexford commonly about 180 by 120 feet (55 × 37 m)) which is surrounded on all sides by a deep ditch, the upcast from which has been used either to raise the interior a few feet above the surrounding land or to construct a bank, usually on the inner side of the ditch. In low-lying areas where streams could be diverted, or where the water table was permanently high, the surrounding ditch was filled with water, thus forming a moated enclosure. In drier areas and on slopes, banks and ditches had to fulfil the defensive function without the help of water. Whether wet or dry, entry must usually have been via either a causeway or a wooden bridge such as was found in the excavation of a site at Kilmagoura, County Cork. Field

---

[1] An issue discussed in K. W. Nicholls, 'Anglo-French Ireland and after' in *Peritia*, i (1982), pp 389–90.

[2] R. E. Glasscock, 'Moated sites' in Stephens & Glasscock, *Ir. geog. studies*, pp 162–8; T. B. Barry, 'Moated sites in Ireland' in F. A. Aberg (ed.), *Medieval moated sites* (London, 1978), p. 57.

[3] George Hadden, 'Some earthworks in Co. Wexford' in *Cork Hist. Soc. Jn.*, lxix (1964), pp 118–22.

observation suggests that modern tracks used by animals to get into these sites, invariably midway along one side of the enclosure, perpetuate the position of the original entrance.

Barry has recently furthered our knowledge of these little-known sites with his work on the south-eastern counties and especially of Wexford and Waterford.[1] He concludes that most of them were defended farmsteads of freeholders, mostly Anglo-Irish, anxious to protect themselves and their stock from marauding raiders. Documentary and archaeological evidence, slight though it is, suggests that moats were dug in the thirteenth and fourteenth centuries, at a period when this type of fortification was common elsewhere in western Europe. It seems certain that the overwhelming majority of examples are in the Anglo-Irish areas of Leinster and Munster; they are to be found in all the south-eastern counties, and in particular they are concentrated in Wexford, Kilkenny, south Tipperary, and east Cork. Their localisation within counties must be explained in terms of particular sets of physical and social conditions. In Wexford, for example, Hadden argued that the moated sites were concentrated in the baronies of Ballaghkeen and Bantry because of the proximity of hostile MacMurrough country to the north. The same frontier distribution may be true in east Cork, yet in Ulster this type of defended site seems to have been almost unknown. The description of many such sites as 'castles' on the ordnance maps of the 1830s suggests that there was still an oral tradition that they were fortifications, and that many of them may have remained in use until the end of the medieval period.

This type of defended dwelling must have been spreading throughout the south and east by the late thirteenth century, the date suggested for the origin of the two examples so far excavated, both in County Cork.[2] There is no evidence yet to suggest that they belong to the first phase of Anglo-Norman settlement, but their locational and chronological relationship to other features such as mottes, castles, and tower houses has still to be worked out. A bigger question-mark still hangs over many other rectangular earthworks which, while banked and ditched, were clearly never surrounded by water. Were they contemporary with the true moated sites of English type, and were all these sites of Anglo-Norman origin or were some Irish?

While the origins of moated sites may be in doubt, more is known about the stone castles which, by 1300, were to be seen throughout much of the country, especially in the Anglo-Irish areas. By then they were of various types for, in over a century of castle-building, designs had changed considerably. The principal change in the century after 1200 was the transfer of the strongest

[1] T. B. Barry, 'The medieval moated sites of County Wexford' in *Old Wexford Soc. Jn.*, vi (1976), pp 5–17, and 'The moated sites of County Waterford' in *Decies*, x (1979), pp 32–6.

[2] P. David Sweetman, 'Excavations of a medieval moated site at Rigsdale, County Cork, 1977–8' in *R.I.A. Proc.*, lxxxi (1981), sect. C, pp 193–205, and R. E. Glasscock, 'Kilmagoura, Co. Cork' in *Medieval Archaeology*, xii (1968), pp 196–7.

Map 5 STONE CASTLES OF NORMAN TYPE, BEFORE *c*.1320,
by R. E. Glasscock

See below, ix, map 36, and note, p. 104.

defensive element of the castle away from a central keep to a perimeter curtain wall with angle towers and a strong gatehouse.

Shortly after the initial acquisition of territory the more powerful Anglo-Norman lords augmented the network of mottes by building stone castles. Some of the earliest castles may have been erected on the sites of demolished mottes, but generally the stone structures were too heavy for earthen foundations and most castles were subsequently built on rock outcrops. Mottes were then gradually abandoned; while their timberwork could be reused, the earthen mounds had no obvious use and as a consequence they have survived as relict features in the present landscape. By comparison with mottes there were far fewer castles in 1300, as building in stone was expensive and could be undertaken only by the most powerful landholders.

The emphasis in late twelfth and early thirteenth-century castle-building was on a strong central point, usually a tower-keep, as seen in the rectangular examples at Trim and Carrickfergus, and in the more advanced circular keeps at Dundrum and Nenagh. Carrickfergus, built c. 1180–1190,[1] was probably among the last tower-keeps built in the British Isles, for by the early mid-thirteenth century they were replaced by rectangular hall-keeps, less defensive and more residential in function; good examples of this type may be seen at Athenry, County Galway, and Greencastle, County Down. At Castleroche, County Louth, c. 1230–36,[2] the hall is fitted into one corner of the castle precinct and the idea of a separate keep was abandoned in favour of a massive curtain wall and a strong gatehouse. Several other keepless castles, rectangular in plan, were built between about 1240 and 1280: examples include Castlegrace, County Tipperary; Quin, County Clare (where the foundations may be seen below the later Franciscan friary); and Liscarroll, County Cork.[3] At Liscarroll the shorter sides were defended by an additional tower on the north and a strong gatehouse on the south, but as Leask observed, the corner towers must have been rather inadequate for the defence of the longer east and west curtains. This weakness in design seems to have been overcome elsewhere in the late thirteenth century. In the 1280s, for example, the castle at Roscommon was entirely redesigned and, as a royal castle, it presumably reflected the latest military thinking. The castle is rectangular in plan with D-shaped angle towers and with the longest sides defended on the west by a small rectangular tower and on the east by a massive twin-towered gatehouse. In addition, the curtain was surrounded by a moat, now gone. These elements (symmetry, moat, angle towers, the emphasis on the gatehouse) all closely resemble those of the contemporary castles of Edward I in Wales; the similarity of the plan of Roscommon to that, say, of Harlech, begun shortly afterwards, is striking. Elsewhere in the British

---

[1] T. E. McNeill, *Carrickfergus castle* (Belfast, 1981), especially pp 41–2 and 53.
[2] R. A. Stalley, *Architecture and sculpture in Ireland, 1150–1350* (Dublin, 1971), pp 43–5.
[3] Leask, *Castles*, p. 71.

Isles, about 1300, older castles were being redesigned with the addition of curtain walls, angle towers, and gatehouses.

At about the same date a new castle was built at Ballymote, County Sligo; with an almost square plan it is the most symmetrical, and in some ways the finest, example of a castle of late thirteenth-century type in Ireland. The angle towers are round, and as at Roscommon there is a strong gatehouse, in this case midway along the north curtain. Unlike Roscommon, however, additional towers were added midway along the other three sides, D-shaped on the west and east, and rectangular, covering a postern gate, on the south. Although smaller, the castle is almost identical in plan to the main ward at Beaumaris, Anglesey, another of Edward's Welsh castles, begun about 1295. In Ireland such symmetry of plan was rarely achieved; the curtain walls of most thirteenth-century castles are polygonal or irregular in outline and follow breaks of slope and the edges of rock outcrops, as at Trim, Castleroche, Carrickfergus, and Carlingford.

Ballymote comes almost at the end of the line of the larger medieval castles of Ireland. Castle-building spilt over into the early years of the fourteenth century, for example, at Ballymoon, County Carlow, built about 1310, and Ballintober, County Roscommon, possibly a Gaelic Irish copy of Roscommon castle of early fourteenth-century date. In the landscape of 1300 almost all the large castles stood occupied, essential and 'living' elements within the country in contrast to their ruined and often desolate appearance today. By 1300 those castles built a century before must already have been thought of as old; others were newly built, their stone still unweathered and fresh with the marks of masons' chisels.[1]

Castles were only one indicator of the increase in the number of stone buildings over the previous century. The Anglo-Normans, equally concerned about their spiritual well-being, had from the outset granted land to the monastic orders and endowed the building of their houses. By 1300 this initial movement was over; the Cistercians, for example, had almost fifty foundations, fifteen of them pre-Norman, their expansion completed with the acquisition from the Benedictines in 1272 of Hore abbey, County Tipperary. Their houses, while generally austere, reflected the changing architectural style of the previous century. This is probably best seen at Boyle, County Roscommon, colonised by monks from Mellifont and built in the late twelfth and early thirteenth centuries. By 1300 three fine lancet windows had replaced earlier and smaller lights in the early presbytery of the 1160s. In the nave, the round arches at the east end on the south side are supported by cylindrical piers, probably of the 1180s, which show stray parallels to those at Buildwas in Shropshire. A few years later fashion had changed and the corresponding piers of the north arcade have attached shafts and support pointed arches. By the time of the completion of the west end of the nave (*c.* 1230?) the piers are square with triple

[1] The architecture of castles is also considered below, pp 753–6, 767–9.

shafts on their inner faces. At Boyle these architectural details are a visual reminder of the constant flow of new ideas (and also of stone-masons?) from England and Wales to Ireland in the thirteenth century. By 1300 many buildings combined both Irish workmanship and external architectural influence, as for example did the abbey at Corcomroe.[1]

The same was true of the cathedrals and town churches which, despite the wishes of both Anglo-Irish and Gaelic Irish bishops for new and grand buildings, were modest in scale by comparison to their English and French counterparts. Though Irish sees lacked the resources to build on a really grand scale, many cathedrals were rebuilt in the contemporary Gothic of western Europe—a style that demanded considerable skill both in design and in execution. The details of some churches show very clear parallels with English work and there seems to be no doubt that English masons were brought in to do some of the finer work, especially in Dublin.

Although a new diocesan framework had been worked out before the arrival of the Anglo-Normans it was only in the late twelfth and thirteenth centuries that the parochial system was organised on the ground. Parishes were normally coincident with manors, and as new tenants moved in so older churches became too small and new churches were built. Most of these were unpretentious rectangular buildings with nave and chancel, built of local stone, and with only a little ornament around doors and windows. The spread and building of parish churches seem to have been slow processes; most medieval churches, almost all now ruinous, contain more fifteenth-century work than thirteenth. While some may have replaced thirteenth-century churches, it seems likely that in 1300 many parishes were still using very small churches of eleventh- and twelfth-century date. As there has been very little archaeological work on the forerunners of later medieval churches this is another aspect of the Irish landscape in 1300 where, at this stage, speculation must substitute for fact.

Most stone buildings, whether castles, abbeys, or parish churches, were the principal elements within communities; as the local centres of social and economic activity they tended both to generate and to sustain nearby settlement. Manorial records of the late thirteenth and early fourteenth centuries leave no doubt that the Anglo-Norman 'conquest' of Ireland was backed up by a movement of settlers from England and Wales. The thirteenth century was a time of increasing population in England, and local land and food shortages in particular years may have tempted people to move, especially when the attraction of improved social status was held out to them. The arrival in Ireland of new settlers, and the consequent expansion of old settlements and growth of new ones, should be seen as a local manifestation of trends general to western Europe at the time. Unfortunately we know nothing of how the settlers were impressed or recruited, nor of the ways and means by which they came to

[1] Roger Stalley, 'Corcomroe abbey: some observations on its architectural history' in *R.S.A.I. Jn.*, cv (1975), pp 25–46.

Ireland. One historian has described the movement as a 'large-scale migration of peasants into Ireland to populate the manors'.[1] It is not known what this represents numerically: 10,000, 50,000, or more people? Even by 1300, when records appear to show a predominance of settlers of English and Welsh origin on many manors, we do not know how their numbers related to the native population. It is likely that the displaced Gaelic Irish were still in the majority except in the most intensively settled Anglo-Irish areas of the south-east, in Dublin and Meath, Carlow, Kildare, Kilkenny, south Wexford, and south Tipperary. Not only did enclaves of Gaelic Irish settlement persist in this Anglo-Irish 'province', for example in the Wicklows, but there were local concentrations of Gaelic Irish, most of them betaghs, on almost every manor. Despite some mixing, even by 1300 the incomers must still have been thought of as foreigners, separated by differences of language, custom, and social status from the indigenous population.

The comparative isolation of the newcomers was more marked because they lived in manorial settlements, newly created in the period 1170–1250 along the lines of villages in the English and Welsh lowlands. For some such settlements there are fairly detailed records which give an idea of their social structure about the year 1300. An unusually informative extent for Cloncurry, County Kildare, in 1304[2] indicates that there were approximately 191 tenants of non-Gaelic descent (112 burgesses and 79 others), and 111 Gaelic Irish, almost all of them betaghs or cottars. As these numbers represent heads of households, and as some sub-tenants may not have been named, we may postulate that the total population was probably over a thousand people. In addition to listing the tenants, the size of their holdings and their rents, this is one of the few extents which includes some detail of agricultural practice and of the actual appearance of the manor, which at this time seems to have been very run down, with an abandoned motte, a dilapidated hall, and several other buildings in a poor state of repair. Although the extent does not convey the layout of these buildings, an imaginative reconstruction drawing has already been published, of which almost every detail is open to question.[3] In fairness to the author, it must be admitted that any reconstruction drawings of settlements of this period have to be highly speculative until such time as written records can be backed up by archaeological evidence for house plans, building materials, and the many associated features of a manorial complex.

While records of this type leave little doubt that manors had nucleated settlements, we cannot say as yet how they were planned or laid out. Were the dwelling houses located near to the fortification or to the church? Were they grouped around a central area, and laid out on rectilinear plans similar to those of regulated villages in northern England and to the thirteenth-century *bastides* of south-west France? As yet we do not know of an example of a manorial

[1] Lydon, *Lordship*, p. 84.   [2] *Red Bk Ormond*, pp 27–34.
[3] John O'Loan, 'The manor of Cloncurry, Co. Kildare' in *Dept. Agric. Jn.*, lviii (1961), pp 14–36.

village depopulated in the fourteenth century that has sufficiently clear earthworks to indicate its layout at or about 1300. While there are several deserted
village sites with good earthworks, it is likely that most of these were finally
abandoned in the post-medieval period, and, because such settlements were
constantly adjusting to changing population numbers and to local social and
economic conditions, their earthworks are unlikely to be a reliable guide to
what they were like three centuries earlier.

It is increasingly evident that most of these manorial villages, although
essentially agricultural in function, were founded and given the inflated status
of boroughs in order to attract settlers. The custom of Breteuil, a small
Norman town whose urban constitution acted as a model, was granted,
apparently freely and without royal authority, by lords of the great liberties
and by their sub-tenants. The advantages to the individual included burgage
tenure for an annual rent of twelve pence, a low amercement (fine) for all but
the most serious offences, denial to the lord of rights of wardship and marriage, restrictions on the imprisonment of burgesses, and the right to manage
their affairs through a hundred court and not through the manorial court.
There can be little doubt that the aim was to attract settlers to the manors
and, to a limited degree, it succeeded. Although it will never be confirmed
from surviving documentation it seems likely that the aim on almost all
principal manors was to have agriculturally-based settlements of this type,
referred to from here on as 'rural boroughs' to distinguish them from places
with true urban characteristics, admittedly a distinction not always easy to
define.[1]

An interesting example of a deserted rural borough is Kiltinan, County
Tipperary, referred to as a town with burgesses in 1308–9, and again included
in a list of Tipperary boroughs in 1437.[2] While its date of desertion is not
known, its extensive earthworks were still known locally in the 1830s as those of
a village and recorded as such on the ordnance survey six-inch map of 1840.
Two stone buildings of the medieval village are still there: the castle, modernised and still inhabited, and the church, ruinous, but with its graveyard still in
use. Until their very recent and unfortunate destruction, the earthworks north
of the church suggested that, at the time of desertion, the village had a regular
plan; there were well defined hollow ways which were probably roadways.
Although house foundations were not clearly visible (perhaps because the
house walls did not have stone footings?) it is likely that the houses were
aligned in some way to the roads and that traces of them might be found to lie
under the adjacent irregular ground surfaces. Despite the levelling of this
impressive site, excavation might still recover the plans of the dwellings and
tell us whether or not the houses which date from the final abandonment were

---

[1] See, for example, the discussion of boroughs in Ulster in McNeill, *Anglo-Norman Ulster*,
pp 89–94.
[2] *Ormond deeds, 1172–1350*, p. 164; *1413–1509*, p. 95.

of the same type as the earlier medieval houses, and whether or not there had
been changes in their alignment and location.

There are numerous other examples of rural boroughs which are known to
have been flourishing about 1300 but which were later deserted. At Glenogra,
County Limerick, an extent of 1298 shows that the manor had about 120
burgages (deduced from the burgage rent of 119s. 6d.).[1] As at Kiltinan, all that
remain today is the ruins of the castle and church; on the first edition of the six-
inch map a fair green is marked, a sure indicator of Glenogra's former importance as a central place. In this case, however, there are no signs on the ground
of where 120 burgesses (or a total population of not less than 500) may have
lived; the fields nearby are flat with only slight surface irregularities. The same
is true at Moyaliff, County Tipperary, where only the site of a castle and a
ruined church indicate the whereabouts of the medieval settlement where 62
burgesses and some other tenants were recorded in 1305.[2] Already under
pressure from the Gaelic Irish in 1338, this manorial settlement may have been
deserted in the fourteenth century.

The records of other boroughs reinforce the view that many Anglo-Irish
settlements, now deserted, were flourishing about 1300. Ardscull, County
Kildare, was a sizeable place with 162 burgesses in 1282;[3] now only a sharp
bend in the road where it skirts the impressive motte (probably an earlier
feature reused by the Anglo-Normans) reminds us of the site. In the north,
always an Anglo-Irish frontier area, there were fewer attempts at manorial
settlements of this type; one at Greencastle, County Down, a strategic rural
borough at the mouth of Carlingford Lough, was in decline by 1333.[4] Except for
a motte and the thirteenth-century castle there is no sign of the whereabouts of
the medieval settlement. The new town of Leix, which disappeared so
completely that its exact location is uncertain, was another borough which
apparently declined fairly rapidly around 1300, its recorded burgesses dropping from 127 in 1283 to only 40 in 1324.[5] Boroughs of this type were founded
not only by the settlers. In 1238 David mac Cellaig Ó Gilla Patraic, bishop of
Cloyne, founded a borough at Kilmaclenine, County Cork.[6] This community of
burgesses, cottars, and betaghs must still have been in existence in 1300, for
there is mention in 1341 of 30 burgesses, all of English origin except three. The
settlement seems to have survived until the 1380s, when it disappears from the
records. All that now remains are the walls of a castle and a ruined church;
presumably the settlers' houses were somewhere between the two where there
are flat green fields today.

[1] *Cal. doc. Ire., 1293—1301*, pp 254—5.
[2] *Red Bk Ormond*, pp 64—7.   [3] *Cal. inq. post. mort.*, ii, 251.
[4] See E. M. Jope (ed.), *An archaeological survey of County Down* (Belfast, 1966), pp 103, 106—7.
[5] A. J. Otway-Ruthven, 'The medieval county of Kildare' in *I.H.S.*, xi, no. 43 (Mar. 1959), p. 184.
[6] *Rotulus pipae Clonensis*, ed. Richard Caulfield (Cork, 1859), pp 16—17. See Edmund Curtis,
'Rental of the manor of Lisronagh, 1333, and notes on "betagh" tenure in medieval Ireland' in
R.I.A. Proc., xliii (1936), sect. C, p. 68.

There are many other examples of places where depopulation was never total but where the present settlement is only a shadow of its former self. At Odagh, County Kilkenny, where there were 110 burgages in 1307[1] there is now little more than the castle and church. There are only a few houses at Ardmayle, County Tipperary, where burgesses are mentioned in 1338,[2] and Lisronagh in the same county is very small by comparison to its size in 1333 when, to judge from the number of tenants named in a rental,[3] the total population probably exceeded 400.

Attention has been drawn to these examples of deserted and shrunken Anglo-Irish settlements because in all probability they hold within the ground the key to the future discovery of the exact nature of thirteenth-century settlements, and perhaps to something of their economy. Unlike those places that have since flourished and where later buildings have either destroyed or obscured the vestiges of their medieval forerunners, abandoned sites offer the best opportunities to fill the tantalising gaps left in the documentary record.

Need for Archeology

AT least one-third of the country in 1300 remained free from the direct impact of the Anglo-Irish, whose influence, especially in frontier areas, was by then beginning to weaken as the scatter of new settlers were either killed, driven eastwards under Gaelic Irish pressure, or absorbed into Gaelic society.[4] The most remote areas, which remained untouched on account of their distance and inaccessibility from the centre of power in Dublin, were north-west Ulster (except Inishowen), the extreme west of Connacht, and the peninsulas of south-west Kerry.[5] All these were rugged areas of limited agricultural potential; had they been more attractive economically the Anglo-Irish would surely have made greater efforts to bring them effectively under their control. As happened in Scotland, where the highlands were difficult country, the infiltration stopped at their margins. The newcomers did, however, penetrate the more fertile lowland areas of the west: the Shannon lowlands, east Thomond (occupied by the de Clares in the last quarter of the thirteenth century), and much of Galway, Mayo, and Sligo, although their occupation of these areas was limited to a network of strongpoints (castles and fortified towns) and was not accompanied by widespread manorial settlement.

Even in the east of the country the Anglo-Normans, after their initial penetration of wooded areas and bogland, did not make strenuous efforts to retain control over areas of low economic potential. The Wicklows, despite their nearness to Dublin, reverted to being a Gaelic Irish stronghold throughout the middle ages; the bog-covered parts of Leix and Offaly were not held,

---

[1] Orpen, *Normans*, iii, 87.   [2] *Cal. inq. post. mort.*, viii, 119.
[3] Published in Curtis, 'Rental of the manor of Lisronagh, 1333'.
[4] For a study of the complex relationship between Irish chiefs and Anglo-Norman lords in a frontier area see Katharine Simms, 'The O'Hanlons, the O'Neills and the Anglo-Normans in thirteenth-century Armagh' in *Seanchas Ardmhacha*, ix (1978), pp 70–94.
[5] See map of the Gaelic areas *c.* 1297 in Nicholls, *Gaelic Ire.*, p. 13.

and most of Roscommon, Longford, and Leitrim remained largely in Gaelic Irish hands. In Ireland, as in Wales, the Anglo-Normans kept to the fertile lowlands; the hills and bogs became refuges for displaced Irish, and for the survival of Gaelic culture; their margins became local frontiers between native and foreigner, and between Gaelic and Anglo-Irish society.

If, as seems likely, the distribution of population in medieval Ireland reflected the fertility of the land, then almost all of the Gaelic areas must have been thinly populated. There is no means of calculating numbers nor of knowing whether in the Gaelic areas, as in the rest of Ireland, there had been population increase in the thirteenth century. Whatever the number it seems certain that the population was relatively low, and unevenly distributed. Settlements were small and impermanent and reflected the turbulent nature of Gaelic society. Whereas the Anglo-Irish areas were equipped in 1300 with an infrastructure of towns and manorial centres, the main places within Gaelic Ireland were still the ecclesiastical centres, which carried on their long-standing roles as centres of spiritual, social, and economic life. Some, such as Armagh, Derry, and Clonfert, were almost certainly large and influential enough to be thought of as the precursors of later towns.

In the open country settlements were small and few and far between, probably a few dwellings of related families clustered together for mutual dependence where water was easily available, where there was reasonable shelter from the elements, and where there was land suitable for both cultivation and grazing. Cultivation was important, especially for oats which, when made into cakes, was the main cereal element in the diet. A little wheat may also have been grown, even in the most westerly areas. To judge from recorded exports of linen cloth, flax must have been grown in some places. Larger pieces of land were probably ploughed, with either oxen or horses being pooled for the common plough-team; smaller patches would have been spade-dug. Stones cleared from the land were either thrown on to mounds or were used for walls, thereby creating small, enclosed fields.

Despite the importance of cultivation, some of it temporary, the mainstays of the economy were cattle and sheep. For large Gaelic landowners they formed the basis of a commercial economy in hides, wool, and meat; for the small man a few animals provided all the necessities of life: hides and tallow, wool for coarse woollen garments, meat, milk, and butter. Life for most people revolved around the stock, and herding cattle and moving with them from place to place was a widespread custom. To eke out the grazing, cattle were driven up to the more remote hill pastures in summer and looked after by herdsmen who built temporary shelters in the hills for the summer months. The custom of the seasonal movement of stock (booleying) survived in parts of the country into the nineteenth century.[1]

A few of the more permanent groups of dwellings may have resembled the

[1] See below, p. 413.

farm clusters (clachans) that were so widespread in the late eighteenth and
early nineteenth centuries.[1] Most clachans in the Gaelic areas are almost certainly of late origin and were a response to post-medieval population growth;
whether or not any single example has its origins as early as the thirteenth
century is still a matter of debate. To date, the only excavation of a nineteenth-
century clachan, undertaken with a view to finding its origins, was at Murphys-
town in the anglicised peninsula of Lecale in south-east County Down. The
results were inconclusive, and while there was some evidence that the site had
been occupied in the later middle ages no conclusions were drawn about the
exact form of the settlement at that time. There is virtually no evidence for the
nature of the medieval house in Gaelic Ireland. We must presume that most
dwellings were small, crudely built, and impermanent; the more substantial
ones may have been rectangular with sound walls, the poorer ones merely
circular or ovoid huts of clay and branches with thatched roofs, as the drawings
on sixteenth-century maps would suggest.[2]

   A related problem is whether or not ring-forts were still occupied in 1300. On
the evidence presently available the commonest settlements of the first millennium A.D. were small, circular, embanked enclosures, the 'forts' of country
people (usually, and wrongly, attributed by them to the Danes), and to the
archaeologists 'ring-forts', an unfortunate label which perpetuates the myth of
their military origin. A large number of these, usually estimated at 30,000,
survive in the country and their distribution poses fascinating problems to
historical and archaeological inquiry, problems to which answers will not be
forthcoming until many hundreds more have been excavated.[3]

   In the context of this chapter the main question that concerns us is whether
ring-forts were still places of habitation in 1300 or whether they had been abandoned by this date. Were they still an element within the settlement pattern or
had they already become monuments to the past? As less than a hundred sites
have been scientifically excavated, answers to these questions remain highly
speculative. Moreover, as over half of these excavations have been in the three
counties of Antrim, Down, and Cork, there are still large parts of the country for
which hardly any hard facts are available. Added to these difficulties, ring-forts
seldom yield many datable artifacts. Having said all this, there is little doubt that
most of them were, at one time, habitation sites; occupational layers and charcoal
spreads indicate occupation over considerable periods of time. Only a few excavated ring-forts have failed to produce any evidence of habitation; perhaps they
were enclosures for cattle or for some specialised activity such as metal-working.

   While the majority of ring-forts are still ascribed to the period A.D. 400–
c.1000, there is an increasing school of thought which believes that some

[1] Mapped by Desmond McCourt in R. H. Buchanan, Emrys Jones, and Desmond McCourt
(ed.), *Man and his habitat* (London, 1971), fig. 4, pp 138–9.
[2] See discussion and illustrations in F. H. A. Aalen, 'The evolution of the traditional house in
western Ireland' in *R.S.A.I. Jn.*, xcvi (1966), pp 47–58.
[3] Buchanan, Jones, and McCourt, op. cit., fig. 6, pp 154–5. Cf. below, p. 405.

continued to be occupied in the later medieval period. The evidence is fragmentary, in all senses, and normally consists of sherds of glazed pottery which can be dated with certainty to the thirteenth and fourteenth centuries. Writing in 1972[1] Barrett listed twelve ring-forts which have yielded late material; but for only six of these, all in the north, is the archaeological evidence strong enough to warrant an interpretation that the site had either been continuously occupied or had had a secondary phase of occupation in the later medieval period. With the exception of Thady's fort and Garrynamona, two ring-forts in County Clare, there is no evidence to suggest that ring-forts were constructed in the later middle ages; Rynne's suggestion that these two ring-forts were constructed in the fifteenth century has remained highly controversial since its publication in 1963.[2]

There is no doubt that the Anglo-Normans recognised the potential for their own purposes of many ring-forts situated in dominant positions which could be raised to form mottes or motte-like fortifications. Excavations in County Down have revealed that several ring-forts were heightened for this purpose. There is no evidence that the settlers systematically destroyed ring-forts, although in this regard the comparative lack of them in the area of the Pale is very puzzling. Were there never as many ring-forts here as further west, or have the majority been destroyed either in the process of settlement or by 'improving' farmers in the post-medieval period? It is evident from aerial photography that many ring-forts have been ploughed out, as for example in County Louth where a recent study has increased the number of known examples by 36 per cent.[3] It is to be hoped that work of this sort will demonstrate the continued need for systematic aerial photographic survey of the landscape. Alternatively, are the large numbers of ring-forts in Gaelic areas to be explained because they continued to be occupied, and even constructed, in Gaelic Ireland in the later middle ages? There is nothing to suggest that the Irish abandoned ring-forts with the coming of the Anglo-Normans; and it has been suggested at various times, without strong supporting evidence, that in certain areas ring-forts continued to be occupied in the middle ages, for example, in the counties of Clare and Armagh. The curious archaeological dilemma is that until now (and before the use of radio-carbon dating) the case for late occupation has been based almost entirely on finds of glazed pottery of Anglo-Norman type, an indicator that in any case one would not expect to find in the Gaelic areas, where the late occupation of ring-forts is therefore even harder to prove. In examining this question as it relates to the frontier area of Meath (where, as in the counties of Down and Cork, there is a striking difference between the number of

[1] Gillian F. Barrett, 'The ring-fort: a study in settlement geography with special reference to southern Donegal and the Dingle area, Co. Kerry' (Ph.D. thesis, Q.U.B., 1972), p. 162.
[2] Etienne Rynne, 'Some destroyed sites at Shannon airport, Co. Clare' in *R.I.A. Proc.*, lxiii (1962–4), sect. C, pp 245–77.
[3] Gillian F. Barrett, 'Aerial photography and the study of early settlement structures in Ireland' in *Aerial Archaeology*, vi (1980), pp 27–38.

ring-forts in the Gaelic and the Anglo-Irish areas), Graham concluded that the difference probably results from the late occupation and perhaps construction of ring-forts by the Gaelic-Irish, coupled with more widespread destruction of sites due to intensive agriculture in the eastern, Pale area.[1]

At present the question must be left open. There seems to be an increasing amount of evidence for the occupation (but still very little for the construction) of ring-forts in areas outside Anglo-Irish control c. 1300. In the Anglo-Irish areas most sites had probably been abandoned by this date, and some had been adapted for mottes and manorial centres. Crannogs, on the other hand, appear to have been continuously occupied throughout the middle ages.

SETTLEMENTS, whether Anglo-Irish or Gaelic Irish, were relatively small and easily overrun. Insubstantial dwellings with roofs of branches, sods, and thatch were easily burned; if abandoned they collapsed very quickly. Such houses have left hardly a trace in the written record and little enough archaeologically. Unless stone was used for wall footings there are few traces left on the surface of the ground; below ground, excavation occasionally reveals post-holes and the outlines of floors. Only in waterlogged conditions is timber present.

As yet we know next to nothing of the dwellings of the majority of people in medieval Ireland. The same was true of England until the post-war upsurge of interest in medieval archaeology; now, as a result of over thirty years' work, much more information is available about the medieval peasant house and its variations from place to place. In England, excavations have shown that the ordinary medieval house was broadly one of three basic types.[2] First there was the very small house, measuring externally about 25 × 12 feet (c. 8 × 4 m), usually of one room but sometimes divided into two. The second type was the long-house, having a living area at one end and a byre for cattle at the other, the two parts usually separated by a cross-passage with opposite doorways. The width externally was up to 20 feet (6 m); if extra space was required the building was lengthened at the living end up to a maximum of about 90 feet (c. 28 m). In the third type, the so-called 'farm', the dwelling and the animal quarters were separated into two distinct buildings, with the byre usually set at right-angles to the dwelling house, thereby forming two sides of a rectangular courtyard plan. While excavations continue to reveal examples of all three types, they also show considerable variations in the details of houses from place to place, a reflection of the availability of building materials, regional building traditions, and differences of social status between occupants.

While we should not expect exact parallels in Ireland, the corpus of evidence

---

[1] B. J. Graham, 'The settlement pattern of Anglo-Norman Eastmeath, 1170–1660' (Ph.D. thesis, Q.U.B., 1972), pp 235–8.
[2] J. G. Hurst in Maurice Beresford and J. G. Hurst (ed.), *Deserted medieval villages* (London, 1971), pp 104–13.

now available from England is helpful in any discussion of the types of house that might have been found in Ireland around 1300. This is especially so of the Anglo-Irish areas, where English and Welsh settlers had probably brought with them their own building traditions, later to be modified both by the local availability of materials and by the influence of traditional Irish building methods. It has been suggested, for example, that mud-walling may have been an Anglo-Norman introduction. As there has been so little excavation of medieval houses in this country, discussion must remain speculative and, in lieu of other evidence, must be generated from the nature of later houses and the possibility of their origins in the medieval period.

The one-roomed dwelling (*bothán scóir*), built variously of sods, dry-stone, and clay-mortared stone, survived in Ireland until comparatively recently.[1] It was the commonest type of house in many parts of the country when dwellings were classified in the census of 1841. Many thousands of these small houses had been built in the eighteenth and nineteenth centuries in a period of rapid population growth. It is unlikely that any actual nineteenth-century example was built in the medieval period, but it seems probable that the tradition of the single-room house was an ancient one and that houses of this type were built in the medieval period. The width of nineteenth-century examples, about 12 feet (*c.* 4 m), was exactly that of the small medieval house in England; the length, although less constant, was usually between 17 and 20 feet (*c.* 5–6 m). Another similarity between the two was the position of the door, not, as might be expected, in the middle of the longer side but towards one end and usually away from the hearth. The widespread distribution of this type of small house in early nineteenth-century Ireland was probably a reflection of poverty. Presumably the poorer people of thirteenth-century Ireland lived in similar small dwellings: houses without pretension, the walls made of the nearest materials to hand, pieces of wood, sods, clay, and stone, maybe mud, with the roof supported on a simple wooden frame, covered with sods and thatch, and maybe with a hole left for the smoke from the fire. Many unfree and landless tenants must have lived in houses of this type; if it is hard to imagine them as family dwellings, it is worth noting that there were families of six in similar houses in County Limerick in 1841.

The long-house survived until recently in upland Wales and it is now clear from both aerial photography and excavation that they were common throughout much of lowland England in the later middle ages. The long-house also had its parallels in Ireland; the byre-house, as it is frequently called, was common in Mayo and north-west Donegal in the late nineteenth century and some were in use until a few years ago.[2] These houses, with dwelling and byre

---

[1] Caoimhín Ó Danachair, 'The *bothán scóir*' in Etienne Rynne (ed.), *North Munster studies* (Limerick, 1967), pp 489–98.
[2] Caoimhín Ó Danachair, 'The combined byre-and-dwelling in Ireland' in *Folk Life*, ii (1964), pp 58–75.

under the same roof, were usually about three times as long as they were wide, with the byre at the lower end separated from the rest of the house by a cross-drain and opposite doorways, as in excavated English medieval examples. In a small byre-house with a one-room dwelling the hearth was usually at the gable; in houses divided into two rooms the hearth was usually central to the living part of the house, again as in English examples. Until recently the long-houses of Wales, Ireland, and western Scotland were believed to be Celtic in origin, because they were found exclusively in these upland, western areas. Recent excavations in eastern and southern England have shown that long-houses formerly had a widespread distribution and that the surviving examples in the highland zone should be thought of as survivals of a wider tradition in the medieval period. In much the same way, folk memory in Ireland testifies to a wider distribution of the byre-house in earlier times, for example, in mid- and south-east Ulster and in south-west Munster. We may conjecture that this type of house may have been widespread in eastern Ireland in the late medieval period and that it disappeared from the lowlands some time at the end of the middle ages when animals began to be housed separately in byres built at right-angles to the dwelling house. This may be the origin of the courtyard farms of eastern Ireland of which so little is known.

It may be that many of the more prosperous tenants on medieval manors lived in long-houses, although there is as yet no historical or archaeological evidence to support this view. The documents are silent on the ordinary houses and there has been little archaeological research on them. The only excavation of medieval peasant houses was that by Ó Ríordáin and Hunt at Caherguilla-more, County Limerick, where two houses were excavated out of a dozen or so clearly visible as earthworks on the surface. Both houses were of the rectangular, central-hearth type, with clay-bonded stone wall-footings. The earlier and larger of the two (House I), measured externally 43 × 20 feet (c. 13 × 6 m), and had walls with a wattle lining, an internal partition, and a doorway near one end of the long side. There was a second doorway (possibly blocked when House II was built) on the opposite side at the other end, a most unusual arrangement. The corners of the house were rounded, a feature that has been found on excavated examples of late seventeenth-century houses, for example at Liathmore-Mochoemog, County Tipperary. Finds, of both coarse and glazed pottery, suggested a span of occupation for these houses from the fourteenth to the sixteenth century; the excavators found no trace of earlier medieval houses beneath. The report[1] describes these houses as of the long-house type, but this description is used only in the general sense of their ground plans; there is no archaeological evidence for the existence of byres.

While it is possible that long-houses with an end-byre for cattle were widespread in eastern Ireland around 1300, there is no evidence of the type of house,

[1] S. P. Ó Ríordáin and John Hunt, 'Medieval dwellings at Caherguillamore, Co. Limerick' in *R.S.A.I.Jn.*, lxxii (1942), pp 37–63.

now characteristic of the eastern part of the country, where a central doorway leads towards the hearth, from which it is separated by a jamb wall. Such an arrangement is not suited to the moving of cattle in and out, nor is there any tradition of sheltering cattle in dwelling houses of this type. By implication, cattle, if sheltered at all, would have had to be kept in a separate building. Writing in 1937, Åke Campbell, pioneer investigator of the nature of the Irish house, regarded this type of dwelling, where door and hearth are in close relationship, as non-Irish in origin, and probably an introduction from England.[1] Following recent work on English medieval houses we are now in a position to hazard a further guess that this type of house may have replaced earlier byre-houses and may date from the change-over from the byre-house to the farm with its separate dwelling and byre, a change that perhaps took place some time at the end of the middle ages. Excavations in parts of southern England have shown that a similar change was taking place in the thirteenth century. In other parts of England this did not occur until the sixteenth century; the pace of change varied from place to place and according to social organisation, local attitudes, and peasant prosperity. As noted above, the change from the byre-house was not completed in upland Wales and parts of western Ireland until this century.

Until more work is done in this field, it can only be suggested that the medieval population in *c.* 1300 lived either in small, single-roomed or two-roomed dwellings, or in long-houses with the byre under the same roof. Round dwellings known from prehistoric and early Christian contexts may have survived in Gaelic areas.[2] For the most part the medieval house was rectangular (probably with stone footings in areas where field stones were easily gathered), and of one storey. Walls were of stone, wattle-and-daub, tempered clay, or even of sods and turf.[3] Roofs were of sods and/or thatch. In the eastern lowlands, especially north of Dublin, the courtyard farm may already have made its appearance by 1300, but this is pure speculation. The testing of this hypothesis lies in archaeology rather than in history, as the evidence for the ordinary house is below the ground rather than in the written record.[4]

ALTHOUGH there were many changes in Ireland between 1100 and 1300 none was more striking and of more lasting importance than the development of towns and the spread of urban life.[5] In western Europe the period 1100–1250 was one of population growth, increased production, and expanding trade. It

[1] Åke Campbell, 'Notes on the Irish house' in *Folkliv*, i (1937), p. 221.
[2] Discussed in F. H. A. Aalen, *Man and the landscape in Ireland* (London, 1978), pp 124–6.
[3] E. Estyn Evans, 'Sod and turf houses in Ireland' in John Geraint Jenkins (ed.), *Studies in folk life* (London, 1969), pp 80–90.
[4] Medieval housing is also discussed below, pp 403–4, 756–8.
[5] For general accounts see B. J. Graham, 'The towns of medieval Ireland' in R. A. Butlin (ed.), *The development of the Irish town* (London, 1977), pp 28–60, and 'The evolution of urbanisation in medieval Ireland' in *Journal of Historical Geography*, v (1979), pp 111–25.

Map 6 PRINCIPAL TOWNS AND MANORS, *c*.1300,
by R. E. Glasscock and K. W. Nicholls

See below, ix, map 37, and note, p. 104. Dots indicate location only, and not size of settlement.

was in this economic climate that the Anglo-Normans, already committed to the idea of town life, arrived in Ireland, then a country in which the opportunities for taking advantage of an economic boom were still very limited. It is not surprising, therefore, that both for strategic and for commercial reasons the Anglo-Normans rapidly took over the ports of Scandinavian and earlier origin in the south and east, and in the next sixty years proceeded to extend urbanism to all parts of their colony. To some extent the Normans had done the same in England, although there, where they had inherited a more developed urban network of Roman and late Saxon origin, they were more concerned to fill the gaps in an existing framework. By contrast Ireland had hardly any towns in a legal sense. While a number of inland places such as Armagh, Downpatrick, Kells (Meath), Kildare, Cashel, and Clonmacnoise almost certainly retained their early importance as monastic and regional centres, the development of port towns by the vikings, and their subsequent importance in international trade, had tended to transfer much economic activity from the inland centres to the coast. By the twelfth century wealth was no longer reckoned in terms of precious metalwork and other loot but in terms of the profits to be made from production and regular trade, for which Ireland was well placed midway along the Atlantic coast route between the northern lands and the Mediterranean.

As port towns of Scandinavian origin already existed on the east and south coasts, the Anglo-Normans were saved the trouble and expense of building their own. Dublin, Wexford, and Waterford, all in their hands by 1171, met their primary needs, and with new charters and organisation they were brought increasingly into the framework of north-west European feudal society. As the colony expanded so did urban development. By 1250 towns had been founded all over the south-east; with some later additions they were to form the basis of the present urban network.

By the late thirteenth century Dublin, with a population variously estimated at between 10,000 and 25,000,[1] retained the pre-eminence it had had since the mid-ninth century. The last two decades have seen a dramatic increase in our knowledge of medieval Dublin, firstly through excavation and secondly through an increased awareness of the historical importance of the medieval town within the context of the modern city. A new map showing the main features of medieval Dublin has been published[2] and recent papers have reconstructed the topographical development of the town.[3] Located midway along the east coast, it was the administrative centre of the Anglo-Irish lordship and

---

[1] Hollingsworth, *Hist. demography*, p. 169; the problem is also discussed in Gearóid Mac Niocaill, 'Socio-economic problems of the late medieval Irish town' in *Hist. Studies*, xiii (1981), pp 18–19.

[2] Ordnance Survey, 1:2,500: 'Dublin *c.*840–*c.*1540: the medieval town in the modern city', with an introduction by H. B. Clarke (Dublin, 1978).

[3] Best summarised in H. B. Clarke, 'The topographical development of early medieval Dublin' in *R.S.A.I. Jn.*, cvii (1977), pp 29–51, and Anngret Simms, 'Medieval Dublin: a topographical analysis' in *Ir. Geography*, xii (1979), pp 25–41.

was ideally situated to take advantage of trade with Britain, France, and the Mediterranean. Its links with Bristol were particularly strong and are recorded not only in the written evidence of documents but in the large quantities of Bristol-made and Bristol-type pottery found in the recent excavations of the medieval city. The first Anglo-Irish coins were minted in Dublin in the 1180s,[1] and the existence from then on of a coinage acceptable to foreign merchants not only helped the development of the city but was instrumental in the whole expansion of Irish trade in the thirteenth century. By 1300 coins had also been minted, if intermittently, at Kilkenny, Waterford, Cork, Limerick, Downpatrick, and Carrickfergus.

While Dublin had emerged as a city of international standing, the other ports, although having some international trade, were principally important as regional centres. Wexford and Waterford served the south-east, Cork the south-west, and Limerick the Shannon lowlands. In the early thirteenth century Wexford and Waterford, despite their nearness, had both prospered, a sure indicator of the importance of the south-eastern corner of the country as a landfall for coastal shipping. Its position relative to south Wales, Bristol, Plymouth, and the French ports gave the south-east commercial advantages over the west and north. However, with the addition of New Ross, with its better access to hinterlands in the Nore and Barrow valleys, Wexford began to decline in importance and by 1300 its trade had decreased and many of its burgages were lying waste. Waterford also declined in importance from the early fourteenth century.[2]

New Ross was planned and laid out about 1200 by William Marshal. Ross, now Old Ross, in the hills five miles (8 km) to the east, was of little strategic or commercial importance and a new port was developed below the confluence of the Nore and the Barrow. Within a few years the town was being called after its new bridge, *Nova Villa de Ponte de Ross*. With new towns all along both valleys the new port could hardly fail and it is not surprising that, despite the continued opposition of Waterford, New Ross had become one of the leading ports in the country by 1300.[3] Access to its hinterland via two important navigable rivers and its location over 20 miles (34 km) from the open sea gave it great advantages over most other ports, including Waterford at the mouth of the Suir. It was especially important in the early years of the colony; by 1300, when more of the country had an urban network, there are signs that the concentration of trade through the south-eastern ports was weakening.[4]

In creating a new port as a commercial speculation William Marshal was only following a well established process that had been successfully tried

---

[1] Below, p. 818.

[2] James Lydon, 'The city of Waterford in the later middle ages' in *Decies*, xii (Sept. 1979), pp 5–15.

[3] Eamonn McEneaney, 'Waterford and New Ross trade competition, *c.* 1300' in ibid., pp 16–24. Cf. above, pp 166–7.

[4] Otway-Ruthven, *Med. Ire.*, p. 123.

elsewhere. For example, there were no ports on the Humber when, about 1140, the earl of Aumale took part of the parish of Preston in order to lay out his new town of Hedon, a port that flourished until it was overshadowed by another new port, Kingston-upon-Hull, planted by Edward I in 1293.[1] The creation of new ports was part of the wider movement of founding new towns which gathered momentum in twelfth-century England and was to transform the urban geography of Wales and Gascony in the thirteenth century. New Ross was laid out about the same time as Stockbridge in Hampshire, a new *burgus* on the Winchester-to-Salisbury road. Whether in the Hampshire countryside or on an estuary in south-east Ireland the motive was the same: to create a community of traders and to profit from the increasing flow of commerce. King John must have been equally convinced of the gains to be made, for in 1207, as New Ross was getting on its feet, he acquired some land alongside a tidal creek of the Mersey and created by charter the new borough of Liverpool, ultimately to become the most successful of all the ports founded at this time.

A similar development took place on the east coast, where the de Verdons did not develop the early Anglo-Norman settlement at Castletown (now marked by a huge motte) but put all their energies into the founding of the new town of Dundalk on a tidal estuary nearer the sea.[2] As it was neither at the mouth of a large river, nor at the heart of extensive Anglo-Irish territory, Dundalk never had the commercial opportunities of New Ross; nevertheless, along with both Dublin and Drogheda (a town founded by Hugh de Lacy, possibly early in the 1180s and originally consisting of two boroughs on opposite banks of the Boyne[3]) it retained some importance in the later middle ages when the Anglo-Irish colony had shrunk to the confines of the Pale.

Further north Carrickfergus, which had also developed about 1200 alongside its massive castle, was by 1300 the established port for Belfast Lough, a role it retained until it was overtaken in importance by Belfast in the mid-seventeenth century. Elsewhere ports were developed by the settlers, for example, Coleraine, Galway, Sligo, Youghal, and Dungarvan; all were relatively more important to the Irish economy in 1300 than they have been in more recent times.

Except for their physical setting the appearance of all these ports must have had much in common. There was only limited quayage and many boats must have anchored offshore while their cargoes were transferred to and from smaller boats. The principal exports were of basic commodities, especially wool, grain (oats and wheat), hides, timber, linen, and fish. Ships coming into the ports discharged wine from Bordeaux and, perhaps by 1300, from Libourne (a planned town of the English in Gascony and the most successful of Edward I's *bastides* in France), salt from Chester, Bourgneuf Bay, Spain, and

[1] Maurice Beresford, *New towns of the middle ages* (London, 1967), pp 510–11.

[2] A. J. Otway-Ruthven, 'The partition of the De Verdon lands in Ireland in 1332' in *R.I.A. Proc.*, lxvi (1968), sect. C, p. 407.

[3] John Bradley, 'The topography and layout of medieval Drogheda' in *Louth Arch. Soc. Jn.*, xix, no. 2 (1978), pp 98–127.

Portugal; spices, silks and other luxuries from the Mediterranean; woollen cloth, food and miscellaneous supplies, including iron and building stone, from Bristol and Chester. From open wharves these goods were either trans-shipped to smaller boats for upstream distribution, or were carried up narrow streets to the commercial quarters of the town where the frontages were occupied by craftsmen and merchants. In every port there were masons, carpenters, smiths, tanners, shoemakers, weavers, millers, butchers, and bakers. Above and behind their premises were the town houses, almost all of wood, some perhaps on stone footings; sheds and outhouses stretched back along the narrow burgage plots.

Almost all the inland towns of importance in 1300 were situated on the larger rivers, which, in addition to their historic role as territorial divides, took on a new importance as the main arteries of trade in a period of increased commercial activity. In the south there were strings of towns along the Barrow (Graiguenamanagh, Leighlinbridge, Carlow, and Athy), the Nore (Inistioge, Thomastown, and Kilkenny, the most important of the inland towns), the Suir (Carrick, Clonmel, Cahir), and the Blackwater (Youghal at its estuary, Lismore, and Mallow). On the Liffey system no town of any size competed with Dublin (perhaps because the river was less navigable), but Navan and Trim were both important centres on the Boyne with their outport at Drogheda. Athlone dominated the middle reaches of the Shannon. In the west and north the primary centres were almost all on the coast, a reflection not only of the more limited river systems but, more importantly, of the very tenuous hold that the Anglo-Irish had on the inland areas.

All the larger towns were defended, either by ditches and banks with timber palisades, or (increasingly by 1300) by walls with angle towers and gates. A number of towns had been walled in the previous century, the actual date varying from place to place according to need and to the wealth of the community. Walling a town was expensive; money for it was usually raised through a murage grant which gave citizens the right to levy tolls on goods passing through the town.[1] Many smaller boroughs were not walled until the fourteenth century and others never had the resources to build substantial defences.

Below the primary towns in the urban hierarchy were numerous small boroughs created by leading Anglo-Irish sub-tenants in speculative moves to attract both settlers and trade. Given the rights to hold weekly markets and annual fairs many of them became important sub-regional centres with true urban characteristics, unlike the 'rural boroughs',[2] which remained agricultural in function, although it must be admitted that without adequate documentation it is frequently hard to categorise many such places. Almost all the smaller towns

---

[1] For a discussion of the process at New Ross, see Hugh Shields, 'The walling of New Ross: a thirteenth-century poem in French' in *Long Room*, xii–xiii (1975–6), pp 24–33; see also above, pp 166–7, and below, pp 718–19, 758.
[2] Above, pp 222–5.

were located along smaller rivers, which although not navigable provided water power for milling. The small Owenree (King's River) in County Kilkenny was one of this type. Callan, another foundation of William Marshal, whose motte still stands boldly on the north bank of the river near the modern bridge, was a small town in 1300. Although it was never walled it served as the market centre for an agricultural region, and in the fifteenth century attracted an Augustinian friary. Six miles (9 km) to the east, along the same river, was Kells-in-Ossory, where the buildings of the Augustinian priory survive but not those of the town, a late twelfth-century foundation by Geoffrey fitz Robert de Monte Marisco whose motte is still there. His town was burned by the de Berminghams in the 1250s and never fully recovered; it disappeared some time after the fourteenth century and its exact location is now something of a puzzle. The borough was probably somewhere between the ruins of the medieval parish church and the motte, and not, as is sometimes supposed, within the walls of the remarkable fortified priory. Midway between Kells and Callan, there may have been another attempt at town-building, for in a field at Newtown Earls there is a well defined hollow way leading from the medieval church (now, unhappily, a ball-court) down to the river. It is possible that there was a settlement here which did not survive the early competition from Kells and Callan.

Fethard, situated on the small Clashawley river in south Tipperary, is a small town for which a murage grant of 1292 (which lists commodities upon that tolls of murage could be taken) gives an impression of the range of goods that were the staple commodities of the commerce of any small Irish town about 1300.[1] They included horses, mares, oxen, cows, sheep, goats, and hogs; hides, salt meat, butter, cheese, onions, and garlic; sea fish, salmon, lampreys, and herring; skins, wool, hides, linen, and other cloth; salt, wine, honey, soap, alum, and wood; coal, firewood, lead, iron, nails, and horseshoes. We must presume that at Fethard trade was good and the murage was raised, for the town was walled in the fourteenth century, after which it hardly grew at all. The first edition of the ordnance survey map, surveyed in 1840–41, shows that the town was still confined within the line of its walls, stretches of which still survive, as do remains of the Augustinian friary founded shortly after 1300.

Small boroughs such as Fethard had grown up throughout the Anglo-Irish territory by the end of the thirteenth century; by 1299, thirty-eight market towns were recorded in east Cork alone.[2] A recent list suggests that in the country as a whole the number of places with some claim to be medieval boroughs was between 225 and 250.[3] Throughout the country these must have been in part a response to more intensive agricultural production made possible by an organised manorial system, in which, given relatively peaceful conditions, it was

[1] Lydon, *Lordship*, pp 97–8.

[2] *Cal. justic. rolls Ire., 1295–1303*, pp 265–6.

[3] Geoffrey Martin, 'Plantation boroughs in medieval Ireland, with a handlist of boroughs to *c.* 1500' in *Hist. Studies*, xiii (1981), pp 23–53, and especially pp 27–8.

possible to produce a surplus, at least on demesnes if not on peasant holdings.[1] But by 1300, when there are signs of recession, it is not surprising that a number of smaller towns and 'rural boroughs', founded in the first wave of colonisation before 1240, began to fall on hard times. The hopes of their founders that they would thrive and generate wealth were short-lived. Their location, which might have seemed advantageous in 1220, looked very different eighty years later. From the outset many had not attracted settlers in great numbers, nor were they sufficiently established by the 1260s to carry them through a period both of increased pressure from the Gaelic Irish and of decreased economic activity. Some struggled on, surviving even the Black Death, eventually to peter out in the sixteenth and seventeenth centuries: Bannow and Clonmines both as a result of the moving sands of the Wexford coastline; Newtown Jerpoint overtaken by nearby Thomastown and Kilkenny. Bunratty, County Clare, was similarly eclipsed by Limerick. At Kilbixy, a medieval borough in Westmeath, only a motte and a field of earthworks indicate its former presence.

For Anglo-Irish towns there is seldom evidence of their size about 1300. The 'town' of Athassel, County Tipperary, was reportedly burned in 1319 and again in 1329; only the magnificent ruin of the Augustinian priory remains. At Rindown, County Roscommon, on the shores of Lough Ree, a remarkable wall was built across the neck of a peninsula, presumably to protect a town, but there is no evidence that the place was ever populated; the fields may have been as green in 1300 as they are today.

In 1300, the justiciar John de Wogan visited the towns of the south and east to raise a subsidy in order to carry on the war in Scotland.[2] If the sums he raised are a general reflection of urban wealth then Drogheda (the two boroughs) and Cork, both with 260 marks ($£173$. 6s. 8d.) were the wealthiest provincial towns. Surprisingly they contributed more than Dublin, whose 200 marks is almost certainly a nominal amount and not a true reflection of its position. Waterford managed 100 marks, and New Ross, Youghal, and Kilkenny all paid £40 (Youghal giving five hundred of fish to add an extra £5). On the next rung of this incomplete urban ladder came Limerick (curiously low), Cashel, and (?) Kilmallock with £20. From some towns the justiciar could raise only 40s., and others managed only a mark or two. While the bigger towns survived, many of the smaller boroughs were to disappear almost entirely from the urban scene in the troubled century that was to follow.

[1] For a discussion of the impact of the manorial system on the agricultural production of a particular area see Empey, 'Medieval Knocktopher', pp 335–6.

[2] Cal. justic. rolls Ire., 1295–1303, pp 303–4.

CHAPTER IX

A land of war

JAMES LYDON

FROM the very beginning of the Anglo-Norman settlement the settlers had to fight for land and defend it when it was settled. Incastellation was a feature of the feudal landscape. The English system of local defence, based on the popular obligation to serve in arms, was introduced. The settlers naturally brought with them many customary military institutions and applied a familiar terminology to familiar situations. The progress of the conquest gradually opened up new frontiers and soon whole territories were in dispute and being fought over. These were the marches (*marchie*), a term we find in use from early in the thirteenth century. In 1215, for example, when Thomas fitz Anthony was given custody of the counties of Waterford and Cork, he had to guarantee to 'guard at his own cost the said counties, castles, and the king's lands in the march and elsewhere'.[1] As the frontier expanded, the march changed. A distinction was drawn, too, between the land of peace (*terra pacis*) and the land of war (*terra guerre*).[2] It is noticeable that in the second half of the thirteenth century the terms 'Irish enemies' or 'Irish rebels' appear and become increasingly common. Another military term that became widely current in the 1270s was 'ward', a slightly ambiguous term since it could mean either a place that was being temporarily guarded or the men who formed the guard.

This increasing use of military terminology in the second half of the century is in itself a useful reminder that war was becoming endemic in the lordship. Initially the Anglo-Normans had enjoyed a marked military superiority, which is very well illustrated by the conquest of Connacht, especially the attack by sea on the islands of Clew Bay and the reduction of the island fortress in Lough Key with siege engines.[3] The whole enterprise shows how irresistible the Anglo-Normans were when they cooperated and put their full energy jointly into some great forward movement. The Irish won the occasional pitched battle; but the advantage lay very heavily with the other side. When and why

---

[1] *Cal. doc. Ire., 1171–1251*, no. 576.

[2] 'Land of peace' is first mentioned in 1248, 'land of war' in 1272 (ibid., no. 2978; *Cal. doc. Ire., 1252–84*, no. 930); Robin Frame, 'Power and society in the lordship of Ireland, 1272–1377' in *Past & Present*, no. 76 (1977), pp 3–33, is a brilliant examination of the structure of the English colony and the sources of power wielded by magnates as heads of lineages.

[3] See the vivid account in *A.L.C.*, i, 329.

exactly the balance was altered is not quite clear. The importation of Scottish mercenaries, the galloglass, in increasing numbers in the second half of the thirteenth century obviously helped the Gaelic lords. They profited, too, from experience gained in alliance with the Anglo-Normans. They were no longer to be terrified by charging knights on huge horses and they learnt how to make the most of a terrain that was naturally unsuited to the traditional French type of warfare. Quarrels among the settlers, too, were to their advantage. And the increasing inability of governments, weakened by the exploitation of Edward I, to cope with disorder enabled many a Gaelic lord to assert independence and win back lost lordships. Whatever the cause, there is no doubt that in the second half of the thirteenth century the land of peace began slowly to contract as a Gaelic resurgence enlarged the land of war. Marchlands appeared in areas that formerly had been deep in the land of peace, some of them perilously close to Dublin itself.

In trying to define precisely the origins of this resurgence, or 'rally' as he called it, Eoin MacNeill suggested that it was instigated by a growing sense of nationality and a deeply felt sense of oppression.[1] There is evidence that something new was stirring in Gaelic Ireland, in the attempt in the 1250s to revive the high-kingship and in appeals during the era of the Bruce invasion to national sentiment in an attempt to whip up support against the English. It is possible, too, that rebellions in Wales and the later success of the Scots had an effect on Gaelic Ireland. A remarkable letter of 1282, from Thomas fitz Maurice to the bishop of Bath and Wells, contained the news that 'because of the war in Wales the Irish in parts of Ireland are more elated than is their custom and some are stirred by the war, others are prompted to make war'.[2] But such evidence, interesting as a sign of a growing self-consciousness in Gaelic Ireland, is less important than the racist attitudes apparent from early in the thirteenth century. The notorious conspiracy of Mellifont among the Cistercians manifested racism in a particularly violent form.[3] Deriving from an understandable aspiration to retain familiar features of old-style Gaelic monasticism in the face of Cistercian conformity, it soon led to a more general xenophobic attitude and Gaelic exclusiveness. The inevitable reaction, when it came, displayed a strong antipathy towards all things Gaelic. It was natural for the Cistercian visitor Stephen of Lexington, who had the misfortune in the circumstances to be an Englishman, to protest in 1228 that he had no racial bias. But almost unconsciously he showed his instinctive feelings of superiority as the product of a culture that was far in advance of the backward and indeed uncivilised Gaelic Ireland that he found in his travels here. When he said that the Irish were 'bestial',[4] meaning that they were ruled by emotion rather than by reason,

[1] Eoin MacNeill, *Phases of Irish history* (Dublin, 1919; reprint 1968), p. 325.

[2] *Facs. nat. MSS Ire.*, ii, plate lxxvi (2).

[3] B. W. O'Dwyer, *The conspiracy of Mellifont, 1216–31* (Dublin, 1970); An tAthair Colmcille [Conway], *Comhcheilg na Mainistreach Móire* (Dublin, 1968); and see above, pp 154–5.

[4] B. W. O'Dwyer, 'The impact of the native Irish on the Cistercians in the thirteenth century' in *Jn. Relig. Hist.*, iii (1965), p. 295.

he was exemplifying the attitude of the conquering Anglo-Normans. Early in the fourteenth century Edward II used the very same term in describing the Irish: they were, he said, 'bestial and uneducated' (*homines siquidem bestiales et indoctos*).[1] Giraldus Cambrensis was not unique in his dislike of what he did not understand and his detestation of what he regarded as inferior. Later in the thirteenth century the lord of Trim, Geoffrey de Geneville, remarked that before Henry II 'reduced the land and its inhabitants to obedience', the Irish 'as if unbridled, strayed over the plains of licence'.[2]

Racism in the church (it was rampant among the Franciscans, for example) may have been ameliorated by the instinct of all churchmen to defend ecclesiastical liberties; but it was there none the less. In a more pernicious form it showed itself too in the exclusion of all Irishmen (except those who purchased charters of denizenship) from the benefits of common law.[3] That this often worked to the disadvantage of Irishmen cannot be denied. It produced some horrific results. There was the preacher, for example, who told his flock that it was no more a sin to kill an Irishman than to kill a dog, a sermon that was not only condemned by the Gaelic appeal to Pope John XXII in *c*.1317, but was attested to by no less an authority than the great archbishop of Armagh, Richard FitzRalph. The exclusion of all Irishmen from apprenticeship in the towns was also condemned by FitzRalph as repugnant.[4]

Examples of this kind abound. It was not all one-sided, of course; Gaelic Ireland was just as racist in many respects. But among those Irishmen who had been willing to accept the Anglo-Norman settlement and who seemed anxious to coexist peacefully with their neighbours (such as those who tried to purchase a massive extension of the common law to Gaelic Ireland in the 1270s)[5] exclusion naturally promoted a sense of grievance. The feeling of being oppressed was generated by loss of lands and the apparent insatiable greed of many Anglo-Normans for further conquests. The levying of head money by the government, the toleration of notorious murders (such as the massacre of the O'Connors by de Bermingham in 1305) only served to increase the frustration and added to the grievances. The 'remonstrance' to John XXII in *c*. 1317 made much of this sense of grievance, and while we must allow for special pleading, there is no doubting the genuine note of grievance which runs through the whole document. The venom against the settlers is especially noticeable. These call themselves the 'middle nation' (an interesting example of the settler mentality, with its inevitable identification with the adopted land) and they are

[1] Watt, *Ch. in med. Ire.*, p. 80.

[2] *Cal. papal letters, 1198—1304*, p. 513.

[3] In general see A. J. Otway-Ruthven, 'The native Irish and English law in medieval Ireland' in *I.H.S.*, vii, no. 25 (Mar. 1950), pp 1–16; Hand, *Eng. law in Ire.*, pp 187–213.

[4] Katharine Walsh, *A fourteenth-century scholar and primate: Richard FitzRalph in Oxford, Avignon, and Armagh* (Oxford, 1981), pp 285, 325, 342.

[5] A. J. Otway-Ruthven, 'The request by the Irish for English law, 1277–80' in *I.H.S.*, vi, no. 24 (Sept. 1949), pp 261–70; Aubrey Gwynn, 'Edward I and the proposed purchase of English law for the Irish' in *R. Hist. Soc. Trans.*, 5th ser., x (1960), pp 111–27.

'so different in character from the English of England and from other nations that with the greatest propriety they may be called a nation not of middle but of utmost perfidy'. They have massacred and murdered, failed to protect the church, depriving it of lands, liberties, and possessions. The 'holy and dove-like simplicity' of the Irish people has been 'surprisingly altered into a serpentine craftiness through daily life with them and through their bad example'. They have deprived the people of all law and oppressed them with their own law. They have pursued a policy of racial exclusiveness in the church. 'Lusting eagerly for our lands', they have kept the Irish apart from the kings of England 'lest of our own free will we should hold from the king directly the lands that are rightfully our due'. There is much more in the same vein, all justifying the repudiation of the lordship of the English and the acceptance of Edward Bruce. The unknown author makes it plain that

there is no hope whatever of our having peace with them. For such is their arrogance and excessive lust to lord it over us and so great is our due and natural desire to throw off the unbearable yoke of their slavery and to recover our inheritance wickedly seized upon by them, that as there has not been hitherto, there cannot now be, or ever henceforward be established, sincere good will between them and us in this life. For we have a natural hostility to each other arising from the mutual, malignant and incessant slaying of fathers, brothers, nephews, and other near relatives and friends so that we can have no inclination to reciprocal friendship in our time or in that of our sons.[1]

Grievances, a sense of oppression, and a natural hostility generated by the attitude of superiority of many of the settlers—all of these undoubtedly helped to produce the kind of environment that made a Gaelic revival and a sense of nationality a possibility. But perhaps a much more potent fact was the perilous economic state of many Gaelic communities. Living on the worst land, barely above subsistence level, they were at the mercy of unseasonable weather and subject to famine. There is no doubt that much of the raiding on the rich manors of the feudal area, which became a feature of the second half of the thirteenth century, was occasioned by sheer economic necessity. Economic pressures, too, may have caused some of the population movements which produced an explosive situation in parts of Leinster. We shall never know for certain. Finally, the ambitions of Gaelic lords, or aspirants to lordship, was a powerful incentive to rebellion. Outstanding leaders appeared in Gaelic Ireland in the mid-thirteenth century and broke with the attempt of their predecessors to find their future within the framework of feudal relationships with the English king and the mesne lords which successive conquests had introduced. They put their faith in the sword, not the charter, and in the old Gaelic institutions that had sustained their ancestors.

[1] The text of the remonstrance can most conveniently be read in translation in Curtis & McDowell, *Ir. hist. docs*, pp 38–46.

It is of some significance that at the end of the remonstrance of *c.* 1317 Domnall
Ó Néill laid claim to be the 'true heir' to the kingdom of Ireland and in a seemingly self-effacing gesture publicly surrendered his right to Bruce and set him
up as king. There was, of course, no real historical basis for Ó Néill's claim.
But about sixty years earlier Brian Ó Néill of Tyrone had in fact been accepted
as king by Fedlimid Ó Conchobair and Tadg Ó Briain at a famous meeting at
Cáeluisce, near Belleek, on the Erne. According to the annals they gave him
'the kingship of the Gaels of Ireland'.[1] This was the climax of the O'Neill rise to
power in Tyrone, where they had successfully replaced the older MacLochlainn dynasty. Of themselves they would never have achieved the final eclipse
of the MacLochlainns and it was only with O'Donnell help that Brian Ó Néill
was finally installed as king in Tyrone in 1241. Brian cleverly freed himself from
dependence on the O'Donnells and astutely made a marriage alliance with his
former MacLochlainn rivals, winning their support in his future military
engagements. Soon he was strong enough to interfere in both Tír Conaill and
Connacht, tried to force the O'Donnells into some sort of submission, campaigned against the O'Reillys, and earned for himself the title of 'high-king of
the north of Ireland'. Then in 1255 there came a significant development, when
Áed Ó Conchobair, son of King Fedlimid of Connacht, 'went into Tyrone and
made peace between his own father and northern Ireland'.[2] It was the beginning of the diplomacy that resulted in the meeting at Cáeluisce.

This new alliance with the O'Connors, confirmed in another meeting the
following year, persuaded Brian Ó Néill that the time had come to strike at the
earldom that hemmed him in to the east. He had already made a number of
raids: in 1253, for example, he had destroyed the castle of Mag Coba. He had,
too, submitted to the justiciar on occasion and is recorded on pipe roll 45
Henry III (where he is styled *regulus*) as owing 3,092 cows of a fine, arrears of
rent for his land, and £100 of an aid that had been granted for the war in
Gascony.[3] But his ambition led him to look for greater power. According to the
evidence available to Henry III he 'presumptuously bears himself as king of the
kings of Ireland',[4] and we may suppose that his decision to invade the earldom
once more in 1260 was the first step towards making that title a reality. This
time he was supported by Áed Ó Conchobair and the men of Connacht, as well
as other allies closer to home. But not far from Downpatrick, on Sunday
16 May, he was totally defeated by 'the commonalty of the city and the county'.[5]
He was killed, together with many of the leaders of contingents in his army.[6]

---

[1] *Ann. Conn.*, p. 127. There is a brilliant analysis of the manner in which the Dublin government
dealt with the military and police problem posed by the Irish in Robin Frame, 'English officials
and Irish chiefs in the fourteenth century' in *E.H.R.*, xc (1975), pp 748–77.

[2] *Ann. Conn.*, p. 113.   [3] *Facs. nat. MSS Ire.*, ii, plate lxxiii.

[4] *Close rolls, 1259–61*, p. 64. When he was killed later, the Annals of Connacht called him 'king of
the Gaels of Ireland' (*Ann. Conn.*, p. 131) and the Annals of Inisfallen record that it was to him that
'the Gaedil gave hostages' (*Ann. Inisf.*, p. 361).   [5] *Cal. doc. Ire., 1252–84*, no. 661.

[6] Brian's death was noted in the Dublin chronicle, indicating its importance from that perspective (*Chartul. St Mary's, Dublin*, ii, 316). It was also recorded in the Kilkenny chronicle, one of only

His court poet Mac Con Mide wrote a great lament for the dead king, mourning his death, bewailing the loss to Ireland, and depicting the hero and his army dressed in linen and pitting themselves fearlessly against the massed iron of the enemy.[1] But even if Ó Néill's army was not in heavy armour (and he may well have enjoyed galloglass support, since in 1259 his ally Áed Ó Conchobair had married the daughter of Mac Sumarlaide and acquired her dowry of 'eight score warriors' who were probably galloglass),[2] it does not say much for its potential that it could suffer such a heavy defeat at the hands of local levies. There is some support for the tradition that he was opposed by a section of his own people who preferred to have his rival Áed Buid as king.[3] Áed, indeed, was not only an ally of the O'Donnells, but was supported by the government and by the Anglo-Irish of Ulster, and with their help he did succeed Brian in Tyrone. It was not the first or last time that a Gaelic lordship was weakened by the political rivalry of opposite branches of one dynasty. The remonstrance of c. 1317 was bitter on the subject. Domnall Ó Néill attributed it to the cunning of the settlers, and in a letter to a MacCarthy he pointed out the pernicious results of this divisive tendency of Gaelic Ireland:

so that we, being weakened by wounding one another, may easily yield ourselves a prey to them. Hence it is that we owe to ourselves the miseries with which we are afflicted, degenerate, and manifestly unworthy of our ancestors, by whose valour and splendid deeds the Irish race in all past ages has retained its liberty.[4]

It is hard to know how serious a threat was posed by Brian Ó Néill before he was defeated. That the government feared his success is evident in the fact that in 1252 the borough of Drogheda (Uriel) supplied food for one day to 200 *satellites* (infantry) 'who were sent to Keneleon to fight Brian Oneale and his accomplices'.[5] The possibility of Scots 'seeking confederacies with the Irish' at this time seriously alarmed the government and must have added to the fear of what Ó Néill was doing in Ulster.[6] The fact, too, that the dead king's head was sent to London, instead of to Dublin as was normal, indicates that the victory was regarded as especially important. So the death of Brian must be seen as not just another local victory over a local chieftain, but as the end of a challenge

two such records, where Brian is styled *regulus* (Clyn, *Annals*, p. 8). For a brief account of his career see Katharine Simms, 'The O'Hanlons, the O'Neills, and the Anglo-Normans in thirteenth-century Armagh' in *Seanchas Ardmhacha*, ix (1978), pp 70–94.

[1] *The poems of Giolla Brighde Mac Con Midhe*, ed. N. J. A. Williams ([London], 1980; Irish Texts Society, li), no. XIII (pp 136–61).

[2] *Ann. Conn.*, p. 131.

[3] *Ann. Inisf.*, p. 361, where it is stated that he 'was slain by the Gaedil themselves and some of the foreigners'.

[4] Herbert Wood, 'Letter from Domnal O'Neill to Fineen MacCarthy, 1317' in *R.I.A. Proc.*, xxxvii (1926), sect. C, p. 143. It has recently been argued that this letter is a forgery, but I do not find the argument wholly convincing; see Diarmuid Ó Murchadha, 'Is the O'Neill-MacCarthy letter of 1317 a forgery?' in *I.H.S.*, xxiii, no. 89 (May 1982), pp 61–7.

[5] Lambeth Palace, Carew MSS, no. 635, f. 132ᵛ.

[6] Letter of 29 Apr. 1260, *Cal. doc. Ire., 1252–84*, no. 652.

that had implications beyond Ulster. Nevertheless, he can hardly have hoped to revive a kingdom of Ireland. Not only did he lack the support of any of the other provinces except Connacht, he was even denied recognition within the northern province. Ó Domhnaill, Mac Mathgamhna, Ó Ragallaig, Ó Ruairc, and most other northern lords spurned him. His title was an empty one, and the ease with which he was contained suggests that he lacked the resources to go very far, even in Ulster. His successor, Áed Buidhe, was certainly more realistic, accepting the overlordship of the de Burghs, helping the seneschal of the earldom to keep the peace in the marches, and generally cooperating with the Anglo-Irish.[1] He gained materially from this. For example, de Mandeville helped him to defeat the O'Donnells in 1281.[2] As we saw, he also formally acknowledged that he held his kingship from the earl of Ulster.[3]

For many years, then, after the battle of Down, the O'Neills were subservient to the earls. Generally relations were amicable and not in any substantial way to the disadvantage of Ó Néill. But for some reason in the early fourteenth century Domnall Ó Néill incurred the disfavour of Richard de Burgh, at the very time when the O'Donnells were becoming a danger to him in the west. The territorial expansion of the earldom under Richard de Burgh seemed to go beyond what was tolerable. Once more, therefore, an Ó Néill revived a claim to the high-kingship, only this time to resign it in favour of Edward Bruce, brother of the king of Scotland. There seems little doubt that from Ó Néill's point of view the Bruce invasion was intended to free him from the threats posed by Ó Domnaill and de Burgh. But in this he was not entirely successful, since after the collapse of Bruce's kingdom Domnall was dethroned and banished by the Anglo-Irish.[4] Even though he recovered his kingship in the same year, it was not until after the collapse of the earldom following the murder of the last earl of Ulster in 1333 that the O'Neills were able to assert their authority in Tyrone and begin that expansion of power that led Richard II to refer to Niall Ó Néill at the end of the century as the 'great Ó Néill'.

In Connacht, too, the de Burghs were able to exercise immense influence and to force the O'Connor kings to accept their overlordship. They regularly acted the part of king-maker and exploited fully the fatal weakness of the vicious feuds among the O'Connors. We saw the anxiety of Cathal Ó Concho-bair to work within the system imposed by the settlers and thereby to secure the inheritance of his son.[5] But his failure and the expansion of de Burgh, and even Geraldine, interest in Connacht saw the gradual erosion of O'Connor power. King Fedlimid Ó Conchobair tried to arrest this process in mid-century; but while he occasionally broke out of the restraints imposed by the feudal

[1] Edmund Curtis, 'Sheriffs' accounts of the honour of Dungarvan, of Tweskard in Ulster and of County Waterford' in *R.I.A. Proc.*, xxxix (1931), sect. C, pp 10–11.

[2] *Ann. Conn.*, p. 173.

[3] *Report on the manuscripts of Lord De L'Isle and Dudley, preserved at Penshurst Place* (H.M.C., 6 vols, London, 1925–66), i, 31–2.

[4] *Ann. Conn.*, p. 255. [5] See above, p. 161.

structure within which he was enmeshed, on the whole he acquiesced in the
status quo and pinned his faith on a personal relationship with Henry III. He
not only kept in contact through ambassadors, but he met Henry on at least two
occasions. His attitude is well illustrated in a letter written shortly after the
defeat of Brian Ó Néill at the battle of Down, in which he said:

For no promise made to him by the Irish had he receded, or would he recede, from the
king's service. He places himself, his people, and all he has under the protection of the
king and of the Lord Edward; and confides to the Lord Edward from then until the
arrival in Ireland of the latter, all his property and all his rights, if any he has, in
Connacht.[1]

It was his son Áed who, even before he became king, lost patience with the
diplomatic policy of his father and resorted to the more direct method of force.
He tried to win back something of what had been lost to the settlers and to
compensate for the rest by a policy of aggrandisement towards Bréifne in particular. It is significant that Áed coincided with the advent of leaders in a
number of Gaelic lordships who were to shake off the more compliant policy of
the last generation and take to the sword. Gofraid Ó Domnaill, who won a significant victory at the battle of Credran Cille in 1257 which effectively halted
the Geraldine advance northwards from Sligo, and Fíngen Mac Carthaig of
Desmond, who halted a similar expansion in the south, are only two of the
greatest names among a number of ambitious Gaelic lords who in the 1250s
were ruthlessly preventing the further expansion of feudal Ireland. Circumstances favoured them. A remarkable series of deaths in mid-century removed
some of the greatest names in Anglo-Ireland. We have already noted the
extraordinary extinction of the Marshal family in the male line, with the death
of Anselm in 1245, and the subsequent partition of the great lordship of
Leinster. Early in 1241 Walter de Lacy died and Meath, the second great lordship in Ireland, was divided between his granddaughters. Such partitions were
inevitably a source of weakness. Hardly less dangerous were minorities, when
lordships fell into the king's hands. This happened with Connacht and parts of
Munster when Richard de Burgh died in 1243 in Poitou and left a minor as heir.
And when Hugh de Lacy died around the same time the great earldom of
Ulster escheated to the king. The resultant weakness in the settlement was
worsened by the failure of the Lord Edward to discharge adequately his
responsibilities in Ireland after 1254.

Áed Ó Conchobair, then, was typical of the new Gaelic Ireland. Even as
early as the 1240s he had shown his mettle. In 1249, when Piers de Bermingham
(who had been given custody of the de Burgh lands during the minority)[2] led 'a
troop of young mounted men' into Connacht, they were successfully ambushed
by Áed, who then invaded and sacked de Bermingham's own lands. This
provoked an all-out war, with the justiciar assembling 'the Galls of Meath and

[1] *Cal. doc. Ire., 1252–84*, no. 713.   [2] Ibid., *1171–1251*, no. 2975.

Leinster, a great host' and Maurice FitzGerald 'with the Galls of Munster and Connacht'.[1] Áed's precipitate action had embroiled his father in a situation outside his control. He was deposed and only restored in 1250 at the cost of a diminution of his lands.[2] It was not the last time his position was to be compromised by his son's refusal to accept the restrictions of the world of the settlers. In 1253, as we have seen, he negotiated a peace with Brian Ó Néill, who three times attacked Ó Ragallaig of Bréifne in the same year. This suited Áed's policy of hostility towards Bréifne. There was then a confusion of attacks and counter-attacks in which Áed was implicated, which weakened both the O'Reillys and O'Rourkes and left Bréifne more susceptible to attack from the west across the Shannon. It was certainly his interest in Bréifne that prompted him to go to Cáeluisce and agree to confer the kingship of Ireland on Brian Ó Néill, an occasion when, the annals say, 'the hostages of Muintir Raigillig and of all the Uí Briuin from Kells to Drumcleff were delivered to Áed'.[3] The price Ó Néill had to pay was to allow Ó Conchobair a free hand in Bréifne. Another meeting between the two took place at Devinish on Lough Erne in 1259, when once again Ó Conchobair interest in Bréifne was confirmed.[4] Áed on that occasion was on his way back from Derry, where he had married the daughter of the Mac Sumarlaide lord of the Isles. She brought eight score warriors with her, probably the first recorded band of the formidable galloglass to be imported into Ireland. Nothing better illustrates the capacity of Áed Ó Conchobair to recognise what might be of value to him and to exploit it to the full. His complete ruthlessness is equally well shown by his blinding of a possible rival Ó Conchobair and hostages in the same year and of yet another rival in 1265.[5]

Áed joined Ó Néill in the fatal hosting that was to lead to the battle of Down in 1260. Although he escaped with his life, many of the nobility of Connacht were left dead on the field of battle.[6] There was a massive government reaction in 1262, when Connacht was invaded.[7] The O'Connors had cautiously moved their great herds of cattle northwards into safety. There was much plundering by both sides before peace was concluded. Ó Conchobair fines for having peace were recorded in pipe roll 46 Henry III, so it looks as if the O'Connors were forced to come to terms.[8] Áed soon broke out again and once more Connacht was plunged into war. Not even Athlone escaped: in his account for 1262–6 Richard de la Rochelle recorded 'nothing for the issues of five acres of land outside the bailey of the castle for the whole of that time because the land was devastated by Fethel' OKonether king of Connacht and his son'.[9] But the

---

[1] *Ann. Conn.*, p. 99.
[2] *Cal. doc. Ire., 1252–84*, nos 35, 223–6, 228.
[3] *Ann. Conn.*, p. 127.
[4] Ibid., p. 131.
[5] Ibid., pp 131, 145.
[6] Ibid., p. 133.
[7] Ibid., p. 139: 'the Galls of Ireland raised an immense army to attack Fedlim Ó Conchobair and his son, Áed na nGall.'
[8] Orpen, *Normans*, iii, 240.
[9] P.R.O.I., R.C. 11/2; calendared in *P.R.I. rep. D.K. 35*, p. 48.

great Geraldine–de Burgh quarrel of 1264 and the civil disturbance unleashed by the capture of the justiciar in the same year gave Áed his chance to take the offensive in a decisive way in Connacht. He succeeded his father as king in 1265 and continued his systematic plundering of the settled lands. He acted the part of king-maker in Bréifne in 1266.[1] No decisive action was taken against him until 1268, when he was summoned to Athlone. According to the annals he came with an army and enjoyed a huge success, killing many.[2] It was not until 1269 that the government made positive moves in Connacht. The new justiciar, Robert d'Ufford, now began the building of a royal castle at Roscommon, and in 1270 his deputy led an army across the Shannon to join forces with Walter de Burgh. There was some negotiation with Ó Conchobair before they were forced to retreat, constantly harried by the Irish. Attempting to ford the Shannon at Áth in Chip, near Carrick on Shannon, the army was utterly routed by Ó Conchobair.[3] Áed followed up this great victory by destroying castles and burning towns. The new castle of Roscommon was knocked down. There was no stopping Áed now, and the unexpected death of Walter de Burgh in 1271 removed the one man who had provided any serious opposition. The English hold on east Connacht was now seriously shaken. Áed raided as far east as Granard and burnt Athlone, the gateway to Connacht, destroying the bridge. But on 3 May 1274 Áed died, 'a king who wasted and desolated Connacht in fighting the Galls and Gaels who opposed him; a king who inflicted great defeats on the Galls and pulled down their palaces'.[4] It was an accurate enough obituary.

Áed's death plunged Gaelic Connacht into civil war which destroyed much that he had achieved. His successor as king lasted only three months before he was killed; the king after him survived a mere fortnight before being murdered. This fatal weakness in the Connacht kingship made impossible any real, permanent, Gaelic recovery. Between 1274 and 1315 there were no less than thirteen kings of Connacht, of whom nine were killed by their own brothers or cousins and two were deposed. This is a terrible record for any kingdom. It was naturally exploited by the de Burghs, Geraldines, and the government. The real weakness of the O'Connors is well demonstrated by their failure to capitalise in any lasting way on the great disturbances caused by the continuous Geraldine–de Burgh quarrel and the lesser faction fights that this engendered. Even the upheaval of the Bruce invasion was misused, one Ó Conchobair using it simply to score off his rival, so that they were decisively defeated at the battle of Athenry, which secured Anglo-Irish dominance for another generation. As in Ulster it was the death of the last earl of Ulster in 1333 which made possible a great Gaelic recovery in which the O'Connors were to share.

---

[1] *Ann. Conn.*, p. 147.   [2] Ibid., p. 151.
[3] *Ann. Conn.*, pp 155–7. It is significant that this is one of only two battles recorded in the Kilkenny chronicle in the mid-thirteenth century (Clyn, *Annals*, p. 9).
[4] *Ann. Conn.*, p. 163.

Nevertheless the achievements of Áed Ó Conchobair must not be too easily written off. If his successors failed to carry on what he had begun, they did cause enough trouble to involve the government in expensive operations in Connacht. The three royal castles of Athlone, Rindown, and Roscommon had to be regularly maintained and repaired. In his enrolled account for 1270–72 the justiciar, James de Audley, records an expenditure of over £1,600 on the three castles.[1] In 1272 Áed Ó Conchobair had knocked down Roscommon and Rindown and damaged Athlone. Geoffrey de Geneville commenced rebuilding in 1274 and also started on a stone bridge at Athlone (where he had a galley built for the king, presumably to patrol the waters of the great Lough Ree).[2] But in 1277 Roscommon was destroyed again and both the other royal castles damaged. Rebuilding commenced almost immediately. And so it went on, a relentless round of destruction and reconstruction. In his account for 1278/9 the justiciar, Robert d'Ufford, was charged with a total of £5,167. Of this he was allowed no less than £3,200 on works at the three castles.[3] This gives a very clear indication of how heavily the government was committed in Connacht at this time. Because of the continuous disturbances it was impossible to disengage, especially since the minority of the earl of Ulster had brought the lordship of Connacht into the king's hand. All attempts through regular diplomatic activity had failed to secure any sort of stable relationship with the O'Connors, and even after de Burgh returned to Ireland in 1286, the government still found it impossible to get out of Connacht, though it tried to cut down on expenditure. After de Burgh and fitz Thomas had settled their differences and the earl was left in the ascendancy in Connacht, he seems to have been able to pacify the areas in which he was dominant. His supreme importance is well exemplified by his petition of 1305 to have the land of Síl Muiredaig, which had been forfeited by the O'Connors. An inquisition examined the proposal, and in supporting it the jurors said that the earl had 'a great force of English and Irish adjoining that land, by which he would be better able to chastise the Irish of that land than another'.[4] With de Burgh interest so dominant the government was able to concentrate on the king's cantreds along the Shannon. But even here, because of increasing commitments elsewhere in the land of war, the king's interests were not well maintained. For example, an inquisition taken in June 1301 revealed that certain royal lands in Roscommon and near Athlone 'were absolutely worth nothing' until 1299 'on account of continual war' and it suggested that this was because the government 'abandoned the custody of the king's castles of Roscommon and Rindown'.[5] The castles, of course, were not

---

[1] *Cal. doc. Ire., 1252–84*, pp 147–8.
[2] Pipe roll 7 Edw. I in *P.R.I. rep. D.K. 36*, p. 40. He spent nearly £430 on Athlone and £440 on Rindown (R.I.A., MS 12.D.10, p. 59).   [3] Pipe roll 8 Edw. I in *P.R.I. rep. D.K. 36*, p. 49.
[4] *Cal. justic. rolls Ire., 1305–7*, p. 134.
[5] *Cal. doc. Ire., 1293–1301*, p. 367. Other lands had already been surrendered to the king by Richard d'Exeter 'as well on account of the high farm of these lands as on account of the common war of the Irish of Connacht'.

'abandoned'; but the government's hold on them became increasingly precarious and the three king's cantreds which they protected were gradually lost to the king. With the escalation of war elsewhere in the lordship, and with increasing demands from Edward I for support in his wars abroad, it became impossible for the Dublin government to find the time or resources to deal adequately with its own problems in Connacht.

JUST about the time that Brian Ó Néill was making his bid for control of the north, and the O'Donnells and the O'Connors were likewise beginning to challenge the expansion of feudal Ireland, the attempt to expand the settlement in Desmond was halted for good. Many parts of Munster had been successfully feudalised in the late twelfth and early thirteenth century, and as usual the settlers made use of Gaelic rivalries to intrude themselves into new lands. It was in this way that Desmond was rapidly invaded and incastellated, with the Geraldines very much to the fore. Intermarriage with the leading Gaelic families followed and a remarkable compromise was reached by which the new settlers were tolerated and the lordship of Mac Carthaig in the Gaelic areas was recognised. There were, of course, plenty of minor disturbances; but on the whole this proved to be one of the most peacefully settled areas in feudal Ireland. Relations with the MacCarthys remained good. Indeed Cormac Finn Mac Carthaig was one of the Gaelic lords summoned by Henry III in 1244 to join his expedition to Scotland.[1] It was on his death that trouble began.

The settlers became enmeshed in a succession quarrel and widespread disturbances followed. In 1249 the justiciar led an expedition against Fíngen Mac Carthaig 'and thirteen other knights in Desmond', which involved an attack by sea.[2] Fíngen was subsequently murdered by his uncle Domnall, who then succeeded to the kingship.[3] But in 1252 he in turn was murdered by John fitz Thomas and this had the most serious consequence. Domnall was the man supported by the government in the succession dispute and fitz Thomas was clearly acting independently in his own interest. But now he had Domnall's son Fíngen to contend with, a man cast in the same mould as Áed Ó Conchobair. To revenge his father's death he went on the rampage and over the next few years ravaged the settled areas with fire and sword. The long peace was at an end and Desmond became a land of war. Fíngen made a special point of destroying the castles which were the shield of the settlement and by 1261 the situation was so critical that government intervention was necessary. The justiciar proclaimed a royal service and money was borrowed from merchants to further augment the royal army.[4] The fact that the barons of Desmond

[1] *Cal. doc. Ire., 1171–1251*, no. 2716. [2] N.L.I., MS 1 (Harris Collectanea), f. 167.
[3] *Ann. Inisf.*, p. 355. Domnall paid £100 'pro regalitate Desmonie habenda' (pipe roll 33 Hen. III, T.C.D., MS 671 (F.3.13), f. 3ᵛ).
[4] A. J. Otway-Ruthven, 'Royal service in medieval Ireland' in *R.S.A.I. Jn.*, xcviii (1968), p. 41; *Cal. close rolls, 1271–9*, p. 240. The money was borrowed 'in order to hire the king's army', which suggests that a large paid force was raised. It was provisioned from Waterford, which may have been the place of muster (*P.R.I. rep. D.K. 35*, p. 49).

promised to repay this loan is a sure indication of how desperate the situation was in the south-east. When the great army moved into Desmond, the Geraldines were prominent among the leaders. On 24 July it came face to face with Fíngen's army, at Callan near Kenmare, where the rough mountain terrain was not suited to the knight and his way of fighting. The slaughter, according to the annals, was 'unspeakable' and many of the leaders in the royal army were killed. Chief among these was John fitz Thomas of Shanid and his son Maurice. The annals say that in addition eight barons and twenty-five knights fell on that day. Certainly the ease with which Fíngen followed up his victory, destroying the settlement on all sides, does argue for Callan being a great turning point in the history of Desmond. Even though Fíngen himself was killed soon after in a raid on Kinsale, and his successor Cormac Mac Carthaig was routed by another royal army which advanced on Desmond in 1262, there was no way in which the settlement could be restored. When Thomas fitz Maurice came of age in 1282 an inquisition revealed that, while his lands in Kerry and Limerick were still valuable, those listed in Desmond were worth either 'nothing, for they all lie in the power of the Irish' or were worth a fraction of their former value 'as nearly the whole has been destroyed by the war of the Irish'.[1] Gaelic Desmond was thus made secure to the end of the middle ages and a massive contraction of the land of peace had taken place in the south-west of Ireland.

Further north in Thomond things were moving too. As with so many Gaelic lordships, that of the O'Briens had been substantially reduced as a result of grants made by the king at different times. Pushed into the modern County Clare, with a new capital at Clonroad near Ennis, the O'Briens had tried to hold on to their diminished lordship as loyal tenants of the king, paying an annual rent and generally keeping the king's peace. Even so, new grants further eroded their position and feudal settlements were made across the Shannon. The most important of these were centred at Bunratty and Clare (the latter uncomfortably close to the O'Brien capital) and so successful were they that in 1253 Robert de Muscegros was granted an annual fair of five days and a weekly market in both places.[2] Still the O'Briens held firm. Suddenly in 1257 violence erupted. The immediate cause of this is unknown, but it is significant that in the southern annals it is recorded as if it resulted from settler expansion into Thomond.[3] There can be little doubt that Tadg Ó Briain had lost patience with the propitiatory attitude of his father. The following year he went to Cáeluisce and the famous meeting with Brian Ó Néill, which shows his determination to force the O'Briens into opposing the feudatories. It is noteworthy that in this same year his father ravaged northwards into Galway, where Geraldine manors were destroyed.[4]

Tadg did not live long enough to exploit the situation he had created. He

[1] *Cal. doc. Ire., 1252—84*, p. 429.   [2] Ibid., no. 155.
[3] *Ann. Inisf.*, p. 357.   [4] Ibid., p. 359.

died in 1259. In the southern annals his death is recorded as 'good news to the foreigners' and 'a fortunate event for the Galls', which shows that the impact had been great.[1] Parts of Thomond, particularly the border areas around Limerick, were now in a disturbed state, and when Brian succeeded his father Conchobar Ó Briain in 1268 the situation worsened. Not only did Brian attack the feudal settlements north of the Shannon, but opposition to his own rule soon led to civil war. This great split among the O'Briens, between those who supported Brian, the son of Conchobar, and the adherents of his nephew Toirrdelbach, son of Tadg, was to dominate the politics of Thomond for many years. Not only did it involve Gaelic Thomond, but Anglo-Irish as well were ranged on opposite sides. Most important of all was the intrusion of Thomas de Clare, brother of the earl of Gloucester and close friend of the king, who was granted the whole of Thomond in January 1276.[2] His arrival was intended to lift Thomond from a state of anarchy and bring it back within the frontier of the land of peace. But de Clare was to become the victim of Anglo-Irish animosities, which helped to tear Thomond apart.[3]

Faced with the challenge of his rival Toirrdelbach, Brian appealed to de Clare for help and an alliance was formed. While this alliance had Geraldine assistance (de Clare was married to Juliana, a daughter of Maurice fitz Maurice), the opposition under Toirrdelbach soon procured de Burgh help from Connacht. Sides had now been taken, and henceforth the issue between the two O'Brien factions was complicated by this intrusion of Geraldine–de Burgh rivalry. There was little real sympathy among the allies on either side, each party using the occasion to further its own interests. This was made clear in a notable incident which was later quoted in the Ó Néill remonstrance to John XXII as an indictment of the 'middle nation' in Ireland. Toirrdelbach and his allies defeated Brian in battle and forced him to fly to the safety of Bunratty castle, the principal seat of his ally de Clare. There, for some reason which has never been satisfactorily explained, he was executed by de Clare. The horror expressed later in the remonstrance is partly at the deed itself, but mainly because de Clare was turning on his 'gossip', someone with whom 'as a token of closer confederacy and friendship he had communicated of the same host divided into two parts'.[4]

There was naturally an immediate reaction from the sons of Brian but they were in no position to dispense with de Clare. By 1278 the alliance was renewed and the war with Toirrdelbach pursued. Gradually the initiative was passing to

---

[1] Ibid.; *Misc. Ir. annals*, p. 103.

[2] *Cal. doc. Ire., 1252—84*, nos 1194–5.

[3] For the wars in Thomond see Orpen, *Normans*, iv, 53–97; T. J. Westropp, 'The Normans in Thomond' in *R.S.A.I. Jn.*, xxi (1890–91), pp 284–93, 381–7, 462–72; Katharine Simms, 'The battle of Dysert O'Dea and the Gaelic resurgence in Thomond' in *Dal gCais*, v (1979), pp 59–66.

[4] Curtis & McDowell, *Ir. hist. docs*, p. 42. For comment, and the wars in Thomond generally, see Aoife Nic Ghiollamhaith, 'Dynastic warfare and historical writing in north Munster, 1276–1350' in *Cambridge Medieval Celtic Studies*, ii (1981), pp 73–89.

Toirrdelbach and eventually in 1281, as a result of government intervention, an agreement was reached whereby the two O'Briens, Toirrdelbach and Donnchad (son of Brian), consented to a partition of Thomond and accepted the lordship of de Clare.[1] But the peace was short-lived and soon the O'Briens were at war again. Until his death in 1287 de Clare managed to protect his own interests, even to the extent where Toirrdelbach Ó Briain was willing to hold his land at an annual rent of £121.[2] By then Toirrdelbach had gained an ascendancy in Gaelic Thomond, and while willing to acquiesce in the de Clare lordship, he continued to enlarge his prestige by military enterprises. This was important in thirteenth-century Gaelic Ireland, when the men of letters were putting the ideal of the warrior-hero in place of the culture-king that earlier generations had praised.[3] Toirrdelbach, like many other aspirants to leadership in Gaelic Ireland, was anxious to display his prowess as a warrior and win renown. In late 1287, for example, he raided deep into Ormond and Limerick, thus revenging himself on the Butlers who had supported the attack on him in 1281. Toirrdelbach was fortunate, too, that he continued to enjoy de Burgh support, all the more important after the return of the powerful earl of Ulster to Ireland in 1286. He was careful not to attack the new English settlements of de Clare; though in 1298, when it was in the king's hand, he did lay siege to Bunratty castle.[4]

When Toirrdelbach died in 1306, he was succeeded by his son Donnchad. This gave rise to yet another civil war among the O'Briens. By the time Richard de Clare had inherited Thomond in 1308, the O'Briens and their allies were once more rigidly split into rival groups supporting either King Donnchad or his opponent Diarmait Cléirech, grandson of the former King Brian. By 1311 Donnchad was supported by the de Burghs and Richard de Clare backed his rival Diarmait. With two of the greatest magnates in Ireland now involved on opposite sides the scale of the war escalated. A battle took place near Bunratty and the losses on both sides were heavy. William de Burgh was taken prisoner, King Donnchad was forced to take flight and soon after was killed near Corcomroe. This de Clare success had an immediate result in the elevation of Diarmait to the kingship. So secure did de Clare now feel that he released de Burgh. This was a mistake since it led to a new invasion of Thomond, with the backing of the earl of Ulster. King Diarmait was defeated and deposed, and the brother of the late King Donnchad was installed in his place. The round of civil war was beginning again.

The interest of the de Burghs in Thomond was pernicious in its effects and served to keep alive the succession hopes of one branch of the O'Briens, while at the same time seriously undermining the power of the de Clares. On this

[1] Orpen, *Normans*, iv, 72–3.
[2] *Cal. doc. Ire., 1285–92*, p. 208.
[3] Nic Ghiollamhaith, 'Dynastic warfare', p. 80.
[4] *Cal. doc. Ire., 1293–1301*, no. 521.

occasion, for example, the invasion of Donnchad was heavily supported, if not actually instigated, by the earl of Ulster. He arranged a conference with de Clare at which he proposed a division of Thomond between the rival O'Briens, though it was not until 1314 that a partition was actually made. Clearly Richard de Burgh was protecting interests of his own in Thomond and not merely perpetuating the age-old animosity towards the Geraldines by striking at de Clare. What exactly those interests were it is hard to say, though the position of Thomond as a bridge between de Burgh lands in Galway and Limerick was one obvious reason for intervention. But he can hardly have calculated that the effect would be so disastrous even in Galway that a collector of customs could find no revenue there because of 'the war recently developed between Richard de Burgh and Richard de Clare in the parts of Thomond'.[1]

Partition was no solution. War soon broke out again and in 1315 a new complication was added with the Bruce invasion of Ireland. The question was, which side would engage the support of the Scots to upset the balance in Thomond? The energies of both de Burgh and de Clare were quickly diverted towards meeting the Scottish menace, and in Thomond itself the O'Briens waited to see how Bruce would fare before committing themselves to his side. Naturally they made use of the disturbance caused by the invasion, and when Richard de Clare returned to Thomond he found Donnchad Ó Briain in control. This should have suited him since Donnchad had been his protégé, a member of the dynasty that had always enjoyed de Clare support. But because Donnchad had now seemingly thrown in his lot with the Scots, de Clare broke with custom and threw his support behind the rival Muirchertach. Donnchad was forced into exile in Connacht and fought with the O'Connor alliance at the battle of Athenry in 1316. He was one of the few to escape from that terrible defeat, but his power was broken. His rival Muirchertach had fought on the opposite side and naturally now enjoyed the support of all those who opposed the Scots. When the Bruces arrived at the Shannon in 1317, expecting to join the army of Donnchad Ó Briain, they found Muirchertach there instead, ready to do battle with them. The forced retreat of the Scots was yet another blow to Donnchad and it was with considerable relief that he agreed to a truce. But in the early autumn fighting broke out again, and finally Donnchad was defeated and killed in battle near the Cistercian abbey of Corcomroe in the rocky Burren country. This was a decisive victory for Muirchertach and broke for good the power of the other branch of the O'Briens. From now on Muirchertach and his house were to be virtually unchallenged as the leaders of Gaelic Thomond.[2]

Muirchertach had played his cards well. Fighting on the Anglo-Irish side at

---

[1] J. F. Lydon, 'Edward II and the revenues of Ireland in 1311–12' in *I.H.S.*, xiv, no. 53 (Mar. 1964), p. 45, n. 20.
[2] Opposition did not wholly die, and the other O'Brien segment occasionally offered a stern challenge (Nic Ghiollamhaith, 'Dynastic warfare', pp 76–7).

Athenry, opposing the Scots, enjoying the support of de Clare at a time when the earl of Ulster's power was neutralised by the circumstances of the Bruce invasion, he had brought himself to this position of supremacy. Now he was to go further and challenge the power of de Clare himself. An excuse was found in de Clare's support of Mathgamain Ó Briain. After a succession of irritating raids on Mathgamain, Muirchertach launched a full-scale attack on him and then banished him. Richard de Clare was forced to intervene. Not well prepared, he was caught in an ambush near Dysert O'Dea and killed.[1] The slaughter that ensued was terrible. The few survivors fled to Bunratty and then, pursued by Muirchertach, they fled Thomond altogether. It was the virtual end of feudal Thomond, for though Quin was held for a brief period and Bunratty was kept up by the government, they were both taken by the O'Briens within a few years. To the end of the middle ages the O'Briens remained in control of Thomond.

THE great Gaelic recoveries in a huge area in the western half of the island were alarming enough to involve the government on many occasions. But in distant Dublin the growing menace must often have seemed of small account because of the growth of a more serious problem much closer to home. For there were large Gaelic enclaves in Leinster too, occupying much of the land over the 600-foot contour line and holding vast stretches of bog and densely forested land in areas that hemmed in the rich river valleys which were among the most densely settled parts of feudal Ireland. From the mountains in the east of the province and the bogs and mountains to the west the Gaelic lords began to raid and devastate the rich manors of the land of peace, creating a security problem which successive governments were unable to solve permanently, and draining away scanty resources in fruitless military expeditions.

Much of the mountainous land south of Dublin, originally part of the bishopric of Glendalough, had passed to the archbishop of Dublin, with the manor and castle of Castlekevin as its centre. Further south, Glenmalure and the surrounding area had been given by Archbishop Fulk de Sandford to the O'Tooles in the mid-thirteenth century, and it was from here, seemingly, that the trouble began.[2] For a long time, under the successful administration of the archbishop's bailiffs, the area was quiet. But there was a prolonged vacancy in the archbishopric between 1271 and 1279, which meant that the government now became responsible for the administration of this area. Perhaps it was the intrusion of new officials that caused a rising among the Irish. More likely, however, they were driven by starvation. In the poor mountainous land they were barely able to live and it was hard to resist the temptation to raid rich

---

[1] Simms, 'Dysert O'Dea', pp 64–5; *Chartul. St Mary's, Dublin*, ii, 358, reporting news of the battle reaching Dublin, adds the interesting detail that 'it was said that the said Richard [de Clare] out of hatred was cut into tiny pieces'.

[2] *Alen's reg.*, p. 136.

manors within easy striking distance. Bad weather aggravated the situation and probably made the starving Irish desperate. The annals in 1271 record 'very bad weather' and 'a great famine in the same year so that multitudes of poor people died of cold and hunger and the rich suffered hardship'.[1] There is no doubt that this year witnessed one of the great famines of the thirteenth century. It can hardly be a simple coincidence that the same year saw the beginnings of trouble in Leinster. In the summer the royal keeper of the temporalities of the vacant see spent money on garrisoning and provisioning Castlekevin and he spent 59s. 7d. in maintaining two O'Tooles, one Harold and one O'Byrne as hostages from 25 July to 26 December following.[2] Clearly the trouble had begun by then. Raids by the Irish became more frequent and more dangerous, the royal demesne manors south of Dublin suffering particularly. The tenants of Saggart, in a petition to the king, complained of one such raid which happened while they were in the fields, when their stock was stolen and forty men were killed. A petition of Roger Owen, king's sergeant, in late 1274 or early 1275 referred to Saggart as being 'near the land of war' (*iuxta terram guerre*), which shows how bad the situation had become.[3] Yet another petition, probably somewhat later, from the tenants of Saggart, Irish as well as English, painted a black picture of relatives killed, houses devastated, lands wasted and lying idle, and complained of the loss of stock, produce, clothes, and household utensils: 'and we are nearer the mountains, having always the first injuries'.[4] The government was forced into military action. But the mountains and the difficulties of communication posed great problems which stretched resources to the limit and produced a succession of disasters.

   In 1274 the justiciar, Geoffrey de Geneville, led the first of his expeditions into the mountains. The only record of this in the Dublin annals is the doleful fact that the prior of the Hospital 'and many others were captured at Glenmalure and many were killed there'.[5] That long narrow valley, with its steep sides, was to be the graveyard of many an army sent out from Dublin, and de Geneville, accustomed to fighting in the French style, and for all his experience gained on crusade, was unable to cope with the problems posed by mountain fighting. Among the other prisoners taken with the prior was Oliver le Gras, sheriff of Limerick, which suggests that the army sent to Glenmalure was drawn from many parts of the lordship and that royal service had probably been proclaimed. The prisoners were soon released in exchange for hostages in Dublin castle. So the Irish had gained a great victory and had forced a return of valuable hostages.

[1] *Ann. Inisf.*, p. 371. The Annals of Connacht describe 'hunger and great destitution throughout Ireland' (*Ann. Conn.*, p. 157). Clyn records 'a great famine and grave pestilence in Ireland' (*Annals*, p. 9), and the Dublin annals similarly record pestilence and famine (*Chartul. St Mary's, Dublin*, ii, 290, 317).

[2] *Cal. doc. Ire., 1252–84*, p. 313.

[3] P.R.O., S.C. 1/20/200, in Otway-Ruthven, *Med. Ire.*, p. 201; Richardson & Sayles, *Admin. Ire.*, p. 230.

[4] Sayles, *Affairs of Ire.*, no. 41.

[5] *Chartul. St Mary's, Dublin*, ii, 318; *P.R.I. rep. D.K. 36*, p. 37.

By 1275 the situation was really serious. The MacMurroughs had now joined the rebels and had emerged as the leaders of a coalition of Leinster mountain lords. Their depredations were so fierce that more than sixty years later the tenants of Saggart tried to excuse themselves from payment of huge debts to the king by appealing back to the 'time of the war of Art MacMurrough' and its devastation as an excuse for non-payment.[1] And so in 1276 the government made a supreme effort. King Edward himself brought pressure on his old friend de Geneville to root out the rebels. But the justiciar, after the bitter experience of the 1274 fiasco, was less sanguine. He told the king that he was willing to try to raise the necessary men, but that he would need the help of the magnates. He also warned that an expedition would likely end 'in disgrace and heavy loss' and even said that it might bring 'great danger to the land'.[2] He seems to have been the victim of opposition in Ireland, where vested interests may have resented his intrusion. Writing to the king in April 1276 he referred to 'secret and malicious' opposition and warned him that many carry lies from Ireland to the council in England. Before listening to such reports, the king should first get in touch with the Irish justiciar and council.[3] De Geneville found it impossible, however, to get the king to devote real attention to Ireland, even when he urged immediate action.[4]

By Irish standards the army assembled by de Geneville must have been huge. He himself led 2,000 *satellites* (infantry) from his lordship of Trim; Maurice fitz Maurice led another contingent from Connacht; and Thomas de Clare led another contingent: he had a vested interest in the success of the campaign, since he had been promised a grant of royal service to 'pacify' his newly acquired land of Thomond 'after those of Glindory [Glenmalure] are in the king's peace or jurisdiction'.[5] Wards seem to have been established at various places to the west of the mountains: Baltinglass, Dunlavin, Ballymore, Saggart, and the vale of Dublin. And there must have been some action in this region, since the escheator paid compensation for horses lost at Ballymore.[6] But the main action was on the other side of the mountains. The army seems to have used Newcastle as its base. It was fortified and it was there that supplies were concentrated. Wicklow and Arklow, too, were both heavily defended.

Once again the result seems to have been disaster. One of the Irish annals records the defeat of the royal army, the death of many, the wounding of de Geneville, and the taking of prisoners. It also depicts the army reduced to starvation in Glenmalure, so that the horses had to be eaten, which suggests that

[1] Robin Frame, 'The justiciar and the murder of the MacMurroughs' in *I.H.S.*, xviii, no.70 (Sept. 1972), p. 228.

[2] *Facs. nat. MSS Ire.*, ii, plate lxxiv, no. 3.

[3] Sayles, *Affairs of Ire.*, no. 17.

[4] Ibid., no. 11. In 1289, in reply to de Sandford's urgent request that he submit 'counsel to the state of Ireland', Edward replied that he was 'occupied on arduous affairs of his kingdom' and would attend to Ireland 'as soon as he can' (*Cal. doc. Ire., 1285—92*, p. 250).

[5] *Cal. pat. rolls, 1272—81*, p. 134.

[6] *P.R.I. rep. D.K. 36*, p. 33.

the army may have been trapped in the glen for a time. The Anglo-Irish annals are silent, except for Clyn who more than seventy years later recorded the Kilkenny tradition of a 'great killing of the English'.[1] But there is some confirmation of a defeat in the appointment of a new justiciar, who led another great expedition to Glenmalure in 1277.

This time, and more sensibly, Castlekevin was used as a base. Nearly £350 was spent by the justiciar on bread, beer, and other victuals, as well as iron, nails, timber, and some other materials necessary to fortify the castle. The wages of the workmen alone came to over £150.[2] Contingents came from many parts of Ireland. Once again Thomas de Clare was prominent, anxious to secure his promised service to Thomond. We know nothing about the conduct of the war, except that it succeeded in the immensely difficult task of cleaning the rebels out of Glenmalure. D'Ufford was able to report to the king that 'the thieves who were in Glenmalure have departed, many of them having gone to another strong place'.[3] And this is confirmed by a royal letter of 29 July in 1278, which granted royal service to de Clare, 'the men of Glenmalure being now pacified and quelled'.[4] There is, too, the evidence of recovery in the prosperity of the manor of Castlekevin, which is very significant. The receipts for 1272–7 came to a miserable £8. 14s. 6¾d. But for about a year and a half after the end of the campaign in late 1277 there was a spectacular increase to over £118.[5] Late in 1287 an unknown correspondent from Ireland could write that the country 'was so pacified these days that in no part of the land is there anyone at war or wishing to go to war, as is known for sure'.[6]

Still the government was very worried about the presence of both Art and Muirchertach Mac Murchada in Ireland, which presented a continuing threat to the peace. It prevailed upon their lord, Roger Bigod, earl of Norfolk, to 'deal with them tactfully, lest any disturbance of the king's peace be plotted by them'.[7] Bigod did his best to placate the brothers with fees, gifts, and robes, and they remained in the king's peace. There is a degree of uncertainty about what happened next, though the evidence suggests a breakdown in friendly relations with the government. The brothers were still dangerous, even if they were in the king's peace. Stephen de Fulbourn, the new justiciar, felt that drastic action was called for and arranged for the murder of the brothers in Arklow on 21 July 1282. This was an event that rocked even the Anglo-Irish world: Clyn recorded it in his chronicle and as late as 1305 a man knew his daughter's birthday because she was born 'on the day when Art McMurth was slain. . . . And it is known in the whole country that twenty-three years are passed since Art McMurgh was slain.'[8] A subsidy to reward the killer was raised in Leinster, and

---

[1] Clyn, Annals, p. 9.
[2] Cal. doc. Ire., 1252–84, p. 267.
[3] Ibid., no. 1400.
[4] Ibid., no. 1476.
[5] P.R.I. rep. D.K. 36, pp 36, 42.
[6] P.R.O., S.C. 1/31/169.
[7] Frame, 'Murder of the MacMurroughs', p. 224.
[8] Ibid., p. 228.

supposedly brought in £300;[1] the effect achieved was out of all proportion to the cost. For with the removal of the two MacMurroughs peace was restored in Leinster. It was not until 1295, when another MacMurrough emerged to lead the Gaelic communities, that war broke out again. So if de Fulbourn's cure was drastic, it worked. That, to the long-suffering tenants of Leinster, was sufficient justification.

It is surely no coincidence that when Gaelic Leinster once more rose in rebellion, it was in the year of another great famine. Clyn records that on 20 July 1294 there was a great storm which destroyed the corn, 'so that many people perished of the hunger'.[2] The Dublin annals also record 'great scarcity and pestilence throughout Ireland in this year and the two years following'.[3] This was also the year when the great quarrel between fitz Thomas and de Burgh reached its climax, with the latter thrown into prison in Lea castle, an event which the annals say, almost in a deliberate understatement, 'led to confusion throughout Ireland'.[4] What better opportunity for a new rising in Leinster? That trouble was expected is certain. The seneschal of William de Valence discussed the situation with his council and the likely effect on the liberty of Wexford, as a result of which provisions were seized to stock the castle of Ferns 'for fear of the disturbance had in Ireland on account of the taking of the earl of Ulster'.[5] But as the notorious event did not take place until 11 December, it was unlikely to have had any serious effect in Leinster until the following year. It was then that the burning and destruction really got under way and that the government once more had to take military action. Mac Murchada was forced into submission, 'with all his nation and following', and was formally received into the king's peace on 19 July by the acting chief governor. Fortunately a record has survived of the terms of submission. The hostages to be surrendered by Mac Murchada, the O'Byrnes, and the O'Tooles are named, and were to be delivered in five days at Castlekevin, with pledges for the payment of 600 cows 'for depredations done by them'; satisfaction was also to be made 'for damages done to betaghs and other tenants of the king, or to the archbishop, or elsewhere' (clearly the tenants on the royal and archiepiscopal manors were still the ones who suffered most); the betaghs and others were to make 'like satisfaction'. And the leading Mac Murchada swore that 'with all his power' he would make war on his kinsmen if they broke the agreement.[6]

This insistence on mutual satisfaction for damage caused is a good example of the care the government was now taking to maintain the principle of one

---

[1] Carlow and Kilkenny raised £60 each, and in Wexford, Kildare, and Dublin 2s. was levied on each carucate of land (*Cal. doc. Ire., 1285—92*, p. 6; Frame, 'Murder of the MacMurroughs', pp 226—7). It is significant that one is called 'king' in the annals (*Ann. Conn.*, p. 173; *Ann. Inisf.*, p. 381).

[2] Clyn, *Annals*, p. 10.

[3] *Chartul. St Mary's, Dublin*, ii, 323.

[4] *Ann. Inisf.*, p. 193.

[5] *Cal. justic. rolls Ire., 1295—1303*, p. 148.

[6] Ibid., p. 61. It is notable that the 'covenant' was formally authenticated by Mac Murchada with his seal.

peace and one war, and to control the truce-breakers and trouble-makers in the land of peace, or in the march. But it was too late for this kind of control to be within reach of the hard-pressed government, more especially when much of its attention, energy, and resources had to be devoted to the king's needs abroad during the last, war-filled decade of Edward I's reign. The situation in Leinster certainly showed no signs of improvement. Indeed the mountains now became John Wogan's nightmare, demanding regular policing and frequent expeditions, at a time when the government could least afford it. In Michaelmas term 1306 the total issues of the exchequer came to £2,238, of which £1,799 went on the war in Leinster.[1] The raids and warlike activities of the Irish of the mountains became more daring and began to impinge seriously on the rich manors to the south of the capital. The Dublin annals reflect this new awareness of the distinct danger presented by the Irish of the mountains: they distinguish between the 'mountain Irish' (*Hibernici montani*) and other Irish.[2] As the attacks became more daring, they reached the suburbs of Dublin and encompassed a wider area: Dunlavin was burned in 1307, Athy in 1308. As always, the manors near at hand suffered greatly. Stock was driven away, crops destroyed, men killed. Whole communities lived in fear. The vill of Haughstown in County Kildare was plunged into terror on a night in 1312 by a rowdy crowd of trouble-makers pretending to be a band of O'Tooles. A court record tells us how they 'of malice shouted in a loud voice Fennok abo, Fennok abo, which is the war cry of the O'Tooles, and by this cry of malice made all men and women of the town fly out of their houses', in the belief that the Irish were descending on them.[3]

It is clear, too, that unscrupulous opportunists exploited the situation to make a handy profit. In this kind of situation the law was often helpless, since the thieves moved from one jurisdiction into another, from the land of peace into the land of war. During the 1297 eyre of Kildare one jury after the other complained of this.[4] But a community might employ a go-between to negotiate for the return of stolen goods; at a price, of course. One such was a woman of the O'Tooles, 'Grathaghe ynyne Otothyl', who was regularly employed, going into the mountains 'at the request of faithful men of peace ... to search for cattle carried off by men of her race'.[5] It was, of course, forbidden to individuals or communities to negotiate without licence with the Irish. In 1302 John Lyvet parleyed for the recovery of stolen horses; but later he got rid of them 'on account of the danger ... from the king's court for treating with felons'.[6] But

[1] P.R.O., E. 101/234/17 (issue roll 1306–7), m. 2.

[2] *Chartul. St Mary's, Dublin*, ii, 340, for example, where the annalist records the death of William de Rupe of Dublin *de ictu sagitte unius Hibernici montani*.

[3] *Cal. justic. rolls Ire., 1308–14*, p. 244.

[4] See *Cal. justic. rolls Ire., 1295–1303*, p. 169, for example.

[5] *Cal. justic. rolls Ire., 1305–7*, pp 480–81. Grathaghe eventually appeared in court in Dublin accused of being a 'common spy' and that 'by her spying the men of Saggart were robbed by the Irish of the mountains of divers goods'. She was found guilty of this and many other crimes and was hanged (P.R.O.I., KB 1/2 (justiciary roll 11 Edw. II), m. 1 (pleas of the crown at Dublin)).

[6] *Cal. justic. rolls Ire., 1295–1303*, pp 368–9.

a blind eye was often turned, and with the escalation of the problem licences to treat, or pardons after the event, were readily issued.[1]

Before the death of Edward I in 1307 the permanent threat of Irish raiding parties was a fact of life in the land of peace (now rapidly assuming the character of a march) around the mountains. In 1306 William de Moenes, a baron of the Irish exchequer and a man of some importance in the Dublin administration, surrendered land which he held of the king in the royal manor of Saggart 'because he was so often preyed upon there by Irish felons that he could not plough, sow, or make any use of the land'.[2] In 1307 the council referred to the O'Tooles as 'robbers continually depredating'. The only solution it could propose was to make a grant of a portion of land held by an O'Toole to an O'Byrne in the hope that 'dissension may be moved between the said families'.[3] Such poverty of thought shows how desperate the situation was. The local communities themselves were doing what they could. A case heard by the justiciar at Swords in December 1306, in which a William Dunheved claimed £20 compensation for a horse lost at Ballymore 'in fighting the Irish of the mountains' preserved the record of a decision taken not long before at Carlow in a meeting presided over by the justiciar and attended by the seneschals of the liberties of Wexford, Kilkenny, and Carlow and by 'the country people . . . as well free tenants as others' of Leinster: that the local community should pay compensation of £10 to 'any of the men at arms who should lose his horse in fighting the Irish felons of the mountains of Leinster in a feat of arms'. The record added that this was agreed to 'for the utility of the state'.[4]

Regular military expeditions, then, were having little effect and were certainly not providing a solution to the problem of the Leinster mountains. On 8 June 1308 John Wogan was heavily defeated in Glenmalure. Many were killed and the Irish almost immediately attacked and burned Dunlavin and other towns to the west of the mountains.[5] The arrival of the king's favourite, Piers Gaveston, as lieutenant in 1308 marked a new attempt to deal with the mountains. He was accompanied by a large household and was liberally endowed. More important, the statute of Winchester of 1285 was promulgated in Ireland to coincide with his appointment.[6] It is strange that this important statute, which provided a framework for popular obligation to help in peace-keeping operations, had not been sent to Ireland long before, and it seems that it was intended to help Gaveston in dealing with the menace of the Leinster mountain Irish. They now threatened the very environs of Dublin, so that it was no longer safe to leave money in the exchequer, outside the protection of the walls of the castle, for the duration of the term as had been customary; instead, it now

[1] *Cal. justic. rolls Ire., 1305–7*, pp 503–4; Hand, *Eng. law in Ire.*, p. 34.
[2] P.R.O.I., EX 2/1 (cal. mem. rolls, 31–5 Edw. I), p. 162.
[3] *Cal. justic. rolls Ire., 1305–7*, pp 353, 354.
[4] Ibid., p. 325.
[5] *Chartul. St Mary's, Dublin*, ii, 336–7.
[6] *Stat. Ire., John—Hen. V*, pp 244–57.

had to be escorted under guard from the safety of the castle each morning and back again at the close of business each day.[1] Gaveston was no mere idler. According to contemporary opinion in England he made a big impression in Ireland because of his extravagance and gifts, and his colourful way of life. But the impression given in Anglo-Irish annals is very different. They credit him with great achievements in Leinster: subjugating the O'Tooles, rebuilding Newcastle McKynegan (which was a crucial point in the defence of the royal road south from Dublin through Bray to Wicklow and Arklow) and Castle-kevin, and cutting a pass between there and Glendalough.[2] Gaveston himself seems to have been satisfied that the danger was being contained, for he was soon busy arranging for a large expeditionary force to sail to Scotland, led by the earl of Ulster, and containing most of the important tenants in chief among the leaders. Huge sums of money were advanced to help them raise their retinues: £1,000 to de Burgh, £200 to Butler, 200 marks to fitz Thomas; nearly £2,000 in all.[3]

But the mountains were not to be pacified so easily, and the rebellion of the de Cauntetons, with Ó Broin and other allies, quickly brought to the forefront a most sinister escalation of the danger. From now on the government had to contend with the rebel English problem in addition to the Gaelic one. Huge lists of Anglo-Irish and Gaelic tenants were pardoned for trespasses and felonies in return for service against

Maurice de Cauntetoun and his accomplices, notorious felons, who slew Richard Taulun, and afterwards, Maurice de Cauntetoun and his accomplices having combined with Doulyng Obryn and other Irishmen from the mountains of Leinster, openly put themselves at war with the king with standards displayed, doing many murders, robberies, and other evils.[4]

This new danger was to some extent balanced by the Gaelic allies that the government was able to employ, most notably Mac Murchada, who was even paid a retainer.[5] But no amount of juggling with dissident elements among the

[1] P.R.O., E. 101/253/13: 'propter iminentiam guerram Lagenie' in Trinity term.

[2] Chartul. St Mary's, Dublin, ii, 338, 293. His clerk of the wages received £834 from the exchequer, as against £285 spent on William de Burgh's expedition of the previous year (P.R.O., E. 101/235/20).

[3] James Lydon (ed.), 'The enrolled account of Alexander Bicknor, treasurer of Ireland, 1308–14' in Anal. Hib., no. 30 (1982), pp 38–40. It is an indication of the bitterness felt towards Gaveston in England that when Bicknor was having a view made of his account before the barons of the exchequer and he claimed this amount on his account, the barons refused to accept a warrant from Gaveston. Bicknor then argued that he had been instructed by the king to carry out Gaveston's orders, to which the barons replied 'that he might therefore pursue the matter against the king if it seemed advantageous' (P.R.O., E. 368/100 (L.T.R. mem. roll 18 Edw. II), m. 167).

[4] Cal. justic. rolls Ire., 1308–14, p. 200. See also pp 145–6, 237, 247.

[5] The issue roll of 1313–14 records the payment of 20 marks to Muiris Mac Murchada 'in subsidium expensarum reprimendo maliciam Hibernicorum felonum de montanis Lagenie' (for his expenses in repressing the malice of the Irish felons of the mountains of Leinster), which was part payment of 40 marks which he received annually from the king 'iuxta ordinacionem consilii sui in Hibernia' (according to the ordinance of his council of Ireland) (P.R.O., E. 101/236/7).

Gaelic lordships of Leinster could compensate for the constant strain that the mountains now placed upon government resources. These were already stretched to the limit, and indeed revenues had declined to such an alarming degree that it is questionable if the government could maintain an adequate defence around the land of peace near the mountains. A system of warding was employed, which was expensive, and it was only by disengaging at some points in other parts of Ireland that it was able to carry on. For on the other side of Leinster and in the midlands there was another Gaelic revival which was hardly any less a threat to the land of peace.

THE first Gaelic rising requiring government intervention came in 1272. In that year the justiciar, Maurice fitz Maurice, led an expedition into Offaly.[1] We know no more than that. A succession of expeditions later make it plain that this critical midland region was in a chronic state of war and, as we shall see, there was danger of it spreading into the comparative quiet of Meath. It needed strenuous action by the government and the local magnates to contain it.

What exactly led to this outbreak of war is not clear. The famine of 1271 may well have been one cause, pushing Gaelic communities into the land of peace in search of food. There is evidence, too, that the Irish of the Slieve Bloom mountains had tried to push out their O'Dempsey neighbours, which may have caused some sort of chain reaction. In the escheator's account on the pipe roll of 4 Edward I (which covers the years 1272–6) he is allowed sums paid to a member of the justiciar's household, William Cadel, 'to succour Odymsy against hostile attacks'.[2] The absence of a resident lord of Offaly (Maurice fitz Gerald was drowned in 1268) and disputes over the custody of the vacant lordship undoubtedly created the circumstances that allowed a Gaelic expansion to occur. Whatever the cause, there is no doubt of the serious nature of the Gaelic revival in this part of Ireland, which turned into marchland a huge area of what had once been part of the land of peace. Taken in conjunction with the incessant trouble in the mountains to the east, it marked a decisive turn in the fortunes of the Anglo-Irish colony. The threat to the land of peace was no longer far distant in Connacht, Munster, or Ulster; it was now endangering the heart of feudal Ireland. Small wonder that strong government action was necessary.

We shall never know the full story of how the trouble escalated. Defective records allow only fleeting glimpses of military actions. Some time before 1276 Thomas de Clare led an expedition against the 'enemies' of the Slieve Bloom mountains.[3] Around the same time Roger Mortimer, lord of Dunamase in Leix, had incurred 'grievous and continuous costs about the defence of his lands', so that in January 1278 he and his tenants had to be excused from contributing to the subsidy the government was raising for the war, in itself a sure indication of

[1] *P.R.I. rep. D.K.* 36, p. 24.
[2] Ibid., p. 33.   [3] Ibid., p. 33.

how serious the situation was becoming.[1] Soon, in an official communication, Offaly was described as a land 'in a state of war'.[2] The justiciar, Robert d'Ufford, had contracted with a local magnate, John de Dunhevet, to supply him with a large force of thirty heavy cavalry and 200 foot 'to subject the king's dominion and reduce to the king's peace all that rebel land'; but in the event he had to do it himself 'with a large force of armed men and with much labour and expense'. But the peace was short-lived. In 1279 and again in 1280 there was action in Leix and the following year further north in Tethmoy in Offaly.[3] A vivid illustration of the devastation caused by these wars is provided by the inquisitions taken in various places as to the value of the lands of John fitz Thomas in 1282. A *theodum* of land in Offaly, which in time of peace was worth more than £90 a year, 'is worth £45 a year and no more, because the whole was destroyed and laid waste by the war of the Irish'.[4] Demesne land on the rich Carbury manor in County Kildare lay 'uncultivated on account of the war of the Irish'.[5] Even as far away as Kilkenny, land which used to be worth fifty marks a year was now reduced to twenty marks in value, because 'the greater part lies waste and uncultivated owing to the war of the Irish'.[6]

A sinister development was the involvement of Gaelic Meath in the mid-1280s. The annals record that 'there was great warfare' in Leinster and that Lea castle was burnt by the Irish of Leinster and Meath.[7] The Anglo-Irish annals record the capture and burning of the castle of Lea 'by the kinglets of the Offaly men' in 1284; the burning of Norragh and Ardscull in 1286 and the capture of In Calbach Ó Conchobair in the same year in Kildare.[8] The same Ó Conchobair was obviously one of the ringleaders of the rebellion, and together with Ó Mórda of Leix and 'the Irish of Slievebloom', he was for a time forced to pay a fine for having the king's peace.[9] But before long he and the others were on the rampage again and the government of John de Sandford was forced into massive intervention in order to prevent the war from engulfing an even larger area than before. The fortunate survival of a long account in journal form of 'expenses of divers journies to divers parts of Ireland' in 1288–90 by de Sandford enables us to see in detail the great effort that was made.[10] He caused a royal service to be proclaimed on 9 September 1288 at Kildare 'against the Irish of Offaly and Leix etc. who were in a state of war'. On that day elaborate provision was made to guard the marches; the seneschals of Kildare, Wexford, Carlow, and Kilkenny were made responsible for guarding marchlands strung out in a line along the Barrow, and were told that 'as long as the service should last they should remain in those parts, which were then very hostile'. But when the forty days' service were up, and with 'the war still

---

[1] *Cal. close rolls, 1272–9*, p. 435. The text in *Cal. doc. Ire., 1252–84*, no. 1410, is defective.
[2] *Cal. doc. Ire., 1285–92*, no. 4.   [3] *Cal. doc. Ire., 1252–84*, no. 2291.
[4] Ibid., p. 424.   [5] Ibid., p. 448; see also p. 544.   [6] Ibid., p. 425.
[7] *Ann. Inisf.*, p. 385.   [8] *Chartul. St Mary's, Dublin*, ii, 319.
[9] *P.R.I. rep. D.K. 36*, p. 24; *rep. D.K. 37*, pp 27, 46.
[10] *Cal. doc. Ire., 1285–92*, pp 265–77.

continuing', new arrangements for warding the marches had to be made. This proved to be costly. Quite small wards cost large sums. At both Reban and Maddenstown, for example, five squires and twenty foot cost over £136 each for a year; at Morett twelve squires and forty foot cost £310. But despite all, the Irish 'remained so hostile that no peace could be established in the marches of Leinster, but the king's lieges were daily killed, their houses burned, and intolerable depredations were made'. De Sandford regularly parleyed with them, but to no avail. Finally, preparations were made for an all-out war. Not only English lieges were summoned, but Irish from the mountains as well, and the men of Leinster and Munster generally. The war lasted for only twelve days, 23 September to 5 October 1289. The result, according to the record, was total victory: 'and be it known that by this expedition the Irish as well of Offaly as Leix came to the king's peace and were never hostile again'.

De Sandford's vast warding system, stretching from Athlone via Tethmoy, Rathangan, and Maddenstown as far south as Kilkenny, was designed to place as much as possible of the burden of defence on the local magnates. Clearly designed to protect the vital Barrow valley, it was a development of the concept of warding that went far beyond the system as applied in the mountains to the east. Its apparent success justified the great expense involved. But as always, success was shortlived. Mainly owing to the widespread disturbances caused by John fitz Thomas, the 'Irish enemies' in the 1290s were a sore threat to the peace of Kildare, Leix, and Offaly. So much was revealed in the great 1297 eyre of Kildare, with communities at the mercy of rampaging Irish. During the eyre juries in different places regularly referred to Offaly as a distinct 'land of war' (*terra guerre*), a place of refuge from the land of peace, so that criminals who flee there cannot be distrained. Already the land of peace had greatly contracted. In 1297 the abbot of the Cistercian abbey of Monasterevin, on the banks of the Barrow in County Kildare, was pardoned for receiving Irish felons of Offaly, because, the jurors said, 'his house is situated in the marches outside the land of peace' and he did not willingly receive them.[1]

The most sinister development during the 1290s was undoubtedly the exposure of the rich settlements along the Barrow to attack. In 1297 Leighlin and other towns were burnt by the Irish.[2] These came from Slievemargy, northwest of Carlow, in what was O'More country. If ever the Irish from this area were to act in conjunction with the MacMurroughs and other Irish from the east side of the Barrow, then the main thoroughfare through Leinster to Munster would be caught in a vice that could strangle the rich settlements along the valley. In the future this threat was to become a reality. But now, in 1297, the government had to take action that would protect this and other prosperous regions of the colony. In 1297 Wogan summoned his famous parliament to deal with the problem, promulgating a series of ordinances 'to estab-

---

[1] *Cal. justic. rolls Ire., 1295–1303*, p. 199.
[2] *Chartul. St Mary's, Dublin*, ii, 327.

lish the peace more firmly'.[1] Popular obligation in defence and peace-keeping operations, both at community and individual level, was clearly defined, and general principles regulating the conduct of war, the making of truces, and the preservation of peace were laid down.

But by 1299, following the destruction of Rathangan and raids on the neighbourhood in 1298, there was a new war which seems to have engulfed part of Meath as well. A meeting of the council at Rathwire, in the present County Westmeath, decreed that 400 foot were to be provided by both Meath and Kildare for Piers de Bermingham, and another 400 for John fitz Thomas.[2] Both fitz Thomas and de Bermingham conducted campaigns against Offaly with some measure of success. But the danger was now continuous. Late in 1303, for example, the justiciar had to order a ward to be set up by the sheriff of Kildare, while he himself led an expedition further south, because he feared that 'the Irish of Offaly, in his absence, would destroy the lands of the king in the parts of Kildare'.[3] By now the local magnates were learning to live with the danger, making agreements, trying to stir up one rival family against another, retaining the services of local lords. In 1303, for example, fitz Thomas contracted with 'Nigellus Omorth' (Niall Ó Mórda), in return for a grant of Morett and other lands, for his service 'against all men'.[4] There were always dissidents available for hire and from now on exchequer records contain evidence of *dona* (rewards) and payments of various kinds to Irishmen for services rendered. Head money, too, was paid for the heads of Irish felons. This naturally encouraged the setting of traps. The most notorious instance occurred in 1305, an event which is bitterly recounted in the O'Neill remonstrance to Pope John XXII in c.1317. It describes how the Anglo-Irish

from of old have had this wicked unnatural custom . . . when they invite noblemen of our nation to a banquet, during the very feast or in time of sleep, they mercilessly shed the blood of their unsuspicious guests, and in this way bring their horrible banquet to an end. When this has been thus done they have cut off the heads of the slain and sold them for money to their enemies, as did the baron Peter Brunechelame [de Bermingham], a recognised and regular betrayer.

It tells how he invited the leading O'Connors for a banquet on Trinity Sunday and 'as soon as they had risen from the table he cruelly murdered them with twenty-four of their following and sold their heads dear to their enemies'.[5] De Bermingham himself, according to an Irish annalist, is reported to have said, when he was reproached with the murder, that 'he was not aware that there was a foreigner in Ireland who had not undertaken to slay his Gaelic neighbour'.[6] In a poem eulogising de Bermingham after his death he is praised for being an

[1] *Stat. Ire., John—Hen. V*, p. 195.
[2] *Cal. justic. rolls Ire., 1295—1303*, pp 286—7.
[3] Ibid., *1305—7*, p. 242.
[4] *Red Bk Kildare*, no. 76, p. 70. It is remarkable that there is no reservation of fealty to the king.
[5] Curtis & McDowell, *Ir. hist. docs*, p. 42.
[6] *Ann. Inisf.*, p. 395.

inveterate foe to the Irish, hunting them out 'as hunter doth the hare', so that 'for terror they would quake'.[1] Among his exploits chosen for special praise is this murder of the O'Connors. And at a council meeting which was held in Kildare shortly after the murder, it was agreed that de Bermingham should have £100 'which was granted to him for the beheading of the captains of the races of the Oconoghors of Offaly, felons, who now sent here the heads of the said captains and sixteen heads of others of their company'.[2]

It looks, then, as if the government had incited de Bermingham to commit the murder, as a way of ending the endemic problem created by the O'Connors. But the effect was to start yet another war in Offaly. John fitz Thomas had to leave Dublin hurriedly for Offaly, 'to fortify the marches of those parts which now are much disturbed by the death of the captains of the Okoneghors slain by said Peter [de Bermingham]'.[3] Soon the lands of fitz Thomas in Kildare began to feel the effect. Geashill had to be heavily garrisoned with twenty men at arms and one hundred foot, partly at the expense of the government and partly by means of a local subsidy.[4] But despite this, in 1307 it was destroyed by the Irish, as was the castle of Lea.[5] From then on there was sporadic trouble, right down to 1315 and the time of the Bruce invasion. By then Kildare was subject to relentless pressure, and the arrival of the Scots was a catalyst that might have forged a union of the Leinster Irish and destroyed the settlement on the rich lands near Dublin. That it did not was no thanks to the government. Right through the fourteenth century the pressure was maintained, necessitating constant government intervention which was climaxed by the great expedition of Richard II in 1394–5.

FROM the middle of the thirteenth century, then, a Gaelic revival was taking place under the initiative of a new generation which spurned the compromising attitude of their fathers. Its success was marked by a gradual recovery of lands that had been feudalised and by the assimilation of many settlers in varying degrees to the Gaelic way of life. A whole complex of problems was thus created which the government had to face. The erosion of the land of peace had consequences which themselves contributed to the further undermining of the settlement. For one thing, there was a flight from the land of war in some places, with settlers seeking refuge in the towns or in more secure areas deep in the land of peace. This did not become endemic until the fourteenth century, when it was aggravated by the terrible effects of the Black Death and by the emigration of labourers and skilled workers to England, so that whole areas were virtually depopulated. But even a century earlier some tenants had abandoned their tenements, and undefended lands were already appearing on the

---

[1] Seymour, *Anglo-Irish literature*, p. 84.
[2] *Cal. justic. rolls Ire., 1305–7*, p. 82.
[3] Ibid., pp 77–8.   [4] Ibid., pp 270–71.
[5] *Chartul. St Mary's, Dublin*, ii, 335.

map of feudal Ireland. The problem of absentees, which to many generations was the greatest single cause of weakness in the settlement, had already emerged. Late in 1254, when the pacification of Ulster was a matter of concern to the advisers of the young Lord Edward, and measures were taken to see to its defence, the danger of undefended land was noted. A mandate to the seneschal of Ulster stated that 'war has, in large measure, been caused by Ralph fitz Ralph having left his lands of Dufferin undefended' and ordered that he be forced 'to defend these and his other lands in the marches, otherwise the Lord Edward will take them into his hand'.[1] Undefended lands were notoriously a source of danger. Even as early as 1228 the government had given orders that 'all those who hold lands in the marches of Ireland' were to 'fortify those lands within one year from Easter; and if they do not the justiciar shall take the lands into the king's hand'.[2] This was to be the classic remedy to the problem, the confiscation of undefended lands. But by the time the government tried to apply it in the fourteenth century it was too late.

It was inevitable, too, that as the Gaelic revival gained momentum, the settlers should come under the influence of the culture of Gaelic Ireland. Some degree of assimilation had already taken place, the result of intermarriage and of close contact with Gaelic neighbours in the land of peace. Many families must have been bilingual. The arts of Ireland found patronage on many a manor. And the pervasive influence of the Irish language can be seen at many levels of society. Nicknames, for example, tell their own story, such as Walter *Slab* who was indicted in the archbishop's court at Ballymore.[3] Many, like William Beg or Henry Óg, combined English and Irish elements in their names. Especially interesting is a Michael Galgeyl who seems defiantly to proclaim his mixed ancestry.[4] The use of Irish words in the famous Anglo-Irish compilation of poems in the British Library manuscript Harley 913 is good evidence, for this compilation in places shows a strong bias against Gaelic practices, especially in 'The land of Cokaygne', which is a vicious satire on gaelicised Cistercians. In a version of the celebrated 'Abbot of Gloucester's feast' the Latin word *currinum* is used for wine cup, which is a direct borrowing from the Irish *cuirín*, the diminutive form of *coire*. An even closer borrowing from the same Irish term is the English 'corrin' in another poem which is a satire on the people of Kildare. And in form and content 'The land of Cokaygne' itself shows a strong Gaelic influence—it could only have been written in Ireland.[5]

[1] *Cal. doc. Ire., 1252–84*, no. 411.
[2] Ibid., *1171–1251*, no. 1576. There had been complaints, such as that of William Pippard in 1226, that although lands had originally been given in fee to tenants in the marches, 'on condition that they fortify them and so render the marches safer', the tenants had done nothing (ibid., no. 1445).
[3] *Alen's reg.*, p. 107.
[4] *Cal. justic. rolls Ire., 1308–14*, pp 184, 300.
[5] P. L. Henry, 'The land of Cokaygne: cultures in contact in medieval Ireland' in *Studia Hib.*, xii (1972), pp 120–41; and see below, pp 727–8.

What worried the government much more was the influence of Irish law on the settlers. The earliest settlers had brought with them a body of customs which coalesced into the 'custom of Ireland' and which modified in some degree the common law of England as it developed here.[1] But apart from that, native custom deeply influenced some fundamental aspects of the imported law, so as to suit Irish conditions. The Rochford agreement of 1299, for example, highlighted the dangers of daughters inheriting, leading to partition and possibly absenteeism. This agreement of 1299 stated that the Rochford barony of Ikeathy in County Kildare should not be partitioned in default of male heirs in the main line, but it should go to

the most noble, worthy, strong, and praiseworthy of the pure blood and name of Roche-fordeyns, issued from the blood of Sir Walter de Rupeforti and Eva de Hereford his wife ... unless the four nearest of our blood and name choose to elect one better and more worthy of the Rochefordeyns to whom so elected the whole barony of Okethy with all appurtenances indivisible shall remain; so that the inheritance shall never pass to daughters.[2]

Thus the law of primogeniture was put aside. Such extremes cannot have been common. More extensive was the influence of Irish custom on criminal law. Even in the royal courts, fines were exacted for murder in place of the death penalty demanded by the common law. For example, the receipt roll of 1291 records 53s. 4d. from a Walter fitz Nicholas 'of a fine for the death of an Englishman'.[3] By the end of the thirteenth century the taking of fines was so normal that a rate had been fixed and it is noticeable in the surviving records that very few criminal offences led to the gallows. Indeed a petition of c.1318 complained to the king that fines were being taken for the murder of Englishmen, a fact that caused concern in some quarters.[4] So, too, did the growing prevalence of 'march law', which seems to have become more widespread as the land of peace shrank. It tolerated customs of Gaelic origin, derived mainly from military needs, for the maintenance of troops and the upkeep of the lord's establishment. An important petition from the mayors and commons of the boroughs, which seems to date from the 1350s, complained of all this and drew attention to the danger of the existence of separate legal systems:

Since the conquest there have been two kinds of people in Ireland and there still are, the English and the Irish, and amongst them three kinds of law had been used, each of which conflicts with the other: common law, Irish law and marcher law; and it seems to us that where there is diversity of law the people cannot be of one law or community.[5]

---

[1] Hand, *Eng. law in Ire.*, p. 177, and see in general pp 172–86.
[2] *Cal. justic. rolls Ire., 1295–1303*, p. 326.
[3] *Cal. doc. Ire., 1285–92*, p. 432.
[4] Sayles, *Affairs of Ire.*, no. 137.
[5] G. J. Hand, 'English law in Ireland 1172–1351' in *N.I. Legal Quart.*, xxiii, no. 4 (winter 1972), p. 413, dates this to early in the reign of Edward III: but Frame, *Eng. lordship*, p. 4, n. 12, argues convincingly for a date in the 1350s.

Altogether, then, Gaelic customary law had a growing influence on the settlers. The condemnation of Edward I in 1277 that 'the laws which the Irish use are detestable to God and so contrary to all laws that they ought not to be deemed laws' had little effect.[1] The gradual assimilation of many settlers to the Gaelic way of life went on apace. It led to what the parliament of 1297 condemned as degeneracy. It was only one of the problems that by then beset the lordship and that are reflected in the legislation of that parliament. It gives the impression of a society beleaguered by hostile enemies. Many of the problems that became endemic in the later middle ages were already in evidence.

The purpose for which the parliament was summoned was firmly stated at the outset: 'to establish peace more firmly'.[2] Each of 'the chief persons of the land' received an individual summons. They, with the council, were the essential element in any parliament. But the gravity of the situation required that the local communities, too, should be represented. Accordingly, the sheriff of each shire and the seneschal of each liberty were to supervise the election of two knights to represent the community. Significantly, these were to have 'full power' (plena potestas) to bind their communities to whatever was enacted in parliament. It was this insistence on plenipotentiary power, and the widely representative character of the attendance, which made 1297 a milestone in the history of the Irish parliament. The commons, as they were later to be called, were only occasionally summoned. It was the great prelates and the magnates who were obliged to attend, and for them this was a burden and not the privilege it later became. Only very gradually did the representative character of parliament become established. In 1299 'two of the most worthy citizens and burgesses of each city and borough' that was frequented by merchants using German coins were summoned to regulate the coinage, and to a later session of the same parliament representatives of the shires were summoned to discuss labour services on the manors.[3] The following year representatives were again summoned, with full power, to assent to a subsidy for the Scottish war.[4] From that time on they were summoned more frequently and by the end of the fourteenth century had established their right to be present at any assembly that was a parliament.

The first piece of legislation that emerged from the 1297 parliament attempted to improve the quality of local government by shiring the former liberty of Kildare and creating new counties in Ulster and Meath.[5] After that the parliament got down to the business of defence and peace-keeping. Absentees were ordered to guard their lands in the march, as through their neglect 'many marches are either altogether destroyed or are for the greater part ruinous, and the English inhabitants either obey felons or are driven as it were

[1] Cal. doc. Ire., 1252–84, no. 1408.
[2] The full text of the legislation is in Stat. Ire., John–Hen. V, pp 195–213.
[3] Ibid., pp 213, 215.   [4] Ibid., p. 231.
[5] See A. J. Otway-Ruthven, 'The medieval county of Kildare' in I.H.S., xi, no. 43 (Mar. 1959), pp 181–99.

into exile'. This dire picture is supported by other enactments. Because residents in the localities have no armed horses for the pursuit of felons, they are able to escape with their booty. Each tenant according to his station must have an armed horse or hobby always ready in future. Some tenants, 'as if exulting in the damage and ruin of their neighbour', let felons pass unmolested. In future they shall go in pursuit. That many of the tenants had their own grievances is clear: they were 'much aggrieved by armies which great men have led without warrant through the midst of a land of peace and of marches where there was no war', and by kern being quartered on them. Private armies must remain on the land of their lord, and nothing was to be taken against the will of the owner. The difficulties of exercising control in the localities was exacerbated by the prevalence of local truces with the Irish. At peace with one community, felons attacked a neighbouring community without fear of reprisal from those with whom they had a truce. Such truces in future were to be universal. The principle of one war and one peace was being proclaimed, though it would be impossible to sustain.

That the Irish, too, had their grievances that might lead to war was admitted. Those at peace were frequently attacked by English neighbours, 'led by covetousness' or for revenge, and had their cattle stolen and men held for ransom. Because the Irish are 'excitable', they immediately rush to war and it is the innocent who suffer. No Irishman at peace is to be attacked in future.

The inability of local communities to defend themselves when the justiciar was unable to help meant that the marches were open to sudden Irish raids. Now it was enacted that in any county or liberty, when the occasion required, all men were to rise to war 'at their own expense'. The obligation to defend the marches was a long-established one in Ireland, even though, as we saw, the English statute of Winchester, which formally defined the nature of that obligation and the means by which it was to be discharged, was not sent to Ireland until 1308. When Walter l'Enfaunt petitioned the king in 1290 for compensation for horses lost in service with the justiciar, the king tartly replied that 'if they went to the defence of the marches, they did their duty'.[1] But now in each county and liberty two magnates were to be assigned to treat for peace in the absence of the justiciar. But the ability of the Irish to make unexpected raids was helped by the terrible deterioration in the condition of the king's highways, so overgrown now that they were almost impassable on foot. The Irish were adept at using paths through forest and bog; the settlers needed the highways. These were now to be cleared, at the expense of the communities, and bridges and causeways were to be repaired and maintained in future.

Finally, parliament turned to the problem of those 'degenerate' English who dressed like Irishmen and wore their hair in the shape of a *culan*, so that they were impossible to distinguish and were frequently killed. This gave rise to enmity, rancour, and family feuds. It was decided that all Englishmen 'wear, at

[1] *Cal. doc. Ire., 1285–92*, p. 250.

least in that part of the head which presents itself most to view, the mode and
tonsure of Englishmen', so that they would not be mistaken for Irishmen.

Altogether, then, the statutes of 1297 show a government unable to cope
with an increasing burden of defence and peace-keeping in the marches and
trying to make the local communities assume responsibility. To some extent
it was falling back on what for long had been a common practice, in some
localities at least. For example, the obligation now placed on every holder of
twenty librates of land to possess a horse, and suitable arms as well, can be
matched by an exactly similar custom in the liberty of Meath.[1] The duty of
the tenants to rise in arms against hostile Irishmen was just a restatement of
the age-old popular obligation to serve in arms in time of war. When John de
Sandford went to raise men in Connacht in 1289, he gathered no fewer than
4,500 local levies.[2] There is evidence that this obligation was imposed
through arraying the men and viewing arms. For example, the prior of Kilmainham and two others arrayed the service of Leinster on 9 September
1288.[3] But the weakness and corruption of local government in Ireland made
impossible the regular imposition of popular obligation to arms, and the 1297
solution to the problem facing the Irish government was, almost inevitably, a
failure. Later parliamentary legislation makes that clear. Besides, the increasing pressure on the government to meet the royal demands for the wars in
Scotland crippled it and diverted the energies of the civil servants into the
war effort. Starved of money, the Irish government in the early fourteenth
century found it impossible to hold a frontier that in many places had collapsed under the pressure of the Gaelic revival.

That collapse can most easily be seen in the abandoned villages and tenements which formerly had been vigorously cultivated by tenants. The once
great and prosperous Bigod lordship of Carlow is a good example of neglect
and desertion. The records of the 1307 extents present a depressing picture.[4] In
Carlow itself the castle and hall were so defective that 'no one would rent
them'. The same picture of decay was evident on the other manors, with rents
falling for lack of tenants. The extents of the tenements held by the earl of
Gloucester were hardly any better. With the exception of the city of Kilkenny,
they too show decay and neglect rampant, so that again and again the jurors on
manors returned that they 'can be extended at no price because nothing can be
got of them'.[5]

Yet life went on as if nothing had changed. In Kerry people jousted, as they
always had, with no notion that they were already surrounded by a land of war
which was to cut them off from a receding land of peace.[6] In Drogheda on the

[1] *Gormanston reg.*, p. 182.
[2] *Cal. doc. Ire., 1285–92*, pp 268–9. He also brought the king of Connacht 'with all his force'.
[3] Ibid., p. 265.
[4] *Cal. doc. Ire., 1302–7*, no. 617.
[5] Ibid., nos 653, 655, 657–9, 663, 666–7, 670.
[6] *Cal. justic. rolls Ire., 1305–7*, p. 415.

side of Uriel the building of a new quay symbolised the optimism of the mercantile community.[1] When the council met at Dublin on 9 April 1307 and dealt with no less than nineteen separate items of business, mostly arising from petitions, they were mainly concerned with mundane matters of grace and favour. If the war in Leinster was an item on the agenda, it came at the end of a long list of routine matters and does not appear as critical or even particularly urgent.[2] In retrospect the state of the colony seems to have been deteriorating fast at the end of the reign of Edward I. But contemporaries seem unaware or unconcerned. The annals compiled by John Clyn in Kilkenny later in the fourteenth century hardly indicate trouble in the Leinster mountains. Apart from the bald entry for 1274, 'the death of English at Glenmalure', the capture of Diarmait Mac Murchada in 1280, and the deaths of the Mac Murchada brothers in 1282, there is nothing to suggest that anything was amiss.[3] A few scattered entries do hint at problems on the other side of Leinster, though nothing that would suggest any real deterioration.[4] For Clyn in Kilkenny it was the period after the Bruce invasion of 1315 which marked the critical change. An earlier Kilkenny chronicle reflects the same attitude. At the end of Edward's reign it is more interested in the affairs of France and the papacy, the 'full conquest of Scotland' and the great fire of Dublin, than in any aspect of the Gaelic recovery. When in 1305 it baldly records that 'Calwach [In Calbach Ó Conchobair Failge] with his brothers was killed', it gives equal prominence to the only other noteworthy event of that year: 'the sickness called *pokkis* prevailed in the land.'[5]

[1] *Cal. justic. rolls Ire., 1305–7*, p. 189.
[2] Ibid., pp 350–55, which seems to be a unique early council roll.
[3] Clyn, *Annals*, p. 9.
[4] Ibid., pp 9–11.
[5] Robin Flower (ed.), 'The Kilkenny chronicle in Cotton MS Vespasian B. XI' in *Anal. Hib.*, no. 2 (1931), p. 334.

CHAPTER X

The impact of the Bruce invasion, 1315—27

JAMES LYDON

WHEN Edward I died in 1307, he was leading yet another army against the Scots, now led by Robert Bruce. As always, the Dublin government was involved in this expedition. It was the murder of John Comyn by Bruce in February 1306 that forced Edward to begin preparing yet again for another intervention in Scotland, and it is a measure of the shock that the murder caused that the news was immediately sent to Ireland as a matter of great urgency. Almost immediately the king began looking for victuals in Ireland and a stream of writs followed, urging haste in gathering supplies.[1] But it soon became apparent that there was no money available in Dublin to meet the royal demands, unless payment of arrears of wages owing to the earl of Ulster and others was postponed.[2] Shortage of ready cash was becoming a problem. In late April the king ordered that wool custom receipts should be recovered from the Frescobaldi because, he said, 'the exchequer stands very much in need of money'.[3]

There were other signs that the Irish exchequer was finding it increasingly difficult, if not impossible, to meet the demands now being placed on limited resources. At a time when the treasurer was paying out nearly £2,500 to royal purveyors for supplies for Scotland, he was trying to find well over £2,000 for the clerk of the wages appointed for Wogan's 1306 expedition to the Leinster mountains.[4] Together these two sums ate up most of the receipts of the exchequer and left little over for the ordinary expenses of government. Something had to be skimped. The escalation of war in the colony, the contraction of the land of peace and the economic decline that necessarily resulted meant that even less money flowed into the Dublin exchequer. A financial crisis resulted. Figures for the last years of the reign of Edward I show a fall from £6,112 in 1301—2 to as little as £3,641 in 1305—6. There was a brief recovery to

[1] Lydon, 'Edward I, Ireland and Scotland', p. 54.
[2] *Cal. justic. rolls Ire., 1305—7*, pp 268—9.
[3] *Cal. doc. Ire., 1302—7*, no. 515.
[4] Lydon, 'Edward I, Ireland and Scotland', p. 56.

£5,893 in 1306–7 and £5,237 in 1307–8. But thereafter the decline continued year by year: £3,477, £2,586, £3,003, £2,865.[1]

Shortage of cash meant an increase in assignment (that is, the exchequer began to operate a system of credit based on anticipated receipts from specified sources of income) which almost inevitably meant that debts began to pile up. It is noticeable, for example, that even the fees of officials (many in arrears) were being paid by assignment.[2] With the fees of constables in arrears, even the royal castles began seriously to deteriorate. In the summer of 1313 the earl of Ulster complained that the walls and houses of the castles of Roscommon, Athlone, and Rindown were 'mostly ruined for want of repair'.[3] A year later Wogan informed the council in England that Limerick castle, 'situated in the dangerous march between the Irish and English', was 'threatened with ruin and fallen down and broken on all sides'.[4] This kind of deterioration was alarming and demanded some attempt at reform that would improve the flow of revenue into the exchequer and increase the ready cash available to the government. But the best it seemed to be able to do was to initiate an inquiry into old debts that were still being recorded on the pipe rolls, and to try to flush out debtors through intensive local investigations, such as were conducted by the chancellor, Walter of Thornbury, during tours that he made in 1308 and 1309.[5]

It was not local Irish needs, however, that immediately prompted this attempt to increase revenues but rather the great need of Edward II to meet the demands of the renewed war in Scotland. In 1310 he explained to Wogan how urgently he needed money, and soon the English council, weary of the failure of the Irish administration to collect debts, took the unprecedented step of sending its own agents over to urge on the work. But it was all to no avail. The disturbed condition of the country and the continuing wars there were all in favour of the debtors. The Irish council, too, was increasingly worried about the problem of defence. In August 1311 it decided that all revenue from customs, which again had been assigned to the Frescobaldi, should be paid instead into the Dublin exchequer and be applied 'to the safety of Ireland'.[6] The last phrase was not lightly used. A letter from the king to Wogan and Bicknor, the treasurer of Ireland, ordered all revenues to be applied 'in reforming the state of Ireland and towards the safety of the same'. Once more the English council took a hand and devised an ordinance for imposing an extraordinary procedure for levying debts in Ireland. It is clear that the ordinary machinery for levying through local government officials had altogether

---

[1] Lydon, 'Enrolled account of Bicknor', p. 13.

[2] P.R.O.I., RC 8/6 (mem. roll 5 Edw. II), *passim*.

[3] P.R.O.I., RC 8/9 (mem. roll 7 Edw. II), p. 9. Two years previously the Irish council had ordered an inquiry into such defects, but nothing had been done (RC 8/6 (mem. roll 5 Edw. II), pp 221–2).

[4] *Cal. close rolls, 1308–13*, p. 484.   [5] *P.R.I. rep. D.K. 39*, p. 32.

[6] For this and what follows see Lydon, 'Edward II and the revenues of Ireland'.

broken down, which is a good indication of the erosion of central control of the localities. But not even the extraordinary procedures devised in England were sufficient to overcome the delinquency of Irish sheriffs, and there seems to have been little to show by way of increased revenue for all the effort.

In 1311, too, the famous ordinances initiated a programme of reform in England which also had repercussions in Ireland. It was almost certainly the ordainers who were responsible for the remarkable letter that came to Ireland in the name of the king and that announced a revolutionary change in policy, whereby in future all Irish revenues were to be spent in Ireland on maintaining the peace. But all too soon the king reverted to his customary policy of exploitation. In 1312 and again in 1313 huge quantities of supplies were sent to castles threatened by Bruce.[1] In 1314, when preparing for the campaign which preceded Bannockburn, the king ordered the Irish treasurer to hand over all the money then in the exchequer and all the issues of Ireland during the next four months to the agent sent to raise troops for Scotland.[2] But already the Irish exchequer was so short of money that it could only find a few hundred pounds to meet the king's wishes. By now Edward was aware of this and seems to have taken steps to subsidise the war effort in Ireland: in 1314 we hear that a 'great sum of money' which he was sending to Ireland was stolen on its way through Wales.[3] This marked the beginning of a momentous change in Anglo-Irish relations whereby Ireland, no longer capable of paying her own way, gradually became a charge on the English exchequer. In February 1315, when the Irish justiciar was ordered to raise troops for Scotland, the king made the unprecedented promise that he would send sufficient money to pay their wages.[4] The invasion of Edward Bruce soon made it impossible for Irish troops to go to Scotland, even though the king had sent money for their wages, and eventually an appeal had to be sent to England for £500 to help fight the Scots in Ireland.

For some years after the havoc of the Bruce wars Ireland was in no condition to help the king. By 1322, however, the lordship had recovered sufficiently to send large quantities of food to Scotland.[5] But the difficulties the administration encountered in finding the necessary supplies, and the impossibility of paying for them from an impoverished exchequer, forced the king to call a halt and no further demands were made on Ireland to the end of the reign. The disturbed condition of Ireland would in any case have made it impossible to raise armies for Scotland, even though a small army did serve there in 1322.[6]

[1] P.R.O., E. 101/236/3; 236/7.
[2] P.R.O., R.C. 8/6 (mem. roll 5 Edw. II), pp 255–6; *Rot. Scotie*, i, 124.
[3] *Cal. pat. rolls, 1313—17*, p. 234.
[4] *Rot. Scotie*, i, 138. In July a clerk was sent to Ireland 'with divers sums of money' for wages (*Cal. pat. rolls, 1313—17*, p. 333).
[5] P.R.O., E. 101/238/1, 238/6.
[6] P.R.O., E. 101/16/16. With the earl of Louth, it included 4 bannerets, 6 knights, 63 men at arms, 189 hobelars, and 93 foot. Of the £1,249 received for wages, only £526 came from the Irish exchequer.

Quarrelling factions gave plenty of scope to those who wanted an outlet for martial spirit. The increase in the number of 'rebel English' and the continuing wars with Gaelic lords maintained a steady demand for troops at home. Lawlessness was on the increase, and when the Kilkenny parliament of 1310 heard the report of a special commission appointed to investigate the recent steep rise in prices, it laid the blame squarely on 'those of great lineage' who regularly robbed merchants of their goods as they travelled through the country or held them to ransom, and who also were in the habit of taking 'bread, wine, beer, flesh, and other victuals and things saleable, wherever they be, without making reasonable payment'.[1] The failure of the central government to maintain the rule of law was exposed even more in the decision of the parliament that each magnate ('chieftain of great lineage') should be responsible for the punishment of errant members of his family. This was a notable extension of an Irish statute of 1278 which made the heads of Gaelic lineages responsible for bringing lawbreakers to justice.[2] Before the end of the reign of Edward I this practice had spread to the Anglo-Irish lineages. In 1290 one of the most important magnates, Eustace le Poer, assembled his lineage before the sheriff of Waterford and swore that they would bring his cousin Robert le Poer to justice.[3] It seems that the justiciar formally licensed some heads of lineages to arrest those of their families found breaking the law. In 1306, when Philip Christopher was accused of wrongfully imprisoning Geoffrey Christopher, he defended himself by appealing to a licence from the justiciar 'to arrest those of his race whom he should find malefactors'.[4] So the 1310 parliament was giving statutory force to what had become an established practice. It also invoked the sanction of excommunication against defaulters, which seems to have been effective, since the magnates at the 1324 parliament requested absolution from the sentence.[5]

The 1310 parliament was notable for the large number of magnates (eighty-seven) individually summoned and for the procedure adopted.[6] Its legislation, too, was extensive, concentrating on what by then had become endemic problems in the colony. The defence of the marches was highlighted and the quartering of private armies on local communities was forbidden. It is significant, too, that the four counties of Leinster were treated as a single unit, which mirrors the growing concentration of the government on this important and most densely settled part of the colony. Perhaps most important of all, the parliament enacted a statute that provided that if 'any man enfeoff another of his land, with the intent of going to war or commit any other felony', the enfeoffment was to be invalid and the land was to become an escheat.[7] Clearly

---

[1] *Stat. Ire., John—Hen. V*, p. 265.   [2] Richardson & Sayles, *Ir. parl. in middle ages*, p. 292.

[3] Henry Cole (ed.), *Documents illustrative of English history in the thirteenth and fourteenth centuries* (London, 1844), p. 71.

[4] *Cal. justic. rolls Ire., 1305—7*, p. 252.

[5] *Stat. Ire. John—Hen. V*, p. 307.

[6] Richardson & Sayles, *Ir. parl. in middle ages*, p. 129.

[7] *Stat. Ire. John—Henry V*, p. 271.

this practice, which was to become so notorious an abuse in the later middle ages, was already widespread and indicates the serious nature of the problem facing the government.

Altogether the legislation of 1310, and the huge number of people summoned to the parliament, are a measure of the determination of the government to deal vigorously with the more acute threats to the rule of law in the lordship. But making the statutes was easy enough: enforcing them was seemingly beyond the capacity of any administration. As the Dublin chronicler put it: 'many provisions were made as statutes, of much use to the land of Ireland if they had been observed.'[1] The cynicism was justified and the writer recounts that even at that Kilkenny parliament itself 'great discords arose between certain magnates of Ireland'. By now the warlike state of Ireland encouraged dissidents among the settlers to rise in rebellion in pursuit of illegal gain. These 'rebel English', who appear in increasing numbers from the early fourteenth century on, not only aggravated the government's problem of enforcing the law but confused relations with Gaelic Ireland as well. In the Wicklow mountains, for example, Harolds and Archbolds allied with O'Byrnes and O'Tooles; further south de Cauntetons not only joined forces with O'Byrnes and other Irish from the mountains, but were willing to help a harper gain his revenge upon men who had refused him traditional hospitality;[2] in the south Maurice fitz Thomas, later first earl of Desmond, was allied with Ó Briain and MacCarthaig. In Meath the de Lacys went into open rebellion, and in Munster Barrys, Cogans, and Roches were only some of the great names listed as rebels.

Such rebels were motivated in many different ways, though personal gain was always the main driving force. Mainly they seem to have been people who had little or no hope of fortune, being younger brothers or from cadet branches of lineages. One of the most notorious examples is the rebellion of Maurice de Caunteton in south Leinster. It started with the murder of Richard Talon on 17 June 1309.[3] It soon escalated and de Caunteton, in alliance with 'Dulyng Obryn and other Irishmen from the mountains of Leinster, openly put themselves at war with the king with standards displayed, doing many murders, robberies and other evils'.[4] The government had to mount a major campaign in September, when the clerk of the wages received a total of £440 for those serving for pay.[5] The huge number pardoned for service in this campaign is also impressive, not least for showing the large number of Irish who served in the royal army.[6] De Caunteton was killed, but the remnants of his force continued to roam the countryside as a danger to law and order.[7] The rebel's lands were

---

[1] *Chartul. St Mary's, Dublin*, ii, 194.
[2] Hand, *Eng. law in Ire.*, p. 172.
[3] *Chartul. St Mary's, Dublin*, ii, 294.
[4] *Cal. justic. rolls Ire., 1308—14*, p. 200.
[5] P.R.O., E. 101/235/24.
[6] *Cal. justic. rolls Ire., 1308—14*, pp 145–6, 199–200, 247.
[7] *Rot. pat. Hib.*, p. 14, no. 222.

naturally confiscated, though the government was unable to prevent the manor of Glascarraig in Wexford from being devastated by the MacMurroughs.[1] In the end, therefore, it was the Leinster Irish who benefited.

Surprisingly, the king had been willing to take de Caunteton into his peace, but he was killed long before the royal command reached the justiciar.[2] His son, however, regained the royal favour and served the king in Scotland in 1312.[3] This is a useful reminder that nowhere, least of all in Ireland, could the king afford to alienate magnates, a fact that is well illustrated in another great rebellion in Ireland at this time.[4] It began in 1312 when Robert de Verdon, the younger brother of Theobald de Verdon, and some others on 21 February began what the Dublin chronicle calls 'the riot of Uriel'.[5] Soon they were openly at war with the king, 'appropriating to themselves as if by conquest the demesne land of the king, administering the oath of fealty as well to free tenants and betaghs of the king as to other inhabitants of the said country, and taking homage'.[6] The justiciar, John Wogan, had to send an army against them. At this point the community of Louth made a significant request of the justiciar: because they feared the damage that would be caused by the royal army, they asked to be let protect the country themselves with a force to be led by two brothers of Robert de Verdon, Nicholas and Milo. Wogan must have been convinced by the argument of their appeal (which amounted to an extraordinary indictment of the conduct of royal armies), for he disbanded his army. But the two de Verdons joined their rebel brother, and Wogan had to send another royal army against them from Ardee. This, according to the Dublin annalist, was 'miserably destroyed' by the rebels, a sore blow to the fast-diminishing prestige of the government.[7] Eventually, through the strong action of Roger Mortimer, whose interests were involved, Robert de Verdon and the others made peace on good conditions (they were guaranteed safety of life and limb) and the community of Louth was forced to pay a fine of 500 marks.

THE failure of the government was never more cruelly exposed than in this defeat of a royal army in the spring of 1312, and with a reforming baronial party in control in England some attempt had to be made to provide better government in Ireland. On 7 August 1312 Edmund Butler was installed as acting justiciar,[8] and according to the Dublin chronicle he quickly enjoyed a spectacular success against the Irish in Glenmalure.[9] His achievement subsequently in making Ireland quiet was such that he was supposedly able to

---

[1] *Cal. justic. rolls Ire., 1308—14*, pp 159–60.
[2] *Cal. close rolls, 1307—13*, p. 181.
[3] Ibid., pp 413, 416, 422.
[4] The main outline is in Otway-Ruthven, *Med. Ire.*, pp 222–3.
[5] *Chartul. St Mary's, Dublin*, ii, 340.
[6] *Cal. justic. rolls Ire., 1308—14*, p. 278.
[7] *Chartul. St Mary's, Dublin*, ii, 341. Many were killed by the rebels.
[8] Richardson & Sayles, *Admin. Ire.*, p. 83, and below, ix, 472.
[9] *Chartul. St Mary's, Dublin*, ii, 341.

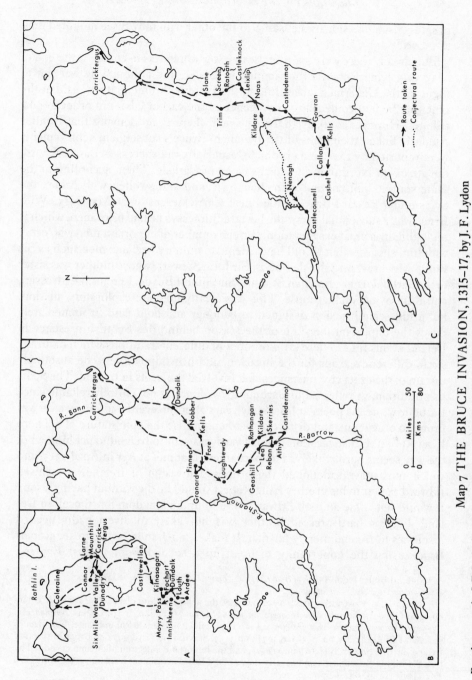

Map 7 THE BRUCE INVASION, 1315–17, by J. F. Lydon

Based on maps by J. F. Lydon in Peter McNeill and Ranald Nicholson (ed.), *An historical atlas of Scotland, c.400—c.1600* (St Andrews, 1975), pp. 168–9.

progress from one side of the island to the other with only three mounted men as escort.[1]

But already there were signs of the disaster which was to come. At the end of May 1313 King Robert Bruce landed in Ulster, and although he was put to flight by the Ulstermen, according to the Dublin chronicle, it was said at the time that he had come ashore by licence of the earl of Ulster in order to take tribute.[2] However unlikely that may seem, there is no denying that rumour regularly linked the names of the two men. Bruce's subsequent achievements were reported by the same chronicle, especially the success at Bannockburn, the attack on Northumbria and the siege of Carlisle. Then, according to the same source, 'not content with their own land and swollen with pride', the Scots under Edward Bruce landed near Carrickfergus on 26 May 1315.[3] With Bruce was a substantial army: the best tradition says he had 6,000 men, which is undoubtedly a great exaggeration. But the number of important men who came with him suggests that he did have adequate military backing: men such as Sir Philip Moybray, Sir John de Soulis, Sir John Stewart (whose mother was sister to the earl of Ulster), Sir Alan Stewart, Sir Gilbert Boyde, Fergus of Ardrossan, and Ramsay of Auchterhouse. This was clearly no mere exploratory mission, but a full-scale invasion designed to conquer and hold land. It immediately raises the important question of the reason behind this Scottish presence in Ireland at this time. There are a number of different traditions which naturally stress different reasons for the invasion, and it is impossible to be absolutely certain of the exact circumstances that involved the Scots in Ireland. The Scottish tradition, as reflected in Barbour's *The Bruce*, is not entirely reliable since Barbour wrote his poem at least sixty years after the event and in any case was prone to exaggerate and distort so as to emphasise the epic stature of his hero King Robert. His suggestion that Edward was sent to Ireland to get him out of the way seems hardly likely. The parliament that met at Ayr in April 1315, and which must have sanctioned the proposed invasion of Ireland, recognised Edward as heir to his brother King Robert should he die without having a son.[4] It would not come amiss if Edward were to find a kingdom for himself in Ireland, but his hard-pressed brother was not likely to divert badly needed resources to Ireland merely for that. It makes much more sense to see Robert Bruce using the opportunity to open up a second front against England

[1] Richard Butler (ed.), *Annals of Ireland by . . . Thady Dowling* (Dublin, 1849), p. 19.

[2] *Chartul. St Mary's, Dublin*, ii, 342.

[3] Ibid., p. 344. Most authorities accept Larne as the actual landing place. There is a basic narrative in Olive Armstrong, *Edward Bruce's invasion of Ireland* (London, 1923); Orpen, *Normans*, iv, 160–206; Otway-Ruthven, *Med. Ire.*, pp 224–51. Especially important is Robin Frame, 'The Bruces in Ireland' in *I.H.S.*, xix, no. 73 (Mar. 1974), pp 3–37. See also J. F. Lydon, 'The Bruce invasion of Ireland' in *Hist. Studies*, iv (1963), pp 111–25, and the important collection of documents edited by J. R. S. Phillips, 'Documents on the early stages of the Bruce invasion of Ireland, 1315–16' in *R.I.A. Proc.*, lxxix (1979), sect. C, pp 247–70.

[4] G. W. S. Barrow, *Robert Bruce and the community of the realm of Scotland* (2nd ed., Edinburgh, 1976), pp 411–12.

in Ireland. It would at least prevent Ireland from being used as a source of supply for future campaigns in Scotland, and with a bit of luck might even cause English resources to be diverted from Scotland to meet a perilous situation in Ireland.

It is quite likely that Bruce himself had made the first diplomatic contacts with Gaelic Ireland. He was, after all, the son-in-law of the earl of Ulster; he had been in Ulster twice before 1315; some of his agents had been captured in Ulster years before; one of the Bissets of the glens of Antrim accompanied Edward Bruce to Ireland in 1315. Apart from that, there was continuous traffic between Ulster and Scotland, and ever since the first galloglass had been imported in the thirteenth century there had been a continuous Scottish military presence in Ireland. One English chronicler, who had a special interest in Scotland, records that Edward Bruce was invited to Ireland by 'a certain magnate of Ireland with whom he had been educated in his youth'.[1] This suggests close contact, though not necessarily with Gaelic Ireland. There is the evidence, too, of the letter written by King Robert 'to all the kings of Ireland, the prelates and clergy, and to the inhabitants of all Ireland, our friends'.[2] It was sent at some date prior to Edward's expedition, perhaps in the early part of 1315 when seven Scots, as well as a certain Henry, 'messenger of Robert le Bruys', were taken prisoner and held captive in Dublin castle, and its clear purpose was to make diplomatic contact easier by appealing to Gaelic national sentiment.[3] 'Whereas we and you, and our people and your people, free in times past, share the same national ancestry and are urged to come together more eagerly and joyfully in friendship by a common language and common custom', the king says that his agents bearing these letters will treat on his behalf 'about permanently strengthening and maintaining inviolate the union of special friendship between us and you, so that, God willing, our nation may be restored to her former liberty'. Bruce obviously did not lightly use phrases of this kind. He was appealing to sentiments that he knew existed in Ireland and posing as a possible deliverer. It is in this guise that he is depicted in the annals: in 1317 he is recorded as coming to 'expel the Galls from Ireland'.[4] The deliberate linking of Scots and Irish into one people (which is what he meant by *nostra natio*, our nation) was calculated to appeal to Gaelic sensibilities, and especially to such anti-English sentiments as might be aroused.

The Irish tradition places the initiative firmly in the hands of Domnall Ó Néill of Ulster, who invited King Robert to Ireland. His hope, apparently, was

---

[1] Phillips, 'Documents', p. 269.

[2] The text will be found in R. G. Nicholson, 'A sequel to Edward Bruce's invasion of Ireland' in *Scot. Hist. Rev.*, xlii, no. 133 (Apr. 1963), pp 38–9. A convenient translation is in Barrow, *Robert Bruce*, p. 434. But by rendering *nostra natio* as 'your nation' Barrow has completely altered the meaning of Bruce's appeal.

[3] *Hist. & mun. doc. Ire.*, pp 377–8.

[4] *Ann. Conn.*, p. 249. In a letter to the king, Nicholas de Verdon also reported that the Scots intended to conquer Ireland with the aid of the Irish (Phillips, 'Documents', no. 15).

to revive the high-kingship of Ireland in the person of Bruce and later, in the address to Pope John XXII, where he claims to be speaking on behalf of Gaelic Ireland, he grandly renounces his own supposed claims to the title. His address, too, lays great stress on the common language and common ancestry that binds both peoples: 'besides the kings of lesser Scotia, who all drew the source of their blood from our greater Scotia, retaining to some extent our language and habits, a hundred and ninety-seven kings of our blood have reigned over the whole island of Ireland.'[1] In due course Edward Bruce was inaugurated king of Ireland in the traditional manner and he certainly began to king it in Ulster at least.

But one can hardly suppose that Domnall Ó Néill, like a latter-day patriot, was willing to sacrifice all for Ireland. He, too, was to benefit from the invasion. As we have already seen, his own situation was becoming increasingly precarious in the north, with pressure from Ó Domnaill from the west and the earl of Ulster favouring his rival Énrí and threatening Domnall to the north and east. By 1315 the situation was desperate, and it was this that forced Ó Néill to appeal to Bruce. What he was doing, in fact, was continuing the well established policy of importing Scottish galloglass, only now on a gigantic scale.[2] Handing a supposed kingship of Ireland to Edward Bruce was a small price to pay for his own security in the north.

Both sides, then, had much to gain. Robert Bruce would have a friendly Ireland at least, and possibly a useful ally as well; Ó Néill would have his enemies toppled and possibly the enlargement of his kingdom too. But if anything lasting was to be achieved the support of Gaelic Ireland was necessary and, if possible, the defection of some of the Anglo-Irish as well. Even though a substantial force accompanied Edward Bruce, it can hardly have been intended to achieve more than the acquisition of a permanent foothold in Ulster. A real conquest would demand much larger forces, and this, of necessity, meant that other Gaelic lords would have to rise in support of the invader. Domnall Ó Néill said as much in his letter to Mac Carthaig:

When we were about to shake off the heavy yoke and tyranny of the English, we took counsel with you and with many other magnates in Ireland . . . as to how far you would assist our efforts in that matter with active assistance and help, nor was the hope thereof vain, seeing that by offering your forces you are bearing part in the undertaking.

He then describes how Bruce is to be king of Ireland, and he sends letters from Bruce confirming that he will drive the English from Ireland, and reminds Mac Carthaig of the damage that has been caused by Gaelic lords fighting among themselves, 'so that we owe to ourselves the miseries with which we are afflicted, degenerate and manifestly unworthy of our ancestors, by whose

---

[1] Curtis & McDowell, *Ir. hist. docs*, p. 46.
[2] The annals in recording the invasion of Robert Bruce in 1317 say that he brought 'many gallowglasses with him' (*Ann. Conn.*, p. 249).

valour and splendid deeds the Irish race in all the past ages has retained its liberty'. They must now stop fighting each other: 'it is necessary for us to be at harmony at home and to prosecute the war with our united forces, if we would regain our liberty'.[1] But whatever promises Ó Néill or Bruce had managed to procure from Gaelic lords such as Mac Carthaig it is apparent that very many of the Irish refused to have anything to do with the Scots, and Bruce's plans were therefore completely frustrated. Even in Ulster the Gaelic lords were divided, and if the likes of Ó Catháin, Ó hAnluain, Mac Giolla Mhuire, Mac Artáin, and Ó hÁgáin (each of them an *uirrí* of Ó Néill) sided with the Scots, others held aloof. In descending from Ulster to the plains of Louth and Meath, Bruce and his army were attacked by the local Irish as he tried to get through the Moyry pass near Newry. One of these seems to have been that same Mac Artáin who had pledged support to Bruce soon after he had landed. The only Irish to remain true to Bruce were Ó Néill and his immediate supporters.

The other circumstance that ruined Bruce in Ireland was that his invasion coincided with the worst famine of the middle ages. Very wet weather meant a series of bad harvests, and famine inevitably followed in a society where so many people lived at a bare subsistence level. Ireland suffered as much as any other part of western Europe, and Gaelic Ireland suffered more than most. What the annals call 'intolerable, destructive bad weather' had made the harvest a complete failure and soon even reports of cannibalism were recorded.[2] Sober official records confirm the effect of the bad weather. In his account of the temporalities of the archbishopric of Dublin, the escheator was allowed for 'loss because of meadows that could not be mown on account of the rainy season and of turf that could not be cut . . . for the same reason'.[3] The Irish annals record the famine and deaths in 1315, 1316, 1317, and 1318, when one annalist wrote of 'snow the like of which had not been seen for many a long year'.[4] A stark entry for 1315 sums it up: 'Many afflictions in all parts of Ireland: very many deaths, famine and many strange diseases, murders, and intolerable storms as well.'[5] This meant that at no time was Bruce able to live off the country through which he passed, but was dependent on what he could procure from Gaelic allies, and that was little. More than anything else it was starvation that caused him to retreat. He ravaged widely, but it was houses and property (as well as people, of course) which suffered most from the Scots. Conditions grew so bad in 1317 that the Ulster army 'were so destroyed with hunger that they raised the bodies of the dead from the cemeteries' and ate them, 'and women ate their children from hunger'.[6]

[1] Herbert Wood, 'Letter from Domnal O'Neil to Fineen Mac Carthy, 1317' in *R.I.A. Proc.*, xxxvii (1926), sect. C, p. 143. This was not the first time an appeal had been made. In the mid-thirteenth century Gilla Brigte Mac Con Mide addressed a poem to Ó Domhnaill appealing for unity between Cenél Eoghain and Cenél Conaill against 'the foreigner' (Mac Con Midhe, *Poems*, pp 12–21).
[2] *A.L.C.*, i, 579.
[3] Pipe roll 9 Edw. II in *P.R.I. rep. D.K. 39*, p. 65.
[4] *Ann. Conn.*, p. 253.   [5] Ibid., p. 241.   [6] *Chartul. St Mary's, Dublin*, ii, 345.

AFTER he landed in Larne, Bruce sent his ships back to Scotland and pressed on for Carrickfergus.[1] He was immediately opposed by the local magnates, with Mandeville, Savage, Logan, and a loyal Bisset prominent. The Scots won an easy victory, giving a frightening sign of their power. A quick surrender of the town of Carrickfergus gave Bruce a secure base; the castle held out for a year. It was there that he established his court. In a matter of days he had secured an important section of the earldom of Ulster. Now he began to engulf the rich settlement stretching away towards Lough Neagh. Next he attacked the settlements further south, in the modern County Down, which made his base in Ulster more secure, as well as providing him with badly needed victuals. There was no compromise with those who refused to accept the new order. The bishop of Down was subsequently granted a pension by the Irish council because he refused to accept Edward Bruce, but fled to Dublin 'leaving his men, lands, goods, rents, and all his possessions in his bishopric of Down'.[2] With a safe retreat Bruce could now afford to move out of Ulster. The difficult Moyry pass was successfully negotiated, despite local Gaelic opposition, and Dundalk was taken on 29 June. All of the extant sources record the ruthless slaughter and destruction: Barbour says that the streets ran with blood, and Clyn recounts the burning of the town and the looting of the Franciscan friary.[3] So terrible was the destruction that the Dublin government took the unprecedented step of awarding nearly £50 to the community to help repair the vill 'recently robbed and burned by the Scots'.[4] This pattern of destruction and death was to be repeated wherever the Scots went. It was probably now, too, that Bruce was formally inaugurated high-king of Ireland near Faughart. Then the surrounding countryside was ravaged. Louth and Ardee were burned and many were killed. The destruction was such that even a generation later many parts of the area had not recovered. The worst atrocity reported was the burning of a church in Ardee that was full of men, women, and children seeking sanctuary.

These early weeks of the war had shown the Scots to be ruthless, destroying everything in their path, and seemingly invincible. The Dublin government was not slow to react, even if the only opposition was local. By 22 July, according to the Dublin chronicler, the justiciar 'collected a great army from Munster and Leinster and other parts, and the earl of Ulster, as if in opposition, came from Connacht with an innumerable army and they both came to Dundalk and consulted together so as to kill the Scots'.[5] The chief governor's intention was to pursue the Scots into Ulster. A royal service had been proclaimed for

[1] For a detailed account of the invasion and Edward's first campaign see Diarmaid Mac Iomhair, 'Bruce's invasion of Ireland and first campaign in County Louth' in *Ir. Sword*, x (1971–2), pp 188–212.
[2] P.R.O., E. 101/237/4.
[3] Clyn, *Annals*, p. 12.
[4] P.R.O., E. 101/237/4.
[5] *Chartul. St Mary's, Dublin*, ii, 345.

Greencastle and in official records the force raised by the government is called the army of Ulster. But de Burgh refused to allow a royal army into the earldom. For one thing he felt that Ulster was his responsibility and he was confident of his capacity to defeat the Scots on his own. But a more convincing reason for his refusal is offered by an Irish annalist who said that it was 'because he feared the ruin of his lands' by a government army. This was a reasonable fear. The same annals, after recounting the damage sustained by Dundalk at the hands of the Scots, adds that 'excepting homicide, however, deeds not less evil were done by the army drawn from different parts of Ireland to do battle with them, in the districts through which they passed'.[1] There is plenty of evidence in official records to support this. Dublin was granted £240 by the king 'on account of the damage caused by the men at arms who came there, on their way to Ulster and other parts of Ireland, to repel the Scots rebels'.[2] Damage at Finglas, Clondalkin, and other places is also recorded. So the earl seems to have had plenty of justification for his stand. But the result was disaster. Bruce made a tactical retreat northwards, drawing the earl after him. Fedlimid Ó Conchobair and the Connachtmen were lured away, thus greatly weakening de Burgh's army. When the two forces finally met at Connor in Antrim, on 10 September, the earl's army was no match for the Scots and he suffered a heavy defeat. This important victory secured Ulster for the Scots, and Bruce was now able to turn his attention to the siege of Carrickfergus castle.

By now the English government had taken note of the serious situation in Ireland. As early as 21 June 1315 the king ordered the Welsh coast to be defended and the castles to be provisioned because of the arrival of the Scots in Ireland.[3] And on 10 July letters were sent to the leading Anglo-Irish magnates requesting information about the Scots and commanding them to resist the invasion with all their power.[4] Edward II was clearly worried. He told the king of France on 18 September that he could not help him because 'of his late troubles with the Scots, who have since entered Ireland plundering and burning', so that he has sent his ships there 'to harass them'.[5] On 1 September the council met at Lincoln and after discussing the invasion of Ireland, decided to send John de Hotham, the chancellor of the exchequer, as a special envoy to Dublin.[6] He was given wide powers, was particularly to investigate the revenues of the lordship, and was to convey a special message from the king to an assembly of the magnates. The English government can hardly have been

[1] *Ann. Inisf.*, p. 419.
[2] Pipe roll 10 Edw. II in *P.R.I. rep. D.K. 39*, p. 71.
[3] *Cal. close rolls, 1313—18*, p. 186.
[4] Phillips, 'Documents', p. 249.
[5] *Cal. doc. Scot. 1307—57*, no. 448.
[6] For de Hotham's embassy, and the Bruce invasion in general, see the important paper by J. R. S. Phillips, 'The mission of John de Hothum to Ireland, 1315–16' in Lydon, *Eng. & Ire.*, pp 62–85.

reassured by the news sent by de Hotham in February of the following year and by the urgent appeal for money that came shortly afterwards. According to de Hotham the Scots seemed to be irresistible: he said that they and their allies 'had passed far into your country doing damage at their will without being arrested'.[1]

Things had indeed taken a turn for the worse in Ireland. In the weeks following Bruce's landing the Dublin government had done its best to bring together an army against him. Nicholas de Balscot was appointed clerk of the wages and was paid just short of £2,000 in Trinity term 1315.[2] The victuals supplied by the royal purveyors for Scotland were used for the castles of Dublin, Carrickfergus, and Northburgh, and the vill of Dundalk, as well as to help pay the wages of the army.[3] But this expenditure achieved nothing, since the army raised by the government never encountered Bruce. He was allowed to consolidate his position in Ulster and then to move south in winter, reinforced by new men from Scotland. His success, and the discomfiture of de Burgh, had encouraged risings in Connacht and Meath which further endangered the position of the settlers and increased the problem that the already hard-pressed government had to face. It was Roger Mortimer, the lord of Trim, who had to oppose the Scots when they advanced on Kells. He was quickly defeated and forced to flee to Dublin. The way was now left open to the Scots to advance further into the old lordship of Meath, and having burned Kells they pressed on westwards as far as Granard. This, too, was burned, as was Finnea and Loughsewdy, where Bruce spent Christmas. These were all important English centres, and their deliberate destruction was a deadly blow to the feudal settlement. By now the de Lacys of Meath had joined the Scots, and it was they who led Bruce through hostile Irish territories into Tethmoy and Kildare.

The progress of destruction continued, the Scots never bothering to waste time besieging well-garrisoned castles. The aim was to move rapidly, destroy as much as possible, and probably try to rouse Gaelic Ireland into rebellion. So far the resistance encountered had easily been swept aside. But by the time the Scots had ravaged through Castledermot, Athy, and Reban, another royal army was waiting to oppose them. By this time Bruce's men must have been tired and hungry. The army which they met was not only larger, but fresher. By all accounts the Scots should have been beaten when battle was joined at Skerries, near Ardscull. De Hotham in his report to England admitted as much and said that 'by bad luck they kept the field'. The Scots won an important victory. The impact on Gaelic Ireland was immediate. Far away in Desmond, when the Irish heard of the victory they rose in rebellion. Maurice fitz Maurice had to rush from Dungarvan to protect Limerick and Kerry. He found settlers in flight for

---

[1] Phillips, 'Documents', p. 251.

[2] P.R.O., E. 101/237/2 (issue roll 1314–15). Total receipt for the year came to only £2,968 (E. 101/237/1; receipt roll 1314–15). So money was scarce.

[3] *Hist. &mun. doc. Ire.*, pp 327–8, 334–7, 340–52.

fear of the Irish and a jury told the justiciar in 1318 that but for his prompt action the whole of Kerry and Limerick, up to the gate of the city, would have been destroyed.[1]

The Dublin chronicler, however, says that the leaders on the government side quarrelled and allowed the Scots to win.[2] Butler, the justiciar, seems to have been unable to hold the Anglo-Irish in check. He had failed with de Burgh and now he failed again with fitz Thomas and Power. So when the disconsolate leaders reached Dublin they had to put their seals to a solemn declaration in which they swore

to defend the king's rights in Ireland, certain traitors and the Scottish rebels having entered that land and having leagued with them all the Irish and a great part of the English. They agree that their bodies, their lands and chattels shall be forfeited if they fail in their loyalty, and to render hostages to the king for the fulfilment thereof, who are to be put in Dublin castle or elsewhere at the king's pleasure.[3]

We can hardly take at its face value this horrific picture of wholesale Irish and English defection to the Scottish side. But it does emphasise how serious the situation was in the eyes of the magnates. The hostages were delivered, some to Dublin castle and others to castles in other parts of Ireland and England, and for the next few years, until the danger in Ireland was averted, payments for their upkeep figure on the issue rolls of the Irish exchequer and in the records of the king's wardrobe. Some never returned. In 1324 the eldest son of John fitz Thomas died in England, still a hostage.[4]

Meanwhile Bruce continued on his campaign of destruction. He destroyed the important Geraldine castle of Lea. But by now the scarcity of food in the famine-stricken countryside was beginning to take its toll and the Scots retreated to Ulster in mid-February 1316. Bruce had successfully probed deep into feudal Ireland, had tested the government and magnates and had found them wanting, and had wreaked havoc over a wide area. He had also experienced the inadequacy of his army for conquest and the failure of support from Gaelic Ireland. Reinforcements from Scotland and positive help from the Gaelic lords of the south were necessary if a campaign or conquest were to be attempted in the future. It was probably now that Ó Néill began to negotiate with the Gaelic lords, urging them to unite and to join Bruce against the English, while the earl of Moray was sent back to Scotland to find the necessary reinforcements.

Bruce in the interim was kept busy in Ulster, taking the great castles which had held out against him (such as Greencastle and Northburgh) and establishing his own administration there. But the most important fortress in the

---

[1] P.R.O.I., KB 1/2 (plea roll 1312–18), m. 17. Fitz Thomas later told the king that the Irish in Desmond had united against him because of the invasion (Phillips, 'Documents', no. 14).

[2] *Chartul. St Mary's, Dublin*, ii, 347.

[3] *Cal. close rolls, 1313–18*, p. 189. The full text is in Phillips, 'Documents', no. 5.

[4] Clyn, *Annals*, p. 16.

north, Carrickfergus castle, defied all his efforts. It was victualled successfully by sea in April 1316 and again in July eight ships were loaded with supplies in Drogheda and set out for the castle. But they were diverted by the earl of Ulster to Scotland in exchange for the release of his cousin William de Burgh. The situation in Carrickfergus then became so desperate that it was reported that the garrison was reduced to eating some Scots they had held prisoner! There was little they could do except surrender, which they did in September 1316.[1] This really made Bruce master of Ulster.

By this time the position of the Dublin government was extremely precarious. Outbreaks in Gaelic Leinster and elsewhere had added to the confusion, and the acute shortage of money made it difficult to plan a successful resistance to the Scots. De Hotham in his report had informed the king that the financial situation was desperate, mainly because the army that had been mustered in 1315 had cost so much.[2] An ominous sign was not only that receipts began to fall and that the government was overspending, but that assignments began to increase. Even so the amount of money available for the war against the Scots was pitifully small. The council decided in 1316, for example, that £4,000 should be made available to de Balscot, clerk of the wages in the justiciar's army; all he got was £578. For putting Dublin castle in a state of defence £400 was allowed; but only £145 was provided by the treasurer.[3] Much attention was devoted to preparing defences in the area around Dublin, where the administration largely fell back on the popular obligation to defend.[4] Despite this some of the Leinster Irish managed to penetrate right into the city and, as events were to show, even the defences of Dublin itself were hopelessly inadequate. Altogether the government was failing miserably in its fitful preparations to meet the next Scottish onslaught out of Ulster, being perhaps misled into complacency by the long sojourn of Edward Bruce there from February 1316 to February 1317.

But Bruce was making careful preparations. He went to Scotland himself to confer with his brother. He succeeded in persuading him to come to Ireland, and by February 1317 King Robert was in Ireland. He must have considered a heavy investment in the Irish enterprise worthwhile, and this can only be as a result of the success of Edward up to this, particularly the exploratory campaign of 1315–16. Scottish control of the sea between Ulster and Scotland made this intervention possible. Thomas Dun was the man who was responsible. He had kept an open passage available to the Scots, so that the necessary reinforcements could be shipped to Carrickfergus. At one time he controlled

---

[1] G. O. Sayles, 'The siege of Carrickfergus castle, 1315–16' in *I.H.S.*, x, no. 37 (Mar. 1956), pp 94–100.

[2] Phillips, 'Documents', no. 47.

[3] P.R.O., E. 101/237/4 (issue roll 1315–16). The following year only £262 was given to de Balscot and £40 to Adam de la More, clerk of the wages in the Leinster army (E. 101/237/5 (issue roll 1316–17)).

[4] *Hist. & mun. doc. Ire.*, pp 372–86.

the sea right down as far as Holyhead, so that the main sea route between Ireland and England became dangerous. When John de Hotham came on his mission to Ireland he was protected by no less than eight ships and eighty *satellites* and crossbowmen 'to have a safe passage because Thomas Dun and divers other enemy robbers daily perpetrate and commit many and divers injuries on the sea between the lands of England, Wales and Ireland'.[1]

Confident of success, the Scots moved out of Ulster early in February 1317. According to Barbour they were determined to march throughout Ireland from one end to the other. It is significant that they made their way towards Dublin for the first time. Once again the army ravaged the rich country of Meath as it moved south. There is one dubious tradition that says that the earl of Ulster ambushed the rear of the army at Ratoath before he fled to Dublin. But there is no doubt about what happened next. The mayor of Dublin arrested the earl on 21 February and imprisoned him in Dublin castle. What provoked such an extreme action was the suspicion that de Burgh had acted in collusion with Bruce and the fear that he might yet betray Dublin. He was, after all, the father-in-law of King Robert, and had been closely associated with him in the past, as far back as 1286, when, as a young man, the earl had been party to a remarkable alliance involving Bruce, his father, and a number of leading Scots.[2] Rumour had linked the two men in 1310 and again in 1313. In England it was said that Bruce had made himself king of Ireland 'with the connivance of the earl of Ulster'.[3] It was remembered, too, that it was his diversion of the relief ships which had brought about the fall of Carrickfergus castle. It is hard to believe that de Burgh was in any way involved with Bruce, but he was kept a prisoner a long time before he was allowed to go to England.

Meanwhile Dublin was in a panic, and with good reason. The defences were in a hopeless state, with great breaches in the walls in places. That they could be penetrated by the Leinster Irish did nothing to reassure the apprehensive citizens. Shortly before this complaints had been made by the 'common folk' about the inadequacies of the defensive system, suggesting measures to be taken to provide armed men to protect the city.[4] But the mayor and bailiffs had done nothing. Now, with the Scots approaching from Meath and with no one to bar their way, the men of Dublin faced the prospect of capitulation. So they took measures into their own hands. A number of buildings, including churches, were torn down and the masonry used to construct a new wall facing the river. Then when Bruce arrived at Castleknock on the other side of the river on 23 February, the Dubliners set fire to the suburbs facing him, so that they could not be used to provide shelter during an assault on the city from that side. The fire got out of hand and a huge area (including the houses of the

[1] P.R.O., E. 101/309/19, m. 3, now in Phillips, 'Documents', p. 267.
[2] Barrow, *Robert Bruce*, pp 25–6.
[3] *Adae Murimuth continuatio chronicarum*, ed. E. M. Thompson (Rolls Series, London, 1889), p. 30.
[4] *Hist. & mun. doc. Ire.*, pp 359–65.

exchequer) was destroyed.[1] As it happened, this may have been a fortunate accident, causing Bruce to turn away from Dublin in the belief that a siege would be long and costly.

We can only speculate on the motives of Bruce in passing Dublin by in this way. It is noteworthy that, with the exception of Carrickfergus, the Scots never involved themselves in long sieges. On this occasion they had made no attempt to take Drogheda as they moved south and now they were to leave more walled towns behind them as they progressed through the country. Naas, Castledermot, Gowran, Callan, and Kells were all plundered. But Kilkenny was left alone as the army moved on through Cashel and Nenagh towards the Shannon, causing terrible destruction in Butler's lands on the way. It was now clear that Bruce was hoping to link up with the Irish of Thomond and possibly Desmond as well. He had no time to spare for lengthy sieges and so ignored the walled towns he could not take by storm.

It seems, too, that the government for once had anticipated what Bruce was trying to do and tried to prevent or at least meet it. The fortunate survival of a view of the account of John of Patrickschurch, clerk of the wages in the army of the justiciar, enables us to follow Butler as he moved rapidly through Munster raising men.[2] From 24 February, when he went to Cork for this purpose, to 17 April when his retinue 'assaulted the Scots as they were crossing the bog of Ely', Butler remained in touch with the Scots without actually bringing them to battle. For a time he had as many as 920 paid troops with him: 220 men at arms, 300 hobelars, and 400 foot. The Scottish army must have been formidable if Butler hesitated to meet it in the open. Had Bruce succeeded in his plan to link up with Donnchad Ó Briain, he would have been able to press on with the business of conquest. But instead he found Donnchad's great rival, Muirchertach Ó Briain, waiting for him across the Shannon, ready to give battle. Now it was Butler who suddenly held the advantage and there was little the Scots could do except retreat. From Castleconnell on the Shannon, not far from Limerick, they moved through Kildare and into Meath, reaching Ulster on 1 May. Later that month King Robert returned to Scotland. The hope of winning Ireland for his brother was now ruined, and when control of the sea was lost in July, with the capture of Thomas Dun by the Irish admiral John of Athy, there was the added problem of getting help to Edward in the future.

Robert Bruce was probably helped in his decision to retreat from the Shannon by the news that Roger Mortimer had landed in Ireland. Backed by powerful interests in England, Mortimer had been appointed lieutenant of Ireland and brought a small military force with him. It is significant that for the first time the king agreed that his expenses would be met by the wardrobe and not, as hitherto had been the case, out of the Irish exchequer. In addition the

---

[1] Sayles, *Affairs of Ire.*, no. 140.
[2] P.R.O., S.C. 6/1239/13, now edited by Robin Frame as 'The campaign against the Scots in Munster, 1317' in *I.H.S.*, xxiv, no. 95 (May 1985), pp 361–72.

government contracted with a certain Antonio de Passagno for the provision of 1,000 Genoese mercenaries who were to be in Ireland by July 1317. The Genoese certainly received money, but there is no evidence that any of the mercenaries ever arrived in Ireland. Nevertheless the English government was finally taking the Irish problem seriously. Absentees were ordered to return to defend their lands. But by now, in fact, the crisis had broken in Ireland. Edward Bruce remained in Ulster for the next year and a half, and the Dublin government was able to devote its energies to the restoration of order in the rest of the country. The release of the earl of Ulster was procured; the de Lacys were put to flight; and the problem of the Leinster Irish was tackled with some measure of success.

At the same time attention switched to Avignon, where a new pope, John XXII, had been elected in August 1316. A diplomatic war followed.[1] Edward II had complained that some of the Irish prelates were 'countenancing and resetting the Scots and preaching against him and his realm'.[2] The Franciscans, in particular, had been active promoters of Bruce, and in August 1316 the minister of the Irish province was sent to Avignon to complain of this to the minister general of the order. At the same time Edward II kept the pressure on the pope, who issued a general condemnation of the supporters of Bruce. The Irish reply was the famous remonstrance from Domnall Ó Néill.[3] This, inevitably, failed to provide papal recognition of Bruce as king of Ireland, though the pope did tell Edward II to act justly and instructed his legates in England to keep urging the Irish case of injustice on the king.

What exactly Bruce was doing in Ulster since May 1317 is a mystery. Perhaps he was hoping to get more help from Scotland. But the long silence was broken at last when on 14 October 1318, according to the Dublin chronicler, 'war commenced between the Scots and the English of Ireland two leagues from the vill of Dundalk'.[4] There is nothing to suggest what Bruce's motives were in thus moving south again. But the evidence indicates that he may have had some reinforcements from Scotland: the annals mention that 'Mac Ruaidri, king of the Hebrides, and Mac Domnaill, king of Argyle, and their Scots were killed with him.'[5] All the evidence, too, suggests that his army was considerable, with de Lacys prominent amongst the leaders. An army, led by John de Bermingham, and including Milo de Verdon, together with the archbishop of Armagh and many local magnates, as well as the men of Drogheda, opposed the Scots near Faughart. There was a major battle between the two armies and Bruce was killed, 'by dint of fierce fighting'.[6] Many Scots died with him.

[1] J. A. Watt, 'Negotiations between Edward II and John XXII concerning Ireland' in *I.H.S.*, x, no. 37 (Mar. 1956), pp 1–20; Watt, *Ch. & two nations*, pp 183–9.

[2] *Cal. doc. Scot., 1307–57*, no. 480.

[3] For a view of this important document in another context see James Muldoon, 'The remonstrance of the Irish princes and the canon law tradition of the just war' in *Amer. Jn. Legal Hist.*, xx (1978), pp 309–25.

[4] *Chartul. St Mary's, Dublin*, ii, 359.   [5] *Ann. Conn.*, p. 253.   [6] Ibid.

A special messenger was immediately dispatched to inform the Dublin exchequer of the 'great victory' and the death of Bruce.[1] His head was sent to the king by de Bermingham, who was rewarded with a grant of the new earldom of Louth. The rest of Bruce's body was quartered. His heart, hand, and one quarter were brought to Dublin and the other quarters were sent 'to other places'.[2] Thus, ignominiously, did the great Bruce enterprise come to an end.

BRUCE'S death was greeted with remarkably unanimous approval in nearly all the Gaelic sources. He was 'the common ruin of the Galls and Gaels of Ireland' and 'never was there a better deed done for the Irish than this, since the beginning of the world and the banishing of the Fomorians from Ireland'.[3] Those who supported him were roundly condemned and he was blamed for the famine, death, and destruction which gripped the whole of Ireland during those years. He reduced Ireland to 'one trembling surface of commotion'.[4] Another near-contemporary writer graphically compared the Scots to an 'overwhelming wave, broken-topped, hoarsely rumbling, virulent in destructiveness, scorching terribly and giving off lively sparks; an earnest of enduring malice and ill-will, breaking down all embankments, all hills and every hoary rock'; they were like a 'black cloud with vaporous-creeping offshoots and dark mist . . . [which] covered our Ireland's surface'.[5]

It is true that the Scots left a trail of destruction and desolation behind them whenever they moved through the country. All the sources support that. For example, the earl of Norfolk later complained of the losses suffered in his liberty of Carlow, where stewards, treasurers and many free tenants had been killed in successive raids.[6] There was, too, a significant fall in rents from many of the royal manors for which the escheator later accounted, because of damage caused by the Scots and the Irish. Hugh Lawless, who farmed the royal manor of Bray, received only £85 in rents during five and a half years after 1314 because the lands were devastated after the Scots arrived and, he claimed in 1320, were now lying waste and uncultivated.[7] This is matched by a fall in the value of many ecclesiastical benefices for the same reason. The valuations for the purpose of ecclesiastical taxation make this clear. For example, the archdiocese of Dublin shows a fall from £2,800 in the late thirteenth century to £800 after the invasion. In the diocese of Ossory, ten prebends fell from £56 to

[1] P.R.O., E. 101/237/9. The news was then added to the Red Book of the exchequer (*Chartul. St Mary's, Dublin*, ii, p. cxxviii, n. 2).

[2] *Chartul. St Mary's, Dublin*, ii, 360.

[3] *Ann. Conn.*, p. 253.

[4] John O'Donovan (ed.), *The tribes and customs of Hy Many, commonly called O'Kelly's country* (Irish Archaeological Society, Dublin, 1843), p. 137.

[5] *Caithr. Thoirdh.*, ii, 83.

[6] Sayles, *Affairs of Ire.*, nos 127–8.

[7] *Hist. & mun. doc. Ire.*, pp 456–62.

£28 and fifteen others from £58 to £27.[1] So severely had the area around Carrickfergus suffered that as late as 1327 it was proposed that the lands which had been lying waste since 1315 should be colonised from Wales and England.[2] But if the Scots were destructive, so too were the armies of the lordship, especially the men of Ulster, who seem to have caused havoc wherever they went. There are many entries of allowances for such damage in different accounts on the pipe rolls: for example, to Henry Kempe, who 'was injured by the Ulster army who came there with the king's banner to pursue Edward de Bruys and his men and who robbed Henry of divers goods to the value of £20'.[3]

The devastation of the armies, coupled with the terrible famine and associated deaths, must have left much of Ireland in a frightful state. It is easy, therefore, to understand the universal condemnation of Bruce, though it is ironical that he should have been held responsible for the famine which played havoc with his own plans for a conquest of Ireland. The general attitude of condemnation suggests, too, that Gaelic Ireland in general did not support Bruce, despite the assertion of the usually reliable Friar Clyn that there adhered to the Scots 'all the time they were in Ireland almost all the Irish of the land, with very few keeping their faith and fealty'.[4] Outside of Ulster the Scots failed to find the Gaelic support which was vital to success. The Gaelic lords used the occasion to secure advantages for themselves. Whatever hopes Bruce had of securing support from Connacht were dashed by the Anglo-Irish triumph at Athenry, and the great design for an alliance with Donnchad Ó Briain was ruined by the ascendancy of his arch-rival Muirchertach. Bruce, in fact, fell victim to the ambitions and rivalries of the Gaelic lords, and so in retrospect we can see that his attempt to revive a kingdom of Ireland was doomed to failure.

This is not to say that the Scots did not for a time pose the greatest of threats to Anglo-Ireland. Until the end at Faughart they were never defeated in battle. They secured the sympathy, at least for a time, of many churchmen, and no small number of the settlers joined them, especially in Ulster, of course, where many of them had little choice. Such were the defections that nervous suspicions of the loyalty of many leading magnates were generated, and this atmosphere of distrust was not conducive to efficient resistance to the Scots. We have already seen that it led to the imprisonment of the earl of Ulster. Many leading magnates had to leave hostages with the government. Rumour played with the good name of even the greatest. Edmund Butler was one who suffered, so that in 1320 the king had to publish a formal declaration 'to clear the fair name of Edmund le Botiller, who has been accused of having assisted the Scots in Ireland, that he has borne himself well and faithfully towards the king'.[5] During the war a petition asked for the removal of Richard

---

[1] G. J. Hand, 'The dating of the early fourteenth-century ecclesiastical valuations of Ireland' in *Ir. Theol. Quart.*, xxix (1957), p. 273.

[2] Sayles, *Affairs of Ire.*, p. 128.   [3] Pipe roll 12 Edw. II in *P.R.I. rep. D.K. 42*, pp 33–4.

[4] Clyn, *Annals*, p. 12. See, too, the letter of Maurice fitz Thomas that reported that all the Irish were united by the invasion and were ready for war (Phillips, 'Documents', no. 14).

[5] *Cal. pat. rolls, 1317–21*, p. 535.

d' Exeter, chief justice of the common bench, who was suspect because of his association with the rebel Walter de Lacy, who had married his daughter, and with many others who were hostile to the king.[1]

The disturbed state of the country was very evident and resulted in a collapse of the rule of law in some localities. The courts became less active. The Dublin bench adjourned cases in 1316 because it was impossible for parties to get to the city without peril to their lives on account of the dangerous conditions on the roads to the city and the continuous presence of enemies. It is noteworthy that the very size of the plea rolls reflects a fall in the volume of business before the courts, since there was a dramatic reduction in the number of membranes required to preserve the record: in Hilary term 1316 there were only fourteen, compared with forty-three for the preceding Michaelmas term. Though there was some recovery after the wars, it was only marginal, and the business of the court continued to be very much less than it had been in the first decade of the century. This evidence of a contraction in the land of peace, where the royal justices were active, is matched by the evidence of the number of Irish cases that appeared in the king's bench in England, for they almost disappear from now on. The emergency powers granted by the government to the Lawless family who lived 'in a narrow part of the country between Newcastle McKynegan and Wicklow' show the same failure to impose the common law: they were empowered to deal with the Irish who harassed them 'in the manner of the marchers'.[2] Nor could the government afford to take too strict a view of infringements of the law during the period of invasion. In 1319 no less a person than the treasurer, Walter of Islip, thought it prudent to obtain a royal indemnity for misdemeanours during the war; and when the citizens of Dublin were similarly indemnified for burning their suburbs, it was because the 'urgent necessity of war' excused infringement of the common law.[3]

The years of the Bruce invasion, then, were traumatic in the life of the island. The destruction of the armies, coupled with the great famine and followed by devastating epidemics among livestock which were shattering in their effect on an economy in which the pastoral element was so pronounced, resulted in sore loss of life. The hardship was worsened by outbreaks of smallpox and influenza in the 1320s which were calamitous. There was crop failure again, too, in 1321, and in 1328 when there was 'much thunder and lightning, whereby much of the fruit and produce of all Ireland was ruined and the corn grew up white and blind'. During the summer there was a 'great intolerable wind . . . with scarcity of food and clothing'.[4] These calamities naturally had a devastating effect on the population, which seems not only to have been seriously dislocated in places, but to have declined as well. An economic recession was the inevitable result.

---

[1] Sayles, *Affairs of Ire.*, no. 151.
[2] Hand, *Eng. law in Ire.*, pp 35–6, 141.
[3] Ibid., p. 36.
[4] *Ann. Conn.*, pp 263, 265.

It is impossible now to be sure of the extent of this decline, for it seems to have got worse as new calamities such as the Black Death hit the lordship later in the century. Some facts gave the impression of a recovery. For example, the enormous quantities of grain shipped to Scotland for the campaign of 1322 suggest that tillage was again flourishing in some parts at least. The building of new stone bridges across the Liffey at Kilcullen in 1319 and across the Barrow at Leighlin in 1320 implies that traffic was once more heavy on the highway from Dublin to Carlow and Kilkenny.[1] The general mood of optimism that prevailed is indicated by the foundation of a university in Dublin in 1320, the realisation of a plan first mooted in 1311 when the archbishop of Dublin procured a bull from Pope Clement V. But its lack of success for want of adequate endowment suggests that the optimism was misguided and that Dublin was not capable of supporting a *studium generale*.[2]

A less favourable view of Ireland after Bruce is given by the statutes of the Dublin parliament of 1320. We see a people 'greatly distressed and well nigh destroyed' by the magnates and their armies, suffering from corrupt officials, and at the mercy of the many 'idle men' who enjoyed the protection of magnates so that it was impossible to bring them to justice.[3] This picture of a society where the rule of law is beginning to break down is reinforced by the ominous decision of the parliament of 1324 that the 'grandees of great lineage' should, as far as lay in their power, 'take and cause to be taken the felons, robbers, and thieves of their own family and surname, and their adherents'.[4] This virtual repetition of an earlier statute of 1310, with its emphasis on the importance of blood relationship, highlights the loosening of the feudal bond which was evident all over the lordship. Even in the thirteenth century something like a clan system was emerging in feudal Ireland. But it was the confusion of unending raids and wars and the lack of adequate governance that made the family bond important again. With it went 'bastard feudalism', which produced a new family based not on the ties of blood, but on service and fees. No wonder society groaned under the oppression of private armies and the magnates who employed them.

The best example of such a magnate is Maurice fitz Thomas, created earl of Desmond in 1329, whose notorious career of crime and rebellion spanned the years from 1319 to 1346.[5] In the former year, perhaps encouraged by the failure of the government to cope adequately with the disorders of the period of the Bruce war and its aftermath, he raised a small army which grievously oppressed not only his own tenants in his vast lordship, but those of other lordships as well. According to later indictments of Maurice, this had the effect of

---

[1] *Chartul. St Mary's, Dublin*, ii, 361.
[2] Aubrey Gwynn, 'The medieval university of St Patrick's, Dublin' in *Studies*, xxvii (1938), pp 199–212, 437–54.   [3] *Stat. Ire., John—Hen. V*, pp 281–91.   [4] Ibid., p. 307.
[5] G. O. Sayles, 'The rebellious first earl of Desmond' in *Med. studies presented to A. Gwynn*, pp 203–27. An indispensable commentary is provided by Frame, *Eng. lordship*, especially pp 157–95.

attracting to him dissidents, English as well as Irish, 'from Connacht and Thomond, from Leinster and Desmond. And Maurice received them and avowed them'.[1] Such avowries were one of the most pernicious causes of public disorder in Ireland, since they gave the protection of a powerful magnate and all the influence that he could control to the man avowed, so that he was hardly amenable to the ordinary processes of the law. This was certainly true in the case of fitz Thomas. As the number of his armed retainers increased they became well known as 'mac Thomas's rout' and they ravaged widely. Soon other magnates joined with him and the scale of destruction increased. On 16 May 1321, for example, they came into the district around Pomeroy in County Cork and burned the vills and houses they found, including a church which they had robbed of goods to the value of 100 marks, and they forced David Roche to hand over two members of his family as hostages. Some atrocious crimes were committed. In 1325, for example, the constable of Bunratty castle, Richard of Harmston, was taken by some of the 'rout', who cut out his tongue and put out his eyes. They seized the vill and castle of Bunratty and killed two men in the castle. On another occasion Maurice seized William fitz Nicholas and put out his eyes because he had killed Mac Carthaig, and then he took William's men who had been party to the killing and 'some he beheaded, others he hanged, and more he tore apart with horses'.[2] The catalogue of crime was endless.

But matters did not end there, for Maurice became ambitious and according to those who later indicted them he 'had filled his heart with such pride and ambition that he thought to obtain the whole of Ireland for his own and to crown himself as a false king'.[3] There seems to be some substance to this fantastic accusation. In July 1326 a meeting was held in Kilkenny, at which the earl of Kildare, the earl of Louth, the future earls of Ormond and Desmond, together with the bishop of Ossory and a number of lesser magnates, and Brian Ó Briain, were present. They agreed to rebel against the king, assume control of Ireland, elect and crown Maurice fitz Thomas king, and share Ireland among themselves in proportion to the contribution each man made to the conquest.[4] It is very likely that events in England, which were to lead to the deposition of Edward II, prompted this plot in Ireland. In any event it came to nothing. But there were to be later plots to make fitz Thomas king of Ireland, involving powerful Gaelic as well as Anglo-Irish lords and even a restoration of some of the old provincial kingdoms.

The story of Maurice's high ambitions belongs to a later period for the most part. But the development of his 'rout', the illegal burdens placed on his tenants and then on other communities, the crime and civil disturbance, are all

---

[1] G. O. Sayles, 'The legal proceedings against the first earl of Desmond' in *Anal. Hib.*, no. 23 (1966), p. 8.

[2] Ibid., pp 8–9, 17–18.

[3] Ibid., p. 8.

[4] Ibid., p. 6. For the date see Frame, *Eng. lordship*, p. 180, n. 101.

typical of what was happening in many parts of Ireland during this period of change. The feudal structure of society, which in any event had never been really suited to Irish conditions, was beginning to change, and already the new lordships, based on family, personal loyalty, and service, were appearing. The social map of Ireland as it was to be in the later middle ages was being drawn. Naturally the upheaval was hard. The illegal impositions of the likes of fitz Thomas were bound to engender quarrels with his neighbours. His forays into east Cork and Waterford were more than simple raids, they were more in the nature of military campaigns: we read of his army moving forward with standards raised and flags flying. They brought him into violent conflict with Barrys, Cogans, and Roches, and ultimately with the Powers. Maurice had allies from those parts, too, and doubtless they were using him to work off old scores against local rivals. And it seems, too, that high politics were not without effect. Events in England were helping new alignments to take place in Ireland, and these were another potent factor in the creation of civil disturbance. There seems to be little doubt, for example, that the Despensers had an Irish ally in Arnold le Poer, seneschal of Kilkenny, and that his war, for such it was, with fitz Thomas in the summer of 1325 was to some extent a reflection of the great Mortimer–Despenser quarrel in England. It is even possible that the vicious attack on le Poer by the bishop of Ossory, who involved him in the notorious charges of witchcraft made against the wealthy Kilkenny woman, Alice Kyteler, may have had a similar political motive. But the root cause of the quarrels was in Ireland, where local rivalries had long histories and were always liable to erupt into violence.[1]

After the successful Mortimer coup in England in the autumn of 1326, the political alignments in Ireland became less clear-cut.[2] Fitz Thomas, the Butlers, de Berminghams, le Poers, and de Burghs were involved in factions. Civil war followed in 1327, causing widespread devastation of lands and castles. If we are to believe the Dublin chronicler, the Dublin government was rendered so powerless by all this that at one stage fitz Thomas, Butler and de Bermingham 'ordered the council of the king to come to Kilkenny and there they would clear themselves that they had plotted no evil against the king's lands, but only to avenge themselves on their enemies'.[3] It is hard to imagine such an open declaration of the right to make private war being made in a period of strong rule.

The popular belief at the time, as reported in Dublin, was that this war had been caused by personal animosity between fitz Thomas and le Poer. We are told that late in September 1327, 'because the Lord Arnold [le Poer] came to the aid of the de Burghs [les Bourkeyns], and because of the monstrous words used by Arnold in calling him [fitz Thomas] a rhymer [rymoure]', fitz Thomas

[1] Frame, *Eng. lordship*, pp 169–73.
[2] Ibid., pp 176–82.
[3] *Chartul. St Mary's, Dublin*, ii, 365.

went to war against him.¹ And certainly we cannot rule out the personal element. But it is noticeable that it was fitz Thomas and his allies who were later rewarded by the triumphant Mortimer faction in England, anxious to win new allies in Ireland, while le Poer was imprisoned in Dublin castle and left to die there. In October 1328 Butler was made earl of Ormond and in the following August fitz Thomas was created earl of Desmond.

Nothing better illustrates the failure of the government to maintain its control in the localities than the massacre that occurred at Braganstown in County Louth in June 1329.² John de Bermingham, earl of Louth, his brother Peter, many close relatives, some friends (including Richard Talbot of Malahide) and more than 160 others were killed by a mob which attacked his manor. The incident was sparked off by the murder of an inhabitant of Ardee by de Bermingham's kern on 9 June 1329. The incensed townsmen turned on the kern, killed fifteen of them on the spot, and pursued the remaining twenty-two as far as the local Carmelite church where they sought sanctuary. But the mob broke the sanctuary and slaughtered nineteen of the kern in the church. The three who escaped, together with other de Bermingham kern who were in the area and were now terrified of the mob, fled to the earl in his manor. Then hue and cry was raised in the county and an even larger mob (which technically was the *posse comitatus*) pursued the kern, stormed the manor, and slaughtered the inhabitants. Only a few, including the wife of the earl and some children, escaped.

It is clear that while resentment against the kern boiled over, there were deeper reasons for this attack by the Louth tenants. Clyn says simply that 'all of his county conspired against him, not wishing that he should rule over them'.³ This may well be the truth. De Bermingham was an outsider, imposed on them by the king after the trauma of the Bruce invasion. He may well have imported into Louth customs and habits that sustained him in Tethmoy but that were alien to the less tolerant Anglo-Irish of his new earldom. But whatever the reason for the hatred, the savagery of the attack by townsmen and local gentry well illustrates the extent to which the forces of disorder could get out of control.

Many stories later grew up around the massacre, including one that told of the earl taking a daughter of one of the de Verdons against her will and thus sparking off the whole affair. There was a woman involved, too, in another famous and much more disastrous murder in 1333, that of the young earl of Ulster.⁴ He had imprisoned and starved to death his cousin Walter de Burgh in 1332 and it was Walter's sister, Gyle, married to Richard de Mandeville, who instigated the murder in revenge. The consequences were momentous in Irish

¹ *Chartul. St Mary's, Dublin*, p. 364.
² James F. Lydon, 'The Braganstown massacre, 1329' in *Louth Arch. Soc. Jn.*, xix (1977), pp 5–16.
³ Clyn, *Annals*, p. 20.
⁴ Orpen, *Normans*, iv, 245–9.

history, leading ultimately to the collapse of the great de Burgh lordship in Ulster and Connacht. But these two murders, and many less important ones, show how fragile the feudal bond had become by now. Fealty had little place in the new world of the fourteenth century. Men were bought, and not even the royal officials were above corruption. When it was proposed to John Darcy in the summer of 1328 that he should go as chief governor to Ireland, he replied by stating a number of conditions, among them that his own nominees should fill the more important offices in the Irish administration; he clearly placed no faith in the existing holders of these offices.

Even more important, however, was another demand made by Darcy that he should be paid more than the normal fee which the chief governor received ('for he cannot live on his fee in the state in which the land is now'), money for his expenses, money in advance, and 'because there is nothing in the treasury, according to what he has heard', he must have £1,000 for an army.[1] A new era in Anglo-Irish relations had been inaugurated. Chief governors could bargain before taking up office, control from England was weakened, and most important of all the English taxpayer was beginning to accept responsibility for the cost of maintaining the king's peace in Ireland. A new pattern was emerging in Ireland, too, in which the Dublin government counted for less than the powerful local lord in many parts of the lordship. Already the tendency to focus governmental attention on what later became known as the four loyal counties in the east was manifest. And as the process of assimilation to the Gaelic way of life continued, many of the Anglo-Irish lordships were becoming hardly distinguishable from those ruled by Gaelic lords. The settlers in many places had already been swallowed up or displaced. In the west, especially, gaelicisation was widespread. There is a remarkable statement by the court poet of the O'Maddens in a passage on Bruce, where writing of 'our own foreigners' he says that 'the old chieftains of Erin prospered under those princely English lords who were our chief rulers, and who gave up their foreignness for a pure mind, their surliness for good manners, and their stubbornness for sweet mildness, and who had given up their perverseness for hospitality'.[2] This is a far cry from the attitude displayed in the Ó Néill remonstrance of c. 1317.

The success of the Gaelic revival was evident on many levels. It had gained a momentum of its own now and was impossible to check in the old way by employing brute force, treachery, and exclusion. Even John Darcy realised this when he demanded as one of his conditions of service in Ireland that all Irishmen who wished to live under English law should be permitted by statute of an Irish parliament to do so: there should be one and the same law for all Ireland. But it was too late. The Irish had their own laws and were not now interested in the benefits of English law. It was no longer a disadvantage to most of them to be outside the law, since the land of peace had contracted so much that the

[1] J. F. Baldwin, *The king's council in England during the middle ages* (Oxford, 1913), p. 473.
[2] *Hy Many*, p. 139.

king's justice could be available in only a small part of the island. The change could be violent and even sudden. In 1342, according to Clyn, Laoighseach Ó Mordha 'violently ejected almost all the English from their lands and inheritance' and in one night burned eight of their castles, as well as destroying Roger Mortimer's 'noble castle' of Dunamase. 'He usurped to himself the dominion of that country, from a serf becoming a lord, from a subject a prince.'[1]

There is one event which perhaps can be taken to symbolise the success of the Gaelic revival and which shows how much Ireland had changed in a couple of generations. In 1327 'the Irish of Leinster came together and made a certain king, that is Donal son of Art MacMurrough. Who, when he had been made king, ordered that his banner should be placed within two miles of Dublin and afterwards to travel throughout all the lands of Ireland.'[2] This was the first inauguration of its kind in Leinster since the twelfth century and it marks a significant advance in the revival of old Irish institutions. It is important not only because it was done in a formal and public way, but because the leading lords of Gaelic Leinster seem to have been party to it and to have acquiesced in the choice of Domnall as king. And he for his part immediately declared his intention of marching on Dublin itself and then leading a conquest of Ireland. That he did not succeed, and indeed was ignominiously captured and imprisoned in Dublin castle, hardly matters, though the fact that his captor was rewarded with the huge payment of £100 is a sure indication of the fright he had given the government.[3] The alarm in Dublin was worsened by the news that Robert Bruce had landed in Ulster and had forced the seneschal to accept a truce for one year and recognise him as king of Scotland.[4] There were also rumours that Bruce intended to invade England via Ulster with Irish help. But the Dublin government believed that the real danger lay in a possible rising in Ulster and sent the chancellor northwards to persuade the Anglo-Irish to resist the Scots, should they land in the future.[5]

But in Leinster, the important thing was that the Irish had a king who was ready to challenge the English. From now on the Leinster Irish were to be more of a problem than ever to the government. They could not be suppressed. They grew more menacing all the time. Like the other great Gaelic lords of Ireland, the MacMurroughs were part of the new pattern that had emerged from the breakup of the old feudal structure which the settlers had imposed. The Dublin government, the English king, and the *Gaill* and *Gaedhil* alike now had to find a way of living within the new structure that was shaping Ireland.

---

[1] Clyn, *Annals*, p. 30.

[2] *Chartul. St Mary's, Dublin*, ii, 365–6.

[3] Ibid., p. 366.

[4] R. G. Nicholson, 'A sequel to Edward Bruce's invasion of Ireland' in *Scot. Hist. Rev.*, xlii (1963), p. 32; Frame, *Eng. lordship*, pp 138–41.

[5] Ibid., p. 141. More important, the king's castle of Leixlip was garrisoned 'contra Scotos felones et inimicos' (P.R.O., E. 101/239/5).

CHAPTER XI

Approaches to the history of fourteenth-century Ireland

J. A. WATT

HALF a century or so ago, F. M. Powicke observed of Curtis's *History of medieval Ireland* (1923) that 'it may well be regarded as the beginning of a new period in Irish historical study'.[1] There can be little question that time has proved the forecast correct, not least in the particular field of fourteenth-century Irish history. Much of the advance in our understanding of this period has been achieved by way of a critical dialogue with Curtis. His book, it is to be noticed, was supplemented in his *Richard II in Ireland* (1927), summarised in chapters of his general *History of Ireland* (1936) and updated in a second edition which appeared in 1938. Some account of his work, at least in its broad outline, and an estimate of the major interpretative trends in relation to it, is an essential prologue to any attempt to resynthesise the significance of the reigns of Edward III and Richard II in Irish history.

In the forewords of both editions of his *Medieval Ireland*, Curtis acknowledged his especial debt to two men: Goddard Orpen, author of the classic exposition of the Anglo-Norman invasion and consequent settlement, and Eoin MacNeill, whom he lauded as 'the acknowledged pioneer and exponent in a whole new and scientific study of the continuous Gaelic ethos of Ireland as it stood intact in 1100 and continued in part up to 1603'. For the fourteenth century, however, Orpen ceased to be a guide. Indeed it almost seems as if he dismissed the period as beneath the attention of the serious historian:

the murder of the young earl of Ulster [in 1333] may fairly be regarded as marking the close of the feudal period introduced by Strongbow and Henry II, and signalising the opening of a new epoch, distinguished by the recrudescence of Celtic tribalism and its spurious imitation by many of Anglo-Norman descent. The door was now finally closed on a century and a half of remarkable progress, vigour and comparative order, and two centuries of retrogression, stagnation and comparative anarchy were about to be ushered in.[2]

The apparent condescension to the indigenous Gaelic culture and the implicit suggestion of its inferiority to Anglo-Norman feudalism, revealed in this

[1] *History*, ix (1925), p. 331.
[2] Orpen, *Normans*, iv, 249.

and similar passages, could not, in the Ireland of 1920, escape unfavourable comment. It was Eoin MacNeill, he who had masterminded the Gaelic League in 1893 and became its first secretary, and whose academic work had taken the study of early Irish literature to a new level of professional competence, who took up the cudgels against Orpen's alleged 'Celtophobia'.[1] For MacNeill terms such as 'Celtic tribalism' denoted an intolerable degradation of a civilisation which 'was probably as high a development of rural life as any country had produced in any [medieval] age'.[2] His own concern with the period 1260 to 1433 was to discover 'evidence of real life, growth, development, purpose and spirit in the Irish nation'.[3] And this he found particularly in the growth of 'a very definite national rally of the free Irish' which brought the conquest to a standstill.[4] The chief element in this process of Gaelic resurgence MacNeill saw as 'national sentiment', and its most characteristic expression was to be found in its literary tradition.[5] Since he did not actually provide any detailed literary exposition to demonstrate this thesis, MacNeill's own contribution to later (as distinct from early) Irish medieval history was limited. But he had made the case, once and for all, that in the study of medieval Ireland the indigenous native culture must have its proper place. He had, too, with his concept of the 'Irish rally' or 'Gaelic resurgence', changed the perspective within which the later middle ages was to be viewed.

What Curtis set out to do, then, was to steer a course between the Charybdis of Orpen's alleged Celtophobia and the Scylla of MacNeill's apparent Celtophilia. His main achievement was to prevent the hardening of an unnatural dichotomy which was developing in the historiography of his day between the study of the colony and of the Gaelic world. Curtis set out to write about both cultures with impartiality. If his work was inevitably an interim report (and later research has shown up its deficiencies in the terms in which it was conceived), it has not been wholly superseded.

Curtis made the Irish resurgence the main theme of what was a predominantly political approach to fourteenth-century history. This process he detailed chronologically and topographically ('the native victories were won by single chiefs or confederacies of chiefs in hundreds of local battles') and he sought to enliven the telling with a sprinkling of 'local heroes' whose deeds were listed in the Annals.[6] Here Curtis was filling in the detail of the picture of which MacNeill had sketched the broad outline. But where MacNeill had nothing positive to say about the colonists, Curtis descried the emergence of a new nationality, or at least a 'half nationality', that of the Anglo-Irish, 'Irish to the English and English to the Irish'.[7] This theme was expanded in the second edition of *Medieval Ireland*, especially in relation to the colonists' attitudes to

[1] MacNeill, *Phases*, p. 314.
[2] Ibid., pp 353–4.   [3] Ibid., p. 347.
[4] Ibid., p. 326.   [5] Ibid., p. 346.
[6] Curtis, *Med. Ire.* (2nd ed.), p. 213.
[7] Curtis, *Med. Ire.* (1st ed.), p. 258.

their home government: 'an Anglo-Irish "patriot party" formed itself, and we hear the first utterance of the spirit that was behind Swift and Grattan'.[1] The patriots, Curtis argued, were a constitutional party, upholding legality against the attempts of the crown to impose arbitrary power on them. The middle nation had produced its own brand of self-identity, and it had assumed political significance.[2] With this hypothesis, Curtis achieved his most distinctive and original contribution to the interpretation of the significance of the fourteenth century in Irish history.

If one of the principal merits of Curtis's work had been to expand Mac-Neill's concept of the Irish rally and, so to say, gather medieval Gaelic Ireland into the fold of historical scholarship, one of its principal demerits was its failure to make an advance in a direction where progress might have been expected. Orpen's *Ireland under the Normans* undoubtedly provided a foundation for the study of colonial Ireland which had previously been lacking. But he neglected the institutional framework within which the lords of Ireland and their representatives administered the country, made their governmental decisions, and sought to implement their policies. His history fails to give his readers any adequate account of the structure of government. The deficiency was not remedied by Curtis.

The materials for examining the colonial system of government are relatively bulky, despite the losses of 1922. Since these institutions were modelled on those operative in England, there is considerable help on hand for those who seek to analyse them, in the writings of those who have studied the English government at work in the various periods of the middle ages. And indeed the study of the Irish transplants of English institutions can throw a powerful beam of light on the nature of those institutions. Hence it is not surprising that the progress of research into medieval Irish history has been especially where earlier scholars were weakest. It was in 1929, with their 'The Irish parliaments of Edward I',[3] that H. G. Richardson and G. O. Sayles began their incomparable contributions to the history of colonial Ireland of which the high points are *Parliaments and councils of medieval Ireland* (1947), *The Irish parliament in the middle ages* (1952, 2nd ed. 1964), and *The administration of Ireland, 1172–1377* (1963). Independently and concurrently with these last-cited books, A. J. Otway-Ruthven has supplemented this work, especially on the level of local administration. A comparison of her *A history of medieval Ireland* (1967) with Curtis's 1938 edition is the measure of the change that this extended study of civil institutions has made in our understanding of the English colony in Ireland, not least in its fourteenth-century phase.[4]

There has been no comparable surge of activity in the study of fourteenth-

[1] Curtis, *Med. Ire.* (2nd ed.), pp 206–7.
[2] Ibid., pp 209, 215–16, 224–5, 249, 256.
[3] *R.I.A. Proc.*, xxxviii (1929), sect. C, pp 128–47.
[4] See further the excellent relevant chapters in Lydon, *Lordship*, and *Ire. in later middle ages*; and Frame, *Colonial Ire.*

century Gaeldom. For MacNeill, the essential element in Irish history in this period was its literary tradition. Characteristically, he found the spirit of the Irish rally typified in that festive concourse of poets which assembled in Uí Mhaine in 1351, an event celebrated in a commemorative poem.[1] Curtis claimed for the fourteenth century a revival in the fields of medical, legal, and historical writing as well as of poetry and imaginative literature; a revival he thought contrasted markedly with the silence of the two preceding centuries. But the detailed studies that would convert such suggestions into something weightier have not so far appeared. The literature, laws, and institutions of early Irish society continue to attract attention, but their evolution in the later middle ages remains understudied. Celticists have for the most part preferred the earlier medieval centuries, and it is only very recently that the first exploratory probes into the Gaelic world of the later middle ages have begun to appear.

One other major aspect of the study of medieval society has been so far unmentioned, that of religious history. By and large, the central tradition of Irish medieval historiography, if one may so describe the approaches of the historians mentioned above, has been concerned with the church in only an incidental way. No systematic account of the fourteenth-century church has yet appeared.[2] Perhaps the most characteristic emphasis of the work that has appeared is on the province of Armagh, material for which begins in this period to become more substantial than for other provinces. Serious scholarly interest in fourteenth-century Armagh goes back to Reeves's work (1850) on Archbishop John Colton,[3] and Lawlor's (1911) on Archbishop Milo Sweetman.[4] Until very recently, it had been left to Fr Aubrey Gwynn to continue this tradition, with his work on Archbishop Richard Fitz Ralph.[5]

It is appropriate to conclude this very brief review of trends in the historiography of fourteenth-century Ireland by taking notice of a criticism directed against historians of Ireland in general. 'It must be admitted', Professor Estyn Evans has written, 'that Irish historians have had little regard for environmental studies. They have been more document-bound than most historians.'[6] Perhaps, if true, this was because 'source-dominated caution'[7] was essential to wrest Irish history from propagandists. But the rebuke, whether merited or not,

[1] MacNeill, *Phases*, pp 344–5.
[2] Preliminary work appears in Aubrey Gwynn, 'Anglo-Irish church life: fourteenth and fifteenth centuries' in Corish, *Ir. catholicism*, ii, fasc. 4 (1968); Canice Mooney, 'The church in Gaelic Ireland', ibid., ii, fasc. 5 (1970); Watt, *Ch. & two nations*, and *Ch. in med. Ire.*
[3] *Acts of Archbishop Colton in his metropolitan visitation of the diocese of Derry*, ed. William Reeves (Ir. Arch. Soc., Dublin, 1850).
[4] H. J. Lawlor, 'A calendar of the register of Archbishop Sweetman' in *R.I.A. Proc.*, xxix (1911), sect. C, pp 213–310.
[5] Aubrey Gwynn, 'Richard FitzRalph, archbishop of Armagh' in *Studies*, xxii (1933), pp 389–405, 591–607; xxiii (1934), pp 395–411; xxiv (1935), pp 25–42, 558–72; xxv (1936), pp 81–96. See now Katherine Walsh, *A fourteenth-century scholar and primate: Richard FitzRalph in Oxford, Avignon and Armagh* (Oxford, 1981).
[6] E. Estyn Evans, *The personality of Ireland: habitat, heritage and history* (Cambridge, 1973), p. 19.
[7] Ibid., p. 20.

is a timely reminder of the medievalist's need to avail himself of work done in adjacent disciplines. No doubt he must expect to wait longer for the five companion volumes to the admirable *Archaeological survey of Northern Ireland: County Down* (1966), and longer still for the twenty-six further volumes which would add a whole new dimension to our knowledge of medieval Irish civilisation. But the historical geographers are active and contributing a body of work on the landscape of both colonial and Gaelic Ireland which the general historian of medieval Ireland will ignore at his peril.

One basic fact emerges inescapably from even the most superficial reflection on the course of Irish history after the Anglo-Norman invasion. It was profoundly conditioned by that fundamental cultural duality which was the result of the colonisation process set in train by the twelfth-century adventurers. The invasion had divided the country between two cultures, Irish and English; two nations, each with its own language, customs, and traditional way of life. Perhaps the simplest account of medieval Ireland is that which tells of the unceasing struggle of these cultures for supremacy, where, whatever temporary lulls expediency or exhaustion might suggest or enforce, the essence lay in the Gaelic Irish wish to expel the foreigner and the Anglo-Irish wish to extend and complete the conquest. The detailed accounts of both Irish and Anglo-Irish Annals leaves us in no doubt that *Gaedhil* and *Gaill* slaughtered each other with remorseless zeal throughout the fourteenth century, just as they had done in earlier centuries. There is this important difference, however, for our period. In the thirteenth century, a hypothetical detached observer of the Irish scene would almost certainly have thought future success lay with the colonists, though, if he were particularly acute, he might have detected some major weaknesses in their position. In the fourteenth century, however, he would observe a pronounced shift in the equilibrium in favour of the Gaelic Irish; though witnessing successive attempts by the lords of Ireland to tilt the balance back in the English favour, he might not have been so convinced that the colony was inevitably doomed, as contemporary colonists professed to believe.

The period of Irish history with which we are here concerned has been likened to a third act in the drama of post-invasion Irish history. The dramatic tension is between a colony in decline and a Gaelic Ireland in resurgence. The act opens in earnest in 1330, when Edward III, free of the tutelage of his mother and her paramour, who as lord of Trim was a figure to be reckoned with in Ireland, began, as almost the first major policy decision of his personal rule, the mounting of a major expedition to Ireland. Preparations were nearly complete when the representations of parliament and Pope John XXII dissuaded him from setting off, and thereafter first Scotland and then France were given higher priorities. The act concludes with Richard II, the only English monarch before Victoria to show himself twice as such in Ireland, losing his throne while engaged in a fruitless bid to reestablish the reality of power as lord of Ireland.

The main theme of the act is the colonists' growing sense of desperation at their plight, and their forcing on the home government (all too prone to look the other way where Ireland was concerned) an awareness of the gravity of the crisis and of its duty to bestir itself to do something about it. Something was done: too little and too late, it is easy to say with hindsight. The act closes with ominous forebodings of worse to come for the colonists and for the authority of the crown.

This perspective on the history of the fourteenth century lays especial emphasis on the significance of the period in the long narrative of an essentially political analysis of Anglo-Irish relations. The theme will be reviewed here, freshened by the additional knowledge that the further exploitation of record evidence still continues to yield. However, to exaggerate this theme risks over-simplification. For there was an important social aspect of relations between Gaelic and Anglo-Irish; there was more to the relationship of the two nations than simply confrontation. The two cultures did not merely collide, they also interpenetrated: each nation assimilated people from the other. Each culture, of course in different degrees at different times and to unequal extents, was affected by the other. The historian must concern himself with the pheno-menon that the anthropologists have taught him to call acculturation: changes that take place when two different cultures coexist in close and continuous first-hand contact.

It is in the study of the acculturation process that the realities of medieval Irish society begin to reveal themselves in all their complexity. The terms 'native Irish' and 'Anglo-Irish' or their variants, commonly used by historians when describing the dichotomy of that society, are perfectly adequate as purely ethnic classifications. But they can conceal wide divergencies in the social and cultural positions of those so labelled. The extremes of variation may be seen as ranging, on the one hand, from urbanised and anglicised Irish to tribalised and hibernicised English on the other. For example, in one Robert de Bree, a Dublin merchant and property-owner of the later thir-teenth century, who became mayor of the capital city and whose family came to form part of the Dublin patriciate in the fourteenth century, we seem to have a typical immigrant success story, that of an obscure Englishman rising to fortune in the bourgeoisie of a new expanding colonial society. However, it transpires he was a Gaelic Irishman, for there is extant his petition to Edward I asking that he might enjoy the status at law of an Englishman,[1] a request we might be permitted to see as the medieval equivalent of taking out naturalisation papers. In the same period, a Hugh of Kent, 'liege burgess of Galway', collector of customs in that important port, proves also to have been a Gaelic Irishman, since he found it necessary to ask the king for letters patent 'enabling him and his children in life and in death to use English law

---

[1] *Hist. & mun. doc. Ire.*, pp xxx–xxxi. A Maurice de Bray was given a grant of English law in 1296 (*Cal. doc. Ire., 1293–1301*, no. 19).

in Ireland'.[1] Again, in Cork, at about the same time, the local Anglo-Irish showed themselves resentful of infiltration of this sort.[2] That they thought they should impede Gaelic Irishmen from holding posts in the customs suggests, with the Dublin and Galway evidence, that the phenomenon was common enough in the colonial towns of the later thirteenth century.

This type of bourgeois Irishman can be contrasted with others in the different ethnic and social groups that went into the making of medieval Irish society. His position, with his English name and speech, dress, and fine town house is, for example, very different from that of a fellow countryman still living the traditional Gaelic way of life, untouched by the new foreign influences. For an insight into that way of life we may have recourse to an outside observer detached enough from the hostilities of the Irish scene not to share the Anglo-Irish fear and distrust of the Irish of these remote parts. In the winter of 1397, Raymond, viscount of Perelhos and of Roda in Roussillon, an experienced traveller, made a pilgrimage from his native Pyrenees to St Patrick's Purgatory in Loch Derg in Ulster. He was taken under the protection of Ó Néill, stayed with him on the way to the Purgatory and spent Christmas with him on the way back. His account of his journey (extant in Provençal) is one of the earliest travellers' accounts of Irish manners and customs we possess. Some of what he saw impressed him. He thought the Irish the handsomest men and the most beautiful women he had seen anywhere. But the main trend of his report was to highlight a way of life as unlike that of urban society as it was possible to be: that of a warrior society, living in poverty close to the cattle on which their sustenance for the most part depended. It was in matters of dress that he found their customs most different from anything he had met in his experience. All the men, he said, irrespective of social position, whether king, bishop, or any other dignitary, went bare-legged and barefoot. What struck him most forcibly, however, was the different standard of modesty in dress obtaining among the Irish of this area, who 'show all their shameful parts, the women as well as the men' (*mostro totas las partz vergonhozas, tant las femnas quant los homes*). The women attendants of Ó Néill's wife apparently 'showed all they had and with as little shame as they show their faces' (*mostravo tot quant avien an tan pauca de vergonha coma de mostra la cara*).[3] Perhaps Raymond exaggerated in this particular respect. But his account as a whole, superficial though it is in many ways, conveys an

---

[1] He was keeper of the new custom of Galway in 1282 (*Cal. doc. Ire., 1252–84*, no. 1907), and obtained his charter of English law in 1297 (*Cal. doc. Ire., 1293–1301*, no. 19). See also M. D. O'Sullivan, *Old Galway: the history of a Norman colony in Ireland* (Cambridge, 1942), p. 32.

[2] In 1279–80 they petitioned Edward I for the removal of one Stephan Brendan, found by a jury to be a native Irishman who had been appointed *concustumarius* of Cork by the Lombard firm entrusted by the king with collection of customs in Ireland. Text printed in MacNiocaill, *Na buirgeisi*, ii, 351–2.

[3] Alfred Jeanroy and Alphonse Vignaux, *Voyage au purgatoire de St Patrice. Visions de Tindal et de St Paul. Textes languedociens du quinzième siècle* (Toulouse, 1903), p. 17. See J. P. Mahaffy, 'Two early tours in Ireland' in *Hermathena*, xviii, no. 40 (1914), pp 3–9.

authentic impression of an observer seeking to communicate to his reader the impression of a society outside the range of ordinary European *mores*.

The lot of the anglicised Irish of the comfortably-off urban middle class contrasts markedly also with that of the hibernicised 'English by blood' of the march areas, straggling precariously across both cultures. These were the men whom the Irish parliament had in mind when in 1297 it referred to individuals who were in a condition 'as if degenerate', *quasi degeneres*;[1] the sense is that these people had abandoned, or were in process of losing, the characteristic traits of their nation: they were *de genere*, out of their *genus* or proper national place. Parliament had begun the process of adding a new word to the English language. Much was to be heard of this sort of 'degeneracy' in the fourteenth century. Its growth in Ireland not merely galled the *amour propre* of the English but convinced them that the phenomenon was at the root of the decline of the colony. It was to be left to Edmund Spenser to hit the right note of amazed resentment at the condition. We may perhaps cite him as giving the best literary expression of a sentiment that had its birth in the fourteenth century:

EUDOXUS: what is this that ye saie of soe manye as remayne Englishe of them? why? are not they that weare once Englishe abiding Englishe still?

IRENEUS: no for the most part of them are degenerated and growen allmoste meare Irishe yea and more malitious to the Englishe then the verye Irishe themselves.

EUDOXUS: what heare I? and is it possible that an Englisheman broughte vp naturallye in suche swete civilytie as Englande affordes can finde suche likinge in that barbarous rudenes that he shoulde forgett his owne nature and forgoe his owne nacion? howe maie this be?[2]

This was written in the last decade of the sixteenth century. It is, however, a reasonably safe conclusion that such thoughts would not have sounded strange to the framers of the statute of Kilkenny, promulgated in 1366, precisely to arrest the hibernicisation of the English.

The pronounced cultural variants of Irish society that lie behind the simple fourteenth-century differentiation between 'pure Irish' (*meri Hibernici*) and 'pure English' (*mere Anglici*) had been fashioned by political developments and conditioned by geographical factors. It has been calculated that before the Anglo-Norman invasion there were in Ireland probably no less than 150 minor kingdoms.[3] This political disunity, to which the geographical fragmentation of the country powerfully contributed, favoured the invaders' initial advance. By the beginning of our period, however, it was clear that far from having overcome the prevailing divisions of Gaelic polity, they had added a new dimension of fragmentation of their own. The Anglo-Normans had progressed in a series of individual uncoordinated initiatives. Military success had been limited,

---

[1] *Stat. Ire., John—Hen. V*, p. 210.
[2] 'A vewe of the present state of Ireland' in *The works of Edmund Spenser: Spenser's prose works*, ed. Rudolf Gottfried (Baltimore, 1949), p. 96.
[3] F. J. Byrne, *Irish kings and high-kings* (London, 1973), p. 7.

settlement unevenly distributed both in territorial breadth and in numerical depth. The colony was the patchwork result of piecemeal conquest, and politically and socially did not form a single coherent entity. The Tudors, who used the plural form 'the colonies' in speaking of the English settlements in Ireland, were nearer the mark. 'The lordship was above all a land of numerous frontiers.'[1]

Despite the apparently unplanned and somewhat haphazard nature of Anglo-Norman colonisation, the invaders had shown a singularly acute eye for the best land, settling it the more thoroughly the better its quality. And despite the losses of fringe areas and the wastings of other parts, they proved tenacious in hanging on to it. There is a revealingly close relationship between the geographer's map of the physically best-endowed land of Ireland and the territorial spread of the colonists.[2] The nucleus of the settled area was that compact eastern zone where the fifty-mile break in the island's mountain rim, extending from Dundalk to Dublin, extends inland over the bog-free boulder clay plains which enjoy Ireland's lowest rainfall. There were extensions northwards and, particularly, southwards into the lowlands of the river systems converging on Waterford Harbour.[3]

An analysis of place-names has provided impressive confirmation of what documentary evidence has to say of the extent of colonial occupation of rural areas.[4] It has been calculated that of Ireland's 62,000 townland names 8,800, or fourteen per cent, are English in origin, and these mostly of the medieval period. Of these English names, one particular element is especially interesting. Some 2,684, or thirty-one per cent, of these English names carry the suffix 'town'. 'No other name element', writes Professor Jones Hughes, 'has such a widespread, compact, and continuous distribution and such sharply defined limits.'[5] This 'town zone' has areas of particularly high incidence and these give us the heartlands of the colony: north County Dublin, Meath, Louth, the eastern part of Westmeath, east Kildare, south-east County Wexford (especially the Bargy and Forth baronies), Kilkenny, south Tipperary, and east Limerick. This is the area where the 'English by blood' kept their national identity longest.

The negative evidence of the place-name map is also revealing. The town zone, as has been said, had sharply defined limits. Outside it lay the most part of Ulster, Connacht, and west Munster. Using documentary evidence it is possible to be somewhat more specific. Clearly, some parts of these areas were more exposed to colonial influence than others. On the whole, the more

---

[1] Frame, *Eng. lordship*, p. 328.

[2] Cf. A. R. Orme, *The world's landscape 4: Ireland* (London, 1970), map 1, p. 2.

[3] Evans, *Personality of Ire.*, p. 24; J. H. Andrews, 'A geographer's view of Irish history' in Moody & Martin, *Ir. hist.*, pp 19–22.

[4] Thomas Jones-Hughes, 'Town and baile in Irish place-names' in Stephens & Glasscock, *Ir. geog. studies*, p. 247.

[5] Ibid., p. 247.

inhospitable the terrain, the more independent were the Gaelic Irish. Hence extensive mountain and bog regions remained to a high degree culturally autonomous, though many of the 'nations of the Irish', to use the contemporary term, were forced or cajoled into some degree of political subjection. The most important of these areas were, in the north, Ulster (apart from most of the territory east of a line joining Dundalk and Coleraine), and in the south, the mountainous region of south Kerry and west Cork. Connacht was a congeries of Irish nations with a colonial presence here and there, of which east County Galway was the most populous. This delineates broadly the area where the customs and traditions of the Gaelic world best preserved their integrity even beyond the medieval period.

Faced with all the complex cultural and political variables of this overall situation, Orpen was led to declare that there was 'little or no history common to the whole country'.[1] He was certainly right to emphasise that the history of Ireland should not be written mainly in terms of the nominal central government. The temptation so to write it must always be there, because of the relative abundance of sources of this provenance. But the influence of central government was far from all-pervasive, and its effectiveness, often very limited even in the thirteenth century, was diminishing in the fourteenth. He was right, too, to stress the importance of writing the history of Ireland with proper regard for regional differences. But Orpen's view, if pushed too far, would make of Irish history nothing but the sum total of a collection of local histories. The history common to the whole country, its shared experience, was that of the evolving consequences of the duality of its cultures and of their mutual interaction.

There remains one final consideration in any identification of particular approaches to the study of medieval Irish history. Extending the horizon beyond regional and national limits, there can be observed an international dimension to the history of medieval Ireland. It has been asserted: '. . . few ask what it must have meant to put a colonial movement into motion seven hundred years ago. Neither is there any study of what a twelfth or thirteenth-century "colony" looked like, how it lived and how it developed as a colonial establishment.'[2] But in fact virtually any study of medieval Ireland, whatever its angle of approach, is a contribution to the history of medieval colonialism, an aspect of the recreation of what happened when a colonial movement went into motion seven hundred years ago. Historians of medieval Ireland are not dealing with phenomena for which the use of the word 'colonialism' might be debated, phenomena like the Norman conquest of England or the establishment of the crusader kingdoms in the Middle East. These were essentially military ventures leading to the establishment of new states, independent of the countries where the conquerors originated. They were not dependencies of

---

[1] Orpen, *Normans*, iv, 130.
[2] Joshua Prawer, *The Latin kingdom of Jerusalem: European colonialism in the middle ages* (London, 1972), pp xi–xii.

a mother country. Ireland became a country to which Englishmen of all levels of society, save the very highest, emigrated and settled in large numbers, expropriating the lands and towns of the indigenous population, building a new society in the image of the one they had left. It was also a society which the home government retained and maintained as a dependency, exercising firm control over the policies and personnel of the oversea administration it had established and continued to develop. Thus medieval Ireland fulfils the strictest criteria semantics can impose on the word 'colony'[1] as Gascony, to take a further example,[2] which did not receive substantial emigration from England or know dispossession of its native ruling class, does not.

To make the permanent dependency of an immigrant society on a mother country the essence of the definition of the term 'colony' should not, however, lead us to narrow the history of the colony merely to the history of its relationship to its controlling parent. There is some truth in the suggestion that 'the history of colonies is surely the history of the ways in which the power, prestige, and profits of some countries were enhanced (or so they believed) by external dependencies of migrant settlers'.[3] But that is only part of the story. Another part, and it is the more important part, since its influence remains after the bond with the mother country weakens or has been severed, is what has happened to a country when its inhabitants, indigenous and settlers, are caught up in a colonial movement. Such is the all-dominating theme of Irish history. The essay that follows is a small part of a big story: an attempt to trace a colonial development in a short period of the medieval phase of Ireland's colonial experience.

[1] M. I. Finley, 'Colonies—an attempt at a typology' in *R. Hist. Soc. Trans.*, xxvi (1976), pp 167–88, is the most valuable discussion. But medieval Ireland is not considered.

[2] Margaret Labarge, *Gascony, England's first colony, 1204—1453* (London, 1980). R. I. Burns studies the Spanish *reconquista* as a colonial movement; *Medieval colonialism: post-crusade exploitation of Islamic Valencia* (London, 1975), and continuation volumes.

[3] Finley, 'Colonies', p. 174.

CHAPTER XII

Gaelic polity and cultural identity

J. A. WATT

GAELIC society, its economy, and its literature are discussed elsewhere in this volume. The relevant chapters cover in a single chronological sweep the period from the Anglo-Norman invasion to the Tudor period and expose in general outline the distinctive features of the culture of medieval Gaeldom. There is no intention here of covering that ground again. But it is not possible to write a meaningful general history of Ireland in this period, or even of the purely colonial aspects of it, without making an attempt to capture something of the specifically fourteenth-century Gaelic ethos. How far it is possible to do this depends of course on the nature of the source material available for the period. Something must be said, therefore, by way of preface about this material, tentative classification suggested, and a brief analysis attempted.

Irish rulers have left none of the administrative records that were the characteristic products of fourteenth-century governments elsewhere in Europe. Some types of record at least must have existed, for there is abundant evidence that the leading Irish kings were quite capable of conducting correspondence in Latin and in concluding legal agreements of many kinds with a variety of authorities in both Latin and French. But if there are no extant records of government except those that have left their trace in the archives of colonial and papal administration, there is a literature of Irish kingship or, more precisely, a literature that Irish kings endowed and patronised. This work, though essentially literary in nature, is concerned with kingship in action and therefore throws some light on the primary political institution of Gaelic Ireland. This is the literature produced by the families that preserved and transmitted through their generations the traditional learning of Gaelic Ireland. Three products of this hereditary tradition, whose prolonged existence down the centuries is in itself a most notable feature of Gaelic culture, are especially significant for the historian: the laws, the Annals and the praise-verse of the court poets. Of these, the first is virtually unavailable to the general historian. As has been authoritatively stated, 'Irish law in the later middle ages is almost completely unexplored.'[1] Where it has

[1] Gearóid Mac Niocaill, 'The contact of Irish and common law' in *N.I. Legal Quart.*, xxiii (1972), p. 16.

been investigated for this period, historians have been concerned more with the interaction of Irish and feudal law than with the law in its own right. It is quite otherwise with the Annals. These have long been exploited by historians, though neither the so-called Annals of Connacht (particularly informative for the fourteenth century) nor the Annals of Ulster can be said to exist in satisfactory modern editions and translations. The Gaelic Irish Annals (as also their Anglo-Irish counterparts) are usually jejune, in historical and literary ambition falling a long way short of chronicle status. They are to a considerable degree necrologies, and since the deaths they record are preponderantly the casualties of battle, they are preoccupied with apparently unending tribal war. The Annals, with their emphasis on genealogy, royal succession, and the martial exploits of kings, stand in close relationship to the praise-verse. This literary genre, the most popular of the fourteenth century, is undoubtedly to be ranked among the most distinctive features of Celtic civilisation, in Wales and Scotland as well as in Ireland, and it was speedily adopted by the Anglo-Irish baronage. The poets, highly skilled practitioners of a traditional art of declamatory verse passed on down the generations of the same families, existed to establish and maintain the honour of their aristocratic patrons.[1] They preserved the genealogies that recorded their patrons' status in society, officiated at their inaugurations, exhorted them to courage on the eve of battle and above all, boosted their esteem by glorifying their success in war. It is the work of these men that alone has preserved something of the intellectual outlook of the native Irish ruling class in this period. Its horizons were not limited to war, but fighting was an integral part of the lives of the ruling class; and for the poets, the recording of martial deeds was their professional concern. Prowess in war was the acme of aristocratic honour and achievement, and the exploits of warriors dominate the works which the hereditary literary caste of medieval Gaeldom composed and compiled, and whose wholesale adoption by the Anglo-Irish constitutes one of the most obvious features of the fourteenth-century acculturation process.[2] The poets did not, however, confine their praise to mere men. They praised God, his mother, the saints. They wrote religious poetry as well as martial verse, and the historian of religion must not overlook that fact.[3]

---

[1] Osborn Bergin, *Irish bardic poetry: texts and translations together with an introductory lecture*; with a foreword by D. A. Binchy; compiled and edited by David Greene and Fergus Kelly (Dublin, 1970); E. C. Quiggin, 'Prolegomena to the study of the later Irish bards, 1200–1500' in *Brit. Acad. Proc.*, v (1911–12), pp 89–143; Ó Huiginn, *Poems*, i; J. E. Caerwyn Williams, 'The court poet in medieval Ireland' in *Brit. Acad. Proc.*, lvii (1972), pp 1–51; Myles Dillon and Nora Chadwick, *The Celtic realms* (2nd ed., London, 1972), p. 318.

[2] Examples from the very beginning of our period of poems written in honour of Richard de Burgh and William de Bermingham, *B.M. cat. Ir. MSS*, i, 338–9. The classic case of literary acculturation in the fourteenth century was Gerald, third earl of Desmond, justiciar of Ireland 1367–9; cf. below, pp 697–8.

[3] For brief comment and illustration, see my *Ch. in med. Ire.*, pp 212–14; further literature, p. 228.

Unquestionably the most outstanding encomiastic composition of the fourteenth century is 'Caithréim Thoirdhealbhaigh' ('The triumphs of Turlough'),
possibly written *c*. 1330 and almost certainly before mid-century. A prose
narrative, liberally interspersed with lengthy poems, it has been described as
'the most vivid picture that has come down to us of the life of medieval Ireland
at war'.[1] It certainly conveys extremely vividly the reality of that incessant
small-scale warfare, *Gaedhil* against *Gaedhil*, *Gaedhil* against *Gaill* with complex variations of combinations of each, which characterised Irish society at
this time. The composition details a twofold struggle. One of its main themes is
a typical Gaelic dynastic contest among the O'Briens, chief of the tribes of
Thomond, and the other their relationship with the de Clares, established
somewhat precariously at Quin and Bunratty. The two conflicts were inseparably interconnected and all neighbouring families, Anglo-Irish as well as
Gaelic Irish, were inevitably drawn into the fighting. The story begins in mid-
thirteenth century and moves to a dramatic double climax with a battle fought
near the Cistercian abbey of Corcomroe in August 1317, which established the
supremacy of Clann Toirdelbaig over Clann Briain Ruaid, and the battle of
Dysert O'Dea in May 1318, at which Richard de Clare and his son were killed.
This latter victory brought about the precipitate abandonment of Bunratty and
led to the extinction of Anglo-Irish settlement in Thomond.

T. J. Westropp long ago vindicated the 'Caithréim' 's claim to be regarded as
an authentic source for political narrative when previously it had often been
dismissed as a work more of imagination than history.[2] Its substantial reliability, when read with the obvious safeguards, was accepted by both Orpen and
Curtis, and it continues to be exploited as a valuable source for the history of
family rivalries, the very stuff of Thomond's politics. There is, however,
another way in which the book has its relevance for the historian, which has not
perhaps always been so well appreciated. As the product of the pure Gaelic
tradition, it reflects the assumptions and aspirations of its culture in a detail
unparalleled by any other fourteenth-century source. The Irish Annals form an
essential complement and may be read similarly with the accent on what they
reveal of a particular civilisation, rather than on the narrative detail of dynastic
history. If to these sources are added works of a related type, products of the
same literary tradition, there is available in print and in translation a body of
specifically fourteenth-century Irish material from which to delineate some at
least of the characteristic features of fourteenth-century Gaeldom.

To supplement these sources of Gaelic Irish provenance, three further sorts
of source material can be drawn on. The largest and most straightforward of

---

[1] Robin Flower, in the introduction to *Caithr. Thoirdh.*, i, p. xvi.
[2] T. J. Westropp, 'On the external evidences bearing on the historic character of the "Wars of
Torlough" by John, son of Rory MacGrath' in *R.I.A. Trans.*, xxii (1903), sect. C, pp 133–98. Cf.
further, L. F. McNamara, 'An examination of the medieval Irish text "Caithréim Thoirdhealbhaigh" ' in *N. Munster Antiq. Jn.*, viii (1961), pp 189–92; Brian Ó Cuív, 'Literary creation and Irish
historical tradition' in *Brit. Acad. Proc.*, xlix (1963), pp 233–62.

these is the material scattered through the different types of administrative records and the Anglo-Irish annals. The Gaelic Irish sources have something to say about relationships between the Irish kings and the colonists, but on the whole the colonial sources offer the chance of a more detailed picture. One category of especial importance relates to the politico-military accommodations made between Irish chiefs on the one hand and the crown, or individual Anglo-Irish lords, on the other. Goddard Orpen always emphasised the irreconcilability of two systems, 'Norman feudalism' and 'Celtic tribalism'. For him, 'feudalism and tribalism could not coexist'.[1] In fact, a long series of compositions (*conventiones*) and indentures (*indenturae*) testify that such coexistence was one of the ordinary features of Irish social and political life.[2] Contractual relationships involving services to a lord with the obligation of affording protection in return, frequently involving also a money payment or grant of a fief, were the accepted methods whereby Irish rulers and such potentates as the earls of Ulster,[3] Ormond,[4] and Kildare,[5] as well as the Dublin administration,[6] allied with each other. These sworn agreements show also another aspect of acculturation: the mutual adjustment of two legal systems, Irish brehon law and English common law. Professor Binchy has given us an excellent generalisation to serve as a working hypothesis about this process:

For the centuries-old relations between the native princes and their powerful neighbours of Norman descent, who governed their territories by a curious amalgam of Irish and feudal law, had eventually led to the extension of a somewhat similar system to the purely Gaelic districts also.[7]

The detailed examination of the adjustment, however, has still to be done. Professor Mac Niocaill has used the Kildare and Ormond deeds to good effect to demonstrate fourteenth-century aspects of this interaction. Such men as the earls of Ormond and Kildare were, so to say, 'legally ambidextrous, employing common law or Irish law as circumstances dictated'. On the other hand, words

---

[1] Orpen, *Normans*, iv, 306, and *Camb. med. hist.*, vii, 546.

[2] Earliest examples are printed in *Report on the manuscripts of Lord de L'Isle and Dudley, preserved at Penshurst Place*, i, ed. C. L. Kingsford (H.M.C., London, 1925), pp 30–33.

[3] G. H. Orpen, 'The earldom of Ulster, part IV: inquisitions touching Coleraine and military tenures' in *R.S.A.I. Jn.*, xlv (1915), pp 131–8, 141; for additional important information, A. J. Otway-Ruthven, 'The partition of the de Verdon lands in Ireland in 1332' in *R.I.A. Proc.*, lxvi (1968), sect. C, p. 406; Otway-Ruthven, *Med. Ire.*, pp 215–16, on the issue more generally.

[4] *Ormond deeds, 1170–1350*, nos 682, 700; ibid., *1350–1413*, nos 22, 34, 35, 36, 38, 46, 48, 74, 219, 347, 374.

[5] *Red Bk Kildare*, nos 139, 166–70.

[6] Now studied in detail for the early part of the period in the excellent Ph.D. thesis of R. F. Frame, 'The Dublin government and Gaelic Ireland in the late thirteenth and fourteenth centuries' (University of Dublin, 1972). For the use of Irish troops by one justiciar, see his 'The justiciarship of Ralph Ufford: warfare and politics in fourteenth-century Ireland' in *Studia Hib.*, xiii (1973), pp 45–6.

[7] D. A. Binchy, 'The linguistic and historical value of the Irish law tracts' in *Brit. Acad. Proc.*, xxix (1943), p. 227.

like 'quest', 'attorney', 'executor', 'feofment', even 'livery of seisin' make their appearance in the Irish language.[1]

There is another facet of the adjustment process which can be documented in the colonial records. Just as the Irish chiefs were impelled to work out a *modus vivendi* with powerful Anglo-Irish lords, so they were often impelled also to reach an understanding with the ecclesiastical leaders of the other nation. It is especially the Ulster experience of this process that can be studied, because of the relatively abundant Armagh source material for the fourteenth century.

A third type of source material is very restricted in both quantity and quality. From Giraldus Cambrensis to modern times Ireland has been afflicted with the inquisitive stranger writing up *curiosa* for the entertainment of his fellow-countrymen. Three foreign travellers in later fourteenth-century Ireland set down their observations on the country and its inhabitants. Raymond of Perelhos, the Aragonese pilgrim to St Patrick's Purgatory, has already been mentioned. Another was Henry Chrysted, an English knight captured while in the service of the earl of Ormond, who married a daughter of his captor, learned Irish, was employed because of this knowledge by Richard II on his first Irish expedition, and told something of his story to Froissart.[2] The third, a Frenchman, Jean Creton, accompanied Richard II on his second Irish expedition and wrote a metrical account of the events leading up to the deposition of that king, beginning in the period Richard spent in Ireland.[3] These three men were not trained social anthropologists seeking to analyse the inner mechanisms of Gaelic society. Their accounts are subjective, superficial, and sometimes inconsistent. But that is no reason for ignoring them. Used carefully, they have their value, not least in conveying impressions of attitudes of the Irish chiefs to their own culture and to the English.

Many of the sources so far mentioned present some degree of technical difficulty for the general historian, and sometimes it is a considerable degree. But the fourth category is perhaps the most hazardous of all for him. What can be learned of the economy of Gaelic Ireland in the fourteenth century? Written sources will provide some important clues but little detail. Recourse to the archaeologist meets no very encouraging response, for medieval Ireland has been neglected for the earlier periods: 'thanks to intensive archaeological fieldwork we probably have more firm facts about conditions of life in the neolithic period than in medieval Gaelic Ireland.'[4] Nor is the historical geographer in a position to lend very much help: 'we have to face the fact that we still do not know the nature of settlement in Ireland between 1100 and the Tudor

---

[1] Mac Niocaill, 'Irish and common law', p. 23. It must be said, however, that it might be argued that the introduction of these words was post-fourteenth century.

[2] *Oeuvres de Froissart*, ed. J. M. B. C. Kervyn de Lettenhove (25 vols, Brussels, 1867–77), xv, 168–81; *Froissart's chronicles*, ed. and trans. John Jolliffe (London, 1967), pp 362–70.

[3] 'Histoire du roy d'Angleterre Richard', ed. and trans. John Webb in *Archaeologia*, xx (1824).

[4] Evans, *Personality of Ire.*, p. 13.

plantations.'[1] Nevertheless it is the historical geographers and archaeologists who have been asking the right sort of question in this branch of Irish history; and, if their work has been directed primarily to other periods, it can be used to throw some fitful light on a particularly dark corner of fourteenth-century history.

AT the focal point of the whole Irish social and political scene stood the *ri*, the tribal king, 'captain of his nation' (*capitaneus nacionis sue*, as English officialdom usually latinised his status). Sometimes, it is true, the English described him as *rex*, but he was not a king in the sense that fourteenth-century Europe generally understood that word, for he was not anointed and crowned in church in a religious ceremony. But then, at the very beginning of our period, neither were the kings of Scotland. Traditionally, the king of Scotland was inaugurated, not crowned, into his kingship in an open-air ceremony of which the central acts were his being placed on the celebrated stone of Scone and being proclaimed king, with a recitation of his genealogy, by his principal court poet.[2] This type of royal inauguration was common to the Gaelic world and was of immemorial antiquity. Throughout the preceding century, the Scots had been trying to persuade the papacy to update their manner of bestowing the royal status, and finally managed to persuade Pope John XXII to concede that privilege. It cost them 12,000 gold florins, and in 1329 David II became the first Scottish king to be crowned and anointed.[3] In the highlands, however, inauguration of the traditional type persisted among the clan chiefs, and it was the rule in all the *tuatha* of Ireland.

The sources are uninformative about how selection of the king was made. Presumably the principle known to the Irish law of an earlier period still had relevance, and selection from the common descent group, the *derbfhine*, the family of four generations, from the descendants, that is to say, of a common greatgrandfather who had been king,[4] was still regarded as the norm. But in practice, as is clear from the Annals, there was much succession from father to son and, in some cases at least, association of the son with the kingship during the father's lifetime. Inevitably political stability was at risk on the death of a king, with factions forming to involve alliance and counter-alliance with neighbouring families, including those of the Anglo-Irish. One of the fullest accounts of such a situation is in the Annals of Connacht for the year 1310.[5]

---

[1] R. E. Glasscock, 'The study of deserted medieval settlements in Ireland (to 1968)' in Beresford & Hurst, *Deserted med. villages*, p. 280.

[2] Cf. Gordon Donaldson, *Scottish kings* (London, 1967), pp 11–12, 30–31.

[3] W. C. Dickinson, Gordon Donaldson, and I. A. Milne (ed.), *A source book of Scottish history* (3 vols, London and Edinburgh, 1952), i, 140–43.

[4] D. A. Binchy, *Celtic and Anglo-Saxon kingship* (Oxford, 1970), pp 24–6; Kathleen Hughes, *Early Christian Ireland: introduction to the sources* (London, 1972); Byrne, *Ir. kings*, pp 122–3, for a very informative dynastic diagram; Donnchadh Ó Corráin, 'Irish regnal succession: a reappraisal' in *Studia Hib.*, xi (1971), pp 7–39.

[5] *Ann. Conn.*, pp 222–3.

It must be quoted in full for it contains a number of different points of interest:

Maelruanaid Mac Diarmata, seeing the exclusion of his foster-son from his patrimony and the heavy exactions on each tuath about him, and much resenting the action of the Galls in restricting and diminishing his power—for the Galls felt sure that if this one man were weak the whole province of Connacht would be in their own hands—determined, like the warrior he was, to take his foster-son boldly and make him king by force. So he carried him to Carnfree and installed him on the mound according to the practice of the saints, and of Da Conna of Assylin in particular; and he, Fedlimid mac Aeda meic Eogain [Ó Conchobair], was proclaimed in a style as royal, as lordly and as public as any of his race from the time of Brian son of Eochu Muigmedoin till that day. And when Fedlimid mac Aeda meic Eogain had married the province of Connacht his foster-father waited upon him during the night in the manner remembered by the old men and recorded in the old books; and this was the most splendid kingship-marriage [*banais rige*] ever celebrated in Connacht down to that day.

We may notice first the emphasis given to fosterage in this passage, an importance that can be paralleled in many other annalistic contexts.[1] The institution, common to the Gaelic world as a whole, constituted a major social bond, was much feared by fourteenth-century English officialdom when the Anglo-Irish took it up as a means of cementing long-term alliances with princely families, and was recognised in the same circles as an especial factor in the enduring strength of the Irish social fabric. Clearly its roots lie in the remote past and its rationale as an institution may well be connected with hostageship, though it has been suggested also that it helped to remove tension from the homes of chiefs where there would be many sons, often of different wives.[2] Fosterage tended to be customary between certain families, and that of the O'Connors by the MacDermots, mentioned in this passage, was one such.

A tradition of another sort is recalled by the place-name Carnfree and the word *carn*, 'mound'. For, as Professor Byrne has pointed out, there is a close association between royal inauguration sites and neolithic or bronze-age burial cairns, arguing, of course, for a strong continuity within the native tradition.[3] Fourteenth-century men were themselves conscious of this continuity. The O'Dowds in County Sligo had Carn Amhalgaidh as one of their two inauguration sites, and the poets handed down the memory, going back to the origins, that

it was Amhalgaidh, the son of Fiachra Ealgach, that raised that cairn for himself, in order that he himself, and all those who should obtain the lordship after him, might receive the style of lord upon it. And it is in this cairn that Amhalgaidh himself is interred, and it is from him it is named.[4]

[1] James Henchy (Séamas Ó h-Innse), 'Fosterage in early and medieval Ireland' (Ph.D. thesis, N.U.I. (U.C.D.), 1943).
[2] Kathleen Mulchrone, 'The rights and duties of women with regard to the education of their children' in *Studies in Ir. law*, p. 187.
[3] Byrne, *Ir. kings*, p. 27.
[4] *Hy Fiachrach*, p. 444, where the spelling 'carn' is used.

The account of the 1310 Ó Conchobair inauguration is ambiguous about the constitutive act of the inauguration. 'Practice of the saints' might suggest that it was the clergy who played the dominant role. Such, however, was not the case:

And it is Ó Maol Chonaire [*ollamh* or poet of Ó Conchobair] who is entitled to give the rod of kingship into his hand at his inauguration, and none of the nobles of Connacht has a right to be with him on the mound save Ó Maol Chonaire who inaugurates him and Ó Connachtáin who keeps the gate of the mound.

This information about the poet's role in the Connacht inauguration comes from a tract which, with a poem, was addressed to another Feidhlimidh Ó Conchobhair, king of Connacht, who died in 1474, recalling for his benefit the deeds of his earlier namesake and referring specifically and in detail to his inauguration in 1310.[1] These texts give a fuller account than the Annals of Connacht of the respective roles of the different classes and individuals. The tract begins with the origin-myth (meaning a statement of events in the remote past that are seen as a justification of existing institutions) that it had been St Patrick who had laid down how the kings of Connacht were to be inaugurated. Twelve bishops had been present when he had made Dauí Galach king. Their successors or coarbs should be present, but not as taking the primary role, as the tract went on to make clear in the passage cited. But the clergy were a necessary element in the ceremony, and one of them had a particular role. This was not the bishop of Elphin, the only one of the twelve listed still to be a bishop in the fourteenth century; it was the coarb of the church of Assylin (near Boyle, County Roscommon) who had a particular role, though the specifically Christian nature of it is not immediately clear: 'his [Ó Conchobair's] horse and his raiment to the coarb of Da Chonna, and he shall mount that horse from Ó Conchubhair's back.'[2] The tract then goes on to detail the ritual conferring the gifts of livestock on Ó Conchobair's sub-kings. The meaning of this seems to accord exactly with a statement of 'Caithréim Thoirdhealbhaigh':

Now in time of old it was the custom that whoso, being ruler whether of a cantred or of a province, accepted another chief's gift or wage did actually by such acceptance submit to the giver as to his chief paramount, and in virtue of the same take on himself to do him suit and service, to pay him rent and tribute.[3]

There is a second list, that of the stipends payable to officeholders within the royal household. These were the heads of lesser subject families, and they carried a whole range of responsibilities from military and naval commands to the charge of the royal latrines. Professor Binchy sees the influence of Anglo-Norman feudal ideas in this part of the tract.[4]

The key role of the poet, presenter of the rod of kingship to the new ruler, is

---

[1] Edited with translation, though without interpretative comment, by Myles Dillon as 'The inauguration of O'Conor' in *Med. studies presented to A. Gwynn*, pp 186–202.

[2] Ibid., p. 197.

[3] *Caithr. Thoirdh.*, ii, 3.

[4] Binchy, *Celtic and Anglo-Saxon kingship*, p. 50.

also demonstrated in the account of the method of inaugurating the Ó Dubhda [O'Dowd]. The part of the clergy and sub-kings as participants in the proclamation is also well brought out:

And the privilege of first drinking was given to Ó Caomhain by Ó Dubhda and Ó Caomhain was not to drink until he first presented it to the poet, that is, to Mac Firbis; also the weapons, battle-dress and steed of Ó Dubhda, after his nomination, were given to Ó Caomhain, and the weapons and battle-dress of Ó Caomhain to Mac Firbis, and it is not lawful ever to nominate the Ó Dubhda until Ó Caomhain and Mac Firbis pronounce the name, and until Mac Firbis brings the body of the rod over the head of Ó Dubhda; and after Ó Caomhain and Mac Firbis every cleric and coarb of a church, and every bishop, and every chief of a district pronounce the name.[1]

Here it is not the coarb who has the special prerogative of receiving the new king's horse and raiment, but his chief sub-king. The later medieval evidence suggests that such local variations were common. It is to be noticed that neither the O'Connor nor the O'Dowd texts make any mention of a stone being used, so notable a feature elsewhere, as with the Ó Néill inauguration at Tullaghogue in County Tyrone, for example.[2] But all have as their common element the preponderant role of the poet.

The kingship rod may in its origins have reference to fertility. The symbol of fertility occurs in another way. The Annals of Connacht entry speaks of Fedlimid Ó Conchobair 'marrying' the province of Connacht and describes his inauguration as a 'kingship marriage' (*banais rige*). The poet of the later text about this inauguration used a similar metaphor, 'gather thy servants around thee and celebrate thy marriage!'[3] It was still the practice of the court poets of the fourteenth century to write of their kings as if they were the incarnation of the spirit of fertility: 'each hazel is rich from the hero' proclaims one, meaning that the worthiness of the ruler has made the tree fruitful.[4] Perhaps by this period men did not take this ruler-fertility link as literally as in pagan times. But if, possibly, by the fourteenth century it was no more than a literary convention, it was a very expressive one, carrying live memories of the very origins of kingship in Europe:

> Fertility has come in the land
> In thy time, O ruddy face of brown eye-brows,
> As thou hast brought down every moistening shower,
> Thou hast given milk to our milch cows.
>
> O son of Domhnall of Dun Guaire [Tadhg Ó Dubhda, 1417–32]
> Oft have we been relieved from distress
> By the rent of Ceara to us distributed,
> Which the trees and the soil confessed.[5]

---

[1] *Hy Fiachrach*, pp 440–42.
[2] G. A. Hayes-McCoy, 'The making of an O'Neill: a view of the ceremony at Tullaghoge, Co. Tyrone' in *U.J.A.*, 3rd ser., xxxiii (1970), pp 89–94.
[3] Dillon, 'Inauguration of O'Conor', p. 201.
[4] *Hy Fiachrach*, pp 252–3.   [5] Ibid., p. 287.

More than on fertility, however, did the leader's prestige depend on successful prosecution of war. It was in war that he established and maintained his claim to have his authority accepted. The act of making war in itself promoted the cohesion of tribes within themselves and in relation to associated kindreds. It was as if the ceremony marked the *de iure* inauguration into office, but the making of war, if it were successful, the *de facto* inauguration into power. This was the more important when there had been disputed succession, a frequent occurrence.

Hardly less frequent as a *casus belli* was the situation where a sub-king had defaulted in his obligations and the only effective redress was a reprisal raid into his territory to levy compensation in the form of livestock: 'woe to him, how great soever his numbers be, that rises against his supreme chief: he will not be long-lived, and shall be left without kine, against whom long-enduring keen-edged wrath shall be directed [i.e. by the chief].'[1] Often the foray would have less legality and its objective would simply be plunder. Cattle raids and the pursuit to recover stolen cattle are often recorded in the Annals almost as if it were a sport, though a highly dangerous one, between two sets of profes-sionals.[2] It apparently had its own rules for it allowed sanctuary in church, as one of the very few conversational exchanges reported in the Annals makes clear. In 1342 Ó Conchobhair took sanctuary in the church of Elphin from Ó Broin: 'Cathal O'Byrne struck O'Conor on the shoulder with a stick as he was going through the doorway of the church, saying "To your sty, hog". "May it bring no good to my swineherd," answered O'Conor.'[3] But this warfare could be much more than aristocratic sport. 'Caithréim Thoirdhealbhaigh' is par-ticularly evocative of the atmosphere of wanton destruction of lives and property that was often the ugly reality:

... they stormed the Dunalach's strong boolies, and on that clan did grievous killing that played havoc with them: women and boys and whole families included; whereby that murderous, far-secluded area became a mere heap of carnage thickly stacked. There in abundance they had young men lying on their faces, women in lamentation, kine that bellowed deafeningly; and by this red raid Clancullen effectually relieved Kineldunal of all care in respect of their cattle and young people.[4]

The events which led to the inauguration of Fedlimid Ó Conchobair as king of Connacht in 1310 were sparked off by the actions of William de Burgh. The Anglo-Irish generally figure prominently in the Irish sources and in ways which reveal the fundamental ambivalence of the attitude of Irish chiefs to their opposite numbers of the other nation. 'Caithréim Thoirdelbhaigh' has a strong vein of anti-foreign feeling running through it. It polarises round de Clare, 'man of unjust judgements, of deadly treachery, of mind unrighteous'.[5] It

[1] *Caithr. Thoirdh.*, ii, 156.
[2] Gaelic warfare has been much neglected by historians, but see Katharine Simms, 'Warfare in the medieval Gaelic lordships' in *Ir. Sword*, xii (1975–6), pp 98–108.
[3] *Ann. Conn.*, p. 289.   [4] *Caithr. Thoirdh.*, ii, 71.   [5] Ibid., p. 55.

exempts, however, the earl of Ulster, 'pillar of sense and noble knight'.[1] Again, in the context of the Bruce invasion, the Ó Néill remonstrance virulently denounced the greed and treachery of the Anglo-Irish to Pope John XXII and proclaimed the utter impossibility of ever living in peace with men so evil.[2] In the same context, however, the O'Maddens could praise the Anglo-Irish as 'those princely English lords'.[3] The poets even joked about the ambivalence the practice of their profession now imposed on them:

There are two kindreds for whom poetry is composed in Ireland of the cool springs—the Gaels, known to fame, and the English of Britain's dewy isle. In poetry for the English we promise that the Gael shall be banished from Ireland, while in poetry for the Gaels we promise that the English shall be hunted across the sea.[4]

The political expression of this ambivalence was the shifting patterns of alliance and counter-alliance. Irish chiefs pursued their individual objectives. Sometimes they saw these as best served by attacking the Anglo-Irish, sometimes by allying with them. There might well be consistency of purpose but an apparent inconsistency of method. In 1395 all the Irish princes who mattered, not least those of Ulster, had personally submitted, in particularly solemn form, to King Richard II.[5] Raymond of Perelhos, however, reports how in 1397 his Anglo-Irish escort of one hundred cavalrymen dared go no further than five miles from Dundalk for fear of the Gaelic Irish.[6] A classic illustration of ambivalence can be found in the composition of the armies recruited by the justiciars, particularly those for service in the Leinster mountains, an especially sensitive area because of its proximity to Dublin and other major colonial centres. These armies invariably contained a Gaelic Irish contingent, sometimes amounting to as much as a third of the whole. Which 'nations' they were drawn from, however, varied considerably; today's ally was tomorrow's enemy. When Ralph d'Ufford was justiciar in 1344–6, there served in his armies, at various times, a certain 'McCuly *hibernicus*' in Ulster, Ó Mórdha and Mac Murchadha in Leinster, Diarmaid Mac Con Mara in Munster.[7] But these were not tribes in permanent royal service. They were fighting against the crown in other years, though in some cases that did not stop them assuming a more or less permanent entitlement for payment for service.

The detail of the incessant, intense, localised, and usually indecisive warfare, with all its complex shifts and changes of allegiance, is suffocatingly tedious. Those who compiled annals recording this detail made no attempt to stand

[1] *Caithr. Thoirdh.*, p. 19.

[2] The remonstrance is analysed below, pp 348–50; cf. above, pp 242–3.

[3] Cf. above, p. 301.

[4] The poet is Gofraidh Fionn Ó Dalaigh (d. 1387) and the translation that of Eleanor Knott (Ó Huiginn, *Poems*, p. xlvii).

[5] Edmund Curtis, *Richard II in Ireland, 1394–5* (Oxford, 1927); the submissions are discussed below, pp 344–5, 350–51.

[6] Jeanroy & Vignaux, *Voyage au purgatoire*, p. 15.

[7] Frame, 'The justiciarship of Ralph Ufford', pp 20, 23, 25–6, 45–6.

back from the turmoil of their times to make an overall national assessment of the situation. But, trying to see the wood despite the trees, it appears that there were three major long-term developments in process. Firstly, it is clear that the power of the crown had diminished and was still diminishing despite some quite sustained efforts to increase it. The justiciar, for example, has disappeared from the Annals of Connacht by the early fourteenth century, and the record of an Anglo-Irish role in Connacht dwindles as the century wears on. In Ulster, save for an eastern coastal strip, the story is similar.[1] The crown's efforts become increasingly dominated by the critical position in Leinster and parts of Munster. Secondly, within these substantial parts of Ireland where the governmental and Anglo-Irish presence had been or was being eliminated, or at least reduced to minimal importance, a power struggle was being fought out among the Irish rulers. Though a degree of contact with the Anglo-Irish in some form or other was never totally irrelevant, Gaeldom was here making its own polity. In Ulster, in particular, large-scale changes followed the breakup of the earldom after 1333. By the end of the century, it was clear even to a visitor like Perelhos that the O'Neills had emerged, as they had been threatening to do for many decades, as the leading Gaelic Irish dynasty. One has only to contrast the Annals of Connacht for the thirteenth century with those for the later fourteenth to gain some idea of the significance for that province too of the removal of the strong hands of the earls of Ulster. The third aspect of long-term development sees the Gaelic Irish with somewhat less freedom of manoeuvre in relation to the Anglo-Irish. The resilience of the area later to be called the Pale was a curb to the ambitions of the Leinster Irish, troublesome though the latter were to the colonists. In Munster, where the earls of Ormond and Desmond were steadily consolidating their power, the Gaelic Irish again found themselves restricted; though in some important areas of the province, Thomond being a notable example, the Gaelic Irish enjoyed virtual independence. It was especially in these latter two provinces of Leinster and Munster that the Irish chiefs often found it necessary to make accommodatory agreements with the crown or the earls. The observance of such agreements by both parties varied with the promptings of the instinct of self-preservation, an instinct necessarily finely tuned in this particular political climate. They were therefore easily made and even more easily broken. But there were, too, elements of continuity and stability in relationships.

From the very beginnings of colonial settlement, the English kings and the occupying baronage had struck such bargains as they thought necessary with the various 'nations of the Irish'. The process was still at work in the fourteenth century, and for this period there is important and detailed documentation from the earldoms both of Kildare and of Ormond.

The Red Book of the earls of Kildare contains a number of *conventiones* or *indenturae* (the terms are those of the documents themselves) between the earls

---

[1] Cf. Curtis, *Med. Ire.*, pp 238–40; Nicholls, *Gaelic Ire.*, pp 127–40.

and leaders of 'nations of the Irish' within or adjacent to the earldom. They are
of different types and their general natures may be briefly summarised. In 1318,
the first earl of Kildare made a compact with Áed Og Ó Tuathail whereby the
latter should rent land from him at Robertstown and its 'Irishtown' (*villa
Hybernicorum*). Áed was to be held responsible to the earl if any of his men
damaged his interests. If any of Áed's *nacio* or their supporters injured the earl,
Áed would help to destroy them, 'even though they were of his own people'.[1] In
1349 the fourth earl granted lands to Muircheartach Og Ó Conchobhair.
Because of his 'good and praiseworthy service' the rent was to be quite nominal
(one cow payable annually at Christmas) and the tenure was to last as long as the
relationship between the two men remained amicable.[2] By an agreement of 1350
Muircheartach Sinnach, *rex* of Fear Tethba, and Fearghal Mág Eochagáin, *dux*
of Cenél Fhiachach, became *homines* of the earl for life, promising him counsel
and aid against everyone, the king and Mortimer excepted. They were obliged
to service as needed anywhere in Ireland. If, however, when the earl was at war
with any of the Irish, these his 'men' were not able to join him because of the
danger in getting to him, they would discharge their obligation to service by
fighting elsewhere against any other Irish who had risen to help the earl's
enemies.[3] The agreement signed between the earl and Donnchadh Ó Ceallaigh
in 1358 was an even closer one, for it was the earl who appointed Donnchadh as
capitaneus nacionis sue; probably it was in fact a confirmation of his headship
rather than a direct nomination. The new ruler and his heirs were to hold their
lands of Ballykelly and elsewhere free of rent for two years, after which period
the rent was to be eight silver pence for every acre ploughed annually. He was
required to assist the earl 'to the best of his ability', which presumably was
primarily in war, and to be respondent to the earl's court at Lea. This agreement
has the ring of long standing custom and at least semi-permanence about it.[4] On
the other hand, that made in 1368 between the earl and certain of the
O'Dempseys reads like an *ad hoc* arrangement in a particular war situation. The
Irish bound themselves on oath to assist the Ó Diomusaigh and his sons and his
subjects (*oireacht* or *aireacht*, latinised as *irraghtus*), and to strive against their
enemies day and night until peace was achieved. For this strenuous effort they
would receive sixty-four marks but were required to surrender hostages to the
earl, returnable when peace was made.[5] To round off a picture suggestive of
these earls being in a fairly commanding position in relation to many Irish
nations, are property agreements between different Irish parties, drawn up at
Kildare, which the earl undertook to enforce.[6]

---

[1] *Red Bk Kildare*, no. 139.
[2] Ibid., no. 166.
[3] Ibid., no. 168.
[4] Ibid., no. 167.
[5] Ibid., no. 169. I am indebted to Kenneth Nicholls for information concerning the Irish of
irraghtus and helpful comment generally.
[6] E.g. ibid., no. 170.

A very similar pattern of relationships is revealed with additional information about the variety possible in the type of agreement agreed to, in the more extensive extant Ormond records of the period 1336–1403. Agreements for military service to be rendered to the earls of Ormond in return for grants of lands to Irish 'nations' were frequent. In that there is a certain standardisation of the actual forms in which these agreements were drawn up, they have the appearance of being renewals of relationships already well established. The Irish *capitaneus* will bind himself to service for life in return for land grants which carry customary services and dues. His military force will serve the earl at the chief's expense if it is possible for the men to return home at night. When this is impossible, the earl will pay. There were agreements of this kind with Ó Ceinnéidigh,[1] Mac Con Mara,[2] and Mac Braoin (this latter, incidentally, described as kinsman of James Butler).[3] Money payments as well as land might be involved. Thus in 1359, when the earl of Ormond was justiciar, he made a two-year agreement with Ó Braonáin for payment of five silver marks and expenses when service was in distant marches.[4] In 1400, however, payment went the other way. Ó Braonáin swore that he and his heirs would be the 'faithful men' of the earl and his heirs, six marks being payable *in signum et redditum dicti homagii*.[5] These agreements exemplify the utter compatibility of English feudal ideas and Irish clientage: service and tribute to an overlord or overking, in return for protection, being in both systems the essence of a contract. Tribalism and feudalism (to echo Orpen's distinction, but rejecting his dichotomy) have effortlessly coalesced.

Most of the agreements detailed above were solemnised with oaths sworn on gospel books and saints' relics, and carried sanctions of excommunication and interdict for violation. In addition, there was often the taking of hostages, frequently a son of the Irish party to the agreement.[6] The enforcing of agreements by exaction of hostages was so common a feature of fourteenth-century Irish society that it deserves a more particular word. Professor Binchy has stressed how the taking of hostages, found almost universally in primitive societies, was a method of enforcing allegiance that was highly favoured in early Irish society: 'he is no king', as one law text had it, 'who has not hostages in fetters' (though in practice the fetters were probably only used when the hostage's life had become forfeit through violation of agreement).[7] In the middle ages, his royal status was the higher, or so the poets thought, if 'he never sees hostage nor fetter', for not to find it 'necessary to take hostages or have recourse to fetters' showed how dreaded a ruler he was.[8] But for the ordinary run of chiefs and

---

[1] *Ormond deeds, 1172–1350*, nos 682, 700; ibid., *1350–1413*, nos 34, 35, 46, 48.
[2] Ibid., no. 36.   [3] Ibid., no. 219.
[4] Ibid., no. 347.   [5] Ibid., no. 1400.
[6] Cf. ibid., no. 74, for a typical example of both hostage-taking and sanction of excommunication.
[7] Binchy, *Celtic and Anglo-Saxon kingship*, p. 21.
[8] *Hy Many*, p. 141.

barons, the taking of hostages was the characteristic method of ensuring that agreements were honoured.

A more than usually detailed indenture of 1358 between the earl of Ormond and 'Esmon' (Éamonn) Ó Ceinnéidigh illustrates how hostageship might be arranged in these situations of mutual accommodation between leaders of the two nations. 'Esmon' had been detained in England; whether as a hostage for an agreement made between the earl and Ruaidhrí Ó Ceinnéidigh two years earlier, or as a prisoner of war to be ransomed, is not clear. His return to Ireland and release from captivity was to be conditional on payment of three sums of money, one of £100 and two of 100 marks at stipulated times. As surety for the first payment he was required to hand over his brother as hostage if he could not satisfy the earl with any other security. For the two hundred marks, the designated hostages were his six sons. Further, two sons of his brother were to be surrendered as hostages against the future loyalty of the O'Kennedys to the earl. 'Esmon' himself was to be responsible for the expenses of these hostages. The agreement then proceeded to detail payments required for O'Kennedy lands, their military obligations to the earl and the damages to be payable in the event of trespass.[1]

There is one last feature of these agreements which calls for comment. They reveal an important facet of acculturation, for they are drawn up in terminology that derives from both Irish and English law. Three aspects of this mixture of laws may be singled out as illustrative of the amalgamation process. The first concerns punishment for murder. Irish law did not exact capital punishment as the appropriate penalty; rather it looked to exact compensation from the murderer or his kin, payable to the kin of the dead person. An agreement of 1336 between the earl of Ormond and Ó Ceinnéidigh shows the reciprocal adoption of the principle, which, from the evidence of other sources, may well have been becoming fairly general in colonial Ireland. If any of the earl's men, whether of English or Irish descent, were killed, the guilty were to be handed over to the earl, from whom they would be redeemed by their own kin. If the guilty party could not be found, his chief or his kin would make the redemption on his behalf, paying one part to the earl and two parts to the murdered man's kin (*parentela*). The same principle applied in reverse when Ó Ceinnéidigh's men were killed.[2]

An Irish law principle of another sort was adopted in the Ormond–Ó Ceinnéidigh compact of 1358.[3] The agreement was that if a trespasser on the earl's property was not surrendered to him within fifteen days of the offence, Ó Ceinnéidigh would pay the earl 5*d.* for every pennyworth of damage. On the other hand, when the trespass went the other way, the earl allowed Ó Ceinnéidigh to

---

[1] *Ormond deeds, 1350—1413*, no. 46.

[2] Ibid., *1172—1350*, no. 682. Cf. Gwynn & Gleeson, *Killaloe*, pp 340—41; Mac Niocaill 'Irish and common law', pp 20—21.

[3] *Ormond deeds, 1350—1413*, no. 46; Gwynn & Gleeson, *Killaloe*, pp 343—4; Mac Niocaill, 'Irish and common law', pp 21—2.

distrain the trespasser's goods. This latter concession was proscribed by English officialdom, but it seems unlikely that the Ormonds took much notice of that.

The third feature of these agreements singled out for comment shows perhaps the adoption of English inquest or jury procedures in these situations. The final clause of the 1336 Ormond–Ó Ceinnéidigh agreement states that the earl 'grants to O'Kennedy and his brothers in so far as it is a matter for him so to do all the lands from Belacharri [?Ballincurry, north County Tipperary] to the Shannon by rendering to the lords of these lands so much rent as three on the part of the English and three on the part of O'Kennedy shall wish to determine'. In the similar 1356 compact there is provision for a panel of four drawn from each nation to settle responsibility for offences against the earl. Should a casting vote be needed, a person acceptable to both sides was to be chosen.

IN the later Elizabethan period, English observers often noted the Irishman's concern for his 'gentility', an observation to be interpreted, after Fynes Moryson, as implying a disdain for any occupation other than the aristocratic one of training for or making war.[1] It is not very likely that this attitude had been newly acquired at this late stage in the history of Gaelic society, and it was almost certainly as characteristic of the Irish upper class in the fourteenth century as in the sixteenth. Certainly the literary men patronised by these warrior aristocrats did not earn their keep by singing the praises of kings in terms of their devotion to husbandry or their success as gentlemen farmers dedicated to increasing the productivity of their fields and flocks. Their encomia were conventionally of a strongly martial flavour, and for that reason often have a strictly limited value for the historian. When a characteristic apostrophe of chiefly merit could run, for example, on these lines, 'then the Irish Hector, the Hercules of noble achievements, the solid-weaponed Achilles, the well-tented Pyrrhus, the unique hero of this age, without peer among the Irish: lordly Murtough . . .',[2] there is little in such material to encourage the economic historian. Nevertheless it is the poets who give the all-important clue to the essential nature of the Gaelic economy. For what they make abundantly clear, and their evidence is amply confirmed by many other types of source, is that cattle-raiding, by highly-skilled fighting men on horseback, was the chief occupation of the Irish aristocracy. The economy of fourteenth-century Gaeldom was dominated by the horse and the cow. It was also heavily conditioned by the harshness of the terrain in which for the most part the Gaelic Irish were forced to live: a land, Chrysted reported, which 'abounds in deep forests and in lakes and bogs and much of it is uninhabitable'.[3]

There is a view current that the Irish mounted soldier or *hobelar*, as he

---

[1] Quinn, *Elizabethans & Irish*, pp 38–40, 46–7.
[2] *Caithr. Thoirdh.*, ii, 83.
[3] Froissart, *Chronicles*, trans. Joliffe, p. 369.

tended to be called outside Ireland, rode an 'ambling pony'.[1] Jean Creton
watched Art Mac Murchadha at full gallop: his horse went at a speed, said
Creton with great emphasis, such as he had never in his life seen, whether from
hare or deer or any other animal.[2] All Irish chiefs of any standing kept studs of
these unusually excellent and highly trained horses. Ó Briain once sent
Ó Néill a hundred horses by way of stipend, at which Ó Néill, furious at the
suggestion that this implied he was Ó Briain's subject, sent back two hundred
horses 'wearing gold-adorned white-edged bridles'.[3] Raymond of Perelhos,
writing much later than this incident, estimated that Ó Néill had three
thousand horses, but historians generally assume that medieval men were
psychologically incapable of counting accurately. With the keeping of horses
went a technology which could equip their riders with lances, swords, coats of
mail, and iron helmets. A pad, probably of wool, was used instead of a saddle.
The rider would be barefooted. This would not necessarily prevent his wearing
spurs. Raymond said they put spurs on bare heels,[4] much, one supposes, as the
gauchos of Argentina, themselves extremely skilful horsemen, still do today.

Creton added that Mac Murchadha's horse, which he so admired, had cost
him four hundred cows, 'for there is little money in the country, so usually they
trade only in cattle'.[5] There is abundant evidence that the cow figured prominently in all manner of business transactions in fourteenth-century Ireland,
and this in itself is important evidence of its crucial role in the economy.[6]
Compensation to injured parties was, in Irish law, ordinarily payable in cows
according to an established tariff. For example, a member of the O'Mulconry
family, chief poets of the O'Connors, was accidentally killed in County Roscommon in 1400, and one hundred and twenty-six cows were paid for his *eraic*,
the Irish equivalent of Anglo-Saxon *wergild*.[7] Pardons were granted on payment of cows; cows were paid as rent or in token of subjection to an overlord;
parties to agreements bound themselves under pain of forfeiture of cows.[8] In
1331 the English government thought fit to pass legislation ordering fines by
Gaelic Irishmen to be payable in money not cows.[9] But the practice was so
integral a feature of society that it was not to be eradicated simply for the
administrative convenience of bureaucrats.[10] It should not be thought,

---

[1] A. E. Prince, 'The army and navy' in *The English government at work, 1327–36*, i (Cambridge,
Mass., 1940), p. 339.

[2] *Archaeologia*, xx (1824), p. 306.   [3] *Caithr. Thoirdh.*, ii, 3.

[4] Jeanroy & Vignaux, *Voyage au purgatoire*, pp 16–17.   [5] *Archaeologia*, xx (1824), p. 305.

[6] The whole subject has been very under-studied. The only discussion in print seems to be A. T.
Lucas, 'Cattle in ancient and medieval Irish society' in Vincent Grogan (ed.), *The O'Connell School
Union record, 1937–58* (Dublin, [1958]), pp 75–85, 87, with a wide selection of source references.

[7] *Ann. Conn.*, pp 374–5.

[8] For an interesting example in an ecclesiastical context, cf. Gearóid Mac Niocaill, 'Irish law
and the Armagh constitutions of 1297' in *Ir. Jurist*, vi (1971), p. 341.

[9] Ordinance of Westminster parliament (1331) in *Stat. Ire., John–Hen. V*, pp 326–7.

[10] It featured prominently also in the highest Anglo-Irish circles. In making a marriage treaty in
1401 with the third earl of Ormond in order to marry Ormond's daughter Elizabeth, Theobald fitz
Walter de Burgh bound himself to pay 240 cows and 40 horses; *Ormond deeds, 1350–1413*, no. 353.

however, that even in Gaelic Ireland hard cash had no place in the economy. In the indentures noted above, money payments figured more prominently than cows, and even in Ulster, where such agreements between the Gaelic Irish and monied men had become less common, there is ecclesiastical legislation of 1379, enacting under pain of excommunication and interdict that one groat of Scottish money should be treated as the equivalent of three English pence.[1] Nevertheless, despite a steady trickle of money into Gaelic Ireland, its economy tended to be a pastoral, subsistence one.

Given Ireland's abundance of grass, the reliance on cattle-rearing is hardly surprising. Though the Gaelic Irish had been driven from much of the best land for arable farming, there remained almost everywhere else abundant grazing, even in difficult areas of mountain, forest, and bog. The exploitation of this grazing often called for a form of transhumance wherein stock would be transferred in the summer months to upland pastures,[2] which has given rise to the somewhat misleading judgement that Ireland was largely a country of 'wandering pastoralists'. By the sixteenth century, English observers were calling this process 'booleying' from the Irish *buaile*, 'cattle enclosure', or, as Liam Price translated it, 'summer dairying place'.[3] The study of place names including a booley element from many areas has provided very strong presumptive evidence of widespread seasonal movement of livestock in medieval times. Perelhos, who noted the phenomenon in Ulster, stated that the Ulster Irish grew no wheat and did not eat bread. But he did receive a gift of oatcakes from Ó Néill. The cultivation of oats was often complementary to transhumance. The absence of stock in the summer and autumn months allowed the growth on infields of spring-sown oats. When the crop had been harvested the land was free for the use of the returned cattle. Thus well-manured land would not need to be left fallow to regain its productivity. Booleying, then, as Aalen succinctly expresses it, 'as well as being a natural response to the seasonal availability of mountain and bog grazing, could serve also as a means of integrating livestock-keeping with open-field cultivation'.[4] It would seem that with this type of farming there might well be associated a characteristic settlement pattern, that of irregular clusters of farm houses and outbuildings. It is known from the abundant nineteenth-century evidence of the ordnance survey and the censuses that these clusters, often called clachans, were widespread at that time, particularly in the areas which in medieval times were most traditionally Gaelic. Typical of the clachan was distant seasonal grazing and turf-cutting in

---

[1] H. J. Lawlor, 'A calendar of the register of Archbishop Sweteman' in *R.I.A. Proc.*, xxix (1911), sect. C, p. 291, no. 254.

[2] J. M. Graham, 'Transhumance in Ireland' in *Advancement of Science*, x (1953), pp 74–9; Evans, *Ir. folkways*, p. 27; F. H. A. Aalen, 'Transhumance in the Wicklow mountains' in *Ulster Folklife*, x (1964), pp 65–72.

[3] *The place-names of County Wicklow, vii: the baronies of Newcastle and Arklow* (Dublin, 1967), p. 497; and see below, pp 413–14.

[4] Aalen, 'Transhumance', p. 69.

mountain and bog outfield, with an infield of common open cultivated land, with each individual family, all likely to be relatives, holding both some of the good and some of the poorer land. The system can be traced back to the seventeenth century.[1] It is not difficult to envisage much earlier origins.

There seems no reason to reject the substantial accuracy of what Perelhos says of the diet of the O'Neills, for Archbishop Richard FitzRalph had said somewhat the same, though in less detail, some decades earlier: 'their food is of beef and the great lords drink milk and others beef broth [*del broet de la carn*] and the common people water and they have excellent butter since all their meats are of oxen and cows and good horses.'[2] This diet was supplemented with food made of oats, which presumably were used sometimes as animal feed. There is apparently no fourteenth-century reference to the practice of taking blood for food from a live cow, which Spenser spoke of and which, on the evidence of the ordnance surveyors of the 1830s, was still practised in at least some of the Ulster counties.[3]

We would do well not to try to reduce the whole of Gaelic Ireland to a single uniform economic pattern. There must have been variation, if only because of the considerable variation of climatic and physical factors in the island as a whole. But in the fourteenth century, outside the areas that had been manorialised by settlers from England, subjected to the techniques of English agriculture and integrated into an English type of trading pattern between towns, it is difficult to believe that the landscape had changed more in kind than degree from that of much earlier periods as it appears to the palaeobotanists: a countryside 'which was a mosaic, areas of virgin forest alternating with tillage patches, rough pastures and secondary forest in various stages of regeneration'.[4] In these circumstances, there prevailed an economy of herding by men who were to an extent cultivators, of a type particularly well adapted for survival in areas where both natural and political factors made more ambitious economies impracticable.

In some parts of the country, as has been seen, Irish rulers might raise their standard of living (whatever ways the chosen improvement might take) with the help of Anglo-Irish money. Some of them, indeed, might find themselves modifying their traditional way of life quite substantially because of trading opportunities they could exploit. Henry Chrysted told Froissart that the inhabitants of the more remote regions knew nothing of commerce, but 'those who live on the coast opposite England are more like ourselves and are used to

---

[1] V. P. Proudfoot, 'Clachans in Ireland' in *Gwerin*, xi (1955), pp 110–22; R. H. Buchanan, 'Field systems of Ireland' in A. R. H. Baker and R. A. Butlin (ed.), *Studies of field systems in the British Isles* (Cambridge, 1973); Glasscock, 'Deserted medieval settlements', pp 284–6; Evans, *Personality of Ire.*, pp 53–6; above, p. 227.

[2] Jeanroy & Vignaux, *Voyage au purgatoire*, p. 17.

[3] Evans, *Ir. folkways*, p. 37.

[4] G. F. Mitchell, 'Post-boreal pollen diagrams from Irish raised bogs' in *R.I.A. Proc.*, lvii (1956), sect. B, p. 242; Evans, *Personality of Ire.*, p. 36.

trade'. Feidhlimidh Ó Tuathail of Wicklow complained to Richard II, when he was in Ireland, that notwithstanding holding a royal licence allowing him to trade in English towns, his men were attacked when they attended a fair at Ballymore in Kildare; and he petitioned that he might have letters patent permitting him to trade in fairs and towns: 'for without buying and selling I just will not be able to carry on' (*quia sine empcione et vendicione nullo modo potero permanere*).[1]

An expressive phrase of the Irish language speaks of one chief 'going into the house' of another, meaning making submission to him.[2] Rulers' dwellings are referred to in other contexts, notably in the dispensing of hospitality, the royal quality so much prized by the poets. Professor Carney cites elsewhere in this volume the most celebrated fourteenth-century manifestation of royal patronage of the arts and entertainers, commemorated in Ó Dálaigh's poem 'Filidh Éireann go haointeach' ('The poets of Ireland to one house'). In the economy of which the general sketch has just been outlined, what did these 'houses' look like?

It would be extremely imprudent to make a very positive answer to this question. The consensus of opinion among archaeologists and historical geographers is that from prehistoric times to the twelfth century, or at least in the first millenium of the Christian period, the ordinary dwelling of the Irish chief was the rath, a circular earthwork with banks and ditches (the ring-fort), generally called a cashel when stone was used in the construction. It is estimated that some thirty thousand of these still survive in identifiable form. For the answer to the question just posed, the critical point at issue is how many of these were still occupied throughout the middle ages.[3] But this is still very much an open question, and will remain a difficult one for technical reasons even when considerably more excavation has taken place. However, some of the limited number of digs have produced evidence of medieval occupation, notably in the form of pottery. There is good evidence of the continued occupation of crannogs or lake dwellings in some parts of Ireland (it seems, incidentally, that Henry Chrysted's father-in-law occupied one) until a comparatively late date.[4] The literary evidence is sparse and difficult to interpret. 'Caithréim Thoirdelbhaigh' states that in the 1240s Donnchad Ó Briain 'made a circular fort and princely palace of earth' at Clonroad, and other evidence from the same work shows the apparent continued occupation of the traditional chiefly homes into the fourteenth century. But it speaks also of one of its heroes preparing for himself 'six white castles of stone'.[5] Poetic hyperbole? Were these

[1] Curtis, *Rich. II in Ire.*, p. 126.
[2] Binchy, *Celtic and Anglo-Saxon kingship*, p. 31.
[3] Barthelet's picture of Tullaghogue fort in 1601 (*Ulster and other Irish maps*, ed. G. A. Hayes-McCoy (Dublin, 1964), map V) shows an inhabited ring-fort. I owe this reference to Kenneth Nicholls. Cf. above, pp 227–9, and below, p. 405.
[4] Lloyd Laing, *The archaeology of late Celtic Britain and Ireland* (London, 1975), pp 160–61.
[5] *Caith. Thoirdh.*, ii, 2.

traditional castles, or castles of the Anglo-Norman model? At Magh Bealaigh (Longford O'Madden?), Ó Madadháin is described as erecting as his seat 'a strong castle of stone and fine timber, the like of which has not been erected by any sub-chief in Erin' in a context that suggests emulation of his Anglo-Irish allies.[1] The Annals too refer occasionally to the erection of castles by Irish rulers, who certainly occupied the stone houses of the Anglo-Irish which were in this period beginning to fall more frequently into their possession. The scanty evidence may be sufficient to indicate an architectural dimension to the culture contact of Gaelic and Anglo-Irish, with the fourteenth century as a transitional phase during which some chiefs were making the change from the traditional rath or cashel to the castle or tower house of the Anglo-Irish style, as certainly happened in some parts in the fifteenth century.

No doubt in many other parts of the country the Irish kings stuck to their traditional dwellings just as they adhered closely to their own way of life in general. But there is at present no way of making any generalisations based on solid evidence. As a working hypothesis, R. E. Glasscock has suggested that the survival of such a large number of raths suggests that they continued to form an important element in the settlement patterns of medieval Gaelic Ireland.[2] General considerations of the essential conservatism of Gaeldom in many areas might well be thought to incline one to the same feeling. It must be pointed out however that with this hypothesis the positing of a second seems inescapable. The mapping of the distribution of raths and excavations of some of them indicate that they were occupied by single families. Given that these were of the upper classes of society, it would seem to follow that the lower and unfree classes, the people who did the bulk of the actual work, lived otherwise. The obvious inference is that they occupied settlements nearby. Archaeology has not been able as yet to substantiate this hypothesis, and the inevitably flimsy nature of such dwellings may make the recovery of their traces in the medieval period very unlikely.

NOT the least characteristic feature of Gaelic society was its art and architecture, particularly as dedicated to the service of religion. This feature, hitherto little enough explored for the later middle ages, is treated elsewhere in this volume. But something must be said here about the church as a distinctive element in Gaelic society.

In 1395, according to Froissart's account, Richard II entrusted the four leading Irish kings, Ó Néill (Ulster), Ó Conchobhair (Connacht), Ó Briain (Thomond) and Mac Murchadha (Leinster), to Henry Chrysted's charge in order that they should learn and adopt something of the English style of courtly

---

[1] *Hy Many*, p. 140.
[2] Glasscock, 'Deserted medieval settlements', p. 282; see above, pp 226–9. For further discussion of the problem of rath occupation continuity, see V. B. Proudfoot, 'The economy of the Irish rath' in *Medieval Archaeology*, v (1961), pp 94–122; *An archaeological survey of County Down*, ed. E. M. Jope (London, 1966), pp 112–17; Buchanan, 'Field systems', pp 613–16.

life. Chrysted recalled that on one occasion he questioned his royal protégés about their religious faith. The four Irishmen made it clear that they thought this an impertinent question, and responded warmly that their belief in God and the Trinity was just as strong as any Englishman's. The question was an odd one since Gaelic Ireland, as Chrysted must have known from his seven years enforced stay among the Gaelic Irish, was an integral part of the Latin church, equipped with all its characteristic cults, institutions, and laws, and open to all the usual processes of papal government. It may be added that in this period of the great schism it belonged, like England, to the Roman obedience. The province of Tuam (Connacht) with eight dioceses was ruled almost entirely by Gaelic Irish bishops, while of the twelve dioceses of the Armagh (Ulster) province only a half had any prelates of the other nation. Two of the nine Cashel (Munster) dioceses invariably had Gaelic Irish bishops in the fourteenth century, and in two others the bishop was sometimes Gaelic Irish and sometimes not. No Gaelic Irishman was bishop in the five dioceses of the Dublin (Leinster) province in this period.[1] Thus, of thirty-three dioceses, over half were ruled by Gaelic Irishmen: *ecclesia inter Hibernicos*, as the contemporary term had it. These dioceses were organised in the conventional Latin way: cathedrals with chapters, deaneries, parishes. It is true that there were regional variations in institutional forms, as was universally the case in the medieval church, but these were of no great consequence. Similarly, the church *inter Hibernicos* cherished the religious orders, endowing and maintaining them for the same spiritual reasons as animated the patrons of the rest of Christendom, though the fourteenth century, unlike the thirteenth and later fifteenth centuries, was not a period of expansion for the religious orders in Ireland.[2]

Fourteenth-century Gaelic Ireland does not emerge from the sources as a land of saints and scholars. Like other countries, and possibly rather more than some, it knew violence, immorality, superstition, and clerical disciplinary laxities; but generally speaking, the *ecclesia inter Hibernicos* was unexceptional enough by the standards of the fourteenth-century Latin church.

This point being made for purposes of right perspective, it has to be said that there were some features of the fourteenth-century Irish church that were distinctive and must be accorded due importance in any sketch of medieval Gaeldom. Perhaps the most fundamental of these was the close integration of the church into that kinship structure which gave Gaelic Ireland its coherence and powers of endurance. Just as the lawyers and poets were members of hereditary castes which had specialised in a particular calling over long periods of time, building up for themselves an established, traditional, privileged status in

[1] See episcopal succession lists below, ix, 264–332. The Gaelic preponderance in Tuam and Armagh was in fact greater than the above figures suggest, as several non-Gaelic bishops spent much of their time as suffragans in England.

[2] Relevant information is to be found in Aubrey Gwynn and R. N. Hadcock, *Medieval religious houses: Ireland* (London, 1970).

society, so too the trend was for the clerical profession to be subject to similar pressure of hereditary family right.

The strength of ecclesiastical families is often obvious enough simply from episcopal succession lists: the O'Farrell family, providing bishops for Ardagh in 1343–67 and 1373–8 and then virtually monopolising the succession in the fifteenth century, is a typical example of a phenomenon common in many dioceses of Armagh and Tuam. The position was clearly similar in respect of religious houses, though the evidence for this is somewhat less accessible. Sometimes abbatial appointments too had significance for promotion to bishoprics, as the example of the MacCraith family shows with its link between its hereditary abbacy of the Augustinian house at Clare, near Ennis, and succession to the diocese of Killaloe between 1389 and 1443.[1] That clerical marriage and succession from father to son or near relative was an integral part of this system needs no emphasis. However, it is instructive to try to piece together something of the ramifications of such an ecclesiastical family, for the examination takes us to the core of the distinctively Gaelic church organisation.

The term coarb (*comharba*, 'heir') has already been encountered when considering the ecclesiastical presence at the inauguration of kings of Connacht. It is a term of great antiquity, common to all Gaelic Ireland. With the passage of time and many ecclesiastical reorganisations, a considerable regional variation had grown up as to the precise practical implications for the holder of the office of heir to the founder of individual monasteries and sees. As yet no satisfactory comprehensive study of this institution and the closely related one of erenagh (*airchinneach*, 'superior') has appeared.[2] The case history now to be related may be regarded as typical, revealing common characteristic elements, but it is still an individual case and its pattern is not one repeated uniformly in all its details across the country as a whole.[3]

Tuamgraney, west of the Shannon in County Clare, has a parish church which is one of the oldest in the country still used for worship, with a holy well which is still a place of devotion. Its long Christian history began with the foundation of a monastery by St Cronan, though whether he was of the sixth century and from nearby Inishcaltra, or of the seventh century and from Clonmacnoise, is debated. The monastery did not become an episcopal centre in the twelfth-century diocesan reconstruction; it became a parish church. In 1184, the Irish Annals record through an obit that the coarb of St Cronan was of the O'Grady family. They were still to be in possession in the sixteenth century.

---

[1] Gwynn & Gleeson, *Killaloe*, pp 385, 452–4; below, ix, 301.

[2] An excellent summary is in Mooney, 'Church in Gaelic Ireland', pp 10–16, with bibliographical note at p. 15.

[3] Compiled from D. F. Gleeson, 'The coarbs of Killaloe diocese' in *R.S.A.I. Jn.*, lxxix (1949), pp 160–69; John Barry, 'The lay coarb in medieval times' in *I.E.R.*, 5th series, xci (1959), pp 27–39; Gwynn & Gleeson, *Killaloe*, pp 29–32, 323, 370, 373; Watt, *Ch. & two nations*, pp 210–11; A. B. Emden, *A biographical register of the university of Oxford to A.D.1500* (3 vols, Oxford, 1957–9), s.v. O'Grady. I am very grateful to Mr Kenneth Nicholls for information from unpublished Irish genealogies.

It might well be thought that the heir of the founding saint would be the parish priest. Perhaps sometimes he was. However, though the evidence is late, it is clear that in Tuamgraney, as in very many parishes throughout the country, the office of coarb had more to do with the administration of lands formerly belonging to the monastery than with pastoral mission. These were the so-called termon lands (Tearmonn Uí Ghráda; the place-name in itself is very instructive) for which dues were payable to the local ordinary, the bishop of Killaloe. This is brought out in a letter of Pope Martin V when in 1429 he was trying to resolve a dispute over the Tuamgraney coarbship. The treasurer of Killaloe had complained to the pope that the O'Gradys had defaulted on the obligation to pay rent to the bishop for the ecclesiastical land they farmed at Tuamgraney. The treasurer had petitioned that

a district of lands called the comorbanship [*comierbiatus*] of St Cronanus de Tomegreyne in the diocese of Killaloe, wont to be held from the church of Killaloe in fee, sometimes by laymen sometimes by ecclesiastics, under a yearly cess to the bishop has, after the death of Thomas O'Grady layman of the said diocese who held it in fee from the said church, been lawfully granted to no one, but that Donatus O'Grada, Benedictine monk, professed of St Mary's, Vienna, in the diocese of Passau, who has abandoned his habit and order and returned to the world, engaging in secular affairs, has unduly detained possession of the said district or comorbanship for a number of years, and has dilapidated and pledged and otherwise alienated the greater part of the said lands and has not paid the said cess, to the injury of the bishops. . . .

Judges-delegate were appointed to investigate these allegations, and if the treasurer were to be found correct he was to be made coarbs of St Cronan. As is so often the case, the sources do not allow us to know whether Donnchadh (whose profession in Vienna and subsequent abandonment of his monastic vocation to take up the family position is surely a very remarkable matter) was ousted. But certainly the O'Gradys (of Tarmony Grady, in the English records) remained hereditary coarbs of St Cronan into early modern times.

As a family with close connections with the diocese of Killaloe, it is no surprise that O'Gradys are frequently to be discovered as members of the diocesan chapter. But they came to cut a more than local figure, becoming indeed in the fourteenth century one of Gaeldom's most distinguished ecclesiastical families. The archbishop of Cashel from 1332 to 1345 was Eoin Ó Gráda; another Eoin Ó Gráda was by 1359 canon and prebendary of Ardfert, Cashel, Cloyne and Tuam, and then archdeacon of Cashel. He was archbishop of Tuam from 1365 to 1371. Brother Donnchadh Ó Gráda was lector of the Franciscan house of Nenagh in 1371, while Seaán Ó Gráda ruled Elphin from 1407 to 1417.

In the fourteenth century, few episcopal appointments were made in Ireland without the papacy playing some part in the process. The papal records show that these O'Grady appointments all required a papal dispensation allowing them to be bishops despite *defectus natalium* (illegitimacy): they were all sons of

¹ *Cal. papal letters, 1427–47*, p. 81.

men in major orders. When precise relationships are investigated in the Irish genealogies, it transpires that the Eoin Ó Gráda who became archbishop of Tuam, described unspecifically in papal documents as the son of an archdeacon, was in fact the son of the Eoin Ó Gráda who became archbishop of Cashel. And also that the Seaán Ó Gráda who became bishop of Elphin was the son of Eoin Ó Gráda, archbishop of Tuam. The O'Gradys were not unique in their abandonment of clerical celibacy. It is clear that they merely illustrate the common practice of the *ecclesia inter Hibernicos* and that the system of the ecclesiastical family was a fully accepted fact of Irish medieval society.

Obviously the O'Gradys were fully integrated into their own culture, one facet of which their family history brilliantly illuminates for the historian. It is not the least interesting feature of their position, however, that they were apparently scarcely less at home in English circles. Since they were from Thomond, where, as has been seen, the removal of the de Clares had restored power to the Gaelic Irish, their pronounced English connection was far from inevitable. The link took two forms, one academic, the other political. Nicol Ó Gráda, who became archdeacon of Killaloe in 1355, was a canon law graduate of the university of Oxford. His archdeaconry was a royal appointment made by Edward III[1] under a principle long established in English law that during an episcopal vacancy (Killaloe being vacant at the time) the right of presentation to benefices, ordinarily in the right of the bishop, lay with the crown.

Other O'Gradys benefited from royal approval. It is evident that both the Dublin administration and Edward III had played a significant part in the promotion of Eoin Ó Gráda to Cashel in 1332. The king told Pope John XXII that the see of Cashel was a cause of great concern to him since it had suffered much from attack by the Gaelic Irish. His ministers in Ireland had recommended a prelate for this see who, it was anticipated, would be able to contain these very violent enemies. This cleric was Eoin Ó Gráda, and when the pope duly provided him to Cashel the king arranged through his proctor at the papal court that the fee known as common service (*servitium debitum*), due to the curia from every newly appointed bishop, should in his case be substantially cut.

Archbishop Eoin Ó Gráda of Tuam was another member of the family to graduate in canon law at Oxford. His intimate association with the colonial world is best exemplified by his presence at the duke of Clarence's parliament in 1366 which promulgated the statute of Kilkenny, notorious for its clauses forbidding priests and religious of Gaelic Irish birth from ministering in the Anglo-Irish area. The archbishop underwrote these provisions with the sanction of full canonical condemnation of those who ignored them.

There were of course very many ecclesiastical families of much humbler status than the O'Gradys. Such were the erenagh families. In the usage of the early Irish church the word *airchinneach*, 'superior', denoted an abbot or sometimes the administrator of monastic lands. The erenaghy of the medieval Irish

---

[1] *Cal. pat. rolls, 1354–58*, p. 264.

church was in essence stewardship of church lands and fulfilment of the duties that went with it. In this respect there was a close similarity of function between erenagh and coarb, though this latter, as heir of some saintly founder, was of higher status. In the administration of the church lands of Gaelic Ireland, the erenagh was even more ubiquitous than the coarb, and likewise equally liable to regional variations in the precise form his office took.

Let us try to see the role of the erenagh and his relationship to his bishop in a specific context. The principal in this particular case-history is an Englishman, John Colton, who has his own niche in Irish history as the only man to hold medieval Ireland's two top jobs: justiciar and archbishop of Armagh, primate of all Ireland. His career has more to tell us of Irish society than merely of his known relations with erenaghs, but for the moment it is with that topic that we are concerned.[1]

As metropolitans of the province of Armagh, the archbishops had guardianship of the spiritualities in each of the suffragan sees whenever they were vacant. In the Gaelic Irish dioceses under their jurisdiction they had the right, too, to guardianship of the temporalities of the vacant diocese, and this principle was recognised by the crown, though Edward I had opposed it and the kings of England did not recognise it as operative in the English dioceses of the Armagh province. In 1397 the see of Derry was vacant and Archbishop Colton resolved that by a personal visit he would vindicate in practice his theoretical rights over the see during vacancy.

On 8 October 1397 he left Termonmaguirck *en route* for the town of Derry, accompanied by a group of his clergy of both Gaelic and Anglo-Irish nationalities. Not the least important member of his party was Richard Kenmare, a priest of the Meath diocese, who was a public notary and whose function was to compile the formal legal record of all the acts relevant to the vindication of the archbishop's jurisdictional position. It is from Kenmare's records, or the surviving parts of them, that an account of this archiepiscopal foray into a purely Gaelic diocese can be constructed, with all its revealing detail. The erenagh figures quite prominently.

The archbishop spent ten nights away from home, and the notary carefully recorded how his expenses were met. Five of the nights were spent with the Augustinian canons at Derry, partly at their expense and partly at the expense of the dean of Derry. For the other five nights, erenaghs of various parishes were responsible. The archbishop's party spent its first night at Ardstraw, where the erenaghs provided milk, butter, and beef, found straw and oats for the horses and supplied night watch over the party. From neighbouring Cappagh, too small to provide for such numbers, the erenaghs sent beef. On leaving Ardstraw, the erenaghs supplied seven fresh horses. This pattern of the erenaghs finding supplies for men and horses, keeping guard overnight and

---

[1] Based on *Acts of Colton*. For a sketch of his career, J. A. Watt, 'John Colton, justiciar of Ireland (1382) and archbishop of Armagh (1383–1404)' in Lydon, *Eng. &Ire.*, pp 196–213.

providing fresh horses was repeated in the other parishes along the route to
Derry. At Banagher, the archbishop settled a dispute as to the lawful occupant
of the erenaghy. It was made clear to all the erenaghs concerned, in case they
did not appreciate the fact (there is no hint of any opposition to the archbishop
or reluctance to do their duty), that these dues customarily paid to the bishop of
Derry were being paid to the archbishop simply because, during the vacancy,
he was acting in the bishop's place. The record of Colton's assertion of his
jurisdictional rights in a Derry vacancy makes it abundantly clear what was the
reality of the erenagh's position: he was the farmer of episcopal mensal lands
for which rent was paid and which also carried the obligation of paying the
prelate's expenses at visitation times. This latter charge may be regarded as the
ecclesiastical equivalent of *cuid oidhche*, 'cuddy', which an Irish king could in
analogous circumstances exact from his subjects.[1] It may be added that evidence of a later date indicates that it was usual, at least in Armagh, for the
erenaghs to bear a proportion of the costs of church maintenance.

The survival of the Colton Derry *acta* and of registers for Milo Sweetman
(1361–80) and Fleming (1404–16), each of which contains material from other
pontificates, puts Armagh comfortably ahead of the other three provinces in
extant fourteenth-century source material. This documentation relates to a
region of Ireland where, on the one hand, Gaelic civilisation was at its most
tenacious and most powerful politically, and on the other, where the English
way of life was most stubbornly defended. It has therefore much to tell us of the
tensions of the two-nation situation, particularly as it affected the church, and
of the problems of coexistence posed by cultural differences.

A formula of distinction between an *ecclesia inter Hibernicos* and an *ecclesia inter
Anglicos* is found to be already established in the terminology of the earliest
register.[2] It is applicable to two contexts: the province of Armagh and the
diocese. The anglicised dioceses were Meath (comprising broadly the lordship
of Trim), Down and Connor, the area roughly of the Anglo-Irish remnant of
the earldom of Ulster. Among the Gaelic Irish lay six dioceses: Raphoe, Derry,
Clonmacnoise, Kilmore, Dromore, and Clogher, each corresponding to the
territory of a ruling family, a member of which often became bishop. The area
of the diocese of Armagh which lay *inter Anglicos* was that of the medieval
county of Louth and was divided into three deaneries, each based on an
important town of the colony; Dundalk, Drogheda, and Ardee. *Inter Hibernicos*
were two deaneries: Tullaghogue, inauguration site of the O'Neills, and Erthir,
subject to the O'Hanlons and including Armagh itself.

There were two major power shifts in fourteenth-century Ulster, both of
which began in the 1330s, one civil and the other ecclesiastical. The de Burgh

---

[1] On which see Katharine Simms, 'Guesting and feasting in Gaelic Ireland' in *R.S.A.I. Jn.*, cviii
(1978), pp 79–86.
[2] See further my '*Ecclesia inter Anglicos et inter Hibernicos*: confrontation and coexistence in the
medieval diocese and province of Armagh' in Lydon, *English in med. Ire.*, pp 46–64.

earldom collapsed when Earl William was murdered in 1333. In the power struggle that followed, the Irish kings created a quite new balance in the respective strengths of Gaelic and colonial Ireland. The consolidation of the power of the O'Neills was the leading feature of this new situation. But while Gaelic Ulster wrested back its political ascendancy, possession of the see of Armagh shifted away from it. Succession of Gaelic Irishmen to the primacy had been fairly certain since the invasion, but after the death of Archbishop David Mág Oireachtaigh in 1346 no other Gaelic Irishman became archbishop before the reformation.

Raymond of Perelhos stated that for the men of Ulster their pope was the archbishop of Armagh. No doubt this is a considerable overstatement; yet there can be little doubt that whatever the nationality of the archbishop, his office, the coarbship of St Patrick, ensured respect for him. On the Sunday of his Derry visitation, John Colton was asked to celebrate mass for 'the thousands of people assembled out of respect for him', and an outside altar had to be erected. But the position of the English or Anglo-Irish primates in relation to their Gaelic Irish subjects was more complex than these scraps of evidence suggest.

It has been seen that Colton could command the service of the erenaghs. Detailed examination of his actions in Derry shows his authority sought, recognised, and obeyed in a number of pastoral contexts. He had been thorough: he reconciled cemeteries and churches polluted by bloodshed; conducted a searching visitation of the Derry Augustinian canons, appointing a new abbot and issuing a set of reform constitutions for the better observance of the rule and of the vow of chastity; made visitation of the Derry chapter, whose early and unsustained opposition he overcame easily with the help of one of his Irish suffragans, Conchobhar Mac Carmaic Uí Domhnaill, bishop of Raphoe; heard matrimonial cases; appointed to a rectory; settled a dispute concerning episcopal property; and excommunicated a number of prominent local laymen for usurpation of church lands.

It would be a mistake, however, to assume simply from the Colton notarial record that the distinction between an *ecclesia inter Hibernicos* and an *ecclesia inter Anglicos*, which was so well established in the vocabulary of later medieval Ireland, had no administrative significance. That English law insisted that Gaelic Irish priests ministering *inter Anglicos* should obtain charters of denization is evidence enough of its reality. For the archbishops to exercise their jurisdiction *inter Hibernicos* was not always as relatively easy as Colton had found it in 1397. In 1390 he had not been able to get into Armagh itself because of war between Gaelic and Anglo-Irish. He had deemed the situation sufficiently typical to take the trouble to obtain a papal exemption from the canon law ruling that a metropolitan might not return on visitation to a diocese before he had completed visitation of all the other dioceses of his province, and this was renewed by Archbishop Swayne in 1418. An earlier papal permission concerning visitation allowed the archbishops to appoint commissaries to act for them. In fact,

the personal appearance of Colton in Derry in 1397 seems to have been exceptional. The usual practice was for the archbishop to appoint commissaries from
within the diocese to be visited, as far as the *ecclesia inter Hibernicos* was concerned. For the Anglo-Irish dioceses, the visitation was done in person. There
was a parallel practice for the Armagh diocese. This meant that in one important respect the archbishop's jurisdiction operated at one remove and was the
less secure and efficient for that. In all other respects, however, no distinction
in principle was made between the two areas, as far as the relationship of
metropolitan and suffragans were concerned. Oaths of canonical obedience
were sworn and provincial councils attended by bishops of both nations, while
the metropolitan court heard cases from all dioceses. This is not to say that the
archbishop was never resisted or that his degree of control was as tight as he
would have wished. It was, however, at least the ordinary assumption of the
Gaelic Irish dioceses of the Armagh province that their metropolitan was,
whatever his nationality and the attitudes of officialdom, the authentic successor of St Patrick and entitled to the traditional *de iure* position of that office,
however vigilant and skilful he might have to be to maintain its substance in
practice. But then, that applied, too, to his position in relation to his Anglo-
Irish subordinates.

The archbishops' position *inter Hibernicos* was not, however, simply a matter
of their relations with their suffragans and the Gaelic Irish clergy of their own
cathedral chapter and diocese. Hardly less important for the reality of their
authority was their standing among the Irish princes of the province. They had
need of their goodwill on a number of counts. One of the major problems was
persuading them, or attempting to coerce them by spiritual sanctions, to refrain
from helping themselves to the possessions of the see of Armagh and from
molesting those who served it. The registers have a long tale to tell of the
making and breaking of promises sworn on the gospels and 'on the cross
carried before the archbishop as it was carried before St Patrick', and of
excommunication and interdict inflicted and lifted in connection with despo-
liation of ecclesiastical lands and their tenants. Armagh stayed poor. But it was
not only for their economic position that the archbishops depended on the
cooperation of Irish rulers. They were the only secular arm available in Gaelic
Ireland, and were essential auxiliaries in such matters as protection of the archbishop's commissaries, stewards, and messengers, in helping to bring the more
notoriously scandalous clergy to justice, and in lending support in action
against concubinary priests.

These are the negative and positive aspects of the relations of the ecclesiastical and civil powers, and have their parallels in all medieval societies. In these
contexts, as with prelates elsewhere, the archbishops of Armagh sometimes
had their successes in getting what they wanted and often their failures. A more
distinctively Irish problem, and a more fundamental one, concerns attitudes to
the endemic strife between Gaelic and Anglo-Irish. In 1349, Archbishop

Richard FitzRalph told Pope Clement VI in Avignon that in his province 'the two nations are always opposed to one another from a traditional hatred, the Irish and Scots being always enemies of the English: so much so that daily they rob and slay each other. . . .'[1] Did the archbishops, acknowledged spiritual leaders for both nations, try to use their position to mitigate this conflict?

The pastoral responsibility was explicitly acknowledged. It was first framed definitively, so far as is known, by Milo Sweetman and achieved permanent form in a provincial decree adopted and reiterated by his successors. Quite simply, this instruction, shorn of that heavy emphasis on penalties for non-observance so characteristic of this form of canon law, made it obligatory on all the bishops 'to labour to their utmost to bring about and preserve peace between the English and Irish of our province of Armagh, preaching peace between them. . . .'[2] There is no very considerable body of evidence to show how far this constructive principle was put into practice; but there is enough, perhaps, to show that sometimes it went further than mere pious aspiration.

We may usefully distinguish two methods of *cura spiritualis et officium pastorale* as exercised in the cause of establishing peace between Gaelic and Anglo-Irish. One, through direct exhortation, sought peace by activating men's consciences to awareness of the overriding importance of justice and charity in human relations. The other, through practical intervention in the world of affairs, sought peace by way of negotiation, mediation, conciliation.

Richard FitzRalph provides a striking example of the former method. Though as theologian and anti-mendicant polemicist he cut a more considerable figure outside Ireland than inside, he did make his presence felt forcibly in his own diocese; not least by vigorous denunciation of the vices endemic among his fellow countrymen in the towns and villages of County Louth. Among these he numbered especially their wicked practices against the Gaelic Irish, such as preventing them from making wills and excluding them from religious confraternities; practices that violated the law of Christian charity, *lex dileccionis proximi*. He reserved his severest censures for the common practice of using the so-called law of the march as a general sanction for killing and despoiling Gaelic Irishmen and breaking the peace at will, and for confessors who tolerated it. For FitzRalph, the *lex marchie* was *lex dyaboli*.[3] How far this attitude was characteristic of the prelates of the period it is unfortunately impossible to say, for FitzRalph's is the only collection of sermons extant from a medieval Irish source.[4]

By contrast, there is appreciably more evidence of the archbishops acting as mediators between Gaelic and Anglo-Irish leaders. From Milo Sweetman's making of peace in 1373 between Mág Aonghusa, Mac Mathghamhna, and

[1] Aubrey Gwynn, 'The Black Death in Ireland' in *Studies*, xxiv (1935), p. 31.
[2] *The register of John Swayne*, ed. D. A. Chart (Belfast, 1935), pp 11–12.
[3] Aubrey Gwynn, 'Richard FitzRalph, archbishop of Armagh' in *Studies*, xxv (1936), pp 81–96.
[4] Freshly discussed by Walsh, *Richard FitzRalph*, pp 318–50.

Mac Domhnaill on the one side, and the justiciar, sheriff of Louth, and other Anglo-Irish notables on the other, and protesting how much he had laboured and suffered in the cause of peace,[1] to John Mey's complicated negotiations with the O'Neills which finally brought them to terms with Richard, duke of York in 1449,[2] the known occasions are relatively numerous. One example must suffice here as illustrating the part an archbishop of Armagh might play in this most characteristic role.

From October 1394 to May 1395, Richard II was in Ireland, at the head of the largest army ever to land there in the medieval period, with the general aim of restoring the fortunes of the sorely pressed colony. One of the essentials for his success was the subjugation of the leading Irish rulers and their acknowledgement of his lordship. In the event, without any great military effort on his part, some eighty Irish *capitanei* swore oaths of homage to him pledging themselves in large fines, and sometimes with hostages, to loyalty, obedience, and peace; in the short term at least, a considerable success for the king. Niall Og Ó Néill, exercising what the Gaelic Irish called the kingship of Ulster because of the advanced age of his father, was the first to submit. It had been on John Colton's advice that he had summoned together his subjects to discuss what his attitude to Richard should be. A letter from Ó Néill himself (extant letters from Gaelic Irish sources are very rare), written to his 'spiritual father', Colton, makes it clear that he was reluctant to make the submission and that he was under considerable pressure from many of the leading Gaelic Irish of Munster and Connacht not to do so. However, Ó Néill explicitly acknowledges that he rejected this course of non-cooperation on Colton's advice and went on to influence and even threaten others to follow his example.[3] John Colton was on hand in January 1395 when, in the Dominican house at Drogheda, Ó Néill swore his oath of fealty. He negotiated too, on Ó Néill's behalf, between the king and the newly appeared earl of Ulster, Roger Mortimer, earl of March, whom Ó Néill distrusted deeply. There is nothing here, or indeed in any other comparable series of negotiations, to suggest that it was the archbishop who was the dominant figure or that the peace accomplished was exclusively of his making. Ó Néill was faced with a strong military presence, sufficiently strong to force him to give a son into captivity as a hostage (for whose release Colton subsequently negotiated). He may have been in receipt of an annual pension from the archbishop, as his descendant was in Archbishop Mey's time. There were too many factors at work of self-preservation and self-interest to make him act

---

[1] Lawlor, 'Sweetman's reg.', p. 222, no. 10.

[2] *Registrum Iohannis Mey: the register of John Mey, archbishop of Armagh, 1443–56*, ed. W. G. H. Quigley and E. F. D. Roberts (Belfast, 1972), nos. 141, 171, 167, 168, 173, 176, 172, 178, 162 (putting the texts in the correct chronological order, which the register does not follow). The text of the agreement itself has been published: Edmund Curtis, 'The "bonnaght" of Ulster' in *Hermathena*, xxi (1931), pp 87–91. On the relationship more generally, see now Katharine Simms, 'The archbishops of Armagh and the O'Neills, 1347–1471' in *I.H.S.*, xix, no. 73 (Mar. 1974), pp 38–55.

[3] Curtis, *Richard II in Ire.*, pp 143–6.

as he did for us to suggest that the archbishop's moral influence was the decisive factor. Nevertheless, it is clear that Colton did influence him and affect the course of events. The archbishop was something more than just a cleric brought along to threaten excommunication for violation of the oath. An archbishop of Armagh might, and often did, play a significant role as the mediatory agent bringing hostile leaders together, helping in the formalities of treaty-making, striving to uphold the peace concluded. That in practice these peaces were fragile, short-lived affairs means that much effort was wasted. But in sum, the effort was not without significance in the gradual, if stormy, adjustment of men united within a common ecclesiastical structure but severely divided on national and cultural grounds.

RAYMOND of Perelhos related how Ó Néill was anxious to hear from him about the customs and way of life of the kings of France, Aragon, and Castile. But he noted from what Ó Néill said that he did not feel he had anything to learn from them, since the Gaelic Irish held their own customs to be 'the best and most perfect in the world' (els teno las lors costumas melhors e plus perfieytas del mon). Chrysted's account of the attitudes of the four kings under his tutorship, without being so explicit, suggests the same tenacious adherence to the Gaelic way of life. This evidence of the two outside observers comes as no surprise. Even the most cursory of examinations of the source material reveals the continuing vitality of Gaelic culture in fourteenth-century Ireland and the fidelity of the population to it. It is true that some Gaelic Irish in the colonial areas became anglicised. Some thirteenth-century examples have been noted above, and the fourteenth-century evidence will be considered later. It is also true that the Gaelic Irish took advantage of certain aspects of English culture, depending on the particular circumstances of different regions: the use of money, participation in trade, imitation of building styles, some adaptation of certain legal principles, a trickle of English words filtering into the Irish language, are examples. But the substance of the Gaelic way of life, its language and traditional literary forms, its kingship and attendant social and legal structure, its economic system, remained intact.

It is pertinent to ask how far, behind Ó Néill's satisfaction with his own culture, there lay any kind or degree of national sentiment. Orpen argued that the Gaelic Irishman knew no nation but his tribe. Against him, MacNeill urged that the existence of the colony had enhanced men's awareness of the uniqueness of their own culture and thus contributed to the growth of a national consciousness. He posited a 'national sentiment, intensified and supplied with a more definite political form under a sense of national oppression' and did not hesitate to speak of the 'sentiment of nationalism'.[1]

Glanmor Williams has done well to remind us that 'it can be an extremely dangerous anachronism to talk too facilely of a sense of nationality among the

[1] MacNeill, Phases, p. 325, apparently with Orpen, Normans, i, 20–28 in mind.

men of the middle ages'. Nevertheless, he has argued to the conclusion that 'the persistence of concepts of nationality, through centuries of hardship, disappointment and setback, is one of the most extraordinary things in the history of medieval Wales'.[1] The historians of medieval Ireland, despite MacNeill's lead, have been slow to consider the possible medieval origins of national consciousness. In a period spanned by the careers of Robert Bruce and Owen Glendower, both of whom have an acknowledged place in the history of their countries as nationalist leaders, there is certainly a case for asking how far the phenomenon of nationalism did in fact exist in Ireland in the same period.

It has already been noticed how, in the late 1270s, the citizens of Cork objected to the appointment of a Gaelic Irishman as collector of customs in the city. Their petition to Edward I stated baldly that those of Irish speech were enemies of the king and his subjects (*Hybernica lingua vobis et vestris sit inimica*). Edward I was to hear more of this hostility in the years following. Nicholas Cusack, a Franciscan who occupied the see of Kildare from 1279 to 1299, warned the king that certain Gaelic Irish members of religious orders were holding secret meetings with Irish kings and assuring them that it was perfectly lawful according to both human and divine law to fight for their native land and to attack the colony with all their strength.[2] In 1285 an English governmental commission appointed to investigate malpractices in the Dublin exchequer recommended that it would be expedient to the king if no Gaelic Irishman should ever be an archbishop or bishop, because the Irish

always preach against the king and always provide their churches with Irishmen . . . so that choice of bishops shall be of Irishmen in order to maintain their own language [*ad sustinendam linguam suam*] . . . similarly the Dominicans and Franciscans make much of that language [*lingua*].[3]

The phrase 'to maintain their own language' is significant. It was not simply a matter of favouring fellow countrymen as an end in itself. The object of these clerics, canons of cathedrals and friars, was to preserve their *lingua*. This word certainly incorporates the connection between language and nationality. It connotes more than merely 'language', and a translation 'way of life' or even 'culture' may be perhaps nearer the real meaning of the word.[4] There can be little doubt that English administrators in Ireland and the king of England knew they were faced with a deliberate effort on the part of the Gaelic Irish to uphold their own culture. This awareness increased during the period of the Edward Bruce invasion and its aftermath.[5]

[1] Glanmor Williams, 'Language, literacy and nationality in Wales' in *History*, lvi (1971), pp 1–3.

[2] Fitzmaurice & Little, *Franciscan province Ire.*, pp 52–3.

[3] Text published in Watt, 'English law and the Irish church: the reign of Edward I' in *Med. studies presented to A. Gwynn*, pp 150–51.

[4] Aubrey Gwynn considered that 'the medieval use of the word *lingua* corresponds more closely with our words *custom* or *race*' ('Nicolas Mac Maol Iosa, archbishop of Armagh (1272–1303)' in *Féil-sgríbhinn Eoin Mhic Néill*, p. 397).

[5] Cf. Watt, *Ch. & two nations*, pp 184–97; *Ch. in med. Ire.*, pp 78–84.

Turning to the Irish sources, it soon appears that the Annals, which record a considerable amount of fighting between Gaelic and Anglo-Irish, offer little in the way of evidence of any burgeoning national sentiment. Of the Irish poets, MacNeill would certainly have said of them what has been said recently of their Welsh counterparts: 'they were the sentinels of a patent sense of nationality closely linked with language.'[1] A thorough examination of the whole corpus of Irish poetry from this point of view might be revealing. Perhaps something of the flavour of the national sentiment preserved in this type of literature in the fourteenth century is shown in a poem addressed to Tomás Mág Shamhradháin (d. 1343), whose family territory lay in County Cavan. The theme is Ireland and her self-inflicted wounds; instead of uniting to expel the foreigner, rivalry among the Gaelic Irish themselves has brought ruin to the whole country. The poet used the traditional mythological names for his native land:

Eire is ruined by rivalry among Gaoidhil; not mutual love in peace is their policy; their anger keeps them apart; sad they cannot agree!

Their rivalry in desire for Banbha's land has deprived them of thick-grassed Fodla; instead of attacking Goill, every troop of Conn's race is in turmoil.

What ruins Fodla is that neither young nor old desire peace; 'tis Eire herself which has ruined this isle of ours; we find the land too tempting an object of attack.[2]

This theme, the shattered unity of the nation, is absent from 'Caithréim Thoirdhealbhaigh'. But there are other themes present, relevant to the study of national sentiment, which command attention. In the first place, it communicates a wealth of anti-foreigner hate, always the seed-bed of nationalist sentiment. The foreigners, the author says, sought to inflict on the Irish 'injustice, tyranny, violence, and oppression, taking from them where they could their blood and their land'. Of Tadg Ó Briain, it was said there was 'no created thing under heaven that he hated and loathed more than an Englishman's progeny', while to Muirchertach Ó Briain 'it was as a violent mortal sickness that ever his faithful natural friends should come to lie under their merciless oppression.'

To this hatred of the invader (it was of course the de Clares that the O'Briens had especially in mind) and sense of oppression at his hands, the 'Caithréim' added a second of the ordinary ingredients of nationalism: a sense of the uniqueness of the nation based on a history of its distinctive origins. The work begins with a reference to the Irish tribes being of the blood of Milesius the Spaniard, and elsewhere there is reference to the Spanish origins of the Irish. The theme is here underdeveloped, but it is clearly part of an established interpretation of the national history, of common occurrence in medieval Irish

[1] Williams, 'Language, literacy and nationality', p. 2.
[2] *The book of Magauran: Leabhar Meig Shamradhain*, ed. Lambert McKenna (Dublin, 1947), p. 362. James Lydon has drawn attention to Domnall Ó Néill's awareness of the pernicious results of divisions among the Gaelic Irish; above, p. 245.

writing. We will see shortly how in this period it was knitted into a nationalist manifesto.

A third theme present in the 'Caithréim' which reveals a sentiment transcending the merely tribal is to be found in its assumption of the existence of the office of king of the whole of Ireland. In 1258, it was recorded here and also in the Annals, Tadg Ó Briain and the men of Munster met Brian Ó Néill and the men of Ulster on Lough Erne to select a king of Ireland. Though the account of the 'Caithréim' is somewhat prejudiced towards the O'Briens and is reluctant to recognise that the O'Neills prevailed, English sources show that Ó Néill did account himself king of Ireland. Again, in 1286 according to the 'Caithréim', the kingship of all Ireland, portrayed in the book in the traditional marriage symbol of a beautiful maiden, was thought to be within the grasp of Toirrdelbach Ó Briain, though, the narrative continued, he allowed himself to be talked out of his opportunity by the earl of Ulster.

These three themes (the usurpation and oppression of the foreigner, a myth of the origin of the nation, a political expression of the unity of the country) are quite clearly enunciated in the 'Caithréim'.[1] Since the subject matter of the book was essentially dynastic and regional, they are expressed somewhat incidentally. They are not welded into a single, emphatic, coherent whole. They are, however, to be found so welded in the celebrated remonstrance addressed in *c.* 1317 to Pope John XXII by Domnall Ó Néill in the name of the Irish kings and people.[2] This is a document similar in both form and content to the better-known declaration of Arbroath which Robert Bruce and the Scottish nobility and people addressed to John XXII in 1320.[3] Both documents, in essence, are pleas to the pope to uphold the birthright of national freedom from English oppression. Scottish historians are virtually unanimous in appraising it as a major document in the history of nationalism: 'the most impressive manifesto of nationalism that medieval Europe produced', its most recent expositor has claimed.[4] There seems no reason why the remonstrance should not be assessed likewise as a manifesto of nationalism, despite the reluctance of Irish historians to do so.

The specific object of the remonstrance was to persuade the pope to recognise Domnall Ó Néill's renunciation of the right he claimed to succeed to the

---

[1] *Caith. Thoirdh.*, ii, 1, 2–4, 28–9, 111, 128.

[2] The text has been preserved in the continuation of Fordun's *Scotichronicon*, ed. Thomas Hearne (Oxford, 1722), iii, 908–26, and Walter Goodall (Edinburgh, 1759), ii, 259–67. There are translations by Robert King, *Primer of the history of the holy catholic church in Ireland* (3rd ed., Dublin, 1845–51), ii, 1119–35, and Charles McNeill in Curtis & McDowell, *Ir. hist. docs*, pp 38–46.

[3] James Fergusson, *The declaration of Arbroath* (Edinburgh, 1970); A. A. M. Duncan, *The nation of Scots and the declaration of Arbroath* (London, 1970).

[4] R. G. Nicholson, *Scotland: the later middle ages* (Edinburgh, 1974), p. 101. Cf. G. W. S. Barrow: 'Certainly we shall find no clearer statement of Scottish nationalism and patriotism in the fourteenth century. Equally certainly, no finer statement of a claim to national independence was produced in this period anywhere in Western Europe' (*Robert Bruce and the community of the realm of Scotland* (London, 1965), p. 430).

kingship of Ireland in favour of Edward Bruce, whom the Gaelic Irish, it was said, had recognised as their ruler. The argument to this end began with an account of the beginnings of Irish history and of the political liberty which the Irish enjoyed throughout this whole period, lasting until 1170, the year when the hitherto independent Irish were 'violently reduced to the deep abyss of miserable bondage' under English misrule. The myth of the Spanish origins of the Irish was woven into the claim to political independence. It was linked directly to the succession of native kings from pre-Christian to post-Patrician times: 197 kings in all, in the 3,500 years since between the departure of the three sons of Milesius from Spain and the granting by the English pope Adrian IV of the lordship of the country to the English king Henry II.

After this proemium, the remonstrance argued a well constructed case. Henry II had been granted his lordship conditionally on the fulfilment of four obligations which Adrian IV's *Laudabiliter* had lain on him. They were that Henry and his successors would extend the bounds of the Irish church and preserve its rights, bring the Irish people under the rule of law, implant virtues among them, root up vices, and make an annual payment of Peter's pence. None of these conditions, it was urged, had been observed. Therefore, Henry and his four successors, having violated the terms of the papal grant, had forfeited their claim to the obedience of their Irish subjects.

The bulk of the argument concerned the second and third of these conditions, and it was very detailed. Far from being brought under the rule of law, the Irish had been subjected to legal procedures that were manifestly unjust to them. The framers of the remonstrance listed the specific injustices that the English legal system had imposed on those of Gaelic Irish descent. It has been demonstrated that this section of the document presented a reasonably accurate statement of the salient features of the disabilities of the Gaelic Irish at English law.[1] Further, the argument proceeded, far from introducing virtues, the English now inhabiting Ireland had introduced vices of their own, thereby cutting out virtues already planted there. Another detailed catalogue of specific accusations follows, this time levelled at the conduct of the 'middle nation', here carefully distinguished from the 'English of England', towards the Gaelic Irish. Many of these charges can be authenticated in other sources.[2] The condemnation of both the operation of the English legal system and of the viciousness of the Anglo-Irish led to the remonstrance's defiant climax:

Hence because of these wrongs and of numberless others which it is beyond the power of the human mind to readily understand and also on account of the kings of England and their officials and the perennial treachery of the English of the middle nation who were bound by decree of the papal curia to rule our nation with justice and moderation

[1] G. J. Hand, 'The status of the native Irish in the lordship of Ireland, 1272–1331' in *Ir. Jurist*, i (1966), pp 102–8; Hand, *Eng. law in Ire.*, pp 187–213.
[2] Light has been thrown on one of the more serious of them by R. F. Frame, 'The justiciar and the murder of the MacMurroughs in 1282' in *I.H.S.*, xviii, no. 70 (Sept. 1972), pp 223–30.

and have made its destruction their wicked objective, and in order to throw off the cruel and intolerable yoke of their slavery and to recover our native liberty which for a time through them we had lost, we are forced to wage war to the death against them, impelled by necessity to put our manhood to the test of war in defence of our just rights rather than any longer submit like women to their appalling outrages.

The pope was then asked to ratify the choice of Edward Bruce as king of Ireland, and the remonstrance concluded with a reference back to the theme with which it started, namely that of the long history of Irish freedom before 1170.

It seems difficult to find any word more accurate than 'nationalism' to describe the principles and emotions that found expression in the remonstrance. But the perspective within which we should view the attitude of Irish kings to the lords of Ireland demands that the position adopted towards Edward II in 1317 be compared with that adopted towards Richard II in 1395.

With this king's first Irish expedition, Gaelic Ireland faced the most powerful military force ever assembled against it before the Tudor period. Nationalist ideology evaporated in the chill wind of political reality. In January 1395, at the Dominican house in Drogheda, the two Niall Ó Néills, father and son, grandson and great-grandson of the Domnall Ó Néill of the remonstrance, swore homage and fealty to Richard II. In March 1395, at the same place, the younger Ó Néill, on bended knees before the king, repeated the act in more solemn form and was admitted to the kiss of peace.[1] At his persuasion, Ó Briain, Ó Conchobhair, Mac Carthaigh, and 'many others of the southern parts' who were of a mind to resist Richard, followed suit[2] and thereafter virtually all the Irish rulers of any significance did likewise. All became the king's liegmen (*ligei*), promising fidelity and service for the future, with many protesting that not merely they but also their ancestors had always recognised English lordship and that they held their territories of these English lords of Ireland.[3] Ó Néill, with Mac Murchadha, Ó Conchobhair, and Ó Briain, accepted knighthood, albeit reluctantly, from Richard II, and temporarily suffered conversion to English dress, court-style, eating habits, and way of horse-riding, as Chrysted so vividly reported.

The contrast between the attitudes of the Ó Néill of 1317 and the O'Neills of 1395 is instructive. It is a perfect demonstration of that political ambivalence which was the norm in fourteenth-century Ireland, the product of the interaction of the two Irelands, Gaelic and colonial. The urge of Gaelic Ireland to preserve its own culture and freedom was inevitably curbed by realistic appreciation of the perennial necessity to achieve coexistence. The circumstances of the Edward Bruce invasion had apparently given hope of radical change in the lordship of Ireland. The armed might of Richard II brought

---

[1] Texts in Curtis, *Rich. II in Ire.*, pp 68–9, 105–6.
[2] Ibid., pp 143–4.
[3] E.g. Tadhg Mac Carthaigh, ibid., p. 67; Mág Aonghusa, ibid., p. 89; Ó Cearbhaill, ibid., p. 95; Ó Ceallaigh, ibid., p. 110.

recognition of the *status quo*. His ability to take sons as hostages and to offer a counter-balance to the pressures of the Anglo-Irish forced accommodation with the lord of Ireland, not his rejection. This political ambivalence,[1] here demonstrated in relation to the highest level of authority, was paralleled over and over again on the different regional and local levels in the independence–coexistence relationships of Irish chiefs, Anglo-Irish lords, English officials and churchmen of both nations. Nationalism was stirring, but coexistence and accommodation were often the stronger force in practical life.

[1] There was a parallel in Wales; Glyn Roberts, 'Wales and England: antipathy and sympathy, 1282–1485' in *Welsh Hist. Rev.*, i (1965), pp 375–96.

CHAPTER XIII

The Anglo-Irish colony under strain, 1327–99

J. A. WATT

THAT the English colony in Ireland had in its social composition, economic institutions, legal system, and structure of government developed as a mirror image of the home country has been made abundantly clear earlier in this volume. A smaller version of England had been transplanted overseas and had flourished, producing its own magnate class, its squirearchy, bourgeoisie, urban artisan class, and peasantry. Not least, there was a steady procession of English officials, some merely serving a term in a career of government service but others remaining to put down roots. Whatever the ethnic origins of colonists, it was the pattern of English society that was recreated.

Nevertheless, despite the fundamental kinship of the two societies, English and colonial, by the opening decades of the fourteenth century it was already clear that the colonists were not, to adapt a well known dictum, as English as the English themselves. Both the Gaelic Irish and the English were agreed on that and they often agreed too, though for very different reasons, in not liking what they saw of the distinguishing features of the colonists' individuality. The remonstrance of c.1317, as has already been noticed, referred to them as 'the middle nation', different in character from the English of England because of their treachery and savagery. On the English side, a distinction appeared in the legislation of this period between the 'English by birth' and the 'English by blood', always in a context that makes it clear that there was animosity between them. The 'degeneracy' or gaelicisation of some sections of the colonists was often at the root of this hostility, but so too was resentment at the policies and actions of English officials. Already, by the beginning of our period, the 'English in Ireland' (the term is a contemporary one) were recognisably a distinct breed, preserving and developing an identity of their own which they were to keep into early modern times, as the later label 'Old English' testifies. This individuality (Curtis chose to call it a 'half nationality', but the term does not seem a good one) was produced when a transplanted society was conditioned at once by its cultural, political, and psychological attachments to the mother country and by the insistent pressures of coexistence with a generally hostile indigenous population of significantly different culture.

The colony had produced its own upper class. Few men had come to Ireland from Britain, or further afield, from the higher echelons of society, with the backing of any very considerable resources at home. They made their way in their new world largely by their own efforts, and by the beginning of our period five families, all of which had been in Ireland since the twelfth century, had risen to the top. Their position had been officially marked by the royal conferment of the title 'earl'. A brief glance at these dynasties is an instructive introduction to the ethos of the Anglo-Irish world.[1]

First in rank among the earls, and first too in general esteem, even among the Irish, was Richard de Burgh, the Red Earl, lord of Connacht, third earl of Ulster (the second de Burgh earl); 'the best of all the Galls in Ireland' is the Irish annalist's obituary comment in 1326. Then came, in order of creation, John fitz Thomas FitzGerald, fifth lord of Offaly, created earl of Kildare in 1316; John de Bermingham, lord of Athenry, created earl of Louth in 1319; James Butler, created earl of Ormond in 1328; and finally another Geraldine, Maurice fitz Thomas, created earl of Desmond some time in 1329.[2]

It was inevitable that all these men were closely interrelated by marriage, partly because of the relative isolation and smallness of their society and partly because an inordinate amount of baronial feuding made marriage a device of reconciliation. The Red Earl had six daughters: Aveline married the earl of Louth, John de Bermingham; Joan married Thomas fitz John, second earl of Kildare, while Katherine secured the first earl of Desmond, Maurice fitz Thomas. There were other de Burgh marriages of potential consequence. Another daughter, Elizabeth, became the second wife of Robert Bruce, then earl of Carrick, later King Robert I of Scotland. Dynastic aggrandisement by marriage brought its complications in this Scottish context, however, for her sister Maud had married Gilbert de Clare, lord of Kilkenny and earl of Gloucester and Hereford, who fell to the Scots at Bannockburn, while her father found himself arrested by the citizens of Dublin, suspicious of his Scottish connection, at the time of the Bruce invasion of Ireland. This connection also included the marriage of the earl's sister to James, high steward of Scotland, a Stuart ancestor. Finally, there must be noted the marriage of one of his sons to a daughter of Toirrdelbach Ó Briain, king of Thomond. That one family in one generation forged such a range of links by marriage is exceptional. That such links could be made readily and unexceptionably was, however, an ordinary feature of Anglo-Irish society.

Such marriages were the consequence of the Red Earl's way of life, which, in common with that of the European nobility of his time, was essentially the making of war at the behest of his king and for his self-aggrandisement. His career of royal service had begun with Edward I in Wales in 1284; it took him to Scotland on numerous occasions between 1295 and 1314 and had him summoned for duty

---

[1] See now the excellent detailed analysis of Frame, *Eng. lordship*, pp 13–51.
[2] *D.N.B.* and G.E.C., *Peerage*, give basic information on these men.

in Gascony in 1294 and Flanders in 1297. He played a part, too, in English politics, being occasionally summoned to parliament in England. His role was not negligible, since in 1318 he was one of the guarantors on the king's side of the treaty of Leake between Edward II and the turbulent Thomas, earl of Lancaster, an important event in the political disturbances of this reign.

For all these activities, the earldom of Ulster and his lordship of Connacht, in theory amounting to virtually half of Ireland, provided the men and money. But the Red Earl was no absentee, merely drawing on his Irish resources to squander them elsewhere. He was active in Ireland in very many directions. Castle-building in Inishowen, Sligo, and Galway testifies to his continuous efforts to consolidate his authority in Gaelic Ireland. The Annals have much to say about his expeditions, if not always recording his complete success.[1] His influence with the O'Briens, with whom he made a marriage connection, as evidenced by the 'Caithréim Thoirdhealbhaigh', has already been noticed. So too have his connections with the Ulster kings, who all recognised him as their lord and provided him with fighting men. These soldiers were used by the earl in Scotland and on at least one occasion were due to serve on the Continent.

Through war, politics, tenurial bonds, marriage ties (even through literature, for the Red Earl was a patron of the bards, and therefore almost certainly an Irish-speaker) the de Burghs were linked as inescapably to the Gaelic world as they were in comparable, if different, ways to the Anglo-French world of England and Scotland. So too, though generally on a smaller scale of operation, were their fellow earls, and so too were all the English of Ireland, to a greater or lesser extent. They lay between two cultures, attracted and repelled to different degrees by each, and thus fashioning an identity of their own.

The earldom of Ulster, so imposing in the Red Earl's time, shattered with remarkable suddenness, victim of the colony's propensity to self-inflicted wounds. Richard de Burgh was succeeded by his grandson William who, aged twenty in 1333, was murdered in some obscure family feud by his own men, including his seneschal.[2] He left only an infant heiress. It has been noticed already how Orpen considered this a great turning-point in Irish medieval history. The blow followed hard on another important dynastic incident in an adjoining area. In 1329, the newly created earldom of Louth had been extinguished in war between the de Verdons and the de Berminghams, in which the earl and many of his close relations were killed.[3] The balance of power between the nations in Ulster had swung dramatically in favour of the Irish kings. They had not substantially weakened, nor had their capacity for making war diminished in the period of de Burgh rule. Indeed, their considerable employment as

---

[1] Nor always to his credit: 'the earl marched into Tir Conaill against Toirrdelbach Ó Domnaill and plundered the whole region, its churchmen and laymen, leaving neither altar-cloth nor missal nor chalice in any church of Cenel Conaill, and carried this booty into Connacht' (*Ann Conn.*, p. 185 (1291); see also, for similar attacks on churches, ibid., pp 197, 231).

[2] *Chartul. St Mary's, Dublin*, ii, 378–9; Clyn, *Annals*, pp 24–5.

[3] *Chartul. St Mary's, Dublin*, ii, 369–70; Clyn, *Annals*, p. 20.

fighting auxiliaries by the earls, and by the justiciars too, had had the effect of preserving the authority of the Irish chiefs in the traditional forms of Gaelic life, and probably also of improving their military efficiency. The way to Ulster was never in the future to be fully secure, and the earl's former vassal sub-kings established a new balance between themselves in which the earldom had an ever diminishing part to play. For there was not to be a resident earl again, though with the title surviving in the female line there were to be fitful but futile attempts to regain territory and authority. The great days of the Red Earl had gone for good.

While the earldom of Louth died out and that of Ulster was reduced to little more than a title, the earls of Kildare, Ormond, and Desmond continued to lay the foundations of their considerable power in the later middle ages.

The Kildares survived a double minority after the death of the second earl in 1328. The career of Maurice fitz Thomas, the fourth earl (d. 1390), reveals most of the salient features of the life-style of an Anglo-Irish magnate. As a young man, before he had been confirmed in his earldom, he commanded a force at the siege of Calais in 1347. He was active in the public life of the colony, serving as justiciar in a number of short spells: a total of about twenty-one months in six periods of office between 1355 and 1376.[1] He was active in consolidating his lordship, being busy in war in the Leinster and Munster marches. The other side of this coin, his treaties and accommodations with Irish chiefs, has already been noticed earlier. Some royal service overseas, sporadic terms of office as chief governor or deputy, considerable local engagements in war against the Gaelic Irish and the concomitant treaty-making, regular attendance at great councils and parliaments, constituted the very similar career of his contemporary, James Butler, second earl of Ormond (d. 1382). In the last quarter of the fourteenth century, the earls of Ormond played an enhanced role in the administration of the colony: the second earl was justiciar from 1376 to 1379 and the third filled the office in 1384–5, 1392–4, and again in 1404. This increase in public service at the highest level reflected their success in building up their lordship. For the Butlers, the crowning step in this process came in 1393 when, after two years of negotiation, they secured the entire Kilkenny possessions of the absentee Hugh le Despenser and Kilkenny castle became their *caput*.[2]

By contrast with the solid and relatively unspectacular advances of the Kildares and Ormonds, the Desmonds were more inclined to extremes. No fourteenth-century earl lived more dangerously than the first earl of Desmond. For Edmund Curtis the career of Maurice fitz Thomas was

memorable for that Anglo-Irish movement which he formed and led, not against the English crown but against the domination of English-born officials and the ruling of Ireland from Westminster. He is the first of the 'patriot leaders' in the long history of Anglo-Ireland.[3]

[1] This information and that which follows about tenures of the justiciarship are taken from Richardson & Sayles, *Admin. Ire.*, pp 84–91 (covering the period 1315–79); see also below, ix, 472–5.
[2] *Liber primus Kilkenn.*, p. 2.   [3] Curtis, *Med. Ire.* (2nd ed.), p. 224.

Desmond's reputation as a patriot leader of a constitutional party has not, however, survived the detailed accounts of his political attitudes and activities that Professor Sayles brought to light in 1961.[1] The earl had been twice proceeded against by justiciars, who had gathered sworn evidence against him—from eight juries, from Clonmel, Limerick, Cashel, Waterford, Cork, and Youghal between 1330 and 1334, while twenty juries from these towns and in addition from Tralee, Fethard, Buttevant, and Kilmallock had sworn their indictments between 1342 and 1345. When in 1351 Desmond came to petition the king against sentence of outlawry passed on him in Ireland in 1345, all these records were sent from Dublin to London, and found a place on the plea roll of the court of king's bench, where they were discovered by Professor Sayles.[2] The very least they show is that, for the minor landowners and townsmen of English Munster, Desmond was a tyrant, a traitor, and a felon.

As early as 1612 Sir John Davies had credited Desmond with being 'the first English lord that imposed coign and livery upon the king's subjects; and the first that raised his estate to immoderate greatness, by that wicked extortion and oppression'.[3] The Munster juries charged that even before 1320 Desmond had created a private army for himself, 'Routi-mac-Thomas'. To this force had come the criminals of Ireland to be empowered by the earl's letters patent, in an Anglo-Irish adaptation of the Irish *coinn mheadh*, to live off the country. 'Mac Thomas's rout', as this force was called, allied with that of Brian Ó Briain of Thomond and with help from Diarmait Mac Carthaig, had terrorised Munster. They had exacted protection money from towns such as Clonmel and Tipperary but had still allowed them to be pillaged by the Gaelic Irish. From Bunratty, which Desmond had seized, obviously aiming to establish himself as successor to the de Clares, he controlled Limerick city and county.[4] Desmond's much publicised feud with Arnold le Poer, in which the *Poerini* and other gentry suffered considerably, had its origins in these activities.[5] A host of small rural boroughs from Limerick to Waterford were at the mercy of one or other of the two 'routs', Desmond's or Ó Briain's. These depredations, allied to a supreme contempt for royal authority, were on a scale and of an intensity to persuade the middling classes of Munster that Desmond's political ambitions had become megalomaniac and that he was plotting, along with the highest in the land, to make himself king of Ireland. A Limerick jury in 1331 testified that Desmond had been scheming for five years to achieve this ambition and had made no secret of his willingness to kill the whole of the king's council in

---

[1] 'The rebellious first earl of Desmond' in *Med. studies presented to A. Gwynn*, pp 203–29.

[2] And published: 'The legal proceedings against the first earl of Desmond' in *Anal. Hib.*, no. 23 (1966), pp 1–47.

[3] Davies, *Discovery* (facsimile of 1st ed.; introduction by John Barry, Shannon, 1969), p. 206; see also p. 190.

[4] Sayles, 'Legal proceedings', p. 10.

[5] Ibid., pp 6–7. For the quarrel in general, Orpen, *Normans*, iv, 221–6; Otway-Ruthven, *Med. Ire.*, pp 245–8.

Ireland if that would win him the kingship.[1] Again, in 1332, a Clonmel jury alleged that in July 1326 a group of magnates, including the earls of Kildare, Louth, and Ormond, with Brian Ó Briain, had met in Kilkenny and plotted to make Desmond their king.[2] Another Limerick jury of about the same time claimed that under Desmond's kingship Ireland was to be divided, with Munster and Meath going to Desmond himself, while de Burgh would have Connacht, de Bermingham Leinster, and de Mandeville Ulster.[3] Though it is not easy to accept all these details of the plot itself, there is such a wealth of names, places, and dates which fit with annalistic references (though these are scanty), that the substantial veracity of the charge that Desmond was pursuing personal ambition ruthlessly and violently can hardly be gainsaid.

In August 1331, Desmond was compelled to submit by Anthony de Lucy, the justiciar, and he was imprisoned until 1333. In 1335 he took a force to Scotland and in 1339 he was credited with conspicuous success against the MacCarthys and O'Dempseys in Kerry.[4] But when Ralph d'Ufford arrived as justiciar in 1344 he found that the Desmond leopard had not changed his spots. His 'rout' was again on the rampage, especially in Cork and Tipperary, this time in alliance with Mac Carthaigh. Once again he was believed to be involved in a grandiose scheme to make himself king of Ireland. A Tralee jury alleged in 1346 that he had sent letters to all the Gaelic Irish throughout Ireland urging them to rise against the king and his subjects and help to make him king. It was stated further that he had even written to the pope and sent messengers to Avignon in 1344 to argue that Edward III had no right to the lordship of Ireland since he had not observed the laws and customs of that country as Pope Adrian had laid down should be done. Desmond, it was said, offered the pope two thousand marks a year to be his vicar in Ireland. He had too, it was claimed, written to the kings of France and Scotland to form an anti-English alliance.[5]

Early in 1344 Desmond seems to have summoned a meeting of magnates at Callan and arrived there with a considerable body of troops. D'Ufford, in the king's name, banned this 'conventicle', whereupon the magnates 'sent their apologies to Maurice and stayed at home'.[6] In June Desmond was a conspicuous absentee from the Dublin parliament. D'Ufford turned to strong measures. In September and October he seized Desmond's two strongholds of Askeaton and Castle Island and proceeded to drastic action against his supporters. D'Ufford died before he could see the affair to its conclusion. Desmond was allowed to plead his case in England before the king; the Dublin annalist

---

[1] Sayles, 'Legal proceedings', p. 8.

[2] Ibid., p. 6.

[3] Ibid., p. 13.

[4] Clyn, *Annals*, pp 26, 29.

[5] Sayles, 'Legal proceedings', pp 20–21.

[6] *Chartul. St Mary's, Dublin*, ii, 385; Clyn, *Annals*, p. 30. An excellent study of d'Ufford is R. F. Frame, 'The justiciarship of Ralph Ufford: warfare and politics in fourteenth-century Ireland' in *Studia Hib.*, xiii (1973), pp 7–47.

thought he had been victimised by d'Ufford.[1] His case kept him in England until 1350. Duly pardoned, his outlawry annulled, his possessions restored, his term of office as justiciar in 1355–6 marked his final acceptance as fully respectable politically. No doubt it was a consummation that astonished the surviving members of the Munster juries of the 1330s.

All the earls, to a greater or less extent, moved in the two worlds of the Anglo-Irish baronage and of the Irish *capitanei*, and each fashioned for himself a pattern of behaviour he judged appropriate to the circumstances of each milieu. Gerald fitz Maurice, the third earl of Desmond (1359–98), was an example, unusual in the fourteenth century for a man from this level of society, with intimate connections with the Gaelic world. It would not be accurate to say he had become gaelicised, because for over twenty-five years he filled a variety of posts under the crown, including that of justiciar (1367–9). But he was a writer of poetry in Irish, 'a witty and ingenious composer' as an Irish annalist was to describe him in a particularly fulsome obituary.[2] This literary activity obviously involved him in very close personal relations with a variety of Irishmen. It is therefore not altogether a surprise to find in 1388 he had his son fostered with Conchobhar Ó Briain.[3] By this date such fosterage was illegal as a principal cause of 'degeneracy'; but Desmond took the precaution of getting Richard II's permission. Despite being a man very much at home in both cultures, Desmond's political relations were often far from smooth. His career was punctuated with very damaging feuds with his father-in-law, the earl of Ormond,[4] while in 1370 or 1371 he had to be ransomed after being captured near Limerick by Brian Ó Briain.[5] Such vicissitudes were unexceptional events in the lives of Anglo-Irish barons.

The earls topped that class of men whom contemporaries categorised in rather general terms as the *maiores terrae* or *les grantz de la terre*, the great men, the magnates. They were the greater land-owners. These terms, like *pieres de terre* (peers of the land) which was beginning to establish itself in the early 1340s, were used especially in a parliamentary context. If we wish to know who precisely in our period were looked on as the colony's leading figures, the best indication is provided in the lists of those who were called to parliaments and great councils by individual writs of summons. It has been made clear that as yet there was no hard and fast rule defining who was a 'peer', and therefore no legal doctrine of peerage.[6] For this period, it would seem, there was no certain demarcation line between one who came by personal summons and one who came as a representative of the knights, elected in the county court: 'on

[1] He was going to England 'suam iusticiam super iniuriis sibi illatis per dominum Radulphum de Ufford' (*Chartul. St Mary's, Dublin*, ii, 389).

[2] *Ann. Clon.*, p. 319; *A.F.M.*, pp 760–61.

[3] *Rot. pat. Hib.*, p. 139.

[4] References in G.E.C., *Peerage*, iv, 244.

[5] *Ann. Conn.*, pp 337–9.

[6] Richardson & Sayles, *Ir. parl. in middle ages*, pp 119–20.

different occasions a man might serve in either capacity'.[1] This fact, however, important though it is for the history of parliament as an institution, does not materially affect the value of the individual unit of summons as an indicator of who were *les grantz* of the fourteenth century. Lists of those who were summoned personally are not over-numerous for the period as a whole, but they would be an adequate basis for a study of the fluctuating composition of the magnate class. This study, which would be in effect an analysis of the colonial ruling class, cannot be undertaken here. Some illustrative careers, supplementing those of the earls, will however throw some further light on the structure of colonial society and particularly on its tensions.

In 1375 a parliament met in January at Dublin; a complete list of those summoned is extant.[2] Forty-two laymen were summoned individually: the three earls, twenty knights, and nineteen others. A further ten received writs of summons; these were the members of the king's council in Ireland. There were summoned also representatives of shires and towns, but with these latter we are not here concerned, since they did not belong to *les grantz*.

Two of the knights in this category were Robert and Patrick de la Freigne. Neither of them figures in the standard histories of medieval Ireland. They are in fact important men of the second rank, members of one of the oldest families of the colony, which in the fourteenth century had risen steadily in fortune and esteem in the service of the earls of Ormond.[3]

Patrick begins to appear fitfully in the records of the 1340s in a variety of roles: itinerant justice, custodian of lands, commander in the field against Mac Murchadha. He was knighted in 1373 and became seneschal of Kilkenny liberty in 1374. His two brothers Roger and Oliver had both held the post before him, and another brother had been sheriff of Kilkenny. Their father, Fulk, had been sheriff in 1327 and seneschal, for the first time seemingly, in 1331. His father had been seneschal before him in the opening decade of the century. Robert was the son of Oliver and in the 1370s was a leading figure in the earl of Ormond's household. In 1380 he became 'chief seneschal, steward and surveyor' of all the earl's lands and lordships in Ireland.

The Ormond deeds show the family consolidating its position and building up its properties, though these do not seem to have become considerable. Annals of a Kilkenny source, from the pen of the Franciscan John Clyn, show something of what it meant to be the right-hand man of a fourteenth-century Anglo-Irish earl. It was warfare all the way. The keynote is sounded by Clyn in his obituary of Fulk de la Freigne the younger, clearly something of a hero to the friar: 'he was a man devoted to war and the military life from his boyhood'.

---

[1] H. G. Richardson and G. O. Sayles, *Parliament in medieval Ireland* (Dublin Historical Association; Dundalk, 1964), p. 18.

[2] Text in *Ir. parl. in middle ages*, pp 302–5.

[3] Cf. *Knight's fees in Counties Wexford, Carlow, and Kilkenny*, ed. Eric St John Brooks (I.M.C., Dublin, 1950), pp 182–7; *Ormond deeds, 1172–1350* and ibid., *1350–1413, passim*; Clyn, *Annals*, pp 26–30. Cf. Hore, *Wexford town*, vi, 13.

War was just about as much against the Anglo-Irish as against the Gaelic Irish, and there was always the possibility of an overseas expedition for good measure. Clyn's somewhat jejune entries give a glimpse of the hazards of this sort of life.

The elder Fulk was killed in 1320 by William and Sylvester de Marisco and 'other mercenaries [*satellites*] of Edmund Butler' (presumably a relative of the lord in whose service he was). His son Fulk was killed by the Gaelic Irish in 1349; through trusting too much in treacherous promises, said Clyn. This Fulk had been knighted by the earl of Ormond in 1335 during a successful campaign against the O'Byrnes of the Duffry in County Wexford. The following year saw him in action against Ó Mórdha of Leix who had succeeded in rallying considerable forces of the Gaelic Irish of Munster as well as Leinster to his support. Only Mac Giolla Pádraig and Ó Riain held to the Anglo-Irish side, Clyn noted. But if he still had Gaelic Irish friends he had his Anglo-Irish enemies. In 1338 Fulk and his son Oliver were suddenly arrested and imprisoned in Kilkenny castle by Eustace le Poer, then seneschal of Kilkenny. It is likely that this family rivalry was of long standing, and the prize at stake the seneschalship of the liberty. The de la Freignes escaped and lived to fight another day. In 1344, when Fulk was himself seneschal, he expelled the Tobins, for their criminal activities, from their territory of Cumsy in County Tipperary. It is in this year that there occurs a record of his membership of the justiciar's privy council (*secretum consilium*),[1] a sure sign of his status in the colony. In 1346 Clyn records a considerable success against the O'Carrolls, the O'Mores and those Anglo-Irish of Ely O'Carroll (Éile Uí Chearbhaill) who supported them. Fulk served with the earl of Kildare at the siege of Calais in 1347. This was a bad year for the family as both his sons Roger and Oliver died, each after brief spells as seneschals of Kilkenny. The following year, whilst the earl of Ormond remained in England, Fulk had complete charge of his lands. He was still apparently waging war successfully, this time recapturing Nenagh and reducing the Gaelic Irish of the district to their former subjection: 'which everyone had thought impossible', said Clyn. Perhaps it was the Gaelic Irish of these parts who had their revenge in 1349.

That Robert and Patrick de la Freigne were compelled to cope with the same problems of Gaelic and Anglo-Irish disorder as Fulk we may take as certain. Whether they were able to emulate his feats of arms must remain unknown to us, for there was no one in the Kilkenny Franciscan friary who thought fit to note the deeds of the de la Freignes where John Clyn left off. Patrick de la Freigne, like others of his family, continued to act as keeper of the peace (*custos pacis*). This was perhaps the most characteristic Anglo-Irish office in this period, an almost routine duty for earls, magnates, seneschals, and gentry. In England, from the later thirteenth century, the active military function of the office had gradually evolved into a primarily judicial one; the keeper of the

---

[1] Richardson & Sayles, *Ir. parl. in middle ages*, p. 30.

peace was transformed into the justice of the peace. Inevitably in Ireland the essentially military and police aspects of the keeper's role persisted. The *custodes pacis* in Ireland continued throughout the fourteenth century to assess to arms, muster local levies, act as commanders in the field in the incessant march warfare, negotiate truces.[1] On their ability to fulfil their duties efficiently the very survival of the colony came to depend. The last references to Patrick de la Freigne are to his appointments as *custos pacis* and finally, in 1391, as deputy justiciar restricted in operation to County Kilkenny, an enhanced version of the same office.[2]

Men from other parts of the colony were making their way to the top by different routes. Among the ten councillors summoned to parliament in 1375 were two knights, one of whom was Robert Preston. The ascent of this family,[3] relative newcomers to Ireland, lay through trade, the legal profession, and a judicious eye for the advantageous marriage. Robert Preston was of only the second generation of his family in Ireland. His two uncles, merchants of Preston, had settled in Drogheda in the early decades of the fourteenth century, prospered, and begun to acquire land in the vicinity. Their brother Roger, a lawyer, joined them in Drogheda in 1326 and obtained a post as justice of the justiciar's bench. He continued to sit as a judge at different levels of seniority for the next twenty years or so. His son Robert followed in his footsteps and from 1349 to 1377 held a variety of legal posts, including that of chief justice of the common bench. In 1388–9 and again in 1391–2 he was keeper of the great seal,[4] a temporary post until the appointment of a chancellor, who ranked next to the justiciar in the hierarchy of the Dublin administration. In 1353 he had married into one of the colony's leading families, his wife being the daughter and eventual heiress of Walter de Bermingham, lord of Castlecarbury (Kildare) and Kells (Kilkenny) who had been justiciar 1346–9. In 1363, when considerable pressure was being exerted on absentee landlords to meet their responsibilities for defence in Ireland,[5] and some preferred to be rid of the burden, Preston bought the lordship of Gormanston from Amaury St Amand. Robert Preston's son Christopher served with him as his deputy in the chancery in 1388–9 and was probably also a lawyer. He married the daughter and coheiress of one of those summoned to the 1375 parliament, William of London, lord of Naas, another long-established Anglo-Irish family, which, with William's death in 1386,

[1] Cf. R. F. Frame, 'The judicial powers of the medieval Irish keepers of the peace' in *Ir. Jurist*, ii (1967), pp 308–36. The ordinance of Kilkenny (1351) made it obligatory for every county to have four keepers drawn from the 'most substantial of the county' and defined their duties. The law was repromulgated in the statute of Kilkenny (1366) (*Stat. Ire., John—Hen. V*, pp 383–5, 454–5).

[2] *H.B.C.*, p. 152.

[3] *Gormanston reg.*, esp. pp iv–xii; Richardson & Sayles, *Admin. Ire.*, under Preston.

[4] A. J. Otway-Ruthven, 'The medieval Irish chancery' in *Album Helen Maud Cam*, ii (Louvain, 1961), pp 131–2.

[5] Absenteeism in general has now been properly investigated for the first time: Frame, *Eng. lordship*, esp. pp 52–74.

became extinct in the male line, to the profit of the Prestons. Even as the main branch of the family became landlords of substance, Prestons continued to trade as merchants of Drogheda in the fifteenth century.

There was yet another route by which a man might join the ranks of the colonial ruling class: by way of the church. There were seven archbishops of Dublin in the century 1317–1417. All of them served in the administration as treasurers and chancellors. Alexander Bicknor (1317–49) became acting justiciar in the early months of 1341 and Thomas Cranley (1397–1417) for a short time in 1414. Of the ten people who held the office of chancellor in Richard II's reign, only one was a layman. The 1375 summons list records four councillors as being clerics. The two most important were William Tany, prior of the hospital of St John of Jerusalem, Kilmainham, chancellor 1372–7 and 1381–3, justiciar 1373–4; and the then treasurer, John Colton, whose role as archbishop of Armagh in Gaelic Ulster has already been examined.

Priors of Kilmainham were commonly members of the Dublin administration; four of the fourteen chancellors in the fifty years of Edward III's reign were such. Senior officials were inevitably involved in war, which is sufficient explanation of the prominence of the Hospitallers; Kilmainham was one of the bastions of the colony. It is, however, difficult to learn anything very much about these men. For John Colton's career, there is rather more information available.[1]

It had three phases. The first turning-point came in 1361, when he went to Ireland, apparently for the first time, as being papally provided to the treasurership of St Patrick's cathedral, Dublin; and the second in 1381, when he was appointed to the see of Armagh, a position he was to resign shortly before his death in 1404.

The first phase was passed in a world very different from that of Dublin and Armagh. Colton has his own personal niche in the history of the university of Cambridge, where he had incepted in canon law, probably in 1348. In 1349 he became chaplain to William Bateman, bishop of Norwich (1344–55) and an important figure in the development of the university. It was he who founded Trinity Hall as a college for a master and twenty fellows and scholars in canon and civil law. He had too an important part to play in the origins of Gonville and Caius college, for as executor of the will of Edmund Gonville he had by 1353 completed the foundations of Gonville Hall. His chaplain had become its first master in 1349 and presumably had responsibilities for the actual implementation of the founder's and executor's plans. Colton held the mastership until 1360.

Quite why he left the university and in what circumstances he was offered the treasurership of St Patrick's is not known. But his career prospered in

---

[1] Useful summary in A. B. Emden, *A biographical register of the university of Cambridge to 1500* (Cambridge, 1963), pp 150–51. Cf. also W. M. Mason, *The history and antiquities of the collegiate and cathedral church of St Patrick near Dublin. . .* (Dublin, 1820), pp 126–8; Watt, 'John Colton' in Lydon, *Eng. & Ire.*

Ireland, in both the ecclesiastical and civil spheres. Despite the by-now-traditional rivalry of Armagh and Dublin over the primacy, which was very much alive in this period, he became chamberlain to Archbishop Milo Sweetman of Armagh in addition to his Dublin office. In 1373 he became treasurer of the Dublin administration (there is no information about any junior posts at any earlier stage), a post he held for three years. During his tenure of office he saw service in the field. When Robert of Ashton was justiciar (1372–3), Colton was with him on campaign against the O'Mores of Leix and distinguished himself in prompt action against them at Athy, as he was to do again later against the O'Byrnes. The treasury was apparently empty at this time, and when the O'Byrnes turned their attention to Newcastle Mackinegan, Colton sold possessions of his own to raise a force from Dublin which, at any rate temporarily, held the castle there.

In 1374 he became dean of St Patrick's, and in 1380 chancellor of Ireland. He was holding both these offices when Milo Sweetman died in August 1380 and Colton was entrusted with the temporalities of the see. Before that was promulgated, however, the sudden death of Edmund Mortimer, earl of March and king's lieutenant in Ireland, was to bring Colton elevation of a different sort. What ensued in Cork in this emergency[1] is of wider interest than merely as an episode in Colton's career.

Once more it is revealed how those responsible for the government of the colony were forced to shifts and expedients by shortage of money in the treasury. The earl of March had died on 26 December 1381. John Colton and John Keppok, who was chief justice, hurriedly summoned the treasurer (Alexander de Balscot, bishop of Ossory) and the earls of Ormond and Desmond. But before they could get to Cork, the Mortimer family had decided to pull out their troops and return to Meath, leaving Cork and its neighbourhood, the councillors thought, perilously vulnerable to attack by the Barretts and other Anglo-Irish rebels as well as by the Gaelic Irish. There were therefore summoned in addition other magnates and prelates as well as representatives of the counties and cities of Cork and Limerick. This group assembled in the church of St Peter's, Cork, on 9 January 1382.

Both the earls flatly refused to undertake the justiciarship, pleading that to do so would leave their own lordships denuded of protection. It was then agreed, on the prompting of Gerald Barry, bishop of Cork, that an experienced English knight was better suited for the position than anyone of the colony. It was suggested that the post be offered to Lord Thomas Mortimer, both on account of his personal worth and because it was thought that the retinue of the deceased would rather serve under him than under anyone else's command. Some sort of approach must already have been made to him for Bishop Gerald revealed that Mortimer would only serve as justiciar if the retinue of which he had drawn up a schedule was to be chargeable on the Irish exchequer. The

---

[1] The source has been published by Richardson & Sayles, *Parl. & councils med. Ire.*, i, 115–20.

treasurer's reaction to that condition was to say that there was not at the present time, nor had there been at any time during his period of office, money for any expenses beyond those of existing commitments. It was then suggested that those present and the communities there represented should undertake the charge of Mortimer's retinue, just for a year or even only part of a year. The assembly declined to accept the responsibility, considering that the whole colony should bear the burden. Since it would take time to arrange this, and delay was dangerous, the council turned back to Ormond and Desmond, who again refused. Then the treasurer was proposed for the vacant office, but he pleaded physical incapacity and suggested Colton. When he too declined, he and the treasurer fell into prolonged altercations. The *impasse* was broken when the other members of the council proposed that the assembly should choose between them. It was concluded that Colton's excuses were less cogent than de Balscot's. Colton accepted, on condition that the two earls and all there assembled should provide him with maximum help, that he might give up the office at the next parliament and that the treasurer sound out Thomas Mortimer about the possibility of keeping his retinue available until that parliament. On these terms, Colton held office until March 1382. He was already archbishop-elect of Armagh but was not consecrated until the following year.

More lay behind Ormond's adamant refusal of the justiciarship than fear for the security of his own lordship if he were to take on wider responsibilities. He had already had experience of the financial difficulties that the poverty of the administration in Ireland and the parsimony of the government in England could bring to a justiciar. In 1379 he was still trying to collect the fee for his term of office which had begun in October 1376. He had also to recover the sums he had disbursed from his own resources to finance war against the Gaelic Irish, most notably a sum of £550 necessary to raise a force to combat a particularly serious threat from Mac Murchadha. It was finally agreed in the English exchequer that 1,000 marks was the sum owed to Ormond. The method of payment chosen reveals the shifts and expedients of government finance in this period. Half the sum was to be found in Ireland: 200 marks a year for two years from the fee-farm payable to the crown from the city of Dublin; another twenty-five marks from the farm at Waterford; and the remaining twenty-five from the fee paid on the weirs of Limerick. If payment should fail in Ireland, a most likely contingency, the deficiency was to be made up in the English exchequer. The other half of the debt was to come from England: two hundred marks direct payment and the remaining three hundred from the dues payable on wool and hides in the port of Chester (some of which, perhaps most, would be levied on Irish trade).[1] Such

---

[1] *Ormond deeds, 1350—1413*, pp 158–66; *Cal. pat. rolls, 1377–81*, p. 382. In 1393 the earl of Desmond was not able to get from the mayor and bailiffs of Cork the twenty pounds of the farm of the city which he had been promised as part of what he was owed for service in the king's wars (*Proc. king's council, Ire., 1392—3*, pp 126–8).

makeshift and lengthy arrangements would hardly enhance the appeal of the office of justiciar to an Anglo-Irish magnate.

It is appropriate to conclude this all-too-impressionistic picture of the Anglo-Irish ruling class in this period with a glance at the men who by definition headed it, the chief governors, or justiciars as was the commonest of the various titles given to them. The justiciar was the king's *alter ego*: 'he was at one and the same time the military chief of the colony, the head of its civil administration and its supreme judge'.[1] Something will be said later of the sort of policies these officials were required to implement. Here our concern is with the men themselves and the extent to which their connections with Ireland were permanent or merely phases in careers of royal service.

Justiciars came and went with some celerity.[2] Too much celerity, all too often, as two examples indicate: in 1346 and again in 1357 four different men held the office in the course of a year. From 1324 to 1379 there were thirty chief governors. Ten of these, whose periods of office totalled in all about fourteen years, were Anglo-Irish. As has already been seen, eight of them were earls. One, Walter de Bermingham, was of the magnate class. The other, John Keppok, listed among the council members of the 1375 parliamentary summons list, was of a well-established County Louth family. Like his colleague Robert Preston, he had climbed the promotion ladder of the colonial administration on the judiciary side and from the late 1350s to the 1380s was rarely without a post, though shortage of extant documentation leaves him a somewhat anonymous figure. Six of the thirty chief governors were prelates: three priors of Kilmainham, one bishop of Hereford, one bishop of Limerick (who was Anglo-Irish), and one archbishop of Dublin. In the colony's earlier days, churchmen had often brought with them to Ireland a flock of relatives and followers who settled in the country. The William of London, mentioned above, was of the family whose origins go back to the appointment of Henry of London as archbishop of Dublin in 1213 and who had served as justiciar in 1213–15 and 1221–4. Such immigration in the wake of the higher clergy seems to have virtually disappeared in the fourteenth century. In fact, though officials on lower levels continued to marry and settle in Ireland, the senior officials and justiciars were apparently not interested in building the family fortune in Ireland. There was one notable and interesting exception to demonstrate that it could still be done.

John Darcy,[3] of a modest Lincolnshire family, was in the service of Aymer de Valence, earl of Pembroke and absentee lord of Wexford, continuously from 1307 to 1323. As a retainer of that loyal servant of Edward II, his passage into royal service was not difficult and from 1317 he held a number of posts under

[1] Otway-Ruthven, *Med. Ire.*, p. 145.
[2] Names and dates below, ix, 469–85.
[3] R. F. D'Arcy, *The life of John, first Baron Darcy of Knowyth* (London, 1933); and, for his service with Pembroke, J. R. S. Phillips, *Aymer de Valence, earl of Pembroke 1307–24: baronial politics in the reign of Edward II* (Oxford, 1972), pp 203, 229–31, 268, 310.

the crown. In 1323, with some years of experience in the military and diplomatic activity of the Scots war behind him, he was appointed justiciar in Ireland. He was to become the century's longest serving justiciar, holding the office for some thirteen years in the twenty-year period 1324–44. For considerable stretches of the later years of his tenure, however, he was an absentee and a deputy served in his place. In 1337–*c*.1340 he was steward of Edward III's household[1] and even after March 1341, when the king appointed him justiciar for life, he was retained in England. In 1341, and again in 1342, the king explained that a deputy continued to be needed as he could not dispense with Darcy's presence at his side.

Despite his absences, however, he established a dynasty in Ireland, with estates chiefly in County Meath, which was connected with the colony's leading families. For in 1329 he married Joan de Burgh, daughter of the Red Earl, who was the widow of the second earl of Kildare. The daughter of this marriage was to marry the second earl of Ormond.

Some of the distinctive features of Anglo-Ireland have begun to emerge from this summary attempt at an anatomy of the colonial ruling class through a cross-section of it. To reveal more of the conditions of life in the colony and the attitudes of the colonists, it is now necessary to examine that state of chronic insecurity which became so characteristic of the colonial world in this period.

THAT the colony was under considerable pressure during this period is an impression conveyed by many different types of source. The Irish Annals particularise, though often rather obscurely, the local gains of numerous Irish chiefs. Anglo-Irish Annals, in somewhat random manner, record the shrinkage of Anglo-Irish territory in a catalogue of Gaelic Irish successes. Thus Clyn noted the spectacular success of Laoighseach Ó Mórdha (d. 1342) who in one evening burnt eight English castles, recovered the lordship of Leix and 'from a serf became a lord, from a subject became a prince' (*de servo dominus, de subiecto princeps effectus*).[2] Inquisitions *post mortem* of Anglo-Irish estates, though they are not numerous, reveal a melancholy state of wastage of lands due to Gaelic Irish attacks. One type of source supplies a more consistent picture over a longer period. We would expect any serious contraction of the power of the crown in Ireland to be reflected in the revenue for which the treasurers of the Dublin administration accounted, and which was recorded on the receipt rolls. Calculations are fraught with methodological hazards, but meaningful comparisons can be made in order to estimate trends. Thus, the average annual revenue in the period 1278–99 was £6,300. For the period 1368–84 it had fallen to £2,512.[3] The sums are pitifully small in themselves; there had been a serious

---

[1] *H.B.C.*, p. 75.

[2] Clyn, *Annals*, p. 30.

[3] H. G. Richardson and G. O. Sayles, 'Irish revenue, 1278–1384' in *R.I.A. Proc.*, lxii (1962), sect. C, pp 93, 100.

decline, and the downward trend was to continue. Definitive conclusions from the financial evidence must await that detailed study of the Irish exchequer which is the outstanding desideratum of colonial institutional history. But there is no difficulty in accepting the judgement of Richardson and Sayles that the burden on the English treasury for Ireland became increasingly serious in the later fourteenth century until in the fifteenth 'the incapacity of the English government to find ready money reduced any subvention from this source to vanishing point'.[1] This had dire consequences for the defence of the colony.

The type of evidence, however, that makes the most immediate impact on the reader of the sources is that of the colonists' own protestations about their worsening position. A steady and vehement tide of complaint flowed out of Ireland to the king's court in England. In 1341,[2] for example, the 'prelates, earls, barons, and commonalty of Ireland' assured Edward III that 'the third part and more of your land of Ireland which was conquered in the time of your progenitors is now come into the hand of your Irish enemies and your English lieges are so impoverished that they can hardly live'. In 1360[3] messengers were sent from a Kilkenny great council to spell out to the king why his land of Ireland was 'en poynt d'estre perdu' and succeeded in persuading him that this was so. Exceptional measures were taken and Lionel, the king's son, was despatched to mount a relief campaign and reform the administration. His three years and six months of chief governorship (1361–4, 1365–6), and all the emergency steps taken, make it the more significant that in 1368 a Dublin parliament assured the king that his lordship was for the most part ruined and destroyed.[4] Very much the same thing happened again before the end of the century. Despite the crisis remedies of Richard's two expeditions (1394–5 and 1399), the Irish council had to report in 1399 that 'la terre est en peril de final destruccion'.[5] There can be no doubt at all that the colonists felt themselves to be under heavy pressure and persuaded the crown that this was so.

The towns were the main centres of English population, the administrative foci and economic backbone of Anglo-Ireland. Before examining their particular complaints and the impact of the recoil of English power on them, some general observations about the towns are in order. Constitutionally, like all other colonial institutions, they followed English models, as examination of the charters and custumals of the Irish towns speedily makes clear.[6] This was a period when towns were updating their charters, and it is possible to detect the introduction of a certain degree of standardisation where previously there had

[1] *Admin. Ire.*, p. 57. For a revealing instance of an attempt to improve the Irish revenue, see Frame, *Eng. lordship*, pp 301–9.
[2] *Stat. Ire., John–Henry V*, pp 332–63; *Cal. close rolls, 1341–3*, pp 509–16.
[3] Richardson & Sayles, *Parl. & councils med. Ire.*, i, 19–22.
[4] *Cal. close rolls, 1364–68*, pp 499–500.
[5] *Proc. king's council, Ire., 1392–3*, pp 261–9.
[6] Charters and custumals are now conveniently assembled in volume i of Mac Niocaill, *Na buirgéisi*.

been significant differences in the privileges conferred on individual towns. It is perhaps also possible to detect in these changes the origins of that position which occasioned comment in Tudor times: that Irish towns enjoyed greater liberties under their charters than did English towns.

Politically, too, the towns were enhancing their status. In the earlier part of the century they could unite to make collective representations to the justiciar and to the king and council in England. They were prominent, as will be seen, in 1341 in the course of the first major confrontation between Anglo-Ireland and the crown. The regular presence of town representatives in parliament seems well established by the 1370s, though they were frequently present before that.[1] The principle that the commons, of which the towns were of course a part, must be present for a grant of parliamentary taxation was first put forward in 1371 by the Anglo-Irish magnates. They had a vested interest in establishing such a principle; but it seems to have been accepted by the justiciar and king. The commons themselves seem to have considered that they had the right to refuse a royal request for subsidy.[2] The towns which had emerged by the 1370s as being of parliamentary status were Athenry, Cork, Drogheda, Dublin, Galway, Kilkenny, Limerick, New Ross, Waterford, Wexford, and Youghal.

Economically, trade was the life-blood of the towns. Information for this period continues to be sparse, but some general features of at least some of the overseas trade emerges. There was a busy short-range trade between a multiplicity of small ports from Carrickfergus to Limerick and the numerous ports, large and small, ranging from Preston to Bristol, with the ports of the Dee, Mersey, and Severn estuaries especially favoured. There was in addition a significant longer-distance trade: in cloth with Hanse merchants trading through London, in wine from Gascony, in hides and woolfells with Flanders. Information is most plentiful from Chester and Bristol,[3] where extant customs accounts supply details of the provenance of merchants and ships and of the precise nature of the merchandise. To Chester, the leading north-western port for the Irish trade until it began to lose ground to Liverpool in the next century, came especially merchants from Drogheda, Dublin, Malahide, and Rush carrying the typical products of an agricultural economy. Hides and skins were particularly important, sustaining the flourishing Chester leather industry and its glove-making speciality. Hides and fish were Ireland's main contribution to the trade of Bristol and other ports in the Bristol Channel, with merchants of Kinsale, Waterford, Cork, Youghal, and Wexford predominating.

Socially, no doubt, this trade gave ample opportunity for self-betterment, though our knowledge of the Irish merchant families in this period is most

[1] Commons participation is analysed by Richardson & Sayles, *Ir. parl. in middle ages*, pp 75–8.

[2] J. F. Lydon, 'William of Windsor and the Irish parliament' in *E.H.R.*, lxxx (1965), pp 257–8, 259.

[3] J. P. Bethell, 'The Dee estuary: an historical geography of its use as a port' (M.Sc. thesis, University of Wales, 1952); *Chester customs accounts, 1301—1566*, ed. K. P. Wilson (The Record Society of Lancashire and Cheshire, cxi, 1969); Carus-Wilson, *Overseas trade of Bristol*.

disappointingly meagre. Much was possible by way of rising in the social scale in the Irish towns, as the spectacular change in the fortunes of John Husee, a butcher of Athenry, testifies. William Burke and the de Berminghams had won an outstanding victory against the Irish just outside the town in 1316.[1] Husee was asked by the lord of Athenry to look for Tadg Ó Cellaig, king of Uí Maine, among the slain. Suddenly Ó Cellaig himself emerged from the shadows, calling Husee to join him and promising that he would become a great lord among the Gaelic Irish. Husee refused, in his turn calling on Ó Cellaig to surrender. But his servant urged him to comply to save themselves because the Gaelic Irish were the stronger. Whereupon Husee slew first his own servant and then Ó Cellaig and the king's bodyguard and bore off their three heads to his lord. Richard de Bermingham rewarded him with ample lands and made him a knight, 'as he well deserved', observed the annalist.[2] Not all the success stories of townsmen were so dramatic. Trade, the professions, royal service, steady acquisition of properties, sensible marriages were the normal pattern of advancement, as has been seen in the case of the Prestons of Drogheda. Another typical burgess/minor-landowner ascent is that of the Dowdalls of Dundalk and related families such as the Plunkets of County Louth.[3] We know of these families in detail through the chance survival of the Gormanston register and the Dowdall deeds, but we can be sure that their stories could be paralleled in all the main towns of the colony.

On the whole, however, the story of the towns in this period is not that of success; for they were the first to suffer from the various 'routs' whether led by Anglo-Irish barons or Irish chiefs. These became increasingly difficult to withstand in this period, especially in south Leinster and Munster. It has been seen already how Clonmel and other towns in County Tipperary paid protection money to the first earl of Desmond. It became common practice for similar sums to be paid to Irish chiefs. Symptomatic of the deteriorating security situation in Leinster and Munster was the royal instruction, issued in 1345, that the exchequer and common bench should be removed from Dublin because of its remoteness and the difficulty of access to it from the south.[4] No move was apparently made at this time, but Carlow became the alternative administrative centre in 1361 and remained so for some two decades. Yet it was hardly a change for the better. In 1349 the citizens of Carlow had protested that frequent Gaelic Irish invasions threatened their town with total destruction and that they were ready to pull out altogether. Carlow was always especially vulnerable to attack from the Mac Murroughs and O'Mores. In 1373–4 their complaints were the same: 'Irish enemies' had destroyed the countryside right up to the city walls and had killed many townsmen, and the final destruction of the city itself seemed imminent.[5]

[1] *Ann. Conn.*, pp 245–7.   [2] *Chartul. St Mary's, Dublin*, ii, 351.
[3] *Dowdall deeds*, ed. Charles McNeill and A. J. Otway-Ruthven (I.M.C., Dublin, 1960), a mine of information on fourteenth-century Dundalk.
[4] *Cal. close rolls, 1343–6*, p. 672.   [5] Hore, *Wexford town*, i, 190, 200; v, 119.

It is to be remarked that when towns protested their poverty and destruction they were looking for some financial concession from the crown: exemption from fines inflicted by a justiciar, restraint on some rival town, waiving of arrears of fee-farms, overseas trading privileges, and so on. Nevertheless, even allowing that it was to the towns' interest to paint as black a picture as possible, town petitions in the period from the 1340s to the end of the century are substantial evidence of how vulnerable some of the major cities had become. In March 1375, for example, the citizens of Waterford, looking for financial relief from the king, stated that recently the king's enemies (Gaelic Irish? Anglo-Irish? it is symptomatic of the state of the country that it could be either or both) had killed their mayor, bailiff, sheriff and coroner, and twenty-six others of the leading men of the city. Eighty merchants of Coventry, Dartmouth, and Bristol had also lost their lives, and six weeks later another twenty-four leading citizens were also killed. It was stated in a rather touching protestation of loyalty that 'if all the king's land of Ireland were gained by his enemies it could be better regained by means of their city, which only contains seven acres of land within the walls, like a little castle, than by any other city in Ireland'.[1] Again, in July 1388 the citizens of Cork, petitioning for dispensation from four years' arrears of farm, pleaded their 'almost complete destruction by frequent invasions of Irish rebels, the burning of the suburbs of the city, the capture in war and impoverishment of many citizens loyal to the royal house and the withdrawal of many to other places of abode . . .'.[2] New Ross carried a double burden. Its commercial existence was threatened with extinction by the enmity of Waterford, and its physical existence by the attacks of the Gaelic Irish, despite the citizens paying an annual sum of ten marks to Art Mac Murchadha 'for their defence'.[3] But despite their perils, these towns had resilience. Limerick, as has been seen, suffered badly earlier in the century from Desmond and his Ó Briain ally. In 1369 it was burnt by another Ó Briain, and a Mac Con Mara took control of the town.[4] But though always living precariously on the 'frontiers of the king's Irish enemies' with all the dangers that involved, it continued to trade with the Gaelic Irish and in English and continental ports.[5]

The petitions of towns form one important type of evidence for the colonists' own view of their predicament. Another and similar source is the complaints and reports formulated by the Irish privy council or parliaments and great councils and sent to the king and council in England. These came from a wider section of Anglo-Irish society, sometimes indeed from what was coming to be called the whole community of Ireland, and are more comprehensive in their coverage. In sum, they tell what the colonial community and officialdom thought was wrong with the state of the *terre Engleis* and what should be done

[1] *Cal. pat. rolls, 1374—7*, p. 145.
[2] *Cal. pat. rolls, 1385—9*, p. 495.
[3] Hore, *Wexford town*, i, 208, 210, 213–17.
[4] *Ann. Conn.*, p. 339.
[5] *Cal. pat. rolls, 1388—92*, p. 496.

about it. They provide therefore at once another angle of approach to the nature of fourteenth-century colonial society, an introduction to the relationship of colony and mother country, and essential background to a study of the policies adopted by the crown towards Ireland in this period.

It was in 1341 that there was the first major formulation of colonial grievances on a general scale, and the circumstances in which they were drawn up are of considerable interest and importance for the understanding of the colonial mind. The Dublin annalist, who, in the silence of John Clyn on this whole episode, is our only source for contemporary opinion, considered that at this time 'the land of Ireland stood on the point of being lost from the hands of the king of England' and that 'at no previous time had there been such a remarkable and overt division between the English born in England and the English born in Ireland'.[1] The cause of the crisis was Edward III's instruction in July 1341, in the wake of his far-reaching shake-up of his administration in England, that there should be a general resumption of all grants made in Ireland during the reign of Edward II. This was followed by an order that all officials with personal and property connections in Ireland should be replaced by Englishmen with lands and benefices in England. The king and council, it was stated baldly, considered that such men would serve the crown better.[2] The colonists were outraged at what was both a slight on the loyalty on which they prided themselves and an encouragement of precisely the sort of exploiting, grabbing official they most resented. Their anger burst out in a parliament of October 1341. The Dublin annalist makes it clear that initially it was the townsmen, *maiores civitatum regium* ('mayors of royal cities' or possibly simply 'the leading men of royal cities'), who took the initiative. The justiciar and his ministers were excluded from the discussions, decisions were taken, and the parliament adjourned to Kilkenny the next month. The justiciar and his ministers absented themselves from this assembly. The annalist recorded the discussion and decision to make representations to the king in general terms only: there was a denunciation of justiciars who in a land of war knew nothing of warfare, and of English officials who came to Ireland merely to line their own pockets. The precise nature of the petition sent to the king in the name of the 'prelates, earls, barons and the commonalty of the land of Ireland' is known from other sources. The twenty-seven articles came back from the king and council with individual and generally sympathetic replies to each specific article. There was a covering letter asking for a 'band of our good men of Ireland' to join the king's projected expedition to France, and the obnoxious instructions about grants and the qualifications of officials were quietly dropped.

[1] *Chartul. St Mary's, Dublin*, ii, 383–4.
[2] *Cal. pat. rolls, 1340–43*, p. 207 (March, 1341); *Cal. fine rolls, 1337–47*, p. 234 (24 July 1341); *Cal. close rolls, 1341–3*, pp 184–5 (27 July 1341). See Frame, *Eng. lordship*, pp 242–61, the first thorough investigation of the Irish dimension of the crisis of 1341–2, and his 'English policies and Anglo-Irish attitudes in the crisis of 1341–2' in Lydon, *Eng. & Ire.*, pp 86–103.

Essentially the petition was a declaration of the colonists' loyalty to the crown and a detailed criticism of those

who are sent out of England to govern them, who themselves have little knowledge of your land of Ireland and have little or nothing at their coming there by which they can live and maintain their position until they are supported by extortion under colour of their offices, to the great destruction of your people.[1]

The clauses of complaint were therefore about ministerial fees, administrative procedures, the rectification of mismanagement in all branches of government and defence. The custody and maintenance of royal castles received special notice, for obvious defensive reasons. The Gaelic Irish, while not featuring prominently, were not ignored. It is the awareness of their insistent presence that made governmental corruption and inefficiency a more serious matter than their actual attacks themselves:

Likewise, sire, although there is in every march of your land of Ireland enough and more of the Irish enemies to trouble your English people who have no power to stop them, save the grace of God which maintains them, sire, still more do the extortions and oppressions of your ministers trouble them than does war with the Irish.[2]

It is merely confusing to label the Kilkenny assembly of November 1341 a 'patriot parliament'. The historical labels of modern periods are rarely appropriate for very different medieval contexts. It is even more confusing to associate the first earl of Desmond with its leadership, even if we ignore for the moment the dubious credentials of his patriotism, for the sources give no justification for dubbing it 'Desmond's parliament'.[3] But in rejecting these descriptions we should not fail to observe the significance of the Anglo-Irish reaction. There was here a distinct manifestation of the colonial mind which reflects its self-identity, though, despite the annalist's words, separatism was not mooted as a serious practical course of action.

In 1376 the colonists were again to dig in their heels, when they considered that the crown was pushing them beyond acceptable limits. The crisis came at the end of the five troubled years of William of Windsor's chief governorship (1369–72 and 1374–6).[4] During this period Windsor had put the colonists under unprecedented pressure to vote subsidies for the financing of his military needs in Ireland. He summoned seven parliaments and five great councils during this time, in all of which request for subsidy was the main business. The colonists alleged that he did not scruple to use coercion to achieve his ends, sometimes by imprisoning representatives and once by the rather more subtle method of summoning parliament to a remote, tumble-down village, Ballydoyle, near Cashel,[5]

---

[1] *Stat. Ire., John—Hen. V*, pp 344–5.   [2] Ibid., pp 360–61.
[3] As does Curtis, *Med. Ire.*, p. 215.
[4] M. V. Clarke, 'William of Windsor in Ireland, 1369–76' in *Fourteenth-century studies* (Oxford, 1937), pp 146–241; Richardson & Sayles, *Ir. parl. in middle ages*, pp 83–5; Lydon, art. cit.
[5] R. E. Glasscock has published an aerial photograph of the site ('Deserted medieval settlements', plate 31).

in order that sheer lack of amenities would hasten a decision favourable to him. Attempts to levy subsidies thus declared illegal were resisted, and the colonists were able to have the whole conduct of Windsor's administration investigated in London. Cleared and reappointed in 1373, he pursued the same financial policy, with similar reactions from the aggrieved colonists. At length, when, in 1375, parliament actually refused to vote a subsidy, the government was ready for just such an eventuality. Nicholas Dagworth, the king's special commissioner acting in place of Windsor, produced a royal mandate that sixty representatives of counties, towns, and dioceses should present themselves before king and council in England, there to give consent to taxation. The representatives were able to present a common front to this unprecedented development. They claimed that according to the 'liberties, privileges, rights, laws, and customs of the land of Ireland' they were under no obligation to go to England. However, because of their reverence for the king and the gravity of the situation in Ireland they agreed to go. But in most cases the communities refused to give their representatives full power to bind them to such decisions as would be taken in London. This was done so as to leave them free to refuse any grant of taxation accepted by their representatives in England, if circumstances should warrant such a course of action. In the event this issue was not to arise. But again the colonists had made a corporate stand against the king. There is much to be said for Miss Clarke's judgement that 'the episode is important as the first struggle between the home government and the Anglo-Irish which can be properly called both political and constitutional',[1] for the 1341 episode was essentially political, without the basic constitutional implications that consent to taxation raised.

In the history of the fourteenth-century colony, however, these brushes between the colonists and their English rulers, revealing though they are of certain attitudes, are of secondary importance. The real problem was how to stem the Gaelic Irish advance, and for this the colonists were only too aware of how dependent they were on receiving help from England. They were no longer able to defend themselves from their own resources, and they knew it. Those assembled in Kilkenny in 1341 assured the king that 'your English people have no power to stop the Irish'. A great council held in Kilkenny in July 1360 gave renewed expression to the same fundamental belief. The earl of Ormond (who was justiciar), the Irish council, prelates, peers, and commons told the king that the Gaelic Irish throughout the whole English land, united among themselves 'd'un assent et covyn', had seized the initiative and would soon empty the land of the Anglo-Irish unless relief and succour were sent quickly from England. Seeing the loss and destruction of lives and possessions, they asked the king 'as a work of charity' to fulfil his princely duty to his subjects and command quickly that there be sent to them from England 'a good well endowed leader, well stocked and fortified with men and treasure'. The

---

[1] Clarke, 'William of Windsor in Ireland', p. 172.

colonists again complained of the oppressions and maladministration of the king's ministers and an empty treasury which, with the effects of plague and the failure of absentee landholders to provide for defence, had made them incapable of adequate self-defence.

It was the common assumption of all colonial pleas for help from England that it was English neglect and exploitation that was responsible for the lamentable insecurity of English Ireland. There was some justice in the claim. The first duty of a king to his subjects was that of providing adequate protection, and this was rarely forthcoming. As has been well observed,

Regarded by the English kings as a source of profit and then as an embarrassment which could neither be surmounted nor relinquished, the country was denied the resources which alone could ensure effective and stable government. The overweening ambition of Edward I was the primary cause of the decline from the promise of the thirteenth century; and Edward I had for successors like-minded kings in Edward III and Henry V.[1]

On the other hand, not very long after the failure of William of Windsor to make the colony pay what the home government thought was the going rate for its own defence, the colonists themselves were taxed with their own shortcomings. In 1378 Richard II's regency government protested about the factions and divisions among the colonists 'and the absence of mutual goodwill and of any effort to provide in common for the safety of the state against the common enemy'.[2] There was some justice in this charge, too. The career of the first earl of Desmond was not different in kind from that of all too many Anglo-Irish magnates and gentry.[3] Professor Otway-Ruthven is undoubtedly right in emphasising that 'one of the major factors weakening the colony from the early fourteenth century was certainly the constant state of warfare among themselves into which certain of the settlers had fallen'.[4]

These views are not mutually exclusive. We will, however, be in a better position to appreciate the various factors contributing to the weakening of the colony after an examination of the practical measures with which Edward III and Richard II sought to halt the Gaelic revival.

By the beginning of our period the relationship of the crown to the colony in Ireland was based on three principles which were present in embryo in Henry II's time and had become axioms in the course of the thirteenth century. In the first place, it was expected that the colony should be at once self-sufficient financially and able to defend itself from its own resources and yet be a source

---

[1] Richardson & Sayles, *Admin. Ire.*, pp 68–9.

[2] *Cal. pat. rolls, 1377—81*, p. 271.

[3] Our period ends with another Desmond causing serious unrest: 'Mac Murchadha is at open war, and he has now gone to Desmond to help the earl of Desmond destroy the earl of Ormond, if they can, and to return afterwards with all the power they can raise in Munster in order to destroy the country.' This is from a report of the chief governor in 1399 (*Proc. king's council, Ire., 1392—3*, p. 262).

[4] *Med. Ire.*, p. 271.

of men, supplies, and revenue to the crown for its needs outside Ireland. As has been seen earlier in this volume, Edward I especially had taken full advantage of the relative wealth of the colony for his wars in Wales and Scotland. A second expectation was that the structures of government, the law and legal system, the relationship of church and state would be the same in Anglo-Ireland as in England itself.[1] The principle had been fully implemented in thirteenth-century practice, and the colony was well integrated with the English governmental system. This position led directly to the third basic principle governing the relations of this 'little England' to its mother country. The latter exercised a considerable degree of supervision over colonial affairs. This control manifested itself in many of the routine procedures of government.[2] It was the king and his council in England who appointed and dismissed justiciars and the senior officials of the Dublin administration. It seems likely that in our period, though the evidence comes from only one document, a justiciar might sometimes discuss or even bargain with the council about his policies and as to who his chief officials should be.[3] But, essentially, personnel and policy were for the crown. Colonial officials were of course empowered to act in the king's name and provide for the good government of the king's subjects; but they had a special responsibility for the well-being of the king's revenue. From c. 1285, the treasurer of Ireland was required to make periodical account at Westminster for his receipts and expenditure. Such routine scrutiny of the focal point of the administration, involving close supervision of its honesty and efficiency as a whole, led readily on occasions into investigations into the conduct of officials. A third dimension of control lay in the dispensation of justice. The English kings, borrowing a phrase long established in the usage of the papal chancery, could describe themselves as 'debtors of justice' to their subjects in Ireland.[4] With the colony subject to English common law and to royal legislation, both general and that which had been specifically framed for it, it was entirely logical that the court of the English king exercised an appellate jurisdiction over the whole of the colonial judicial system, from the justiciar's own court downwards. Sometimes, though by no means always, these appeals would be heard in parliament. But parliament was something more than a mere law court and was concerned also with requests and complaints of a non-judicial nature. Edward I, as Richardson and Sayles have made clear, consciously promoted the role of his parliament as a central court (judicially and extrajudicially) for all his dominions.[5] The development of procedure by petition, a vehicle for the presentation of a host of issues great and small of both individual and collective relevance, brought much Irish business to England in the later years of the thirteenth century.

[1] Hand, *Eng. law in Ire.*; Watt, *Ch. & two nations*.

[2] Richardson & Sayles, *Ir. parl. in middle ages*, pp 244–68.

[3] J. F. Baldwin, *The king's council in England during the middle ages* (Oxford, 1913), pp 473–5, with reference to John Darcy (Aug. 1328).

[4] Cf. *Stat. Ire., John—Hen. V*, p. 406.   [5] *Ir. parl. in middle ages*, pp 246–7.

None of the axioms of the relationship was abandoned in the course of the fourteenth century. But, inevitably, their actual implementation was modified with changing circumstances. Enough has been said already to make it apparent that the financial situation had changed very markedly. From being a source of revenue at the beginning of the century, from the 1360s Ireland became a charge on the English exchequer.[1] After some real but ineffective attempts to halt that trend, the English government became less and less inclined to devote scarce resources to the defence of the colony. It was a matter of priorities. Just occasionally, for a year at the beginning of Edward III's personal reign, in Lionel's period of Ireland in the 1360s and again when Richard II made his two expeditions, Ireland was promoted in the order of government priorities. Generally it ran a bad third to France and Scotland. Thus began a vicious circle. Because there was little or no money to meet the real needs of the government in Ireland, the numbers and quality of administrators declined sharply and an inadequate administration was increasingly unable to restore the diminishing revenue. In 1345 the justiciar and his council sent the king a damning indictment of the staffing and efficiency of the Irish exchequer and chancery.[2] It is clear that nothing happened in the next fifty years to remedy this permanently. A similar critique of 1399 was to report very much the same state of affairs, especially in the exchequer.[3] Service in the Irish administration had ceased to offer attractive careers, and the reluctance, and even outright refusal, of prominent men to serve as chief governors was apparently paralleled on the lower levels of officialdom. The 'default of good government' of which the colonists perennially complained was essentially 'default of officers'. Nevertheless, accountability of ministers for their conduct in office did not disappear, as the prolonged investigations into William of Windsor and his officials illustrates, and it remained a live, if not very frequently implemented, principle of English supervision of the Irish administration.

For a certain time, Edward III continued the policy of looking to Ireland for troops for his wars; there were Gaelic Irish and Anglo-Irish in Scotland in 1335 and a force from Ireland at the siege of Calais in 1346. Thereafter the government seems to have appreciated the danger to Ireland if magnates left the country,[4] and there seems to have been no significant Irish contribution to English armies in the second half of the century. The presence of Irish troops at the siege of Rouen in 1419, however, shows that English kings had not entirely lost the ability to exploit Irish manpower in the hundred years war.

[1] The *nature* of the charge has been well analysed by Philomena Connolly, 'The financing of the English expeditions to Ireland, 1361–1376' in Lydon, *Eng. &Ire.*, pp 104–21. Her particular conclusion is very revealing of the general trend: 'Between 1361 and 1376 a total of £91,035 was spent on army wages in Ireland, of which £71,572 came from the English exchequer, £16,398 from Ireland and the remaining £3,065 was provided out of their own resources by Windsor and Ashton [the lieutenants]' (ibid., p. 117).

[2] *Proc. king's council, Ire., 1392–3*, pp 314–22.

[3] Ibid., pp 261–9.

[4] *Cal. close rolls, 1349–54*, pp 587–8.

Anglo-Ireland in the fourteenth century continued to be governed by the laws and customs of England in the usual way. From time to time, it was necessary to remind administrators of details that should be observed: that, for example 'by the law and custom of England no pleas ought to be held before the barons of the exchequer except those which touch the king and his ministers and their servants', or that common pleas should not be pleaded in the exchequer.[1] But this was a superficial matter by comparison with a development that began to attract attention in this period. It was first ventilated in the petition addressed by the mayors, bailiffs, and communities of the cities of Ireland to the justiciar and to the king and his council:

Since the conquest there has been two sorts of people in Ireland, the English and the Irish, and there are still, and three types of law have been used among them, each of which conflicts with the other: common law, Irish law, and marcher law. It seems to us that where there is diversity of law the people cannot be of one law or one community.[2]

The townsmen had the unity of the colony in mind and the use of the three laws by the colonists. It was in this sense at least that eventually, in 1351, an Irish great council legislated against this mixed law usage and the weakening of the principle of the primacy of common law:

It is commanded that if dispute arises between English and English of the peace, neither party should distrain or take pledge or distress on the other nor take vengeance on the other whereby the king's people might be troubled; they must sue one against the other at common law. And because before this time in such disputes between English and English it has been the practice to use the law of the march and the brehon law, which is not law and ought not to be called law, and not by the law of the land, it is agreed that neither march nor brehon law be used between English and English but that they be ruled by the common law.[3]

In 1360 this practice was again condemned,[4] while in 1366 the 1351 instruction was reiterated as clause 4 of the statute of Kilkenny[5] as one of a number of measures to eradicate the 'degeneracy' of some of the colonists. It has been seen at an earlier stage that Anglo-Irish magnates and Irish kings were in the habit of adopting a mutually convenient blend of common, march, and brehon law. This is not the practice being condemned in this legislation, which applied specifically to legal proceedings between Anglo-Irish parties. But in a society where legal ambidexterity of this sort was increasing rather than diminishing from mid-fourteenth century onwards, it is highly probable that the condemned practice persisted. The principle of the primacy of the common law had become less secure among the colonists in this period.

There was yet another way in which the three basic principles of the colonial

[1] *Cal. close rolls, 1349–54*, p. 292; *Stat. Ire., John–Hen. V*, p. 413.
[2] Mac Niocaill, *Na buirgéisí*, ii, 336. For comment, G. J. Hand, 'English law in Ireland, 1172–1351' in *N.I. Legal Quart.*, xxiii (1972), pp 413–14.
[3] *Stat. Ire., John–Hen. V*, pp 388–91. This ordinance is discussed in more detail below, pp 382–4.
[4] *H.M.C. rep. 10*, app. v, p. 260.
[5] *Stat. Ire., John–Hen. V*, pp 434–7.

relationship underwent modification in the course of this century. Petitions in
the English parliament from Ireland fell off after Edward I's time, as they did
from other sources. The principal reason for this was a change in parliamentary practice. But there was in any case a falling-off in the Irish legal business
after the early years of Edward II's reign.[1] It was established in 1341 that those
charged with felonies and trespasses committed in Ireland should not have to
answer in England, a matter 'contrary to common law and right reason', the
colonists claimed.[2] Exception was made of charges of treason and of offences
touching the king's person, so that it was still open for a rebellious earl of Desmond and the like to be tried in England. After 1355 there was probably a further decline in the Irish jurisdiction of the English courts, when liberty to sue
for lands taken into the king's hands before the justiciar and chancellor in Ireland, rather than before the king in England, was allowed. Likewise complaints
of errors in the records and processes of Irish courts could be heard and corrected in parliaments in Ireland.[3]

The established relationship principles, then, were modified with the passage of time. But the fourteenth century was to bring a new dimension to English policy towards Ireland. The colony declined, the Gaelic Irish thrived, the
colonists demanded help from the mother country. What was its response?
This period is bounded by a projected royal expedition and two actual ones.
They form two appropriate *termini* for an unusually important period in the
history of English policy in medieval Ireland.

Edward III's assumption of personal government in October 1330 came
when there was a lull in both Anglo-French and Anglo-Scottish hostilities.
There is no information available as to Edward's reasons for deciding on an
Irish expedition. The need for some decisive English intervention was clear
enough and, with Scotland and the Continent temporarily closed to English
warriors, Ireland had plenty to offer to a young king anxious to flex his muscles
in war. Preparations for the expedition were set in train in the Westminster
Michaelmas parliament of 1331. 'Want of custody' of Irish lands by absentees
was, it was said, a frequent complaint of the colonists, so the earl of Norfolk and
twenty-five other English magnates with titles to land in Ireland, without being
resident there, and who had lost them to the Gaelic Irish, were instructed to
send troops to recover them.[4] The Irish chancellor was given permission to
summon such absentees to the defence of their lands as he saw fit. The earls of
Ulster and Ormond, Walter de Burgh, William de Bermingham, and Alexander Bicknor (archbishop of Dublin and Irish treasurer) were summoned to
England to advise the king on measures necessary 'for the reformation of Ireland's estate and the establishment of peace'. It was perhaps on their advice

[1] Hand, 'English law in Ireland', p. 411.
[2] *Stat. Ire., John—Hen. V*, pp 350–51.
[3] Ibid., pp 406–7.
[4] *Cal. close rolls, 1330–33*, pp 400–01.

that, in November of 1331, the king issued an ordinance of twenty-two articles whose stated purpose was 'the improvement of the state of our land of Ireland and the quiet and tranquillity of our people there'.[1]

It would be an exaggeration to describe this ordinance as setting out a reform and restoration programme. But it does highlight some of the problems of the colony at this time and offers some of the solutions that were to become part and parcel of English policies for the rest of our period. Of the twenty-two articles, seven deal with different aspects of improving the state of the king's Irish revenues. For the most part they were simple prescriptions, such as that the king's wardships and marriages should be sold for profit, and not just given away by the justiciar, or that sheriffs and other officers should account annually. No drastic changes were envisaged. Another seven articles had to do with the king's officers and their spheres of action. The simple principle that all king's officers should be investigated annually by the justiciar and his council, and that the inefficient (insufficientes) be replaced, was the most far-reaching. Five articles were about defence and peace-keeping. Two of these attempted to remedy long-standing grievances of the colonists. The first of these was about absentees: all who had lands in Ireland should, under penalty of forfeiture, either reside on them or place guard in them. The second forbade the maintenance of kerns or persons called 'Idelmen' except in their own marches. The problems of absenteeism and arbitrary exactions for the maintenance of private armies were, however, long to defy repeated attempts to solve them. The remaining three articles of the ordinance had specific reference to the Gaelic Irish. They were to pay fines in money, not cows, and it was declared felonious to break a truce between Gaelic and Anglo-Irish. Finally (the one radical change envisaged) it was proposed that one and the same law be applied to the Gaelic as to the Anglo-Irish, betaghs (villeins) excepted. Of this important matter more must be said later.

While these preparations were being made in England, a new justiciar was making his presence felt against the double threat to good order in the colony, rebellious Anglo-Irish and predatory Gaelic Irish. In August of 1331 Anthony de Lucy arrested in Limerick the first earl of Desmond and clapped him in Dublin castle, where he remained until 1333. In February 1332 he captured the earl's henchman, William de Bermingham, at Clonmel, took him to Dublin and hanged him.[2] It was the Gaelic Irish of Leinster who were always the most troublesome, especially in this period when Mac Murchadha was letting it be known he was king of Leinster. There emerged a special strategy for dealing with this problem. The justiciar was not powerful enough to conquer and reduce to permanent subjection the MacMurroughs, O'Byrnes, O'Tooles, and O'Mores, nor yet the marcher dynasties like the Lawlesses, Archbolds, and

---

[1] Stat. Ire., John—Hen. V, pp 332–9.

[2] Chartul. St Mary's, Dublin, ii, 375–7. The detailed study of the Leinster problem in this period has been one of the distinctive features of the research of R. F. Frame.

Harolds, all of whom allied and quarrelled among themselves on a turn-and-turn-about basis. When the 'nations of the Irish' could be enlisted into military service with the crown, they were, sometimes with their *capitanei* receiving the justiciar's official confirmation as their chiefs. Coercion, with exaction of hostages, fines, excommunication, and interdict, alternated with cajolery in the form of payments, nominally for services, in reality to buy them off. From about this time Mac Murchadha seems to have been paid an annual fee by the Dublin administration. His successors would appear to have become adept at collecting it, and similar payments, from other Anglo-Irish sources, while not being seriously deflected from any course of action they wished to pursue.

Throughout July and August of 1332, the king was collecting archers from most of the English counties and recruiting troops from Wales; purveyance for their supplies was in progress and ships were being organised for a September sailing from Holyhead.[1] Then suddenly the English diplomatic situation changed because of developments in Scotland. Robert Bruce had died in 1329, leaving a five-year-old son, David II, against whom there had been English support for the disinherited Scottish barons whose leader was Edward Balliol. On 12 August 1332 Balliol won the important victory of Dupplin Moor. In his September parliament, Edward III called off his Irish expedition. Once again an English king was enmeshed in the toils of a Scottish war, and a huge army, with a substantial contingent from Ireland, went to try to take advantage of Balliol's assumption of the Scottish throne. But there were to be further developments. In 1337 the king opened negotiations with the Flemish cloth towns, which were to lead to his assumption of the title of king of France and to an expedition to support his claim. In 1338-9 the French were attacking ports along the south coast of England and an invasion was expected. Edward led his army to Flanders in 1339. In all these circumstances, it was obviously unrealistic to expect any major English initiative on behalf of the beleaguered colonists in Ireland.

From the cancellation of Edward III's personal intervention in September 1332 to the appointment as justiciar of Sir Thomas of Rokeby in July 1349, there was appallingly little continuity of government in Ireland. Justiciars and their deputies were being continually changed, and a tenure period of a year or more was exceptional. Only one justiciar in this time made any real impression on the colonial scene: Ralph d'Ufford (July 1344–April 1346), who made his mark as the man who brought the first earl of Desmond to heel. Thanks to Dr Frame's skilful exploitation of the surviving financial records his period of office is known in some detail. His itinerary shows him to have been a vigorous commander in the field, engaged in 'endless small-scale military expeditions'. The rewards of his energy were a demonstration that the Dublin administration was not a negligible force, and a modest increase in the revenue. But any radical attempt to solve the colony's deep-seated problems was beyond his

[1] *Cal. close rolls, 1330—33*, pp 483–5, 487–8; *Cal. pat. rolls, 1330—34*, p. 321.

powers. He could hold his own in the tactics of Leinster campaigning-negotiating, but without hope of enduring peace. His intervention in Gaelic Ulster, which had him giving governmental support for the supplanting of Énrí by Aodh Ó Néill in 1345, was, though in its way remarkable, of necessity of only short-term significance. The real weakness of his position lay in the limited force he could deploy. His retinue as justiciar was to be counted in dozens of soldiers rather than hundreds. To muster a force of one thousand men for a campaign anywhere in Ireland was a major, but temporary, achievement. For supplementation of his retinue he was dependent on two uncertain quantities, the support of the colonists in men and money and the loyalty of his Gaelic Irish mercenaries. If comparison is made between the size of his armies and, say, the fifteen thousand estimated as the size of the English army in Scotland in 1335 or the twelve thousand in France in 1351, some idea is gained of the government's order of priorities in this period.[1] The justiciars in Ireland were barely equipped for policing; conquest was beyond them.

Thomas de Rokeby[2] is the only other justiciar of this period to emerge as a vigorous and efficient chief governor; he was to prove himself one of the few who held his office of whom the colonists had a good word to say. De Rokeby was a tough north-Yorkshireman, a seasoned Scottish campaigner with a wealth of administrative experience in northern England and the Borders. He was to hold the justiciarship for the unusually long period of five years and five months in 1349–55, with a further four months' service in 1357. In these years it is possible to see something of the characteristics of English policy towards the deteriorating Irish situation as it had evolved by mid-fourteenth century.

Like d'Ufford, de Rokeby was an indefatigable campaigner. Of the police operations he conducted against the Gaelic Irish, eight were in Leinster, three in Munster, and two in County Louth. Like d'Ufford, too, he seems to have managed to do this without imposing undue strain on the Irish exchequer; the revenue in his time showed no particular rise but there was no catastrophic fall. The home government had allowed him a few more soldiers for his retinue than was customary and he raised the usual troops under Irish chiefs. There is no indication that he was being subsidised from the English exchequer. There is little doubt that the justiciar's court was functioning in different parts of the colony, but so far the scattered and limited legal records of this period have not been systematically examined.

There was also an attempt to improve the quality of the administration. One of de Rokeby's first acts was to put the treasurer under arrest and have him sent in custody to England. An enquiry into the working of the administration,

[1] A. E. Prince, 'The strength of English armies in the reign of Edward III' in *E.H.R.*, clxxxiii (1931), pp 353–71; J. W. Sherborne, 'Indentured retinues and English expeditions to France, 1369–80' in *E.H.R.*, lxxix (1964), pp 718–46.

[2] *D.N.B.*; A. J. Otway-Ruthven, 'Ireland in the 1350s: Sir Thomas de Rokeby and his successors' in *R.S.A.I. Jn.*, xcvii (1967), pp 47–59; Otway-Ruthven, *Med. Ire.*, pp 277–81; Frame's thesis lists his campaigns.

whose results were reported back to England, produced a royal ordinance in March 1351. It was hardly a radical measure, being concerned largely to bring the procedures of the Irish exchequer and chancery into line with English practice and to regulate the fees of some lesser officials.[1] More relevant to the realities of the colonial situation had been the discussion in the Westminster parliament of 1350 about the defence of the lands held by absentees. These, it was said, were careful enough in collecting their rents, but quite ignored their responsibility for the defence of the colony. They and their agents in Ireland were warned about the need to help the justiciar and supply men and money when necessary. The most striking legislative attempt to cope with Irish problems, however, came from the colony itself. Though he did raise subsidies from local *tractatus*, de Rokeby apparently felt no great need for full colonial assemblies, summoning only one parliament and three great councils in his period of office. But the ordinances of 1351, the work of two great councils held in Dublin and Kilkenny, were to be one of the few major colonial legislative acts of this century, standing second only to the statute of Kilkenny of 1366, to which, however, it contributed over half the clauses.[2]

The ordinances owe much to 'the grievous complaints of the commons' mentioned in the proemium, and it is a safe assumption that many of them were based on petitions presented by the commons to the justiciar and council. Hence the unordered arrangement of the legislation, its very diverse nature, and the inclusion of certain articles that were essentially pleas for the implementation of existing law, rather than new and precise formulations by professional legal draftsmen. The 'routs' of such as the first earl of Desmond, which all knew to be illegal, would not be eliminated by clauses 15 and 20 of the ordinances, which were a declaration of their illegality, but by vigorous enforcement of the existing law. These imperfections apart, which are in any case common enough in medieval legislation, the ordinances did go some way towards giving precision to, and codifying, acknowledged solutions to the colony's problems of external attack and internal disorder.

There were twenty-five clauses. One was the conventional acknowledgement that the church should be free and that Magna Carta should be observed in all its articles. Another introduced to the colony an unspecified English statute of labourers (there was one of 1351). There were detailed regulations about the fees of marshals of the benches and exchequer and of constables of castles. The last four were concerned with sheriffs, with a view to making their accounting more efficient and to relieving those under their jurisdiction of oppressive practices. The remaining eighteen ordinances may be divided into two categories: eleven were concerned in one way or another with the protection of the king's lieges from abuse by their fellow colonists, and seven dealt with matters of war, peace, and defence in relation to the Gaelic Irish.

[1] *Cal. close rolls, 1349—54*, pp 292–3.
[2] *Stat. Ire., John—Hen. V*, pp 374–97.

Several of the first group have been encountered already, notably the attempt to restrict the plague of kerns and 'idlemen' living off the country, and the insistence on the use of the common law for the settlement of disputes in place of private distraints and vengeances. Clause 5 is of great interest as a feature of peace-keeping peculiar to Ireland, which was probably a result of acculturation. This made every 'chieftain of lineage' (*chevetyn de lynage*) responsible for arresting any of his 'lynage, de sa aherdance [*sic*] ou de sa retenance' who had committed any trespass or felony and holding them until they could be tried. Failure to do so would bring the arrest and punishment of the chieftain himself. This procedure seems to be the adoption of the brehon law principle of *cin comhfhocuis*, kin-liability, which had been first applied to the Anglo-Irish in 1310.[1] De Rokeby himself had put the principle into practice in 1350 in County Wicklow. It was first necessary to establish who was the legal *chevetyn* or *capitaneus*. Walter Harold was chosen as head of the Harolds by a group of his relatives, with others of his *aherdance*, members of the Lawless, Howell, and Walsh families. He then swore on oath to remain in the king's peace and to arrest, and hold until the law demanded delivery, any of his family, kin, and adherents who had committed felony or robbery.[2] The principle was still part of the Irish legal system in the seventeenth century.

Much in the ordinances that relate to containment of the Irish has a familiar ring. Two clauses were complementary to the recent royal decree about absenteeism: those resident in Ireland and not living in the march were to ensure that their march possessions were properly defended; those resident in England were to contribute to the defence of their Irish lands. The increased importance of keepers of the peace in the circumstances was brought out in new rules concerning their numbers and duties. Parleying between marchers and those Gaelic or Anglo-Irish who were against the peace was not to take place without leave of the justiciar or in the presence of a sheriff or keeper of the peace. Two weaknesses of the defensive system were pinpointed, not for the first time. There was to be no local particularisms about who was at peace and who was at war: there should be 'one peace and one war' throughout the whole country. The work of the justiciar, keepers of the peace, and sheriffs often went to waste when their hard-won truces and peaces with the Gaelic Irish were broken by the colonists; this was to be severely punished. Finally there was one ordinance which was new and which was to be expanded in the future. Clause 11 stated that no Anglo-Irish should make any sort of alliance (marriage and fosterage were specifically mentioned) with Gaelic or Anglo-Irish not at peace, without the justiciar's permission. A veto on marchers marrying Gaelic Irish who were in open rebellion (*qe sount contre le fey et la pees*) had already been recommended to the king by the town spokesmen earlier in the century.[3] In 1357 the 1351 ordinance

[1] Hand, 'English law in Ireland', pp 407–8, 417–18.
[2] The text has been printed by Edmund Curtis, 'The clan system among English settlers in Ireland' in *E.H.R.*, xxv (1910), pp 116–17.   [3] Mac Niocaill, *Na buirgéisí*, ii, 337.

was tightened in a royal decree which withdrew the qualification of such marriages needing authorisation. Now they were forbidden absolutely, and the justiciar was instructed to make enquiries about such relationships and punish them. It is to be noticed that the 1357 ordinance makes it clear that the reason for the ban is a security one. Marriage and fosterage led to 'forewarnings and espials', and thereby the justiciar's expeditions were often impeded.[1] The ban was not, in 1351 or 1357, seen as an aspect of an Anglo-Irish 'degeneracy' which had to be eradicated.

There were, then, good intentions enough. But, despite de Rokeby's efforts, all the indications were that in the years 1355–7 he was being swamped by numerous Gaelic Irish attacks in the whole length and breadth of the colony and was not always assured of the full cooperation of those best able to help him. On his removal from office, the citizens of Cork urged strongly on the king that he be reinstated, sincerely believing, they said, that he could act more quickly and less expensively than anyone else.[2] The Dublin annalist spoke of him as one 'who subdued the Irish well and paid well for his victuals and said "I wish rather to eat and drink from wooden vessels and pay gold and silver for my provisions, clothes and soldiers" '.[3] But a royal ordinance, issued just six months after de Rokeby's death in Ireland which cut short his second tour of duty, told a different story. Its proemium spoke of the default of good government in Ireland and the neglect and carelessness of royal officers there, of the parlous state of the marches deserted by their inhabitants, laws not observed, the people oppressed, and more in the same vein.[4] No doubt this is in part conventional rhetoric, but it forms an apt comment on how little Rokeby had been able to improve the general condition of the colony.

It was not to be very long, however, before another and more sustained attempt to do so was to be made. The urgent plea from the Kilkenny great council of 1360 arrived in England at an auspicious time, in that a temporary peace in the hundred years' war was beginning. On 15 March 1361 Edward III announced that because Ireland is 'now subject to such devastation and destruction . . . that it will soon be plunged into total ruin', he was sending his son Lionel, who had been earl of Ulster since 1347, to the relief of the colonists, ordering all who held lands in Ireland either to go there in person or to provide a substitute, and summoning to a colloquium at Westminster the more notable of these absentees. So there began what was to prove the biggest relieving operation yet mounted for the embattled colonists, second in ambition only to those of Richard II in 1394–5 and 1399.

Lionel's expedition and his lengthy spell as chief governor (September 1361 to April 1364; December 1365 to November 1366) were to have three distinguishing

---

[1] *Stat. Ire., John–Hen. V*, p. 412.
[2] Otway-Ruthven, 'Ireland in the 1350s', p. 53.
[3] *Chartul. St Mary's, Dublin*, ii, 392–3.
[4] *Stat. Ire., John–Hen. V*, p. 408.

features. There was for the first time a genuinely sustained effort to translate into practice the much reiterated legislation about absentee landlords making provision for the defence of the colony; there was despatched, again for the first time, a sizeable English-raised and English-financed army; there was produced, in the statute of Kilkenny, the most celebrated, even the most notorious, of Irish medieval legislative acts, which was to remain in force down to the early seventeenth century.

Dr A. J. Otway-Ruthven is very right to argue that 'as much as anything else the passing of so much authority all over Ireland into the hands of absentee lords in this century, and the fragmentation of lordships by division among coheiresses, was to bring about the decline of the colony'.[1] The colonists had long appreciated the danger and the home government had responded to their complaints. But much of their response seems to have been merely on paper. For once, in 1361, it looked as if the government meant business about absentees. It named them: some thirty-four lords, nine women (the coheiresses of Dr Otway-Ruthven's judgement), eight religious houses, and a small assortment of obscure clergymen.[2] In the event, nine of the thirty-four magnates actually accompanied Lionel with retinues of their own, and a further five entrusted the issues of their Irish lands to help to defray the costs of someone who did cross the Irish sea.[3] Others were forced to pay their revenues to the expedition's wages clerk. A few got rid of their lands.[4] Some of the remainder were to be pressured again in 1368 to meet their obligations.[5]

English financial records offer some indication of how Ireland had moved temporarily higher in the order of royal priorities. Calculations of very precise sums is a matter for those with particular expertise in treasury book-keeping,[6] but it is clear that expenditure was of an exceptional order for Ireland. The English treasurer accounted for the sum of £14,733 in expenses for army and transport costs in 1363–4.[7] The accounts of William of Dalby, clerk of wages to Lionel's expedition and later Irish treasurer, have not yet been systematically discussed in print, but sums laid out in soldiers' pay and shipping costs and other expenses were substantial and came from English sources.[8] The expenditure was such as to suggest that the king had fulfilled his promise of sending 'a great army' to Ireland. In fact the number of troops sent was modest indeed by the standards of the fourteenth-century English armies that served in Scotland and France. The biggest contingent was led by Ralph, earl of Stafford,

---

[1] Med. Ire., p. 251.

[2] Rymer, Foedera, vi, 318–20.

[3] P.R.O., E. 101/28/14, 15, 20.

[4] The Preston acquisitions have already been mentioned above, p. 361. For other examples, see Dowdall deeds, p. x.

[5] Rymer, Foedera, vi, 594–5.

[6] Now successfully tackled by Philomena Connolly, 'Financing of expeditions', pp 104–11.

[7] Cf. T. F. Tout and D. M. Broome, 'A national balance sheet for 1362–3 with documents subsidiary thereto' in E.H.R., xxxix (1924), pp 404–19.

[8] P.R.O., E. 101/28/21.

a veteran captain who through his wife, daughter and heiress of the earl of Gloucester, was absentee lord of a part of the partitioned liberty of Kilkenny. His force was of nineteen knights, seventy-eight men-at-arms, and one hundred mounted archers. He had also a force of Staffordshire foot archers. Lionel's own contingent was somewhat smaller, and other retinues, smaller still, had been recruited by William of Windsor, John of Carrew, and Ralph de Ferrers. All told, these various retinues totalled something in the region of fifty knights, three hundred men-at-arms, and four hundred and fifty mounted archers. There were to have been in addition eight hundred foot archers from levies in Wales and the English western counties, but there seem to have been problems about getting a full muster of these men. The most optimistic reading of Dalby's accounts would put the size of the army at less than two thousand; there were in addition some soldiers under the earl of Ormond and some small Gaelic Irish contingents.[1] Such a force could only be for police and garrison duties. It could not conquer or even overawe the Gaelic Irish. It is difficult to credit Lionel with the success of clearing out the marches of invading Gaelic Irish, though he did capture Art Mac Murchadha who died in his custody.[2]

The abiding monument of Lionel's period in Ireland was the statute of Kilkenny. The most recent editor of the statute has divided it into thirty-six articles.[3] The last two are enforcement clauses. Clause 35 established a procedure whereby enquiry could be made twice a year in each county by two lawyers and two leading men from the locality as to violations of the statute. The last clause added ecclesiastical censures (there were three archbishops and five bishops present in parliament) on the violators. Of the remaining thirty-four clauses, no less than nineteen were taken almost in the same words from the de Rokeby ordinance of November 1351. It is, therefore, at once clear that the first intention of the legislators was to complete a codification of the standard remedies for colonial problems in so far as it seemed appropriate to legislate about them. Of the six ordinances of 1351 missing from the statute of Kilkenny, one, concerning sheriffs hearing pleas of withernam, was simply omitted. So too were the two clauses on absentee lords, presumably because it was being otherwise dealt with. The clause enforcing the English statute of labourers was replaced by new legislation. The biggest change was in the replacement of clauses 11 and 12 of the 1351 ordinance; these concerned security aspects of relations with the Gaelic Irish, and of the fifteen new clauses added to the ordinance eight were concerned with this issue. We may, then, conclude that such originality as the statute possessed lay primarily in its attempt to deal comprehensively with that relationship.

The proemium to the statute makes it clear at once that the problem was

---

[1] These calculations are based on the P.R.O. material cited above.
[2] *Ann. Conn.*, pp 320–21.
[3] H. F. Berry, in *Stat. Ire., John–Hen. V*, pp 430–69. James Hardiman, 'A statute of the fortieth year of King Edward III . . .' in *Tracts relating to Ireland* (Ir. Arch. Soc., ii, 1843), numbers thirty-five.

being tackled on a more fundamental level than in any previous legislation. The statute, like the 1351 ordinance and its precursors, was certainly *in toto* about 'the good government of the land and quiet of the people and for the better observance of the laws and punishment of evil-doers'. But in particular (and this was new) the proemium argued that the reason why the colony was 'decayed and the Irish enemies exalted and raised up' was because

many English of the land forsaking the English language, dress, style of riding, laws, and usages, live and govern themselves according to the manners, dress, and language of the Irish enemies and also had contracted marriages and alliances with them whereby the land and the liege people thereof, the English language, the allegiance due to our lord king, and English laws there are put in subjection and decayed. . . .

The statute was describing the phenomenon that came to be known as degeneracy, in the sense of being changed from a higher stock to a lower. The phenomenon of Anglo-Irish colonists 'degenerating' into Gaelic ways was not in itself new in the 1360s. Legislation in the Irish parliament in 1297 had referred to colonists being mistaken for Gaelic Irishmen because, *quasi degeneres*, they had adopted Gaelic dress and hair style with consequent legal complications if they were killed.[1] If killing of a colonist was to be punished differently from killing of a Gaelic Irishman, then a colonist must look like one. Conversely, if a Gaelic Irishman were given a charter of English liberty, he must cut the hair of his 'culan' to look like a colonist.[2] In 1297, parliament made no attack on degeneracy as such, nor was there, so far as is known, any such attack before 1366. It was apparently first singled out as a grave social evil and the cause of colonial ills and perils in 1360. A royal decree was then issued which in substance was a follow-up of de Rokeby's 1351 legislation against the colonists using march and brehon law, and the 1357 royal ordinance against the fosterage of Anglo-Irish children among the Gaelic Irish. But the 1360 decree went much further. It deplored the fact that 'large numbers of the English nation both in the marches and elsewhere in our land of Ireland have recently become Irish in their way of life [*condicio*]'. It explicitly attacked the use of the Irish language by the colonists in Ireland, a quite new development. Fosterage was now forbidden not because it conduced to 'forewarnings and espials' but because it led inevitably to the learning of Irish. It was the use of Irish that was now identified as the hall-mark of degeneracy and on this was blamed the decline (*diminucio*) of the colony: 'through use of this language our plains people [*populus campestris*] of English stock [*genus*] have become for the most part Irish, to the manifest decline of our authority in the land of Ireland'. It was therefore forbidden, under pain of losing English liberty (that is, having only the status of the Gaelic Irish at English law) for anyone of English stock to speak Irish to another person of English stock; all Anglo-Irish

---

[1] *Stat. Ire., John—Hen. V*, p. 210.
[2] Richardson & Sayles, *Parl. & councils med. Ire.*, i, no. 13, p. 17.

were to learn English; no Anglo-Irish child was to be reared among the Gaelic Irish.[1]

It is in the context of the 1360 decree that the new clauses of the statute of Kilkenny are to be viewed. The change in attitude that had then revealed itself was to be reiterated, developed, and established as part of the norm of right living for a colonist. The gist of the matter was put in this way in clauses 2 and 3:

Also, it is ordained and established that no alliance by marriage, gossipred, fostering of children, concubinage or sexual liaison or in any other manner be made henceforward between English and Irish on one side or the other. . . . Also, it is ordained and established that every Englishman use the English language, and be called by an English name abandoning completely the Irish method of naming and that every Englishman use English style in appearance, riding and dress, according to his position in society, and if any English or Irish living among the English use the Irish language among themselves contrary to this ordinance . . . [penalty stated]. . . . And that no Englishman worth one hundred shillings a year in land, holdings or rent shall ride otherwise than on a saddle in the English style. . . . And also, that beneficeholders of holy church living amongst the English, use the English language. . . .

It is abundantly clear then that the first purpose of the new clauses in the statute was to preserve the Englishness of the colonists, thereby shoring-up that loyalty to their mother country, enfeebled by their 'degeneracy'. It is appropriate to mention at this point that following complaints of dissension between English born in Ireland and English born in England, clause 4 ordered that the one should refrain from calling the other 'English yokel' (*hobbe*) and the other from retorting with 'Irish dog', for it was perhaps 'degeneracy' that lay at the root of the tension. Four further clauses related to matters of security and defence in relation with the Gaelic Irish (clauses 10–12, 15). Thus, in a variation on the 'one war, one peace' theme (specifically the subject of clause 21), it was enacted that war should only begin on the decision of the council taken with local advice and should only conclude on terms acceptable to both the councillors and local people. There was a grim addition to this provision, designed to discourage the making of peace on too easy terms which would have the effect of further encouraging the Gaelic Irish to go to war: in the event of their breaking an agreed peace, execution of hostages should follow without delay or favour. Clauses 10 and 11 were attempts to remove provocations to war: debts due from Gaelic Irish at peace should be levied only on the principal debtor, not on any of his fellows or followers; every peace between men of the two nations was to include the provision that the Gaelic Irish should not pasture their cattle on lands that were not theirs. Then, because Gaelic Irish musicians and entertainers coming among the colonists were said to be spies, it was forbidden to employ them. Clause 6 was designed to foster the martial spirit and expertise of the colonists. They were forbidden to play certain games

[1] *H.M.C. rep. 10*, app. v, pp 260–61.

which seem to have been early versions of hockey[1] and quoits (*coitings*), and were to practise archery and use of the lance instead. The clause was an adaptation to Ireland of a law often promulgated in fourteenth-century England: for example, a writ of 1363 issued to the English sheriffs forbade among other sports the allegedly useless and dishonest sports of bowls, football, and cockfighting in favour of the *ars sagittandi*.[2]

There was a third purpose in this group of eight clauses in the statute that in one way or another concerned the relations of the colonists with the Gaelic Irish. This was to ensure that all the clergy of the colony should be of English stock. The legislators framed the principles very starkly in clauses 13 and 14:

Also it is ordered that no Irish of the nations of the Irish be admitted into any cathedral or collegiate church by provision, collation, or presentation of any person whatsoever, or to any benefice of holy church amongst the English of that land. . . .

Also it is agreed and established that no house of religion which is situated among the English, exempt or not, shall in the future receive any Irishman to their profession but receive Englishmen without consideration of whether they were born in England or in Ireland. . . .

Though the meaning of these clauses seems only too clear, there are difficulties about taking them at their face value. In the first place, earlier in the statute (clause 3) it was stated specifically that there were Gaelic Irish living among the colonists and, implicitly, that this was perfectly legal. If some Gaelic Irish, why no priests and religious? Further, in the same clause, reference was made to beneficeholders, living among the colonists, being required to learn English. It is not certain that by this it was Gaelic Irish priests who were intended, but there is a strong presumption that they were. Thus the statute seems inconsistent, or at least clause 3 does not seem to accord with clause 13. Another difficulty is that the principles set out in clauses 13 and 14 ran contrary to what had been official policy throughout the century. It is true, as the framers of the 1317 remonstrance had claimed, that in 1310 legislation had been passed in a Kilkenny parliament forbidding the reception of Gaelic Irish into Anglo-Irish religious houses. But this had been quickly quashed from England. Other occasions of tension between religious of the two nations do not show such a policy of exclusion being officially advocated. As far as the diocesan clergy was concerned the customary position had been restated as recently as March 1360. There had been a royal instruction imposing a ban on Gaelic Irishmen being appointed to offices in towns, to canonries and prebends in cathedrals, and to benefices of other types. Representations had been made in the English parliament, from Gaelic

---

[1] The statute used the word 'horlings' which is generally understood as meaning the Irish game of hurling. There are two objections to this reading: (i) the text spoke of a stick-and-ball game played 'sur la terre', and hurling is most conspicuously not played 'on the ground'; it is essentially a game played through the air; (ii) the link between 'horlings' and hockey in the Anglo-Irish context is clearly established in a Galway statute of 1527: 'the horlings of the litill balle with hockie sticks or staves'; *H.M.C. rep. 10*, app. v, p. 402.

[2] Rymer, *Foedera*, vi, 417. There is another example from 1365; ibid., p. 468.

Irish clergy living among the colonists, that this was unjust to those of them who had ministered peacefully for many years and were of proven loyalty. The petition was favourably received and the veto lifted, with the king's protestation that it had never been his intention to penalise such men, who included religious as well as diocesan clergy.[1] Clauses 13 and 14 obviously professed a different attitude, though it seems highly likely that it was the 1360 doctrine that prevailed in practice. It will be necessary to return to the whole question of the position of the Gaelic Irish living *inter Anglicos*.

The codification that was the statute of Kilkenny was to be Lionel's particular contribution to the diagnosis and solution of the colony's problems. As with de Rokeby, so with Lionel; it was a report from Ireland about the state of the country shortly after he left it that insinuates strongly the note of failure. In 1368, Edward III, basing himself on what an Irish parliament had told him, announced that the 'loss and destruction of Ireland are more than ever manifest' so that 'if remedy and succour be not speedily applied the land was like to be ruined'.[2] The longest-serving justiciar between Lionel's departure from Ireland and the end of the reign of Richard II was William of Windsor, perhaps the most experienced of all commanders against the Gaelic Irish, who served some five years in two spells of office (1369–72; 1374–6). As has been seen, his terms are full of interest and significance as far as the attitudes of the Anglo-Irish were concerned. But his efforts to persuade the colonists to pay more for their own defence led him personally into serious trouble and the colony into political crisis.[3] He was no more successful than de Rokeby or Lionel in even halting, much less reversing, the steady erosion of the crown's strength and the colony's security. Perhaps the aptest comment on his permanent success in driving back the Gaelic Irish and strengthening its financial position is the decision of the parliament held at Castledermot in March 1378. Murchadh na Raithne Ó Briain of Arra had invaded Leinster with a large force from Munster. He could not be repelled by force, so his withdrawal was bought at a cost of one hundred marks. Characteristically, parliament could not, or would not, itself find this modest sum and Murchadh refused to move until he got his money in full.[4]

After Windsor's withdrawal from the Irish scene, colonial government entered a particularly drab phase of its history with a dreary succession of ineffectual heads, mostly of very short-term appointments which often owed more to royal whim and English court politics[5] than suitability for this taxing position. Underfinanced, short of troops,[6] without adequate policy direction

---

[1] Ibid., pp 321–2; *Stat. Ire., John—Hen. V*, pp 420–21.

[2] Rymer, *Foedera*, vi, 594–5, 605; *Cal. close rolls, 1364—8*, pp 482–3, 499–50.

[3] See now Sheila Harbison, 'William of Windsor, the court party and the administration of Ireland' in Lydon, *Eng. & Ire.*, pp 153–74; Connolly, 'Financing of expeditions', pp 111–14.

[4] *Stat. Ire., John—Hen. V*, pp 472–5.

[5] Anthony Tuck, 'Anglo-Irish relations, 1382–93' in *R.I.A. Proc.*, lxix (1970), sect. C, pp 15–31.

[6] P.R.O., E. 101/30/2 (particulars of Windsor's account in Ireland) is revealing about the small size of the forces at his disposal.

and support from the home government, they were as unable to ward off the hostile Gaelic Irish as to suppress Anglo-Irish marauding and the debilitating feuds among the magnates, of which that between Ormond and Desmond was the most scandalous. There is one source which gives a sudden glimpse of how the colony's position had deteriorated by the 1390s. There has survived a single roll of petitions, some of which were presented to the Hilary parliament held at Kilkenny in 1393, others to the council on other occasions in the preceding year. Some of these petitions divulge in an incidental way how serious the position was for the towns, the lynch-pins of the colony. The road between Kilkenny and Carlow was impassable without strong military escort, while Carlow itself had been laid waste and plundered so that most of its inhabitants had fled. This was the acting seat of government. The country round Cork, Youghal, and Limerick had been laid waste and travel between Cork and Limerick was extremely hazardous. Castledermot had been forced to buy off Mac Murchadha, giving a prominent citizen as pledge of payment, and was having great difficulty in raising the required eighty-four marks. When Ó Raghallaigh raided Meath and put Kells in great jeopardy, the justiciar and the primate persuaded him to accept eighty-four marks (apparently the recognised fee) to withdraw, and a prominent citizen to hand over his son as surety. Again, finding the money posed an acute problem.[1]

It was Richard II himself who was to try to stop the drift of English policy. The colonists had asked for him personally in 1385,[2] and now with peace in France and Scotland, there was the opportunity to devote the whole of English military strength and expertise to the problems of Ireland. There was the by-now-customary attempt to round up absentees; an army, up to the usual size of English armies on the Continent in the latter part of the century, was raised;[3] and substantial sums of money were ear-marked for the task in hand. A swift and well coordinated sortie flushed out Mac Murchadha and forced him to surrender, and thereby Gaelic Ireland was persuaded to turn away wrath by due protestation of loyalty. How the eighty or so Irish kings and sub-kings submitted has been told often and well, and it is not necessary here to repeat the narrative of events.[4] It is important, however, to see the whole episode in the context of English colonial policy and to estimate its real significance.

That most interesting analyst of the shortcomings of the Irish policies of the medieval English kings, Sir John Davies, took it as '. . . the plaine and manifest

---

[1] *Proc. king's council, Ire., 1392–3*, nos 160, 5, 109, 114, 162.

[2] *Stat. Ire., John—Hen. V*, pp 485–7.

[3] J. F. Lydon, 'Richard II's expeditions to Ireland' in *R.S.A.I. Jn.*, xciii (1963), pp 141–2; Sherborne, 'Indentured retinues', pp 735–6.

[4] Curtis, *Rich. II in Ire.*; Otway-Ruthven, *Med. Ire.*, ch. x; Lydon, *Lordship*, pp 231–40 and *Ire. in later middle ages*, pp 109–24. There is a good summary of Curtis's reconstruction of events in his 'Unpublished letters from Richard II in Ireland, 1394–5' in *R.I.A. Proc.*, xxxviii (1927), sect. C, pp 277–83. See now Dorothy Johnston, 'The interim years: Richard II and Ireland, 1395–1399' in Lydon, *Eng. & Ire.*, pp 175–9; 'Richard II and the submissions of Gaelic Ireland' in *I.H.S.*, xxii, no. 85 (Mar. 1980), pp 1–20.

trueth ... that the kings of England in al ages, had bin powerfull enough, to make an absolute conquest of Ireland, if their whole power had been employed in that enterprize'.[1] He was very likely right. But the experience of Richard II shows that it was not enough merely to employ the whole of English power. There had to be a long sustained and intelligent follow-up programme. Paper submissions meant little in themselves. They might or might not prove a basis for something enduring in the pacification of the country and the eventual integration of the two nations into a stable society. But in the event, there was no significant consequence. There was not even a plan by which victory might be consolidated. The one new idea produced at this time, that Art Mac Murchadha and all his sub-kings should give up their lands in Leinster, be engaged as royal mercenaries against the rebel Irish of other areas, taking possession of such lands as they might conquer,[2] was impracticable. No Irish king, much less the king of Leinster, with pretensions to the kingship of Ireland, would submit meekly to such a scheme.

Richard II went home apparently convinced he had scored a triumph. But Mac Murchadha was not paid his promised annuity nor had his Anglo-Irish wife's barony of Norragh been restored to him as promised. War broke out again in Leinster: the familiar pattern had reasserted itself after a minimum of disruption; Roger Mortimer, earl of March and heir to the English throne, was killed in an obscure skirmish against the Gaelic Irish near Carlow in June 1398. Richard II's retaliatory campaign in 1399 was all anticlimax. Defied politically and embarrassed militarily by Mac Murchadha, there was to be no repetition of the capitulations of the first expedition. Henry Chrysted had observed to Froissart of these submissions, 'l'onneur y est grant, mais le prouffit y est moult petit'.[3] In 1399 the honour was as little as the profit; the 'rough rug-headed kerns'[4] had won convincingly.

Alexander de Balscot, bishop of Ossory (1371–86) and of Meath (1386–1400), had served thirty strenuous years in Ireland as bishop and top civil administrator. It has been seen how he managed in 1382 to avoid selection as justiciar when John Colton reluctantly accepted the post. But he was justiciar for short spells in 1387 and 1391, and now, with an absentee chief governor, he found himself keeper (*custos*) in the period after Richard's departure. It fell to him with his council to report to Westminster on the state of Ireland. His restrained and objective appraisal conveys, better than any of the other documents of its kind in the fourteenth century, the grim realities of the situation.

It was reported how the enfeebled colonists felt themselves no match for the confident and powerful Gaelic Irish. More specifically they feared Mac

---

[1] Davies, *Discovery* (1969), p. 77.
[2] Text in Curtis, *Rich. II in Ire.*, pp 80–85. For the view that Richard II did not envisage a complete evacuation of Leinster by Mac Murchadha, see Johnston, 'Richard II and the submissions of Gaelic Ireland', pp 15–16.
[3] Ed. Kervyn de Lettenhove, xv, 171.
[4] Shakespeare, *Richard II*, II. i. 156.

Murchadha in Leinster and Ó Néill in Ulster, both in arms and threatening major offensives. The earl of Desmond could expect Mac Murchadha's support in the destruction of the earl of Ormond. Other Anglo-Irish families (Butler, Power, de Bermingham were the most powerful of those named) were in open rebellion and more oppressive to the faithful Anglo-Irish even than the Gaelic Irish with whom they allied. There were neither soldiers nor money for defence. The army brought by the earl of Surrey had been discharged and the money granted to him sent for from England. The king's Irish revenue had dwindled to nothing: there were no fees of justice because no officer dare put the law into execution; most of the counties were now liberties from which the king got nothing; the exchequer lacked the expert staff to perform its function. In short, the colony stood on the brink of 'final destruction'.[1] The whole report is a commentary not only on the failure of Richard II's Irish policy but on that of English policy generally throughout our period.

THIS essay has so far been concerned with both Gaelic and colonial Ireland and their relationships, and with the English politicians and administrators who influenced or sought to influence the course of events in this country. There is one further segment of society that needs consideration to round off the survey of the fourteenth-century Irish scene: that composed of those of Gaelic Irish stock who lived among the colonists.

They were not of one single type. At the bottom of the social scale was the betagh, the *biatach* of Gaelic society[2] whom, in economic function and legal status, the invaders had no difficulty in equating with the villein of English feudalism. The occasional occurrence of the term 'betagesland'[3] or similar, testifies to their presence as a socially cohesive and distinctive section of the colony. At the other end of the social scale, Irish ruling families tended, for the most part, to be in the margins only of colonial society, preserving their own way of life, making different types of clientship arrangements with Anglo-Irish magnates as the situation called for, sometimes entering into marriage and fosterage alliances with them, even occasionally renting land and property in a small town.[4] In closer proximity to the colonists stood a third category of Gaelic Irish, of a more heterogeneous character. What they had in common was that they had become anglicised, at least to the extent of possessing recognised English legal status. Often they had become culturally as well as legally assimilated. This class of person is generally to be discovered in an urban context. Some thirteenth-century examples have already

---

[1] *Proc. king's council, Ire., 1392—3*, pp 261–9.
[2] Gearóid MacNiocaill, 'The origins of the betagh' in *Ir. Jurist*, i (1966), pp 292–8.
[3] G. H. Orpen, 'The earldom of Ulster', part 5 [*recte* 6] in *R.S.A.I. Jn.*, li (1921), p. 73; Edmund Curtis, 'Rental of the manor of Lisronagh, 1333, and notes on "betagh" tenure in medieval Ireland' in *R.I.A. Proc.*, xliii (1936), sect. C, pp 41–76.
[4] Cf. *Ormond deeds, 1350—1413*, no. 374, for the renting by 'Thomas Carach O'Rean' from the earl of Ormond of a site in 'Hagardstrete', Gowran.

been noticed. In the fourteenth century, cases still occur to reveal a Gaelic Irish background to an established colonial family.

One such is that of the Neill (Neale) family of Clondalkin, County Dublin. By the fifteenth century this was a prosperous commercial and farming family. William Neill, who made his will in 1471, owned a tannery and had farming interests; another member of the family had shops and land in New Street, Dublin.[1] Their Gaelic Irish origin is revealed when in 1355 Simon Neill brought an action of trespass against a person he accused of breaking into his close at Clondalkin. The defendant pleaded that he should not have to answer, as Neill was a Gaelic Irishman. Answer was made that Neill was one of the 'five bloods', namely of the O'Neills of Ulster who, by grant of former kings of England, enjoyed English liberty and were held to be free. When this was denied, a jury found the facts to be as Neill had pleaded.[2]

Among other points of interest in this unusual case is its forcible reminder that the Gaelic Irish living among the colonists were still, in the fourteenth century, disadvantaged at English law. It was the law that had translated into concrete terms the attitude of conqueror to conquered. By decision taken in the colony's earliest days, there was not to be one and the same law, within the colonial areas, for both Gaelic and Anglo-Irish. The latter were accorded secondary status. Their principal legal disabilities[3] were that causing the death of a Gaelic Irishman was not regarded as felonious, though compensation for it was due to his lord; a Gaelic Irishman bringing a real or personal action could be blocked by the defendant's objection that he was not obliged to answer since the plaintiff being Gaelic Irish was 'not of free blood'; dower was refused to Gaelic Irish widows; there was testamentary incapacity. As has been seen, English status was accorded to members of the 'five bloods', the five leading Gaelic Irish families, to the higher clergy and to individuals who obtained a grant of 'English liberty' for themselves and their progeny.

Early in the reign of Edward I, there had been a move to bring about a general enfranchisement of the Gaelic Irish living among the colonists, but this had not been successful. When our period opens the position in theory and, as far as can be seen, in practice, was still that of the later years of Edward I. But there were signs that English opinion was altering. In 1328, when John Darcy was discussing with the council the personnel and powers he could have as justiciar, he asked that the king and his council should assent to all the Gaelic Irish of Ireland having English law if they so wished, a statute to this effect to be promulgated in the Irish parliament.[4] An instruction was issued asking that the

[1] *Register of wills and inventories of the diocese of Dublin . . . , 1457—83*, ed. H. F. Berry (Dublin, 1898), pp 94–9, 220.

[2] *Cal. Carew MSS*, v, 452; Davies, *Discovery* (1969), pp 103–4 (based on the original plea roll, now destroyed).

[3] The most recent and best analyses of this difficult subject are by G. J. Hand, 'The status of the native Irish'; *Eng. law in Ire.*, pp 187–218; 'English law in Ireland, 1172–1351', pp 405–7.

[4] Text in Baldwin, *King's council*, p. 474.

king be informed of the view of the Anglo-Irish magnates, the matter having been discussed in parliament. No record of any such debate has survived. On earlier occasions when they had been consulted on this issue, they had not been in favour of abandoning the system of individual grants; it is possible that they had changed their minds. At any rate, the English parliament in November 1330 decided that 'one and the same law be applicable for the Irish as well as for the English except for servitude [servitutus] of betaghs in relation to their lords on the principle established in England for villeins'.[1]

If this general extension of English law came into effect in practice, it has left virtually no trace so far discovered in the legal records. On the other hand, it has been shown that the established system of granting individual charters of liberty continued, and that the numbers of such grants shows little apparent decline during the fourteenth century, with a tendency to rise quite sharply from the early fifteenth century.[2] The charter of liberty itself, as it had become standardised by the end of the century, spoke of granting the recipient, his family, and his descendants freedom from all Irish servitude (servitutus), conceding them the use of English law in exactly the same way as the colonists in Ireland enjoyed it. It specifically mentioned freedom in connection with all property transactions including succession, and, with an obvious reference to clause 13 of the statute of Kilkenny, freedom to accept any ecclesiastical benefice both within and without collegial and cathedral churches.[3] It may be taken for granted that if the statute of Kilkenny envisaged all Anglo-Irish using an English name, English speech, and English styles in dress and other things, then the same would be expected of those Gaelic Irish who were given charters of English liberty. How many Gaelic Irish in all sought such charters and how many lived and worked among the colonists with or without them is impossible to say.

When discussing the position of the clergy among the colonists it is necessary to make a distinction between Gaelic Irish clergy who ministered among the 'nations of the Irish', who were within the colonial sphere of influence, and those who held benefices among the colonists themselves. The former would usually be subject to an Anglo-Irish bishop and there was an attempt to use this situation to the advantage of the colonists. A Dublin provincial council, held under Archbishop Thomas Minot at Kilkenny near to the time of the parliament which promulgated the statute of Kilkenny, instructed such clergy under pain of suspension to restrain Irish rulers from rising in war 'against the church and the peace of the king and his faithful people' and to withdraw their pastoral services should they refuse to obey. It was also ruled under pain of excommunication that all ordinands of Gaelic Irish nationality were to take an oath not to

[1] Stat. Ire., John—Hen. V, p. 324.
[2] Bryan Murphy, 'The status of the native Irish after 1331' in Ir. Jurist, ii (1967), pp 116–28; further discussion, R. F. Frame, 'The immediate effect and interpretation of the 1331 ordinance "Una et eadem lex": some new evidence' in Ir. Jurist, vii (1972), pp 109–14.
[3] There are two good examples in Proc. king's council Ire., 1392–3, nos 45, 132.

go to war nor to aid or encourage those who did.[1] The second category was numerous and influential enough to be able successfully to petition an English parliament to withdraw the ban on their holding benefices *inter Anglicos*. Clause 13 of the statute of Kilkenny seemed to cancel that victory. But in practice Gaelic Irish clergy did continue to hold benefices and be members of religious communities, though apparently often finding it advisable to get a charter of English liberty or some formal recognition of their loyalty.[2]

Shortage of source material about the policies and attitudes of town authorities and citizens is a severe limitation on knowledge of the real situation of the Gaelic Irish in the colony in the fourteenth century. There is a little evidence to suggest that there was not necessarily a uniform view in all the towns at all times. Thus in the important matter of admitting young Gaelic Irishmen into apprenticeships in the towns, Drogheda in 1358 seems to have had a fairly open policy,[3] while in 1414 Limerick decreed that no Gaelic Irishman was to be admitted to apprenticeship.[4] In Waterford it was enacted in 1469–70 (though it is likely to have been a rule of longer standing) that no apprentice of Gaelic Irish blood should be admitted to the franchise of the city until he could produce a charter of English liberty, and he was required to be of 'Inglish aray, habite, and speche'.[5] Perhaps, however, the continuing psychological gulf between townsmen and Gaelic Irish, all bridges and mitigations apart, is revealed in the Waterford statute decreeing that compensation be paid to the victim, when anyone living in the city 'shal curse, diffame, or dispice ony citsayn of the saide citie in calling him Yrishman'.[6]

[1] Text in Aubrey Gwynn, 'Provincial and diocesan decrees of the diocese of Dublin during the Anglo-Norman period' in *Archiv. Hib.*, xi (1944), pp 100–01; Watt, *Ch. & two nations*, pp 204–6.

[2] *Proc. king's council Ire., 1392–3*, nos 72, 103; *Swayne's reg.*, pp 45, 114.

[3] *Dowdall deeds*, no. 212. Walsh, *Richard FitzRalph*, pp 342–3, tentatively links Drogheda attitudes with the pastoral influence of the archbishop.

[4] MacNiocaill, *Na buirgéisí*, i, 245–6. For dating this to 1414, see *Cal. pat. rolls, 1413–16*, p. 180. The charter is misdated in *Cal. charter rolls, 1341–7*, p. 463, where the roll is correctly identified as 1 Hen. V.

[5] *H.M.C., rep. 10*, app. v, p. 308.

[6] Ibid., p. 282.

CHAPTER XIV

Gaelic society and economy in the high middle ages

KENNETH NICHOLLS

A FIFTEENTH-CENTURY French herald, in a series of brief descriptions of the countries of the world,[1] paints a picture of Ireland (outside the lands of the Pale, which were ruled by the king of England) as a land of bogs, without either roads or permanent settlements, inhabited by a scattered population of pastoral nomads who reckoned their wealth entirely in cows, practised no trades and used no money, all their transactions being by barter. Wildly exaggerated and inaccurate though it might be, this picture was nevertheless grounded upon a kernel of truth. Late medieval Gaelic (and gaelicised) Ireland was thinly populated, its economy was predominantly a pastoral one, and its forms of settlement were for the most part scattered and impermanent. To a traveller from the typical lands of contemporary western Europe, from France, Germany, or England, with their pattern of permanent nucleated villages surrounded by the arable fields of peasant cultivators, it must indeed have seemed another world. The Catalan traveller Raymond, viscount of Perelhos, an eyewitness who visited Gaelic Ulster on pilgrimage to St Patrick's Purgatory in 1397, has left us a description which recalls, in more detail, that quoted above.[2] The failure of crops brought about by the inclement autumn of 1397 may have led Perelhos into overestimating the reliance of the people of Ulster on a diet of pastoral products (indeed, certain parts of his description suggest just this sort of abnormal destitution), but the remoteness of the economic pattern of Gaelic Ireland from the contemporary western European norm cannot be doubted.

Socially, too, Ireland differed widely from western Europe in general. The society of Gaelic and gaelicised Ireland was characterised by a continuing proliferation of the ruling and other dominant lineages within a stable, or perhaps declining, population, with the result that there was a recurrent process of replacement of the constituent elements of society from the top downwards, as

[1] Giles le Bouvier, dit Berry, *Le livre de la description des pays*, ed. E. T. Hamy (Paris, 1908), pp 122–3. I am grateful to Professor D. B. Quinn for bringing le Bouvier to my notice.
[2] English translation by J. P. Mahaffy, 'Two early tours in Ireland' in *Hermathena*, xviii, no. 40 (1914), pp 3–9. Cf. above, pp 309–10.

top downwards, as junior branches of the ruling lineages took the place of former chiefly houses and were in their turn supplanted by more recent off-shoots, the immediate offspring and kinsmen of the ruling lords. The displaced elements, pushed down the social ladder, would in turn replace their former inferiors and eventually descend into the propertyless bottom layer of the population. This proliferation, helped by Irish legal practice, which took little account of legitimacy and permitted the affiliation of children upon slender grounds, was a feature of Gaelic Irish society from its earliest recorded period down to its final annihilation at the beginning of the seventeenth century.[1] It was commented on by the seventeenth-century Irish genealogist Dubhaltach Mac Fir Bhisigh in a passage which has been frequently quoted.[2] Coupled with the defective nature of the mechanisms of succession to rule, it was a primary cause of the extreme political instability of native Irish society and of the endemic disorder which afflicted it.

It is not correct to assume that Gaelic Ireland did not produce records that, had they survived, would have enabled us to speak of its society and economy with more certainty than the vague speculation to which we are now so often confined, but it is probably true that it did not produce them in anything like the usual western European quantity. The question is, however, an empty one, as thanks not only to the destruction wrought by the wars of the sixteenth and seventeenth centuries but also to a process of archival destruction which has continued down to the present day, they have not survived, except for scattered fragments. In consequence the historian of Gaelic Irish society is confronted, as regards his sources, with a historiographical situation more characteristic of Asia than of Europe, carrying with it the need to hazard probabilities from scraps of evidence so fragmentary that it would be highly dangerous to base any generalisations upon them. Any attempts at quantification are out of the question, and an even more serious consequence of the paucity of documentation is the virtual impossibility of tracing changes in the economy and in institutional structures during the period under review. By far the greater part of the evidence that has come down to us dates from the second half of the sixteenth century; how far we are justified in assuming that the essential features of the Irish economy had remained largely unchanged during the two preceding centuries must remain open to discussion. As regards the century and a half immediately following the Anglo-Norman 'invasion', economic and social information regarding the Gaelic Irish world outside the limits of the colony might be said to be for practical purposes non-existent, and only a few deductions can be hazarded. Thus we need have no doubt about the largely pastoral emphasis of the Gaelic economy, at least in Connacht; even a cursory reading

---

[1] See Nicholls, *Land, law and society in sixteenth-century Ireland* ([Cork], 1976; O'Donnell Lecture, XX), pp 7–9. See also Katharine Simms, 'The medieval kingdom of Lough Erne' in *Clogher Rec.*, ix (1977), pp 132–3.

[2] E.g. by the present writer in *Gaelic Ire.*, pp 10–11. For the original, see *Genealogical tracts*, ed. Toirdhealbhach Ó Raithbheartaigh (I.M.C., Dublin, 1932), p. 26.

of the thirteenth-century parts of the Annals of Connacht, which of all the Irish annals approaches for this period the nearest to a chronicle, makes this clear. But one would like to be able to go beyond such vague generalisations. Was tillage perhaps more important on the church lands[1] than on the secular ones? We cannot say more than that it is possible, in fact probable, that this was the case. Did the purely Gaelic regions, like the colony, experience an upsurge of population in the thirteenth century, with a consequent tendency to an increase in the extent of cultivation? Again it seems possible that they did, but on the other hand the constant insecurity in the frontier districts would have been a factor operating against any such increase in these regions. It is unlikely that future research will shed much light on these questions.

Like the economy and the social structure, the settlement patterns of Gaelic Ireland differed widely, as has been said, from the western European norm. The permanent nucleated villages of the typical western European landscape were, of course, quite foreign to Gaelic settlement patterns, and, apart from the survival in gaelicised regions in the later middle ages of some boroughs and manorial villages from the high colonial period, agglomerations of dwellings were rare and for the most part confined to ecclesiastical centres. The ecclesiastical sites constituted a special case, with a long tradition of agglomeration. Long before the Anglo-Norman 'invasion' considerable urban settlements had grown up at such important religious centres as Kildare and Clonard, and in the later medieval period this tradition lived on in such episcopal cities as Armagh. In 1517 the episcopal see of Rosscarbery, in a purely Gaelic area, was a walled town with two gates and nearly two hundred houses.[2] Other episcopal 'cities', such as Clonfert and Clogher, were certainly much smaller, but appear to have been walled, probably with earthen ramparts, which may have followed the line of the early 'monastic' enclosures.[3] The wars of the sixteenth century, even before the greater violence imparted by the Tudor reconquest and the religious divisions of the Elizabethan period, had a severely destructive effect on many or most of these places: Ardagh was in ruins as early as 1517, as a result of the wars between the late bishop, Uilliam Ó Fearghail, and his kinsmen, and then consisted of four wooden houses and the half-ruined cathedral.[4] Armagh itself was laid in ruins after the 1550s, and its desolation is vividly shown on Barthelet's map of 1601, when the great cathedral is shown as partially

---

[1] For the church lands, which were in many ways set apart from the areas which surrounded them, see below, pp 433–5.

[2] Theiner, *Vetera mon.*, p. 529.

[3] At Clogher, thirty-two houses, besides the bishop's palace and abbey, were destroyed in the disastrous fire of 1395 (K. W. Nicholls (ed.), 'The register of Clogher' in *Clogher Rec.*, vii (1971–2), p. 390). The mention of a *capitalis platea* (ibid., pp 382–3), suggests an earthen rampart (see below, p. 405). The 'walls' of Clonfert are mentioned in a papal bull of 1496 (Archivio Vaticano, Registrum Lateranum, 1097, f. 142).

[4] Theiner, *Vetera mon.*, p. 521. Compare the similar desolation at Clonmacnoise, where there were only twelve wattle-and-daub houses surrounded by forest (ibid., p. 518).

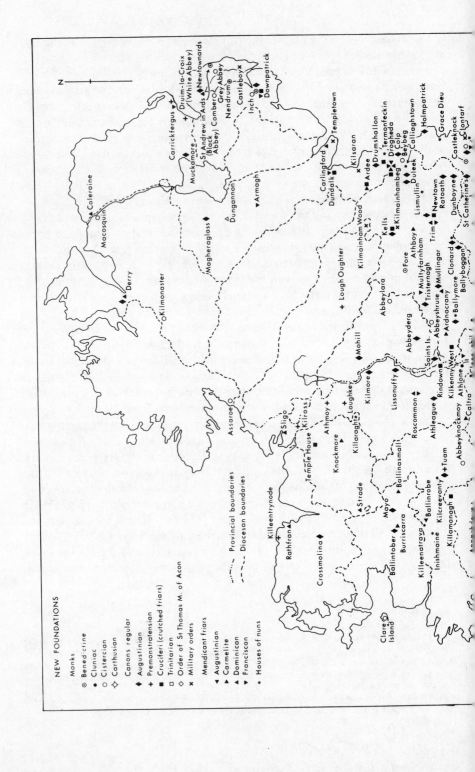

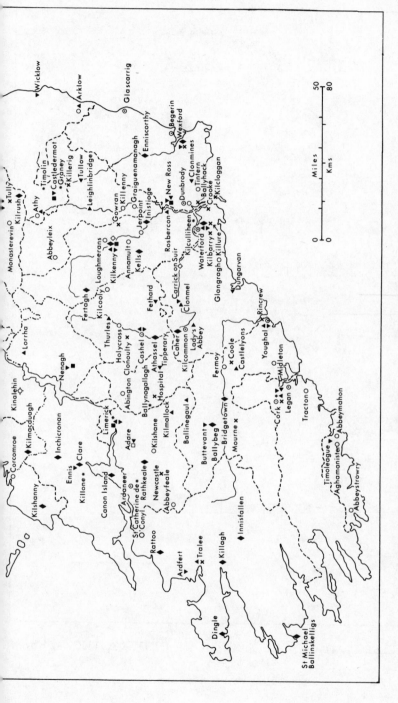

Map 8 THE SPREAD OF THE RELIGIOUS ORDERS, 1169-1320, by F. X. Martin

Gwynn & Hadcock, *Med. relig. houses.*

N

Woodburn +

Cross ♦

Ardnaree ◄
Errew ♦

Cavan ▲

Cloonshanville

Mayo ♦
Burriscara ◄

Longford ▲

Skreen ▲

Ballynahinch ►

▼ Ross

◄ Creevaghbaun

* Fooran

Cloncurry ►

Eglish ◄

Kilconnell ◄

Monasteroris ▼

Naas ▲

Galway ►

Meelick ▼

Kinalehin ▼

Portumna ▼

Kilcormac ▼

Aghaboe ▼

▼ Quin

▼ Askeaton

Knocktopher ►

Carrick on Suir *
Carrickbeg ▼

Horetown ▼

Youghal *

Kinsale ►

| 0 | Miles | 50 |
| 0 | Kms | 80 |

Map 9 **THE SPREAD OF THE RELIGIOUS ORDERS, 1320–1420,** by
F. X. Martin
Gwynn & Hadcock, *Med. relig. houses.*

unroofed, the other stone buildings totally ruined, and the house-plots (*areae*) of the city vacant except for heaps of rubble, recording the former presence of stone houses.[1] The immunity from secular violence enjoyed by churches and their lands, although frequently violated in practice, also attracted settlers to minor ecclesiastical sites, and the agreement of 1297 between the archbishop of Armagh and bishop of Clogher, on one side, and Mac Mathgamna and the chiefs of Airghialla on the other, suggests strongly that craftsmen in particular tended to make their residence there.[2]

Putting aside the ecclesiastical sites as a special case, Gaelic Irish settlement patterns of the later middle ages must be seen in the light of the twin factors of a highly mobile population and of the flimsy and insubstantial nature of the typical Irish dwelling, which, representing a minimum of investment in either labour or materials, could be erected with facility and abandoned without regret.[3] Of the mobility of the Irish population in the later middle ages there is little doubt.[4] Canny has demonstrated the movement of farmers in the 1560s between areas as supposedly culturally remote as Tyrone and the English Pale,[5] and the descriptions attached to the names of persons in the Elizabethan fiants for pardons also show a remarkable mobility, if only between different parts of the sept-lands as these were periodically redistributed under the Irish system. The Gaelic Irish house, even when the dwelling of a person of some consequence, tended to be of an insubstantial nature, which reflected this mobility. In the early thirteenth century Abbot Stephen of Lexington referred scornfully to Irish 'kings' who dwelt in little huts made of wattle, and nearly four centuries later we find the same scorn in the remarks of Fynes Moryson about 'a poor house of clay, or ... a cabin made of the boughs of trees and covered with earth, for such are the dwellings of the very lords among them'.[6] The armada fugitive, Captain Cuellar, similarly says of the Irish that 'they live in huts made of straw'.[7] More substantial houses of wattle-and-daub or of all-timber construction, however, also existed, while stone houses are recorded not only from the episcopal towns above referred to but also on church lands in some stony areas of the west.[8]

[1] *Ulster maps, c.1600*, plate iii.

[2] Nicholls, 'Register of Clogher', pp 416–18.

[3] For a later period see J. H. Andrews, 'Ireland in 1685' below, iii, 465–6; Arthur Dobbs, *An essay on the trade and improvement of Ireland* (2 vols, Dublin, 1729–31), ii, 6.

[4] Nicholls, *Land, law and society*, pp 9–11.

[5] Nicholas Canny, 'Hugh O'Neill, earl of Tyrone, and the changing face of Gaelic Ulster' in *Studia Hib.*, x (1970), pp 7–35.

[6] O'Dwyer, *Conspiracy of Mellifont*, p. 31; Falkiner, *Illustrations*, p. 231.

[7] Hugh Allingham (ed.), *Captain Cuellar's adventures*, with Cuellar's narrative trans. by Robert Crawford (London, 1897), p. 61.

[8] The basic study of Irish dwellings is Caoimhín Ó Danachair, 'Representations of houses on some Irish maps of *c.* 1600' in [John] Geraint Jenkins (ed.), *Studies in folk life: essays in honour of Iorwerth C. Peate* (London, 1969), pp 91–103. Cf. also Gernon's description in Falkiner, *Illustrations*, p. 355, and above, pp 229–32. For stone houses see, e.g., *Cal. papal reg. letters*, viii, 501; *Cal. pat. rolls Ire., Jas I*, pp 4, 381; Representative Church Body library, MS J/7, pp 41–2.

Such dwellings might be erected in isolated or temporary positions; Bishop Lyon of Cork and Cloyne, writing in 1596, declared that the Irish commonly dwelt 'in dispersed dwellings abroad . . . the people of the country, especially in Munster, dwell scattered by bogs' and woods' sides and such remote places'.[1] His reference to Munster suggests interesting regional variations in settlement patterns, but in 1608 a proclamation against scattered habitations in Ulster was issued at Armagh by the lord deputy, Chichester, in which he declared that the temporary dwellings in which the people of Tyrone passed the summer months, while following the herds, were not placed 'together in form of a town, but scattering and single, here and there'.[2] The opposite extreme is represented by Lifford in County Donegal in 1601, where beside the O'Donnell castle there were 'some eighty houses . . . compassed with an old ditch'.[3] Here the ditch implies a tradition of settlement, though not necessarily of continuous occupation; such a site, like the castles, could be abandoned in time of war. The four or five hundred Irish houses that existed on the island of Inch in Lough Swilly at the same date probably represent a settlement of refugees from the wars seeking the added safety of an island. The twenty houses around the castle of Longford O'Madden in County Galway that were burned in 1570[4] were probably more typical than Lifford of a castle-centred 'village' in Gaelic Ireland, the difference in size perhaps reflecting the comparative difference in power and importance between O'Donnell and O'Madden. At Cavan a real town, a trading centre of some importance, grew up in the sixteenth century under the protection of the O'Reillys and perhaps as a result of the initiative of the merchant family of MacBrady. In 1558 the then lord, Maolmórdha Ó Raghallaigh, in consideration of Bernard MacBrady (described as a merchant of Navan, although a native of the Cavan area) having paved one of the streets of Cavan at his own expense, granted him the vacant sites for another street and for a watermill.[5]

The permanent element in Gaelic Irish settlement patterns was, however, provided in general by the earthen forts or stone castles which were the residences of persons of substance,[6] but even these, around or within which a group of huts of the kind referred to would be erected by dependants and family members, might be abandoned in time of war or trouble. The Elizabethan state papers are full of records that such and such an Irish lord, before going into rebellion, 'broke' his castle. The castle of Strabane, which Turlough Luineach O'Neill had erected, was afterwards 'broken' by him 'for fear of the

[1] *Cal. S.P. Ire., 1596–7*, p. 19.   [2] Bodl., MS Rawl. A. 237. f. 115.
[3] *Cal. S.P. Ire., 1600–01*, pp 93–4.
[4] Bodl., MS Carte 57, f. 537.
[5] Gearóid Mac Niocaill (ed.), 'Cairt ó Mhaolmhordha Ó Raighilligh, 1558' in *Breifne*, i (1959), pp 134–5.
[6] Much of Iain A. Crawford's discussion of Gaelic settlement patterns in the Scottish highlands ('The present state of settlement history in the west highlands and islands' in Anne O'Connor and D. V. Clarke (ed.), *From the stone age to the 'Forty-five: studies presented to R. B. K. Stevenson* (Edinburgh, 1983), pp 350–67) is, I suspect, applicable to Ireland also.

English', subsequently rebuilt and broken again after the builder's death by his son Sir Art, at the instigation of Hugh O'Neill, when he joined the latter in his rising.[1] The motive of such destruction was, of course, to prevent the garrisoning of the place by hostile forces. In spite of the controversy regarding the 'medieval ring-fort',[2] and of the many references to the use and occupation of earthen forts in the later medieval period,[3] there has been as yet no systematic investigation of the subject, and even such a basic question as to whether the late medieval earthen fortification was usually a circular ring-fort, like the fort at Tullaghogue in Tyrone, still inhabited in 1600,[4] or of a rectangular shape, must remain uncertain. It is probable that regional or even local variations existed in this respect, and that both shapes occurred, but one would like to know, for instance, whether the 'bawns of sods' erected by native Irish grantees under the Ulster plantation were of round or rectangular form.[5] The names applied to such fortified enclosures in late medieval usage may sometimes have served to conceal their identity from modern readers: they are variously referred to as bawns (*badhbhdhún*, *badhún*, a term in modern usage appropriated exclusively to the stone-walled courts of castles),[6] as gardens (*garrdha*),[7] or as chief (or head) places (*cenn ait*).[8] The earthen bank is in one instance referred to as planted with quicksets,[9] and it seems likely that this was a usual practice, as a thick thorn hedge on the crest would much increase the defensive capacities of the earthen bank and ditch. In Barthelet's picture of Tullaghogue fort tall trees are shown growing on the encircling bank, as in a modern hedge. Another very ancient form of fortification within which dwellings were erected, and which likewise remained in use down to the wars of 1641, was the crannog

---

[1] T.C.D., MS 578 (E. 3. 10), p. 172.

[2] The best discussion to date is that by B. J. Graham, *Medieval Irish settlement: a review* (Lancaster, 1980; Historical Geography Research Series, 3), pp 34–9, which provides a useful corrective to the views of some archaeologists. See also above, pp 226–9.

[3] Two other references besides those cited here: a lessee in Co. Kilkenny in 1548 covenanted to 'mounde or compace the chiefe dwellyng place with a wall of grene soodes so it shalbe defensyble' (*Ormond deeds, 1547–84*, no. 11); a list of places of strength in Co. Roscommon taken by the rebels in 1597 groups them as 'castles' and 'earthen forts' (P.R.O., S.P. 63/183/59).

[4] Ó Danachair, 'Representations of houses'.

[5] See Pynnar's survey in George Hill, *An historical account of the plantation in Ulster . . . 1608–20* (Belfast, 1877; reprint, Shannon, 1970), pp 450–590.

[6] In the early fifteenth century the dwelling-place of Ruaidhrí Mac Mathghamhna of Oirghialla is described as a bawn (*bawona*) (*Registrum Johannis Mey*, p. 211).

[7] See e.g. *A.U.*, iii, 118, 192; O'Donovan's note in *A.F.M.*, iv, 998–9, n. v; and the following two notes.

[8] For the term *cenn ait* see *A.F.M.*, vi, 2,082; T.C.D., MS 1429 (I. 6. 12), no. vii; *Anal. Hib.*, no. 20 (1958), p. 5 ('a house towne or kynnad'). An award regarding Cloonihea (in Drangan Parish, Middlethird), Co. Tipperary, 1577, refers to 'the whole garden or chief place thereof (excepting one good house within the said garden)' (N.L.I., MS 2068, f. 124ᵛ), and a deed of 14 Apr. 1600 mortgages 'one acre of arable land of great Irish measure. . . . with his portion of the head place belonging to the said acre' in Monalin, Co. Wicklow (N.L.I., Wicklow MSS, unsorted collection).

[9] *Ormond deeds, 1584–1603*, nos 31, 32, where lessees in Co. Tipperary covenant to build 'a strong defensible garden, with a gate and strong ditches set with quickset'.

or fortified lake-island, not always artificial in origin.[1] References to these 'islands' are frequent in Elizabethan sources as well as in the Irish annals.

The erection of the stone tower-houses or 'castles' so common in most parts of Munster and Connacht seems to have begun on any appreciable scale only in the mid-fifteenth century, and most of them are probably of sixteenth-century date.[2] An accurate map of their distribution has yet to be made, since many of those that existed have perished completely,[3] but the evidence suggests a radiation of distribution outwards from certain centres, perhaps the port and other trading towns, in which case the actual distribution may reflect rather the moment of arrest of a gradual process of spread than deep-rooted regional distinctions. They were, however, almost but not entirely absent from Gaelic Ulster. These 'castles' were for the most part of a standard type which varies only in detail, normally with two or three lofted storeys over a vaulted basement; some, however, have two vaults and there is at least a single example with a vaulted stone roof, at Buolick in County Tipperary, erected in 1453.[4] Normally the roof would have been covered with thatch or wooden shingles. There are also larger and more elaborate examples of tower-houses, as at Bunratty and Blarney, and the subsidiary buildings could also differ in elaboration and extent. The normal accompaniment of each tower-house was a stone courtyard or bawn, within which would stand a hall and other subsidiary buildings of timber or wattle-and-daub, as well as smaller cabins or huts of the usual Irish type described above.[5] In some cases there might be two bawns, while it was probably frequent in the case of the less important 'castles' for the bawn to be of earth rather than stone. This might be due to the castle having been set down within an existing earthen fort. Castles were also erected within crannogs.[6] Timber castles are occasionally referred to, especially in the upper Barrow valley where building stone must have been scarce.[7] The method of their construction is uncertain.

[1] The crannog at Monaghan is illustrated by Barthelet (*Ulster maps, c.1600*, plate xi; cf. also plate v). That at Augher had a castle erected in it (ibid., no. x). For the crannog in Scotland see Crawford, 'Settlement history', p. 356.

[2] This conclusion is strongly supported by a list of the builders of 'castles' in MacNamara's country, Co. Clare, preserved in an English translation in R.I.A., MS 24.D.10, p. 70 (the surviving half of the Irish original is printed by Gwynn & Gleeson, *Killaloe*, p. 523, with a misleading description), the names in which seem reliable (see the remarks of George C. MacNamara in *N. Munster Antiq. Jn.*, iii (1913–15), pp 263–4). See also below, pp 767–9.

[3] The marking of sites on the ordnance survey maps can be erratic. Leask (*Castles*, p. 159) lists from this source 24 castles of all kinds in Co. Roscommon, but the state paper list of 1573 names 73, of which two are really in other counties and two are duplicates, leaving a total of 69 (P.R.O., S.P. 65/45/35, i). I know of one more erected between then and 1610.

[4] Myles Dillon (ed.), 'Laud Misc. 610 (contd)' in *Celtica*, vi (1963), pp 146–7. There is no published description of any of the remains at Buolick. For Irish castles in general the standard authority is Leask, *Castles*.

[5] Quinn, *Elizabethans & Irish*, p. 73; Ó Danachair, 'Representations of houses'; K. W. Nicholls, *The O'Doyne manuscript* (I.M.C., Dublin, 1983), pp 40, 42.

[6] As at Augher (*Ulster maps, c.1600*, plate xi) and at Lough Coura in Co. Offaly.

[7] *Ann. Conn.*, p. 734; *Ormond deeds, 1547–84*, no. 11; *Fiants Ire., Eliz.*, no. 589; Carte MS 568, f. 734.

In the late medieval period the whole of Ireland, with the exception of some waste areas of mountain and bog, was divided into a network of named and defined land units, the antecedents of the modern townlands, with which, in spite of many changes, amalgamations, and especially subdivisions, their boundaries in many cases still essentially correspond.[1] The essence of the townland system, the existence of a network of named and bounded units which retain their identity largely irrespective of the patterns of settlement and land-utilisation which may be imposed on them at any given time, is not peculiar to Ireland, although only in Ireland were these units recorded so thoroughly by the nineteenth-century surveyors of the ordnance survey. The same system can be traced also in parts of Scotland, where the difference in land-name patterns between 'Scotia' (the land north of Forth and Clyde) and Galloway on the one hand and Lothian and Strathclyde on the other is very clear in medieval records. In the former, we have a multitude of unit-names, corresponding each to a single large farm in size, while in the latter lands are normally defined as lying within a larger seigneurial or village unit.[2] In Ireland, it seems likely that not only do most of these units predate the Anglo-Norman arrival (although the latter certainly led to the creation by subdivision of many new ones, based on the holdings of the lesser free tenants) but they may in many cases go back to a much earlier age. If one might hazard a guess, the period of relatively high population and intensive reclamation that seems to have preceded the great plagues of the late seventh century seems a possible date for the formation of at least many of such units, but an even earlier origin is possible in some cases. Their boundary ditches, which even today can be often distinguished from the later field ditches by their greater size, may also in some cases be of very great antiquity. During the later medieval period these townland units were marshalled into an elaborate system of assessment, whose terminology varied widely and confusingly between area and area.[3] The assessment units would from the evidence appear to have been imposed, with a rough-and-ready reckoning, on the existing units, so that the latter, in spite of individual variations in size, normally emerged as a whole unit, or at least a

---

[1] There is now at last an excellent introduction to the townland system by Thomas McErlean, 'The Irish townland system of landscape organisation' in Terence Reeves-Smith and Fred Hammond, *Landscape archaeology in Ireland* (British Archaeological Reports, British Series 116; Oxford, 1983), pp 315–40.

[2] I have based this statement on a cursory study of the evidence contained in the *Register of the great seal of Scotland* (*Registrum magni sigilli regum Scotorum*) (Edinburgh, 1882–). It will be seen that I differ from the opinion of McErlean, who believes that the Irish townlands 'are the same type of small land units as the vills, trefs, towns, and townships etc. of Britain' ('Irish townland system', p. 333).

[3] For example, in Munster the *gniomh* (gneeve) was one-twelfth of the ploughland, corresponding to a nominal 10 acres; in Connacht, however, it was one-sixth of the quarter, i.e. a nominal 20 acres, but in Westmeath *gniomh* denoted the ploughland of 120 acres itself. There is a list of assessment units (with some slight errors) in McErlean, op. cit. A useful early list (though not exhaustive) is to be found in Lambeth Palace, Carew MS 614, f. 197.

simple and easily-handled fraction, in the assessment system.[1] Thus in Connacht, where there are some indications that the assessment system, based on the *baile* of four quarters, may have been created by the twelfth-century O'Connor king, Toirrdelbach or his son Ruaidrí, it would seem that the existing units, normally the holdings of separate septs or lineages, were each taken as a *baile*. Where, however, the holding was clearly too small to be assessed as a *baile* it became a *leathbhaile* or half-*baile*;[2] where too large, a *dhabhaile* or double *baile*.[3] In other areas the assessment system was probably of later date, but, once fixed, it remained unchanged, with the result that by the seventeenth century enormous anomalies had evolved as a result of clearance and reclamation. An extreme contrast is provided by the enormous 'quarters' in the woodland region in Killian barony, in north-east County Galway, and the tiny ones to be found in the districts east of Galway Bay and Lough Corrib. In some regions the assessment units formed an elaborate hierarchy; this was most developed in Connacht, where one might (theoretically at least) find the half-cartron of A in the cartron of B in the half-quarter of C in the quarter of D in the *baile* of E, each with its separate name, but in other areas it was much simpler. Every assessment unit notionally contained a fixed number of customary acres, though for the reason stated this might bear little relation to its actual size, as was evident when actual surveys were carried out in the seventeenth century.

Although any kind of precise demographic information is lacking, we can safely say that Ireland shared in the general European phenomenon of depressed population levels during the century and a half that followed the Black Death of 1348–9. Research in recent years has tended to date ever later the beginning of the secular upsurge of population which succeeded this period of demographic inertia and which is so characteristic of the sixteenth century and carried on into the early seventeenth,[4] and it now seems established that English population, following with a short timelag the trend of continental Europe, did not begin to rise rapidly until at least the second or third decade of the sixteenth century.[5] In Ireland, probably as a result of the incessant war and destruction that prevailed during the period of the Tudor

---

[1] It need hardly be said that the ideas of Helmut Jäger ('Land use in medieval Ireland: a review of the documentary evidence' in *Ir. Econ. & Soc. Hist.*, x (1983), at pp 52–3), which assume a continuous revision of the assessment system, which (as broken fractions of units were extremely rare) must necessarily imply a frequent alteration in unit boundaries, are mistaken.

[2] *Leathbhailes* do not occur in pairs, as would be the case if they resulted from division of entire units.

[3] *Dhabhaile* occurs as early as 1223 (Sheehy, *Pontificia Hib.*, i, 231, where 'Danaly' should be read 'Daualy').

[4] Ian Blanchard, 'Population change, enclosure and the early Tudor economy' in *Econ. Hist. Rev.*, xxiii (1970), pp 427–8, and references cited at p. 427.

[5] Bruce M. S. Campbell, 'The population of early Tudor England: a reevaluation of the 1522 muster returns and 1524 and 1525 lay subsidies' in *Journal of Historical Geography*, vii (1981), pp 145–54. This would appear to controvert the suggestions of John Hatcher, *Plague, population and the English economy, 1348–1530* (London, 1977), pp 65–6.

reconquest, the rise was to be delayed for three-quarters of a century. The seventeenth century was to be the age of a rapidly rising Irish population. If we are to accept the testimony of contemporary observers, as well as circumstantial evidence, late Elizabethan Ireland was still severely underpopulated. That usually acute English official, Andrew Trollope, estimated in 1581 that the Irish density was only one-eighth that of England (halving, in the course of writing his memorandum, his original estimate of a quarter!) and although this is a mere guess, and probably an exaggerated one, it records the impression of a contemporary.[1] The lack of people in this period is borne out by the frequent reference in documents to the shortage of tenants and cultivators, for whose services landlords competed and who wandered from place to place and master to master, apparently driven not by want but by restlessness and the inducements held out to them.[2] One response of the Irish lords to this shortage of labour was to claim that their subjects in general (and not just, as has been imagined, a hypothetical service class, for whose existence there is no documentary evidence) were bound to remain in their service and had no right to leave;[3] another can perhaps be seen in the imposition of agricultural labour services (ploughing, reaping, and the like) on the hereditary landowners with their territories.[4]

A further development of modern English population research has been a downward adjustment of the population level in the late fifteenth and early sixteenth centuries. A figure of 1.8 millions in 1524, with a suggestion that 'at its nadir the population may have been less than 1.5 millions, possibly little more than 1 million', has recently been suggested.[5] If this is accepted, then it would seem inevitable that estimates of population for such countries as Ireland and Scotland,[6] which were certainly less economically developed and more thinly populated than England, must be similarly adjusted downwards. We might then suggest that the Irish population in the early sixteenth century was below half a million, perhaps well below that figure, and that as a result of the severe conditions created by war it remained around that level until after 1600. Since there are certain indications suggesting the possibility of a phenomenal explosion of the population in the early seventeenth century, such a figure does not seem irreconcilable with recent estimates for the population in 1660.[7]

[1] P.R.O., S.P. 63/86/39.
[2] Nicholls, *Land, law and society*, pp 9–11.
[3] Ibid., pp 21–2, n. 11.
[4] Nicholls, *O'Doyne MS*, pp xiii–xiv.
[5] Campbell, 'Population of early Tudor England', p. 154.
[6] The Scottish population in the late sixteenth century has been (on what appears to be very scanty evidence) estimated at *c.* 800,000, giving a density of 11 per km² (Ian Whyte, *Agriculture and society in seventeenth-century Scotland* (Edinburgh, 1979), pp 8–9). One's confidence in the accuracy of this conjecture is hardly increased by the quotation in the same work of Helleiner's estimate of the Irish density as 27 per km², a figure which it need hardly be said is based on no Irish evidence whatsoever.
[7] I intend to discuss Irish population, 1349–1649, in a coming article.

Throughout the later middle ages Ireland was, of course, harried by endemic local war and disorder, the intensity of which seems to have experienced a marked increase in the sixteenth century, even before the Tudor reconquest injected a new element of more directed violence into an already violent situation. Such accounts as Sir Henry Sidney's description of the desolation of Munster in 1567, Spenser's account of the same unhappy province after Grey's scorched-earth policy during the Desmond rebellion, or Moryson's narrative of the similar situation of Ulster after the similar policy of Mountjoy in 1601–2, all combine to paint a situation in which a static or even declining population is easily comprehensible.[1] In the fifteenth century, Ireland, besides experiencing excessive war, had shared in the recurrent epidemics which characterised that unhealthy century. Subsequent to the great plagues of 1348–9 and 1361, the Irish annals record serious outbreaks of epidemic disease in 1383–4, 1392–3, 1397–8, 1401, 1406, 1408, 1414, 1419–20, 1446, 1466, 1470–71, 1478, 1488–9, 1519–20, and 1536, besides merely local visitations of pestilence. Serious famines are recorded in 1380, 1397, 1433, 1445, 1446, 1447, 1461–2, 1465, 1468, 1497, and 1545. That of 1497, the result of the exceptionally bad summer and autumn of 1496 which led to widespread mortality among livestock as well as to crop failure, was especially severe, 'for there was scarce an angle or recess in all Ireland wherein died not many persons of that hunger'.[2] And while Gaelic Irish lords, unlike Elizabethan soldiery in Ireland, do not seem to have gone in for the wholesale slaughter of noncombatants, the destruction of food supplies that characterised Irish warfare must have caused widespread mortality through starvation in the aftermath of local wars. Given all these factors, and also the more recondite possibility of a sex ratio heavily skewed towards males,[3] a low level of population in late Gaelic Ireland does not seem inconceivable.

The low population of Gaelic Ireland was reflected in a low intensity of land-utilisation, which commonly took the forms of grazing and of shifting (long-fallow) cultivation. The tendency to rely upon stock-rearing was, as always, reinforced by considerations of social pride; the herdsman, as everywhere, despised the dull laborious toil of the cultivator, and sixteenth-century English observers record the distaste for manual labour of those Irish who belonged, or claimed to belong, to distinguished lineages, a section who, from the process of lineage proliferation already referred to, constituted no small proportion of the population. Again, the endemic violence of the country was to some extent both a cause and a consequence of the pastoral economy; cattle, which could be

[1] It seems to me that the effects of both the local, but destructive, native wars and the more total variety practised by Elizabethan soldiers on the Irish economy and population have been grossly underestimated. I intend to discuss this factor in the article on Irish population I have referred to in a preceding note.

[2] *A.U.*, iii, 423.

[3] Possible changes in the sex ratio, and the possible effects of diet on that ratio, seem to have been traditionally ignored by demographers. A serious excess of males in the population would be consistent with certain features of sixteenth-century Irish society.

driven off to a place of safety, were less vulnerable to enemies than cornfields and granaries, easy targets for an incendiary's torch; while, conversely, the temptation to raid a neighbour's herds, always present in pastoral societies, breeds a climate of ready violence.

The picture of Gaelic Ireland as an entirely pastoral economy is, however, a grossly inaccurate generalisation. Although pastoral products probably provided, on balance, the larger portion of the Irish diet (Estyn Evans has remarked that the staple diet was probably butter and oatcake rather than oatcake and butter[1]), the Gaelic Irish practised agriculture on a fairly extensive scale, growing large quantities of oats, and a little barley and wheat, for food, and a considerable amount of flax for the making of linen. As has been observed, a long-fallow system, under which land was tilled for two or three years and then abandoned to pasture for a much longer period, was probably commoner than a regular course of rotation. The three-course rotation, of winter corn, spring corn, and fallow, which had become general in the Pale by the sixteenth century, is also found in some neighbouring Gaelic and gaelicised regions[2] (although the possibility of a lengthened fallow period cannot be entirely ruled out) and its influence was probably spread more widely, although the practice of always tilling newly-broken land for two successive years, which is widely authenticated,[3] may have been rather based on the greater ease of ploughing stubble than grassland. Land was occasionally manured with sand, not only sea-sand; in a deed of mortgage from a purely Gaelic region of central Tipperary in the mid-sixteenth century it is provided that if the mortgagee should manure the land with sand he could not be dispossessed by redemption until he had taken three crops,[4] presumably implying that after such a manuring it was usual to cultivate the land for three years running. In coastal areas where seaweed was abundant a much more intensive agriculture, based on its use as a fertiliser, was no doubt practised.[5] In general Irish fields lay open and unenclosed, the crops being surrounded for their protection, where necessary, by temporary fences of stakes and wattle which had an estimated life of two years. Only between different townlands were boundary hedges or ditches

---

[1] Estyn Evans, *Irish folk ways* (London, 1957), pp 81–2.

[2] The reckoning of tithes in 'couples' (a 'couple' being a unit composed of an acre of winter corn and an acre of spring corn) is a clear indication of a rotation of these crops. In 1543 the tithes belonging to the priory of Kilkenny West in Westmeath are reckoned in 'couples' in most of the Dillon and Dalton lordships and in a few townlands in the O'Ferrall country, the present Co. Longford; reckoning in acres is general in the latter, but extends also to a considerable area around Ballymore, in the present Co. Westmeath (inquisition in P.R.O.I., RC 9/9). Reckoning in acres suggests to me a monoculture of oats, and differences in soil may be the decisive factor. For further details and discussion see my forthcoming article 'Agricultural practices in sixteenth-century Ireland'.

[3] E.g. deed of mortgage of Pembrokestown, Co. Waterford, 10 Jan. 1578, in MSS of the marquis of Waterford, Curraghmore (here definitely a rotation of winter and spring crop) (K. W. Nicholls, 'Gaelic landownership in Tipperary' in William Nolan (ed.), *Tipperary: history and society* (Dublin, 1985), p. 98). Cf. *Civil Survey*, x, 85.

[4] Nicholls, 'Gaelic landownership', pp 100–01; cf. below, p. 473.

[5] See e.g. O'Flaherty, *West Connaught*, pp 57–9.

usual.[1] There is little information on the actual processes of agriculture. From the time of the Anglo-Norman arrival at least, and probably earlier, the Gaelic Irish ploughed with horses, not oxen, the horses being hitched to the plough by the hairs of their tails. The plough used in Gaelic Ulster, and perhaps in parts of the west as well, was of a cruder type than that found in the old colonial regions, requiring the services of a third man, the 'beamholder', who held down the front of the plough, in addition to the ploughman and driver.[2] The standard food crop, oats, provided not only food for men and horses but also malt for the making of ale, and even in the sixteenth-century Pale dredge malt, a mixture of oat and bere malt, was the standard material for brewing.[3] Horses were fed on unthreshed oats in the straw. For human consumption the grain was burned out of the straw, a peculiarly Gaelic practice,[4] and ground into meal which was usually consumed in the form of cakes based on a hot iron plate or 'griddle'. Querns were still widely used in the late medieval period, but the country also possessed numerous watermills, which in the Gaelic areas were usually of the small horizontal type in which the water drives a turbine wheel fixed in a vertical shaft which passes, above, without the need for gearing, through the grinding stones. Wheat, which was the standard food crop of the Pale (the Ulster annalist, in his notice of the famine of 1497, mentions the inflated price of wheat and ale in Meath and of oats 'among the Gael'[5]), may have been as important a crop as oats in south-eastern regions like County Kilkenny; it is mentioned as cultivated around Rosscarbery, County Cork, in 1517 and was grown on a small scale in many other parts of the country, where it figures in renders to lords.[6] Differences of soil and local climatic conditions would of course have affected the crops grown. In 1601 Inishowen grew oats and barley, as well as flax, but not wheat or rye.[7] The last-named, although grown for bread in the Pale, was obviously a crop of little interest to an oatcake-eating Gaelic population. In the mountainous regions of south Kerry in the seventeenth century we are told that the (spring sown) 'small' barley (*hordeum distichon*) was the form grown, but in areas of better soil it was probably less frequent than the autumn-sown bere (*h. vulgare*).[8] The latter was the standard barley of the Pale.[9] References to flax-growing are curiously rare, but as linen

[1] For a discussion of fencing practices see my forthcoming article, 'Agricultural practices in sixteenth-century Ireland'.

[2] A. T. Lucas, 'Irish ploughing practices', pt 2, in *Tools and Tillage*, ii, no. 2 (1973), pp 67–83; pt 3, in ibid., ii, no. 3 (1974), pp 149–60; pt 4, in ibid., ii, no. 4 (1975), pp 195–210.

[3] *Anal. Hib.*, no. 2 (1931), pp 158–9; cf. 'Acts of the privy council in Ireland, 1556–1571', ed. J. T. Gilbert, in *H.M.C. rep. 15*, app. iii (London, 1897), p. 49 and *passim*.

[4] For details of the process see A. Fenton, 'Net-drying, pot-drying and graddaning: small-scale grain drying and processing techniques' in *Saga och Sed* (Uppsala, 1982), pp 92–101.

[5] *A.U.*, iii, 422.

[6] Theiner, *Vetera Mon.*, p. 529; Lambeth Palace, Carew MS 625, f. (B), 20–23; T.C.D., MS 656 (F. 4. 25), f. 74; MS 1429 (I. 6. 12), no. xvii.

[7] R. A. Butlin, 'Land and people, *c.* 1600', below, iii, 161.   [8] *Civil Survey*, x, 85, 98, 108.

[9] For details of crops and cultivation in general see my forthcoming article, 'Agricultural practices in sixteenth-century Ireland'.

was an important Irish product and furnished in this period a considerable export trade, its cultivation must have been extensive, at least in the north and west. Its absence from records may be due to the sparsity of documentation from these regions. In the old colonial regions such as Kilkenny and Tipperary, agricultural production was of a more varied nature than in the purely Gaelic ones of the north and west. Hay-making, which seems to have been unknown in most parts of Ireland at this period, is recorded from this area, and orchards were probably more numerous here than elsewhere; there are, however, occasional references to their existence in the purely Gaelic regions.[1]

Cattle were of course the primary element in the Irish pastoral economy, providing not only milk and its derivative products—butter, cheese, and sour curds—but also meat and blood, which was drawn from the living cattle to serve as a foodstuff, and the hides which came to form the largest item in Ireland's exports. The great herds of cattle possessed by the lords and their kindred, together with their herdsmen and guards—for defence against the *creach* or cattle-raid necessitated a substantial body of guardians—were known by the collective term of *caoruigheachta* (a term that seems to have originally denoted the human personnel alone), anglicised as 'creaghts', 'keriaghtes', etc. Cattle were a highly mobile form of wealth and economic resource which could be quickly and easily moved to a safer locality in time of war or trouble, as well as moving in search of fresh pasture within a smaller radius. There has probably been too much readiness to identify the movement of the herds with a simple transhumance from winter quarters in the lowlands to upland summer pastures. True transhumance or booleying,[2] as it was later called, was to be found in all the mountainous regions of Ireland,[3] but it must be remembered that large stretches of the country were quite devoid of upland grazings and it is certain that, in the thinly peopled state of the country, similar movements occurred from the home pastures around the settlement site to other more distant lands, not necessarily at a higher altitude, which were lying waste or unoccupied. Gaelic legal custom favoured this practice in permitting the grazing of unused or unoccupied lands either by the lords or by the 'kinsmen and neighbours' of the nominal owners, if they were ready to pay the tribute due out of the lands. The distinction need not have been a rigid one. The custom in any case was of great economic importance, permitting a wide range of movement and often, especially in times of waste and destruction, rendering the nominal ownership of the land of little importance.[4] In time of war,

[1] See e.g. *Cal. pat. rolls Ire., Jas I*, pp 64, 80, 280, 438; Nicholls, *O'Doyne MS*, pp 40, 42. An interesting reference from Co. Kilkenny will be found in *Ormond deeds, 1547–84*, no. 11.

[2] From the Irish word *buaile*, which in its later significance denoted a shieling or summer milking place. Its earlier meaning would, however, appear to have been more general; cf. *Misc. Ir. Ann.*, p. 170; *A.F.M.*, iv, 1134.

[3] J. M. Graham, 'South-west Donegal in the seventeenth century' in *Ir. Geography*, vi (1970), pp 41, 144; J. M. Graham, 'Rural society in Connacht, 1600–1640' in Stephens & Glasscock, *Ir. geog. studies*, pp 196–9.

[4] Nicholls, *Land, law and society*, pp 16–17.

however, it is clear that whole communities frequently left their lands with all their cattle and movable property, sometimes migrating considerable distances, and subsisting for long periods of time by grazing their cattle on other people's lands.[1] The rhymers or poets (*fileadha*), who enjoyed a quasi-sacred status, could wander with their herds through hostile territories in a way not open to others who did not enjoy the same immunity from attack. The wealth of the poets in cattle was noted by Thomas Smyth in the sixteenth century,[2] and Flann Mac Conmidhe, 'head of a great *caoruigheachta*', was presumably one of the great Ulster poetic lineage of that name, though his slaying by Scots in Clandeboye in 1536,[3] as well as other examples of raids upon poets recorded in the annals, shows that their exemption from attack, like that of the church, was not always real.

A statute of 1430 was directed against the 'Irish rymers, outlaws and felons' who brought their 'keryaghtes', horses, cattle, pigs, sheep, and goats to graze on the borders of the 'Maghery', the area subject to the Dublin administration.[4] It is possible that the statute, passed during the ascendancy of the Talbot faction in the absence of the White Earl of Ormond from Ireland, reflects a covert attack on the latter's patronage of Irish men of learning. A later statute of 1474, aimed against the 'Irish rymers and hermits' who settled on lands in County Kildare without the consent of the lords of the soil, arouses interesting speculations when it expressly exempts those who will settle within three miles of Ballymore, (Old) Kilcullen, or Kilgowan.[5] If these were the Dublin mile of 2560 yards rather than the English one, then the sixteenth-century settlements of the poetic family of Mac Eochadha (MacKehoe) along the frontier would have fallen within the prescribed limits.[6] The three places named were frontier lordships of the Eustace family, with whom the Mac Eochadhas were already intermarrying,[7] and the implication is of a Eustace patronage of the latter in this area.

'Creaching', or cattle raiding, always remained a favourite recreation of the Gaelic ruling classes, and its destructive effects upon the economy should not be underestimated; not only was it commonly accompanied by the burning of houses and corn-ricks but the plundered cattle, if for some reason they could not be carried off, might be wantonly and uselessly slaughtered.[8] A further effect of the frequency of the *creach* would have been to concentrate the ownership of stock in the hands of those strong enough to guard it effectively; it would have been the weaker elements in society who would be the obvious

[1] Katharine Simms, 'The medieval kingdom of Lough Erne' in *Clogher Rec.*, ix (1977), pp 139–40. Dr Simms perhaps lays more emphasis on regular seasonal migrations and less on irregular ones than I have done here.

[2] *U.J.A.*, 1st ser., vi (1858), p. 166.　　　　　　　　　　　　　　　　[3] *A.U.*, iii, 608.

[4] *Stat. Ire., Hen. VI*, pp 34–7.

[5] *Stat. Ire., 12–22 Edw. IV*, pp 214–17.

[6] Nicholls, 'Anglo-French Ireland and after' in *Peritia*, i (1982), p. 399, n. 5.

[7] T.C.D., MS 1346 (H. 4. 4), p. 72.

[8] *A.U.*, iii, 350.

targets for raids and it is clear that two or three such at close intervals would have reduced even a prosperous group to beggary. Their only recourse would have been a similar raid on some other victim.

The Gaelic Irish, as has been observed, did not make hay, and the customary practice was to leave certain lands unused during the summer in order to utilise the standing herbage as winterage for cattle.[1] Given that most cattle were not housed but merely brought into bawns or enclosures at night[2]—it is indeed unlikely that housing would even have been possible for the enormous herds possessed by the Irish lords and prominent persons—a heavy mortality of cattle, with consequent dearth or famine, could be expected in the case of a severe winter and delayed spring. In old colonial areas like the Butler lordship, however, hay continued to be made and we hear of cattle being housed in considerable numbers.[3] According to sixteenth-century English observers, Irish cattle were of small size, a statement supported by what little information we have on dead weights—the average beast provided for the victualling of English soldiers in Ireland was expected to produce 200 lb of prime beef, besides neck and shin, but could, as Lord Chancellor Gerrard complained, work out at as little as 141 lb.[4] The milk yield seems also to have been low; five gallons of butter (c. 40 lb) would seem to have been the expected yearly production per cow.[5] Cows were let out by the lords and others in return for a render of butter, which in the Ormond territories appears to have been three and a half gallons per cow.[6] In such cases the renter would have had the benefit, not only of the surplus of butter, but of the buttermilk and the calf.

Sheep and pigs played a much more subordinate role in Irish pastoralism. As there was in the early sixteenth century a fairly considerable export of wool from the south-eastern ports, we may assume that sheep were of greater importance in the southern regions than in the north and west. In 1581 John fitz Edmond, dean of Cloyne, complained of having been robbed over the previous three years of over twenty thousand head.[7] The evidence suggests that the native Irish sheep resembled the present Shetland breed; it produced a long coarse fleece, plucked instead of shorn, which served for the manufacture of the friezes and rug mantles which figured as an Irish export. We also hear of herds of goats in the south.[8] Herds of swine, fed upon acorns in the woods in the usual European manner,[9] seem to have been of less importance in the

---

[1] *Cal. S.P. Ire., 1588—92*, pp 481-2; P.R.O.I., chancery pleadings, bundle S, no. 63.

[2] Those who had only a few beasts could, however, bring them into their dwelling (Moryson, in Falkiner, *Illustrations*, p. 220; Hanmer, in P.R.O., S.P. 63/214, f. 231).

[3] *Ormond deeds, 1509—47*, no. 178 (4); *1547—84*, p. 70.

[4] *Anal. Hib.*, no. 2 (1931), pp 143, 158.

[5] B.L., Lansdowne MS 159, f. 109.

[6] Graham, 'South-west Donegal in the seventeenth century', p. 149; N.L.I., MSS 2506, f. 112; 2507, ff 84, 84ᵛ.

[7] P.R.O., S.P. 63/83/29.

[8] Ibid.; *Ormond deeds, 1547—84*, p. 3.

[9] Uppsala University Library, MS H.248, f. 14ᵛ; B.L., Lansdowne MS 159, f. 109ᵛ.

economy than one might expect. The great herds of mares kept by the lords and other great persons seem to have been solely for the purpose of breeding; there is no evidence that they were ever milked, and the Irish disliked riding mares.[1] Fynes Moryson noted with amazement that some Irishmen were ready to eat horse-flesh,[2] but this was probably exceptional except in case of war or famine. Besides supplying home needs, in war, agriculture, and transport (the pack-horse, as over most of Europe, was the normal and indeed the only means of transportation: in 1581 it was said that 'the manner of carrying wine in Ireland is in little barrels on horses' backs', and when Hugh Roe O'Donnell made preparations for revolt in 1596 he levied 600 horses for transport, with two baskets for each),[3] horse-breeding also provided for a considerable export trade to England and the Continent.[4]

The hunting of wild beasts and inland fisheries also contributed to the Gaelic economy. Hunting provided not only venison and the flesh of other edible animals and birds but also the furs which formed a substantial item in Ireland's export trade.[5] The most valuable fur was that of the pine marten, which was hunted with packs of dogs to obtain it.[6] The skin of the squirrel, used to make purses, was in demand,[7] while wolves and otters also provided skins for export. Deer, besides being hunted with hounds, were also taken in springalds made by tying down the branches of trees.[8] Another forest product were the goshawks, whose eyries were regarded as an important asset and which were likewise exported.[9] Most Irish rivers had their fishing weirs, and the eel-fisheries of the midland rivers—the Shannon and its tributaries, especially the Inny—were of some importance economically, attracting merchants from Dublin and the Pale.[10] In 1452 we learn that a convoy of merchants, conveying fish from Athlone, the centre of the eel-fishery region, to Trim under the escort of some of the local Irish, were attacked, massacred, and plundered by Fearghal Óg Mág Eochagáin; 'and no man living shall give an account of the multitude of eeles lost or left therein, wherefore that defeate was called *maidm-an-esg*' (the defeat of the fish).[11] The estuarine salmon fisheries, such as those of the Bann and Shannon—the former a surviving asset of the earldom of Ulster and always worked by English and Anglo-Irish, the latter belonging to the citizens of Limerick—were of considerable value, while the sea fisheries of the

---

[1] Moryson in Falkiner, *Illustrations*, pp 284–5; Payne in *Tracts relating to Ireland* (Irish Archaeological Society, 2 vols, Dublin, 1841–3), i, 7.

[2] Moryson, pp 228–9; *Cal. S.P. Ire., 1601–3*, p. 251.

[3] *Cal. S.P. Ire., 1574–85*, p. 321; *1596–7*, pp 152–3.

[4] A. K. Longfield, *Anglo-Irish trade in the sixteenth century* (London, 1929), pp 99–101.

[5] Ibid., pp 62–6.

[6] Uppsala University Library, MS H.248, f. 16; *Cal. Carew MSS*, i, 32.

[7] Ibid.

[8] Falkiner, *Illustrations*, p. 323.

[9] Longfield, *Anglo-Irish trade*, pp 94–5. I hope some day to publish a short note on the references to the goshawk in Ireland.

[10] Below, iii, 19.

[11] 'Annals of Ireland, from 1443 to 1468 . . .' in *Ir. Arch. Soc. Misc.*, i, 234–5.

southern and western coasts, although worked by foreigners rather than natives, brought in a considerable revenue to the local lords in dues for the use of port and shore facilities.[1]

On local industrial production there is hardly any information and on internal trade very little. A considerable amount of linen cloth was produced for export as well as for home use, principally in the north and west, and pieces of linen seem to have served as a medium of exchange in Galway in the fifteenth and early sixteenth centuries.[2] The export trade in linen declined in the sixteenth century, yarn replacing the finished cloth, perhaps as a result of increasing war, in which looms would be vulnerable to destruction.[3] The Irish dress of the sixteenth century used large quantities of linen: thirty or forty yards are mentioned as being used in a lord's shirt,[4] while the two smocks looted from a woman in 1575 by the men who arrested her husband contained between them twenty-eight yards and her kerchief or turban twenty-four.[5] Sixteenth-century statutes directed against Irish costume severely cut down the amount of cloth permitted to be used in garments.[6] Coarse woollen cloths, such as friezes and—most importantly—the famous Irish mantles, were also produced from the native wool, the mantles forming a considerable item of export.[7] The mantle was, of course, the most famous item of the native Irish dress and, if we are to believe observers from Perelhos in 1397 to Trollope in 1581, often the only one.[8] In Ireland, as in the medieval Arab world, the weaver's trade was regarded as a degrading one,[9] and it appears to have been practised by the very poor; Bingham, writing of Connacht in 1592, refers to a scheme for encouraging trade whereby 'the gentlemen and the rest shall sell . . . their cows and garrans, and the poor their linen cloth and yarn'.[10] Artisans and craftsmen are rarely mentioned in the surviving records, but the Annals of Ulster occasionally record the deaths of wrights (sair) who are obviously persons of high social

[1] Below, iii, 36–7.
[2] The will and inventory of John Blake of Galway, 1468, expresses certain debts in *lineos* (O'Flaherty, *West Connaught*, p. 206); that of Dominick Lynch, 1508, leaves legacies in *linteamentas* to various persons (*Ir. Arch. Soc. misc.*, i, 79). Cf. Gearóid Mac Niocaill, 'Meabhran dlí Ó Mhuintír Eoluis' in *Galvia*, iv (1957), pp 25–6.
[3] Longfield, *Anglo-Irish trade*, pp 86–92.
[4] H. F. McClintock, *Old Irish and Highland dress* (Dundalk, 1943; 2nd ed., 1950), pp 80–81, 102.
[5] Bodl., Carte MS 55, p. 251.
[6] McClintock, *Old Irish dress*, pp 84–5. For an example of the enforcement of laws against Gaelic Irish dress (in Cork, 1578), see *Cal. Carew MSS*, ii, 142.
[7] Longfield, *Anglo-Irish trade*, pp 81–5; McClintock, *Old Irish dress*, pp 51–3.
[8] Ibid., pp 96–100; Mahaffy, 'Two early tours in Ireland', p. 7; *Cal. S.P. Ire., 1574–85*, p. 318. The Irish term for the mantle, from the thirteenth to the seventeenth century was *falaing*, not, as McClintock thought, *brat*.
[9] See the remark of Conall Mageoghagan: 'This Shane [O'Conor] was the son of a woman that could weave, which of all trades is the greatest reproach amongst the Irishry, especially the sons and husbands of such tradeswomen . . .' (*Ann. Clon.*, pp 314–15). For the parallel prejudice against weavers in the medieval Arab world see Robert Brunschvig, 'Metiers vils en Islam' in *Studia Islamica*, xvi (1962), pp 50–55, and S. D. Goitein, *A medieval society*, i (Berkeley, Cal., 1967), p. 92.
[10] *Cal. S.P. Ire., 1588–92*, p. 563.

status and who sometimes achieved the ancient and honorific rank of *ollamh*[1] in their profession. Augustin Ó Carmaic, who died in 1431, was *ollamh* in wrightship (or carpentry) of all Fermanagh (*ollamh sairsi Fermanach uile*),[2] and Mathew Ó Mailruanaigh (died 1471) was *ollamh* in metalwork (*cerda*) to Mág Uidhir and is described as a skilled goldsmith (*sai oircerdna*: the term *sai* is that usually employed to denote distinction in any learned profession).[3] The existence of these goldsmiths and metal workers, 'who make their chalices, houps, buttons for their sleeves, and crucifixes and such like',[4] is well attested by the surviving examples of their work. It may not be entirely due to the choice of the Fermanagh compilers of the Annals of Ulster that we have these unique notices of craftsmen; it is possible that Fermanagh was especially rich in them, as it was in scholars and clerics.[5] Sometimes a wright might also be a cleric, as in the case of Eóghan Ó Diarmada, *saer* and Augustinian canon regular.[6] In 1478 we hear of wrights (*sair*) being sent for from Fermanagh to build engines for the siege of the Rock of Loch Cé in Connacht.[7] To the same class of master-wrights would have belonged, in an ecclesiastical context, the masters of the works (*magistri operum*) of the primates of Armagh,[8] and the sept of the Dowgans who were the bishop's carpenters at Raphoe, and held lands in the termon there.[9] We know of the presence of stonemasons and of monumental sculptors, such as the O'Tunney family in the Butler territories,[10] from their surviving works. More humble craftsmen, such as smiths and shoemakers, were, like the weavers, found everywhere; in the O'Doyne lordship in the late sixteenth century they had to pay a render to the lord in horseshoes and brogues respectively.[11] Although iron was one of the staple Irish imports, some smiths carried on local smelting on a small scale, and a question as to the possible existence in some places of small manufacturing communities is raised by the occurrence in 1612 of an annual render of 'thirty wooden dishes and six stone of iron' paid to O'Hara out of a now unidentifiable townland in Leyny, County Sligo.[12]

[1] For the *ollamh* see Gearóid Mac Niocaill, 'À propos du vocabulaire social irlandais du bas moyen âge' in *Etudes Celt.*, xii (1970–71), pp 523–7.

[2] *A.U.*, iii, p. 116. The translation (p. 117) is a mere wild guess. Cf. the obit of a probable descendant, Mathghamhain Ó Carmaic, 'an honoured well-to-do wright' (*saer maith onórach*), in 1533 (ibid., p. 592).

[3] Ibid., p. 266. The translation is again erroneous.

[4] Thomas Gainsford, in Quinn, *Elizabethans & Irish*, p. 167.

[5] Simms, 'Medieval kingdom of Lough Erne', pp 136–7.

[6] *A.U.*, iii, 106; cf. p. 152.   [7] *Ann. Conn.*, p. 580.

[8] The master of the works at Armagh held lands in return for his services. In the fifteenth century we find the office occupied by various persons, some—if not all—of them priests, but by the sixteenth century it had become hereditarily vested in the family of MacGillamura. See *Registrum Johannis Mey*, pp 103–6, 344; Gwynn, *Med. province Armagh*, pp 94–6, 266.

[9] *Cal. pat. rolls Ire., Jas I*, p. 380; *Inq. cancell. Hib. repert.*, ii, app. v.

[10] John Hunt, 'Rory O'Tunney and the Ossory tomb sculptures' in *R.S.A.I. Jn.*, lxxx (1950), pp 72–8; Edwin C. Rae, 'Irish sepulchral monuments of the later middle ages, pt II: the O'Tunney atelier' in ibid., ci (1971), pp 1–40, and below, pp 774–5.

[11] Nicholls, *O'Doyne MS*, p. 7.   [12] *Cal. pat. rolls Ire., Jas I*, p. 259.

We have even less information on internal trade. We have evidence that merchants from the port towns would travel the countryside, selling their imported merchandise and collecting local products for export. An unsigned letter formerly in the Blake collection, addressed to John Blake (died 1468), a Galway merchant, and his wife Juliane French, asks them to come with their wine to the writer's town of Roscommon, where they would be able to conveniently sell all their merchandise, and where the writer had the linen cloth that he owed to them ready and awaiting their arrival.[1] In the early sixteenth century we find Galway merchants trading in Tír Conaill, though they had arrived by sea.[2] In any case, the wills and inventories of fifteenth-century Galway and Limerick merchants show the extent of their commercial dealings with the Gaelic and gaelicised population.[3] Foreign trading ships dealt not only with the port towns but directly with the rural population at many small havens along the western and south-western coasts: in 1420 we hear incidentally of an English ship in the harbour at Ballyshannon, County Donegal, and another source explicitly calls it a trading ship, while in the sixteenth century many Spanish ships were trading in the lordships of the southwest.[4] There were probably always local merchants resident in the interior as well. In the 1560s there were native Gaelic merchants at Armagh who travelled on business through the O'Neill territories,[5] and this is unlikely to have been a recent development. It seems a likely supposition that some at least of the many merchant families of Gaelic origin who established themselves in the chartered towns during the fifteenth century—such as the Dorsey family (Ó Dorchaidh, later Darcy) in Galway, or the Ronaynes in Cork and Kinsale—had been already operating as rural merchants, or at some of the smaller ecclesiastical centres, before their immigration to the towns. In the sixteenth century we find such a pattern followed by that branch of the Breifne erenagh lineage of MacBrady whose members appear as merchants within the Pale at Navan and Drogheda, as well as being instrumental in promoting the urban development of the town of Cavan in their native region.[6] Cavan was one of a number of Gaelic centres (others being Longford and Granard) whose development as markets by their lords in the fifteenth century aroused the jealousy of the Irish parliament, concerned to protect the markets of the Pale, in 1480.[7] The expressions used in this case suggest that this was a recent development, but markets

[1] Copy in N.L.I. MS 4140, pp 154–5. The original was destroyed in 1922. See also below, p. 503.

[2] See e.g. *S.P. Hen. VIII*, iii, 140.

[3] Mac Niocaill, *Na buirgéisí*, ii, 502–3, 519–21.

[4] *A.U.*, iii, 84–5; *Ann. Conn.*, pp 452–3; Longfield, *Anglo-Irish trade*, p. 59.

[5] P.R.O., S.P. 63/29/32.

[6] See above, p. 404, n. 5. Patrick Brady, mayor of Drogheda in 1641, was a nephew of the Bernard mentioned in that note (see the genealogies in R.I.A., MS 23. E. 26, p. 284; T.C.D., MS 3397 (N.5. 12), f. 18). An earlier Patrick Brady, described as of Tonemore (Tonaghmore on the termon of Kilmore), merchant, in 1601 (*Fiants Ire., Eliz.*, no. 6559) was a brother of Brian and an uncle of the mayor.

[7] *Stat. Ire., 12–22 Edw. IV*, pp 818–21.

as well as fairs appear to have been held at some ecclesiastical sites, such as Eastersnow (*Disert Nuadhan*) in County Roscommon, where it is recorded in 1590 that a Saturday market had traditionally been held beside the church 'when there is peace'.[1] Again, there is little information on them. It seems to have been a usual practice for merchants to purchase from a lord the exclusive right of trading within his territory; statutes in restraint of this practice, declaring that it did not cover hawks nor could be exercised over ports and havens, were passed by the Galway town council in 1530 and 1532.[2] Lords might also claim a monopoly in important products such as hides, as well as general rights of preemption within their territories.[3] In 1576 Lord Roche was exacting a 5 per cent duty on all goods purchased by merchants within his country.[4]

The decline of the colonial lordships in Ireland in the later fourteenth century left the port towns of the southern and western coasts in an increasingly isolated position, and after 1400 they passed almost entirely outside the control of the Dublin administration, developing into virtually autonomous urban republics controlled by merchant patriciates, a surprising number of whose members bore Gaelic surnames. By the sixteenth century not only municipal government but almost the entire ownership of urban property had been engrossed by the patriciates, whose genealogical multiplication parallels that of the Gaelic and gaelicised lineages in the countryside. Their rise must have involved a serious social and economic depression of the craftsman element, resembling that which occurred in contemporary Scotland, and a restriction of social mobility within the urban population.[5] The oligarchies, however, did not become completely closed bodies; the Dorsey family had been settled in Galway for five generations—without appearing in the surviving records—before the time of James Riabhach Dorsey, a man of great wealth who in 1578 became the first of his name to hold municipal office.[6] It is reasonable to assume that the position of his ancestors had been a fairly modest one, but in the early seventeenth century his sons and grandsons were among the leading persons of the town. By 1640 the surname had been changed to Darcy. The Dorseys illustrate the fact that in all the towns families of Gaelic origin were to be found, even at the highest level. The law of the western towns, at least, was Roman, not common law, though by the second decade of the sixteenth century

---

[1] Inquisition of 2 May 1590 (P.R.O.I., RC 9/15).

[2] Hore & Graves, *Southern & eastern counties*, p. 245; *H.M.C. rep. 10*, app. v, pp 404–5.

[3] Hore & Graves, *Southern & eastern counties*, pp 164, 246; *Celtic Soc. Misc.*, pp 103–4.

[4] Hore & Graves, *Southern & eastern counties*, pp 273, 279.

[5] Little has so far been written on the Irish towns, although a foundation has been laid by Professor Mac Niocaill, 'Socio-economic problems of the late medieval Irish town' in *Hist. Studies*, xiii (1981), pp 7–22. See also Nicholls, 'Anglo-French Ireland and after', pp 376–7. 'The Irish town in the sixteenth and seventeenth centuries' in R. A. Butlin (ed.), *The development of the Irish town* (London, 1977), is a useful assemblage of factual information. For references to individual towns see below, iii, 1–38.

[6] *Hy Fiachrach*, pp 46–51; *H.M.C., rep. 10*, app. v, p. 428.

the latter seems to have been reestablishing itself in Galway.[1] The high-water mark of the towns' prosperity, to judge by their buildings, would seem to have been the early years of the sixteenth century, after the growth of the Atlantic trade; they appear to have declined somewhat in the second half of the century. The staples of the Irish import trade which passed through them were wine, iron, and salt; the staple exports, as has been seen, cloth, hides, sheepskins, and furs. In the early sixteenth century a trade in timber grew up in the south-east. The trade in hides probably always played the dominant role in the export trade, as witness the numbers of Irish hides imported into Italy from the 1460s onward;[2] in the later sixteenth century, with the decline of the cloth industry, this dominance must have increased. The profits which the towns derived from their monopolistic position in overseas trade were relatively very large when compared with the poverty of Ireland as a whole—'the poorest land in the world', as Le Bouvier called it[3]—and although all the Irish towns were small by European standards they were well built, largely of stone, though their exposed position was reflected in the castle-like architecture of the larger houses, many of which, indeed, were simply urban tower-houses.[4]

A word must be said here on the position of the gaelicised lordships, that is, those ruled by lords of Anglo-Norman surname: the *Gaill* as they are called in the Gaelic learned tradition to distinguish them from the *Gaedhil*, the original inhabitants of Ireland. Two streams of Irish historical myth, the one—which incidentally owed much to the deliberate myth-making of medieval Gaelic scholars[5]—stressing the archaism and unchanging quality of Gaelic Irish society,[6] the other seeing the 'Anglo-Norman invaders and settlers [and their agnatic descendants after many generations of Gaelic Irish mothers] in the role of alien invaders'[7] have come together to assert that the lordships ruled by lords of Anglo-Norman descent must have differed fundamentally in their nature and organisation from those of the *Gaedhil*. The available evidence lends little support to such an assumption. One must however look at the terminological divisions, found in sources of the period, on which it would appear to be grounded.

The anonymous early sixteenth-century writer of the well-known tract on the 'regyons' of Ireland,[8] having listed the sixty or so 'chief captaynes' of 'the

[1] See especially *Stat. Ire., 11–22 Edw. IV*, pp 572–3; M. J. Blake (ed.), *Blake family records, 1300–1600* (London, 1902), pp 53–5.

[2] M. E. Mallett, 'Anglo-Florentine commercial relations, 1465–91' in *Econ. Hist. Rev.*, xv (1962–3), pp 258, 263.

[3] Le Bouvier, *Description des pays*, p. 122.

[4] T. G. Delaney, 'The archaeology of the Irish town' in M. W. Barley (ed.), *European towns: their archaeology and early history* (London, 1977), pp 48–64.

[5] See Donnchadh Ó Corráin, 'Nationality and kingship in pre-Norman Ireland' in *Hist. Studies*, xi (1978), pp 1–13; Nicholls, 'Anglo-French Ireland and after', pp 392–3.

[6] Ó Corráin, loc. cit.; Nicholls, *Land, law and society*, pp 2–3, 21.

[7] Frame, *Colonial Ire.*, p. ix; the words in brackets are of course the present writer's. Cf. also my remarks in 'Anglo-French Ireland and after', p. 371.

[8] *S.P. Hen. VIII*, ii, 1–31.

kinges Iryshe enmyes' and described the polity of the Gaelic world, goes on to say that 'ther is more than 30 greate captains of thenglysshe noble family that folowyth the same Iryshe ordre and kepeith the same rule'. He then lists 'the countyes that obey not the kinges laws' and says that 'all thenglysshe folke of the said countyes ben of Iryshe habyt, of Iryshe language and of Iryshe condytions, except the cyties and the walled tounes'. There is little evidence here that the writer saw any serious cultural or political difference between the existing condition of the two groups; the distinction, as he draws it, is a legal one based on descent. 'Thenglysshe' are those who are by agnatic descent subjects of the king, even if they are in fact oblivious of his laws or authority; if they chose to submit to the latter, they would be automatically received as subjects. The Gaelic lords, on the other hand, were in legal theory the king's 'Irish enemies'; aliens outside the system. The actual condition of the two is immaterial in this theoretical framework. In a rather similar manner, the distinction drawn in Gaelic writings between *Gaedhil* and *Gaill* is based on theoretical reasons, but here antiquarian, not legal. The classic Irish historical tradition, formulated before the eighth century and enshrined in its definitive form in the *Leabhar Gabhála* or 'Book of Invasion' well before the coming of the Anglo-Normans, had laid down firmly that the 'last' legitimate conquest of Ireland was that by the sons of Míl of Spain, from whom the Gaelic ruling classes claimed descent.[1] This being the case, the descendants of subsequent invaders, no matter how Gaelic in cultural identity, could only be accepted, as it were, on an 'associate' basis. In each case the distinction is one of descent, rather than of condition. And of course we must not forget that in each case, likewise, the descent was a purely agnatic one. The mother, paternal grandmother, and—if later genealogical tradition is correct—paternal great-grandmother of Piers Ruadh, earl of Ormond and Ossory, were all of Gaelic Irish birth. To an outsider arriving in Ireland, the differences in any region between the lordships of Anglo-Norman and of Gaelic surname would have appeared imperceptible.

This is not of course to say that the same outside observer, as he travelled across autonomous Ireland, would not have noticed wide regional variations in the economic conditions and human geography of the districts he passed through. The two extremes would have been the Butler lordship in Kilkenny–Tipperary on the one hand, where survivals of the thirteenth-century colonial economy and settlement pattern were at their greatest outside the Pale and South Wexford,[2] and Gaelic northern and eastern Ulster on the other, where the tendency towards a mobile pastoral society was at its most pronounced. But in between there would have been areas in varying degrees of an intermediate condition. And in Gaelic Ulster itself, Fermanagh, peace-loving by Irish standards and full of clerical and learned families—the two were usually identical—

[1] Ó Corráin, 'Nationality and kingship', pp 5–7.
[2] C. A. Empey, 'The Butler lordship' in *Butler Soc. Jn.*, iii (1970–71), pp 174–87, gives a good account, but overstresses the 'Englishness' of the area.

and of craftsmen, gives the impression of a society very different from that of neighbouring Tyrone.[1] But none of these differences invalidate the thesis that the system of government and, in spite of regional variations, the basic social and economic conditions were everywhere essentially the same. And as the fifteenth and early sixteenth centuries progressed, the process of political, economic, and cultural assimilation continued as such magnates as the earl of Desmond and Lords Roche and Barry adopted increasingly Gaelic forms of taxation and administration and, on another level, the manorial villages and, in west Munster and in Connacht, the isolated borough towns gradually fell into decay. The fate of such places as Claregalway, still a borough in 1430, but a mere castle in the Elizabethan period, and Loughrea, the last remnants of whose municipal organisation disappeared in the 1560s (when its houses or stonework were partly destroyed and ruinous: '. . . it had ben within this 30 yeares a good mercat towne, but now there is none'), may serve as examples.[2]

As is well known, the Irish lords were chosen by a system of election within the ruling lineage, a system referred to by English writers of the reconquest period as tanistry. The tanist (tánaiste, literally 'second') was normally an appointed successor, chosen within the lord's lifetime and automatically succeeding on his death. The term, however, may also have been applied to persons holding an acknowledged position as second in rank within the lordship but without the right of succession, while on the other hand it was possible for there to coexist two (and perhaps more) persons, each of whom, if he survived, would automatically succeed by seniority.[3] These would be styled adhbhar righ or righdhamhna, terms meaning 'materials of a king'.[4] Elective succession of the Gaelic kind was practised in the late medieval period not only in the lordships of purely Gaelic origin but also, from the late fourteenth century, in those ruled by lords of Anglo-Norman descent in Connacht and on the Westmeath frontier—Dillons, Daltons, Delameres, and perhaps Tyrrells—and among the Burkes in north Munster.[5] Almost all the other Anglo-Irish lordships of Munster, however, still adhered throughout the later medieval period to the rule of primogeniture, a custom which greatly strengthened the political power of their lords, who did not have to contend with the claims of rival kinsmen, though this did not entirely protect them from segmental opposition

[1] Simms, 'Medieval kingdom of Lough Erne', especially pp 135–7. For the craftsmen see above, pp 417–18.

[2] P.R.O., S.P. 63/45/35, I, ad finem. For the borough of Clare(-Galway) in 1428 see Fitzmaurice and Little, Franciscan province Ire., p. 185.

[3] See my forthcoming Late medieval Ireland: studies in law and society, ch. I.

[4] Gearóid Mac Niocaill, 'The "heir designate" in early medieval Ireland' in Ir. Jurist, iii (1968), pp 326–9; Mac Niocaill, 'À propos du vocabulaire social irlandais du bas moyen âge' in Études Celt., xii (1970–71), pp 517–19.

[5] The evidence, to be found in annals and genealogies, is too long to summarise here. Note however the chancery bill (c. 1588) of Shane Delamar of Culvin, which shows the acceptance of the derbfine entitlement to succeed: he, as great-grandson of a previous chief, 'is by custom enabled to be cheiftayne' (P.R.O.I., chancery pleadings, bundle E, no. 214).

within the lineage. Where we do have the case of a brother succeeding before a
son, as with the Butlers of Cahir in the late fifteenth century or the Condons in
the third quarter of the sixteenth,[1] this was probably on account of the son's
youth, and in each of the instances cited the son in fact subsequently succeeded. In the early fifteenth century, however, Thomas fitz John, sixth earl of
Desmond, was ousted by his uncle James, subsequently dying without issue.[2]
But apart from the actual principle of primogeniture, it was of course quite
possible for a son to succeed his father directly under the practice of elective
succession, and examples of this are frequent, even in successive generations of
the same house; all that would be necessary to allow this to happen would be
for the father to have outlived all those who might be considered stronger candidates than his son. In theory, succession went to the 'eldest and worthiest'
among the descendants of former lords within four generations—the *derbfine*
group of early Irish law—but in practice, just as in the pre-invasion period, it
was possible for individuals outside this circle to succeed.[3] This was not, however, very frequent, and it was commoner indeed for competition to be
confined to the most immediate kinsmen of the late chief. There is no reason to
assume the existence of a formally defined mechanism of election—though
there was a formal rite of acceptance or inauguration, highly archaic in character—but we know that, in the case of a lordship or chieftaincy subject to an
overlord, the choice of a successor was made by the overlord and the notables
of his territory as a whole, rather than by the group immediately involved. In
general, succession would go to the contender with the best command of
resources and support, not necessarily within the lordship itself; but there is
some evidence that on occasion a less powerful candidate might be admitted to
the nominal lordship on the ground of his seniority, while effective power
remained with a more influential junior. If there were two or more candidates
of evenly matched strength—a common occurrence—there might be a bloody
conflict for the succession and, even if this was avoided, the successful candidate would as often as not find himself confronted with the permanent hostility
of the defeated faction, who would automatically ally themselves with his
enemies and so with the hereditary external enemies of their own territory. The
more distant the genealogical relationship between those who could reasonably hope to achieve the lordship, the greater the possibility of such factional

---

[1] Richard, second son of Piers fitz James Gallda Butler, was chief of the Cahir sept in 1485, in
succession to his brother Thomas (died 1478) (*Ormond deeds, 1413–1509*, pp 260–61: a very bad
rendering of N.L.I., MS D. 1854). Thomas's son Edmond eventually succeeded. Richard Condon,
a younger brother of the previous lord, David, was 'captain and chief of his name' in 1564 (P.R.O.,
S.P. 63/14/52). David's son Patrick eventually succeeded; see the genealogy in Lambeth Palace,
Carew MS 635.
[2] K. W. Nicholls, 'Late medieval Irish annals: two fragments' in *Peritia*, ii (1983), p. 89.
[3] Examples (among many) in the latest period are Cú Chonnacht Óg Mag Uidhir, 'an
comharba', lord of Fermanagh (1527–37), and Cathaoir mac Airt Mac Murchadha, king of Leinster
(1547–54). For the earlier period see Donnchadh Ó Corráin, 'Irish regnal succession: a reappraisal'
in *Studia Hib.*, xi (1971), pp 7–39.

conflict; and it is noticeable that the strongest and politically most coherent lordships, such as those of the O'Donnells and O'Briens in the late medieval period, were those in which succession to the chieftaincy remained restricted to a small and closely connected group. In this respect the contrast in the early part of the sixteenth century between the two Burke families of Connacht, Clanricard and MacWilliam, is instructive. The weakness of the MacWilliam Burkes in the first half of the sixteenth century can plausibly be ascribed to the fact that the chieftaincy was passing between second, third, and eventually fourth cousins, thus preventing any continuity of government and creating alternative centres of power in the septs who had lately produced a chieftain and who hoped to provide another before long. Conversely, among the Clanricard Burkes succession was still confined to a narrow group; only in the 1530s do we find it passing between cousins, and this development was to be arrested by the creation of the earldom in 1544. A recurrent pattern in Irish local history in the later middle ages is the strong refounder who by a long reign succeeds in excluding all collaterals from the succession and among whose descendants a strong chieftaincy is maintained for three or perhaps four generations. At this point the proliferation of the ruling house reaches a critical stage and severe succession disputes begin, often followed by actual or virtual fragmentation of the lordship.[1] The late fourteenth century was characterised by a number of such founders or refounders in the political situation arising from the 'Gaelic reconquest', and the last decades of the fifteenth century and the opening years of the sixteenth were thus a crisis period for many Irish lordships, such as those of the Maguires, MacMahons, and O'Kellys. Again, the emergence of well established septs or segments of the ruling house in particular areas within the territory was a source of weakness, not strength, to the lordship to which they belonged; their members, even if themselves without hope of rising to the lordship, would feel themselves born to share in power and thus be more ready to resent and reject the authority of their ruler than had been the old chiefly lineages of independent origin whom they had displaced. The principle is well illustrated by the junior septs of the O'Neills of Tyrone in the late fifteenth century, but it was of general application.

It would be impossible to deal adequately in the space available here with the fiscal system of the Irish lordships in the late middle ages.[2] Irish lords levied tribute from the territories subject to them, tributes heavy in time of peace and virtually unlimited in time of war. While part of these revenues consisted of fixed tributes in money, cattle, or foodstuffs, assessed proportionately according to the assessment units described above, the more important element probably always consisted in the taking of free board and lodging, known in

---

[1] Compare the similar situations in Africa described by Professor Audrey I. Richards, 'African kings and their royal relations' in *Royal Anthropological Institute Journal*, xci, no. 2 (1961), p. 141.

[2] See a brief survey in Nicholls, *Gaelic Ire.*, pp 31–7, and a full treatment in my forthcoming *Late medieval Ireland*, ch. III.

Irish by the generic term of *coinnmheadh*, embodied as 'coyne'[1] (probably more accurately to be read as 'coynue') in the well-known hybrid term 'coyne and livery'. In practice it was known by a bewildering variety of local names, usually referring to the specific persons who exacted it or the circumstances in which it was exacted. Even the bishops in the Gaelic areas received a great, and perhaps the greater, part of their revenues in the form of the 'noctials' or free entertainment provided for the bishop and his train by his tenants and clergy.[2] The taking of free entertainment as a form of taxation cannot be clearly distinguished in practice from its provision as hospitality, as there will always be a borderline area in which elements of compulsion, social pressure, and voluntary hospitality come together. The whole subject has recently been exhaustively and stimulatingly discussed by Dr Katharine Simms.[3] We can probably find a clue to the origin of many such exactions in the statement regarding the ninth earl of Kildare that he 'used to give many horses to gentylmen, and to evy man . . . that he gave eny suche horse, if the man were able to receave hym, he wold be wth hym ii days and twoo nights, to have bothe mete and drinke with hym'.[4] If the times in Kildare had not changed, how many of these entertainments would not have become permanent obligations on the heirs of those who gave them, long after the horse had been forgotten? Similarly, a County Cork jury in 1576, speaking of the custom of the lords levying their daughters' dowries from the country, says that they did it 'some by waye of peticion, which the freeholders dare not denye, and some by compulsion'.[5] Taxation in the form of the taking of free entertainment might be regarded as an unsophisticated form of fiscal exploitation, and it is an interesting commentary on fifteenth century Irish conditions that during this period it was introduced and became universal throughout the Anglo-Irish areas, right up to the marches of the Pale and even within it. Furthermore, there are some slight indications that its incidence in this period may have been increasing in the purely Gaelic areas, and that fixed rents or tributes in cattle, money, and foodstuffs may have provided a larger proportion of the lords' revenues at an earlier date than they did in the sixteenth century.[6] The variety of different names and headings under which exactions were being taken in the final period also suggests that a gradual process of accretion had taken place, as more and heavier burdens were imposed; it is possible that this was both a symptom and to some extent a contributory cause of the general economic and social collapse of Irish society that seems to have taken place in this period. Early

---

[1] It must be noted that 'coyne', derived from *coinnmheadh* (the Scots 'conveth') has of course no connection with the word *cáin* (plur. *cána*, the Scots 'kain'), originally meaning a law, later a fine or payment.

[2] *O.S. memoir, Londonderry*, i, 50; K. W. Nicholls, 'The episcopal rentals of Clonfert and Kilmacduagh' in *Anal. Hib.*, no. 26 (1970), pp 132–4.

[3] Katharine Simms, 'Guesting and feasting in Gaelic Ireland' in *R.S.A.I. Jn.*, cviii (1978), pp 67–100.

[4] Hore & Graves, *Southern & eastern counties*, p. 161.

[5] Ibid., p. 272.   [6] See my forthcoming *Late medieval Ireland*, ch. III.

Gaelic society, like Germanic, did not possess a system of public law, and crimes such as theft and homicide were simple torts to be resolved by the payment of compensation under voluntary arbitration. From the twelfth century at least, however, we find instances of the death penalty being inflicted for crimes that outraged public opinion. Thus in 1197 a sacrilegious thief who had stolen sacred vessels from the church of Derry was hanged—at a place called, significantly, *cros na riagh*, the cross of execution—'in reparation to [St] Columcille, whose altar had been so profaned'.[1] A little later we find the O'Connor kings of Connacht using the penalty of mutilation to enforce public order,[2] thus establishing as it were a 'king's peace'. The germ of this could possibly have been found in the Irish legal institution of *comairce* ('comrick'), the protection which a great man was entitled to extend to an inferior, any offence against the latter being thereafter taken as an offence against the protector himself. If the person so protected committed an offence, the protector was bound to see that he rendered satisfaction, failing which the protection could (in theory at least) be violated with impunity.[3] The O'Connor kings may have seen themselves as extending their *comairce* to all their subjects. Be this as it may, law enforcement of this kind does not seem to have survived, but the execution of those guilty of crimes that outraged public opinion,[4] and those unable to pay the composition for their offences, remained standard practice throughout the late medieval period. The two categories were combined in the case when a lord or other great person was murdered by a menial or other of low rank, and for this burning alive is more than once recorded as the punishment.[5] Besides all this, however, there had evolved by the end of the thirteenth century[6] a system by which crimes against public order rendered the offender liable for the payment not only of compensation to the injured party but also of a fine to the lord of the country. This provided in such cases a strong incentive for the lord to use his authority to compel the offender to accept arbitration—which in theory could only take place by mutual consent—but in other cases this would be left to the resources of the injured party himself. If the defendant refused to agree to arbitration, the plaintiff would seek to enforce him by seizing upon some of his property—or that of his kindred, under the rule of *cin comhfhocuis*, 'kincogish', or collective responsibility among the kindred—as a pledge for justice. This was at the root of the practice of private distraint which was one of the most characteristic features of the Gaelic Irish polity and one that aroused the greatest hostility among English legislators. Besides the collective liability of the kindred, a

[1] *A.U.*, ii, 226–7.

[2] *Ann. Conn.*, pp 2–5.

[3] Gearóid Mac Niocaill, 'Irish law and the Armagh constitutions of 1297' in *Ir. Jurist*, vi, no. 2 (1971), p. 340.

[4] Gearóid Mac Niocaill, 'Notes on litigation in later Irish law' in *Ir. Jurist*, ii, no. 2 (1967), p. 301, n. 8.

[5] *Ann. Conn.*, p. 580; *A.U.*, iii, 350–51, 596–7.

[6] As has been demonstrated by Gearóid Mac Niocaill. See above, n. 3, and his 'Aspects of Irish law in the late thirteenth century' in *Hist. Studies*, x (1976), pp 25–42.

master was liable for the acts of his servants, while in late medieval practice an outsider would treat a whole township or territory as responsible for a wrong done or debt due by one of its inhabitants. A bill against private distraint introduced in the Irish parliament of 1534 declares that persons were in the habit of seizing and taking away horses or other animals which they might find grazing by the roadside 'and in case the owners make sharpe pursuyt and chaunce by fastenes[1] or otherwise to come to the sight of his good, the taker thinketh sufficient to say that sume person of that town or cuntrey did hym summ injurie.'[2] To secure the performance of the arbitrators' award it was common, and perhaps usual, to make the parties swear in advance to abide by it, and a further method of enforcing performance was to appoint sureties, usually persons of importance, who would bind themselves to intervene to enforce the award, and who were sometimes entitled by its terms to levy a fine from a recalcitrant party.[3] In the case of what was probably the commonest Irish offence, cattle-theft, the person or persons to whose land the track of the stolen beasts had been traced was obliged to demonstrate that it led out again or accept responsibility for the theft. This was the custom of the 'tract', accepted into English law in Ireland in the sixteenth century.[4] In general, the thief was obliged to pay to the injured party double the value of the theft (*cinn agus aithghein*, 'offence and equivalent'), along with the reward which had been paid for information leading to his (the thief's) identification or the recovery of the stolen property. This was called *fiacha faisnéisí* ('information charges', or in sixteenth-century semi-translation, 'fastness money').[5] This was in addition to the heavy fines which might be levied by the local lord. A thirteenth-century tract gives a scale of fines varying from seven cows down to one, in proportion to the rank of the lord, not the seriousness of the offence, and the same seven-cow penalty is also recorded in the sixteenth century.[6] In the Butler and Power countries, and in Counties Kildare and Carlow, we find a fine of five marks (equivalent to ten 'legal' cows).[7] Failure to restore the stolen cattle or to pay the compensation awarded for them involved the delinquent in the severe penal interest of head for head for every year they so remained unpaid.[8] Nevertheless, the political division of the country and its endemic local wars received juridical recognition in the rule that if cattle were carried off by theft or spoil from one lordship to another which was at war with the former, the original owner could

[1] Irish *faisneis*, 'information'. For 'fastness money' (*fiacha faisnéisí*) see *Anal. Hib.*, no. 2 (1931), p. 115.
[2] *Anal. Hib.*, no. 10 (1941), pp 140–41.
[3] Mac Niocaill, 'Notes on litigation', pp 299–307.
[4] Mac Niocaill, 'Irish law and the Armagh constitutions of 1297', pp 343–4; idem, 'Aspects of Irish law', p. 36; G. J. Hand's note in *Anal. Hib.*, no. 26 (1970), p. 206.
[5] Mac Niocaill, 'Irish law and the Armagh constitutions of 1297', p. 341; 'Aspects of Irish law', p. 38; N.L.I., MS 2551, f. 2ᵛ.
[6] Mac Niocaill, 'Aspects of Irish law', p. 35; O'Flaherty, *West Connaught*, p. 403.
[7] N.L.I., MS 2551, f. 2ᵛ; *Southern & eastern counties*, pp 162–3, 186–7.
[8] See my *Late medieval Ireland*, ch. v.

make no claim to them if they were brought back either by a counter-theft or by purchase.[1] Homicide involved the payment of a wergild (*eraic*), calculated in accordance with the social standing of the victim, to his kindred and to the lord whose subject or under whose protection he was.[2]

Arbitrations were normally made by members of the hereditary lineages of jurists or brehons, who sat for the purpose in the open, on the usual Irish assembly-place of a hill or rath. In the sixteenth century, however, lay arbitrators are found sitting along with them, or even alone,[3] and the bishops and their ecclesiastical judges (officials) seem to have tried cases arising on church lands.[4] Every lordship had its official judge or judges, appointed by the lord with the primary function of deciding cases that affected the lord's interests or those of the territory as a whole, and who may have received a retaining fee for doing so. In addition, the brehons who conducted an arbitration were entitled to a fee (*aile dheag*) equivalent to an eleventh part of the sum awarded by them.[5]

By the late medieval period the early Irish law texts had become a purely antiquarian study, understood with difficulty or not at all by the jurists who continued to gloss and transcribe them and who quoted rules and tags from them, more or less out of context, in their pleadings and adjudications.[6] Of much more relevance to the actual legal practice of the late medieval period was Roman law (including under this term both civil and canon law), whose study was widespread in Ireland and whose influence was so strong that Lord Deputy Sussex, in 1562, could say that brehon law was 'a corrupt kind of civil law', and Conall Mageoghagan, writing in 1627, a generation after the final decease of the native legal system, declared that the law administered by the brehons had been simply Roman law in an Irish dress.[7] Legislation was promulgated on occasion by Irish lords: Eoghan Ó Raghallaigh, ruler of east Bréifne (1418–49), was the author of the statutes 'by which the men of Brefny abide',[8] and in 1478 James Butler, deputy for the earl of Ormond in the latter's Irish territories, promulgated at Kilcash an ordinance laying down the law to be followed in cases of theft and other offences against public order in Counties Kilkenny and Tipperary. Unfortunately the surviving text is very largely illegible.[9] Lesser lords also issued statutes or proclamations, usually concerned

---

[1] Mac Niocaill, 'Aspects of Irish law', pp 39–40.

[2] Ibid., pp 32–4; cf. Mac Niocaill, 'Á propos du vocabulaire social irlandais', p. 525.

[3] Mac Niocaill, 'Notes on litigation'.

[4] *O.S. memoir, Londonderry*, i, 51.

[5] The term *aile dheag* means literally 'twelfth', and the jurists' fee may have been originally that; four independent sixteenth- and seventeenth-century sources, however, say that it was an eleventh (a twelfth of the total including itself?).

[6] Daniel Binchy, 'Ancient Irish law' in *Ir. Jurist*, new ser., i (1966), pp 84–91, and 'Distraint in Irish law' in *Celtica*, x (1974), pp 22–61. See also Mac Niocaill, 'Notes on litigation'.

[7] *Cal. Carew MSS, 1515–74*, p. 331; *Ann. Clon.*, p. 280.

[8] James Carney (ed.), *A genealogical history of the O'Reillys* ([Cavan], 1959), pp 19–20, 49, 95–6.

[9] N.L.I., MS 2551, f. 2ᵛ. I hope to publish the decipherable portion of the text.

with protecting their own financial interests or enforcing monopolies. The execution of the lord's orders was the function of the *ceithearn tigh* ('keherynty' or 'kernty') or household troop, who acted as a sort of police; their leaders, and probably the ranks as well, were usually hereditary.[1]

The Irish land system of the late medieval period can only be clearly understood in the light of the social and economic conditions of the country, such as the absence of a true settled peasantry and the low intensity of land utilisation. The forms of land proprietorship in any society must in the end depend both upon the prevailing social and political structure and upon the use that is being made of the land. In late Gaelic Ireland, owing to the absence of a centralised legal system as well as to the low population and other factors which made land of itself less valuable than the men and stock necessary to utilise it,[2] most rights in land were subjective and could therefore be, on occasion, contradictory. A striking example is provided by the rights of the Munster lords over unoccupied lands as they are recorded in the late sixteenth century. The exactions that the lords imposed on the lands within their territories might often amount to the greater part of the value, and for this reason, or because they found themselves unable to obtain tenants or labour, the owners might throw up possession. The lord was then at liberty to take possession of the land and graze his herds upon it, or even set it to tenants for cultivation. Nevertheless, the original owners still remained owners in theory, and could return at any time to reoccupy the land if they felt themselves able to support the lord's exactions. This custom was to pose very considerable problems in the period of the reconquest for English lawyers, who found themselves quite unable to reconcile the rights of the two parties concerned in terms of English law or to decide which should be regarded as the true proprietor. Where the land had remained in the lord's hands under this system for a considerable period, he might come to regard it as his own and pass it on as inheritance to his sons, an occurrence of which we have documented examples. In some areas of Connacht it is recorded that the 'kinsmen and neighbours' of the true owners might similarly graze upon unoccupied land.[3]

Of the details of landholding in Gaelic Ireland at the time of the Anglo-Norman arrival and during the two centuries which followed it, we know next to nothing. Such scraps of evidence as are available suggest—perhaps misleadingly—that the overall picture was not very different from that found in the fifteenth and sixteenth centuries. A few tracts,[4] certainly describing a twelfth-

---

[1] For the *ceithearn tigh* see my forthcoming *Late medieval Ireland*, ch. II. Compare the description of the *fircheithearn* (i.e. the leaders of the *ceithearn tigh*) of Ó Néill (Myles Dillon (ed.), 'Ceart Uí Néill' in *Studia Celt.*, i (1966), pp 10–11).

[2] Katharine Simms, 'Warfare in the medieval Irish lordships' in *Ir. Sword*, xii (1976), pp 99–100; Nicholls, *Land, law and society*, pp 10–11.

[3] Nicholls, *Land, law and society*, pp 14–17.

[4] O'Flaherty, *West Connaught*, pp 368–72 (another version of this tract is to be found in *Bk Ballymote*, p. 90, c–d); *Hy Fiachrach*, pp 149–73; *Crichad an Chaoilli: being the topography of ancient Fermoy*, ed. Patrick Power (Cork, 1932).

century situation, which set out to name the landowning lineages and their lands in certain districts, seem to show a pattern in which particular lineages of 'freeholders'—as they would have been called by English lawyers of the Tudor or Stuart period—held large townlands or groups of townlands as allodial owners. This exactly parallels the situation in the sixteenth century, but one has the impression that in the earlier period the proportion of the soil in the actual possession of the royal and chiefly lineages was less than it was in the later. The tracts in question, however, are not detailed enough to establish this with certainty, and we do not in any case know how extensive the proliferation of the ruling lineages was at this particular period. More precise dating of these tracts, if this were possible, might throw further light on the question. On the other hand, it would seem from the evidence that the major Irish kings of the twelfth century were coming to regard themselves as *domini terrae*, with a right to grant away the land in their kingdoms to whomsoever they pleased in the same way as the contemporary kings of Scotland. The evidence for such a view rests in the extensive grants of land made by them to churches and monasteries, without any apparent reference to the rights of the actual occupiers. As Ó Corráin has observed, it is unlikely that 'the free commoner families who were allodial owners in severalty were consulted about the transfer. It is likely that they were simply transferred with the land to their new masters'.[1] In one instance, indeed, Diarmait Mac Murchada's grant of Balidubgaill (Baldoyle, County Dublin) to the monastery that was to become All Hallows, Dublin, we find the inhabitants ('Melisu Mac Feilecan and his sons and grandsons') explicitly conveyed along with the land.[2] I have suggested elsewhere that there is no need to assume that Mac Feilecan belonged to a special category of serfs; it seems more likely that he was simply the former allodial owner.[3] Nor may King Diarmait, in conveying him and his lands to the church, have felt that he was conveying more than his royal rights to the tribute and service of land and people. Whether the same kings were granting lands in the same way to lay individuals must, in the absence of evidence, remain doubtful, but a curious record in the 'Book of Lecan' records that a twelfth-century Donnchad Mag Aireachtaigh acquired 'the chieftaincy (*taisigeacht*) of Clann Taidc and Clann Murrthaile, between lordship (*tigernus*) and stewardship (*maeraigecht*)'.[4] The last term can only mean the collectorship of royal tribute. Clann Taidg was around Athenry, far away from the Mag Aireachtaigh homeland of Muintear Radhuibh around Roscommon, and Clann Murrthaile may have been in the same area. Are we dealing here with a grant from Toirrdelbach Ó Conchobair

---

[1] Ó Corráin, 'Nationality and kingship', pp 24–5.

[2] Richard Butler (ed.), *Registrum prioratus omnium sanctorum iuxta Dublin* (Dublin, 1845), pp 50–51.

[3] Nicholls, 'Anglo-French Ireland and after', p. 378. The analogy between the status of Irish landowners at this period and that of the native 'king's thanes' of contemporary Scotland (see G. W. S. Barrow, *The kingdom of the Scots: government, church and society from the eleventh to the fourteenth century* (London, 1973), p. 50) is suggestive.

[4] *Bk Lec.*, p. 65 rb.

or his son Ruaidrí to a favoured subject? There is an early seventeenth-century reference to a charter then existing by which 'Cahell O'Connor sometyme lord or rather kinge of the province of Connaght' granted the *baile* of Leamore in County Roscommon to one Cahell O'Multully, ancestor of the physician family of that name;[1] as Leamore was in the area ruled in the fourteenth and fifteenth centuries by the MacDavid Burkes, the king can only be the great Cathal Crobderg, who died in 1224. The question of royal rights over land in the pre-invasion period must therefore remain open, but there is no reason to suppose that Irish land titles at that time were less subjective than in the sixteenth century; indeed the converse is more likely to be true.

In sixteenth-century Gaelic and gaelicised Ireland land would normally be the hereditary property of a lineage group which, for this as for some other legal purposes, can be taken as forming a corporate body. The land would be divided between the adult males of the group in shares which would normally be periodically redistributed among the members on systems which varied widely between region and region—and very probably sometimes between one lineage group and another within the same area. In Connacht and Thomond in the late sixteenth century it was usual to make a new distribution among the members on May day every year, but in other areas, such as parts of the midlands, redistribution took place only after a death among the coheirs. In most areas the division into shares was made by the most junior of those entitled to participate, his seniors then choosing their shares in order of their seniority, but in Munster and in Offaly—and probably in some other districts as well—it was made by the most senior, the chief (*ceannfine*), who could take the best portion for himself.[2] It is easy to see how this could lead to the chiefs being in possession of disproportionately large shares of the lands of their lineages, as was in fact so often the case in Munster. If the coheirs under the system failed to agree among themselves they might decide to avoid future disputes by making a permanent division, and this could take place even in the first generation, but the mooting of a permanent division could itself be a cause of violent dissension within the lineage.[3] This system of land division was the 'Irish gavelkind' (or, more usually and correctly, 'custom in nature of gavelkind') of English writers. By the beginning of the sixteenth century at least it was already universal in the gaelicised regions of Connacht and the Westmeath frontier and was rapidly spreading into those of Munster, where intermediate systems—allowing the younger sons a share in the estate but not an equal dividend—must have differed little in practical effect from the practice in the adjacent Gaelic territories where, as we have seen, the chief was in effect allowed to take the largest portion.

[1] P.R.O.I., chancery pleadings, bundle A, no. 134 (bill of William Floodie, alias O'Multully of Dublin, chirurgeon).

[2] Nicholls, *Land, law and society*, p. 18. The article on 'The custom in nature of gavelkind' there referred to will now appear as ch. VII of my book, *Late medieval Ireland*.

[3] E.g. the episode referred to in *A.U.*, iii, 480–83.

The practice of periodic redistribution was on the one hand a reflection of the low intensity of land utilisation and the impermanence of settlement—it is difficult to see how it could have worked if either dwellings and settlements had been permanent, or the occupation of the arable land at all complete—but on the other it was itself a cause, as English critics noted, of economic under-development, in the disincentive that it gave to the erection of permanent buildings or even fences, the planting of orchards, or other improvements.[1] The whole system must be seen as essentially one of joint proprietorship by the lineage group as a whole rather than as a matter of partible inheritance of the usual European type. Women, whose children would of course not belong to their mother's lineage, were entirely excluded from inheritance, although they could and did hold land in pledge, even from their own immediate kinsmen: a daughter might be assigned part of her father's land in pledge for her dowry, to be redeemed by the male heirs on its subsequent payment to her or her repre-sentatives.[2]

The system of pledge or mortgage—analogous to the Welsh *prid*—was the standard method by which land changed hands in Gaelic Ireland and by which rising and expanding groups would peacefully oust declining ones. By the system, money or cattle would be paid for land which thereupon passed into the hands of the person advancing the sum, but could be redeemed, usually under very strict restrictions and conditions, on repayment by the pledger or his heirs. A feature of the system was that the pledgee in possession would con-tinue to advance further sums to the pledger on the security of the land, thereby increasing his own security of tenure, especially as it was a normal condition that all the sums advanced must be repaid in a single payment. All kinds of debts and charges, such as criminal damages, could be and were converted into pledges on land.[3] Eventually it might happen that the sum for which the land was in pledge was so great that the heirs of the pledger would have no hope of repaying it.[4] In such a case, or if the heirs in question had died out, fallen into poverty or emigrated from the district, the land would remain in the un-disturbed possession of the heirs of the pledgee.

The church or termon (*tearmonn*) lands formed to some extent a distinct element set apart from the rest of the countryside, though this distinction, based upon the wide immunities that the Irish church claimed not only for itself but for its tenants (the term *personas ecclesiasticas*, occurring in the bull *Clericis laicos* (1297) which laid down the immunity of the church from secular taxation, had in fact been understood in Ireland as denoting the inhabitants of church lands), was blurred at the close of the later middle ages through the increasing infringement of these immunities by the secular lords. The church

---

[1] Cf. Nicholls, *Land, law and society*, p. 19.   [2] See *Late medieval Ireland*, ch. vii.
[3] Gearóid Mac Niocaill, 'Land-tenure in sixteenth-century Thomond: the case of Domhnall Óg Ó Cearnaigh' in *N. Munster Antiq. Jn.*, xvii (1977), pp 43–50; Nicholls, 'Gaelic landownership', pp 97–102.
[4] See e.g. N.L.I., MS D. 2989.

lands had originally been the endowments of monastic establishments or cells which, for the most part, had become at an early date the hereditary perquisites of particular ecclesiastical lineages from whose members the heads of the establishments were chosen.[1] As one of the consequences of the twelfth-century reforms the lands, together with the old ecclesiastical establishments themselves, were transferred to the bishops within whose newly formed dioceses they lay.[2] In the case of Connacht we know that this transfer was carried out at a provincial synod in 1210.[3] In the Gaelic areas, however, this did not mean the dispossession of the former ecclesiastical lineages, who continued in possession subject to the payment of a rent to the bishop and to the obligation of providing free entertainment (*noctiales*) for himself and his train during his visitations and circuits.[4] The chief of the lineage in possession was appointed or at least confirmed by the bishop and bore the title of erenagh (*airchinneach*; Latin *herinacius*),[5] which had originally denoted the head of a monastic establishment. A single church with extensive lands might have several erenaghs, each the head of a separate lineage occupying particular parts of its lands. If an erenagh lineage became extinct, the bishop could—and indeed was supposed to—install another in its place, and in the sixteenth century we find a number of lineages that descended from late medieval bishops installed as erenaghs, such as the Sliocht an Easpaig Maguires at Aghalurcher in Fermanagh and the Sliocht an Easpaig MacDonaghs at Toomour, Sligo. The members of these erenagh lineages enjoyed, as they had done in the pre-reform period, a quasi-clerical status, and from them the greater part of the actual clergy in the purely Gaelic areas were recruited. The coarb (*comharba*; Latin *converbius* or *comorbanus*) was literally the 'successor' or representative of a patron saint and enjoyed as such an indefinable but very considerable spiritual prestige. His office was distinguished by this prestige rather than by any specific functions, but the coarb would normally be simultaneously erenach of the church lands in possession of his family; thus the O'Farrellys were both coarbs of St Maedhóg and erenaghs of Drumlane.[6] In a number of places, however, the office of coarb had become by the fifteenth century a simple ecclesiastical benefice corresponding to that of rector and was no longer the hereditary preserve of a particular line. The probable explanation of the change in these cases is that the coarbships in question had acquired an endowment in tithes, and that this had led to their being treated as

[1] Hughes, *Ch. in early Ir. soc.*, pp 157–72.

[2] A few exceptions to this rule existed: certain of the old termon lands were vested in monasteries, while the archbishop of Armagh and the bishop of Clonmacnoise obtained possession of certain churches (and their lands) which had belonged to the former *paruchiae* of these centres, but were situated in other dioceses.

[3] *Ann. Clon.*, p. 224.

[4] See above, p. 426.

[5] Note, however, the late medieval use of *airchinneach* in Munster and Connacht to denote 'archdeacon'.

[6] *A.F.M.*, ii, 876–7; *Acts of Colton*, p. 26 n.

ecclesiastical benefices subject to the general rules of the canon law. Where this had not occurred, their original nature would have persisted unchanged.

Tithes were everywhere, of course, the basic economic foundation of the church. In Ireland their introduction as a general institution had been one of the consequences of the twelfth-century reform,[1] but the payment of tithes on anything but the actual produce of the soil would appear to have been resisted in the Gaelic areas. In Gaelic Ulster at the close of the sixteenth century tithes were paid in kind on field crops, wool, and fish, while cattle and swine paid a fixed tariff per head, and no other tithes of any kind were paid. It is unlikely that the situation in other Gaelic areas was greatly different. The Cashel provincial synod held at Limerick in 1453 attempted to decree the payment of tithes on the income arising from trades and professions, and on the profits of mills, but admitted that the existing custom was that none of these was titheable.[2] It is unlikely, therefore, that the general incidence of tithes in Ireland was heavy. In the province of Tuam, and part of that of Armagh, there existed the archaic custom of quadripartition or tripartition, by which the bishop received a share of all the tithes within his diocese.[3] The mortuaries or duties levied by the church on the estates of deceased persons must have represented a heavy burden on the poor, since they were paid at a fixed rate irrespective of the assets of the deceased once these had passed a very modest level. The rate varied from diocese to diocese. Early seventeenth-century sources mention a bewildering variety of minor ecclesiastical taxes, including the 'dues of St Patrick' which appear to have been first-fruits paid to the use of the metropolitan cathedrals in their respective provinces, but the evidence is seldom or never localised enough to give a coherent picture.

In general, the earlier Irish forms of monastic organisation disappeared after the reform movement of the twelfth century had introduced the religious orders of western Europe, though a few communities of Culdees (*Céile Dé*) survived under that name at Armagh, Devenish, and perhaps some other locations, and some other older monastic establishments survived unreformed into the fourteenth century. Mayo, for example, was only converted into a house of Augustinian canons regular in 1386; and Muiredach Ó Conchobair, coarb of St Commán at Roscommon in the mid-thirteenth century, although styled prior of Roscommon in official Anglo-Irish records, is given instead the title of provost in papal documents, strongly suggesting that the establishment over which he presided was not regarded at Rome as a monastic house.[4] At many of the more important early monastic sites, the twelfth-century reform saw the establishment of houses of Augustinian canons of the observance of

---

[1] Nicholls, 'Register of Clogher', p. 371, n. 2.

[2] David Wilkins (ed.), *Concilia magnae Britanniae et Hiberniae* (4 vols, London, 1737), iii, 567, 569.

[3] Nicholls, 'Register of Clogher', p. 371, n. 2; and K. W. Nicholls, 'Rectory, vicarage, and parish in the western Irish dioceses' in *R.S.A.I. Jn.*, ci (1971), p. 65, n. 10.

[4] *Cal. papal letters, 1404–15*, pp 274–5; K. W. Nicholls, 'A list of the monasteries in Connacht, 1577' in *Galway Arch. Soc. Jn.*, xxxiii (1972), p. 42.

Arrouaise, which became remarkably popular in Ireland,[1] and in a number of instances (as at Clones and Ballysadare) we find the endowments divided between them and the original surviving erenagh families, suggesting a compromise between those of the original community who supported reform and those who did not. The same would apply to those cathedral cities where an Augustinian abbey coexisted with a chapter of secular canons.[2]

The reform also saw the introduction to Ireland of the Cistercian order, largely due to the efforts of St Malachy (Máel Máedóc Ua Morgair) of Armagh and later of the Premonstratensians, though the spread of the latter was severely limited. A feature of the earlier Cistercian houses is that many of them came to be known by names not of places but of the territories within which they were erected;[3] and only two, Monasterevin and Boyle, can be clearly established to occupy the site of a previously important church. Among the Cistercians, assimilation to native Irish customs set in early, in the form of monks erecting separate eremitical cells within the monastery precincts and the erection of dependent cells of nuns attached to the monasteries, or even occasionally the admission of women to the houses themselves. The well-known Derbforgaill, benefactress of Mellifont, died at that monastery in 1193. Giraldus Cambrensis denounced the admission in 1181 of a benefactress to the Cistercian abbey of St Mary's beside Dublin and hurled allegations of immorality at the double monastery of Augustinian canons and nuns at Termonfeckin, County Louth.[4] The community of canons at Termonfeckin was dissolved shortly after (perhaps as a direct result of Giraldus's charges!) and the particularly Irish practices already mentioned among the Cistercians, departing from the general rule of the order, were the target of the reform campaign conducted by the English abbot Stephen of Lexington, a campaign that had strong national and racial overtones and resulted for a period in the subjection of the Gaelic Cistercian houses to those of Anglo-Norman origin.[5] Although double houses disappeared in Ireland, the admission of women into otherwise male monasteries is recorded from the later period; thus Ailbhe, daughter of Aodh Mág Uidhir, had retired a year before her death in 1477 into the monastery of Lisgoole, a house of Augustinian canons.[6]

Both those Cistercian monasteries and those houses of Augustinian canons founded by the Anglo-Normans represented a different tradition from those of

---

[1] M. T. Flanagan, 'St Mary's abbey, Louth, and the introduction of the Arrouaisian observance into Ireland' in *Clogher Rec.*, x (1980), pp 223–34.

[2] K. W. Nicholls, 'Medieval Irish cathedral chapters' in *Archiv. Hib.*, xxxi (1973), p. 102.

[3] E.g. Abbeyleix (*Mainistir Laoghis*), Abbeydorney (*Mainistir ua dTorna*), Abbeymahon (*Mainistir Ua mBadhamhna*), Fermoy (*Mainistir Fhear Mhuighe*), and Corcomroe (*Mainistir Corca Modhruadh*).

[4] *Gir. Camb. op.*, iv, 178–81, 183. The Arrouaisian monastery in Airghialla that he refers to must be Termonfeckin (Flanagan, op. cit., pp 229–30).

[5] O'Dwyer, *Conspiracy of Mellifont*. The basic documentation is contained in 'Registrum Epistolarum Stephani de Lexinton' in *Analecta Sacri Ordinis Cisterciensis*, ii (1946), pp 1–118; and *Stephen of Lexington: letters from Ireland, 1228–1229*, ed. B. W. O'Dwyer (Kalamazoo, Mich., 1982).

[6] *A.U.*, iii, 262.

Gaelic origin and were often violently hostile to the Gaelic Irish and forbidden by their statutes to admit them as members. By the fifteenth century, however, such distinctions of origin had largely disappeared, and monasteries in general acquired the racial and cultural colour of the areas in which they lay; for example, the earliest Gaelic Cistercian house, Mellifont, became purely Anglo-Irish, while the violently anti-Gaelic Granard, having been forced by the pope in 1400 to admit Gaelic Irish, quickly passed under the control of the local ruling family of Ó Fearghail.[1] All the houses of the older orders, except a handful in the Pale, shared in a general collapse of standards in the fifteenth century, accompanied by the sudden appearance (c. 1418) of the delator at Rome[2] and by the reemergence of the hereditary principle so typical of the pre-reform period. Thus in 1414 the abbot of Mellifont, acting as deputy for the abbot of Citeaux as head of the Cistercian order, removed Eóghan Mac Donnchadha from the abbacy of Boyle as unfit to rule and substituted in his place one of the monks, Cormac MacDavid, who was, however, the son, born during his father's abbacy, of a previous abbot. Among a number of delators who attempted subsequently to displace Abbot MacDavid in their own favour was one Muirgheas Mac Donnchadha, generally accepted as son of the previous abbot Eóghan but believed by some to be really the son of Abbot MacDavid himself![3] The Ó hIffearnáin family provided three generations of Cistercian abbots in the fifteenth century: father, son, and grandson.[4] The practice of papal provision led to the appointment as commendatory abbots and priors of ever more secular individuals, and the last generations of commendators before the dissolution in the sixteenth century seem to have been little better than laymen, local lords or men of war.[5] The extensive rebuilding which we find at some Cistercian houses in the late fifteenth century shows, however, that not all abbots were totally neglectful of the welfare of their monasteries, though such expenditure on the fabric may well have been a substitute for the maintenance of a true conventual life.

The other side of Gaelic Irish religious life in the later middle ages was provided by the friars. Although the earliest foundations of the mendicant orders in Ireland, as elsewhere in Europe, were urban and associated with the more important Anglo-Norman boroughs, they attracted from the beginning

[1] Cal. papal letters, 1396—1404, pp 331, 346. For the anti-Gaelic attitude of Granard see the 'Remonstrance' of Domnall Ó Néill in c. 1317 (Curtis & McDowell, Irish hist. docs, pp 38–46).

[2] See the remarks of G. G. Coulton, Scottish abbeys and social life (Cambridge, 1933), pp 216–18.

[3] Cal. papal letters, 1404—15, p. 435; John O'Donovan (ed.), 'The Annals of Ireland, from the year 1443 to 1468' in Ir. Arch. Soc. misc., p. 202.

[4] Cal. papal letters, 1455—64, pp 2, 195; 1471—84, p. 531.

[5] See e.g. Nicholls, 'List of monasteries in Connacht', pp 28–39; 'The Lisgoole agreement of 1580' in Clogher Rec., viii (1965), pp 27–33; Nicholls, 'Visitations of the dioceses of Clonfert, Tuam, and Kilmacduagh, c. 1565–67' in Anal. Hib., no. 26 (1970), pp 144–58; and, in general, Gaelic Ire., pp 108–9.

patronage from Gaelic lords and kings,[1] and the second wave of foundations from the mid-fourteenth century on was rural and the work of Gaelic and gaeli-cised lords. The observant movement gave further impetus to their spread, and by the sixteenth century the friars were the dominant factor in Irish spiritual life.[2] It is, however, to be remarked that neither Franciscans nor Dominicans made any effort during this period to introduce into Ireland their dependent orders of nuns.

Late medieval Gaelic Ireland shows by European standards a remarkably low level of economic and technological development, contrasting with its achievements in the cultural sphere, such as in literature. The comparison with Ethiopia, made by the present writer in a previous work,[3] still seems in many respects a valid one, but in any case the marginal nature of Irish society and the economy in western European terms cannot be overemphasised.

[1] See e.g. Ambrose Coleman (ed.), 'Registrum monasterii Fratrum Praedicatorum de Athenry' in *Archiv. Hib.*, i (1912), p. 213.

[2] Brendan Bradshaw, *The dissolution of the monasteries in Ireland under Henry VIII* (Cambridge, 1974), pp 8–16.

[3] Nicholls, *Gaelic Ire.*, p. 3. Cf. a review of this work by G. J. Hand in *Ir. Independent*, 1 July 1972.

CHAPTER XV

Colonial society and economy in the high middle ages

KEVIN DOWN

WHOEVER would attempt to write an account of the economic and social history of medieval Ireland is immediately confronted by two serious problems: a lack of records and a consequent backwardness in research and serious publication which contrast strongly with the considerable production in English economic and social history and in other fields of Irish history. Two aspects have, however, been more fully covered than others, trade and feudal organisation; the former by Professors Carus-Wilson and M. D. O'Sullivan and Dr William O'Sullivan, and the latter by the numerous articles of Professor A. J. Otway-Ruthven. Towns, too, have not been neglected, largely through the pioneering efforts of Professor O'Sullivan in the case of Galway, of Dr William O'Sullivan for Cork, and of Professor Gearóid Mac Niocaill whose *Na buirgéisí, XII—XV aois* (Dublin, 1964) covers all aspects of medieval towns in Ireland. There has, moreover, recently been a considerable revival of interest in Irish urban history.[1]

Much less fortunate than the towns has been the countryside, for comparatively little has been written about the manorial economy and agrarian history of medieval Ireland. This is largely the result of the paucity of surviving records dealing with this subject. Where England can produce numerous examples of estates throughout the country with a wealth of documentation including long runs of manorial accounts, Ireland has very few with substantial collections of manuscripts, and, when they exist, it is in strictly limited areas of time and place with the shortest of runs. No Irish manors are as well covered by ministers' accounts as are those of the Bigod earls of Norfolk in the lordship of Carlow, but the longest run, for the manor of Forth (County Carlow), contains only nine accounts, those for the years 1279 to 1288.[2] In the absence of copious records and studies of the various regions of the country it is necessary to point out that there is an inevitable temptation to construct a picture of the medieval

---

[1] R. A. Butlin (ed.), *Development of the Irish town* (London and Totowa, N.J., 1977); *Hist. Studies*, vii (1981), entitled *The town in Ireland*.
[2] P.R.O., S.C. 6/1237/40–55.

economy of the lordship of Ireland from such fragmentary information as we
have and to pretend that the result is valid for the whole area of the colony.
Clearly there were considerable regional differences, such as those between the
comparatively fertile, well settled, and peaceful counties of Leinster and the
rough and troubled west. So, too, conditions in the late thirteenth century differed considerably from those that resulted from the Gaelic revival, the Bruce
invasion and the Black Death. In view of these difficulties it is necessary to bear
in mind that the conclusions which follow are largely restricted to the times
and places to which they refer and should be extended only with caution to the
area of English conquest as a whole.

As has been mentioned above, the fullest picture available of an estate in Ireland is to be had from the ministers' accounts of the Bigod earls of Norfolk in
the late thirteenth century, but a later set of accounts gives a fairly wide coverage of the lands of Lady Elizabeth de Burgh in Ireland in the mid-fourteenth
century in Kilkenny, Tipperary, Meath, Connacht, and Ulster.[1] A considerable
amount of material for the period up to 1307 is printed in the *Calendar of documents relating to Ireland*, and for the time after 1307 in the various calendars of the
English records. A large category of documents is the inquisitions *post mortem*,[2]
but these are not very reliable as they tend to undervalue estates; and there are
also important collections of purveyors' accounts and customs accounts.[3] Cartularies in Ireland are few, but there are some collections of documents belonging to individual families.

The country to which the Anglo-Normans came was not undeveloped.
According to Giraldus Cambrensis, who tends to contradict himself in his
descriptions of Ireland, the country was mountainous and hilly, watery,
wooded and boggy, a hostile terrain; but he goes on to add that it was fertile,
with rich crops, though more pastoral than agricultural, and sustained plenty of
cattle and wild beasts.[4] Modern research suggests that Giraldus underestimated the extent of arable farming. From the middle of the sixth century there
had been a great expansion of monasticism, which had led to growth in agriculture and horticulture and the introduction of more advanced techniques.
There are indications that there was extensive clearance and colonisation of
forest and waste land. By the ninth and tenth centuries it was a land of mixed
farming where cereal growing was extensive and economically important. The
arable, enclosed in small fields of one or two acres, was ploughed in March, so
that only one corn crop could be sown each year. Vegetables and corn were
grown on ridges and were manured from the farmyard. The main cereals grown
were wheat and oats, barley, and rye. Much of the heavy labour was carried

---

[1] Bigod ministers' accounts: P.R.O., S.C. 6/1237/1–6, 12–22, 32–55; S.C. 6/1238/1–9, 24–61;
S.C. 6/1239/1–12. De Burgh ministers' accounts: P.R.O., S.C. 6/1237/8–11, 23–6, 29–31; S.C.
6/1238/10–16, 21–2; S.C. 6/1239/13–33.

[2] P.R.O., C. 132–6.

[3] Purveyors: P.R.O., E. 101. Customs: P.R.O., E. 122.

[4] Giraldus, *Topographia* (1982), pp 34–5.

out by slaves, who were sometimes prisoners of war and sometimes brought from England by viking entrepreneurs. Heavy traction was done by oxen; horses, again often imported from England, were too light for heavy work.[1] The Scandinavian occupation, which by the twelfth century was based on extensive Norse colonies, settled with farming communities, did not alter this. Perhaps a greater impact on Ireland was made when the Norse invaders founded towns on the coast at Dublin, Wexford, Waterford, Cork, and Limerick, from which they expanded trade with the world overseas, especially with England, Normandy, southern France and Spain, northern Europe and the east. It is probable that they captured the wine trade early, and they also dominated the textile, hide, and slave trades, commodities for which they traded with the native Irish.[2] It was through the trade between Dublin and Bristol that Diarmait Mac Murchada came to know Bristol merchants, particularly Robert fitz Harding. Internal trade benefited from the good road system, which was to be of considerable use to the Anglo-Normans during their 'conquest' of the country.

By western European norms Ireland before the Anglo-Norman advent was underdeveloped, but it was moving nearer to the general economic and social pattern of much of western Europe. Irish society was not feudal or manorial, for theoretically land was held inalienably by families, while military, political, and administrative support had to be bought by superiors with cattle in what was a largely pastoral economy. Feudalism and the manorial order, on the other hand, were based on tenancy of land conditional upon services, military, administrative, or legal, so that the structure of the state depended on landlordship. By the early twelfth century, however, Irish society was exhibiting characteristics both in its social stratification and in land tenure that resembled the feudal system on a small and localised scale.[3] Conquest by Anglo-Norman adventurers in the late twelfth century and its expansion during much of the thirteenth century drew large areas of Ireland into the European order of society and imposed Anglo-Norman feudalism. Wherever the conquest spread, the land was divided into manors, all held ultimately of the lord of Ireland through the process of subinfeudation.

For our knowledge of the introduction and organisation of feudalism into Ireland by the Anglo-Normans, we are reliant on the comparatively small number of surviving charters and on two narrative works, the 'Expugnatio Hibernica' of Giraldus Cambrensis, who was a contemporary witness and a kinsman of some of the invaders, and the somewhat later 'Song of Dermot and the earl'. The feudalisation of Ireland began not with Strongbow's inheritance of Leinster from Diarmait Mac Murchada but with its grant to him as a fief by Henry II in 1171, to be held by the service of one hundred knights. The great

---

[1] Donnchadh Ó Corráin, *Ireland before the Normans* (Dublin, 1972), pp 45–58.
[2] Ibid., pp 105–7; J. I. Young, 'A note on the Norse occupation of Ireland' in *History*, xxxv (1950), p. 12. [3] Ó Corráin, op. cit., pp 171–2.

difference between the 'conquest' of Ireland and that of England a hundred years before was that it was begun and carried out without the constant involvement of the crown; it lacked the single-minded drive and total commitment of forces that accompanied the conquest of England, and it is in the founding of the colony that the clue to its ultimate weakness is to be found. By handing over large areas of land to a few great lords and then making speculative grants in Gaelic areas in return for homage, the crown was in reality weakening its control over the newly-acquired country, for vast areas were either in liberties, controlled by powerful lords in a very independent manner, or conquered by private enterprise, which tended to buttress the strongly independent outlook of the noble settlers.

There was an early organisation of the newly conquered lands along feudal lines. Henry II, on his way to Ireland, granted to Strongbow the kingdom of Leinster, with the exception of the Norse cities of Dublin, Wexford, and Waterford, and the coastal land around them, which Henry kept for his royal demesne. Before leaving Ireland in April 1172, Henry granted Meath to Hugh de Lacy to hold by the service of fifty knights. The process of conquest and occupation continued rapidly so that by the arrival of John in 1185 most of the eastern and southern seaboard from Drogheda to Cork was under Anglo-Norman rule, while Hugh de Lacy had advanced the area of his lordship west to the Shannon, and a substantial part of the north-east had been successfully conquered and held by John de Courcy in 1177. Expansion gained fresh impetus from grants made to new men. Lands in Clare, Offaly, Limerick, and north Tipperary were granted to Theobald Walter (le Botiller), the founder of an important Irish dynasty, while much of south Tipperary was given to Philip of Worcester and William de Burgh. In the north, grants to Piers Pipard and Bertram de Verdon closed the gap between de Courcy's lordship and Meath to make a continuous belt of occupation from north to south. Finally in 1235 Richard de Burgh conquered Connacht, thereby bringing the colonised area to its fullest extent, about three-quarters of the island.[1]

The large fiefs of the tenants-in-chief were held by military service on conditions of tenure sufficiently favourable to permit them in turn to subinfeudate their lordships by dividing them into a larger number of knights' fees than the service they themselves needed to fulfil their commitment of military service to the king. In Leinster, therefore, the actual number of knights' fees was one hundred and eighty, while in Meath it was one hundred and twenty, a considerable profit for their lords. By the early thirteenth century there were about four hundred and thirty knights' fees, enough to provide the knightly nucleus of the army of the lordship or its equivalent in scutage, which was known in Ireland as 'royal service'.

Organisation of the newly won lordships began at once with the subjugation of a district, based on the building of castles in its important centres and its

[1] See above, pp 164–6.

subinfeudation. These castles were of the motte-and-bailey type, built of wood, and were in some cases replaced with stone at a later date. Those who could not afford the considerable capital expenditure of building a castle made do with a house surrounded by a stockade and perhaps a ditch.[1] Naturally this process of feudalisation met with resistance from the Gaelic Irish which was never effectively eliminated, and even in the conquered districts there remained fairly large areas occupied solely by the Gaelic Irish, for the colonists rarely settled on land higher than six hundred feet, and it was from the unconquered areas all over the country that the Gaelic counter-attack was to come.

The usual unit of subinfeudation in the first instance was the knight's fee—in theory, at least, the amount of land needed to support one knight—and they were normally coincident with ecclesiastical parishes. They appear from royal charters under Henry II and John to have been in Ireland a known fixed area, though they were not of uniform size everywhere. Ten ploughlands was normal in County Dublin, while in the more peaceful part of the lordship of Meath, which is the modern county, a knight's fee was twenty ploughlands. In the western section of the same lordship, presumably because the disturbed conditions of the frontier made it more difficult to run economically, the number was thirty, and in the march, where war with the Gaelic Irish was virtually permanent, several fees were often granted for the service of one. The services owed by the tenant, in addition to the obligation of service for forty days or the forty shillings royal service (*scutage*), were suit at the court of the fief, counsel to the lord when desired, and the accepted aids.

Information about the settlement of Ireland is not plentiful, and most of it concerns the grants of great lordships and subinfeudation which in Leinster was virtually complete by 1200 and in Meath by about 1250.[2] Both these processes in many cases involved thousands of acres which no lord could hope to cultivate directly; it was necessary, therefore, to find tenants and a peasantry to fill out the conquest if it was to become anything more than a military occupation. By the reign of Edward I, for which records are fairly plentiful, most of Leinster and Meath and much of Munster and eastern Ulster were occupied by a new class of small free tenants who in some districts may have outnumbered the native population.[3] Who, then, were these new small tenants, whence did they come and how were they recruited?

Since there is no direct evidence about this, it is necessary to take the records that become available from the second half of the thirteenth century onwards and to work backwards on the basis of surnames. The problem here is that, by the date from which records have survived, many Gaelic Irish had taken

---

[1] *Song of Dermot and the earl*, lines 3222–5; Giraldus, *Expugnatio*, pp 190–91, 194–5.

[2] For the process in Meath see B. J. Graham, 'Anglo-Norman settlement in County Meath' in *R.I.A. Proc.*, lxxv (1975), sect. C, pp 223–48.

[3] A. J. Otway-Ruthven, 'The character of Norman settlement in Ireland' in *Hist.Studies*, v (1965), p. 77.

English names, but it is likely that they were a minority. Dr A. J. Otway-Ruthven has shown convincingly from surnames that tenants-in-chief enlisted many men in their own English and Welsh lordships,[1] but many have names which give no indication of origin. Although the majority appears to have come from England, the large number of Welsh place-names and surnames suggests that many came from Wales and the marcher lordships. The frequency with which the surname *Flemming* or *Flandrensis* is encountered possibly indicates a large group from Flanders, though this is equally likely to have been via England and Wales and after a considerable lapse of time. Flemings from Pembroke formed a sizeable contingent among the first adventurers. Although there is no direct evidence, it may be that recruiting agents (*locatores*) were employed, as in other European enterprises of colonisation, to find a new tenant and peasant population for Ireland, or that publicity and offers of franchises and privileges were used for the same purpose. This would explain the creation of many small military tenures which were neither military nor financial, but which were probably intended to confer a higher social status with less onerous terms. The large number of boroughs created by various lords, many of which were in reality rural settlements with little in common with towns, was probably for the same purpose, with burgage tenure as the bait. It is likely that some settlers were soldiers who took part in the conquest and were rewarded with grants of land. Undoubtedly a prime inducement to settle in Ireland would have been the availability of land there at a time when there was increasing pressure on it in England resulting from the growth in population. It is impossible to know exactly the success of these efforts and the number of the humbler settlers, but the process of settlement and the organisation of manors in many parts of Ireland seems to have been reasonably complete and successful by about 1200 because King John, from early in his reign, could obtain a large surplus from his Irish exchequer and the Irish pipe roll shows a picture of successful manorialisation and agriculture.[2]

Clearly the settlement considerably altered the situation of the pre-conquest population, both Irish and Norse. In conquered areas the native lords and superior tenants were generally displaced by the newcomers and either retreated further afield or found themselves with a lower status on what had been their former possessions. The bulk of the population was needed by the new landlords to work the land as serfs and it is no doubt to these that the treaty of Windsor (1175) refers when it specifies that Ruaidrí Ua Conchobair, the high-king, should, if requested, ensure the return of those Irish who had fled from the lands of Anglo-Norman barons in Ireland. As well as the Irish of servile condition, there remained in colonised areas many free Irish who held

[1] Otway-Ruthven, 'The character of Norman settlement in Ireland', pp 78–9.
[2] *The Irish pipe roll of 14 John, 1211–1212*, ed. Oliver Davies and D. B. Quinn in *U.J.A.*, 3rd series, iv (1941), supplement.

land by one of the higher tenures. Within the lordship there were parts, however, that the conquerors left to native princes, as Strongbow assigned Ferns and much of Uí Felmeda to Muirchertach, nephew of King Diarmait; this was an arrangement that survived for centuries. Similarly, Domnall Cáemánach kept much of the rougher parts of Uí Chennselaig, for which he served the earl as 'seneschal of his Irish of Leinster', and this too persisted until the end of the thirteenth century. Indeed, much of the rougher and mountainous land was left for Irish lords who often held it as vassals of Anglo-Norman barons. In one case at least, an Irish lord himself became a feudal tenant; this was Domnall Mac Gilla Mo Cholmóc, Strongbow's brother-in-law, the ancestor of the Fitz-Dermots. Two of these cases of survival, those of Muirchertach and Domnall Mac Gilla Mo Cholmóc, must have been due to their relationship with Earl Richard. The dispossession of the Irish was not carried out all at once, but proceeded by stages; a crucial one, according to Giraldus, was during John's visit in 1185, for it provoked many faithful Irish to join the hostile Irish,[1] and the process continued as more humble settlers were recruited from England. The servile position of Irishmen was not, however, irrevocably decided, and grants of English law and manumissions occur regularly right up to the sixteenth century.[2] Also affected were the Norse inhabitants of the towns and their hinterlands, the Ostmen. On the whole they were more fortunate than their Irish fellows, held on to some of their property and mostly avoided the servile status of the Irish, so that many, like 'Gylmihel Maclotan', an 'estman' mentioned in an inquisition held at the archbishop of Dublin's manor of St Sepulchre's in the middle of the thirteenth century, had the law of the English.[3] When their cities passed into Anglo-Norman control, the Ostmen in some cases seem to have been moved out of them, as the Dublin men moved north of the river to the modern Oxmantown. In spite of these changes, they continued to play a part in the affairs of their former cities for long after 1170 and seem to have preserved some group consciousness before becoming submerged in the Gaelic and Anglo-Irish population; the Ostmen of Wexford, indeed, even in 1283, were still considered to be a separate group.[4]

Professor M. M. Postan has pointed out that behind most economic trends in the middle ages are to be discerned the effects of rising and declining population.[5] He goes on to warn that 'our evidence being what it is, a close and a clear view of demographic trends is impossible; least of all is it possible to measure the total size of the population at any given point of time'. He is writing about England, and adds that the difficulties have not prevented historians from attempting to estimate the totals at various times in the middle

[1] Giraldus, *Expugnatio*, pp 236–9; above, p. 123.
[2] *Reg. Swayne*, pp 45, 114; Curtis, *Med. Ire.* (2nd ed.), pp 420–21.
[3] *Alen's reg.*, p. 101.
[4] Hore, *Wexford town*, p. 22. For Waterford, see P.R.O., C. 133/31 (1), inquisition *post mortem* of John fitz Thomas.
[5] M. M. Postan, *The medieval economy and society* (London, 1972), p. 27.

ages. What Professor Postan has said about the problem in England is even more true of Ireland. In demography, as in many aspects of Irish medieval history, there is an absence of relevant records. Medieval England, in the Domesday Book and the poll tax returns of 1377, at least has sources with which an attempt at a population estimate can be made; medieval Ireland has no such surviving documents. This lack, however, has not deterred historians, particularly Professor J. C. Russell,[1] from estimating the size of the population of medieval Ireland. Professor Russell makes his Irish calculation on the basis of a comparison with Wales. Arguing that Ireland is four times as large as Wales, had four times as many clergy and four times the number of political units (cantreds), he draws the conclusion that it must, therefore, have had four times the population of Wales. In 1100, therefore, the population of Ireland, according to Russell, was about four hundred thousand; at the end of the twelfth century about 500,000, and, on the assumption of faster growth in the thirteenth than in the twelfth or fourteenth centuries, something near 750,000 around the year 1300. Because of political troubles under Edward I, Russell suggests that the growth in population was held back and that an estimate of about 675,000 'might be hazarded' for the years 1275–85. The figure just before the Black Death is put somewhere around 800,000. As well as an estimate based on his population figure for Wales, Russell uses another approach: Ireland in 1320 had about 2,400 parishes which had existed from the twelfth-century reorganisation of the Irish church; assuming that the Irish parish had the same number of inhabitants as the English one and taking that number from the Domesday Book as 210 to 230 per parish, he arrives at an estimate for Ireland in the twelfth century of from 500,000 to 550,000. He extends this method for the end of the thirteenth century: around 1291 the 2,400 churches of Ireland equal one-quarter of the taxed churches in England. Thus, if the population of England around 1275 was two and a half million, the Irish population should have been about 650,000. The figures arrived at by the latter method are reasonably near those estimated by the first.

Dr A. J. Otway-Ruthven prefers a somewhat higher estimate based on F. W. Maitland's Domesday Book figures: '. . . the population of England at the time of Domesday Book has been estimated as perhaps 1,375,000, and it is reasonable to suppose that two or three generations later the population of Ireland was of much the same order.' The Domesday Book figure has more recently been raised by H. C. Darby to an estimate around 1.5 million.[2] Thus around 1200 the two estimates are approximately 500,000 and 1,375,000, a difference of 875,000 and at its highest point Russell's estimate never reaches one million. Can any of these figures be accepted and is it really possible, as the authors of these attempts must claim, to calculate such a figure? It seems unlikely that such precise estimates are possible. As has already been pointed out, for

[1] J. C. Russell, 'Late-thirteenth-century Ireland as a region' in *Demography*, iii (1966), pp 500–12.
[2] Otway-Ruthven, art. cit., p. 77; H. C. Darby, *Domesday England* (Cambridge, 1977), pp 87–91.

Ireland no documents, such as Domesday Book or the poll tax returns, survive on which an estimate can be based; and even if they had, they would only refer to the area of the conquest and would tell nothing of the Gaelic parts of the country. It seems, then, that the attempted estimates should be treated with a great deal of caution. Dr Otway-Ruthven's estimate appears to be based on the supposition that the population of Ireland at the end of the twelfth century would have caught up with Maitland's Domesday figure, 1,375,000, but as no evidence is put forward in support of this contention, it seems unwise to accept it. This leaves Russell's figures. The obvious objection is that his method of comparison with England and Wales presumes considerable uniformity between Ireland and the other two countries and that Gaelic Ireland followed the pattern of the colony closely enough to permit a comparison. The use of Wales in this way is especially doubtful because it too lacks information on which to construct an estimate. Furthermore Russell has consistently used in his calculations the 3.5 multiplier which is regarded by many historians as too low,[1] so that even if his comparative method were to be accepted, it would probably be necessary to increase his figures to take account of a multiplier of between 4.5 and 5.0. The objection to his argument from the number of parishes is the same as that to comparison with Wales; it presupposes that the distribution of the population of Ireland was uniform with that of England. His argument from the ratio of Irish to English parishes begs the question because it both misrepresents the date and process of formation of the parochial system in Ireland and presumes that Irish parishes in the late thirteenth century were all as heavily populated as those in England.[2] In view of the increasing evidence of the absence of tenants on many manors in Ireland, often because of warfare with the Gaelic Irish, from the end of the thirteenth century, and the impossibility of knowing the distribution of population in the Gaelic west, a direct comparison with England seems inadvisable.

Although it is not possible to arrive at an accurate estimate of the population of Ireland at any point in the middle ages, it seems reasonable to suggest trends. These suggestions, however, because of the nature of the evidence, must be only tentative. The first problem is that the right sort of documents are not available in a quantity sufficient to allow any form of precise quantification even for small areas like individual manors, and they lack continuity from which to assess movement and make comparisons. Thus court rolls are few, and none are earlier than the fifteenth century. Population movement has to be deduced from occasional references to the absence of tenants on certain manors, departures for England and the government's efforts to counter them, references in chronicles to mortality resulting from plagues, and mention of assarting and colonisation.

[1] J. Z. Titow, *English rural society, 1200—1350* (London and New York, 1969), pp 66–71.
[2] K. W. Nicholls, 'Rectory, vicarage, and parish in the western Irish dioceses' in *R.S.A.I. Jn.*, ci (1971), pp 53–84.

During the eleventh, twelfth, and thirteenth centuries there was rapid population expansion in western Europe, and if pre-conquest Ireland was in line with the rest of Europe its population should have been rising. Apart from this analogy, there is no evidence for this. But it offers a probable explanation for the totally unexpected rise to power of Connacht in the twelfth century and the concomitant expansion of Bréifne. Although settlement in the wake of the conquest must have caused some increase in the population, it should probably not be exaggerated, for there are signs that there was a shortage of men rather than land; this is suggested by the treaty of Windsor's provision for the return of fugitive Irish and by charters of the first half of the thirteenth century which specify the return of betaghs belonging to the lands granted.[1] Immigration evidently continued, for by 1280 the Anglo-Irish formed a large proportion of the population of Leinster, eastern Ulster and much of Munster, and in some areas may have outnumbered the Gaelic Irish. This was the time of the colony's greatest extent, with perhaps its greatest population, but even then there is no indication that there was any serious shortage of land, although it may be possible to speculate that one of the factors behind the Gaelic resurgence in the later part of the thirteenth century was a corresponding growth in the Gaelic population with accompanying pressure on pasture. It seems probable, however, that Ireland never experienced the land hunger that England knew in the thirteenth century; there was always room for the expansion, if it could be won, though it would have meant absorption of less suitable land.[2]

If the lordship's fullest extent was in the reign of Edward I, that period also saw the beginning of decline. Although it is common to explain it by reference to the Bruce invasion and the accompanying famines, there are ample signs before 1315 of failing prosperity and possibly declining population in widespread areas of English occupation, largely because of Irish attacks. It happened as early as 1252 on Geoffrey de Costentin's land at Kenkelly, County Longford, and by 1282 wide areas of Offaly and Kilkenny were waste and uncultivated because of war.[3] At Bray, County Wicklow, in 1311 the earl of Ormond could take nothing from his wood 'because of robbers and war', while on his manor of Ardmayle, Tipperary, in 1305 there were a hundred acres of arable land lying waste 'because now no one has dared to lease them'.[4] Similar references to loss of arable land, though not necessarily because of warfare, recur about the same time in Kilkenny, Limerick, and Tipperary.[5] To a certain extent this fall in the occupation of arable land may be partly a reflection of the pestilence that hit Ireland in 1271.[6] Existing difficulties were exacerbated, however, by the Bruce invasion of 1315 to 1318 in which there was such destruction

---

[1] Otway-Ruthven, art. cit., p. 77.
[2] Frank Mitchell, *The Irish landscape* (London, 1976), pp 185–8.
[3] Inquisitions *post mortem*, P.R.O., C. 132/14 (12) and C. 133/31 (1).
[4] *Red Bk Ormond*, pp 24, 63.
[5] Ibid., pp 60, 62, 70, 131, 154.
[6] *Liber Primus Kilkenn.*, p. 62.

that many areas suffered considerable depopulation and never recovered. This probable fall in population was not the result of war and disorder alone; the bad weather of 1314 and 1315 combined with warfare to cause poor harvests resulting in the famine that persisted in Ireland until 1318.¹ Perhaps as a consequence of famine, there was an outbreak of plague among the Scots in Ulster which no doubt also affected the population at large.²

Clearly it is not possible to assess exactly the effects of the upheavals of the second decade of the fourteenth century on the population, but the result of the combined problems of those years is apparent from the regular accounts of shortage of population for one reason or another in different areas. Moreover, it was not just a question of recovery from past difficulties, for the endemic warfare and Irish attacks continued to drive away the inhabitants of more disorderly areas and to deter new settlers, and the statement that lands 'lie waste and uncultivated for lack of tenants' becomes a commonplace in documents from the 1320s onwards. Even on the archbishop of Dublin's manors near Dublin, St Sepulchre's, Tallaght, Rathcoole, Ballymore Eustace, and others, in 1325 it is frequently stated that the tenants have left because of the Irish, and the same problem occurs two decades later on manors of Lady Elizabeth de Burgh in Kilkenny, Tipperary, and Meath.³ These references suggest that the main reason for the drop in population on many manors before the Black Death was the Gaelic revival. That this was not merely a movement of population within Ireland, but an important emigration, is confirmed by legislation: the statute of Kilkenny (1366) and an Irish statute of Henry IV⁴ make provisions against labourers leaving, while absenteeism at a higher level of society was also forbidden by legislation. The success of these laws can be judged by the large number of Irishmen in England, particularly in important towns like Bristol and Coventry.⁵

Irish attacks on the lordship were not, however, the only important factor in the decline of population; more crucial was the Black Death, which first appeared in Ireland at Howth in July and August 1348. From there it spread swiftly to Dublin and Drogheda and then to the rest of the country. The general view of the chroniclers was that the Anglo-Irish suffered most—no doubt because they were more likely to be gathered together in towns and villages.⁶ By analogy with other countries the probable mortality in the lordship was around twenty-five to thirty-five per cent, a serious loss from which

¹ Lydon, *Lordship*, p. 147.
² *The Annals of Ireland by Friar John Clyn and Thady Dowling*, ed. Richard Butler (Irish Archaeological Society, Dublin, 1849), p. 8.
³ *Alen's reg.*, pp 170–71, 181, 184, 186–7, 189–90, 194–5; and ministers' accounts, P.R.O., S.C. 6/1239/15, 16, and 18.
⁴ 11 Hen. IV, c. 1.
⁵ *The register of the Guild of the Holy Trinity, St Mary, St John the Baptist and St Katherine of Coventry*, ed. M. D. Harris (London, 1935; Dugdale Society Publications, xiii), pp xxi–xii, 4, 9, 16, 19, 23, 31, and others. It begins some time after 1340.
⁶ J. F. D. Shrewsbury, *A history of the bubonic plague in the British Isles* (Cambridge, 1971), pp 46–50.

recovery was made more difficult by further outbreaks in 1357, 1361, 1370, 1373, 1382, and 1384; and it has been argued that the Black Death and its successors probably reduced the population of the colony by forty to fifty per cent.[1] So it is probable that by the end of the fourteenth century there was serious depopulation in the lordship and that its contraction and the decline in its revenue and prosperity were to a considerable extent due to it.[2] The persistence of complaints about absenteeism in the fifteenth century suggests that recovery in numbers did not come very quickly, and it is only by the questionable process of extending some European trends to Ireland that any increase towards the end of the century can be suggested.[3]

THE 'conquest' brought about a great redistribution of land into four main blocks: the possessions of the crown; the lands of the church; the estates of the tenants-in-chief; and the areas that remained in the possession of the Gaelic Irish. The latter portion was not the only example of continuity, for the crown, in reserving for itself the Norse cities, was taking over areas already outside the Gaelic system; the earls of Leinster claimed their lordship, however incorrectly, by right of inheritance from Diarmait Mac Murchada through his daughter Aífe, and the post-conquest church continued to enjoy a large part of its pre-conquest possessions. This continuity should not, however, disguise the drastic change in the ownership of land which has been noticed already; at the highest levels the Gaelic Irish gave way to Anglo-Normans and the Gaelic system of land tenure was superseded by the feudal arrangement. In the early days of the colony it seems to have been the intention to retain much land in royal demesne,[4] but in 1235 Henry III ordered Maurice FitzGerald, justiciar of Ireland, to let the Irish demesne lands to farm for greater profit, and by the middle of the thirteenth century there were only five demesne manors: Crumlin, Newcastle Lyons, Esker, and Saggart (Dublin) and Newcastle Mackinegan (Wicklow). To these might be added the lands of Othe (Uí Theig), Obrun (Uí Briúin), and Okelli (Uí Chellaig), also in County Wicklow. As all these lands, with the exception of Crumlin and Esker, were in positions very vulnerable to attack from the Irish of the Dublin and Wicklow mountains, defence may have been the reason for their retention. The manors were usually farmed to the actual occupants of the land and during the thirteenth century the rents went up steeply, at Saggart from £30 to £112. 18s. 4d. and at Newcastle Lyons from £40 to £147. 5s. 8d.; but this was seriously overdone, for the tenants, in their exposed position, could not pay, and early in Edward III's reign petitioned for relief which they received in the remission of arrears and the reduction of rents.[5]

---

[1] Maria O'Kelly, 'The Black Death in Ireland (1348)' (M.A. thesis, N.U.I. (U.C.C.), 1973), pp 64–7, 78.

[2] Richardson & Sayles, 'Irish revenue, 1278–1384' in *R.I.A. Proc.*, lxii (1961–2), sect. C, pp 99–100.

[3] Postan, *Med. econ.*, p. 39.   [4] *Alen's reg.*, p. 31.

[5] *Cal. doc. Ire.*, *1171–1251*, no. 2254; *Cal. close rolls, 1231–4*, p. 553.

Before 1169 the church already possessed considerable holdings of land and the advent of the Anglo-Normans increased them. Giraldus asserts that the newcomers were mean to the church and stole its lands;[1] Hugh de Lacy, John de Courcy, and William de Burgh were accused of plundering churches and, later, William Marshal was excommunicated for trying to absorb lands of the see of Ferns into his huge lordship; but all were founders or considerable benefactors of monasteries. There were disputes about particular pieces of land, but on the whole the possessions of the church remained intact, and the newcomers added to the endowment of the church in three principal ways. They made grants to existing foundations, though some of these, such as King John's to Christ Church, Dublin, were really confirmations of pre-conquest grants;[2] secondly, the greatest magnates among the conquerors, and their more important sub-tenants, founded new monasteries or made them benefactions. Finally, grants of land and tithes of churches in Ireland were made to English religious houses, as Hugh de Lacy and his sub-tenants endowed the two Llanthony priories with possessions in Meath, Westmeath, and Louth.[3] Thus by continuity or fresh endowment the church in colonial Ireland held a vast amount of land which, in contrast with its position in England, was held, with a few minor exceptions, in frankalmoign or fee farm, and churchmen were, therefore, not required to render military service to the crown.[4] These immense church possessions were not distributed among the various institutions with anything approaching equality; while some of the many bishoprics and monasteries possessed vast estates, others held comparatively small amounts of land which often, for various reasons, yielded smaller incomes than land in England, so that many individual Irish churches were poorer than comparable English institutions.[5] The better-off institutions were very great landlords, and among the greatest were the archbishopric of Dublin and St Mary's abbey, Dublin, a Cistercian house. Of the total acreage of the modern County Dublin (222,710 acres) the church held nearly a half, at least 104,000 acres, at the end of the middle ages, of which the archbishop in turn possessed about 53,200 acres, St Mary's abbey 17,125 acres, Christ Church 10,538 acres, St Patrick's and monastic houses the remainder.[6] The absence of great Benedictine estates in this list constitutes a conspicuous difference between the Irish and English church estates.

The archbishop of Dublin's lands were formed into manors in two groups north and south of the Liffey, in what were called his crosses; these became eventually the baronies of Nethercross (north) and Uppercross (south). Most

[1] Giraldus, *Expugnatio*, pp 154–7, 242–3, 263–4.
[2] *Alen's reg.*, pp 28–9.
[3] *Ir. cartul. Llanthony*, pp 81–120, 213–27.
[4] A. J. Otway-Ruthven, 'Knight service in Ireland' in *R.S.A.I. Jn.*, lxxix (1959), p. 2.
[5] Otway-Ruthven, *Med. Ire.*, p. 129.
[6] A. J. Otway-Ruthven, 'The medieval church lands of County Dublin' in *Med. studies presented to A. Gwynn*, pp 54–72.

of this was held by the church before the conquest and much was probably originally monastic property which had been in the possession of the see of Dublin only since the synod of Kells (1152). Some additions were made by John, but the estates were virtually complete by about 1200 and only minor changes occurred during the rest of the middle ages.[1] Like many other land-holders in County Dublin, the archbishops from the fourteenth century had the problems of the Irish of the mountains; even the manor of St Sepulchre's was said in 1326 to have suffered 'because near evildoers', the labour services of some betaghs at Boly Minor were not valued because they were in the march and dared not stay there at night, and several holdings are described as being waste for want of tenants. The extents of other archiepiscopal manors in 1326 tell the same story, which is further confirmed by the papal permission granted on 19 March 1352 to Archbishop John of St Paul to hold three or more bene-fices to make good the losses to the revenues of his see resulting from Irish raiding parties and high mortality, presumably the Black Death.[2] The position of the archbishop of Armagh as a landholder reflected his ecclesiastical posi-tion; his lands were divided between the Gaelic and Anglo-Irish areas, though not equally. Apart from his two manors at Dromiskin and Termonfeckin (Louth), he held little land in the colony and his principal holdings were in the counties of Armagh and Tyrone with a concentration of mensal lands around the city of Armagh and much of his income dependent on a variety of cus-tomary payments deeply embedded in tradition.[3]

The formation of monastic estates in the colony followed the same course as the two episcopal examples quoted above. A good example of a successful monastic estate is provided by St Mary's abbey, Dublin, the leading Cistercian (from 1147) house in both wealth and influence, founded *c.* 1139. Its landed property was mainly in County Dublin with a great deal in the city itself in the manner of the great English houses, but there were also extensive holdings in Kildare, Louth, Meath, Westmeath, and Galway, as well as substantial posses-sions in the west later lost to the Irish. St Mary's began with a pre-conquest nucleus to which were added a few gains soon after the conquest, mainly con-firmations like those of Strongbow. The period of great advance was from 1182 to 1236, after which little was gathered until the considerable acquisitions between 1423 and 1460 which included the purchase of the Irish lands of Little Malvern Priory. This last gain is an indication of the abbey's continuing pros-perity, which was possibly the result of the effective concentration of its lands within the Pale.[4] The growth of the Christ Church estates was similar, with substantial holdings from Irish and Norse grants before 1169, confirmations

[1] A. J. Otway-Ruthven, 'The medieval church lands of County Dublin' in *Med. studies presented to A. Gwynn*, pp 58–9.
[2] *Alen's reg.*, pp 170–71; Walsh, *Richard FitzRalph*, p. 265.
[3] Gwynn, *Med. province Armagh*, pp 86–94.
[4] Colmcille Conway, 'The lands of St Mary's abbey, Dublin' in *R.I.A. Proc.*, lxii (1962), sect. C, pp 21–5.

and less important grants after the invasion and further acquisitions around 1250; nothing in the fourteenth century, but further gifts in the fifteenth for chantry purposes.[1] St Patrick's, because a latecomer, was endowed with much less land than those mentioned above and relied mainly on tithes and ecclesiastical rights; similarly, churches and their tithes were an important part of the estate of the two Llanthony priories which built up their Irish possessions bit by bit up to about 1270, often with purchases to consolidate holdings.[2] The contraction of the colony in the fourteenth century meant that many monasteries and their estates tended to become purely Irish, and others lost outlying areas. An example of this from St Mary's, Dublin, has already been quoted, and a further example is afforded by Llanthony Prima which was unable to get rent owed by the *Domus Dei* of Mullingar at the beginning of the fifteenth century.[3] Those houses which did not lose land often suffered loss of income as a result of hostile attacks and it was probably because of problems of this nature that Llanthony usually let the outlying lands of its parish churches. In spite of the difficulties caused by warfare, plague, depopulation, mismanagement, depredation by superiors, and secular encroachment, many houses clearly continued to enjoy some prosperity during the fourteenth and fifteenth centuries, as is suggested by their purchase of land revealed in the inquisitions *ad quod damnum* and by the successful management of the estates of Holy Trinity, Dublin, in the 1340s and of Llanthony Secunda towards the end of the century, for it was stated in 1381 that the proctors of that house could in any year send to England £80 clear profit.[4]

Throughout those parts of Ireland that were occupied by the colonists, that is, over two-thirds of the country in the late thirteenth century, the standard area of occupation was the manor, a direct transplant from England rather than a native institution. The manors grew out of the conquest, in that they often began with a fortified place, sometimes on the site of an old centre, which became the nucleus of a new manor. Originally built of wood, many, like Carlow and Trim, were rebuilt in stone and their presence is commonly recorded in extents and inquisitions, where, by about 1300, they are often described as being ruinous; it is, however, difficult to assess the reliability of these frequent pictures of dilapidation and collapse.[5] Settlement and organisation followed, often based on pre-conquest landholdings, and almost certainly some clearance, for the colonists increased considerably the amount of land under the plough. Coming to Ireland at a time when the direct exploitation by lords of their demesnes was becoming profitable, it is possible that on Irish

[1] Otway-Ruthven, 'Medieval church lands of County Dublin', pp 60–61.

[2] *Ir. cartul. Llanthony*, pp 110, 113–14, 223.

[3] Ibid., pp 135–8.

[4] Ibid., p. 311; Brendan Bradshaw, *The dissolution of the religious orders in Ireland under Henry VIII* (Cambridge, 1974), pp 27–35.

[5] *Red Bk Ormond*, pp 25, 27, 52, and 64; P.R.O., S.C. 6/1237/8–11, 33–4, 48, and 50 for Bigod examples; C. 135/36, mm 12 and 14.

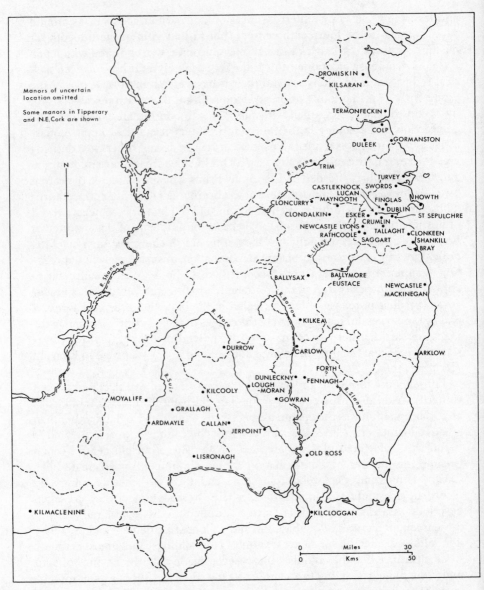

Manors of uncertain
location omitted

Some manors in Tipperary
and N.E.Cork are shown

N

DROMISKIN
KILSARAN

TERMONFECKIN

COLP
DULEEK GORMANSTON

R. Boyne TRIM

TURVEY
CASTLEKNOCK SWORDS
LUCAN
CLONCURRY MAYNOOTH FINGLAS HOWTH
CLONDALKIN DUBLIN
ESKER ST SEPULCHRE
CRUMLIN
NEWCASTLE LYONS TALLAGHT CLONKEEN
RATHCOOLE SHANKILL
SAGGART BRAY

R. Liffey

BALLYSAX BALLYMORE
EUSTACE
NEWCASTLE
MACKINEGAN

R. Barrow

R. Nore KILKEA

DURROW ARKLOW
CARLOW

FORTH
DUNLECKNY ?
LOUGH FENNAGH
MOYALIFF -MORAN
R. Suir KILCOOLY GOWRAN
GRALLAGH
ARDMAYLE CALLAN
JERPOINT

R. Slaney

LISRONAGH
OLD ROSS

KILMACLENINE
KILCLOGGAN

R. Shannon

| 0 | Miles | 30 |
| 0 | Kms | 50 |

Map 10 MANORS IN LEINSTER IN THE HIGH MIDDLE AGES,
by Kevin Down
The manors shown are those mentioned in chapter XV.

manors lords kept demesnes in hand from the outset of the colony. Unfortunately, for the first century of Irish manorial history no extents or accounts are available and nothing approaching a full picture emerges until Edward I's reign, so that it is mainly from then that any account of the manorial economy of Ireland has to be constructed. Most of the manors about which we have information were divided into two sections: the lord's demesne, which was cultivated directly by the lord, and the larger portion which was let by various tenures to his tenants. On the majority of manors was a group of buildings from which the manor and demesne were run; these were usually the principal building, a castle in some cases or a manor house, like that on Walter de la Hide's manor of Maynclare within the liberty of Trim; this had 'a stone tower, a hall, a chamber, a bakehouse, a granary, and a dovecot roofed with straw'; it must have resembled Stokesay castle in Shropshire, a fortified house of the late thirteenth century.[1] Others boasted a stone surrounding wall and sometimes a chapel.[2] These buildings were regularly surrounded by a ditch and near them were often the gardens and orchards.[3] As time went on, lords of many Irish manors were increasingly absentees and their non-residence may at least in part explain the dilapidated state into which so many of these buildings seem to have fallen; or perhaps both lords and manorial officials were unwilling to diminish profits by ploughing any portion of them back into non-productive installations.

As has been seen above, much of the land in the colony was held of the king by tenants-in-chief in fiefs of varying size; these great lords in turn sub-infeudated their possessions to lesser barons and knights, usually their followers, who in return for their lands owed their lords homage, fealty, suit of court and military service, which in Ireland was commuted at an early date to a cash payment, 'royal service'. Lords of manors let them to their tenants on several different tenures. The population of those Irish manors about which there is information was composed mostly of peasants—free tenants, farmers, gavillers, cottars, burgesses, and betaghs, distinguished by inequalities of wealth, by free or unfree status, and by their tenures, though these distinctions were not rigidly exclusive and often tenants held land by more than one form of tenure.

Free tenants covered a wide spectrum of wealth and position and sometimes were themselves lords of lesser manors within a large one, with substantial free tenants of their own. They held lands in perpetuity by what amounted to a form of military tenure, were liable to 'royal service' when proclaimed, and in some, though not all, cases paid a money rent, as well as the other customary feudal incidents. Others held in fee-farm and paid a fixed rent. Most of them owed

[1] P.R.O., C. 135/75 (3); Nikolaus Pevsner, *Shropshire* (The Buildings of England, Harmondsworth, 1958), plate 40b.
[2] P.R.O., C. 135/36.
[3] *Red Bk Ormond*, pp 62, 64.

suit to the lord's court, generally once a fortnight, but sometimes less frequently; and some, for example on the archbishop of Dublin's manor of Finglas in 1326, were required to perform labour services, in this case ploughing and carrying at harvest.[1] Most free tenants were of English or Welsh origin, but some, especially in the later middle ages, were Gaelic Irish.[2] Usually mentioned next in extents are the tenants-at-will and farmers, who held land on a lease for a set term in return for rent. Some of them held large areas of land,[3] but generally their holdings were small and in some cases were evidently intended to augment the land which they held by other tenures. When more land became available from the early fourteenth century onwards, lords had increasing recourse to farming to dispose of it profitably, especially in difficult areas and on former betagh land, and it became perhaps the most common form of tenure on many manors in the lordship.[4]

In some cases, as in 1326 with farmers on Dublin manors of Christ Church and the archbishop of Dublin, they owed suit of court and even labour services.[5] Tenants-at-will of a lower status were the gavillers (*gavillarii*, *gablarii*); they are not found on all manors, but there are references to them over a wide area including manors in Counties Dublin, Kildare, Wicklow, Leix, Offaly, Kilkenny, and Tipperary, mostly from the late thirteenth and fourteenth centuries, although there is a late mention of them in 1427.[6] Archbishop Alen, writing in the sixteenth century, gives the impression that he is commenting on an obsolete tenure: he says that they were farmers at will or by deed, 'copyholders' all of whose children succeeded as heirs; although he adds 'not gavelkynd, as in Kent, nor Borowgh Inglis, as at the town of Nottinghame, . . .', there is a resemblance to Kentish gavelkinders.[7] They paid a money rent, but it does not seem certain that they were liable for labour services. Some held substantial amounts of land, while others appear indistinguishable from cottagers. Among them at Kilkea (Co. Kildare) in 1311 were clergy, widows, and a bailiff; at Cloncurry in 1304 two appear to be Gaelic Irishmen, while at Callan (Kilkenny) in 1307 there were burgess gavillers.[8] Like other classes, during the course of the fourteenth century their numbers appear to have decreased in some places, for example Lisronagh where in 1351–2 much of their land was in the lady's hand untilled.[9] At the bottom of the economic scale

---

[1] *Alen's reg.*, p. 174.

[2] *Red Bk Ormond*, pp 20 and 30.

[3] Ibid., pp 31–2.

[4] Edmund Curtis, 'Rental of the manor of Lisronagh, 1333, and notes on "betagh" tenure in medieval Ireland' in *R.I.A. Proc.*, xliii (1936), sect. C, p. 75; *Alen's reg.*, p. 181.

[5] *Account roll of the priory of the Holy Trinity, Dublin, 1337–1346*, ed. James Mills (Dublin, 1891), R.S.A.I., extra vol. for 1890–91, pp 189–91; *Alen's reg.*, p. 173.

[6] *Reg. Swayne*, p. 56.

[7] *Alen's reg.*, p. 179; Edward Miller and John Hatcher, *Medieval England: rural society and economic change, 1086–1348* (London, 1978), pp 119–20.

[8] *Red Bk Ormond*, pp 11, 33; P.R.O., C. 133/130, 'burgens(es) gavelar(ii)'.

[9] P.R.O., S.C. 6/1238/14.

were the cottagers (*cottarii*, *cottiers*), smallholders who held their cottages and a small piece of land in return for a money and poultry rent and labour services, especially reaping. They were of mixed origin; most of those at Cloncurry in 1304 had Irish names, but the names of the cottagers at Lisronagh in 1333 were mainly English.[1] The cottagers were the manor's farm labourers who, because their holdings were small, had to work for the lord or better-off neighbours in their villages to make a living.

On many, but not all, manors were village communities, often quite small, which had been given by their lords a borough constitution. For their burgage plots, a share in the pasture, and about three acres in the fields the burgesses paid a low fixed rent, frequently 12*d.*, sometimes performed labour services, and owed suit to their own hundred court rather than to the court of the manor.[2] Most were of English origin, but several manors had a few Gaelic Irish burgesses.[3] It is clear that most of these small boroughs were not urban but agrarian communities, principally concerned with agriculture or small-scale rural industry, such as the tanners on the bishop of Cloyne's manor of Kilmaclenine who were, unusually, betaghs.[4] Many boroughs were founded by Anglo-Norman barons in the early days of the colony, perhaps to provide an inducement for settlers in the form of favourable burgage tenure and its accompanying privileges; or they may have hoped that in due course they would become profitable market centres. The Gaelic revival destroyed many small rural boroughs in much the same way as it ruined and depopulated manors in its path; by 1326 the burgesses at Shankill (County Dublin) had fled because of the Irish, and between about 1366 and 1382 Kilmaclenin may have been destroyed by the raids of Murchadh Ó Briain, and by coyne and livery and other exactions by the local Anglo-Irish lords.[5] Others, however, survived to become moderately important towns in modern times.

MOST members of the classes of manorial society discussed above were personally free; the betaghs (*betagii*, *betaci*, *nativi* or perhaps more significantly *Hibernici*) were unfree, customary tenants who provided much of the labour which cultivated the lord's demesnes on many, though not all, manors, and who could be sold or given away with their holdings. The equivalent of villeins, they were almost universally Gaelic Irish, the conquered population, which the colonists gathered indiscriminately into one class. The English form of their name comes from the Irish *biatach*—'one who gives food [*biad*]'—and refers to the typical pre-conquest free commoner who owed services to a lord.[6] Where

---

[1] *Red Bk Ormond*, pp 33–4; *Lisronagh rental*, p. 48; *Alen's reg.*, pp 186, 189.

[2] Otway-Ruthven, *Med. Ire.*, pp 112–13; *Alen's reg.*, pp 187, 190.   [3] Gormanston reg., p. 112.

[4] 'The pipe roll of Cloyne' in *Cork Hist. Soc. Jn.*, xx (1914), pp 88–91; *Rot. pip. Clon.*, pp 15–16.

[5] *Alen's reg.*, p. 195; Thomas Olden, 'On some ancient remains at Kilmaclenine, with illustrations from the Pipa Colmani' in *R.I.A. Proc.*, xvi (1879–88), pp 126–7.

[6] *Alen's reg.*, p. 176; *Ir. cartul. Llanthony*, p. 253; Gearóid MacNiocaill, 'The origins of the betagh' in *Ir. Jurist*, new series, i (1966), pp 292–8.

betaghs are found with English names it is possible that some men of English descent either degenerated to this status, or, perhaps more likely, were personally free but held land by betagh tenure and so were associated with or counted among them.[1] The number, however, is too small for significance. In extents from the first century or so of the lordship the betaghs are generally referred to as a group holding their land in blocks for which they paid a joint rent and were liable for labour and a variety of other services, sometimes a render in kind, perhaps a relic of their pre-conquest status as providers of food.[2] At Cloncurry in 1311 they had $341\frac{1}{2}$ acres of land between sixty-three of them, about five acres each on average, which makes them a great deal better off than the cottagers there, who mostly had only their cottages and just over half a stang of land each.[3] This greater prosperity is, however, merely comparative, for five acres was hardly adequate to provide even a bare subsistence living, and was perhaps below the acreage of the majority of peasant holdings in England, which (for Warwickshire and Worcestershire) R. H. Hilton puts at less than fifteen or twenty acres in arable, but it may be that this apparently low acreage merely reflects a larger Irish acre.[4] On the other hand, labour services and customary payments seem to have been lighter in Ireland than in England, so that the ultimate condition of betaghs and English villeins may not have been that much different.

Towards the end of the thirteenth century their conditions in some ways improved. Gaelic Irish attacks, famine, plague, and consequent depopulation created a greater availability of land and eased the pressure on that of the betaghs, so that some were able to acquire larger holdings, either from land deserted by other betaghs or from that no longer occupied by Anglo-Irish tenants, and much former betagh land was let because they had gone away.[5] The change is clearly seen on the manors of the archbishop of Dublin which were prone to attack from the Gaelic Irish. At Boly Major on St Sepulchre's in 1326 betaghs' land was let to others 'because the betaghs are undone by evildoers'; at Boly Minor five betaghs held sixty acres, a higher average, and their labour was not valued because they were in the march and dared not stay there at night. Similar conditions obtained at Finglas, while poor betaghs at Swords held, if it was equally averaged, between ten and twenty acres each.[6] At Callan, County Kilkenny, they acquired land that was worn out and much used, and which, had they not taken it, would have been waste; better betaghs than no tenants! Much the same picture is revealed on the earl of Ulster's estates in

[1] *Red Bk Ormond*, pp 14, 128; *Lisronagh rental*, pp 46, 47, 61; 'The pipe roll of Cloyne' in *Cork Hist. Soc. Jn.*, xix (1913), p. 161; xx (1914), pp 88–9, 91.

[2] P.R.O., C. 135/36, m. 23.

[3] *Red Bk Ormond*, pp 32–3.

[4] R. H. Hilton, *A medieval society* (London, 1966), p. 115; Titow, *Eng. rural society*, pp 89–90; M. M. Postan, *The Cambridge economic history of Europe* (2nd ed., Cambridge, 1966), pp 618–24. See below, p. 460, n. 2.

[5] *Red Bk Ormond*, p. 54.

[6] *Alen's reg.*, pp 170–71, 173, 176.

Connacht and Ulster by William de Burgh's inquisition *post mortem* of 1333–4, where some betaghs are shown to have returned with the earl's permission to the jurisdiction of an Irish king.[1] In the later fourteenth and fifteenth centuries betaghry was dying out in the colony and by 1500 had become rare. The suggestion of Edmund Curtis that their disappearance was the result of the replacement of agriculture by grazing does not seem valid for the remaining English areas, because in the Pale arable farming remained important.[2] It seems more likely that the fall in population and the ensuing shortage of labour improved their conditions and status and that those who remained in the colony were able to sell their labour at a higher price.

There are indications, even before the advent of manorial accounts, that some demesnes were cultivated directly by their lords. The Irish pipe roll of 14 John (1211–12) shows the demesnes of the crown both directly cultivated and farmed; the income from the leasing of some manors is recorded, while references to sales of produce, lists of stock, and the use of grain from various manors for seed, wages, and military supplies indicate direct cultivation.[3] Demesne cultivation, however, seems to have been normal on a large scale on the manors of the great Marshal lordship of Leinster, as indicated by the command in 1224–5 to the barons of the Cinque Ports not to impede persons conveying to London one thousand crannocks of wheat that had been bought from William, Earl Marshal, in Ireland by Richard Renger, mayor of London, and John Travers.[4]

It appears from the evidence of inquisitions *post mortem* that in the thirteenth century large areas of arable land were held in demesne and cultivated by tenants-in-chief, and it is clear that at the same time a considerable amount of land was brought under the plough and improved agricultural methods were introduced with a consequent expansion in the production of cereals, so that by the middle of the century a large surplus was available for export. Henry III was able to use this in the 1240s as a source of supplies for his Welsh wars, and the same situation during the next two reigns gave royal purveyance extensive scope in Ireland.[5] In the second half of the century the direct cultivation of demesnes was widespread and flourishing in the areas of peace, as is seen from the ministers' accounts of the estates about which we know most, those of the Bigod earls of Norfolk in the south-east. These reeves' accounts show successful cultivation of cereals and raising of stock on a fairly large scale for the market and for the earl's household.[6] The Bigod demesnes, however, were not necessarily the most successful, nor were they the largest; indeed the earls of

[1] P.R.O., C. 135/36, m. 23.
[2] *Lisronagh rental*, pp 74–5.
[3] *Pipe roll Ire., 1211–12*, pp 21, 32–5, 38–41, 56–7.
[4] *Cal. doc. Ire., 1171–1251*, no. 1285. The crannock is the usual Irish equivalent of the English quarter: of wheat eight bushels, of oats sixteen.
[5] Orpen, *Normans*, iv, 268; *Close rolls, 1237–42*, p. 325.
[6] *Cal. doc. Ire., 1252–84*, no. 2009, and ministers' accounts *passim*.

Ulster and the de Clare earls of Gloucester and Hertford had huge areas under their ploughs.[1] The average amount of demesne arable during the period when direct cultivation was at its height was about 300 acres, and it ranged in size over a scale from 125½ acres on the Ormond manor of Cloncurry, County Kildare, in 1304 to 570 acres in 1333 at Toolooban, a part of the earl of Ulster's great manor of Loughrea in Galway, and 660 acres on the archbishop of Dublin's manor at Swords in 1326.[2] In the second half of the thirteenth century lords continued to build up their directly-cultivated demesne arable, and the surviving records contain many examples of its augmentation. At Forth in County Carlow, a Bigod manor, it appears that in the mid-1280s there was a definite policy of purchasing small parcels of land to consolidate the demesne arable and of transferring larger areas of land from farm in the borough of Forth castle to increase the manor's demesne arable, a process that seems to have been accompanied by a steady programme of manuring.[3] The total acreage was further enlarged by renting a carucate of arable land from Baltinglass abbey. The process evidently continued, for by the death of Roger Bigod, the last earl of Norfolk of that name, in 1306, there had been an immense increase in the demesne arable of some of his Irish manors, an increase confirmed by the growth of the area sown with cereal crops at Forth between 1279 and 1288.[4] A similar picture of piecemeal augmentation is indicated by the 1305 extent of the Ormond manor of Ardmayle, where sizeable additions had been made by purchase about the middle of the thirteenth century, probably to consolidate the demesne arable and possibly to introduce a third course for crops.[5] In addition to purchase, lords also added to their arable by assarting land, probably often on the edges of their existing fields. This must have been done on a large scale in the period after the coming of the Anglo-Normans, since it seems certain that the invaders increased greatly the area of land under the plough. At Fennagh, a Bigod manor in Carlow, in 1280–81, the year of the first bailiff's account, there was expenditure on four new ploughs and two harrows for the oxen for new land made and on assarting land before the plough. Moreover, there are further indications in the account that the demesne there was only then coming into normal operation: in the issues of the grange only six crannocks of oats appear and these were received from Forth, another Bigod manor nearby, and mostly sown on eleven acres; the income was mainly from foreign

[1] P.R.O., C. 133/30 (69, 71, 73, 76).

[2] *Red Bk Ormond*, p. 28; C. 135/36, m. 21, inq. *post mortem* of William de Burgh, earl of Ulster; *Alen's reg.*, p. 175. No doubt the size of acre varied greatly from place to place; James Mills calculated that in the Dublin area the medieval acre was equivalent to about two and a half statute acres ('Notices of the manor of St Sepulchre, Dublin, in the fourteenth century' in *R.S.A.I. Jn.*, xix (1889), 35–6). This larger acre may be reflected in the apparently high rate of seed sown per acre and the low expectation of a day's ploughing on some manors. Actual information on what constitutes an acre appears to be lacking.

[3] P.R.O., S.C. 6/1237/45, 46, 51, 53.

[4] P.R.O., C. 133/127, Bigod's inquisition *post mortem*, and reeves' accounts, *passim*.

[5] *Red Bk Ormond*, pp 62–3; *Ormond deeds, 1172–1350*, nos 80, 271.

receipts; the livestock was being built up by purchase or acquisition from else-where; the land of the betaghs was measured; and the manor remained under the supervision of a bailiff rather than the usual reeve.[1] It may, however, be that this was merely a resumption of activity after devastation by the Gaelic Irish, because the 1280–81 account states that 'scarcely anyone wanted to stay there for fear of Art'. There are other examples: a rath was levelled at Forth manor in 1285–6; Geoffrey de Tourville, bishop of Ossory (1244–50), granted to his burgesses of Durrow (Leix) pasture in Lanath wood until it should be assarted and cultivated; and Henry of London, archbishop of Dublin, about 1220 made a grant of sixteen acres of land which had been assarted from wood near Dublin by Robert Blund, a smith.[2] There are, moreover, frequent references to new land throughout the area of conquest. Not all reclamation, of course, was for expansion; some was to compensate for land going out of cultivation because of deterioration due to overuse, and there is plenty of evidence for this. After about 1300 such replace-ment seems to have been unnecessary because of the lack of labourers and tenants, resulting from Gaelic Irish attacks; the problem on most large estates from then on was finding enough tenants, and it may be that from about that time, on some manors, deterioration was more often reversion to scrub due to breaks in cultivation rather than soil exhaustion caused by overuse.[3]

From about the beginning of the fourteenth century on many Irish manors the amount of demesne arable cultivated directly was reduced and ever greater areas of it were let at farm.[4] The change was gradual and never complete, and direct cultivation continued on many demesnes, especially on ecclesiastical manors and those on the eastern seaboard. On the Dublin manors of the arch-bishop of Dublin in 1326 direct cultivation persisted, though some of the land was exhausted and poor; war had reduced the acreage cultivated, as it had also diminished rents, and there was a marked movement towards leasing substan-tial areas of demesne arable, turning it over to pasture and sometimes enclosing it.[5] It is likely that to some extent these Dublin manors were victualling the archbishop's household and that supplies were a more important considera-tion than cash in this case. The same is true of some manors of Christ Church, Dublin, in the 1340s when the account roll shows cultivation of the demesne mainly for internal use with little corn for sale, and it may be that until their dis-solution religious houses generally kept some arable permanently in demesne to supply their needs for food; there is a hint of this in the possessions of Ardee priory in 1470.[6] Direct cultivation was still the norm for the earl of Kildare's

[1] P.R.O., S.C. 6/1237/32, 36.

[2] P.R.O., S.C. 6/1237/51; *Ir. mon deeds, 1200–1600*, pp 213, 215; *Reg. St John, Dublin*, no. 338.

[3] *Alen's reg.*, pp 170, 181, 186; inquisition *post mortem* of Joan, late wife of Gilbert de Clare, 1307, P.R.O., C. 133/130, (69) Rosbargon, (71) Loughmetheran, (76) Callan; C. 133/127, (32) Dunleck (Bigod, 1307); C. 134/84 (1). m. 71, Odagh (Aymer de Valence, earl of Pembroke, 1324).

[4] *Red Bk Ormond*, pp 1, 52, 60.

[5] *Alen's reg.*, pp 170, 173, 175–6, 181, 185–6, 194.

[6] *Account roll of Holy Trinity, Dublin*, pp 30–31, 43, 49–58, 78–83; Reg. Octavian (Armagh Public Library), f. 74ᵛ.

eastern manors about 1330, but by 1331 it had broken down on his Limerick manors because of warfare, Irish incursions, and the consequent lack of tenants to provide either a work-force or lessees.[1] By the middle of the fourteenth century the receivers' accounts of the de Burgh manors in Kilkenny, Tipperary, and Meath indicate that the demesne arable was mostly let, and because of the combination of disorder and plague it was proving difficult to find tenants for much of it, as at Callan in 1351; while at Lisronagh in the same year much land was in the lady's hand, untilled, and the rent of the demesne and of the gavillers was halved because the land could not be let.[2] In some cases former officials of the lord farmed the demesne, as happened at Loughmoran (Kilkenny) between 1351 and 1354; jurisdiction, however, normally remained in the possession of the lords.[3] The few surviving fifteenth-century documents indicate that the demesnes were mostly let, though there are signs on some manors of the earls of Ormond and Kildare that parts were kept for the lord's direct use.[4]

The change from direct cultivation of demesnes to farming them occurred in England between about 1300 and 1348, especially after the bad harvests of 1315–17: rising costs resulting from higher wages and the stability or fall of agricultural prices induced landlords to seek the stabilisation of their incomes by leasing their demesne lands for rents which were reliable, predictable, and adjustable.[5] It has been seen that a similar process took place in Ireland, but there additional factors encouraged the tendency towards change; the effects of the bad harvests of 1315–17 were exacerbated by the ruin caused by the Bruce invasion. In the growing disorder of the fourteenth century the regular absenteeism of lords was an important instigator of change in running estates.

Direct management was easier in times of peace and stability when lords could exert minute control over their officials even at a distance. The breakdown in order and the growing hazardousness of communications made control at a distance more difficult and the transport of produce both within and out of Ireland more of a risk, so that it paid absentees to leave their demesnes to the enterprise of their officials and tenants, with a lease favourable to themselves, in order to assure a regular and reliable income from more easily transferred cash. This was the policy pursued for the Irish estates of Lady Elizabeth de Burgh in the middle of the fourteenth century.[6] Absenteeism also meant a reduction in defence and less resistance to the attacks of the Gaelic Irish, which must have reduced and often wiped out profits and finally deterred lords from capital expenditure. Efforts were made to defend vulnerable areas against the Gaelic Irish or rebel Anglo-Irish by contributing towards the

[1] *Red Bk Kildare*, pp 99, 102, 104, 110, 112, 118–19, 123.
[2] Callan, P.R.O., S.C. 6/1237/11; Lisronagh, S.C. 6/1238/14.
[3] P.R.O., S.C. 6/1238/16.
[4] *Red Bk Ormond*, 119, 123, 125, and P.R.O., S.C. 6/1237/7 for Ormond manors *c.* 1415 and *c.* 1480; S.C. 6/1238/17, 19, 20 for three Kildare manors *c.* 1450.
[5] Postan, *Med. econ.*, pp 105–6.
[6] P.R.O., S.C. 6/1239/14, 16.

armies of the colony or by buying off the enemy, as Richard Tobin was paid to spare the lady's tenants at Lisronagh; but it is likely that the energetic presence of a great lord would have been much more effective.[1] The tendency towards absenteeism was encouraged by the failure in the male line of many noble families and the consequent division of their Irish estates between heiresses. These were usually married to English lords who were more interested in their substantial lands in England than in Irish estates which were difficult to run and sometimes so diminished by partitions as to be insignificant beside their English interests. A good example of this situation is provided by the fate of the liberty of Thomond, which was built up, together with landed property in England, by Thomas de Clare, a landless member of a comital house.[2] After his death in 1287, his elder son Gilbert was little in Ireland and probably neglected the estates; his younger son, Richard, was continuously in Ireland, but his defeat and death at the hands of the Gaelic Irish at the battle of Dysert O'Dea in 1318 was the virtual end of the Anglo-Irish overlordship of Thomond, because the husbands of Thomas's two heiresses were not interested in Ireland, and the Gaelic Irish took over until the Tudor reconquest. The lordships of Kilkenny, Carlow, Wexford, and Leix were similarly left by their absentee lords to their practical occupiers, Gaelic or Anglo-Irish; little was done about the earldom of Ulster and lordship of Connacht after the death of Lionel of Clarence in 1368; and the de Verdon lands in Meath and Louth, which had been partitioned between four heiresses in 1332 leaving none of them with an adequate working unit, were, by the 1380s, all sold by uninterested English inheritors to local residents.[3]

THE labour for the cultivation of the demesnes of Irish manors came from two sources: labour services, generally of unfree tenants, and the paid work of the estate servants (*famuli*) and hired labour; of these sources the latter was the more important. It is generally agreed that in Ireland labour services played a comparatively small part in the cultivation of the demesne and were lighter than was usual in England; nowhere in Ireland did services approach the hundred days or more each year that the English villein commonly owed to his lord, and English week-work, perhaps the peasants' greatest burden, appears unknown. It may be that these lighter conditions were part of the concessions necessary to attract settlers and keep betaghs from going off with their animals to the Gaelic areas.[4] On Irish manors the typical unfree tenant was obliged to plough each year one acre for wheat and one acre for oats if he had a complete

[1] Ibid.; P.R.O., E. 101/505/29, in Richardson & Sayles, *Admin. Ire.*, p. 234.
[2] Michael Altschul, *A baronial family in medieval England: the Clares, 1217–1314* (Baltimore, 1965), pp 194–7.
[3] Curtis, *Med. Ire.* (2nd ed.), p. 234; A. J. Otway-Ruthven, 'The partition of the de Verdon lands in Ireland in 1332' in *R.I.A. Proc.*, lxvi (1968), sect. C, p. 417.
[4] A. J. Otway-Ruthven, 'The organization of Anglo-Irish agriculture in the middle ages' in *R.S.A.I. Jn.*, lxxxi (1951), pp 9–10; Lydon, *Lordship*, p. 86.

ploughteam, and if not, to join with neighbours to do it; to reap one or two days, perhaps to cart hay, corn, or fuel, and sometimes to dig turf. The heaviest services noted by Dr A. J. Otway-Ruthven were on the Ormond manor of Baly-bothy in Tipperary in 1415–16; there each tenant was required to plough one acre for wheat and one acre for oats, and owed the lord five days reaping, five days weeding, and five days carting grain.[1] On some manors labour services were expected of burgesses, as in 1326 at Swords and at Clondalkin where they were to plough, save hay, and reap corn; while at Moyaliff in Tipperary they were obliged to carry iron and salt from Cashel whenever the bailiff required it.[2] By the late thirteenth century labour services were frequently commuted to money payments, but they persisted, mainly where lords continued direct cultivation of their demesnes, and were included in the terms of leases until the end of the middle ages.[3]

Boonworks were supposedly voluntary, but in practice they were com-pulsory and differed from ordinary day-labour only by the lord's provision of food. They survived at least into the middle of the fourteenth century on some manors of Christ Church and the archbishop of Dublin, and were an additional burden on some tenants at those times of the year when their own land required their greatest efforts.[4] The importance of services, especially at times of labour shortage and competitive wages, is underlined by the Irish ordinance of 1299 which attempted to peg wages and reimpose services, because agricultural workers were refusing customary services 'on account of the fertility of the year'; but, more than that, it shows how far the process of commutation had gone, and the heavy reliance on hired labour, which by the early fourteenth century was making the major contribution to demesne culti-vation.[5]

At the times of greatest agricultural activity, Irish demesnes relied mainly on piece-work carried out by hired labourers and the constant employment of the permanent manorial servants (*famuli*). On the Bigod manors, for example, between 1279 and 1289, it seems to have been usual to hire a great deal of labour, especially for the hay and corn harvests; and although the betaghs did about half the reaping at Fennagh and helped at Old Ross, hired labour was mainly responsible for the harvests at Ballysax and Forth, apparently without help from betaghs, but with a considerable contribution from the *famuli* at Forth.[6] The demesnes of Christ Church, Dublin, too, were by 1343–4 mainly dependent on hired labour for their cultivation; so much so that at Clonkeen

[1] Otway-Ruthven, 'Anglo-Irish agriculture', p. 9. *Red Bk Ormond*, p. 123.

[2] *Alen's reg.*, pp 177, 187; *Red Bk Ormond*, p. 66.

[3] *Lisronagh rental*, loc. cit., p. 69; betaghs on lands of Sir Thomas de Clare in his vill of Youghal: *Red Bk Ormond*, pp 49–50; *Account roll of Holy Trinity, Dublin*, pp 207–9; Otway-Ruthven, 'Anglo-Irish agriculture', p. 10.

[4] *Account roll of Holy Trinity, Dublin*, p. 58; *Alen's reg.*, p. 189.

[5] Lydon, *Ire. in later middle ages*, p. 6; *Early statutes*, p. 215.

[6] Fennagh, P.R.O., S.C. 6/1237/37–9; Old Ross in Hore, *Wexford town*, i, 28; Ballysax, P.R.O., S.C. 6/1237/1–6; Forth, S.C. 6/1237/40, 42, 43–4, 47, 49, 51, 53, 55.

(Kill of the Grange, County Dublin), in 1344, out of 562 days' reaping 471 were done by labourers at 1*d.* a day and only 91 by customary tenants.[1] The *famuli* were the essential group of regular farm workers who toiled on the demesnes throughout the year. Usually they numbered around ten, though this figure varied from place to place; on the earl of Norfolk's manors, for example, the number ranged from five at Fennagh in 1282–3 to nineteen at Old Ross in 1283–4.[2] Normally they were divided into two groups by their responsibilities and pay. In the better-paid class were the *tentores* (ploughmen who guided the plough) and the master carter; the other, more numerous, grade consisted of the hayward, the *fugatores* (ploughmen who drove the plough-animals), the undercarters, shepherds, swineherds, cowmen, door-keepers, and dairymaids. The former were paid six shillings a year on the Bigod manors in the 1280s and at Cloncurry in 1304, and five shillings at Clonkeen (Christ Church) in 1344–5; the latter received four shillings in all three cases. In addition to their wages, they were given maintenance or an allowance of food worth 4*d.* a week to Bigod servants, 3½*d.* to those of the earl of Ormond at Cloncurry.[3] Various part-time workers were also taken on for seasonal tasks or as the need arose: watchmen, sowers, harrowers, the woman at Clonkeen 'drying malt and doing other necessary work within the manor', carpenters and smiths to make and repair ploughs.[4] Drawn from both the Anglo-Irish and Gaelic Irish sections of the population, they were usually found from among the ranks of the cottagers and small tenants who had not sufficient land to live off, like those at Dunleckny (County Carlow) in 1287–8 who each held a cottage and curtilage for a rent of 8*d.* to 10*d.* a year; or the four betaghs at Gowran who held burgages from their lord to find four *famuli* for his work; the fourth of them, Robert O'Gillinan, is said to be himself *famulus adhuc in Grangia*.[5]

The immediate responsibility for running a demesne rested on a reeve or a bailiff, and it is from the accounts which they rendered annually for their charges that most of the information about agriculture in the lordship of Ireland can be obtained. In charge of a single manor, and not always his native one, was the reeve, possibly one of the more prosperous farmers or gavillers or lower free tenants. Although Bigod reeves were paid only 6*s.* a year, the wages of the higher grade of *famuli*, and received the same weekly food allowance of 4*d.*, they were probably much better off than those they directed. It is likely that they were let off their rent, and their favourable position gave them opportunities for personal gain while in office (often by using the lord's possessions for their own purposes), and for improving their condition in the future by

[1] *Account roll of Holy Trinity, Dublin*, pp 23, 64–7.

[2] Bigod ministers' accounts, *passim*; Hore, *Wexford town*, i, 30–31.

[3] Bigod ministers' accounts, *passim*; *Red Bk Ormond*, p. 29; *Account roll of Holy Trinity, Dublin*, pp 50, 52.

[4] Bigod ministers' accounts, *passim*; *Account roll of Holy Trinity, Dublin*, pp 29–30, 35, 62.

[5] P.R.O., S.C. 6/1237/27–8; *Red Bk Ormond*, p. 50.

being able to increase their own holdings, as David de Bonham, reeve of Bally-sax, did when he acquired the farm of Ballysax mill.[1] They were normally heavily in debt to their lords, often for years after leaving office, but this was largely because of the debts owed in turn by their creditors, particularly the arrears of their predecessors. The length of tenure of office varied, but most of the known Bigod reeves served for only one or two years apiece, with one instance of four and a half years. Unlike the *famuli* with whom they worked, the reeves on the earl of Norfolk's manors in the 1280s, with one exception, had English names; and fifty years later, between 1340 and 1355, the same was still largely true of Callan, a rural borough, and other manors of Lady Elizabeth de Burgh in Kilkenny and Tipperary.[2]

The immediate link between a lord's administration and the various reeves was usually provided by a bailiff, normally a free man and often a professional farm manager, who was put in charge of a group of manors or even, as was the case with the Christ Church estates, an individual manor. In addition to super-vising the work of lower officials, he put into practice the agricultural policy laid down by the lord's steward or auditors. During the period covered by their surviving ministers' accounts, the manors of Ballysax, Fennagh, and Forth were all supervised by a single bailiff, one Thomas de Clene, who seems to have been concerned only with the agrarian side of the manors around which he rode. This arrangement was probably temporary and connected with the abnormal conditions at Fennagh, and by 1293 the post appears to have given way to a purely military one in response to the threat of war from the neigh-bouring O'Byrnes and O'Nolans.[3] For his work, in addition to living in the manor-house at the lord's expense, he was paid 100 shillings a year and given the same robes as the higher officials of the liberty; and it is likely that his position gave him various advantages and perquisites, among them perhaps the fifty-two acres at Ballysax which he farmed at a lower rent than the other farmers, together with the farm of the mills there.[4]

The overall direction of estates, particularly important in Ireland where so many lords were distant and permanent absentees, was usually in the hands of a steward (*senescallus*). In the late thirteenth century the stewards of the earl of Norfolk were knights experienced in administration. In addition to running the earl's estates and looking after his Irish interests, the steward presided over the chief court of the liberty, was its principal military commander and an impor-tant royal officer. For his services he received robes and a yearly salary of £100, a seventh of the lordship's gross income of around £770. He was assisted by a treasurer, who dealt with the financial business of the liberty, two lawyers (*nar-ratores*), a sheriff, constables of castles, clerks and a chief serjeant.[5] Supervision

---

[1] P.R.O., S.C. 6/1237/6. For all this, see Bigod ministers' accounts, *passim*.
[2] De Burgh ministers' accounts, P.R.O., S.C. 6/1237/15–29.
[3] For Fennagh, see above, pp 460–61; P.R.O., S.C. 6/1239/1 & 9.   [4] P.R.O., S.C. 6/1237/1–6.
[5] James Mills, 'Accounts of the earl of Norfolk's estates in Ireland, 1279–1294' in *R.S.A.I. Jn.*, xxii (1892), pp 51–2; W. F. Nugent, 'Carlow in the middle ages' in *R.S.A.I. Jn.*, lxxxv (1955), pp 67–73.

from England was exercised through the auditors on their annual visits, when they travelled about the liberty auditing accounts and directing every aspect of its economic life. Stewards of the Christ Church estates in the middle of the next century were usually canons of the house who directed its home farms, received rents and presided over its manorial courts, while the English house of Llanthony Secunda supervised its Irish possessions through a proctor, one of its canons.[1] At about the same time, the widespread estates of Lady Elizabeth de Burgh in Ireland were run by a knightly chief keeper and by her chief receiver in Ireland. Under them the liberties of Kilkenny and Tipperary and the estates in Meath, Ulster, and Connacht were supervised by stewards, who in some cases, for example at Lisronagh and Grallagh, were in charge of a single manor. Cash surpluses were collected by the chief receiver from the sub-receivers, who appear to have replaced reeves in charge of the demesnes, which were by now mostly farmed, and from the farmers of entire manors; he in turn transmitted the cash to the lady's receiver in England.[2]

The essential concomitant of the manorial organisation that was introduced into Ireland after the coming of the Anglo-Normans was the open-field or common-field system,[3] cooperative agriculture in which the village arable was divided into two or three sectors made up of a differing number of fields throughout which were scattered the demesne arable and the strips which con-stituted the holdings of individual villagers. Between these sectors or courses the crops were rotated annually to preserve the land's fertility. Where the two-course system obtained, each year half the land was sown with whatever crops were considered suitable for it and the remainder was left fallow. Under the three-course system the growing land was increased because the fallow was reduced to about a third of the total, thus leaving two-thirds to be divided between winter corn (wheat or rye) and spring corn (oats and barley). The three-course cycle was begun by sowing winter corn, which was both more dif-ficult to grow and more valuable, on the land fresh from fallowing; then spring crops replaced winter corn in the second sector, and the third was left fallow to be grazed, manured, and ploughed. The satisfactory cultivation by individuals of strips scattered about the fields in each sector of rotation, with various tasks to be done at different times of the year, clearly required the unified approach resulting from common control, and this was provided and enforced by the manorial court.[4] The open-field system which prevailed in most of the colonised area of Ireland in the thirteenth and fourteenth centuries was vir-tually the same as that which is found on those 'typical manors' characteristic of the arable plains of central and southern England, and there is plenty of evidence to show that the system of cultivation of the fields was the same. At the

---

[1] *Account roll of Holy Trinity, Dublin*, p. xviii; *Ir. cartul. Llanthony*, pp 281–6.
[2] P.R.O., S.C. 6/1238/13; 1239/14, 16, 26, 29.
[3] See Titow, *Eng. rural society*, pp 20–23.
[4] Postan, *Med. econ.*, p. 50; Titow, op. cit., pp 20–22.

edges of this area, however, near the Gaelic Irish, this pattern, which required peace and orderly running, was probably modified considerably and, as may also have been the case in the hillier regions, replaced by pastoral husbandry.

On those manors for which most evidence survives, the arable land was cultivated mainly in open fields, throughout which were dispersed unfenced strips of varying shape which made up the individual holdings. It is debatable whether the demesne arable was interspersed with peasant land in the common fields or was separate from tenant holdings. Evidence on this is slight, but in Ireland, as in England, there are some indications of both arrangements: it is quite clear from a comparison of the names of the locations of demesne acreage at Lisronagh in 1333 with those of the tenants' holdings that, before it had been let to farmers, the demesne arable had been separate from the holdings of the gavillers and of the three free tenants, two of whom held separate knights' fees and had tenants of their own.[1] The position of the land of the burgesses and cottagers, however, is not stated, and it may be that it was in the demesne fields. At Duleek, County Meath, a grange of the priory of Llanthony Secunda, in 1381 the demesne arable appears to have been dispersed among that of the tenants. That some acres are described as *simul iacentes* argues that others were not; and this is borne out by others that are said to be *iacentes diversimode*.[2] The land of the betaghs, which they may have cultivated by their own native methods, possibly using the infield and outfield system, may also have been apart from that of the other tenants, and sometimes the betaghs are described as holding definite townlands, or, as at Lisronagh, 'granges' which they held in mainly family groups.[3]

Although the demesne arable and the tenants' holdings were cultivated in two or three sectors, the acreage was often divided between a larger number of fields and locations: for example, at Lisronagh the 358 acres and $1\frac{1}{2}$ stangs of demesne arable were divided at various times into twenty-six or twenty-eight different parcels, of which at least four were fields and some were probably enclosures; and the gavillers' land was similarly divided into fourteen denominations.[4] A memorandum of the lands of St Thomas's abbey, Dublin, in 1268 divides its 105 acres into fourteen units, all in fields or furlongs except for seven acres of arable in the wood; and a similar large number of divisions is revealed by the extent of the Llanthony grange at Duleek in 1381.[5] It seems possible that this large number of fields was the result of piecemeal augmentation

[1] *Lisronagh rental*, pp 42–3, 45–6, 48–50; accounts of the receiver of Lisronagh, 1350–52, P.R.O., S.C. 6/1238/13 & 14.

[2] *Ir. cartul. Llanthony*, pp 291–2.

[3] *Lisronagh rental*, pp 45–7; Otway-Ruthven, 'Anglo-Irish agriculture', p. 3; R. H. Buchanan, 'Field systems of Ireland' in A. R. H. Baker and R. A. Butlin (ed.), *Studies of field systems in the British Isles* (Cambridge, 1973), pp 609–10.

[4] P.R.O., S.C. 6/1238/13 & 14, where the fields appear clearly, as they do not in *Lisronagh rental*, pp 42–3; *Red Bk Ormond*, p. 155 (Carkenlis, 1300); *Red Bk Kildare*, pp 97–9 (Maynooth, 1328); *Alen's reg.*, p. 175 (Swords, 1326).

[5] *Reg. St Thomas, Dublin*, p. 3; *Ir. cartul. Llanthony*, pp 291–2.

of demesnes by clearance and purchase, but this complicated pattern is by no means standard, and at Turvey, County Dublin, Cloncurry, County Kildare, and Gowran, County Kilkenny, in the early fourteenth century all the demesne arable was divided between three areas or fields.[1] It is clear, too, that there was no uniformity in the arrangement of humbler holdings; charters show that some tenants, like the Lisronagh tenants-at-will and gavillers, had their land dispersed among several fields or, more likely, furlongs (*culture*), sharing good and bad land, while others held in comparatively large blocks. In the latter case, however, it is difficult to be certain whether this was so from the time when the holdings were laid out or whether it was the result of thirteenth-century consolidation of holdings, a practice that became increasingly common from the fourteenth century onwards.[2]

The system of agriculture for which there is most evidence in the Anglo-Irish area of Ireland was triennial rotation of crops, but the documents are few and relate mainly to a group of manors fairly near Dublin: Cloncurry (1304), Turvey (1311), Maynooth (1328), and five of the archbishop's manors, Cullen (Colonia), Finglas, Swords, Tallaght, and Clondalkin (1326).[3] Three-course rotation is also found on the Ormond manors of Gowran (1306), Ardmayle in Tipperary (1305)—where the third sector appears to be the result of piecemeal purchase—and possibly at Callan (1307).[4] Their common factor is that they are all in fertile areas which have a good depth of soil.[5] The sectors in these examples were roughly equal in size, but their acreage varied considerably from manor to manor and ranged between three sectors of 43, 48, and 34 acres apiece at Cloncurry and of 220 acres each at Swords. Although extents give the impression that the sectors were static in size, it is clear from the Bigod reeves' accounts that the acreages sown in each course changed much from year to year, and, as has been seen above, they were not necessarily confined to one field. In most of these Irish examples of triennial rotation the crops sown were wheat in the winter course and mainly oats in the spring one, with a little barley (including *hastivellum*), beans, and peas. This arrangement was not always strictly followed; for example, in 1326 at Swords 200 acres were said to be sown by the archbishop with wheat and only five acres with oats, while 201 acres in the other sector were sown with wheat and peas by the archbishop and the king. There is very little evidence for two-course rotation in the lordship, one of the few examples being the old town of Jerpoint, a de Clare manor, where in 1307 of 135 acres of arable only 38 acres were sown with wheat and 30 acres with oats. There are, however, indications that a two-field system may have been followed by the first colonists, and this impression is supported by the suggestion

[1] *Red Bk Ormond*, pp 27, 28, 34.
[2] P.R.O., S.C. 6/1238/13 and 14; Otway-Ruthven, 'Anglo-Irish agriculture', pp 2–4.
[3] *Red Bk Ormond*, pp 27, 28; *Red Bk Kildare*, pp 97–9; *Alen's reg.*, pp 170, 173, 175–6, 181, 185–6.
[4] *Red Bk Ormond*, pp 34, 63; P.R.O., C. 133/130 (76). At Gowran, a three-course rotation may be planned rather than in operation.
[5] John O'Loan, 'A history of early Irish farming' in *Dept. Agric. Jn.*, lx (1963), pp 193–4.

that some third fields were built up by gradual acquisition.[1] Although the paucity of evidence does not permit certainty, it is probable that in the lordship, as in many parts of England, two-field and three-field systems coexisted. The reason for the adoption of a particular system was the condition of an area's soil; where soils needed to be rested every year, half of the arable was left fallow, as happened in the Cotswolds; where the soil could be cropped for two successive years, a three-sector system, which takes more out of the soil, was possible.[2] In view of the absence of anything but negative evidence to the contrary, it seems not unreasonable to suggest that the same was true of the English area of Ireland. Moreover, there appears to have been a two-course system in 1408 on many tenant holdings of Llanthony Prima's manor of Colp in County Meath; of some holdings listed to show the value of their tithes, about half, or just over half, of the arable acreage is said to be sown in any year.[3] Similarly, at Gormanston, County Meath, of the two carucates of land (240 acres) that Christopher Preston had in demesne, 126 acres (63 of wheat, 63 of oats) were sown in 1408, 69 acres (6 of wheat, 63 of oats) in 1409, and in 1410 again as in 1408, so that presumably almost half was left fallow each year; and several other tenants of the priory in that area appear to have followed the same practice.[4] Unfortunately, the extents are not detailed and are principally concerned with the payment of tithes, so it may be that they mention only that part of a tenant's arable which he cultivated himself and take no notice of what he may have let to his tenants; but it is at least possible that there is here a picture of the two systems of rotation coexisting in close proximity. However, even for a two-course system, some holdings are under-cultivated, perhaps because of the probable fall in population, and it may be that, as the number of acres cultivated declined, some farmers found it convenient to revert to a two-course rotation.

The crops grown on Irish manors were very much the same as those found on their English counterparts. Wheat and oats were the largest crops, with barley, rye, beans, peas, and leeks occupying much less of the arable. The recorded acreages under wheat and oats, most of them belonging to demesnes, were, allowing for annual variations, roughly equal; but some accounts of cereal quantities suggest that oats may have been the bigger crop, as is indicated in the earlier years of the lordship by the issues of the royal granges of Meath in 1211–12; and this preponderance may be attributed to their cultivation on the more readily available rougher land, mountain, and even marsh.[5] On the earl of Norfolk's demesnes, the wheat and oats acreages were more or

[1] P.R.O., C. 133/130 (74); Otway-Ruthven, 'Anglo-Irish agriculture', p. 9.
[2] Hilton, *Med. society*, p. 113; Titow, *Eng. rural society*, p. 39.
[3] *Ir. cartul. Llanthony*, pp 180–81.
[4] Ibid., pp 188–91.
[5] *Pipe roll Ire., 1211–12*, pp 32–3; Hore, *Wexford town*, i, 26, 28; Gearóid Mac Niocaill (ed.), 'Documents relating to the suppression of the Templars in Ireland' in *Anal. Hib.*, no. 24 (1967), p. 204. Measurements varied in quantity according to the cereal; above, p. 458, n. 2.

less equal with perhaps a slightly greater area devoted to oats, particularly at
Forth, and with very little land given over to barley; but according to their 1326
extents, the opposite was true of the archbishop of Dublin's manors, where the
recorded wheat acreage was more than twice that of oats, barley, beans, and
peas combined.[1] In the surviving accounts of Irish manors, wheat is virtually
the only winter corn and very little rye appears to have been grown, at least on
demesne land, probably because it was not suited to Ireland's high rainfall. It is
to be found in County Wexford at Old Ross in 1283–4, where it shared only
twenty-eight and a half acres and a piece of marsh with mixed corn, and in 1308
at Kilcolgan, a Templar manor where six acres were sown with it, but it does
not appear on the demesnes of the earl of Norfolk in Carlow or Kildare in the
1280s, of the archbishop of Dublin in 1326, or of Christ Church in 1344–5; however, if a petition of the commons of Ireland in 1471 is to be taken literally, its
cultivation persisted.[2] The principal leguminous crops were beans and peas, of
which small areas are normally found alongside the greater cereal crops in the
demesne arable. Leeks too were sometimes cultivated in the fields; for
example, at Kilsaran, the Templars' manor in County Louth, where in 1308
there were found to be seven and a half selions (ridges) of them; but it appears
to have been more usual to grow them in the walled or fenced gardens which
were a feature of many manors.[3]

Yields were low, by modern standards very low, even on the arable land of
well-run demesnes, but they were comparable with English ones. At Cloncurry, according to the 1304 extent, wheat yielded $2\frac{1}{2}$ crannocks an acre and oats
2 crannocks from seed sown at the rate of 5 bushels of wheat and 12 bushels of
oats to the acre.[4] In 1297, land near Duleek was said to have produced 2 crannocks of wheat to the acre and the same yield of oats.[5] It was usual on the earl of
Norfolk's demesnes to sow about half a crannock of seed to the acre, a little
more at Cloncurry and sometimes less at Colp in 1408, where 3 bushels were
considered adequate for wheat.[6] With this rate of sowing, yields were fourfold
for wheat in both the cases cited and two and two-third times for oats at Cloncurry. These figures are confirmed by the estimates of yields of the earl of
Norfolk's demesnes in the 1280s, which average about fourfold of wheat and
threefold of oats before deductions for the following year's seed, but with tithes
probably subtracted. Low quality of seed, shallow ploughing, bad drainage,
insufficient control of weeds, and inadequate manuring all contributed to low
yields; and in the case of the peasants' land, on which yields were probably

[1] Bigod ministers' accounts, *passim*; *Alen's reg.*, pp 170, 173, 175, 180–81, 185–6.

[2] Hore, *Wexford town*, i, 28, 30; Mac Niocaill, 'Suppression of the Templars', p. 201; *Anc. rec. Dublin*, i, 172.

[3] Mac Niocaill, 'Suppression of the Templars', p. 196.

[4] *Red Bk Ormond*, pp 28–9. The acre was possibly more than double the statute acre. See above, p. 460, n. 2.

[5] *Cal. justic. rolls, Ire., 1295–1303*, pp 106–7.

[6] *Ir. cartul. Llanthony*, p. 180.

lower than these demesne estimates, it is necessary to add that generally the villagers had less livestock to provide manure for what was often the inferior arable of the manor, and that they lacked capital to compensate with other forms of manure.[1]

In spite of poor yields, large surpluses of cereals were available for sale on the home and export markets. In John's reign, after royal needs, mostly military, had been met, the surplus of wheat and oats was sold; and late in the same century most of the earl of Norfolk's crops, except what was required for animal fodder, were produced for the market.[2] At the same time, it is evident from the accounts of the purveyors gathering provisions in Ireland for the Scottish and Welsh wars of Edward I and Edward II that up to about 1324 large surpluses were being produced by some lords and their free tenants even after the catastrophic Bruce invasion.[3] Purveyance, indeed, provided a ready market for surplus grain and possibly stimulated Irish agricultural production for some time, so that it could perhaps have led to an agricultural boom, but over-exploitation ensured decline. Frequency of purveyance, uneconomic prices or lack of payment, due to the inability of the Irish exchequer to find adequate cash for its needs in the face of Gaelic Irish attacks and Anglo-Irish rebellion, brought about resistance and the collapse of the system.[4]

Unfortunately there are no figures to form even an impression of whether yields declined naturally in Ireland as in England in the thirteenth and early fourteenth centuries, but it is clear that, as the country became increasingly disordered in the fourteenth century, agriculture suffered and in many areas warfare, rather than deteriorating arable land, was a more potent reason for declining cereal production. It is clear from the port books of Bristol and other towns of the west of England that the export of grain had ceased almost completely by the late fifteenth century, when the trade in cereals appears to have been in the opposite direction; Irish boats took aboard cargoes of beans, barley, malt, and even occasionally oats, possibly for export to Ireland.[5] This decline in production is suggested by the 1471 commons' allegation, not borne out by the port books, that exports of grain were causing great dearth and famine; and it seems that in the later middle ages, in many parts of what had been the lordship, there was a reversion to pastoral husbandry, which is reflected in the large cargoes of sheepskins and hides recorded on ships from Ireland entering English ports.[6] In many parts, however, and especially in the late medieval

---

[1] Postan, *Med. econ.*, p. 62.

[2] *Pipe roll Ire., 1211–12*, pp 31–5.

[3] Purveyors' accounts, P.R.O., E. 101/16/7, 8, 20, 21.

[4] A full account of purveyance is given in J. F. Lydon, 'Ireland's participation in the military activities of English kings in the thirteenth and early fourteenth century' (Ph.D. thesis, London, 1955), summarised in Lydon, *Lordship*, pp 89–90, 127–36.

[5] P.R.O., E. 122/199/1 (Bristol); E. 122/115/7, 11, 12 (Plymouth, Fowey, and other west country ports). E. M. Carus Wilson (ed.), *The overseas trade of Bristol in the later middle ages* (Bristol, 1937), pp 268–9, 286 (P.R.O., E. 122/19/14).

[6] *Anc. rec. Dublin*, i, 172; Bristol port book, 19–20 Henry VII, P.R.O., E. 122/199/1.

Pale, the Anglo-Norman pattern of agriculture survived, but Ireland never again became the important source of grain that it had been in the thirteenth and early fourteenth centuries.[1]

Attempts were made to obtain better yields or at least to keep up their level. On the Bigod demesnes it was usual to procure a certain amount of seed-corn for sowing each year either by purchase or from the issues of another of the earl's manors, perhaps in the belief that seed grown on other land was more efficacious than that raised in a manor's own fields, though it was never a very large proportion of the seed sown in any year. The principal effort to raise yields, however, lay in manuring. Three means of improving the fertility of the soil occur in the ministers' accounts of the Irish estates of the earl of Norfolk: spreading and digging in animal dung; sanding; and burning the land. The use of animal dung, the only effective manure known to the medieval farmer, was undoubtedly the most widespread method, particularly in the inland parts of the lordship, and because it was readily available, it was the cheapest method. The accounts seem to make a distinction between merely spreading the dung, at between $1\frac{1}{2}d.$ to $2d.$ an acre, and the more expensive business of digging it in, which cost $4d.$ to $12d.$ This manure was probably the mixture of straw and animal droppings collected in the farmyards; it would never have been very large in quantity because during much of the year it was lost while the beasts fed in the open, and it was, therefore, adequate for manuring only a few acres each year. This was in addition to the normal practice of folding sheep on the stubble after harvest so that they would tread in their dung; and not only the lords' flocks were used for this, but by the *jus faldae* tenants too were expected to fold their sheep on the demesne arable rather than on their own land, which accordingly suffered by its loss. The second method, sanding, was used at Fennagh, Forth, and Old Ross. Scattering sand cost $2d.$ an acre, but the total cost per acre at Fennagh and Forth is given as $2s.$ and probably included the cost of its purchase, transport, and digging in. The accounts of Old Ross in 1283–4 show that the total expense could be as much as $8s.$ an acre, but this was probably because the sand had to be transported up river by boat from the tidal estuary of the Barrow.[2] Whether or not the sand for Fennagh and Forth was brought from so far afield, it is impossible to say, but there may have been a local source like the sand-pit that in 1312 was put at the disposal of the Hospital of St John Baptist without the New Gate, Dublin, to sand its land at Fingal in north County Dublin.[3] A somewhat desperate attempt to improve land by burning the turf at $16d.$ an acre and spreading the ashes, at $3d.$ or $4d.$ an acre, was used at Old Ross.[4] This method, which is said to be *more patrie* and was

[1] *Ir. cartul. Llanthony*, pp 180–92, 290–311; *Red Bk Kildare*, p. 170; *Extents Ir. mon. possessions*, *passim*.

[2] Hore, *Wexford town*, i, 27, and Bigod ministers' accounts, *passim*.

[3] *Reg. St John, Dublin*, p. 144.

[4] Hore, *Wexford town*, i, 27, 38.

therefore perhaps in use before the conquest and inherited by the Anglo-Normans from the native population, seems to have been used also as a means of conditioning the rougher type of meadow and pasture. It adds to the potash in the soil and for a time gives increased yields, but ultimately it is ruinous because it destroys the humus and impoverishes the soil. The use of meadow for this purpose meant a further loss of valuable grazing, a consequent reduction in the number of livestock, and a proportional loss of natural manure for the arable. The fairly frequent references to the absence of beasts in connection with land that was poor and worn out tends to confirm this.[1] Using all of these methods or any combination of them, only a fairly small proportion of the Bigod demesne arable was manured in any year, and the amount of manure available for tenant holdings must have been even less.

The agricultural methods followed in the lordship of Ireland were similar to those currently in use in England. The earliest, albeit somewhat limited, evidence of the pipe roll of 14 John about agricultural techniques indicates that on demesnes in Ireland the principal plough-animal was the ox; against a total of 906 plough-oxen on various manors, there were only twenty-three horses, five of them cart-horses and eighteen draught-horses (*affri*, there called *aures*).[2] On the earl of Norfolk's manors oxen outnumbered horses (*affri*), at Forth and Old Ross by a fairly large number; but it is clear that horses were employed in ploughing, probably to supplement the teams, and on at least one occasion in 1284–5 they had to be used when the Ballysax oxen were distrained at Dublin for the earl's debt.[3] In no recorded case on Bigod demesnes, however, were horses the majority, and generally they were many fewer than the oxen; for example, at Old Ross in 1283–4 there were 36 oxen to 4 horses, and about the same time there were rough averages of 13 to 7 at Ballysax, 14 to 10 at Fennagh and 20 to 6 at Forth. Similarly, in 1308 the Templars' manors are recorded as having a large preponderance of oxen over horses, usually six to two.[4] On manors of the earl of Kildare around 1330 and of Christ Church in the following two decades both animals were used for the plough, but the relative proportions varied from manor to manor.[5] During the remainder of the middle ages in the area of English influence, according to the admittedly scanty evidence, it appears that both oxen and horses were kept for ploughing; in 1402 there is a mention of the plough-oxen and *affri* which the prior of the *Domus Dei* of Mullingar had in County Meath, and in 1470 among the goods of Ardee priory were eleven oxen and thirteen horses for the plough.[6] The size of the team varied a little from place to place, but eight, the figure given in the pipe roll of

[1] *Alen's reg.*, p. 186, for example.
[2] *Pipe roll Ire., 1211–12*, pp 38–41; *aures* should perhaps be *avres*, presumably a form of *avra*, an alternative of *averus* or *affrus*.
[3] P.R.O., S.C. 6/1237/1–6, 32–9, 40, 42–4, 47, 49, 51, 53, 55; Hore, *Wexford town*, i, 29.
[4] MacNiocaill, 'Suppression of the Templars', pp 188–91.
[5] *Red Bk Kildare*, pp 102–3, 105. *Account roll of Holy Trinity, Dublin*, pp 22–3, 28, 35–6, 62.
[6] *Ir. cartul. Llanthony*, p. 136; Reg. Octavian (Armagh Public Library), f. 74ᵛ.

14 John, seems to have been the normal figure for oxen, a figure repeated by the 1304 extent of Cloncurry; on the Templars' manors in Louth, Waterford, and Wexford in 1308, however, teams were mostly of six oxen and two horses.[1] The ratio of plough-horses to oxen in the small number of heriot payments recorded in the Bigod ministers' accounts suggests that among the peasantry horses were more numerous than oxen, and the lists of animals acquired by the earl from tenants in others ways (for example, goods of felons and suicides and various perquisites) give roughly equal numbers. The earl of Norfolk's minis-ters' accounts underline the advantages that the English medieval agricultural writers say that oxen had over horses: horses were more expensive to keep because they ate more oats; indeed on the Bigod demesnes the *affri* usually consumed oats during the winter at the rate of half a bushel a night, more than twice the amount allowed for an often greater number of oxen, which in many accounts appear to have made no demands on the stock of oats. Moreover, oxen, which did not need to be shod and for which harnesses were cheaper, were stronger and invaluable for reclamation work on heavy ground, which may account for the notable preponderance of them at Forth.[2] Horses, which are quicker than oxen, possibly came into their own more in Ireland where a wet and uncertain climate meant that work had often to be done with speed to avoid agricultural disaster.

The agricultural year began with ploughing for the winter corn. At Clon-curry, according to the 1304 extent, it was necessary to plough three times for wheat, but only once for oats, no doubt because the wheat was to be sown on land that had just been fallowed and which accordingly needed regular plough-ing to keep down weeds; the extent adds that a plough with eight oxen, driven well, could plough there each year 25 acres in any season, the equivalent of the half-acre a day that a demesne plough was supposed to cover on some Kil-kenny manors at about the same time, a smaller area than many English assessments, but perhaps a reflection of a larger Irish acre.[3] The heavy plough (*carruca*), with an iron share and coulter, iron-bound wheels and mould-board, was employed; the iron used for the cutting parts, however, was very brittle and a large number of new ploughs was necessary after a hot, dry summer.[4] Harrows were normally drawn by horses, at the rate of an acre a day at Bally-dowel and Jerpoint but only half an acre at Cloncurry; oxen, however, were used to harrow newly assarted land at Fennagh.[5] After the winter sowing, the sector for spring corn was ploughed during the winter to be ready for sowing in Lent, but at that time of year bad weather could delay progress seriously, as the Annals of Inisfallen record under 1282, when frost and snow prevented all ploughing or harrowing between Christmas and the beginning of February.[6]

[1] *Red Bk Ormond*, p. 28.   [2] P.R.O., S.C. 6/1237/32.
[3] *Red Bk Ormond*, p. 28; P.R.O., S.C. 11/791, extent of (?) Ballydowel; S.C. 11/794, Jerpoint.
[4] MacNiocaill, 'Suppression of the Templars', p. 218; P.R.O., S.C. 6/1237/6, 35–8.
[5] P.R.O., S.C. 11/791, 794; *Red Bk Ormond*, p. 28; S.C. 6/1237/32, 37.
[6] *Ann. Inisf.*, p. 381.

Once the Lent sowing was over, weeding and hoeing had to be carried on continuously; then there was the hay harvest, and finally, at the height of summer, the corn harvest, which, in 1344 at Clonkeen, a Christ Church demesne, lasted for a month, from 5 August until 4 September.[1]

Arable land in medieval conditions was inadequate without pasture for the livestock which was used in its cultivation and manuring, and meadowland to provide hay for its winter fodder. Meadow (grassland that was good enough for regular mowing for hay and which was usually low-lying and damp, often adjacent to rivers and streams) was normally a small proportion of the total pasture, most of which was made up of the wastes, sections of the open fields unsuitable for the plough, woodland, mountain, and moor. The amount of meadow and its proportion to the acreage of demesne arable appears to have varied considerably from manor to manor, but at a rough estimate in the most favourable circumstances meadow seems to have stood at about one-tenth of the arable, the approximate figure for several Ormond manors in the early fourteenth century in various counties.[2] The amount of meadow revealed by inquisitions *post mortem* in the first half of the fourteenth century is very low, and in many places it may have been unwisely reduced to increase the arable acreage during the period of highly profitable cereal cultivation. This shortage is reflected by the relatively high value of meadow, usually the same value per acre as the best demesne arable; other pasture was much cheaper and a great deal more plentiful. The movement of land was not, however, always in the direction described, and sometimes arable was intentionally turned over to meadow or pasture; for example, around 1200 Hugh Tyrel gave to St John's Hospital, Dublin, some of his demesne arable at Castleknock to remain forever uncultivated for the common pasture of the hospital's livestock.[3] Meadow was, however, lost in other ways than by conversion to arable; burning it to provide fertiliser must have been as destructive as digging sods, perhaps for the same purpose, which was responsible for the ruin of much of the archbishop of Dublin's meadow.[4] Using meadow to provide manure in this way must have had in the long run an adverse effect on the arable because the loss of grazing inevitably meant a reduction in livestock with a proportional loss of natural manure, the medieval farmer's only real fertiliser.

However scarce meadow was on the demesnes, even less was available for tenants. Villagers who held land in the common fields had a small share of meadow proportionate to their arable holdings, pasturing rights over the commons and over the meadows when they became commonable after the hay harvest. Although there may have been a general shortage of good meadow, there cannot have been in Ireland by the early fourteenth century the shortage

---

[1] *Account roll of Holy Trinity, Dublin*, pp 64–7.
[2] *Red Bk Ormond*, pp 24, 26, 28–9, 34.
[3] *Reg. St John, Dublin*, pp 200–01.
[4] *Alen's reg.*, pp 170, 184, 186, 189.

of pasture found in England at the same time. As has been shown above, large areas of many manors, demesne and tenant land alike, were uncultivated and fallow for lack of population, or waste as a result of warfare. No doubt the meadows suffered as much as the arable, and pasture, which was often in out-lying parts of manors, was particularly vulnerable to the attacks of the nearby Gaelic Irish. Proximity to the Gaelic Irish is frequently given as the reason for the inability to let pasture on some manors, and this is sometimes related to the lack of livestock. The overall trend, however, from the early fourteenth century onwards was towards a considerable increase in the total amount of pasture, and this may at least partly explain the shift to animal husbandry in the later middle ages.

Not all the agricultural land in the lordship was divided between open fields, meadow, and pasture; some came to be separated into smaller enclosed sec-tions.[1] These enclosures had their beginnings as early as the thirteenth century when small arable holdings, held in separate closes and crofts, were created outside the common fields by clearance, and at the same time strips of arable land were being consolidated into fairly large unified holdings, often bounded by ditches, like William le Bret's twenty-six acres of his demesne at Kilcooly, County Tipperary, enclosed on all sides with ditches, which he gave to St John's Hospital, Dublin, around 1200. Ditches, sometimes banked, which were the normal form of division between the larger holdings, rather than walls, fences, or hedges, appear to have been the usual means of effecting these early enclosures as well as being used at the edges of open fields.[2] Reference to enclosed land become more frequent in the fourteenth century: at Youghal in 1321, of two carucates of land in demesne containing 240 acres of arable, eighteen acres lay *in parco*, a normal expression in medieval Ireland for enclosed land and not to be confused with those large tracts of land kept by lords as game preserves, like the earl of Ulster's park containing seven caru-cates at his manor of Loughrea.[3] Similarly at Callan by 1350 and Duleek by 1381 several enclosures had been made, but the greatest number of references occur during, and particularly towards the end of, the fifteenth century; it is unlikely, however, that, even in the first two or three decades of the sixteenth century, they occupied a large part of the Irish landscape.[4]

In addition to the horses and oxen, which have been discussed above, most manors had much other livestock which made important contributions to the

[1] A. J. Otway-Ruthven, 'Enclosures in the medieval period' in *Ir. Geography*, v, no. 2 (1965), pp 35–6.

[2] *Reg. St John, Dublin*, p. 332. See also p. 260, where mention is made of *fossatum de le hegge* as a boundary.

[3] P.R.O., C. 134/67 (2), m. 15, inquisition *post mortem* of Thomas, son of Richard de Clare; C. 135/36, m. 21, inquisition *post mortem* of William de Burgh, earl of Ulster, 1333.

[4] P.R.O., S.C. 6/1237/8, receiver's account; *Ir. cartul. Llanthony*, pp 291–2, 299; *Extents Ir. mon. possessions, passim*.

manorial economy with its meat, milk, skins, or all-important dung. The pipe roll of 14 John shows that by 1211/12 many manors in northern Leinster had built up large herds of cows and pigs and flocks of sheep; one lord alone, Richard de Tuit, had on his manors at the time of his death 96 oxen, 96 cows, 750 sheep, and 199 pigs.[1] During the 1280s the earl of Norfolk's manors in southern Leinster were equally well-stocked. The proportions of the various types of animal differed from manor to manor, and manors appear to have specialised to a certain extent in raising particular livestock, which they frequently supplied to the earl's other manors. Ballysax, which specialised in sheep, had very few pigs and no cows, not even breeding stock.[2] Fennagh, on the other hand, had no sheep and during the first half of the 1280s concentrated on breeding pigs, of which there were 31 in 1280/81; in 1285/6 all the pigs were sold and thereafter the herd of cows and calves was steadily built up. At Forth in 1279/80 pigs were the principal livestock, but in 1281/2 twenty-eight pigs were transferred to Ballysax, perhaps the ones which the reeve there supplied with other livestock and provisions for the earl marshal in Wales, and from 1282/3 no more pigs were kept.[3] Thereafter it seems to have been the policy to build up the number of cattle, so that by the last account available (that for 1287/8) there was a good number of cows, steers, yearlings, and calves, probably kept as breeding stock to ensure the supply of oxen. Bulls were kept only intermittently and not on all cattle-rearing manors, and it is likely that, whenever necessary, a tenant's beast was used for breeding. The most richly stocked of the earl's manors was Old Ross, which had in 1289, according to its stock account, in addition to 13 horses and 56 oxen, one bull, 38 cows, 4 steers, 11 yearlings, 33 calves, and many sheep.[4] Many of the horses appear to have been bred from the manor's own stock, but some lords had large separate studs, like the earl of Kildare's three at Kildare, all with Irish stud-keepers, which had, probably in 1328, 9 stallions, 184 mares, and 64 foals.[5] Poultry and other fowl, including ducks, geese, swans, and peacocks, were found on most demesnes, and pigeons and rabbits were often kept for their meat.

On those manors for which lists of stock have survived the largest single category of livestock was sheep. Most of the Bigod manors had flocks of sheep of varying sizes; the figures given of those remaining at the end of accounts of some manors are as follows.

	1280/81	1282/3	1283/4	1284/5	1285/6	1286/7	1287/8
Ballysax	365						333
Forth		287	388	352	129	280	475

[1] *Pipe roll Ire., 1211–12*, pp 36–42.
[2] P.R.O., S.C. 6/1237/1–6, Ballysax; S.C. 6/1237/32–9, Fennagh; S.C. 6/1237/40, 42–4, 47, 49, 51, 53, 55, Forth.
[3] *Cal. doc. Ire., 1252–84*, no. 2009.
[4] P.R.O., S.C. 6/1238/55.
[5] *Red Bk Kildare*, p. 104.

The largest flocks, according to the figures for those remaining, were at Old Ross, which had 821 sheep in 1280/81, and 1,894 in 1289.[1]

These figures, which vary considerably from place to place as flocks or large sections of them were moved from manor to manor, remain fairly static during the 1280s and, although there are great fluctuations in the numbers during the decade, there are no indications that these figures were abnormal or recently built up; indeed, the large Cistercian flocks in the early days of the colony and the evidence of the pipe roll of 14 John suggest that they were not. There appears to be no support in the Bigod accounts for the view that the number of sheep in Ireland increased greatly between 1280 and 1290 to meet a growing demand resulting from an outbreak of sheep-scab in England,[2] and there are signs that Ireland was similarly afflicted. At both Ballysax and Old Ross in 1280/81 there were heavy losses of sheep, perhaps part of the great losses of livestock that the Annals of Inisfallen say occurred in 1280 as a result of severe weather and which increased the normally high mortality among sheep.[3] Another opinion which the Bigod accounts make it necessary to qualify is that the economy of the manor was more dependent on sheep than on anything else.[4] No doubt this is true of manors, for example Old Ross, that specialised in sheep; and in that they were providers of manure, it is true of other manors, but from the point of view of production as a cash crop, in the second half of the thirteenth century, they were by no means as important as cereal crops on 'typical' arable manors. On the earl of Norfolk's manors, the proceeds from sale of corn were invariably much greater than all the other issues of the manor combined, including sale of livestock, sheepskins, and wool; for example, at Forth and Old Ross the figures are as follows.[5]

		issues of the manor			sale of corn		
		£	s.	d.	£	s.	d.
Forth	1285/6	10	5	8¾	52	15	0¾
	1286/7	8	5	1¼	30	4	11
	1287/8	11	18	5	19	9	10¼
Old Ross	1283/4	28	0	5	35	13	8

At Fennagh and Ballysax, too, cereals make up a much greater proportion of income than all other produce. This may not be true for other estates; the reason for it on the Bigod ones is that, because the earl was virtually an absentee, very little of the produce of the manors was required for direct consumption by his household; the greater need was for cash. The accounts of estates which, like those of Christ Church, were producing for the table tell a different story.[6] The number of sheep on the Bigod manors is by no means

[1] P.R.O., S.C. 6/1238/42 & 55.   [2] Lydon, Lordship, p. 90.
[3] Ann. Inisf., p. 375.
[4] Lydon, Ire. in later middle ages, p. 11.
[5] P.R.O., S.C. 6/1237/51, 53, 55; Hore, Wexford town, i, 30.
[6] Account roll of Holy Trinity, Dublin, p. 56.

abnormal, and other instances can be cited of large flocks: at Dunfort in the early fourteenth century the earl of Gloucester had 500 sheep and in 1331 there were 440 belonging to the earl of Kildare at Kilcork.[1] There is little evidence about the livestock of the peasants, but some indication is given by the peasants' goods confiscated by the earl of Norfolk: a felon in Offelin had 5 *affri*, 2 cows, and 13 ewes, and one William de Brone, who drowned himself, had at least 4 *affri*, 13 ewes, 14 lambs, and 16 pigs, while a king's betagh, Clement Ocathyll, is recorded in the Irish memoranda roll for Michaelmas 1303 as having 4 cows with calves, an ox, 3 draught horses, 30 sheep, and a piglet.[2]

The disturbances that severely devastated arable cultivation also affected animal husbandry. References are common to land being impossible to let because of the lack of animals, and on the Dublin manors of the archbishop the absence of beasts from the pasture may be explained by the nearness of the Gaelic Irish.[3] Serious livestock mortality, at least partly confirmed by ministers' accounts, is recorded by the Annals of Inisfallen in 1280, in 1297, and in 1321, when the 'murrain' mentioned was probably the *Máel Domnaig* which was prevalent about 1323–5.[4] In the later middle ages there was probably an increase in pastoral husbandry, the continuation of the trend detected by Professor Lydon in figures of the customs levied on wool, woolfells, and hides exported from Ireland from 1275 onwards and underlined by the ending of the export trade in cereals and the subsequent predominance of hides and woolfells in the trade between Ireland and the ports of western England and Europe.[5]

It remains to ask whether the situation described above really justifies calling it, in the words of Professor Lydon, 'an agricultural revolution'.[6] There can be no doubt that the Anglo-Normans' settlement of most of Ireland brought with it considerable changes in the agrarian economy, but it is important not to underestimate the development of the country before their arrival. As has been seen above, modern research suggests that there had been extensive arable farming; that the expansion of monasticism had brought a growth in agriculture and the introduction of more sophisticated techniques; and that there was widespread clearance of forest and wastes, helped no doubt by the heavy plough already in use, so that by the tenth century Ireland was a land of mixed farming where cereal growing was extensive and economically important. What the Anglo-Normans brought to Irish agriculture was not so much a revolution as the extension and development of the existing situation. In the course of the thirteenth century a great deal more land was cleared and brought under the plough, and large open fields replaced small enclosed ones of only one or

[1] P.R.O., C. 47/10/19 (13), m. 2; *Red Bk Kildare*, p. 105.
[2] P.R.O., S.C. 6/1237/32 & 42; Philomena Connolly, 'The Irish memoranda rolls: some unexplored aspects' in *Ir. Econ. & Soc. Hist.*, iii (1976), p. 73.
[3] *Alen's reg.*, pp 170, 175, 184, 186, 189, and 194.
[4] *Ann. Inisf.*, pp 375, 391, 435.
[5] Lydon, *Lordship*, pp 90–91.
[6] Ibid., p. 90.

two acres. The introduction of winter corn and triennial rotation made it possible in suitable conditions to obtain more and larger crops in a year, but did not of itself lead to revolutionary consequences; more important was the expansion of areas under tillage which, combined with the manorial system, intense direct cultivation of the demesne for cash crops, and the Anglo-Normans' high degree of knowledge of agricultural technique, made possible a quality and quantity of agriculture previously unknown in Ireland. The result of this was to be seen in increased production, cereal surpluses, and great quantities of wool for export, staples of the lordship's extensive foreign trade. Little of this would have been possible, however, without the influx of capital, at first Jewish but later mainly Italian, which followed the Anglo-Normans to Ireland. It is unlikely that this capital would have been attracted without the more secure communications and comparative peace that the central government was able to ensure in thirteenth-century Ireland, and which made investment reasonably safe. The availability of this capital was a considerable stimulus to production because it enabled landlords to borrow for agricultural improvements and to purchase equipment, stock, and more land. It was also invested in trade, which, by providing profitable outlets for agricultural surplus, encouraged production. All of this represents a great expansion of the Irish economy which may perhaps be called revolutionary, but it must not be understood as the sort of agricultural revolution envisaged by Lynn White, who has made claims for the revolutionary effects of a change to horse-ploughing, triennial rotation, and the cultivation of large crops of legumes.[1] The criticisms of these theories which have been made with respect to England apply equally to Ireland.[2] As has been seen, in Ireland as in England, at the height of the period of greatest cereal production the ox remained on demesnes the favoured plough-animal. Although there is very little sign of two-course rotation in Ireland, the small amount of evidence for the three-field system makes it not unreasonable to suggest that both systems are as likely to have existed side by side in Ireland as in England. Finally, on no Irish manor for which records have survived was the acreage under legumes of any size. Having said this, it is perhaps necessary to reiterate that agricultural growth in the lordship from the 'invasion' until the fourteenth century was spectacular; it was reflected by the success of Irish trade in the same period.

Already before the Anglo-Normans' arrival the characteristics of Irish trade for the remainder of the middle ages had been laid down by the Norse inhabitants of the coastal towns, Dublin, Wexford, Waterford, Cork, and Limerick, who were immersed in flourishing trade with England, and especially Bristol, with Normandy, southern France and Spain, northern Europe and the east.

---

[1] Lynn White, *Medieval technology and social change* (Oxford, 1962), ch. II, 'The agricultural revolution of the early middle ages', especially pp 57–76.

[2] Titow, *Eng. rural society*, pp 37–42; R. H. Hilton and P. H. Sawyer, 'Technical determinism: the stirrup and the plough' in *Past & Present*, no. 24 (Apr. 1963), pp 90–100.

With the exception of slaves, the commodities too remained the same: wine, hides, and textiles, traded for with the Gaelic Irish. After 1169 the Norse towns were granted royal charters, and by 1250 important new coastal towns had been added and given charters by the king or the greater magnates; those that were to become most prominent in external trade were Carrickfergus, Dundalk, Drogheda, New Ross, Youghal, and Galway. The relative economic importance of these towns by the last quarter of the century can be gauged from the amount collected from customs in each of them after Edward I had been granted the 'great custom' on wool, woolfells, and hides in 1275. Until the last years of Edward I, New Ross and Waterford each regularly produced twice as much as any other port; Cork and Drogheda came next, then Dublin; next was Youghal, which began well but declined somewhat towards 1300, and Galway, which did not have extensive trade until the next century; at the end of the list came Limerick and the Ulster and Kerry ports.[1] These towns were intended by their founders to be centres of trade in their lordships, outlets for the surpluses of the manors which they were then organising. William Marshal, who seems to have been interested in the advance of trade, made his principal contribution to the economic development of Leinster by establishing boroughs in his lordship; the preeminence in trade that New Ross enjoyed over its rivals was in large part due to the free passage past Waterford which he obtained for ships bound for his own port, and later, as *rector* of England, he continued to favour Leinster merchants.[2] Irish merchants also received royal encouragement: Henry II granted the burgesses of Dublin freedom from tolls throughout his empire; in 1204 John helped to establish fairs to attract foreign traders to Ireland; Henry III encouraged the trade between Dublin and La Rochelle; and government helped further by providing an adequate official coinage and by attempting to regulate the diversity of weights and measures.[3] As a result of these efforts the successful pre-conquest trade appears to have survived the invasion, or at least to have been resumed. Already in Richard I's reign there are records of customs collected in Ireland, and from the time of John onwards there is evidence of the export of cloaks and cloth to England and elsewhere; by 1275 Irish trade was clearly flourishing.[4]

Internal trade in the lordship was largely based on the many towns that developed around the castles of the new nobility; the ones that became commercially important were those that stood on navigable rivers or main roads and in easy communication with coastal trade. Rivers were widely used for transport, especially for heavy goods, and during the comparative peace of the thirteenth century the government tried to improve communications by clearing rivers and making new roads.[5] Most of the heavy carrying for the estates of

[1] Otway-Ruthven, *Med. Ire.*, p. 123; O'Sullivan, *Econ. hist. Cork city*, pp 29–31.
[2] Sidney Painter, *William Marshal* (Baltimore, 1933), p. 167.
[3] Lydon, *Lordship*, pp 96–8; see below, pp 818–20.
[4] Orpen, *Normans*, iv, 276.
[5] Lydon, *Lordship*, p. 96.

1. Cistercian abbey, Knockmoy, Co. Galway, from east

2. (*a*) Cistercian abbey, Jerpoint, Co. Kilkenny: nave

2. (c) (d) (e) Cistercian abbey, Jerpoint, Co. Kilkenny: capitals from eastern part of nave

2. (f) Cistercian abbey, Baltinglass, Co. Wicklow: capital from eastern part of nave

2. (b) Cistercian abbey, Boyle, Co. Roscommon: transept chapels

3. (b) Cistercian abbey, Mellifont, Co. Louth: detail of lavabo

3. (a) St Mary's cathedral, Limerick: nave

3. (d) St Flannan's cathedral, Killaloe, Co. Clare: chancel

3. (c) Christ Church cathedral, Dublin: arch in chancel

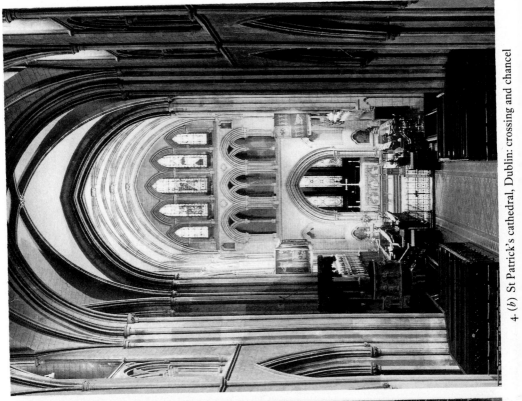

4. (a) Christ Church cathedral, Dublin: north wall of nave

4. (b) St Patrick's cathedral, Dublin: crossing and chancel

4. (d) St Canice's cathedral, Kilkenny: west doorway

4. (c) St Canice's cathedral, Kilkenny: interior

5. (*a*) St Canice's cathedral, Kilkenny, from south-west: engraving by Worthington G. Smith, 1872

5. (b) St Patrick's cathedral, Cashel, from north-east

6. (*a*) Church of Dominican friary, Athenry, Co. Galway, from north-east

6. (*b*) Dominican friary of Holy Trinity, Kilkenny, from south-east

7. (*a*) Carrickfergus castle, Co. Antrim

7. (*b*) Trim castle, Co. Meath

8. (*a*) Cathedral, Kilfenora, Co. Clare: figures from chancel windows

8. (*b*) Augustinian abbey, Ballintober, Co. Mayo: capitals in chancel

8. (c) Christ Church cathedral, Dublin: capitals in nave

8. (d) Franciscan friary, Kilkenny: figures beneath vault in tower

9. (*a*) Sepulchral slab associated with Domnall Mór Ua Briain, St Mary's cathedral, Limerick

9. (*b*) (*left*) Cross slab, St Nicholas's church, Galway; (*c*) (*right*) Sepulchral slabs, Old St Mary's churchyard, Kilkenny

10. (a) Effigy of bishop, St Aidan's cathedral, Ferns

10. (b) Effigy of Sir Thomas de Cantwell, Kilfane, Co. Kilkenny

10. (c) Effigy of lady of Hackett family, St John the Baptist's cathedral, Cashel

10. (d) Kilcorban Madonna, Loughrea, Co. Galway

11. (*a*) Cistercian abbey, Holycross, Co. Tipperary, from east (restored)

11. (*b*) Augustinian friary, Callan, Co. Kilkenny: sedilia and piscina

11. (c) Cistercian abbey, Holycross, Co. Tipperary: section of cloister arcade

11. (d) Cistercian abbey, Jerpoint, Co. Kilkenny: cloister arcade

SCALE OF FEET

SITE OF STORES.

CLOISTER GARTH.
50'0" x 45'6".

SITE OF
WEST ARCADE

CLOISTER WALK 6'6" WIDE.

UNDERCROFT OF REFECTORY.

PROBABLE SITE
OF DAY STAIRS.

CHAPTER ROOM.
26'3" x 15'0".

SACRISTY

CHOIR.
44'0" x 21'4".

MONUMENT.

TOWER.
14'5" x 21'4".

MONUMENT

ROOD SCREEN.

NAVE.
74'6" x 21'6".

TRANSEPT.
33'0" x 21'0".

AISLE.
50'0" x 15'0".

12. (b) Dominican friary, Sligo: plan (Office of Public Works)

12. (a) Cathedral, Clonmacnoise: Dean Odo's doorway

13. (*a*) A reconstruction of an Irish friary, late fifteenth century: drawing by George Foster

3. (*b*) Church of Franciscan friary, Quin, Co. Clare: west end

13. (*c*) Franciscan friary, Quin, Co. Clare: cloister walk

14. (*a*) Dominican friary, Sligo: nave

14. (*b*) Church of Franciscan friary of the third order, Rosserk, Co. Mayo: chapels in transept

14. (*c*) Dominican friary, Sligo: cloister garth

14. (*d*) Manor church, Killeen, Co. Meath: east window

15. (a) Cahir castle, Co. Tipperary

15. (c) Clara castle

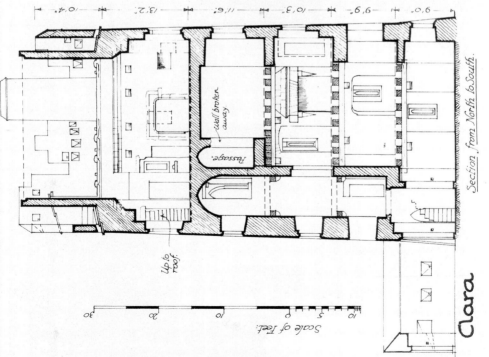

Clara

Section from North to South.

Up to roof.

Passage.

wall broken away.

Scale of Feet.

15. (b) Clara castle, Co. Kilkenny: section (Office of Public Works)

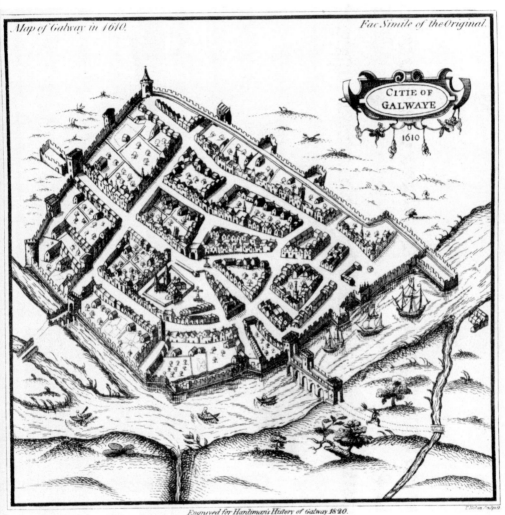

Map of Galway in 1610.   Fac Simile of the Original.

CITIE OF
GALWAYE

1610

Engraved for Hardiman's History of Galway 1820.

16. (c) Galway and its fortifications, 1610, from James Hardiman, *History of the town and county of the town of Galway* (Dublin, 1820)

17. (b) Rothe house, Kilkenny

17. (a) Lynch's castle, Galway, from Hardiman, *Galway*

17. (c) Ormond castle and mansion, Carrick-on-Suir, Co. Tipperary

18. (a) Cross slab of William Cantwell and Margaret Butler, c. 1528, Cistercian abbey, Kilcooly, Co. Tipperary

18. (b) Galway–Bultingfort tomb, St Mary's cathedral, Limerick

18. (d) Wall tomb, Franciscan friary, Adare, Co. Limerick

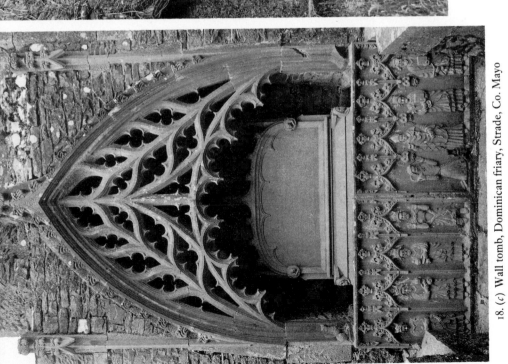

18. (c) Wall tomb, Dominican friary, Strade, Co. Mayo

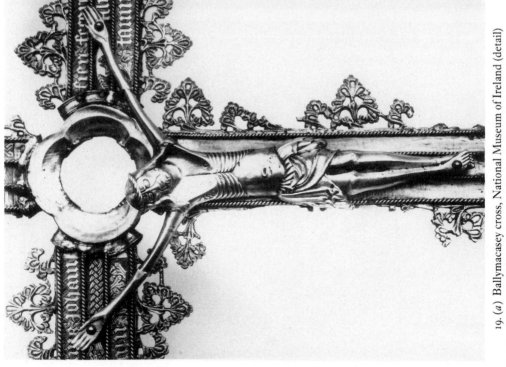

19. (a) Ballymacasey cross, National Museum of Ireland (detail)

19. (b) Crosier of Bishop Conchobhar Ó Deadhaidh, St John's cathedral, Limerick (detail)

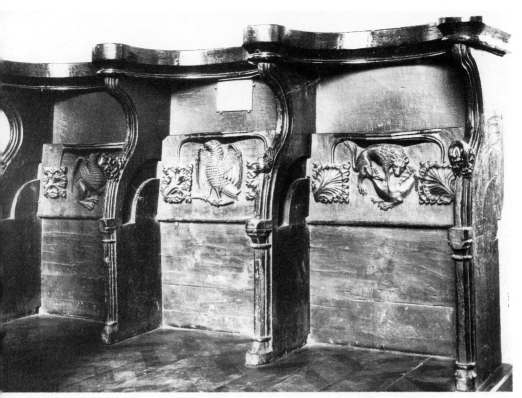

20. (*a*) Choir stalls, St Mary's cathedral, Limerick

20. (*b*) 'Resurrection', and figure of a donor(?), MacMahon tomb, Franciscan friary, Ennis, Co. Clare

20. (c) Mensa monument, manor church, Killeen, Co. Meath

20. (d) Mensa monument, manor church, Killeen, Co. Meath (detail)

21. (*a*) Tomb of James Rice and his wife Catherine Broun, Holy Trinity cathedral, Waterford

21. (*b*) Tomb of Piers Butler, eighth earl of Ormond, and his wife Margaret FitzGerald, St Canice's cathedral, Kilkenny

22. (a) Apostles, from tomb of James Shortall, St Canice's cathedral, Kilkenny (now detached)

22. (b) St John the Evangelist, from mensa tomb, St Canice's cathedral, Kilkenny

22. (*d*) Virgin Mary with Infant Jesus, probably from tomb, Piltown, Co. Kilkenny

22. (*c*) Virgin Mary with Infant Jesus, from west end of Rice tomb, Holy Trinity cathedral, Waterford

23. (a) Crucifixion, from tomb of James Shortall, St Canice's cathedral, Kilkenny; now part of a Butler monument

23. (b) 'Ecce homo', from tomb of Bishop Walter Wellesley, St Brigid's cathedral, Kildare

23. (c) Effigy of Bishop Walter Wellesley, St Brigid's cathedral, Kildare

23. (d) Abbot and lady, from cloister arcade, Cistercian abbey, Jerpoint, Co. Kilkenny

24. (b) Members of Plunket family, from cross in meadow, Killeen, Co. Meath

24. (a) Cistercian abbey, Jerpoint, Co. Kilkenny: details from cloisters

24. (d) Baptism of Christ, from baptismal font in St Peter's protestant church, Drogheda, Co. Louth

24. (c) Baptismal font, now in St Andrew's church, Curraha, Co. Meath

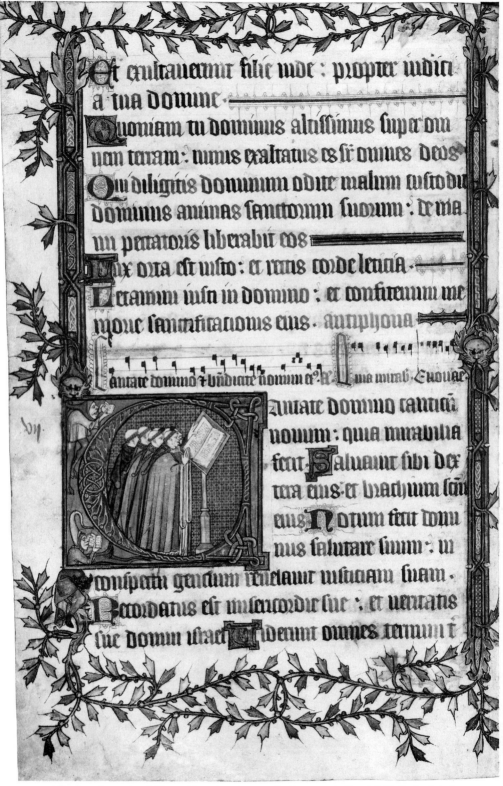

25. Psalter, formerly of Christ Church cathedral, Dublin (Bodl., Rawl. MS C 185, f. 81ᵛ)

26. (*a*) Charter roll of the city of Waterford: mayors of Waterford

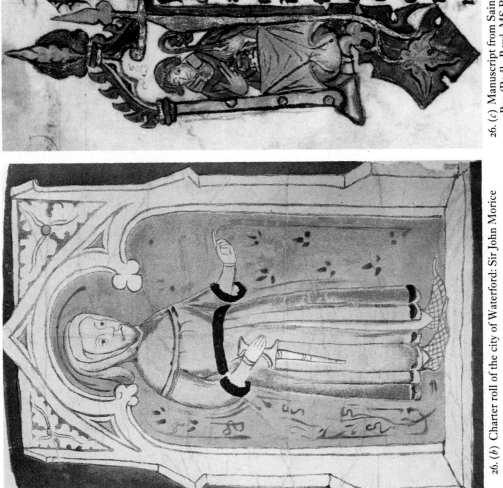

26. (c) Manuscript from Saints' Island, Lough Ree (Bodl., Rawl. MS B 505, f. 191ᵛ)

26. (b) Charter roll of the city of Waterford: Sir John Morice

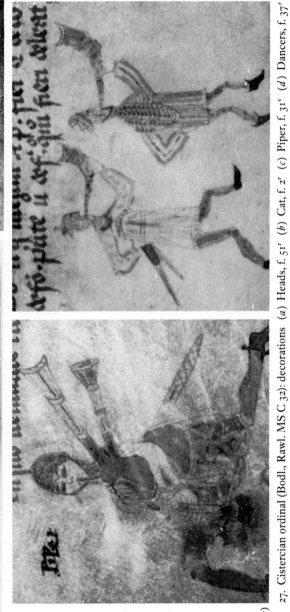

27. Cistercian ordinal (Bodl., Rawl. MS C 32): decorations (a) Heads, f. 51ʳ (b) Cat, f. 2ʳ (c) Piper, f. 31ᵛ (d) Dancers, f. 37ʳ

28. (b) Book of the White Earl (Bodl., Laud MS 610, f. 60ᵛ)

28. (a) Leabhar Breac (R.I.A., MS 23.P.16): crucifixion

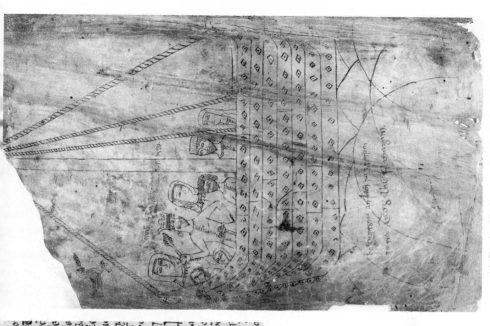

29. (c) Book of Ballymote (R.I.A., MS 23.P.12): p. 2

29. (b) Yellow Book of Lecan (Bodl., Rawl. MS B 488, f. 3ʳ)

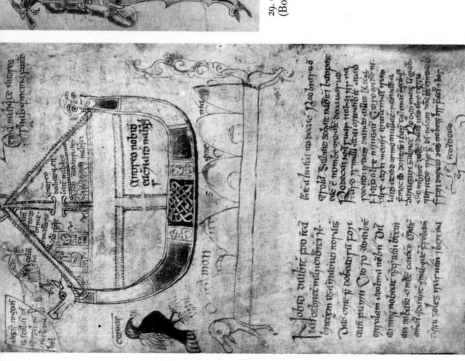

29. (a) Building of Noah's ark, by Ádhamh Ó Cianáin (N.L.I., MS G.3, f. 16ᵛ)

(a) Initial, p. 13

(b) Initial, p. 275

(c) Animal, p. 292

(d) Animal, p. 399

30. Book of Ballymote (R.I.A., MS 23.P.12): decorations

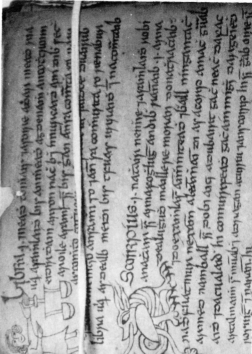

31. (b) King's Inns (Dublin) MS 17, f. 5ᵛ: spade and flail

31. (c) National Library of Scotland, Adv. MS 72.1.2, f. 3ᵛ: Libra and Scorpius

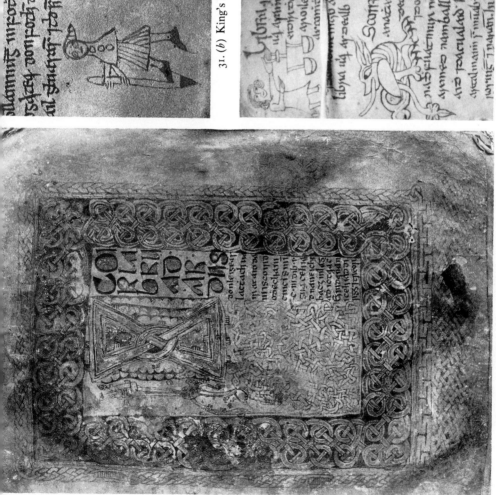

31. (a) King's Inns (Dublin) MS 17, f. 1

32. (b) Book of the Burkes (T.C.D., MS 1440 (F.4.13), f. 18ᵛ): carving of the cross

32. (a) St Columba (Bodl., Rawl. MS B 514, facing f. 1ʳ)

the earl of Norfolk was by riverboat; sand was transported from the coast up the Barrow to Old Ross for manure, wool from Ballysax was carried by boat to Ross, and millstones from the Island to Carlow.[1] During the thirteenth and fourteenth centuries many towns were given the right to hold fairs and markets, which were encouraged by their lords as valuable sources of revenue. In spite of this encouragement, in many cases they came to nothing; but the more successful ones, which became important centres for the sale of agricultural produce, attracted merchants and traders not only from Ireland, but also from Europe, and the ubiquitous Italians were to be found at all the important towns and at the great fairs. The commodities of internal trade can be gathered from murage grants allowed to various towns, and they can be divided roughly into the produce of the country and imported goods brought from the ports. Livestock, cereals and other foodstuffs, hides and skins, wool and woolfells, cloth, and timber were in the former group; in the latter were wine, salt, metals, fine cloths, dyes, spices, and a variety of luxury goods.[2] The disturbed state of the country in the fourteenth century made internal trade more difficult. In 1340 the justiciar complained that merchants dared not trade in Ossory and elsewhere for fear of being set on and robbed, and it was usually necessary to pay the Gaelic Irish for safe conduct from place to place.[3] This danger in the interior and the devastation of their hinterlands made it difficult for coastal towns loyal to the crown to obtain supplies; to solve this problem they were given permission in 1450 to import corn by sea from Dublin and Drogheda. The extensive export trade, however, of the coastal towns in the fifteenth and early sixteenth centuries in commodities that were obtained from the Gaelic Irish shows that, in spite of the troubled conditions, internal commercial activity continued to flourish, based, at least in part, on native requirements of imported goods.

If Irish trade was prospering in 1275, there can be no doubt that a great deal was owed to the stimulus provided by the arrival on the scene of Italian merchants and bankers. During the course of the thirteenth century they were closely involved in the collection of both papal and royal revenue, particularly the customs; they largely controlled the mint and supervised the various attempts at mining; they dominated trade and acted as purveyors for the royal campaigns in Scotland, Wales, and France; and, of the utmost importance to the economic development of the colony, they lent money to the crown, to lords ecclesiastical and lay, and to the townsmen.[4] Heavy debts to Italian bankers were incurred by the greatest lords, among them the earl of Norfolk, some of whose wool was handed over direct to the merchants Galardus Maubin and Gillot the merchant of Lucca, to repay his debts. The 1287 account of the debts

[1] P.R.O., S.C. 6/1237/6, 19.
[2] Otway-Ruthven, *Med. Ire.*, p. 124; O'Sullivan, *Old Galway*, p. 16; Lydon, *Lordship*, pp 97–8.
[3] *Liber primus Kilkenn.*, pp 11, 12; P.R.O., S.C. 6/1239/29, 31, 32.
[4] O'Sullivan, *Italian bankers*, p. 26.

owed to the Riccardi of Lucca by Joan, the widow of Sir Theobald Butler, shows that she had borrowed from them as much as £341 19s. 10d. for a variety of expenses which included her husband's funeral, her own transport, food and luxury goods, livestock, grain, and wages.[1] The Italians began to arrive in numbers during the reign of Henry III, and under Edward I they were given official positions in the administration of the lordship; early in the reign the greatest companies of Florence and Lucca, especially the Riccardi, had agents all over the colony, with the result that more capital was available and better markets were found for Irish produce.[2] In 1275 they were appointed collectors of the customs on wool, woolfells, and hides, with extensive powers through which they were able to control the wool trade. They had their collectors at the important ports and were able to appoint members of their own firms to the various customs posts. With a few intervals, and in spite of doubts about their honesty and physical attacks on their persons from time to time, the Italians, at first the Riccardi and later the Frescobaldi, kept the collection of the customs until the early fourteenth century when, as a result of the ordinances of 1311, it passed to natives. The increasingly turbulent condition of the colony after 1300 and the consequent economic decline made Ireland much less attractive to foreign bankers, and the activity of the Italians had almost entirely ceased there before many of them were ruined by their credit dealings with Edward III.[3] This did not mean the end of Italian trade in Ireland; Italian merchants, especially Genoese, were still making the journey in the fifteenth century, and one Ambrogio Lomellini is recorded at Nantes in the middle of the century with a boat laden with leather and cloth en route between Ireland and Lisbon.[4] Nor did merchants from Lucca entirely leave off commercial activity in Ireland; among the early chancery proceedings is a case in the 1490s about an obligation of two haberdashers of London made at Dublin to two such merchants, George Morevelle and Sebastian de Giglys, who was perhaps related to Silvestro Gigli, another Lucchese, absentee bishop of Worcester.[5] After 1311, however, there was never again the alien control of Irish commerce which had obtained under Edward I.

One of the main stimulants of agricultural growth in thirteenth-century Ireland was a ready outlet for its products in external trade with England and Europe. During the period when the direct cultivation of demesnes was at its height in the thirteenth and early fourteenth centuries, considerable surpluses of cereal crops were sold on the home and export markets. From early in Henry III's reign Ireland appears to have been supplying England's needs. In 1224–5 one thousand crannocks of wheat, bought in Ireland from William

---

[1] P.R.O., S.C. 6/1237/1, 4; *Ormond deeds, 1172–1350*, pp 111–12.

[2] O'Sullivan, *Italian bankers*, p. 63.

[3] Ibid., pp 136–7.

[4] Henri Touchard, *Le commerce maritime breton à la fin du moyen âge* (Paris, 1967), p. 222. See below, p. 494.

[5] Early chancery proceedings, P.R.O., C. 1/203/5–9.

Marshal, were imported into London by its mayor; throughout the century religious houses and individuals were given permission to export grain from Ireland for their own needs or for profit, not only to English ports, but also to Gascony, whence the boats could return with cargoes of wine.[1] The main centre of the trade in grain appears to have been Ross, which, situated on the Barrow and Nore, was a particularly well-placed outlet for the produce of the manors of the south-east, especially for those of the earls of Norfolk. Second only to Ross in the amount of corn shipped abroad was Waterford, at the mouths of the Barrow, the Nore, and the Suir. Another considerable market, although because of preemption and prisage not usually as profitable as the open market for the producers, was created between around 1240 and 1324 by purveyance for the royal armies, particularly those of Edward I. Extant accounts, which are not complete, show that in 1297 alone something well in excess of 11,600 quarters of wheat and 1,850 quarters of oats were shipped to the army in Gascony; and between 28 May and 7 November 1299, at a time when Ireland was the king's only source of supply, it sent to Carlisle 3,113 quarters of wheat, 6,964 quarters and $2\frac{1}{2}$ bushels of oats, 1408 quarters and $1\frac{1}{2}$ bushels of malt of oats, 708 *dolea* and 1 pipe of flour and meal, $176\frac{1}{2}$ carcases and 1 quarter of beef, 669 bacons, 24 *dolea* of dried fish, 1,136 dried fish and 351 tuns of wine.[2] Purveyance continued under Edward II, but supplies of this size could not be kept up, particularly when, early in the fourteenth century, agricultural production suffered severely because of the troubled state of the country. The abuses of the system, in which merchants often waited long for payment by the crown and purveyors did not always pay for the victuals, inevitably brought about resistance which, combined with the devastation of Irish agriculture, ended purveyance after 1324. Commerce possibly benefited from purveyance by the development of ports, shipping and trade links and by its creation of a ready market for agricultural surpluses; but in the long run, it appears to have hastened the decline of the corn trade by over-exploitation and artificial prices. Furthermore, Edward I's heavy demands on the Dublin exchequer reduced the resources required by the Irish government to preserve the peace and order essential for the booming agriculture that produced the surpluses. Thus, although the Irish export trade on the whole possibly benefited, the part that cereals played in it declined until by 1437 Bristol was shipping grain to Ireland. In 1471, because of the shortage of corn in Ireland, the Irish parliament petitioned for a ban on its export. This was granted in 1475, and during the last quarter of the century and early in the next there were regular shipments of corn and beans from Bristol and other west-country ports.[3]

[1] *Cal. doc. Ire.*, *1171–1251*, no. 1285; ibid., *1285–92*, no. 1069; ibid., *1252–84*, no. 2044; O'Sullivan, *Italian bankers*, pp 114–15.

[2] Lydon, *Lordship*, pp 89–90; Lydon, 'Ireland's participation', pp 194–5, 230. The *doleum* varied: a *doleum* of wine was equivalent to a tun, which generally was about 252 gallons (9.54 hl).

[3] E. M. Carus Wilson, 'The overseas trade of Bristol' in Eileen Power and M. M. Postan (ed.), *Studies in English trade in the fifteenth century* (London, 1933), p. 199; P.R.O., E. 122/199/1 (Bristol port book 1503–4), E. 122/115/11 and 12 (western ports, 1504 and 1507–8).

As the falling-away of the corn trade reflected the declining fortunes of Irish agriculture, so the movement towards pastoral husbandry appears to be mirrored in the growth of the export of hides and animal skins. The increase in the number of cattle meant that hides, which had been exported before the conquest and in great numbers from the early thirteenth century onwards, became a very prominent commodity of the Irish export trade and probably more important than wool or cloth. As well as hides, other skins and furs were exported, those of wild beasts, which are listed by the author of 'The libelle of Englyshe polycye' (*c.* 1436).

> And marterns gode bene in here marchaundye;
> Hertys hydes and other hydes of venerye,
> Skynnes of oter, squerel, and Irysh hare,
> Of shepe, lambe, and fox is here chaffare,
> Felles of kydde and conyes grete plente.[1]

The main market was Europe: regular shipments were sent to Flanders, Calais, Normandy, Brittany, Bordeaux, and Lisbon, and huge quantities went each year to Italy, where the leather industries of Pisa alone took 34,000 in one half-year (1466/7) and over 24,000 in another (1482/3).[2] With England too the trade was substantial, based mainly on Bristol, where almost every vessel coming in from the various ports of Ireland brought its quota of hides. From there shiploads passed in Bristol boats to the ports of southern England, France, and Flanders.[3] Southampton also was importing hides and cloth from Ireland around 1300, and in 1426 two Southampton men in partnership sent a ship loaded with salt and wine to Ireland to effect an exchange for fresh salmon and hides, one incident in a trade that continued throughout the fifteenth century.[4]

Wool and woolfells were another raw material which Ireland exported in large quantities throughout the middle ages to England, France, Flanders, and other parts of Europe. The trade was in existence in the early thirteenth century; in 1216 Henry of London, archbishop of Dublin, sold fifty-one sacks for export. Already the Italians were established in it and they virtually controlled it after 1275 while they were in charge of the customs on wool.[5] They secured their supplies by taking wool in repayment of debts, like those of the earl of Norfolk, and by a policy of forward buying from the Cistercians, whose flocks, even in the early years of the colony, were large. There seem to have been particularly close commercial relations with Bruges, whence Italian merchants shipped wool to feed the cloth industry of Italy, and a list of wool and other

---

[1] *The libelle of Englyshe polycye*, ed. George Warner (Oxford, 1926), p. 34, lines 660–64. Bristol port books, P.R.O., E. 122/199/1 (1503–4) & E. 122/21/7 (1533–4).

[2] O'Sullivan, *Econ. hist. Cork city*, pp 37, 52; O'Sullivan, *Old Galway*, p. 58; Lydon, *Ire. in later middle ages*, p. 13.

[3] Carus Wilson, 'Overseas trade of Bristol', p. 198.

[4] Colin Platt, *Medieval Southampton: the port and trading community, A.D. 1000–1600* (London, 1973), pp 82, 153, 157.

[5] O'Sullivan, *Italian bankers*, pp 102, 122.

goods arrested in Flanders some time after 4 June 1274 shows that substantial amounts of cloth and wool at Bruges were the property of Irish merchants.[1] The trade continued in the later middle ages, but it is perhaps not entirely without significance that 'The libelle of Englyshe polycye' does not include wool specifically among the products of Ireland, and on the evidence of the customs accounts of Bristol and nearby ports it appears that in the fifteenth century the trade with England went over almost entirely to woolfells rather than wool, though some was exported as flocks. It may be, however, that the decline in the export of raw wool was the result of the growth of the Irish cloth industry reflected in the buoyant export trade in cloth and mantles, especially with the west of England.

There was a cloth industry at various centres in Ireland in the thirteenth century, and cloth and cloaks were exported to England and elsewhere from the time of John onwards.[2] During the fourteenth century the Irish woollen industry appears to have made great steps, and, using the coarse Irish wool, produced cheap cloth which was exported in considerable quantities to England and Europe; finer cloths, however, had to be imported, principally from England, and became by 1400 Bristol's chief export to Ireland.[3] In addition to cloths, the industry produced heavy Irish mantles and whittles, or heavy blankets, which were brought to Bristol and the havens of the west country in very large numbers in both Irish and Bristol boats.[4] No less important a place in the Irish textile trade was occupied by linen. Its manufacture flourished particularly towards the end of the fifteenth century, when it was widely known in Europe and large amounts were exported to England, where in one year alone at Bristol there was a recorded import of over 20,000 yards.[5]

DURING the middle ages fish from its rivers and the sea surrounding it was perhaps one of Ireland's most valuable natural resources, both as an important source of protein and as a substantial contribution to its wealth through the export trade. Already, by 1217, an Irish fishing-fleet, made up of crews from the coastline from Derry round to Waterford, was operating on a large scale in the Manx herring fishery, and later in the century the Irish fisheries were taking their share in victualling the royal armies.[6] By the end of the fourteenth century Ireland was exporting a great deal of fish to Bristol, which remained its principal port of entry.[7] The main centre of the trade in Ireland was Waterford, a large port opposite Bristol, with a wealth of herring off its coast; but boats from

[1] Miscellanea of the exchequer, P.R.O., E. 163/5/17.

[2] P.R.O., C. 133/16 (6); *Ir. cartul. Llanthony*, p. 140; *Register of the priory of the Blessed Virgin Mary at Tristernagh*, ed. M. V. Clarke (I.M.C., Dublin, 1941), p. 81; Orpen, *Normans*, iv, 276.

[3] Carus Wilson, 'Overseas trade of Bristol', p. 187; Touchard, *Commerce maritime breton*, p. 222.

[4] P.R.O., E. 122/199/1, E. 122/21/4, E. 122/21/7 are typical for Bristol; E. 122/115/7, 10, 11, 12 for west-country ports.

[5] Carus Wilson, 'Overseas trade of Bristol', p. 199.

[6] Dolley, *Anglo-Norman Ire.*, p. 119.

[7] P.R.O., E. 122/16/21.

many other ports from Wexford to Dingle were prominent in the trade. During the fifteenth and sixteenth centuries the Irish banks were much frequented by continental fishing fleets, especially those of France and Spain, but it is difficult to know whether they made any contribution to the Irish economy. It may be that they took supplies aboard in the havens of the south coast in return for cargoes brought with them, as happened in 1534 when some merchants of Dingle on passage from Bordeaux loaded twenty tuns of wine on a Breton ship to be landed at an Irish port, after which the ship was to fish about Ireland and take the produce to La Rochelle.[1] The principal customer for Ireland's fish, however, appears to have been England, Bristol in particular, and it is probable that fish was the Irish product most valued there.[2] The Bristol customs accounts do not always indicate whether the boats bringing fish had bought it from Irish fishermen or had caught it themselves off Ireland, and where the cargo was wholly salt-water fish it may be that it was the result of a fishing expedition. Among salt-water fish, herring was first in quantity, and vast amounts were exported fresh, salted, or smoked to Bristol and the west of England, particularly during the autumn.[3] Other sea-fish, fresh and salted, were exported to Bristol, mainly members of the cod family, hake, pollock, and whiting, but again in some cases it may have been brought straight from the fisheries rather than imported from an Irish port. More highly priced than salt-water fish was salmon, which the Irish ports exported to Bristol and, salted, to Bordeaux.[4] Much of the fish exported to ports like Bristol and Chester was subsequently either sold to inland towns of England, like the six butts of salmon sent by a Drogheda merchant to Chester and finally sold at Shrewsbury; or reexported to the Continent, especially to Spain.[5] Apart from fish, foodstuffs seem not to have been exported by Ireland in any great quantity in the later middle ages; there are a few references to butter, bacon, and meat, but they are hardly significant.[6] Livestock too occupied a very small place in the total volume of trade: in the earlier years of the colony some horses were exported, but few are recorded in the later middle ages, and hawks of various kinds seem to be the most commonly recurring group of live exports met in the customs accounts.[7]

The final export of significant size was timber. During the thirteenth century it was shipped to England as sawn timber for building and ships, or in manufactured form as oars and as brattices sent to Wales and Gascony.[8] Timber continued to be shipped from Ireland in the fifteenth and sixteenth centuries to

[1] Jacques Bernard, *Navires & gens de mer à Bordeaux vers 1400—vers 1500* (3 vols, Paris, 1968), iii, 217.
[2] Carus Wilson, 'Overseas trade of Bristol', p. 196.
[3] Ibid., pp 196–7.
[4] Ibid., pp 197–8; Bernard, *Navires & gens de mer*, p. 186.
[5] Carus Wilson, 'Overseas trade of Bristol', pp 195–6.
[6] Ibid., p. 198.
[7] P.R.O., E. 122/115/12 (m. 15); E. 122/199/1.
[8] Orpen, *Normans*, iv, 278.

both England and France for a variety of purposes, often in the form of barrels for herring; but the vast bulk of it that entered England, mainly through the west country ports, was as boards, and sometimes oars, probably for the local shipbuilding industry.[1]

Raw materials made up the greatest part of Ireland's exports; its imports were mainly luxury goods and those commodities that the country did not produce for itself, at least in any quantity. Throughout the middle ages the greatest import was wine, already an important item in Ireland's pre-conquest trading. Under the Anglo-Normans the wine trade increased considerably; by 1185 it flourished, paid for with hides. Most of the wine that came to Irish ports during the early Anglo-Norman period came direct from La Rochelle and Rouen, but some came via England, especially from Bristol.[2] After Edward I in 1275 had granted a charter of privileges to Gascon merchants, Gascon wines predominated, coming from Bordeaux and Bayonne, carried mainly in Gascon ships. Not all of it was consumed in Ireland; large quantities were reexported, with other supplies, to royal armies and castles in Wales and Scotland. The Gascon trade remained important, but in the late fourteenth century the trade in wine with Spain and Portugal, largely based on Galway, came to rival it.[3] Galway, which was not an important port until the fourteenth century, probably benefited more than others from Richard II's permission, given in 1380, for Portuguese merchants to come to Ireland and for Irish merchants to go to Portugal. Taking advantage of a geographical position that was well suited to trade with the Iberian peninsula, it built up in the following century the substantial commerce in Spanish wine upon which much of its wealth and prestige rested, and became Ireland's principal supplier of wine. Another necessity that Ireland had to import, either direct from the Continent or from Bristol, was salt, essential for preserving meat, fish, and sometimes hides, for little seems to have been produced in Ireland.[4] Metals too had to be imported. There were in Edward I's reign attempts at mining in the counties of Tipperary, Kerry, Limerick, and Waterford, but they appear to have come to little. In spite of that, the prospect of great mineral wealth in Ireland was still held out to the English in the 1430s:

> For of sylvere and golde there is the oore
> Amonge the wylde Yrishe, though they be pore,
> For they ar rude and can thereone no skylle;
> So that, if we had there pese and gode wylle
> To myne and fyne and metall for to pure,
> In wylde Yrishe myght we fynde the cure.[5]

[1] P.R.O., E. 122/115/7, 11, 12; E. 122/116/4, *passim*.
[2] O'Sullivan, *Italian bankers*, pp 103–4.
[3] O'Sullivan, *Old Galway*, pp 38–9.
[4] McNeill, *Anglo-Norman Ulster*, p. 41.
[5] *Libelle*, p. 35, lines 686–91.

A similar view was put forward by the parliament and council of Ireland for Sir Gilbert Debenham and his companions to use in trying to get help from England in the 1470s, but in both these cases Irish ore deposits were being used as an inducement and their actual output, if any, appears to have been minimal.[1] A similar picture is given in 1503 at the beginning of the Red Book of the earls of Kildare, where gold, silver, lead, iron, and alum sources are listed, but again it seems to be more a matter of hearsay and small quantities than of actual production.[2] The bulk of Ireland's metal requirement was imported; some iron came direct from the Continent, but most of it was brought from Bristol, the source also of the earl of Norfolk's lead in the 1280s.[3] In addition to these large commodities, Ireland imported a variety of manufactured goods and luxury items: spices, dried fruits, drugs, perfumes, and the finer cloths. For example, in 1468–9 at La Rochelle ships took on cargoes for Ireland which included wine, iron, steel, salt, resin, pitch, cork, nails, liquorice, and saffron; and in 1503–4 ships leaving Bristol for Ireland carried, among other things, cloth, worked silk, corrupt wine, coal, saffron, pepper, verdigris, knives, aniseed, alum, paper, and books.[4]

The evidently flourishing state of Irish commerce during the later middle ages, reflected in the prosperity of its towns, was partly the result of a successful response to the change in emphasis of the rural economy in large areas of Ireland from agriculture to pastoral husbandry. The great exports of the cereal surpluses of Irish manors, the fruit of the comparative peace and order of the thirteenth century, were replaced in the late fourteenth and the fifteenth centuries by increasing shipments of the products of Irish herds: hides, wool, woolfells, and cloth, staple raw materials of much late medieval industry which, with Irish fish, were in great demand in England and on the Continent. The central government's inability to enforce its rule in most of the country may have contributed to the decline of the manorial economy, but it does not appear to have harmed external trade, which may even have gained from being untrammelled by governmental restrictions. In the new situation brought about by the Gaelic revival and failure of government from Dublin this prosperity was of necessity based to a considerable extent on economic cooperation between the two nations in Ireland, in that the traders of the coastal towns were largely dependent on their often Irish-dominated hinterlands for the principal commodities of trade. It is perhaps not without significance that Ireland enjoyed this substantial prosperity while the connection with England was at its weakest and when the preoccupation with France and trouble at home distracted the attention of the government of England from Ireland, which had ceased by then to be a source of revenue and supplies. This did not go entirely

[1] P.R.O., C. 47/10/29.
[2] *Red Bk Kildare*, pp 12–13.
[3] O'Sullivan, *Italian bankers*, p. 108, n. 2; Carus Wilson, 'Overseas trade of Bristol', p. 200; P.R.O., S.C. 6/1237/39.
[4] Touchard, *Commerce maritime breton*, p. 182; P.R.O., E. 122/199/1.

unremarked in England, and Ireland's potential as a source of wealth was stressed by the author of the 'Libelle', writing in the 1430s with the aim of showing the English council, at a time when the English position in France was seriously threatened, the political and commercial advantages of securing command of the sea. Forty years later the Irish parliament and council followed a similar line of argument in the instructions that they gave to Sir Gilbert Debenham as part of their attempt to interest Edward IV in the defence of the colony. When in the next century efforts were made to recover Ireland, with the result that Irish commerce lost its freedom, the glowing prospects held out for England by the fifteenth-century propagandists proved to be illusory and Ireland ceased to play a prominent part in the trade and industry of Europe.

CHAPTER XVI

Overseas trade

WENDY CHILDS AND TIMOTHY O'NEILL

> I caste to speke of Irelonde but a lytelle.
> Commoditees of it I woll entitell
> Hydes and fish, samon, hake and herynge;
> Irish wollen and lynyn cloth, faldynge,
> And marterns gode bene in here marchaundye;
> Hertys hydes and other hydes of venerye,
> Skynnes of oter, squerel, and Irysh hare,
> Of shepe, lambe, and fox is here chaffare,
> Felles of kydde and conyes grete plente.
> . . . .
> For they have havenes grete and godely bayes
> Sure, wyde, and depe . . .
> . . . .
> It is fertyle for thynge that there do growe
> . . . .
> So large, so gode, so plenteouse, so riche . . .

THUS the author of the 'Libelle of Englyshe polycye', impressed by its potential wealth and its political vulnerability, described Ireland's commercial advantages.[1] The much more prosaic author of the 'Noumbre of weyghtes' also noted plenty of hides, linen, iron, marten and otter skins, black lamb which was 'ffelow to bogy' (i.e. like 'budge', a fur of lambskin or kidskin), and the gentle horses called hobbys. He emphasised that 'Also att Slegoy^e [Sligo] is grett plente of heryng and att bame [Bann] is grete plente of salmon and grete chepe', hence the proverb 'heryng of Slegoy^e and salmon of bame heis made in brystowe [Bristol] many a ryche man'.[2] This well-known fifteenth-century view of the richness of Irish trade is, however, difficult for the economic historian to substantiate in detail. The disappearance not only of essential quantitative sources but also of many other Irish records has been a great hindrance to studies of Ireland's overseas trade; but scholars' careful use of the remaining central and municipal records, together with those of England and other European areas where Ireland dealt, has gradually clarified its pattern, and modern

---

[1] *Libelle*, lines 656–64, 674–5, 682, 743.
[2] B.L., Cotton MS, Vesp. E IX, ff 101–101^v.

Map 11 EUROPEAN PORTS TRADING WITH IRELAND,
by Timothy O'Neill

work is becoming ever more precise. The geographical extent of the trade, governed by Ireland's position, current political problems, and the nature of Irish produce, is quite clear. The overall scale of the trade, however, remains somewhat obscure, although its general trends are becoming clearer. The mercantile organisation and shipping supplies of the trade need much more attention, but here too the general outline is quite apparent.

IRELAND'S position in the far north-west of Europe, although by no means isolating her, meant that direct contacts with the more distant Mediterranean and Baltic markets were limited. Italian merchants had, of course, been common in Ireland in the late thirteenth century, but these representatives of Lucchese and Florentine banking companies had come more as English royal administrators than as speculative traders, although once in Ireland they encouraged the export of wool. However, as their governmental role declined they gradually withdrew, and the compendious fourteenth-century merchant manual of Pegolotti, the Bardi representative in London, does not even mention Ireland, although wool was still being sent to the Bardi there in 1338.[1] Thereafter direct contact was known but slight: a Venetian carrack was loaded with salt and iron in Guérande for Dublin in 1431; Ambrogio Lomellini of the Genoese family domiciled in Lisbon, but himself living in Nantes, dealt in Ireland in 1454; and in 1492 Leonard Lynch of Galway sued James Adurnus of Genoa for the price of some linen.[2] Ireland was never on the route of the official Italian state fleets to the north. Her market size and her goods were not attractive enough to divert large and expensively run carracks and galleys from the liner services to Southampton and Bruges. Even Bristol, visited by some Genoese in the later fourteenth century, could not keep their interest. It is noteworthy that the portulan charts, which became increasingly informative about current Irish landfalls, remained none the less much less accurate in the delineation of the Irish coastline than in the regularly sailed English Channel.[3]

Direct contact with the Hansards increased at the end of the fourteenth century when the Hansards themselves pushed into the Atlantic, seeking Bourgneuf salt but also visiting Iberia and Bristol. Ireland was part of this westward expansion, and ships of Danzig and Kampen came to Ireland in 1384; the *Katherine* of Danzig had already been to Waterford and probably before that to Portugal when she arrived at Southampton in 1407; and a ship of Lübeck loaded goods at Galway before setting off to pay customs at Kinsale in 1415.[4] The Hansards made little permanent impact in these waters in the face of English and Spanish hostility, and in the fifteenth century their large fleets tended to go only to Bourgneuf. With the formally Hanseatic area of Iceland Ireland had a little contact, since the trade in English and Dutch ships often passed her shores and some Irishmen such as Nicholas Abbot took part in the trade.[5] But the links were fragile in this small, expensively licensed market across a dangerous sea. Elsewhere in Hanseatic as in Mediterranean areas the Irish themselves made no impact. The sheer distance to these destinations with no friendly staging posts en route, and the near-monopoly of the highly organised Italian and Hanseatic merchants, together with political and military

---

[1] *Cal. close rolls, 1337—9*, p. 419.

[2] *Cal. pat. rolls, 1429-36*, p. 199; Touchard, *Commerce maritime Breton*, p. 222; *Blake family records, first series, 1300—1599*, ed. M. J. Blake (London, 1902), p. 46.

[3] T. J. Westropp, 'Early Italian maps of Ireland from 1300 to 1600, with notes on foreign settlers and trade' in *R.I.A. Proc.*, xxx (1913), sect. C, pp 366—7.

[4] *Cal. pat. rolls, 1381—5*, pp 500—01; *Cal. close rolls, 1405—09*, pp 209—10; *Rot. pat. Hib.*, p. 212, no. 92.   [5] *Stat. Ire., Hen. VI*, p. 697; see below, p. 520.

pressure in the Hanseatic case, made it economically impossible for a small alien merchant to operate competitively in such areas.

Not surprisingly Ireland's main trading links were with her nearer neighbours, and probably her greatest single market, and certainly the best documented, was England, also her political overlord. Although trade with the Gaelic Irish was restricted and Ireland was seen as a foreign area in so far as trade between the two countries was taxed as foreign trade, the settlers in Ireland were full English subjects who paid only English rates of customs and whose trade with England was fully encouraged. Naturally enough the trade was predominantly to England's western ports of Bristol and Chester, and later Bridgwater, and mainly through Ireland's eastern ports from Drogheda to Waterford. Chester's particular interests lay in Drogheda and Dublin and their outports, while Bristol and Bridgwater dealt mainly with Wexford, Waterford, and the south coast to Kinsale. However, there are enough references to show that Bristol also maintained a steady interest in western Ireland, with merchants holding property and renting fishing rights there, and ships sent to Dingle, Limerick, Galway, and Sligo. Limerick's recorded trading links seem to be quite as strong with Bristol as with Iberia. Some Irish trade went to Wales, some to Devon and Cornwall, and a little to the south coast and London, but direct seaborne trade was modest outside the main western ports of England.

The area beyond England which proved particularly attractive was Flanders, which provides the earliest and most plentiful references outside the English trade. Bruges and its port of Sluys were usually open to Irish and English merchants despite intermittent political troubles, and Irishmen were offered privileges there in the fourteenth century. In difficult times Irish activity along with English might shift northwards to Middelburg in Zeeland. Irish wool and hides were most acceptable in Flanders, but probably hides had become the more important of the two by the later fourteenth century. There were inconveniences in the trade, since ships putting into England for any reason were not infrequently delayed while their masters proved payment of customs in Ireland and swore good intentions towards the Staple regulations, but the trade was worth while. The writer of the 'Noumbre of weyghtes' wrote 'many men lay ye hyd' in Ireland and sellyth yem in fflaunder for xviiij li. a last for is ye best uttrauns off yem',[1] and cases throughout the period confirm his claim that hides sold better in Flanders than in England. Many hides were carried by English and Welsh ships but they attracted carriers from all over Europe. Carriage by Flemish and Hansard shipping reached its peak at the end of the fourteenth century, by which time Spanish and Portuguese ships appear more often. Only on rare occasions, as in 1397 when the *Mary* of Kinsale was at Sluys, is there reference to Irish shipping active in Flanders, and this case is not a happy one. The ship, which belonged to Patrick Galuay and John Scot of

[1] B.L., Cotton Vesp. E IX, f. 101. A last of hides consisted of two hundred.

Kinsale and had a Bristol master, was freighted by a Catalan, Bernard Fons, to take his goods to Valencia (a rare instance of an Irish ship being bound for southern seas). In the event, somewhere in the Bay of Biscay, on Saturday 6 October 1397, perhaps for fear or dislike of the extended journey, the crew threw Bernard Fons and two other merchants overboard, drowning them, and sailed off with their goods. They transferred some to a Dartmouth ship off the Race of St Matthew in Brittany, and sailed on to the Scilly Islands where they sold more to a Bristol merchant and to the constable of the islands' castle. At last they arrived at Waterford, where they bought the *Pycard* to send the rest of the goods for sale in Dublin. By this time, 23 November, orders were already out for their arrest, and the case rumbled on into the following year.[1]

Northern French trade, except that with the Calais staple, became difficult with the hundred years war. Before this, Norman trade had been reasonably regular: Drogheda and Dublin merchants chartered a ship at Dieppe in 1319, a Cork vessel visited Dieppe in 1330, and one of Howth went to Normandy in 1335,[2] but thereafter traders had to rely on safe-conducts and truces. For some these were adequate; Thomas Borton of Limerick visited Harfleur apparently in safety in 1397, but in 1384 Thomas Melantaun of Cork and others had their goods, valued at £3000, arrested by men of Dieppe and Harfleur despite the current truce.[3] After the war contacts possibly strengthened, but Mollat's work on Norman trade shows little evidence of such direct contact before the early sixteenth century. Breton trade with Ireland, which seems to have been sparser than Norman before the war, faced the same problems. The difficulties of navigating in the Biscay area with enemy shores so close are illuminated by a complaint of 1356: during Anglo-Spanish truces Robert Droup, then mayor of Cork, and seven other Irish merchants loaded the *Ste Marie* of Castro Urdiales at Bordeaux with wines and other goods, including, they claimed, gold and silver worth altogether 2,000 marks, to be taken to Cork. Then the master, John Dyes, 'scheming to defraud them', as they claimed, deliberately and unnecessarily sailed into Audierne Bay to the king's Breton enemies and the confiscated goods were shared out between them.[4] None the less, references to Breton contacts are numerous in the fifteenth century, and the expansion of Breton trade, especially of Breton carrying services, described by Touchard, meant increased contacts, although, as with Normandy, the densest evidence for this comes from the early sixteenth century. Similarly trade with La Rochelle was limited until then, although the *Mary* of Waterford was hired by Peter Morice of La Rochelle to take wine to Scotland under truce in 1395.[5]

Bordeaux was quite a different proposition, since it was an English posses-

---

[1] *Cal. misc. inq. 1393–9*, no. 220; *Cal. pat. rolls, 1396–9*, pp 311, 366; *Cal. close rolls, 1396–9*, p. 364.

[2] *Cal. pat. rolls, 1317–21*, p. 373; *Cal. close rolls, 1330–34*, p. 138; *Cal. pat. rolls, 1334–8*, pp 147–8.

[3] Michel Mollat, *Le commerce maritime Normand à la fin du moyen âge* (Paris, 1952), p. 9; *Cal. close rolls, 1381–5*, p. 478.

[4] *Cal. close rolls, 1354–60*, p. 276.   [5] *Cal. pat. rolls, 1391–6*, p. 634.

sion and Irish goods, men, and ships were welcome. M. K. James's work[1] and frequent references in the patent and close rolls testify to the direct Irish–Gascon links, and Irish exports of corn and hides were particularly useful in an area specialising in viticulture. The Bordeaux wine customs accounts allow an assessment of Irish activity there, although since they give no destination for departing ships the amount of wine actually sent to Ireland is unknown.[3] In the early fourteenth century activity was marked: in 1303–4 eighteen Irish ships (five each from Cork and Ross, four from Waterford, two from Wexford, and one each from Dublin and Dundalk) carried out 1,648 tuns of wine and in 1307–8 another eighteen (seven from Ross, six from Cork, two each from Waterford and Youghal, and one from Drogheda) took 1,657 tuns. In Bordeaux's total trade, running then at some 100,000 tuns carried by 600 to 900 ships, the Irish role is small, but the amount would be useful to Ireland. Thereafter, as the Bordeaux trade itself declined, so did Irish activity within it, dropping to one to five ships taking 200 to 300 tuns a year if any; and the Cork, Ross, and Waterford ships lost their lead to Dublin vessels, which were the only regular carriers in the fifteenth century, with some support from Kinsale ships. After the English loss of Gascony, Irish shipping disappeared from Gascony altogether (none show up in the one surviving account for 1481–2), but the notarial records calendared by Bernard for Bordeaux show shipments to Ireland to have continued, although not at a particularly high level even in the expansion of the early sixteenth century.[2]

Spanish trade was also troubled by Anglo-French politics but, even so, Spain was often open to subjects of the English crown under truce and safe-conduct; only between 1369 and 1388, when Spain actively supported France, was the breach sufficient to cause a clear stoppage of direct trade. Spanish contacts with Ireland seem to start about the mid-fourteenth century, although her trade with England was old by then. Ireland was included in the Anglo-Spanish commercial treaty of 1351 simply as one of the king's several territories, not because of her trading importance,[4] but soon, in 1354 and 1356, come references to the Spanish carriage of goods of Irish origin from Bordeaux and to and from Flanders and to triangular voyages like that of the *Gracedieu* of Dartmouth, freighted to sail from Flanders to Spain and back to Ireland in 1402.[5] Such activity continued in the fifteenth century, when ships of Laredo and Bermeo bought safe-conducts to trade in Ireland.[5]

[1] M. K. James, *Studies in the medieval wine trade*, ed. E. M. Veale (Oxford, 1971).
[2] P.R.O., E. 101 (Constable of Bordeaux) *passim*; B.L., Add. MS 15524; 'Registre de la Comptablie de Bordeaux, 1482–3', transcribed by M. G. Ducaunnes Duval, in *Archives Historiques du Département de la Gironde*, l (1915), pp 1–166. An interesting statement from Winchelsea in 1327 shows that one-third of its spring fleet to Bordeaux, perhaps 1000 tons of shipping, intended to take wine to Ireland (*Cal. mem. rolls, 1326–7*, no. 892 (n)).
[3] Bernard, *Navires & gens de mer*, and 'The maritime intercourse between Bordeaux and Ireland, c. 1450–c. 1520' in *Ir. Econ. & Soc. Hist.*, vii (1980), pp 7–21; for further estimates of the wine trade, see below, p. 507. [4] Rymer, *Foedera*, III, i, 228–9.
[5] *Cal. pat. rolls, 1354–8*, p. 73; *Cal. close rolls, 1354–60*, pp 276, 367; *Cal. pat. rolls, 1401–5*, p. 134; see below, p. 521. [6] *Cal. pat. rolls, 1441–6*, pp 201, 247, 287; P.R.O., C. 1/19/22; C. 76/123, m. 15.

Portugal was even more open as a friendly power; only for a few confused years in the 1370s and 1380s, when she allied with Spain, were there difficulties, so that in 1380 a general safe-conduct for the merchants of Portugal and Lisbon to visit Ireland with wines and other goods was thought necessary.[1] The Portuguese trade seems to begin later than the Spanish, when the *St Mary Olyver* was sent to Waterford from Lisbon in 1374; and in 1377 Ellis Spelly's *John* of Bristol was heading from Lisbon to Dublin or England when it was blown to Kinsale, where officials insisted on viewing it as an enemy ship because its crew included four or five Spaniards.[2] Portuguese contacts continued through the fifteenth century and by mid-century the Irish were certainly visiting Lisbon. Of the twenty-four subjects of the English crown for whom Portuguese royal safe-conducts survive, seven were Irish: Richard May, a member of the Irish family based in Bristol and London (1452), Richard Alford of Dublin (1462), John and Dominic Lynch, Thomas Faute, and Patrick, for whom no surname is recorded (1465), and Geoffrey Galway of Limerick (1488).[3] But general safe-conducts make it clear that merchants of Bristol and London were the usual visitors.

It has been said that Iberian contacts, especially those of Portugal, were greater in Galway and the west than in the east of Ireland but, while this is possibly true, it must be remembered that most of the firm evidence is from the sixteenth century, when considerable changes were taking place in European trading patterns. The larger and numerous ports of the east, en route for the west of England, must have remained attractive.

BESIDES the constraints of geography and politics, Irish trade was, of course, influenced by the goods that the country produced and needed. Exports were largely agricultural products, together with textiles, furs, and fish—all useful but not unique. England also produced wool, woolfells, and hides, as did Spain; Portugal was a hide producer; all three had their own fishing fleets. England and Flanders produced a greater variety of woollen cloth, and Germany and the Low Countries good linen. Northern Hanseatic areas produced corn, timber, fish, and furs. Moreover, contemporaries did not reckon Irish wool, hides, or cloth among those of the best quality: the Bruges ordinance of 1282 rated Irish wool below English and Scottish;[4] Pisan customs tariffs placed Irish hides below Spanish in 1474;[5] Irish textiles were rated low in Bruges in 1497.[6] Such goods would not attract merchants from great distances, and

[1] *Rot. parl.*, iii, 86a.   [2] *Cal. close rolls, 1374–7*, p. 13; ibid., *1377–81*, p. 24.

[3] P.R.O., PRO 31/8/153; P. de Azevedo, 'Comercio anglo-portugûes no meado do dec. xv' in *Academia das Sciencias de Lisboa: Boletim da Segunda Classe*, viii (1913–14), *passim*.

[4] Cited in J. H. Munro, *Wool, cloth and gold: the struggle for bullion in Anglo-Burgundian trade, 1340–1478* (Brussels, Toronto, 1972), p. 2.

[5] M. E. Mallett, 'Anglo-Florentine commercial relations, 1465–1491' in *Econ. Hist. Rev.*, 2nd ser., xv (1962), p. 258, n. 6.

[6] Cited in Mac Niocaill, *Na buirgéisí*, ii, 521–2.

MAJOR PORTS
OTHER PORTS

N

CARRICK-FERGUS

ARDGLASS

ASSAROE
Lower
L. Erne

R. Bann

R. Foyle

CARLINGFORD

SLIGO

DUNDALK

R. Shannon

Clogher Head
DROGHEDA

R. Boyne

SKERRIES
Lambay I.
MALAHIDE
HOWTH
DUBLIN
DALKEY

R. Liffey

GALWAY

Aran Is

Wicklow Head

R. Barrow

R. Nore

KILKENNY

R. Slaney

LIMERICK

THOMASTOWN

NEW
ROSS
WEXFORD

CLONMEL

R. Suir

WATERFORD
Tuskar Rock

DINGLE

R. Blackwater

YOUGHAL

R. Lee

CORK

KINSALE (Endleford)

Miles   50

Kms   80

0

0

Kenmare R.

BALTIMORE

Map 12 IRISH PORTS IN THE LATER MIDDLE AGES,
by Timothy O'Neill

indeed the Irish complained, when home staples were set up under Edward II and Edward III, that their trade suffered badly as foreign merchants did not come in great numbers to their ports; and in the troubled mid-fifteenth century they complained again that neither did the English come as they once had.[1] This is not to say that the goods were not welcome and did not sell well enough all over Europe from Lübeck to Pisa, but it is not surprising that most of Ireland's trade remained with her closest neighbours in the Atlantic and the English Channel, who could easily supply her with the essentials she lacked and some of the luxuries she craved.

The greatest Irish exports in the thirteenth and fourteenth centuries, and the only ones listed in the extensive Flemish list of commodities of the period, were undoubtedly wool, woolfells, and hides, but these were probably run close and perhaps later surpassed by fish exports. Wool, as in England, was produced by the secular and religious landlords and its export was often handled in the thirteenth century by Italians, although Flemings, such as Giles de Courtray of Bruges, who had wool and hides stored at Kilkenny and Thomastown in 1295,[2] also came to fetch it. Its main destinations were probably the cloth manufacturing centres of Flanders. It was coarser than much English wool and, like Spanish wool, best when mixed with wool of higher quality, but serviceable cloth could be made from it. A little Irish wool was imported through Chester for the looms of Coventry, but demand in England was low: a consignment of 46 sacks sent by Robert Droup of Cork and five other Irish merchants to Plymouth and Dartmouth remained unsold five years later in 1356, since merchants 'refused to buy on account of its poor quality', and the request to ship it on to Flanders was allowed.[3] England gave a warmer welcome to woolfells, and both sheep- and lamb-skins were exported to Bristol in the fifteenth century when imports ranged from 16,500 to 48,000 skins worth £70 to £150 in a year. Otherwise Bristol's only dealings in the wool trade were tiny amounts of waste wool, or 'flocks'.[4]

The bulk of wool exports, according to customs receipts, left through southern ports, especially Waterford and Ross, conveniently situated on a river system passing through south Leinster and south-east Munster. The Suir, Nore, and Barrow rivers also flowed through the lands of ten major Cistercian abbeys, thus facilitating the transport of their wool through Waterford, and Waterford clearly hoped to benefit from it by new and unusual regulations for weighing and customing wool in 1355.[5] When home staples were set up in 1326 Waterford was rather oddly omitted, but it had been added to Dublin, Drogheda, and Cork by 1354.[6]

[1] *Cal. pat. rolls, 1354–8*, p. 434; *Stat. Ire., Hen. VI*, p. 663.
[2] *Cal. doc. Ire., 1293–1301*, pp 109–11.
[3] *Cal. pat. rolls, 1354–8*, p. 405.
[4] P.R.O., E. 122 (Bristol), *passim*.
[5] *Cal. close rolls, 1354–60*, p. 144.
[6] *Stat. of realm*, i, 332.

Hides passed through the same ports as wool, and also went predominantly to Flanders. Amounts were high. Four Drogheda merchants hired a Spanish ship in 1353 to take 3,700 hides to Flanders and John Toky hired a ship of Sluys to take 13,000 there from Limerick in 1382.[1] William Canyngs and Richard Spicer were each allowed to reexport 12,000 hides in 1370 from Bristol to Calais, from which they would have reached Flanders, and Canyngs and John Barstaple planned to take 8,000 there in 1378.[2] Drogheda men had also loaded 12,115 hides on three ships of Danzig, Kampen, and Bristol in 1384, only to find them all stolen by the Hanseatic crews.[3] Proof of customs payment in Ireland before reexport from Southampton and Bristol in 1340 showed hides coming through Carrickfergus, Drogheda, Wexford, Waterford, Cork, Youghal, Galway, 'Kilchet', and Kerry, and the St Antoyne of Castro Urdiales had hides customed at Cork, Waterford, and Dublin, wool at Carmarthen, and other goods at Bristol on her voyage to Flanders in 1384.[4] These amounts taken to Flanders far surpass the meagre quantities taken to Bristol, where usually fewer than 150 hides worth less than £12 were recorded annually. They are, however, rivalled by fifteenth-century imports to Pisa where often 2,000 to 8,000 Irish hides arrived in a half-year, and peaks of 34,000 and 24,000 were reached in 1466–7 and 1482–3 respectively. Whether this was a new or traditional market is unclear, as is whether they came direct from Ireland or through an intermediary.[5]

The hide trade shows the vital interdependence of town merchants and hinterland suppliers, despite laws forbidding trade with the Gaelic Irish, and municipalities recognised its importance with their attempts at regulation. Fifteenth-century wills show extensive trade in hides with the local Gaelic Irish around Galway, and that town, rather than forbid such dealings, tried to regulate them, as in 1515, by forbidding citizens to buy hides outside the liberties, thus forcing the trade into the town's marketplace.[6] In the east, merchants of Waterford and New Ross went inland to buy in Counties Kilkenny, Carlow, and Tipperary, and sent hides back by river.[7] At Waterford municipal authorities regulated prices, and it is clear that profits were good. Fresh hides could be bought for £8. 6s. 8d. the last in 1469–70 and £11. 13s. 4d. in 1485–6, and salt hides for £10 and £13. 6s. 8d.,[8] and these could be sold in Flanders for £18, according to the writer of the 'Noumbre of weyghtes'.[9] The returns of the customs show that total exports of wool, woolfells, and hides fell dramatically between the late thirteenth century and the

---

[1] *Cal. close rolls, 1349–54*, p. 578; ibid., *1381–5*, p. 47.
[2] Ibid., *1369–74*, pp 161, 169; ibid., *1377–81*, p. 150.
[3] *Cal. pat. rolls, 1381–5*, pp 500–01.
[4] *Cal. close rolls, 1339–41*, pp 591–2 ('Kilchet' remains unidentified); ibid., *1360–64*, pp 22–3.
[5] Mallett, 'Anglo-Florentine . . . relations', p. 265.
[6] O'Flaherty, *West Connaught*, pp 198–201, 205–10; *H.M.C. rep. 10*, app. v (1885), p. 396.
[7] Hore, *Wexford town*, i, 228–9.
[8] *H.M.C. rep. 10*, app. v (1885), pp 306, 318. A last consisted of 100 hides.
[9] See above, p. 495.

mid-fourteenth century, but while there is no reason to suppose that raw wool recovered, the frequency of references to hides indicates that these did better.

Linked with this trade was the more modest one in lighter-weight skins of kid, goat, and the wild animals mentioned in the 'Libelle' and the 'Noumbre of weyghtes' (coney, deer, fawn, hare, squirrel, marten, fox, and otter). These are rarely listed in general cargo descriptions, indicating a minor constituent, but customs accounts show Irish coneyskins being reexported from London in 1389, and these lighter skins enjoyed some popularity in Bristol in the early fifteenth century, when 13,252 various skins worth £56. 10s. 7d. arrived in 1403–4, and 14,877 in 1437–8. Thereafter such skins sagged to under 500 a year except for minor surges in 1485–6 (720) and 1517–18 (1,555).[1]

Irish cloth exports were undoubtedly helped, as were English, by the unforeseen tax protection given by Edward III's heavy wool taxes, but the industry was not then new. Irish cloth had been exported in the thirteenth century, and experienced Irish cloth workers had settled in England by the mid-fourteenth century. Much of the cloth was of the rougher sorts—frieze and serge—and some wool was made into heavy Irish mantles, many of which were exported through Waterford. These, although of apparently rough quality, were used by the upper classes too: the papal tax collector bought five in 1382; the earl of Warwick had two in 1397; and in about 1440 the archbishop of Armagh considered a mantle a suitable gift for the bishop of Bath and Wells.[2] Irish cloth could be sold by a Lincoln merchant in Normandy in 1327; transported by Hansards from Hamburg to Oslo in 1360; and reexported from Southampton, Sandwich, and especially London at the end of the century.[3]

The advance of industry is difficult to chart but exports of cloth to Bristol certainly increased during the fifteenth century, although reexports from the east of England seem to decline. To Bristol in 1403–4 Ireland sent a variety of items: frieze, narrow frieze, old and new ware, old and new faldyng (a type of coarse cloth similar to frieze); but this was low in value at £24. 5s. 6d. and low in quantity at a few pieces and some 80 dozen yards (unlikely to be the equivalent of much more than 40 English broadcloths, if that). By 1492–3 variety and quantity had grown. Mantles were now the major constituent, with imports of 1,012 worth £102. 4s. 0d., and checkers (a wool cloth woven with a checked pattern) are now first mentioned with imports of 2,000 yards worth £60. 12s. 0d. But even in this year, the highest for the middle ages, total cloth values reached only £265. 19s. 9d., in the same range as the skin and hide trade and far below the value of fish.[4]

[1] P.R.O., E. 122/71/13 (London, 1389); E. 122 (Bristol), *passim*; *Bristol town duties*, ed. Henry Bush (Bristol, 1828), pp 17–25.

[2] *Cal. close rolls, 1381–5*, p. 55; ibid., *1396–9*, p. 161; N.L.I., MS 2689, no. 191.

[3] *Cal. close rolls, 1327–30*, p. 175; *Hansisches Urkundenbuch*, iii, ed. Konstantin Höhlbaum (Halle, 1882), p. 291, no. 537; *Cal. pat. rolls, 1377–81*, p. 281; P.R.O., E. 122/71/13 (London, 1389); 126/3 (Sandwich, 1378–9); 138/11, 16, 20 (Southampton, 1383–4, 1387–8, 1391–2).

[4] P.R.O., E. 122/17/10, 20/7; tabulated in W. R. Childs, 'Ireland's trade with England in the later middle ages' in *Ir. Econ. &Soc. Hist.*, ix (1982), pp 19–20.

Linen appeared at Bristol in the fifteenth century as a regular import but little is known of the areas of production in Ireland. There was perhaps a centre in the Galway region, where wills show Gaelic Irishmen owing hundreds of linen cloths to merchants of that town; and Carus-Wilson suggested that the activity of Kilkenny merchants in the trade might indicate a centre there.[1] The highest amount sent to Bristol (20,000 yards worth £100 in 1477–8) was run close by nearly 16,000 yards in 1437 and over 18,000 yards in both 1485–6 and 1486–7, but it was a trade which fluctuated like others and in 1492–3 Bristol received only 525 yards worth £2. 12s. 6d.[2]

Ireland's other main agricultural product, corn, was an export in the thirteenth and early fourteenth centuries, but many references are to transactions outside the open market, to licences to individuals or to religious houses to provide for their own needs, or more importantly, to purveyance for the Edwardian wars, in which the Irish supplies were most valuable.[3] Some corn was certainly sold on the open market and some went regularly to Bordeaux in exchange for wine, but Ireland's role as exporter does not seem to have lasted long past the mid-fourteenth century, no doubt due partly to growing internal political difficulties. As the area peacefully held by the Anglo-Irish landowners decreased and endemic raiding increased, livestock would undoubtedly seem a safer proposition than standing corn. In the fifteenth century Ireland had become a grain importer, but the amounts sent from England were not large; although Ireland no longer had a surplus for export she could normally feed herself, and imports indicate a minor trade to tide over local shortages. Bean exports to Ireland also became more frequent in the late fifteenth century. Bristol's usual shipments were 100 to 250 weys[4] a year, worth some £50 to £160, and Bridgwater's, drawing on the fields of Somerset, were somewhat larger, usually worth £100 to £200 a year, reaching a peak of £300 in a half year in 1496.[5]

Ireland's production of butter, bacon, and meat rarely swelled exports. Her famous gentle horses seldom appear in customs accounts, but a fifteenth-century lawsuit shows thirty-four horses loaded on a ship of Sluys to be taken to Brittany to be sold in return for salt.[6] Hawks are recorded occasionally in ones or twos, and probably constituted gifts more often than trade. Timber exports were larger and more regular and found in Flanders, Normandy, and England, but total amounts to England were low, and overall their economic importance compared with other exports was very small.

Fish was a different matter and was one of Ireland's main exports by the late

---

[1] *Blake family records*, pp 46, 48; O'Flaherty, *West Connaught*, p. 207; E. M. Carus-Wilson, *Medieval merchant venturers* (2nd ed., London, 1967), p. 25.

[2] P.R.O., E. 122/19/13, 20/5, 7, 9; *Bristol town duties*, pp 17–25.

[3] See above, pp 397–438; Timothy O'Neill, 'Irish trade in the later middle ages: a survey' (M.A. thesis, N.U.I.(U.C.D.), 1979), pp 49–76; Lydon, 'Ireland's participation', pp 192–7, 226–9.

[4] The wey varied, but was usually about six quarters.

[5] P.R.O., E. 122 (Bristol and Bridgwater), *passim*.

[6] P.R.O., C. 1/45/25.

fourteenth century and probably much earlier. Indeed, by the sixteenth century exports were so great that an attempt was made in 1515–16 to reserve one-third of fish catches for Ireland's consumption.[1] Herring was the most important sea-fish export and came from two areas. The Irish Sea fishery, closely linked with the ports of County Dublin and the Pale, enjoyed plentiful herring supplies throughout the period. Scottish fishing boats from Rutherglen near Glasgow were trading herring in Dublin and Drogheda in 1306; herring boats were taxed for using Bullock Harbour, Dalkey, in 1345–6, and at Clogherhead in 1475–6.[2] The herring remained plentiful in the sixteenth century, the fishing grounds round Ardglass being particularly valuable. In 1535 the English fleet operating round Carlingford numbered 600 vessels and the fishermen offered to make 3,000 fighting men available for two to three days to supplement the lord treasurer's forces campaigning in the area.[3] The concentration of towns in the Pale meant a good local market for fish, but much was exported, and a statute of 1355 forbidding forestalling and unlicenced exports gives a glimpse of the organisation of the fish merchants, the fish shambles, and the brokers.[4]

The second fishery was of a different nature. The apparent migration of the herring shoals in the fifteenth century, while not destroying the old centres of fishing in the North Sea and Baltic, saw a marked increase, if not wholly new appearance, of herring shoals off the south and west of Ireland. Much fishing was done by English and foreign fleets, especially Spanish, who might take their catches directly home, but some was done by ships of Irish ports such as Wexford and Waterford, through which some of the fish was reexported. Fishermen paid duties to the local lords to fish and use the havens and bays of the Irish coast for refitting, revictualling, and landing their fish for salting, which had to be done, then as now, in twenty-four hours if the catch was not to lose its flavour. Such payments annoyed the government when the recipients were Gaelic Irish, and legislation was passed in 1449–50 to prevent fishing off Baltimore in West Cork because of the profit in victuals and arms it brought Fínghin Ó hEidirsgeóil; in 1465 foreign vessels were forbidden to fish 'among the king's Irish enemies' without licence because the Irish were being 'much advanced and strengthened, as well in victuals, harness and armour, as divers other necessaries; also great tributes of money' were given by every vessel; and early-sixteenth-century records refer to Spaniards paying £300 a year to 'Mac Fineen Duff' of Ardee for liberty to fish in Kenmare Bay.[5] Hake came closely after herring in importance and some way ahead of cod, ling, haddock, pollock, 'salted fish', porpoise, and seals.

---

[1] *Red Bk Kildare*, p. 171. We are grateful to Dr Cosgrove for this reference.

[2] *Cal. justic. rolls Ire., 1305–7*, p. 279; *Chartul. St Mary's, Dublin*, i, 307–10; *Stat. Ire., 12–22 Edw. IV*, p. 389.

[3] *Cal. Carew MSS, 1515–74*, p. 85.

[4] *Stat. Ire., John–Hen. V*, p. 399.

[5] *Stat. Ire., Hen. VI*, p. 191; *1–12 Edw. IV*, p. 353; A. E. J. Went, 'Foreign fishing fleets along the Irish coast' in *Cork Hist. Soc. Jn.*, liv (1949), pp 18–19.

Salmon completes the range of fish and came from both the west coast and the famous Bann fishery of the north. It was taken by river and tidal weirs owned by religious houses, the crown, great landowners such as the earls of Ormond and Desmond, and some prominent merchant families such as the Lynches of Galway. Monastic and royal weirs were almost invariably leased, which leaves no doubt as to their value. Merchants from as far as Bristol were attracted to rent west coast fisheries, as did Richard Panys for £10 a year in Galway in 1386–7.[1] Irish and English merchants shared the export of salmon, which was already well established by the late fourteenth century, but there may have been some increase in English activity when over thirty licences were sold to Bristol men between 1400 and 1415 to fetch Irish salmon. Thomas Clerk, master of the crayer *Trinity* of Bristol, was typical: in 1400 he and four others were allowed to take the ship to Sligo with 20 tuns of corrupt wine, six lasts of salt, and five packs of cloth to sell to the king's lieges in exchange for salmon for salting there before they brought it back to England.[2] Although Sligo is mentioned only in this permit it is probable that most of the permits were for the western fisheries. Certainly a lawsuit of 1436 between Bristol merchants over the ownership of seven pipes of salmon said to have been bought from Ó Domhnaill, lord of Lassery (Assaroe, County Donegal) shows the western trade to have continued.[3] The Bann fishery seems to have slipped into the hands of Drogheda and Dublin merchants with the decline of the Ulster colony in the fifteenth century. Two Drogheda merchants rented the fishery in 1386–7, and licences similar to those above for the Bristol men were issued to Drogheda men to trade for fish in 'the parts of Ban' in Ulster.[4]

The amounts of fish were huge. The quantities sent directly home by foreign fleets can never be known, and the form of the Chester customs accounts obscures the exact volume there while making plain that herring was the major import,[5] but Bristol accounts make the volume and value there clear.[6] In the late fifteenth century, fish worth from £1,001 to £2,843 a year made up on average 80 per cent of Bristol's Irish imports by value, and there had been little change over the century if the figures for 1403–4, the only surviving earlier year, are typical. In that year fish worth £1,754 made up 84 per cent of the total Irish import value. Herring was the most important, with some 338 lasts worth over £994 imported in 1403–4, and 370 lasts worth £1,233 in 1479–80; amounts and values then slipped back to under half that but recovered to £1,440 in 1504–5. Most herring was white salted herring but normally some 14 to 16 per cent of

---

[1] *Rot. pat. Hib.*, p. 131, no. 29.

[2] *Cal. pat. rolls, 1399–1401*, p. 260. A last of salt was 420 bushels, or *c.* 148 hl. A pack of cloth was usually ten 'pieces', each of which was usually 24 yards (*c.* 21.95 m) by 7 quarters (*c.* 1.60 m).

[3] P.R.O., C. 1/43/251.

[4] *Rot. pat. Hib.*, p. 135, no. 162; p. 193, no. 162.

[5] *Chester customs accounts, 1301–1566*, ed. K. P. Wilson (Liverpool, 1969; Record Society of Lancashire and Cheshire, cxi), *passim*.

[6] Childs, 'Ireland's trade with England', pp 19–20. Figures for 1479–80 include those in a separate account for Bristol's creeks, not included in Carus-Wilson, *Overseas trade of Bristol*, no. x.

the value was made up by red smoked herring; in the peak year of 1479–80 red herring worth £174 made up 14 per cent of the herring imports. Hake imports often ran at between 600 and 900 hundreds a year, worth some £300 to £400, and reached 1,235 hundreds worth £649 in 1479–80. Salmon reached a peak of 495 pipes worth £733 in 1479–80 but had dropped to some 364 pipes worth £600 in 1485–6 and fell further to £205 and £173 in value in 1486–7 and 1492–3. Altogether Ireland exported some three to four million seafish and many thousands of salmon to Bristol alone, and the value of the trade there compares well with the value of the hide trade in its important markets. For instance, typical cargoes for Flanders of 4,000 hides would be worth £160 to £200, and exceptional ones of 12,000 hides some £480 to £660, if sold at the Waterford selling prices known for the fifteenth century.[1]

In return for these goods Ireland imported cloth, wine, salt, metals, and a miscellany of other necessities and luxuries. Cloth from England went mainly through Bristol and Chester and was sent in a wide variety of qualities, weights, and colours, although these are concealed by the form of the customs accounts. These list cloth simply as *panni sine grano*, *panni in dimidio grano*, and *panni in grano* according to whether it is dyed without, partly, or wholly with the expensive kermes dye (grain). Those in which kermes was used paid a higher rate of duty on the assumption that they were better quality cloths. The others were dyed in a wide variety of greens, blues, blacks, greys, browns, and even reds (using madder). They might also include undyed cloth, but the term *sine grano* does not itself mean that the cloth was undyed and unfinished.

Part of the cloth trade was organised by the London mercers despite the lack of direct sea contact with Ireland. They probably sent most cloth through Bristol or Chester. A number of them appointed Dublin cloth merchants as their attorneys, several of whom in the early fifteenth century were named White,[2] possibly indicating a family specialising in this trade. Another strong branch of the trade was dominated by the Coventry merchants, exporting through Chester mainly midlands cloth, including some of Coventry, possibly partly made from imports of Irish wools and yarns.[3] A third branch was organised by the Bristol merchants. Only the trade through Bristol can be quantified from surviving customs accounts. In the 1370s Ireland took an average of 483 cloths of assize or their equivalent, about 20 per cent of Bristol's exports; between 1391 and 1404 this rose to 877 (ranging in fact from 480 to 1,237 cloths and 17 to 35 per cent of the exports). By the late fifteenth century Ireland took only half of this: in the peak recorded year only 528 cloths were sent, and between 1485 and 1505 consistently between 380 and 399, worth at customs valuations some £800. By now a measurable amount of miscellaneous goods

---

[1] See above, p. 501.

[2] *Cal. pat. rolls, 1396—9*, pp 79, 531; *1401—5*, pp 373, 395; *1416—22*, pp 236, 303.

[3] K. P. Wilson, 'The port of Chester in the later middle ages' (Ph.D. thesis, University of Liverpool, 1965), *passim*.

was sent, but this rarely exceeded £500 a year, thus not making up for the drop in cloth exports. The miscellaneous goods were mostly foodstuffs (beans, corn, malt, old wine, and salt), some alum for the cloth and leather industries, and a few manufactured goods, mostly batteryware (metal goods, often brass or copper, hammered into pots, pans, kettles, and the like). Large reexports of wine, salt, iron, and spices are conspicuously absent from Bristol accounts.[1]

Most of the wine consumed in medieval Ireland came from France, some from the ports of Normandy, Brittany, and La Rochelle, but much without doubt, given English domination of the area, from Bordeaux. A victualling order by Edward I appeared to expect 3,000 pipes of wine to be available in Ireland, and Irish exports from Bordeaux mentioned above would justify such expectation, but in the mid-fifteenth century wine imports from Bordeaux must have been much lower. It is clear that by then England itself, in taking 9,000 to 14,000 tuns a year, absorbed most of Bordeaux's total exports of 10,000 to 12,000 tuns a year and needed supplements elsewhere,[2] and little of this appears to have been reexported to Ireland. Imports by Irishmen themselves active in Bordeaux brought no more than 200 to 300 tuns a year, as shown above, and wine brought to Ireland by other nations active in Bordeaux might not have been much more: Professor Bernard's collection of notarial material for Bordeaux shows that only 22 out of 591 surviving contracts for the period 1455–99 mentioned Irish destinations or merchants, and in the busiest year, 1499, still only 300 tuns were recorded for Ireland. However, it must be recognised that surviving notarial registers provide records far from complete for trade.[3]

Supplies from La Rochelle as well as Bordeaux may have increased towards the end of the century with the Anglo-French truces after 1463 and the Anglo-French peace of 1475,[4] and more Spanish and Portuguese wine would have been available with the Iberian trade developments, but figures are absent. It has been suggested that the Iberian wine trade was concentrated in Limerick and Galway, and certainly ships sailed this route. In 1402 a Dartmouth ship, about which we have little detail, freighted by English merchants in Flanders, had been sent first to Spain, then to Ireland, where it was attacked twice by Irishmen and ransom paid. This may be the same ship as the *Gracedieu* of Dartmouth which arrived at Athenry in 1402 with wine and salt; two captains of Galway bribed the master of this ship with $207\frac{1}{2}$ marks to take the ship on to Galway while the merchants aboard slept. There the merchants were seized (two being killed) and held for ransom. Then the charters exchanged after this was paid were not honoured, and the merchants were plundered and ransomed a second time. The *Julian* of Bristol sailed from Lisbon to the west coast in 1453 with less trouble, and two Portuguese ships each with 50 tuns of 'fine Portuguese wines

[1] P.R.O., E. 122 (Bristol), *passim*; Childs, 'Ireland's trade with England', pp 16–18; Longfield, *Anglo-Irish trade*, pp 216–18.

[2] James, *Wine trade*, pp 41–2, 55–9.   [3] See above, p. 497.

[4] James, *Wine trade*, pp 48–50.

called Oseys' were present in Limerick in 1475.[1] However, while such instances indicate the presence of the trade they cannot indicate its scale. The western ports were relatively isolated and their Iberian links, which were so manifest in the sixteenth century, should not be pushed back too far without firmer proof; their role in the wine trade, as M. D. O'Sullivan indicated, may well have been overstated.[2] The apparent inability of Spanish and Portuguese vineyards to fill the gap left by the Bordeaux wines at Bristol, and the Spaniards' eagerness to move into the Bordeaux trade in the 1480s, warn against overestimation of their trade. The Iberian contribution to Bristol's wine trade, already some 300 tuns in 1391, did not exceed 600 until 1486, and imports at south-coast ports and London were lower.[3]

Salt, necessary for preserving both fish and hides, came to the east coast from Chester until about 1450, when it disappears from Chester records.[4] Ireland must then have relied entirely on her continental sources. Salt came from south-west Spain and Portugal and in abundance from the Bay of Bourgneuf. From early in the fourteenth century Irishmen such as Ralph Kenefeg of Drogheda were buying in the Bay, and a ship of Limerick and two of Wexford were loading salt in the Bay port of Le Collet in 1383.[5] Bretons too were active, such as the four, one of whom, Garcianus de Mon Reall, lived in Ireland, who loaded three small ships with salt and other commodities worth 700 marks for Ireland in 1412, and who found themselves captured at sea by John Penkeston, a Dublin citizen, who had letters of reprisal granted against Bretons by the king's lieutenant in Ireland.[6] Englishmen also joined the suppliers: Thomas de Byndon of Southampton was sending 1,000 quarters of salt to Galway in 1335 and in 1435 John Gayncote of Dartmouth joined a group of five Drogheda merchants in a plan to bring eight 200-ton ships from Brittany loaded with salt, iron, and other goods.[7] Ireland probably sought most of her salt directly, given that reexports through Bristol were so small and her needs for the fishing industry so great: the largest amount recorded from Bristol was some 69 tons worth £59 in 1479–80. This would have been enough to salt a maximum of 90,000 herrings,[8] much less than the quantity of fish sent to Bristol itself.

Despite contemporary reports of Ireland's richness in ores she had to import metals, but the volume remains totally unassessable. The rich iron mines of Biscay and Guipuzcoa which provided most of England's imports were near, and the voyages to Spain for iron and salt for Ireland were planned by London, Bristol, and Dublin merchants.[9] Some iron, possibly reexported from Spain,

[1] *Cal. pat. rolls, 1401–5*, pp 134, 186–7; Carus-Wilson, *Overseas trade of Bristol*, pp 106–9; *Stat. Ire., 12–22 Edw. IV*, p. 379. [2] O'Sullivan, *Old Galway*, pp 37, 45.

[3] W. R. Childs, *Anglo-Castilian trade in the later middle ages* (Manchester, 1979), pp 132–6.

[4] Wilson, 'Port of Chester', p. 84.

[5] R.I.A., MS 12. D. 12, p. 84; Touchard, *Commerce maritime Breton*, p. 389.

[6] *Cal. pat. rolls, 1408–13*, p. 474.

[7] *Cal. close rolls, 1337–9*, p. 27; *Rot. pat. Hib.*, p. 257, nos 39, 68.

[8] A. R. Bridbury, *England and the salt trade in the later middle ages* (Oxford, 1955), pp 3, 160.

[9] *Rot. pat. Hib.*, p. 257, nos 33, 48.

was available from Gascony. Reexports from Bristol were minimal: the highest recorded export was 6¾ tons valued at £27 in 1492–3. Manufactured metal goods were no more important, with the largest amount, exported in 1479–80, being only 12¾ hundredweights valued at £25. 10s. 0d.

Luxuries such as silks and spices were certainly available in Ireland, as they appear in tariff lists, but there is little evidence about their arrival, apart from some mention in customs accounts of the northern flavourings of saffron and liquorice. Amounts would have been modest and are no doubt included in the phrase 'and other things' so often used to describe a cargo when piracy or robbery was reported. Reexports from Bristol were slight, although silk featured occasionally, and the small exports of one to four pounds of silk had risen to 98 pounds worth £65. 6s. 8d. in 1492–3 and to 243 pounds worth £162 in 1504–5. Perhaps many such luxuries were brought direct from the great international entrepôt of Bruges.

THAT Ireland's foreign trade was extensive in area and in variety of goods is clear, but, in the absence of good Irish quantitative records, its total scale is not, whether in terms of volume, value, or numbers of men and ships involved. However, a combination of Irish and external sources suggests some order of magnitude for some aspects of the trade even if figures cannot be precise.

Records of total receipts at the Irish exchequer from the ancient custom on exports of wool, woolfells, and hides survive for various years between 1275 and 1345, conveniently tabulated by Mac Niocaill.[1] They do not differentiate between the three commodities, which paid at the rates of 6s. 8d. a sack of wool, 6s. 8d. on 300 woolfells, and 13s. 4d. on 200 hides, but they provide figures of possible maxima. The trade was at its height in the 1270s and 1280s with a maximum possible average export of 4,000 to 4,500 sacks of wool a year, or 400,000 to 450,000 hides; the busy period of April 1277 to September 1278 with receipts of £2,026, noted by Lydon, would represent 6,078 sacks or 607,800 hides or 1,820,000 wool-fells.[2] The exports dropped dramatically in the 1290s and by the mid-fourteenth century ran at about one-quarter of their peak, at something over 1,000 sacks or 100,000 hides a year. It is difficult to suggest reasons for the initial fall in the 1290s recently shown by McNeill.[3] Possibly Edward I's emphasis on corn supplies encouraged some Irish landlords to swing towards arable farming; but more likely it reflects the fall of the Riccardi, whose period of untroubled control of the customs collection precisely coincides with the

[1] Mac Niocaill, Na buirgéisí, ii, 523–8.
[2] Lydon, Lordship, pp 90–91.
[3] McNeill, Anglo-Norman Ulster, pp 42, 132–5. While the calculation there used of monthly averages and estimates for part-years is not always wise for such seasonal commodities, his graph and tables certainly, and no doubt correctly, highlight the plunge in exports of the 1290s; but his failure to show on the graph that there are no figures for 1291, and on the graph and in his table that the 1292 figure is still high, is misleading; the fall may well be as late as 1293 or even 1294, and not immediately after 1290 as the graph implies.

peaks of wool exports at Waterford and New Ross from 1275 to 1290. In 1294 the Riccardi fell dramatically, losing all their offices and having their goods confiscated. R. W. Kaeuper disagrees with M. D. O'Sullivan's suggestion that they were in trouble from 1290, and has no doubt that they were still in a strong position in 1294,[1] and, despite McNeill's presentation of the material, the actual customs receipts would not in fact be at variance with this. Figures for 1278–90 show receipts at £1,200 to £1,700 a year; there are no figures for 1291, but receipts still reached some £1,460 in 1292;[2] even 1293, although beginning to show a fall, whether receipts were £956 or £887, is not out of line with 1276–7 and might have been no more than a short fluctuation. However, in 1294 the fall is clear.

The Riccardi were clearly heavily engaged in the wool trade: their English buying included very large individual purchases up to 120 sacks; they had export licences for 1,080 sacks from England in 1273, which made them the second biggest Italian exporting company even before they acquired their privileges; the initial seizure of foreign wools in 1294 showed them then as the biggest single company. Part of their confiscated Irish wools sold in 1298 for over £1,996, and probably amounted to 662 sacks; there was still in Ireland in 1301 confiscated Riccardi wool, which the king proposed to sell to the Frescobaldi.[4] Although the fall of the Riccardi cannot account for the whole fall in receipts, the removal of a company possibly dealing in well over 1,000 sacks a year could account for a substantial single part of it. No other Italian company took over their position until the Frescobaldi in 1304. By that time, given complaints of internal disturbances and dislocation because of the French war,[5] it may have proved too difficult to resurrect trade on the Riccardi scale.

Although it remains difficult to explain fully the initial fall of the wool and hide receipts, that they should remain low in the 1340s is not surprising and can well be explained by Edwardian wool taxes and staple policies which would have hit Irish wools hard. The frequency of references in the later fourteenth and fifteenth centuries to hides and decreasing references to wool suggests that by then, if not before, hides rather than wool were the major export. Whether this later trade ran at mid-fourteenth-century levels (the last for which we have any figures) or had improved or declined further is unknown. However, exports of some 100,000 hides (as implied by the mid-fourteenth-century receipts) would fit perfectly well with the fragmentary later information on the size of shipments of hides to Flanders and Pisa mentioned above. No sources provide any indication of total exports of goods other than wool, fells, and hides.

[1] Richard W. Kaeuper, *Bankers to the crown: the Riccardi of Lucca and Edward I* (Princeton, 1973), pp 214–19; M. D. O'Sullivan, 'Italian merchant bankers and the collection of the customs in Ireland, 1275–1311' in *Med. studies presented to A. Gwynn*, pp 174–7.

[2] Mac Niocaill, *Na buirgéisí*, ii, 523–8.

[3] Ibid.; McNeill, *Anglo-Norman Ulster*, p. 134.

[4] Kaeuper, *Bankers*, pp 37, 44–5, 222–3.

[5] Ibid., pp 178, 183.

Total import figures are even more difficult. Wine prise figures for 1267–1366 are again tabulated by Mac Niocaill,[1] but they are patchier and harder to interpret than ancient custom receipts. The king's wine prise was taken at the rate of one tun from ships carrying 10 to 19 tuns and two tuns from those carrying 20 or over (those carrying under 10 were exempt). Dublin was clearly the busiest port and 56 tuns were taken as prise for the two years 1301–3; this would represent an import of between 560 and 1,064 tuns if all the prise was taken from cargoes between 10 and 19 tuns, or of 1,120 tuns upwards if all came from cargoes of 20 tuns upwards. In fact, at this time Irish ships loading at Bordeaux took on average some 90 tuns apiece;[2] thus we should perhaps think of the 56 tuns as two tuns from each of 28 larger vessels carrying about 90 tuns each, representing an import of 2,520 tuns for the two years, or some 1,260 tuns a year. Drogheda wine imports on similar tentative calculations may have been about 1,000 tuns a year at this time. It must, however, be strongly emphasised that these figures, like those of possible wool exports, calculated from tax returns, provide us with a possible order of magnitude and not precise trade figures. Wine prise figures, like wool, drop towards the mid-fourteenth century so that on the above calculations Dublin's imports for 1335–8 and 1346–66 might have been 180 tuns a year, Drogheda's for 1348–66 under 90, and Waterford's some 180 for 1335–8 and 90 for 1348–66. This fall is due to the same reasons as in England: prise was no longer taken from aliens after 1303 and, more importantly, Bordeaux's wine exports were severely cut back after 1336 with the outbreak of the hundred years war.[3] Supplements of wine came from La Rochelle, Spain, and Portugal, but individual shipments, where known, rarely exceeded 50 tuns. It seems unlikely, whatever happened in the sixteenth century, that Ireland's wine imports ran greatly in excess of 1,500 tuns a year in the fifteenth.[4]

It is equally difficult to approach the scale of Irish trade through its particular geographical branches, given a similar dearth of quantitative material and the form of that which does survive abroad. But it does seem clear that Ireland's trade was limited. For Portugal and Spain there are only minimal scraps of customs accounts for some Guipuzcoan ports for a few months in the 1290s which show no Irish activity.[5] The local accounts for Dieppe survive much better and are tabulated for 1470–80 but show no trade with Ireland.[6] Three surviving pilotage accounts for Bruges, where one might expect more involvement given the trade in Irish hides, show a Breton cargo of Irish hides in 1486–7, three ships which might be English or Irish in 1499, but no links with

---

[1] Mac Niocaill, op. cit., p. 512.

[2] In 1303–4 the actual cargoes of the eighteen ships were in tuns, 142, 147, 50, 120, 136½, 70, 99½, 70½, 100½, 84, 72, 152½, 61, 86, 62, 71, 60, 63½ (P.R.O., E. 101/158/10).

[3] James, *Wine trade*, p. 32; they fell from over 74,000 tuns in 1335–6 to some 16,500 in 1336–7 and rarely rose over 20,000 thereafter.

[4] Above, pp 489, 507–8.

[5] Printed in Mercedes Gaibrois Riaño de Ballesteros, *Historia del Reinado de Sancho IV* (3 vols, Madrid, 1922–8), i, pp iii ff.

[6] Michel Mollat, *Comptabilité du port de Dieppe au XVᵉ siècle* (Paris, 1951), *passim*.

Ireland in 1500.[1] The accounts for Pisa show the arrival of Irish hides but no Irish carriage. The Bordeaux wine accounts do show a significant but declining activity in the period, but give no inkling of the total trade bound for Ireland.

Only in England do the comparatively full customs accounts allow more accurate assessment, and even here there are problems: while the Irish merchants' activity is reasonably although not completely identifiable, English merchants trading with Ireland are much more difficult to pick out except at Bristol where destinations and last ports of call of ships are consistently given.[2] It is clear that Irish merchants' activity outside Chester, Bristol, and Bridgwater was limited. Even in nearby Wales, Lewis's work showed little Irish activity, although admittedly here sources are very sparse;[3] away from the Irish Sea Irish participation was severely limited. Devon and Cornwall had one or two Irish ships in a year, but many accounts record no activity at all and further east the numbers drop fast. Only two Irish ships appear in Southampton's accounts for the fourteenth century and none for the fifteenth. In a few cases cargoes on English ships are specified as Irish, as with the ten lasts of white Irish herring at Exeter in 1358, but most are not, and fish cargoes are not necessarily from Ireland. Overall the discernible Irish sea-trade seems small with the south-western ports and negligible with Southampton, Sandwich, and London, despite the presence of Irish cloth for reexport there.[4] Although London merchants were prepared to invest heavily in the sea-route (if the claim is true that the 320-ton *Mary* of London, sent to Ross for pilgrims for Santiago in 1477, carried goods worth 6,000 marks for trade in Ireland),[5] it is likely that many contacts were overland through Bristol or Chester, where the accounts show the trade to be overwhelmingly concentrated. Unfortunately even here there are problems.

The form of Chester's accounts makes the scale and balance of her trade less easy to determine than Bristol's. Ireland certainly played little part in Chester's wine and iron trade but was overwhelmingly important in her general trade. In 1404–5 over 80 per cent of the entrances and exits, where provenance and destination are discernible, concerned Ireland and from 1422, when details of incoming shipping appear, over two-thirds of it is Irish. Yet it remains impossible to quantify the trade or compare it with Bristol's since most cargoes are unspecified and given simply by the horse or cart load.[6]

At Bristol, where the substantial Irish connection was already evident in the

[1] Jules Finot, *Étude historique sur les relations commerciales entre la Flandre et l'Espagne au moyen âge* (Paris, 1899), pp 217, 232–3.

[2] Tabulated information on commodities and shipping from the customs accounts of Bristol, Bridgwater, and Chester are given in Childs, 'Ireland's trade with England'.

[3] E. A. Lewis, 'A contribution to the commercial history of Wales' in *Y Cymmrodor: the magazine of the Honourable Society of Cymmrodorion*, xxiv (1913), pp 86–188.

[4] P.R.O., E. 122, *passim*; S.C. 6 (Haveners' Accounts for Cornwall); Devon Record Office, local customs accounts; Southampton Civic Centre, local port books.

[5] *Cal. pat. rolls, 1476–85*, p. 78.

[6] *Chester customs*, *passim*.

naming of Irish Mead[1] and in the attempts to get rid of Irish immigrants in times of economic difficulties,[2] the trade can be fully assessed. Ireland's total exports to Bristol, carried by Irish and other ships, amounted to a customs valuation of £2,091 in 1403–4, reached £3,100 in 1479–80, dropped to between £1,400 and £1,800 for the rest of the century, then rose to £3,143 in 1504–5. Details for particular commodities have been given above. The imports made up 40 per cent of the value of Bristol's imports in 1403–4 (excluding wines, which might be valued at another £5,000) but dropped to 33 per cent by 1479–80 and below 20 per cent thereafter. In return Ireland took, as shown above, some 877 cloths a year in the fourteenth century, but under 400 at the end of the fifteenth century together with about £500 of other goods by that date. The cloth then made up only 7 to 11 per cent of Bristol's total cloth exports.

The balance of this trade was consistently although not enormously in Ireland's favour. This was partly offset by trade in the smaller ports of the Bristol Channel, as at Bridgwater, where trade between England and Ireland was always in England's favour. But this trade was on a much smaller scale: cloth exports at Bridgwater were usually under 20 a year, and miscellaneous exports worth under £100. It was not uncommon for ships from Ireland to unload at Bristol, leave with little or no cargo, but call at Bridgwater or Axwater for beans and a few cloths on the return journey. The constant trade of ships of Tenby, Minehead, and the like between Ireland and Bristol, sometimes sailing in from their homeports with fish and Irish cloth, indicates a similar coasting trade. However, whether all these taken together would redress the balance at Bristol is unknown.

Although records make it clear that all nations were involved in the supply of shipping for Ireland's trade, only at Bristol is a full analysis possible, and on this route, not surprisingly, the shipping is overwhelmingly Irish and British. Between 1376 and 1404 in 71 recorded entrances from and 276 exits to Ireland only two foreign ships appear, one Breton, one Norman. Between 1465 and 1493 among 400 recorded entrances from and 240 exits to Ireland the only foreign ships noted are four from Brittany, two from Lisbon, and one from Spain. Nor is there much evidence for the triangular trade which included Ireland, as most ships sailed directly back from their recorded destination. Half the ships in the fourteenth century and two-thirds in the fifteenth were English and Welsh, mostly from Bristol, but joined by increasing numbers of west country and Welsh ships in the fifteenth century, especially from Minehead and Milford. The Irish shipping, which dropped from a half to one-third over the period, came from all ports from Drogheda to Limerick, but mainly from

[1] Now Rosemary Street, but known as Irish Mead (*pratum ybernicum*) since c. 1200; see M. D. Lobel and E. M. Carus-Wilson, 'Bristol' in M. D. Lobel (ed.), *The atlas of historic towns*, ii (London, 1975), p. 8.
[2] Harassment was intermittent and worst in the first half of the fifteenth century; Carus-Wilson, *Merchant venturers*, p. 20. For the general English context of legislation against Irish immigrants, see Cosgrove, *Late med. Ire.*, pp 32–6; see also below, pp 518–19.

the five southern ports of Waterford, Cork, Kinsale, Youghal, and Wexford in that order of frequency. At Bridgwater the picture was similar in the fifteenth century with Irish ships making up a third of those involved, and with only one foreign ship, a Portuguese. The same Irish ports were busy but led in this instance by Youghal and Wexford. At Chester we can trace only incoming shipping and the pattern of involvement by Irish ports was naturally different. Most ships came from Dublin, Malahide, and Howth; Drogheda made the only other significant contribution. As at Bristol, there was a drop in the active Irish shipping.[1]

There is no evidence that this drop was offset by an increase in the size of ships, and indeed this would be against the European trend towards more economical small vessels. The accounts in fact give little information on the type and tunnage of vessels. At Bristol most are called *navis* or *batella* and are probably typical northern square-rigged, clinker-built vessels; cargoes unloaded rarely exceeded 20 to 30 tons, indicating that most were small.

Despite the drop, Irish shipping was still busy. Usually between 13 and 24 Irish ships a year brought goods to Bristol and at Bridgwater 6 to 18 Irish ships could be found annually. At Chester 10 or 11 still appeared each year to the end of the century. At these three ports one can identify for the decade 1480–89 an Irish fleet of 100 to 120 ships and at least 120 active working shipmasters.

With such materials the precise charting of overall changes in Ireland's overseas trade remains difficult, but some trends appear likely. The trade in corn dropped. The trade in wool, woolfells, and hides also dropped to a quarter of its former size between the 1270s and 1340s. This happened just when internal troubles might have been expected to encourage a move from arable to pasture, but, if this was so, the encouragement was more than offset by the withdrawal of Italian buyers, the swing away from sheep-rearing by the Cistercians, the inconveniences of the staple system, the Flemish industrial troubles, and the greater difficulty Irish wool probably had in supporting the high wool taxes of Edward III. It is likely, however, that in the overall decline there was a shift from wool to hides.

Whether the dramatic losses were offset by other gains is doubtful. The lighter furs did not become a major trade; although the growth of the textile industry must have helped, it was not a growth from nothing; and both woollen and linen exports to England, while rising, remained modest into the sixteenth century. The scale of the fish trade is impossible to discern for the fourteenth century with so few figures, but certainly in the fifteenth century the trade to Bristol shows fluctuations but no growth, despite the increase of herring shoals around south-western Ireland.

Ireland's imports of salt from Chester ceased about 1450, and her imports of cloth from Bristol dropped by half in the fifteenth century. Whether such losses were made up by imports from Bourgneuf and by her own cloth industry

[1] Childs, 'Ireland's trade with England', pp 26, 28–9.

remains unclear. Wine exports by Irishmen from Bordeaux dropped by four-fifths over the period and Ireland's total wine imports no doubt dropped as did England's. Irish shipping activity in the Irish Sea was declining and it is unlikely that it was increasing much elsewhere. Trade with Iberia may have been a bright spot, with growth in the fourteenth and fifteenth centuries, but Norman and possibly Breton trade seems to have remained low into the sixteenth.

The overall picture, admittedly still obscure, seems to be of a trade flourishing in the late thirteenth century but already dropping steeply by the mid-fourteenth century even before the disruptions of the Black Death. Perhaps it stabilised at a lower level after the Black Death, but in the late fifteenth century, to judge simply on the English evidence, may have drifted further downwards in the 1480s and 1490s. There was potential for expansion, as the Bristol account for 1504–5 analysed by Longfield shows; but if this is a part of a general increase, it is an expansion lagging a generation behind the rest of Europe, where growth is visible from the 1480s in general trade.

The difficulties and lack of recovery of the mid-fourteenth and fifteenth centuries should certainly be seen against the general northern European developments of the time, where a lower volume of trade followed the Black Death, with a reduced demand for basic agricultural products; although supplies for luxury industries might have been in increased demand it is unlikely that these would have made up for losses in more general demand. Added to this general problem were ones specifically relating to Ireland's political dependence on England. It is possible that the English king's changing relations with the Riccardi had first encouraged and then struck hard at the export of Irish wool; it is certain that warfare between England and her nearest neighbours, France and Scotland, hit Ireland quite hard in cutting off some markets and making voyages more dangerous; it is probable that Edward III's wool taxes hit the inferior Irish wool harder than it hit the English; and it is likely that the staple system based on Calais was indeed, as Irish merchants complained, much more inconvenient for them than for Englishmen. Further problems were added by Ireland's internal political unrest which no doubt made maintenance of trade levels, let alone recovery, more burdensome. The troubles led at times to emigration sufficiently high to worry English governments, who legislated to send the Irish home, but, in general, English government policies did little to resolve Irish problems. The general pattern of internal difficulty seems to be in line with evidence for the particular case of Waterford recently presented by Lydon,[1] and no doubt similar cases could be put for Youghal which complained of frequent sea and land attacks by 'English rebels' in 1462,[2] Cork which cited suburban churches destroyed by rebels over the last 50 years, also in 1462,[3] and Drogheda which was granted the honour of

[1] Lydon, 'Medieval Waterford', pp 5–15.
[2] *Cal. pat. rolls, 1461–7*, pp 225–6. [3] Ibid., p. 214.

having a sword carried before the mayor for its active help against John Orailby (O'Reilly?), a leader of the hostile Gaelic Irish.[1]

The complaints of men killed, countryside burned, ships plundered, and money diverted to defence and taxes certainly left fewer resources in time, men, and money for investment in trade; yet, as Lydon pointed out in the case of Waterford, the picture cannot be entirely gloomy. Trade was not restricted to the dwindling Anglo-Irish centres: the 'Irish enemies' and 'English rebels' had produce to sell and a need for imported goods, and peaceful trade, both licensed and illicit, took place. Further, the new building in Irish ports indicates some spare wealth. Moreover, the complaints are likely to be exaggerated, and medieval merchants on all routes had to face a level of piracy and robbery quite unacceptably high by modern western European expectations. Profits seem to have been good enough to encourage all nationalities to persist in the Irish trade; and yet there may well have been a greater risk to Irish trade, not just of damage, but in the unsettled areas of failing to obtain justice and reparations through the law courts when damage was done. In the absence of Irish records there is no way of estimating this, but it is noticeable that in the cases pursued into the English chancery or council the complaints of merchants rarely cite specifically Irish political troubles but more often the normal problems of fraud, broken contracts, and foreign piracy.

MUCH remains to be done on the organisation of Ireland's overseas trade, but some general comment is possible. The trade was protected and controlled by legislation passed in England and applicable to Ireland, despite the claim of the Irish parliament in 1460 to be bound only by its own laws, a claim prompted by the English civil war when the duke of York took refuge there from a conviction for treason passed in the English parliament in 1459. Irish merchants were expected to pay the same duties as in England, to have their dealings with alien merchants regulated by the Carta Mercatoria of 1303, and to accept the inconveniences of the staple system, although here they were allowed some concessions. They had to run their businesses in accordance with the common law, borough customs, and the law merchant; their goods had to comply with standards and weights and measures ordained in England. In one way, however, they were hampered as their English contemporaries were not, being forbidden to trade with the Gaelic Irish; this prohibition would have robbed the Anglo-Irish merchants of a large and increasing part of their hinterland if it had ever been fully obeyed.

The wealth and status of merchants actively involved in Ireland's overseas trade require closer study, but it is clear from Bristol records that they included men of a wide variety of fortunes. At one end of the spectrum were merchants such as William Canyngs and Richard Spicer, who might handle cargoes worth over £200 a year; in the middle range were men handling cargoes worth £50 to

[1] *Cal. pat. rolls, 1467–77*, p. 193.

£100; and at the other end were men with cargoes worth 2s. 6d. or even 1s. 8d., who were probably simple crewmen.

Mercantile organisation on Irish routes was similar to that in most of northern Europe. The merchants did not need the elaborate techniques of the Italian companies with great investments in long-distance routes and networks of overseas branches; and in comparison with such companies their techniques look elementary. However, the techniques were sophisticated enough for the scale of their trade. Merchants trading regularly in ports over short distances had less need of permanent representation there except perhaps through an occasional factor; they could easily build up a circle of contacts; and the organisation of medieval ports, with their customs collectors, weighers, porters, and innkeepers, as well as official brokers, provided plenty of middle-men to put buyer and seller in touch. It was also possible to find fellow country-men who had emigrated and who might provide contacts for men from home. In 1412 Garcianus de Mon Reall was described as 'now dwelling in Ireland' and was still trading in Breton salt with three other Bretons, Alan Corre, Martin Lorgle of the Ile de Batz, and John Gychard of Nantes.[1] Jenico Marks of Gascony, who had come to Dublin aged eight, remained for the rest of his life, and in the other direction one Bernard d'Irlande was an active merchant of Bordeaux in the 1440s.[2] William Waleys of Lancaster and Robert Langherst of Newcastle-upon-Tyne described themselves as Drogheda residents when they complained that Richard Walter, master of the *Christopher* of Dartmouth, had deliberately run down the *George* of Wells with their goods in a strong wind off Dartmouth in 1440.[3] Thomas Archibald, born in Ireland, was a citizen of Lon-don in 1477;[4] and Denis Galway, a Bristol shipmaster experienced on the Andalusia route, and Henry May, a substantial Bristol merchant, were only two of many Irishmen in the port who made careers despite occasional harass-ment.[5] John Bannebury of Bristol died in 1404 holding two watermills and other tenements in Limerick as well as his Bristol property, and Richard Boys of Coventry held a shop in Dublin at his death in 1471.[6] Wilson's study of Chester has shown the particularly strong links of Coventry and Dublin men who traded through Chester: Christopher Hegley married a Dublin woman, and in Chester, in 1474–5, of sixteen new members of the gild merchant, seven were also freemen of Dublin.[7] In the small world of medieval commerce it was not hard to find an acquaintance to vouch for reliability or stand as formal guarantor or help to store goods.

[1] *Cal. pat. rolls, 1408–13*, p. 474.
[2] *Stat. Ire. Hen. VI*, p. 399; Bernard, 'Maritime intercourse', p. 13.
[3] P.R.O., C. 1/43/33, 44/278.
[4] *Cal. pat. rolls, 1476–85*, p. 16.
[5] See above, pp 512–13; below, pp 518–19.
[6] *Notes or abstracts of the wills contained in the volume entitled the Great Orphan Book and Book of Wills*, ed. T. P. Wadley (Bristol, 1886), pp 70–71; *Register of wills and inventories of the diocese of Dublin . . . 1457–83*, ed. H. F. Berry (Dublin, 1898), pp 8–11.
[7] Wilson, 'Port of Chester', pp 87–94.

Some more formal organisation for cooperation might be found in gilds for visiting merchants, exemplified in Dublin, where merchants from England, and especially those of London, Coventry, and Chester, had by 1460 acquired a royal charter for a fraternity by which, it was claimed, they intended to control shipping for England. By 1479 this gild had a chapel and by 1481 it was incorporated. The gild clearly upset the Dublin merchants but it may have been partly in response to the trading restrictions in their own gild merchant regulations of 1452. Their gild had existed at least since the reign of Henry V, but its restrictions may have become tighter in the difficult times of the mid-fifteenth century.[1]

The businesses were carried on by single merchants, some travelling, some remaining at home, with family, servants, or temporary agents to help them. In the absence of private papers and account books the terms of family cooperation, employment, and agency are unknown, but glimpses of the daily routine can come from lawsuits, grants and licences, and wills. An informative case is that of Thomas Mustard of Bristol, who exported 15 great sacks of wool from Clonmel in 1319 by his servant Walter atte Strode of Waterford. Walter was to use the sale price of the wool, £100, to buy wine in Bordeaux, but his purchase of 33 tuns (partly for cash and partly for goods) was incomplete when he died. Because he died intestate the goods and money were seized, and Mustard had to sue for their return. His proofs of ownership show how close the circle of merchants was. He found at Bordeaux one Waterford merchant who had been present at Waterford when Walter was engaged, and again when the wool was handed over and instructions given, and who had heard Walter in Bordeaux often say that all the goods were Mustard's. Another Waterford merchant then in Bordeaux had been frequently told that Walter was of Mustard's livery and had himself heard from Walter how the business was going.[2]

The Mays of Bristol show something of the sweep of family association. From 1432 Henry May, originally from Ireland, traded through Bristol to Iceland, Bordeaux, and Portugal and owned at least one ship, the *Trinity* of Bristol. A lawsuit in 1443, involving Portuguese merchants whom he had helped against pirates, reveals his association with Richard May of London, possibly a brother, who was trading in Lisbon and who was arrested there to put pressure on Henry during the lawsuit. Richard was still trading in Lisbon in 1452 with a Portuguese safe-conduct and was certainly receiving Iberian cargoes in London in 1442–3 and 1456–7. By this time Henry May was also in dispute with the mayor of Bristol. In 1456, now describing himself as twenty-two years a commoner and freeman of Bristol, he sued Richard Hatter (mayor 1455) and John Shipward (mayor 1456) for 'discommoning' him and depriving him

---

[1] *Register of wills*, ed. Berry, p. 194; *Stat. Ire.*, *12—22 Edw. IV*, pp 769 ff; Charles Gross, *The gild merchant* (2 vols, Oxford, 1890), ii, 61 ff.

[2] *Select cases concerning the law merchant*, ed. Charles Gross and Hubert Hall (3 vols, London, 1908–32; Selden Society, xliii, xlvi, xlix), ii, 150–51.

of the freeman's right to trade, and for doing the same to four of his supporters (some possibly Irishmen), George Roche, Thomas Fraunces, Thomas Walsshe, and Nicholas Hoker. Shipward's defence was simply that the town council had absolute rights to admit and dismiss from the freedom of the town, but clearly May won the support of chancery and it ordered his reinstatement. However, although this was done on the Monday after St Valentine's day, by the following Friday he had again been ejected and men had been sent by the council to board up his shop windows and stop his trading. The original reason for the dispute seems to have been over the high admission fee to the freedom of the town proposed for Henry's apprentice, another Richard May, born in Ireland. The council claimed that admission depended on a proven seven-year apprenticeship, abstention during this time from trading in the apprentice's own name, adequate testimony from a burgess, and payment of a discretionary sum, and alleged that Richard had not presented his indentures proving his seven-year training nor paid the fee. Henry alleged that indentures did not have to be produced, that oath of the master would do, that it was common practice for apprentices to trade for themselves with their master's permission, and that the fee charged should be 2s. as for English-born candidates and not the outrageous 104s. demanded on the strength of a recent ordinance of the town council because he was born in Ireland. Henry refused to let Richard present himself at this price. It seems that in the end Henry won, as he was still trading in Bristol in 1460, as was Richard May in 1461; however, it is not clear whether he won proudly or had to rebuy his freedom 'with the blood of his purse and with weeping eye', as Ricart's *Kalendar* puts it with gusto.[1] Neither Henry nor Richard appears to have traded with their home country, but John May, who was also associated with Henry and probably of the same family, did so. John May's trade stretched beyond Ireland as his goods were aboard the *Julian* of Bristol when she reached Southampton after a voyage to Portugal, Ireland, and Plymouth on the way to Normandy or Zeeland.[2]

Joint-stock arrangements are revealed in the lawsuit between two Coventry men who invested jointly in a voyage between Brittany and Ireland to pay off their ransom there. Such arrangements explain too the identical cargoes for five Bristol merchants aboard the *Katherine*, arrived from Ireland on 15 September 1486, when each man had 10 pipes of salmon, one last and 12 dickers of hides, and 1,300 yards of Irish linen worth £42. 16s. 8d. Similar joint cargoes can be found in Bristol in 1480, when three merchants each exported to Ireland 10 cloths without grain, 3 tuns of corrupt wine, 4 tuns of salt, 2 barrels of honey, 1 cwt of alum, and 40 lbs of dyed hair (probably coarse wool) worth £12. 13s. 4d. excluding the cloth.[3]

[1] Robert Ricart, *The maire of Bristowe is kalendar*, ed. Lucy Toulmin Smith (London, 1872; Camden Society, v), p. 41.

[2] Many family details in Carus-Wilson, *Overseas trade of Bristol*; see also P.R.O, E. 122 (Bristol), *passim*; C. 1/17/30, 17/213–15, 19/409; PRO. 31/8/153, f. 642; E. 159/210, Recorda, Michaelmas, mm 34–5d.

[3] P.R.O., C. 1/11/506; E. 122/20/5; Carus-Wilson, *Overseas trade of Bristol*, p. 269.

The inventory of the goods of Richard Boys of Coventry, who died in Dublin in 1471, illustrates English dealings there. Boys's main property and family remained in Coventry, but he had a shop in Dublin and stored goods in the houses of other merchants, one of Drogheda and one of Navan 'otherwise of London'. His main business was selling cloth of various qualities—10 dozens of superior cloth were valued at £30 and 6 dozens of lesser quality at £13. He sold for cash, but also for credit secured by 'a paper written by the hand of the said Nicholas' (Nicholas Bourke of Dublin), and he was also owed smaller amounts in goatskins and linen, which may indicate barter. The wills of John Oge Blake in 1420 and of John Blake in 1468 seem to show that barter was widespread in the west, with long lists of Gaelic Irish debts expressed in hides.[1]

Disputes over bargains and credit show the international flavour of Ireland's trade. Walter Mannyn, an immigrant from Dartmouth to Drogheda, master of the barge *Marie de Martha* (*sic*), contracted a debt of 15 marks in Bordeaux to Piers Belenguey, a butcher there, and found himself sued by Belenguey's wife and imprisoned in London. William Bargayn, a Breton merchant, bought £50 of goods in Ireland from Geoffrey Lynch, an Irish mariner, and bound himself by his 'bill of his hand writyng' to pay Geoffrey when he returned from selling in Portugal. This, he claimed, he did within a short time of his return to Ireland, but, 'not havyng mys trust of any deseit', he neglected to have the bill returned or cancelled and found Lynch suing him in a Bristol court for the full amount again.[2] Clearly credit on this sort of international scale implied steady trading with regular contacts, but voyages to more distant areas could call for more *ad hoc* arrangements, as Nicholas Abbot's well-known voyage to Iceland shows. Abbot of Drogheda, Richard Byrne of Dublin, Jenkin Alderseye and John Glover of Chester, and John Symkoke and Robert Preston of Drogheda freighted a Drogheda ship in February 1457 to sail from there to Westmony in Iceland with Irish goods well suited, as they said, to trade in Iceland; but when it arrived the season for fish was past and all fish had already been taken by English merchants. Abbot, Byrne, Alderseye, and Glover were there in person and Symkoke and Preston had sent factors. These consulted, and Abbot agreed to stay over in Iceland to sell their goods and have ready a return cargo for next season, and the others agreed to send a ship the following May. Unfortunately they did not, and Abbot, when he finally returned, sued them in parliament for his losses of £45 and his labour because he ran into the usual problem of overseas traders, that contracts made abroad were not admissible in common law courts.[3]

Professor Bernard's examination of Bordeaux documents for the late fifteenth century confirms the presence of all these practices in Irish trade there: consignments of cargoes to servants or agents or shipmasters; temporary

[1] *Register of wills*, ed. Berry, pp 8–11; O'Flaherty, *West Connaught*, pp 198–201, 205–10.
[2] P.R.O., C. 1/16/67, 31/65.
[3] *Stat. Ire.*, 1—12 Edw. IV, pp 696–8.

partnerships; payments in cash and kind; credit transactions; and elementary insurance schemes.[1]

The merchants probably had little difficulty finding suitable shipping since shipowning was attractive to all classes. Most owners were merchants or working owner-masters, but members of the upper classes, such as Sir Edmund Mulso and Lord Talbot, hired out ships for trade.[2] Some vessels were jointly owned. Some investment took place in other towns: Maurice Wyse of Bristol owned the *John* of Waterford.[3] Non-working owners might employ a regular master for their ship, or alternatively employ a variety of masters, each for a single voyage. They might even split a voyage to get the most experienced master on a particular route, as when Richard Bye hired one master to take his ship from Zeeland to Winchelsea and another to take it on from Winchelsea to Bordeaux and then to Ireland.[4] The terms of each voyage were carefully laid down in charter-parties between the merchants and the masters, determining destinations, turnaround times, and freight charges, with clear penalties for default. Flexibility was often allowed in destinations to take account of weather or market conditions. This is seen in the charter-party negotiated by Chester merchants in 1393–4 for a voyage to either Bordeaux or La Rochelle where the ship would wait for 21 days before sailing to Dalkey; there it would be decided whether to go on to Drogheda or not. Similarly the *Julian* of Bristol, after her voyage to Lisbon and Ireland in 1454, was to put in to Plymouth for the final decision on whether to go to Normandy, Brittany, or Zeeland.[5]

The master was responsible for the ship in port, for victualling, for the hire and discipline of crews. These crews were often enough an international mixture, as was that of the *Mary* of Kinsale,[6] which included 15 westcountrymen of England, four Irishmen, two Welshmen, two Spaniards, a Fleming, and a Gascon. Discipline was covered by such codes as the Laws of Oleron and was probably fairly good at most times, but the crew of the *Mary* of Kinsale did mutiny and kill the merchants aboard, and the crew of the *Gracedieu* of Dartmouth at Athenry was persuaded for a bribe of $207\frac{1}{2}$ marks to seize the ship and take it on to Galway.[7]

Navigation was the master's responsibility on the open sea, while merchants usually hired the local pilots. Sometimes they hired long-distance pilots too. John Richeman of London hired William Cokke of Bristol to pilot his hired ship to Iceland, but when adverse winds held it too long in Scilly and the destination was changed to Cork, Cokke was discharged and the ship sent to

---

[1] Bernard, 'Maritime intercourse', pp 18–19.
[2] P.R.O., C. 1/25/207, 43/35; see below, pp 523–4.
[3] *Cal. pat. rolls, 1452–61*, p. 119.
[4] Cited in James, *Wine trade*, pp 134–5.
[5] Ibid., pp 134–6; Carus-Wilson, *Overseas trade of Bristol*, no. 127.
[6] Above, pp 495–6.
[7] *Cal. misc. inq., 1393–9*, no. 220; *Cal. pat. rolls, 1401–05*, pp 186–7; Athenry had its own port at Stradbally (below, iii, 13, n. 1; above, p. 507).

Mount's Bay to pick up a pilot for Ireland. It is unlikely that a Bristol pilot could not navigate from Scilly to Cork, and more likely that Cokke refused the change of destination, since he had goods of his own aboard and probably hoped for better profits in Iceland; certainly John Richeman, who hired the ship, objected strenuously to the change and alleged that the ship's owner, John Payn of Southampton, had deliberately plotted the change to his own profit and had sold Richeman's goods in Ireland as his own.[1] The Hansards also knew Cornwall as a place to find pilots for Ireland, and sailed to Falmouth from La Rochelle in 1387 to pick one up.[2] Charts were not much used in northern seas and even Italian portulan maps, while indicating familiarity with place-names, did not provide an accurate delineation of Irish coastlines. The northern sailor had rather ruttiers (route guides) to serve as memory aids. Sailors from southern England to Ireland had plain directions to help them ('Lands End and tower of Waterford, north-north-east and south-south-west' and 'from Tuskar to Skerries Head, going clean of all the ground between Tuskar and Dalkey, the course is north-east and south-south-west') together with soundings, sightings, and tidal information.[3]

The risks of sea trade were considerable. It could be simply time-wasting to be driven into English ports with staple goods aboard and have to prove that duty was paid and Calais the destination; it could be more irritating to be driven off course, as when Ellis Spelly's ship heading for Dublin was blown to Kinsale where officials arrested it as an enemy vessel because its crew included five Spaniards, or when destinations changed as drastically as from Iceland to Ireland because of the weather; it could mean total disaster if shipwreck occurred, as when Reymund Maugnel of Cork claimed that Cornishmen not only stole cargo washed ashore but cut the remains of the ship into little pieces and carried off the timber.[4] Wrecks often resulted in long and costly lawsuits. None the less, although weather caused some diminution of sailing in winter, it did not stop it, and Bristol and Chester customs accounts show that the fish trade brought particularly heavy sailings from January to March.

A further menace was the frequency of attack by the king's enemies and pirates. Possibly the incidence was higher around Irish coasts because of the political instability, and possibly it was harder to gain restitution of goods where the king's writ no longer ran, but many of the known cases were not immediately derived from Ireland's internal troubles. Scottish warships continued to prey on Irish Sea shipping, and while the government of Edward III attempted to protect the vital victualling convoys, later governmental efforts to protect shipping were fitful. The merchants either tried to protect themselves with safe-conducts, as did those of Drogheda who arranged safe-conducts

[1] P.R.O., C. 1/43/275–8.
[2] *Cal. close rolls, 1385–9*, p. 364.
[3] *Sailing directions for the circumnavigation of England*, ed. James Gairdner (Hakluyt Society, London, 1889), pp 17–20. 'North-east' should clearly be 'north-north-east'.
[4] *Cal. pat. rolls, 1338–40*, p. 488.

through the archbishop of Armagh for their trade between Ulster and Scotland, or they suffered and paid the ransoms asked.[1] The Anglo-French wars made the English Channel dangerous and, in the fifteenth century, piracy by Breton and Spanish shipping increased. When Drogheda and Waterford petitioned for help in repairing fortifications in 1442, they complained of damage by Scots, Bretons, and Spaniards and especially of a recent Breton piracy; indeed it appears that Breton trouble was so frequent that a recognised system had been established for the collection of ransom money.[2] The late fifteenth century saw sporadic efforts to deal with the problem, possibly stimulated by the shocking abduction in Dublin Bay in 1453 of the archbishop of Dublin by pirates who took him to Ardglass. Governmental plans were made to guard the area north of Wicklow Head in 1454–5 and 1460, to fortify Lambay Island in 1467, and to build a fortified harbour at Skerries in 1496–7, but the plans came to nothing.[3]

If the government's power to counter piracy was weak in the Irish Sea, it was practically non-existent along the coast west of Waterford. Kinsale seems to have become something of a haven for sea-rovers in the fifteenth century.[4] Further west, around Baltimore, lurked 'the nation of O'Driscolls, Irish enemies, who constantly remained upon the western ocean', preying on passing ships. Admirals appointed for the ports of County Cork in 1381–2 were to direct their attention to the O'Driscolls.[5] The harbour of Dingle was one of the few safe anchorages for shipping on the west coast south of Galway, but problems arose through theft: the *Trinity* of Bristol en route for Limerick was robbed of goods worth 1,000 marks there in 1401, and although the earl of Desmond controlled Dingle, no redress was forthcoming, no doubt because the White Knight, the sheriff of Desmond, and other notables were involved.[6] Galway Bay, according to Hardiman, was kept free of pirates in return for an annual tribute from the town to the branch of O'Briens who held the Aran Islands, but the value of this protection may be doubted, since in 1400 a licence was issued to recruit a naval force in Bristol to free the city from William de Burgh and to take the Aran Islands 'which always lie full of galleys for the spoiling of the king's lieges'.[7] The O'Malleys, whose lordship lay further north in the region of Achill and Clew Bay, also indulged in profitable sea-roving.[8]

Piracy by Englishmen should have offered easier remedy through the king's English courts, but it could prove difficult to obtain judgements and to exact compensation. One of Sir Edmund Mulso's ships, the *Mary* of Dublin of 70 tons, was seized with a cargo worth £137. 3s. 3d. on 26 November 1451: this was

[1] N.L.I., MS 2689, no. 351; *Rot. pat. Hib.*, p. 42, no. 17.

[2] *Cal. pat. rolls, 1441–6*, pp 58, 97; *Stat. Ire., Hen. VI*, pp 483–9.

[3] Ibid., pp 311, 671; *Stat. Ire., 1–12 Edw. IV*, p. 467; R.I.A., MS 24. H. 17, p. 211.

[4] *The little red book of Bristol*, ed. F. B. Bickley (2 vols, Bristol, 1900), ii, 232; *Cal. pat. rolls, 1452–61*, p. 61; *1476–85*, p. 79.

[5] *Rot. pat. Hib.*, p. 114, no. 196; *P.R.I. rep. D.K. 55*, p. 118; *Cal. Carew MSS.*, v, 470–71.

[6] *Cal. pat. rolls, 1399–1401*, p. 451.

[7] Ibid., p. 254; cf. below, p. 535.

[8] *A.U.*, iii, 33.

composed of $6\frac{1}{2}$ lasts of hides at 41 marks 8s. $10\frac{1}{2}d$. the last; $7\frac{1}{2}$ hundred yards of Irish frieze at £3 the hundred (£22. 10s.); 80 Irish mantles at 4s. each (£16); 2 pipes, 1 hogshead, and 2 barrels of tallow (£12); and one Breton prisoner, whose ransom was worth £20. The value of the ship was put at £100 and Mulso reckoned his total losses at £400. The perpetrator of the offence was Thomas Bodulgate (a Cornishman who often held the king's commission on local enquiries), and Mulso failed to obtain restitution from him at common law in Cornwall over three years. At last he appealed to chancery and Bodulgate put up a flurry of defences: it was a common law matter and should not be removed to chancery; the ship and goods were not of the value stated; anyway he was not guilty; and moreover the goods and ship did not belong to Mulso at the time they were taken. Whether this multiplication of defences was effective is unknown, as there is no indication of who won the case.[1] It is, however, a case which shows the size of investment in shipping and goods which was made on the routes to Ireland. Clearly the risks of the trade were worth taking for high profits could be made. Hides bought at Waterford for £8 or £11 and sold in Flanders for £18 the last showed a good return even after costs were paid; and a Coventryman claimed that £80. 14s. 8d., used to buy not only wine and iron to trade with but also the small boat to carry them from Brittany to Ireland, had made a clear profit of £17. 18s. 10d., a high return of about 22 per cent.[2] Most ships moreover did arrive, most merchants honoured their obligations, most goods found ready buyers. Even in its difficulties in the fifteenth century, Irish overseas trade ran at a level high enough to employ hundreds of merchants, seamen, shipbuilders, and port officials. The constant cries of distress and economic ruin voiced by citizens of Irish ports, while no doubt valid, are also partly belied by the descriptions of the beauty of the same towns by sixteenth-century travellers. The profits of trade had still been sufficient for municipalities to build in stone, and for merchants to embellish their local churches and die wealthy. The potential for even greater trade was there, and with the relative stability and the general European economic expansion of the early sixteenth century, Ireland's trade was able to take off again, albeit for only a few decades more.

---

[1] P.R.O., C. 1/25/207.
[2] Ibid., 11/506.

CHAPTER XVII

England and Ireland, 1399–1447

ART COSGROVE

THE attempts to reduce Ireland to obedience to the English crown culminated in the expeditions of Richard II. The expenditure of a large sum of money on the army of 1394–5 had appeared briefly to offer hope of an improvement in the Irish situation; but the ephemerality of Richard's success was succinctly pointed out by the chronicler, Adam of Usk: 'Yet he gained but little; for the Irish, then feigning submission to his will, straightaway after his departure were in revolt, as all men know.'[1] The king's second expedition in 1399 achieved even less, and while Richard struggled to come to grips with Art Mac Murchadha in Leinster, Henry Bolingbroke invaded England and usurped his title to the kingship of England and the lordship of Ireland.

Richard II's experiences in Ireland were not such as to encourage his successors to emulate him; yet the ultimate failure of the king's Irish policy does not mean that it was entirely without merit. His plans for Ireland envisaged the building-up of a body of loyal subjects among the Irish chieftains, or 'Irish rebels' as he termed them, by granting them a status roughly equivalent to the leaders of English blood, and in particular by involving them in the government of the country through participation in the councils and parliaments of the king. The plan failed; but in many of its features it anticipated the policies of his successors, particularly the scheme of surrender and regrant put forward under Henry VIII almost a century and a half later.[2]

Allied to the scheme for the anglicising or 'civilising' of the Irish chieftains was a plan for recolonisation or plantation to strengthen the most loyal province, Leinster. Here, too, Richard was proposing a solution that was later to be more widely adopted. But at the time, its implementation proved to be beyond his resources, for the king was unable to secure the necessary prerequisite for any successful scheme of recolonisation—the transfer from the Gaelic Irish landholders of the territories granted to new colonists. The difficulties which this created are apparent in the reaction of one grantee:

The king has granted me a parcel of land in the country of the Irish rebels, which, if it were in parts of London, would be worth by the year 50,000 marks, but in faith, I have so

---

[1] Adam of Usk, *Chronicon*, ed. E. M. Thompson (London, 1904), pp 9, 151.
[2] Below, iii, 48–51.

much trouble holding on to it that I would not like to lead such a life for long even for a quarter of the land.[1]

With England's population itself in decline because of the effects of plague, there was no large-scale influx of new settlers to bolster the declining colony. Instead, as the fifteenth century advanced, the area under effective control decreased, and the colonists sought in vain for an effective intervention from England to check the Gaelic Irish resurgence.

Richard II's successors had little new to offer as a solution to the Irish problem. Unwilling to undertake the vast expenditure that a conquest of the island would demand, they preferred to mount sporadic expeditions which, at best, could only hope to maintain rather than extend the area of 'English ground'. Under Henry IV the limited expenditure involved in such a policy could not be met, and the commons in parliament were increasingly unwilling to sanction the outlay of money in Ireland, complaining in 1406 that vast sums had already been expended on the war in Ireland without any apparent improvement in the situation.[2] In Ireland, as in other disturbed areas, such as the marches of Wales,[3] stress was inevitably laid on the duty of local magnates to provide for defence needs. It was up to them to reside on their estates and resist the rebels.

Such was the thinking behind the succession of absentee acts from 1368 onwards. Shortly after his accession, in December 1399, Henry IV ordered the implementation of the absentee act of 1380. This demanded that all who held lands, benefices, or offices in Ireland should go to reside there and defend the land against the 'Irish rebels'; all who had castles and fortresses in Ireland were enjoined to repair and defend them. Those who were absent 'with reasonable cause' were to find capable substitutes to defend their possessions. If these provisions were not met, then two-thirds of the profits accruing from such lands or offices would be forfeited to the Irish exchequer to meet the costs of defence inside Ireland. In the case of clerks who were absent from their benefices in the king's service or for the purpose of study at a university, the levy would be at the rate of one-third of the value of the benefices.

This act was directed against the 'king's faithful lieges' of Ireland, those colonists of English descent who remained loyal to the crown and who were now to return to the country of their birth to defend the colony. It is doubtful if the act made much impact. Licences of exemption from it could be and were granted both by the English administration and, after 1402, by the Dublin government. For many of those who nominally held lands in Ireland, the loss of two-thirds of the issues represented no great sacrifice since the occupation of

---

[1] Edmund Curtis, 'Unpublished letters from Richard II in Ireland, 1394–5' in *R.I.A. Proc.*, xxxvii (1927), sect. C, p. 296.

[2] *Rot. parl.*, iii, 573, no. 33; 577, no. 40.

[3] Cf. ibid., p. 610, no. 17.

their lands by others precluded them from drawing any revenues from them in any case.

In June 1394, prior to his first expedition to Ireland, Richard II had ordered that all Irish-born living in England were to return home by the following autumn. Those who did not comply had to pay for the privilege of remaining in England. As late as 1410 one Robert Sygn, who had been born in Kilmallock, County Limerick, was still suffering the consequences of his failure to return to Ireland in 1394. In his complaint to the king he claimed that he had been brought from Ireland by William of Windsor when he was fourteen years of age and that he had lived for over forty years in Yorkshire, where he had acquired ten acres of land. Now the escheators of the county levied 6s. 8d. yearly from him, as if his land had been forfeited to the king for failure to comply with the order of 1394, and he petitioned the king successfully for leave to remain in England and enjoy the revenues from his property.

Of course, not all of the inhabitants of Ireland could be counted among the king's faithful lieges. In Ireland, according to one chronicler, there were

two races speaking two languages [*ii generacions et deux langaiges*]; the one speak bastard English and dwell in the good towns, cities, castles, and fortresses of the country and in the seaports . . .; the other are a wild people who speak a strange language . . . and dwell always in the woods and on the mountains of the country, and have many chiefs among themselves, of whom the most powerful go barefoot and without breeches and ride horses without saddles.

Equally, readers of Froissart's chronicle would have been made aware of the distinction to be drawn between the two peoples inside the island.

Now the inhabitants of the more remote parts of Ireland . . . neither know nor wish to know anything about commerce, since they live quite simply, like wild beasts. But those who live on the coast opposite England are more like ourselves and are used to trade.[1]

And Froissart regaled his readers with descriptions of the unusual and, in his view, outlandish habits, dress, and methods of warfare among the Gaelic Irish population. His descriptions were based on information received at second hand, and were doubtless embroidered in the telling for the amusement of his audience; but the distinctiveness of the Gaelic Irish, in warfare at least, is confirmed by another source. Those who accompanied Thomas Butler, prior of Kilmainham, to the siege of Rouen in 1418 attracted the attention of a French chronicler.

The king of England had in his army numbers of Irish, the greater part of whom were on foot, having only a stocking and shoe on one leg and foot, with the other quite naked. They had targets, short javelins, and a strange sort of knives. Those who were on horseback had no saddles, but rode excellently well on small mountain horses, and were mounted on such panniers as are used by the carriers of corn in parts of France. They

[1] *Chronicque de la traison et mort de Richart II*, ed. Benjamin Williams (London, 1846), pp 28, 171; Froissart, *Chronicles* (ed. Joliffe), p. 369.

were, however, miserably accoutred in comparison with the English, and without any arms that could much hurt the French whenever they might meet them. These Irish made frequent excursions, during the siege, over Normandy and did infinite mischiefs, bringing back to their camp large booties. Those on foot took men, and even children from the cradle, with beds and furniture, and, placing them on cows, drove all these things before them, for they were often met thus by the French.

And Butler was ordered by the king to rebuke those among his Irish followers who contravened the normal laws of army discipline.[1]

Richard II had attempted to categorise the Gaelic Irish population into 'Irish rebels', those who had at some stage accepted English authority in Ireland but had then rebelled against it, and 'wild Irish', who had never submitted to the English crown.[2] But it is doubtful if such a distinction was generally made in England,[3] where it was easier to accept the plea of the 'poor Irish lieges', made in the parliament of 1416, that the land was divided into two nations, English and those of English descent on the one hand, and the Irish nation, enemies of the king, on the other. And the accusation that one was a 'wilde-hirissheman' and an enemy of the king could have serious consequences, as an Irish chaplain, Nicholas 'Hogonona', discovered in 1401.

Nicholas was passing through England on his way from Ireland to Rome, a pilgrimage he had vowed to undertake, when he met up with an Austin friar at Oxford. According to his own account, Nicholas gave the friar 40 pence to conduct him to London and also entrusted to him 60 shillings for safe-keeping. When they reached London, however, the friar refused to return the money and, instead, denounced Nicholas as a wild Irishman (*un wilde Irisshman*) and an enemy of the king, an accusation that resulted in Nicholas's arrest and imprisonment. Subsequently the Irish chaplain petitioned the king's council to be released on the grounds that the charge was false, since he was a loyal subject, and on 25 August 1401 the council directed the sheriffs of London to release him if he was being held only on the charge of being a wild Irishman and an enemy of the king.[4]

The case demonstrates how difficult it could be for the English government to distinguish between people of Irish birth on the basis of loyalty to the crown. There were rebels among those of English descent, and many of the 'Irish enemies' were not, to English eyes at least, markedly different from the loyal Anglo-Irish. Particularly was this true in the universities. In 1408 the king instructed the chancellor of the university of Oxford to enquire into a report

---

[1] *The chronicles of Enguerrand de Monstrelet*, trans. Thomas Johnes, i (London, 1840), p. 404; *Gesta Henrici Quinti*, ed. Benjamin Williams (London, 1850), p. 125, n. 1.

[2] For a recent interpretation of Richard II's categorisation of the population in Ireland, see Johnston, 'Richard II and the submissions of Gaelic Ireland', pp 6–8.

[3] 'And these rebelles of Ireland bith called "wilde Irisch men" ': *The Brut*, ed. F. W. D. Brie (2 vols, London, 1906–8), ii, 357.

[4] 'Per suggestionem quod ipse fuit Wildehirissheman Hibernicus et inimicus noster' (P.R.O., C. 54/248, m. 6; *Cal. close rolls, 1399—1402*, p. 370; *Select cases before the king's council, 1243—1482*, ed. I. S. Leadam and J. F. Baldwin (Selden Society, 1918), pp 85–6).

that 'certain rebels of Ireland, asserting themselves to be the king's faithful lieges' were using their position as students as a cover for espionage; for it was stated that these rebels daily revealed, either by letter or by going in person to Ireland, the plans made in England to counteract rebellion in Ireland.[1] And it may have been as a consequence of this enquiry that the Irish parliament in 1410 forbade any Irishman, adhering to the king's enemies, to go out of the country 'by color of going to the scooles of Oxford Cambridge or els where'.[2]

But trouble continued at Oxford. In 1422 it was claimed that many crimes in Oxford and the surrounding counties were committed by students from Ireland 'of whom some were lieges of the king, but others were enemies to him and his kingdom called wylde Irishmen'. In future all of Irish birth who wished to enter either Oxford or Cambridge were required to have letters of recommendation from the chief governor of Ireland; otherwise they would be treated as rebels.

This restriction followed close upon the complaint of the Anglo-Irish in the previous year that able men of good family in Ireland were being refused admission to the inns of court to study law. Not until March 1440[3] did the Dublin government secure a satisfactory undertaking that Irish-born students would be admitted to the inns on the same basis as those born in England. And it would seem that legislation originally designed to provide for the defence of the colony in Ireland was also being used to rid England of undesirable Irish residents. The statute of 1413, which ordered the expulsion of Irishmen from England under pain of losing their goods and being imprisoned, had the twin objectives of stocking the land of Ireland and securing quiet and peace within the realm of England.[4] Exempted from the operation of the statute were university graduates, serjeants and apprentices of the law, professed religious, those who had inheritances in England, and merchants of good report, along with their apprentices. In consequence of the statute, all sheriffs were ordered on 6 September 1413 to make proclamation throughout their shires that all Irish-born were to return to Ireland by Christmas Day 1413. Similar measures were taken against the Welsh-born.

Had the act been strictly enforced, there would have been a sizeable exodus from England in the last months of 1413. But in December 1413 its terms were relaxed somewhat to allow all clerks of Welsh or Irish birth to remain at the university of Oxford; and, as with Richard II's order of 1394, many others were able to purchase licences from the king allowing them to stay in England.

But though the effectiveness of such proclamations in improving the defences of the colony in Ireland may be doubted, they were a continuing feature of English policy over the next thirty years. In March 1417, just before

---

[1] *Cal. pat. rolls, 1405—8*, p. 482.

[2] *Stat. Ire., John—Hen. V*, p. 527.

[3] P.R.O., E. 28/63/61. Thomas Chace, then chancellor of Ireland, was later rewarded for bringing back this 'full and effectual response under the privy seal of England' (*Rot. pat. Hib.*, p. 263b, no. 21).

[4] *Stat. of realm*, ii, 173.

his departure with a large army to Normandy, Henry V ordered that all Irish lieges, with the usual exceptions, should return to their own country by the end of June 'to provide for the safe guard of Ireland against the rebel Irish'. A similar proclamation was made in 1430 at the request of the commons in the English parliament, on the grounds that the Irish rebels and other enemies of the northern parts were banding together to invade Ireland and lay waste the country. In 1431, 1432, and again in 1439 further expulsion orders were made against Irish-born residents in England.

In all these cases there is evidence of licences being purchased from the king exempting individuals from the requirements of the proclamation, evidence that supports the contention of one contemporary chronicler regarding the act of 1413: 'And against the Welsh and the Irish he sent forth an edict, that each man should get him to his own country; and thereby from them, for leave to remain, he gathered to himself much treasure.'[1] Certainly the numbers who returned to Ireland made no significant difference to the strength of the colony, and the proclamations were probably more effective as a means of increasing royal revenue at the expense of those Irish-born who wished to remain in England.

Irish immigrants were further penalised in 1440 when they were included among those liable to be assessed for the poll-tax on aliens. In August 1441 the Dublin government requested that the Anglo-Irish (the English born in Ireland) should enjoy the same status in England as native Englishmen and thus be exempt from the tax,[2] and it may have been in response to such pressures that the formal classification of the Irish-born as aliens was officially abandoned in December 1442. Nevertheless, continuing attempts were made in London and other areas to include the Irish-born within the scope of the tax, and failure to find general acceptance as equals in England must only have served to widen the gulf between the Anglo-Irish and the English at a time when the English government was already regarded as guilty of neglecting the interests of the colony in Ireland.[3]

What was really needed, the colonists claimed, was generous financial assistance from the English crown. In the early years of Henry IV's reign some attempt was made to provide this. Faced with the serious revolt of Owen Glendower in Wales, the king was forced to consider the possibility of a union against him by Welsh and Irish dissidents, a possibility that Glendower himself attempted to exploit in 1401 when he sent messengers to some Irish chieftains

---

[1] Adam of Usk, *Chronicon*, pp 120, 299.

[2] The petition to the king asked that those of English birth in Ireland should have 'suche fredomes ... lyke unto English men borne within his said noble Roaume' (N.L.I., MS 4 (Harris Collectanea) f. 337b).

[3] See Sylvia L. Thrupp, 'A survey of the alien population of England in 1440' in *Speculum*, xxxii (1957), pp 262–72; and 'Aliens in and around London in the fifteenth century' in A. E. J. Hollaender and William Kellaway (ed.) *Studies in London history* (London, 1969), p. 254. For useful general comments on Irish residents in England see Ralph A. Griffiths, *The reign of Henry VI: the exercise of royal authority, 1422—61* (London, 1981), pp 134–5, 142–3, 167–8.

urging them to make common cause with him against the English. The messengers were captured and beheaded, and Glendower did not secure any help from Ireland. But the incident clearly demonstrated to the king the possible strategic dangers that an unreduced Ireland might hold for him, and may explain the comparatively large outlay that was sanctioned for use in Ireland in the early years of the century. Even then, however, the king was not always able to match his promises with the actual money, and the administration in Dublin could still find itself in acute financial difficulties.

The continuing decline of the colony brought little improvement in this situation. That decline was recognised not only by the English but also by their French enemies. At the council of Constance, called in 1415 to attempt to heal the schism in the church, the English delegation claimed the right to sit as one of the four 'nations' into which the council was divided. Among the arguments put forward by the French delegation against this claim was that England could not legitimately represent Ireland, since only two out of forty-eight dioceses in that country were subject to the king of England, and the rest of the country did not recognise his lordship. This exaggerated the extent of the colony's decline (there were, in fact, only thirty-three dioceses in Ireland and almost half of these still maintained some link with the Dublin administration), but it shows that the weakness of the English position in Ireland was recognised internationally. The French, however, did not attempt to exploit Irish disaffection as a weapon against England as they had done in Wales in 1405, and with the passing of the menace from Glendower and the reopening of the war on the Continent in 1415, the affairs of Ireland inevitably assumed a less prominent place in the English scale of priorities.

It was in vain for the earl of Ormond to protest in the 1430s about this neglect of Ireland, and to argue, with unrealistic optimism, that, if what were spent on one year on the French war were applied to Ireland over a number of years, a complete conquest of the country could be made. Preoccupied with the war against the French, and aware that Ireland presented no real strategic threat, the English government was unprepared to devote the time and money necessary to remedy a situation whereby, as the author of the 'Libelle of Englyshe polycye' put it,

> our grounde there is a lytell cornere
> To all Yrelande in treue comparisone.

That work, written about 1437, pointed out that the king of England was lord of Ireland too, and that the Anglo-Irish and English had a common interest in defending these islands against any enemy and particularly in maintaining command of the sea between them. Now 'the wylde Yrishe' had gained control of so much territory that he feared they might set up a king of their own, with a consequent loss of English authority over the entire country. But the author's appeal for more attention to be paid to Ireland on strategic grounds drew little response in the 1430s. It was only as the French war drew to a close and England itself began to split into rival Yorkist and Lancastrian camps that force was given to the author's warning:

> To kepen Yreland that it be not loste,
> For it is a boterasse and a poste
> Undre England and Wales is another.
> God forbede but eche were othere brothere,
> Of one ligeaunce dewe unto the kynge.[1]

[1] *Libelle*, lines 700–04; cf. Griffiths, *Reign of Henry VI*, p. 412.

CHAPTER XVIII

The emergence of the Pale, 1399–1447

ART COSGROVE

THROUGHOUT the first half of the fifteenth century the area under the control of the administration declined in extent as more territory passed into the hands of 'Irish enemies' and 'English rebels' (hostile Gaelic Irish and rebellious Anglo-Irish). The earliest known use of the term 'Pale' occurs in 1446–7 when the Irish leader Aodh Ruadh Mac Mathghamhna promised 'to carrie nothing owte of the inglishe pale contrarie to the statutes'.[1] But the concept of a geographically defined limitation on English authority in Ireland was clearly present in the mind of the writer of the gloomy report of 1435 that told the king that

his land of Ireland is wellnigh destroyed, and inhabited with his enemies and rebels, so much so that there is not left in the nether parts of the counties of Dublin, Meath, Louth, and Kildare, that join together, out of the subjection of the said enemies and rebels scarcely thirty miles in length and twenty miles in breadth there, as a man may surely ride or go in the said counties, to answer to the king's writs and to his commandments.[2]

Since the Irish council was at pains to stress the serious nature of the situation in order to convince the king that he should come to Ireland himself, it is possible that the report somewhat exaggerated the plight of the colony. But the observation of Archbishop Swayne of Armagh that the territory under effective control of the administration amounted to little more than one shire, and the estimate of the 'Libelle of Englyshe polycye' that the proportion of the land still held by the English was the equivalent of two or three shires as a proportion of England, both reflect a similar view. Certainly the previous thirty-five years had seen the increasing fragmentation of the colony and outlying areas could not, in many instances, be visited by officers of the administration unless they were accompanied by a sizeable military escort. The two collectors of the Irish customs appointed in April 1400 for all the ports of Ireland were permitted to serve the office by deputy on the grounds that 'the administration of these

---

[1] Cal. Carew MSS, i, 290; E. P. Shirley, Some account of the territory or dominion of Farney (London, 1845), p. 24.

[2] Betham, Dignities, p. 361.

offices lie in divers ports among the king's enemies and they cannot continually go thither in person except by sea, and this with a force of fencibles'.[1] The difficulties in communication were further underlined by the exemption, in the same year, of the mayor of Waterford from his duty of taking the oath of office at the chancery in Dublin, because of the dangers involved from the Irish enemies in such a journey. And in June 1400 it was claimed that both the city and the county were continually harassed by the attacks of the Powers and other English rebels.

Other Munster towns faced similar problems. Arrears of £229. 6s. 8d. were remitted to the city of Cork in 1400 in consideration of the great losses that it had sustained through the invasion of Irish and English rebels and as an encouragement to provide sterner resistance to the king's enemies. But the impoverishment of Cork continued, and in 1423 the mayor and citizens complained that they could no longer pay the annual render or fee-farm of 86 marks due to the crown, since they were continually beset by Irish rebels who exacted tribute from all entering or leaving the city. Limerick, too, was on the frontier of the king's Irish enemies, and was, it was claimed in 1427, 'the only place of resistance in those parts',[2] when the mayor and citizens successfully petitioned the king for custody of the great castle there, on which the security of the city depended. Four years earlier the castle had been entrusted to James, earl of Desmond, but dissatisfaction with this arrangement is evident in the complaint of the mayor and citizens that the castle, when granted to outsiders, had often through their negligence been on the point of capture. Lying on the Shannon, the castle had the great advantage that it could be supplied by water without any aid from land, a factor that must have been of considerable importance in the circumstances of 1450, when it was claimed that the city was so surrounded by 'Irish enemies' and 'English rebels' that all supplies had to be brought in by sea.

Waterford was menaced not only by 'Irish enemies' and 'English rebels' but also by sea-raiders from Brittany, Scotland, and Spain, and in 1430 a grant of £30 (almost half the yearly fee-farm of the city) for a three-year period had to be made towards the repair of ruined fortifications. Twelve years later, following the capture of a cargo valued at 4000 marks by Breton pirates, the concession was extended for a further thirty years; and since a similar grant of 25 marks was made around the same time to the dean and chapter of Waterford because of spoliation of their lands by hostile Gaelic and Anglo-Irish, this meant that well over half of the annual revenue from the city's fee-farm of 100 marks had been diverted from the central government for local usage. In this Waterford resembled many other cities and towns which had formerly contributed towards the revenues of the Irish exchequer but which could no longer do so. Increasingly isolated from Dublin, Waterford had to look to its own resources

---

[1] *Cal. pat. rolls, 1399—1401*, p. 257.
[2] *Cal. pat rolls, 1422—9*, p. 390.

to provide for its defence.[1] Even within the Pale area the costs of defence were onerous, if one can believe the claim of the Drogheda citizens in 1442 that repair of the town's fortifications against various enemies cost over £140 a year.

Connacht was even more isolated from the authority of the central administration. The chief western town of Galway was in the hands of William de Burgh (or Burke) in March 1400, when it was proposed that a force led by Nicholas Kent, a burgess of the town, and certain citizens of Bristol should cross to Ireland and attempt to recapture the town and also the Aran Islands 'which always lie full of galleys for the spoiling of the king's lieges'.[2] But the expedition seems never to have got beyond the planning stage, and de Burgh was still in possession of the town in 1403 when his position was formalised by his appointment as royal deputy in Connacht, an office he continued to hold on the grounds that chief governors were too busy elsewhere to be able to go to Connacht. His activities were rewarded in August 1415 by an official recognition of his right to enjoy the customs revenue of the port of Galway, from which he received a grant of 80 marks. This made little difference to royal finances, since it had been reported a month earlier that there was no royal collector of customs at the port in any case. Nine years later de Burgh's increasing authority inside the area was marked by an extension of the grant to one of £40 from the customs of Galway and Sligo, a reward for past service to the deputy, James, earl of Ormond, and as an inducement to have 'a happier mind in helping the deputy in his present needs'.[3] In effect, governmental functions, in so far as they could be exercised, were abdicated to de Burgh, over whose conduct the Dublin administration exercised little control.

In the north-east the main stronghold of the colony was the castle at Carrickfergus. But the town had been completely burnt by the king's enemies in 1403, and a year's customs revenue had to be diverted to its rebuilding. With the continuing decline of the old liberty of Ulster, the pressure upon the castle probably increased. In 1428 the constable was granted £10 towards the cost of its defence when he reported that Ó Domhnaill had sent to Scotland for a large force of men to aid him in an attack upon it.

An index of the overall decline of the administration's authority in Ulster is provided by the surviving registers of the archbishops of Armagh. Normally the archbishop, like other prelates, looked to the administration as the 'secular arm' to enforce his decrees upon those who proved unamenable to the discipline of the church. If, for example, a man was excommunicated and remained unrepentant, the archbishop could inform the secular authorities of his obduracy and have him arrested. Increasingly, however, the archbishops of Armagh were forced to recognise that the real power in many parts of the province lay with the Irish chieftains rather than with the Dublin government,

[1] James Lydon, 'The city of Waterford in the later middle ages' in *Decies*, xii (1979), pp 5–15.
[2] *Cal. pat. rolls, 1399–1401*, pp 254, 285.
[3] *Rot. pat. Hib.*, p. 233a, no. 15.

and requests for aid by the 'secular arm' had to be addressed to Ó Néill and other Irish 'captains of their nations' who had supplanted the authority of the government.[1]

It is not possible to strictly delineate the extent of the Pale area itself. At its northern extremity, the town of Carlingford probably represented its outer limit, but the town and the lordship of Cooley were already becoming detached from the main colonial area, as the inhabitants graphically explained to the Dublin government in March 1410:

The town and lordship are situated on the frontier of the marches of County Louth in a valley between the sea and the mountains . . . and are cut off from the rest of the county by high mountains and wooded passes as well as by the arm of the sea flowing backwards and forwards, so that they are not able to be helped against the Irish and Scots and on account of that they are often burned and devastated.[2]

To the south of Dublin, Wicklow was situated among the O'Byrnes, the king's Irish enemies, and in 1416 it was claimed that it was far distant from any aid from the colonists; clearly one could not travel far to the south of Dublin without entering hostile territory.

Inland the frontier was a shifting one, but the balance of advantage clearly lay with the enemies of the colony. Early in the century, the town of Kilcullen, little more than twenty miles from Dublin, was burnt by the Gaelic Irish; the other Kildare town of Naas was reported to be surrounded by 'Irish enemies and English rebels' in 1414, when a grant was made by the Dublin government towards its defence. In Meath the town of Drumconrath was granted a weekly market in 1412 because its position on the frontier had led to frequent burnings of it by the Gaelic Irish.

To the north, the influence of the administration might stretch further inland. In 1420 Domhnall Ó Fearghail demolished the castle at Granard in County Longford to prevent its reoccupation by the colonists, an action that suggests that his control of the area was not yet unchallenged. In the southern midlands, the expedition by John Talbot, Lord Furnival, against Ó Mórdha of Leix in 1415 led to a strengthening in the position of Athy, where the subsequent repair of the bridge and the erection of new fortifications in 1417 gave the inhabitants greater security than they had had in the previous thirty years. And seventeen years later it remained the 'greatest fortalice and key town of the area'.[3]

But such advances were few, and did little to compensate for more serious losses elsewhere. The writer of the 1435 report pointed in particular to the domination by enemies and rebels of the county of Carlow, where, according to his estimate, one hundred and forty-eight castles and other fortified positions

[1] See Katharine Simms, 'The archbishops of Armagh and the O'Neills, 1347–1471' in *I.H.S.*, xix, no. 73 (Mar. 1974), pp 42, 51–2.
[2] *Rot. pat. Hib.*, p. 196a, no. 75.
[3] Ibid., p. 251b, no. 23.

had been lost in the previous sixty years; and the loss of this key area had severed the line of communication between Dublin and outlying parts of the colony in Kilkenny and Tipperary. Increasingly the inhabitants of this area were forced to fend for themselves. Under the leadership of their Butler lords and particularly of James, fourth earl of Ormond (1405–52), Anglo-Norman traditions became intermingled with Gaelic Irish practices in the administration of the lordship.[1]

Even if we allow for undoubted exaggeration both in reports made to England and in the complaints of individual towns, who were, after all, attempting to escape payment of royal dues, it is still clear that the area under the effective control of the Dublin administration contracted during the first half of the fifteenth century. The basic reason for this decline was the inability to put sufficient forces in the field for a long enough period to achieve any lasting expansion or even stabilisation of the frontier. And that inability was itself directly linked to the fact that money was not consistently available for the purpose.

The effects of parsimony towards Ireland were made apparent early in the century during the lieutenancy of Henry IV's son, Thomas of Lancaster. Appointed in May 1401 with a salary of 12,000 marks per annum, he secured so little in payment that by the following February many of his captains had already departed and others were threatening to follow suit because of non-payment of their wages. By August 1402 he was reported to be 'so destitute of money that he has not a penny in the world, nor can borrow a single penny, because all his jewels and his plate, that he can spare of those which he must of necessity keep, are spent and sunk in wages'. His soldiers had already left him, and even the members of his household were on the point of departure because of his poverty.[2]

In part, Thomas was a victim of the system of financing adopted by a practically bankrupt Lancastrian government. Unable to raise enough ready cash to meet his commitments, Henry IV resorted increasingly to the method of assignments, whereby revenue not yet collected was allocated to settle crown debts. Instead of giving the crown appointee the actual money, the exchequer issued a tally authorising him to collect what was due to him from a particular source of royal revenue. Thomas, for example, was granted an assignment on the customs of Kingston-on-Hull in 1403. Anticipation of revenue in this fashion was a feature of medieval financing, but clearly there was a limit to its application, and too frequent recourse to it could lead to financial breakdown. Under Henry IV, such an overanticipation of the revenue occurred; too often the holder of a tally who arrived to tap his assigned source of revenue found that it had already dried up, and he was forced to return to the exchequer and seek

---

[1] See C. A. Empey, 'The Butler lordship' in *Butler Soc. Jn.*, iii (1970–71), p. 185; K. W. Nicholls, 'Anglo-French Ireland and after' in *Peritia*, i (1982), pp 400–01.
[2] *Royal and historical letters of Henry IV*, ed. F. C. Hingeston (2 vols., London, 1862–6), i, 73–6.

an alternative method of payment. At best, this system led to long delay in the satisfaction of crown debts; at worst, to a failure to meet them either in whole or in part.

Like other royal officials, Thomas of Lancaster and some of his successors as chief governors of Ireland suffered from this lack of ready money. But financial stringency alone will not altogether account for the comparative neglect of Ireland during the first half of the fifteenth century. Money could be, and was, made available for other purposes, and the fact that Ireland could attract little of it is a pointer to its low position in the scale of English priorities, where it ranked far behind France, Scotland, and Wales in terms of the expenditure of royal revenues.

In these circumstances the chief governorship could impose severe burdens on its holder, and it is not surprising to find that in March 1404, after the departure of both Lancaster and his deputy, Stephen le Scrope, the earl of Ormond sought to avoid acceptance of the office of justiciar or temporary chief governor. In a petition to the king, he asked to be excused the responsibility on the grounds that he simply could not afford it; he had already incurred heavy expenses in the governmental service under both Henry and his predecessor, Richard II; the Irish treasury was so feeble and reduced that it could afford him little assistance; and he therefore requested the lords of the privy council to urge the king to make new provisions for Ireland which would allow him to be discharged. An unusually generous subsidy from the Irish parliament[1] helped to tide the earl over the emergency, but left the fundamental financial problem unsolved.

Even when the stipend paid to the lieutenant was scaled down, the crown could not always meet its commitments. Lancaster was reappointed as deputy in 1408 at a salary of 7,000 marks per annum, but by 1411 the amount owed to him exceeded £5,000. John Talbot, Lord Furnival, appointed lieutenant in 1414 at a reduced salary of 4,000 marks for the first year and 3,000 marks per annum thereafter, had similar difficulties, and had to interrupt a vigorous and largely successful campaign against the Gaelic Irish in 1416 to go in person to England to seek payment of what was owed to him. Failure to secure adequate reimbursement forced him to pass on his debts to others, and when he left Ireland in 1420 he was castigated by one chronicler for his failure to pay what he owed for victuals and other necessities. In the parliament of 1421 it was reckoned that his debts 'amounted to a great summe' and he was accused of having committed

several great and monstrous extortions and oppressions . . . against your said lieges . . . and took their goods and chattels, paying them little or nothing therefore, by which your said lieges in that part have been greatly injured and impoverished.[2]

---

[1] The subsidy was granted to Ormond as 'soldier and governor of the wars' (*soldario et gubernatori guerrarum*) rather than as justiciar, so that the grant might not set a precedent for future justiciars. See Richardson & Sayles, *Ir. parl. in middle ages*, p. 155, n. 72.

[2] Marlborough, *Chronicle*, pp 28–9; *Stat. Ire., John—Hen. V*, p. 571.

Sir John Stanley, who acted as lieutenant during 1400–01 and again for a three-month period prior to his death in January 1414 (a death allegedly caused by the curses of Irish poets against him), was similarly criticised by the 1421 parliament, which sought to make his heirs and executors responsible for his debts in Ireland. And in both instances resentment at the non-payment of debts was increased by the fact that neither Stanley nor Talbot had resources within Ireland that could be made responsible for their liabilities.

Such criticism could not be levelled against James Butler, fouth earl of Ormond, who was appointed lieutenant in February 1420. But the granting of the office to an Anglo-Irish earl with extensive properties marked a further stage in the attempts to scale down English financial commitments to Ireland. Not only was Ormond to have a reduced salary (2,500 marks per annum) but payment of it was no longer to be the sole responsibility of the English exchequer. Instead the earl was expected to find the bulk of his remuneration from money collected within Ireland. Only when it was demonstrated that Irish revenues were insufficient to meet the lieutenant's salary would the shortfall be made up by the English exchequer. At the same time, the practice of allowing lieutenants to freely dispose of Irish revenues was discontinued. Closer supervision from England was promised in the regulation that the treasurer of Ireland should present periodic accounts at the English exchequer, a return to the procedure operative before 1379.

The arrangements made in 1420 worked satisfactorily throughout the two-year term of Ormond's lieutenancy, primarily because the earl was able to generate increased revenue within Ireland. It is not surprising, therefore, that, when Ormond was reappointed lieutenant in 1425 after the sudden death in Ireland of the earl of March, a return was made to the 1420 arrangements. And for the next twenty years all lieutenants of Ireland were required to hold office under similar terms.

But the initial success of the new procedures was not to be repeated. Ormond himself was able to secure a fair proportion of his salary as lieutenant from Irish sources during 1425–6, but the Englishmen who succeeded him[1] could derive only a very small percentage of their salaries from revenue collected within Ireland. Lacking the ability to stimulate income at the Irish exchequer, they remained preponderantly dependent on its English counterpart. The latter, in turn, did not pursue the aim outlined in 1420 of exercising closer supervision over Irish revenues, and thus the attempts to make the Irish lordship contribute more to the costs of its government and defence ultimately achieved little. The failure of these arrangements was tacitly recognised in the return to older procedures in the reappointment of John Talbot, now earl of Shrewsbury, as lieutenant in 1445. It was agreed that Talbot should receive exactly the same salary as in 1414 and that the English exchequer should be

[1] For the succession of chief governors see below, ix, 476–7.

fully responsible for it. The only difference was that Talbot now found it even more difficult to gain actual payment.

Concentration on the difficulties experienced by lieutenants should not obscure the fact that, for almost two-thirds of this period, the responsibility for the government of Ireland rested with others. Lieutenants normally enjoyed the power of serving the office by deputy, and often exercised it. In cases of emergency where the lieutenancy or deputyship was vacated by the death or departure of the holder, or where the appointment lapsed owing to the death of the king, a temporary chief governor, or 'justiciar', was appointed, usually by the Irish council, to head the administration until a new appointment was made.

Neither the deputy lieutenant nor the justiciar normally had direct access to revenues from the English exchequer. Deputies tended to make their own financial arrangements with lieutenants, but the indications are that they were expected to defray their expenses from local resources. Thus the fact that an absentee lieutenant was paid his full salary does not necessarily mean that the financial situation within Ireland was improved. Justiciars traditionally received a salary of £500 per annum and, in some instances, were also provided with a small defence force of twelve men-at-arms and sixty archers. But both the salary and the cost of the force had to be derived from Irish revenues. There were many occasions, therefore, when the lordship was thrown back upon its own resources.[1]

Annual receipts at the Irish exchequer averaged about £1000 for the period 1420–45, and this revenue barely sufficed to meet the normal recurrent demands upon it. In the absence of any subvention from England, a chief governor had at his disposal only what he could raise from scutages and taxation.

The old feudal levy of scutage, or royal service, as it was termed in Ireland, survived as a method of raising money long after it had disappeared in England. It still made an important contribution to Irish finances in the first half of the fifteenth century, and the frequency of its incidence in the period 1415–52 is an indication of the Irish administration's increased dependence on its own resources. But repeated impositions seem to have provoked opposition, and a statute of 1445 banning royal service for the following ten years began a progressive decline in its importance.[2]

Income from taxation was limited. The parliamentary subsidy estimated to levy only 700 marks per annum and the collection probably fell considerably short of this target. Recourse to frequent local subsidies negotiated with individual counties reflects a continuing inability to provide protection in any other

[1] The foregoing is based on the excellent analysis by Elizabeth Matthew, 'The financing of the lordship of Ireland under Henry V and Henry VI' in A. J. Pollard (ed.), *Property and politics: essays in later medieval English history* (Gloucester, 1984), pp 97–115.

[2] Steven G. Ellis, 'Taxation and defence in later medieval Ireland: the survival of scutage' in *R.S.A.I. Jn.*, cvii (1977), pp 5–28, especially p. 17.

way. And even these expedients could not prevent many chief governors from contracting large debts in their efforts to meet the colony's defence needs.

The parliament of 1428 made a general request that all the lieutenants and deputies who held office under both Henry V and Henry VI should pay what was owed by them for themselves and their soldiers. These debts were considerable, if we can believe the estimate of Archbishop Swayne of Armagh in the same year.

All the lieutenants that have been in this country, when they come there, their soldiers live on the husbandmen, not paying for horse meat nor man meat, and the lieutenants' purveyors take up all manner of victuals, that is to say, corn, hay, beasts, and poultry, and all other things needful to their household, and pay nothing therefor to account but tallies, so much so that, as it is told me, there is owing in this land by lieutenants and their soldiers within these few years £20,000. And more also, at parliaments and great councils the lieutenants have great subsidies and tallages granted to them. And all this the poor husbandry bears and pays for, and the war on the other side destroys them.[1]

The indignation expressed in this statement is understandable. But any chief governor who wished to maintain a force in the field was probably driven to rely on such unorthodox methods of supporting it. The stipend promised to him was inadequate and sometimes remained unpaid. Royal revenue inside Ireland itself dwindled as the issues from sources like the customs and the fee-farms of towns and cities were increasingly devoted to local defence. Those faced with the burden of parliamentary taxes undoubtedly viewed them as 'great subsidies and tallages', but the actual amount derived from the parliamentary subsidy was modest. And even this became more difficult to collect as the area under the control of the administration decreased and, with it, the taxable capacity of the colony, already further strained by demands for local subsidies to meet the menace of the Gaelic Irish in particular areas. Increasingly, therefore, the administration found itself caught in a spiral of declining authority and diminishing revenue from which it was difficult, if not impossible, to escape without recourse to unpopular means of financing military campaigns.

But the inevitability of such exactions did little to assuage the colonists' resentment of them. The practice of quartering armies on the local countryside had long been a feature of Gaelic Irish areas, where local lords claimed a traditional entitlement to this method of supporting their forces. The adoption and adaptation of this system by Anglo-Irish lords led to widespread condemnation of it under the general title of 'coyne and livery'. The word 'coyne' derives from the Irish terms *coinneamh* and *coinnmheadh*, both meaning billeting or quartering. Under its operation soldiers would exact food and lodging and, in some instances, wages from the local population. In 1416 it was reported that coyne was being levied at a weekly rate of twenty pence per man. Livery referred to

[1] *Reg. Swayne*, p. 108. Spelling and punctuation have been modernised.

the practice of similarly supporting horses and grooms without payment.[1] The use of such exactions to maintain private armies was already creating difficulties for many of the colonists. Even within the county of Dublin, it was reported in 1409, several people kept 'kernes, coynes, hobelers, and idlemen' in defiance of the 1366 statute of Kilkenny which permitted men to maintain such forces only in the border areas and at their own expense.[2] Attempts to stamp out the abuse had little hope of success if the government itself resorted to it as a means of supporting its forces, and the commons in parliament made strenuous but ultimately unavailing efforts to prevent this from happening.

The subsidy granted to the third earl of Ormond in 1404 was made conditional on his renunciation of coyne and livery as long as he remained justiciar. A petition in the parliament of 1410 demanded that any chief governor or any others who put any manner of coyne and livery upon the king's faithful people should be treated as traitors and open robbers of the king and his subjects. The reply to this, that former statutes on these matters should be observed, can have brought little satisfaction to the petitioners.

The parliament of 1421 secured a much firmer undertaking from the then lieutenant, the fourth earl of Ormond, who promised to make due payment for anything he required and, as a security against non-payment by the crown, pledged the rents of certain of his own lands as satisfaction of any debts outstanding at the end of his term of office. Thanks were also conveyed to the lieutenant because he 'abolished a bad, most heinous and unbearable custom, called coigne'.[3] But such a respite can only have been temporary, and the complainants against the many extortions and non-payments, by lieutenants and other governors, were still vainly seeking a remedy from the king in 1435.

The strength and quality of the forces at the disposal of the Dublin government depended, of course, on the availability of resources to support them. At times, the military power of the administration was sufficient to overawe the Irish chieftains and enforce submissions from them. On other occasions the colonists found it difficult to muster adequate forces for their own defence, and a campaign might only be brought to an end by the payment of a bribe or black rent to the Irish chieftain involved. Since neither the submission nor the agreement to pay black rent was regarded as permanently binding, each resulted only in a temporary cessation of hostilities and brought little prospect of a more lasting peace. And if the colony was unable to gain any permanent advantage from the campaigns, its enemies were sufficiently disunited to ensure that there

[1] On the evolution of the system of coyne and livery see C. A. Empey and Katharine Simms, 'The ordinances of the White Earl and the problem of coign in the later middle ages' in *R.I.A. Proc.*, lxxv (1975), sect. C, pp 178–87. The writer of the report entitled 'State of Ireland and plan for its reformation' (*c.* 1515) defined coyne and livery as 'takeing horsse meate and mannes meate of the kinges poore subgettes by compulsion, for nought, withoute any peny paying therfor' (*S.P. Hen. VIII*, ii, 12).

[2] *Rot. pat. Hib.*, p. 193a, no. 168.

[3] *Stat. Ire., John—Hen. V*, p. 573.

would be no combination large enough to threaten its survival. Warfare, therefore, was generally on a small scale, piecemeal, confused, and indecisive. It is not surprising that after 1415 the larger theatre of war in France held a much greater attraction for fighting men, even from within the colony; for if the hazards of war were greater there, so too were the prospects of booty and a share in the glory that bathed the victors of a great and decisive battle.

The vicissitudes through which the administration's relationship with an Irish chieftain's family might pass are well illustrated in its dealings with Mac Murchadha in Leinster. Art Mac Murchadha's renewed campaign against the colony, which had been the main reason for Richard II's return to the country in 1399, ended with the government order of 1 April 1400 confirming to him the annuity of 80 marks and the restoration of his wife's inheritance in the barony of Norragh, originally conceded by Richard II in 1395. But Art did not remain at peace for long. In 1401 his attack on County Wexford drew a retaliatory expedition from Dublin against him, and many of his hired kern from Munster were killed. Four years later, however, he was again waging 'a great war with the Galls' in which not only the county of Wexford suffered but Carlow and Castledermot were burnt also. On this occasion there does not seem to have been sufficient force to repulse him, and eventually he was again brought to peace by an agreement by the commons of County Wexford to pay him 80 marks. On 11 June 1409, the Dublin government, in its anxiety to preserve the fragile peace in the area, ordered the seneschal of the liberty of Wexford and the chief men of the towns of New Ross and Wexford to investigate charges of bad faith made by Mac Murchadha against the people of Wexford and to enquire how far the promised payment of 80 marks was in arrears. The enquiry seems to have been successful in at least postponing a further outbreak of hostilities, but in 1413 Mac Murchadha again attacked Wexford and continued his campaign in the following year. Then came another volte-face. By 24 July 1415 Art had again become the king's faithful subject, and his son Gearalt was issued with letters of safe-conduct to come to England to take an oath of fealty to the king on his father's behalf. If Gearalt went to England in pursuance of these letters, he can hardly have met Henry V, who was already at Southampton preparing for the departure of his forces to France on 7 August. But whatever negotiations took place that year, they had little lasting effect. A raid by Mac Murchadha on Wexford in the following year resulted, according to one annalist, in the death or capture of 340 of the colonists and the taking of great booty by the attackers.

On Art's death in 1416/17, he was succeeded by his son Donnchadh. The latter's capture by Talbot in May 1419 represented a minor triumph for the colony, and he remained a prisoner firstly in the Tower of London and later in Talbot's own custody until 1427. But his place was soon taken by his brother Gearalt; and after Gearalt had burnt and pillaged Wexford in 1422, the council agreed that he should be paid an annual fee of 40 marks, half of what had been paid by the government to his father and brother, to keep the peace. This arrangement endured for only three years and in 1426 Gearalt was again at war. As the situation deteriorated in the course of 1427, the decision was taken to release Donnchadh in the hope that he would provide an effective counterpoise to his brother, and in July 1427 the government granted him 80 marks for his efforts to bring the Leinster Irish to peace. The manoeuvre met with little success. Gearalt, with the support of a great number of kerns and other 'Irish enemies', was in too strong a position to be overthrown, and Wexford secured peace only by the payment of the large sum of 213 marks.

Donnchadh did regain his position after Gearalt's death in 1431, and seems to have been more disposed towards a policy of cooperation with the Dublin government; provided, of course, that the administration continued to pay him to keep the peace. But he remained a force to be reckoned with, and when his son Muircheartach was killed by the colonists in County Wexford in 1442, he levied an *éraic* or compensation-fine of 800 marks from the whole county.

The complex and, at times, bewildering shifts in policy towards the Mac Murchadha family reflect the ebb and flow of the colony's own resources. When the administration had adequate forces at its disposal it could enforce submissions by Irish chieftains with comparatively little difficulty. During the autumn and winter of 1401–2, before Thomas of Lancaster's financial difficulties became acute, Ó Conchobhair Failghe, Ó Broin, Mac Mathghamhna, and Ó Raghallaigh all submitted and promised to be the king's faithful subjects. The campaign of John Talbot, Lord Furnival, in 1415 was even more successful, and a large number of chieftains in the midlands and Ulster, including 'the greate O'Nele pretending himself to bee kinge of the Irish in Ulster'[1] were forced to submit and give hostages. The arrival of Edmund Mortimer, earl of March, with a large force of English and Welsh troops in the autumn of 1424 sparked off another series of submissions which continued under Talbot and Ormond, despite Mortimer's sudden death from the plague in January 1425. In October 1426 Ormond was still holding hostages from Ó Néill, Ó Domhnaill, Mac Mathghamhna, and the English rebel, Meiler de Bermingham, when he was granted 50 marks towards their upkeep.

Such successes demonstrated what might be achieved by a sizeable force under a competent commander. But failure to consolidate these victories in the field meant that their effects were ephemeral, and periods of military triumph were interspersed with others when the colony was thrown back on the defensive. In the autumn of 1422, William fitz Thomas, prior of Kilmainham, then justiciar, had to pay 160 marks out of his own pocket to Gearalt Mac Murchadha to secure freedom from attack for the inhabitants of the counties of Dublin and Kildare; and six years later he was still seeking recompense from the government. Fitz Thomas's successor as justiciar, Richard Talbot, archbishop of Dublin, could field only the traditional force of twelve men-at-arms

---

[1] Sir Henry Ellis (ed.), *Original letters illustrative of English history*, 2nd series (4 vols, London, 1827; reprinted, 1969), i, 58.

and sixty archers to deal with the menace from the O'Tooles in 1423, and when
Ó Conchobhair Failghe and Ó Raghallaigh also rose in rebellion in the same
year, only the intervention of the earl of Desmond with a large force from Munster prevented greater disasters for the colony. Again, in 1427 Archbishop
Swayne complained bitterly of the lack of provision made to deal with the
Gaelic Irish in the north, and pleaded in vain for the dispatch of 400 archers to
put down the latest rising.

A real difficulty in the way of a more stable settlement was the fact that the
Irish chieftains felt themselves bound by their submissions only for as long as
they could be enforced. Once the military power which had secured them was
withdrawn, there was no guarantee that warfare would not be resumed. Even
the surrender of hostages or, as Richard II had secured in 1395, a commitment
to forfeit large sums of money to the papacy if they broke their agreements, was
not sufficient to ensure observance of the terms of their submissions. Thus the
'king's faithful liege' could quickly become again the 'king's Irish enemy'. The
growing exasperation of the colonists with what they considered breaches of
faith prompted parliament's impractical request to the king in 1421 that he
should ask the pope to launch a crusade against the 'Irish enemies', on the
grounds that their leaders had broken their oaths of allegiance made to the
crown in 1395 and had not forfeited to the papacy the large sums of money
which they had promised if they failed to keep faith. The Irish chieftains could
of course, plead, with some justification, that the colonists were not always
scrupulous in their observance of agreed terms. But it is hard to escape the
conclusion that a submission was regarded by an Irish chieftain more as a tactical manoeuvre than as a firm undertaking governing future conduct. A letter
to the king in 1418, urging him to maintain a strong army in Ireland, asserted
that 'your Irish enemies and English rebels yf they may espie the contrary,
although they have putt in hostages and are otherwise strongly bound to the
peace, yet they will rise agayne unto wars'.[1]

Thus even military successes brought little enduring benefit for the colony.
The occasional successful sortie into enemy territory temporarily checked the
Gaelic Irish advance and presumably raised morale. But the underlying problem remained the defence of the frontier of the shrinking area under the administration's control. Parliament did encourage individuals to build fortresses
along the frontier. Anyone who undertook to erect a castle in the border area
was permitted to levy a subsidy in the surrounding county or liberty to help
finance it. And there is evidence that this led to a strengthening of the colony's
defences, though some projects had to be abandoned through an inability to
collect the required subsidy.

Increasing concentration on the defence of the emerging Pale involved, however, a greater neglect of the outlying areas. The writer of the 1435 report
thought that the major cause of the decline of south Leinster and Munster was

[1] Ibid., i, 60–61. On the importance of hostages see above, pp 327–8.

the failure of chief governors over the previous thirty years to visit these parts except 'for a sodan journay or an hostyng'; they never stayed long enough to punish rebels in accordance with the law, and the residents of these areas had little contact with the administration since, apart from a parliament in Kilkenny in 1425, 'the kyngs courtes, parlementz and great conseilles have not been holden there this 30 yere'. The situation was worse in Ulster and Connacht, which, according to the writer, had not been visited by a chief governor in the previous forty years except 'for acteying, hosteyng, or a sodan journey'.[1] And clearly the writer was correct in his inference that isolated military forays were no substitute for the effective exercise of government authority.

A strong and united administration might have been able to counter this continuing erosion of the government's authority despite the handicap of inadequate resources. But for much of this period the administration itself was divided. Shortly after the arrival of John Talbot, Lord Furnival, in Ireland in 1414 a feud broke out between himself and the fourth earl of Ormond which lasted for nearly thirty years and led to the disruptive growth of two factions within the colony. The effects of this quarrel were summed up by Archbishop Swayne in the late 1420s:

When my lord Talbot was in this country there was great variance between him and my lord of Ormond, and yet they be not accorded. And some gentlemen of the country be well willed to my lord of Ormond; they hold with him and love him and help him and be not well willed to my lord Talbot nor to none that love him. And they that love my lord Talbot do in the same manner to my lord of Ormond. So all this land is severed.[2]

The conflict between the two men seems to have had its basis in a personal antagonism which extended beyond Irish affairs. In the English parliaments of 1424 and 1425, the king's uncle, the duke of Bedford, intervened in the quarrel and secured a temporary reconciliation of the protagonists. But the accord was a brief one, and in any event, even when the two principals were absent from Ireland the quarrel continued to be waged by their followers. The main issue at stake was the control of the Irish administration, and although the struggle may be 'devoid of the enlivening interest of the great conflicts of political principle',[3] the documents enshrining the wearisome series of charges and counter-charges made by the two parties do throw some light on the workings of the Irish administration and on its relationship with the English government.

Richard II was the third and last reigning king to visit Ireland in the middle ages. His successors were unable or unwilling to accede to the requests from the colonists that they should come to Ireland, and the functions of the absentee

[1] Betham, *Dignities*, pp 362–3.
[2] *Reg. Swayne*, p. 111. Spelling and punctuation have been modernised.
[3] Margaret C. Griffith, 'The Talbot–Ormond struggle for control of the Anglo-Irish government, 1414–47' in *I.H.S.*, ii, no. 8 (Sept. 1941), p. 376. See also A. J. Pollard, 'The family of Talbot, lords Talbot and earls of Shrewsbury in the fifteenth century' (Ph.D. thesis, University of Bristol, 1968), pp 110–34; Griffiths, *Reign of Henry VI*, pp 14, 80, 162–4.

lord of Ireland were always delegated to others, chief governors with the varying titles of lieutenant, deputy lieutenant, or justiciar.

Like the king in England, the chief governor ruled with the advice of a council composed of the chief officers of the administration, and, on occasion, leading members of the Anglo-Irish aristocracy. He also had the power to summon
great councils or parliaments which now normally included, as well as the
leading lay and ecclesiastical magnates, representatives from the towns,
liberties and shires, the commons, and also, unlike England, proctors from the
clergy of the Irish dioceses. The day-to-day administration of the colony
rested, as it did in England, on the great departments of state, the chancery and
the exchequer, and the whole apparatus of government and dispensation of
justice was modelled closely, though necessarily on a much smaller scale, on
that current in England.

The Irish administration was a separate but subordinate one. A steady
stream of directives issued to it from England and a consistent control was
exercised over it within the limitations imposed by the time and hazards
involved in a journey to Ireland. The latter could, on occasion, be considerable.
In 1437 one Walter Dolman, 'carrying letters under the great and privy seals
and the signet' to the lieutenant and chancellor of Ireland, was captured at sea
by a Breton warship and carried off to the port of St Pol de Léon in Brittany.[1]
But such mishaps apart, English oversight of Irish affairs was normally sufficient to ensure compliance with the king's wishes.

That vigilance in this regard was necessary is clear from an incident at the
opening of Henry IV's reign. The new king had assumed office on 30 September 1399; yet, more than ten weeks later, on 15 December, he was forced to
write to the chancellor and treasurer of Ireland ordering that the seals of the
administration be amended to bear his name rather than that of the deposed
Richard II. The excuse given for the delay in doing this—that the administration had not yet been made aware of the new king's accession—is difficult to
accept, and it seems more likely that the Irish administration, if not actually
sympathetic to Richard II, was at least waiting to see if Henry IV could establish his position before transferring its loyalty to him. The chancellor and
treasurer presumably complied with this directive, and nothing further is heard
of the matter; but the incident is of interest as foreshadowing the more serious
differences that were to arise between the two administrations when succession
to the crown was disputed later in the century.

Although the financial risks involved in the chief governorship remained
considerable, the office itself seems to have become more attractive to Anglo-
Irish magnates as the century progressed. The willingness of the fourth earl of
Ormond in 1421 to pay any debts contracted during his lieutenancy, out of his
own pocket, contrasts with his father's reluctance to undertake the chief governorship on a temporary basis in 1404. Again, in 1442, he accepted the office of

[1] *Cal. pat. rolls, 1441–6*, p. 418.

lieutenant despite the refusal of the English administration to grant the terms he requested.[1] And one must conclude that the power and prestige attached to the office were sufficient to outweigh the possible costs involved in its exercise. The addition of the king's delegated authority to his own personal power inside Ireland clearly made the fourth earl of Ormond a formidable figure, and fears that he was becoming too powerful, and too independent of royal control, lie behind some of the charges made against him.

There were, of course, checks on the lieutenant's authority. From 1420 onwards his control over the officers of the administration was not absolute, since his patent of appointment normally prohibited him from dismissing the chancellor or treasurer, and in some instances the chief justices and chief baron of the exchequer were also exempted from his control. There was thus an opportunity for officers independent of the lieutenant to act as a counterbalance to his authority within the administration, and the impatience that might be felt at these restraints is clearly illustrated by Ormond's strenuous, if ultimately unsuccessful, attempts to remove a hostile treasurer and chancellor from office during 1442–4. In more general terms, the lieutenant's conduct was subject to review by the English council. From 1423 onwards, patents of appointment specifically stated that if the lieutenant or his deputy did anything unlawful, the council in England was to correct and reform the matter, and the numerous appeals made to the English privy council in the course of the Talbot–Ormond dispute confirm its role in this regard.

One of the issues raised in 1428–9 was royal control of the lieutenant. The petition from the parliament of 1428, which was pro-Ormond in its outlook, made the not unreasonable point that frequent changes in the lieutenancy and deputyship had been to the disadvantage of the colony, and requested that such changes should not be made in future so long as the conduct of affairs was satisfactory. But the riposte to that document by the rival faction inside Ireland sought to underline the lieutenant's dependence on the crown by claiming that the request was illegal in its attempt to circumscribe the power of the king. The exchanges also turned on the question of how complaints against chief governors should be transmitted to the king and council in England. The 1428 petition alleged that unfounded and unsubstantiated charges against the chief governor, motivated by malice and ill-will, were brought before the English council without any prior investigation inside Ireland; and it recommended that in future, before any such accusations were entertained by the English council, they should be notified to the council in Ireland and examined in parliament or great council there. Such complaints had been made in the fourteenth century, and an ordinance of 1357 had laid down a procedure not unlike that which was now requested for dealing with false and untrue suggestions made in England against officers of the Irish administration. But the pro-Talbot group opposed any such restriction on access to the English council,

[1] Matthew, 'Financing of the lordship of Ireland', p. 103.

and claimed that the truth would never be discovered if the charges were submitted to parliament or great council for investigation; for, it was argued, 'those
who are sent to parliaments and councils are chosen not for the good of the
king and his lieges but at the will of the nobles and magnates'.[1] This fear, that
charges against the chief governor would be smothered by the Irish council and
parliament, seems to have been shared by the English government, and complaints from unofficial sources continued to come before the English council
throughout the century.

The general charge, that the elected representatives of the Irish parliament
were under the influence of the magnates, was later made more specifically
against Ormond. He was accused in the 1440s of having had members of his
own household elected as knights of the shire so that parliament might be completely under his control. The charge was also made against him that he had
Gaelic Irishmen illegally elected to parliament; for the assembly remained
essentially a colonial body, despite Richard II's attempt in 1395 to include the
Irish lords within it, and the Gaelic Irish were not qualified for election to it.
Occasionally a Gaelic Irish bishop or abbot might attend, but parliament's
main relevance to the 'Irish enemies' was a negative one. According to one
chronicler, parliament's meeting was a signal for the Gaelic Irish to take advantage of the absence of those in attendance from their localities, and to launch an
attack.[2]

The role of the elected representatives inside parliament was a subordinate
one. It was necessary to secure the consent of the knights, burgesses, and clerical proctors to a grant of taxation, but since the annual parliamentary subsidy
formed a comparatively small proportion of the chief governor's income, and a
refusal to grant it would only lead to a more widespread use of illegal exactions,
the influence conferred on the commons by their control of taxation was
limited. At best they could hope to extract a promise from the chief governor
that he would not resort to the practice of coyne and livery, and such promises,
as we have seen, were not always honoured. In the making of legislation the
commons had a formal role in the presentation of the bills and petitions upon
which statutes were later based. But the chief governor rarely encountered any
opposition to the presentation of government-sponsored bills, and any difficulties experienced with the commons were usually the result of pressure upon
them by magnates opposed to the administration. And, of course, the decision
as to whether any bill or petition should become law depended on its approval
by the upper house, composed of the council and the magnates, and its acceptance by the chief governor. But while the legislative and fiscal functions of the
Irish parliament were less important than those of its English counterpart,
parliament did provide a forum for the increasingly embattled Anglo-Irish

[1] 'Ex gracia procerum et magnatum' (*Rot. pat. Hib.*, p. 248a, no. 13).
[2] 'In which time the Irish burned all that stood in their way, as their usuall custome was in times
of other parliaments.' (Marlborough, *Chronicle*, p. 25, 1413.)

community, through which it could express its concern about the deteriorating state of the colony in Ireland. And the series of petitions seeking more effective royal intervention, and predicting dire consequences of it was not forthcoming, doubtless had the full support of the commons in parliament.[1]

The idea that the elected representatives of the shires and the diocesan clergy had a more important parliamentary role than earls or bishops, at least in the granting of taxation, finds expression in the tract known as the 'Modus tenendi parliamentum'.[2] A copy of this document was found in the possession of Sir Christopher Preston when he was arrested, along with the earl of Kildare, by the deputy lieutenant, Sir Thomas Talbot, in 1418.

Both Kildare and Preston had expressed open dissatisfaction with the deputy's conduct of affairs, particularly his handling of the quarrel between Walter Burke[3] and Thomas Butler, prior of Kilmainham. The latter was a half-brother of the earl of Ormond, then absent in France, and Kildare was Ormond's father-in-law; Thomas Talbot had been appointed deputy by his brother John, Lord Furnival, before the latter's departure to England in the spring of 1418. It seems probable that the quarrel was part of the general Talbot–Ormond feud, and if, as one report stated, Kildare and Preston were planning to seize Talbot and replace him as chief governor, their arrest had ample justification.[4] Subsequently the two men were brought before the English council and part of the evidence in the case was the copy of the 'Modus' found in Preston's possession.

The tract, a summary of the procedure of parliament, has caused much controversy among historians as to its dating and significance. Most of those who have examined the texts have argued that the 'Modus' was originally composed in England in the reign of Edward II and that the Irish version is a modified copy of that English original. Notable dissidents from that view were H. G. Richardson and G. O. Sayles in a work first published in 1952,[5] but almost thirty years were to elapse before Sayles elaborated the reasons for that dissent. Cogent arguments have now been advanced in favour of the contention that the Irish 'Modus' is the original, the English the derivative text, and that the Irish version cannot be dated earlier than the reign of Richard II.[6] But even Sayles finds it difficult to establish the reasons for the composition of the tract, admitting that 'we cannot be sure of the purpose of the "Modus" ' and that 'if in late

[1] Art Cosgrove, 'Parliament and the Anglo-Irish community: the declaration of 1460' in *Hist. Studies*, xiv (1983), pp 34–6.
[2] M. V. Clarke, *Medieval representation and consent* (London, 1936; reprint, New York, 1964), p. 388; Nicholas Pronay and John Taylor (ed.), *Parliamentary texts of the later middle ages* (Oxford, 1980), pp 77–89.
[3] See below, p. 581.
[4] A. J. Otway-Ruthven, 'The background to the arrest of Sir Christopher Preston in 1418' in *Anal. Hib.*, no. 29 (1980), pp 71–94.
[5] Richardson & Sayles, *Ir. parl. in middle ages*, pp 137, 142.
[6] G. O. Sayles, 'Modus tenendi parliamentum: Irish or English?' in Lydon, *Eng. & Ire.*, pp 122–52, esp. p. 147. For a summary of other views of the 'Modus' see ibid., pp 122–3, 148.

fourteenth-century Ireland it was intended as a political squib, it proved a damp one'.[1] In 1419 the English council seem to have attached little importance to the document as evidence against Preston, and both he and Kildare were soon released from custody. And it has yet to be demonstrated that the 'Modus' exercised significant influence in any political crisis in England or Ireland in the later middle ages. But the debate continues.[2] Despite the attribution by the 'Modus' of greater importance to elected representatives, as the voice of the whole community, than to magnates, who only represented themselves, it is clear that parliament, and more particularly the commons in parliament, generally acted in accordance with the wishes of the chief governor. Ormond's attempts to manipulate the election of knights of the shire in the 1440s probably owed as much to a desire to overwhelm Talbot's supporters inside parliament as to any fear that the commons might begin to act independently of the administration.

The settlement of the Talbot–Ormond feud, by a marriage between Ormond's daughter and Talbot's son in 1444, removed the need to build up a party inside the commons. Thereafter, parliament, with the members in attendance dwindling as the colony itself shrank, was normally under the control of successive chief governors. And the crown was clearly correct, in its own interests, not to restrict reception of complaints against the chief governor to those authorised by parliaments, which normally provided chief governors with whatever testimonials they wished. For the issue of the extent of royal control over the chief governor survived the resolution of the Talbot–Ormond quarrel. The charge against Ormond in 1444, that he had disobeyed many of the directives sent from England, points to the practical difficulty in enforcing crown authority inside Ireland, if the chief governor chose to take an independent line. There remained, too, areas of potential friction between the two administrations, particularly when an appointment to the same office could be made by both, or where petitioners seeking to dislodge an incumbent might appeal to the superior authority of the English government. The settlement of 1444 meant that such issues were placed in abeyance; but they were to reemerge and trouble relations between the two administrations later in the century.

A stock charge by both sides in the Talbot–Ormond dispute was that their opponents had been guilty of treasonable complicity with the 'Irish enemies'. Officially, relations with the Gaelic Irish were still governed by the 1366 statute of Kilkenny, which was repromulgated in the 1402 parliament.

But, of course, the strict segregation envisaged by that measure could not be enforced. Numerous licences were issued to those living on the border of the colony, permitting them to negotiate with the neighbouring Gaelic Irish and

[1] Ibid., pp 138–9. Earlier he had contended that the 'Modus' was 'what H. W. C. Davis termed a *jeu d'esprit*, though, if we are to resort to French, perhaps the *mot juste* is *blague*' (ibid., p. 123).

[2] Sayles's view has been rejected by Michael Prestwich, 'The *Modus tenendi parliamentum*' in *Parliamentary History: a yearbook*, i (1982), pp 221–5. He contends that 'in spite of Sayles's arguments, it remains most probable that it was written in the early fourteenth century' (ibid., p. 224).

also, on occasion, to trade with them. In June 1403, for example, the citizens of New Ross, which was surrounded by 'Irish enemies', were allowed to treat with these enemies and also to sell them all manner of victuals and other goods, even during time of war. In 1405 Thomas Bath, who lived in the march area of County Meath, was licensed not only to trade with Gaelic Irishmen and rebels but also to foster their children. Similarly, in April 1406, permission was granted to William, son of Henry Betagh, to give his daughter Elizabeth in fosterage to 'Odo' O'Reilly, despite the prohibitions against fosterage in the statute of Kilkenny.

Intermarriage between the two 'nations' continued with or without the sanction of the administration. On occasion, opposition to such marriages might be expressed by the community. In 1448 it was stated in the ecclesiastical court of Armagh that John Brogeam's marriage to a Gaelic Irishwoman called Katherine 'Odobuy' had greatly displeased his friends. They did not think it fitting that John, the son of a good father, 'should marry such an Irishwoman'.[1] But intermarriage was also encouraged as a means of promoting peace. In his submission to the papacy in 1426 seeking a licence for Roger MacMahon to marry Alice White, Archbishop Swayne gave as one of the reasons in support of the grant of the licence that 'therefrom probably peace will be strengthened between the English and Irish'.[2] The archbishop's expression of this as only a probability was justifiable: marriage alliances of this kind did not always contribute towards the promotion of a lasting peace. In a rootedly patrilineal society, where wife and children adopted the 'nationality' of the husband and father, frequent intermarriage failed to break down the distinction between *Gaedhil* and *Gaill*, natives and foreigners, which the annalists continued to make throughout the century, and indeed beyond. The administration, too, differentiated between 'Irish enemies' and 'English rebels' on much the same basis; but the distinction, based as it was on descent, did little to determine political attitudes and alliances outside the Pale area, and intermarriage and fosterage, which the government could do little to control, were rightly seen by it as factors disposing the colonists to adopt Gaelic ways and consequently eroding their loyalty to the English crown.

Licences to receive Gaelic Irish tenants on their estates underline the difficulty experienced by many Anglo-Irish landholders in finding men of English descent to undertake tenancies, particularly in the border areas. Even within the earldom of Ormond, where the majority of the tenants were of English descent,[3] the earl decided to employ a judge skilled in brehon law, to settle disputes in accordance with that law. In his agreement with Donald Macglanghy (Domhnall Mac Flannchadha), the earl granted this expert in Irish law lands

---

[1] 'Quod talem Hibernicam in suam haberet uxorem' (Reg. Prene, ff 54–54ᵛ, T.C.D., MS 557, v, 213–15); cf. Art Cosgrove, 'Marriage in medieval Ireland' in Art Cosgrove (ed.), *Marriage in Ireland* (Dublin, 1985), p. 35.
[2] *Reg. Swayne*, pp 45–6.
[3] Empey, 'The Butler lordship', p. 184.

within the earldom in return for his services. But Donald had to undertake that any damage done to the earl's tenants by visitors to his new domicile would be made good at his expense.[1]

There were problems, too, in maintaining a sufficient work-force on estates. The parliament of 1410 claimed that so many labourers and servants had gone abroad that 'the husbandry and tillage of the same land is on the point of being altogether destroyed and wasted'; and it laid down that in future any mariner who was discovered conveying a labourer or servant abroad, without licence from the administration, should forfeit his ship. Officers were appointed to enforce this statute, but not, it would seem, with a great deal of success. The task of patrolling the Leinster coast would have been far beyond the administration's resources, and those who were determined to cross to England must have found it comparatively easy to do so. By 1421 the colonists were complaining that 'tenants, artificers, and labourers . . . daily depart in great numbers . . . to the kingdom of England and remain there', and they asked the king to provide some remedy for this drain on the colony's resources. But in 1429 many labourers and servants were reported to be emigrating without licence, and parliament passed a further statute attempting to restrain them.

It was difficult, too, to find suitable clergy of English descent to fill vacant ecclesiastical benefices. Even benefices in royal patronage were passing into Gaelic Irish hands, since no one in Ireland had power to fill them and they were of insufficient value to encourage anyone to journey to England to petition for them. And the parliament of 1428 requested, therefore, that the king should delegate the exercise of his right of patronage to the chief governor. The overall situation was summed up by Archbishop Swayne, who claimed in 1428 that 'there is mo gone out of the londe of the kyngis lege pepyll then be in'.[2]

Yet in spite of the colony's continuing decline and the growing prevalence of Gaelic customs and habits, there remained a number of Gaelic Irish who wished to formally anglicise themselves by securing charters granting them the right to use English law. Although the statute of 1331 had laid down that there should be one and the same law for the Gaelic and Anglo-Irish inside Ireland, its provisions seem to have had little practical effect in the fifteenth century. In general, Gaelic Irishmen seem to have been regarded as outside the scope of the English common law; their position, it has been convincingly argued, was analogous to that of aliens, and if any of them wished to enjoy the benefits of that law they had to secure a charter of denization. The usual form of that charter was as follows:

A.B. and all his issue (born and to be born) shall be of free estate and condition and free of all Irish servitude, shall answer and be answered in all courts in Ireland, shall use and enjoy English law in all respects in the same way in which Englishmen in the king's land

---

[1] *Ormond deeds, 1413–1509*, no. 66, pp 49–50.
[2] *Reg. Swayne*, p. 108. For the view that the records of the central government may exaggerate the extent of emigration and ignore regional variations, see Empey, art. cit., p. 186.

of Ireland use and enjoy it, shall have power freely to acquire lands, tenements, and possessions and also goods and chattels and to dispose of them at their will and to succeed to them as the English do in the aforesaid land of the king, and to accept church benefices as well in cathedrals and collegiate churches as elsewhere, their Irish condition (or any statute or ordinances) notwithstanding.[1]

Throughout the first half of the century the Irish chancery issued a steady stream of such grants to Gaelic Irish applicants, usually, it would seem, in return for payments that varied between half a mark and 20 shillings. About one-third of these were to clerics, and presumably were made to allow them to hold benefices or enter religious houses in the colonial area despite the prohibition imposed on Gaelic Irish clergy by the statute of Kilkenny. The few grants to Gaelic Irish women were probably made in connection with their marriages to men of English descent to ensure that no doubts should exist about the English status of their offspring.[2] In a rare case a specific reason is given for the grant. In 1423 Philip McKeown, a clerk who was to have a long and successful career in the employ of the archbishop of Armagh, was admitted to English law as a reward for his services to John Talbot and other lieutenants in the wars in Ulster, and more particularly for acting as interpreter between the colonists and the Gaelic Irish. Other grants to Gaelic Irishmen were made at the request of prominent members of the colony like the mayor of Limerick or Thomas, son of the earl of Desmond. In some instances the government accepted the claim of the applicant that he and his ancestors had been faithful subjects of the king since the time of the conquest. On these grounds Robert, son of Philip Holhane and Margaret de Barry, was admitted to English law in 1425 despite the fact that he had 'a surname of the Irish nation viz dez Holhaganes'.[3]

Applications for a grant of English law, indicating as they do a desire to become equal members of the colony, presumably came from those Gaelic Irish who had decided to make their careers in areas under the administration's control. Without such a charter they would have been liable to harassment, if not positive discrimination. A grant of denization would have been essential to any Gaelic Irishman wishing to advance himself in Limerick after 1414, when it was laid down in the charter granted to the city by Henry V that Gaelic Irishmen were to be excluded from the mayoralty and all other civic offices as well as from entering into apprenticeship there.[4]

---

[1] Bryan Murphy, 'The status of the native Irish after 1331' in *Ir. Jurist*, ii (1967), pp 116–38; G. J. Hand, 'Aspects of alien status in medieval English law with special reference to Ireland' in Dafydd Jenkins (ed.), *Legal history studies, 1972: papers presented at the Legal History Conference, Aberystwyth, 18–21 July 1972* (Cardiff, 1972), pp 129–35.

[2] Cf. *Ormond deeds, 1413–1509*, no. 230, pp 205–6.

[3] *Rot. pat. Hib.*, p. 235b, no. 6.

[4] The regulation demonstrates that a peculiar, and presumably inferior, status was indicated by the Latin term for Irishman, *Hibernicus*: '. . . quod nullus qui de sanguine et nacione Hibernicus existit, intelligendo et capiendo hunc terminum *Hibernicus* prout in terra nostra Hibernie intelligi

The process of admitting Gaelic Irishmen to full rights did cause some qualms among the colonists, who feared that conversion to an English way of life might not be either total or lasting. The parliament of 1410 urged that no Gaelic Irishman should receive a 'charter of denizen' until he had given sufficient guarantees that he would not afterwards adhere to the 'Irish enemies'. Such fears were a natural outcome of the colony's own preoccupation with security. In 1407 worries were expressed even about the safety of Dublin castle, and the constable was ordered to guard against the possibility that it might be taken 'by deceit of untrue men, strangers, and others dwelling in the marches of Ireland, who flock thither and enter the castle'.[1] The English parliament of 1416, at the request of the colonists, confirmed a statute banning Gaelic Irishmen from church promotion, on the grounds that Gaelic Irish bishops and abbots brought with them to the Irish parliament servants who discovered the secrets of the English and reported them to the king's Irish enemies. And an Irish statute of 1431 urged the capture of the many Gaelic Irish who came and resided among the colonists for the purpose of espionage.

Considerations of security probably lie behind, too, the sporadic attempts at stricter enforcement of the statute of Kilkenny. In 1415 two officers were appointed to apprehend all the children, both male and female, of 'Irish enemies' and 'English rebels', who were being fostered by the faithful English in the marches or elsewhere. Twenty years later an attempt was made to deal with minstrels and other entertainers who, after they had displayed their talents for the benefit of the colonists, went back to the 'Irish enemies' and acted as guides for them in their attacks on the colony. William Lawless, described as the marshal of the 'faithful English' entertainers in Ireland, was ordered to capture all these 'clarsaghours, tympanours, crowthores, kerraghers, rymours, skelaghes, bardes and others'.[2] There is little to suggest that either measure had much effect. Continuing gaelicisation among the colonists in the border areas and the admission of a number of Gaelic Irish to English law blurred the line between friend and foe and made it difficult to distinguish those who were loyal and those who were not. The parliament of 1447, faced with the problem that there was no difference in dress between the Gaelic and Anglo-Irish in the march areas, attempted to impose an alternative means of ready identification. Any man who wished to be accounted of English descent was to shave his upper lip at least once every two weeks so that he would not have a moustache. Those who failed to comply with this statute were liable to have their persons and goods seized and to be ransomed as 'Irish enemies'.

To such expedients was the colony driven in its attempts to maintain itself against the rising tide of the Gaelic resurgence. Depleted in numbers and

et capi consuevit, sit maior nec aliquod aliud officium exerceat infra civitatem predictam . . .' (Mac Niocaill, *Na buirgéisí*, i, 245). For Waterford attitudes, see above, p. 396.

[1] *Cal. close rolls, 1405–9*, p. 178.
[2] *Rot. pat. Hib.*, p. 258a, no. 86.

resources, increasingly harried by the 'Irish enemies' and 'English rebels' along the borders of the Pale, the colonists looked towards the king to provide for their salvation. If he could not come himself, then let him send some great lord from England. The appointment of Richard, duke of York, as lieutenant in 1447 gave a promise of better things to come, and the extent of his welcome when he arrived in 1449 was a measure of the hopes that he might revive the fortunes of the colony after the disasters of the previous half-century.

CHAPTER XIX

Anglo-Ireland and the Yorkist cause, 1447–60

ART COSGROVE

ON 30 July 1447 Richard, duke of York, was appointed lieutenant of Ireland with effect from 9 December following. The appointment, for a ten-year period, was made at a time when he was not only the most powerful landowner in England but also, by virtue of the duke of Gloucester's death in the previous February and Henry VI's failure, as yet, to produce a child, heir-presumptive to the English throne. He was thus a natural focus for the growing opposition to the weak and immature king, now under the influence of his wife, Margaret of Anjou, and the leader of the Beaufort or Lancastrian faction among the aristocracy, William de la Pole, marquis, and by 1448 duke, of Suffolk. York had been appointed lieutenant-general of the English forces in France in 1440, but was formally replaced by Edmund Beaufort in December 1446. The decision to send him to Ireland was subsequently interpreted by some English chroniclers as a deliberate attempt by Suffolk to send the duke into virtual exile.[1] It is probable that Suffolk and his adherents would have welcomed York's absence from England. As military failure and concession in France increased the government's unpopularity, York could well have become the leader of those critical of the ruling clique. But, in fact, no effort was made to enforce York's departure. Not until July 1449 did he set out for Ireland and there is evidence to suggest that he came to this country of his own volition, not at Suffolk's behest.[2]

In fact the delay in taking up his commission may have been caused by his attempts to raise sufficient money to finance his expedition. He can have had few illusions about the efficacy of the government system of assignment as a means of meeting its commitments, since he was still seeking payment of what was owed him for his previous services in Normandy.[3] As late as September 1449 he was requesting permission from the king to sell or mortgage part of his own property to meet the costs of his office. This was probably a wise precaution

---

[1] *Incerti scriptoris chronicon Angliae de regnis Henrici IV, Henrici V et Henrici VI*, ed. J. A. Giles (London, 1848), p. 35; G. L. and M. A. Harris, 'John Benet's chronicle for the years 1400 to 1462' in *Camden Miscellany*, xxiv (London, 1972, Camden Society, 4th series, ix), p. 195.

[2] Griffiths, *Reign of Henry VI*, pp 420, 439, n. 105, pp 508, 672.

[3] Ibid., p. 674.

in view of the fact that his stipend was fixed at 4,000 marks for the first year, with £2,000 annually for the remaining nine years of his term as lieutenant. Such a sum was now the fixed rate for the position, but it compared unfavourably with the 12,000 marks a year granted to Henry IV's son Thomas of Lancaster in 1401, and contrasted starkly with the £20,000 a year assigned to York as commander in France. But in the extent of the powers given to him, if not in the salary, York's appointment did hark back to that of Thomas of Lancaster. His agreement with the king allowed him full control over all offices in the Irish administration, and he could dispose of all the revenues he received without accounting for them to the crown.

Whatever the reasons that prompted York's dispatch to Ireland, it was clear that many of the Anglo-Irish would welcome him. The colony had often requested the king, as it did in 1441, to 'ordayne a mightie lord of . . . your realme of England for to be your lieutenant of the said land'. And the address to the king from the Irish parliament in that year had argued that the people would favour and obey a nobleman of English birth more than anyone born in Ireland, since Englishmen 'keep better justice, execute your lawes, and favour more the common people there, and ever have done before this tyme'.[1]

For York himself, Ireland was not without its advantages. Through his descent from Edward III's son Lionel, duke of Clarence, who had married Elizabeth de Burgh, the daughter of the last resident earl of Ulster, he was heir to the earldom of Ulster and the lordship of Connacht. The death in Ireland in 1425 of his uncle Edmund Mortimer also conferred on him the lordships of Trim and Leix. Most of this property, with the exception of the Trim lordship and the eastern strip of the old liberty of Ulster, had now passed into the hands of 'Irish enemies' and 'English rebels'. But clearly a successful military campaign in Ireland would be to York's personal benefit if it resulted in any reclamation of property or reassertion of his rights in the areas nominally under his lordship.

Initially, such success seemed assured. Prompted, perhaps, by a letter from Archbishop Mey of Armagh, York abandoned his original intention of a foray into Wicklow and turned his attention to the north. Because of the difficulties there Mey had been unable to comply with York's request for a contribution to his army. Ó Néill, with his sons and followers, had so hindered the archbishop's visitation of his diocese that he had publicly excommunicated them in the market-place at Dundalk and placed their lands under interdict. The borders of Louth were still secure,[2] but there were fears and uncertainties about the truce concluded between the colonists and the Gaelic Irish, before York's arrival, by his deputy Richard Nugent, baron of Delvin, and the earl of Ormond.

---

[1] *Stat. Ire., Hen. VI*, p. 50.

[2] In the parliament of 1450, Mey and Thomas White were given leave to levy £100 spent in resisting attacks on Louth, shortly before the lieutenant's arrival, by Ó Néill, Mac Mathghamhna, Mag Aonghusa, Ó hAnluain, and others (*Stat. Ire., Hen. VI*, p. 209).

York's march northwards soon had its effect. By 15 August Mág Aonghusa, Mac Mathghamhna, Mac Uidhilín, and Ó Raghallaigh had submitted to York along with a number of leaders of English descent within the earldom of Ulster. Twelve days later, at Drogheda, Énrí Ó Néill, son of Eóghan, captain of his nation, submitted on behalf of his father, sons, brothers, and all his subjects, and entered into an elaborate agreement with York defining the future relationship to be observed between them. Énrí undertook to become Richard's man or vassal and to restore all property seized by the O'Neills from the earldom of Ulster as it existed in the time of Walter and Richard de Burgh. In addition he bound himself to provide the 'bonnaght' or military service traditionally owed by the O'Neills to the earls of Ulster, and more specifically to place at the duke's disposal 500 cavalry and 500 foot-soldiers for any war conducted by the duke inside Ulster. He also promised to restore lands and properties seized by the O'Neills from other Anglo-Irish in Ulster, particularly the territory known as the Fews, in Armagh, which belonged to Sir John Bellew. Archbishop Mey's complaints about Ó Néill's incursions into church property were met by an undertaking that he would surrender all ecclesiastical property held by his family and, in future, that he would pay or cause to be paid tithes and other ecclesiastical dues to their rightful recipients. Ó Néill's agreement to discipline all Gaelic Irish rebels against the duke's authority in Ulster was matched by York's promise to investigate any offences committed by his subjects in Ulster against Ó Néill, and to do justice according to the laws and customs of the earldom. As an earnest of his homage and fealty, Ó Néill undertook to give 600 fat cattle to the duke, who remitted 300 of these as a reward for future services on Énrí's part. Finally Énrí swore on the gospels and on a piece of the wood of the True Cross, enclosed in a small golden cross, that he would observe the terms of the agreement under pain of excommunication and interdict.

Clearly the 1449 indenture was a further attempt to regularise the relationships between the earls of Ulster and the O'Neills by making Énrí a mesne tenant of the earl, holding his lands in return for specified military service. As such, it recalled the similar undertakings entered into by Énrí's father, Eóghan, in 1425 with the earl of Ormond; and like the former treaty it had little lasting effect.

But it did give an immediate impetus to York's campaign in the midlands and south Leinster later in the summer. Ó Broin of Wicklow not only submitted and agreed to be the king's true servant, but also undertook for himself, his children, and his chief followers that they would wear English clothes and learn the English language. His surrender was followed by that of Mac Murchadha and most of the other Leinster chieftains, who flocked to York to make submissions in a manner reminiscent of Richard II's expedition of 1394–5. So impressed was one of York's entourage that he gave his opinion in the autumn of 1449 that 'with the myght of Jesus ere twelvemonth come to an end the wildest Yrishman in Yrland shall be swore English'.[1]

An antidote to such euphoria was soon provided by a report to York from the citizens of Cork, Kinsale, and Youghal, who requested that the lieutenant and council should come to Cork to quell the disorder inside that county. In particular they complained of the dissensions among the lords of English descent, which had become so widespread that much of the county had passed into the hands of the Gaelic Irish. Unless measures were taken to end these destructive quarrels, they claimed, 'we are all cast away, and then farewell Munster for ever'.[2] If York and the council refused to act, then they would complain directly to the king.

There is no evidence that this petition elicited any response. York himself certainly did not go to Cork. The great council summoned to Dublin by him in October was more concerned with the misconduct of those of English descent living on the edge of the Pale. Many of those on the border of Dublin and other counties kept more soldiers than they could afford and supported them illegally by the exaction of coyne from the surrounding countryside. Particularly resented was the adoption of the Gaelic custom of 'cuddies',[3] whereby, at certain times of the year, the leaders of these forces extorted food and entertainment for the night (*cuid oidhche*) for themselves and their miscellaneous followers from the inhabitants of the area. The exaction of coyne and these 'cuddies' was prohibited, and, in an effort to enforce some discipline on these marauding bands on the border of the colony, it was laid down that everyone who kept troops should do so at his own expense, and that he should give the sheriff or justices of the peace of the county concerned a list of names of those in his following. It is unlikely that this legislation proved any more effective than earlier similar enactments. What was needed, as the memorial from Cork had pointed out, was a strong reassertion of governmental authority. York's campaigns of 1449 had seemed to presage such a development, but the fleeting nature of his successes had become apparent by the spring of 1450.

It was customary for 'the Irish enemies . . . to go to war immediately after the feast of Easter'.[4] And the parliament that York summoned to Drogheda in April 1450 faced the prospect of an early resumption of hostilities. Like many chief governors before him, York was gravely hampered by the failure of the English government to pay him his stipulated salary. To help him over his financial difficulties, parliament authorised him to collect a scutage, the commutation paid by military tenants of the crown in lieu of personal service, even though the parliament of 1445 had forbidden the levy of scutage for the following ten years.

---

[1] Cited in Edmund Curtis, 'Richard, duke of York, as viceroy of Ireland, 1447–60' in *R.S.A.I.Jn.*, lxii (1932), p. 168; cf. Katharine Simms, ' "The king's friend": O'Neill, the crown and the earldom of Ulster' in Lydon, *Eng. & Ire.*, pp 222–4.

[2] Gilbert, *Viceroys*, p. 357.

[3] Cf. Empey and Simms, 'Ordinances of the White Earl', p. 184; and above, p. 340.

[4] *Stat. Ire., Hen. VI*, p. 259.

But this was not sufficient to enable him to deal effectively with renewed up-risings by the Irish chieftains, particularly Mág Eochagáin of Meath, who, despite his submission of the previous autumn, had allied himself with three or four Gaelic Irish chieftains and a great number of Anglo-Irish rebels, and attacked and burnt the town of Rathmore and nearby villages. In a letter written on 15 June 1450 to his brother-in-law, the earl of Salisbury, in England, York recounted these events and urged the speedy payment of his salary to enable him to resist these attacks. Otherwise many others would follow Mág Eochagáin's example. The duke stressed his dire need and claimed that if money was not sent for the defence of the colony

my power cannot stretch to keep it in the king's obedience. And very necessity will compel me to come into England to live there upon my poor livelihood. For I had liever be dead than any inconvenience should fall thereunto by my default: for it shall never be chronicled nor remain in scripture, by the grace of God, that Ireland was lost by my negligence.[1]

The final sentence shows York's concern that he should not be accused of surrendering territory in Ireland at a time when concessions in France had made Henry VI's government markedly unpopular. Suffolk had never escaped from the obloquy that had been heaped upon him after the cession of Maine to the French in 1446; the surrender of Rouen in October 1449 was also laid at his door, and rumours circulated, even in Ireland, that he had sold the town to the French. Formal charges against him by the English parliament resulted in his banishment from England in April 1450, but the ship carrying him abroad was intercepted and Suffolk himself murdered. Aware of the anger that Suffolk's conciliatory policy towards the French had aroused in England, York was naturally anxious to dissociate himself from any implication that he was guilty of similar concessions in Ireland. But his plea for funds from England met with no effective response,[2] and he was forced eventually to compromise with Mág Eochagáin and make peace on terms favourable to the Irish chieftain.

Events in England provided a not unwelcome distraction for the lieutenant in these straitened circumstances. Suffolk's murder had sparked off a series of disorders which culminated in the rising led by Jack Cade in Kent in 1450. Cade remains a mysterious figure, but the writ for his arrest claimed that he had been born in Ireland, and he maintained that his name was John Mortimer and that he was a cousin of the duke of York, whose recall from Ireland was one of the rebels' demands. There is no evidence to link York directly with the Cade rising, but it was inevitable that he should be suspected of complicity with it. And although the rising was speedily put down and Cade himself

[1] Gilbert, *Viceroys*, p. 362.
[2] Although the king ordered the exchequer, on 17 May 1450, to pay what was owed to York, this did not result in any speedy transfer of funds to the duke. See R. A. Griffiths, 'Duke Richard of York's intentions in 1450 and the origins of the wars of the roses' in *Journal of Medieval History*, i (1975), pp 195–6.

captured and killed, knowledge that accusations of treason were being made against him may have been one of the factors that determined York to leave an unpromising situation in Ireland and to return to Britain towards the end of August 1450.[1]

York's stay in Ireland had done little to advance the fortunes of the colony. But the duke clearly won widespread personal popularity among the Anglo-Irish, and the links established with many of the leading families were to endure and to prove of considerable value when Yorkist hopes were dashed by defeat in England in the autumn of 1459. One bond that did not last was that made with the Butler family of Ormond. Shortly before his departure, in July 1450, York reached an agreement with the ageing but still powerful fourth earl of Ormond, whereby the latter undertook to serve the duke in peace and war, both in England and Ireland, in return for an annual fee of 100 marks.[2] And it was Ormond whom York chose to act as his deputy in his absence. But Ormond's death in August 1452, after a vigorous military campaign which belied his advancing years, not only removed a dominant figure from the Irish scene but also conferred the earldom on his absentee son, the earl of Wiltshire, a strong Lancastrian partisan. Indeed, when the Lancastrian party strengthened its grip on the English administration in the spring of 1453, the new earl of Ormond displaced York as lieutenant of Ireland and subsequently nominated John Mey, archbishop of Armagh, as his deputy. York, however, continued to dispute Ormond's tenure of the lieutenancy and in February 1454 the situation became so confused that it was decided that the sums of money assigned to Ireland should be paid to the treasurer of England until it had been legally determined 'who is and ought to be lieutenant'. In the following April, York, now protector of England during the king's insanity, was sufficiently strong to have the dispute resolved in his favour.[3]

The new earl of Ormond did not come to Ireland either to act as lieutenant or to reside upon his Irish estates; and the absence of a resident lord of Ormond seems to have resulted in increased disorder among the cadet branches of the Butler family. Ormond's claim to the manors of Maynooth and Rathmore against the Fitzgeralds of Kildare was pursued vigorously by his cousins, Edmund and William Butler, and in June 1454 the people of Kildare complained to York that the struggle between the two sides had caused more destruction in Kildare and Meath within a short period than had been done by Gaelic and Anglo-Irish enemies for a long time before. Such was the disorder

[1] York landed at Beaumaris on the island of Anglesey and had reached the Welsh mainland by 7 September. See R. A. Griffiths, 'Richard, duke of York, and the royal household in Wales, 1449–50' in *Welsh Hist. Rev.*, viii (1976), p. 14. The decision to return may also have been influenced by news of the arrival in England, on 1 Aug. 1450, of his rival, Edmund Beaufort, duke of Somerset. Nevertheless, as Griffiths admits, the 'timing of York's arrival [in England] is not easy to explain' (*Reign of Henry VI*, p. 687).

[2] *Ormond deeds, 1413—1509*, no. 177, pp 167–8.

[3] P.R.O., E. 28/83/1; Herbert Wood, 'Two chief governors of Ireland at the same time' in *R.S.A.I. Jn.*, lviii (1928), pp 156–7.

in the area that many refused to appear in the royal courts, or even to travel to market towns, for fear of being robbed or killed. The parliament held by the earl of Kildare as York's deputy in October 1455 was informed that various members of the Butler families of Paulstown, Dunboyne, and Tipperary had allied themselves with Mac Murchadha and burnt and destroyed the county of Wexford continuously for a period of four days and nights.[1] These collateral branches of the Butler family, in contrast with the absentee main line, had frequently intermarried with Gaelic Irish families, and the campaign of 1455 revealed the extent of their gaelicisation as well as their opposition to Kildare as deputy. Parliament ordered them to appear by the following Easter to answer for their offences under pain of being adjudged traitors, but the administration was not strong enough to compel their attendance, and the parliament of 1458 revoked the sentence of treason against them on the specious grounds that they had all been too ill to appear. But the quarrel between the Butlers and FitzGeralds continued and, like many similar private feuds in England, became entangled with the wider conflict between Lancastrians and Yorkists, with Kildare supporting York, and the Butlers, by and large, taking the Lancastrian side.

Beset by attacks from both Gaelic Irish and rebel Anglo-Irish, it is not surprising that the colonists sought further to entrench the Pale area. In 1454 commissioners were appointed to recruit 'labourers and workmen ... to make trenches and fortresses upon the borders and marches' of the four Pale counties of Meath, Louth, Kildare, and Dublin.[2] That further defences were necessary is clear from the threat presented to Dublin itself by the proximity of the colony's enemies. In 1455 orders were issued for the building of barriers and towers on the bridges of Lucan and Kilmainham and beside the wall of St Mary's abbey to repel the 'Irish enemies' and 'English rebels' who 'enter into Fingal by night and there kill, rob, and destroy the liege people of the king'.[3] Attempts were made, too, to limit the number of Gaelic Irish entering the colonial area by sea. The master of any ship who was discovered transporting Gaelic Irish men and women into 'any English land occupied and tilled by Englishmen' was to be fined 6s. 8d. for each passenger. For it was alleged that so many Gaelic Irish, most of them strong young men and women, had entered the colonial area under the guise of beggars that there was scarcely sufficient to feed both them and the residents. And these immigrants exacerbated the situation in the autumn by cutting and stealing corn, threshing it, and carrying it off to the Gaelic Irish.[4] This was a loss the colony could ill afford at a time when it was reported that many had been forced to leave Ireland because of the scarcity of corn, and in 1456 the government placed a year-long embargo on the export of corn without special licence.

[1] These campaigns are referred to by the scribes of the Gaelic MS Bodl. Laud Misc. 610, who accompanied their lord Edmund Butler; see below, pp 692–3.
[2] *Stat Ire., Hen. VI*, p. 299.   [3] Ibid., pp 315, 403.   [4] Ibid., pp 417–19.

The 1455 parliament also appealed to England for help. Six messengers were selected to travel to England to impress upon the duke of York the gravity of the situation, for it was claimed that the colony was likely to be finally destroyed unless aid was speedily sent from England. York, however, had more pressing problems. The antagonism between the Lancastrian and Yorkist factions had finally erupted into open warfare at the battle of St Albans in May 1455. By his victory in that battle York established an uneasy superiority, and the king's relapse into insanity allowed him to become protector of England again in November 1455. But the opposition to him, led by the queen, remained, and the recovery of Henry VI in the spring of 1456 marked the beginning of a Lancastrian resurgence. In these circumstances York could devote little attention to the affairs of Ireland. In March 1457 his commission as lieutenant of Ireland was renewed for a further ten years, and there is some evidence to suggest that an Irish expedition was contemplated in the following autumn.[1] But it was not until the autumn of 1459 that York eventually returned to Ireland; and then he came as a fugitive from the victorious Lancastrians after the rout of the Yorkist army at the battle of Ludford Bridge on 12 October.

York's decision to seek refuge in Ireland demonstrated his confidence in the continuing loyalty of the Anglo-Irish to him. And his reception in Ireland fully justified that confidence. According to one English chronicler he was welcomed by the Irish 'as if another messiah had descended to them and was going to live among them'.[2]

The English parliament of November 1459 attainted York of treason, and thus all his offices, including the lieutenancy of Ireland, were stripped from him, and the earl of Ormond and Wiltshire was appointed to replace him as lieutenant on 4 December. The attainder had meant, too, that all York's lands were forfeited to the crown, and on 27 January 1460 the treasurer of Ireland was ordered to take all York's Irish possessions into the king's hands. But none of the measures against York could be made effective inside Ireland. The parliament that he summoned to meet at Drogheda in February 1460 confirmed his tenure of the office of lieutenant and made it a treasonable offence for anyone to challenge his authority. That this was no idle threat was made clear by the conviction and execution of a messenger sent from England with writs ordering York's arrest.

The parliament then proceeded to declare that

the land of Ireland is and at all times has been corporate of itself, by the ancient laws and customs used in the same, freed of the burden of any special law of the realm of England, save only such laws as by the lords spiritual and temporal and the commons of the said land had been in great council or parliament there held, admitted, accepted, affirmed, and proclaimed according to sundry ancient statutes thereof made.[3]

[1] Cf. *Cal. pat. rolls, 1452—61*, p 388.
[2] *Registrum abbatiae Johannis Whethamstede*, ed. H. F. Riley (London, 1872), pp 367–8.
[3] *Stat. Ire., Hen. VI*, p. 645.

The significance of this claim, that Ireland was a separate entity bound only by those laws that were accepted and passed by her own parliament, has been disputed among historians. One older authority, Edmund Curtis, saw it as 'a declaration of independence' which marked the apogee of a period of 'aristocratic home rule' by the Anglo-Irish. Subsequent writers on the issue view the claim in a very different light. Richardson and Sayles argue that it 'was a mere measure of protection devised by the duke of York' and that the 'assertion had no basis in history', and A. J. Otway-Ruthven agrees with them that the claim 'had no validity in law or custom'. More recently, however, J. F. Lydon, while rejecting the anachronistic terms in which Curtis couched his arguments, has revived the view that the declaration was an expression of Anglo-Irish separatism and has argued that 'there was some historical justification for the 1460 claim'.[1]

There is no doubt that in the thirteenth and fourteenth centuries English statutes were regarded as binding on Ireland without any need for reenactment. And the royal directive of 1 February 1412, ordering the implementation in Ireland of the English statutes against provisors, was based on the same assumption; the administration in Ireland was simply directed to enrol the statutes in the records of the Irish chancery and courts and to publicly proclaim them in cities, towns, and other suitable places. It has been argued that when such proclamation was made by the Irish parliament the distinction between publicisation of statutes and their acceptance became blurred, and that this practice afforded a precedent for the 1460 claim. But more important than the question of historical precedents is the claim itself and the reasons that lay behind it.

On one level the 1460 declaration can be seen as a stratagem to protect York by the refusal to accept that the English legislation convicting him of treason was applicable in Ireland. Similarly, the concurrent enactment invalidating all writs summoning people to answer charges outside of Ireland, unless such writs were endorsed by the Dublin administration under its own great seal, legalised York's own refusal to obey such a writ. But to see these measures merely as Yorkist manoeuvres would be to underrate their significance; for they also raised the question of the relationship to be observed between the English and Irish administrations, as well as the wider issue of the attitude of the Anglo-Irish in general towards the English government.

The immediate purpose behind the prohibition on English writs summoning people out of Ireland may have been to protect York and his Anglo-Irish supporters against such a summons. But the act also appealed to ancient custom, claiming that Ireland always had its own seal to which Irish subjects owed lawful obedience, and asserting that it was unheard-of that any persons

[1] See Curtis, *Med. Ire.* (2nd ed.), pp 309–24; Richardson & Sayles, *Ir. parl. in middle ages*, pp 92–3, 260, 263; Otway-Ruthven, *Med. Ire.*, pp 190, 387, n. 19; Lydon, *Lordship*, pp 263–6, and *Ire. in later middle ages*, pp 144–5.

'inhabiting or resident in any other Christian land so corporate of itself'[1] should be summoned abroad except by the proper seal of the land. The language in which the act was couched denotes a consciousness of the separate character of the Irish administration, and its implementation would clearly have restricted the king's control over that administration. For charges against his officers in Ireland could only be heard in England if the Irish administration agreed to this procedure. Such a brake on royal jurisdiction was in line with earlier attempts to prevent the reception in England of complaints against the administration unless they had first been investigated and substantiated inside Ireland.[2]

Relations between the two administrations continued to be troubled by disputes over appointments. Petitioners in England could and did secure appointment to offices in Ireland 'by sinister information' or 'by craft',[3] and the ability of tenacious litigants to exploit the differences between the two administrations is best seen in one dispute over the offices of chancellorship of the green wax and clerkship of the common pleas of the exchequer, which began in 1446 and was not resolved until 1455. And fear of unwarranted or unjustified interference from England prompted the Irish parliament, on occasion, to confirm appointees in their offices, despite any writs from the king to the contrary.

Such administrative friction was, in part, the natural outcome of a situation where two separate bureaucracies claimed the right to appoint to the same offices. But the desire to secure more independence of English control also owed something to the growing feeling of 'separateness' among the Anglo-Irish themselves. Three hundred years in Ireland had not made the colonists indistinguishable from the Gaelic Irish, in their own eyes at least, but they could now be clearly distinguished from the English. Even those who remained loyal, and still participated in the governing institutions of the colony, must have felt that there was a less sympathetic understanding of their problems than they would have wished in England, where they were often regarded, and sometimes treated, as aliens. Differences in dialect and accent accentuated their distinctiveness, and while such differences existed between regions inside England itself in the fifteenth century, no region had a separate administration and parliament to give expression to them. And the existence of these institutions afforded the opportunity to the Anglo-Irish aristocracy to secure a greater freedom from the control of the English king.[4]

But whatever the gains that the Anglo-Irish leaders hoped for from the legislation of 1460, the immediate beneficiary was the duke of York. His position as lieutenant of Ireland had been secured against any challenge from

---

[1] *Stat. Ire., Hen. VI*, p. 646. Cf. ibid., pp 664–5, for a further assertion of Ireland's separateness in the act establishing a distinct Irish coinage.

[2] See above, pp 548–9.

[3] *Cal. pat. rolls, 1446–52*, p. 204; *1452–61*, p. 245.

[4] Cf. Art Cosgrove, 'Parliament and the Anglo-Irish community: the declaration of 1460' in *Hist. Studies*, xiv (1983), pp 25–41.

England, and his control over the country was further strengthened by measures against Lancastrian supporters inside Ireland. These included Thomas Bathe, whom the earl of Ormond and Wiltshire had appointed as his deputy, and one Richard de Bermingham, who was accused of having gone to England to recruit an army to oppose York in Ireland. The 1455 sentence of treason against the Butlers, revoked in 1458, was reaffirmed, though the final session of the parliament in July exempted Edmund Butler from the statute and recognised him as the lawful heir to the barony of Dunboyne. York clearly enjoyed the support of the great majority of the Anglo-Irish, and from his Irish sanctuary prepared for his return to England. Envoys from Scotland arrived to discuss a marriage alliance with the Scottish king, James II, and in the early summer of 1460 the earl of Warwick was able to visit him in Ireland to concert plans for the overthrow of the Lancastrian regime.[1] Anglo-Ireland remained nominally loyal to Henry VI, but, in fact, by throwing in its lot with the duke of York, it had adopted a different allegiance from that still held, however shakily, by England. And in this situation, as the author of the 'Libelle of Englyshe polycye' had predicted, the strategic importance of Ireland soon became apparent.

Henry VI's government was clearly aware of the danger to its security that Ireland now presented. In April 1460 an order was issued to arrest all boats that were accustomed to cross from England to Ireland and to keep them in custody until their masters gave sufficient pledges that they would not cross to Ireland without royal licence. More positively, attempts were made to counteract York's influence in Ireland by enlisting Gaelic Irish lords on the Lancastrian side. Parliamentary measures against four men, accused of having brought letters from England inciting the Gaelic Irish to rise against York, tend to confirm the veracity of the charge, made in the Yorkist propaganda manifesto issued from Ireland by York and Warwick, that

dyvers lordes have caused his hyghnenesse to wryte letters under his privy seale unto his Yrisshe enemyes, whyche never kyng of England dyd heretofore, whereby they may have comfort to entre in to the conquest of the sayde londe: whyche letters the same Yrysshe enemyes sent un to me the sayd duke of York, and merveled gretely that any suche letters shuld be to theym sent, speking therinne gret shame and vylony of the seyd reme.[2]

But, as the manifesto implied, this unparalleled attempt to involve the Gaelic Irish in an English political struggle met with no success, and York's position in Ireland does not seem to have been seriously threatened in the period prior to his departure to England in the autumn of 1460.[3]

The situation in England had been radically altered in York's favour by

[1] Griffiths, *Reign of Henry VI*, pp 813, 854–6.
[2] *An English chronicle of the reigns of Richard II, Henry IV, Henry V and Henry VI*, ed. J. S. Davies (London, 1856; Camden Society, 1st series, lxiv), p. 87.
[3] He arrived in England 'a lytelle before' 8 October (ibid., p. 99). His arrival is dated 'around 8 September' in 'John Benet's chronicle', p. 227.

Warwick's successful invasion from Calais and his defeat of the Lancastrian army at the battle of Northampton on 10 July. Shortly afterwards York began to prepare for his departure and in the final session of the 1460 parliament, which opened on 21 July, various people who wished to accompany the duke to England were given permission to do so. York may also have brought with him the force of archers levied earlier in the year by parliament to serve him.

In England his claim to the throne was not accepted, and in October a compromise settlement was reached whereby Henry VI was to retain the crown for his life but was to be succeeded by York and his heirs. This settlement failed to last, and renewed Lancastrian opposition resulted in York's death on 30 December 1460 at the battle of Wakefield, after which his head, mockingly crowned by his opponents with a paper cap, was impaled on the walls of York. But the Yorkist cause did not die with him, and victory at the battle of Towton in the following March ensured its eventual success and the accession to the throne of York's son as Edward IV.[1]

York's two sojourns in Ireland had done little to improve the position of the colony. Later tradition went so far as to attribute a further decline in the north to him because he attracted so many of the colonists from that area to join him in England and give their lives there, that the reconquest of Ulster was made easy for Ó Néill and his followers. Whatever the truth of that view, there is much to be said for a later annalist's opinion that 'he was not able to achieve anything of note, to conclude peace or to overcome the Irish'.[2]

The Yorkist victory in England had precluded the possibility of a confrontation between a Lancastrian England and Yorkist Anglo-Ireland. It also prevented the Anglo-Irish leaders from demonstrating how far they would have gone in support of the Yorkist cause to separate themselves from the jurisdiction of the English crown. But attachment to the Yorkist cause by an increasingly independent-minded Anglo-Irish aristocracy survived as a problem to trouble relations between the two islands later in the century.

[1] Griffiths, *Reign of Henry VI*, pp 866–75.
[2] Dowling, *Annals*, pp 29–30.

CHAPTER XX

Ireland beyond the Pale, 1399–1460

ART COSGROVE

THE increasing area of the country lying outside the jurisdiction of the Dublin administration comprised a network of autonomous or semi-autonomous lordships, Gaelic and Anglo-Irish, whose relationships with one another were little affected by the politics of the Pale. To concentrate, therefore, on the happenings in the colonial area is to present an unbalanced picture of late medieval Ireland. Some parts of the country, like the O'Donnells' territory in the northwest, had never experienced Anglo-Norman or English settlement. In other areas, Irish chieftains had reclaimed lands from their former conquerors and revived their claims to lordship over them. And many of the lords of English descent, like the Burkes or de Burghs of Connacht, conducted their affairs with little reference to the government at Dublin, and in a way that could hardly be distinguished from that of their Gaelic neighbours. Even in the great Anglo-Irish earldoms of Ormond and Desmond, the influence of Gaelic customs and practices was already marked by the opening of the fifteenth century and continued to grow as the century progressed.

That political developments in this, the greater part of the country, have tended to be neglected by historians is due, in part, to the comparative scarcity of source material and the difficulties involved in using what there is. But lack of evidence is but one obstacle in the way of a coherent picture of political happenings in the area of the country outside the administration's control. For the Gaelic resurgence of the fifteenth century failed to express itself as a politically unifying force, and the most immediately striking feature of Gaelic and gaelicised Ireland is the fragmentation of authority which resulted in the numerous political divisions inside the country. Struggles for power tended, in the main, to be localised.[1] The ruling groups, whether of English or Irish descent, opposed or allied with each other on the basis of immediate local advantage. Descent was no determinant of political allegiance; even though the division

[1] It is worth noting here the observation of a Welsh historian that 'the outstanding feature and informing principle of much of English historiography [has been] the belief that strong centralised government is a prerequisite of civilised life and human progress'. See R. R. Davies, *Historical perception: Celts and Saxons* (Cardiff, 1979), p. 12.

between *Gaill* and *Gaedhil*, foreigner and native, continued to be made by the genealogists and annalists, the struggles in fifteenth-century Ireland were not based on national origins. There is some evidence, indeed, that the 'foreigners' were now accepted as Irish. An entry in the Annals of Connacht describes how Thomas Bachach Butler, prior of Kilmainham, the illegitimate son of the third earl of Ormond, brought a force of men, 'noble Galls and Gaels' to France in 1419 to aid Henry V. After initial successes, 'an attack of dangerous sickness came upon the Irishmen in the strange land and killed many of them, the earl of Ormond's son himself dying of it'.[1] And the Irish annalist's acceptance of both *Gaill* and *Gaedhil* as Irishmen affords a striking parallel to English chroniclers' usage of the term *Hibernienses* to describe all the inhabitants of Ireland whether they were 'English lieges' or 'wyld Irish'.

The absence of any consistent antagonism between *Gaill* and *Gaedhil* only adds to the complexity of political groupings, since it makes it impossible to attribute any national significance to the various struggles for power, and we are thrown back to the politics of localities. It is true that, on the Gaelic Irish side, the old chimera of a high-kingship of all Ireland continued to have an attraction for the learned classes. The obit of Niall Óg Ó Néill in 1403 praised him as a man 'who the learned and pilgrims of Ireland thought would take the kingship of Ireland on account of the prowess of his hands and the nobility of his blood'.[2] But this was the view of an intensely conservative group, intent on preserving an anachronistic tradition rather than analysing current political realities. The acceptance of the high-kingship by Edward Bruce had marked its swan-song; his defeat and death in 1318 revealed its sterility as a practical concept. Even the very limited unity he had achieved among the Gaelic Irish in opposition to the colonists was not to be repeated. Paradoxically, perhaps, the decline of the colony removed the need for any united front on the Gaelic Irish side. As the colony itself fragmented, so, too, did the opposition to it. And the appeal of Owen Glendower to the Irish chieftains in 1401, calling, like the Bruces almost a century earlier, for an alliance against the English, struck no responsive chord.

Effectively, therefore, the summit of political ambition for an Irish chieftain was the kingship of a province. Throughout this period the MacMurroughs consistently claimed the kingship of Leinster, and in the north the O'Neills were usually accorded the title of king of Ulster. Neither hegemony, of course, extended over the whole of the province concerned, nor was it undisputed, and the extent of the authority exercised depended on the military strength available to enforce it. In the west, the Ó Conchobhair family, debilitated by its own internal feuds, found it increasingly difficult to give any substance to its traditional claim to the kingship of Connacht; while jurisdiction over the whole of

---

[1] 'Co tanaig teidm galair guasachtaig forna hErennchaib' (*Ann. Conn.*, pp 442–3). Cf. Cosgrove, *Late med. Ire.*, pp 72–98.

[2] *A.U.*, iii, 50–51.

Munster had ceased to be even an aspiration in a situation where the struggles for supremacy involved not only the old royal families of Ó Briain and Mac Carthaigh but also the powerful Anglo-Irish earls of Desmond and Ormond.

From the point of view of those dwelling within the Pale, the most consistently serious threat was presented by the Mac Murchadha family. The foundations of their authority lay in the strong kingdom established by Art Mac Murchadha in Wexford and Carlow; and despite tergiversations in their attitude towards the Dublin administration, his successors maintained their hold over this territory and continued their raids on the colonists of Wexford if their black-rent was not paid. Their claim to the kingship of Leinster received some recognition from the Ó Broin and the Ó Tuathail families to the north of their territories, but they seem to have exercised little influence over the main Gaelic families of the midlands, the Ó Mórdha family of Leix and the Ó Conchobhair family of Offaly.

The advance of Ó Mórdha on Kildare was checked by his defeat by John Talbot in 1415, and the subsequent rebuilding of Athy provided a greater defence for the colonists in that area against him. But he was again at war in 1421, when the earl of Ormond led a large army into his territories and wasted them for four days 'until the Irish were glad to sue for peace'.[1] Two years later Ó Mórdha was again raiding Kildare and Dublin, when the administration found it difficult to field a sufficient army against him. Subsequently, however, chief power among the Gaelic families of the midlands seem to have passed to Ó Conchobhair of Offaly under the long and successful kingship of An Calbhach Ó Conchobhair (1421–58).

In the year after his succession, An Calbhach had to face a strong challenge from the earl of Desmond, who brought a large army to the aid of the colonists in Meath and ravaged the neighbouring territory of the Anglo-Irish de Berminghams of Carbury. But 'O'Connor came with an army and faced them, defying them to attack him in his own territory. So they turned back without concluding a peace or exacting pledges.'[2] And in the following year, 1423, An Calbhach renewed his attacks on Meath, this time with the assistance of Ó Raghallaigh of Cavan, the de Berminghams, and a great number of other 'Irish enemies' and 'English rebels'. It was in the course of this campaign that an incautious clerk of the Irish chancery, one Adam Veldon, was captured and had to pay £10 to Ó Conchobhair for his release.

In March 1425, An Calbhach, 'captain of the nation of Offaly', submitted to John Talbot and agreed to become the king's faithful subject, undertaking to restore lands seized from the Anglo-Irish, to renounce his black rent on Meath and to pay 1,000 marks for pardon for past offences. But the agreement meant little and Meath was again under attack the following year. In September 1427, with the connivance of one Hubert Tyrell, he burned and robbed the

---

[1] Marlborough, *Chronicle*, p. 32.
[2] *Ann. Conn.*, pp 464–5.

town of Mullingar, and over the next thirty years he posed a constant threat to the colonists of Meath and Kildare. When he died in 1458, he was reputed to have been the man 'that wrested most from the foreigners of Ireland' and 'who got back more of Leinster from Galls and Gaels opposing him than any man since the time of Cahair Mór [supposed king of Ireland, A.D. 122–51]'.[1] He was succeeded by his son Conn, who faced sterner opposition than his father; and his defeat by the earl of Kildare in 1459 signalled the emergence of the Kildare family as a potent influence in the politics of Leinster.

In the north the main opposition to Ó Néill dominance came from the O'Donnells of Tír Conaill, who attempted to exploit quarrels inside the Ó Néill family to their own advantage, only to find themselves hoist with their own petard, as the O'Neills capitalised on Ó Domhnaill succession disputes to reassert their authority over them. The absence of a stable system of succession was a continuing weakness in the Gaelic polity. Attempts to have the kingship descend in a direct line from father to son inevitably ran into opposition from the collateral branches of a royal family, who claimed an equal right to the kingship, which was traditionally open to any male within the four-generation group descended from a king. The efforts of the Ó Néill family to maintain a system of primogeniture were frustrated by the death of Niall Óg's eldest son, Brian, in 1403. This allowed the kingship to pass to Niall Óg's nephew, Domhnall, recently released from captivity by the English in return for a large ransom and the surrender of other hostages, including his brother Aodh, who spent ten years in prison before his escape from Dublin in 1412.[2]

From the outset of his reign in 1404 Domhnall had to contend with opposition from his cousin, Eóghan, son of Niall Óg. And when Domhnall was captured by Brian Mac Mathghamhna in 1410 and handed over to Eóghan, the latter assumed the powers of the kingship and exercised them for four years until he in turn was captured by Domhnall's brothers. An exchange of prisoners was agreed and Domhnall's authority recognised, but the settlement did not last, and in 1419 Eóghan, now in alliance with Toirdhealbhach Ó Domhnaill, king of Tír Conaill, renewed his attack on Domhnall who 'was driven to the foreigners of Ulster with dishonour'.[3] From his base among the Anglo-Irish population of east Ulster, Domhnall negotiated his return, but in 1420 he was again expelled by Eóghan and forced to seek refuge with Brian Ó Conchobhair, lord of north Connacht. By 1422, however, Domhnall had regained his position and joined with Eóghan and Ó Domhnaill on a raid into Connacht. In the following year the same forces descended upon the colonists of Louth and ravaged that area until they were frightened off by the arrival of a large force of men-at-arms and archers from Dublin under the leadership of the mayor of that city.

---

[1] *Ann. Conn.*, p. 499; *A.U.*, iii, 195.
[2] *Cal. pat. rolls, 1401–5*, p. 183; *Ann. Conn.*, pp 414–15.
[3] *A.U.*, iii, 83.

The cooperation between Eóghan and Domhnall in the campaigns of 1423 indicates an improvement in their relations. But the Anglo-Irish seem to have regarded Eóghan as the more dangerous of the two. When both O'Neills and a number of other northern chieftains were captured by John Talbot in 1425, it was Eóghan who was forced to make an agreement recognising his status as a tenant of the earldom of Ulster and undertaking to perform the traditional services due to the earl. But the differences between the two cousins were formally composed in 1426 when Eóghan submitted to Domhnall, 'and they proceeded to recover by force all the lands which had been alienated during their contentions'.[1]

In 1430 Eóghan led a successful campaign outside Ulster. After attacking the colonists of Louth and burning Dundalk, he and his army made a circuit of the midlands and enforced submission on a number of Gaelic and Anglo-Irish lords. An Calbhach Ó Conchobair and other midland chieftains accepted wages (*tuarastal*) from Eóghan as a sign of their dependence on him; Ó Fearghail of Anghaile in County Longford surrendered as a hostage his son, who was brought back to Dungannon; and the Nugents, Plunketts, and Herberts among the Anglo-Irish families of Meath had to pay a tribute to Ó Néill to secure peace. This striking demonstration of Ó Néill power beyond the bounds of Ulster further underlined Eóghan's military ability; and when Domhnall was killed by Ó Catháin in 1432, Eóghan was the natural successor. The Annals of Ulster claim that he was unanimously made king of Ulster and that he went to Tullaghogue, the traditional inauguration site of the O'Neills, to be 'crowned on the flagstone of the kings there by the will of God and men, bishops and ollams'.[2]

Eóghan's accession was the signal for a fresh outbreak of war between Ó Néill and his sometime allies, the O'Donnells. And in the course of 1433, Ó Néill, with the support of a Scottish fleet, faced a combination comprising Niall Garbh Ó Domhnaill, Mac Uidhilín from the district of north-east Antrim known as the Route, and the Anglo-Irish of Meath. Peace was made at the close of 1433 and Niall Garbh Ó Domhnaill was allied with Ó Néill in the following year in an attack on the colonists, when he was captured by Sir Thomas Stanley. He was later sent to England and died in captivity in the Isle of Man in 1439. His successor, his brother Neachtan, attempted to exploit dynastic dissension within the Ó Néill family by supporting Brian Óg Ó Néill as a rival to Eóghan, but the latter's forces proved too strong and Brian Ó Néill was captured and rendered unfit to present any further challenge for the kingship by having a hand and foot removed.

By 1442 Eóghan's power was sufficient to enable him to bring Neachtan into submission and to force him to admit Ó Néill's claim to tribute from Inishowen and jurisdiction over the area known as Cinéal Moen, on the borders of the

---

[1] *A.F.M.*, iv, 869.
[2] *A.U.*, iii, 119.

modern counties of Tyrone and Donegal, which had both been long-disputed between the two families. Subsequent rivalries within the family further weakened the position of the O'Donnells. Neachtan himself was killed by his nephews, sons of Niall Garbh, in 1452, and Eóghan Ó Néill's son Énrí was the arbiter of the settlement that allowed Neachtan's son, Ruaidhrí, to take the kingship but gave half of Tír Conaill to the sons of Niall Garbh. One of these sons, Domhnall, killed Ruaidhrí in 1454, but was himself slain in battle by Énrí Ó Néill in 1456; and afterwards Énrí made Toirdhealbhach, son of Neachtan, king over Tír Conaill on condition that he recognised Ó Néill's jurisdiction over him.

The reduction of Tír Conaill to obedience gave real substance to Énrí's claim to be king of Ulster. He had succeeded to the title on the resignation or deposition of his father Eóghan in 1455, and among those who attended his inauguration at Tullaghogue was the archbishop of Armagh, John Mey. Later on the same year, in an appeal to Ó Néill to act as the secular arm in the case of a contumacious excommunicate, the archbishop termed him 'the most powerful chieftain in these parts of Ulster'.[1] Mey's attitude was indicative of the new spirit of cooperation between Énrí and the Anglo-Irish colony. From the time of his inauguration until his abdication in 1483 Ó Néill cooperated with the Dublin government and mounted no attacks upon the colonial areas.[2]

The politics of Ulster involved not only the Gaelic Irish and the Anglo-Irish colonists in the east of the province, but also the 'Scottish enemies' so frequently mentioned in the records of the Dublin administration. For the narrow strip of water separating the north-east from the western isles of Scotland was less a barrier than a link between two parts of one cultural and linguistic world. The practice of recruiting Scottish mercenary soldiers, or galloglass, for warfare in Ireland went back to the thirteenth century and some of these galloglass families had settled in Ireland. But Ireland continued to provide an outlet for the surplus military potential of the western isles, now governed as a practically autonomous area by their MacDonnell lords, a branch of whose family had already established itself in the Glens of Antrim.[3]

In 1400 many of the colonists were slain or drowned in a naval engagement with the Scots off Strangford. Four years later a force of Scots, in alliance with the Irish chieftains Mág Aonghusa and Mac Giolla Muire, burnt Downpatrick, Coleraine, and the abbey of Inch, wreaking such havoc in the area that the Dublin government was compelled to despatch an emergency force of 800 foot-soldiers to the north to recover those parts devastated by Irish, Scots, and 'other enemies from the outer isles'.[4] Later in the same year fears were

---

[1] 'Cum in hiis partibus Ultonie non vobis maior existit princeps'; *Registrum Johannis Mey*, p. 336.
[2] Simms, ' "The king's friend" ', pp 214–36, esp. p. 224.
[3] See K. A. Steer and J. W. M. Bannerman, *Late medieval monumental sculpture in the west highlands* (Edinburgh, 1977), pp 201–13; J. W. M. Bannerman, 'The lordship of the Isles' in J. M. Brown (ed.), *Scottish society in the fifteenth century* (London, 1977), pp 209–40.
[4] *Rot. pat. Hib.*, p. 178, no. 77 (c).

expressed that the colony would never recover from this attack unless those who had fled could be returned to their lands in time to harvest the grain sown that year. A subsequent expedition may have helped to stabilise the situation, and when John Dongan, bishop of Down, was appointed keeper of the liberty of Ulster in June 1405 he was authorised to negotiate with both Gaelic Irish and Scottish enemies. Later, in September 1407, the bishop, along with Janico Dartas, admiral of Ireland, was commissioned by the English government to seek a final peace and a treaty of friendship with Donald, lord of the Isles, and John his brother, and these negotiations were still continuing in May 1408. There is no record of any formal treaty between the two sides, but the 1410 grant of a royal licence to Janico Dartas's son and daughter to contract marriages with the daughter and son of John of the Isles suggests improved relationships between the colonists and the islanders. In June 1411 Donald was again negotiating with the English court, probably in an attempt to secure support for his claim to the earldom of Ross against the son of the then governor of Scotland, Robert, duke of Albany.[1] The struggle between the two sides culminated, in July 1411, in the great battle of Harlaw, the outcome of which was apparently indecisive.[2] Donald continued to claim title to the earldom of Ross and his independent position as lord of the Isles is attested by his appearance in the Anglo-French truces of January 1414 and October 1416 as an ally of both sides.[3]

Donald's involvement in Scottish affairs must have limited the extent of his intervention in Ulster. But Scottish recruits continued to play a part in Ulster wars, particularly in the armies of the O'Neills of Clandeboye, who seem to have been the main beneficiaries of the destruction of the colony in east Ulster and posed a serious threat both to the colonists and to the senior line of the O'Neills in Tír Eóghain.

Hitherto the Scottish crown had taken little interest in the activities of its subjects inside Ireland. But in 1425 the returned Scottish king, James I, was forced to consider Ireland as a possible threat to his own security. In that year James Stewart (son of the former regent of Scotland, Murdoch, duke of Albany) fled to Ireland after an unsuccessful rebellion and thus escaped the fate of his father and brothers, who were executed in May 1425. He remained a dangerous focus of disaffection to the Scottish king, and fears that he might attempt an invasion of Scotland prompted the Scottish parliament of 1426 to issue strict regulations controlling the passage of ships between Scotland and Ireland.[4]

[1] *Cal. pat. rolls, 1405—8*, pp 361, 487; *1408—11*, p. 183; E. W. M. Balfour Melville, *James I, king of Scots, 1406—37* (London, 1936), p. 46. The Scottish king remained in captivity in England until 1424.
[2] The controversy about the outcome and significance of the battle is discussed by Ranald Nicholson, *Scotland: the later middle ages* (Edinburgh, 1974), pp 232—7. The Scottish Gaelic view that it was a struggle between the highlands and the lowlands, with victory going to the former, is reflected by the Connacht annalist who claims that 'Mac Domhnaill of Scotland won a great victory over the Galls of Scotland' (*Ann. Conn.*, pp 410—11).   [3] *Cal. close rolls, 1413—19*, pp 108, 369.
[4] '. . . sene the kings notouris rebellours ar reset in Erschry of Yrlande. And for that cause passingers passande fra thyne mycht do preiudice to this realm'.

A secondary purpose of the legislation was to prevent Irish subjects of the king of England from spying out the secrets of the Scottish realm; it was emphasised, however, that these measures were not intended to break 'the alde frendschip betuix the king of Scotlande ande his lieges ande the gude alde frends of Erschry of Yrlande'.[1]

We know little of James's doings inside Ireland, but the report in March 1428 that O'Donnell had sent to Scotland for a large force to attack Carrickfergus castle may be connected with his presence in the north. There was clearly a danger, too, that James might attempt to link up with the disaffected western islanders; and this could explain the vigorous campaign by the Scottish king in the western highlands and isles in the summer of 1429. For the Irish Annals state that a Scottish fleet arrived in Ireland that year 'to convey him home that he might be made king'.[2] But James died shortly after the fleet's arrival; and in June, Alexander, lord of the Isles, was forced to surrender unconditionally to the Scottish king after a decisive defeat in battle. The projected attack on Carrickfergus seems to have been abandoned, and in July 1429 Niall Ó Domhnaill and his followers were issued with a safe-conduct to come to England to do fealty and allegiance to the English king.[3]

The immediate effect of James I's reassertion of control over the western highlands and isles was to divert larger Scottish forces towards Ireland. The proclamation of 4 March 1430, ordering Irish residents in England to return home, warned of the danger from enemies of the northern parts who were 'purposing with all their strength to invade Ireland',[4] and that such a warning was justified is clear from a report by the Irish council, later in the same year, that a great multitude of Scots had come from Scotland to assist the Gaelic Irish in their attacks on the colony. Three years later, a large fleet came from the Isles to aid Eoghan Ó Néill in his war against Niall Ó Domhnaill. After the joint forces had burnt the town of Ardglass, the Scottish fleet sailed to Inishowen to link up again with Ó Néill's army, which had journeyed overland to the rendezvous, and together they enforced a peace on Niall Ó Domhnaill's sons and subsequently on Ó Domhnaill himself. The 1433 expedition seems to have been the last large-scale intervention by Scottish forces during the first half of the fifteenth century, though sporadic Scottish raids by land and sea continued to add to the troubles of the colony in the north.

In the west, Connacht, now almost entirely outside the jurisdiction of the Dublin government, was rent by quarrels among the Ó Conchobhair family over the succession to the kingship of the province. After the death of Ruaidhrí Ó Conchobhair in 1384, the two rival claimants to the succession, Toirdhealbhach Ruadh, representing the descendants of Fedlimid Ó Conchobhair (died

[1] *The acts of the parliaments of Scotland*, ed. Thomas Thomson and Cosmo Innes (12 vols, Edinburgh, 1814—75), ii, 11.
[2] *A.F.M.*, iv, 875.
[3] *Cal. pat. rolls, 1422—9*, p. 542.
[4] *Cal. pat. rolls, 1429—36*, p. 42.

1316), the line later known as Ó Conchobhair Ruadh, and Toirdhealbhach Óg, descended from Fedlimid's brother Toirdhealbhach (died 1345) and progenitor of the Ó Conchobhair Donn line, conducted a long and indecisive war over the kingship. In this struggle the Ruadh faction normally had the support of the O'Kellys of Uí Mhaine, the MacDermotts, and the gaelicised de Burghs or Burkes of northern Connacht. Allied with the Donn branch of the family were the MacDonaghs, the O'Connors of Sligo (a cadet branch of the royal family), and the Burkes of Clanricard in southern Connacht, who still maintained a tenuous link with the Dublin administration and claimed the right to exercise royal jurisdiction within the province.[1] These dispositions reflected the continuing rivalry between the Burkes of northern and southern Connacht (the lower and upper MacWilliams), as well as the conflict in the south of the province between the Burkes and the rising power of the O'Kellys, and that between the O'Connors of Sligo and the northern Burkes for supremacy in north Connacht. Local differences between the neighbouring MacDonaghs and MacDermotts dictated their stance also, but although these more localised antagonisms probably outweighed any sense of loyalty to one or other of the competing Ó Conchobhair factions, the alliances remained fairly constant throughout the first half of the fifteenth century.

The murder of Toirdhealbhach Óg (Donn) by the son of Toirdhealbhach Ruadh in December 1406, after he had been 'twenty-one years in co-sovereignty',[2] ended the first phase of the struggle. But the dead man's cousin, Cathal Donn, immediately laid claim to the kingship and renewed the challenge to Toirdhealbhach Ruadh. In a clash between the two sides in 1407, the forces of Cathal and Burke of Clanricard were defeated and Cathal himself taken prisoner. The price of his release was the surrender to Toirdhealbhach Ruadh of the castle of Roscommon,[3] but the Donn faction refused this condition and successfully defended the castle against an almost continuous siege by their opponents. Attempts to starve the defenders into submission were foiled by the ability of Cathal Donn's allies to provision the castle in spite of the besiegers. In 1409 Brian Ó Conchobhair of Sligo—perhaps the ablest military leader on either side—and Conchobhar MacDonnchadha mounted such an expedition to relieve the defenders. They expected the aid of Burke of Clanricard, but when the forces assembled at Ballintober, Burke was accompanied only by a few horsemen, and the absence of any large Clanricard force seemed to presage abandonment of the expedition. But Mac Donnchadha and Ó Conchobhair of Sligo decided to press on, though the dangers were clearly seen by Mac Donnchadha, who persuaded Burke to stay behind on the grounds that 'if we are slain, it is agreeable to us that you should live for our children after us to maintain them'.[4] Despite their depleted forces, the attackers defeated the besiegers

[1] See above, p. 535.   [2] A.L.C., p. 121.
[3] For the castle's earlier history see R. A. Stalley, *Architecture and sculpture in Ireland, 1150–1350* (Dublin, 1971), pp 52–7.   [4] A.L.C., pp 129–31.

and succeeded in getting stores and provisions into the castle without the losses envisaged by Mac Donnchadha.

Three years later the O'Connors of Sligo carried the war into their enemies' territories. While Brian successfully raided northern Connacht and burnt the castles at Castlebar and Lough Mask, his brother Domhnall invaded Toirdhealbhach Ruadh's lands in Roscommon and carried off many cattle and prisoners. But these successes failed to secure the release of Cathal Donn, and Roscommon castle remained under siege. In 1413 a further expedition to relieve the defenders of the castle by Ó Conchobhair of Sligo and Mac Donnchadha was defeated by the forces of Toirdhealbhach Ruadh and Ó Ceallaigh, and though the castle continued to defy the besiegers, the erection of a small castle opposite it by Ó Ceallaigh in 1418 demonstrated the continued determination of the attackers to capture this key fortress. In the same year, however, Ó Conchobhair and Mac Donnchadha again broke through the besiegers, and though they failed to take or destroy Ó Ceallaigh's castle, they did succeed in provisioning the Roscommon garrison.

Frustrated in their efforts to take Roscommon castle, the O'Connors Ruadh and their allies turned their attention southwards, and in 1419 a large army composed of the O'Kellys, the Burkes of north Connacht, the MacDermotts, and Toirdhealbhach Ruadh's son, Cathal Dubh, invaded Clanricard with the intention of expelling William (Uilleag or Ulick) Burke from his territory. But William was able to call upon the help of Tadhg Ó Briain, son of the lord of Thomond, and the combined armies of Thomond and Clanricard proved too strong for the invading force. This decisive victory not only secured William Burke's dominance in southern Connacht, but it also brought into his hands many valuable prisoners; and in 1420 two of these, an Ó Ceallaigh and an Ó Conchobhair Ruadh, were exchanged for Cathal Donn, released by the northern Burkes after thirteen years captivity, with the castle of Roscommon still intact. Six years later Toirdhealbhach Ruadh Ó Conchobhair, after disputing the kingship of Connacht for forty-two years, died, to the surprise of the Connacht annalist, in his bed; and this 'Cú Chulainn of his times', as the annalist exaggeratedly styled him, was succeeded as undisputed king of Connacht by Cathal Donn.[1]

During the thirteen years of Cathal's rule there was, if not comparative peace, at least a decline in the scale of warfare. But sporadic clashes between the two factions, such as that which resulted in the death of Aodh Ó Conchobhair, son of Toirdhealbhach Ruadh, in 1430, showed that the old animosity still smouldered; and on Cathal's death in 1439, it flared again into open warfare between the rival claimants to the succession, Tadhg (Ruadh), son of Toirdhealbhach Ruadh, and Aodh (Donn), son of Toirdhealbhach Óg.

The death of Brian Ó Conchobhair of Sligo in 1440, after thirty-seven years of lordship, removed the mainstay of the Donn faction, and the subsequent

[1] *Ann. Conn.*, p. 469, 1425. Both *A.F.M.* and *A.U.* give 1426.

quarrels within his family not only added further confusions to Connacht politics but also gravely weakened the defences of northern Connacht against incursions by the O'Donnells. Hitherto the O'Connors of Sligo had been the main barrier to any advance by the O'Donnells into Connacht. Occasionally allied with Ó Néill against Ó Domhnaill, they were also strong enough to defeat a combined expedition by Ó Néill and Ó Domhnaill into Connacht in 1422. Ten years later Énrí Ó Néill again sought their aid in his war against Ó Domhnaill and concluded a formal treaty of friendship with them. But in the 1440s the rupture of the alliance between Ó Conchobhair and Mac Donnchadha, and dissension within both families, allowed Neachtan Ó Domhnaill to make greater inroads into Connacht than his predecessors. In 1445, in company with Eóghan Ó Conchobhair of Sligo, who opposed the succession of his uncle Toirdhealbhach Carrach to the lordship of north Connacht, Ó Domhnaill burnt the town of Sligo and killed Tomaltach Mac Donnchadha and many others. In the following year Ó Domhnaill's forces penetrated further into Connacht, sweeping in an arc through Roscommon to link up with the army of the northern Burkes in south Mayo. Seemingly oblivious of the menace from the north, the Donn and Ruadh factions of the royal family continued their vendetta, and the quarrels within the Mac Donnchadha family could only be composed by the division of their territory between two rival claimants.

Untroubled by the crippling succession disputes that beset most of their Gaelic neighbours, the Burke families, northern and southern, now emerged clearly as the leading powers within the province.[1] In the south the O'Kellys of Uí Mhaine, the main rivals to the supremacy of the Clanricard Burkes, were themselves the victims of internal dissension and were forced to submit to Aodh Ó Conchobhair (Donn) in 1451. In the north the troubles of the Mac-Donaghs and the O'Connors of Sligo continued. Cathal Mac Donnchadha was killed by his own father in 1451, and in the following year Muircheartach Ó Conchobhair of Sligo was murdered by his own kinsmen, Domhnall and Cathal. These dissensions aided not only the northern Burkes but also their allies, the O'Donnells;[2] and the increased vulnerability of Connacht to attacks from the north was demonstrated in 1458 when Ó Néill and Ó Domhnaill carried away hostages from much of northern Connacht after a successful campaign in the area. The main Ó Conchobhair line, now permanently split into the warring Donn and Ruadh branches, was unable to reassert its authority, and after the death of Aodh Ó Conchobhair (Donn), 'half-lord of Connacht', in 1461 it ceased to have any pretensions to the kingship of the province.

The politics of Munster were dominated by the two great Anglo-Irish earldoms of Desmond and Ormond, the latter of which stretched across provincial

---

[1] E.g. the headship of the northern Burkes or Lower MacWilliam passed peacefully from Thomas (died 1402) to his son Walter (died 1440) and thence in turn to Walter's brothers, Edmund (died 1458) and Thomas (died 1460).

[2] Neachtan Ó Domhnaill (died 1452) was married to Edmund Burke's daughter.

boundaries to embrace the counties of Tipperary and Kilkenny 'under one government and one lord'.[1] Throughout most of this period each earldom had a single ruler. James Butler, the fourth or 'white' earl of Ormond, succeeded to the title in 1404 and survived until 1452; his namesake James FitzGerald of Desmond secured the earldom by the expulsion of his nephew, Thomas, in 1411, succeeded to it by right after Thomas's death in France in 1420, and held it until his death in 1462/3.

Within both territories the first half of the fifteenth century saw an increase in Gaelic custom and practice, though in Ormond's territories English language and traditions seem to have survived to a greater extent. Both earls had recourse to the practice of coyne and livery to support their armies, and in their alliances with other Gaelic or gaelicised lords their conduct differed little from that of, say, the Burkes of Connacht. But, unlike the Burkes, both earls retained contact with the Dublin administration. Ormond, indeed, as we have seen, was appointed to head that administration on a number of occasions during this period. Desmond was less closely associated with the government, but in times of emergency the large army he could raise proved invaluable in the struggle against the 'Irish enemies'. In 1415, for example, a subsidy was raised in County Meath to compensate Desmond for the expenses incurred in bringing an army of 5,000 horse and foot to the midlands and campaigning there for thirteen days to counter the menace presented to Meath by Ó Conchobhair of Offaly and the Anglo-Irish rebel, Meiler de Bermingham. His services in the wars in Munster were rewarded in 1423 by his appointment as constable of Limerick castle, and in 1429 he was granted £100 by the administration because 'for a long time he had retained many men-at-arms to resist the malice of Irish enemies in parts of Munster and Connacht'.[2]

Despite their links with the administration, however, both Ormond and Desmond tended to rule their territories as autonomous units with as little interference from Dublin as possible. One cause of Ormond's resentment of John Talbot was the latter's interference in the internal affairs of the Ormond lordship, and particularly his attempts to support his troops by levying coyne and livery from Ormond's tenants. Ormond himself, like most Gaelic and Anglo-Irish lords, used such exactions to maintain an army, though in the statutes he drew up for his lordship he attempted to regulate their imposition. It was one thing for a lord to tax his own tenants in this fashion; quite another for such resources to be tapped by the chief governor, particularly one as hostile to Ormond as John Talbot. And Ormond himself, when chief governor, seems to have made sincere efforts to avoid the use of such irregular impositions outside his own territories as a means of supporting governmental forces.

Desmond enjoyed a similar position of near-autonomy in the administration

---

[1] 'Sub uno regimine vel uno domino', from the Ordinances of Fethard, 1428/35, printed by Empey and Simms, 'Ordinances of the White Earl', p. 185.

[2] *Rot. pat. Hib.*, p. 252a, no. 28.

of his territories. The increasing gaelicisation of his family must have made it hard to distinguish him from the rebellious nations of Geraldines, Powers, and Burkes, whose oppressions caused much complaint among the Munster towns, and it is hardly surprising that his tenure of the office of constable of Limerick castle was opposed by the mayor and citizens of the city. Significantly, too, when he was issued a safe-conduct to visit the king in England in March 1437, he was licensed to bring a retinue of 24 persons 'rebels or otherwise',[1] and the campaigns in Munster which earned him governmental rewards were probably motivated as much by self-interest as by any desire to protect the colony.

Conflicts between the two earls broke out sporadically throughout the first half of the fifteenth century. In 1401 the third earl of Ormond sought to secure his flank by a marriage alliance with Theobald Burke of Clanwilliam in County Tipperary, whose territories were strategically situated between the two earldoms. Under the terms of the agreement the earl gave his daughter Elizabeth in marriage to Theobald, who undertook 'to aid the earl in all his wars and disputes and those of his people, saving only more ancient friendships'.[2] This Burke family, descended from Sir Edmund de Burgh, younger son of the Red Earl of Ulster and, as such, to be distinguished from the two Burke lords in Connacht, seems to have honoured this undertaking by going to Ormond's aid in the war against Desmond the following year.[3] But the alliance did not endure with all of the Burkes of Clanwilliam, for in 1407 Walter Burke, in company with an inveterate enemy of the Butlers, Ó Cearbhaill of Ely (in the south of modern County Offaly), raided County Kilkenny until the deputy, Sir Stephen le Scrope, advanced against them and routed their forces in battle near Callan. According to the Anglo-Irish chronicler, Tadhg Ó Cearbhaill and 800 others were killed, and the victory was marked by a miraculous event; for many testified that the sun stood still in the sky while the victorious army journeyed a distance of six miles.

Walter Burke was reported to have been captured in the battle of 1407; but two years later he was again at large, when with Ó Cearbhaill and a great number of 'Irish enemies' he burnt much of County Kilkenny and eventually had to be bought off by a payment of fifty-five marks. And one of the charges made by Ormond against Talbot in 1422 was that he had given aid and comfort to Walter Burke in his attacks on Ormond's tenants and property. The specific accusation was that Talbot had ordered Ormond's brother, the prior of Kilmainham, to disband his forces in Kilkenny on the grounds that Walter Burke had made peace. But within ten days of his doing this, Walter, along with Tadhg Ó

---

[1] *Cal. pat. rolls, 1436—41*, p. 17.

[2] *Ormond deeds, 1350—1413*, no. 353, pp 250—52.

[3] So I interpret the statement that 'the two MacWilliam de Burghs' (*A.U.*) or 'the two MacWilliams' (*A.F.M.*) 'went to assist the earl of Ormond'. It seems improbable that the Burkes of Connacht would have joined together to aid Ormond, and it is more likely that one of those referred to is Burke of Clanwilliam, and the other Burke of Clanricard. *A.F.M.* dates the conflict 1402. *A.U.* and *A.L.C.* give 1403.

Briain, 'the grettest rebell of all Mownester', and William Burke of Clanricard, 'the grettest rebell of Conaght', invaded Ormond's territories, killed a number of the earl's followers and caused damage to the tune of £6000. And afterwards Walter was well received by Talbot and suffered no punishment for this offence.[1]

Whatever the veracity of such charges, it is clear that the attempted alliance between Ormond and the Burkes of Clanwilliam had failed. And preoccupation with these enemies as well as the feud with Talbot may have prompted the effort at *rapprochement* with Desmond indicated in the grant by Ormond to Desmond in 1422 of custody of his lands in Imokilly, County Cork. Seven years later, even closer ties between the two families were envisaged by the proposed marriage of Ormond's daughter Ann to Desmond's son Thomas, and the two earls undertook 'to maintain, love, cherish, and defend each other and either of the two children'.[2] The terms of the alliance were not fulfilled in that the marriage never took place, but peaceful relations seem to have been maintained between the two earls until the 1440s.

Both, of course, had other enemies to contend with. In 1432 Ormond mounted a punitive expedition against Ó Cearbhaill of Ely and demolished Ó Cearbhaill's two castles. Desmond's power was constantly opposed in the south by the two branches of the Mac Carthaigh family, Mac Carthaig Mór and Mac Carthaigh Riabhach. In 1430 he invaded the lands of Mac Carthaigh Riabhach, captured the castle of Kilbrittan (County Cork), deposed the reigning lord of the territory, and replaced him briefly with his brother Donnchadh Mac Carthaigh, who eventually succeeded to the lordship in 1442. The other royal line in Munster, the O'Briens of Thomond north of the Shannon, were more closely associated with the politics of Connacht through their alliance with the Burkes of Clanricard. Tadhg Ó Briain, whom Ormond described in 1422 as the greatest enemy of Munster, as we have seen, intervened decisively on the side of William Burke in 1419. Succession disputes subsequently weakened Ó Briain power, and in 1446 Burke of Clanricard was called upon to restore order in Thomond after a civil war among members of the Ó Briain family. Not until the succession of Tadhg, son of Toirdhealbhach, in 1459 did the O'Briens begin to extend their power in Munster through the subjugation of the Clanwilliam Burkes.

Desmond was again campaigning in the midlands against Ó Conchobair of Offaly in 1440, but the issue to him in 1445 of a licence to be represented in parliament and great councils by a proctor marked a further stage in his divorce from the administration. And in 1446 war broke out again between himself and Ormond, who had finally resolved his feud with Talbot through a marriage alliance two years earlier. According to reports in the following year from the people of Counties Kilkenny and Tipperary, Desmond, with the aid of three

[1] See Margaret C. Griffith, 'The Talbot–Ormond struggle for control of the Anglo-Irish government, 1414–47' in *I.H.S.*, ii, no. 8 (Sept. 1941), pp 393–4.
[2] *Ormond deeds, 1413–1509*, no. 88, p. 72.

Gaelic Irish lords, ravaged and burnt both counties so that the inhabitants reckoned that the 'counties never took such rebuke of our sovereign lord's Irish enemies as they did by the earl of Desmond'.[1]

But the two earls seem to have been reconciled again before Ormond's final campaign in 1452, a campaign which gave the lie to earlier charges that he had grown 'unlustie and unwieldie'. In the space of six weeks he traversed the country from Limerick to Ó Néill's territory in Tír Eoghain, enforcing submission on a number of the midland and northern chieftains before he confronted Énrí Ó Néill and made him put away Edmund Burke's daughter, recently widowed by the death of Neachtan Ó Domhnaill, and return to his lawful wife, who was the earl's own niece.[2] It was a striking demonstration of the power which a great magnate like Ormond, with numerous connections among both Gaelic and Anglo-Irish families, could bring to the office of chief governor. But he died on the return journey from the north, and his successors chose a role in English politics in preference to the more complicated task of establishing their supremacy inside Ireland. Butler power was dissipated among the collateral branches of the family, and the earl of Desmond seized the opportunity to become the greatest power not only in Munster but also, for a brief space, throughout the country.

Overall, the picture of Gaelic and gaelicised Ireland that emerges is characterised by the stress placed on local autonomy by both Gaelic and Anglo-Irish lords, and the frequency of warfare between these independent or semi-independent units. It would be mistaken, however, to place too much emphasis on these conflicts, descriptions of which make up the majority of annalistic entries. Warfare had limited objectives, was usually on a small scale, and confined to the summer months. The methods used in an attempt to secure an enemy's submission were the traditional ones of harrying and plundering. The former involved a purely destructive raid on an opponent's territory in the hope that the extent of the devastation would enforce his surrender. More usual was the plundering of an enemy's cattle, and the success of a raid would be measured by the number of cattle seized. The acquisition of booty could, of course, be an end in itself, but more ambitious leaders used it as a means of gaining the submission of those attacked. In the latter instance, the stolen cattle, or a proportion of them, might be returned if their owners agreed to surrender hostages or pay a tribute to the victorious raider.[3] But such submissions, as the Dublin government repeatedly discovered in its dealings with Gaelic Irish lords, provided no firm guarantee of future loyalty.

If it is true that, 'while the war-lord elsewhere might fight to gain possession of land, an Irish lord fought for dominion over people',[4] it is not surprising that

---

[1] Richardson & Sayles, *Ir. parl. in middle ages*, p. 165.
[2] Her parents were Mac Murchadha and the earl's sister.
[3] Katharine Simms, 'Warfare in the medieval Gaelic lordships' in *Ir. Sword*, xii (1976), pp 98–108.
[4] Ibid., p. 99.

territorial aggrandisement was a less usual objective of hostilities. Thus adjustments in land holding were the result of steady pressure of an expanding group rather than of a decisive military victory. Most gains during this period were made at the expense of the colony, by the O'Neills of Clandeboye in the north, Ó Conchobhair of Offaly in the midlands, and Mac Murchadha in the south; and the 1449 report from Cork averred that quarrels among the lords of English descent had allowed the Gaelic Irish to recover much territory within that county. Nevertheless, no lord, Gaelic or Anglo-Irish, achieved effective control even over one province. And particularly amongst the Gaelic lords, the attempt by any individual to expand and consolidate his territory was always liable to be frustrated by conflicts within his own family, the outcome of a succession system that stubbornly resisted the application of the more unifying principle of primogeniture.

One institution whose organisation took little account of this welter of conflicting authorities was the church. Its diocesan boundaries had been fixed, in the main, in the late twelfth and early thirteenth centuries, and had not changed to accommodate subsequent political developments. The main dividing line—between the church *inter Anglicos* and that *inter Hibernicos*—cut across provincial and diocesan borders. The diocese of Armagh was itself split by the frontier between the 'English' and 'Irish' areas, the northern half with its centre at Armagh lying among the 'Irish enemies', while the southern part in County Louth was within the Pale area. Of the suffragan dioceses of the province only Meath and parts of Down and Connor (united as one diocese in 1453) were within the colonial area, and because of the difficulties involved in a visitation of the province the archbishop held a papal privilege which allowed him to revisit one of his dioceses without having completed his tour of all the other sees. The disturbances within Ulster could make visitation a dangerous if not impossible task, and that strife could interfere with other church business is clear from the plea of the bishops of Ardagh and Raphoe that they could not attend in person at the provincial council of 1427 'because of war'.[1] Nevertheless, successive archbishops of Armagh did their best to overcome the difficulties of a divided province. In the period 1417–71 all the dioceses under their jurisdiction, with the exception of Dromore and Ardagh, which were considered too dangerous, were visited personally by each of the primates on at least one occasion.[2]

The split between Gaelic and Anglo-Irish areas affected not only the province of Armagh but the church throughout Ireland, and it had been accorded statutory recognition by the Kilkenny legislation of 1366, which had forbidden the appointment of any Gaelic Irishman to a benefice, or the reception of any Gaelic Irishman into a religious house, among the Anglo-Irish. The

[1] *Reg. Swayne*, p. 74.
[2] See Anthony Lynch, 'The province and diocese of Armagh, 1417–71' (M.A. thesis, N.U.I. (U.C.D.), 1979).

NEW FOUNDATIONS

Mendicant friars

◄ Augustinian
► Carmelite
▲ Dominican
▼ Franciscan
△ Franciscan third order regular

✻ Houses of nuns

〰 Diocesan boundaries

N

Ballymacswiney △
Rathmullan ▼
Serade Kaill
Bonamargy ▽

Killydonnell △
Balleeghan △
Landmore △
Glenarm △

Corickmore △
Pubble △
Inver △

Scarvagherin △
Donegal ▼
Massereene △
Holywood △

Ballysaggart △
Magherabeg △
Omagh △

Ballynasaggart △
Dungannon △
Lambeg △

Dromahair △
Monaghan ▼

Moyne ▼   ◄ Scurmore
Rosserk △   Kilcumin ▲   Court △   Ballindoon ▲
Banada ◄   Ballymote ▲
Bofeenaun   Cloonameehan △

Burrishoole ▼
△ Urlaur   Elphin ▼   Caldragh △
Murrisk   Ballyhaunis △   Clonrahan △
Annagh ▼   Toomona △   Tulsk ▲   Slane △   ✻ Kellystown
Dunmore ▼   Toberelly △   Ballynasaggart △
Killeenbrenan △   △ Beagh   Kilmacahill △
Toombeola ▲   Ross ▼   Cloonyvornoge △
Tisaxon △   Bellaneeny ▼
Galway ▼   Temple-   Clonkeen-
moyle-   kerrill
Kiltullagh △   Kilboght △
Aran Islands   Kilcorban △
   Kilcullen ▼
Roscrea ▼   Stradbally △
   Graney ▼   ✻ Wicklow

Lislaughtin ▼
Adare ▼   △ Friarstown   Enniscorthy △
   ► Milltown
Kilshane △   Killeennagallive △   Callan ▼
   Galbally △

Glanworth ▲

Muckross ▼

Kilcrea ▼   ✻
Ballymacadane △

Bantry ▼

Goleen ▼   Sherkin Island ◄

| 0 | Miles | 50 |
| 0 | Kms | 80 |

Map 13 THE SPREAD OF THE RELIGIOUS ORDERS, 1420–1530,
by F. X. Martin

Gwynn & Hadcock, *Med. relig. houses*.

full implementation of the statute in this, as in other respects, proved to be impossible or, at least, impracticable. Even within the dioceses of the Pale area there was a growing need for clergy who could minister in Irish-speaking districts, and licences had to be issued permitting the appointment of Gaelic Irish clergy to serve in these regions. There were other practical difficulties in the way of rigorous enforcement. The statute of 1366 had laid down that if a Gaelic Irishman was appointed to a benefice within the colonial area, the appointment was to be declared void and the right of presentation would pass to the crown. But most of these benefices were of such little value that there were few applicants to the king for them, and hence the petition of 1428 that the king should allow the lieutenant or deputy to act for him in this regard.

As the area under the administration's control diminished, so too did crown influence over the church. In an increasing number of dioceses the royal right to custody of the temporal property of a bishopric during vacancy could not be enforced. By 1460 the dioceses in the north-east and south-west of the country had been added to those in the north and west which had long passed out of royal control.[1] Thus, in most of the country beyond the Pale, the statutes against papal provisions were unenforceable, and appointments to these bishoprics could be made without reference to the crown. Some appointees still took the precaution of securing a pardon from the government for their offence in accepting a papal provision. Thaddaeus Mág Raith, appointed by the pope to the diocese of Killaloe, received such a pardon in September 1431 along with a grant of denization making him of English condition.[2] The latter concession was an unusual one, since it was normally assumed that a bishop, even if he was of Gaelic Irish descent, enjoyed English legal status as well as the right to attend great councils and parliaments by virtue of his office. That some bishops 'of Irish nation' did attend parliament is clear from the complaint made in England in 1416 that they brought with them servants who spied out the secrets of the colonists and reported back to the 'Irish enemies'. But, as the century progressed, fewer bishops from the outlying areas, whether Gaelic or Anglo-Irish, responded to the summons to attend parliament. In 1456 John Cantwell, archbishop of Cashel, was charged with securing papal appointment to the see without the king's licence, and with failure to answer writs of summons to parliament or council. Four years later Donatus Ó Muireadhaigh, archbishop of Tuam, was condemned by the crown for his refusal 'to come to the king's parliaments and councils and to obey the laws of the land'.[3]

The denunciation of Ó Muireadhaigh came in the course of the crown's efforts to secure the see of Annaghdown for Thomas Barrett, provided by the

---

[1] Cf. R. D. Edwards, 'The kings of England and papal provisions in fifteenth-century Ireland' in *Med. studies presented to A. Gwynn*, p. 176.

[2] *Rot. pat. Hib.*, p. 255b, no. 122. Mág Raith's anxiety to secure royal support can be explained by the fact that his claim to the bishopric was disputed by another candidate; see Gwynn & Gleeson, *Killaloe*, pp 402–9.

[3] *Cal. pat. rolls, 1452–61*, p. 655.

pope in 1458. Involved in the dispute was the whole question of the status of Annaghdown as an independent diocese. In 1327 the pope had ordered the amalgamation of Annaghdown with the diocese of Tuam, and subsequently the two dioceses had been loosely united, though Annaghdown retained its own cathedral and chapter and occasional independent appointments continued to be made of bishops of Annaghdown. But when Ó Muireadhaigh was provided to Tuam in 1450 he simultaneously secured appointment to Annaghdown and was clearly determined to make the union of the two dioceses a reality. Not surprisingly, therefore, he vigorously opposed Barrett's attempts to gain possession of Annaghdown after 1458. In 1460 it was stated by the crown that 'Donatus, named archbishop of Tuam, born of the Irish race adverse to the king, destroys the lands of the said bishop (of Annaghdown) and of his men and tenants, and wages war against the bishop, who is born of the English nation.'[1] The king ordered William Burke of Clanricard and Thomas de Bermingham, 'lords of their nations', to cease their aid to the archbishop and to give obedience and protection to Barrett. But the latter could make little headway and eventually retired to England, probably to seek employment as an assistant bishop in an English diocese, a common practice among English appointees to Irish dioceses, which led in the early 1430s to a situation where there were no less than four absentee bishops of Dromore plying their episcopal trades as assistants in various English and Welsh dioceses.

The Annaghdown incident demonstrates clearly the inability of the crown to make its authority effective in the province of Tuam. But it also shows the persistence of animosity between Gaelic and Anglo-Irish within the church. Though the conflict can be seen as a mainly jurisdictional one, the fact that Ó Muireadhaigh was 'of the Irish race' and Barrett 'of the English nation' was clearly of importance as well. Recrudescence of the old hostility between the two nations could still occur, as in 1421, when John Geese, bishop of Waterford and Lismore, charged in parliament that his metropolitan, Richard O'Hedian, archbishop of Cashel, 'made very much of the Irish, and that he loved none of the English nation, and that he bestowed no benefice upon any English man, and that he counselled other bishops not to give the least benefice to any of them'.[2]

In the increasing area outside the control of the Dublin government, the unimpeded exercise of papal jurisdiction was not an unmixed blessing. Too often papal judgements tended to endorse abuses already prevalent in the Gaelic and gaelicised regions rather than attempting to eradicate them. In many districts benefices, and even bishoprics, had become the preserve of particular families, passing from one incumbent to his nephew or, in some cases, his son; and papal policy, by regularising this practice through dispensation

[1] *Cal. pat. rolls, 1452–61*, pp 655–6. Cf. Ruth Edwards, 'Ecclesiastical appointments in the province of Tuam, 1399–1477' (M.A. thesis, N.U.I. (U.C.D.), 1968), pp 8–14.
[2] Marlborough, *Chronicle*, p. 30.

and manipulation of canonical rulings, encouraged its continuance. Indeed the whole practice of 'Rome-running', as it was later termed, was mainly motivated by material self-interest; the desire to retain a benefice within the family, or to secure one from a rival by denouncing him at the papal curia, sprang from no concern with the welfare of souls but from an ambition to enjoy the benefice's income. Naturally this meant that many of the secular clergy took little interest in their spiritual ministrations, and when it was not unheard-of for a bishop to be married it was consequently difficult to stamp out concubinage among the clergy, though in some areas efforts were made to discourage the practice by seizing the property of such concubines or placing them in jail. In Waterford in 1430–31 it was ordained that 'no preste sholde have no wif or concubyne within the citie, and if they may be founde, the fynders shal have al their clothes and ther bodies to the jayle of the said citie unto tyme thei shal mak a fyne'. And an Irish tract of the mid-fifteenth century, 'Riagail na sacart' equally stressed the duty of the secular authority to act against priests with concubines.[1]

Many monastic houses had also fallen prey to the greed of local families, particularly among the older religious foundations of the Augustinian canons and the Cistercians; and here, too, the secular value of the property outweighed any spiritual considerations, with a consequent decline in fervour. The Cistercians, in particular, fell upon bad times in the fifteenth century, with many abbeys losing contact with the mother-house at Mellifont and becoming prizes to be fought over by local families. The abbey of Knockmoy in County Galway was the subject of a long dispute between the Burkes of Clanricard and the O'Kellys of Uí Mhaine, and lent an ecclesiastical dimension to their long-standing rivalry in secular matters. When William Burke gained possession of the abbey, he was denounced by his opponents at Rome in 1460 as 'an open and notorious fornicator, a dissolute vagabond guilty of enormous crimes'.[2] And even if one allows for the normal exaggeration of such denunciations, the whole dispute was a far cry from the way of life envisaged by the Cistercian rule. Such instances could be multiplied, and any strict observance of the rule in the houses outside the Pale must have been rare. An entry in the Armagh registers under 1439 tells its own story. One Henry Avell was dispensed for defect of birth, being born of a professed Cistercian monk and a married woman.

In contrast to those older orders, the friars were entering upon a period of renewal, particularly associated with the Observant or reformed branches of the Franciscans, Dominicans, and Augustinians. The movement within these orders for a stricter observance of the original rule had begun in the late fourteenth century and reached Ireland in the early fifteenth century, when the first

[1] *H.M.C. rep. 10*, appendix, part v (1885), p. 293; *Irisleabhar Muighe Nuadhad*, 1919, pp 73–9.
[2] *Cal. papal letters, 1458—71*, p. 87. The terms of such denunciations had become commonplace in the fifteenth century. Burke himself had been the subject of similar charges by Ó Ceallaigh four years earlier (ibid., *1455—64*, pp 264–5). For other examples see ibid., *1447—55*, pp 664, 665–6.

houses of Observant friars were founded. The Franciscan Observants were the last to become established, but were to become the most influential in bringing about a religious revival later in the fifteenth century. Even before the advent of the Observants, there were signs of a resurgence among the Franciscans in the foundation of some new houses, and the order, now containing many houses of mixed nationality where Gaelic and Anglo-Irish lived together, gained its first Gaelic Irish minister-provincial, Uilliam Ó Raghallaigh, in 1445. But old animosities died hard, and in 1451 a group of Anglo-Irish friars persuaded the king to withdraw recognition from Ó Raghallaigh and to reissue orders that Franciscan houses were not to receive those born among rebels until they had given satisfactory proof of their allegiance. Subsequently Ó Raghallaigh was able to gain confirmation by the pope in his position, and there is no evidence that any disturbance inside the order ensued.

The incident, however, demonstrated continuing English control over the affairs of the Irish Franciscan province, and both the Augustinians and Dominicans were similarly subordinated to English direction. One of the attractions of the Observant movement was that it provided an opportunity to gain independence of English control, as the Observant Franciscans did in 1460 when Nehemias O'Donohue was appointed first vicar-provincial. But although the Observant movement made its greatest impact in Gaelic areas, it also attracted support among the Anglo-Irish, and one should not overlook Anglo-Irish objections to being ruled from England. In the late fourteenth century the movements for independence among the Dominicans and Augustinians had been endorsed by the Anglo-Irish friars of the Pale area; and the same tendency is evident among an order, entirely Anglo-Irish in composition, the Hospitallers of St John of Jerusalem, who fought a tenacious and largely successful battle to free themselves from subordination to the English branch of the order.[1]

The activities of the friars, particularly the Franciscan Observants, did much to compensate for the laxity so evident elsewhere in the Irish church. Lack of evidence prevents us, however, from painting any detailed picture of their effects upon the laity, the largest section of the church but the one about whose attitudes and practices we know least. The annalists mention the routine practices of religion only incidentally, as when we are told that Catherine, the wife of Mac Fir Bhisigh, was drowned in a torrent while on her way from her house to Sunday mass. Pilgrimages were clearly popular expressions of devotion, whether to shrines within the country like that at St Mary's, Trim, or overseas to Rome or the shrine of St James at Compostella in northern Spain; and returning pilgrims were sometimes the source of annalists' information about events in contemporary Europe. But it was the unusual, not to say the outlandish, which attracted most attention, like the holy crucifix of Raphoe which was reported to have poured out blood from its wounds in 1411, or the miracles

[1] See C. L. Tipton, 'The Irish Hospitallers during the great schism' in *R.I.A. Proc.*, lxix (1970), sect. C, pp 33–43.

attributed to the image of the Blessed Virgin at Trim, which in 1444 was credited with curing the blind, dumb, and crippled, as well as inducing a woman to give birth to cats! Popular religion easily shaded into even more popular superstition in Ireland, as elsewhere.

Among the aristocracy it was difficult to enforce respect for church property. In 1447 the earl of Desmond was reported to have spared neither women nor churches on his raid into Kilkenny and Tipperary.[1] Énrí Ó Néill was excommunicated in 1454 by Archbishop Mey for his depredation on ecclesiastical possessions in Armagh diocese. Church laws on marriage also proved difficult to enforce. In Ireland, as elsewhere in Europe, clandestine marriages presented problems for a church which urged a formal celebration of matrimony but which was forced by its own teaching to recognise unions where the consent of the two parties had been legitimately expressed without church involvement.[2] And in Gaelic Ireland these problems were increased by the survival of marriage customs derived from the brehon law of earlier times rather than the canon law of the church.[3] But the continuing influence of brehon law was but one aspect of the resurgence of Gaelic customs and habits which, by 1460, predominated over most of the country and threatened to engulf even the Pale itself.[4]

---

[1] For similar accusations against Desmond see *Cal. papal letters, 1447—55*, p. 499. The Cistercian monastery of Graiguenamanagh described the earl of Ormond and his associates as 'more cruel than Pharaoh' in their subjugation of the house to their own jurisdiction and their exaction of various subsidies and tributes from it (ibid., p. 498).

[2] Cf. R. H. Helmholz, *Marriage litigation in medieval England* (Cambridge, 1974), pp 26–31.

[3] Katharine Simms, 'The legal position of Irishwomen in the later middle ages' in *Ir. Jurist*, new series, x (1975), pp 96–111, and Cosgrove, 'Marriage in medieval Ireland', pp 28–34.

[4] I wish to thank Dr Katharine Simms, who read the original version of these chapters in typescript and saved me from a number of errors.

CHAPTER XXI

Aristocratic autonomy, 1460–94

D. B. QUINN

THE Scot, John Major, in his *Historia majoris Britanniae* (Paris, 1521), wrote of Ireland: 'The southern part, which is also the more civilised, obeys the English king. The more northern part is under no king, but remains subject to chiefs of its own.' In so far as he describes the north, the great lordships of Ó Néill and Ó Domhnaill, Major is undoubtedly correct, and it is perhaps the most important single feature of Irish life in the last period of the middle ages, since the military power and political influence asserted by the northern lords dominated much of the pattern of Irish politics in this period. And if it would be incorrect to accept what Major says about the south without qualification, yet the permeation of English influence, whether emanating from London or from Dublin, was a major element, if a somewhat fluctuating one, in the affairs of the rest of the island. From Galway to Carrickfergus, around the southern Irish coasts, pockets and areas of English influence existed. If the hinterland behind Galway was little affected, and that behind Limerick only peripherally, English influence around Cork, Kinsale, and Youghal was not negligible; in the area behind Waterford and Wexford it was considerable, and between Dublin and Dundalk dominant, though thinning out rapidly towards Carrickfergus. The great Gaelic or gaelicised lordships such as those of the Burkes (de Burghs) and O'Briens might well have contacts with Dublin and London, but they were much more directly influenced in their external relations by the activities of the northern lords than by the centres of English authority. There was indeed— and this is basic—no single focus of authority in Ireland. Dublin remained only one such focus, even though it was the most prominent at most times. The springs of action frequently lay elsewhere, and we must recognise that the rulers of all the major lordships, whether of Anglo-Norman or Gaelic origin, operated inside systems of relationship that had a considerable degree of independent momentum, untrammelled by the force of a centralised authority.[1]

Between the centre of the administration in Dublin and the great Irish lordships of the west and south-west lay the extensive Ormond territories in the south midlands, the Talbot lands in Wexford, and the growing and ultimately

[1] I have been substantially helped in the revision of this chapter by Steven G. Ellis. See his *Reform and revival: English government in Ireland, 1470–1534* (forthcoming), and *Tudor Ireland* (London, 1985), pp 73–84.

N

Coleraine

Carrickfergus

ULSTER

Downpatrick
Ardglass

Greencastle
Carlingford
Dundalk

LOUTH
Ardee

Kells   Drogheda

Navan
MEATH
Mullingar   Trim

Maynooth   Dublin

Naas   DUBLIN

Kildare   Ballymore
KIL-
DARE   Wicklow

Athy   CARLOW

Carlow

CONNACHT

Galway   Athenry

Kilkenny
KILKENNY
Cashel   Callan
TIPPER-
Limerick   ARY
Clonmel
LIMERICK   New Ross   Wexford
Kilmallock   WEXFORD

KERRY   Waterford

Tralee   Dungarvan

Dingle

CORK

Youghal

Cork

Kinsale

Miles   0   50
Rosscarbery
Kms   0   80
Baltimore

Map 14 COUNTIES AND LIBERTIES, 1460, by K. W. Nicholls
See below, ix, map 44, and note, p. 108.

overpowering lordship of the FitzGerald earls of Kildare, gradually eating into the authority of the central administration in Dublin over its lands in Kildare and Carlow, and proliferating into landholdings and marriage connections in many other parts of the island. The lordship of the earls of Desmond in the south was for the most part more nearly autonomous than other Anglo-Irish territories, except for the almost wholly gaelicised territories of the Burkes, but the earls retained friendly ties with the earls of Kildare, cooperated with the anglicised urban centres on their coasts, and retained intermittent contacts with both the administration in Dublin and the English king. Both the Butlers and the earls of Kildare were strongly anglicised, even though they had many connections with, and even roots in, Gaelic Ireland, while superficially the earls of Desmond were much more nearly absorbed by the native culture. But all three of these lordships faced two ways: on the one hand towards Dublin and London, and on the other towards their friendly or hostile neighbours, in whose shifting alliances and recurrent wars they were closely involved. It is of course too simple to suggest that because a particular earl of Kildare or earl of Ormond had closer cultural connections with England or retained a greater measure of English custom and law than his neighbours, that he was therefore more likely to subordinate his own or his family's interest to that of the Dublin administration or the king. Decisive factors were family self-interest and tradition rather than cultural ones. There is thus no single political history to be written in Ireland at this period: much of Irish history is the record of fluctuating relationships between aristocratic local rulers, often influenced but rarely dominated by policies evolved in London and Dublin.

The position of the English king as regards Ireland after 1460 was that he was concerned to maintain his lordship of the island within the limits of what was practicable to him. This meant that he retained the right to appoint his representative in Ireland and to supersede him at any time, if he was a member of the Anglo-Irish aristocracy, by an English appointee unless a term of years was specified in his appointment. The Irish parliament and the Irish administration at Dublin remained subject to his authority, if and when he cared to exercise it. But the authority of those officers and institutions that he commanded was limited by their effective power in Ireland. Edward IV, Henry VII, and Henry VIII were all challenged in the exercise of their authority in Ireland, but seriously only once or twice in each reign; in 1462, 1478, 1487, and 1534. The king was often kept in the dark about what was done in Ireland and on occasion was seriously misled, but this was not inherent in his position as lord of Ireland. On almost all occasions his authority was respected when it was asserted vigorously. The king did not always ensure that his control over the appointment of high officials, where this was part of the chief governor's contract with him, was maintained efficiently. Moreover, the appointment of an Englishman as chief governor, because of the growing poverty of royal resources in Ireland, involved equipping him with an army supplied by and paid for from England. It might, on occasion, be worth doing this, but before 1534 no English king did it for longer than he could help. He might send some English troops for an Irish-born governor or make it possible to pay with English money troops raised in Ireland, or he might arrange, or try to arrange, for the specific allocation of some of his limited Irish revenues for military purposes. More often it was easier to give authority and in effect control of the Irish revenues to a great magnate who lived in Ireland and who had already a retinue of his own. He could supplement his own resources from the royal revenues; that is, from such sums as might be left over after the officials had been paid. And he was, in his own interests, concerned to maintain effective authority not only in his own lands, but in those adjoining them.

Occasionally there is a suggestion of a 'reconquest' of Ireland. This remained a hope, almost an ideal, of the official families and smaller gentry of the Pale. But it was never seriously contemplated under Edward IV, though from the time of Richard III's accession it advanced somewhat further towards being a realistic objective. Henry VII was tempted several times to attempt it, and Henry VIII eventually undertook it, but in 1460 these changes remained far away. Edward IV realised that he had some influence but little effective author-ity in Ireland outside the normal range of the Dublin administration. If a royal deputy, such as the earl of Kildare, carried royal authority somewhat further afield than was usually possible, or if an English chief governor made a few exceptional excursions to parts of Ireland which were normally outside the range of the Dublin officials, this was to be welcomed but not taken as a sign of fundamental change. The king was bound to recognise that he was powerless to affect much of what went on in Ireland, though his formal and informal con-tacts through towns, liberties, and individual lords, Gaelic as well as Anglo-Irish, outside the Dublin orbit, were by no means negligible.

Provided he could basically depend on his representative in Ireland to serve his interests, the king was better served by having a powerful Anglo-Irish mag-nate as his representative rather than one of the minor Anglo-Irish lords or an Englishman. Such a man as one of the earls of Kildare could, through his own power, bring a touch of the king's authority much further afield than would otherwise be possible. This was to extend his authority perhaps rather by shadow than by substance, but it was not entirely so. If the system created vested family interests, the king did gain to some extent by the influence and power of his magnates in Ireland, even as they themselves gained, more substantially, from having the king's authority behind them. The result was a system by which the royal rights were maintained, provided a certain degree of responsibility for their enforcement, within whatever narrow limits, was accepted by the chief governors appointed by the king in Ireland.

In the history of the great Anglo-Irish lordships in this period, the dominant position is held by that of the earls of Kildare. The seventh earl, Thomas (1456–78) may well have been undervalued for his contribution to the building-up of the territorial resources of the family, for his exercise of power as the frequent representative of the king in Ireland, and as a bridgemaker between Gaelic and Anglo-Irish, though he was helped by the virtual disappearance of Butler competition and by the retirement of the earls of Desmond from Leinster affairs after 1468. Gerald, the eighth earl (1478–1513), clearly deserves the title of 'the great earl': he combined immense skill and force as a diplomatist and administrator with formidable military capacity. He could consequently mono- polise for a large part of his life the representation of the king in Ireland, though it was only by trial and error in the maze of political changes which dominated the later fifteenth century that he found the correct balance of policy which enabled him to be both trusted by the Tudor monarchs and allowed to go sub- stantially his own way in Ireland. At the same time it is worth while remarking that both he and his successor, Gerald, the ninth earl (1513–34), operated very frequently as secondary participants only in the intrigues and wars of the great Irish lords of the north and west. Dynastic interests of O'Donnells, O'Neills, and O'Briens often tended to override the concerns of the earls of Kildare. The ninth earl, able, resilient, and ingenious as he was, had a less stable and con- trolled personality than his father. Though he too was a considerable soldier and administrator, he lacked the realism that had distinguished his father. He was, too, presented with much more complex issues in his relations with the English crown than his predecessors had been.

The heirs of James, fifth earl of Ormond, were excluded from their territories for long enough after 1460 to render them incapable of playing a major positive part in Irish affairs. The activities of Sir James Butler (known as Sir James Ormond) between 1491 and 1497, and the success of his rival Sir Piers Butler after 1497, revived the family as a force both in the Gaelic and Anglo-Irish com- munities. Piers Butler of Polestown, from his father's death in 1487, as the trusted associate of the absentee seventh earl, Thomas (1477–1515), as earl of Ormond, 1516–28, and finally as earl of Ossory from 1528 onwards, showed himself well able to match the earls of Kildare in the use of force and dip- lomacy. Though for geographical reasons he was unable to dominate the Dublin administration as the Kildare earls so often did, his power in the southern midlands enabled him to wield great influence throughout Munster as well as in Leinster. The FitzGerald earls of Desmond had a very extensive patrimony in Kerry, Limerick, Cork, and part of Waterford, even though they had to share authority with a large number of lesser Anglo-Irish families. Thomas, the eighth earl (1463–8), made a bid for wider power and influence in Dublin but was cut down in 1468. Thereafter, Desmond influence was confined to the south. James, the ninth earl (1468–87), and Maurice, the tenth earl (1487– 1520), concentrated mainly on their Munster territories, building up formid- able military forces, which they sometimes used with effect against MacCarthy lords in the south-west, sometimes against the O'Briens, often against the Butlers, though less decisively in support of pretenders to the English throne.

The principality they dominated was more self-contained than any other and through its ports it looked to Europe rather than to elsewhere in Ireland. The eleventh earl, James (1520–29), had ambitions to play a European part in his dealings with Francis I and Charles V, but his great armies were levies which could take the field, half-armed, for a few months only and were no equal of the professional continental armies, or indeed of those of the Butlers. In the end, they were sufficiently weakened by the latter to encourage the twelfth earl, Thomas (1529–34), to revert to more realistic dealings with his immediate neighbours.

Ireland as a whole was somewhat cut off from Europe, or else made contact with Europe indirectly through England. The most important independent channel of connection was through the papacy. Many of the Irish lords kept in touch with the successive popes in order to secure church appointments for relatives and friends. There were pilgrimages to Rome as the centre of the church. Members of the religious orders and secular clergy came and went to Rome in the course of their ecclesiastical business. Papal tax collectors operated in Ireland. Papal nominees who were Italians, for example Octavianus de Palatio (Spinelli), archbishop of Armagh (1478–1513), occupied an occasional benefice in Ireland from which they were not absentees. And these contacts generated others outside the religious sphere. The earls of Kildare, for example, developed ambitions to link their family with the Gherardini of Florence and built up a correspondence with this family. There was contact also through trade. Irishmen were familiar with a considerable stretch of the French coast, notably with the wine-producing areas in the west. Similarly, they had many trading links with western Spain and Portugal. Ships from these countries and from the Netherlands and from Hanseatic *kontors* farther east came to Irish ports. Spanish and French fishing vessels came in large numbers to fish off the Irish coast. Contacts with them established a line of communication between the outlying ports of Ireland and the Continent. A Waterford wool merchant, Sir John Hacket, in virtue of his international trading connections, was to become a diplomat in the service of Henry VIII.[1] Independent attempts at political contacts with European powers by Irish lords were rare. Inevitably there were some during the period of Yorkist intrigue and activity against Henry VII, but thereafter those of the earls of Desmond with France and the Empire were exceptional rather than typical.

Warfare was a commonplace of later medieval Ireland. Gaelic Irish warfare was traditionally seasonal and was rarely very widely destructive. Much the same might be said of the military activities of many of the Anglo-Irish lords. But such a measure of disorder, or one approaching it, was not confined to Ireland alone in the Europe of the fifteenth and early sixteenth centuries. Centralisation in countries like France, England, and Scotland had only begun to curb, not stop, it, though perhaps disorder was more frequent in Ireland than in any part of the British Isles except Scotland. The country had, indeed, learned

[1] E. F. Rogers, *Letters of Sir John Hacket* (Morgantown, W. Va, 1971).

to accommodate itself to a substantial degree of warfare. Under screens of defence of one kind or another, most parts of late fifteenth-century Ireland, both Gaelic and Anglo-Irish, were prospering. The maintenance and enhancement of town life, the construction of tower castles that were genuine houses as well, the building of many new and elaborate friaries, the rehabilitation of older monastic foundations and secular churches, perhaps some modest improvement in the lot of the smaller farmers, all indicated that a *modus vivendi* had been reached between the purveyors of force and the proponents of peace and quiet. The picture was not always and everywhere favourable. Devastation and burning by enemies did take place, economic hardship was the legacy of an appreciable number of local affrays, epidemics still swept urban and rural populations alike.

The overall picture became less favourable in the early sixteenth century. It may well prove that the increased use of firearms rendered warfare more lethal; possibly, too, the very continuance of a measure of economic prosperity enabled the lords to devote more money for a time to arming and deploying their forces. Certainly war became more devastating. The relative strength, too, of the Gaelic Irish who bordered the Pale—and lived off it to some extent by plundering its agricultural and urban riches—increased in proportion greater than that of the Anglo-Irish defenders. The decline of the Pale, which had long, with some hypocrisy, been lamented, became a reality, and it might appear that other Gaelic and Anglo-Irish districts suffered too. A balance attained in the late fifteenth century began to be upset, even overturned, as the sixteenth century proceeded. No one in Ireland seemed to be able to find a remedy. Lords, both Gaelic and Anglo-Irish, became more predatory and added to the decline of prosperity by the oppression of their own tenants. Much of the oppression and decline was blamed on the adoption of Gaelic Irish military customs by the Anglo-Irish lords, greater and lesser. It was perhaps a symptom rather than a cause. What became clear was that in a period when kingly power in western Europe more and more set store on order and good government, the failure of Ireland's leaders to find a new equilibrium tempted the English crown to new and ultimately permanent intervention in the Irish lordship, though for most of the period down to 1534 Ireland was left to try to solve many of its problems for itself.

IN 1459–60 Richard, duke of York, had attempted to build up a power base in Ireland from which he could influence affairs in England. With the aid of both the earls of Kildare and Desmond, he got the backing of the Irish parliament and its support in legislating against outside authority—in this case the legitimate government of Henry VI in England.[1] But Irish backing proved of little importance in Richard's intervention in England in September 1460, and with

---

[1] Otway-Ruthven, *Med. Ire.*, p. 388, says 'It is clear that the great majority of the Anglo-Irish were solid in supporting York.'

his death at Wakefield on 30 December, direct Irish influence on English affairs was, for nearly a generation, at an end.

Edward IV was indeed heir to the earldom of Ulster and knew well his father's reliance on his Irish supporters, but throughout his reign, he did not consider Ireland to be of major importance to him. He concentrated on the political and administrative reconstruction of England, and left Irish affairs largely, though by no means wholly, to take their own course. At the same time, he relinquished none of his rights, and he kept in contact with his officials in Ireland. He considered the lieutenancy of Ireland of sufficient importance to put it normally into the hands of one of the royal princes, and it was not wholly a sinecure although its practical significance tended to decline. The lieutenant was expected to exercise some general superintendence, from a distance, over the Irish lordship, as well as nominally to appoint the deputies who governed the lordship for the king. Generally, Edward relied on the Anglo-Irish magnates or officials to act as deputies. During the early part of the fifteenth century the favoured family had been that of the Butlers, occupying a central position in colonial Ireland, and best able for this reason to safeguard the interests of the Lancastrian kings. But though the fifth earl of Ormond had briefly held the lieutenancy in 1453 against Richard, duke of York, the Butlers had then left the scene. Identified with Henry VI, they had been attainted, and their lands had been left to the rivalry of cadet branches of the family. In the absence of the Ormond earls it was natural that Edward should rely much more largely on the earls of Kildare. Not only had they consolidated their hold on Kildare itself but they had expanded their lands into many other parts of the Pale and its borders and even farther afield. Under the capable Earl Thomas, they supported the Yorkist interest in the years before Edward's accession. The only original feature of Edward's policy in his early years was his attempt to bring the eighth earl of Desmond to take his turn with Kildare in the deputyship. This was a novel departure, as no member of his family, since the time of the third earl, had occupied the position of king's representative. It made sense. The family exercised wide powers in the south and south-west and could be brought to authority at Dublin to redress the shrinking of effective English authority in the south which had come with the downfall of the Butler earldom. At the same time to do so was to break with tradition, to offend deeply vested interests in the English Pale, and to lead to intrigue which perhaps, though by no means certainly, led Desmond himself into possible disloyalty to the crown. In any event his execution in 1468 eliminated the influence of the Desmond principality on the English administration in Dublin for several generations. Alternatively, an Englishman like William Sherwood, bishop of Meath from 1460 to 1482, might occasionally be called on to act as chief governor; or, exceptionally, an English nobleman, though only twice in the reign, could be sent to Ireland to govern temporarily when conditions appeared to demand it.

A thin though consistent trickle of royal orders and charters showed that

Edward retained an effective link with Ireland.[1] A similar trickle of money, rewards, payments for special services, and occasionally major payments for contingents of English troops required in Ireland, indicate something of the nature and limitations of his commitment.[2] Edward's advisers on Ireland are not clearly distinguishable and it is highly probable that his Irish policy was Edward's own. The geographical range of his contacts extended round the coast from Galway to Carrickfergus and was not confined, as has often been suggested, to the official channels of the Dublin administration. He thought of himself as the effective ruler of his lordship of Ireland, even though, apart from exceptional circumstances, he allowed the great Anglo-Irish families, or, occasionally, English officials in Dublin to carry on the greater part of the day-to-day administration.

The earl of Kildare and Lord Portlester successively held the fort for Edward in 1461–2, but in 1462 Edward had to face a Butler insurrection in the midlands. Sir John Butler (or Sir John Ormond), who was the heir to the fifth earl and who regarded himself as the sixth earl of Ormond, put in a claim to effective control of the earl's territories, the fifth earl having been executed in the English wars in 1461. With a Butler rising in the midlands, an invasion of Lancastrian Englishmen under Sir John in the south, and the capture by this force of Waterford and New Ross, there was a rising also in Meath under Philip de Bermingham. The earls of Desmond and Kildare were both threatened by this insurrection. Thomas FitzGerald, eighth earl of Desmond, who had probably just succeeded to the title, proceeded to attack and demolish the Butler insurgents in the south, while Kildare did his best to imitate him in the Pale. The final blow came with FitzGerald's victory at Piltown, near Carrick-on-Suir. Ormond went into exile, though he was later reconciled to Edward IV and came back to live in England, where he died in 1477. Once the struggle was over, the deputyship was assigned to the earl of Desmond on 1 April 1463.[3] His years in office, 1463–7, were distinguished by a much closer linking of the outlying areas of the former colony with the Pale than had been usual for many years, and the occasional appearance in Dublin of many representatives of the outlying parts of western and south-western Ireland. Desmond's parliaments were held inside the Pale and in Wexford and Waterford, and there is no reason to believe that his policy was peculiarly favourable to the Gaelic Irish. Some acts were passed directed against the invasion of Gaelic Irish custom and requiring the lapsed settlers to conform to English social practices. It was even proposed that they should pay their black rents (or blackmail) to the royal exchequer in exchange for protection instead of to the bordering Gaelic Irish

---

[1] Mostly to be traced in *Cal. pat. rolls* and *Rot. pat. Hib.* A few scattered directives for Ireland under the privy seal and signet are also to be found.

[2] See Quinn, *Guide finan. rec.*

[3] Warrant 30 March, 3 Edw. IV. (P.R.O., E. 28/89); commission 1 April, *Cal. pat. rolls, 1461–7,* p. 270. Thomas FitzGerald succeeded his father to become eighth earl in 1462 or early 1463.

lords. There was certainly a wider range of legislation during his deputyship than in most of those before or immediately after.[1] Yet the great expansion of armed power needed to overcome the rising of 1462 had to be paid for, and the price was a great extension of Irish methods of raising and providing for military forces. The institution of coyne and livery, the quartering of troops in traditional Irish fashion on the landowners in the settled areas of the Pale, was in itself a considerable, if not wholly novel, invasion of Gaelic custom, and a very burdensome one. Desmond, through the authority that he exercised in the south of Ireland, was able to impose such burdens on the Pale, and his example was later copied by Kildare. The Anglo-Irish population of Meath was hostile to these developments, and they found a leader in the person of William Sherwood, bishop of Meath. Sherwood regarded Desmond's friendship with Irish lords outside the Pale as sinister, and the practice of coyne and livery outrageous. In 1466, too, Desmond was defeated by the O'Connors in Offaly and this indicated that his military capacity was declining, and that he might not prove fully capable of defending the Pale.

In 1464, Desmond and Sherwood had come to England to discuss their differences with Edward IV, and the earl of Kildare was left as deputy during these months, indicating the close association at this time of the two earls. Desmond returned with assurances of the king's confidence in him. In 1464, John Tiptoft, earl of Worcester, was appointed chancellor of Ireland, but he did not go to Ireland at this time (Desmond making his own appointment of Kildare as chancellor), though it was proposed that he should bring over some English troops in 1465. This was countermanded, but he was eventually chosen in 1467 to replace Desmond. It may have been thought that the divisions between the gentry of Meath and the lord deputy were opening the way for fresh Lancastrian intrigues. Worcester had a retinue of 500 English archers, and he was, therefore, a power in the land from the time of his arrival in mid-October 1467. He opened parliament at Dublin on 11 December and occupied it busily with bills for reinforcing the king's authority and for holding Gaelic customs at bay. It might appear that he found Desmond and Kildare somewhat uncooperative, and it is almost certain that he received reports of their potential treachery and hostility—whether these were true or not it has never been possible firmly to establish. Nevertheless, when parliament was recalled to Drogheda in February 1468, a bill was rushed through declaring that both Desmond and Kildare, with the former seneschal of Meath, Edward Plunkett,[2] were traitors and

---

[1] A higher proportion than usual of the 108 acts on the rolls of the parliament of 1463 were public rather than private acts (*Stat. Ire., 1—12 Edw. IV*, pp 40–271).

[2] K. W. Nicholls identifies him as Edward Plunkett of Balrath, Co. Meath, and son of Christopher, first Lord Killeen. It is alleged in the annalistic fragment in University College, Oxford, MS 103, ff 53r–53v, edited and translated by Brian Ó Cuív in *Celtica*, xiv (1981), pp 83–104, that Tiptoft 'had Edward Plunkett, one of the nobles of the foreign youths of Ireland, flogged through the streets of the town [of Drogheda] like a villain or a scoundrel'. He died 8 July 1474. (See *Stat. Ire., 1—12 Edw. IV*, pp 431, 445, 465, 499, 501, 555; *Stat. Ire., 12—22 Edw. IV*, pp 2–5, 44–7, 360–61;

should suffer for their crimes; and when similar action was taken against Lord Portlester, the treasurer, it was clear Worcester was challenging the Anglo-Irish aristocracy as a whole. Moreover, within ten days of the passing of this act, Desmond was seized at the Dominican convent in Drogheda and executed summarily on Worcester's orders. This execution was a shock to the Anglo-Irish of the Pale, but even more so to the great principality which he ruled in Munster. It alienated the Desmond branch of the FitzGerald family from the English crown for several generations. It also shook the western and northern Gaelic Irish lords, who had thought highly of him. The earl of Kildare, who was also accused, managed to evade Worcester long enough to affect a reconciliation, which also covered Portlester.

Worcester's action was very much in character. He had won a reputation amongst the Lancastrians as 'the butcher'. But if his summary execution of Lancastrian enemies had been unusually rigorous, it was almost a commonplace of the English civil wars at this time. Desmond's death at his hands was a loss that could not easily be made good; he was an able young man who had wide interests and considerable capacity. Nevertheless it is clear that Worcester was able to enforce his authority in Ireland, though we know little about the circumstances under which he did so. There was one devastating reprisal raid through Meath and Kildare by Gerald FitzGerald, brother of the late earl, which did considerable damage to property and caused appreciable loss of life.[1] Worcester was able to continue his parliament in further sessions, Kildare's attainder being reversed, while he also received a pardon from Edward IV.[2] Worcester remained in Ireland until 1470, being appointed lieutenant after his return to England. His period of power in Ireland indicated that royal authority could prove effective when it seemed worthwhile for an English king to make it so. It could be argued that in this case overviolent action—in alienating one of the major lordships and so paving the way for later recalcitrance—could be counterproductive.

THE decade 1460–70 had seen the activities of the English king and of the Dublin administration involve a much wider area of Ireland than the Pale. The years that follow, 1470–78, in contrast, saw the Pale very much contract into itself. The great lordships, Gaelic and Anglo-Irish, went on in their own way: major campaigns were waged by MacCarthys and O'Donnells, for example, but

Ann. Conn. ('best of all the Meath Galls'); *A.U.*; T.C.D. MS 594 (E. 3. 33), f. 4). Art Cosgrove, 'The execution of the earl of Desmond, 1468' in *Kerry Arch. Soc. Jn.*, viii (1975), pp 11–27, has conclusively revised earlier accounts.

[1] Attempts at reconciliation, by recognising Desmond's son as his heir and sending commissioners to him, do not appear to have had much result (P.R.O., P.S.O. 1/31, 1626; N.L.I., MS D 1805; *Ormond deeds, 1413–1509*, pp 209–10).

[2] An entry in a contemporary chronicle (that by William Worcester, in *Liber niger scaccarii nec non Wilhelmi Worcestrii annales*, ed. Thomas Hearne (2 vols, Oxford, 1728; 2nd ed., London, 1771), ii, 513) suggests that the execution of Desmond met with Edward IV's displeasure ('in Hibernia comes Wigorniae fecit decollari comitem Desmund, unde rex in principio cepit displicenciam').

these scarcely impinged on the Pale. The administration in Dublin was concerned very much with internal quarrels and issues, though the need for defensive military measures, now that the Pale was largely isolated, took a serious place in its debates. Edmund IV continued, after his restoration, to take a measure of responsibility for smoothing out controversies and in providing some money for defensive purposes, but, although there was at least one project for reviving his authority on a large scale, generally these years saw a purely defensive and local view prevailing.

From the latter part of 1468 to the summer of 1471, England was faced with a renewal first of Lancastrian intrigues and then of revolt against the authority of the Yorkist king. Edward IV was eventually pushed off his throne, the restoration of Henry VI took place, and Edward reasserted himself against the earl of Warwick and Henry VI only in April 1471. During the greater part of this period, Ireland was left to itself. Wages were sent for Worcester's men in the spring of 1469, but thereafter he had to advance money out of his own pocket, and Edward was more than £4,000 in his debt by March 1470. It might seem that this latter date marks the time of Worcester's final departure from Ireland. He left an English deputy behind him, Sir Edmund Dudley,[1] who was acting in Dublin in May and June 1470, but who left Ireland later in the summer, possibly about the time of the successful Lancastrian invasion of England in September 1470. Ireland was left isolated, and nothing is known of what precisely its contacts were with the restored Henry VI and the earl of Warwick during the latter part of 1470 and the early months of 1471. The council elected the earl of Kildare justiciar before 13 October 1470 and held a parliament in Edward's name shortly afterwards, though King Edward was by then a refugee on the continent. This passed a reasonable tally of acts, several of them referring to the late earl of Worcester, as he had been executed by the Lancastrians on 18 October. There was little animus exhibited against Worcester, though he was said to have compelled the archbishop of Dublin, unfairly, to hand over to him Lambay Island. Moreover, Kildare had parliament declare all laws that were derogatory to himself and his family annulled.[2] The appointment of George, duke of Clarence, as lieutenant of Ireland by the Lancastrians in February 1471, with Kildare as his deputy, appeared to indicate that they were intending at last to move against the Yorkists in Ireland, but Edward's return and his victory in April saved Ireland from involvement in the English struggle. Kildare duly submitted to Edward IV after his restoration, and presumably held office as justiciar until after Edward adopted Clarence as his lieutenant on 16 March 1472, when he became deputy once more. On our present limited information the English crisis of 1470–71 appears to have had little direct effect on Ireland.

---

[1] There has been some obscurity about his identity. In *H.B.C.*, p. 155, he appears as Edmund Dudley, but he is also noted as Sir Edward Dudley who was testing in Dublin in May and June (see *Stat. Ire., 1—12 Edw. IV*, p. 593); but see *Cal. close rolls, 1468—76*, no. 536.

[2] *Stat. Ire., 1—12 Edw. IV*, pp 650–711.

Kildare was certainly unable to get any financial or military help from England in the period after 1471 when Edward was in financial difficulty. But Worcester's retinue of English archers was missed. A force of eighty men was now to be levied and put under Lords Portlester and Gormanston to act as a mobile defence nucleus in the Pale. Kildare was to pay for half of it, forty archers costing as much as the twenty men-at-arms a chief governor was expected to pay from his fee of £500, and the rest of the money was to be raised by parliament. This was an enactment of a parliament that met intermittently at Dublin between November 1471 and October 1472.[1] There were a number of restorations and readjustments of offices following the political disturbances, and it is clear that the Pale had suffered numerous raids and that in particular the southern part of County Dublin had been seriously disturbed by Gaelic Irish attacks.There is evidence also of the emergence of a difference of opinion in the Pale about the government of Meath. Earlier, Edward had revived the liberty of Meath, which took the liberty out of the control of the Dublin exchequer and to an appreciable extent out of the purview of the royal courts there. The precise reasons for this action are unclear, though it seems to have had the support of the gentry of Meath, and to have been opposed by Kildare. None the less the liberty was again revived in 1472 at the king's request, and its restoration and suppression were several times dealt with by parliament during the next ten years. Another parliament held at Naas in December 1472 was perhaps intended to strengthen Kildare's position, as it was held within his own sphere of influence in Kildare. It gave him possession of the goods and other chattels of the earl of Worcester in Ireland without citing any royal authority for such a transfer; and indeed a number of its acts were reversed in the next session held in Dublin in March 1473. We cannot say that this was the result of royal intervention, but it may well have been so.[2] In the Dublin session, a retinue of 160 archers and 63 mounted spearmen—all parliament could afford to finance—was created to operate for three months in the Pale. It might appear that Kildare was struggling to maintain the wide autonomy he had exercised during 1470–71, and that thereafter Edward was trying to limit his power, though without antagonising him.

Late in 1473, or early in 1474, Sir Gilbert Debenham, James Norris, David Keting, and Sir Robert Bold were sent to Ireland by the king.[3] Debenham was Edward's trusted servant and was evidently sent as the result of requests for assistance to meet attacks on the Pale. He is likely to have been there when parliament met in Dublin in March 1474, and to have welcomed on the king's behalf, as a sign of self-help, the creation of a military order, the Fraternity of St George.[4] This was to be administered by a guild consisting of the chief men

[1] Ibid., pp 712–897.
[2] Cf. ibid., pp ii, 1–187.
[3] Quinn, *Guide finan. rec.*, p. 30.
[4] *Stat. Ire., 12–22 Edw. IV*, pp 189–95.

of the Pale, headed by Kildare, and financed from the new poundage on imports and exports which was introduced by parliament. It was to consist of 120 archers and 40 horsemen. Such a device, spreading responsibility for a permanent force amongst the great landowners and not concentrating it in the hands of Kildare alone, was perhaps one which suited the circumstances of the time. Parliament proposed that Debenham should carry to Edward proposals for a general reconquest of Ireland, suggesting that after the earldom of Ulster had been restored a revenue of 100,000 marks would be available.[1] This was, as has been suggested, an occasional gambit of the Pale gentry, but it was too venturesome and too expensive to appeal to Edward IV. All the king would do was to meet immediate emergencies in Ireland. Debenham was equipped with 400 archers for one year from September 1474,[2] and he was given the second highest office under the crown in Ireland, that of chancellor.

Little is known of Debenham's activities in Ireland. It appears that he carried out a campaign or campaigns in the south of Ireland, in Wexford and Waterford in particular. It is also evident that there was some degree of friction between him and Kildare, probably because Kildare was unwilling to share the military command with an English official. Kildare gave place as deputy to William Sherwood, bishop of Meath, in 1475, and further reinforcements of 100 archers were sent in that year. Parliament met under Sherwood in July 1475 at Drogheda and subsequently at Dublin, in various sessions up to June 1476, though nothing much was done there. It seems probable that Debenham's force was reduced before the end of 1475 and probably withdrawn with him early in 1476. It must have been felt that the military situation had been to some extent restored. Sherwood was left to see what he could do with parliament. The parliament that assembled on 6 December 1476 at Drogheda was a more important one (it lasted until October 1477). In the session that opened on 14 January 1477 at Dublin, it was decided that poundage, the mainstay of the Fraternity of St George, but said to be harmful to trade, should go. Sherwood may have been lukewarm in its defence as he may not have been confident he could control it. Now persons required to fight to defend the Pale were to do so at their own cost.[3] The result was to weaken the capacity of the Pale to defend itself. Sherwood had been on a series of campaigns in 1476 and had injured various parties in Munster who had appealed to the king against him, but was supported by parliament in rebutting their complaints.[4] This sparse sequence of information suggests that the gentry of the Pale, to spare their pockets, had brought about a substantial deterioration in the military effectiveness of the Anglo-Irish. Obscurity deepens in the period immediately after 1476. At the request of parliament, Sherwood went to England in 1477, leaving Robert

[1] P.R.O., C. 47/10, 29, no. 1, printed in Donough Bryan, *Gerald FitzGerald, the great earl of Kildare* (Dublin & Cork, 1933), pp 17–22.

[2] Quinn, *Guide finan. rec.*, pp 30–31, 46–7.

[3] As they may well have had to do earlier (*Stat. Ire. 12–22 Edw. IV*, pp 478–81).

[4] Ibid., pp 476–9.

Preston, Lord Gormanston, as deputy. The Pale, we are told, was again threatened by 'the Irish enemies and English rebels who purposed to have destroyed them' and so he was obliged to hire and retain professional soldiers.[1] But he was not able to find all their wages, £360 of which had to be made up by parliament later. There were evidently continued quarrels between the magnates in the Pale, particularly between Sherwood and Kildare. In June 1477, Edmund Connesburgh, archbishop of Armagh, and Alfred Cornburgh were sent by the king to arbitrate in these quarrels.[2] It might seem that they reported there was need for more effective exercise of royal authority in Ireland. When Sherwood came back later in the year, he was given the assistance for a time of 200 archers, though the king had decided to intervene in Ireland as soon as he had an opportunity to do so. A curious situation had arisen. The duke of Clarence had been reappointed lieutenant of Ireland by 1472, having been reconciled to Edward after his flirtation with the Lancastrians. Early in 1478, however, Edward had him attainted of treason, and Sherwood was informed that his own patent as his deputy would require renewal. What happened in Ireland was that the council, without waiting for any instructions from England on who should succeed, elected its own justiciar, in the person of Thomas, earl of Kildare. He can have done little more than take up office when he died on 25 March 1478. His son Gerald succeeded as eighth earl and was almost immediately elected justiciar in his turn. This takeover of Irish administration by the Kildare family was something that Edward had evidently hoped to avoid. There may well have been some sympathy felt for Clarence in Ireland, and Edward possibly suspected that the Kildare earls, first father and then son, were in contact with elements hostile to himself. The young earl proceeded to hold parliament at Naas in May and adjourned it to Dublin, and subsequently it met at Connell, County Kildare, where it was dissolved in September.

It was claimed later that the king had sent letters under the signet either to forbid Kildare to hold parliament (or to command him to dissolve the parliament he had called), and also removing him from office. But it is unlikely that he could have received them before July and possibly not before parliament was dissolved in September. Meantime, on 6 July, Henry, Lord Grey of Ruthin, was appointed deputy by the king. Equipped with 300 archers, he was to be subsidised from England for two years. But he was slow in coming to Ireland, and may not have arrived before October. It is not unlikely that Kildare deliberately kept out of Grey's way in fear of arrest for having acted against the king's authority. His supporters resisted the king's deputy in a protest that was only a hairsbreadth from open rebellion. Sir James Keating, prior of Kilmainham, constable of Dublin castle, refused Grey admission to the castle, while Lord Portlester as treasurer and, he claimed, chancellor, did all he could to sabotage the collection of money and the issue of sealed documents. It is very

---

[1] Ibid., pp 548–53.
[2] Richardson & Sayles, *Ir. parl. in middle ages*, p. 264.

difficult to know whether these events represented a reaction by the FitzGeralds against the gentlemen of Meath who had backed Sherwood, or an attempt by the young earl to assert himself against the crown. Grey was able to hold parliament at Trim and Drogheda and finally at Dublin between November 1478 and May 1479.[1] The acts passed at Trim and Drogheda were unfavourable to the FitzGerald faction. Grey appears to have acted with great restraint, and there is no record that he made any attempt to use his English soldiers against Kildare. It may indeed have been he who suggested to Edward that an attempt should be made to settle the matter by direct recourse to the king.

Consequently, it was arranged that Lord Gormanston should be left as deputy, and he was acting as such in the early months of 1479.[2] Grey accompanied the chief justice, de Bermingham, Kildare, Keating, the archbishop of Dublin, and the prior of All Hallows to London with safe conducts (where Sherwood seems to have preceded them) and there were discussions with the king in March and April. Once Edward was forced to give serious attention to Irish matters, he was not afraid to alter his plans for keeping Grey in Ireland. Edward, like his successors, was ultimately willing to accommodate himself to existing conditions in Ireland and to work with the earl of Kildare rather than attempt to destroy him. Kildare had remarkable personal gifts, and this was only the first occasion in which he was able to talk himself out of an awkward situation when he came to London to confront an English king. As a result, he was restored as deputy, and Portlester was allowed to keep his authority as treasurer, though Sherwood was to be chancellor, and certain other offices were to be decided later by the king. Compromises were also reached about the exact tenor of acts of resumption passed in the two parliaments of 1478. The parliament which met after Kildare's return was one that carried out the orders of the king,[3] and it would seem that, in general, Edward's authority to dictate to the Irish parliament was not questioned, though Kildare may occasionally have evaded the responsibilities undertaken in England. This he may have done, for example, in failing to carry out the restoration of the seventh earl of Ormond in 1477 to his Irish estates, which was delayed. The parliament which put these agreements into effect was held at Dublin on 10 December, and all was conscientiously done. The rift between Meath and the rest of the Pale was patched up and the later sessions of parliament in 1480 were peaceful.

The agreements of 1479 were such that Kildare and Portlester were bound to accept the royal decisions. It seems probable that some temporary arrangement

[1] See Gilbert, *Viceroys*, pp 592–9; Bryan, *Great earl of Kildare*, pp 26–40; Otway-Ruthven, *Med. Ire.*, pp 397–9. Documentation for the events of 1478–9 is slight; see *Stat. Ire.*, *12–22 Edw. IV*, pp 584–679; Quinn, *Guide finan. rec.*, pp 48–9.

[2] Gormanston occupied the post for some months, having his patent renewed from 8 May to 30 September, and being provided with a retinue (P.R.O., E. 28/92, 1, 3; Quinn, *Guide finan. rec.*, pp 31–2).

[3] Printed in *Stat. Ire.*, *12–22 Edw. IV*, pp 680–81, and followed by the acts, pp 682–835.

was made about money, and that the surviving indenture of 12 August 1480[1] was
the first to commit Edward IV to a firm financial arrangement with Kildare.
The deputy was to maintain a standing retinue of 80 foot and 40 horse, presumably in addition to the Fraternity of St George which was to be restored and
paid for by reviving poundage. It was estimated that this retinue could be maintained for £600 a year, which was the estimated amount of the return of the normal subsidy from the Pale; but if Kildare did not have as much clear revenue as
this he was to be able to get the remainder by furnishing evidence to the king,
who would in turn make it available from the English exchequer. Thus Kildare,
if he wished to keep to the terms of the agreement, had to furnish some sort of
annual return of Irish receipts and expenditure, and so restore in a manner the
old financial links with England which had been broken in the 1440s. It appears
that Kildare did apply annually for a grant in aid from the exchequer and he
was paid £100 a year towards his expenses in the years 1481–3.[2] This was to set a
pattern for the more disturbed years that followed.

Edward's final programme for Ireland was now clear. It was to maintain a
strong deputy, for which purpose the earl of Kildare was the only effective candidate, but also to provide means by which he could have some professional
military force equipped from the royal revenues in Ireland and financed in addition from England if necessary. The main purpose of this force was to preserve
the Pale from further attrition. To maintain his links with the Irish administration, Edward tried to see that some members at least of the ministerial council
were his own nominees, though they remained a minority. In many ways this
was a satisfactory outcome from Edward's point of view, since it stabilised the
limited but genuine stake that he had in the government of Ireland.

From Kildare's point of view, the arrangement had similar advantages. It
gave him the backing of royal authority, which could count for much in Dublin
and in the Pale, and for something in areas farther south. It left him free to do
most of the things he wanted to do. Politically, he managed to curb Portlester's
intransigence, one of the causes of his earlier difficulties. He was able to exercise considerable authority in Meath after Sherwood's death in 1482. Because
he could also influence parliament very strongly, and had a controlling influence in his council, he could gradually extend his control over what had been
the king's rights and properties in Ireland. It sems probable that his greatest
asset was the control of adequate military forces. The retinue provided under
the arrangement of 1480, together with the Fraternity of St George and the
'rising-out' of the able-bodied men of the Pale, formed the nucleus of a substantial force. On the other hand, they were not adequate to carry out the major
interventions which he was soon accustomed to attempt in other parts of Ireland. He installed a band of galloglass in County Kildare and hired kern who
were paid for by coyne and livery, namely by quartering and payments in kind.

[1] P.R.O., C. 47/10/27, 8–9; see Bryan, *Great earl of Kildare*, pp 44–6.
[2] Quinn, *Guide finan. rec.*, pp 30, 50.

This was acceptable in an emergency, for example when there were raids into County Dublin from the south, or when the borders in Meath or Louth were seriously in danger. The existence of these exactions was recognised from time to time in acts of parliament, particularly when religious houses pleaded to be exempt from their impact. But there is no evidence that they had been used since 1467 as normal and year-round exactions. Their revival meant that Kildare gained a stranglehold on the prosperity of the Pale, and in effect acquired a powerful means of exercising pressure on any possible opponents there.

There is no clear evidence that Edward IV clearly understood that this was happening. Kildare concentrated much of his military power so as to take over lands in Counties Kildare and Carlow that had fallen into hostile, mainly Gaelic Irish, hands. He invited their absentee owners to return, and when they did not do so he transferred them to himself by act of parliament in 1483. It is significant that this parliament was held in Limerick, indicating that Kildare was using his authority under the crown to extend the normal range of official activity. He was also building up his family territory in this county. The arrangements of 1479–80 lasted effectively while Edward IV was still active. Problems arose again during the brief reigns of Edward V and Richard III and the replacement of the Yorkists by Lancastrians in 1485.

The political crisis of 1478, and its solution in 1479 by the installation of Kildare in a position of strength, brought to an end the short period during which the authority of the king's deputy was ineffective outside the Pale. With Kildare in the saddle the Dublin government entered on a new phase of activity, involving itself in a much wider area. Kildare was young, energetic, and ambitious. He was determined to use the authority derived from the crown effectively over as wide an area as he could command. That he used his power to build up his estates and extend his family's alliances throughout the island did not appear to him in any sense illegitimate.

DURING the five years from 1483 to 1488 the English lordship in Ireland was in a state of flux. The catastrophic changes of the years from 1483 onward in England produced conditions under which the earl of Kildare, as lord deputy in Ireland, obtained a degree of freedom which he exercised with a mixture of astuteness and rashness, illustrating very well both the strength and, ultimately, the weaknesses of a powerful representative of the king, even of one who had a strong backing in Ireland, but who lacked strong support in England. Within his own limits, Kildare could often act almost as an independent sovereign in relation to the king. Yet Kildare, however cautiously he began, eventually overstepped the limits of what it was possible for him to effect. His initiatives in 1486–7 nearly brought him to disaster. His task during the following years, 1488–94, was to try to minimise the effects of his mistakes. By 1494, it appeared that he had finally failed to do so.

The death of Edward IV in 1483 and the accession of Edward V, followed within two months by the usurpation of Richard III, did not in themselves create any vitally new problems between the administrations in London and Dublin, but the growing insecurity of Richard's position, and the lack of power from which his regime ultimately suffered, enabled Kildare to enlarge the range of his own initiatives. At the same time, it is possible for E. R. Jacob to say with some confidence that 'in Richard's time, Ireland was quiet, and . . . the house of York had had some hold on the Irish people',[1] though it may be queried, however, whether the phrase 'the Irish people' meant more than 'much of the Anglo-Irish aristocracy'.

   The accession of Richard III gave Kildare the opportunity to demand rather better terms for the continuance of his support for the new sovereign than he had obtained from Edward IV. At the same time, he was to show himself very wary of putting himself in Richard's power by coming to England, and he was faced with the possibility that Richard might intervene more actively in Ireland, even to the extent of coming to Ireland in person. On the news of Edward's death, the council had elected Kildare justiciar to Edward V, and it is probable that on the news of Richard's usurpation a further election was held. Richard sent over instructions to Ireland on 19 July by William Lacy,[2] who had previously been in Ireland on business for Edward IV. Kildare was to be confirmed as deputy to Edward, Richard's son and heir, as lieutenant, but the confirmation of Kildare was for one year, and officials were to hold office at pleasure only. Richard was clearly reserving his right to formulate something more than an interim policy in due course, Lacy's instructions stating that 'the king will always be at his liberty to the intent the relief of that land by his immediate authority, whensoever he may have first leisure thereunto'. Kildare was instructed to come to England or send a representative to determine the details of his indenture with the king for the year October 1483–October 1484. Kildare responded by sending John Estrete, the king's sergeant, to bargain for him, Richard's replies indicating the terms he proposed. He asked for a fixed term, nine or ten years, as deputy, with a guarantee of £1,000 a year from England, and also the constableship of Wicklow castle, which was in the custody of an Englishman, and the manor of Leixlip, normally assigned for its support. He would come to England, but only if he had a safe-conduct attested by a number of English magnates as well as by the king. Clearly he thought of himself as in a strong position so long as he remained in Ireland, but he was not prepared to assume that the king would necessarily accept his demands if he put himself into his power. Richard took these requests more calmly than his violent reputation might indicate; Estrete brought back with him reassuring answers, extolling Kildare's merits as deputy and assuring him of the king's good faith.[3] At a more prosaic level he was told that his specific requests would

   [1] *The fifteenth century* (Oxford, 1961), p. 629.
   [2] *L. & P. Rich. III & Hen. VII*, i, 44–6; Quinn, *Guide finan. rec.*, p. 32.
   [3] *L. & P. Rich. III & Hen. VII*, i, 91–3 (placed *c.* 1486).

be granted and that he would be subsidised if he came to England by 1 August, bringing with him an account of Irish revenues to justify his case. The earl duly appeared, and though the indenture he made with Richard is not extant, it almost certainly provided for some royal subsidy. The parliament which Kildare held at Dublin and Naas between March and August 1484[1] transferred a considerable part of the royal revenues to him. These were in the form of contributions to his castle-building at Kildare, Lackagh, and Castledermot; and if they strengthened the Pale against attack, they also made it easier for Kildare to claim that the Irish revenues were declining and must be more largely augmented from England.

The king, however, saw this rapprochement as a first step only. Thomas Barrett, the absentee bishop of Annaghdown, was commissioned in September[2] to sketch out a wider ranging policy of royal activity in Ireland which would extend the range of royal influence, though perhaps within the orbit of Kildare's power as his representative. Barrett was to enlist Kildare's cooperation in obtaining for the king some effective control over his earldom of Ulster. Edward IV had maintained some direct contact in the early part of his reign with the Anglo-Irish inhabitants of Lecale, but had gradually ceased to take any active part in the administration of the residual part of the earldom. Richard now aspired to establish effective control over Ulster and made the novel suggestion to Kildare that the cooperation of both Ó Néill and Ó Domhnaill might be sought in reinstating the ancient position of the earl of Ulster.

The king had instructed Barrett to carry letters to representatives of the Anglo-Irish throughout the rest of Ireland. To the earl of Desmond he was to bring a collar of gold, a letter apologising for the execution of the eighth earl by Worcester in 1468, and a promise to find him a wife in England if he would come there, having given up the Gaelic Irish costume and customs. Lord Barry, another of the Munster magnates, was told that his old claim to a family inheritance in Wales would be looked into if he wished to make contact with the king, while the heads of the Power family were encouraged to be loyal to him, as was Lord Roche. Letters were also carried to old families in Connacht, to Lords Stanton, Nangle, Dexter, de Bermingham, and Barrett—the last of them probably relatives of the bishop—and the Burkes 'descended of the auncien blood and lynage of our auncestres of Wolster', as well. These were the first direct communications known between the lord of Ireland and the western province of Connacht for many years. In addition, Barrett was to make personal contact with the lesser magnates of the Pale, Lords Gormanston, Delvin, and Portlester, and Sir Oliver and Sir Alexander Plunkett, the two latter being commended for their loyalty in repelling the king's enemies. A significant omission was that of the Lancastrian Butlers and their dependants in the midlands. To follow Barrett on his mission would be a fascinating exercise, but

[1] P.R.O.I., R.C. 13/8.
[2] *L. & P. Rich. III & Hen. VII*, i, 67–98.

unfortunately his journal, if he kept one, has not survived. Whether Richard could have maintained these contacts and have built on them cannot be told since his reign was too short, but there are some indications that after this mission Kildare himself was more careful to foster his own links with the Munster magnates and possibly with others.

Barrett undoubtedly talked with Kildare about his financial situation in relation to the king. A consequence of his visit was the appearance in England, apparently about Easter 1485, of a roll of the Irish revenues.[1] This contained a great list of sources of revenue which had long passed out of the king's hands, such as 32,000 marks from Ulster and Connacht, and fee farms and customs duties long assigned to outlying towns for defence, or else simply abandoned. Much of the remaining hereditary revenue was shown to have been alienated and a total of only some £750 was shown to be leviable, all of which was needed for the day-to-day expenses of the administration, leaving none for the deputy's salary and military expenses. From one point of view this document looks like an attempt by Kildare to obtain the whole of his salary, set out in the lost indenture, from England, but the inclusion of so many items lost to the king by past neglect could be construed to lend support to Richard's policy of looking again for potential profits to be revived by his personal attention to Ireland beyond the Pale. It was perhaps, therefore, not wholly a Geraldine document.

Kildare held parliament again at Dublin and Trim in March, June, and August, and at Dublin on 24 October,[2] the last date falling well after the battle of Bosworth on 22 August had swept away Richard, his line, and his policies. There is evidence in Kildare's acts that he was beset by problems, by plague as well as hostile forces, money being granted him to hire kern for the defence of the Pale. Acts passed in June that resumed the right of electing a justiciar *ad interim* to the ministerial council, and declaring that the chief officers should hold their posts for life and not at pleasure as Richard had earlier ordered, may be seen as defences against a more active policy of intervention by Richard.

Though short, therefore, Richard's reign had opened up the prospect of wider activities by the king in his lordship of Ireland, either in friendly cooperation with his powerful representative, or in competition, probably in conflict, with him; but it left Kildare substantially where he had been in the last years of Edward IV. We have no knowledge of when news of the battle of Bosworth was known in Ireland, but it was probably some time in September 1485. It seems probable that Kildare and the council temporised during October and that the latter reelected the earl as justiciar. The earl of Lincoln, Richard's lieutenant, accepted Henry VII as king and was not at once displaced, and it is not unlikely that Kildare took his cue from him and sent over some form of recognition to the

[1] Quinn, *Guide finan. rec.*, pp 17–27. It is clear that scutage was an occasional addition to this. Light is thrown on this and other means of providing resources for defence in S. G. Ellis, 'Taxation and defence in late medieval Ireland: the survival of scutage' in *R.S.A. I. Jn.*, cvii (1977), pp 5–28.

[2] P.R.O.I., P.R.O. 7/1.

new sovereign which was acceptable for the time being. But the appointment of Jasper Tudor, duke of Bedford, as lieutenant in March 1486 meant that Kildare came under a Lancastrian prince, and it was probably on receipt of this news, and a confirmation of his own deputyship with it, that he sent John Estrete to England to negotiate a new indenture. Estrete brought with him a rather perfunctory, and now incomplete, account of the current Irish revenues, and was rewarded by the king on his return to Ireland.[1] It may well be that no indenture was made at this time. Anglo-Irish sympathies might remain with the Yorkists but in the first year or more of the reign there was no appearance of resistance to the new English establishment.

According to our not very reliable chronicle sources,[2] Lambert Simnel was brought to Ireland late in 1486 or at the beginning of 1487 by Richard Symonds, an Oxford priest, who passed him off as Edward, earl of Warwick (son of George, duke of Clarence, who had been born in Dublin in 1449), escaped from the Tower, where he had been placed by Henry. The pretender was taken under the wing of Sir Thomas FitzGerald of Lackagh, the chancellor and Kildare's brother, and was given for a time covert support by Kildare and other officials. Once communication had been established with Lincoln in England and with Margaret of Burgundy in the Netherlands, arrangements were made to bring him into the open against Henry. Lord Howth apparently informed Henry in January of Simnel's arrival; Henry thereupon took protective measures against the Yorkists and exhibited the young earl in London in February to convince doubters. He did not arrest Lincoln, however, who made his way to Flanders, and with Margaret raised a body of German mercenaries under Martin Schwartz. By April they were in touch with Kildare, Lincoln perhaps being regarded by him as still rightfully lieutenant of Ireland and heir to the English throne. A fleet arrived in Dublin on 5 May with some 2,000 men, including Lincoln and some other English Yorkists. During the next few weeks most of the Anglo-Irish in the Pale were induced to accept the pretender. He was eventually crowned at Christ Church on 24 May, in the presence of a large force of kern introduced to overawe Lancastrian supporters. 'Edward VI', with his 'cousin' Lincoln at his side, proceeded to organise an Irish force to upset the Tudor monarch. Sir Thomas FitzGerald resigned his chancellorship to Portlester to take command of the Irish contingent. This was mainly, if not wholly, composed of kern, with a few Anglo-Irish amongst the officers, Maurice FitzThomas and one of the Plunketts of Killeen being amongst them. The expedition set sail for England on 4 June and the speed of the campaign,

[1] The account is in Quinn, *Guide finan. rec.*, pp 27–8, the reward p. 38.

[2] On the Simnel affair see *Cal. Carew MSS*, v, 188–9, 472–3; *L. & P. Rich. III & Hen. VII*, i, 95–6, 383–4; Bernard Andreas, *Historia . . . Henrici septimi*, ed. James Gairdner (London, 1858), pp 49–55; *A.F.M.*; *Anal. Hib.*, no. 10 (1941), pp 33, 51; Sir James Ware, *Annales* (London, 1664), pp 5–14; *The Anglica historia of Polydore Vergil*, ed. Denys Hay (London, 1950), pp 20–27. The fullest modern accounts are Mary Hayden, 'Lambert Simnel in Ireland' in *Studies*, iv (1915), pp 622–38, and Bryan, *Great earl of Kildare*, pp 99–123. See also S. B. Chrimes, *Henry VII* (London, 1972), pp 75–8.

through Lancashire and Yorkshire to its end at Stoke in Lincolnshire on 16 June, was impressive, though the defeat of the invaders by Henry at the battle of Stoke was decisive. Sir Thomas FitzGerald and Lincoln alike were killed and the Irish kern, fighting valiantly, undefended by armour and armed with little but darts, were apparently almost wiped out.

Kildare had held a parliament in the name of 'Edward VI' and later, after news of the pope's support for Henry became known, a great council which attempted to buy off papal censures. In the north Octavianus de Palatio, archbishop of Armagh, and John Edmund de Courcy, bishop of Clogher, had refused to accept the revolution, and there was resistance in the south, though it would seem that Desmond, murdered later in 1487, came out for Kildare. Though at first coins were minted at Waterford in the name of 'Edward VI', the city later refused recognition and aid to Kildare when he asked for help. The recorder, William White, paid a visit to England in March and got from Henry VII money to buy bows, bowstrings, and arrows for the defence of the city.[1] From Waterford, resistance spread to the midlands: the Butler territories, including the town of Kilkenny, declared against Kildare. At that time, Thomas, earl of Ormond, high in Henry's favour in England, was trying to assert his own influence in the Butler lands. Kildare was at least checked in his attempt to consolidate his authority as the lieutenant of the new 'king'. When news of the disaster at Stoke reached him, probably before the end of June, he might well have reacted to his failure to act as the kingmaker by attempting to set up an independent Yorkist regime in Ireland. But opposition in the south and midlands, and even, it would seem, in the Pale, where the city of Dublin rapidly came out for Henry VII, forced him to temporise after an interval. But as late as 20 October Henry was writing to Waterford, declaring that Kildare and his supporters had still made no submission. Yet, during the winter, contacts with the king were made and submissions offered, and pardons were promised to Kildare and to a long list of his fellow Yorkists on 25 May 1488. Before this time, Sir Richard Edgecombe had been sent out with royal ships to see whether the southern approaches to the channel were free of hostile shipping, and it is probable that he made a few calls at southern Irish ports before he returned before the end of May to say that the way was clear. The Yorkist earl of Desmond had been murdered in December 1487 and his successor, Maurice, appears to have made friendly contact with Henry, as on 18 April he was recognised as earl, and as constable of Limerick castle. Shortly afterwards he was given a commission to act against rebels in Counties Limerick, Cork, Waterford, and Tipperary. Lord Roche at this time was also given authority to represent the king in County Cork. Florence MacCarthy (Fínghin Mac Carthaigh Riabhach of Carbery) was to be given the privileges of English law and a grant of the royal customs west of the Old Head of Kinsale, while he and

---

[1] Quinn, *Guide finan. rec.*, pp 33, 51, and see S. G. Ellis 'The struggle for the control of the Irish mint 1460–c. 1506' in *R.I.A. Proc.*, lxxviii (1978), sect. C, pp 17–36.

Cormac mac Taidhg Mac Carthaigh, lord of Múscraighe (Muskerry), were to pay homage to the king. These, and further grants to Waterford, suggest that Henry was busy creating a party in the south before coming to grips with Kildare. Edgecombe was equipped to make a major expedition in June. Setting out with four ships and 500 men from Cornwall late in the month, he went first to County Cork. Landing at Kinsale, he took the oaths of the townsmen and then of Lord Barry and Lord Courcy and of the O'Sullivans. The technique was to require adhesion to oaths of loyalty and then the acceptance of a bond and obligation. Waterford, as might be expected, gave him a very friendly reception, but requested, in view of the king's intention to accept Kildare once more as chief governor, that Waterford should be exempt from the jurisdiction of Dublin and should remain directly under the crown. On 2 July, Edgecombe set sail for Dublin. Landing to the north of the city, he was at first rather isolated, since Kildare had kept out of his way, but gradually the major officials came to see him and to make their personal submissions, as did the Dublin citizens, while he remained at the Blackfriars. With Kildare and the council, after the deputy arrived on 12 July, there were long discussions. There was resistance to the posting of bonds in particular. This involved further meetings at both Maynooth and at Dublin and finally, on 21 July, great public oathtakings and signatures of documents which bound almost all those who had been in rebellion to the king's service. Edgecombe refused to pardon James Keating, and he installed Richard Archbold in Dublin castle, from which Keating had kept him. Only after much pleading and discussion would he accept the submission of Thomas Plunket, chief justice of common pleas, on 30 July. He left Dublin the same night but managed to reach Fowey only on 8 August.[1]

The Edgecombe mission gave Henry valuable information on various parts of his Irish lordship and a report in detail on acceptable and unacceptable members of the Dublin administration. It was impossible to forecast whether this quite efficiently conducted expedition meant much or little. Henry had combined radical concessions to the former rebels with a show of strength and a respect for ceremonial which were not unimpressive. It seems clear that thereafter the majority of the Anglo-Irish of the Pale were reluctant to risk openly treasonable activity against the lord of Ireland. At the same time it left the general situation somewhat unsettled, and it remained so. Kildare never fully reconciled himself to English intervention and was to demonstrate that he would resist it covertly, if not openly, when he was next faced with it.

It seems, however, that for the time being, after Edgecombe's mission, Kildare felt safe enough to come to England, early in 1489, along with a number of

---

[1] The principal narrative of the Edgecombe mission is printed in Walter Harris, *Hibernica* (2 vols, Dublin, 1747–50), i, 29–38, and is represented in T.C.D., MSS 842 (F. 3. 16) and 664 (F. 4. 30). Oaths and recognizances appear in Dublin City Records, MS 36/2, 18; P.R.O., C. 1/10, 27 (10); Bodl., Laud MS 614, pp 13–33. See also *Materials for a history of the reign of Henry VII*, ed. William Campbell (2 vols, London, 1873–7), ii, 309, 315–19, 321, 496; Quinn, *Guide finan. rec.*, pp 33, 52; *Ormond deeds, 1413–1509*, pp 263–6.

the lords of the Pale. They were entertained at Greenwich, and the earl of Ormond joined them at dinner with the king. One symbol in the banquet was the humiliation of the visitors by having Simnel wait on them at table. One fruit of the visit was the pardon of James Keating on 27 January. We know nothing of the new indenture that was, almost certainly, drawn up to embody terms in detail of Kildare's deputyship.

The situation in Ireland appears to have been peaceful in the year following, but in July 1490 the king decided that he wished once again to discuss with Kildare the terms of his continuing responsibility as chief governor, and invited him to come to England within the next ten months. For some reason Kildare did not care to do so. He appears to have made no answer until June 1491. Then, when he was holding parliament in Dublin, he induced the fifteen spiritual and temporal lords who made up the upper house of parliament on this occasion, to excuse him for not leaving Ireland, and wrote himself also to the same effect to the king. Amongst the signatories of the lords was the archbishop of Armagh, who had no reason to love Kildare. The reason given was that there was too great a danger to the Pale from its enemies to permit the chief governor to leave the country. Kildare claimed that he had been called in to arbitrate between Desmond and 'Lord Burke of Connacht' (Burke of Clanricard), and he promised to bind all parties in the disputes that were current in Connacht to the king's service. From the earl of Desmond, Lord Roche, Lord Courcy, and Sir Piers Butler came a letter on 10 July from Limerick, urging that Kildare be allowed to carry through his conciliatory measures. The letter implied, though it did not state, that Kildare was already in Munster.[1]

It may be that there were already plots in the air. In November 1491 Perkin Warbeck, claiming to be Richard, duke of York, escaped from the Tower, arrived in Cork from Portugal, accompanied by some Yorkist agents. He appears to have been well received there, and is said by Ware to have written to both Desmond and Kildare asking for their support. He probably received encouragement from Desmond and some help, though Kildare is not certainly known to have responded to him. However, Kildare's failure to come to England earlier in the year, and the obvious danger that Henry might be involved with a further rising in the Pale, made him act rapidly.[2] James Ormond was sent to secure the midlands and south for the king and for the earl of Ormond. An illegitimate nephew of the earl, he is said to have been the seventh earl's representative after 1485 and to have played an active part against Lambert Simnel, but there is no certain record of this or his presence in Ireland before 1491, when he is described as one of the esquires of the king's body. Thomas Garth, at the same time (7 December), was commissioned for three months to take a force of 200 soldiers and the necessary sailors to Ireland.

[1] L. & P. Rich. III & Hen. VII, i, 377–84.
[2] For the events of 1492–4, see Agnes Conway, Henry VII's relations with Scotland and Ireland (Cambridge, 1932), pp 42–62.

Ormond and Garth were jointly to act as captains and governors on their campaign and to withdraw Kilkenny and Tipperary from the deputy's control. Ormond had evidently strong connections in Ireland already: he was able to call in Ó Briain and Burke of Clanricard to help him dominate the other Butler families,[1] especially that of Piers Butler, and remove Kildare's supporters in Kilkenny and Tipperary. Garth's force apparently operated mainly with Ormond in the midlands and also to protect Waterford. Its prime function was to drive a wedge between Desmond and Kildare and so prevent their cooperation in favour of the Yorkists. In February the royal ship *Margaret* was sent to patrol the Irish coasts. Garth and Ormond between them were empowered to supersede Kildare as and when they found it necessary, and this authority appears to be the origin of the title of 'governor of Ireland' (intended, it might seem, to divide the authority of the chief governor) which Ormond retained after the emergency was past. At any rate, whatever support Perkin had mobilised, or Desmond had mobilised for him, had been dissipated by the following spring. Yet Henry had not, in spite of assertions by Kildare of his continued loyalty, regained his confidence in the earl. On 11 June 1492, therefore, under the guns of Garth's men, Kildare was removed from the deputyship and Portlester from the treasurership. The deputyship was given to the archbishop of Dublin, Walter FitzSimons, apparently on the assumption that there was now a pro-Henrician party in the Pale, and the treasurership was consigned to Sir James Ormond, who now attested documents alongside the deputy as 'governor and treasurer'.[2] Later in the year, at harvest time, Ormond brought some of his Irish army to Dublin, and there were fights between them and Kildare's men, in and around the city. Meanwhile, Garth had had a successful campaign against the O'Connors on the western borders of the Pale, and in revenge for his killing one of them, Kildare had Garth's son hanged, an act that Henry does not seem to have avenged. Kildare's letter of February 1493 to the earl of Ormond complained that Sir James Ormond was setting himself up as earl (the object being to alarm Earl Thomas), that Kildare's messengers to the king had not been allowed to reach him, and that he, the earl, had had nothing to do with Warbeck. An attempt was made to conciliate Kildare by the issue of a pardon to him on 30 March—if he sent his son to the king within six months— and others were issued to Desmond and his relatives in April. Parliament between June and August[3] took protective action on behalf of Waterford and punitive measures against Portlester. But FitzSimons, even with Ormond at his side, was evidently not in a strong enough position; he gave way to Lord

---

[1] *A.F.M.* For the period 1491–6 as a whole, see S. G. Ellis, 'Henry VII and Ireland' in Lydon, *Eng. & Ire.*, pp 237–54.

[2] S. G. Ellis, 'Henry VII and Ireland', p. 251, suggests that Sir James Ormond had a separate patent to divide the chief governorship with FitzSimons (though the suggestion in the text may, in the absence of a patent, be regarded as a simpler explanation). He also indicates that, after 11 June 1493, Sir James was acting as treasurer, as substitute for the earl of Ormond.

[3] P.R.O.I., R.C. 13/9.

Gormanston in September. Under his auspices, a great council at Trim in September 1493 was intended to seal the reconciliation once more of the Anglo-Irish with the king. They were to eschew Gaelic customs, to keep the peace, and to answer complaints about their misdeeds since 25 July: as pledges to keep these ordinances, Kildare and fifteen other lords and gentlemen gave recognizances (Kildare in 1,000 marks). Henry Wyatt, sent over specially from England, and Thomas Garth were there as the king's commissioners.

The great council at Trim marked an attempt by Henry VII to impose some formal obligation on the Anglo-Irish of the Pale to maintain the laws in the marches, and to concert measures for the punishment of offenders and for defence.[1] In particular it was provided that there was to be no coyne and livery imposed within the Pale, and that it was to be used by marchers only on their own tenants. The ordinances appear to have had some success. Though a parliament which followed at Drogheda was afterwards declared to have been irregularly called, it may also have helped in the pacification. By the end of 1493 it had proved possible to withdraw all but one hundred of the English soldiers, and to bring Kildare, Sir James Ormond, Lord Gormanston, and a representative group of Anglo-Irish clerics and laymen to England for prolonged discussions with the king and his ministers which continued well into 1494. The object was the establishment of some more secure regime in Ireland, the reconciliation of Kildare with Ormond being an essential factor.

The end of the year 1493 marks something of a turning point. From 1483 onwards the successive rulers of England had tried to follow the pattern of Irish policy marked out by Edward IV. Like him, in his later years, they had to deal primarily with Kildare. Kildare had been involved there in maintaining and developing his own wealth and influence, but it is clear that he preferred to rest his authority over the Dublin administration on the backing of a secure royal power in England. Although Kildare had favoured the Yorkists, Richard III had some doubts about his willingness to serve him, while in 1485 and afterwards Kildare had some substantial doubts about whether Henry VII—if he continued to hold his crown against Yorkist plotters—would give him sufficient backing in his deputyship. It was probably this, more than a desire to be a king-maker, that seems to have led Kildare into the rather ridiculous Simnel enterprise. Thereafter, as Henry appreciated, he was bound to the Lancastrian monarch in some degree by a sense of shame at having been so innocent in this affair. Yet, during the years which followed, Henry could not establish a firm basis for a relationship with Kildare, so that the appearance of Perkin Warbeck as a new pretender meant that fresh suspicions between them were bound to arise. The sending over of English troops in 1491 and the following years upset Kildare's carefully balanced system of relations with Gaelic and Anglo-Irish alike. The result was continuing friction. The replacement of Kildare by minor magnates such as the archbishop of Dublin and Lord Gormanston

[1] *Stat. Ire., Hen. VII & VIII*, pp 88–91.

(Gormanston's son, William Preston, took over from him for a time in 1493, when he was in England), was basically ineffective. Such men ruled with the assistance of an English force, it is true, but to a large degree on sufferance from Kildare. Continuing friction led to the eventual determination to send an effective English deputy to Ireland and to fill the administration with English appointees in all the principal posts. We may ask, did Henry think of a complete conquest of Ireland? How far he thought ahead, beyond a determination to destroy opposition in Ireland, and to provide a more secure framework inside which his limited lordship of Ireland could be effectively run, we cannot say. Henry was a realist and did not hope for too much too soon.

1494 is not an unimportant date in the relationship between England and Ireland. It marked the beginnings of the reorganisation of the system of government and administration in the course of which there was some reshaping of the formal relationship between the English crown and its Irish dependency; and it was on the foundations of what was accomplished then that Henry VIII was later to build.

CHAPTER XXII

'Irish' Ireland and 'English' Ireland

D. B. QUINN

APART from the skein of continuity that the government of the Pale and its English associations provides, it is not possible to write a history of Ireland in this period, only a series of local histories. But these local histories, whether at a provincial or a regional level, are interlocking ones: they interact with each other to provide, if not a total history, at least a series of changes through time which convey some indirect sense of movement. Inside each major unit or grouping, internal tensions and conflicts alternately establish and upset an equilibrium: between the major groupings their interaction is of greater importance through time, because in it are expressed long-term changes in the balance of forces throughout the island. We have far too few facts at our disposal to do more than indicate some of the ways in which these interactions were taking place in the period 1460 to 1534, but something at least can be conveyed. It will be seen that the main changes take place round the periphery of the island, most of them independently of what was happening inside the Pale, but that, at the same time, many of the interactions between the smaller Gaelic units and the Pale have some significance for the major units, while they themselves have each, at any one time, some policy, even if only a shadowy one, towards the Pale. And whenever a major Anglo-Irish lord, Desmond, Kildare, or Ormond, is in control of the Pale, its affairs have an importance for the major Gaelic Irish lordships that they do not have when the king's representative in Ireland is an Englishman or a member of the minor gentry of the Pale. This is why the considerable continuity, which the intermittent rule of the seventh, eighth, and ninth earls of Kildare provides, brings the Pale into the picture more often and more significantly in this period than it otherwise would have done. Reciprocally, the earls of Kildare, through their long continuance in power in the Pale, developed the resources to make their presence felt outside its borders. Thus, though O'Neills, O'Donnells, Burkes, O'Briens, Mac-Carthys, earls of Desmond, earls of Ormond, MacMurroughs and the rest have their own momentum inside their regional context, they are repeatedly brought into contact with the influence and power of the ruler who has the Pale at his

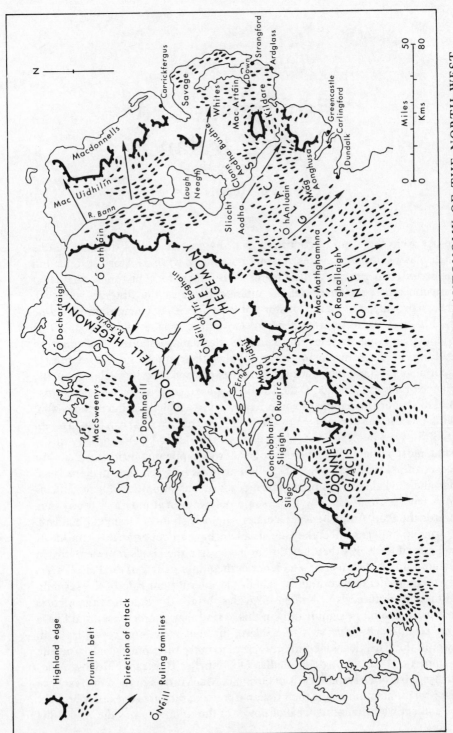

Map 15 THE PHYSICAL AND STRATEGIC BASIS OF THE AUTONOMY OF THE NORTH-WEST, 1460–1534, by D. B. Quinn

command. To ignore either the regional interactions or the dynamic influence of the Pale when led by an earl of Kildare is fatal. Both orders of activity and development must in some degree be kept in view.[1]

THE most important single fact in the history of Ulster in this period was the continued clash between the O'Donnells and the O'Neills, but the most novel one was the consolidation of the O'Donnell lordship, which made it an effective force outside Ulster in the west of Ireland. The decisive turning-point was the elimination in 1461 of Toirdhealbhach Cairbreach Ó Domhnaill from the lordship by Aodh Ruadh. This led to the reconciliation between Ó Domhnaill and the Mac Sweeneys of northern Tír Conaill which was to provide almost unbroken support for successive O'Donnell lords by the strongest galloglass groupings in Ireland. Continuity given to O'Donnell rule by the two remarkable soldiers and politicians, Aodh Ruadh (1461–1505) and Aodh Dubh (or Aodh Óg) (1505–37), had much to do with this. The use of the consolidated O'Donnell power was seen alike in the revival of the old raids into north Connacht and in the new range of activity undertaken by Ó Domhnaill in his great raid through the western marches of the Pale in 1475. The appearance of Mac-William Burke[2] and Ó Domhnaill in Dublin as guests of the earl of Desmond in 1464 is significant of their prestige as leading rulers of the north and west, though we do not know the terms of the treaty they made with him. The influence of O'Donnell policy on the west, however, can only be seen in a study of the history of Connacht.

The Ó Néill–Ó Domhnaill rivalry centred on the Foyle valley around Strabane (Cenél Moén) and on Inishowen, which had formerly been an O'Neill territory but, since the fourteenth century, had been in the hands of the O'Dohertys who were normally linked with Ó Domhnaill. Later in the period the O'Neills were to extend their claims—either attempting to revive archaic ones or giving a spurious cast of age to newer, invented, ones—so as to claim the overlordship of Tír Conaill as a whole. Occasionally, and briefly, when it happened to suit their interests, Ó Néill and Ó Domhnaill are to be found in alliance; more normally they are to be seen stirring up opposition in the enemy camp by backing some rival branch of the ruling family for the succession to the lordship or in order to evade the performance of its duties to its overlord.

To the east the O'Neills had to suffer the hostility of the O'Neills of Clandeboye (Mac Uí Néill Bhuidhe) who were rapidly expanding in the late fifteenth century in what is now northern County Down and southern County Antrim. They were frequently allied with the O'Donnells against Ó Néill, which

---

[1] The outline of political events in Kenneth Nicholls's *Gaelic Ire.*, pp 126–77, has been generously supplemented from his unpublished work placed at my disposal. It can be read with advantage in association with our combined chapter below, iii, 1–38; and see below, ix, 140–76.

[2] 'Mac Uilliam Burc' (*Ann. Conn.*, 1464, par. 24), where this form normally implies the Mac-William Burke. If Desmond's mother was of the MacWilliam, rather than the Clanricard, house, he would have been Desmond's uncle.

enabled them to resist pressure from him and to expand eastwards at the expense of the remaining Anglo-Irish settlements. The town of Carrickfergus and its Pale, the Savages of the Ards (who frequently held the seneschalship of the earldom of Ulster, that fading entity), and the Whites of Dufferin were, when they stood together, able to offer some effective resistance, especially when given some help from the Pale. But Savages and Whites were rivals for the seneschalship and so frequently divided to support opposing sides in the recurring conflicts. Scottish mercenary forces, drawn from the MacDonnell lordship of the Isles, were also employed by the rival forces in their summer campaigns.

If we look briefly at the history of the O'Neills of Clandeboye, we can see how the pattern changed almost from year to year. Thus, Conn Ó Néill in 1468 defeated his uncle Muircheartach Ruadh and took over the lordship from him against an alliance which included the Anglo-Irish of Ulster and their Scottish mercenaries. This victory was followed by an incursion by Ó Néill, accompanied on this occasion by both Ó Domhnaill and Mág Uidhir, but Conn maintained himself against all comers, eventually capturing, blinding, and castrating the seneschal, Pádraig Óg Savage, in 1481 and dying himself in 1482. Niall Mór, who succeeded in 1482, revenged himself for an earlier imprisonment in Carrickfergus by invading the town and capturing its mayor in 1507, before dying in 1512. Aodh Buidhe ruled from 1512 to 1524, when he was killed by an army from the Pale led by the earl of Kildare. During the last decade of the period, the lordship gave signs of having passed its peak and begun to decline. Farther south the Magennises were expanding in Iveagh. Aodh Mág Aonghusa, lord of Iveagh, in 1487 handed on his lordship to four sons in succession who continued his expansionism. Another son, Glaisne, concentrated on gaining power, lay and ecclesiastical, in south and east County Down, becoming abbot of Newry, prior of both Down and Saul, and persuading Kildare to expel Roland Savage from the Ards and instal him as seneschal, so that even the nominal representative of the earl of Ulster (the English king) was Gaelic Irish. He was killed in 1526.

Inside the territories of Ó Néill of Tír Eóghain a notable feature in the late middle ages (after the death of Eóghan Ó Néill in 1456) was the expansion of the O'Neill family groups in lands taken over from clients or conquered from enemies. The descendants of Aodh were installed in the Fews in lands largely taken from the Anglo-Irish Bellews; those of Muircheartach to the north in Clann Chonnchadha, those of Art in Omagh and the Derg valley, and those of Feidhlimidh in Arachta. From the next generation, the descendants of Domhnall (died 1509) occupied the MacCawell (Mac Cathmhaoil) lands of Ceneal Fearadhaigh and Learga, around Clogher. In a third generation, descendants of Seaán (died 1517) held Kinard, and those of Art Óg the lands of Fintona on the Fermanagh border, Munterlinny in the north-west, and territory that they took from the Sliocht Airt. These scattered O'Neill septs can scarcely be said to have strengthened Ó Néill's power, since they so frequently allied with Ó Domhnaill or Ó Néill of Clandeboye against him, and contributed by their alignments to make disputed successions even less easy than usual to resolve.

On the O'Donnell side there were parallel problems in that there were usually one or two powerful branches of the family in opposition, ready to contest the authority of the ruler, especially in the case of a succession, and often prepared to ally with Ó Néill against him. The O'Donnells, however, had not proliferated into as many significantly powerful septs as had the O'Neills. In 1461, as we have indicated, the family of Niall Garbh O'Donnell, in alliance with Ó Néill, overthrew the ruling Ó Domhnaill and established Aedh Ruadh mac Néill Ghairbh (Hugh Roe) in his place, a change which was to have long-enduring consequences. On the O'Neill side, nephews of Énrí Ó Néill (in power 1456–83) with their centre at Omagh castle—the Sliocht Airt—were to give trouble to him and to his successors over some fifty years, and frequently sided with Ó Domhnaill. But other permutations could take place. For example, in 1470–71 the Sliocht Airt were in alliance with dissident O'Donnells against an alliance of Ó Néill and Ó Domhnaill. By 1472 the traditional pattern had reasserted itself, and Ó Néill invaded Tír Conaill, while in 1474 Ó Domhnaill retaliated on Tír Eóghain. Then, honours being even, each left the other alone for several years. Between 1477 and 1480 there were again annual offensives on one side or the other, and after that, once more, a period of relative peace.

By this time Conn Ó Néill, Énrí's son, was the leading figure on the O'Neill side. By his marriage to Eleanor FitzGerald he became brother-in-law to the eighth earl of Kildare at the time of the earl's rise to supreme authority in the Pale. This tended to involve the lord deputy intimately in the affairs of central Ulster. After Conn succeeded his father in 1483 he was able to call on Kildare for aid, though Ó Domhnaill on his side was able to raise an unusual number of the O'Neill septs against Conn. There were further hostilities during 1490–91, and on this occasion, Kildare, his own position being precarious in the Pale, tried to achieve a measure of stability in Ulster by taking up an arbitral position, though his mediation soon proved ineffective. But Conn was killed by his half-brothers, the most senior of whom, Énrí Óg, stepped into his place, though Ó Domhnaill set up a rival candidate, Domhnall Clárach, who eventually took over in 1498 and ruled until 1509.

Meantime, Aodh Ruadh Ó Domhnaill had been plagued with family rivalries and resigned in favour of his son Conn in 1497, but resumed his position when Conn was killed, later in the year, in Connacht. Aodh Ruadh continued to administer Tír Conaill with the aid of another son, Aodh Dubh (or Aodh Óg), who finally succeeded in 1505. In 1498 the newly-restored earl of Kildare joined Ó Domhnaill to secure Domhnall Ó Néill from the opposition of other members of his family, and they jointly took Dungannon castle with the help of artillery brought from the Pale, and then went on to Omagh to force the Sliocht

Airt to recognise Domhnall. But only two years later it was Ó Domhnaill who carried out a raid against Domhnall as far as Dungannon.

Art mac Aodha Ó Néill of the Fews succeeded Domhnall in 1509, ruling to 1513. Conn's sons called Kildare to revenge the capture of Art Óg, eldest son of Conn, by the Sliocht Airt, and he duly destroyed Omagh castle. In 1511 Art mac Aodha invaded Tír Conaill while Ó Domhnaill was on pilgrimage at Rome— he called on Henry VIII on his return journey. In 1512 Ó Domhnaill, after his return, burned Dungannon and rebuilt Omagh castle for the Sliocht Airt. When Art Óg Ó Néill succeeded in 1513, he took the offensive against Ó Domhnaill and the Sliocht Airt, and burnt Omagh. Though he also invaded Tír Conaill he was subsequently weakened by internal dissensions. In 1516 the ninth earl of Kildare and his council tried to intervene in the north to bring about some settlement between the contending parties, but failed to do so. In 1517 Kildare, in the interest of his nephew Conn Bacach, attacked Art Óg, Conn's half-brother in Dungannon. When Conn Bacach eventually succeeded in 1519 a new phase of O'Neill history began.[1]

In Conn Bacach Ó Néill, Tyrone obtained a ruler who had a gift for diplomatic intrigue as well as some capacity for military organisation, but his ambitions were rather greater than his resources, weakened by continued internal dissensions, could support. He asserted and planned to impose his suzerainty on Tír Conaill, reviving, as is shown in 'Ceart Uí Néill',[2] a claim relevant perhaps to a period three hundred years or more earlier. On the whole Ó Domhnaill proved too much for him. He failed to prevent Maghnus Ó Domhnaill erecting the powerful castle of Lifford on the disputed border, though in 1527 he did force Ó Domhnaill to make several concessions to him, including a grant of the tribute of east Fir Manach. In 1531–2 he deployed his diplomatic talents in building up a great coalition of Ulster and Connacht lords against Ó Domhnaill, but when Ó Domhnaill won a major battle against its soldiery, MacWilliam Burke deserted Ó Néill and the confederacy collapsed. Conn Bacach was left with little to satisfy his pretensions.

It will be seen from this northern chronicle, simplified as it is, that it is difficult to plot meaningful developments for the political history of the area as a whole. The relationships between Ó Domhnaill and Ó Néill find, over a period, a reasonably stable equilibrium, but this is not necessarily apparent from the sequence of events. On the other hand much depended on the personality and staying power of the rulers, and on accident. The newest factor during the late fifteenth and early sixteenth centuries is the capacity of the O'Donnells to affect the life of other parts of Ireland than Ulster.

---

[1] It may be noted that in Conn Bacach's time the Sliocht Airt were his allies, through their enmity to Art Óg's sons.

[2] 'Ceart Uí Néill' in *Lr. Cl. Aodha Buidhe*, pp 41–7, and translated by Miles Dillon in *Studia Celt*, i (1966), pp 1–18. Another translation, with a detailed commentary, is given by Éamon Ó Doibhlin, 'Ceart Uí Néill' in *Seanchas Ardmhacha*, v (1970), pp 324–57.

For Connacht the period after 1460 was one of continued political disintegration over much of its extent. The old royal house of Ó Conchobhair had been split since 1384 into rival lines of Donn and Ruadh. Of the more prominent personalities Tadhg Ó Conchobhair Ruadh (d. 1464), was continually opposed by rivals of his own line: Feidhlimidh Geangcach Ó Conchobhair Donn (d. 1474) achieved a brief dominance, while Feidhlimidh Fionn Ó Conchobhair Ruadh held a similar position from 1488 to 1490. Thereafter, the O'Connor lines ceased to have much political importance in Connacht except when their internal divisions provided a pretext for the intervention of external magnates like the earls of Kildare.

The dominant families were those of the Burkes. The extensive lordship of the MacWilliam Burkes, in the modern counties Mayo and Sligo, declined during the period, both from internal weakness and from being subjected to repeated and destructive assaults from Tír Conaill, which, after 1500, took place almost annually. On the one hand these reflected the capacity of the O'Donnells to act in their own interests outside Ulster irrespective of their continued engagements with the O'Neills there; on the other it reflected the interest of the O'Donnells in intervening in the affairs of Fir Manach, Bréifne, the north-western borders of the Pale, County Galway, and even to some extent in Clare, Tipperary, and Limerick. The MacWilliams bore the brunt of this expansionism.

The other principal branch of the Burkes, that of Clanricard, retained and appreciably improved its position, though with some ups and downs, in this period. Society in this lordship was increasingly gaelicised, and it is evident that internal disorder was tending to increase steadily. This was leading to the decay of such urban centres as Claregalway, Athenry, and, somewhat later, the chief centre of their authority, Loughrea. Throughout this period the Burkes of Clanricard, or occasionally one of their dependants, the MacHuberts, held the nominal sheriffdom of Connacht. How active an office it was, and what practical avantages it brought to its holder, are not known. The name of the sheriff of Connacht was almost always entered among the lists of sheriffs in the exchequer memoranda rolls, but he seldom made his semi-annual proffer before the barons in Dublin. Though the Burkes retained by prescription the cocket of hides of the port of Galway, the town was determined to keep their influence at bay. The townsmen dealt with them on equal terms, and, except on one occasion, succeeded in denying them any effective footing there.

The affairs of Connacht saw something of a turning point in the years 1466–79. Ricard Ó Cuarsge Burke was effective ruler of the MacWilliam lordship under his uncle Richard (Risdeárd), whom he succeeded in 1469. From 1466 onwards he was intervening in the complex affairs of the O'Connor lordship of Sligo, where the ruling family was sharply divided. In 1467 he was at war with the lord of Clanricard, who defeated him, but called in Ó Domhnaill to prevent the latter pressing home his victory. In 1468, however, both MacWilliam and

Clanricard, acting separately or in alliance, were unable to prevent or defeat a devastating O'Donnell incursion across Sligo. Then, in 1469, MacWilliam Burke joined Ó Domhnaill in invading Clanricard, when the town of Clare-galway was burnt and apparently did not recover. This was followed by divisions between the allies over Sligo, MacWilliam backing one Ó Concho-bhair, Ó Domhnaill another. Sligo was taken by Ó Domhnaill in 1470, when the still-surviving 'Leabhar na hHuidhre' passed into his keeping, and was retaken by MacWilliam in 1471. In 1476 they agreed to divide the O'Connor territory into two spheres of influence, but over the next few years Sligo castle changed hands twice when conflict broke out anew. After Ricard's death the MacWilliam Burkes were preoccupied with internal disputes and left the field open for Ó Domhnaill.

The ruler of Clanricard, Uilleag Ruadh Burke, had an exceptionally long period in power (?1430–85), and his son Uilleag Fionn continued from 1485 to 1509 to maintain an exceptionally stable regime. Uilleag Ruadh's last years were much preoccupied with intervention in northern Connacht, especially in Sligo, as were the early years of his successor. Forces from Clanricard and Tír Conaill were commonly on opposing sides. This intervention focussed on Sligo castle in the 1490s, which changed hands with bewildering rapidity until in 1497 Ó Domhnaill again imposed a division of lands on rival O'Connor fac-tions. In this year, however, Conn Ó Domhnaill, in association with Ó Con-chobhair Sligigh, was defeated and killed by the MacDermots of Mag Luirg, who seized the 'Cathach' psalter of St Columcille which had always accom-panied the O'Donnells into battle.

The eighth earl of Kildare, as part of his policy of intervening from time to time in the outlying parts of Ireland, crossed the Shannon in 1499, to set up, in association with Ó Ceallaigh, his own candidate as Ó Conchobhair Ruadh. In this year too Aodh Ruadh Ó Domhnaill took his revenge on Mac Diarmada, forcing him to return the Cathach. Uilleag Fionn had been closely associated with Sir James Ormond since 1492 and had, in particular, backed him against Kildare in 1497. His alliance with Ó Briain, and the extent of O'Brien influence to the east of the Shannon, meant that MacWilliam too could intervene there with effect. In 1503 he defeated the O'Kellys, who were linked with Kildare, and his penetration and temporary domination of the town of Galway provided the occasion for Kildare's celebrated incursion into Connacht in the Knockdoe campaign of 1504, which marked a decisive assertion of Kildare's authority outside the Anglo-Irish areas. In one of his last campaigns in 1512 Kildare was again active in northern Connacht. There Aodh Dubh Ó Domhnaill had defeated the MacWilliam Burke, Edmund son of Ricard, when Kildare, apparently in alliance with Ó Domhnaill, arrived to attack and defeat Mac Diarmada. Thus, if northern Connacht was frequently dominated by invaders from Ulster, both central and northern Connacht could at times be invaded from the Pale, even if the presence of the earl of Kildare was a less pervading one than that of Ó Domhnaill.

O'Donnell raids into Connacht continued regularly until 1516, but during these years Sligo castle was successfully held against them. After it fell in 1516, it remained in O'Donnell hands until 1533. Thereafter, the O'Donnells obtained a wider and continuing influence in the territories of the MacWilliam Burkes and MacDermots, acting as a disintegrating influence and exacerbating local rivalries. Apart from them, there was no longer any strong power in north Connacht.

In the south the lordship of Clanricard remained powerful, though when, in 1522, Ricard Mór Burke led a great Connacht confederacy against the O'Donnells in Sligo, he was defeated. His ally Conn Bacach Ó Néill had tried to cooperate with him by a simultaneous attack in Ulster, but he too was repulsed. The ninth earl of Kildare, maintaining his father's policies, found time in 1526, at the height of his controversies with Ormond and Henry VIII, to intervene in Connacht in favour of Ó Conchobhair Ruadh against Ó Conchobhair Donn. The MacWilliam Burkes, MacDermots, and O'Connors Sligo were mostly left to the untender care of the O'Donnells; only in 1533 did Tadhg Ó Conchobhair recover, by treachery, Sligo castle, and with this the turning of the tide of O'Donnell influence in Connacht had begun.

Only some outlying parts of Connacht (for example, the lordship of the O'Flahertys in Iar-Chonnacht) were self-contained, but the Burke influence to the east of the Shannon was occasional only. The main, unwelcome, link of Connacht with the rest of Ireland was through the O'Donnell presence.

MUNSTER was in many ways self-contained. The size of the dominions of the earls of Desmond, stretching from western Kerry to western County Waterford, meant that most of the problems which arose in Munster were internal to the earldom. Few earls of Desmond were without some opposition from one or more members of their family, but, on the other hand, it was only occasionally that such quarrels had any considerable impact externally or were of such a nature as to disrupt the principality. Ó Briain remained a considerable influence in Munster affairs outside Thomond, especially in Counties Limerick and Tipperary and, outside it, in Connacht, but his effect on affairs to the east of Shannon remained somewhat peripheral. The old Desmond–Ormond rivalry continued to smoulder, but rarely burst into a major conflagration. The nibblings by Desmond at the southern fringes of the Butler liberty of Tipperary, and the intermittent offensive ripostes that they produced, were usually only of local significance. Though Ormond held the liberty of Tipperary and dominated the O'Kennedy lordship in Ormond to the north of it, Kilkenny remained the centre of the Butler influence, though Butler politics were nearly as often Munster- as Leinster-oriented. The three MacCarthy rulers, Mac Carthaigh Mór, Mac Carthaigh Riabhach, and Mac Carthaigh Múscraighe, are often to be found associated with or taking part against the earls of Desmond, but at most times Mac Carthaigh Mór kept his attention to his own territories, and the other two, though active, were rarely able to influence events except in alliance with one of Desmond's enemies. The growth in the autonomy of the FitzGerald dependency of the Decies meant that the eastern frontier of the Desmond territories was unsettled for much of this period. Over the whole period, however, Munster remained relatively strong, moderately peaceful, and prosperous compared with a declining Connacht and a war-torn Ulster. The spheres of interest of the O'Briens of Thomond, the FitzGerald earls of Desmond, and the Butler earls of Ormond met in the border region of Counties Limerick and Tipperary, which was from 1466 onwards a dependency of the O'Briens and constituted an O'Brien wedge between the territories of Desmond and the Butlers.

Tadhg Ó Briain initiated a phase of expansion after 1461. The earl of Desmond's absence as lord deputy in Dublin provided an opportunity for the O'Briens lasting for some five years and culminating in the distraction caused by his defeat by the O'Connors in 1466 and his subsequent death at the hands of Tiptoft. An O'Brien expedition across the Shannon, assisted by the Mac-Carthys and other Irish allies from Munster, enabled Tadhg to occupy lands on the Limerick–Tipperary border. Desmond was forced to acquiesce in this occupation, and the county of Limerick granted an annual tribute of £40 a year to Ó Briain, which was paid throughout the period with which we are concerned. Tadhg's ambitions are said to have soared towards the idea of reviving the high-kingship of Tara, but he died without further ventures in the same year. His successors continued to hold castles and exercise overlordship in the territory he had occupied. One consequence of this was the decline of the hitherto important Burkes of County Limerick. Another was the domination by the O'Briens of the Macnamara country in Clare, Bunratty castle (built about 1467) coming into O'Brien hands about 1500. Conchobhar Ó Briain (1466–96) remained powerful for a time, but was eventually challenged by his nephew Toirdhealbhach Donn, who appears to have been in control in eastern Thomond by 1486. He allied with the earl of Desmond against Tadhg in 1488 and married Desmond's sister Eleanor in 1490.[1] Conchobhar was, however, succeeded not by him but by his own brother Toirdhealbhach Óg (1496–8).

The Desmond earldom had shown its strength at the battle of Piltown in 1462. The victor, Thomas FitzGerald, appears to have been in control of the earldom before his father's death. His preoccupations as the king's deputy (1463–7) allowed, as we saw, the eastward expansion of O'Brien influence to take place, while his execution divided as well as weakened his family. His brother Gerald had been installed in the most easterly Desmond territory, the Decies, and in 1468 he attempted to assert a claim to the earldom. Desmond's widow, Alice Barry, successfully resisted his claim on behalf of her son James, who was proclaimed earl in Cork, probably in 1469, and was able to assert his

[1] Eleanor FitzGerald had previously been married to Thomas Butler, baron of Cahir, and to Piers Butler's elder brother Edmond.

authority gradually over most of the family's land, but the friction with the Decies remained and was to last a considerable time.

Gerald FitzGerald's ally, Cormac Mac Carthaigh Riabhach, established himself as joint ruler of Cairbre (Carbery) with his uncle Diarmaid, but was overthrown in 1478, and Cairbre came under the control of Fínghin mac Diarmada Mac Carthaigh by 1484 after a series of military struggles. Fínghin married a daughter of Earl Thomas. He entered into direct negotiations with Henry VII in 1487–91, receiving a charter of denization from him as did the strong and active Cormac mac Taidhg Mac Carthaigh of Múscraighe (1461–95). These examples show it was not only the Anglo-Irish of Munster who were occasionally responsive to direct English influence. Múscraighe had in fact expanded eastwards against the Anglo-Irish Barretts and Lombards, Tadhg apparently building Blarney castle about 1480 on what had until recently been Lombard land. Domhnall Mac Carthaigh Riabhach (1506–31) made an alliance with Sir Piers Butler in 1513 in which he reserved his 'duty' to the eighth earl of Kildare whose daughter Eleanor he had just married on rather unusual terms, giving her a veto on his appointment of officials in his lordship and agreeing to banish his MacSweeney galloglass if they would not obey her.

The earls of Desmond were strongly fortified in the divide between the Connabride and Blackwater rivers and from there encroached on Tipperary during the long period of the absenteeism of the earls of Ormond, but Sir Piers Butler of Polestown revived and reorganised the Butler power, and, well before his recognition as earl of Ormond in 1516, began to retaliate. His alliance with Mac Carthaigh Riabhach and Mac Carthaigh Múscraighe in 1513 was linked with a devastating raid into Desmond's territories in the same year. Both earlier (1510) and later (1516), both MacCarthys were to be found on Desmond's side in these exchanges.

James, ninth earl of Desmond, was murdered in 1487 and was succeeded by his brother Maurice, who proved to be less willing to be involved in Lancastrian causes than James had been, so that the main sphere of Desmond activity shifted to meet the O'Brien expansion to the north. Maurice raided as far as the Éile Uí Chearbhaill (Ely O'Carroll) country in 1489 and did considerable damage to the O'Brien lands and clients. On the other hand, he had to confront an alliance of FitzGerald of Decies with the Muskerry MacCarthys. When Toirdhealbhach Donn Ó Briain raided Desmond lands in Limerick in 1501 he also attacked Kildare's lands in the neighbouring Cois Máigh, in County Limerick, as well. In 1506, with the help of other branches of his family, he built 'O'Brien's bridge' over the Shannon at Portcrush, a little way below Killaloe, in order to give him more effective access to Tipperary and Limerick. Kildare had been hostile to the O'Briens ever since their alliance with Sir James Ormond from 1492 until his death in 1497. In 1510 Kildare mounted a major offensive against Ó Briain which built up into a major war, drawing in contingents from distant parts of Ireland. Kildare was joined both by Ó Domhnaill and by the earl of Desmond's forces under his son James. Ó Briain mustered beside him Burke of Clanricard and other assistance from Connacht. The result was that in a major battle near Limerick, Kildare was defeated and Ó Briain and the Connacht men had their revenge for Knockdoe.[1] This defeat was a factor in the decline of the eighth earl, who was to die three years later.

The ninth earl of Kildare speedily fell out with James of Desmond, who was now administering the lordship for his father. Desmond allied with Ó Briain in 1514 and administered a check to Kildare. An internal struggle between James and his uncle John attracted Ó Briain to intervene against him, in alliance with Sir Piers Butler and the O'Carrolls, and to defeat him at Lough Gur (1515), where the MacCarthys were found on the Desmond side. In 1521 James, after he had formally succeeded to the earldom, was defeated by the MacCarthys of Muskerry and his uncle Sir Thomas FitzGerald, at Mourne Abbey, and as a result Mac Carthaigh Múscraighe established himself in the barony of Kerry-currihy, which was a significant encroachment on the Anglo-Irish area of County Cork.

Piers Butler in the 1520s, after he had become earl of Ormond, came into conflict with the O'Briens on the borders of Tipperary; to begin with Kildare aided them against him, but in November 1523 he agreed to relinquish his support. Another occasion when Ormond intervened in affairs outside his territory was when James, earl of Desmond, was in controversy with the Fitz-Geralds of Decies over their refusal to accept the earl's galloglass sometime in the early 1520s. On this occasion Desmond was besieged in Dungarvan castle by a force that included Ormond, Mac Carthaigh Múscraighe, and Sir Thomas FitzGerald. He escaped only with difficulty by sea. On the succession of Sir Thomas FitzGerald to the earldom in 1529, he renounced most of his family claims over the Decies and ceded to its lord the barony of Kilsheelan.

Earl James had entertained the envoys of Francis I of France in 1523 with a review of his assembled allies and galloglass, backed by grandiose assertions of his military potential. Earl Thomas was to do the same a little later for the representatives of the Emperor Charles V. The power and potentialities of the Desmond principality were substantial, but they were deployed in practice to consolidate rather than extend the earldom, and were rarely used outside Munster itself. The earls of Desmond may after 1468 have relinquished much of their potential influence on the Dublin administration, except for their flirtations with the pretenders Lambert Simnel and Perkin Warbeck, but they had gained rather than lost by their preoccupation with their local territorial interests.

It is difficult to deal with the Butlers on a provincial basis, since their lands and their interests were very much divided between Munster and Leinster; but it is probable that under Piers Butler their orientation towards the Pale and to

[1] Ann. Conn., pp 614–17.

the south-east was greater than towards the south and south-west. Their links with Waterford were close, and they had considerable influence in the eastern part of the county. With Wexford too and the residual palatinate of the earls of Shrewsbury they had ties, but in the south-east they had also to meet the rivalry of the earls of Kildare, who, when they had consolidated their footholds in Carlow, were anxious to maintain some control of the river valleys which led down to Waterford harbour.

The Butler territories were left without effective leadership in the period after 1460, and it is clear that, as a result, the three leading cadet branches of the Butler family all extended their influence. The Butlers of Polestown, of whom Sir Piers was to be the leading figure after 1490, the Butler barons of Cahir in the south, and the Butler barons of Dunboyne, were all of considerable strength at the time of the restoration of Earl Thomas in 1477. The Butlers of Cahir were for long enemies of the other two major branches. Under Edward IV and Henry VII alike, Earl Thomas was able, while remaining an absentee and visiting his Irish lordship only occasionally, to play off skilfully one cadet branch of the family against another, so that none became dominant, while he still contrived to obtain a substantial income from his lands. He continued to appoint the seneschal of the liberty of Tipperary and various officials in Kilkenny, though how far he administered County Kilkenny on similar lines to Tipperary is not clear. A key appointment was that of the earl's deputy. This office James Butler of Polestown held as early as 1474 and continued to do so after the earl's restoration,[1] but it then appears to have been handed to Sir James Ormond, a son of the sixth earl, who was to act so vigorously in his own interests, as well as those of Earl Thomas and Henry VII, in the years 1492–7. His deadly rivalry with Piers Butler in these years, resolved only when Sir Piers killed him in 1497, brought severe dissensions amongst the Butler families, but Earl Thomas, once he had reached agreement with Sir Piers, was content to allow the latter to increase his own authority so long as the earl continued to receive his rents and to assert a measure of influence on local appointments. Though Sir Piers built up his power in and around Kilkenny, it was not until after he was recognised by Kildare as earl in 1516 that he was able fully to dominate the cadet branches. During the following years (remembering that his title after 1528 was earl of Ossory during Thomas Boleyn's assumption of the title of earl of Ormond) he forged effective links with Irish lords in the midlands like the O'Carrolls and MacGillapatricks, while he and his wife Margaret concentrated on reviving Kilkenny and Carrick-on-Suir as centres of Anglo-Irish influence. Though he served Henry VIII several times as lord deputy, continued absence in Dublin was an embarrassment to him as a territorial magnate in southern Leinster and Munster. He was by no means always successful in his contests with Kildare where their interests clashed, and he had to cope with continuing if uneven Desmond pressure on the south, but in general

[1] N.L.I., MS 2551, f. 2ᵛ.

his work of consolidation inside the Butler lordships was remarkably successful. When Kildare left Ireland in 1534 the Butler dominions were for several
years the mainstay of English authority in Ireland.

THE Gaelic Irish groupings that bordered the Pale were for the most part
composed of smaller lordships, whose significance lay less in their own
power than in their interaction with the Anglo-Irish to whom they were
neighbours. The northern borders were indeed dominated by Ó Néill and his
dependants, and it was to him that a substantial black rent was paid from
County Louth. But MacMahons, O'Reillys, O'Rourkes, O'Connors,
O'Mores, MacMurroughs, O'Byrnes, and O'Tooles were all significant small
or intermediate-sized lordships, with a substantial degree of independence
and with a vested interest in the fortunes, or more usually the misfortunes, of
the Pale.

The MacMahons, like Ó Néill, took a black rent from County Louth, but
their territory of Oriel (Oirghialla) nevertheless had moderately friendly
relations with the administration at Dublin from which they leased lands,
namely the lordship of Farney (though a renewal of the lease after 1451 has
not been traced). At some later date they took the border manor of Stonetown
in County Louth from the Anglo-Irish family of Darcy.

Feidhlimidh mac Briain Mac Mathghamhna, who founded the Franciscan
house at Monaghan in 1462, died in 1466. Second in succession from him a
cousin, Réamonn, was challenged by his nephews in 1475, who occupied
Farney with the help of the Anglo-Irish of Louth. When Réamonn raided
Louth in revenge, he was taken prisoner and held at Drogheda until his death
in 1484. Dartry was occupied by his nephew Seaán Buidhe (d. 1492), whose
descendants thereafter treated it as an independent lordship. Descendants of
Réamonn and other septs contested the succession, so that Ó Domhnaill
intervened in 1496 to set up Brian mac Réamoinn, but he was soon killed by
Mág Aonghusa while attempting, with the Whites of Dufferin, to retake
Erenagh castle, thus showing the involvement of MacMahons in Ulster
affairs as well as those of the Pale. While Aodh Óg Mac Mathghamhna was
deposed in 1496, Rossa Mac Mathghamhna (d. 1513) held Monaghan against
the Clann Réamoinn. Rossa was succeeded by Réamonn (1513–21) and Brian
(d. 1550, acting as lord under his brother Glaisne, the nominal lord), while
Fearnmhagh (Farney) and Dartraighe (Dartry) remained independent under
other MacMahon septs. The lordship was rarely in this period able to act as
a single unit—and is a good example of its kind in this respect—though on
the other hand its divisions did not involve disintegration into non-viable
segments.

Bréifne, the part of Connacht to the east of the Shannon, had become in
course of time involved more with Ulster and the pale than with Connacht
itself. The O'Rourkes in west Bréifne (modern County Leitrim) were in close

contact with the O'Donnells, and their territory formed part of the south-western O'Donnell glacis: they had some contacts also with the western borders of the Pale. The O'Reilly lordship of east Bréifne (modern County Cavan) was a strong political unit, partly involved with the O'Neills to the north and partly with the Pale to the south and east. Most of the important changes of this period were the result of intervention from outside. Seaán Ó Raghallaigh and many of his followers were killed by the Drogheda men in 1460 while raiding County Louth. An attempt by Ó Ruairc, with O'Donnell backing, to revive a kingdom of all Bréifne in 1470 was defeated by Toirdhealbhach Ó Raghallaigh with assistance from the Pale. The seventh earl of Kildare inter-vened shortly after to settle a dispute about the O'Reilly succession, and it may have been then that he arranged to receive tribute from one of the O'Reilly septs which was still being paid to the ninth earl in the 1520s. The eighth earl similarly intervened in 1491, but his fall from power soon led to his opponent there, Seaán Ó Raghallaigh, winning unchallenged authority in 1495. In 1514 the ninth earl invaded the O'Reilly lordship and defeated and killed the ruling lord, Aodh Ó Raghallaigh. Again, in 1526, he intervened to settle a further disputed succession. The association of Bréifne with the Pale was thus close and continuous, but, far from being paid black rents by the Pale, several O'Reilly septs were, before the end of the period, paying tributes to Kildare, largely to limit his intervention in their affairs and to provide security for their good behaviour.

The position of the O'Connors of Offaly was very different. They were paid a black rent of £40 a year from the exchequer, and their other exactions are said to have been greatly in excess of what was paid to any other Irish lordship, while at the same time they maintained the most continuous pressures of any Irish group on the borders of Counties Kildare and Meath. Offaly was strong from a strategic aspect. Its heartland was an island surrounded by almost impenetrable bogs and forests. The great bog of Allen stretched unbroken to the south for over twenty miles to the Slieve Bloom mountains and to their nearest powerful neighbours, the O'Mores. They were only a little less well protected in other directions. Nor was any of their Gaelic Irish neighbours strong enough to confront them in their own territories, while they had brought those with whom they were in closer contact under their control, namely the O'Dunnes of Uí Riagáin (Iregan), the O'Dempseys of Clann Maolughra (Clan-maliere), and the MacMorishes of Aireamh (Irry) who were an O'Connor sept. To the west the O'Molloys of Fir Cheall (Fercall) were politically of little importance.

An Calbhach Mór Ó Conchobhair, a strong lord of Offaly, ruled for more than thirty-five years, and died in 1458. His son and successor Conn was defeated and captured by the seventh earl of Kildare in 1459. It was probably on this occasion that Kildare recovered Rathangan, an important border castle, which had been in O'Connor hands for some years. In 1460 Conn, once more at

liberty, raided Meath and killed the baron of Galtrim. In a further raid a year
later he was allied to Edmund mac Richard Butler, when they may have been
attempting to further the Lancastrian cause against Edward IV. An attempt by
the earl of Desmond to destroy him in 1466 led to disaster to the forces of the
Pale which were ambushed, John FitzGerald, a prominent member of the
family (head of the MacThomas sept), being killed and the earl of Kildare captured. Kildare was subsequently rescued by a marriage connection of his own,
Tadhg Ó Conchobhair, Conn's brother (who had married his sister Margaret).
Tadhg died, however, in 1471 and Conn's son Cathaoir succeeded in 1474. He
was drawn in 1471 into a war amongst the Anglo-Irish marchers, in which
another of the MacThomas sept was killed. In 1493 he was defeated by Séamus
Mág Eochagáin, lord of Kineleagh. In 1511 Cathaoir was at war with a number
of dissatisfied kinsmen, including the sons of his uncle Tadhg, one of whom
killed him at Monasteroris, Brian mac Taidhg gaining the lordship which he
held at his death in 1517, being succeeded by another brother, An Calbhach.
But by 1525 Cathaoir's son Brian was able to obtain the succession. Brian met
further opposition from inside his family, but was able to maintain himself
against it. At the same time, it is clear that the influence of the ninth earl of Kildare had penetrated substantially into Offaly, since his rental shows that in the
1520s many of the septs of the O'Connors were paying him tributes for their
protection. Up to 1534, then, it appears that the offensive capacity of the
O'Connors against the Pale, or at least against Kildare's liberty in County Kildare, was being checked.

To the south the O'Mores occupied a compact block of territory in Leix. It
too was heavily forested and had a number of smaller bogs, the bog of Allen
extending protection to the north. We lack a continuous history of their rulers,
but it is clear that while they frequently raided County Kildare in the late fifteenth century, they were then a nuisance rather than a menace. Their power
grew in the early sixteenth century, perhaps by their early adoption of firearms,
and their rulers, especially Conall Ó Mórdha, played a major part in weakening
the ninth earl of Kildare's hold on his patrimony. By 1534 they had come to
rank alongside the O'Connors in strength.

To the north lay a mixture of small Gaelic Irish and gaelicised territories.
One of the more important of the latter was the de Bermingham lordship of
Carbury in north-west Kildare. The family and their territory had come to be
known as the Clann Fheórais. Their lordship formed something of a buffer
state between the O'Connors and Meath, and they were at times enemies and
at others allies of the O'Connors. John de Bermingham was lord by 1465 and
retained his position until 1488. One of his close associates was Piers de Bermingham of Carrick, who acted as intermediary to Tadhg Ó Conchobhair for
the ransom of certain prisoners from the Pale taken in 1463. A certain amount is
known of the internal history of Clann Fheórais, as it appears to have been in
the fifteenth century a favourite resort of Irish men of learning, so that the

de Berminghams might appear to have been good patrons and an interesting example of cultural assimilation. Nearby was Cenél Fiachach (Kineleagh), the territory of the Mageoghegans, who had built their lordship on the ruins of the western Meath manors and were perpetually raiding their Anglo-Irish neighbours. The chiefs over a considerable period were able men who, on occasion, were able to take on and defeat the O'Connors. A number of the marcher families, Dillons, Daltons, and others, had become more Gaelic than Anglo-Irish, and the question of allegiance along the western borders of Meath had become very confused, a number of the families acting as if they were independent Gaelic Irish lords rather than defenders of the Anglo-Irish territory subject to royal officials in some degree.

The MacMurrough country of 'Low Leinster' illustrates many aspects of the linking of Gaelic and Anglo-Irish interests. As kings of Leinster the MacMurroughs maintained a considerable degree of formality in their dealings with their neighbours. They were sufficiently influenced by their long contacts with the Anglo-Irish to issue charters, for example, that are scarcely distinguishable in form from those used by the earls of Ormond and Kildare. They continued also to intermarry frequently with the Butlers. By this fact, and by the geography of their territory, they were frequently brought into conflict with the earls of Kildare. They acquired both Arklow and Tullow during this period from the Butlers and held them in spite of Kildare. It appears that the O'Byrnes recognised their overlordship at this time, though specific evidence is lacking. The earls of Kildare, however, were penetrating their territory down the eastern side of the Slaney valley, where they held the castle of Clonogan ('Wogan's castle'). But they too were able on occasion to take the offensive. The eighth earl of Kildare had purchased the castle of Dromroe (Mount Loftus, County Kilkenny) from Teabóid (Tibbot) Butler, but by 1526 it had passed into the hands of the MacMurroughs, though perhaps these were tenants from a friendly sept.

Donnchadh Mac Murchadha, king of Leinster since 1417, was still ruling c. 1455, but long before his death in 1478[1] he had been succeeded by a nephew, Domhnall Riabhach (d. 1476), and he in turn was succeeded by a grandson of Donnchadh, Murchadh Ballach (d. 1511). An able ruler, married to Joan, daughter of Butler of Polestown, he obtained control of the important Cistercian monastery of Duisk by installing his son Cathaoir as abbot. Cathaoir received a charter of English liberty from Ormond in 1522.[2] At Murchadh's death his sept continued to occupy the northern part of the lordship, Uí Dróna (Idrone, north of Borris), while the lands to the south were in the hands of Domhnall Riabhach's sept, and to which succeeded in turn three of his sons, Art Buidhe (d. 1517),[3] Gearalt (d. 1523), and Muiris (d. 1531). Muiris was Piers

[1] K. W. Nicholls, 'Late medieval Irish annals: two fragments' in *Peritia*, ii (1982), p. 99.
[2] T.C.D., MS 578 (E. 3. 10), p. 15 (from the Register of Duisk).
[3] B.L., Egerton MS 1782, in *Z.C.P.*, viii (1910–12), p. 111.

Butler's uncle and agreed in 1525 to surrender Arklow to him, though reserving a life interest. Kildare intervened in the succession in 1531 to support, successfully, his candidate Cathaoir against Dúnlang. The Leinster kingdom was thus very much of a buffer state between Kildare and Ormond interests and suffered from intervention from both sides, though the earls of Kildare were usually the aggressors.

The O'Byrnes and O'Tooles completed the circle of Irish lordships around the Pale; the O'Byrnes, largely, and the O'Tooles, almost wholly, found their *raison d'être* in being able to raid County Dublin, and their history appears sufficiently in the story of the Pale's attempts to deal with them.

An English chief governor in the Pale, or a member of one of the lesser Anglo-Irish families as if he was acting, had little capacity to operate effectively against the encircling Gaelic Irish lordships, part of whose living and prosperity came from the cattle and other things they stole from the Pale. The earls of Kildare, on the other hand, had sufficient local forces to carry out punitive raids in retaliation which could be effective for a time, but in the longer term the eighth and ninth earls found it was more effective to attempt to impose sanctions, agreements obliging the Irish to pay tributes and the like, which proved a rather better insurance than the black rents paid to them from the exchequer or by the counties of the Pale. At the same time, these lordships too could become instruments of, say, O'Neill policies against the Pale in the north or perhaps, on the southern side, pawns in the struggle of Ormond and Kildare.

IN one sense the Pale has no history beyond that centred on the administration in Dublin and its chief governor. But while it is true that major developments in the Pale are subsumed in the development of the central policies and major activities of the government, it must be remembered that each of the districts inside the Pale had a life and historical perspective of its own. The affairs of the marchers, especially those of Meath, were very different from those of the more settled areas. Inside their own confines the families of the Pale marchers were expanding or contracting their estates in direct response to the pressures from the Gaelic Irish lordships outside, whose major activities have been followed already, or were themselves imposing pressures on those lordships. There was a process of attrition going on in this period, when a few Anglo-Irish families were expanding, but many more were contracting or were being swallowed up. There was another process going on also. A few of the marchers were maintaining rigorously their Englishness in language, customs and laws; others had become almost wholly Gaelic in law, custom, and behaviour; still others were riding both English and Irish horses, mixing cultural and legal prescriptions as suited their local, family, or personal interests or preferences. The marchers of the Pale were thus in a state of movement, even though the force and direction of those movements would need to be plotted on a microscopic scale in order for them to be at all sharply observed.

In contrast to this the more settled areas of the Pale had less history. Life was more stable, was being lived at a family and local community level, mainly peacefully and with relatively little alteration in social balance. Much of County Dublin, the southern part of County Louth, a substantial part of Meath, and the eastern part of County Kildare had this kind of history. Some families were growing richer, some poorer, but change was not catastrophic, or, over the seventy-four years with which we are concerned, at all rapid. There were plenty of problems for the propertied groups in the areas—taxation, the imposition of military forces quartered at times on their lands, the obligation to serve on defensive or offensive missions against Irish enemies or those whom the earls of Kildare, perhaps, regarded as rivals who must be humbled. This history must be sought in studies of families, monasteries, localities, in large part not yet written, or impossible to write fully. The history of these settled areas of the Pale has its totality also, but it is more important in this context to state that it exists than to attempt to follow it in detail. Only when we know much more than we do about the social and economic conditions of life in the Pale will it be possible to make these developments meaningful.

It must not be forgotten that Dublin had a peculiarly important part to play in this period of Irish history. It was the most important urban nucleus in the country, even though, compared to English and continental cities, it was small; it had the largest single concentration of the Anglo-Irish population; its citizens were far from being politically inert and exercised, at times, a considerable influence on events; as the seat of government offices and institutions it was involved directly and indirectly in the business of government; as a major port it was Ireland's most important single link with England and an inlet too for continental ships, products, and ideas.

What we must remember finally is that the Pale was a fulcrum for action. He who held the Pale had the strategic advantage of the interior movement and could affect a large number of the lordships lying outside it. But the Pale was also an anvil, struck repeatedly from almost all sides by Gaelic Irish lordships whose well-being depended to an appreciable extent on what they could steal from the Pale. The greater rivalries of the peripheral lordships were in the long run, if only in the long run, affected by these circumstances.

CHAPTER XXIII

The hegemony of the earls of Kildare, 1494–1520

D. B. QUINN

THE years 1494–6 were significant ones in the history of the English lordship
in Ireland and its relations with the English king. Armed intervention in these
years effectively removed the external threat that Ireland offered to the Tudor
line as a base for its dynastic enemies. But it did more than that in setting a
pattern which was to be influential both in the period down to 1520, when the
restored authority of the earls of Kildare was to be paramount in the lordship,
and also in the more confused period, down to 1534, that followed.[1] These years
made clear the seriousness with which the Tudors were to regard the retention
of their Irish lordship. The military, diplomatic, legislative, and administrative
successes of 1494–6 were such that they could be repeated, it was thought, at
will. None the less, expansion of the area in which royal authority could be
effectively exercised, until it ultimately comprised the whole island, remained
the long-term objective. The activities of 1494–6 can be seen as an attempt to
lay foundations for doing this directly, but the arrangements of 1496 and thereafter can be construed as part of a policy of doing it indirectly. The overriding
theme of this chapter is, therefore, not the autononmy which the eighth earl of
Kildare came to exercise but the extent to which he carried out the mission of
expanding the English lordship entrusted to him by Henry VII, and, of course,
the assumption of a continuing responsibility for this policy by his son after
1513. To take this overall view is not to underestimate the foundations of
aristocratic power both in the great Anglo-Irish lordships and in the Gaelic
Irish ones. The previous chapter will have shown quite clearly that the centri-
fugal forces operating in Irish politics tended to cancel out any policies originating and directed from outside the island, except in unusual and temporary
episodes of direct English intervention. But in the longer term the decisive
forces which worked on Ireland were those emanating from the English king,
however much they were mitigated by delegation, by ignorance of the cultural

---

[1] Steven Ellis has generously helped me with the revision of this chapter, particularly with its
later passages. His researches have added precision to what I myself had written. See his *Tudor Ire.*,
pp 75–107.

unities of Gaelic Ireland, and by temporary unwillingness to penetrate either the mysteries or the territories of the island.

In June 1494 the first new dispositions for Ireland were made. Sir James Ormond was sent back with the gift of manors in Meath, Kilkenny, and Tipperary, and exchanged his treasurership (or deputy treasurership) for the office of constable of Limerick castle, a key post in the south of Ireland, hitherto held by the earl of Desmond. FitzSimons apparently accompanied him. Gormanston had earlier (by 20 February at latest) taken over the administration from his son. It is probable that there were rumours or even news of further intrigues on behalf of Warbeck. The sending back of the loyal magnates was only the first step. By August, preparations for a major English expedition, which had all the marks also of a political revolution, were under way.

The recent delegation of lords from Ireland had made representations on behalf of both magnates and officials that Henry should send a sufficient army into Ireland to bring laws to the 'wild Irish'. So he informed the king of France in August. On 12 September, Henry, duke of York, became lieutenant (at the age of four) and Sir Edward Poynings his deputy. Poynings was to be accompanied to Ireland by the bishop of Bangor, Henry Deane, who was to be chancellor. Sir Hugh Conway was sent as treasurer, and two new English chief justices, Thomas Bowring and John Topcliffe, were also supplied. The deputy's retinue was not a very large one: 427 men. It could, however, be supplemented by men hired in Ireland, and apparently 226 such soldiers were shortly after employed in his campaign. Poynings landed at Howth on 13 October, and his establishment as deputy marked the most substantial English intervention since the time of Worcester, perhaps of Richard of York himself.

Sir Edward Poynings was primarily a soldier, but he was also a shrewd and skilful politician, who installed himself and his officials in Dublin without undue friction. The new regime was virtually unprecedented in its clean sweep of the Anglo-Irish families from high offices of state and of the judiciary. There may have been some resentment, but the English intervention was probably regarded primarily as a cure for an emergency situation rather than as a sign of a permanent change of policy. But the ministerial council, for example, became almost wholly English in composition. Henry evidently soon had satisfactory reports from Ireland and could state confidently in December that in Ireland both Gaelic and Anglo-Irish among the prelates and lay magnates of the country had come to the deputy and made their homage to the king, so that he hoped for a speedy termination of the Irish difficulties and an access of honour and profit as a result. Though this was in a diplomatic document intended to impress the king of France,[1] there is no reason to think that Henry's assumption of an optimistic outlook on Ireland was insincere. Sir James Ormond

---

[1] Instructions to Richmond king of arms, 30 Dec. 1494 (referring to 'Irlandois sauvaiges'), Conway, *Henry VII, Scot. & Ire.*, p. 200.

reported shortly after[1] that many of the Gaelic Irish had given up lands, or, as we learn elsewhere, members of their family, as pledges for peace, and that some of those who did not had had their lands harried and destroyed.

There seems to have been some major opposition to Poynings beyond the boundaries of the Pale. One result of this was to bring Poynings northwards with a force into Ó hAnluain's country in County Armagh in November. This force contained contingents supplied by both Sir James Ormond and Kildare. Ormond's men carried a devastating trail of fire into Ó hAnluain's country, so that he eventually submitted and handed over his son as a hostage, his ally Mág Aonghusa following suit. The earl of Kildare had had contacts with both of these lords immediately before their submission, and was later accused of trying to keep them in the field against Poynings—the basis for a treason charge which was eventually refuted.[2] Poynings did not think it necessary to venture farther into Ulster. It may indeed be that Ó Néill sent a formal submission that made any incursion into his territories unnecessary, though Ó Domhnaill was too close to the king of Scots for any concessions at this time. How far Poynings ranged westwards and southwards from the borders of the Pale we cannot tell.

By the end of November the situation was peaceful enough for Poynings to call together the famous parliament which met at Drogheda on 1 December 1494.[3] It is probable that the representation of the three orders, lords, commons, and proctors, was wider than usual, if only out of curiosity on the part of the outlying magnates and towns about the new regime, so that it was probably a peculiarly representative body for its time. Desmond, of course, did not appear.

Whether the first thirty or so acts of the parliament which belong to the period between 1 December 1494 and February 1495 were all passed at a single session, is not known. The most famous act, chapter 9, 'Poynings' law', provided that the Irish parliament in future could meet only with the consent of the king and could pass no acts for which the bills had not earlier been approved by his council.[4] Other acts declared that all officials should hold office only during pleasure, and that on a vacancy the deputy should be succeeded by the treasurer. It was also provided that the constables of the king's castles—those at Dublin, Trim, Athlone, Wicklow, Greencastle, Carlingford, and Carrickfergus[5]—should be Englishmen born in England. The distribution

---

[1] *Ormond deeds, 1509—47*, pp 322–3; Conway, *Henry VII, Scot. & Ire.*, pp 149–51.

[2] See G. O. Sayles, 'The vindication of the earl of Kildare from treason, 1496' in *I.H.S.*, vii, no. 25 (March 1950), pp 39–47.

[3] See Edmund Curtis, 'The acts of the Drogheda parliament' in Conway, *Henry VII, Scot. & Ire.*, pp 118–43, 201–19; *Stat. Ire. Hen. VII—Hen. VIII*, pp 91–6.

[4] See for more detail D. B. Quinn, 'The early interpretation of Poynings' law' in *I.H.S.*, ii, no. 7 (Mar. 1941), pp 241–54; R. D. Edwards and T. W. Moody, 'The history of Poynings' law' in *I.H.S.*, ii, no. 8 (Sept. 1941), pp 415–24. The views of Brendan Bradshaw, 'The beginnings of modern Ireland' in Brian Farrell (ed.), *The Irish parliamentary tradition* (Dublin, 1973), pp 69–71, and Ellis, 'Henry VII and Ireland', pp 248–9, should also be taken into account.

[5] Athlone would appear to have been (perhaps briefly) in English hands at this point. It had been

of these castles, incidentally, describes very well the range from Wicklow to Athlone and Carrickfergus which Poynings expected to police with his troops. The extensive act of resumption of all royal lands granted since 1327 had exemptions aimed to conciliate all those who were at that time on good terms with the administration. They included Kildare and most of the other magnates of the Pale so far as lands passed to them by specific grant were concerned, so that it applied mainly outside the Pale, and its effectiveness would depend almost wholly on how far Poynings could extend his range of action there. A great deal of clarification on other matters was achieved; all earlier acts under which, for example, support of Simnel or Warbeck might be countenanced, were declared void. The citizens of the Pale towns were prohibited from taking wages and livery of any gentleman; gentlemen of the Pale were to have their estate and household servants in their retinues and were forbidden to keep others; marchers had to send a list of those whom they had in their retinues and their use of coyne and livery was closely circumscribed; the keeping of firearms by private persons was prohibited. There was to be an end to private war; hereafter only the chief governor could permit the carrying on of any warlike actions in the areas under his jurisdiction. Together with the revival of the statute of Kilkenny against the use of Gaelic Irish customs, such acts, if they were enforceable, could have laid the foundations of a polity reformed to something like its situation in the earlier fourteenth century. It is to be noted that a number of them were specifically limited to the Pale and its marches, though others still applied, in theory at least, to all the areas where the king's writ might run or his army penetrate. Control of officials, parliaments, and castles, if implemented, would give the king the power to influence or command the maintenance of a degree of order and law, under the supervision of men who were sufficiently dependent on him for them to be relied on.

Our information of what was happening in the south of Ireland at this time is incomplete. A pardon had been drawn up in December for the earl of Desmond on the assumption that he would submit to the king, but this hope was not realised. It would appear that there was some hostile shipping operating in the waters off the south and south-east coasts of Ireland early in 1495 and some activity on land on behalf of Warbeck. Kildare too seems to have been restive, and perhaps, if the Book of Howth's accounts are correct,[1] in violent controversy with the bishop and some of the gentlemen of Meath. Finally, on 27 February, he was arrested, charged with treason on the strength of his dealings with Ó hAnluain the previous November, and sent by Poynings to England on 5 March. An immediate reaction to his arrest was the expulsion of the small royal garrison from Carlow castle and its occupation against the king by James FitzGerald, a brother of the earl. This brought Poynings into open

in Ó Ceallaigh's hands (1455–90) and a little later seems to have reverted to the Dillons. Greencastle was lost to Magennis in July 1497 (B.L., Add. MS 33956, f. 92).

[1] *Cal. Carew MSS*, v, 178–9.

conflict with a section of the Anglo-Irish of the Pale and forced him to rely more than ever on Sir James Ormond, who in April was undertaking the siege of Carlow, though after it had been taken it appears to have been put in Ó Conchobhair's care, perhaps as a pledge of his sincerity. But there was no general rising, and probably no major protests, at the downfall of Kildare.

The parliament now appears to have been resumed under the auspices of Henry Deane, bishop of Bangor, Poynings himself being involved in military affairs. Whether the early sessions of 1495 were held partly at Drogheda and partly at Dublin or wholly at Dublin is not known. A number of acts intended to pacify the country were introduced, the specific effect of which is difficult to estimate, but chapter 39 (chapter 22 in the printed version) was novel, ordaining as it did that all statutes of late made within the realm of England, concerning or belonging to the common and public weal, be deemed good in law in Ireland. Did this introduce a whole new body of English statute law to the lordship, or was it declaratory of accepted practice? Or was it a device by which the king might draw on the English statutes against private disorder, such as those against livery and maintenance, passed since 1485, to reinforce the acts of the Poynings parliament against similar dangers in Ireland? Lawyers and historians have never been clear precisely what was intended at the time, though the adoption of a number of English statutes made prior to 1494 was later justified on the basis of this act.[1] The act of attainder of Kildare accused him not only of conspiring with Ó hAnluain, but of causing his brother James to attack and occupy Carlow castle (which we would consider had followed rather than preceded his arrest). The major charge that he had conspired with the king of Scots and Desmond, to send an army to Ireland to destroy English authority, is an indication of how real the threat from Warbeck appeared. Though parliament was not finally wound up until late April, its later acts were of smaller significance.

The breach with Kildare imposed a double test. Firstly on the military ability of Poynings and his English army, and secondly on the Anglo-Irish who had been deprived of the magnate on whom so many had depended for such a long time. It certainly gave Sir James Ormond a further opportunity to build up his own power. There seems little doubt that, for the time being at any rate, the Pale gentry were willing to cooperate with the administration both to enforce the recent acts of parliament and to withstand any intervention by southern insurgents, whether or not these were backed by foreign forces in the interests of Perkin Warbeck. For the time being Poynings had to restrict his activities to the Pale and to the midlands, and was unable (being deprived of Kildare's resources) to exert his influence and military power in the south. Thus he was thrown back on the defensive.

[1] The English judges had already ruled in 1485 that English statutes were binding on Ireland (*Yearbook, 1 Hen. VII* (1679), p. 2, extracted in A. F. Pollard, *Reign of Henry VII*, iii (London, 1914), pp 292–4). For a recent discussion of the issue see S. G. Ellis, 'Parliament and community in Yorkist and Tudor Ireland' in *Hist. Studies*, xiv (1983), pp 51–2.

The immediate need for English troops was stressed by the appearance at long last of a Yorkist fleet and the emergence into the open of many, at least, of Warbeck's supporters. In the north, Ó Domhnaill identified himself with the pretender and with James IV, whom Ó Domhnaill had visited earlier that year. We are told that Ó Néill of Clandeboye and Burke of Clanricard also came out in support of Warbeck against Henry. At the same time, it cannot be said that any of these magnates took any offensive action against the English forces. We may therefore regard their alignment as political rather than military. Indeed, Ó hAnluain and Ó Raghallaigh held the northern approaches to the Pale for Poynings.

More significantly, the city of Cork and the earl of Desmond, with a number of other Munster magnates, notably Lord Barry, declared for Warbeck. It appears that Desmond raised forces to blockade Waterford and also sent raiding forces into the Butler territoriees. The siege began in June, and in July a fleet, under Warbeck's command and supplied by the Emperor Maximilian, joined the blockade of Waterford from the seaward side. Poynings had already been reinforced from England in June, and in August he marched south with the gentry of the Pale and the citizens of Dublin. The Butlers came in force. He had also with him Mac Murchadha and some of the O'Briens. His artillery train enabled the blockading forces to be dispersed and a number of the ships taken. Desmond, retreating from Waterford to his own territories, conveyed Warbeck to safety, and he eventually reached Scotland where he took refuge with James IV. Thereafter Poynings engaged in an effective mopping-up operation, so that by November, at the latest, Henry decided that the external threat, with such internal support as it had attracted, had been fully dissipated.

The next phase was one of attempted conciliation. Desmond made it known that he would relinquish his support of Warbeck and come to terms with the king. Richard Hatton was sent to Munster to negotiate on Henry's behalf in December 1495. The first step was clearly to reconcile the coastal towns to the king. Cork was absolved, and probably Youghal also, for their acceptance of Warbeck. Then Desmond's terms were considered and a petition from him sent to the king. His requests were that Kildare should be allowed to return to his inheritance and that he himself should be confirmed in the lands he had held under Edward IV; he asserted, too, that he would continue to attend parliaments and councils only at his own pleasure. Yet it seems unlikely that he stood out and insisted on specific consent to these rather wide-ranging demands. His full and apparently unconditional submission to the king was made on 15 March, only three days after his petition had been submitted. His son was to remain in the custody of the town of Cork as the king's hostage for three years, and Youghal was to pledge itself, along with Cork, that Desmond would keep the terms of his agreement. During the next few months pardons were issued to almost all those who had taken part in or were suspected of taking part in the rebellion of Munster.

Sir Edward Poynings' primary task of clearing the king's enemies from Ireland and of receiving at least nominal submission from the greater part of the country was now ended. He had, it is true, failed to lay foundations on which his military successes could be followed up by enforcement of the acts of his parliament through the energy and expertise of his officials in the areas outside the traditional limits of the Pale and its rather exiguous subsidiary areas of English influence, so that he was forced to recognise the continuing narrow limits of the effective lordship of Ireland. He was, therefore, withdrawn in December 1495 having made a permanent mark through the legislation of his parliament.

Henry expected to raise a substantial revenue from Ireland to make up for the money he somewhat reluctantly sent from England. The revenue accounts of 1485–6 showed the Irish revenues to have been largely dissipated. Legislation to resume lost revenue sources and to require local officials to perform their money-raising tasks more effectively could start the process of rehabilitation. His trained officials, expert in the management of the English finances, could do more. Sir Hugh Conway, appointed treasurer in 1494, William Hattecliffe, under-treasurer, and John Pympe, treasurer of the wars, following in 1495, were to modernise the administration. Alongside the old exchequer procedure, the newer royal chamber system, with its daybooks, running balances, and declared accounts, was introduced. Hattecliffe's surviving papers show both what was done and how it was achieved.[1] We have no complete figures for the year 1494–5, but for 1495–6 the estimated yield was £2,691 and the total accounted for some £3,055, sums that were much greater than those which had come in for very many years, though the double subsidy accounted for some of the increases. This was done with little if any expansion of the area from which the revenue was customarily derived. None the less a real effort would still be needed to bring money to Dublin from Kilkenny, Tipperary, Wexford, and the Desmond lands, let alone the 'lost' royal territories of Connacht and Ulster, and this it was premature to attempt. It could be seen that by Michaelmas 1496 an internal revenue that supplied a surplus over civil costs of some £1,500 would be available. Set against this, the cost of maintaining a small English force and its hired auxiliaries was running at some £9,000 a year. During 1492–4 some £3,600 was sent from England, but between August 1494 and July 1496 a total of £18,303 (sterling, the equivalent value in Irish money being one-third more) was sent, a substantial item from the still small English revenue.[2] Clearly, at some point, Henry would need to balance the cost

---

[1] B.L. Royal MS 18. C. xiv (extracts in *L. &P. Rich. III—Hen. VII*, i, 297–318). Conway, *Hen. VII, Scot. &Ire.*, uses and illustrates these documents intelligently: she did not, however, make any clear assessment of the financial achievements of the English officials. See Ellis, 'Henry VII and Ireland', pp 244–5.

[2] Ellis, 'Henry VII and Ireland', p. 250, suggests that while £18,303 is correct for 1494–6, the gross total for 1491–6 may have reached £23,000 sterling. His 'The Irish customs administration under the early Tudors' in *I.H.S.*, xxii, no. 87 (Mar. 1981), pp 271–7, should also be taken into account.

and advantages of continued spending on this scale against the feasibility of raising more money in Ireland, or else retrace his steps and revert to a cheaper method of managing the Irish lordship.

Henry Deane, bishop of Bangor, the chancellor, succeeded Poynings, his appointment being dated 1 January 1496. He could still rely on a force of 330 English soldiers and 100 hired kern, Garth and Ormond between them sharing command of about half this force. James FitzGerald, Kildare's brother, was still in the field, and was able to raise various alarms in the Pale in the early months of 1496, but gradually the support which he had was cut away, and in June he was in touch with the deputy to obtain a pardon, which was granted on his submission about 4 July. The possibilities of an invasion from Scotland were still giving rise to some anxiety early in the year, while Ó Domhnaill raided Ó Raghallaigh and sent some of his men to plunder in County Louth. Yet, by the summer of 1496, the country appeared to be peaceful. Money was coming into the treasury steadily, if not in large quantities, and it seemed unnecessary for Henry to maintain his English troops any longer, especially as it was clear that, even if the new revenues could make some contribution to military expenses, they were clearly insufficient to maintain any appreciable number of English troops.

Henry had come round to the view that Kildare could, as Desmond had requested in March, be permitted to go back to Ireland. He had been cleared of his alleged treason by solemn declarations by Ó hAnluain and Mág Aonghusa early in June,[1] and when he was released from custody and brought to court to meet Henry, mutual respect between the two men evidently grew. Whether or not, in a confrontation with Henry, in response to a remark that 'All England cannot rule yonder gentleman', Henry had responded 'No? Then he is meet to rule all Ireland', the story is well found. Kildare, it is clear, combined a hasty, even violent, temper with great personal charm and with a sardonic sense of humour.[2] The famous story told by Campion and Stanihurst that when he was being reprimanded for setting fire to the cathedral at Cashel, he apologised humbly to the king and said that he had only done this because he thought the archbishop was inside, is probably untrue (there is no record of his antagonism to Archbishop David Creagh), but again it is in character. He had a rich interest in the world around him and a statesmanlike view of political realities. In any case, Henry agreed to put him back into what both Kildare and he regarded as his rightful place, as the king's deputy in Ireland.

Kildare had accepted an English wife, Elizabeth St John, a ward of the king. With her he was promised substantial grants of land from the king both in England and Ireland. In return he was to guarantee his wife an extensive jointure from Irish land. This was only the first stage. There were also to be elaborate

[1] Sayles, 'Vindication of Kildare', pp 43–7.
[2] *Cal. Carew MSS*, v, 180; Campion, *Hist. Ire.*, ed. Vossen, p. 117; Richard Stanihurst, *De rebus in Hibernia gestis* (Antwerp, 1584), p. 51.

political arrangements. In July Sir James Ormond and the deputy were called to England, and at Salisbury Sir James, Earl Thomas, and Kildare swore solemnly to bring to an end the enmity between their families. Henry insisted that Kildare should formally undertake to maintain the constitutional framework laid down under Poynings, and to call no parliament, or place any bills before it, without previous authority from Henry. He undertook to defend the whole island against any outside invasion and specifically against any renewal of rebellion by the earl of Desmond, and to forward to Henry any person deemed by him to be engaged in traitorous activities. Kildare was to leave his son Gerald in England under the king's surveillance. After a voyage that lasted, almost incredibly, from 28 August to 18 September, Kildare reached Howth. Sir Ralph Verney accompanied Kildare and his wife to oversee his reinstallation in Ireland. This took place at Drogheda, where Kildare took his place in a great council, one to which members of the commons had possibly been called as well as the magnates. He gave assurances to them that he would rule according to his undertakings, and took solemn oaths in St Peter's church to maintain his obligations. Then since, we are told, 'all the gentlemen of the north and the four counties of Ulster' wished to meet Kildare, he moved to Dundalk where he received submissions early in October from one of the O'Neills (Domhnall), Ó Raghallaigh, Ó hAnluain, several Mac-Mahons, Mág Aonghusa, and representatives of other Irish lordships farther south, those of Mac Murchadha, Ó Mórdha, Ó Diomusaigh, Ó Briain, and Ó Conchobhair. The main oath-taking ceremony seems to have been on 2 October when undertakings of fealty to King Henry were given.[1] There were still some hints of opposition in the midlands and farther south, but Desmond sent encouraging words and agreed to meet Kildare early in November at Waterford.

Kildare's patent had been a succinct and generous one. He was appointed for ten years and thereafter during pleasure. He was to appoint all officers, including the treasurer, except for the chancellor. FitzSimons was given his patent as chancellor on the same day as Kildare, namely 6 August.[2] Kildare was authorised to retain for himself in tail male all the king's lands he could recover from the Irish. He was also given all the revenues of Ireland to be assigned and spent at his pleasure. Moreover, though there was a considerable balance of English money in the Irish treasury, he was given a reward of 400 marks when he was leaving in August, and £600 more was sent after him in October. On the other hand, no arrangements were made to pay him a regular fee from England. Verney remained to watch the turn of events in Ireland in the king's interest. Up to the end of October they were, he thought, favourable. To join him there in December came Lord Daubeney, the king's chamberlain. On 20 December and on 3 January 1497 following, a series of

---

[1] Conway, *Henry VII, Scot. & Ire.*, pp 226–35.
[2] P.R.O., C. 66/578; *Cal. pat. rolls, 1494—1509*, p. 62.

assignments of lands[1] were made to Daubeney, Verney, the undertreasurer William Hattecliffe, who was still in Ireland, and others as trustees for Lady Kildare's jointure which Kildare formally confirmed. Thereafter, Kildare was left unsupervised by English officials, but it should be remembered that the two chief justices were Englishmen (though Topcliffe and Bowring changed places in their courts, and the latter left Ireland in 1497 and was replaced by an Anglo-Irish appointee in 1498).

The intervention of 1494 to 1496 had not been, from Henry VII's point of view, in vain. The last, or at least what he could hope was the last, major Yorkist intervention in that island had been eliminated. Much knowledge of Ireland was gained, and this body of knowledge helped to give the English administration a clearer view of the situation in Ireland, though that clarity was to fade in course of time. Henry's officials knew that the maintenance of the Pale was a task that could be undertaken either by the king, at an appreciable cost, or by Kildare, at no cost, but it had to be done by one or the other. Henry had made valuable contacts in the north of Ireland with important Gaelic Irish lords there, and had somewhat strengthened his hold on the remnants of the earldom of Ulster. He had learnt that the payment of 'black rents' to lords like Ó Conchobhair and Mac Murchadha could be a cheap way of gaining some immunity for the marches of the Pale. He had realized the strength of the Butler lands as a counterpoise to Kildare, and was to encourage the earl of Ormond to maintain even closer links with his estates there. He had himself forged close ties with Waterford and had revived direct contacts with Limerick, Youghal, and Cork. His contacts with Desmond had also some significance: at least he knew enough to anticipate that if Desmond retained his association with Kildare he was not likely to be a serious menace to English interests. Henry gave up altogether his attempt to oversee the Dublin administration in Ireland, but his determination to maintain 'Poynings' law' showed his policy to have been one of ensuring that at least the Irish parliament and the Pale should not be used against him. This policy gave Kildare, as lord deputy, a wider range of autonomy than he had had before. Ties with England through his wife, his English lands, and, for a long time, his son's residence at court, were thought to be enough to keep him basically in line with the policy of the English government. Henry seems to have argued that if anyone could reextend the limits of the confined English Pale and could dominate the Gaelic Irish and the Anglo-Irish outside it, it was Kildare. Thus the positive policy of the years 1494 to 1496 gave way to a negative one. But from the English point of view the system which was got under way in 1496 appeared to work.

IN the years after 1496 and until his death, the eighth earl of Kildare adhered to the terms he had agreed with Henry VII. His relations with the king remained

---

[1] P.R.O., E. 40/A. 15056–65. The manors transferred were estimated by Hattecliffe to have an annual value of £253. 6s. 8d. (B.L., Royal MS 18. C. xiv, f. 216).

continuously friendly and cooperative. They did so, perhaps, because the chain that bound him to Henry was a very light one. But Kildare took on seriously and consistently the task of ruling as great a part of Ireland as he could master in the king's name, even if he was concerned more directly with furthering his personal power and his family's wealth and influence. Any idea that Kildare regarded himself as being in any sense the absolute ruler of Ireland is false. Kildare identified his own interests and power in Ireland with that of the king. Whether his own interest or the king's interest was predominant with him was not again put to the test. The king had sufficient confidence in him to allow him to rule Ireland in the main in his own way.

The years immediately following Kildare's return to Ireland were ones in which Kildare cooperated closely with Thomas, the absentee earl of Ormond; Piers Butler; the earl of Desmond; and the city of Waterford. This cooperation was fostered during the first year after Kildare's return by the problem that Sir James of Ormond presented. He had agreed to renounce his hostility to Kildare in the tripartite agreement between himself, Kildare, and the earl of Ormond on 6 August 1496, but without any intention of keeping his word. His situation was clearly an uneasy one. He had accumulated by royal grant the assistance of both English money and Garth's troops between 1491 and 1496, and by force of arms a position of considerable power, and he had also made alliances with Ó Briain and Irish lords in Connacht. He was now faced with the return of Kildare to a position of authority in Dublin and his almost certain hostility. Consequently, he adopted an independent and aggressive attitude. Piers Butler declared that James claimed to be the rightful earl of Ormond in open defiance of Earl Thomas. Whether this is precisely true or not, it is clear that James tried to mobilise all the Butler areas under him. Allied with Toirdhealbhach Dubh Ó Briain, he soon made himself a predominant force in the area, probably retaining the constableship of Limerick castle. He put considerable pressure on Piers Butler and the other branches of the family to submit to his authority. Piers, at least, conformed with a very ill grace. Kildare, Earl Thomas, and Piers Butler together alarmed the king by their reports, and letters were sent to Sir James of Ormond early in 1497 ordering him to come to England; a second letter was brought to him in May and on each occasion he ignored the summons. He had now put himself outside the pale of the king's protection, though he may not formally have been declared a traitor. Piers Butler accused him, rightly or wrongly, of inciting Perkin Warbeck to come back to Ireland. Warbeck did indeed arrive off Waterford in July 1497, but whether this was by arrangement with Sir James of Ormond or not, there appears to be no evidence. By that time he was dead; he had been attacked and killed by Piers Butler, who wrote a frank account of the killing—we may call it a duel if we like—to the earl of Ormond, and offered to take over the deputyship of the earl's lands. Ormond remained on friendly and cooperative terms with Piers, but he seems to have preferred to manage his properties for some years through a number of different agents, coming himself occasionally to Ireland to oversee his estates. Kildare, in 1498, to indemnify Piers against any possible punitive action for the killing of Sir James, issued a most comprehensive pardon to him.

The situation in the south was an interesting one. Earlier, in 1493, as part of the machinery for strengthening Sir James of Ormond's hand, a legal commission had been authorised to enforce the law in Kilkenny and Waterford. This was now revived and we find John Wise, formerly chief baron of the exchequer and one of the earl of Ormond's correspondents, being made special justice for Kilkenny in 1499. And we must remember too that Kildare had a very substantial interest in the Butler areas, since the earl of Ormond as an absentee paid two-thirds of his revenues to Kildare as lord deputy, who, therefore, was concerned to maintain peace and order throughout the Butler territories. The building of a great new castle at Carrick-on-Suir was intended to provide Piers Butler with a new stronghold from which the cadet branches of the Butler family could be controlled. An active attempt was being made to induce them to give up the practice of coyne and livery, which was liable to cut down drastically the revenues from their lands. Kildare held a council at Kilkenny in 1500 and issued ordinances for the maintenance of peace and order in the areas covered by the special commission and the palatinate of Tipperary. The affairs of this area illustrate the nature of the extended authority which Kildare exercised as the king's deputy, showing that the sphere inside which English law was enforced was enlarged and strengthened, at least for a time.

Kildare's own direct contacts with Henry were not necessarily very frequent, and almost all the correspondence between them is lacking, but Henry continued to speak well of Kildare and of his work in Ireland. Kildare regularly reminded the king of his goodwill by sending him gifts of hawks and horses. The chief justice of common pleas, John Topcliffe, visited Henry in October 1496 and was in England again in April 1498. On the latter occasion he brought a request from Kildare for permission to hold parliament and presented bills drawn up in Ireland to be placed before it. The procedures of Poynings' law led to the production of a document, the first transmiss of its type, which passed the great seal of England on 28 March 1498, and authorised the calling of parliament in August 1498. Bills then approved were largely to alter in detail acts passed in Poynings' parliament. The double subsidy of 1494 was to be replaced by a single subsidy to last for a period of ten years, which suggests that Kildare did not intend to call parliament frequently. A separate transmiss was sent over to exempt the earl of Ormond from certain consequences of the act of resumption of 1494.

Kildare did not, however, hold parliament in 1498, since his preoccupations in the south were too great. Perkin Warbeck had reached Irish waters in July 1497, but was driven away from the approaches to Waterford harbour. Kildare and Desmond took precautionary measures in case he returned, and it may well have been these which led Kildare to postpone the meeting of parliament.

Parliament in the end assembled in March 1499, at Dublin and a further session was held at Kildare's new town of Castledermot, County Carlow, on 26 August 1499. We have an interesting document in connection with this parliament, namely a list of fines imposed on officials who did not sit at one or other of the sessions,[1] and this gives us some impression of how far afield writs were distributed and which areas and groups were represented in parliament. For the first session the sheriffs for the counties of Kilkenny (Piers Butler), Waterford, Cork, and Limerick, and the seneschal of the liberty and cross of Wexford, were fined for not returning writs. The towns of Youghal and Wexford and the abbot of Dunbrody abbey were fined for not being represented at the first session. In the second session, fines for non-attendance were imposed on fourteen persons; on Lords Slane, Delvin, Killeen, and Dunsany, one of the burgesses for Drogheda and one of the knights of the shire for County Meath, which might suggest that the Anglo-Irish of Meath and the earl of Kildare were at variance, and that the former were unwilling to come to his town of Castledermot. But there were other absentees also: the bishop of Ferns and proctors of the Armagh clergy, of the clergy, dean and chapter of Ferns, of the bishopric of Ossory, of the prior of Louth and one of the burgesses for Kilkenny. Whether these fines were ever levied is not particularly material, but the fact that writs were sent as far afield as Cork and Limerick and that a number of representatives outside the Pale proper were clearly expected to be present, is of some significance as a guide to the area that might be influenced by the Dublin administration. The parliament itself does not seem to have raised any problems, since Kildare got it to do what he had expected it to do.

While there are, therefore, indications that Kildare was not wholly without opposition from the Anglo-Irish of the Pale, he continued to exercise a wider range of authority over the Anglo-Irish as a whole than any deputy had done for a long time. It is impossible to distinguish what he did in the king's name from what he did in his own right as a great magnate. He could secure the person of the former mayor of Cork, John Water, Perkin's sponsor, condemned in Poynings' parliament in 1494, to be executed in London; but it was Henry himself who issued a new charter to Cork in 1500 after it had purged itself of its treasonable associations with Perkin.

So far as relations with England were concerned, they had by 1500 settled into a routine. Kildare continued his gifts; messages came to him usually by way of the king's own pursuivant.[2] The earl of Desmond, shrewd politician that he was, kept a direct line of communication open with the king; so did Fitz-Simons, the chancellor, and so too did Piers Butler. Through them and

[1] Ware's extracts from the estreat roll of the Irish chancery, 12 [etc.] Hen. VII (B.L. Add. MS 4797, ff 109ᵛ–110).

[2] To the extracts from the king's 'Daybooks' in Quinn, *Guide finan. rec.*, pp 64–8, can now be added items for 1502–5 from the volume, Phillipps MS 4104, now B.L., Add. MS 59899, for which see D. B. Quinn, *England and the discovery of America* (New York, 1974), pp 119–20.

through the earl of Ormond,[1] Henry was reasonably well informed about Ireland.

In a sense the year 1503 marks the end of another subperiod, for in that year Kildare paid his first visit to England since 1496. We have little direct evidence of the nature of his contacts with the king, but there is no reason to doubt that they were entirely amicable. Kildare's son Gerald had been made much of at court and now, aged sixteen, had been found an English wife in Elizabeth Zouche, a ward of the king. Kildare left for Ireland with his son and his new daughter-in-law at the end of April, after receiving a further grant of land in England. He was now confirmed in his deputyship and apparently had convinced Henry that he was fully justifying the responsibility with which the king had entrusted him in his Irish lordship.

Kildare made good use of the privilege, a very exceptional one, of receiving and spending the revenues at his pleasure. It was his exploitation of this privilege which was perhaps the most distinctive feature of his rule after 1496. We have no record that Kildare at once appointed a successor to Hattecliffe when he left about February 1497. Apparently Gerald Dillon, general receiver of the royal lands, hitherto a subordinate of the vice-treasurer, took charge of revenue and disbursements. In 1501 he was replaced by Sir William Darcy of Platten with the title of receiver general of all the king's revenues in Meath, Louth, Dublin, Kildare, and Drogheda. Darcy appeared before the barons at the exchequer table and accounted in the traditional way. His account for the year ending 18 October 1502 was enrolled in the pipe roll of 18 Henry VII, and we hear of a similar account two years later.[2] For the year 1501–2 the ordinary revenues, passing through Darcy's hands, amounted to only £1,110, and did not include receipts from many of the king's manors. The single subsidy of 1499 was producing a little under £500 a year. The total he was handling was only half of that estimated by Hattecliffe as leviable, and we must consider that Kildare was taking directly into his hands a substantial share of the revenues from royal lands. During the following year this process was taken much further. A receipt roll for the years 1502–6[3] had this note under Hilary term 1505:

It is known that of the feefarm of the city of Dublin and of the town of Drogheda and of the customs of coketts and poundage of the said city and town of Drogheda, Dondalk, Skerrey and Malahyde, nor of the issues and rents of the manors of the lord the king, being in the counties of Meath and Dublin, Louth and Kildare, nor of the subsidies of the county of Kildare nor of Wexford nothing is expressed in this roll, except the parcels above included in this roll, because all such fees [etc.], and the said subsidies of the said counties of Kildare and Wexford therefrom arising have been received by the hands of

---

[1] The surviving Ormond correspondence is in *Ormond deeds, 1509–47*, pp 329–71.

[2] Betham's extracts from the pipe rolls (N.L.I. MS 761, pp 327–32) supply such details as we have.

[3] Receipt roll, 18–22 Hen. VII (R.I.A. MS 12. D. 10, p. 189).

Lord Gerald, earl of Kildare, the deputy lieutenant of the lord the king of his land of Ireland and by his assigns.

It is clear therefore that Kildare was taking over the major part of the royal revenues without allowing them to go through the exchequer.[1]

During his deputyship, and possibly by stages, Kildare built up the county of Kildare as a palatine liberty. The medieval liberty of Kildare had come to an end in 1345, but it was revived by the eighth earl with a seneschal, a justice, an escheator, and a treasurer, and these officials administered the revenues and the laws in the lands comprising the county of Kildare in almost complete independence of the Dublin administration.[2] Such a radical devolution was scarcely contemplated and most probably never known to Henry VII. How far Henry VIII was aware of it still remains to be determined.

The year 1504 saw Kildare's most spectacular act as the king's deputy, the carrying of the armed forces of the Pale—lords, gentlemen, and townsmen—on a major campaign into Connacht.[3] This was primarily directed at Burke of Clanricard and his ally, Ó Briain, and was part of the long and complex struggle for power in the west which has already been touched on. Kildare had, however, a specific reason for intervening at this time on the king's behalf. The town of Galway, after long resistance to the Burkes, had been invaded and absorbed into the lordship of Clanricard earlier in the same year. Galway, however autonomous it might be, was one of the king's towns, and the action of Burke of Clanricard was an act of hostility against the crown. This made the campaign, which culminated in the battle of Knockdoe, not far from Galway itself, on 19 August 1504, a remarkable victory for royal power, even though it was primarily a demonstration of Kildare's capacity to deploy military forces in his own as well as the king's interest.

There is little doubt that Kildare regarded this victory as a vindication of his efforts to extend the influence of the king. He sent the chancellor, Walter Fitz-Simons, to England with the news, and it is probable that this messenger was preceded by correspondence telling the king what had occurred and followed by FitzSimons's report to the king's council.[4] Another grant of lands was made to Kildare for his achievement; so too the king rewarded him in 1505 with the order of the Garter, a proxy representing him at Windsor on 4 May 1505 when his stall was designated and filled.

The battle of Knockdoe and the reception of its news in England was the

---

[1] Kildare's rental (B.L., Harl. MS 3756; extracts ed. H. F. Hore in *R.S.A.I. Jn.*, v (1858–9), pp 266–80, 301–10; vii (1862–3), pp 110–37; viii (1864–6), pp 501–18, 525–46; *H.M.C., rep. 9*, app. ii, pp 265–93).

[2] See below, iii, 5–6. Though the liberty was formally suppressed only by the attainder on Kildare in 1536, the government appointed a sheriff for Co. Kildare in 1535, and it was deemed to have been voided from the date of Kildare's treason in 1534.

[3] *Cal. Carew MSS*, v, 181–6. There is a full account in G. A. Hayes-McCoy, *Irish battles* (London, 1969), pp 48–67.

[4] He was present at meetings on 26 Nov. and 2 Dec.(*Select cases in the council of Henry VII*, ed. C. G. Bayne and W. H. Dunham (Selden Society, London, 1958), pp 34, 43–4, 149–51).

high-water mark of Kildare's prestige in Ireland, both as a great magnate in his own right and as the representative of Henry VII in his Irish lordship. By 1506, however, it would seem that the earl felt himself to be in considerable difficulty in Ireland. The recently constructed 'O'Brien's bridge' over the Shannon was thought to be a threat to his power, lands, and influence in the south and he was in some need of English assistance. It would appear that, in July 1506, he sent over one of his brothers to the king—we have a reward paid to his servant in July 1506—and that he was followed by Christopher Fleming, Lord Slane, a little later. It seems evident that Slane made a full report on a rather serious situation in Ireland and asked for money or men.

We can follow the emergence of this Irish crisis in the council meeting of 3 December 1506.[1] On this occasion, Cardinal Morton, the lord chancellor, spoke in the king's name on the reports and letters that had come from Kildare regarding the war threatened by Ó Briain. The chancellor reported to council that the king considered that 'litell advantage or proffitt hath growne of such armyes and captaynes for the conducte of the same as the kinges grace hathe divers tymes send into the land of Ireland for the reducc[i]on of the same'. The implication here is that troops had been asked for and that Henry, reviewing the events of 1491–6, when troops had been sent to Ireland, had decided against this type of intervention as unsatisfactory. It would appear, however, that he had come to a more significant conclusion, namely that he should go to Ireland in person with an overwhelming force and carry through a reconquest of the whole island. The report states that he had decided in principle 'to make a viage personall in his moste noble personn for the represse of the wilde Irishe and redresse and sure reducc[i]on of all the said land'. At the council were present Lord Slane, representing Kildare, Sir Hugh Conway, the former treasurer of Ireland (1494–6), and the earl of Shrewsbury, though not the earl of Ormond. Thus the meeting contained a few men familiar with some at least of the circumstances in Ireland. The king, through his chancellor, asked the council to advise him what force would be necessary to implement his proposed intervention. After deliberation, the council produced a programme which envisaged a formidable expedition, of 6,000 'well chosen men and noe lesse'. This would be in addition to the members of the king's household and the labourers and seamen required for transport purposes by sea and land. Three great guns and nine hundred other guns would be needed for the army. This was a major force, comparable only with that brought to Ireland by Richard II, and greater in number than any English army hitherto employed in the Irish lordship. The advice of the council may well have been sound, but the scale of the commitments that it suggested Henry should undertake was too high for him to accept, as he was closely involved in marriage negotiations for his daughter with the Emperor Maximilian. His alliances in western Europe were scarcely firm enough for him to risk a major involvement in Ireland. We

[1] *Select cases*, pp 46–7.

therefore hear no more of his ambitious plans, nor do we know precisely what answer he sent to Kildare. That Henry contemplated such an incursion into Ireland at all is significant. It is evidence that he did not regard Kildare as indispensable. At the same time, it does not appear that his plans were in any way conceived in terms of hostility to the lord deputy. If he was in temporary difficulties, then it might be necessary for Henry to take direct action. As it was, Kildare does not appear to have been immediately challenged by the O'Briens, even though their power remained a potential threat to him.

In 1507, indeed, Kildare was able to write complacently to a Florentine correspondent: 'Our house in this region has further increased in numbers by a multitude of barons, knights, and noble persons, who have various possessions, and numerous vassals owing them obedience.'[1] The leading distinction he claimed was that 'through the liberality of our most serene master the king of England, I am vicegerent over all Ireland henceforth, at the pleasure of his majesty'. Writing thus from his castle of Castledermot on 27 May, Kildare was clearly not in considerable danger from his Irish enemies. At this time, too, Henry was still in contact, independently, with the port towns, as is shown by his reward to the mayor of Youghal in January 1508.[2] His English council was next concerned with Ireland in July of the same year.[3] By that time Kildare had sent over draft bills and a request to hold parliament in Ireland. This the council considered on 18 July at a meeting when Sir Edward Poynings, the architect of the new status of the Irish parliament, was present. The council sent to the king for the affixing of the sign manual. To the permission to hold parliament and the draft transmiss of bills the great seal was affixed on 23 July. Kildare's messenger may have been his son, Gerald, treasurer of Ireland since 1504. The main reason for calling parliament was to renew the subsidy for a further ten years, the other bills authorised being unimportant ones. Unless there was opposition to the subsidy it is hard to know why parliament should have met on four occasions between October 1508 and, perhaps, the summer of 1509. Additional lands in England were conveyed to Kildare in 1508, probably on the occasion of his son's visit. Henry died on 21 April 1509, and at that time, the basic relationship established in 1496 was still being firmly maintained. By the passage of time, by his energy and skill in asserting the king's and his own strength, Kildare had ruled, not the whole of Ireland, yet a greater part than many of his predecessors as chief governor.

Henry's death removed the king who had established an effective and mutually fruitful relationship with Kildare. The accession of a new king, with a very different temperament, with new and perhaps more enterprising advisers, was bound in the long run to result in the emergence of a different English

[1] Samuel Hayman and others (ed.), *Unpublished Geraldine documents* (4 vols, Dublin, 1870–81), iii, 59 (from Eugenio Gamurrini, *Istoria-Genealogica delle famiglia nobile Toscane et Umbre*, ii (Florence, 1671), pp 111–38).
[2] Quinn, *Guide finan. rec.*, p. 6.
[3] *Stat. Ire., Hen. VII & VIII*, pp 104–8.

policy towards the Irish lordship. In the short run, however, there was no basic change. With the accession of Henry VIII, Kildare automatically ceased to be deputy and was duly elected justiciar around the beginning of June. The king was informed of this, and on 28 July 1509 instructed Kildare to come to England. It seems probable that some temporising messages were sent, as Kildare's position at this time was not too stable, and it is likely that he thought it wise to consolidate his position before putting himself into the power of the new king. He sent formal apologies for not coming to England in a letter of 5 June 1510, but it was not until 8 November that his patent as deputy was granted.

The long-threatened combination of the Irish enemies of his house had eventually emerged. Kildare raised forces from the Pale and had to call in assistance from as far afield as Donegal since, rather unusually, he was in alliance with Aodh Óg Ó Domhnaill. The latter took his force down to the south-west, combined with the army of the earl of Desmond, and attacked and defeated Mac Carthaigh Mór. He then turned on Ó Briain, but he, making adroit use of his recently constructed bridge, was able to attack the plunder-laden army and to inflict very severe losses on it in County Limerick before retreating across the Shannon. Kildare reorganised his forces and beat a retreat, but he did not attempt to renew the struggle, and it could well be said that the events of 1510 showed that he had passed his peak as an effective military power in Ireland. We have no evidence whatever about the mutual reactions of Kildare and Henry to each other at this time. It is clear that Kildare was being urged to come to England to greet the new monarch, and to inform him of the condition of affairs in Ireland. They were not, indeed, favourable. The severe check that Ó Briain had delivered to the combined forces of Kildare, Desmond, and Ó Domhnaill, had shattered the fame of Kildare as an invincible leader. If Henry was fully informed of what had happened he may well have expected Kildare to ask for English aid in restoring his prestige in Gaelic Ireland. Consequently it is not surprising that we should find Walter Eustace on 29 June 1511 writing to the earl of Ormond: 'my lord depute purpose yn to England hastly and I most yewe hym attendance'.[1] He did not come; Topcliffe, however, did so, and it is probable that there were serious discussions of Irish affairs later in the year.

Hugh Inge came to Ireland as bishop of Meath, and later in the year Rokeby replaced FitzSimons, who had died, as chancellor. Henry insisted that another Englishman, John Rawson, prior of the Hospitallers, should also join the council. If these appointments strengthened the English element in the Irish ministerial council, there is no indication that they involved any major change of policy. Kildare, none the less, was wounded in action in the midlands in 1511 and appears to have gone into a slow physical decline, dying in the end on 3 September 1513.

[1] *Ormond deeds, 1509–47*, p. 367.

His death, though this was not immediately apparent, marked the end of an era in Ireland. It is interesting to note that Philip Flattisbury, a County Kildare gentleman and an exchequer clerk, who spent much of his time compiling cartularies like the Red Book for Kildare, and who was his chronicler,[1] spoke of him first and foremost as the representative of English power in Ireland. He was said to have occupied the place of deputy for thirty-three years and to have excelled all other deputies. He had done so by overthrowing and prosecuting the 'Irish enemies' of the king, reducing them by his strong hand to the king's peace. He was said to have built castles, fortifications, towns, and bridges in many parts of Ireland long devastated, more especially on the Pale borders, for the future protection of the king's subjects. A man as great in stature as in achievements, he had been active, good, and merciful.

To succeed such a man was not easy. He had carried his position as king's representative, and also as the greatest Anglo-Irish magnate of the past century or more, with a strong sense of both his own capacities and of his limitations. In Ireland he did what was best for his own power, but took some care that it did not derogate, and might even enhance, that of the king. His confidence and sense of control may have begun to falter in his last years, but they had not broken. His son was faced with a situation in which, to retain the position that his father had gained and to make further advances from it, he needed not only native ability but a mature sense of the realities of his position, which it was, perhaps, too much to expect from a young man of twenty-five. Gerald, the ninth earl, was almost to live up to his father's example, but it is not surprising that in the long run he failed.

IT should not be forgotten that Gerald, ninth earl of Kildare, had had a thoroughly English education. His long stay at court had not only familiarised him with the classics and the new vernacular literature of the renaissance, but had given him some knowledge of how the English court and government worked. Above all it had brought him intimately in touch with the men who ruled England alongside Henry VII and, more significantly, with the younger men who were to rule alongside Henry VIII. Kildare did not forget the young courtiers with whom he grew up and to whom he sent gifts to remind them of his continuing friendship. Familiarity with the English court may also have bred a measure of contempt. He does not seem to have thought that the power exercised by the boy four years younger than himself, who became Henry VIII, could seriously touch him in Ireland; if it did so his friends at court could speak for him. It is possible, too, that his sense of being able to manipulate affairs in England may have made him careless in his diplomacy and liable to underestimate men like Wolsey, Cromwell, and not least Henry VIII himself. R. Dudley Edwards sums him up as 'A talented man, partly anglicised . . ., he

[1] T.C.D., MS 584 (E. 3. 22).

lacked the charismic quality of his father and never showed himself capable of
rising triumphantly above the great challenges confronting him.'[1]

Inside Ireland the earl applied himself to maintain and develop traditional
associations with lords throughout Ireland and to assert himself as the greatest
of the lords among the Anglo-Irish. At the same time there are indications that
while he was prepared to respect Gaelic Irishmen like Ó Néill, Ó Domhnaill,
Ó Briain, and a few other heads of dynastic families, he was inclined to be contemptuous of the lesser magnates of the Pale. Uneasy at times under his father's
rule, they were liable to break out in opposition to the son, and when they did
so they were rudely and arrogantly pushed aside. Moreover, Kildare showed
too a degree of contempt for his major rival, Piers Butler, which was scarcely
justified. If he had not, like Kildare, been brought up at the English court, he
had had a hardy schooling in Irish war and diplomacy.

The ninth earl was an energetic ruler. In his early years he loved, like his
father, to go on almost regal progresses, carrying the king's law with him, and
showing his power as at once the greatest lord in Ireland and the king's representative. Yet he was less successful than his father, and did not seem to have
the reserve of authority on which his father could call when he was in difficulties. He built up his landholdings in his early years also and looked after
their administration carefully, but there are signs here too that he was not the
shrewd manipulator that his father had been. He did, however, greatly extend
the tributes exacted by his father from Gaelic Irish septs bordering the Pale,
and this may have contributed to enhance his influence in these areas. His
greatest asset was his heredity. The fact that his father and grandfather had
been outstandingly able men, and had spread their family, their lands, and
their alliances so widely, had given him some at least of the perquisites of
royalty. The esteem that came to him as the king's representative alone was
probably less than in the case of both his predecessors; his family name more.

Relations between England and Ireland from 1513 to 1534 were not merely
those between Kildare and Henry VIII on the one hand, and Kildare and his
fellow countrymen, Gaelic and Anglo-Irish, on the other. English policy
towards the Irish lordship was bound to reflect in some degree the course of
events in England. Henry VIII did not pay continuous attention to his Irish
lordship, but, like his father, he did not forget it. He regarded it as a reserve
sphere of influence, which it might be desirable or necessary to govern more
directly than had been done since 1496. Dissensions in Ireland might mean that
his representative was not doing his duty of keeping the lordship in order and
should be replaced. They could arise acutely if it appeared that Henry's European rivals were attempting to use any powerful elements in Ireland against
England. They might also come from the intermittent urge towards reform, the
desire to assert direct royal power more firmly and ultimately more profitably
over the peripheries of his realm. These impulses did not constitute a coherent

---

[1] R. Dudley Edwards, *Ireland in the age of the Tudors* (London, 1977), p. 39.

programme of action before the 1530s but emerged from time to time in Henry's Irish policy.

The transition in Ireland was a smooth one. An afforced council elected the new earl as justiciar; the king confirmed the deputyship to him on 26 November 1513, and appointed an English chancellor, Sir William Compton, to go to Ireland; but he declined to do so and the office was given back to Archbishop Rokeby. Christopher Fleming, Lord Slane, became treasurer, Darcy being left for the time being as undertreasurer. John Kite reached Ireland in May 1514 and settled, not without difficulty, into his archiepiscopal see of Armagh. He found everywhere signs of disorder and licence, and wrote to Wolsey from Termonfeckin that he was telling the people he met that things were so bad that King Henry would need to come to Ireland to reform the state. It is not unlikely that the comparative peace that had characterised the years after 1496 had given place to disorder over which the ninth earl had little control. There were fresh and frequent raids into the Pale, and new seizures of lands on the borders by the Gaelic Irish. There were allegations that the ninth earl was favouring his Gaelic Irish friends at the expense of the Anglo-Irish. The Meath gentry were becoming restive and found their spokesman in Sir William Darcy, whose authority as under-treasurer had been undermined by the new earl. The famous polemical tract, 'The state of Ireland and a plan for its reformation' of 1515 (or a little later),[1] surveyed the land and found almost everywhere decay and Gaelic Irish enemies who were crushing the settlers. Only royal intervention and a new plantation, it was said, could preserve the king's lordship. This gloomy view, on traditional lines, was exaggerated and biased, but it was not wholly unfounded. The rule of the house of Kildare had declined from being government in the interests of the Anglo-Irish community and of the king into rule for the personal and family aggrandisement of the earl, no matter what the social costs to the Anglo-Irish polity.

Early in 1515 Kildare was called to England and in April he set out, leaving Lord Gormanston as justiciar. With him went both Rawson and Rokeby, as well as Sir William Darcy. On 1 May Kildare and Rawson were dining with the king at Greenwich, a preliminary, no doubt, to many discussions on Irish affairs. When the Irish issues were brought before the king's council at Greenwich on 24 June, Darcy courageously set out an indictment of the rule of the earl.[2] Coyne and livery and other Gaelic Irish practices were invading the Pale: they had already removed the protection of the English law from outlying parts of the lordship, and especially so in the territories of the earl of Desmond. The implication was that Kildare must either change his policies or else give place to a chief governor more active in the defence of the interests of the lesser Anglo-Irish and of the king. Agreement on these points was reached in September, when Kildare emerged victorious over his critics as his father had done

---

[1] *S.P. Hen. VIII*, ii, 1–31.
[2] *Cal. Carew MSS, 1515–74*, no. 2.

in 1496, though we have no information on how his victory was achieved. He had returned to Ireland before 20 September. On 7 October he was given extensive grants as signs of the king's favour, notably the residue of the king's lands and rights in the earldom of Ulster (Strangford and Ardglass), the manor of Ardmullan, authority to found and endow a collegiate church at Maynooth, and grants of borough privileges for Kildare and Athy. On the same date he was given authority to hold a parliament. A new patent as lord deputy followed him home in 1516: he was to hold under the same terms—very generous ones—as Poynings in 1494. Rokeby was reappointed chancellor, having stayed on in England for some time; Kite (disgusted with Ireland and probably out of favour for his complaints) was removed. He was replaced, after the usual formalities, by another Englishman, George Cromer, less Wolsey's man than Kite, as he was soon to show by his defence of the rights of his clergy against Wolsey's legatine powers.[1]

A new problem was presented to Kildare at the end of 1515. Thomas, earl of Ormond, died in August, and later in the year Kildare was instructed to facilitate the transfer of the Butler lands to the heirs general, Margaret (Boleyn) and Ann (St Leger), his daughters. Sir Thomas Boleyn, Margaret's son, was already influential enough at court to get the aid of Wolsey and the king. Kildare was still on good terms with Piers Butler, who claimed the title and estates as heir male, and whose wife was Kildare's sister. The result was a period of temporising, Rokeby reporting that he was doing his best to get Piers to appear in Dublin to arrange for the transfer of the estates to the English heirs, but saying that he was calling himself earl of Ormond and had failed to come before the chancellor. Finally Kildare on 16 April 1516 recognised Piers's right to the title, the Irish lands, and the traditional Butler prisage of wines in Ireland.[2] This was something of a challenge by Kildare to the authority of the king, but it may not have been formally communicated to Henry. The heirs general did not abandon their claim and duly entered the English lands. The king left a final disposition of the earldom in suspense.

Had this been only a matter of succession to a title, it would have had little historical significance. As it was, it helped to define the relationship of the two major families amongst the conformable Anglo-Irish for nearly twenty years. Ormond, who had hitherto been on good terms with both earls of Kildare, now found—ironically enough, in view of his recognition by Kildare—that the ninth earl was an intolerable rival, and the two turned against each other. Though we lack documentary confirmation, it appears probable that a major cause of strife was that Ormond refused to compensate Kildare for the two-thirds of the income from the Butler properties he had enjoyed while the title was held by an

[1] The dilemma of papal intervention versus English interests is brought out clearly in Edwards, *Ire. in the age of the Tudors*, pp 23, 34, 36–7, 40.

[2] The Irish patent of recognition of 6 April 1516 and the decision of the court of exchequer on prisage were entered on memoranda rolls 7–8 Hen. VIII, m. 20 (R.I.A., MS 24. H. 17) and 8 Hen. VIII, m. 29 (B.L., MS 4791, f. 194).

absentee. Relations were not made easier by the fact that Kildare had lands of his own in Kilkenny and Tipperary. Moreover, one of the men whom Kildare had dismissed from his service, Robert Cowley, put his legal talents and his able and vindictive pen at Ormond's disposal. Ormond proved willing to carry complaints against Kildare to the English court. He may well have been encouraged to do so by the hope that English recognition of his title would follow as the result of such action.

Kildare received authority in October 1515 to hold parliament, but it did not meet until 25 February 1516 and was adjourned at various times until it was dissolved in October.[1] The bills approved were headed by one to renew the subsidy. Another withdrew licences hitherto granted to absentees. An act was passed that limited the power of persons to sue for letters of privy seal in England for private causes. Others were for regulating trade in traditional ways. We know nothing more.

Though we cannot trace their course in detail, the complaints that made Henry again attempt to bring Kildare to heel developed during 1518. It is in that year too that we find the king carrying on a direct correspondence with Cork and with the earl of Desmond. There had been friction between Kildare and the earl of Shrewsbury over Wexford—the rights that the earl of Shrewsbury had were not too closely defined, while Kildare had lands in the country nearby and was inclined to assume he had full authority wherever he went on progress. This appears to have come to a head in 1519. On 12 January 1519 Kildare was instructed to appoint a deputy and to come himself to England.[2] Thus no very clear picture emerges. Kildare was administering his own lands vigorously, but he appears to have been failing to maintain evenhanded justice.

We know little about the internal administration of the Dublin officials under the ninth earl between 1513 and 1519, but it may be significant that his successor (1520–22) was unable to locate any accounts of revenue received for the years before he was called to England. Sir Bartholomew Dillon, the subtreasurer and receiver general, evaded all inquiries about what he had done with the monies he collected. Since he was also chief baron of the exchequer, he presided over the board that audited his accounts. In the end he remained liable to the crown for some £2,000 of the royal revenues of the Pale, including a subsidy, which he was alleged to have received between 29 September 1517 and 10 March 1520. A collusive action in the court of exchequer later allowed Dillon to produce a pardon from Kildare, dated 12 May 1526, when the earl was once more deputy, pardoning him for all debts and arrears.[3] It would seem that during these years all receipts, including the parliamentary subsidy, were being conveyed directly to Kildare and that this went on for

[1] *Stat. Ire., Hen. VII & VIII*, pp 108–15; *Red Bk Kildare*, pp 168–74.
[2] *L. & P. Hen. VIII*, iii (i), no. 17; *Red Bk Kildare*, pp 188–9.
[3] Memoranda roll 17–18, Hen. VIII, m. 17, P.R.O.I., Ferguson collection, iv, 111[r].

many months after Kildare had left for England about the beginning of 1520.[1] It makes a good illustration of just how far he had come to regard the king's patrimony as his own.

---

[1] Steven Ellis suggests to me that, since Kildare had power to appoint his own deputy during absence, he could also arrange for the continuance of the financial arrangements to which he was accustomed. Consequently, from his point of view (or that of Sir Thomas FitzGerald whom he had left to act for him) there was nothing unusual about the disposal of revenues in this way up to the date on which his successor took the oath as lieutenant. But the situation would appear very different to the English officials who succeeded him, familiar, probably, with the system operating at Hattecliffe's departure, and trained as they were both in English exchequer and in royal chamber practices in accounting.

CHAPTER XXIV

The reemergence of English policy as a major factor in Irish affairs, 1520–34

D. B. QUINN

HENRY VIII stepped into Irish affairs effectivly for the first time in 1519.[1] Like Edward IV and Henry VII, he was inclined to accord Ireland only a secondary concern at most times. But he too, like them, had occasional phases of thinking, as early as the eleventh year of his reign, that conquest of his Irish lordship was not only desirable as a possibility but necessary in terms of his broader policies and commitments. Conquest to Henry did not mean a challenge to an established regime which was organised against him. Conquest meant installing English officials at Dublin who would extend their effective power over the widespread territories of the old lordship, bringing them into some uniform government with the Pale, as the royal organs of government at Ludlow and at York were to be used in later years to override lordly autonomy in his English and Welsh dominions. But what about the Gaelic Irish lordships encapsulated within those of the descendants of the Anglo-Norman conquerors, or situated outside them? Henry knew their rulers were spoken of as 'Irish enemies' but, like his predecessors, he saw them rather as allied chieftains, loose in their loyalties though not necessarily obdurate, who need not be expropriated but should be made to disgorge some at least of the lands of the old conquest that they had regained. If there were to be kings in Ireland beside him, then they must be at least moderately compliant sub-kings, as in his view the lordship of Ireland comprised the whole island.

The first specific statement of the king's way of thinking came in 1519, after Kildare's recall had been decided, when Henry VIII, as his father had done in 1506, debated with his council 'how Ireland may be reduced and restored to good order and obedience'. What advice he had on this point is not known, but early in 1520 his views had crystallised. He would send over a lieutenant,

---

[1] See D. B. Quinn, 'Henry VIII and Ireland' in *I.H.S.*, xii, no. 48 (Sept. 1961), 322–30. Brendan Bradshaw, *The Irish constitutional revolution of the sixteenth century* (Cambridge, 1979), pp 58–83, considers this episode in a substantially different context. See also Ellis, *Tudor Ire.*, pp 108–26.

provided with artillery and with a substantial retinue drawn from the royal guard—four hundred new jackets for whom were ordered so that they would present a uniformed embodiment of the power and majesty of a renaissance monarch, even if this, in itself, did not confer on the retinue any remarkable military potency.

The royal policy was embodied in two sets of memoranda.[1] The members of a great council of Anglo-Irish magnates, assembled first at Dublin and later at Kilkenny or Waterford, were to undertake to make no war against any of the Gaelic Irish without specific authority from the chief governor. Gaelic Irish lords, on their part, were to be required to put in pledges, to swear allegiance to the king and obedience to the chief governor, and were to be rewarded according to their merits. It will be noted that this line of policy was not a partisan Anglo-Irish one. It recognises that a major source of disorder lay in the military initiative of the Anglo-Irish. Intentions towards Gaelic Irish lords themselves appeared benevolent, even if not very realistic, unless the chief governor could charm them by diplomacy or impress them by force. But it had at least the germ of a policy for Ireland and not for the Anglo-Irish alone.

This policy, sketched out in the early months of 1520, was developed and refined in the famous despatch sent to his chief governor in the autumn.[2] By that time the policy of making contact with the great Gaelic Irish lords was under way and the conciliation of differences between them and their Anglo-Irish neighbours was being attempted. Henry was anxious, however, to make it clear that an 'apparaunce oonly of obeisaunce' was not enough. This would be merely temporary and ineffective. Gaelic Irish lords must 'observe our lawes, and resourte to our courtes of justice'. Moreover, they must 'restore suche dominions as they unlaufully detaigne from us'. These requirements could involve a drastic change in the Irish legal and social system and in territorial arrangements for which no bridges had yet been established. Henry appreciated this, and did not advocate the direct and immediate use of force—'whiche thing must as yet rather be practised by sober waies, politique driftes, and amiable persuasions, founded in lawe and reason, than by rigorous dealing, comminacions, or any other inforcement by strength or violence'. Once again there is some attempt to think in terms of conciliation which applied to the whole island, even if there was very little realisation of what the 'restoration' of former royal lands could imply territorially, or how different Irish law was from English. A long patient progression towards a reconciled population extending over the whole lordship was still envisaged, however mistily.

The document carried in it the strong legalism of Henry's own thinking which was to be extended more effectively to Ireland after 1534. It also carried the ultimate sanctions of unlimited power:

It may be said unto theym, in goode maner, that like as we, being their soveraigne lorde and prince, though of our absolute power we be above the lawes, yet we woll in noo wise

[1] P.R.O., S.P. 60/1, 28, 30 (*L. & P. Hen. VIII*, iii, no. 670; and iv, no. 80 (misplaced)).
[2] *S.P. Hen. VIII*, ii, 53–7.

take any thing from thaym, that rightuously apperteigneth to theym; soo, of good congruance, they be bounde, boothe by lawe, fidelitie, and ligeaunce, to restore unto us our oune.

Respect for and obedience to the king, with at least the token return of former royal lands, was to be expected. Should they remain recalcitrant, royal author- ity, bound by no limits of law, would be unloosed to force them into an accept- able mould. In this we can see the mind of the man who was in the 1530s to dominate England as no monarch since the Conqueror had done before.

The selection of Thomas Howard, earl of Surrey, as chief governor to replace Kildare was a good one, and the granting to him of the status of lieu- tenant (not before enjoyed by a resident chief governor since Richard of York left in 1460) a wise move, since it emphasised the significance the king placed on his intervention, and brought the prestige of aristocracy to an essentially aristocracy-ridden island. Surrey was a good soldier, who had served Henry well, and a capable politician also, though perhaps lacking the subtlety often necessary if Irish problems were to prove soluble. His arrival in Ireland on 23 May, with several hundred members of the royal guard and three hundred other soldiers, had perhaps more colour than anything seen in Ireland since Worcester came over as deputy in 1467. Surrey was well received in Dublin and clearly, in his early days, impressed his council and dominated his court. But physical conditions were not satisfactory. Kildare had allowed the official fabric to run down. Dublin castle was in a ruinous state and had to be evacu- ated so that it could be reconstructed. The records were in chaos also. This naturally made administration difficult. Sir John Stile, sent over as Surrey's man of business and appointed under-treasurer, could discover neither revenue nor record of efforts to collect any. It was not until late in 1520 that some degree of order was restored.

Surrey's first task was to show himself, to parade his retinue and to make contacts with both Gaelic and Anglo-Irish lords as quickly and as widely as he could. He thus left official Dublin to the workmen and occupied himself in swift and effective progresses both in the north and the south. Between June and October he made three major progresses: to the north, westwards into Leix and southwards by way of Tipperary to Waterford. During the first of these he beat back an attack by Ó Néill into Louth and later, after a second brief cam- paign, received his submission, and also that of Ó Domhnaill—being greatly impressed by the wisdom of the latter. His raid into Ó Mórdha's country was, as was usual in such encounters, indecisive, and had to be repeated the follow- ing year. His progresses to the south brought him into contact with Desmond (whose first submission was followed by some squabbling with Ormond which required fresh diplomatic manoeuvres), with the Butler territories (where he seized Sir Edmund Butler for oppressing his neighbours and tenants) and with both Mac Carthaigh Riabhach and Cormac Óg Mac Carthaigh of Múscraighe. The last not only offered submission but requested a peerage. But Surrey was not able to use his English retinue quite as had been expected. Enough members of the royal guard accompanied him to give him an English presence, but most were unsuited for Irish campaiging. In July, against Ó Mordha, he was paying 120 Gaelic Irish horse and 300 kern in addition to the Gaelic Irish and Anglo-Irish rising-out from the Pale and those who had come in compliment to his status as the king's special representative. But in all this he was doing no more than Kildare had done regularly before him, making a show of force and of diplomacy, but having no time or resources for the consolidation of a new policy of conciliation, or effective, permanent force.

Surrey was unlucky in that this was a plague year, that revenue was tardy in coming in, Dublin castle in ruins, and his English soldiers unable and unwilling, while communications with England were incredibly slow and money from there late in arriving. The replacement of the decorative guardsmen by effective soldiers—northern horse—also took time and was not very efficiently managed. The cost of the Irish soldiers he had to hire was high. Moreover, he could not count on the willingness of the Pale gentry to turn out for military displays more than once or at most twice a year. He was, therefore, driven during the winter of 1520–21 into a state of inaction. Henry VIII, also, soon retracted his more ambitious and expensive plans for Ireland. Just as Henry VII drew back when he realized that Poynings in 1495 was not able to do more than restore the royal authority to its earlier limits without more English resources than the king was willing, after reflection and experience, to spend, so Henry VIII soon thought less about reconquest than of the ways in which Surrey could be stabilised in a position of moderately effective authority at what seemed like a bearable cost to the crown. The revelation that the royal revenues were so meagre, and that the making of friendly agreements with Gaelic and Anglo-Irish lords was more likely to produce honeyed words than revenue, gradually cooled off Henry's concern with Ireland. It is by no means clear that he or his advisers—who, of course, included Wolsey in particular—had any conception of what would be required under existing conditions in Ireland to 'recover' for the king lost lands of the medieval lordship in Ulster and Connacht. As so often was to be the case later, English policy placed impossible tasks on the chief governor and then threw the blame for lack of achievement on an administration at Dublin which had no resources to do what was expected of it. Consequently, much of the correspondence which marked Surrey's continuance in Ireland in 1521–2 was concerned with ways and means of maintaining an English presence at a reduced, even minimal, cost, rather than with developing the promising military and diplomatic initiatives of 1520.

A parliament was held in June 1521 and was not dissolved until 21 March 1522.[1] It may well have provided a useful opportunity for Surrey to follow up contacts he had already made with Anglo-Irish lords and with the representatives of outlying towns. We do not know, however, whether any Gaelic

---

[1] *Stat. Ire., Hen. VII & VIII*, pp 116–23.

Irish lords attended as observers. There is indeed some mystery about what, precisely, it achieved. We know only that acts defining the burning of corn, ricks, and houses as treasonous, forbidding the export and wool of flocks as injurious to industry in Ireland (an interesting protectionist measure), and modifying the qualifications of jurors were passed. Bills resuming grants of cocketts, customs, and fee farms, and instituting a monopoly to the crown of the import of salt were probably rejected—an unsuccessful attempt to enhance the revenues derived from internal sources so as to reduce Surrey's dependence on English money. We are handicapped by lack of evidence on the significance of this assembly and its legislation.

The lieutenancy had been budgeted for in terms of a total annual cost of £8,000 a year, £3,000 being the lieutenant's salary and the remainder being designed mainly to support some 500 regular troops. While he arrived with the best part of a half-year's income in May 1520, Surrey soon found that Henry expected him to finance the bulk of the £8,000 from revenue obtained in Ireland. Instead, Stile discovered he could not, until after Michaelmas, find even enough from local sources to pay official salaries,[1] and when he did collect a full year's revenue it appeared that it did not amount to more than £2,000 gross or some £1,600–£1,700 net. With the utmost economy in the running of the civil administration, Stile was able to hand over only about £750 a year towards the £8,000 represented by the lieutenant's fee and the costs of the retinue. As Henry VIII spent at least £18,000 in two years—and probably rather more as not all military expenses appear to be on record—it will be clear why Surrey resolutely refused to be bound to meet any appreciable proportion of his costs from Irish revenues and why the king soon came to feel that he was not receiving good value for his relatively high continuing expenditure in Ireland. Surrey, moreover, when the season of raiding attacks on the Pale began in the spring of 1521, was unwise enough to ask for an additional force of 300 horse and 500 foot. Sir John Pechie was sent over in June 1521 to tell him that the king was simply unable to commit himself to such expenditure and to inquire what alternatives were possible. In fact, Pechie had little to suggest to Surrey beyond indicating that the gentlemen of the Pale might be induced to take more energetic measures for their own defence. He returned to report that Surrey had weathered his immediate crisis. Six-month truces had been agreed with leading Gaelic Irish lords on the borders of the Pale. Ó Néill was keeping his engagements, and rumours of a threatened invasion from Scotland had been exaggerated.[2]

When Surrey gave his considered opinion[3] on the implications of an Irish conquest at the end of June 1521 he made a good professional assessment of the

[1] We have Stile's accounts (not complete) for Mar. 1520–May 1522 (P.R.O., E. 101/248, 21). Payments from England are compiled from *L. &P. Hen. VIII*, iii, nos 800, 2750, and pp 1533, 1540, 1543; iv, no. 2216; *S.P. Hen. VIII*, ii, 70–72.

[2] *S.P. Hen. VIII*, ii, 65–73; *L. &P. Hen. VIII*, iii, no. 1252.

[3] *S.P. Hen. VIII*, ii, 73–5.

situation. A piecemeal conquest would involve 2,500 men for many years and was likely to be faced by a combination of all the Gaelic Irish and the hiring by them of many 'Irish Scots' (galloglass); for a rapid conquest (though how rapid he could not forecast) 6,000 would be needed—the number already estimated in 1506—which would need to be regularly supplied and fed from England. The conquest would have to be secured both by encastellation and town-building and also by plantation. The Gaelic Irish, if conquered and then left to themselves, would cling to and revive their old practices; new English settlers—those brought from Europe might not remain loyal—must be made the backbone of the conquered areas. Surrey had clearly no pacification programme that did not depend on force, continued repression, and resettlement, and in this he differed radically from Henry's original plan. At the same time we may perhaps discount his programme a little. A year after he had arrived in Ireland he was already anxious to be recalled and was to step up his pressure to this end as the year advanced. And here time was with him. The development of Henry's European policy was proving unfavourable to an expensive Irish programme. A quick dramatic victory and the effective submission of all Ireland would no doubt have made its contribution to Henry's standing in Europe in 1520. In default of this, the expense of the Field of the Cloth of Gold, the alliance with Charles V in August, and the gradual drift to war with France all warned Henry to concentrate his available revenues on these involvements and not on Ireland. Apart from that, Surrey was lord high admiral of England and would soon be needed in the English Channel. His recall from Ireland thus gradually became inevitable.

Between October 1521 and January 1522 the difficult problem of what to do when Surrey should be replaced was endlessly debated. Lord Ferrers was rejected because he would prove too expensive. Ormond (to whom Henry still refused to grant the title of earl of Ormond and spoke of as Sir Piers Butler) was finally suggested as Surrey's deputy. Surrey paid a brief visit to England early in 1522, returned during March to wind up his affairs in Ireland and left before the end of the month, relinquishing his lieutenancy and having installed Ormond as the king's deputy. Henry, in spite of many other preoccupations, retained his personal involvement in the Irish venture until the end, though Wolsey's opinion was influential in the choice of Ormond. Kildare, though at liberty under bond in England, was slowly rebuilding his connections with the English aristocracy, notably with the marquis of Dorset, whose daughter he was soon to marry; Wolsey was hostile to any suggestion, such as that made at one time by Surrey, that Kildare be restored in Ireland. Piers Butler had been a powerful and friendly associate of Surrey during the latter's two years in Ireland though he had not won recognition of his title as earl of Ormond from the king. He was clearly a possible chief governor: the fact that his strength lay in the midlands and that the lands of the FitzGeralds lay across his route between Kilkenny and Dublin was not yet seen as a weakness because Kildare was not present to exploit it. His association with Surrey had brought him new influence and prestige also.

Surrey's lieutenancy was abortive. He had shown that an English chief governor could win prestige and even military victories, but that this did not give him either power or revenue. It did not remove, but merely staved off, the round of intrigues and raids and changing aristocratic alliances that made up the texture of the Gaelic and Anglo-Irish polities alike. More was needed—persistence, money, bribes perhaps, administrative and diplomatic skill—before the lordship could expand again and reconquest begin. Yet Surrey's short period in Ireland was not all loss from the English viewpoint and that of the Anglo-Irish of the Pale. The quarter-century domination of the earls of Kildare had been broken, the ninth earl was shown to be dispensable, Surrey had brought English soldiers into many parts of the island (though neither into Connacht nor the heart of Ulster) and had encouraged Anglo-Irish sentiment by indicating that the lordship still mattered to the English king. For outlying magnates like Desmond the intervention was too brief to offer any clear indication of whether traditional policies should be maintained or new ones developed. For the great Gaelic Irish lords contact with an English earl was not distasteful, but if they learnt of his instructions to conquer them they must have been somewhat contemptuous of the means by which it was proposed to do so. They were clearly only superficially affected, though they too were reminded that in English eyes the whole island made up a single lordship.

THE period that followed Surrey's recall is a long-drawn-out series of experiments in relations between England and Ireland. It is dominated by a situation in which, by and large, the Anglo-Irish both inside the Pale and in outlying towns and territories find their strength being gradually, but steadily, eroded until a measure of despair comes to predominate in the minds of many of them. It is, especially, a period in which the predatory Gaelic Irish lordships on the borders of the Pale, the O'Tooles south of Dublin and the O'Mores on the south-western flank in particular, seem to have become particularly dependent on plunder and peculiarly adept in taking it from their Anglo-Irish neighbours. It is against this background that the shifting policies of the English crown and the struggles of successive deputies with the 'Irish enemies' must be seen. Henry VIII was anxious to keep out of serious involvement in Ireland, yet was not willing to allow his lordship to slide into faction and disorder without some measure of continuous interference from outside. At the same time, by failing to give the Anglo-Irish of the Pale any effective assistance, he was partly responsible for their worsening plight.

Inside Ireland the main feature of a somewhat tragic period is the inveterate and sometimes senseless rivalry of Kildare and Ormond. Kildare, it is clear, was unwilling to make any serious effort to reach a *modus vivendi* with Ormond, and regarded himself as free to indulge his vindictiveness at his loss of the deputyship in 1519. Ormond must somehow be made to pay for his part in it. Even though twice restored, Kildare made no attempt to use his position as deputy to negotiate a genuine peace with his rival. Ormond was a less transparent personality than Kildare. He appears more cool and detached: he is prepared to let his servants, men like Robert Cowley and latterly Cowley's son Walter, do his dirty work for him, often making it appear that he himself was not too deeply involved. In a period too when Kildare finds it difficult to rely firmly on a number of his Irish allies and is being harassed in his own liberty of Kildare by the O'Mores, Ormond is inclined to flaunt his own Irish allies, notably the O'Carrolls, in Kildare's face, or even before the Anglo-Irish of the Pale, by bringing them to Dublin on occasion to enhance his sense of power and importance. Yet Ormond was the more skilful in the end: he knew better than Kildare how to bend to the changes of fortune and the need to exchange force at times for diplomatic concession. He knew too when it best served his interests to retire to his own territories.

In 1522 the omens for Ormond were not good. Stile wrote on 11 March that 'the lande is moche waste, and the people marvelously pouer'[1]—so much for the social effects of Surrey's chief governorship. Before the end of April he had heard that Kildare was to be allowed to come home, which would, he said, loose Conall Ó Mórdha against the Pale, and be the final ruin of County Kildare, the gentleman of which had already, in his estimation, 'almost destroyed' it by coyne and livery. Ormond's first concern was to be secure himself in the south. After he had taken the oath in Dublin, he left for a meeting with Desmond, on whose neutrality much of his own success might depend. One of his earliest acts as deputy had been to activate a strong judicial commission to go on circuit in the south, empowered to exercise wide authority in the counties of Carlow, Wexford, Waterford, Kilkenny, Tipperary, Cork, Limerick, Kerry, and the crosses (areas of ecclesiastical jurisdiction) of these counties,[2] though how far their range extended in practice is not clear. His honest and forthright report to Surrey[3] declared that the Pale was too weak to be defended without English soldiers, admitted that his own energies were liable to be much divided between his lands in the midlands and the Pale, and requested that his son, James Butler, who had been detained at the English court, should be sent home to aid him in Kilkenny. This letter underlined one of the problems of a Butler chief governorship. Ormond might, with the prestige and force of the deputyship, enforce the king's laws rather farther afield than Kildare could often do; but the price of this was a degree of neglect of the interests of the Pale; in particular, the inability to repel and avenge sudden raids into it from the Gaelic Irish, for which Kildare with his base in Kildare was better placed. Yet such

[1] *S.P. Hen. VIII*, ii, 95.

[2] *Ormond deeds, 1509–47*, pp 74–6. Such commissions were not unknown under Kildare, but he had subserved their judicial aspect in the military-political progresses he made to enhance his authority outside the Pale.

[3] *L. &P. Hen. VIII*, iv, no. 81 (*recte* Mar. 1522).

few indications that there are suggested that Ormond was active and reasonably successful during the remainder of the year. At the same time, the failure of the king to confirm him as earl of Ormond rankled.

On 1 January 1523 the long-heralded return of Kildare took place. Married now to the marquis of Dorset's daughter—who soon became her husband's strong partisan with her English relatives—and reconciled to the king, Kildare's arrival in Ireland was bound to cause difficulties. He later indicated that Ormond had offered him an agreement by which they could cooperate closely, provided Kildare bound himself to support Ormond's claim to recognition. This, he declared virtuously to the king, he refused to do. But it was not unreasonable, placed as he was, that Ormond should at least insist that Kildare would not place his services at the disposal of the Boleyns against him. We learn little of how Kildare reinserted himself into County Kildare. It is clear, at least, that not all his uncles, brothers, and cousins were enthusiastic at his return, though the majority of them reasserted their family loyalty. Kildare was soon alleging that Ormond paid little attention to his council and he was probably also busy intriguing with the old official families in Dublin, themselves members of the Pale gentry, against Ormond, perhaps with some success.

It was characteristic of Kildare that he was totally unwilling to settle down as a subject. He raised an army of his tenants and allies and set out for Ulster without any reference to Ormond. Ostensibly a visitation of his lands in the old Ulster earldom, this turned into a full-scale campaign against Ó Néill of Clandeboye, various Scottish forces, and the town of Carrickfergus, the mayor and other leading men of which, accused of trading with the French, he forwarded to Henry. Moreover, in his letter to the king in May[1] he accused Ormond, who had heard, he said, of an intention to remove him from the deputyship, of potentially treasonable activities, and charged him with taking advantage of his absence in Ulster to seize a number of castles in the marches, either destroying them or handing them over to the Gaelic Irish, of which charge there is no confirmation. Clearly the Irish lordship could not contain two such persons, each acting as if he held the crown's authority.

The particular issue on which differences came to a head was over the levying of men and supplies in County Kildare. Ormond had made an agreement with Surrey before he left that he would take coyne and livery from the Pale only under narrow limitations of time and amount—some such latitude being probably essential if English troops were to be withdrawn. The issue was whether Kildare would allow Ormond to levy it inside the Kildare liberty, and alternatively, whether Ormond would admit that Kildare could impose any coyne and livery for his own purpose within the county or elsewhere. Judging by the complaints that each earl was to make against the other in the next few years, the plight of the poor Palesmen in the face of impossibly high exactions,

---

[1] *S.P. Hen. VIII*, ii, 99–101; see also pp 101–2 and *L. &P. Hen. VIII*, iii, no. 3050.

almost certainly heavier under Kildare than under Ormond, rapidly became intolerable.

The king, faced by complaints from both earls, entrusted the two archbishops, the treasurer, Rawson, and the chief justice of the king's bench, Bermingham, with the task of arbitration. The agreement they concocted on 28 November 1523 is a revealing document:[1] Ormond was to have what we may describe as his official rights to coyne and livery in County Kildare; Kildare what we may equally call his unofficial rights, those he could screw 'voluntarily' from his tenants. Each surrendered some of the enemies of the other to judgement—in one case 'to be judgid within the countie of Kyldayre according unto the lawes of his libertie grauntid by the kinges grace to hym in this behalve', as he claimed. But this had no lasting effect. Traditionally, enmity is said to have revived with the brutal murder of Robert Talbot of Belgard, sheriff of County Dublin, by Kildare's brother, James, when he was on his way to spend Christmas with Ormond in Kilkenny.[2] Though this emphasised the hold by the Fitz-Geralds on the main route between Dublin and Kilkenny, it was not a primary reason for the revival of antagonism. Each earl now poured out charges against the other, Ormond's son James being still at court and available to add point to his complaints, Kildare using his connections with Dorset, and with Surrey. Each was trying to put maximum pressure on the king. Henry finally decided on an arbitral commission to settle all outstanding disputes in the Pale and, above all, those between Ormond and Kildare: it was then to switch deputies, Kildare to take over, though leaving Ormond as treasurer. The personnel of the commission was made up of James Denton, dean of Lichfield, and Sir Ralph Egerton, both rising administrators under the crown, and Sir Anthony Fitzherbert. Landing at Howth on 20 June, they made a good impression on the harassed Dubliners. At the chancery in Dublin, on 12 July, they assembled forty of the major landlords of the Pale and the marches and obliged them to enter into recognizances to maintain no more men than the deputy permitted, and then only at the times and rates laid down by him: they were also to aid the king's officials and keep the king's laws. Ormond and Kildare entered separately into obligations to regulate their manner of raising armed men, and an elaborate settlement was worked out regarding the specific differences between the two earls. All these documents throw much light on conditions inside the Pale and in the midlands.

Finally, on 4 August, Kildare was declared deputy, with Ormond treasurer, and the new lord deputy was presented with an indenture which defined his engagements to the king. This laid down the limits within which Kildare could levy exactions for military purposes inside the Pale and for his personal

---

[1] James Graves and J. G. A. Prim, *The history . . . of the cathedral of St Canice* (Dublin, 1857), pp 221–5; *Ormond deeds, 1509–47*, pp 82–4.
[2] See Dublin chronicle, T.C.D., MS 591 (E. 3. 28); Stanihurst in Holinshed, *Chronicles* (1587), p. 84; memoranda roll, 15 Hen. VIII, m. 11, P.R.O.I., Ferguson collection, iv, 80–82.

expenses during progresses, bound him to allow the courts and the local officials of the crown to operate independently and without interference, while he
also undertook to govern by the advice of his council and cease to pursue his
vendettas against Ormond, Lord Delvin, Sir William Darcy, and others.[1] The
Dublin chronicle[2] gave an impression of the change-over:

they kept the counsayll in Chrischyrche and sodenly the erll of Hostre[3] was deprywide
and therll of Kyldar proclamyde and sworn deputey, and so Honeyll beinge in the con-
sayll housse with them bare the swerde beifore the deputey tyll they went to Thomas
Courte and ther dynede and after dyner had a goodly bancket.

Ó Néill's presence in Dublin was probably not coincidental: he had probably
been briefed to come at this time so as to exhibit Kildare's high standing with
the greater Gaelic Irish lords.

The commissioners acted with the council as an equity tribunal, adjudicated
in a number of outstanding civil disputes, and also had the murderer of Talbot
apprehended. He was brought to London and was subsequently pardoned.
What we do not have are the ordinances that the commissioners commended to
the Irish council as a guide for Kildare's actions, though they probably followed closely the lines of the indenture. The commissioners left in September.

The commissioners had demonstrated that the personal representatives of
the English king would almost always be accepted with respect and deference
in the Pale, but the paper framework they established in 1524 had few lasting
characteristics. True, the members of the council, both English and Anglo-
Irish, found Kildare somewhat more agreeable to them than Ormond had
been, but it might appear that they trusted neither earl to any great extent. Kildare's great asset was his influence amongst the Gaelic Irish, especially those of
the north. This he exploited to as great a degree as possible, having both
Ó Néill and Ó Domhnaill present at meetings of afforced councils in Dublin
and maintaining a network of agreements with both rulers, though he failed to
reconcile them effectively with each other. Kildare appears for a time to have
allowed the officials to go about their business peacefully, according to the
agreements signed, while he concentrated on reentrenching himself in County
Kildare, where his relatives had dissipated much of his personal possessions
and authority. Ormond similarly consolidated himself in Kilkenny. Neither
earl gave much attention to what was happening farther south.

James, earl of Desmond, had remained wrapped up in his own concerns
since his contacts with Surrey in 1520; he had, surprisingly, left Ormond's territories unraided during his deputyship. Yet he was engaged in fostering his own
ambitions with the prospect of an alliance with France. The opening of

---

[1] *Cal. Carew MSS 1515—74*, no. 27; *L. & P. Hen. VIII*, iv, no. 558, pp 243–5; *S.P. Hen. VIII*, ii, 104–
18; memoranda roll, 16 Hen. VIII, m. 9; 17–18 Hen. VIII, m. 11 (P.R.O.I., Ferguson coll. iv, 92,
110); *Ormond deeds, 1509—47*, pp 87–90, 108–9.

[2] T.C.D., MS 543/2 (E. 2. 19), no. 14.

[3] Ossory, Piers Butler's title from 1528 to 1538 (during which the manuscript was written).

hostilities between France and England in 1522 led to the visit of French emissaries to Ireland and the drawing up of an agreement between Desmond, acting as a sovereign prince, and Francis I, which was ratified at Askeaton on 20 June 1523 by Desmond, the latter agreeing to support the French candidate for the English throne, the Yorkist Richard de la Pole.

Desmond was testing Ormond's defence on the Tipperary borders in 1524 and began full-scale raiding late in 1524 and continued in 1525. Ormond bore the brunt of these attacks, and managed to contain Desmond's forces by arousing some of his own relatives and allies against him, notably Sir John of Desmond, his uncle, and Cormac Óg Mac Carthaigh of Múscraighe, the latter of whom recalled his agreement with Surrey in 1520. Kildare made one foray into the south, but did not bring on a major engagement with Desmond. He had no desire to become embroiled in warfare far from the Pale, where he was still concerned in consolidating his own position. The French defeat at Pavia reduced the international complications of Desmond's intrigues for Henry VIII, and it seems probable that English intelligence agents reported that Desmond's activities did not pose any serious threat to English interests. However, a precautionary bill of attainder had been prepared in case it should be needed. At the same time Desmond remained hostile, a potential danger inside Munster, capable of tying down the attention of the Butlers to the defence of the southern border of their own territories and distracting them from affairs farther north.

We lack correspondence from the Irish council to Wolsey and the king in 1525 and 1526, so that we have no means of assessing precisely what was happening to the Pale and on its borders. All we have are the charges and countercharges which Ormond and Kildare began making once more against each other. If Ormond was to be believed, Kildare was breaking his agreements made in 1524, was imposing intolerable military charges on the Pale, and was inciting Gaelic Irish lords against Ormond; if we are to believe Kildare, Ormond was doing almost identical things inside his territories of Kilkenny and Tipperary and was inciting his own allies to impede Kildare's friends and tenants in Kildare. It is not unlikely that there is an appreciable amount of truth in both sets of allegations, even though specific instances may well be exaggerated or even invented. Though most of the surviving documents belong to 1525, it was not until August 1526 that Henry sent for both Ormond and Kildare to appear before his council. Ormond set off at once and reached England in September, being determined to get ahead of his rival. Kildare had more to do before he could leave. On 5 November he attested a grant by the king of certain lands to Ormond which he, himself, had been withholding, constituted his brother, Sir Thomas FitzGerald of Leixlip, as his own deputy, and crossed to England before the end of the year.[1] We have no information on the proceedings

[1] *S.P. Hen. VIII*, ii, 118–25; *L. & P. Hen. VIII*, iv, nos 1352 (12), 2424, 2433, 2751; *Cal. Carew MSS 1515–74*, no. 37; Dublin city records, MS 36/2, recorder's book, p. 235.

in England other than highly coloured stories, passed down by Campion and Stanihurst, of the confrontation of Kildare with Wolsey, in which the former had the best of the argument.[1] These probably represent the version put about by Kildare and his partisans after his eventual return to Ireland, but how far they have a factual basis it is impossible to say. What is clear is that the council failed to find a clear path through the maze of accusations and counter-accusations. Kildare was not cleared, but the duke of Norfolk, as the former earl of Surrey had become, offered to maintain him in his own household for the time being, though he expressed the opinion that Kildare would eventually have to be sent back to Ireland. The opportunity was also being taken to bring to an agreement the long-conflicting claims of the heir male and the heirs general to the Butler lands and titles, though these were not resolved until early in 1528.

It can be suggested that at no time did Henry VIII and Wolsey show less regard for the interests of the Irish lordship than in the years 1526–8. The English government had plenty of evidence (and Norfolk could go on supplying them with more) that the Pale was almost uniquely weak and defenceless, that the government there, in the absence of the two really powerful figures that could sustain it in some effective measure, was vulnerable to every minor attack from outside and that no possible help was at hand. Yet not a single pound nor a single soldier was despatched to assist in keeping the Pale, and the reputation of the Dublin administration with it, intact. Consequently, these are years when the authority of the Dublin government reached its lowest point, and only the forbearance of the greater Irish lords, such as Ó Néill and Ó Briain, allowed it to survive, shattered though it was by the raids of the lesser borderers.

Sir Thomas FitzGerald appeared to have done his best to assist the officials in Dublin to organise the Pale for defence during 1526 and the earlier part of 1527, but he felt he had not the full confidence and support of the other members of the official council, and he resigned his office before 14 September 1527. He was succeeded by Richard Nugent, Lord Delvin. It seems probable that the lesser Meath magnates were now, as they had attempted to do in the past, trying to shake themselves loose from the dominance of the FitzGeralds to which they had submitted since 1496. They would have made a better showing if they had had some English money to hire troops or if Delvin had proved a more competent organiser and soldier. Hugh Inge, archbishop of Dublin, the chancellor, and Patrick Bermingham, chief justice, give us our only picture of the situation early in 1528.[2] Delvin, they said, had neither sufficient lands of his own nor any help from the Irish revenues since the subsidy had run out, and the remainder was scarcely sufficient to pay official salaries. Consequently he was

---

[1] Campion, *Hist. Ire.*, ed. Vossen, pp 119–27; Stanihurst in Holinshed, *Chronicles* (1577 ed.), pp 81–3.
[2] *S.P. Hen. VIII*, ii, 126–7.

forced to oppress the people of the Pale even more than Kildare had done by stepping up coyne and livery for the support of a retinue. He was indeed so desperate for money that he stopped the black rent paid to Ó Néill and Ó Conchobhair Failghe to abstain from raiding the Pale. Rumours were circulating that Kildare had been imprisoned for treason. The Butlers, in spite of James Butler's efforts, were riven by dissensions, James Butler, however, being active in pursuit of the earl of Desmond.

This was written on 23 February; on 12 May Delvin agreed to meet Ó Conchobhair Failghe at a castle belonging to Sir William Darcy; when he did so he was ambushed and taken hostage, the price of his release being the restoration of the subsidy, and the return of Kildare to Ireland, Ó Conchobhair being his sometimes faithful son-in-law and Sir Thomas FitzGerald being also involved in the kidnapping. James Butler, having a safe conduct, was allowed to go free. The council reported this sorry news to Wolsey on 15 May, saying that they had advised Delvin against antagonising Ó Conchobhair in the first place. Inge and Bermingham also wrote to Norfolk, stressing that the Pale was 'destitute of good capitaynes' so that they were forced to bring back Sir Thomas FitzGerald, this time as 'a generall capitaine for thes parties' as the Butlers were too far away and too preoccupied. James Butler, too, was anxious to stress that the whole affair was inspired by 'thErll of Kildare his counsaillours, and band'. In this he appears to have been correct, and Sir Thomas FitzGerald's restoration a symbol of its success.[1]

By this time a solution had been found for the Butler dispute. It would seem that the case of the heirs general against the heir male of the Butler line had been pursued for some time in the courts in England.[2] Eventually, on 18 February 1528, the king imposed an agreement on the parties. Thomas Boleyn, now Viscount Rochford, was anxious to climb further with the aid of the Ormond earldom. Henry favoured him, and consequently the agreement leant on the side of the heirs general. All Butler lands and rights in Ireland east of the Barrow were to pass to them absolutely (which might have the effect of limiting the points of friction between Kildare and the Butlers). Lands to the west of the Barrow were for the most part to pass to the heirs general in title only, but were leased to Piers Butler for a nominal sum for thirty years, with the exception of the castle of Carrick-on-Suir. At the same time, Norfolk leased his extensive, though Irish-occupied, land to Piers Butler at a similarly nominal rent. The other side of the coin was the exchange of the title of Ormond by Piers Butler for that of earl of Ossory in February, and the grant in prospect to him of the manor and lordship of Dungarvan, detained 'wrongfully by intrusion' from the king by Desmond. He was granted possession on 26 February.[3]

[1] Ibid., ii, 127–36, and apology of Sir Thomas FitzGerald, 1529 (*Ormond deeds, 1509–47*, pp 99–101).

[2] *Ormond deeds, 1509–47*, pp 99–101.

[3] *Ormond deeds, 1509–47*, pp 116–29; *L. & P. Hen. VIII*, iv, nos. 3937, 3973, 6085; *S.P. Hen. VIII*, ii, 136–42.

It is hard to estimate the balance of loss and gain, but it would appear that Ossory made appreciable concessions to gain royal approval. One of the main signs of his success in this was the grant to him of the deputyship on 4 August. He made his way home by way of his southern possessions, and came to Dublin only in October. The Dublin chronicler reported

the erll of Hostre came to Oxmantowne gren with a great host of Iryshe men as Hocary-roll, Homore and Hoconnour [Cathaoir Ruadh Ó Conchobhair Failghe, the *tánaiste*, not the head of the family]. The maiour with his company of the cittie went throw them to the Erber [Arbour] Hyll and ther stode a certayne whill waittinge for the deputie, but he dynede in Kylmayname and made no haste, soo that the maiour recullede bake to the cittie and the deputie rode to Saincte Mary Abaye and ther take his oghte.[1]

The snub to the city of Dublin may have been a deliberate one in repayment for its earlier lack of enthusiasm for the Butlers. Ossory was also trying to make it clear that the Pale must learn to live with its Gaelic Irish neighbours if it was to avoid being ruined by them.

It took some months of negotiation before agreement was reached that Ó Conchobhair's 'rent' should be paid, Delvin released, and Sir Thomas Fitz-Gerald (revealed as a party to the complicated blackmail operated by Ó Conchobhair) forgiven. The length of Delvin's imprisonment, and the exploitation of Kildare's Irish marriage connection with the O'Connors to influence the crown's dealings with the earl, illustrate very well the depths to which the Anglo-Irish administration had declined. We have little other information on Ossory's activities. James Butler was deeply involved in border warfare with Desmond in the south, while Ossory spent sevral months putting the Pale defences into some sort of order. Ossory may not have set much store on the deputyship, since the new concessions to the Butler heirs general involved him heavily in the midlands and the south if he was to safeguard his own interests effectively.

On 3 February 1529 there landed at Dublin two men who were to prove very influential in Ireland as representatives of royal policy, the two John Alens. One of them, designated archbishop of Dublin, was an able administrator, who modelled himself very much, in his arrogance and interests, on his master, Cardinal Wolsey. The other John Alen was designated for the humbler post of clerk of the council; but his chief task was to act as an intelligence agent, in association with the archbishop, for the English authorities. He brought £100 with him to be disbursed secretly on the king's service, some of it to persons whom Norfolk reckoned could be useful eyes and ears for the royal court.[2] The Alens were intended to stiffen the limp and weakened Dublin administration. Rawson, the treasurer, who had been away from Ireland for some months, came with them. It appears highly probable that Ossory made strong representations about this time that he could not defend the Pale adequately without

---

[1] T.C.D., MS 543/2 (E. 2. 19), no. 14.
[2] P.R.O., E. 101/420, 11, ff 48–48ᵛ; S.P. 1/67, ff 38–44.

English aid and that this led to further changes in the fabric of government in Ireland. It was decided to release Ossory from the deputyship and allow him to concentrate on the south of Ireland. The first step taken was to appoint Henry FitzRoy, duke of Richmond, as lieutenant of Ireland, and thereafter to continue Ossory only until an alternative arrangement could be made.

The situation in Munster had again become serious. Desmond, in carrying on his campaign of attrition against the southernmost Butler lands, was able to find as allies against Ossory the latter's illegitimate son, Edmund Butler, archbishop of Cashel, and his cousin James Butler, baron of Dunboyne. Desmond's French alliance having come to nothing as a result of the French defeats in 1525, he now turned to the emperor, Henry VIII having become embroiled with Charles V. He attempted to negotiate a pact which would give him arms and other assistance against the English king, or, more particularly, against Ossory and his son James. James Butler showed himself an astute diplomatist, mobilising against Desmond Sir John FitzGerald of Dromana, sheriff of County Cork, and his son Gerald, and Desmond's uncle, Sir Thomas (the heir male to the earldom). Cormac Óg Mac Carthaigh of Múscraighe also took the field against Desmond. The fighting appears to have been concentrated largely in County Waterford, where Richard Power, Desmond's ally, was routed, leaving the way to Dungarvan open to the Butlers. This is the explanation of the grant of Dungarvan to the new earl of Ossory in 1528: if he was able to instal himself there he would have a powerful bulwark against Desmond in the south.

Desmond's dealings with the emperor can be traced from September 1528 onwards. On 12 September he wrote asking for help against Henry, specifically requesting the gift of artillery and desiring a formal treaty which would give him the status of an ally of Charles V. His offer was couched in as extravagant terms as that made to Francis I earlier. He and his ally, Mac Carthaigh Mór, between them could field 35,000 foot and 2,200 horse. Charles was sufficiently interested to send his chaplain, Gonzalo Fernández, to Ireland in February 1529. His report contained interesting indications of what he saw and heard, but the bombastic declaration which Desmond read to him on 26 April was sufficient to raise considerable doubts about his truthfulness or even his sanity. In fact the earl's fortunes varied very much over the year 1528. The Butlers made good headway and eventually defeated him so that he was forced to fly for a time for shelter to Thomond. Though he made a come-back in 1529, he did not survive to continue his struggle. His death on 18 June removed one of the main obstacles to Butler power in the south.[1] The new earl, Desmond's uncle, Sir Thomas FitzGerald, came to terms with his brother, Sir John, recognising his possession of certain lands which had been in dispute. He was shortly afterwards recognised as earl by the king, entered into good relations with Sir

[1] *S.P. Hen. VIII*, ii, 141; *L. & P. Hen. VIII*, nos 3817, 3922, 5084, 5938 (1) [*recte* 1528], 4878, 4911, 4919, 5002, 5322 (1–5), 5501 (see William Thomas, *The pilgrim*, ed. J. A. Froude (London, 1861)), 5756; *Cal. Carew MSS, 1515–74*, no. 33; *A.L.C.*, ii, 269.

William Skeffington, and in 1523 submitted himself to the settlement of continuing disputes about his lands by the arbitration of the Irish council.[1]

Though the Desmond question thus settled itself, it was probably a major influence on the decision in July 1529 to send over Sir William Skeffington to Ireland to report on the Irish military situation. Lord Leonard Grey, Kildare's brother-in-law, and Sir Thomas More were among those recommended to go to Ireland as deputy so as to relieve Ossory of his commitments in the Pale. But Skeffington was chosen simply as the king's commissioner. He brought some equipment and a small sum of money when he arrived, apparently on 24 August, but it would seem that between August and the following March he made a detailed assessment of the Irish situation. It was decided, in an unprecedented step, to put the chief governorship in commission. Archbishop Alen, chancellor, John Rawson, treasurer, and Patrick Bermingham, chief justice, a group similar to that which had held power when Delvin had been captured, were constituted as a 'secret council' which was 'to represent the place, rowme, and auctoritie of the kinges deputie ther'.[2] Skeffington as the king's 'counsellor and commissioner in Ireland' may have presided over the deliberations of the other counsellors while he was still in Ireland. On 4 November he, and they, were seen in action when they worked out an arrangement for the government of the midlands.[3] Ossory, with others to be joined with him, was to be one of the justices of the peace for Kilkenny, Tipperary, and Ormond, and was to administer these areas in the king's name; he was to cooperate closely with the new earl of Desmond and submit disputes with him to arbitration; he was also to see that communications through his territories were unimpeded. Ossory was thus left to digest his new gains and consolidate his somewhat impaired position in the Butler heartland. His removal from the deputyship implied no disgrace, merely the recognition that his primary concerns for the time being were in the midlands and the south.

The 'secret council' acted collectively as the representative of the duke of Richmond and attested patents in his name. Its members seem to have convinced Skeffington that they could carry on the government with the aid of a small English force. He arranged on his return that 100 English soldiers, the first since 1522, should be supplied to them. We do not know the details of his report to the king in the spring of 1530, but it is likely that he stressed the difficulty of controlling and defending County Kildare in the absence of the earl. Since Archbishop Alen was gradually involved in Wolsey's fall and disgrace, his authority as the chief English representative in the council was fatally impaired. He was suspended from the chancellorship and the commission was then left in the hands of Rawson and Bermingham alone. Consequently, it was

---

[1] *S.P. Hen. VIII*, ii, 160–61.
[2] S.P. 1/67, ff 33–6; see D. B. Quinn, 'Henry Fitzroy, duke of Richmond, and his connection with Ireland, 1529–30' in *I.H.R. Bull.*, xii (1935), pp 175–7.
[3] *Ormond deeds, 1509—47*, pp 133–5.

necessary to take fresh steps to restore the administration to effective strength. The decision finally taken in June was to send Skeffington back to Ireland as deputy, and along with it went another major change of policy: Kildare was at last to be allowed to return. This was a crucial step. It may be seen as evidence of the Grey family influence at court, and possibly also as the result of Norfolk's belief that Kildare was at least a necessary evil, but probably it was due in the end to Henry's desire to see whether Kildare's energy and ability could, in any circumstances, be harnessed for the effective restoration of the weakened lordship.

Skeffington's instructions[1] were to take a further 200 horsemen to Ireland, and to employ them in repressing intruders on the Pale; and also to reconcile the outstanding differences between Kildare, Ossory, and Desmond so that the three earls should cooperate in restoring the lordship to a position of strength and tranquillity. Skeffington was to hold a parliament at which it was expected a subsidy would be granted. He was to be careful to act only with the approval of his council. Finally, he was to have the active, not merely the passive, assistance of Kildare, who had promised the king 'to employe . . . hym selfe . . . for the annoyance of the kynges sayd rebellious subjectes of the wyld Irishrey, as well by making excourses upon them, as otherwise'. For this purpose he was to have the use, on specified terms, of such English soldiers as Skeffington was not employing at any particular time. This was to be a fatal provision. Kildare was unable to share power, as he had shown, it might be thought decisively, in 1524–6; now with a commoner as deputy it was almost inevitable that he should attempt to take the reins of government into his own hands.

Before the arrival of the new deputy, the 'secret council' had been engaged largely in routine administration. Skeffington landed on 24 August 1529, accompanied by Kildare, and relieved the commissioners of their responsibilities. In the short run, the cooperation of Kildare with Skeffington was effective. A general hosting was proclaimed in 1530, a force marched against Ó Mórdha, and his country was burnt and devastated. On the other hand, the council agreed on 12 November that Skeffington should continue the payment of Ó Conchobhair's wages. After a quiet winter, Skeffington and Kildare were early in the field against the Ulster lords. Ó Néill eventually offered his submission to Skeffington and so, on 6 May 1531, did Ó Domhnaill. It is difficult to know whether these successes of the 'gunner', as Skeffington was known in Ireland from his expertise as master of the king's ordnance, were due to his leadership, to his English soldiers, or to the prestige that his association with the earl of Kildare, widely welcomed at first after his return to Ireland, brought him.

The parliament that Skeffington was authorised to hold assembled for two meetings at Dublin (15 September and 13 October 1531) and another at Drogheda (27–31 October).[2] Nine bills were put before it: the principal one was

---

[1] *S.P. Hen. VIII*, ii, 147–50.
[2] *Stat. Ire., Hen. VII & VIII*, pp 125–6.

that reviving the subsidy. A bill assuring Lady Kildare the income from certain manors is known to have passed, as did another which threatened the monopoly of landholding of the earls of Kildare in Counties Kildare and Carlow. Lands of absentees in these counties, granted in 1482 to the eighth earl and his heirs were to revert, if still waste, to the representatives of their early owners. Norfolk, the principal claimant, leased his rights in Carlow and elsewhere to Ossory, which inevitably created a new ground for hostility between the earls, by giving Ossory an opportunity to penetrate Kildare's main sphere of influence. Skeffington did not escape effective opposition in this parliament, since he was denied a subsidy by it, though we do not know under what circumstances. The country representatives of the Pale may have insisted that their territories were too weak and poor to pay extra taxes. Ossory was present at the parliament too long for his own welfare, he complained; while one of the knights of the shire for Kilkenny had been kidnapped on his way to the parliament and the two burgesses for Kilkenny on their way back. This may point to reprisals against them from the FitzGeralds on account of the Carlow act (Kildare being afterwards accused of inciting the kidnappers), while these circumstances illustrated vividly once more how Kildare could impede contacts between the Butler territories and Dublin.

Trouble was developing between earl and deputy. Kildare appears to have begun to treat Skeffington less as the king's representative and more as a mere commoner. In order to secure his freedom of action it would appear that the deputy encouraged the feud between the two earls, supported Kildare's kinsmen against him, and built up alliances with the Gaelic Irish bordering the Pale in opposition to Kildare. To the council it seemed that Skeffington favoured Ossory against Kildare, though Ossory professed to believe the opposite.[1] Early in 1532 he accused Kildare of playing off the earl of Wiltshire (as Boleyn had now become) against him in regard to Butler possessions in the east (Tullow and Arklow) to which he had a title, and of stirring up his relative, Sir Edmund Butler, against him in Tipperary. He complained that Kildare had acted in a hostile manner towards his retinue when they were together on a hosting against Ó Néill. Ossory, too, appears to have been left out of the commission constituted by Skeffington on 26 January 1532 to exercise judicial authority in Kilkenny, Waterford, Tipperary, and Cork, though this was probably because he was party to several suits which would come before them. In one he claimed prisage of wines within Desmond's territories: Desmond refused to come to Waterford for the hearing but put his case at Dungarvan to members of the commission. They decided for Ossory. Kildare was afterwards accused of trying to stiffen Desmond's resistance to the Butlers. Ossory, it is significant to note, was now reporting directly to Thomas Cromwell, whom he knew could bypass great nobles like Norfolk and Dorset, stating that Skeffington was

---

[1] *L. & P. Hen. VIII*, v, no. 1061.

very much under Kildare's thumb.¹ Nor was the situation regarded in England as satisfactory. Up until May 1532 nearly £5,000 had been spent in maintaining Skeffington and his troops, while all that was received in England was a further series of complaints and little evidence of pacification.

In April, Kildare, Ossory's son James, Rawson, and Bermingham came over to England for consultations. The king felt that he was not receiving good value for his outlay on Ireland, and in their examinations before the council Rawson and Bermingham did nothing to dispel this impression, deposing that Skeffington lacked thirty of his retinue and fifty horses at the last muster and that he was exploiting his office for his own private gain. The deputy, moreover, had done nothing to compose the feud between the two earls, which had been a major reason for his appointment. Since, on the other hand, Kildare's conduct in the circumstances was considered to have been reasonably satisfactory, the decision was taken to reduce expenditure by reappointing him as deputy. The appointment was made on 5 July and Kildare returned to Dublin in triumph. George Cromer, archbishop of Armagh, was made chancellor and James Butler became treasurer.² It would seem that the king took the advice of Wiltshire and Norfolk and gave the earl what must surely have been regarded as the last chance to come to terms with the Butlers and to administer the lordship with some degree of impartiality. The man in charge of Irish affairs in the king's council from this time onward, however, was Thomas Cromwell, who had Kildare watched closely by his own agents, and was soon to develop an active concern with the king's Irish lordship.

Kildare took the oath on 18 August, and characteristically began his deputyship by settling his score with Skeffington, 'where of great myscheff came'.³ He humiliated Skeffington publicly while taking a muster of his troops and the 'gunner' was then forced to remain in attendance on Kildare while the king decided what to do with the military stores sent to Ireland with him. On 20 October he handed over custody of them to the council.⁴ One result of this clash was to add Skeffington's weight to the campaign begun by the Butlers against the deputy, but the leaving of the ordnance in Ireland was not without consequence for the rebellion that broke out in 1534. Probably the decisive factor in the failure of Kildare's third deputyship and the breakdown which followed was the relationship between the deputy and Henry's new chief minister Thomas Cromwell. Cromwell's intelligence system in Ireland was effective enough but the extent of his understanding of Irish affairs has become a matter of controversy between historians. It can be argued that during the period 1532 to 1534 Cromwell's attempt to tame the earl by close supervision

¹ *S.P. Hen. VIII*, ii, 153–8.
² *L. & P. Hen. VIII*, v, no. 1207 (14–16); Stanihurst in Holinshed, *Chronicles* (1577 ed.), p. 85; T.C.D, MS 543/2 (E.2.19). ³ T.C.D., MS 543/2 (E.2.19).
⁴ Memoranda roll 24 Hen. VIII, m. 15 (St Peter's College, Wexford, Hore MS I, 1178–80), printed by S. G. Ellis, 'An indenture concerning the king's munitions in Ireland, 1532' in *Ir. Sword*, xiv (1980), pp 100–03.

and frequent interference was the foretaste of a radical reforming policy or else that it was merely the continuation by another hand of measures such as had been tried repeatedly since the time of Henry VII. To begin with, Cromwell attempted to arbitrate between the two earls, but it might appear that Kildare did not take his new status in the English administration too seriously, was suspicious of his association with men such as Archbishop Alen, whose hostility to Kildare was of long standing, and preferred to rely on his earlier links with both Norfolk and Wiltshire which had been powerful influences in his re-instatement. The question of whether Cromwell achieved anything before Kildare's recall to England must remain a matter of opinion: it has been argued strongly that he did (though the events of the summer of 1534 appear to show that what he achieved was completely undone), and it has also been urged that the building up of a system of checks and balances to limit Kildare's freedom of action merely provided irritants, detracting from his authority without effectively diverting it into other channels. Norfolk was to make a case later that Cromwell's mishandling of Kildare was one cause of the rising of 1534.[1]

During his last term as chief governor, Kildare's unwillingness to compromise with his political opponents or to tolerate restraints on his control soon created a situation in which faction ran rife. The king's confidence was partly withheld from Kildare and the deputy's authority was consequently undermined. The two factions in Ireland, moreover, quickly identified themselves with the two sides (Cromwell on the one, Norfolk, Wiltshire, and Stephen Gardiner on the other) in the struggle to succeed to Wolsey's position in Henry VIII's counsels. In such circumstances, the attitude of the Irish council was crucial. To begin with, at least, it probably favoured Kildare. The English element was now represented by Cromer, Rawson, Edward Staples, bishop of Meath, and probably Archbishop Alen, who had been pardoned the previous February; while the two chief justices, Bermingham and Richard Delahide, and the chief baron, Patrick Finglas, remained from the previous deputyship. They were joined by James Butler as treasurer (if in fact he took any active part), Lord Trimbleston, a Kildare protégé, and Nicholas Wycombe, whom Kildare appointed clerk of the rolls in place of Anthony Skeffington.[2] Thus with Cromer and Delahide also aligned by preference with Kildare, and

---

[1] There is a conflict of opinion on the nature and extent of Cromwell's actions and influence. Brendan Bradshaw, in 'Cromwellian reform and the origins of the Kildare rebellion, 1533–34' in *R. Hist. Soc. Trans.*, 5th series, xxvii (1977), pp 69–93, and in *Ir. const. revolution*, pt ii, makes out a case for the dominant character of Cromwell's influence and for his early formulation of a policy of radical change in Ireland, while Steven G. Ellis, 'Tudor policy and the Kildare ascendancy in the lordship of Ireland, 1496–1534' in *I.H.S.*, xx, no. 79 (Mar. 1977), pp 235–71, and 'Thomas Cromwell and Ireland, 1532–40' in *Hist. Jn.*, xxiii (1980), pp 497–519, takes a more cautious stance. The poverty (and sometimes ambiguity) of the materials on the discussions between 1532 and 1534 make a definitive treatment impossible, so that final judgements, in the absence of additional evidence, must tend to be ones of opinion rather than of established fact.

[2] Memoranda roll, 22 Hen. VIII, m. 15d, and 24 Hen. VIII, m. 15 (B.L., Add. MS 4791, f. 203; St Peter's College, Wexford, Hore MS I, pp 1176–7); *Cal. pat. rolls, Ire., Henry VIII–Eliz.*, p. 6.

Rawson and Bermingham well disposed to him, at least to begin with, Kildare as deputy was by no means hamstrung by the council. Indeed, he was soon able to strengthen his position when Sir Bartholomew Dillon, second justice of king's bench, deputised from October onwards for the ailing Bermingham and succeeded him on his death in December, and by appointing the lawyer William Bathe as undertreasurer to take effective control of the finances in the treasurer's absence.

Kildare's record in dealing with the Gaelic Irish lords outside the Pale had been his major asset in earlier phases of his career, but this time his good fortune and power appear almost to have deserted him. He countered Ó Domhnaill's attempt to reach an accommodation with Henry VIII, initiated under Skeffington, by maintaining that Ó Domhnaill was not sincere and that the castles he offered to hand over in trust were not worth having, thus indicating his continuing bias in Ó Néill's favour. In December, however, he gained only a Pyrrhic victory over the O'Carrolls, Ossory's allies, for though he took two castles he was, at Birr Castle, 'shot into the bodye with a handgone and ney slayne, but he wase never holl againe, the more pittie', as the Dublin chronicle related.[1] In consequence, he was forced to rely more on his kinsmen (who were at loggerheads with each other) in military campaigns and several reverses followed. Three of his brothers were defeated in a raid on the O'Tooles; the MacMahons defeated another of his brothers; Ó Raghallaigh routed his son Thomas and a rising-out of the Meath gentry, while the O'Byrnes raided Dublin, entered the castle, released some prisoners, and terrified the citizens.[2] While some of these reports emanate from sources hostile to him there seems little doubt that his authority in the military sphere was in decline.

We know little about the course of the feud between Kildare and Ossory in 1532–3 beyond the fact that the first round culminated in the murder, before the end of 1532, of Ossory's son Thomas, by Kildare's retinue. The Butlers reacted with complaints brought by their spokesman, Robert Cowley, to Cromwell, who seems by the summer of 1533 to have come to the conclusion that something more than letters of warning to Kildare was now necessary.[3] By that time also, councillors were growing restive at Kildare's conduct, and a meeting of councillors, reinforced by several peers, equivalent to an afforced council but without the deputy, reported to Henry that disorder was widespread, that Kildare and Ossory were again at each other's throats, and that the colonial area was threatened from various points. John Alen was given the task of bringing both complaints and suggestions to England. The latter would have involved placing considerable restraints on both Kildare and Ossory but also on other lords and gentlemen in the Pale and outside it who were almost out of

---

[1] T.C.D., MS 543/2 (E. 2. 19).
[2] L. & P. Hen. VIII, v, nos 1548, 1560, 1729; vi, nos 39, 105 (i), 299, 551 (ii), 567; T.C.D., MS 543/2 (E. 2. 19).
[3] S.P. Hen. VIII, ii, 162–6.

control. Alen was well received and on 5 July 1533 was appointed the first master of the rolls (hitherto only a clerkship) and a member of the council, for which he had already acted as clerk. At the same time Kildare's opponents were trying to remove the chancellor, Cromer, who was alleged by Archbishop Alen, whom he had replaced, as being of 'great unskylfulnes' and an open partisan of Kildare. He even suggested that the council (which had so recently attempted to demonstrate its neutrality) was 'partley corruptid with affection toward therle of Kildare, and parttely in soche dread of him, that either they will not or dare not do any thing that shuld be displeasante to him'.[1] It is clear, however, that the deputy was not now finding much support from any section of the Anglo-Irish. Even his brother, Sir James FitzGerald, complained that he was being oppressed by the earl, who was finally ruining the counties of Kildare and Carlow by his impositions.

It does not appear possible, at this crucial point, to obtain any clear idea of Kildare's own position. Was he being, as his critics and enemies would suggest, simply irresponsible and unwilling to cooperate with anyone inside the Pale or outside it who would not grovel before him? Or had he possibly a case, at least for his undoubtedly heavy military exactions, and did he try to gain support by concessions to his critics? He held a parliament at Dublin on 19 May 1533 and on 5 June, and dissolved it on 2 October. Curiously, no application, licence, or transmiss for it has been traced in the English records, but its statute roll was later accepted as authentic. The only act of importance known to have been passed was one for a three-year (not the usual ten-year) subsidy. The fact that a subsidy had been rejected in 1531 suggests Kildare could still get some qualified assistance from an Anglo-Irish assembly, even if his critics appear to have been more numerous than his wholehearted supporters.

At the end of August the king sent Kildare a sharp reprimand and, in response to this, he soon began to transfer the royal ordnance out of Dublin castle into his own strongholds, a potentially treasonable action which Cromwell's agents did not fail to report. In September both earls and other councillors were summoned to England, but Kildare procrastinated, sending his wife to bear excuses. By this time it was apparent to Kildare that his deputyship was at stake, while Cromwell learned then or a little later that the earl would not easily be reconciled to its loss. The position of Ireland was becoming complicated by the ecclesiastical schism, which was now almost complete, and by indications that Charles V's ambassador in London was not indifferent to the possibilities of using an Irish counter to his master's difficulties.[2] Cromwell and Henry must ascertain whether Kildare could be trusted to initiate the Henrician reformation

---

[1] *S.P. Hen. VIII*, ii, 168, 179.

[2] The political aspects of these years have been stressed, but the underlying need for Henry and Cromwell to introduce and enforce the ecclesiastical changes of the years 1533–4 in Ireland was also a vital factor, and one of which the agents of Charles V were well aware and were already in process of attempting to counter. See Steven G. Ellis, 'The Kildare rebellion and the early Henrician reformation' in *Hist. Jn.*, xix (1976), pp 807–12.

in religion in Ireland as well as to continue in office in the normal way, so that his presence in England became imperative, though it might not be politic or easy to coerce him to come. It has been argued[1] that he was induced to comply by being allowed to appoint a deputy to hold office for him until his return since this would give him a continuing lien on his own office as deputy. In any event he did so, appointing his son Thomas, Lord Offaly, his deputy, with instructions to take counsel only from those councillors and advisers whom he (Kildare) felt he could fully trust. He reached court about the beginning of March 1534.

At court, Cromwell had already decided on a complete overhaul of the administration. A number of vacancies in Irish offices had given him the opportunity to begin the remodelling of the council and administration so that it would reflect Henrician not Geraldine interests. He now planned to install an English chief governor. Henry, duke of Richmond, whose wife was Norfolk's daughter, should be the king's lieutenant and a policy very like that of 1520 would be revived, this time with a very strict emphasis on the subordination of the earls, and any who might imitate them in a lesser way, to the new adminis-tration. Such an administration would necessarily have been supported by a major establishment and this Henry would not contemplate on account of the cost, so that in May it was decided that Skeffington should return to carry out the new policy. Though it is probable that the published ordinances were not put in print by the king's printer, Thomas Berthelet, until later,[2] they were evi-dently in some rough shape by May since Ossory entered into an elaborate indenture in which he bound himself to maintain no forces or alliances except under direct order of the deputy (though his liberty of Tipperary was not to be interfered with), while he also undertook to enforce the new royal authority over the church within his territories. It is clear that Kildare was offered some very similar document but that he was either reluctant to accept some of the limitations imposed or else rejected it out of hand. We are told he was examined by the king's council and 'manyfold enormyties' proved against him though he was not imprisoned,[3] while two of the new officials—Thomas Cusack and Thomas Finglas—were sent back to Ireland to summon Lord Offaly to court. Kildare took counter-measures to make the Irish lordship ungovernable, instructing his son that he 'shulde play the best or gentilst parte, and that he shulde not trust to the kinges counsaill ther', while his life would be in danger if he came to England.[4]

[1] This is the view put forward with documentation by Ellis in *I.H.S.*, xx, no. 79 (Mar. 1977), pp 255–6.

[2] The only surviving copy is in P.R.O., S.P. 60/2, 26 (*S.P. Hen. VIII*, ii, 207–16), and it is not included in the revised *Short-title catalogue*, ii (1976), where it should probably appear as 14128.2.

[3] *S.P. Hen. VIII*, ii, 194.

[4] Ellis in *I.H.S.*, xx, no. 79 (Mar., 1977), pp 257–8, and his citation of Cromwell's interrogation of Offaly (P.R.O., S.P. 60/2, 159), shows that Bradshaw (*R. Hist. Soc. Trans.*, xxvii, 85) misses the point of the Cusack–Finglas mission which instructed Thomas 'to repair to the kingis counsaile' (in England). Bradshaw says they carried 'instructions from the king which were to be delivered to the

The crucial events took place on 11 June 1534 when Offaly summoned a council to meet at St Mary's abbey: this was ostensibly to debate the king's instructions. Instead, on the advice of his personal advisers, Offaly utilised the occasion for a demonstration of defiance: leading a retinue of horsemen through the city of Dublin, he denounced royal policies before the council, resigned his office, and surrendered his sword of office to Archbishop Cromer as chancellor. Did this mean that he at once 'went into rebellion' or that he was resorting to the extremer measures of putting pressure on the monarchy of which there had been many examples since the Kildare hegemony began in 1478?[1] These conclusions have been and may continue to be argued, but in the face of an English king who was in process, under the guidance of one of his strongest chief ministers, of defying the papacy, such 'pressure' was most unlikely to be treated as anything but open rebellion, as indeed it was. Kildare was imprisoned from June until his death early in September as a sign that no concession would be made. It seems clear, however, that Offaly held his hand from launching a wholesale insurrection until this was certain. His siege of Dublin castle and the killing of Archbishop Alen late in July marked the line of no return.

It has been argued vigorously that Cromwell planned something different from what Henry had attempted earlier. We can concede that the ordinances of 1534—with their laconic opening 'First it is ordeyned that the kinges deputie make no warre . . .'—were more explicit about the precise role of the king's chief governor and of the great Anglo-Irish lords under him than earlier documents of this kind. The statement that 'they passed sentence of death on bastard feudalism in the colonial area of the lordship and decreed the resuscitation of crown government'[2] means little in an Irish context. In form and content—if not in vigorous directness—they varied little from the arrangements that had been proposed on previous occasions when transitions in government were in prospect earlier in the reign. Nor was any extraordinary instrument prepared to put them into effect. A minor official, whose earlier experience of Ireland had not been too happy or successful, was intended to enforce this new and supposedly revolutionary policy, with merely a token force of English soldiers, and at minimum cost. It was only in August that it was realised that a major army and a truly revolutionary policy of direct royal control alone could meet the situation. The Cromwellian solution began to emerge and take effect only when Skeffington eventually arrived in Ireland in October with a force of 2,300 men, the size of army that, alike in 1506 and 1520, had been deemed necessary if Ireland was ever to be reconquered.

Irish council assembled with their acting head, Kildare's son, Silken Thomas'. This appears to be a decisive point.

[1] Compare Bradshaw, 'Cromwellian reform', p. 85; Ellis, 'Tudor policy', pp 259–60.
[2] Bradshaw, 'Cromwellian reform', p. 85.

THE history of the English in Ireland from 1496 to 1520 is mainly Irish history, that is, it is focused on activities by Anglo-Irish rulers, the earls of Kildare, both inside and outside the English Pale. But the history of the years 1520 to 1534 is increasingly the history of relations between the ruler of the Dublin administration, whether he was one of the Anglo-Irish magnates or an Englishman, and the English king. Both Kildare and Ormond in this period had their own policies as lord deputies and their private interests as magnates to safeguard in ways that might or might not be agreeable to Henry VIII and his advisers, but neither was left for any length of time unsupervised. Royal agents or commissioners heard complaints and investigated conditions in the Pale, and policy decisions were based on what was learnt from inquiries, from complaints by Kildare, Ormond, and their friends about each other, and from consultations with officials brought from Ireland. Supervision was not minute, and, except when English money was being spent in Ireland, little attempt was made to oversee the day-to-day administration in the Pale. Kildare was still the most powerful and able single personality in the Anglo-Irish hierarchy, though Ormond was not so very much his inferior in effectiveness and probably superior in political sensibility. At the same time, though it may not have seemed so then, the autonomy of the great magnates was drawing slowly to a close. It would be unwise to say that the installation of an English administration in the place of the Anglo-Irish aristocratic one was inevitable, even if there had not been a FitzGerald rebellion in 1534, but the course of English policy and interests in relation both to the outlying parts of England and Wales, and also to the international situation, was such that a new effort to integrate Ireland more fully into the dominions of the king was becoming increasingly probable. The rebellion of Silken Thomas gives a romantic flavour, spiced with tragedy, only to the last days of a period in which feudal autonomy and aristocratic licence were alike about to give place to the prosaic workings of the expanding bureaucratic English national state. Our knowledge of the social context in which these political events took place is still very limited. Until and unless it can be extended, the effects of such events as have been described on the lives and conditions of all orders of society cannot effectively be estimated.

CHAPTER XXV

Literature in Irish, 1169–1534

JAMES CARNEY

THE immediate reaction of the poets, historians, and learned men of Ireland to the Anglo-Norman invasion can only have been one of shock. Apart from the fact that a foreign element exercised power in many areas of Ireland, the hardest thing to bear must have been that Tara, for centuries an incomparable focus of sentiment, was no longer in the possession of the descendants of Míl. Added to this the church, hitherto an important guardian of Irish historical and literary traditions, virtually abandoned this secondary role. These two factors, the one political, the other ecclesiastical, may well account for the fact that no Irish literary manuscripts have survived from the period 1150–1350. This is not to say that none was written then. But their absence is suggestive of interruption and of a slowing-down in the flow of literature.

Towards the end of the twelfth century, Cathal Crobderg, grandson of the last high-king, Ruaidrí Ua Conchobair, became king of Connacht. It would appear that, with Tara in the hands of foreigners, the kingship of Connacht had now come to be invested, at least for the literary men, with something of the dignity of the high-kingship. Cathal in his time was certainly the premier descendant of Conn and would be a focus of hope. His epithet *Crobderg* (red-handed) was doubtless due to a red mark on his hand, in all probability a birth mark. The early thirteenth-century poet Gilla Brigte Mac Con Mide comments on Cathal's mark in the lines:

> *Táinic an Crobhdhearg go Cruachain,*
> *an comhartha ad-chiú 'na láimh.*

(The red-handed one has come to Cruachain, I see the sign in his hand.)[1]

This mark appears to have been regarded as a messianic symbol and to have identified Cathal with Áed Engach, the hoped-for saviour of Ireland who had long been looked for. That such hopes were current is testified in the Annals of Ulster in 1214 where there is the entry: *Isin bliadhain dobi in t-Áedh breicci frisa raitea an Cabharthach* (in this year the false Áed who was called 'the helper').[2]

[1] James Carney, 'Cath Maige Muccrime' in Myles Dillon (ed.), *Irish sagas* (Dublin, 1959), pp 160–66.
[2] Cf. below, iv, 407.

The general contemporary attitude to the invaders can be seen in a pseudo-prophetic poem, recently published, and preserved in the fourteenth-century Book of Uí Mhaine: *A fir ná suidh arin síth* (Man, do not sit on the mound). Here Cathal and his grandfather Ruaidrí are depicted as noble salmon who have been attacked by monstrous *gairbhéisc* (rough fish) who are defined as the Welsh, the English, and the French (*Bretnaigh*, *Saxain*, *Franncaigh*).[1]

Quite an amount of poetry written within a century of the Anglo-Norman invasion has survived in later manuscripts. This poetry, much of it written by professional poets of great repute, was composed in Early Modern Irish, the classical language that survived in Ireland and Scotland until the seventeenth century. Indeed, so constant was the literary, especially the poetic, language in this period over time and space that linguistic considerations are alone no certain guide to either date or place of composition. The emergence of this well-regulated and consistent language about the year 1200 might at first sight seem to be a result of the invasion. But perhaps it is more likely connected with the increased activity of professional literary families who took over the cultivation of native learning from the church when it gradually abandoned the cultivation of native learning. The regularisation of the language of poetry, and the abandonment—or bare toleration for metrical purposes—of Old and Middle Irish features was doubtless a recognition of linguistic facts that had been in existence for a considerable time.

Before 1200 it is clear that scribes transcribing manuscripts mainly in the Irish language were also competent in Latin. On the other hand in certain Irish manuscripts written by laymen in Connacht around 1400—such as the Book of Lecan and the Book of Ballymote—the scribes show little or no understanding of the occasional Latin passages. It cannot, however, be assumed from this that knowledge of Latin was at a low ebb through the whole of society. The professional medical men, as well as religious writers, were competent in Latin, and what was true of a somewhat later period, when Latin, as Edmund Campion testifies, was spoken in Ireland 'like a vulgar language', would *a fortiori* be true of about 1400.[2]

Contrasted with the virtual absence of manuscripts in the period 1150–1350, the survival of a considerable number in the period 1370–1500 is suggestive of a literary revival that reached its peak in the early years of the fifteenth century. On the other hand it should perhaps be suggested that the survival of manuscripts in great numbers from this period might be partly due to the increased use by the Gaelic Irish of stone houses or castles; these afforded manuscripts better protection, with less risk of destruction by fire. The fourteenth-century revival is best evidenced in the figure of Seoán Mór Ó Dubhagáin. Ó Dubhagáin died in the year 1372; the date of his birth is not known. But as he

[1] See Brian Ó Cuív (ed.), 'A poem composed for Cathal Croibdhearg Ó Conchubhair' in *Ériu*, xxxiv (1983), pp 157–74.

[2] See W. B. Stanford, *Ireland and the classical tradition* (Dublin, 1976), p. 26.

was a scholar of influence and distinction it is not unlikely that he died an old man, and his life-span may reasonably be regarded as beginning with the century, if not indeed sooner.[1]

Ó Dubhagáin was historian to Ó Ceallaigh, lord of Uí Mhaine, an extensive and important lordship in the province of Connacht. He was probably connected with—if he did not originate and organise—the great meeting of learned men who assembled as guests of Uilliam Buidhe, son of Donnchadh Muimhneach Ó Ceallaigh, at Christmas 1351. This meeting, noted in the Annals of Ulster and of Connacht, and elsewhere, is best chronicled in the Annals of Clonmacnoise:

William O'Donogh [leg. m'Donogh] Moyneagh O'Kelly invited all the Irish poets, brehons, bards, harpers, gamesters or common kearoghs, jesters & others of theire kind of Ireland to his house upon Christmas this yeare, where every one of them was well used dureing Christmas holy dayes, & gave contenment to each of them at the tyme of theire departure, soe as every one was well pleased and extolled William for his bounty, one of which assembly composed certaine Irish verses in commendation of William and his house which began thus: *Filidh Ereann go haointeach*.[2]

Ó Dubhagáin wrote a number of poems of learned and antiquarian interest. The most important is his unfinished topographical poem 'Triallam timcheall na Fódla' (Let us travel around Ireland). Ó Dubhagáin treated the northern half of Ireland and Leinster. The poem was finished by one Giolla na Naomh Ó hUidhrín (d. 1420) who begins *Tuilleadh feasa ar Éirinn óigh* (Additional knowledge concerning virginal Ireland); he dealt with Munster and with Leinster, which latter province is therefore covered twice.[3] These two poems constitute a compendium of the topography of Ireland prior to the advent of the Anglo-Normans as seen by scholars who lived about two centuries after the invasion. They typify the whole fourteenth- and fifteenth-century revival, which was not directly creative. Its aim was rather to recreate Ireland as it was in the past, and as it should be in the present if certain events had never happened. Consequently, families of Anglo-Norman descent are not mentioned and Gaelic Irish families are shown as ruling over territories then under effective colonial control.

Amongst the many manuscripts surviving from the period 1350–1500 are some that could be called great books, both from their dimensions and the importance of their contents. These are the Yellow Book of Lecan, the Book of Uí Mhaine, 'An Leabhar Breac' (the speckled book), the Book of Mac Carthaigh Riabhach, the Book of Fermoy, the Book of Pottlerath (Bodl., Laud

---

[1] His declared pupil Ádhamh Ó Cianáin (d. 1373, *A.F.M.*) outlived his teacher by a year. The latter appears to have written N.L.I., MSS G2–3 before 1345 'from an exemplar belonging to or perhaps written by his teacher, Seoán Ó Dubhagáin' (*N.L.I. cat. Ir. MSS*, fasc. 1, p. 13).

[2] *Ann. Clon.*, p. 298. The poem 'The poets of Ireland to one house', written by Gofraidh Fionn Ó Dálaigh (d. 1387), has been edited by Eleanor Knott in *Ériu*, v (1911), pp 50–69.

[3] John O'Donovan (ed.), *The topographical poems of John Ó Dubhagáin and Giolla na naomh Ó Huidhrín* (Dublin, 1862); James Carney (ed.), *Topographical poems by Seaán Mór Ó Dubhagáin and Giolla-na-naomh Ó hUidhrín* (Dublin, 1943).

Misc. 610) and what may be called the Book of Art Buidhe Mac Murchadha Caomhánach (B.L., Eg. MS 1782).

The unity of the Yellow Book of Lecan (T.C.D., MS 1318) is one imposed by the binder. It consists of sections written by Cirruaidh mac Taidhg Ruaidh who probably belonged to the family of Mac Fir Bhisigh, Giolla Íosa mac Donnchaid Móir mic Fir Bhisigh, who wrote in 1391–2, and Murchadh Ó Cuindlis: some medical fragments were written by one Giolla Pátraic Albanach in 1413 and by one Donnchadh mac Giolla na Naemh Ó Duinnín in 1465; a *duanaire* or poem-book was written by Mael Muire Ó Maol Chonaire in 1473. The greater part of the manuscript was written by Giolla Íosa mac Donnchaidh Móir; this contains the most important extant version of 'Táin Bó Cualnge', and other saga material of inestimable worth. Ten folios of this section were in the Phillipps collection in Cheltenham and were unknown when the facsimile was produced.[1]

The Book of Uí Mhaine[2] may well be the earliest great book of the Irish revival. It has also been known as the Book of the O'Kellys and was written for the most part, if not entirely, before the election in 1392 of Muircheartach Ó Ceallaigh, bishop of Clonfert, to the archbishopric of Tuam. The main scribes are Ádhamh Cuisin and Fáelán Mac a' Ghabhann na Scéal (d. 1423, *A.F.M.*).

The Book of Ballymote[3] was written at different times and places by various hands. The name of the book connects it with Ballymote, County Sligo, the seat of Mac Donnchadha of Corann, under whose patronage it seems to have been compiled. The period of writing was that in which Toirdhealbhach Óg Ó Conchobhair Donn held the kingship of Connacht (1384–1406). The principal scribes are Solamh Ó Droma, Robertus Mac Síthigh, and Maghnus Ó Duibhgeannáin.

The Book of Lecan,[4] known in Irish as 'Leabhar Mór Leacáin', was compiled by Giolla Íosa Mór Mac Fir Bhisigh at Leacán, County Sligo in 1417–18. He had the help of two scribes, Ádhamh Ó Cuirnín and Murchadh Ó Cuindlis. Mac Fir Bhisigh was *ollamh* to Ó Dubhda, chief of Uí Fiachrach. Of this MS, 302 leaves are preserved in the Royal Irish Academy (MS 23. P. 2), and nine in the library of Trinity College, Dublin. In content it is closely connected with the Book of Ballymote, and for some texts they shared a common exemplar.

The book now known as 'An Leabhar Breac' may not have received this

[1] The facsimile was published by the R.I.A. (Dublin, 1896) with an introduction by Robert Atkinson. For descriptions of the material, see the introduction to that volume and *T.C.D. cat. Ir. MSS*, pp 94–110, supplement, pp 342–8. For the leaves from the Phillipps collection, see *N.L.I. cat. Ir. MSS*, pp 28–31. The MS was previously numbered H. 2. 16.

[2] Published in facsimile by the I.M.C. (Dublin, 1942), with an introduction by R. A. S. Macalister. For a description see also *R.I.A. cat. Ir. MSS*, fasc. xxvi (1943), pp 3314–56.

[3] Published in facsimile by the R.I.A. (Dublin, 1887) with an introduction by Robert Atkinson. For a description see also *R.I.A. cat. Ir. MSS*, fasc. xiii (1934), pp 1610–55.

[4] Published in facsimile by the I.M.C. (Dublin, 1937) with an introduction by Kathleen Mulchrone. For a description see also *R.I.A. cat. Ir. MSS*, fasc. xiii (1934), pp 1551–610; *T.C.D. cat. Ir. MSS*, pp 112–13, and supplement, p. 350.

name before the late eighteenth century. It was long known as 'Leabhar Mór Dúna Doighre' from being preserved at Dún Doighre (Duniry, County Galway), a home of the MacEgan (Mac Aodhagáin) family. It was brought there from the place of its compilation, Cluain Leathan in Múscraighe Tíre, County Tipperary, where the MacEgans had a law school. The manuscript was in course of compilation in 1411, and parts of it were written at places other than Cluain Leathan; at Clonmacnoise, at Clonsast and Magh Ua Farga in County Offaly, and at Baile Riccín in north Tipperary. The scribe was probably Solamh mac Aodhagáin. It is one of the best preserved of the manuscripts of this period.[1]

The Book of Mac Carthaigh Riabhach, more commonly known as the Book of Lismore,[2] was discovered at Lismore castle in 1814, during the course of building operations. It was compiled, probably at the Franciscan friary of Timoleague, County Cork, for Fínghin Mac Carthaigh Riabhach, son of Diarmaid an Dúna, lord of Cairbre (Carbery), and his wife Caitlín, daughter of Thomas, earl of Desmond. The book is to be assigned to *c.* 1500, or possibly some years earlier.

The Book of Fermoy could also be called the Book of Roche.[3] It is a miscellaneous volume, but a large part of it relates to the Roches, a family of Anglo-Norman descent. The manuscript is in the main fifteenth-century, although some leaves, written by Ádhamh Ó Cianáin (d. 1373), belong to the fourteenth, and some belong to the sixteenth. Amongst the identified scribes are Domhnall Ó Leighin (*fl. c.* 1460), and the sixteenth-century Torna, son of Torna Ó Maoil Chonaire; the latter wrote at Castletown Roche in the barony of Fermoy, County Cork. It is to be regarded as a collection of manuscripts, rather than as a single great book.

The Book of Pottlerath (Leabhar an Rátha), better known from its place in the Bodleian library as Laud Miscellany 610, contains two manuscripts written at different dates.[4] The earlier was compiled for James Butler, fourth earl of Ormond, early in the fifteenth century. It contains copies of 'Félire Óengusso', 'Acallam na Senórach' (defective), and also included a *dindshenchus*, now fragmentary and separated from the main manuscript. In 1453–4 the older book was incorporated in a new volume compiled for Edmund, son of Richard Butler, nephew of the fourth earl. This extension of the original compilation

---

[1] A lithographic facsimile of a transcript of the manuscript made by Joseph O'Longan, with a description and list of contents based on the work of O'Curry, was published by the R.I.A. in 1876. For a description see also *R.I.A. cat. Ir. MSS*, fasc. xxvii (1943), pp 3379–3404.

[2] Published in facsimile by the I.M.C. (Dublin, 1950) with an introduction by R. A. S. Macalister.

[3] See J. H. Todd, 'Descriptive catalogue of . . . the Book of Fermoy' in *Royal Irish Academy: Irish manuscripts, series I* (Dublin, 1870), pp 5–65. Also *R.I.A. cat. Ir. MSS*, fasc. xxv (1940), pp 3091–3125.

[4] The manuscript has been described by Myles Dillon in *Celtica*, v (1960), pp 64–76; vi (1963), pp 135–55. See also R. I. Best, 'Bodleian MS Laud 610' in *Celtica*, iii (1956), pp 338–9, and Anne and William O'Sullivan, 'Three notes on Laud Misc. 610 (or the Book of Pottlerath)' in *Celtica*, ix (1971), pp 135–51.

written in Pottlerath, Kilkenny, Gowran, Carrick-on-Suir, and Dunmore, as well as at other places, while Edmund and his entourage travelled between these various centres of power. The main scribes were Seaán Buidhe Ó Cléirigh and Giolla na Naomh Mac Aodhagáin. In 1462 Edmund Butler, the patron of the book, was taken prisoner at the battle of Piltown by Thomas Fitz-Gerald of Desmond;[1] the book was considered sufficiently valuable to ransom him, and thus passed out of the possession of the Butlers.

The Book of Art Buidhe Mac Murchadha Caomhánach, otherwise Egerton 1782 in the British Library,[2] was written about 1517, the greater part at Cluain Plocáin in County Roscommon, the chief seat of the family of Ó Mhaoil Chonaire. Part of it may have been written in Leinster, and the patron seems to have been Art Buidhe mac Murchadha Caomhánach, who died while the compilation was in progress. The chief scribe was a son of Seaán mac Torna Uí Mhaoil Chonaire. The contents include 'Táin Bó Cualnge', tales of the Ulster cycle, and other early texts.

These great books of Ireland consist to a very large extent of texts composed many centuries earlier, and there is in them, apart perhaps from the Book of Fermoy, comparatively little that was contemporary, even using the word loosely to cover any work composed up to a century before the date of compilation. They show the same spirit of diligent antiquarianism that is found in the compositions of Ó Dubhagáin. None could be read in its entirety by its patron, and many passages would not be intelligible to the learned compilers. For the patron, whether Gaelic or Anglo-Irish, his book had two main functions: it was a type of currency and an object of beauty. It would be shown with the same pride as a wealthy owner in a later age might display a Rubens or a Rembrandt.

In addition to the great books a number of lesser ones have survived, many of them scholars' rather than patrons' books. One such is the Book of Ádhamh Ó Cianáin (N.L.I., MS G 2–3), Ó Cianáin being the pupil of Seaán Ó Dubhagáin, already mentioned above.[3]

A notable survival in Scotland is the Book of the Dean of Lismore, written in the early years of the sixteenth century by James MacGregor. MacGregor was from Perthshire and was dean of Lismore, in Argyll. He made a great collection of verse, acquired apparently from passing travellers, and wrote it down phonetically in contemporary Scots orthography, a fact that contributes equally to the difficulty of the poems and to their interest. Some five or six thousand lines consist of poems known to have been composed in Ireland, some by well-known poets such as Donnchadh Mór Ó Dálaigh and Gearóid Iarla, that is, Gerald, third earl of Desmond.

Towards the end of the period 1260–1550 two matters greatly affected Irish

[1] See above, p. 599.
[2] For description see *B.M. cat. Ir. MSS*, ii, 259–98.
[3] Above, pp 689–90. See also James Carney, 'The Ó Cianáin miscellany' in *Ériu*, xxi (1969), pp 122–47; and cf. below, pp 793–5.

literature: the advent of the printed book, which increased vastly the amount of knowledge available; and the availability of paper, a cheap material which made possible the wider dissemination of literary material.

BARDIC verse, from the earliest times up to the seventeenth century, is a continuum, and its interest as a cultural phenomenon is greater than its detailed expression in any given time or place. In the period from the Anglo-Norman invasion up to about 1550 there were many poets whom the bardic order regarded as great masters of the craft, and some will be mentioned here. These masters achieved a type of excellence but, with rare exceptions, it is a quality that no longer fully communicates itself today. Bardic poetry in this period might be described as a fine, useful, homogenised product, the best of one master's output being indistinguishable from the best of another's; as a consequence of this it is difficult, perhaps impossible, to establish authorship of a given poem on grounds of style alone. Part of the excellence consisted in fulfilling the requirements of the most difficult metres while giving an impression of ease and naturalness. Despite the overall similarity, every poem by a good poet seems different in approach, theme, and construction; the better poets, while adhering to convention, seem to have been determined not to produce totally hackneyed products. Poetic diction was a taught subject, but there are virtually no standard lines or couplets as one might expect in such institutionalised verse.

The poet in constructing a praise poem draws upon a common stock of ideas. The subject, a territorial dynast, might be referred to as *éigne Bearbha* (salmon (= hero) of the river Barrow), or as *géag Gabhráin* (branch (= scion) of Gowran). Even to a contemporary, on account of the geographical proximity of the two places mentioned, there would be hardly a shade of difference between the two descriptions: the geographical element is important, but apart from this the phrases have been determined by metrical considerations. The choice of the defining genitive in such cases is part of a code reflecting the subject's descent, the extent of his power, or some element in his personal or family history. If one of the O'Connors of Connacht were referred to as *oighre Cuirc* (heir of Corc) it would be clear that the poet indicated descent from Corc, the founder of the Eóganacht dynasty of Munster; in such a case one would suspect that the subject's mother or grandmother came of a Munster Eóghanacht family such as that of Mac Carthaigh. Thus the understanding of this verse requires a knowledge of the whole Irish genealogical scheme back, at least, to the fifth century, as well as a good knowledge of Irish topography. These requirements are part of the difficulty encountered in translating such poems into English; without the necessary background knowledge much of the meaning is lost.

Amongst the stock ideas is that the subject is an excellent specimen of manly beauty and physique. He is attractive to women and may secretly father sons on wives of other noblemen. The poet may sometimes affect a female role and speak as if he were his patron's wife or mistress. The subject is of impeccable ancestry and, unless some measure of reproach is intended, is unfailingly generous. The weather, the harvest, the fruits all respond to the justice of his rule. He deserves that his power should spread outside his patrimony. His enemies fear him; his courage in battle is unparalleled; if he were to get his just deserts he would gain possession of Tara and rule all Ireland. The poem may be built up with an apologue, an analogy from the past that can be flatteringly applied to the subject.

Some quotations from a poem to Cailleach Dé, daughter of Ó Mannacháin, a Roscommon chieftain, will illustrate the analogous type of poem when addressed to a woman. The date of this poem, 'Bean ós mhnáibh cáich Cailleach Dé', is early in the thirteenth century.[1]

Woman beyond all women of the world is Cailleach Dé . . . smooth gentle rose-like cheek . . . white-handed . . . smooth stately foot . . . has won love in peace and turmoil . . . has outstripped . . . every lady of the *Gaoidhil* and the *Goill*. . . . Quickly given is her wine and ale, quickly appeased is she . . . quickly forgiven are my folk [i.e. the poets] . . . bright stately lady of curly tresses and black eye-lashes . . . devoted to generosity—it was not more lavish in Eimhear [i.e. Cú Chulainn's wife] . . . she has the hue of berries on her cheek and the hue of coal [in her hair] . . . this majestic swan; wealth of red gold will reward the poem to her—Cailleach Dé is the sun risen high over the wood; all my heart's desires are in her giving; my house stands as a supporting buttress to her castle; to dwell in her house is my only heaven.

This kind of poetry doubtless affected (or drew upon?) a more popular kind of love poetry.

Bardic poems are in the main contemporary historical documents. Any facts alluded to, such as details of immediate ancestry, or battles won over rivals, must be taken as true, for they had to receive the assent of a contemporary audience to whom the relationships and events were well known. A poet could not easily write a lengthy poem without some reference to contemporary affairs. But such references are so vague and so minimal that this fact in itself calls for explanation. Poets were trained diplomats. Even when they exercised the office of *ollamh* to a given prince they travelled and exercised their art for the benefit of other princes. Today's enemy might be tomorrow's friend, so that, while there are exceptions, poets praised one man in such generalised terms that they could not thereby incur the disfavour of another.

It seems that, at least from the thirteenth century on, the poets had doubts as to the morality of their craft. It was, after all, based upon technical lies, one of the most obvious being that old men had to be described as if they were in full possession of manly vigour and beauty. More serious were their political 'lies', and these are referred to frankly in a poem by Gofraidh Fionn Ó Dálaigh to

[1] Lambert McKenna, *Aithdioghluim Dána* (2 vols, Dublin, 1939–40; Ir. Texts Soc., xxxvii, xl), i, 1–5; ii, 1–4.

Gerald FitzGerald, son of Maurice, first earl of Desmond, and later known to the Irish as Gearóid Iarla:[1]

> Flaitheas nach gabhaid Gaoidhil
> geallmaoid dóibh i nduanlaoidhibh;
> a ráthughadh dhúibh níor dhluigh,
> gnáthughadh dhúinn a dhéanaimh.
>
> Dá chineadh dá gcumthar dán
> i gcrích Éireann na n-uarán,
> na Gaoidhil-se ag boing re bladh
> is Goill bhraoin-inse Breatan.
>
> I ndán na nGall gealltar linn
> Gaoidhil d'ionnarba a hÉirinn;
> Goill do shraoineadh tar sál sair
> i ndán na nGaoidheal gealltair.

(In our poems we promise the Gaoidhil a kingdom they never get. You should not pay attention to it, 'tis our custom!

Two races to whom poems are sung are in cool-streamed Éire, the Gaoidhil known to fame, and the Goill of Britain, isle of varied beauty.

In poems to the Goill we promise the driving of the Gaoidhil from Éire; in those to the Gaoidhil we promise the driving of the Goill east overseas!)[2]

In a poem of uncertain authorship and date (but which the editor, on the basis of an attribution in a single late manuscript, attributes to the thirteenth-century Gilla Brigte Mac Con Mide) there were allegations in Ireland that the bardic craft was about to be condemned in Rome.[3] In a poem attributed, but perhaps wrongly, to the fourteenth-century Muireadhach Ó Dálaigh, the poet, about to enter the church and receive tonsure, offers his four-year growth of hair to the Lord in requital for his lying verses.[4]

The best poetry produced at this time is the personal poetry of the bards, laments for members of their own families, wife, child, or children. One such is 'Ar iasacht fhuaras Aonghas' (As a loan did I get Aonghas) attributed to the thirteenth-century Donnchadh Mór Ó Dálaigh; it is a lament for the poet's son in which impassioned sorrow is movingly expressed in correct and disciplined verse.[5]

Very near to being personal poems are some of the religious verses of the bards. In these the poet temporarily releases himself from the strictures of his professional craft, and faces the eternal. But habit does not die easily, and God can readily become the supreme chief who can do the poet many favours. One

---

[1] See below, p. 697.

[2] The full poem, 'A Ghearóid déana mo dháil' (O Gearóid, plead my cause), was published by McKenna in *Ir. Monthly* (Sept. 1919), pp 509–14; see also Mac Cionnaith, *Dioghluim Dána* (Dublin, 1938), pp 201–6. For Eleanor Knott's translation, see above, p. 324.

[3] 'A theachtaire thig ón Róimh' (messenger who comes from Rome) in *Dioghluim Dána*, pp 220–23; see now Mac Con Midhe, *Poems*, pp 204–13.

[4] *Aithdioghluim Dána*, i, 174–6.

[5] *Dioghluim Dána*, pp 211–14.

of the best-known religious poets was the fifteenth-century Franciscan, Philip Bocht Ó hUiginn. A substantial amount of his verse has been preserved, and has been edited by Lambert McKenna.[1] Philip Bocht had obviously been a poet before becoming a member of the Franciscan order. Little in his verse reflects Franciscan ideas; his religious concepts are those of his bardic contemporaries. Of these McKenna, writing on the chief religious ideas of bardic poetry, says:

Some of the concepts and conceits of the bardic style are not merely quite unknown in the religious literature of any other country, but are such as to surprise—even unpleasantly—the ordinary pious mind. . . . The far-fetched analogies, the unnatural and often untheological conceits, and the unfamiliar points of view adopted by the bards make their verses on the Passion very difficult to understand, and destroy almost completely the devotional effect of their poems. The cause of their complexity and obscurity is, perhaps more than anything else, the bard's love of playing with paradoxes, especially those which arise from a confusion—deliberately introduced—between the Persons of the Trinity.[2]

A COLLECTION of love poems by T. F. O'Rahilly,[3] made from various manuscript sources, has had considerable influence on opinions held regarding Irish literature of this period. The earliest of the poems belongs apparently to the fourteenth century; the greater part is of late sixteenth- or seventeenth-century date. This work contained a remarkable essay on Irish love poetry written by Robin Flower. Flower saw this verse as originating in Provence, and penetrating Ireland by means of the Anglo-Norman invasion. He writes:

Their characteristics are fairly clear. The subject is love, and not the direct passion of the folk-singers or the high vision of the great poets, but the learned and fantastic love of European tradition, the *amour courtois*, which was first shaped into art for modern Europe in Provence, and found a home in all the languages of Christendom wherever a refined society and the practice of poetry met together. In Irish, too, it is clearly the poetry of society. . . . The other contributors to this anthology belong to a class which had no representative in England, the bardic order. . . . In this happy union the aristocrats of position contributed the subject, the aristocrats of art the style. By their intermediation the matter of European love-poetry met the manner of Irish tradition.[4]

In the origin of this type of verse Flower sees Gearóid Iarla, or Gerald, third earl of Desmond (d. 1398), as a very important figure:

The first recorded practitioner of the kind is Gerald the Rhymer, fourth [*sic*] earl of Desmond, of that great family of the FitzGeralds—the 'Greeks' and 'Florentines' of Ireland—which played such a part in the history of Irish literature. He was lord chief justice of Ireland in 1367, and in 1398 he disappeared, says the tale, and sleeps below the

---

[1] *Philip Bocht Ó hUiginn* (Dublin, 1931).

[2] Ibid., pp xiv, xviii.

[3] *Dánta Grádha: an anthology of Irish love poetry (A.D. 1350—1750)* (Dublin and Cork, 1926). This is an amplification of an earlier edition which appeared in 1916.

[4] Ibid., pp xi–xii.

water of Loch Gur, whence he emerges every seven years to ride the ripples of the lake.... There can be no reasonable doubt that in men such as this our poetry came into being. Acquainted with both worlds, the French world of the matter and the Irish world of the manner, they were admirably placed for introducing this new thing into Irish verse.[1]

That the Anglo-Normans and Gaelic Irish should mix, and that the mixing should not in some way affect the mood of Irish verse, might be considered unlikely. Yet it may be reasonably questioned if Flower has produced solid evidence to demonstrate that this type of verse is, indeed, a mixture of the efforts of the 'aristocrats of position' (Anglo-Norman) and the 'aristocrats of art' (Gaelic). It is doubtful if a single feature in the whole collection can be shown to be necessarily French in origin. Indeed, since the bulk of the verse is somewhat late, English influence in the Tudor period may have greater claims than the more remote French influences postulated by Flower.

Since Flower's essay the position has been changed by the publication of thirty poems from the Book of Fermoy which were certainly written by Gearóid Iarla.[2] The existence, but not the content, of these poems was known to Flower. If there had been in the thirteenth or fourteenth centuries a marked influence of French, or specifically Provençal, poetry, one would expect to find some traces of it in this substantial collection. There are not, in fact, any discernible French features. Gearóid Iarla was not a great poet and it is doubtful if this collection would have survived were it not for his exalted public position. He could best be described as writing in a sub-bardic tradition. The approach is bardic, the ideas are bardic, but the metrical technique is amateur. He is, as one would expect, a poet without extensive training who does his best to imitate his professional predecessors and contemporaries. He shows a wide knowledge of Irish tales and traditions, such indeed as one would expect from an Irish lord who was a constant recipient of poetry. From these poems we can learn a little about Gearóid Iarla. He was deeply devoted to the Blessed Virgin. She was his chosen saint, and following the example of many Middle Irish poets, he likes to conclude every poem, whatever its subject, with a stanza in her praise. He had such a deep friendship for Diarmaid (d. 1381), son of Cormac Mac Carthaigh, that at some time in their lives he made a compact with him that he would include a reference to Diarmaid in every poem he wrote. Possibly the two were fostered together, but, however it be, this is a well-known bardic practice. He usually couples his stanza to Diarmaid with a stanza or two dealing with the hero of the Fianna, Diarmaid son of Donn Ó Duibhne, lover of Gráinne. It seems clear that in some playful way he identifies Diarmaid Mac Carthaigh with Diarmaid Ó Duibhne, and references to the latter are implicitly references to the former. Any theory of the influence of French verse upon Irish will not rest easily upon the figure of Gearóid Iarla, as revealed in his poems.

[1] *Dánta Grádha: an anthology of Irish love poetry* (A.D. *1350–1750*) (Dublin and Cork, 1926), pp xii-xiii.

[2] Gearóid Mac Niocaill (ed.), 'Duanaire Ghearóid Iarla' in *Studia Hib.*, iii (1963), pp 7–59.

The aristocratic amateur of literature was probably, from the earliest period, a not uncommon phenomenon in Irish society, and the name of Flannacán son of Cellach, king of Brega (d. 896) springs to mind: he has left a poem, 'Innid scél scaílter n-airich' (Tell the tale of the leader), which has a certain general importance for the history of Irish saga.[1] The Gaelic aristocratic figure in the post-invasion period that invites comparison with the Anglo-Irish Gearóid Iarla is Maghnus Ó Domhnaill, lord of Tír Conaill (d. 1563). At least five of his poems have survived.[2] These show him as a graceful poet. In particular his three-stanza lament for his wife or departed lover, 'Cridhe lán do smuaintigh-thibh' (Heart full of thoughts), has a rare gem-like quantity; a comparison of this with a longer poem made by Gearóid Iarla (poem XXI) under similar circumstances leaves no doubt as to the superior talent of Ó Domhnaill. Not merely was Ó Domhnaill a poet but he was a literary figure in a broader sense. As a fairly young man he set about composing a comprehensive biography of his renowned kinsman, St Colum Cille. He conceived of the original 'Life' as having been lost through the depredations of the Norse; by collecting every-thing relevant to the saint that had survived, he could recreate it. It is character-istic of earlier Irish literature that a poem is thought of as a final evidential statement and the name of its creator is commonly attached to it. But prose was not final; it could be changed from scribe to scribe, added to and taken from. Hence it was not a high prestige product and, while there were exceptions, an author's name was rarely attached to it. Ó Domhnaill composed with pride and deliberation, using the first person in his writing. He has left a rare type of statement telling how the work was brought into being. As a man of wealth and position he had secretarial and professional help, but the final shaping he claims as his own:

Bidh a fhis ag lucht legtha na bethad-sa gorab é Maghnas, mac Aeda, mic Aeda Ruaid, mic Neill Gairb, mic Toirrdelbaigh an fina hi Domhnaill, do furail an cuid do bi a Laidin don bethaid-si do cur a n-Gaidhilc, & do furail an chuid do bi go cruaid a n-Gaidilc di do cor a m-buga, innus go m-beith si solus sothuicsena do cach uile.

Et do thimsaig & do tinoil an cuid do bi spreite ar fedh shenlebor Erenn di, & do decht as a bel fein hí, ar fagail t-shaethair ro-moir uaithe, & ar caitheam aimsiri faide ria, og a sduidear cindus do cuirfed se gach en-chuid in a hinad imcubhaid fen amail ata scribtha annso sis.

Et ar n-gabhail baide & brathairsi dó rena ard-naem & réna combrathair genelaig & réna patrun gradhach fen, da raibe se ro-duthrachtach.

A caislen Puirt na tri namat, umorro, do dechtagh in betha-so an tan ba shlan da bliadain dec ar. xx. ar cuic. c. ar. m. bliadan don Tigerna.

(And be it known to the readers of this 'Life' that it was Manus O'Donnell son of Aed, son of Aed Ruadh, son of Niall Garbh, son of Toirdelbach of the Wine, that bade put

[1] Ed. Kathleen Mulchrone in *Jn. Celt. Studies*, i (1950), pp 80–93.
[2] O'Rahilly, *Dánta Grádha*, poems 49–53.

into Gaelic the part of this 'Life' that was in Latin, and bade make easy the part thereof that was hard Gaelic, to the end it might be clear and easy of understanding to all.

And he collected and assembled the part thereof that was scattered throughout the ancient books of Erin, and he set it forth with his own lips. And passing great labour had he therewith. And much time did he give thereto, conning how he might put each part thereof in its own fitting place as it is writ here below.

And having conceived the affection and the love of a brother for his high saint and kinsman by lineage and his dear patron that he was bounden to in steadfast devotion.

In the castle of Port Na Tri Namat [Lifford] in sooth this 'Life' was put together in the year that twelve and a score and fifteen hundred years were fulfilled from the birth of Our Lord.)[1]

THE Anglo-Norman invasion was not followed by any immediate or dramatic abandonment of the older types of Irish narratives. The learned classes still read and copied the early sagas. But with every generation these were becoming less intelligible. Hence new versions were made of 'Táin Bó Cualnge', probably at some time in the period 1200–1400, and these are known as Recension IIb (Stowe) and Recension III. The earliest surviving manuscript of the Stowe version was written in 1633, and in this form approximately the tale has survived into modern times. As its editor (Cecile O'Rahilly) says:

This IIb version of the Táin is of considerable interest, being, as it were, the 'end-product', for it is the version which gained much popularity among later scribes and which is found in numerous manuscripts of the seventeenth, eighteenth, and nineteenth centuries.[2]

'Longas mac nUislenn', the old story of the love of Deirdre and Noíse, and the consequent exile of Fergus mac Roig, was remade in a romantic style, probably at the same period, and in this form, under the title 'Oidheadh Chlainne Uisnigh' (The death of the sons of Uisneach) it has survived into the modern tradition. It came to be combined in manuscripts with two other medieval tales loosely derivative of the mythological cycle 'Oidheadh Chlainne Lir' (The death of the children of Lir) and 'Oidheadh Chlainne Tuirinn' (The death of the children of Tuireann). These three tales are described in late manuscripts as 'Trí truagha na scéalaigheachta' (The three tragedies of storytelling). At some time, perhaps in the fourteenth century, 'Acallam na Senórach' was subjected to revision, and in this form has survived in a single manuscript of the seventeenth century.[3] Similarly in the sagas of the kings there are new versions of old tales. 'Aided Fergusa maic Léiti' (The death of Fergus son of Léite) appears in an amusing, original, and developed form as 'Echtra ríg thuaithe Luchra is Lupracán go hEmhain agus fochonn báis Fherghusa mhic Léide ríg

---

[1] *Betha Colaim Chille: life of Columcille*, ed. Andrew O'Kelleher and Gertrude Schoepperle (Urbana, Ill., 1918), pp 6–7.

[2] *T.B.C. (Stowe)*, p. viii.

[3] *Agallamh na Seanórach*, ed. Nessa Ní Shéaghdha (3 vols, Dublin, 1942–5).

Ulad' (The expedition of the king of the people of Luchra and Lupracan [leprachauns] to Emhain and the cause of the death of Ferghus son of Léide, king of the Ulaid). Tales of central dynastic figures, such as Cormac mac Airt and Niall Noígiallach, are modernised, and Brian Bóruma appears as a character in what are apparently new creations such as 'Leigheas coise Céin' (The curing of Cian's leg).

The Fionn cycle of tales continued to grow, and here may be mentioned some few of the principal compositions. 'Feis tighe Conáin' (The feast at the house of Conáin) is a kind of frame tale and is of some international interest as containing the 'hand down the chimney' motif, an analogue to the Grendel incident in 'Beowulf'. 'Cath Fionntrágha' (The battle of Ventry) is a boisterous picture of Fionn defending Ireland against mythical invaders; it is a blood-thirsty tale and exists in a fifteenth-century manuscript written for a lady named Sadhbh Ó Máille. A tale, 'The chase of Síd na mBan Finn and the death of Finn'—the title is Kuno Meyer's—is found, unfortunately incomplete, in the Book of Art Buidhe mac Murchadha Caomhánach; it is dated by Meyer to the thirteenth or fourteenth century.

Most of these tales tend to be inferior to the best of Old Irish prose narrative. They lack the variety of style characteristic of the older material, the good conversational passages and the direct observation of life and character.

This period is characterised by what may be called a vigorous 'ballad' tradition mostly concerning Fionn and the Fianna. In his *The Ossianic lore and romantic tales of medieval Ireland* (Dublin, 1955), Gerard Murphy considers two possibilities: that the Irish tradition rose independently or that it was the result of the impact upon Irish literature of the west European ballad, mainly represented by the English and the Danish traditions. He proceeds from a definition of the ballad as found in William J. Entwhistle's work *European balladry* (Oxford, 1939): 'any short traditional poem sung, with or without accompaniment, in assemblies of people'. Although the ballad traditions of most countries were not to reach their apogee till the fifteenth and sixteenth centuries, ballads must have arisen at a much earlier period. Various scraps of evidence led Entwhistle to conclude that the origin of English and Danish balladry may with probability be dated to the mid-twelfth century. Certain Irish ballads found in the Book of Leinster would in Murphy's opinion point to a somewhat earlier origin for west European balladry, that is, of course, assuming that Irish balladry arose under the influence of the English and European ballad. Murphy then, allowing for the possibility that Irish ballads developed independently from the speech poems which had been common in Irish prose tales, concludes that in view of the close coincidence of dates in the rise of Irish balladry and of west European balladry in general, 'it seems wiser to regard the Irish movement as connected essentially with the European'.

In the course of this discussion Murphy admits that the early speech poem must have had a close influence on the form of the Irish ballad since they are hardly ever told in the third person: 'they are, as it were, overgrown dramatic lyrics, in which the narrator of the story either takes part in the action or is closely connected with those who did so.'

While Murphy's discussion of this matter is interesting, his conclusions as to the partial derivation of the Irish ballad from the west European tradition are open to doubt. The great mass of *dindshenchus* poems, many of them dating from the ninth and tenth centuries, are ballads within the terms of Entwhistle's definition. Going back further still to the sixth century, the two surviving poems of Luccreth moccu Chiara, 'Conailla Medb míchuru' and 'Ba mol Midend midlaigi',[1] each tell a short traditional story in the third person. From all this it would seem reasonable to conclude that the telling of a short traditional story in verse form, for public recitation, goes back in Ireland to the pre-literary period and, if there is a genetic connection with the balladry of Europe, it must be on a prehistoric level.

This period was dominated by the 'romantic tale', a term which includes compositions referred to above, such as 'Cath Fionntrágha' and 'Feis tighe Conáin'. Here also the question of external influence, and its extent, arises. A lengthy study of these tales, and their partial survival in the modern folk tradition of Ireland and Scotland, has been made by Alan Bruford.[2] To quote Bruford:

These romantic tales are romances not unlike those current in other European countries during the later middle ages: rambling episodic stories of battle and magic, sometimes loosely unified by a quest theme. The favourite continental settings, the courts of King Arthur and Charlemagne, are used for a few of them. But, like the late Icelandic *lygisögur*, they could also draw on an older native tradition of prose writing. In the fifteenth century a Gaelic story-teller had the experience of some seven hundred years of romancing behind him, and scribes were still busy copying tales from the earliest periods into manuscripts for their masters: it is not surprising then that . . . older Irish models had more influence on the style and content of the romances than anything from abroad.

Bruford continues:

The romantic tales were designed to be read by or to members of the leisured classes, and generally to be read aloud, whether in a prince's hall or a lady's bower. The authors were probably professional men of letters, laymen, but trained to write or at least to use words. Their productions would be known at least to those of the Irish and Hiberno-Norman nobility, who, like Gearóid Iarla, took an interest in literature—and since the panegyric poetry which was part of every petty chieftain's public life often quotes from prose tales, probably any chief and his retainers would have some knowledge of them.

Early Irish tales are, generally speaking, restricted geographically to the Gaelic areas of Ireland and Scotland, and to the Irish Otherworld. There is

[1] See above, vol. i.
[2] Alan Bruford, 'Gaelic folktales and medieval romances' in *Béaloideas*, xxxiv (1966 [1969]).

awareness of the island of Britain and of the British; nor did the Roman occupation and the Saxon conquest go unnoticed. There is knowledge of Gaul and Spain, of the Alps, and, in 'Táin Bó Froích', a reference to Lombardy. These references by no means represent the limits of Irish geographical knowledge, but the outer world did not impinge very much on the Old Irish tale. In the period of the romantic tales Ireland opened itself to the wider world of Europe, Asia, and Africa. But apart from the already well-known regions of Britain and western Europe the geography of the tales is vague. There are no problems of colour or communication. Gaelic is universal and the royal dynasties of the world bear Gaelic names. There are mythical kingdoms such as *An Dreolann*, a parallel to the Ruritania of modern English fiction. The discovery of America was ignored, suggesting perhaps that the creative period of Irish romantic fiction did not long survive the year 1492.

THE question of the central position of Connacht in Irish learning in the post-Norman period, the questions of the 'ballad' and of the 'romantic tale' may be affected by certain material, largely unpublished, in the Book of Uí Mhaine. This material is in verse; the items tend to be too long for the use of the term 'ballad' but could properly be called 'metrical romances'. These range over Irish saga, covering both the Ulster–Connacht cycle and the matter of Fionn and the Fianna, and draw too upon biblical and classical history. A date in or about 1300 might be thought of and the question of common authorship may well arise in the case of some of the items. Here it must suffice to mention two.

In the first item, 'Carn Fraoich, soitheach na saorchlann' (Carn Fraoich, goodly house of the noble kindreds) a poet collected traditions concerning Fróech of the Gamanrad of Connacht.[1] Working mainly on the old saga 'Táin Bó Froích' (which tells of the love of Fróech for Findabair), drawing slightly on 'Tochmarc Treblainne' (The wooing of Treblann), another love story concerning Fróech, and supplementing this with *dindshenchus* material and his own imagination, the poet created a useful Early Modern version of the older saga. The poem is intended as a glorification of Carnfree (Carn Froích), the inauguration site of the kings of Connacht. St Patrick makes a brief appearance, when he confers this 'hill of warriors' upon Duach Galach, a fifth-century ancestor of the ruling dynasty.

The second item to be mentioned is the poem 'Fuaid i ceand reisi méidhi' (Stitch the head to the neck),[2] a composition of 179 quatrains. This poem could be called 'The battle of Magh Tadhuirn (Tabhuirn)'. The period is that of Conchobar mac Nessae. Herod (Iruath) and the host of Africa, together with his allies, the kings of Greece and Italy, are in Magh Tadhuirn in northern Britain, ready to challenge the northern peoples, the Irish, the British, and the Northmen (*Lochlainn*). Ireland is for the moment united under Conchobar, and

---

[1] See James Carney, 'Carn Fraoich soitheach na saorchlann' in *Celtica*, ii (1962), pp 154–94.
[2] *Bk Uí Maine*, f. 147ᵛa.

all the greater heroes of the Connacht–Ulster cycle are there. Magh Tadhuirn (Tabhuirn) is the *Campus Taberniae* of Patrician tradition, supposedly St Patrick's birthplace, and victory is won by anticipating his virtues; his birth there is foreseen in vision by the druid, Cathbad. The narration is by Conall Cernach who recounts this battle as the major portion of a lament for the death of his fosterling Cumscraid Menn Macha, son of Conchobar, and his successor in the kingship of the Ulaid.

FROM about 1400 on there was considerable activity in bringing the outer world into the Irish ambience by means of translations into Early Modern Irish. This new form of the language was more or less standardised, being the prose counterpart of the bardic language of the period. Its general characteristics are directness, simplicity, and an avoidance of rhetoric and archaism. These characteristics are found to a greater degree in the religious and scientific material; narrative may tend towards the more elaborate style of the romantic tale. This standardised language was an effective instrument in use over the whole Gaelic world, that in which Irish and Scottish Gaelic lords communicated by letter, and possibly to some extent in speech. Poetry admitted popular or dialect forms, as it were, on a kind of licence. The prose of the period also admitted popular forms, but not necessarily those sanctioned by the poetic schools. A peculiar instance of difference concerns the preposition *dochum* (towards), which in forms such as *chun* has survived into modern speech. For some reason the word was forbidden in poetry, but freely used in prose.

Translation literature is of three types: religious; medical, scientific, and philosophical; and literature intended to be informative or entertaining.

The associated items 'The invention of the holy cross' and the story of Fortibras (Fierebras)[1] may be cited as religious literature, though they might as easily be classed as romance. These are found in manuscripts of the late fifteenth century; a copy of the Latin original, of slightly earlier date, is found in T.C.D. MS 667. The Latin text is thus an intermediary between the Irish text and 'Fierebras', the Old French *chanson de geste* composed about 1200.

One of the most popular religious texts was that edited under the title 'Smaointe Beatha Chríost'.[2] It is a translation of the 'Meditationes vitae Christi' (falsely attributed to St Bonaventura) made in the middle of the fifteenth century by Tomás Gruamdha Ó Bruacháin, a canon of the choir of Cill Aladh (Killala, County Mayo). Other religious tracts of about the same period are a translation of Lothario dei Conti's (later Pope Innocent III) 'De contemptu mundi sive de miserio conditionis humanae'[3] and a translation

[1] Whitley Stokes, 'The Irish version of Fierabras' in *Rev. Celt.*, xix (1898), pp 14–57, 118–67, 252–91, 364–93; xx (1899), p. 212.
[2] Ed. Cainneach Ó Maonaigh (Dublin, 1944).
[3] *An Irish version of Innocent III's De contemptu mundi*, ed. James A. Geary (Washington, 1931).

(perhaps by the same translator) of 'Instructio pie vivendi et superna meditandi'.[1] Both texts are translated from Latin.

No medical or scientific textbooks or herbals have survived from pre-Norman Ireland. But there is evidence of the survival into Christian times of a system of magico-medicine based on a knowledge of herbs. Some Old Irish incantations, which were a part of this system, are found in early religious manuscripts, as well as in medical manuscripts of the fifteenth and subsequent centuries. Very curiously some Old Irish curative formulae, in a somewhat corrupt state, are found in Anglo-Saxon sources. The opening words of one such charm used (in conjunction with a paternoster) when a man or beast swallows a worm, are 'Gono mil orgo mil marbu mil' (I slay a beast, I destroy a beast, I kill a beast).[2]

In the period after the Anglo-Norman invasion, certainly by the fourteenth century, the Gaelic Irish abandoned their ancient system and came under the influence of the Arabian scholastic medicine of western Europe. Among the advantages of this change was the introduction of Arabic numerals into Ireland. A perusal of the copious medical writings of this period led Fr Francis Shaw to feel confident 'that there is no text amongst them that does not derive either directly or at some slight remove from a Latin non-Gaelic original'.[3] He states further that the texts show that the new Irish medical learning was derived, not from the nearer northern universities (Oxford, Paris, Cologne), but rather from the southern schools of medicine such as Montpellier, Salerno, Padua, and Bologna. However, evidence is scanty, and while we know of the presence of an Irishman at Montpellier as early as c. 1330, one 'Johannes de Kylloylac O Kannin',[4] it is not clear that such contacts were either numerous or continuous. Furthermore, the evidence adduced by Shaw may merely reflect the fact that the southern universities were the ultimate source of the Arabian tradition in western Europe generally.

Only a small proportion of the corpus of medical and scientific material has been published, and none of the associated philosophical texts.[5] The more important published material includes: an astronomical work, partly translated and partly adapted from a Latin translation of an Arabic treatise[6] by the eighth-century Messahalah of Alexandria; a version of the 'Rosa Anglica' of the fourteenth-century Englishman, John of Gaddesden;[7] a translation of a handbook of gynaecology and midwifery attributed to the controversial Trotula, a

[1] Ed. John MacKechnie (2 vols, London, 1933–46; Ir. Texts Soc., xxix).

[2] J. H. G. Grattan and Charles Singer, *Anglo-Saxon magic and medicine* (Oxford, 1952), pp 64, 106.

[3] Francis Shaw, 'Medicine in Ireland in medieval times' in William Doolin and Oliver Fitzgerald (ed.) in *What's past is prologue: a retrospect of Irish medicine* (Dublin, 1952), p. 11.

[4] Ibid.

[5] For an account of the manuscript remains of the philosophical material see Francis Shaw, 'Medieval medico-philosophical treatises in the Irish language' in *Féil-sgríbhinn Eóin Mhic Néill*, pp 144–57.

[6] *An Irish astronomical tract*, ed. Maura Power (London, 1914; Ir. Texts Soc., xiv).

[7] Ed. Winifred Wulff (London, 1929; Ir. Texts Soc., xxv).

supposed eleventh-century female professor at the medical school of Salerno;[1] a translation of the 'Regimen sanitatis' of the thirteenth-century Magninus of Milan.[2] All these translations seem to be of fifteenth-century date. From approximately the same period there are fragments of Irish versions of medieval lapidaries[3] and tracts on diseases of horses.[4]

In the category of literature of entertainment and information a notable figure was Fínghin Ó Mathghamhna, a local chieftain from Fonn Iartharthach in south-west Cork, who died in 1496. Ó Mathghamhna translated the Book of Ser Marco Polo from what is known as the 'defective English version', itself a translation from French.[5] In 1475 he translated 'The buke of John Maundeville' for the benefit of 'whosoever would fain know the best way to wend from every country to Jerusalem and the holy places that are thereabout'.[6] His literary interests are referred to in the annalistic notices of his death. In *A.F.M.* (*sub anno* 1496) he is given as *saoi eccnaidhe illaidin & i mberla* (a wise man, learned in the Latin and English languages); under the same year in *A.U.* there is what appears to be an oblique reference to his work on the Marco Polo text where he is described as *eolach i sgelaibh in domain th[s]oir* (learned in the history of the world in the east). Interest in the east is also shown in two Irish versions of the medieval forgery, the 'letter of Prester John'.[7]

To the fifteenth century also may be assigned 'Lorgaireacht an tSoidhigh Naomhtha' (The pursuit of the Holy Grail);[8] the beginning of this substantial text is missing, and the title is that supplied by the editor. The style is, quite suitably, close to that of the romantic tales. This text was apparently translated into Irish from a lost English version of what is known as the Vulgate version of 'La queste del Saint Graal', usually attributed to Walter Map (Gautier de Mapes); the Irish text has some importance in a study of the history of the romance. The editor writes (pp ix–x):

The French romance is followed incident for incident, and although much detail of description and circumstance is omitted, nothing of consequence appears which was not, we feel sure, in the copy the translator had to hand. . . . Above all, the true spirit of the work is faithfully transmitted, and the Irish reader coming to the 'Quest' in translation is in no way hindered thereby from appreciating it as the story of how man may attain to the good life, told allegorically in terms of medieval chivalry.

Somewhat later in the history of translation literature is 'Stair Ercuil agus a

---

[1] Ed. Winifred Wulff in *Ir. texts*, v (1934).
[2] Ed. Séumas Ó Ceithearnaigh, *Leabhair ó láimsgríbhnibh*, ix, xi, xii (Dublin, 1942–4).
[3] David Greene, 'Lapidaries in Irish' in *Celtica*, ii (1952), pp 467–95.
[4] Brian Ó Cuív, 'Fragments of two medieval treatises on horses' in *Celtica*, ii (1952), pp 30–63.
[5] Whitley Stokes, 'The Gaelic abridgement of the Book of Ser Marco Polo' in *Z.C.P.*, i (1897), pp 245–73, 362–438, 603.
[6] Whitley Stokes, 'The Gaelic Maundeville' in *Z.C.P.*, ii (1898), pp 1–63.
[7] See David Greene, 'The Irish versions of the letter of Prester John' in *Celtica*, ii (1952), pp 117–45.
[8] Ed. Sheila Falconer (Dublin, 1953).

bás' (The history of Hercules and his death).[1] This work was translated from an English book, Caxton's *The recuyell of the historyes of Troye*, printed probably in 1474; Caxton's work was itself a translation of Raoul Lefevre's *Recueil des histoires de Troyes*, which was begun in 1464 and printed in 1478. The Irish translation, according to the editor (p. xxv), was probably made in the last quarter of the fifteenth century. The work is known from a single copy in T.C.D., MS 1298, written by Uilliam Mac an Leagha, and the editor is of the opinion that Mac an Leagha was not merely the scribe but also the translator. To the same translator are to be attributed two other works taken from English sources: the romances of Guy of Warwick and Bevis of Hampton.[2] The suggestion is also made (*Stair Ercuil*, p. xxxix), that to Mac an Leagha is to be attributed 'Betha Mhuire Eigiptacdha' (The life of Mary of Egypt); this was taken apparently from a lost English work which was ultimately dependent on a French original.[3]

In all this literature of entertainment and information there is a consistent picture of increasing external influence on Irish from at least the beginning of the fifteenth century onwards; the impact of English is direct and that of French indirect.

[1] Ed. Gordon Quin (London, 1939; Ir. Texts Soc., xxxviii).
[2] Ed. F. N. Robinson in *Z.C.P.*, vi (1908), pp 9–104, 273–338, 556.
[3] Ed. Martin Freeman in *Études Celt.*, i (1936), pp 78–113.

CHAPTER XXVI

Literature in Norman French and English to 1534

ALAN BLISS AND JOSEPH LONG

A NUMBER of different languages were spoken by the Anglo-Norman invaders of Ireland. The rank and file included Welsh bowmen and Flemish men-at-arms whom Henry I had planted in Gower and south Pembroke. It does not appear, however, that either Welsh or Flemish made any extensive or lasting impression upon the dialects of south-east Leinster. It was once believed that the archaic dialect that survived into the early nineteenth century in the Wexford baronies of Forth and Bargy owed something to the influence of Flemish, but this view is now wholly discredited.

The ruling families of the FitzGeralds, Barrys, Carews, and other sharers of the conquest, who had been established for two generations in the south of Wales, brought the Norman French language with them to Ireland. This was the language of the ruling caste in England at the time, and was to remain so for more than a century to come. It was not until the reign of Edward I that the speech of the Anglo-Saxon population became the second language of the English king and of the aristocracy. Up to the reign of Henry IV, the first king whose mother tongue was English, French maintains its position as the language of the court and enjoys a status of prestige, although already losing ground in current use.

The form of French that appears in documents emanating from Irish sources shows similar general characteristics to Anglo-Norman—the spelling of which, it should be pointed out, is highly unstable. It may be possible, when a sufficiently wide body of material of Irish provenance has been analysed, to discern constant features which would define Hiberno-Norman, at least in its written particularities; for the present, it is not possible to speak of Hiberno-Norman as a distinctive form of language.

Medieval Hiberno-English, on the other hand, is quite distinct from the dialects of Middle English to which it is related; some manuscripts of doubtful provenance have been identified as Hiberno-English on the strength of their language alone. The identification of a dialect of Middle English is based on the concurrence in a single text of a number of linguistic features not found in association elsewhere; most, though not all, of the linguistic features found in medieval Hiberno-English occur also in dialects of Middle English, but never all together concurrently. In general, as might be expected, the linguistic character of medieval Hiberno-English resembles that of the Middle English dialects of the south-west counties and of the south-west midlands; individual features occur in Herefordshire, Gloucestershire, Somerset, Devon, Shropshire, and Wales, but the dialect of none of these areas has all the features in combination. A few features are rare or unknown in the dialects of Middle English, and are probably due to the influence of Irish: among these are the confusion in spelling of *t* and *th* (*thyme*, 'time'; *tis*, 'this') and the writing of *w* for *v* (*yewe*, 'give'; *ewill*, 'evil'). In some respects medieval Hiberno-English is a conservative dialect: it preserves *hit*, the older form of 'it'; and the ending *-y* of the infinitive, as in *auordy*, 'afford', survives until the middle of the fifteenth century, long after it had become obsolete in England. Yet in one respect it is a very advanced dialect. The Middle English dialects of the south-west and south-west midlands were rather conservative in their treatment of final unstressed *-e*, which they preserved well into the second half of the fourteenth century, though it was early lost in the dialects of the north and north midlands. Yet in the earliest monuments of medieval Hiberno-English final unstressed *-e* is already wholly lost; it is written at random, without consideration of historical propriety. As McIntosh and Samuels point out,[1] the early loss of *-e* must be due to the mixed dialectal origins of Hiberno-English. Though the Middle English dialects of the south-west and south-west midlands are all conservative in their treatment of final *-e*, they do not preserve it in all positions; each preserves it in only some of the cases in which it should historically appear, and the different dialects have a different distribution of survival. If the Irish colonists, as seems probable, spoke a number of different dialects of Middle English, their use of final *-e* would have been far from uniform; and uniformity could only be achieved by the total loss of the sound.

It is not to be supposed that medieval Hiberno-English was wholly uniform; but it has not as yet proved possible to set up a system of local dialects within Hiberno-English. A number of texts that conform on the whole to the general pattern also display features characteristic of the northern dialects of Middle English; one of them, like a Latin poem in the same manuscript,[2] contains a reference to Richard FitzRalph, archbishop of Armagh. It is possible that the more northerly parts of Ireland were colonised by settlers from Lancashire and neighbouring counties, who may have come either directly or from the Isle of Man.

What is the relationship, historically, between English and French as spoken in Ireland? Or in other words, to what extent and how lastingly did the French-speaking newcomers establish their language in the Irish colony, both as a

---

[1] Angus McIntosh and M. L. Samuels, 'Prolegomena to a study of medieval Anglo-Irish' in *Medium Aevum*, xxxvii (1968), pp 1–11.　　　　　　　　　　[2] See below, p. 734.

spoken and as a literary tongue, before abandoning it in favour of the other vernaculars? Its establishment as the language of administration and government is easier to trace, as its use for this purpose parallels the situation in England, and documents continue to appear down to a late date. It is less easy to survey its development as a living idiom in speech and literature, and to document with accuracy its replacement in these functions by English and Irish. The references to language questions which abound in the English chronicles are not to be found for Ireland, and original texts are extremely few. What evidence there is has been used to draw somewhat exaggerated conclusions, so that Norman French has been hailed as one of 'the three rivals for linguistic supremacy in medieval Ireland'[1] along with Irish and English. This is probably overstating the case. In England, it may have appeared at one time as if French was about to gain the upper hand over the native tongue; it cannot be said that it ever so appeared in Ireland. We shall therefore examine and attempt to reassess the documents available for the external history of Norman French in Ireland.

Little remains of whatever Norman French literature Ireland may have produced. Apart from a few minor fragments, notably some verses attributed to the first earl of Desmond, two pieces of consequence stand out. The first of these is the narrative poem on the coming of the Anglo-Normans which G. H. Orpen published in 1892 under the title of *The song of Dermot and the earl*. The editor places the date of composition between 1200 and 1225, with the reservation that the greater part of the text could well have been written earlier. The other is a poem of some 200 lines describing in humorous vein the fortifying of the town of New Ross in 1265.

These texts indicate that during the generations which followed the invasion, Norman French was able to establish itself as a vehicle for literary expression. It is true that they are not all of equal value as documents to prove this point. The attempt at historiography represented by the 'Song of Dermot' may have been addressed to a limited audience, and the few verses in a personal note from the hand of the earl of Desmond, if they were circulated at all, may not have been intended for more than a few friends. A quite different view, however, must be taken of the unsophisticated verses from the town of New Ross, which are of all the more interest and value as they are precisely dated and localised.

One might object, and it is true, that we have no absolute proof of the author being himself a native of the town or even born amongst the colonists in Ireland, but the brief account of the text given later in this chapter will suffice to show how personally the poet interested himself in the detailed affairs of the town community. Even the most cautious conclusion must allow that conditions are such in the later thirteenth century that incidental verses of this kind came to be written in French; and the piece, if it shows no exceptional talent, is clearly not a once-for-all-time effort by someone quite unlettered. For

[1] Edmund Curtis, 'The spoken languages of medieval Ireland' in *Studies*, viii (1919), p. 235.

example, it is resolved to build as part of the defence works a gate which will be called *la porte des dames*, and to construct the prison nearby. 'Bon serreit estre en prisun de dame' says the poet, and his sadly conventional gallantry at least reveals some familiarity with the commonplace conceits of love lyric. It is clear that at this time not only were trade and industry flourishing in the Anglo-Norman town of New Ross, but literature too was beginning to emerge. It is worth noting, as does a recent editor of the text,[1] that the manuscript remained in local hands in the later sixteenth century, at which time it was in the possession of George Wyse, a member of a noted family of the town of Waterford. The existence of this poem is evidence that verse-writing in French was an object of interest and encouragement, and that there was a public for French literature of a minor genre among the inhabitants of this active centre of trade.

The implantation of Norman French in thirteenth-century New Ross is evidenced by documents of a different nature, for that language figures, along with Latin, in inscriptions appearing on coffin-lid tombstones of the period. One such stone is described as bearing a floreated cross and incised inscription which reads: *Julia ke fu la feme Simon Gaunter git ici Deu de lalme eit merci*. (Julia who was the wife of Simon Gaunter lives here. May God have mercy on her soul.) The Simon Gaunter mentioned may be identified with some probability as one who was provost of Rosponte (that is, New Ross) for the year 1288–9, for this name is to be found on a list of provosts extracted from the accounts and records of the Bigods, earls of Norfolk and lords of the liberty which included New Ross.

Obviously, the use of French on funereal monuments does not allow any inference to be drawn as to its continued use in writing or in speech. In fact, from the end of the thirteenth century on, it becomes increasingly difficult to glean any signs pointing to the survival of French as a living language in the major towns.

Some indications may be gathered from the Red Book of Ossory, which is preserved at the episcopal palace, Kilkenny. Richard Ledred (Leatherhead), who was bishop of Ossory from 1317 to *c.* 1361, was concerned about the great interest displayed by his clergy in 'vile, secular songs', and as a counter-measure he composed himself a number of Latin hymns of more edifying inspiration. Interspersed with the Latin hymns in the manuscript are fragments of eight songs, two in French and six in English, apparently representing the profane compositions that are condemned, and inserted so as to indicate the air to which the sacred songs should be sung. The two French fragments are certainly undistinguished:

> Harrow! ieo su trahy
> Par fol amour de mal amy

(Alack! I am undone by reckless love for a faithless lover)

---

[1] Hugh Shields, 'The walling of New Ross: a thirteenth-century poem in French' in *Long Room*, xii–xiii (1975–6), pp 24–33.

Heu alas par amour
Qy moy myst en taunt dolour

(Alas for love that put me in such sorrow.)

The point is that both vernaculars are represented in these traces of popular songs which were possibly composed, and surely sung, in Kilkenny in the early fourteenth century. This is not to say that the city was bilingual: it is going too far to speak of 'the two languages which we know from the fragments of love songs preserved in the Red Book of Ossory were spoken in Kilkenny at this period'.[1] But it does at least suggest that the earlier language had not entirely disappeared from the streets.

The use of French on a public occasion is attested in a colourful incident which occurred in 1324. The same bishop of Ossory, Richard Ledred, was with great ruthlessness pursuing his case against the celebrated Dame Alice Kyteler, accused of witchcraft, who remains a legend in Kilkenny to this day. Dame Alice, who had married four times, was well connected with persons of influence, including the chancellor of Ireland, and it is probably fair to say that the ecclesiastical persecutions were not unrelated to secular feuds. The hectic affair is recorded in a contemporary Latin narrative, which modern commentators attribute to Ledred himself, and which certainly favours the latter's point of view. On 23 April, the bishop forced his way into the court of the seneschal, Arnold le Poer, bearing the sacrament in a golden vessel and accompanied by his clergy carrying lighted candles. In spite of mistreatment and abuse by the seneschal, the bishop delivered his summation, demanding the aid of the secular power for the arrest of the guilty parties; this summation, of which the Latin text is quoted, he thrice repeated, in English and in French: *quam quidem monitionem dictus episcopus tam in Anglico quam in Gallico coram toto populo tertio replicavit*. The narrator probably means that the requisition was uttered once in each of the three languages. In any event, the bishop used French, not surely 'so that all should understand',[2] but the better to impress his hearers and to discountenance his opponent. Twice previously, he had used a similar tactic, exploiting the dignities of his office to the discomfiture of his enemy; in this instance, in addition to his escort of clergy and liturgical effects, he is availing himself of what was the official language of public law and justice. It is excessive to suggest on the basis of this incident that a state of bilingualism existed in Kilkenny at the beginning of the fourteenth century.

The fact is that we have no unequivocal evidence of French still being used as a common vernacular at this period, even among the inhabitants of the strongest colonial settlements. On the contrary, the ever more frequent condemnations from official sources of the progressive hibernicisation of the colonists testify to a very different situation, which we shall now examine.

---

[1] St John D. Seymour, *Anglo-Irish literature 1200–1582* (Cambridge, 1929), p. 46.
[2] Edmund Curtis, 'Spoken languages', p. 243.

The preamble to the statute of Kilkenny (1366) makes no mention of French, but notes the abandonment of the English language in favour of Irish:

... but now many English of the said land, forsaking the English language, fashion, mode of riding, laws, and usages, live and govern themselves according to the manners, fashion, and language of the Irish enemies. ...

A royal decree issued a few years earlier (1360) to the sheriff of Kilkenny contains a similar statement:

Many of the English nation in the marches and elsewhere have again become like Irishmen ... and learn to speak the Irish tongue, and send their children among the Irish to be nursed and taught the Irish tongue, so that people of the English race have for the greater part become Irish.

The adoption of native ways is not new at this date, but goes back several generations. The parliament of 1297 had already noted the problem.

Englishmen ... attire themselves in Irish garments and having their heads half-shaven grow and extend the hairs from the back of the head and call them *culan* conforming themselves to the Irish as well in garb as in countenance, whereby it frequently happens that some Englishmen reputed as Irishmen are slain, although the killing of Englishmen and of Irishmen requires different modes of punishment.[1]

The statute of 1366 makes it clear that English is the established tongue, whose place is now contested by Irish, and its intention is to legislate on this very question. Although Norman French is to survive for several centuries as a legal jargon, and although it is used as such in this very statute, which is written in that language, it receives no mention; plainly, it is no longer in the field as a spoken idiom and does not have to be considered. The divorce that can exist between the living, spoken idiom of a community and a technical or learned jargon used for special purposes is exemplified in the text of this statute.

As the *lingua franca* of commerce and trade, Norman French is preserved in the numerous documents recording the activities and transactions of the energetic merchants and traders of the Anglo-Norman settlement in Ireland. It appears even to have had some use as a jargon in the conduct of business at the Irish court of the exchequer. The Red Book, or official record volume, of the exchequer contains an ancient drawing, apparently of the early fifteenth century, which depicts the court and its officials in the performance of their everyday tasks and duties. The chequered table occupies the centre of the sketch; to the left are three magistrates, to the right three suitors, and to the rear the remembrancer, the 'clerk of the pipe', and other officers. In the background, the crier is in the act of adjourning the court, exclaiming 'A demain'. One of the magistrates is exclaiming 'Soient forfez', another 'Voyr dire'; facing them across the table, one of the suitors with arms extended is protesting 'Chalange', while another exclaims 'Soit oughte'. This document gives striking testimony

---

[1] *Stat. Ire., John—Hen. V*, pp 210–11; cf. above, p. 387.

to the use of French, not only in the formula of dismissal pronounced by the crier, but even in the regulating of business between suitors and judges.[1]

French was used in acts of parliament from 1310 to 1472, alternating occasionally with Latin. It is only after 1472 that English came to be used in acts of parliament. Prior to that date, government documents generally as well as municipal records, statutes, and ordinances are either in French or in Latin. The case of Waterford city, where English appears in such documents as early as 1365, is exceptional. When French came to be replaced by English, that language was at first used concurrently with Latin, as Norman French had been previously; after 1450 the use of Latin declined, and by 1500 the use of English had become normal. Throughout the fifteenth century and the first half of the sixteenth the English used was still unmistakably Hiberno-English; characteristic dialectal features survived later in Ireland than in England, where a standard uniform official language had developed relatively early.

The earliest municipal archives in English are those of Waterford. The acts and statutes of the city are recorded in Hiberno-English from 1365; a set of 'notable precedentes, used and accustomed for laudable ordenances' begins in 1407. Both of these documents were copied out in about 1525, and it is possible (though hardly probable) that they were originally recorded in Latin or French and translated into English in 1525. The records of the corporation of Kilkenny as preserved in the 'Liber primus' present a more normal picture. The first entry in English is dated 1434, but the use of English does not become regular until 1467; Latin is used concurrently with English up to 1537. In the earlier period, both Latin and Norman French occur, but the French texts are not original recordings of proceedings—Latin is used for that—but citations of pertinent statutes, letters patent, and such documents. The last such article in Norman French is a copy of a statute of 25 Edward III (1350–51). Only one record entry is in French, and that significantly is the earliest and the only one that relates to the thirteenth century: it is an act of the commonalty of Kilkenny concerning the election of sovereigns, provosts and councillors for the town, and is dated 1231.

The Chain Book of the city of Dublin, which is cited in the old municipal records as a standard authority on the laws and regulations of the city, contains under the title of 'Les leys et les usages de la cité de Diuelin' a transcript in an early fourteenth-century hand of diverse regulations and laws, charter clauses and grants pertaining to the city. Similar texts of borough customs exist for Waterford and Cork. The White Book of the Dublin corporation consists of copies of documents connected with the properties and rights of the city, and contains a notable petition in French by which the common folk of Dublin pray the mayor, bailiffs, and commonalty to remedy defects in government grievous to them, especially during the troubles occasioned by the Scottish enemies, and the general war of the Irish, who daily menace the city. The earliest English in the White Book occurs in 1471; in the Chain Book English does not

---

[1] *Facs. nat. MSS Ire.*, iii, plate I.

appear until 1486. The records of the Dublin merchants' guild were kept in English from 1438 onwards. The earliest English document in the Dublin assembly rolls is dated 1447; the earliest in the statute rolls is dated 1450; the Tipperary ordinances belong to the same period. The statutes of the town of Galway, entirely in English, begin in 1485.

Hiberno-English was also used in the fifteenth century for private documents such as deeds, and also for memoranda and letters. The earliest deed seems to be one executed by Thomas Butler, prior of Kilmainham, in 1417; four were executed by the Blake family in Galway between 1430 and 1449. In 1429 the parliament at Dublin sent a memorandum in English to Henry VI. A letter from James Cornwallis, chief baron of the exchequer of Ireland, belongs to the same period. In 1432 the mayor and town of Limerick complained to the exchequer. A letter from the earl of Ormond was written in Kilkenny about 1435; a complaint against the earl of Ormond belongs to 1441, a set of articles against him to 1442. A letter from Richard Wogan to Henry VI is also dated 1442.[1] A memorandum from the county of Kildare to Richard, duke of York, was written at Naas in 1454. A letter from the dean of Dublin to the earl of Ormond is rather later, and a letter from the mayor of Youghal is dated 1475. After 1500 the use of English becomes too commonplace to be worth detailed comment. After the middle of the sixteenth century, however, the English used no longer shows any signs of Hiberno-English dialect characteristics; Hiberno-English has been replaced by standard official English. The fortunes of the spoken language present many problems, which are followed up in a later chapter.[2]

It is impossible to estimate how much of the literature produced in Ireland in Norman French and in English has been lost. Certainly the quantity which has survived is rather small in comparison with what has survived in England. It must, however, be remembered that the survival of medieval literature in any language has been largely a matter of chance; and the virtual supersession of Norman French and English by Irish towards the end of the medieval period must have greatly reduced the chances of survival of works in these alien and obsolescent languages.

In Norman French two substantial works survive. The first of these, probably written between 1200 and 1225, is a poem on the coming of the Anglo-Normans; it is generally known by the title that Orpen devised for his edition, *The song of Dermot and the earl*. The text is preserved in a single manuscript transcribed in all likelihood at the end of the thirteenth century and now among the Carew papers of the archiepiscopal library in Lambeth palace (MS 596). What survives is a fragment; a number of lines are missing at the beginning, and the narrative ends abruptly after 3,459 lines with the arrival of Raymond le Gros

---

[1] A number of letters in English appear in the register of John Mey, archbishop of Armagh 1443–56. See *Registrum Iohannis Mey*, pp 133, 156, 168, 177–8, 262–3, 372–3, 377, 404.

[2] Below, iii, 546–60.

before Limerick in October 1175. The defective opening passage provides our only information about the author of the work and the source of his material, and as it has been the object of conflicting interpretations, it merits quoting here:

> . . . Par soen demeine latimer
> Que moi conta de lui l'estorie
> Dunt faz ici la memorie.
> Morice Regan iert celui
> (Buche a buche parla a lui)
> Ki cest jest endita:
> L'estorie de lui me mostra.
> Icil Morice iert latimer
> Al rei Dermot, ke mult l'out cher.
>
> (. . . By his own interpreter
> Who gave me the account of him
> Which I here record
> Morice Regan was the man
> (Face to face he spoke to him)
> Who related this tale:
> He set forth the history of him to me.
> This Morice was interpreter
> To King Dermot, who held him dear.)

These lines have for long been misinterpreted and understood to mean, not that Morice Regan 'was the man who related this tale', but that Morice Regan 'spoke to him who related this tale'. Thus Orpen supposes that Morice Regan spoke to the author of a lost earlier chronicle, and that he passed on this chronicle to the author of the extant poem. In the introduction to his edition, Orpen considers in some detail the implications of this transmission both for the dating of the composition and for the assessment of its value as an historical document. His interpretation was challenged by J. F. O'Doherty,[1] whose explanations unfortunately served only further to obscure the issue, as they were based on the same misreading of the text. In O'Doherty's view, it was not Morice Regan who provided the composer of our 'Song' with his source material, but an unidentified secretary of an unnamed *bacheler* (who may, he suggests, have been Strongbow); this secretary was allegedly in possession, if not himself the author, of a rhymed chronicle, and the composer of this earlier chronicle had in turn been in communication with Regan, secretary to Mac Murchada. This devious interpretation cannot, however, be reconciled with the text correctly understood. French usage, both medieval and modern, requires that the antecedent to the relative *ki* (line 6) be a demonstrative such as *celui* and not a personal pronoun such as *lui*. The text cannot be read as

---

[1] J. F. O'Doherty, 'Historical criticism of the Song of Dermot and the Earl' in *I.H.S.*, i, no. 1 (Mar. 1938), pp 4–20.

meaning that Morice Regan 'spoke to him who related this tale'; it can only mean that 'Morice Regan was the man . . . who related this tale'.[1]

The punctuation of the text as given above makes the meaning clear: Morice Regan, interpreter or secretary to King Diarmait Mac Murchada, communicated his material directly to our author, who drafted the extant poem. The next question is to know what was the nature of the materials so provided? Did they constitute a full and complete account, or merely a sketch of events? Were they in oral or written form, and in what language? Orpen argues that they must already have been in the form of a French verse chronicle, on the basis of references throughout the text to *la chanson*, *la geste*, *l'estorie*, or *l'escrit* as authority for particular statements. But this may be giving unwarranted weight to such conventional formulae as *Si la geste ne nus ment*, or *selon l'escrit*, which are little more than filler lines or half-lines, most frequently used to supply a rhyme; and it does not tally well with the passage just quoted, which does not suggest that the role of our author was no more than the mere transcribing of a pre-existing French verse narrative. Our writer is, however, at pains to emphasise the fact that he has derived his information, whatever form it took, from so uniquely privileged a source as Morice Regan, secretary to one of the principal personages in the story, in direct personal contact with him—*buche a buche parla a lui*—and enjoying his special favour—*mult l'out cher*—so that we may perhaps assume, in view of this insistence upon the authoritativeness of his source, that he respected the materials supplied to him and reproduced their substance faithfully.

The period covered corresponds to the years 1152–75, beginning with Diarmait's intrigues and his abduction of Derbforgaill, wife of Tigernán Ua Ruairc—whom, according to our poet, Diarmait only pretended to love, his real motive being revenge, whereas her love for him was sincere—down to the assault on Limerick by Raymond le Gros and the king of Osraige. A later event, the taking of Slane castle, which the Four Masters record for the year 1176, is alluded to in an anticipatory fashion in lines 3178–3201.

It is inaccurate to refer to the poem as a *chanson de geste*, as do most commentators. The poem relates to quite a different established genre, that of the vernacular verse chronicle, which in Norman French literature had been most illustriously represented by the works of Wace. The verse form used is not the ten-syllable line in assonanced groupings or *laisses* characteristic of French epic, but appropriately the eight-syllable line in rhyming couplets as cultivated by the chroniclers and by the romance writers. The account is given markedly from the point of view of the Anglo-Norman invaders. The enemies of Diarmait are felons and traitors, and King Diarmait's own worthiness is

---

[1] Joseph Long, 'Dermot and the earl: who wrote "The song"?' in *R.I.A. Proc.*, lxxv (1975), sect. C, pp 263–72.

praised with as much eloquence as the poet can muster, which unfortunately is not very great:

> En Yrland, a icel jor,
> N'i out reis de tel valur:
> Asez esteit manans e richez,
> Ama le[s] francs, hai les chiches.

(In Ireland, at that time, there was not a king of such valour. He was very rich and powerful. He loved the generous, he hated the mean.)

On occasion the bare narrative is given variety by a briefly penned portrait of one of the heroes, such as that of Philip de Prendergast in lines 3044–51, or more frequently by the recording of direct speech, such as Diarmait's address to King Henry in lines 272–91. Otherwise the work appears to be that of a mediocre rhymester, in whose defence it can be said, perhaps, that the text preserved in the manuscript may be a much corrupted copy of the original, which had been written some three generations earlier.

Orpen believed that the poem is not in any way derived from Giraldus Cambrensis, and that it is 'an entirely independent authority for the facts it records'. Although Giraldus and our author generally corroborate one another, they do not always report the same events, and even when they do, it is with just such differences in detail and in treatment as would suggest that they were deriving their material from distinct sources. The poem's reliability on some points of fact is questionable, but it has been much prized by historians, who recognise it as a primary authority for the period of the invasion, and it remains a most valuable document, being the only attempt at Irish historiography in the language of the invaders.

The second substantial work in Norman French is a poem on the entrenchment of the town of New Ross ('Rithmus facture ville de Rosse' according to the title given in the manuscript) dated 1265. It describes the measures taken by the townsfolk to protect their prosperous mercantile port against possible acts of violence occasioned by the feud between 'Sire Morice e Sire Wauter'; that is, between Walter de Burgh, earl of Ulster, and Maurice fitz Maurice, who represented the Geraldines in Connacht. The poet speaks as an eyewitness, and explains in sprightly verse how the labour of digging the trench is shared out, according to each trade and craft: on Monday, the vintners, the mercers, the merchants, the drapers set to work from prime to noon, as many as 1,000 of them, accompanied by flute and drum, their banners leading them out. On Tuesday it is the turn of the tailors, coatmakers, dyers, fullers, and saddlers, to the number of 400; similarly for each day of the week, until on Sunday the ladies of the town come forth to lend a fair hand and to go singing round the fosse. In this way, a labour force of over 3,200 souls is recruited—for the poet constantly quotes figures, with the one exception of the fair ladies, whose numbers are, he says, beyond reckoning. The fosse is twenty feet in depth, its length extends over a league. When the work is completed, the inhabitants will be able to sleep securely, without need for a watch, for not 40,000 enemies coming against them will be able to take their town. As if further to discourage prospective assailants, the poet details the arms available and the defenders to hand: 104 mounted knights, 363 crossbowmen, 1,200 archers, 3,000 men armed with lances or axes—a considerable garrison for the time, if we accept the figures as accurate. But the townspeople are peace-loving, and are not to be blamed for providing their own defence: there is no more hospitable town on mainland or island, and any foreigner is made welcome there and freely allowed to conduct his trade:

> Kar ce est la plus franch vile
> Qe seit en certain ne en yle;
> E tot hom estrange est ben venu,
> E de grant joi est resceü,
> E chater e vendre en pute ben,
> Qe nul hom ne li demandra reen.

The two remaining snatches of Norman French to be considered here occur in the same manuscript as the New Ross poem. Each occupies six lines of writing. The first is a series of proverb-like sentences composed of words beginning with the letter F: 'Folie fet qe en force s'afie'; 'fortune fet force failire', etc. Below this comes the rubric 'Proverbie comitis Desmonie' and the following text:

> Soule su, simple, e saunz solas,
>   Seignury me somount sojorner,
> Si suppris sei de moune solas,
>   Sages se deit soul solacer.
> Soule ne solai sojorner,
>   Ne solein estre de petit solas.
> Sovereyn se est de se solacer,
>   Qe se sent soule e saunz solas.

These verbal acrobatics might be rendered, rather tentatively, in the following manner:

> Alone am I, simple and solace-less,
>   Seignory bids me to stay
> And so I am deceived of my solace.
>   A sage should seek his solace from himself.
> Alone I was not wont to stay
>   Nor sullen be of little solace.
> Sovereign it is to solace self
>   Who feels alone and solace-less.

The attribution in the rubric to the earl of Desmond seemingly refers to Maurice fitz Thomas, created first earl of Desmond in 1329. That event set the seal on his triumph over Arnold le Poer, with whom he had been conducting a feud for many years. It may well be that the newly-created earl found the leisure to indulge in such pieces of verbal jugglery, but the feeling expressed corresponds better to later circumstances. The fall of Roger Mortimer and the reversal of political fortunes in England brought about his undoing and his imprisonment in August 1331 at the hands of the justiciar, first in Limerick and afterwards in the castle of Dublin. The second line suggests just such a predicament: authority bids him to remain where he is. It is difficult to accept the suggestion of St John Seymour that *seignury* means the tyranny of love and that our vigorous earl is therefore writing a melancholy love lyric. In any case, we must note that Maurice fitz Thomas apparently devoted himself to literary exercises before ever he became earl, for it is recorded that his enemy le Poer, amongst other abuse and *enormia verba*, jeeringly called him 'a rymour'.

The manuscript in which the last three items occur, Harleian MS 913 in the British Library, is well worth further consideration, since it also contains seventeen items in English[1] and thirty-one in Latin. It must once have contained at least one more item in English, since an early seventeenth-century transcript of it in Lansdowne MS 418 (also in the British Library) includes the first stanza of an additional poem. The Irish provenance of the manuscript is not in doubt; the evidence is clear and abundant. A list of Franciscan provinces begins with the provinces of Ireland, not with those of England; four Irish towns (Drogheda, Kildare, New Ross, and Waterford) are mentioned by name; one of the English poems lauds the excellence of Piers de Bermingham in the slaughter of the Irish; as we have seen, a set of proverbs in Norman French is attributed to the earl of Desmond; the mythical and idyllic land of Cokaygne is located 'fur in see bi west Spayngne', the traditional position of Ireland according to medieval geography; and finally, at least three Irish loanwords are used in the English texts: *corrine* (Irish *coirín*, 'can'), *eri* (Irish *éraic*, 'compensation'), *keperin* (Irish *ceithearn*, 'band of soldiers'). A fourth word, *russin*, is equivalent in form to Irish *roisín*, 'lunch', but the Irish word may perhaps ultimately be of English origin.[2]

It is also certain that the manuscript has some connection with the Franciscan order: as well as the list of Franciscan provinces already mentioned, two of the Latin items deal directly with St Francis, and a third is the work of the Franciscan archbishop of Canterbury, John Pecham. Further than this it is difficult to go. It has often been claimed that the manuscript is a product of the Franciscan abbey in Kildare: the author of one of the English poems names himself as Friar Michael of Kildare; and Piers de Bermingham, the subject of another poem, was buried in the abbey. On the other hand, the mention of New Ross and of Waterford suggests an origin much further south than Kildare. A marginal note in Lansdowne MS 418, dated February 1608, refers to our

---

[1] The English items are printed by Wilhelm Heuser, *Die Kildare-Gedichte* (Bonn, 1904).
[2] Tomás de Bhaldraithe, 'Roisín/Ruisín' in *Eriu*, xxxi (1980), pp 169–71.

manuscript as 'a smale olde book in parchm. called the book of Ross or of Waterford'; the scribe first wrote 'Cork', then deleted it and substituted 'Ross'. The date of the manuscript can be determined with some confidence. One of the items, already referred to, is the work of John Pecham, archbishop of Canterbury from 1279 to 1292; another is by Theobald, archbishop of Assisi from 1296 to 1319; Piers de Bermingham, whose death is lamented in the poem which bears his name, died in 1308; the first earl of Desmond, to whom the Norman French proverbs are attributed, did not receive this title until 1329. It would seem that the manuscript cannot have been completed until about 1330; and the features of the language in which the English poems were written makes it difficult to date it much later than this.

The later history of the manuscript is rather well documented. On folio 2 is an inscription reading *Iste liber pertinet ad me Georgium Wyse*, and this George Wyse has been plausibly identified with the George Wyse who was mayor of Waterford in 1561 and bailiff of Waterford in 1566. On folio 29 is another inscription, barely legible, which seems to read *Iste liber pertinet ad Ihoe lambard ... Waterfordie*. ... Whether or not the manuscript was compiled in Waterford, it seems certain that it was there in the sixteenth century. In 1608 some seven items from the manuscript were transcribed for Sir James Ware into the 'volume of miscellaneous Irish collections' which subsequently became MS Lansdowne 418. By 1697 our manuscript was in the possession of John Moore, bishop of Norwich, as no. 784 in his library: it was described in Bernard's *Catalogi librorum manuscriptorum Angliae et Hiberniae*, published in that year. In 1705, however, it was in the possession of Thomas Tanner, later bishop of St Asaph. In that year George Hickes, in his *Linguarum vett. septentrionalium thesaurus*, printed 'The land of Cokaygne' from a codex that had been sent to him by Tanner (*quem ad me pro humanitate sua misit, qui ab omnibus antiquorum studiosis, de quibus optime meruit, summo cum honore nominandus est*, Tho. Tanner). Possibly Moore had lent the manuscript to Tanner, who had still not returned it at the time of Moore's death. At all events, it did not pass with the rest of Moore's library to the university of Cambridge; in circumstances unknown it came into the hands of Robert Harley, first earl of Oxford, and passed to the British Museum with the rest of his library in 1754.

The contents of Harleian MS 913 are very miscellaneous, but two clear tendencies are discernible: on the one hand, towards the religious, on the other hand, towards the satirical; the two tendencies are not independent, since the satire is often directed against the clergy. The nature of the Latin satires can be well illustrated by three successive entries in Wanley's catalogue of the Harleian manuscripts.

5 A song against the luxurious abbat & prior of Gloucester, in vile Latin rhythms (but in the manner of hymns) the author using poor Priscian most barbarously, on purpose.

6 *Hore sompnolentiam adversus capitulum*. This is the divine service, villainously altered, by way of abuse upon some slothful & lazy convent.

7 *Missa de potatoribus*, this is even much more villainous (or rather blasphemous) than the former.

The English pieces, as will appear in more detail below, are also mainly religious and satirical. The Norman French items, as we have seen, are of rather a different kind. The English pieces are rather difficult to classify: they are scattered through the manuscript, and are linked together in a complex pattern by their form, by their content, and by the hands in which they are written. They can, however, be divided into three general categories: religious poems apparently of Irish provenance; secular poems apparently of Irish provenance; and poems which are known not to be of Irish provenance, since identical or similar texts also occur in other manuscripts.

The most interesting of the religious poems is the one which gives the name of its author, Friar Michael of Kildare. It is usually called a hymn,[1] but this title is misleading, since it is addressed not to God but to rich men. It is written in a unique and complex metre. The ten-line stanzas rhyme *a a a b a b a b a b*; the *a*-lines have four stresses, the *b*-lines three; the last two *a*-lines have internal rhyme in the middle of the line, so that eight *a*-rhymes in all are called for. The pattern can be illustrated by the final stanza, which gives the author's name:

> þis sang wroȝt a frere [menour],
> Iesus Crist be is socure;
> Louerd, bring him to þe toure,
> 　Frere Michel Kyldare;
> Schild him fram helle boure,
> Whan he sal hen fare!
> Leuedi, flur / of al honur,
> 　Cast awai is care;
> Fram þe schoure / of pinis sure
> 　þou sild him her and þare!　Amen.

(A friar minor composed this song—may Jesus Christ be his help! Lord, bring him to the tower [of heaven], Friar Michael Kildare! Save him from the lodging of hell, when he must journey hence! Lady, flower of all honour, free him from sorrow! From the torrent of bitter torments shield him in all circumstances! Amen.)

The poem begins with two conventional stanzas addressed to Christ, and ends with another conventional stanza followed by the stanza just quoted. The eleven intervening stanzas constitute the core of the poem. They are addressed to 'þe riche men' or to a 'riche man', who is exhorted to remember that life is short, death will come, and wealth will not pass the grave. The descriptions of the plight of the poor man are particularly striking:

> þe pouer man bit uche dai
> Gode of þe, and þou seiist ai:

[1] Heuser, *Kildare-Gedichte*, pp 81–5.

> 'Begger, wend a deuil wai!
> þou deuist al min ere.'
> Hungir-bitte he goth awai
> Wiþ mani sorful tere.

(Every day the poor man begs alms of you, and you always say 'Beggar, go to the devil! You're deafening me.' Pinched with hunger he goes away weeping miserably.)

Though the homiletic content of the poem is commonplace enough, its highly developed social consciousness is unusual, and perhaps reflects the attitudes of the Franciscan order in Ireland; as we shall see, social consciousness is characteristic of many of the poems in this manuscript.

There are four religious poems which, though they do not occur consecutively in the manuscript, seem to belong together in metre, content, and tone; the first two are written by one hand, the second two by another. The titles usually given to them are: 'A sermon', 'Fifteen signs before the judgment', 'The fall and passion', and 'The ten commandments'.[1] All are written in four-line stanzas rhymed *a b a b*—common enough later, but a rare metre at this date. All contain religious instruction of a type popular in the middle ages. Though only the first is commonly called a 'sermon', all take a similar form and include direct exhortations addressed to a congregation. The beginning of 'The fall and passion' is characteristic:

> þe grace of god ful of miȝt
> þat is king and euer was
> Mote amang vs aliȝt
> And ȝiue vs alle is swet grace:
>
> Me to spek and ȝou to lere [*recte* here]
> þat it be worsip, lord, to þe,
> Me to teche and ȝou to bere [*recte* lere]
> þat helplich to ure sowles be.

(May the grace of almighty God, who is and always was our king, descend among us; and may he give his sweet grace to all of us—to me to speak, and to you to hear, so as to do honour to you, Lord; to me to teach and to you to learn, so that it may be helpful to our souls.)

The content of the 'Sermon' bears some resemblance to that of Friar Michael's 'Hymn'. Its sixty stanzas are concerned mainly with the transitoriness of human wealth, and the vanity of human pride and ostentation. Some of its language is crude and vivid:

> Man, of þi schuldres and of þi side
> þou miȝte hunti luse and flee;
> Of such a park i ne hold no pride,
> þe dere nis nauȝte þat þou miȝte sle.

(Man, you can hunt the louse and the flea from your shoulder and your side; I take no pride in such a park: the game you can kill is of no value.)

[1] Ibid., pp 89–96, 100–105, 106–12, 114–16.

Man must consider the coming judgment, described in fearsome terms. The remedy is to honour God and his church, and—as also in the 'Hymn'—to remember the poor; by this means man can come to heaven, full of every comfort, both physical and spiritual. The poem ends with the promise of a seven-year indulgence to all those who have come to hear the sermon. The poem of the 'Fifteen signs before the judgment' is no more than a fragment, since some leaves have been lost from the manuscript. Only twelve of the fifteen signs are described in the surviving forty-five stanzas. The theme was a popular one in the middle ages, and this poem is a free translation of an extant Old French original. 'The fall and passion' links together in a continuous narrative the major episodes of the Old and New Testaments. The first twenty stanzas describe the fall of the angels, the creation, and the fall of man. The treatment is not free from naiveté, as the following stanzas about the serpent show:

> Whi com he raþer to Eue
> þan he com to Adam?
> Ichul ȝou telle, sires, beleue,
> For womman is lef euer to man.

> Womman mai turne man is wille,
> Whare ȝho wol pilt hir to;
> þat is þe resun and skille
> þat þe deuil com hir first to.

(Why did he come to Eve earlier than he came to Adam? I will tell you promptly, sirs—because woman is always dear to man. Woman can turn a man's will wherever she wants to go to; that is the cause and the reason why the devil came to her first.)

The remaining thirty-four stanzas describe the birth, death, burial, and resurrection of Christ. There is only one brief attempt to link the passion with the fall:

> For þe appil þat Adam ete
> Deþ he þolid opon þe tre.

(Because of the apple that Adam ate, Christ suffered death on the cross.)

'The ten commandments' is only one of a large number of treatments of the subject in medieval English, but it is independent of the others, and appears to be older than any of them. The order of the commandments, though not unique, is not that found in the Bible. Eight of the twenty stanzas are devoted to a condemnation of oaths, and particularly of swearing by the limbs of Christ—a sin also reprehended in Chaucer's 'Pardoner's tale'; this passage corresponds to the traditional third commandment. Then come seven numbered commandments, of which the fourth is not one of the biblical ten, but is adapted from Christ's words in Matthew 22: 38:

> þe verþ: loue þi neiȝbore as þine owe bodi,
> Non oþer þou him wil.

(The fourth: love your neighbour as yourself—you must treat him in no other way.)

Finally come two unnumbered commandments, corresponding to the biblical tenth and ninth.

A fifth poem seems to be closely linked with this group. It is not so much a religious as a social poem, yet in metre and in style it closely resembles the four poems just discussed. Like them, it is written in four-line stanzas rhymed *a b a b*; but the resemblance is somewhat obscured at the beginning of the poem by the fact that the first four stanzas rhyme together in pairs, so as to produce what seem to be two eight-line stanzas. Four stanzas—three in one place and one in another—are identical (apart from insignificant verbal discrepancies) with four stanzas from the 'Sermon'. Above all, this poem shows the same concern for the plight of the common people which is characteristic of the 'Sermon', and also of Friar Michael's 'Hymn'. The poem has been entitled 'A song on the times',[1] and also 'A beast-fable' after the nature of its central part. It begins with an attack on the state of society: all is ruled by covetousness, and neither the church nor the king's ministers do anything to protect the poor people who are being plundered. The lion, king of beasts, once summoned the wolf, the fox, and the ass to answer charges of misconduct. The wolf and the fox sent gifts of geese, hens, goats, and sheep. The ass, who ate only grass, trusted in his innocence and sent nothing. The wolf and fox were acquitted, but the ass was condemned and executed for the crime of eating grass.

> þus fariþ al þe world nuþe,
>   As we mai al ise,
> Boþe est and west, norþ and suþe,
>   God vs help and þe trinite!

(This is the way the world goes now, as we can all see, east and west and north and south—may God and the Trinity help us!)

Pride, avarice, and envy rule the world. After some moralising stanzas the poem ends with a quotation from the 'Sermon':

> Anuriþ god and holi chirch,
>   And ȝiueþ þe pouir þat habbiþ nede,
> So god is wille ȝe ssul wirche
>   And ioi of heuen hab to mede.
>   To whoch ioi vs bring
>   Iesus Crist, heuen king.   Amen.

(Honour God and Holy Church, and give to the poor who are in need; in this way you shall do God's will and have the joy of heaven as your reward. May Jesus Christ, the king of heaven, bring us to that joy. Amen.)

Another poem also has connections with the 'Sermon' group, a fragmentary poem on 'The seven sins'.[2] It is written in the same hand as the 'Sermon' and 'Fifteen signs', but it is in a different metre: the introductory section consists of

---

[1] Heuser, *Kildare-Gedichte*, pp 133–9.
[2] Ibid., pp 119–24.

ten six-line stanzas rhymed *a a b c c b*; the main part of the poem is in octosyllabic couplets. Like the poems of the 'Sermon' group, the text of this poem
gives clear evidence that it was intended for use as a rhymed sermon:

> And þat ʒe hit mote vnderstonde,
> þe fend to mochil schame and schonde.
> þis predicacioune.

(May you understand this preaching, to the shame and injury of the devil!)

And again:

> Mi leue frendis, ich ʒou biseche,
> Ʒung, old, pouer, and reche,
> Herkniþ to god is speche!

(My dear friends, I beseech you—young, old, poor, rich—listen to the word of God.)

The poem breaks off when no more than three sins have been discussed, and
the rest of the page is blank. It is perhaps no more than a coincidence that the
three sins discussed are pride, avarice, and envy, the sins that are said in 'A
song on the times' to rule the world; the limitation to three sins can hardly be
authorial, since the introduction expressly promises to name all 'þe heuid
sinnes seuene'.

The seven poems discussed so far all seem to reflect the preoccupation of the
Franciscans with social abuses, and their use of rhymed sermons. Two other
religious poems are of a different type. 'Christ on the cross'[1] is an English verse
translation of a Latin prose original which is given in the manuscript; it is
incomplete, and the remainder of the last page has been left blank. The forty-
two lines that survive are curiously disparate. The first eighteen lines, rhymed
in pairs, are long, with from four to seven stresses; there is a good deal of
alliteration, though it is not used systematically. The remaining twenty-four
lines are in octosyllabic couplets. The treatment is very conventional. The
other poem, 'Nego',[2] is a satire on scholastic discussions. A quotation will illustrate the theme of the poem:

> Now o clerk seiiþ 'Nego',
> and þat oþer 'Dubito';
> Seiiþ an oþer 'Concedo',
> And an oþer 'Obligo'.
> 'Verum falsum' sette þer to—
> þan is al þe lore ido.
> þus þe fals clerkes of har heuid
> Makiþ men trewþ of ham be reuid.

(Now one clerk says 'I deny', and the other says 'I doubt'; another says 'I concede', and
another 'I compel'. Add to this 'Truth is false'—then all learning is destroyed. Thus out
of their heads the treacherous clerks bring it about that men are deprived of truth.)

---

[1] Heuser, *Kildare-Gedichte*, pp 128–9.
[2] Ibid., pp 139–40.

Much the most striking of the secular poems in Harleian MS 913 is the satirical poem 'Land of Cokaygne'.¹ This well-known poem fully deserves its high repu-tation. The theme is one popular in the middle ages and later, that of the 'happy land', where all necessities and luxuries can be had without toil; there are analogues in Old French and Middle Dutch. Our poem differs substan-tially from these, and it has been called a 'parody'² of accounts of the Other World. The land of Cokaygne is explicitly contrasted with the Christian para-dise, much to the disadvantage of the latter:

> þo3 paradis be miri and bri3t,
> Cokaygn is of fairir si3t.
> What is þer in paradis
> Bot grasse and flure and grene ris?
> þo3 þer be ioi and gret dute,
> þer nis met bote frute;
> þer nis halle, bure, no benche,
> Bot watir manis þursto quenche.

(Though paradise is gay and bright, Cokaygne is more beautiful to see. What is there in paradise but grass and flowers and green branches? Though there is joy and great pleasure there, there is nothing to eat but fruit; there is no hall, no chamber, no bench, and nothing to quench a man's thirst but water.)

After fifty lines of description the poet introduces a new note; in the happy land there is an abbey 'of white monkes and of grei', and the fortunate inhabitants of this abbey lead an idyllic existence. The abbey is described at length, in terms derived partly from Celtic legends of the Other World and partly from the Book of Revelation:

> þer is a cloister, fair and li3t,
> Brod and lang, of sembli si3t;
> þe pilers of þat cloister alle
> Beþ iturned of cristale. . . .
> Whan þe monkes geeþ to masse,
> Al þe fenestres þat beþ of glasse
> Turneþ into cristal bri3t
> To 3iue monkes more li3t.

(There is a cloister, fine and well lit, broad and long, beautiful to see; all the pillars in that cloister are turned out of crystal. When the monks go to mass, all the glass windows turn into shining crystal to give the monks more light.)

The monks are gifted with the ability to fly through the air, and amuse them-selves by organising races in the sky. Close by there is another abbey of nuns, of whom the monks have a right to take their pleasure; he who is most efficient at

¹ Ibid., pp 145–50. For an attempt to localise the poem, see P. L. Henry, 'The land of Cokaygne: cultures in contact in medieval Ireland' in *Studia Hib.*, xii (1972), pp 120–41.
² J. A. W. Bennett and G. V. Smithers, *Early Middle English verse and prose* (Oxford, 1966), p. 137.

this sport is certain to become Father Abbot. However, the ordeal awaiting any one intending to reach this happy land is severe:

> Seue ȝere in swine is dritte
> He mot wade, wol ȝe iwitte,
> Al anon vp to þe chynne,
> So he schal þe lond winne.

(He must wade, if you want to know, for seven years up to his chin in swine's dung; thus he shall get to that land.)

A second satirical poem (written in the same hand as Friar Michael's 'Hymn') is commonly known as 'A satire';[1] it is sometimes referred to Kildare, but the satire is more probably on the people of Dublin. The metre is unique: the six-line stanza consists, first, of two long lines rhymed together; then, two unrhymed long lines; then, two short lines rhymed together. In each stanza the poet devotes the two short lines to a eulogy of his own skill, as the following examples show:

> þis uers is imakid wel
> Of consonans and wowel.
>
> Sleiȝ he was and ful of witte,
> þat þis lore put in writte.
>
> Sikirlich he was a clerk
> þat so sleilich wroȝte þis werk.

(This verse is well constructed, both in its consonants and its vowels. He who put this doctrine into writing was cunning and full of intelligence. Assuredly he who composed this work so cunningly was a highly literate man.)

Every stanza starts with the word 'Hail!' The first five stanzas are addressed to Saints Michael, Christopher, James, Dominic, and Francis; next, three orders of religious are apostrophised, followed by an order of nuns and the secular clergy. Then come all the trades in turn: merchants, tailors, cobblers, skinners, butchers, bakers, brewers, hucksters, and woolcombers. Finally the poet addresses his friends and urges them to drink:

> Makiþ glad, mi frendis, ȝe sittiþ to long stille,
> Spekiþ now and gladieþ and drinkeþ all ȝur fille!
> Ȝe habbeþ ihird of men lif þat woniþ in lond;
> Drinkiþ dep and makiþ glade, ne hab ȝe non oþer nede.
>   þis song is yseid of me,
>   Euer iblessid mot ȝe be.

(Make merry, my friends, you are sitting still for too long; talk now, and rejoice, and drink your fill! You have heard about the life of the men who live in the country; drink deep and make merry, you have no other obligation. I have recited this song so that you may always be blessed.)

[1] Heuser, *Kildare-Gedichte*, pp 154–8.

The poem about Piers de Bermingham[1] is of great historical interest. The last stanza refers to a patron who caused the song to be made, and it would seem that he was a cleric:

> He þat þis sang let mak
> For Sir Pers is sake
> Wel wid haþ igo,
> Wid whar iso3t
> And god pardon ibro3t,
> Two hundrid daies and mo.

(He who caused this song to be made for the sake of Sir Piers has travelled far and wide; he has searched everywhere and has brought an indulgence for more than two hundred days.)

Whoever the patron may have been, he was motivated by intense hostility towards the Irish. Piers de Bermingham was lord of Tethmoy in Offaly; he and his associate John fitz Thomas FitzGerald (later earl of Kildare), who is also mentioned in the poem, were engaged in constant warfare against the O'Connors of Offaly; in 1305 de Bermingham treacherously slew twenty-nine of the O'Connors in his own castle. According to the poem, 'þos Yrismen of þe lond' took an oath to kill four English noblemen:

> þe erl of Vluester,
> Sire Emond þe Botiler,
> Sire Ion le fiz Tomas,
> Algate al bi name,
> Sire Pers þe Briminghame,
> þis was har compas.

(The earl of Ulster, Sir Edmund Butler, Sir John fitz Thomas, and above all Sir Piers de Bermingham—this was their plan.)

The plot became known, and the four noblemen determined that when the appointed day came they would pay the Irishmen back in their own coin. However, long before the day arrived three of the noblemen had forgotten all about it. Sir Piers was of sterner stuff, and was ready to meet the O'Connors. He had always been the terror of the Irish:

> An oþer þing also:
> To Yrismen he was fo,
> þat wel wide whare.
> Euer he rode aboute
> Wiþ streinþ to hunt ham vte,
> As hunter doþ þe hare.

(Another thing as well: he was very hostile to Irishmen in all circumstances. He was always riding about in force to hunt them out as a huntsman does hares.)

The defeat and slaughter of the O'Connors is described in somewhat obscure

[1] Ibid., pp 161–4.

terminology, which may have been colloquial; possibly, too, there are topical allusions no longer intelligible or recoverable.

The poem 'Young men of Waterford'[1] is no longer in Harleian MS 913, but its first stanza is preserved in the seventeenth-century transcript in Lansdowne MS 418. It must be mentioned here, since its theme seems to have been comparable to that of 'Piers de Bermingham': it is a warning to the young men of Waterford to defend themselves against the Powers.

> Yung men of Waterford, lernith now to plei,
> For ȝure mere is plowis ilad beth awey.
> Scure ȝe ȝur hāfelis þat lang habith ilei,
> And fend ȝou of the Pouers that walkith bi the wey,
> > Ich rede,
> For if hi takith ȝou on and on
> Fram ham scapith ther never one,
> I swer bi Christ and St Jon
> > That of goth ȝur hede.
> How hi walkith, etc.

(Young men of Waterford, now learn how to fight, for your ploughmares are being carried off. Burnish your weapons that have long been unused, and defend yourselves against the Powers who are patrolling the roads, I advise, for if they catch you one by one never a one will escape from them; I swear by Christ and St John that you will lose your head. How they walk, etc.)

The text may be corrupt, and the translation is uncertain.

One short poem in Harleian MS 913[2] deserves to be quoted in full, since it is such a remarkable *tour de force* of metre; it must be admitted, however, that the language has been so strained by metrical exigencies that translation is scarcely possible.

> Loue hauiþ me broȝt in liþir þoȝt,
> > þoȝt ich ab to blinne;
> Blinne to þench hit is for noȝt,
> > Noȝt is loue of sinne.
>
> Sinne me hauiþ in care ibroȝt,
> > Broȝt in mochil vnwinne;
> Winne to weld ich had iþoȝt;
> > þoȝt is þat ich am inne.
>
> In me is care, how i ssal fare,
> > Fare ich wol and funde;
> Funde ich wiþ outen are,
> > Ar i be broȝt to grunde.

The metrical peculiarity of this poem is that the first word of each line repeats the last word of the preceding line. Since the quatrains are rhymed, it follows

---

[1] Heuser, *Kildare-Gedichte*, p. 11.
[2] Ibid., p. 166.

that the initial words also rhyme, though the initial rhymes form a pattern which is not coterminous with the end-rhymed stanzas. A similar technique was used in French by, for instance, Deschamps and Froissart, but this instance seems to be unique in English.

Of the four poems that are known not to be of Irish provenance, since identical or similar texts also occur in other manuscripts, one is added in a blank space at the end of 'The land of Cokaygne', and in the same hand. It is commonly called 'Five evil things',[1] and reflects the concern with social and religious abuses displayed in many of the other poems:

> Bissop lorles,
> Kyng redeles,
> ȝung man rechles,
> Old man witles,
> Womman ssamles—
> I swer bi heuen kyng:
> þos beþ fiue liþer þing.

(Bishop without doctrine, king without counsel, young man reckless, old man witless, woman shameless—I swear by the king of heaven that these are five evil things.)

Two short poems[2] are in the same hand as 'The entrenchment of New Ross'— this scribe, at least, must have been bilingual. One deals with old age, and is commonly known as 'Elde', after its first word; the other, commonly known as 'Erthe', is a moralising poem marked by a punning repetition of the theme-word erþ (earth), sometimes several times in the same line. In this latter poem each English stanza is followed by a translation into Latin. The fourth poem immediately follows 'The fall and passion' and 'The ten commandments', and is in the same hand; it is a version of a popular lullaby, and is usually known as 'Lullay'.[3] In quite a different part of the manuscript, immediately after the conclusion of 'Erthe', someone has begun to draft a translation of this poem into Latin. The first stanza of the English poem and of the translation will illustrate the style:

> Lollai, lollai, litil child, whi wepistou so sore?
> Nedis mostou wepe, hit was iȝarkid þe ȝore
> Euer to lib in sorow and sich and mourne euere,
> As þin eldren did er þis, whil hi aliues were.
> Lollai, [lollai,] litil child, child, lolai, lullow,
> Into vncuþ world icommen so ertow.
>
> Lolla, lolla, paruule, cur fles tam amare?
> Oportet te plangere necnon suspirare,
> Te dolere grauiter, decet uegetare,
> Vt parentes exules nexerant ignare.
> Lolla, lolla, paruule, natus mundo tristi.
> Ignotum cum maximo dolore uenisti.

[1] Ibid., p. 184. [2] Ibid., pp 170–72, 180–83. [3] Ibid., pp 174–6.

(Hush, hush, little child, why are you weeping so bitterly? You have no choice but to weep, it was decreed long ago that you should always live in sorrow and always sigh and mourn, as your elders did before now, while they were alive. Hush, hush, little child, hush, hush, hush, you have come into an unfamiliar world.)

Literature in medieval Hiberno-English outside Harleian MS 913 is not very extensive, but some of it is of considerable interest; much of it can be accurately localised. Kilkenny is particularly well represented. Two Norman-French fragments from the Red Book of Ossory have already been quoted above, and there are seven fragments in English, the second and third of which occur more than once.[1]

> Mayde yn the moore [l]ay.

(A maiden lay in the moor.)

> Alas, hou shold y syng?
> Yloren is my playng.
> Hou shold y wiþ þat olde man
> To-leuen, and let my lemman,
>   Swettist of al þinge?

(Alas, how can I sing? All my pleasure is gone. How could I live with that old man and abandon my lover, the sweetest of all creatures?)

> Haue mercie on me, frere.
> Barfote þat y go.

(Have mercy on me, friar, that I should go barefoot.)

> Do, do, nihtyngale,
> Syng ful myries,
> Shal y neure for þyn loue
> Lengre karie.

(Sing, sing, nightingale, very beautifully. I shall never again be troubled for love of you.)

> Haue god day, my lemmon, etc.

(Farewell, mistress, etc.)

> Gayneth me no garlond of greene
> Bot hit ben of wythones ywroght.

(A garland of green is of no profit to me unless it be made of willows.)

> Hey how þe cheualdoures woke al nyght.

(Hey, how the knights lay awake all night.)

Three other poems also come from Kilkenny.[2] The first is a brief extract from a poem, otherwise unknown, on 'The old and new dispensations'; it was

---

[1] Theo Stemmler, 'The vernacular snatches in the Red Book of Ossory: a textual case-history' in *Anglia*, xcv (1977), pp 122–9.
[2] St John D. Seymour, 'Three medieval poems from Kilkenny' in *R.I.A. Proc.*, xli (1933), sect. C, pp 205–9.

written about 1300 over a faded list of names in the 'Liber primus Kilkennien-sis'. The other two date from the end of the fifteenth century, and are written on a strip of vellum found among the Ormond manuscripts in Kilkenny castle. One is a macaronic poem in English and Latin on Lucifer, and the following extract will illustrate the style:

> Lucifer was angyll bry3th
> *In arce polorum;*
> For hevest he fell full ly3t
> *At yma baratrorum.*
>
> He walkys euer yn garmentes gent
> *In plateis ville;*
> 'Y ham he, Sir, weryment'
> *Dyxit miser ille.*

(Lucifer was a shining angel in the heavenly citadel; because of pride he fell very swiftly into the depths of the abyss. He is always walking in fashionable garments in the town squares; 'It is I, Sir, assuredly', says that wretch.)

The other is the charming and well-known love-lyric 'Gracious and gay':

> Gracius and gay,
> On hyr lyytt all my tho3th;
> Butt sche rew on me today
> To deth sche hatt me broth.

(Gracious and gay, all my thought is on her; unless she has mercy on me today she has brought me to my death-bed.)

Most of the poem consists of a rather conventional description of the loved one; nevertheless, the material is well handled, and the poem conveys an effect of sincerity.

A striking satirical poem can be localised with confidence in Armagh. It is entered into the primatial register of John Swayne (archbishop of Armagh 1418–39),[1] and consists of a ferocious attack on women's fashions at the end of the fourteenth century—horned headdresses and long trains. It is only twelve lines long and is worth quoting in full:

> Fleshy lustys and festys
> And furres of divers maner of bestys
>   The devyll of hell hame first fonde
> Hole clothes ycout in scheredys
> And the pruyd of women hedes
>   Hath destrude this londe
>
> God that berreth the crone of thornes
> Destru the prude of wome[n] hornes
>   For his der passione,

---

[1] *Reg. Swayne*, p. 139.

> And let never har long taylys
> That beth the devyll of hell is saylys
> Be cause of our conficione.

(The devil of hell was the first inventor of fleshly lust, and feasts, and furs made from various kinds of animals; clothes deliberately cut into shreds, and the pride of women's headdresses, have destroyed this land. May God who wears the crown of thorns destroy the pride of women's horns, for the sake of his precious passion, and may their long trains (which are the sails of the devil of hell) never be the cause of our confusion.)

Another satirical poem,[1] in B.L. Cottonian MS Cleopatra B. II, has also often been localised in Armagh, mainly because it includes a reference to Richard FitzRalph, archbishop of Armagh, who died in 1360 and was a notorious enemy of the friars; but FitzRalph was well known outside Ireland, and it is doubtful if the language can properly be classified as Hiberno-English. The poem has been given the title 'On the Minorite friars', and the reference to FitzRalph runs as follows.

> Thai have done him on a croys fer up in the skye,
> And festned on hym wyenges, as he shuld flie.
> This fals feyned byleve shal thai soure bye,
> On that lovelych Lord so for to lye.
> With an O and an I, one sayd full stille,
> Armachan distroy ham, if it is Goddes wille.

(They have put him on a cross right up in the sky, and have fastened wings on him as if he was about to fly. They shall pay bitterly for this false fabricated belief, for lying in this way about that gracious Lord. With an O and an I (someone whispered) may Ardmachanus destroy them, if it is God's will.)

Any writer attacking the friars, in Ireland or in England, would be likely to refer to FitzRalph's well-known preoccupation, and indeed there is another reference to him in a Latin poem in the same manuscript:

> Armacan, quem cœlo Dominus coronavit,
> Discordes tantomodo fratres adunavit.

(Ardmachanus, whom God has crowned in heaven, to a certain extent united the quarrelsome friars.)

The same manuscript also contains a 'Song against the friars' which has been localised in Ireland, but the origin of this and of the poem 'On the Minorite friars' must remain a matter of uncertainty.

Another satirical poem, certainly of Irish provenance but not localisable, is 'Tutivillus'.[2] It is macaronic in English and Latin, and describes the fate of women who chatter in church:

---

[1] Thomas Wright (ed.), *Political poems and songs relating to English history* (2 vols, London, 1859–61), i, 268–70.

[2] Heuser, op. cit., p. 223.

þos women þat sitteþ þe church about,
þai beþ al of þe deuelis rowte,
  Diuina inpotentes [recte *impedientes*].
But þai be stil, he wil ham quell,
Wiþ kene crokes draw hem to hell,
  Ad pacienciam [recte *puteum autem*] *flentes*.

(The women who sit round the church are all of the devil's company, hindering divine service. Unless they keep quiet he will kill them, drag them to hell with sharp hooks, drag them lamenting to the pit.)

Towards the end of the fourteenth century a 'Treatise on gardening' was added to an English poem on 'The virtues of herbs'.[1] The language of the poem certifies it as of Irish provenance, and its origin is made quite certain by the reference it contains to 'alle of þe herbys of Ierlonde'. The poem has survived in two manuscripts, and one of them also contains a poem 'On bloodletting' and a number of medical recipes; medical recipes were also inscribed on a number of slates, dating from the first half of the fifteenth century, found in a disused church at Smarmore, County Louth.[2] A treatise on gardening, a poem on bloodletting, medical recipes—these are hardly literary documents in the ordinary sense; and in fact after 1400 the creative spring of Hiberno-English literature seems to have run dry; not a single original work in English can be proved to have been written in Ireland during the fifteenth century. Instead, interest shifted first of all to translations, then to the mere transcription of works written in England.

In the latter part of the thirteenth century an Irish Dominican friar named Geoffrey of Waterford, then living in France, translated into French a work entitled 'Secreta secretorum', erroneously attributed to Aristotle. In his preface he claims to have translated it from Greek into Arabic, from Arabic into Latin, and from Latin into French. The work is discursive, dealing with the duties of rulers, the science of physiognomy, the secret of good health, and many other topics; it is therefore peculiarly liable to interpolation and adaptation, and Geoffrey admits that he has treated it with considerable freedom. In the year 1422 Geoffrey's French was translated into English by a Dublin man, James Yonge, at the behest of James Butler, fourth earl of Ormond and viceroy in Ireland. Like Geoffrey, Yonge too treated his exemplar with the greatest freedom, and it is his additions that give the work such interest as it has. About the same time an anonymous translator produced a free rendering of the 'Expugnatio Hibernica' of Giraldus Cambrensis; the translation is not of great distinction, but some local detail is added.

The transcriptions, guaranteed as Hiberno-English by their linguistic forms, throw some light on the tastes of educated Anglo-Irishmen in the fifteenth century. There are no less than three transcriptions of 'The prick of conscience', a

[1] Arne Zettersten, *The virtues of herbs in the Loscombe manuscript* (Lund, 1967).
[2] A. J. Bliss, 'The inscribed slates at Smarmore' in *R.I.A. Proc.*, lxiv (1965), sect. C, pp 33–60.

homiletic work of the most uninspiring kind. This treatise was, in the fifteenth century, commonly attributed to the Yorkshire hermit Richard Rolle of Hampole, and a number of genuine works of Rolle were also transcribed into Hiberno-English; mystical works by Walter Hilton are also represented. Other religious works include the so-called 'Northern passion' and the 'South English legendary'.[1] The only secular works represented are the 'Proverbs of Hendyng', a compendium of traditional wisdom, and the C-text of 'Piers Plowman'. This picture can be somewhat extended from a rather later source: the library of Gerald, earl of Kildare, was catalogued in 1526, and shown to contain over a hundred titles, a sizeable collection for the time.[2] There were thirty-six items in French, thirty-two in Latin, twenty-two in English, and nineteen in Irish. Many of the English works are romances: 'Arthur', 'The siege of Thebes', 'The destruction of Troy', 'Charlemagne', and many others. There are also historical works: 'A nolde booke of the croneklys of Englond', and a work described as 'Cambrensis', perhaps the 'Expugnatio' already referred to. A work described as 'Troillus' is no doubt Chaucer's 'Troilus and Criseyde'. The French works are more varied, and include scripture, hagiography, and philosophy as well as history and romance. The historical works include the 'Chroniques de France' and Froissart; among the literary works are 'Ogier le danois', 'Lancelot du lac', 'Le roman de la rose', and 'Le jardin de plaisance'.

[1] Frances E. Richardson, 'A Middle English fragment from the First Book of Kilkenny' in *N. & Q.*, ccvii (1962), pp 47–8; O. S. Pickering, 'An unrecognised extract from the "South English Legendary" ' in *N. & Q.*, ccxvii (1972), p. 407.

[2] *B.M. cat. Ir. MSS*, i, 154.

CHAPTER XXVII

Architecture and sculpture, 1169–1603

EDWIN C. RAE

THE eleventh and twelfth centuries were a time of great reform and organisa-tion in western Europe. In both church and state, corrective measures which had already been begun were continued, and other reforms were newly insti-tuted. Irish leaders clarified and organised their country's diocesan system in a series of synods held from 1101 to 1152. Fuller implementation followed later. For the most part, the greater Irish cathedrals date from the thirteenth century, and will be discussed in the section on that period. In view of the primary importance of conventual establishments in Ireland in the twelfth century, attention will first be directed to the character of the monastic orders of the time, particularly the Cistercian, and the nature of their architecture. This sec-tion closes with a brief description of how monasteries were founded in twelfth-century Europe and an indication of some of the sources of their support.

Most spectacularly successful of the new reforming orders were the Cister-cians, founded in Burgundy in 1098. Their rule was based squarely on close adherence to a more stringent application of the original precepts of St Bene-dict. Straightforward, unembellished performance of the offices and liturgy, private prayer and pious reading, and manual labour were to be the basic con-stituents of the monk's life. By incorporating lay brothers in their monasteries, the Cistercians were able to ensure that additional labour would be available for the construction of buildings, developing and farming the fields, sheep-raising, and the like: activities which the monks might not be able to perform *plate* fully without neglecting their spiritual duties. Both the life and physical aspect *1* of the monasteries were to be spartan and uniform, although the need for more altar space led eventually to elaboration in the larger English foundations, and in some continental examples to creating a rounded east end.

Unlike their Benedictine forebears, the 'white monks' (Cistercians) made few processions. Their simple liturgy required only a shallow, rectangular chancel ('presbytery' in Cistercian usage). Usually, two or three adjoining, rec-tangular chapels projected from the east side of each arm of the transept (the *2b*

2a transverse member), and narrow aisles flanked the nave (that part of the church west of the transept). Little colour was used for walls or windows. The typical plan for Cistercian churches and conventual groups (living quarters) is seen at Fontenay (Côte-d'Or) in Burgundy, founded 'on the instructions of St Bernard' in 1118–19, most of the present buildings being constructed in the period 1130–49. There were no towers, although the much-quoted prohibition concerning such constructions was not, apparently, applied to the crossing tower, originally very low, which was sometimes added to British Cistercian churches from about the middle of the twelfth century.[1]

The site of the monastery was as remote from human habitation as possible, preferably hidden away in a valley. A supply of water was essential for the kitchen and sanitary uses of the community. The church occupied the highest part of the site. At first the buildings were often primitive: of wood, clay, perhaps even the simple 'wattle and daub' (poles and rods woven together and plastered over with clay), which appears to have been much used in Ireland for ordinary dwellings, wherever the materials were available, throughout the middle ages and later. As soon as possible these temporary shelters would have been replaced by constructions in stone.

The usual Irish Cistercian church was very large compared to most earlier religious structures in Ireland. For instance, the interior space of the eight churches within the enclosure at the Early Christian site of Clonmacnoise, County Offaly, is approximately 5,193 square feet (482.4 square metres); the
1 Cistercian church at Knockmoy, County Galway, contains 8,200 (761.7).[2] The interior was divided by walls or screens to form the monks' choir, which included the space where transept and nave cross and the easternmost bays of the nave. A limited area to the west of this (seldom shown in Irish plans) constituted a retrochoir for the infirm, and the western part of the nave formed a choir for the lay brothers. In Ireland some low dividing walls between these sections still remain at Jerpoint, County Kilkenny, and elsewhere.

In Irish Cistercian houses the claustral ensemble (monks' and lay brothers' living quarters) usually lay to the south of the church. In the east range (block of buildings) the principal features were, clockwise, beginning next to the church, the sacristy and book closet, chapter house (where the rule was explained and certain administrative business of the abbey was done), the parlour (for necessary conversation), and noviciate or monks' work room. This sequence was sometimes interrupted by a slype (passageway) running east and west. The dortor (monks' dormitory), with a latrine structure near the end away from the church, filled the second storey. Let no one assume that amenities in early times were more than minimal. At Clairvaux during the time of St Bernard

---

[1] Peter Fergusson, 'Early Cistercian churches in Yorkshire and the problem of the Cistercian crossing tower' in *Journal of the Society of Architectural Historians*, xxix, no. 3 (Oct. 1970), pp 216–20.
[2] Measurements kindly furnished by Mr R. P. Corrigan, National Parks and Monuments Branch, Office of Public Works, Dublin.

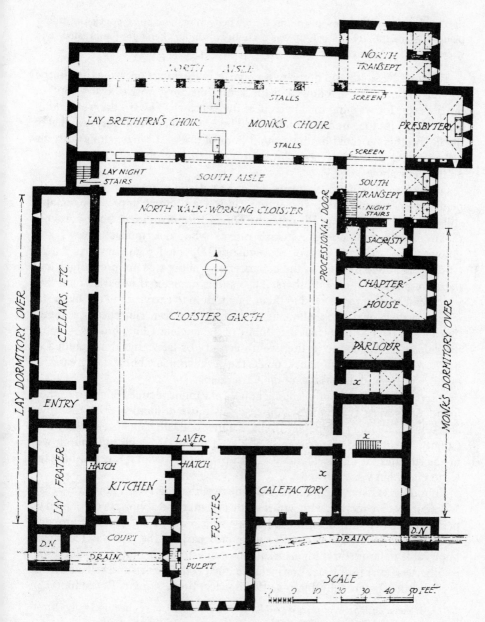

PLAN OF A TYPICAL IRISH CISTERCIAN ABBEY
Based on Jerpoint, Co. Kilkenny. Drawn by H. G. Leask

the dormitory was like a row of coffins, for the beds were mere boxes consisting of four planks. As for the abbot's cell, it was a cupboard under the stairs illuminated by a wretched slit, a hollow in the wall to serve as the seat of government.[1]

Either at the south end of the east range or in the range opposite the church was the warming room, followed by the frater (refectory), with a lavabo (font) or other device for washing the hands near the entrance. Toward the west end of this section was the kitchen, which served both the monks' refectory and that of the lay brothers located on the ground floor of the west range, along with the cellars and various other rooms for their use, the lay brothers' dormitory being on the floor above.

Of the Benedictine monasteries, so powerful and numerous on the Continent and in England, there were but few in Ireland.[2] Some impressive remains still exist at Fore, County Westmeath. The picture is different for the Augustinian canons, or 'canons regular', priests who took monastic vows and followed the brief precepts of St Augustine. Detailed regulations, of varied types, were added by most of the monasteries. Labour was not prescribed, and there were few or no lay brothers. The canons ministered in parish churches which had been appropriated to them, in addition to carrying out the monastic offices in their own establishments. A part of their own churches was sometimes given over to parochial use. Many of the ancient Celtic houses adopted the rule of St Augustine in the twelfth century or later, and these, added to newly founded establishments, made the Augustinian abbeys far greater in number in Ireland than those of the Cistercians.

There was much variation among houses of canons regular. Sometimes their foundations were as large and impressive as those of monks—Irish examples are Athassel, County Tipperary, Kells, County Kilkenny, and Newtown Trim, County Meath—and sometimes small, 'even minute'.[3] Often the church was not aisled, and the chancel tended to occupy a large part of it except where the Cistercian plan was followed.

Founding a Cistercian monastery in the twelfth century was not always easy. Normally twelve monks, with a thirteenth as leader and abbot, accompanied by perhaps some lay brothers,[4] would seek a site. A donor of a piece of property was sometimes readily at hand. But upon occasions the site was too small, impossible to farm, 'fitter for an ark than a monastery'[5] (i.e. subject to flooding), or otherwise inappropriate. For instance, the brothers tried and rejected three previous sites before they finally settled down at Boyle, County Roscommon, in

---

[1] G. H. Cook, *English monasteries in the middle ages* (London, 1961), p. 151, quoting Henry Daniel-Rops, *Cathedral and crusade* (London, 1957).

[2] Gwynn & Hadcock, *Med. relig. houses*, pp 102–9.

[3] M. D. K[nowles], 'Monastery' in *Encycl. Brit.* (1970), xv, 686.

[4] Gwynn & Hadcock, p. 116, indicate that the 'abbot with at least twelve monks' sent out to found new communities from Mellifont were accompanied by 'usually a greater number of lay brothers'.

[5] J. C. Dickinson, *Monastic life in medieval England* (London, 1961), p. 9.

1161. A few attempted foundations failed completely. Sometimes gifts flowed in, as when King Henry II in 1178 paid for replacing with lead the shingled roof at Clairvaux in France, St Bernard's own monastery, or when Cathal Crobderg Ó Conchobair (died 1224), king of Connacht, granted five marks per annum for ever to the great mother church of Cîteaux in Burgundy. At Cistercian Sylvanès in southern France various persons gave the different buildings. Monasteries of other orders might profit from the income from parish churches bestowed upon them, a gift which the early Cistercians, however, rejected. Nor did this order normally seek to raise money through the sometimes amazingly profitable cult of relics. From the thirteenth century onwards they might gain from indulgences (remission of temporal punishment under certain stipulated circumstances), granted in part for contributing to ecclesiastical construction. However, the primary patrons and sources of help for new foundations were usually those who controlled the land; in Ireland the native leaders at first, later joined by the Angevin king Henry II and his acquisitive Anglo-Norman barons.

The architecture of the Cistercian order, established in Ireland at Mellifont, County Louth, in 1142, continued to dominate large-scale ecclesiastical projects for most of the country until the end of the twelfth century. Direct contact with France was definite in the first work at Mellifont and is possible in later buildings. Although a version of native decorative detail persisted for a time, the predominant forms then stemmed from Cistercian buildings in the Romanesque style of Britain and Wales, until Anglo-Norman control and patronage in the eastern part of the country brought the Transitional style of western Britain, followed by the Gothic. The Transitional style also influenced projects sponsored by Gaelic lords in western Ireland, the manner and degree of acceptance or rejection of the new ideas being, as in the political realm, a matter of great interest.

The site at Mellifont is said to have been picked out by St Malachy. St Bernard sent one of his monks to oversee the construction. Donnchad Ua Cerbaill, king of Airgialla, gave not only the land for the abbey but also stone and wood for the building of the monastery, and is credited by the 'Antiphonary of Armagh' (under 1 January 1170) with having supplied in addition agricultural implements and books for use in the choir.[1] This first permanent church was somewhat shorter than the one which replaced it in the thirteenth century. Muirchertach Mac Lochlainn, soon to be high-king of Ireland, was at the celebrated dedication in 1157. He gave to the monastery a townland, 140 cows, and 60 ounces of gold. King Donnchad also gave 60 ounces of gold; and so did Ua Ruairc's wife Derbforgaill, spirited queen of Bréifne. Even before the dedication, however, Mellifont had sent out at least seven daughter monasteries. 'Mellifont was ... one of the cornerstones of the New Ireland which enlightened leaders, lay and clerical, were endeavouring to build in the twelfth

[1] Conway, *Mellifont*, p. 8.

century.'¹ After the invasion, Henry II and some of his followers also became benefactors of Mellifont.

But Cistercianism was in some ways very different from the practices of earlier Irish monasticism. Hence, as might be expected, there was considerable 'backsliding' among the brothers who had joined the new order.

Even as late as 1228 we find complaint being made to Rome and to the general chapter of the Cistercian order that the Irish monks had in many places abandoned their monasteries and built for themselves 'miserable huts' of clay and wattle outside the monastic walls.²

Two monks of Holy Cross were in that year granted their request to become hermits, and an abortive monastery on Clare Island, County Mayo, was kept as a cell of Knockmoy, possibly so that monks who wanted a more secluded life could go there.

One of the earliest Cistercian abbeys of which parts remain above ground is that at Baltinglass, County Wicklow, founded by Diarmait Mac Murchada in 1148. Another is Jerpoint, established on its present site probably about 1163–5, perhaps first as Benedictine, adopted as a daughter of Baltinglass in 1180.³ The eastern parts of both churches seem to have been built chiefly before Anglo-Norman participation took place. Delicate carvings on some of the capitals of 2c, d, e, f the naves stem from native Irish sources,⁴ whereas the shapes of the capitals and of many of the piers are revealingly close to those at the Cistercian abbey of Buildwas in Shropshire, probably finished in 1170. (At the synod of Cashel in 1171–2, Ralph, abbot of Buildwas, attended as one of the representatives of Henry II.) Although parallels to work in France sometimes occur (the original lack of a tower in most of the Cistercian churches descended from Mellifont has been given as an instance), from *c.* 1160 until at least the fourteenth century the architecture of Ireland was on the whole more closely related to that of the western part of Great Britain than to the building of any other area. Much of the charm of Baltinglass and Jerpoint results from the felicitous integration of Norman bigness and power, Cistercian purity and restraint, and Gaelic sprightliness and refinement in detail.

Boyle Cistercian abbey reflects a more chequered situation in the arts. Its majestic eastern part, tower, and especially the stolid piers of a portion of the nave arcade are very close to west-of-England prototypes, although Boyle was far away from the focus of the invaders when this part of the abbey church was built (perhaps begun about 1161, continued *c.* 1180 and later). All the abbots appear to have been Gaelic Irish, and prominent benefactors were the Mac-Dermots of Mag Luirg. Hence, this earlier work at Boyle appears to show

---

¹ Liam de Paor, 'Excavations at Mellifont abbey, Co. Louth' in *R.I.A. Proc.*, lxviii (1969), sect. C, pp 115–16.
² Conway, *Mellifont*, p. 5. See also O'Dwyer, *Conspiracy of Mellifont*, p. 31.
³ Gwynn & Hadcock, *Med. relig. houses*, p. 136.
⁴ Harold G. Leask, *Irish churches and monastic buildings* (3 vols, Dundalk, 1955–60), ii, 26, 29.

acceptance of an exotic method of building, in this case Norman, without political pressure, just as at Mellifont a presumably Burgundian treatment was welcomed. But in the west part of the nave of Boyle are colonnettes (small or slender columns) indicative of the transition to the more delicate Gothic, and they are surmounted by capitals carved in a manner characteristic of western Ireland just before the Gothic triumphed everywhere.

Under the patronage of the ruling dynasty of the O'Briens, there occurred in Thomond (north Munster) in the twelfth century a notable ecclesiastical reform accompanied by important architectural achievements. Domnall Mór Ó Briain, last *de facto* king of Munster, did obeisance to Henry II when the king came to Ireland in 1171–2, but on other occasions he found it expedient to resist. For the most part, King Domnall was able to maintain his position and possession of his capital, Limerick, from the time of his accession to power in 1168 until his death in 1194.

Domnall is credited with founding, or importantly championing by his gifts, nine monastic foundations, six of them Cistercian houses: Holy Cross, Monasteranenagh, Corcomroe—probably primarily by Domnall's son Donnchad—Fermoy, Inishlounaght, and Kilcooly. He also built three cathedrals: Cashel, 1169 (now replaced); Killaloe, County Clare, c. 1180 (now replaced); and St Mary's in Limerick, established in 1172 and constructed primarily c. 1180–94, with many additions in later years.

His cathedral church of St Mary in Limerick is eloquent of its time and place. The use of a Romanesque, round-arched doorway (restored) as the principal entrance in the western wall is a reminder of the final fruition of this style in the 1160s and 1170s. The assertiveness of the doorway contrasts with the 'Cistercian' reticence of the simple nave. Direct influence from continental French prototypes appears clear, not only in the uninterrupted sweep of the roof in the original building from the west gable to the chancel arch (if there ever was one), but also in the complete lack of any tower structure at the crossing or elsewhere. The present tower was inserted later, and the transept, if any, had perhaps only a south arm originally. There were once arches over the aisles from the piers to the outer walls, a feature which also suggests continental prototypes, such as Fontenay and Bonmont in Switzerland; and, in Britain, Fountains, where the nave was built under the direction of a monk from Clairvaux.[1]

3a

Very different from St Mary's was the contemporary rebuilding of the east end of Christ Church, Dublin, possibly begun c. 1175 under Archbishop Lorcán Ua Tuathail but more probably some time after the appointment in 1181 of his successor, John Cumin, first Anglo-Norman archbishop of the see.[2] The east end through the transepts was probably finished by about the year

[1] R. F. Hewson, 'St Mary's cathedral, Limerick: its development and growth' in *N. Munst. Antiq. Jn.*, iv, no. 2 (1944), pp 56–8.
[2] Roger A. Stalley, *Architecture and sculpture in Ireland 1150–1350* (Dublin, 1971), pp 58–60, and *Christ Church, Dublin* (Ballycotton, Co. Cork, 1973), pp 6–9.

This work is part and parcel of the manner seen in the lady chapel at Glaston-bury abbey in Somerset and in the nave of St David's in Pembrokeshire, under construction in the 1180s. Moreover, the lay patrons—Strongbow, Robert fitz Stephen, and Raymond le Gros—came from this area, and Archbishop Cumin was not only familiar with western England but had been a custodian of revenues from Glastonbury just before he became archbishop of Dublin.

3c   Much of the handsome eastern part of Christ Church is a nineteenth-century rebuilding, but enough detail survives, to indicate that it was in all probability the key monument in Ireland of the more highly decorated phase of Transitional architecture.

3b   Quite different, a splendid example of the Transition in a more restrained phase, is the lavabo at Mellifont, probably done about the year 1200. There had been an octagonal structure for the font at Cîteaux, and polygonal lavabos occur at other places on the Continent, but this is one of the finest of all. The lavishing of care on one exquisite object—a piscina (basin for the disposal of the water from liturgical ablutions), window, or door, here the lavabo—while much of the rest of the construction may be plain, is frequently found in Irish medieval work.

Influence from these striking structures at Mellifont and Dublin and of yet others across the Irish Sea soon spread westward. Thirty-six feet (10.97 m) high and suggestive of work at Glastonbury abbey is the dramatic east window of 3d St Flannan's cathedral at Killaloe. Almost all the Killaloe bishops of the time were Gaelic Irish, though the English-born Robert Travers was placed in the see in 1217, deprived in 1221, but apparently in possession as late as 1226.[1] Whether the great window was created by him or by others is a moot question. Some details suggest that this masterwork at Killaloe is related not only to work of the type of the east end of Christ Church, Dublin, but also to achievements such as the east window of the little cathedral of Kilfenora, County Clare, probably *c.*1200. Kilfenora shows a more distinctively Irish approach.

At this time some of the freshest and most unusual work, of Gaelic patron-age, is to be found in Connacht. Here Cathal Crobderg Ó Conchobair, with Anglo-Norman help, managed to have himself recognised as king and was in control for most of the time from the peace of Athlone (1195) until his death in 1224.

One of the most important of the O'Connor foundations, a retreat and rest-ing places for many of the family both in life and in death, was the Augustinian abbey of St Mary at Cong, County Mayo, which had been refounded by the high-king Toirrdelbach in 1134. The character of the hard, grey limestone used for decorative detail lent itself to crispness of carving. Western French parallels have been suggested for some of the work.

A second outstanding example of the piety of the O'Connors is the Cister-1 cian abbey of Knockmoy, County Galway, founded by Cathal Crobderg in

[1] Watt, *Ch. in med. Ire.*, p. 103.

1190, probably 'in thanksgiving for an escape from drowning in Lough Ree' in that year.[1] The church seems to date from between 1202, the year in which Knockmoy was plundered by William de Burgh, and c. 1216. It was colonised from Boyle.

Knockmoy impresses by its massive walls and its generally sparse but fine decorative details. There is little later medieval work—no tower, no important fifteenth-century windows, no elaborated doorway. A marsh lies close by. The nearest house is far away. One senses the pristine asceticism of St Bernard.

The well-restored church of the monastery of canons regular at Ballintober, County Mayo, of c. 1216–c. 1225, founded by Cathal Crobderg, on a Patrician site, brings to a fitting close the series of large monasteries built by indigenous leaders in this period of change. Ballintober is Cistercian in plan. Relations with Knockmoy and Cong are clear in the carved detail, and the same sculptors probably worked at Boyle. Some of the animal heads and serpent forms at the *8b* County Mayo church would seem to stem directly from earlier Irish Roman-esque art in western Ireland.[2]

A continuation and reinterpretation of certain older forms is also evident in the distinctive spartan manner encountered in some little cathedrals and abbey churches, mostly early-thirteenth-century and mostly in the west. They have an aisleless nave and sometimes a short chancel. 'Classically' restrained, the outstanding feature is the paired, narrow, round-topped window, completely enframed, the splay sometimes lined with beautifully fitted and finished stone. Ó hEidhin's church at Kilmacduagh, County Galway, Clonfert cathedral, and Kilfenora are representative examples. *8a*

In conclusion, the outstanding achievement of the later twelfth century in the arts of Ireland was the championing of the Cistercians. By 1171 there were fifteen Cistercian abbeys already in existence in this land, and fifteen more were colonised from the older native Irish monasteries after that date, making a total of thirty. Four of these failed. The Anglo-Normans founded ten abbeys of white monks; seven were colonised from British abbeys, two from St Mary's in Dublin, and one from France.[3] The dimensions of twelve of the largest Cistercian churches follow on the next page. Measurements come for the most part from plans in the office of public works, Dublin. Fontenay church is 66 metres (c. 216.5 feet) in length.

In considering church building in the Gothic manner under the Anglo-Normans attention will first be invited to the general character of the style. This was the cathedral age, and the fruits of the fully operative diocesan system, culminating in an important bishop's seat (cathedral church), are also

[1] Gwynn & Hadcock, *Med. relig. houses*, p. 124.

[2] Stalley, *Architecture*, p. 116.

[3] Gwynn & Hadcock, *Med. relig. houses*, p. 117. Watt, *Ch. in med. Ire.*, p. 50, states that the total number of Cistercian houses in Ireland was thirty-one, though his map indicating the location of the monasteries as of 1228 shows thirty-four.

abbey	foundation[1]	date of whole or greater part of present church	internal length (approx.) feet	metres
Mellifont				
1st church	Ua Cerbaill and others 1142	1157	176	53.65
2nd church[2]		13th–15th cent.[3]	191.5	58.37
Baltinglass	Diarmait Mac Murchada 1148	2nd half 12th cent.	178	54.26
Boyle	Mac Diarmata (1148) 1161	c. 1161–1230	183	55.78
Jerpoint[4]	Mac Gilla Pátraic c. 1160	late 12th cent.; tower 15th.	162	49.38
Monasteranenagh	Ua Briain 1148	late 12th–early 13th cent.	176	53.65
Inch	John de Courcy 1180/87	end 12th cent.–early 13th cent.	161.5	49.23
Grey	Affreca, wife of John de Courcy 1193	c. 1200	123	37.49
Knockmoy	Ó Conchobair 1190	early 13th cent.	194.33	59.23
Dunbrody	Hervey de Montmorency 1182	1st half 13th cent.; tower later.	194	59.13
Graiguenamanagh	William Marshal 1202/7	1st half 13th cent.	204	62.18
Tintern Minor	William Marshal 1200	13th cent.	154	46.94

to be seen in parts of Ireland. In the larger towns, important parish churches were also erected. For a few decades the widespread founding of abbeys continued, some of them being outstanding examples of the first flush of the Gothic in Ireland. However, interest in the conventual branch of the church was soon captured by the friars. The Dominicans and Franciscans, ardent preachers and ministers, quickly spread over western Christendom, winning support from all sectors of society. The friars' architecture, for the most part purely functional, exhibits a simple solution to simple needs.

Gothic architecture originated in France, where it is characterised by the use of the pointed arch, large window areas, the ribbed and groined vault,

[1] Dates based on those given by Gwynn and Hadcock, pp 121–3, as checked, and where necessary amended, by R. A. Stalley.

[2] Gwynn & Hadcock, p. 139: 'After the Anglo-Norman invasion Henry II and later English kings were benefactors of Mellifont'. Conway, *Mellifont*, pp 38, 52, 76–8, indicates that Anglo-Normans made donations by as early as 1185–6 and later.

[3] R. A. Stalley, 'Mellifont abbey: some observations on its architectural history' in *Studies*, lxiv (1975), pp 363–7.

[4] Gwynn & Hadcock, p. 236, indicates that at the time that the nave was apparently being built Bishop Felix Ua Duib Sláine and 'certain Anglo-Normans' helped to increase the endowment.

concentrated supports, and flying buttresses. Gothic forms tend to be more lively, less heavy, than the Romanesque. Of especial interest are the great new windows of stained glass, their vibrant light symbolising the presence and power of God. Paintings, coloured sculpture, and gilt detail added life. Since vaulting occurs regularly in Irish Gothic building only in towers, heavy walls and flying buttresses were not necessary. St Patrick's and Christ Church in   4a, b
Dublin were outstanding exceptions in being vaulted throughout.

The story of Gothic architecture in Ireland may begin with the earlier parts of the Cistercian abbey church of *c.* 1200 or before, which the Anglo-Norman John de Courcy founded at Inch, and that which his wife Affreca set up at Grey, both in County Down. Here, and at Dunbrody, County Wexford (early thirteenth century) and Hore abbey at Cashel, County Tipperary, is experienced that feeling of nobility which results from self-disciplined simplicity, characteristic of the pristine concepts of Cistercianism.

At Graiguenamanagh, County Kilkenny, sponsored jointly by William Marshal and his wife Isabel de Clare (Strongbow's daughter), was built the largest Cistercian church in medieval Ireland. The founding charter (*c.* 1207) mentions serfs and tenants,[1] evidence that the relaxation of the austerity of the order as regards work by the monks and lay brothers had begun. A change of attitude is also apparent in the elaboration of delicate detail seen in the chancel and processional doorway. Perhaps it reflects the personal tastes of Earl William and Countess Isabella, like St Mary's parish church at their newly founded town of New Ross.

Most of the greater thirteenth-century Irish cathedrals and parish churches were constructed in the towns and cities controlled by the colonists, and in a style imported from western Britain. Among the earliest is St Mary's in New Ross, dated on stylistic grounds to the period 1200–20. It was once probably the gayest thirteenth-century parish church in the country, and is the largest extant (155 feet (47.24 m) in length). Much of the decorative stonework is salmon pink in colour, imported from Bristol.

Of the larger Irish cathedrals, significant work from the thirteenth century still remains in Christ Church nave (*c.* 1213–35) and St Patrick's in Dublin,   4a, b, c, d
Cashel, Kilkenny, Kildare, Ferns, and the Victorine priory at Newtown Trim.   5a, b
The existence of two imposing cathedral churches in Dublin has been convincingly explained.[2] The first two Anglo-Norman archbishops seem not to have wished to work with the Augustinian chapter of Christ Church. Archbishop Henry of London (1213–28) accorded full cathedral status to the collegiate church of St Patrick, which had been established *c.* 1190–92 by his predecessor in the see, John Cumin. Soon after his accession, Henry began to

---

[1] Conway, *Mellifont*, p. xxxiii; also, C. M. Butler and J. H. Bernard (ed.), 'The charters of the Cistercian abbey of Duiske' in *R.I.A. Proc.*, xxxv (1918), sect. C, p. 18.

[2] Geoffrey J. Hand, 'The rivalry of the cathedral chapters in medieval Dublin' in *R.S.A.I. Jn.*, xcii, pt 2 (1962), pp 193–206, is one of the more recent discussions.

build the present St Patrick's, 300 feet (91.4 m) in length, the largest medieval church in the land. Success must have attended the preachers to whom King Henry III in 1225 granted protection for four years to collect money throughout the land on behalf of the building of the cathedral church.

The more elaborated phase of the Gothic, however, culminates in the nave
4a of Christ Church, a masterpiece of the school of western Britain. The carved stone came from England, as did the sculptors. From and including the capitals of the nave piers up to the vaults, the north side of the nave consists primarily of the original stonework. The rest of the nave—south wall, west end, vaults—is a careful modern rebuilding. Vigorously carved capitals, banded shafts, and a luxuriant richness of mouldings make Christ Church one of the splendours of the medieval period in Ireland.

4b St Patrick's is simpler in detail. Salisbury has been suggested as a model, but the elevation of other naves seem closer.[1] Much has had to be rebuilt: almost all of the north transept and much of the nave, as well as parts of the choir.[2]

More characteristic of Ireland than either of the two cathedrals in Dublin, is
4c, d St Canice's in Kilkenny. The first Anglo-Norman bishop, Hugo de Rous (*c.* 1202–18) may have begun the present church, anxious to give visual evidence of the recently fortified diocesan organisation and the new government and
5a culture which he represented. St Canice's, 226 feet (68.88 m) in length, and the second longest Irish medieval cathedral, was probably finished *c.* 1275. The presence of a rectangular chancel, transept, crossing tower, aisled nave of two storeys (arcade and row of windows above) and wood roofs, with a fifteenth-century vault under the tower, make St Canice's the archetype of the larger Irish Gothic church, save for the unusual arrangement of the transept chapels. Spacious proportions, plenty of windows, and piers of modest size lend a pleasant, open effect. Chancel, transepts, and nave are to a considerable extent original in form. Glorious fourteenth-century glass once filled the chancel with vibrant colour. In 1648 the papal nuncio Rinuccini unsuccessfully sought to purchase the east window for £700. Two years later it was utterly demolished.

In the north transept is a splendid tomb niche enlivened with pensive faces suggesting real personalities. Below are sixteenth-century carvings. It may commemorate Bishop Hugh de Mapilton (1251–60), whom written records
4d credit with having built much of the cathedral. St Canice's west doorway is another handsome example of British thirteenth-century Gothic. The low central tower replaces a taller one which collapsed in 1332. Two fragments believed to have come from the original wooden roof are preserved in Rothe House museum in Kilkenny.[3]

[1] Stalley, *Architecture*, p. 32.
[2] E. C. Rae, 'The medieval fabric of the cathedral church of St Patrick in Dublin' in *R.S.A.I. Jn.*, cix (1979), pp 29–73.
[3] Peter Harbison, 'Three decorated wooden beams of the thirteenth century' in *Old Kilkenny Rev.*, xxv (1973), p. 38. See also Siuban Barry, John Bradley, and Adrian Empey, *A worthy foundation: the cathedral church of St Canice, Kilkenny* (Mountrath, 1985), pp 25–48.

An example of an important thirteenth-century church built under Gaelic 5b control which shows acceptance of the new Gothic style as regards decorative detail is the cathedral of Cashel. All of its archbishops in the thirteenth century bear names of Gaelic stock. The dramatically situated building was probably begun at the time of Archbishop Mairín Ó Briain (1224–37) and substantially finished by 1289, except for the upper part of the crossing tower and the residential structure at the west end of the nave. But in plan Cashel is very different from the cathedrals at Dublin or Kilkenny. There are no aisles; the chancel is much longer than the very short nave, and the pairs of chapels off the transept arms are suggestive of those of the larger monastic foundations. Though unroofed, the venerable structure seems very much alive, for here the British love of adorning architecture with heads and busts reaches a peak. The exterior of the south transept alone is peopled with twenty-five or more peering faces, and there are many others.

Two fine parish churches demand notice. That at Gowran, County Kilkenny, probably of the period c. 1250–75, presents some attractive heads done in the full-bodied manner of carving seen in Christ Church and some of the work of St Canice's, and the same kind of pier and quatrefoil clerestory as that of the Kilkenny cathedral are used. Gowran church was patronised from the beginning by the Butlers, who became earls of Ormond and chose it as their principal place of burial for the greater part of the fourteenth century. The remains of the spacious parish church at Thomastown, County Kilkenny, on the other hand, display the less elaborated treatment characteristic of St Patrick's in Dublin, the thirteenth-century rebuilding of Mellifont abbey, and the foundations of the mendicant orders

In its struggle in the eleventh and twelfth centuries to achieve relative independence of secular control and to establish its institutions firmly in medieval life, the church had not stressed preaching as a means of religious education and spiritual enrichment of the life of the laity. There was apparently little preaching of any kind in churches toward the end of the twelfth century. But in the growing towns people were asking questions and seeking answers. Heretics were increasing in number.

Thus was the stage set for the arrival of St Dominic and St Francis. The orders they founded, Dominican (1216) and Franciscan (1223), differed markedly from most in an emphasis on evangelism, on preaching, meeting 'the world' on its level and lifting it up. Preaching the Christian doctrine was an especial aim of the Dominicans, 'a task previously regarded as the prerogative and monopoly of bishops and their delegates'.[1] The great scholar St Thomas Aquinas was a Dominican. The Franciscans also produced renowned intellectuals but 'have ever been the order of the poor, and in their preaching and missions and ministrations they have ever attempted to meet the needs of the poor'[2]. Genuine

[1] M. D. K[nowles], 'Dominicans' in *Encycl. Brit.* (1970), vii, 572.
[2] E. C. B[utler], 'Franciscans' in *Encycl. Brit.* (1961), ix, 672.

poverty was a basic and effective tenet of the friars, embraced fervently by the Franciscans, and St Dominic also practised poverty himself and made it a part of the life of his order.[1] Both groups were mendicant, i.e. they depended upon alms for their support, having no income from estates at this early time.

The friars preachers (Dominicans) came to Ireland in 1224, settling first at Dublin and Drogheda, the friars minor (Franciscans) *c.* 1231, being first established at Youghal and Cork. By about 1270 the Carmelites had arrived, and the Augustinian friars by 1282.[2] The friars' foundations spread rapidly. Practically at the start, an Irish province had been set up for the Franciscans.[3] By 1350 there were already thirty-four of their foundations; twenty-six Dominican houses, nineteen friaries of Carmelites, and twelve of Augustinians. Although officially a part of the English province throughout the middle ages, the Irish Austin friars achieved a large amount of self-direction. Policies originating in the west, part of the Gaelic resurgence, dominated their houses *c.* 1440–1540.[4]

Because of their evangelising mission to lead men to a better state of being through preaching, the hearing of confession, and general concern for the people, the ideal location for the friars' houses was considered to be close to a town of importance, or even within it. Of some sixty-nine friaries established by about 1300 A.D., all but eight may be plotted on a map of principal towns and manors *c.* 1300.[5] The great majority of sponsors at this time were therefore those who favoured the growth of towns and a more stable economy—the Anglo-Norman lords and the English settlers. For only thirteen of the approximately ninety friaries established in Ireland before the middle of the fourteenth century are founders bearing Gaelic names definitely indicated. Two, and perhaps four, are credited to the townspeople. Practically all the others are associated with the names of Anglo-Norman persons of importance.[6] But there were indubitably more general contributions to the friars' foundations than these statistics would imply (see Athenry, below). Knowledge that the welfare of the brothers at this time depended almost entirely upon alms must have prompted untold donations in kind, services, and otherwise.[7] Pious King Henry III set a good example. In 1245 he committed himself to make an annual gift of money to buy habits for the friars minor of Dublin, Waterford, Drogheda, Cork, Athlone, and Kilkenny, and the grant continued to be made irregularly until 1372.[8]

---

[1] J. C. Dickinson, *Monastic life in medieval England* (London, 1961), p. 90. For a convincing discussion of Dominican poverty, see R. F. Bennett, *The early Dominicans* (New York, 1971; reissue of 1937 publication).

[2] Gwynn & Hadcock, *Med. relig. houses*, pp 218, 236, 282, 293. See also above, pp 400–01.

[3] Alan R. Martin, *Franciscan architecture in England* (Manchester, 1937), p. 4.

[4] F. X. Martin, 'The Irish Augustinian reform movement in the fifteenth century' in *Med. studies presented to A. Gwynn*, pp 230–64.

[5] Above, p. 233.

[6] Based on the data collected by Gwynn & Hadcock.

[7] Many customary periodic donations are listed in *Extents Ir. mon. possessions* under the names of the various establishments.

[8] Fitzmaurice & Little, *Franciscan province Ire.*, p. xviii.

From the start to *c.*1350 the friary church evolved from simple beginnings to an approximation of its fully developed Irish type, a picturesque but unpretentious, functional building, which persisted until the end of the medieval period. As perfected in the fifteenth century, the whole friary (church and monastic buildings) shares with western work of Transitional style the honour of being probably Ireland's most significant contribution to the history of European ecclesiastical architecture of the Gothic period. The Franciscan establishments, most numerous and fairly well studied, will serve as the general norm.

St Francis had clearly wished that his followers should have only small churches and poor little houses of mud and wood (the latter in tune with what many people in Ireland were living in). The first permanent (stone) Irish friary churches would have consisted usually of a simple rectangle between 100 and 150 feet (30–45 m) in length by perhaps about 23 to 26 feet (7–8 m) in width, but one storey in height. The earliest extant version of the Dominican constitutions limited the height of walls to 30 feet (9.14 m); for the conventual buildings, 12 feet (3.66 m), or 20 feet (6.10 m) if there were a loft.[1] There was no vaulting of any kind. The roof would have been of thatch or other readily available material. Inside, a plain rectangular choir for the brothers in the eastern part, generally somewhat shorter than the nave, was separated by a screen of wood or stone from the remainder of the building, which could have been 50 to 75 feet (15–23 m) or so in length—the people's church. The high altar was in the friars' choir in the east end. Typically, an opening in the middle of the screen afforded communication between the two parts of the church, and there would probably have been a simple altar in the people's area on each side of the opening. Seldom, if ever, had the Cistercians originally planned for ordinary lay people to use a part of their abbey churches, though a chapel for laity was sometimes built nearby. Sparsely employed at first, lancets (simple pointed windows) were soon multiplied, especially in the friars' choir.

But the friary church did not often remain a simple, long rectangle. If well located, the community of friars and the congregation of the people tended to increase. More room for the friars could be achieved by lengthening the choir to the east, as at the Franciscans' church at Kilkenny and Castledermot and the Dominicans' at Athenry. The usual way of adding to the area of the nave was to construct an aisle on the side away from the cloister. In some cases such an aisle may have been constructed from the beginning. This also made space for another altar at its east end, a welcome increment if all of the brethren who were ordained were to find adequate room for their daily masses. Beginning in the late thirteenth century more places for altars were afforded by another kind of extension—a single transept arm placed usually near the east end of the nave, again on the side away from the claustral buildings. It was a distinctively *6a, b, 14b*

---

[1] Daphne D. C. Pochin Mould, T.O.S.D., *The Irish Dominicans* (Dublin, 1957), p. 32.

Irish feature, although known to have occurred also in Britain in friaries at Richmond in Yorkshire, Warrington, and Llanfaes. Frequently this addition was referred to as the lady chapel in deference to the growing cult of the Virgin Mary. Sometimes it would have increased significantly the capacity of the
6b church for preaching, as at the Dominicans' at Kilkenny, where the transept arm is about the same size as the original nave (the original choir has been removed). In some cases, as in the large aisleless Franciscan friary church at Buttevant, County Cork, and the Dominicans' at Kilmallock, the transept arm seems too cut off from the nave for very effective use as an adjunct to services in the latter.

As the desire for greater luminosity increased, closely spaced lancets, sometimes paired, became common. In end walls they were sometimes graded in size from the sides to the middle. Meantime, however, tracery had been developed by grouping lancets under a large arch and filling the top with decorative stone openwork, geometrical at first, characteristic of the English Decorated style, which began *c.*1250. Elaborate mouldings and sometimes naturalistically carved foliage may accompany this development. After *c.*1310 in Britain a substitution of free forms for some of the geometrical curves produced the curvilinear or flowing Decorated, a forerunner (even an exemplification) of the Flamboyant style.

6b A traceried window was frequently the chief glory of a transept arm added in the early fourteenth century. Both geometric and flowing types are an expression of the love of lively, linear surfaces so sumptuously achieved in Hiberno-Saxon manuscript illumination. Such windows became a highly
6a important part of the matrix of Irish culture. At Athenry, the end walls of the choir, nave, and the transept all received windows of Decorated style, that in the east end of the brothers' choir now replaced by a window of sixteenth-century type.

Athenry illustrates well an example of a friary which grew through participation on the part of the people.[1] The *regestum* of the friary[2] relates how both Gaelic and Anglo-Irish worked together toward a common goal. In 1241 Meiler de Bermingham, who had gained control of this part of Connacht, gave the lands and funds toward building the church. Though recently bested by the invaders, Fedlimid Ó Conchobair, king of Connacht, built the refectory (and also founded the Dominican priory at Roscommon in 1253).[3] Cornelius Ó Cellaig contributed the chapter house at Athenry, Eogan Ó hEidin the dormitory. A Dominican archbishop of Tuam, Flann Mac Flainn, built the 'scholar

---

[1] For plans and details, see Leask, *Churches*, ii, 126–9; and R. A. S. MacAlister, 'The Dominican church at Athenry' in *R.S.A.I. Jn.*, xliii (1913), pp 197–222, very valuable despite inexpert analysis of some of the architectural features.

[2] Consult Martin Blake, 'The abbey of Athenry' in *Galway Arch. Soc. Jn.*, ii (1902), pp 65–90, and Gwynn & Hadcock, *Med. relig. houses*, p. 221, or *Archiv. Hib.*, i (1912), pp 201–21.

[3] Whereas most friars' establishments are properly termed friaries (popularly 'abbeys' in Ireland), Dominican houses may be called priories.

house', tangible evidence of the Dominicans' interest in education. Sir William de Burgh (died 1324) built the 'great guest chamber' and lengthened the choir. 'Mac-a-Wallyd' de Bermingham built the lady chapel up to the window sills; it was finished by William Wallys (died 1344), who also built the tower as far as the gable; the tower, in turn, was finished by James Lynch.

The Irish friary tower deserves special attention. One type nearly filled the width of the church, but was much narrower from east to west. Another kind, especially favoured by the Franciscans, was very slender, usually of far less *13a* width than the church. Stepped battlements ordinarily crowned the top. Among preserved examples, seniority is probably correctly awarded to the Magdalen tower at Drogheda, almost the sole remnant of a Dominican priory. It has none of the taper characteristic of later Irish friary towers, and probably dates from the first half of the fourteenth century. The archways on the east and west are narrow, thus allowing for masses of masonry which have proved quite adequate for stability. In all likelihood a screen or doors closed off the lower part of the archway, thus more completely separating the friars' choir from the preaching nave. Towers were often inserted after a friary church had been built, and were sometimes quite self-supporting. A little groined vault often filled the space under the tower.

FORTIFIED buildings constitute some of the most striking monuments preserved from Ireland's past. The Anglo-Norman invaders introduced the motte and bailey (mound and courtyard) as an instrument of conquest and domination, a 'considerable impetus' being given to motte building by a mandate of King John in 1200.[1] Soon they also constructed stone castles consisting of great rectangular keeps with stone curtain walls. A local variant with round *7a, b* towers at the corners of the keep was also developed. The prompt appearance of the circular keep shows that the Anglo-Normans were keeping abreast of the developments elsewhere. Naturally, the king took measures to ensure that the castles were in loyal hands. He took some into his own custody and built others as royal castles in the first place. As the thirteenth century progressed, there occurred a change from the concept of a strong keep, with outlying curtain walls, to a massive and well defended outer wall, with powerful gate structures as the primary element of defence. Also to be considered are the halls and houses built for the ordinary peacetime uses of the upper classes and the homes of the ordinary people. This section closes with some comments about city fortifications.

In a typical motte-and-bailey castle, a ditch was dug around the site selected for defence and a bank was created, at the top of which was planted a wooden palisade. Thus was formed the bailey, sometimes rectangular but often of other shapes, varying from a minimum of 60 by 70 feet (18.29 m × 21.34 m) to a

[1] H. C. Lawlor, 'Mote and mote-and-bailey castles in de Courcy's principality of Ulster' in *U.J.A.*, 3rd ser., ii (1939), p. 54.

maximum of well over twice that amount.[1] One side or end usually impinged upon the second element of the ensemble: the motte, a truncated, conical mound of earth, surrounded by a ditch usually deeper than that of the bailey, and terminating in a flat top of an average diameter of about 60 feet. A natural or previously constructed man-made mound was very often adapted to serve as the motte, and an appropriate fall of ground might take the place of part or all of the surrounding ditches.[2] The top of the motte was fortified by a wooden palisade, and within the enclosure was often placed a wooden hall, tower, or the blockhouse of the commander. Sometimes there was no bailey; only the motte. Where circumstances permitted, the inflammable walls of wood would be eventually replaced by stone, the wooden tower of the commander thus becoming eventually a stone keep or 'donjon' (place of ultimate refuge).

The great age of the castle characterised by an imposing rectangular stone keep began in the reign of Henry II and continued in Ireland into the following 7*a* century. A good example is Carrickfergus, begun some time in the 1180s by John de Courcy, 'conqueror of Ulster', and perhaps continued by his successor Hugh de Lacy and, after Hugh's fall, by King John and others. It was the key to Ulster, and one of the most imposing of all Irish castles. The site is a rocky, largely sea-girt peninsula. An encircling stone wall, altered and repaired at various times, incorporates in its ambit the north-west side of the keep, a squat tower 60 by 55 feet (18.29 m × 16.76 m) and about 90 feet (27.43 m) in height. At the narrow landward end of the peninsula stood a strong gate of the early to mid-thirteenth century. Flanking wall towers, coming into extensive use in western Europe about the time Carrickfergus was built, enabled the defenders to subject the enemy to crossfire should he try to scale or breach the walls. In its final form, provided with a well within the keep and capable of being provisioned from the sea, Carrickfergus seemed impregnable. However, it bowed to Edward Bruce after a year's siege in September 1316.[3]

7*b* Properly paired with Carrickfergus is the castle at Trim. Occupying over three acres (1.2 hectares), it is the largest Anglo-Norman castle in Ireland. The keep was perhaps built by Walter de Lacy, probably some time between 1190 and 1220. But only four years later (1224) Trim surrendered after a seven-weeks' siege by William Marshal the Younger and other nobles. The keep is unusual in having had a tall tower, about 22 feet (6.7 m) on a side, applied to each face of the central block, the sides of which measure approximately 65 feet (19.81 m) in breadth. Because of its many ninety-degree corners, Trim would have been particularly susceptible to undermining, a fate which befell the rectangular keep at Rochester, in Kent, in 1215. However, since siege operations in Ireland were probably less fully developed than in England, this indignity

---

[1] Harold G. Leask, *Irish castles* (2nd ed., Dundalk, 1944), p. 10.
[2] R. E. Glasscock, 'Mottes in Ireland' in *Château Gaillard*, vii (1975), p. 96; and see above, pp 214–19.
[3] Above, pp 289–90.

seems never to have been visited upon Trim. Perhaps the recently-revealed great spreading foundation (plinth) would have discouraged undermining.

The curtain walls, built at some time in the first half of the thirteenth century, show an advance over earlier work in the inclusion of at least two sallyports, originally seven flanking towers, and two strongly fortified gateways exhibiting a drawbridge, portcullis, barbican, and other defensive accoutrements. The future King Henry V lived in the south gate tower for a while in 1399. A moat completed the picture *par excellence* of the medieval castle of its time.

Of circular donjons (keeps), less easy to undermine than structures having right-angle corners, there were several in Ireland. Some still exist in fairly good preservation, as at Dundrum, County Down, of probably the first quarter of the thirteenth century and Nenagh, County Tipperary, of *c.* 1200–20. The former, beautifully sited not far from Dundrum Bay, occupies the location of an earlier motte-and-bailey. The presence of a rocky escarpment and rock-cut ditch made the use of simple curtain walls around the inner bailey adequate. These walls were probably constructed before 1203, perhaps as part of John de Courcy's conquest begun in 1177, and are considered to be 'among the earliest stone defensive works to be built by the English in Ireland'.[1] If de Courcy had indeed initiated the project, he had built too well for his own good fortune. Out of favour with King John, deprived of his lordship in 1205, he attempted to recover Ulster with the help of the king of Man. But Dundrum withstood both assault and siege. De Courcy never regained Ulster. At Nenagh, the slightly tapering circular donjon, about 55 feet (16.76 m) in external diameter at the base, had already been constructed as one of the round towers which guard the curtain wall, suggestive of developments which were to take place later in the thirteenth century. Nenagh, a Butler stronghold, represents a bold Anglo-Norman thrust to the Shannon, as did the castle of Athlone farther north.

Another scheme was developed which also found some favour in Ireland. The keep remained rectangular, but the use of a tower of circular type at each corner eliminated all angles and furnished cross fire for the protection of the walls. Ferns was the largest of these early towered keeps. It was built about the middle of the thirteenth century for descendants of William Marshal. A chapel in the better preserved of the two surviving towers is a fine example of architectural detail of the time, and pleasantly trefoiled window openings remind one of contemporary ecclesiastical work.

More significant for the history of the castle, however, was the popularity toward the end of the thirteenth century of the concept of the heavily defended curtain wall as not only the first but also the principal element of resistance. Dwellings and other shelters could be freely constructed inside the area protected by the wall. The desirability of being able to retire to a place of at least temporary safety in the event that the defence of the periphery should fail was met by the provision of quarters in one or more of the heavily fortified gate

[1] *An archaeological survey of County Down* (Belfast, 1966), p. 119.

structures or towers. This type of castle had made its appearance earlier in the century as part of the defences of towns, as is still evident in the denatured 'King John's castle' at Limerick. Where exigencies of site did not dictate otherwise, the plan is often largely symmetrical. The type was cosmopolitan, occurring in Wales, France, and England as well as Ireland The three outstanding Irish examples, Roscommon (*c.* 1280), Ballintober, County Roscommon, and Ballymote, County Sligo, both *c.* 1300, are all in Connacht, part of an extensive military effort on the part of the colonists to subdue western Ireland. Roscommon was a royal castle, a bold 'signal of the king's intent', commenced under the king's justiciar in 1269.[1] But in 1272 it was 'broken' by Áed Ó Conchobair, king of Connacht[2] and 'thrown down' by his successor, another Áed, in 1277.[3] At this a considerable sum (£3,200 or more) was spent for a stronger castle. It was largely finished, apparently, by not long after 1280. The principal front was converted into a dwelling in the sixteenth century. Richard de Burgh's smaller castle at Ballymote was a gem of symmetry, a 'correction' of Roscommon. It is unclear whether Ballintubber, less perfected in appearance, was a de Burgh creation 'well situated to overawe the O'Connor kings'[4] or built by the O'Connors to counter the invaders.

Where wood was available, the dwellings of the great majority of all persons of Gaelic and gaelicised areas throughout medieval times were probably of wattle and daub or other wooden construction.[5] When it is realised that large numbers of the lower classes of the Gaelic population were highly mobile, their acceptance of such quickly constructed, readily abandoned dwellings is more easily understood. In an architectural sense, the permanent anchors of the society were the stone castles of the lords and the monastic foundations.

To illustrate, in 1171 a building of Irish work in wattles was constructed outside Dublin for Henry II, reportedly at his own request.[6] (But in 1243 Henry III ordered to be built in Dublin castle a structure 'in the style of the hall of Canterbury'.[7]) Ancient Irish literature contains many tantalising references to vanished wooden buidings.[8] 'Never hath there been constructed among fair mansions of the clay or timber of Ireland a stouter rampart face', sings a Gaelic poet concerning a long-disappeared house built by Áed Ó Conchobair, king of Connacht, 1293–1309.[9] Excavations in the most ancient part of the city of Dublin

---

[1] Orpen, *Normans*, iii, 247.

[2] Ibid., 249.

[3] Ibid., iv, 109.

[4] Ibid., iii, 205. See also J. A. Claffey, 'Ballintubber castle, Co. Roscommon' in *Old Athlone Soc. Jn.*, i, no. 3 (1972–3), pp 143–6.

[5] Above, pp 403–4.

[6] Stalley, *Architecture*, p. 5.

[7] See above, p. 175.

[8] Leask, *Churches*, i, 5–9, gives some. See also Arthur Champneys, *Irish ecclesiastical architecture* (London, 1910), pp 26–8.

[9] E. C. Quiggin, ed., 'O'Conor's house at Cloonfree' in *Essays and studies presented to William Ridgeway* (Cambridge, 1913), pp 339, 340. Katharine Simms and Peter Harbison have kindly invited attention to passages such as this.

have revealed that even at this comparatively cosmopolitan centre, engaged in trade with various parts of the world, 'remains of structures built in the post-and-wattle technique have been encountered at all levels',[1] i.e. from the ninth to the fourteenth centuries. In the Dublin houses the poles were fixed in the ground, the 'weft' of wattles being woven between them and even used for floors. Doorways were framed in squared timber, and there were also thirteenth- and fourteenth-century houses of squared beams and uprights. In England, wattle work has been used to fill the interstices between a succession of vertical, squared posts.[2] The same is possible for Ireland. One suspects that the 'huts' that some of the monks of Mellifont chose to inhabit in 1228 were of the simplest type. Wattled buildings could have been a familiar sight within the rath, in Gaelic areas a presumably upper-class farm home-site, surrounded by a ditch and an inner bank. Such buildings are thought to have been used extensively throughout the medieval period in Ireland.[3] Houses of wattle might have been either circular, oval, or roughly rectangular, like one unearthed in Dublin with an open hearth near the centre. As late as c. 1620 a traveller reports 'the baser cottages are built of underwood, called wattle, and covered some with thatch and some with green sedge, of a round form and without chimneys', like beehives.[4]

Since most Irish sites still await investigation, we must turn to England for suggestions as to the kind of buildings which were probably constructed by the settlers who came in the wake of the Anglo-Norman lords.[5] There the wood-framed houses of earlier times gave way with varying degrees of speed and completeness to stone-walled buildings during the course of the thirteenth century, sometimes only the lower part of the walls being of stone, clay and wood being used for the upper part. One of the type plans fully developed in England by the late twelfth or the early thirteenth century is known as the long house, in one end of which was in many cases a cattle byre. The hearth was near the centre of the principal living room. Probably at a much later period a cottage type very similar in essentials to this medieval long house is thought to have been developed independently in western Ireland.[6]

Where there was no stone castle, the focus of the manor by the end of the thirteenth century apparently consisted of rectangular wood and stone

---

[1] Breandan Ó Riordáin, 'Excavations at High Street and Winetavern Street, Dublin' in *Medieval Archaeology*, xv (1971), p. 76.

[2] See *Medieval Archaeology*, xv (1971), pl. XII, for an illustration.

[3] R. E. Glasscock, 'The study of deserted medieval settlements in Ireland (to 1968)' in Beresford & Hurst, *Deserted medieval villages*, p. 282. See also above, pp 229-32.

[4] Falkiner, *Illustrations*, p. 355.

[5] See D. G. and J. G. Hurst, 'Excavations at the medieval villages of Wythemail, Northamptonshire' in *Medieval Archaeology*, xii (1969), pp 167-203. As to the rapidity and extent of acceptance of Anglo-Irish types of buildings on the part of purely Gaelic Ireland, cf. above, pp 403-6.

[6] F. H. A. Aalen, 'The evolution of the traditional house in western Ireland' in *R.S.A.I. Jn.*, xcvi (1966), pp 47-59. See also Caoimhín Ó Danachair, 'Traditional forms of the dwelling-house in Ireland' in *R.S.A.I. Jn.*, cii (1972), pp 77-93.

structures loosely grouped, protected by enclosing walls and ditches.[1] For the modern eye, the presence of these simple fortifications would perhaps have most markedly distinguished the medieval countryside in the colonised areas from that of today.

To date, the only published medieval examples of Irish houses similar to the long house are two found in the abandoned medieval town at Caherguillamore, near Lough Gur, Limerick.[2] There still remain the lower parts of the walls, of stone and clay. The simple, rectangular plans, with central hearth, suggest modest examples of the English type. Artifacts point to a fourteenth-century date.

Through the twelfth century, city walls in the British Isles appear to have been for the most part in the nature of those of the motte-and-bailey castle—earthen defences of banks and ditches and palisades. The banks might be revetted with stone or wood. Properly maintained and adequately manned against a not too numerous or better-equipped foe, such systems often proved effective. In Ireland, Primate Máel Pátraic Ó Scannail in 1264 constructed a ditch (and palisade?) around the city of Armagh. But the efficient type of siege warfare developed in the early thirteenth century helped discredit such simple defences. By the middle of the century in England the construction of city walls in stone was apparently not uncommon, having already been used for gateways in several instances where the rest of the defences continued to be of earth and palisades. Ireland also preserves a sparkling account of the building of a city's defences.

In the year 1265 the citizens of William Marshal's flourishing port of New Ross became alarmed by the chance of attack by warring local gentry and, according to a tale told by the sixteenth-century historian Stanihurst, were also outraged by a brazen theft on the part of an ill-bred rustic. Thereupon, the whole town made a veritable tournament of labour of the entrenchment of the place and the building of its stone defences. Six hundred sailors, as well as the different guilds and tradesmen, banners flying, came *en masse* at specified times to give their labour. Song filled the air. Beautifully clad ladies of importance pitched in.[3] But little of their achievement is now left at New Ross. Still impressive among remnants of town defences in Ireland is the barbican of the St Lawrence gate at Drogheda. Significant remains of walls are to be seen at Fethard, Youghal, Athenry, and Wexford. Galway in 1610, *16c* with its interesting variety of towers and gates and adaptation to the peculiarities of the site, may serve to illustrate fully developed medieval town fortifications.

---

[1] See above, pp 453–5.

[2] Sean P. Ó Riordain and John Hunt, 'Medieval dwellings at Caherguillamore, Co. Limerick' in *R.S.A.I. Jn.*, lxxii (1942), pp 37–63.

[3] As sung by poet Maurice of Kildare, transcribed *c.* 1308 and now part of B.L., Harl. MS 913, *Facs. nat. MSS Ire.*, iii, pt 1, pp iii–v. See also above, pp 167, 710–11, 718–19.

SINCE architectural sculpture has been referred to in the discussion of architecture, it will be mentioned only in passing in this discussion of the sculpture of the period from the late twelfth century to the end of the fourteenth century. Very little freestanding sculpture has survived. Most of it is of wood, often disfigured by frequent repainting. Yet, as the work of local artists these pieces have a rare significance. Also to be considered is a series of medieval cross slabs (coffin lids), some of them as pure and fine in design as the faith they symbolise. *9a, b* Upon occasion patrons commissioned carved effigies. During most of this period connection with England is very close, but the hand of a local sculptor is indubitably present in some cases. Tomb niches in the walls come into use at this time but reach their most impressive development later.

Except for funerary work, much of the medieval figure sculpture of Great Britain and Ireland has been lost. Among preserved carvings are some architectural details of importance at Kilfenora, *c.* 1200, and Corcomroe, where the *8a* sculptor continues to employ to good effect the stylised, awesome faces frequently found in Romanesque times. On the other hand, there comes to full flower the naturalism of the nascent Gothic and its conviction of a more intimate relationship between God, man, and nature, already in the ascendancy in the phase of the Transition represented by the late twelfth-century capitals of the eastern part of Christ Church in Dublin.

In the heads of queens and a bishop on capitals in the early thirteenth- *8c* century nave of the same building the self-assured, lofty idealisation of the 'classical' phase of high Gothic is evident. These visages are a sculptured parallel to the quiet logic of great scholars like Aquinas. Close by is a representative of that liking for caricature which is considered a distinctive aspect of British medieval art. More charming, but also idealised, are some heads of fine quality from a tomb recess in the north transept of St Canice's, Kilkenny. Cashel presents examples of both characterisation and caricature, and some of the heads show a more distinctively Irish treatment in the creation of strong, simple shapes upon which the detail is rather lightly carved. The increased expressiveness associated with later work is exemplified in the figures of some of the confraternity responsible for building the tower of the Franciscan house *8d* at Kilkenny about 1347. The little figures are placed as if holding up the ribs of the vault under the tower.

Indigenous traits are more convincingly revealed in a small number of wooden figures that have been associated together as the product of a school centred in the eastern part of County Galway. Best known is the probably thirteenth-century Madonna from Kilcorban now at Loughrea. Simplicity in *10d* conception, a restrained naturalism, and grace of handling are here the appropriate means for the depiction of Mary as a modest mother. Dignity and the suggestion of queenliness are also engendered by the largely axial, hieratic pose carried over from Romanesque times: she is still the throne of wisdom. The incarnate wisdom itself, the infant Christ, appears in the role of a likeable baby.

Sepulchral slabs constitute one of the most significant types of sculptured objects from the period under discussion as well as later. One such in the cathedral of St Mary, Limerick, may commemorate the founder, King Domnall Mór Ua Briain, who died in 1194. A slender cross, a circle at the intersection of the arms (reminiscent of earlier Irish work) divides the surface into areas occupied by catamounts, whose tails turn into vines and leaves. But this memorial in Limerick stands very much apart from the great body of grave slabs from the first two centuries of the Gothic in Ireland, just as Domnall Mór stood apart from the Anglo-Norman nobles.

9a

A slab at St Nicholas's, Galway, illustrates the characteristic Norman sepulchral art of the new era. Typically, the actual cross, arms approximately the same length, is clearly marked off from the shaft. It suggests the cross shown in the hands of the resurrected Christ to indicate his triumph over death.

9b

Sometimes a sword (common in Britain), eloquent witness of the earthly status of the deceased, is depicted in addition to the cross. Other implements, such as shears, tell us that the grave is that of a woman, shearman, or textile worker. Most specific of all are the frequently encountered inscriptions, sometimes in Norman French in the thirteenth and early fourteenth centuries. They usually tell us in simple terms the name of the person who lies beneath the stone, request our prayers, and pray that God may have mercy on the soul of the departed.

Not infrequently a head or heads appear just above the cross. In some areas of Europe during the twelfth century a full-length sculptured effigy had already gradually begun to emerge from the plane of the slab. The whole process appears to be recapitulated in a trio in the churchyard of the former parish church of St Mary, Kilkenny. The use of a simple engraved line to depict the whole figure also found popularity.

9c

Despite the horizontal position of the effigy, the peoples of northern Europe in Gothic times usually chose to depict the deceased not as a corpse but as a vital being. Wide-open eyes gaze out serenely. A bishop may hold his crosier in one hand and bless with the other; a gentlewoman touches an object around her neck or hooks a finger over the neckline of her dress or cord of her cloak, and with the other hand holds a fold of her garments. (Clothing falls for the most part toward the feet, often reflecting but slightly, if at all, the supine position.) Exceptions tend to occur amongst effigies of churchmen, where the defunct may be shown as a dead body, eyes closed, in the southern European fashion. Such is a bishop at Ferns. An architectural framework, censing angels (suggestive of absolution) and a dragon at the feet (here a symbol of evil overcome by the bishop's faith and good works) project the whole into an otherworldly realm. The effigy may commemorate Bishop John of St John (1223–53) or Bishop Geoffrey of St John (1254–8). Considerable colour remains.

10c

10a

The effect of life inherent in the figure of a bishop (?John of Taunton,

d. 1258) in St Brigid's cathedral in Kildare, probably carved later than his contemporary at Ferns, is more characteristic of the medieval effigy in northern Europe. Wide-open eyes, a pursed mouth and two twisting, censing angels create a very lively impression. At Ferns, the material substance of the bishop sleeps peacefully until the day of the resurrection of the body; at Kildare, it waits in a state of suspended animation. The artist has made much of fine detail in the latter, a characteristic of the better Irish medieval work.

Likewise outstanding are three figures of ladies, members of the Hackett family, now built into the walls of the churchyard of the post-reformation protestant cathedral at Cashel. Seldom is a female effigy more attractively viva- 10c cious, and perhaps never before nor since in medieval Ireland have draperies been in part more deeply carved. All three, like the armoured man of between perhaps 1300 and 1350, who is an integral member of the group, have one leg thrown across the other in a fashion which writers have sometimes sought to reserve for crusaders or for those who died on the field of action. Other Irish examples of cross-legged figures include knights at Hospital, County Limerick, and Jerpoint abbey. Of the little standing knights on the chest (front) of a tomb in Cahir castle from Athassel abbey, County Tipperary, two are in the cross-legged pose. The tomb probably commemorates Walter de Burgh, a scion of the founding family, who died in 1271, and is almost surely of English origin. The crossing of the legs in effigies may usually be interpreted not as an indication of dying nor of death but of vitality.

Free of the awkwardness which the cross-legged pose sometimes involves is the well preserved and highly representative, over life-size (eight feet or 2.42 m) figure in the roofless ruins at Kilfane, County Kilkenny, which may represent a Sir Thomas de Cantwell (one gentleman of this name died about 1321, another 10b not until after 1331).[1] Sir Thomas still favours the long surcoat and long shield often used in the preceding century, and, like the more conservative of his contemporaries in Britain, has not yet adopted plate as part of his armour. The spare elegance is characteristic of much work in Ireland.

Although seldom adorned with much representational sculpture at this time, tombs consisting of broad recesses in the wall, often finished with architectural trim, form another significant type of sepulchral monument. If near the east end of the north wall they may commemorate the principal founder. Along with the piscina and the sedilia (elaborated niche-like seats in the south side of the 11b chancel for officiants of the mass), they often turn an otherwise bare chancel into a thing of interest.

FOLLOWING the devastations of the fourteenth century and the destruction of Anglo-Irish hegemony (which had begun, especially in the west, in the later thirteenth), there had arisen powerful and varied, often highly independent elements in society—resurgent Gaelic Irish, Anglo-Irish nobility, and, in the

[1] *Ormond deeds, 1172–1350*, p. 268. Suggested by Dr Peter Harbison.

cities and the Pale, the loyal colonial population, all active patrons of the arts. For inspiration, Ireland could draw upon Romanesque and Gothic buildings already in the land and upon ideas adopted from abroad. The often distinctive result is well displayed in some of the refurbished abbeys, and especially in the newly founded friaries. Some new work was done almost everywhere in the fifteenth and early sixteenth centuries, if only the addition of a chapel, window, or doorway.

The fourteenth century had been portentous for all Europe, but especially for Ireland. Colonial decline had already started when, during the four years of the wars of the Bruces (1315–18), 'enormous damage' was done 'which gravely weakened the English interest'.[1] County Roscommon, with its new, strong castles, was abandoned; in Connacht, representatives of the de Burghs became thoroughly gaelicised. Also disastrous for the colonial settlement was the Black Death of 1348–9. It affected most severely the urban centres, and may have killed off half of the population of English descent.[2] However, after a time of gestation there occurred that striking efflorescence of the arts which characterises the end of the middle ages in Ireland.

The nature of the patronage was highly significant. Especially in the west, many of the patrons were leaders in the Gaelic resurgence, increasingly able to hold their own against both fellow Gaelic Irish and Anglo-Irish, and increasingly free to indulge in their preferred language and customs and to adopt what they wished from other peoples. The culture of the mighty ones among the Anglo-Irish—Desmond, Ormond, Kildare, and their followers—was often a hybrid of the traditions of *Gaedhil* and *Gaill*. Many of these leaders not only understood but spoke Irish and had adopted Gaelic customs and titles. The Pale, reduced toward the end of this period to territory lying between Dublin and Dundalk, voiced only a gentle murmur of trans-channel culture, quite different from the robust and widespread chorus of Anglo-Norman architecture and sculpture in Ireland two hundred years previously. Although the larger towns, especially the seaports, held the position of outposts of English interests, in Galway in the late middle ages Gaelic terms were becoming part of everyday speech, and a late fifteenth-century mayor of Waterford, James Rice, was complimented for what one might have imagined to be far too common a trait to deserve notice, his championing of the use of English.

The picture as regards monasteries in the century before the dissolution is a chequered one. There had been changes in the practices of the Cistercians, still among the most significant of the orders in Ireland as regards architecture. Labour no longer formed part of the monks' daily activities. The institution of lay brothers, already beginning to decline, had been dealt a lethal blow by the Black Death, which is believed to have resulted in the death of three-fifths of

[1] Otway-Ruthven, *Med. Ire.*, p. 237; and see above, pp 275–302.
[2] Ibid., p. 238; and above, pp 449–50.

all the Cistercians in northern Europe. The order never recovered from this catastrophe.

But some of these abbeys now held productive lands and enjoyed income from parishes and churches, like most of the other monastic orders. Some of the most important projects in this later period consisted of rebuilding parts of already existing monastery churches, especially the east ends. The smaller number of monks probably contributed to emphasising an interest in elaboration and high quality in detail rather than large-scale new enterprises.

Among the principal sources of inspiration for the highly eclectic late-Gothic builders in Ireland were windows and doorways derived from Irish examples of English work of the thirteenth and fourteenth centuries. A frequent use of the round arch was in all likelihood abetted, if not inspired, by the presence of this feature in Irish Romanesque and Transitional work. Cloister *3b* arcades often show clear derivation from Romanesque or early Gothic proto- *11d* types; but whether from southern France or Spain, or from now disappeared *14c* cloisters in the British Isles, is at present difficult to decide. Ideas from afar had probably already played their part, well before the fifteenth century, in establishing the use of the typical Irish stepped battlement. Some influence from continental Flamboyant work in canopies and tracery is surely possible. But although the carvers may have been emboldened in their creativeness by an acquaintance with work elsewhere, the so-called 'Spanish' screens and doorways are best referred to as Irish until such time as it may have been convincingly demonstrated that the specific design, mouldings, and other details are taken from work encountered originally only in Spain.

Prime examples of Irish late Gothic work are furnished by the Cistercian abbeys of Holy Cross, Kilcooly, Jerpoint, and Bective. Surely the most elaborate enterprise of the time was the rebuilding of the east end of the church and *11a, c* the building of the present cloister arcades of Holy Cross.[1] Some work may have been under way by the 1430s.[2] This achievement was in all likelihood made possible in part by gifts presented at the shrine of the famous relic from which the abbey derives its popular name. Also, the monastery was in lands now under the control of the powerful Butlers of Ormond. In 1364 James, the second earl, had become a principal patron, and this concern was continued by the later earls.[3]

Towers were appearing everywhere at this time, sometimes for defence, as at Fore abbey and Kells priory, County Kilkenny, but also as a mark of prestige as well as a place for bells and dovecotes. Holy Cross, Jerpoint, Kilcooly, and *2a, 11a* Dunbrody all received a central tower. The common Irish custom of integrating living quarters with the church also occurs: well-appointed rooms were constructed over the vaulted north transept, chancel, and transept chapels at

---

[1] Leask, *Churches*, iii, 60, suggests the third quarter of the fifteenth century for much of the work.
[2] W. J. Hayes, *Holy Cross abbey* (Dublin, 1971), p. 28; he does not give his evidence, however.
[3] Ibid., p. 26.

Holy Cross, and a similar situation exists at Kilcooly, where there were also rooms for habitation within the tower itself. A structure east of the cloister at Holy Cross is believed to have been the abbot's house, and in the church a larger amount of ribbed vaulting than usual gives the effect of great richness.

Very characteristic of Irish late Gothic is the treatment of the larger windows, usually derived from curvilinear or 'switch-line'[1] work of the four-teenth century, now simplified, now elaborated. Eight different traceried win-
11a dows were installed at Holy Cross, that in the west end of the nave perhaps influenced by the latest English Gothic style, the Perpendicular. Most elabor-ate of all, however, is the window of the chancel of Kilcooly. Here the east end of the church was reconstructed by Abbot 'Phillip O'Molwanayn' (?Ua Lanain) and his family between the time it was burned (1445) and 1463 or a little later. A Butler coat of arms and Butler tombs suggest contributions by members of this influential family also.

The new windows at Holy Cross are only part of the achievement of the late Gothic renovation. A fine vaulted tomb, in all probability unique in Ireland, occurs between the south transept chapels. Most impressive of all are the minutely detailed sedilia (seats for those officiating at mass) in the chancel. They bear the arms of England and Butler, the latter found also on the splen-did cloister arcade which, an inscription states, was made by Abbot 'Dyonisius
11c [Denis] O Congail'. This part of the arcade, probably made about 1450,[2] is the most regal in all Ireland, an elegant fourteenth-century English type, here and there adorned with typically Irish detail of lace-like delicacy. Nor were elabor-
11b ate late-Gothic features exclusive to the great monasteries. In the modest little cathedral at Clonmacnoise, a vaulted loft was inserted, and about 1459 a door-
12a way was created in the north wall at the behest of Dean Odo (Aodh) Ó Maoileoin, 'the most learned man in all Ireland'.[3] The excellence and richness of the decorative work in this doorway make clear why Leask termed it a land-mark for Irish medieval architecture, 'undoubtedly the work of a master'.

In marked contrast is the revival of Romanesque-type round arches, coupled colonnettes and bases, and capitals of thirteenth-century type in the cloister
11d arcade at Jerpoint. On the plates between the colonnettes occurs a menagerie of animals, demons, churchmen, saints, ladies, and several knights, one bearing
23d, 24a a shield which displays what is probably the arms of the Butlers. This family, along with the Graces, Blanchfields, and others whose tombs are in the church, must have been some of the greater patrons of the abbey when the cloister was carved at some time in the fifteenth century.

---

[1] Leask, *Churches*, iii, 115–31, defines and illustrates these terms.
[2] *Cal. papal letters, 1447—55*, pp 389, 653; *1455—64*, pp 2–4, 199–200. These confusing entries sug-gest that Abbot Denis was placed in the abbatial chair by one of the families or groups battling for control of the abbey and its lucrative resources.
[3] Leask (*Churches*, iii, 74) points out that Ó Maoileoin, described thus in *A.F.M.* at his death in 1461, was deprived of his office two years earlier, in 1459, and that 'this work must, therefore, have been executed before or about that year'.

Freed from the associations with decay and retrenchment which beset the older monastic orders, and vitalised by effective reform and developments from within, the great friary movement was the badge of honour of late medieval Ireland. Between 1340 and 1539 some 60 new friaries were founded and in addition 44 houses of the Franciscan third order regular.[1] This flourishing friary movement was often closely associated with the Gaelic resurgence and with Gaelic sympathies among the Anglo-Irish.

Reform impulses of the fifteenth century had led to the organisation of groups of friars, the Observants, committed to following a stricter observance of the rule, in contrast to the Conventuals, who had chosen not to adopt the severer discipline. Beginning in 1460, most of the newly established Irish Franciscan friaries were Observant.[2] Among the Dominicans, the Regular Observance began to win acceptance beginning c. 1426, and among the Augustinians from 1423. Also phenomenally successful and especially popular in areas of Connacht and Ulster where the Gaelic Irish were dominant were the Franciscans of the Third Order Regular, composed primarily of priests and laymen living in conventual establishments under vows of chastity, poverty, and obedience. The members engaged in pastoral work and Christian education, and appear to have had virtually no parallel outside Ireland.[3] Some of their buildings are of admirable craftsmanship.

The conventual buildings of friaries now ordinarily lay to the north of the church, and, like the church itself, were completed as donations came in. The community could now aspire to a stone cloister arcade, sometimes built within the ranges. Although variations are frequent, the sequence of rooms about the cloister followed in general the Cistercian prototype, but typically there were added a recreation room, guest rooms, a library, and lecture and study rooms, for 'the study of theology was in general left to the friars, who maintained their own schools for the purpose'.[4] The incorporation of the cloister walk in the ranges, thus reducing the space for rooms on the ground storey, sometimes led to placing the refectory on the first floor. In the west range arrangements were very flexible. *12b*

13a, 14c

An outstanding example is the fully developed, extremely well preserved Franciscan friary at Quin, County Clare. Founded by the local noble family of Mac Con Mara, the present buildings seem to have been constructed primarily between 1433 and the middle of the century. Eloquent of the new situation in Ireland, the friary is for the most part neatly fitted into what remained of the castle which Thomas de Clare had intruded into Macnamara territory c. 1280, only to have Cú Meda Mac Con Mara burn it out in 1288. The tall, subtly tapered tower of the church forms an organising focal point, and the cloisters *13b, c*

[1] Gwynn & Hadcock, *Med. relig. houses*, p. 9.
[2] Ibid., p. 236. See above, maps 9 and 13, pp 402, 585.
[3] Gwynn & Hadcock, *Med. relig. houses*, pp 263–6.
[4] Nicholls, *Gaelic Ire.*, p. 99.

with their delicate buttresses are more structurally articulate than many. Stone-work of high quality ennobles the tower and transept, whereas there occurs here the frequently encountered roughness of handling in the structurally sound vaulting of the cloister walk. The west end is a masterpiece of restrained expressiveness, worthy of comparison with Cistercian work at its best.

13c
13b

At the Franciscan friary of Askeaton, County Limerick, the chief patron of the time was the Anglo-Irishman James, seventh earl of Desmond. Judging from its fine craftsmanship, the cloister which he gave to the friars, apparently *c.* 1420–40, must have been one of the most costly of the whole century. This Anglo-Irish participation in the great upsurge of building was continued by the earl's daughter, Joan, who, with her husband, Thomas, seventh earl of Kildare, added (probably between 1427 and 1464) the charming, English-inspired, window-type cloister of the Augustinian friars' house at Adare, County Limerick. Equally attractive is the detail of an aisle added to enlarge the capacity of the church.

Acceptable to the Augustinians and to most Dominicans, this decorative detail contrasts with the complete absence of embellishment in the 'poor abbey' at Adare, a Franciscan Observant house to which Earl Thomas and Countess Joan gave the church, dedicated in 1464, and a quarter of the cloister. Various people gave other parts (compare with Athenry, above). Square-headed openings stare from a stern, unvaulted, but gracefully tapered tower. There is not a single sculptured leaf. But inside were fifteen graceful, if simple wall tombs of donors, at least some of the trim coloured, and also painted figures of saints—a compromise with lay frailties.[1]

18d

Not near large towns, but accessible to the country-dwelling Gael, were two flourishing Observant Franciscan friaries in Connacht, Ross, County Galway, and Moyne, County Mayo, both built in the second half of the fifteenth century. Confusion as to who may be credited as the founder of Moyne may reflect the participation of many patrons. A transept and very broad aisle more than doubled the area of the peoples' part of the church, and at Ross the addition of two juxtaposed transept arms approximately doubled the capacity. Remarkably preserved, Ross is the medieval Irish friary at its apogee. Stone claustral buildings stretch north to form a second court in addition to the tiny cloister. Great restraint in carved detail bespeaks the Observant vow, but the handling of the stonework is a matter of great beauty in itself.

Among the several remains of the architecture of the third order regular, that at Rosserk, County Mayo, founded before the year 1441,[2] stands out for its completeness, adroit planning and construction, and genial figure sculpture. A small lady chapel (transept arm), an integral part of the original church, provided deep recesses for two altars, a fine architectural development repeated at Moyne and elsewhere.

14b

[1] Caroline W. and Edwin R. W. Quin, *Memorials of Adare manor* (Oxford, 1865), pp 82–3; and T. J. Westropp, 'Paintings at Adare "abbey", County Limerick' in *R.S.A.I. Jn.*, xlv (1915), pp 151–2.
[2] Gwynn & Hadcock, *Med. relig. houses*, pp 267, 274.

As for cathedrals and larger parish churches, additions were frequent, such *12a* as a new chancel at St Mary's, Youghal, *c.* 1468; new aisles and longer transepts enlarged St Nicholas's in Galway; and chapels crowded the flanks of St Mary's in Limerick. Sometimes parish churches, for instance St Mary's in Callan, County Kilkenny, were built largely or entirely anew. At Callan, details in the north aisle and chancel suggest the later English Gothic, whereas the south aisle is characteristic of the national Irish style, an architectural parallel of Butler policies. In the 1460s the Butlers founded at Callan an Augustinian *11b* friary which became in 1479 the centre of the Augustinian Observants, a movement propelled by the Gaelic areas of western Ireland.

In the Pale itself a distinctive type of manor church was erected for the noble families—Plunkets, Cusacks, Talbots, and others. The church was often distinguished by a residential tower, sometimes over the sacristy, sometimes at the west end. For the lithe, simple mullions and drip (label) moulds typical of the friary, the builders substituted cusped openings, sometimes with tracery approaching the English Perpendicular style in the heads of the arches, although this manner 'influenced Irish architecture only to a limited extent'.[1] Like the friary, the manor church was divided into chancel and nave, although by a simple archway rather than by a tower structure. Fully developed examples of the manor type, such as Killeen and Dunsany in County Meath, *14d* had towers or turrets at or near each corner of the long, rectangular block formed by the nave and chancel. The aisleless, transeptless plan, a doorway in the north wall of the nave and another in the south wall opposite, occurs not only in the Pale but often elsewhere.

IT comes as no surprise that the building of castles flourished during the fifteenth and early sixteenth centuries, a period of only sporadic interest in Irish affairs on the part of the English crown, of resurgent gaelicism, and of powerful, semi-independent, Anglo-Irish lordships. Strategic older fortresses were maintained and improved, sometimes by one faction, sometimes by another. Most characteristic were the tower houses, even today 'quite the most evident ancient features of the Irish countryside'.[2] In the towns the upper classes also found the tower house a solution to prudent living. The lower classes presumably for the most part continued to live in modest homes of wood and clay and thatch. Apparently absent earlier, the charming and highly satisfactory English type of manor house made an appearance in Ireland at the end of the sixteenth century.

Adaptation to propitious topographical features and the incorporation of previously constructed buildings often led to marked asymmetry in the larger late-medieval castles. Towers reminiscent of Norman keeps often dramatised the occupant's power and position, while, inside the walls, halls of wood or

---

[1] Leask, *Churches*, iii, 117.
[2] Leask, *Castles*, p. 75.

stone evidenced the nobler mode of life. Such was the great stone banqueting hall of the Desmond stronghold at Askeaton, 'one of the finest medieval secular buildings in Ireland',[1] built about the middle of the fifteenth century by the seventh earl.

A fuller account is furnished by the picturesque and imposing complex at Cahir. The great tower that forms part of the walls of the inner bailey, and
15a commands the gate, dates perhaps in part from the thirteenth rather than the fifteenth century.[2] Like the Desmond stronghold at Askeaton, Cahir, in Butler hands since 1375, was built on an island in the river. It occupied a strategic position on the edge of Ormond and Desmond lands. The castle's vulnerability to artillery having been demonstrated by the breaching of the walls in Elizabethan times, Cahir wisely capitulated on honourable terms in the face of Cromwell's cannons in 1650 and hence survives, now well restored. A fine hall, strong keep, and entrance defences including a portcullis make it one of the most interesting castles in southern Ireland.

15b, c　　Far less grand and imposing than Cahir or Askeaton were the tower houses of the chiefs and nobles, somewhat comparable to the 'peel towers' of the Scottish border. They bespeak a society where defence of property was largely a matter of the devices of the local proprietors rather than the result of effective action by a powerful central authority.[3] Symptomatic was the issuance of a statute of Henry VI in 1430 awarding a subsidy of £10 to 'every liege-man of our lord the king' who built a tower house of specified minimum dimensions (that at Donore, County Meath, may be an example) in the 'land of peace' of the time, the counties of Louth, Meath, Dublin, and Kildare.[4] The typical tower house, larger and more complex than the '£10' structure, became widespread and continued to be built until down into the seventeenth century. Sometimes—perhaps nearly always—there was also a bawn (walled area) which could be almost any conceivable shape and size, from the little yard attached to one side of the tower at Clara, County Kilkenny, to an enclosure many times larger.

As in so many Irish church towers, the walls of the tower house
15c characteristically batter (incline inward) slightly, with a similarly pleasing result. The ground-level entrance was guarded by machicolations (openings in the floor of a projecting parapet through which missiles would be directed at attackers). Narrow openings, their tops square, round, or ogee-arched (the curve reversed at the peak), irregularly spaced, served as the simple windows, vents, and defensive loops. Paired lights were often used for the principal chambers high in the tower.

The arrangement of the interior does not vary greatly. A typical tower house
15b had four or five principal storeys, and was apportioned vertically into a main

---

[1] Peter Harbison, *Guide to the national monuments in the Republic of Ireland* (Dublin, 1970), p. 146.

[2] As indicated by Mr David Johnson, inspector of national monuments, Dublin.

[3] For their distribution see Caoimhín Ó Danachair, 'Irish tower houses and their regional distribution' in *Béalóideas*, xlv–xlvii (1979), pp 158–63.

[4] Leask, *Castles*, pp 76–7.

part and a subsidiary area which contained the stairs and smaller chambers. At least one and sometimes two storeys were vaulted. The other floors and ceilings were of wood. In the ground storey was a cellar. A little lobby with a 'murdering hole' (aperture) in its ceiling, a guard room, and stairs filled the ground storey of the forepart. Typically the hall would occupy the entire top floor. Garderobes (latrines), fireplaces, flues, secret chambers, storage recesses and window embrasures with seats were formed in the thickness of the walls.

Among the more dramatic and larger of the tower-house type of castle is the great mass of Blarney, an aggressive statement of the Gaelic revival. It was built by Cormac Mac Carthaigh about the middle or end of the fifteenth century. Blarney is nearly as high as the keep at Carrickfergus, 82 feet 6 inches (25.15 m) as against 90 feet (27.43 m). It was probably once adorned with stepped battlements.

Bunratty is among the finest. Its location was important for controlling *16a, b* commerce on the Shannon. Thomas de Clare, who unwittingly laid the foundations of Quin friary, built a stone castle at Bunratty in 1277, successor to an earlier one of *c.* 1250. The Anglo-Irish castles having been destroyed five times, the Gaelic Irish builders of Quin friary, the Macnamaras, took control and built the present Bunratty castle *c.* 1450–67, another example of the achievement of the Gaelic resurgence. There are many subsidiary rooms and garderobes, the four angle towers being almost large enough to constitute separate little castles on their own.

Upper-class town houses of the fifteenth and earlier sixteenth centuries resemble the tower houses of the countryside. Several still survive at Ardglass and elsewhere in County Down and at Dalkey, County Dublin. The greater domiciles of Galway were of particular interest for their elaborate decorative *17a* details. Quite different is the house of the merchant John Rothe in Kilkenny, *17b* begun in 1594. Its commodious rooms, broad windows, and multiple court-yards proclaim the prosperity and relative peace of some of the larger Irish towns at the end of the middle ages.

Also in Butler territory is the mansion which Thomas, tenth earl of Ormond, added to his family's castle complex at Carrick-on-Suir in the 1560s and later. *17c* An extensive, low façade, banks of windows, and a lack of any kind of tower-like structure at the ends suggest a gracious and gentle state of society in this area of 'Black Tom's' domains. He had been brought up at the English court, and was lord treasurer of Ireland. At Carrick a great gallery, ninety feet (27.43 m) in length, fills most of the front of the first floor. Representations of Queen Elizabeth, coats of arms, and mottoes in stucco form a rich decorative ensemble. Possibly an unrealised hope that the monarch might visit Carrick was involved in building the mansion.

Little is known of the housing of the largest part of the population of Ireland during this period.[1] Depending on the type of materials available, the peasants

[1] For a sound and candid summary, see the contribution by R. E. Glasscock in Beresford & Hurst, *Deserted medieval villages*, pp 277–301; see also above, pp 229–32, 403–4.

in areas where colonisation had not been effected can perhaps be pictured as continuing to live in structures of wattle and daub, rounded or approximately rectangular, or in simple, thatched buildings of sods, turf, clay, wood and clay, etc. Huts of stone might have sufficed where there was little else at hand. On the manors where English influence was predominant—much of the east coast, Leinster, and parts of south Munster—greater rectangularity in plan and the use of stone, at least in the base courses, might be found in the dwellings of the free tenants, burgesses, farmers, and perhaps others farther down the social scale.

In English villages 'rebuilding took place once a generation on completely new foundations and often on a new alignment',[1] and the same comparatively rapid replacement may have taken place in Ireland, but without much change in basic type.

THE Irish stone carvers of the end of the middle ages were often skilled designers and good craftsmen. Motifs from earlier Irish art sometimes reappear. A noteworthy achievement was a late form of cross slab. There was also a continuing interest in architectural wall tombs, especially in the west. Little is left of the paintings which were sometimes made on the back wall of the recess or on other parts of the church walls. Representation in sculpture and metalwork ran the gamut from highly abstract to highly naturalistic. A few important monuments in a semi-naturalistic manner occurred in the west, particularly at Ennis, County Clare. In the fifteenth century a well-defined school of funerary sculpture arose in the Meath–Dublin area, to be followed in the sixteenth by clearly characterised ateliers in the lordships of Kildare and Ormond. Here thrived the 'apostle tomb', a highly significant accomplishment. Also to be considered are the fonts and crosses of the manors of the Pale.

A singularly appropriate type of funerary monument was the Irish late-Gothic cross slab. Sometimes it was tapered slightly, suggestive of the thirteenth-9b, c century coffin-lid type. The low relief carving made the slabs almost as suitable as sepulchral brasses for the paving of the floor. There was considerable variation in motif and style of carving, as well as repetition of some patterns. Com-18a monly found in Leinster and Munster is a type with a monstrance-like cross head bearing broad points shaped like fleur-de-lys, mounted on a tall stem with a base. Around the edges of the stone a black-letter inscription in Latin gives much the same information as in the earlier slabs, although often in greater detail, usually the date of death and sometimes a pious plea or admonition. Sacred emblems, the mystic rose, 'IHS', or purely decorative foliage and occasionally some figures may also be present. In several instances, Ireland's best-known medieval stone carvers, the O'Tunneys, proudly and conspicuously added an inscription stating that they had done the work. It does not always follow that a funerary monument was made in the year of the death of the person commemorated. It may have been created before or after that event.

[1] Beresford & Hurst, *Deserted medieval villages*, p. 122.

The wall tomb (tomb niche) continued to find favour. A mensa slab, with or *18b, c, d* without effigy or inscription, might be inserted within the recess. Upon occasion the area below the slab was treated like the side of a chest, with arcading and perhaps sculptured figures. In several instances the arch was quite tall, the upper part filled with rich tracery, framed at the sides by buttress strips, the whole suggestive of an actual canopy. Connections with English work are sometimes clear, as at Youghal and Limerick, whereas similarities to continen- *18b* tal Flamboyant work may be pointed out in a group in Connacht. That at Strade, County Mayo, is one of the most impressive. It has been suggested that the figures refer to pilgrimages undertaken by the kneeling donor: the three kings (if the magi), Cologne; the archbishop (Thomas Becket?), Canterbury; Peter and Paul, Rome.

A word is due on the colour and painting that formerly enlivened the interior of the later medieval church, although it has almost entirely disappeared. Not one medieval stained glass window is known to remain. At times, as on the lavabo and chapter house at Mellifont, colour was even applied to carved architectural detail,[1] and designed tiles garnished the floors of better-endowed foundations. Fortunately, colour and recognisable painting on walls persisted long enough to be seen and recorded. There must have been a considerable amount of it, and most sculpture in stone and wood was in all probability painted, judging from meagre but positive remains. Paintings of the crucifixion and locally popular invocations would have been frequent. One of the chapels in St Nicholas's, Galway, was called the chapel of the Doom, reference to a painted 'Last judgment'. Still visible in the later nineteenth century were a 'trinity' and figures of saints and angels in recesses in the south aisle of St Audoen's in Dublin, and also in the chancel at Knockmoy abbey.

Among the few wall paintings still extant is a hunting scene, probably of the fifteenth century, in the north transept at Holy Cross. This and the work once at Knockmoy are little but enlargements of illuminations in manuscripts such as the corporation roll of the fourteenth century at Waterford. At Knockmoy, thought to have been done *c.* 1541, was a figure with a scales, possibly a St Michael from the 'Last judgment', and, a less common scene, the attempted martyrdom of St Sebastian, a nude youth being shot through with arrows by two bowmen. In another register appeared the popular late medieval moralising theme of the decaying cadaver (encountered also in the Rice tomb at *21a* Waterford). The transitoriness of life is made all too clear as three pleasure-seeking kings out a-hawking meet three grisly cadavers. All are shown in frontal pose, as so often in Irish art, more the presentation of an idea than the representation of an event.

Differing cultural currents are evident in Ireland's late medieval sculpture. The well known St Francis at Ennis suggests folk art. Far more genuinely 'abstract' are some heads from western County Clare, representative of a number

[1] Conway, *Mellifont*, pp 248–9.

of such carvings by skilful artist-craftsmen innocent of any compulsion toward anatomical exactitude. Much of the stark sense of presence of Romanesque Dysert O'Dea and Transitional Kilfenora has been recaptured.

19a   Stylised form of another nature is employed in the brass Ballymacasey cross of probably 1479. In the conventionalised but eloquent form of the corpus true artistry has transformed the bitterness of indignity and cruelty into a profoundly moving and unforgettable experience.

These achievements in a non-naturalistic vein contrast markedly with strongly naturalistic work such as the cosmopolitan mitre and silver-gilt crosier *19d*   of Bishop Conchobhar Ó Deadhaidh in St John's cathedral in Limerick. The crosier is one of the finest from the medieval period in Great Britain and Ireland. It was constructed in 1418, perhaps by 'Thomas O'Carryd', who signed the accompanying mitre. Also in some respects highly naturalistic is the menagerie of motifs on the late fifteenth-century choir stalls of black Irish oak *20a*   in St Mary's cathedral in Limerick. The use of leaves or other motifs flanking the main subject of the carving of the misericordes (under parts of the seats) is characteristically British; the fine linear patterns on the surfaces and the almost metallic effect are fully in tune with Irish ideals.

Much of the work lies between these extremes of 'abstraction' and naturalism. In the fifteenth century there occurred in the west an unexpected and remarkable outburst of figure sculpture dramatically exemplified by the *20b*   canopied 'royal' (MacMahon) tomb of *c.* 1470 in the Franciscan friary at Ennis, now incorporated in a nineteenth-century Creagh memorial. For story-telling, the narrative panels are unmatched in extent by any other Irish Gothic sculpture. Against the wall at the level of the mensa in the reconstruction are Christ and the twelve apostles, perhaps from another monument.[1] Models for some of the Passion scenes were indubitably English alabasters, which spread far and wide over Europe at this time. On the tomb chest, beginning with the west end, are an archbishop (Patrick?) and the 'Betrayal'; on the front, the 'Flagellation', 'Crucifixion', and 'Entombment'. Four flails depicted on a huge scale make the first-mentioned doubly harrowing. There is a greater inclusion of historical personages at Ennis than in most Irish medieval representations of the Crucifixion. A strongly frontal treatment projects some of the figures forcibly upon the spectator. In the 'Entombment', as in many alabasters, the eyeballs, having lost their painted detail, lend a curiously dreamlike appearance. Gross, sullen soldiers make an effective contrast to a beatific Christ in the 'Resurrection' on the east end. At the right is possibly the patroness, Mór Ní Bhriain, holding an open prayer book; or perhaps a representation of a Virtue.[2] She displays the austere beauty latent in severe, stylised form.

Another canopied tomb in County Clare, the Macnamara monument at Quin, bears no figure sculpture, but is representative of fifteenth-century carving at its best.

[1] Hunt, *Figure sculpture*, i, 121.   [2] Ibid., i, 89.

Like the figures on the often splendid Flemish *dalles* (sepulchral slabs) of the period, later Irish representations of the deceased are carved in relief, sometimes low, sometimes fairly high. A good example of the former is the monument of Sir Thomas de Tuite at Kentstown, County Meath, dated by an inscription, unfortunately damaged, to either 1363 or 1463. Costume and some other details suggest the earlier period; the faulty inscription would seem to point to the latter.[1] At the foot of the monument is a dog, symbol of religious faith and perhaps also of other kinds of fidelity.

Most accomplished of all Irish late Gothic achievements in sculpture, however, is the mensa tomb—a freestanding, rectangular structure similar to a sarcophagus. It is composed of the *mensa*, or covering slab, with or without an effigy or other carving on it, and the chest which it surmounts. The sides (surrounds) of the chest are often treated architecturally as blind arcades or niches and in addition are often enlivened with coats of arms, human figures, and various types of decoration. *20c*

21a, b

Among the more important examples of fifteenth-century sepulchral monuments in north Leinster is a sadly damaged and fragmentary tomb or cenotaph of about mid-century at Killeen, County Meath. A partly preserved inscription *20c, d* suggests that it may commemorate a Lady Joan Cusack, who died in 1441, and her husband, Christopher Plunket.[2] She was the heiress of Killeen, and a generous benefactor to the church, as indicated in the book of obits of Christ Church, Dublin. He was a loyal king's man, who acted (1432–4) as deputy to the lieutenant, Thomas Stanley. The coats of arms on the sides of the structure are considered to denote familial relationships of the deceased.[3] This monument was probably the paradigm of the group. For subtlety and fineness of detail it is one of the best of all Irish tombs: the sculptor must surely have been acquainted with sepulchral brasses and delicate work in alabaster. Later examples, such as those at Dunsany and Rathmore, County Meath, and Howth in County Dublin, often include little figures of saints in the low-relief arches on the ends of the chest. Sometimes the effigies on the mensa assumed greater bulk and projection, perhaps through the sculptors' acquaintance with flourishing tomb sculpture abroad rather than from a native evolution.

Most elaborate of extant Irish mensa tombs of the fifteenth century is the

[1] Lord Walter Fitzgerald, 'Kentstown churchyard' in *Ir. Mem. Assoc. Jn.*, viii (1910–12), pp 608–10, reads '1463' and reproduces a rubbing where the questioned fourth 'C' is clearly indicated in the date: MILESIMO CCCC SEXAGESIMO TCIO. Perhaps the carver mistakenly included an extra C, which was later partly effaced. Hunt (*Figure sculpture*, i, 207) is convinced that 1363 is correct.

[2] It is difficult to agree that the reference on the mensa of the monument is to Lord John Cusack (Hunt, *Figure sculpture*, i, 208) rather than to a Lady Joan (Johanna) Cusack, as suggested by Lord Walter Fitzgerald (*Ir. Mem. Assoc. Jn.*, viii (1910–12), p. 404). The inscription was presumably much more legible in Lord Walter's time than it is today.

[3] Hunt (loc. cit.) finds it probable that the sides originally belonged to the fragmentary mensa that now rests upon them. Helen Roe's reading of the heraldry confirms that one of the coats of arms is that of Cusack–Plunket; another is St Lawrence; a third, either Butler or de Paor.

2*1a* monument made about 1482 for James Rice, oft-time mayor of the city of Waterford. In place of the usual life-like effigy, a handsomely carved open-eyed cadaverous figure on the mensa reminds one of the decay of the present life, and an artfully carved inscription in Latin on the horizontal surface presses the point home:

Here lie James Rice, onetime citizen of this city, founder of this chapel, and Catherine Broun, his wife. Whoever you may be, passerby, stop, weep as you read. I am what you are going to be, and I was what you are. I beg of you, pray for me! It is our lot to pass through the jaws of death. Lord Christ, we beg of thee, we implore thee, be merciful to us! Thou who has come to redeem the lost, condemn not the redeemed![1]

One of the grandest, the Rice monument appears also to be the earliest extant fully developed Irish 'apostle tomb'. By this term is meant a *mensa* tomb where most of the figures on the surrounds represent the apostles, often six on each of the longer sides. Sometimes, as here, the figures are placed in an order frequently found in late medieval art in Great Britain and Ireland when each figure is given a scroll inscribed with that portion of the apostles' creed credited to him. (An example is the painted choir screen at Kenton in Devonshire, where the apostles are also paired with prophets who bear quotations appropriate to them.) Reference to the creed may have been intended on the Rice monument as well as intercession for the deceased on the part of the apostles.[2] In the niches of one end are the Virgin Mary with the infant Christ, 22*c* and the saints Margaret of Antioch and Catherine of Alexandria; on the opposite end are Edward the Confessor, the holy trinity, and Patrick.

One of the several local schools of sculpture which flourished in Ireland between *c.*1450 and *c.*1550 appears to have been associated to a large extent with Piers Butler, eighth earl of Ormond, and his closer relations. Figures by 22*b, d* this atelier are full-bodied and charmingly expressive. A major achievement of 2*1b* the school was the mensa monument of the earl and his countess, Margaret FitzGerald, in St Canice's cathedral, Kilkenny, of probably between *c.*1515 and *c.*1530, now unfortunately pieced out with parts of other works. Piers's armour is a practical type, resembling that long since discarded for effigies done for court circles, while Lady Margaret's headdress, superseded as high fashion by other modes, appears to have been retained in south Leinster as a mark of high estate. Both figures are idealised in feature, alert, depicted as if in the prime of life, as they would be at the resurrection.

More characteristically Irish, however, is the work of a group in south Lein-23*a* ster and Munster centred around Ruaidhrí Ó Tonnaigh (O'Tunney), who excelled in finely cut inscriptions. In the now disassembled mensa monument

[1] The inscription deciphered with the help of the late Fr Thomas Clohosey of Mooncoin (Kilkenny) and Dr Ludwig Bieler of University College, Dublin.

[2] E. C. Rae, 'The Rice monument in Waterford cathedral' in *R.I.A. Proc.*, lxix (1970), sect. C, p. 8; E. C. Rae, 'Irish sepulchral monuments of the later middle ages' in *R.S.A.I. Jn.*, ci (1971), pp 10–12.

dated 1507 of James Shortal in St Canice's the work of this shop is highly   22a
stylised and grandly monumental. Reminiscences of the other-worldliness
inherent in the manuscript illuminations of early Christian times abound, and
the best knightly effigies by the O'Tunney circle form elegant and effective
memorials.

As regards naturalism, the culminating achievement of an atelier associated
primarily with work in County Kildare is the tomb of Walter Wellesley (d.
1539), prior of Great Connell and bishop of Kildare, now in St Brigid's
cathedral, Kildare.[1] The style of the incipient renaissance is already present in   23c
some of the figures and motifs. Related to this monument is the tomb of Walter
Bermingham, first Baron Carbury (died 1548) at Dunfierth, County Kildare.   23b
His plate armour shows the fanciful development sometimes encountered in
the sixteenth century. The medieval tradition lingered long in the effigies of Sir
Maurice Fitzgerald of Lackagh (d. 1575) in St Brigid's, the recumbent knight
which does duty for Sir Richard Butler (d. 1571) and the strikingly conventionalised lady on the tomb of Honorina Grace (d. 1597), both in St Canice's.
The Barnewall tomb of 1589 at Lusk, County Dublin, belongs to another era.

Most extensive of all Irish sculptural ensembles of the entire middle ages   11d, 23d,
was the fifteenth-century cloister arcade at Jerpoint abbey. The scope of the   24a
subject-matter is encyclopaedic. But the presence of apostles and so many lay
figures suggests that the Jerpoint carvings may also constitute a kind of
expanded chantry for certain of the local noble families. The vitality of the
stylised figures is contagious.

Less well known but sometimes of high quality are the fonts and later stone
crosses of the fifteenth and sixteenth centuries which, in addition to the sedilia
and perhaps a tomb for the family who controlled the area, enriched several of
the manor and parish churches in north Leinster.[2] Outstanding is the elaborately adorned example from Crickstown, County Meath, now in the church of   24c
St Andrew at Curraha, County Meath, probably created in the first half or
toward the middle of the fifteenth century. To the common subject of the
twelve apostles, authors of the creed to be accepted by the baptised, are added
various other saints, a 'Crucifixion', and an 'Annunciation'. On the chamfer of
the bowl and on the base are some remarkably lifelike grotesques and animals,
an indication of the acceptance of all facets of life on the part of the more
sophisticated patron of the middle ages. A rare depiction of the baptism of   24d
Christ happily survives on the vigorously sculptured font in St Peter's protestant church in Drogheda.

Less appreciated than the fonts are the remains of the late Gothic sculptured
stone churchyard and market crosses. The carvings usually represent either

[1] Some of the pieces of the sides may have formed part of another monument. See E. C. Rae,
'The tomb of Bishop Walter Wellesley at Great Connell priory, County Kildare' in *Kildare Arch.
Soc. Jn.*, xiv (1970), pp 560–62; and Hunt, *Figure sculpture*, i, pp 162–3.
[2] Those of County Meath have been examined by Miss Helen Roe, *Medieval fonts of Meath*
([Navan,] 1968), the source of most of these comments.

apostles or other saints, Mary with the dead Christ (the 'Pietà') or a 'Crucifixion'. Foliage and animals were also acceptable. Exceptional is the second
24b cross stem at Killeen, County Meath, where Thomas Plunket, Marion Cruise,
and their offspring, suggestive of family 'weepers' on English alabaster tombs,
form a guard of honour below the now missing head of the cross. They are
characteristic of medieval Irish sculpture in a lack of interest in copying individual peculiarities of face and pose. Instead, the achievement is more in the
nature of a poetic evocation, a radiant presence.

T H E development of Irish architecture in the late middle ages was in its initial
phase a direct product of the activities of the reforming native churchmen and
sponsorship by the native laity. Although never disciplined by the tradition of a
Roman conquest, and situated apart from the mainstreams of trade and commerce, Irish reformers readily accepted new developments in church organisation and methods and scale of building. These new developments contrasted
markedly with what had formerly been the traditions of the country. A stronger
British orientation was afforded by the subsequent Anglo-Norman presence,
which many welcomed for its better aspects—thorough diocesan organisation
and operation, and the orderliness possible under strong monarchical rule. At
first the new architectural and sculptural forms were sometimes affected by
local colour, but from the middle of the thirteenth century to the middle of the
fourteenth, Ireland was a British province as regards the more obvious aspects
of architecture and sculpture.

During the two centuries which then followed there arose a method and style
of architecture based largely upon the lingering Romanesque and the Early
English and Decorated styles of earlier years in Ireland, fortified by selective
borrowings from contemporary architecture abroad.

This variable but highly successful integration of different attitudes apparent in most of the architecture (that of the Pale tended to be English in style) is
less true of sculpture and metalwork. Highly naturalistic, cosmopolitan
examples contrast with contemporary semi-naturalistic or even highly stylised
work. The incalculable losses, and the dangers inherent in relying largely upon
written references as to the character of the arts, will probably always prevent a
convincingly clear account from emerging.

In any attempt to evaluate the character of a culture, the evidence of the arts
must be interpreted with the greatest care. However, the meaning for history of
the late medieval Irish friary seems clear. As Gaelic and Anglo-Irish self-
assurance found full voice, these little establishments sprang up, often the
primary concern of one family or group, spurred on by a genuine spiritual
reform, as seen in the institution of the strict observance, and a sometimes
quite remarkable social involvement. The latter is particulary evidenced by the
houses of the Franciscan third order regular.

The friary structures, however, are but visual evidence of a healthy and vigorous phenomenon. The greatest contribution of medieval Ireland to her later history which is involved here is of course the spiritual and organisational rebirth itself, which survived the catastrophic events that followed and helped to form the basis of much that is strongest in Irish society today.

GLOSSARY

ARCHITRAVE: Moulded frame around a door or window.

BARBICAN: Advance tower or other defensive work outside a castle or town.

BASILICAN: From *basilica*, a longitudinal building with a wider central part (nave) and side aisles, and a projection (apse) at the end.

BATTER: Inward slope of the face of a wall.

BATTLEMENT: Notched (crenellated) parapet at the top of a wall.

BAWN: Fortified enclosure or outwork of a castle.

CELL: Dependency of a larger monastery; room for an individual monk.

CHAMFER: Diagonal plane created by bevelling off a square edge.

CHANCEL: Eastern arm of a church, used by the clergy in performing services.

CHAPTER HOUSE (ROOM): In a monastery, a room for reading the rules and other business; in a cathedral, a room for meetings of the governing body.

CHEVRONS: In architecture, zigzag mouldings.

CHOIR: Chancel of a church; more accurately the space set aside for monks, canons, or others assisting in the service. Often consists of the space at the crossing of nave and transept (see below), together with the eastern part of the nave.

CLAUSTRAL ENSEMBLE: Cloister garth (see below) and surrounding buildings.

CLERESTORY: Part of a building, pierced with windows and rising above an adjoining part, e.g. the wall of the nave above the aisle roofs.

CLOISTER: Covered passage around a court (garth).

COLONETTE: Little column; often used decoratively, sometimes much elongated, as on doorways and window enframements.

CORBEL: Projection from a wall for the support of a superimposed weight, e.g. a beam or statue.

CROCKET: Decorative foliate or bud-like projection, usually found on top of gables, arches, and the like.

CROSSING: The part of a cruciform church where the transept crosses the axis of the nave.

CUSP: Inward-pointing projection on an arch head, forming a foliation.

DECORATED STYLE: The second style of English Gothic architecture, characterised by traceried windows, elaborated carvings, and increased decoration.

DONJON: Innermost and strongest structure, or central tower, of a castle, serving as a last defence.

DORTER: Dormitory of a monastic establishment.

DRIPSTONE: Moulding or canopy over a door or window to throw off rain running down the wall.

FRATER: Refectory of a monastic establishment.

GARTH: Courtyard surrounded by a cloister walk.

GRISAILLE: Grey; uncoloured.

HOOD MOULD: See dripstone, above.

KEEP: See donjon, above.

LABEL MOULD: See dripstone, above.

LANCET: Tall, narrow, pointed window.

LAVABO: Washing trough, or structure containing a font for washing the hands, in a monastic establishment.

MONKS' CHOIR: See choir, above.

MOTTE-AND-BAILEY: Fortification consisting of a large steep-sided mound (motte) with a flat top, the site of a defensive structure, and an adjacent area (bailey) enclosed with ditch, bank, palisade, or wall.

NAVE: Main body of a church, usually separated from the aisles by columns or piers.

NOVICIATE: Living quarters for novices (trainees) in a monastic establishment.

OGEE: A cyma reversa curve; a double curve, convex above and concave below. The outline of an ogee arch resembles that of an inverted beetroot.

OPE: Window; opening.

PALISADE: Fence of pales or stakes.

PARLOUR: Conversation room in a monastic establishment.

PERPENDICULAR: The third and last style of English Gothic architecture, characterised by accent on the vertical line.

PISCINA: In churches, a basin for liturgical washing of vessels used in the mass; in the Gothic period, often set in an elaborated niche in a wall of the chancel (in the British Isles, the south wall).

PLINTH: Projecting part at the foot of a wall or column.

PORTCULLIS: Strong grating, sliding in grooves on the inner sides of a gateway or passage so as to be lowered as a defensive obstacle.

PRESBYTERY: Chancel (see above), or its eastern part, in which the altar is placed.

QUATREFOIL: Opening, or ornament, so divided by cusps as to give the appearance of four petals or leaflets radiating from a centre.

REFECTORY: Dining room in a monastic establishment or college.

RETROCHOIR: In a Cistercian monastery, a part of the nave just to the west of the monks' choir (see above), set apart for the infirm.

SACRISTY: Room or repository in an ecclesiastical establishment, in which are kept vestments, sacred vessels, and the like.

SEDILIA: Seats in or at the side wall of a church near the altar, for the use of the officiating clergy during services.

SLYPE: Passage; in a monastic establishment, one leading from the east walk of the cloisters to the outside of the building complex.

SPANDREL: Triangular space between the outside of an arch and a rectangular enframement, or between contiguous arches and a horizontal moulding above them.

SWITCHLINE: Type of compound window in which the bars (mullions) between the lights are projected upward following the curve of the arch, their intersections thus forming the tracery in the head of the window. Sometimes enriched with quatrefoils (see above) and other shapes.

TOWER HOUSE: Fortified dwelling in the form of a tower.

TRANSEPT: Transverse part of a cruciform church, considered apart from the nave; one or other of the two arms thus formed.

TRIFORIUM: Gallery or arcade in the wall over the arcade of the nave, transept, and choir.

WATTLE-AND-DAUB: Construction method using interlaced posts, rods, or branches, plastered with clay or mud.

CHAPTER XXVIII

Manuscripts and illuminations, 1169–1603

FRANÇOISE HENRY AND GENEVIÈVE MARSH-MICHELI

It is usual to consider that the coming of the Anglo-Normans marks the end of the 'vernacular' style of decoration in Ireland and that Irish art from this time forward models itself on imported trends. This is nearly true of architecture and, up to a point, of sculpture and metalwork, though there are examples of resurgence of traditional methods and patterns. But the case of manuscripts is different; there, a remarkable duality is immediately apparent. The Anglo-Normans and most of the new monasteries of continental origin imported books from England and the Continent and had them copied in the same style in Ireland. During the troubled times of the thirteenth century scribal art of Irish type seems to reel under the impact. But this is only a short episode, and most of the scribes working outside the Pale soon rallied to the old traditions. For centuries, in fact from the fourteenth to the nineteenth century, Irish and sometimes Latin texts were copied in the same type of script as had been used up to the twelfth century, and were often ornamented with large initials which derive from those of eleventh- and twelfth-century Irish books. The work, however, was not usually done in monasteries, as had been the case so far, but had become the privilege of a professional class of historians, lawyers, and scribes.[1]

A rapid glance at the situation in the twelfth century will help us to appreciate both the continuity of the tradition and the changed conditions in the production of books. Up to the coming of the Anglo-Normans all the extant evidence points to exclusively monastic scriptoria. Of the books that have survived,

[1] It is essential to keep in mind, when reading this chapter, the fact that it deals with the *decoration* of manuscripts; this will explain why some books, important for their text, are rapidly glossed over or even totally omitted. Only the most important decorated manuscripts have been dealt with. References to catalogues of manuscripts have only been given when they are of especial importance, as they can easily be found from the shelf mark.

The decoration of late Irish manuscripts has so far attracted little attention. The only publication that gives reproductions in colour of many of the illuminations concerned is *Facs. nat. MSS Ire.* On the general problems of the manuscripts, see O'Curry, *MS materials*; E. C. Quigg in 'Prolegomena to the study of the later Irish bards, 1200–1500' in *Proc. Brit. Acad.*, v (1911–12), pp 89–143; Robin Flower, *The Irish tradition* (Oxford, 1947); Walsh, *Ir. men of learning*; Brian Ó Cuív (ed.), *Seven centuries of Irish learning* (Dublin, 1961; Cork, 1971); and Liam de Paor (ed.), *Great books of Ireland* (Dublin, 1967). On calligraphy, see below, p. 813, n. 1.

MAGH LUIRG   Ruling families

MAC SUIBHNE

Ó DOMHNAILL

Dungiven

Lifford

OIRGHIALLA
Armagh

Downpatrick

Lisgoole

Lecan
TÍR AILEALLA

MAGH LUIRG
MAC DIARMIDA

Ballymote   Kilronan

Castlefore

TEALLACH
EACHACH

Boyle

R. Shannon

Mellifont

Navan
Rathmore

Duleek

Dunsany
Trim

MACWILLIAM BURKE

Roscommon

Glinsk

Saints' Island

Tuam

UÍ MHAINE

Galway

Clonfert

Kilcormac

Monasterevin

Dublin

Great Connell
Herbertstown

Kilnalahan
Duniry

Lorrha

ÉILE UÍ CHÉARBHAILL

Roscrea

Arklow

Kilkenny

ORMOND
Pottlerath

Gowran

Graiguenamanagh

Inistioge

Cashel

Mealaigh Móir

Carrick-on-Suir

Waterford

Fermoy   Lismore

Cork

| 0 | Miles | 50 |
| 0 | Kms | 80 |

Map 16 PLACES MENTIONED IN CHAPTER XXVIII,
by Françoise Henry

some—gospels, psalters, missals, hymn-books—are meant for liturgical use. A few manuscripts may have been intended as textbooks in the monastic schools. With the exception of some Old Irish hymns, they are all written in Latin. The annals are written in a mixture of Latin and Irish. On the other hand, Irish is used for the great collections of texts: Lebor na hUidre (Book of the Dun Cow), Rawlinson MS B. 502, and the Book of Leinster, though it may be noted that Latin phrases and sentences occur in such texts. In these an essential place is given to secular literature—epics, poems—and to historical and pseudo-historical matter such as genealogies, traditions of places, legendary lore of the 'invasions of Ireland'.

All these manuscripts, whether in Latin or in Irish, are written in Irish script and are illuminated in a style that continues that of the eighth and ninth centuries, though it incorporates also the alterations brought to Irish ornament by contacts with the Norse.[1] Each important section of a book begins with a large initial coming right to the bottom of the page. In some cases an illustration accompanies that ornamental beginning, such as a representation of the relevant symbol for each of the gospels. Elsewhere, the page has remained blank, as the illustration was planned but not executed. The text is often lavishly decorated with smaller initials of two main types: 'ribbon-initials', where the letter is made of the body of an elongated animal, and 'wire-initials' drawn in thick black lines ending in animal heads and paws on a background of vivid colour disposed mosaic-fashion. Indications that a part of a sentence is the continuation of the text above or below ('turn-in-the-path') are also the occasion for decorative motifs.

This picture is true up to the very moment of the Anglo-Norman invasion. When it is possible to survey the situation again, about the middle of the fourteenth century, a drastic change has taken place: the old monasteries have disappeared, either swept away by the tide of the twelfth-century reform, like Kells, or destroyed beyond recovery by the plunderings of the Anglo-Normans, like Durrow, Clonard, Clonmacnoise, or Derry. They have often been replaced by an episcopal see, and in this case canons regular have settled in what is left of their buildings. New communities, Augustinian canons regular, Cistercian monks, then Franciscan, Dominican, Carmelite, and Augustinian friars were established in the country. Their books, like all their cultural activities, were dominated by the example of what was being done abroad, chiefly in England.[2]

There are a good number of liturgical books which can be identified as having been used in Ireland. Most of them differ very little from their English counterparts. The same applies to the surviving examples of books used by the government in Ireland, and to the charters or registers of towns.

However, at the same time, such books of the great Irish monasteries which

---

[1] See Françoise Henry and G. L. Marsh-Micheli, 'A century of Irish illumination (1070–1170)' in *R.I.A. Proc.*, lxii (1962), sect. C, pp 101–64.

[2] See the ordinances of the second synod of Cashel (1172), above, p. 92.

had escaped destruction, especially the collections of miscellaneous Irish texts, were being studied and their matter copied or adapted by members of 'learned families' living, chiefly in Munster and in Connacht, under the patronage of various kings, chiefs or lords, either of the old stock or of the already half-absorbed Anglo-Irish families. And the historians, poets, and jurists of the learned families were producing manuscripts which are an exact continuation of the great collections of the twelfth century. How the transmission took place, we shall have to see later, but it is essential to stress from the start the dual aspect of Irish manuscript writing in the medieval period. And it will now be convenient to examine first rapidly the manuscripts of imported style, as in some cases they lend patterns or a lay-out to the 'vernacular' ones which will be studied in more detail afterwards.

There are, preserved in various libraries, perhaps thirty or forty manuscripts of religious character which fall into the category of 'foreign style'. In many cases, the only indication of an Irish provenance is the inclusion, by the original hand, of feasts of Irish saints in the calendar. Sometimes the feasts have been inserted in a different hand, showing that the book has been used in Ireland but was origin-ally meant for a monastery or a church abroad, generally in England, and is of foreign manufacture. The collections of charters, and the other manuscripts dealing with the administration or the records of a church or its history, are much more likely to be entirely local products. But in general their script is non-Irish, and they are seldom elaborately decorated, so that most of them will only be quoted because they help to complete the general picture.

The earliest of the surviving manuscripts of this category goes back to a time very little removed from 1169. It is a Benedictine gradual, probably meant for the Benedictine monastery founded by John de Courcy at Downpatrick, and has some capitals in a florid style current in the late twelfth century.[1]

But the great bulk of these books belongs to the period from the late thir-teenth century to the sixteenth century. As would be expected, Dublin looms large in the list of places of origin. From the cathedral of the Holy Trinity—Christ Church—come the Book of the Obits, now in Trinity College, the Black Book, the White Book, and a psalter. There are several books pertaining to the Hospital of St John-the-Baptist-without-the-New-Gate.[2] Others come from St Thomas Martyr;[3] from St John-the-Evangelist;[4] from the abbey of St Mary's.[5] But Navan, Clondalkin, Trim, Arklow, Great Connell, Inistioge,

[1] Bodl., Rawlinson MS C. 892.

[2] Charters: Bodl., Rawlinson MS B. 501; register: B.L., Add. MS 4797; and Bodl., Rawlinson MS B. 498 (c. 1340).

[3] Martyrology: T.C.D., MS 97 (B. 3. 5) (fourteenth century); register: Bodl., Rawlinson MS B. 499 (thirteenth century) and Rawlinson MS B. 500 (copied in 1526 by William Copinger of Cork in a chancery hand).

[4] Antiphonal: T.C.D., MS 79 (B. 1. 4).

[5] Annals: T.C.D., MS 578 (E. 3. 10); chartularies: Bodl., Rawlinson MS B. 495 (fourteenth and fifteenth centuries); B.L., Cotton MS Tiberius A. XI (fourteenth century), St Augustine, 'In Genesin', T.C.D., MS 123 (A. 5. 8); Miscellanea, Cambridge University Library, MS Add. 3392. C.

and the Cistercian abbey of Duiske (Graiguenamanagh) are also represented. The Lambeth palace library has some manuscripts that seem to come via Llanthony Secunda (Gloucestershire) from a priory of Augustinian canons founded by Hugh de Lacy in Duleek, County Meath. T.C.D. MS 80 (B.1.5) probably comes from Meath; MS 77 (B.1.1) from the same library, an antiphonal, comes from Armagh and belongs to the early fifteenth century. In 1535 a long inscription in Irish was inserted on f. 48ʳ, relating the squabbles between Primate Dowdall and Conn Ó Néill, and the agreement that ended them.

Most of these books are of a type very common at the time outside Ireland, and their chief ornament consists of blue or red initials accompanied by loose thread-like patterns in the same colours; human heads are often included in the motifs and occasionally there are some figures framed in the loop of an initial. Two or three of them, however, stand out and belong to the luxury production of the time or come very near to its standard. The most remarkable is the psalter in the Bodleian[1] that belonged to Christ Church and dates from 1397. On f. 142, an inscription informs us that Prior Stephen of Derby ordered its production (*Frater Stephanus de Derby, prior ecclesie sancte Trinitatis Dublinie cathedralis, istud psalterium ordinavit et fieri fecit*). But the exasperating man refrains from telling us where he got the psalter made. In England, almost certainly, perhaps in Durham. It is a most elaborately decorated book, which starts with a 'Tree of Jesse' and has a continuous series of blue, red, gold, and buff ornaments and a few magnificent historiated initials such as that on f. 20ʳ which shows the prior kneeling at the feet of the teaching Christ, that on f. 68ᵛ with a choir of musician monks, or that on f. 81ᵛ where monks are shown reading. The early fifteenth-century missal in Lambeth (MS 213), which has an office of St Finnian (written in a different ink from the bulk of the manuscript), though not quite so splendid, has on f. 18 a picture of the holy family, and on ff 100 and 101 elaborate initials and borders. The canon of the mass inserted in the Red Book of the Exchequer in Ireland[2] seems to have been a fragment of such a luxury missal. It was written 'in large, solid, black, blue, and red Gothic characters, with some elaborate coloured initial letters'. On p. 52 it contained 'an illumination representing Christ on the cross, with a figure standing at each side', no doubt Our Lady and St John the Evangelist. To these liturgical luxury books can be added the 'World Chronicle' of Ranulf Higden,[3] which has initials in blue and red, sometimes picked out in gold. Its first page has an elaborate frame which includes the escutcheons of Ireland and Dublin.

This brings us to the non-ecclesiastical manuscripts of colonial origin, such as charters, government and town registers, etc. The earliest and the most

[1] Bodl., Rawlinson MS C. 185.

[2] The Red Book of the Exchequer was destroyed in the Record Office fire in Dublin in 1922. It is known only from old descriptions, of which the most reliable is *Hist. & mun. doc. Ire.*, p. xxii. See R. Dudley Edwards, 'Magna Carta Hiberniae' in *Féilsgríbhinn Eoin Mhic Néill*, pp 308–18.

[3] Bodl., Rawlinson MS B. 179.

handsome is the charter roll of the city of Waterford,[1] which dates from the late fourteenth century and the expeditions of Richard II to Ireland. It is a long roll made of several pieces of vellum, containing copies of earlier charters granted to the city from the time of Henry II, to which are appended illustrations relevant to the text, chiefly 'portraits' of people connected with the charters: Prince John holding a falcon and framed in the door of a battlemented tower; Henry of London, archbishop of Dublin, in blue and yellow vestments under an ogive arch; the four mayors of Dublin, Cork, Waterford, and 'Lymeric', little figures in a variety of blue and red costumes; Sir John Morice, justiciar of Ireland under Edward III, in a hooded coat and pointed check shoes, under a trefoil arch. The figures are natural in their pose and attitude; the colours, now slightly darkened, were bright, and the whole effect is direct and pleasing. It would be interesting to know where the painter came from. His work, with its characteristic mixture of picturesqueness, elegance, and realism, takes its place easily among the works of 'international Gothic' style done around Richard. A comparison with B.L., Harley MS 1319, a 'History of Richard' in French verse, which contains an account of his expedition to Ireland in 1399, will show both the similarities of style and the differences. The manuscript is illustrated by a painter trained in the Franco-Flemish school and master of all its subtleties. The charter roll, where the same mixture of realism and fancy can be found, is much less accomplished in execution, but it shows an eager and incisive flavour which looks forward to those intensely vivid, if sometimes slightly uncouth, figures which will accompany late fifteenth- and sixteenth-century recumbent effigies on so many tombs of the same neighbourhood. It may not be out of place to reflect that it is for a mayor of Waterford, Stephen Rice (d. 1489), that one of the earliest of these monumental tombs was erected.[2] We would be inclined to suggest a local authorship for these paintings.

26a, b appears in left margin

A miniature contained in the Red Book of the Exchequer (p. 32) was only very slightly later than the Waterford roll. It showed the court of the exchequer in the time of Henry IV, seen in plunging perspective, and reminiscent of miniatures in the same perspective showing the English parliament and dating from the fourteenth and fifteenth centuries. It had, however, judging from its reproduction in Gilbert's *National manuscripts of Ireland*, an original, vivid quality very similar to that of the Waterford drawings.

It is necessary to remember at this point that royal charters, written and illuminated in England, were coming into Ireland and that their florid style of decoration and their typical late Gothic initials, combined with ornament and pictures, certainly had some influence. This is manifest in a few pages of the earliest of the town registers that have survived. The Waterford register[3] has

[1] J. T. Gilbert, 'Archives of the municipal corporation of Waterford' in *H.M.C., rep. 10*, app. v, p. 265.

[2] See above, pp 773–4. See also Marie Duport, 'La sculpture irlandaise à la fin du moyen-âge' in *La Revue de l'Art, 38ᵉ année* (1934), pp 49–62.

[3] Municipal Archives, Waterford.

one full-page decoration in pen-and-ink drawing, dated 1566. This includes some text headed by a large initial of charter type, and is a record of admissions when Peter Aylward was mayor of the town, in the time of Elizabeth. The roses which are part of the decoration are topical enough. But the rest is startling for that date: at the top of the page appears a silhouette of the city indicated by its Irish name ('Portlarge'), in the right-hand margin is an abbreviated description of the Last Judgment, and further down walks the Virgin holding the Child. Surprising as this may appear at first, it is in keeping with what is known from other documents of the stubborn catholic atmosphere that prevailed in Waterford to a late date.

The decoration of the Galway registers,[1] if one may venture into a late period, gives a most entertaining example of fanciful decoration. The registers were begun in 1569, but it is in the seventeenth-century section that several decorated pages appear (1632, 1638). Here again, the wild flourishes of the charter initials are the starting-point, but they are freely combined with animals and interlacings which embody here and there memories of traditional Irish ornament. It is the same reversion to type as occurs on the carvings of the contemporary tomb of Sir Peter French, dating from 1631, in Galway Franciscan friary.[2]

All the manuscripts we have examined so far are examples of close contact between Ireland and the outside world, whether they were imported from abroad or imitated more or less freely from foreign models. That the scribes working in the native tradition knew about these books is obvious. Occasionally they have borrowed from them an initial or a flourish; but on the whole, contaminations are few and far between until the sixteenth century.[3] There are, however, several manuscripts which fall into a different category. They are not modelled on a specific type of foreign book, and they are not written for any of the cities under colonial sway or influence. They are in fact written by Gaelic Irish scribes, in some cases as a commission from Irish chiefs, and some of them contain specifically Irish matter. However, they are in Latin and their scribes are mostly monks; so they are written in non-Irish script and given ornaments modelled, up to a point, on those of foreign books. This shows a curious evolution: in the twelfth century, Latin books were written in Irish script and decorated in Irish style. Now they are thought of, in a way, as belonging to the world of the foreigners and divorced from normal Irish production.

Among them are some of the most famous collections of translations into Latin of lives of Irish saints. The oldest is a manuscript emanating probably

[1] University College library, Galway.
[2] See Duport, 'Sculpture irlandaise'.
[3] An example of such contaminations is found recurring with some constancy in the fifteenth-century manuscript known as the 'Liber Flavus Fergusiorum', where capitals made of enlarged Irish characters sprout thin curved lines clearly derived from the current vocabulary of foreign initials (R.I.A., MS 23. O. 48); see Edward Gwynn, in *R.I.A. Proc.*, xxvi (1906), sect. C, pp 15–41.

from the Augustinian monastery of Saints' Island in Lough Ree.[1] It may date from the late thirteenth century. Though the script is of English type, Irish abbreviations are used and sometimes the lower limbs of letters in the last line of a page blossom into flourishes as they do in some Irish manuscripts. The ornaments are the current red and blue thread-like patterns of squiggles and formalised palmettes of continental and English manuscripts. A later manuscript from Saints' Island is based for its text on this early one.[2] It is signed by Matthaeus Ó Duibhidhir (O'Dwyer) and has annotations in Irish. The scribe seems to have also painted the initials and he occasionally introduces, beside the foreign leaf motif, some key-patterns of essentially Irish flavour. It was he *26c* also, probably, who painted a figure of a saint, crosier in hand, under an arcade (f. 191ᵛ) that is obviously adapted from an English manuscript.

Two other fourteenth-century Latin collections of lives of Irish saints are treated in a similar way: the 'Codex Kilkenniensis' or 'Ardmachanus', now in the Marsh Library, Dublin (MS Z3. 1. 5), which has little decoration, and the much more elaborate 'Codex Salmanticensis',[3] which has initials with stylised patterns of palmettes. It was written in Oirghialla by Brother John MacKern.

In the fifteenth century, the Carmelites of the friary founded in 1406 at Kilcormac (or Frankford, County Offaly) seem also to have strained themselves to imitate imported books. To their scriptorium can be ascribed a missal written by Denis Ó Flannagáin in 1458 and a breviary written by Malachy Ó Lachtnáin (Loughnane) in 1489. A collection of 'Clementinae' due to another member of the same family, who signs himself 'Rodericus O'Lacthmain', was written probably in 1477, not very far from Kilcormac, in the Augustinian abbey of Lorrha, County Tipperary, of which Rodericus was prior.[4] These manuscripts have all the same casual and unconvinced approach to the English style of manuscript writing. They are written in a good compressed script and have awkwardly drawn initials of English style, mostly in red and green.

The Loughnanes seem to have worked under the patronage of the O'Carrolls, lords of Eile Uí Chearbhaill (Ely O'Carroll). The O'Carrolls were celebrated for their patronage of poets; but here we find them in their capacity as protectors of monasteries. There is another instance of it, as one Tadhg Ó Cearbhaill (there were several in the fifteenth century) was probably responsible for the restoration from old fragments of the shrine of the Book of Dimma, then at Roscrea, to which was added an inscription in Latin in non-Irish characters.[5] This gives us an insight into a very interesting set-up, of which few

---

[1] Bodl., Rawlinson MS B. 485. See Charles Plummer, 'On two collections of Latin lives of Irish saints in the Bodleian library' in *Z.C.P.*, v (1905), pp 430–54.

[2] Bodl., Rawlinson MS B. 505.

[3] Brussels, Bibliothèque Royale, MS 7672–4. See W. W. Heist, *Vitae sanctorum Hiberniae* (Brussels, 1965).

[4] T.C.D., MSS 82 (B. 3. 1) and 86 (B. 3. 10); Lambeth Palace, MS 46.

[5] Gwynn & Gleeson, *Killaloe*, p. 67. In addition to the Tadhg Ó Cearbhaill mentioned there, who died in 1407, there is another, who was made prisoner in 1454 (*A.F.M.*).

examples have come to our knowledge: the patronage of an Irish chief supplying the needs of local monasteries, some of them founded and most of them supported by his family. Irish chiefs as patrons of scribes are common enough in the history of these late manuscripts. But we shall find them usually commissioning texts in Irish of a very different character from these Latin ones.

To these manuscripts can be added another, which will have to be studied later in more detail for its very arresting decoration. It is a Cistercian ordinal[1] of which the colophon on f. 65 tells us that it is 'Liber sancte marie de rosse UUale quem. Donatus okhellay monachus dicti monasterii sancte marie de rosseuale. scripsit Dompno thome macostela. Abbati rosse uualle, Scripsit, in monasterio Mellifontis.' There follows the usual request of a prayer for the scribe, and the date: 1501. The punctuation is erratic, but it seems obvious that Donnchadh Ó Ceallaigh, monk of Rossevalle, wrote this book for his abbot, Tomás Mac Oisdealbhaigh, in Mellifont, where his exemplar was probably kept. An inscription in a different hand informs us that Ó Ceallaigh was made prior of Rossevalle in 1509. The Cistercian monastery of Sancta Maria de Rosea Valle, variously called Rosglas, Rossevalle, or Monasterevin, County Kildare, founded between 1177 and 1181, was one of the houses still clearly linked with Mellifont in the confusion that had overcome the Irish Cistercian monasteries in the late fifteenth and early sixteenth centuries,[2] and this book comes as a confirmation of the still close relationship between the two abbeys.

The manuscript is puzzling and deserves careful study. It is written in English script and, of course, in Latin, but many of the habits of the scribe and painter are in the Irish tradition. The decoration is most unusual, though in some ways it takes its place beside that of some of the late fifteenth-century manuscripts in Irish. In consequence it will have to be studied with them.

L ET us turn now to those manuscripts that appear as the direct continuation of the late eleventh- and twelfth-century encyclopaedic books. Though there is a gap of nearly a century and a half between the Book of Leinster, the last of the twelfth-century collections, and the earliest of the medieval manuscripts that have survived, the script, somewhat freer in appearance, is of the same type, and the decoration is in the same style as that of any of the twelfth-century books either in Latin or in Irish. The continuity is near perfect, but we know that the whole background has changed. From the monastic scriptorium the manufacture of books has passed to the workshop of a school kept by one of those learned families which have attached themselves, as poets, historians, brehons, to chiefs from whom they expect their living in exchange for the services of their trade.

How change and transmission took place is a problem that has been

---

[1] Bodl., Rawlinson MS C. 32.
[2] Conway, *Mellifont*, p. 154.

examined several times[1] but to which it seems difficult to find a definite solution. A close scrutiny of the entries in the annals for the eleventh and twelfth centuries may, however, yield useful hints, and to get some idea of the problem we must go back to this crucial period.

First of all, what is the origin of these learned families of poets, historians, and lawyers which assume so much importance in fourteenth- and fifteenth-century life? The poets had always been there from pagan times—turbulent, insufferable, indispensable. The early annals record occasionally deaths of notable poets. By the eleventh century such obits appear more frequently. Eight times, at least, in the course of this and the succeeding century, the death of a 'chief poet of Ireland' is recorded. But there are more local glories: poets of the north, chief brehon of Leinster, chief poets and historians of Munster, etc. The poets of Connacht are certainly the most interesting, as the entries are numerous enough to give the impression of a nearly continuous sequence. In 1064 is recorded the death of 'Muircertach Ua Carthaigh, chief author and chief poet of Connacht [*prim ughdar ocus prim ollamh*]' (*Chron. Scot.*). In 1097, 'In druth Ua Carthaigh, ollamh Connacht' was killed by the Connachtmen themselves (*A.F.M.*) and probably replaced by Gilla na Náem Ua Dúnabra, whose death is announced in 1101; the succession then went back to the same family as before, and Ferdána Ua Carthaig, having accompanied Toirrdelbach Ua Conchobair in one of his wars, was killed in an engagement in 1131;[2] the Ua Carthaig name then disappears and the next entries record in 1145 the death of Gilla Oengusa Ua Clúmáin, and in 1170 that of his son Aindíles. But on the whole we find one family which supplies the chief poet of Connacht for long periods and reappears after a spell of disfavour.

Other families are less localised, though the permanence of their calling is again a distinctive feature. This is the case for the numerous dynasty of the O'Dalys. In 1139, the death of Cú Chonnacht Ua Dálaig (*na scoile*) is recorded in the *A.F.M.* He died at Clonard and was from Leacain, in Westmeath. He is, of course, the grandfather of Áengus Ua Dálaig, the ancestor of all the O'Daly poets. They started travelling south at an early date, and the *A.F.M.* have in 1161 an entry on the death of 'Raghnall Ua Dálaigh, *ollamh* of Desmond'. They were finally to reach the south coast. But others went west and north. In 1185 is recorded the death of 'Máel Íosa Ua Dálaigh, *ollamh* of Ireland and Scotland'. In 1244 Donnchad Mór Ua Dálaig was buried in Boyle. His brother, Muiredach of Lissadil (*A.F.M.*, 1213) may have fled to Scotland and become the ancestor of the Scottish poets, the Mac Vuirichs.

So, not only is the existence of *ollamain* of poetry, of history, and of law, attached to some of the rulers of the twelfth century, well established, but that also of a whole dynasty of them. And they seem to flourish especially in Connacht and Munster, the main centres of manuscript writing in later times.

---

[1] Flower, *Ir. tradition*; Proinsias MacCana, 'The rise of the later schools of filidheacht' in *Ériu*, xxv (1974), pp 126–46. [2] *A.F.M.*; 1127 in the *Chron. Scot.*

The status of these men seems to have been very high in the society of the time. They owned land and had a seat of their own, at that time some kind of large house, which was to become a castle in a later period. The description of the death of Ua Baígelláin, chief poet of Ireland (*rig file* in the *Chron. Scot.*; *ard ollamh le dan* in *A.F.M.*; *ard-ollamh Erenn ar dhan* in *A.U.*) gives some idea of their magnificence. He is described as 'a man distinguished for charity, hospitality, and universal benevolence towards the needy and the mighty'. He was killed 'with his wife and two very good sons and also five and thirty other persons, consisting both of his family and guests, in one house' (1119).

In the entries of that period concerning historians and brehons, even scribes, it is sometimes difficult to know whether an ecclesiastic or a lay person is meant. Possibly some of them, in these times of upsets and changes, lived in a sort of dim state pertaining to both estates. What, for example, of Máel Ísu Ua Stuir, whose death is recorded in 1098, and who is described as 'scribe and philosopher of Munster and of Ireland in general' (*scribhnidh 7 feallsomh Mumhan*), or of Cairbre Mac Samuel, 'chief *ollamh* of Ireland in penmanship', who died in Armagh in 1162, or of Mac Raith Ua Forréith (d. 1137), 'a learned historian and an *anmchara* [confessor] of meekness and mildness'. What indeed of that rather formidable person, the brehon Ua Duilendáin, 'erenach of Easdara [Ballysadare, County Sligo], *ollamh* of law and chief of his territory' (*ollamh feineachais 7 taoiseach a thuaithe*' (*A.F.M.*, 1158)?

To complete the picture of these figures which, still half wrapped in ecclesiastical trappings, already seem to join the ranks of the lay learned men living at the expense of the kings, one might evoke two of them, especially well documented. First Flannacán Ua Dubthaig, 'bishop and chief doctor of the Irish in literature, history and poetry and in every kind of science known to man in his time' (1168). He was a member of the ubiquitous ecclesiastical family of Roscommon and Tuam, two members of which, some thirty years earlier, presided with the king of Connacht at the making of the cross of Cong. To him is ascribed the authorship of a genealogical tract on the Síl Muiredaig, the dynasty to which the O'Connors belonged.[1] The other is Áed Mac Crimthainn The often quoted description in the Book of Leinster gives him as 'lector [*fer léigind*] to the high king of Leth Moga, successor of Colum mac Crimthaind [i.e. abbot of Terryglass], chief historian [*prímsenchaid*] of Leinster in wisdom and knowledge and practice of books and learning and study'. Here are two men, one an abbot, the other a bishop, who, once their ecclesiastical quality has been mentioned, are described in terms of territorial dignities and titles. Ua Dubthaig's surviving work shows him as a historian. Áed, however, is of vital importance, as, being chief scribe of the Book of Leinster, he is one of the immediate predecessors of the fourteenth- and fifteenth-century compilers and scribes. He bears a title, apart from that of abbot of Terryglass: 'chief

[1] T.C.D., MS 1298 (H. 2. 7), col. 32b.

historian of Leinster'.[1] But the title may have been purely honorific and does not mean that the Book of Leinster was written for the king. It remains probably, as William O'Sullivan has shown,[2] a brilliant exercise of compilation, done for sheer pleasure, but perhaps helped materially by the honour bestowed by the king.

How far Áed is typical of the twelfth-century compilers we cannot know. We are in complete ignorance about the scribe of Rawlinson MS B. 502, another Leinster compilation written *c.* 1130. As for the scribes of Lebor na hUidre, they are hard to focus.[3] One of them, however, Máel Muire, belonged to that rather mysterious family of Conn-na-mbocht, closely attached to Clonmacnoise, which produced many ecclesiastics but also, it seems, some benevolent laymen, and which traced its ancestry to Torbach mac Gormáin, abbot of Armagh (d. 808), who directed the work of compilation of the Patrician documents contained in the Book of Armagh. He may or may not have been a monk.

So it seems that a slow evolution had set the stage during the twelfth century for the transformations that took place at the time of the Anglo-Norman invasion and partly in consequence of it. The hereditary families of poets, historians, and lawyers attached to powerful rulers existed already, and were ready to absorb the heritage of monastic *fir léigind* and scribes made redundant by the new circumstances.

O F what happened during the thirteenth century we know practically nothing, except for the importation of foreign books and the attempts at hagiography in Latin in an English style of writing on Saints' Island.[4]

It is only in the fourteenth century, when Irish society begins to settle down into a new pattern, that the patronage of scribes and compilers and their family organisation become manifest. But obviously we are then only catching up with the outcome of a slow development whose earlier phases in the thirteenth century escape us. At that time, the regions of greatest activity seem to have been the centre of Ireland (Tipperary, Kilkenny, Offaly) and the north-west (Sligo, Roscommon, Leitrim). Various branches of the Mac Egan family (Mac Aodhagáin) worked in both areas and most of the other scribes seem to have been in some way or other connected with them. But other names appear at an early date, such as that of the poet and scribe Seoán Mór Ó Dubhagáin, who wrote for an Ó Ceallaigh the early part of the Book of Uí Mháine (B.L., Egerton MS 90, ff 20–24) and probably another book, now lost, which his pupil,

---

[1] *Pace* Aubrey Gwynn, 'Some notes on the history of the Book of Leinster' in *Celtica*, v (1960), pp 8–12.

[2] William O'Sullivan, 'Notes on the scripts and make-up of the Book of Leinster' in *Celtica*, vii (1966), pp 1–31.

[3] Tomás Ó Concheanainn, 'The reviser of Leabhar na hUidhre' in *Éigse*, xv (1976), pp 277–88.

[4] One of us (G.M-M.) suggests that perhaps some of the undated manuscripts attributed by us, in a previous article, to the twelfth century may belong in fact to the thirteenth century. The other author (F.H.), chiefly for historical reasons, would be reluctant to accept this hypothesis.

Ádhamh Ó Cianáin, copied.[1] He is described in his obituary notice in the
A.F.M. (1372) as 'chief historian of Ireland, *ollamh* of Uí Mháine'. He is at the
origin of the Ó Cianáin school working in Cavan and Fermanagh, which it will
be convenient to study first, as after the fourteenth century it will be a long time
before Ulster holds our attention again.

The Ó Cianáin were a family group centred on its most prominent member,
Ádhamh, whose death is recorded in the *A.U.* and *A.L.C.* at 1373. Ruaidhrí,
who died in 1387, described by the Four Masters as 'a learned historian and
ollamh of Oriel [Oirghialla]', and Seoán, who, according to its colophon, wrote
the first ten pages of Rawlinson MS B. 506 for Ádhamh, may have been his
brothers. An element of their chronology which has puzzled some historians is
the fact that Ádhamh's master, Seoán Mór Ó Dubhagáin, died only one year
before his pupil; he died at Rindown after seven years of religious retreat (*A.U.*,
1372). As the earliest datable works of Ádhamh go back to 1339, this need not
really be a difficulty. Supposing, for the sake of argument, that Ádhamh was
then about 25 years old, while his master was thirty; his master would have died
at about 63 (in 1372) and Ádhamh at 59 (in 1373), while Ruaidhrí, if he was a year
or two younger than his brother, may have died at 71 or 72. The obit of Ádhamh
has a misleading element: in the *A.U.* he is said to have died 'after being ton-
sured by the canons of Lisgabhail [Lisgoole, near Enniskillen] on gaining
victory from the world and from the demon'. This sounds like one of these *in
extremis* adoptions by a monastery, not uncommon in the middle ages, of a
dying man who may have been connected with it, and it does not mean that he
was, except during his last hours, an ecclesiastic.

The geographical indications given by the mentions of Lisgoole and
Oirghialla is confirmed by the fact that the Magauran *duanaire*, one of their
manuscripts, is written for Tomás Mág Shamhradháin (Magauran or Mac
Govern) whose death is recorded in the *A.L.C.* and the *A.F.M.* at the year 1343,
and who is there styled '*dux* of Teallach Eachach'. Teallach Eachach is the
modern Tullyhaw, in County Cavan.

So we have a family group of scribes who seem to be working together and
whose hands sometimes alternate in the same book. The chief manuscripts
which can be attributed to them are the two manuscripts from the Phillipps
collection in the National Library of Ireland (MSS G. 2–3), which formed
originally one volume (written mostly by Ádhamh); the first section of the
duanaire (written by Ruaidhrí), which was kept for a long time in the library of
the O'Conor Don at Clonalis and is now in the National Library of Ireland; six
pages of MS 23. O. 4 in the Royal Irish Academy, with a colophon by Ádhamh;
and pages 1 to 10 of Rawlinson MS B. 506 in the Bodleian Library, written by
Seoán Ó Cianáin for Ádhamh, according to its colophon.[2]

---

[1] The genealogical manuscript, T.C.D., MS 1298 (H. 2. 7), cols 1–236, was written for him by
Lucas Ó Dalláin in the mid-fourteenth century; see John Bannerman, in *Celtica*, vii (1966), pp 143–6.
[2] Lambert MacKenna, *The Book of Magauran, Leabhar Meig Shamhradhain* (Dublin, 1947); James

Of these manuscripts, the *duanaire* is the most important in many ways: it is the earliest of these collections of texts made for a patron and gathered to enhance his claim to land and prestige. As Tomás Mág Shamhradháin, the patron, died in 1343, the earliest part of the book, the only one that concerns us, is anterior to that date and consequently antedates the late part of the Book of Uí Mháine and the Books of Lecan and Ballymote by half a century. The volume that is now N.L.I. MSS G. 2–3 was not a patron's book, but a collection of miscellanea written for the scribe's own use, a type of manuscript to which the Book of Leinster has introduced us already but of which this is the earliest example in the medieval period. According to Nessa Ní Shéaghdha it was written from an exemplar belonging to the scribe's master and probably by his hand; but the text was brought up to date in the genealogies and can be dated from them to 1345.

As far as decoration goes, N.L.I., MSS G. 2–3 and the Rawlinson fragment are the most interesting. They both have ornamental initials, chiefly of the 'wire' type. In the Rawlinson manuscript, the very lively animals that form them are accompanied by elaborate compartments for a 'mosaic' background, which does not take all its effect, as the colours that they are meant to enclose have been omitted. Occasionally they end in leaf motifs. In G. 2–3 a note of fancy is introduced, represented by 'turns' with foliage frames, human heads in full face or in profile, etc. But by far the most remarkable is that in G. 3 which

29a contains a figuration of Noah's ark (f. 16ᵛ), touched with red and green, and headed: 'Denamh na hairce andseo 7 sliebh Armenia fuithe.' The ark is depicted as on the Irish stone crosses of the ninth and tenth centuries, with a large animal head at the prow; the stern bears a rather ghastly full-face human head; the frame of the boat contains an interlacing. The ark rests not on the traditional three summits of Mount Ararat, but on a much more complicated mountain system described by an inscription as 'Mons Armenia', carried by a sort of animated tray ending in a head, reminiscent of the frames of genealogical tables in twelfth-century manuscripts; its tail is a scroll of foliage of the type found in a twelfth-century Irish psalter in the British Library. The dove and a black raven of death are completely out of proportion to the boat, and, strangely enough, the 'corvus' has some similarity to the eagle of St John in the early twelfth-century gospel-book Harleian MS 1023 in the British Library. A running commentary in Irish and identifications in Latin occupy most of the available space inside and outside the boat. Admittedly, this slightly awkward, timid drawing is very far from the lyricism of some of the scenes represented in the Book of Kells or from the weird illustrations of the tenth-century Cotton psalter (B.L., Vitellius F. XI) but it still belongs to the same atmosphere, and the artist has something of the same unconcern for the literal appearance of

Carney, 'The Ó Cianáin miscellany' in *Ériu*, xxi (1969), pp 122–47; *N.L.I. cat. Ir. MSS*, fasc. 1, pp 12–28. For Rawlinson MS B. 506, see [F. J. Byrne], *1000 years of Irish script: an exhibition of manuscripts at the Bodleian library* (Oxford, 1979), pp 22–3.

things as had the Kells painter. As no twelfth-century manuscript illustration of Irish style has come down to us, except symbols of the Evangelists and the plan of the dining-hall of Tara in the Book of Leinster, the suggestion made by Professor Carney that we have here a copy of an older exemplar, possibly twelfth century, is not easy to verify. One feature, though, may point in this direction: this is the intrusion of a few words of Latin in the commentary of the picture; it seems to show that it was inspired by a picture illustrating a pre-1169 liturgical book written in Latin. It is hardly likely, however, to be a servile copy, and it shows that the traditional Irish style was alive enough in the middle of the fourteenth century to produce a picture that still embodies many of its chief characteristics.

The question of the possible imitation of an earlier picture is connected with that of the sources of these manuscripts. One of them is quoted by the scribe himself (G. 2–3) as the now lost Book of Glendalough, and others seem to be _{29a, c} also of Leinster origin. On the other hand, there are close connections showing the use of similar sources, between MSS G. 2–3 and the Book of Ballymote, written, as we shall see, in Connacht towards the end of the century. So, from the start, we are faced by the extreme mobility of these medieval scribes and the constantly shifting pattern of their movements. A few rolls of vellum, some ink and quills, and a few colours were easily packed in a satchel.[1] Where employment was to be found, the scribe went. Where his source-manuscripts were, he appeared for a while. Some manuscripts or their copies were probably also lent from one school to the other. This makes for a remarkable unification of the styles of writing and decorating and for the near-absence of any really local character.

As for the Ó Cianáin family, they probably continued their activity after the death of Ádhamh, though there is no way of bridging the gap which separates their fourteenth-century manuscripts from the reappearance of a scribe of the same family more than a century later. He was Maoleachlainn Ó Cianáin who wrote in 1491–2, probably in Fermanagh, a book of adaptations from classical stories ('Destruction of Troy', etc.; King's Inns, MSS 12–13), whose decoration is very unspectacular.[2] The Ó Cianáin family remained historians to the Maguires of Fermanagh until one of them, Tadhg, travelled with the earls in 1607 to the Continent and became the historian of their flight. His brother was hanged in Derry in 1615 as part of the persecution of poets and learned men.

In the centre and west of Ireland, as already mentioned, a good deal of activity was centred on the ubiquitous family of Mac Aodhagáin (MacEgan). They were hereditary brehons who became attached to various families in Connacht and Munster, and came to lend their services also to the Clanricard Burkes and to the Barretts of Tirawley.

---

[1] The technique and materials of the painters cannot have been very different from what they had been for centuries; see Françoise Henry, *The Book of Kells* (London, 1974), pp 157–60.

[2] *King's Inns cat. Ir. MSS*, p. 30.

The oldest manuscript from their hands, a fragment of the 'Senchas Már' now in Trinity College,[1] is earlier than 1350, judging from an inscription by Aodh, son of Conchobhar Mac Aodhagáin, dated 1350, in which he says that he is writing this in his father's book. The script is a slightly spiky, large minuscule, handsome and well ordered. There are a number of decorated initials, mostly made of the bodies of animals, surrounded by snakes and coloured in purple and green on a red background, with yellow touches on the snakes. They derive obviously from the tradition of the twelfth-century Rawlinson MS B. 502, though they are on a larger scale. This applies also to various historical and religious fragments in vol. iii of the same manuscript (of which a fragment is in R.I.A., MS D. i. 1), which may be even earlier.

At that time, the great activity of the southern part of the MacEgans seems to have been in Ormond, where they had their chief seat, and was based to a certain extent on material coming from the old monasteries of that neighbourhood. Later, a branch of the family settled at Duniry (Dún Doighre), some distance west of Portumna.

The western branch seems to have worked in close contact with another scriptorium active at Lecan, County Sligo, slightly west of the centre of activity of the western Mac Egans, which was under the direction of the Mac Fir Bhisigh family. They were historians of Tír Fiachrach and gravitated around the Ó Dubhda family. There are obits of members of the Mac Fir Bhisigh family in the *A.F.M.* in the thirteenth and all through the fourteenth century.

To the contact between the MacEgans and the Mac Fir Bhisigh family, to the close relations between the various groups of MacEgans, and to their influence are due some of the greatest manuscripts of the late fourteenth and early fifteenth century, the Great Book of Lecan, the Yellow Book of Lecan, the Leabhar Breac, and the Book of Ballymote.

The close connection between them is shown by the fact that the hand of Giolla Íosa Mór Mac Fir Bhisigh is found in one of the miscellaneous fragments contained in T.C.D., MS 1318, and in the Great Book of Lecan, while the hand of his pupil, Ó Cuindlis, who belonged to the MacEgan circle, appears in the Great Book of Lecan, the Yellow Book of Lecan, and the Leabhar Breac. The latter seems to have worked at Lecan, perhaps in other parts of Connacht, and also in Ormond.[2] Unfortunately, as far as decoration goes, the Great Book of Lecan and the Mac Fir Bhisigh fragments in MS 1318 are of no great interest.

On the contrary, the Yellow Book of Lecan[3] is in this point of view of

[1] MS 1317 (H. 2. 15), vol. ii. Facsimile edited by R. I. Best and Rudolf Thurneysen, *Senchas Már* (I.M.C., Dublin, 1931).

[2] See two papers by Tomás Ó Concheanainn: 'Gilla Ísa Mac Fir Bhisigh and a scribe of his school' in *Ériu*, xxv (1974), pp 157–71; and 'The scribe of the Leabhar Breac' in *Ériu*, xxiv (1973), pp 64–79.

[3] A facsimile was published by the R.I.A. (Dublin, 1896), with introduction and analysis of contents by Robert Atkinson. As indicated in the introduction to the facsimile, only the first section (cols 370–401) of T.C.D., MS 1318 (H. 2. 16) reproduced in the facsimile belongs to the Yellow Book of Lecan proper. Best has summed up in his article 'The Yellow Book of Lecan' in *Jn. Celt. Studies*,

outstanding quality. It exists now only in a few fragments dispersed between the Trinity and Royal Irish Academy libraries in Dublin and the Bodleian in Oxford. But there is enough to show that it was planned with the luxury décor of a patron's book, though the fact that it was still in the possession of the Mac Fir Bhisigh family in the sixteenth century seems to indicate that they did not part with it. It starts with a recension of the Lebor Gabála. The first page has a large initial made of a beast with snake head and interlacings. This is in a very bad state, but the red, yellow, and green in which it was painted can still be distinguished. It is very magnificent, and announces immediately a high standard of book production.

The Bodleian fragment consists of the only surviving copy of the Annals of Tigernach, which are known to have been written in Clonmacnoise.[1] One wonders if the gorgeous red and blue initial made of three interlaced beasts (f. 2ᵛ) drawn in the best twelfth-century style may not have been copied from a *29b* Clonmacnoise exemplar.

There is quite a wealth of small initials, sometimes rather simplified, but always accurately drawn. There are also spaces left blank which have not been filled by the relevant initials. It may indicate that for some reason, perhaps the death of the patron, the manuscript was not finished, and that would explain why it remained in the hands of the scribes. Given the small proportion of the book which has survived, this can be no more than a tentative hypothesis.

The MacEgans and the scribes who worked with them in the centre of Ireland exploited for some of their compilations old manuscripts still kept on the sites of the monasteries of Clonmacnoise, Lorrha, Mona Incha, etc. This forms the basis of the material of the Leabhar Breac,[2] compiled between 1390 and 1410. Nearly entirely composed of religious texts—epitomes of Old and New Testaments, lives of Patrick, Brigit, and Columba, the Martyrology of Óengus—it is based on pre-1169 Latin texts and includes passages in Latin. It must have been made for the use of the members of the MacEgan family, as it was still in their hands in the sixteenth century. It was kept at Duniry until 1629; hence its other name, the Great Book of Duniry. It was then deposited in the Franciscan friary at Ceneal Feichín or Kilnalahan, about eight miles west of Portumna and near to Duniry, where Michael O'Clery consulted it. It is

i, no. 2 (Nov. 1950), pp 190–92, what remains at present of the 165 leaves mentioned in an inscription: 8 leaves in T.C.D., MS 1318 (H. 2. 16 (XII)); 9 leaves in R.I.A., MS D. v. i; 8 leaves in R.I.A., MS D. iv. i; 6 leaves in R.I.A., MS D. i. 3; 26 leaves in Bodl., Rawlinson MS B. 488; a total of 57 leaves. The other sections of T.C.D., MS 1318 (H. 2. 16) are mostly by scribes of the Mac Fir Bhisigh group, but cannot be described as 'Yellow Book of Lecan'. See, however, Hans Oskamp, 'The Yellow Book of Lecan proper' in *Ériu*, xxvi (1975), pp 102–21, where these fragments are dated to 1350–70.

[1] This ends at the year 1178. Although this is the date of the sack of Clonmacnoise by Hugh de Lacy, this circumstance is probably fortuitous, as several folios (which may have continued the annals to the first quarter of the thirteenth century) are now missing.

[2] A facsimile was published by the R.I.A. (Dublin, 1876), with a description and list of contents based on the work of O'Curry.

written in a beautiful regular script and has many coloured initials; some of them of the wire type, with red and yellow mosaic backgrounds, others ribbon-shaped, surrounded by a maze of fine interlace. They are in the best tradition of twelfth-century initials and may well have been closely imitated from some of the exemplars. Two drawings, however, are different. One, in the 'Story of the children of Israel', is a depiction of the Menorah indicated in large, bold lines and described in an inscription as 'the candelabrum which illuminated the tabernacle of Moses and the Israelites' (p. 121). The other, in the Passion according to St Matthew, is a rather awkwardly drawn crucifixion, where *28a* Christ wears an interlaced crown of thorns (p. 166). It has, however, no relationship to pre-Norman representations of the crucifixion, and conforms to all the norms of the time, the most obvious being the use of a single nail for the two feet crossed over each other. It has a close parallel in the crucifixion affixed on the reliquary of the tooth of St Patrick from Cong (*fiacail Phádraig*) which belongs most probably to the original part of the reliquary, made around 1376.[1] This shows a duality of sources of inspiration which is found also in the Book of Ballymote, the figurative scenes being closely imitated from foreign models, even when the initials are thoroughly traditional.

To three pupils of one of the MacEgans of Connacht, Domhnall Mac Aodhagáin, is due the Book of Ballymote.[2] It seems to have been written partly in his house and partly in that of Tommaltach Mac Diarmada, who became prince of Tír Ailealla (Tirerrill) in 1383. It is a large book of 250 folios and contains a remarkably miscellaneous collection of texts, some religious—'Creation of the world', biblical fragments, hagiological texts—others historical or pseudo-historical—kingdoms of Ireland and their genealogies, Lebor Gabála—others legal, such as the Book of Rights; in it are found also metrical treatises and lore of place-names; finally it concludes in a classical mood with the 'Destruction of Troy', a summary of the 'Aeneid' and the 'Life of Alexander'. It is in fact a miniature library collected for the interest and relaxation of the prince who commissioned it or bought it. Part of it is translated from Latin, and the sources must be extremely varied. As we have seen, they include the Book of Glendalough for some texts found also in MSS G. 2–3, written by the Ó Cianáins about half a century earlier. But this is only one item amongst many others.

There were three scribes, Solamh (Solomon) Ó Droma, Robertus Mac Síthigh (Robert MacSheehy), and one of the O'Duigenans, Maghnus Ó Duibhgeannáin, the chief one, it seems. The O'Duigenans were hereditary historiographers to the MacDermots of Mag Luirg, the MacDonaghs of Tír Ailealla, and several other families in the same neighbourhood. They were

[1] H. S. Crawford, 'A descriptive list of Irish shrines and reliquaries' in *R.S.A.I. Jn.*, liii (1923), p. 92.
[2] Published in facsimile by the R.I.A. (Dublin, 1887) with an introduction and analysis of contents by Robert Atkinson.

established at Castlefore, County Leitrim, where in earlier times they had had a school of poetry, and at Kilronan, near Boyle, where they wrote the Annals of Connacht.[1] In the seventeenth century an O'Duigenan (Peregrine) was to be one of the Four Masters. So it appears as perfectly normal that one member of such a family would be the chief scribe of an important book. It seems, however, that the work was shared constantly by the three scribes, and their colophons, which are numerous, give the impression that they were incessantly taking the pen from one another.

The writing of the manuscript can be dated pretty accurately to the beginning of the fifteenth century: according to the Four Masters, Maghnus Ó Duibh-geannáin died in 1452; on f. 106a there is a mention of Toirdhealbach Óg as the then ruling king of Connacht; he reigned from 1384 to 1406. This fits in satisfac-torily enough with the date of 1383 for the inauguration of Tommaltach as prince of Tír Ailealla, but the very last years of the reign of Toirdhealbach are likely to be those when the manuscript was written if we ascribe a minimum of twenty-five years of age to a scribe in the leading position assumed by Maghnus. In fact, the problem of chronology is curiously similar to that encountered à propos of the Ó Cianáin manuscripts, and the pattern is the same: a 'master' hovering in the background, and a young scribe seeming to take the lead amongst his pupils and proving himself—in modern terms, writing his Ph.D.

The book is remarkable for its generous proportions ($15\frac{1}{4}$ in. by $9\frac{3}{4}$ in.). It shows also an obvious intention of ornamental presentation, marred now by the cutting out of what must have been the most spectacular pages. It starts with the tract 'Of the ages of the world', whose first page is missing; this is likely to have been stolen because of some handsome initial. From the surviving text, it is obvious that the missing page contained the story of Noah. A detached page with the picture of the ark, now at the beginning of the volume, is then likely to *29c* have faced that opening of the text. On p. 13, the treatise 'On the creation of the world' starts with a magnificently-coloured initial reaching to the middle of the *30a* height of the page. A stub shows that a page facing it has again been abstracted, and one may assume that it was an illustration. Pages 17–18 (one folio), at the beginning of the Lebor Gabála, are also missing, probably because they proved too tempting to a collector. One may assume here a beginning of text with a large initial, and perhaps an illustration on the left. On page 67, the 'Genea-logies of the kingdoms of Ireland' start with a remarkable initial accompanying a square of text in outsize script. Some, if not all, of this part of the book is due to Maghnus Ó Duibhgeannáin, who has left an elaborate colophon at the foot of p. 55. So we may credit him with this startling and well planned decoration, unless, of course, the painter was a different person from the scribe and was allowed to do the planning.

---

[1] Ed. A. Martin Freeman (Dublin, 1944). For the O'Duigenan authorship, see Walsh, *Ir. men of learning*, p. 23, and Aubrey Gwynn, 'The Annals of Connacht and the abbey of Cong' in *Galway Arch. Soc. Jn.*, xxvii (1956–7), pp 1–9.

In addition to the large capitals, there are similar initials in some parts of the text, though they are very irregularly distributed. The most remarkable series is to be found in the Lebor Gabála, which has spirited little letters of the 'ribbon' type in green, yellow, orange, and red. The large initials on pp 13 and 67 are
30a even more brightly coloured. On p. 13, the animals are dark red, blue, and buff (? perhaps a faded purple) on a background of pale red with a network of yellow snakes. The whole structure of the initial recalls those of the twelfth-century 'Corpus gospels', especially that in the beginning of St Mark's gospel. But here, as in the small initials of the Lebor Gabála, a confrontation with twelfth-century manuscripts reveals a slightly wobbly outline of the beasts for the large capitals and some slackness in the building of the small initials, which occasionally lack the head of the animal. These are the only indications that we are dealing with a derivative art. The exemplar may have been a manuscript of the type of MS Rawlinson B. 502, an early twelfth-century manuscript of Leinster origin. The analogies with the 'Corpus gospels' are of little use here, as the origin of this book is unknown.

In two sections of the book, the scribe seems to follow closely, though in a slightly different way, some early manuscript. One of them is the Book of Rights (pp 267–81), whose scribe is Solamh Ó Droma (colophon at the foot of p. 281), the other the *dindshenchus* (pp 349–410) which may have been written by Maghnus Ó Duibhgeannáin (colophons on pp 443 and 445). Both have very spirited little initials and show a marked tendency to alternation between wire and ribbon initials. As this does not appear in any other part of the book, one may assume that it was a feature of the exemplars from which the texts were copied or adapted. Of surviving manuscripts, the Southampton psalter (St John's College, Cambridge), dating probably from the beginning of the eleventh century, is the earliest to show the alternation used systematically. But it appears already in many sections of the Cotton psalter in the British Library (Vitellius F. XI), which goes back to the early tenth century. So the exemplar could be late tenth- or early eleventh-century. The style of some of the initials, which show the combination of beasts and snakes, points to a date not earlier than the twelfth century. But this in itself is no compelling element in dating, as the fact of the alternation may have been imitated, the initials themselves being of a type invented in the twelfth century and still in use in the early fifteenth.

The decoration of the *dindshenchus* is in fact incomplete; from p. 395 on, the spaces reserved for the initials have not been filled. There is still a good 'turn-in-the-path', but otherwise the painter, who may have been a different man from the scribe, has failed.

As for the picture of the ark, it compares strangely with that of the Ó Cianáin
29c manuscript: it shows a boat made of large planks resting again on a complicated mountain system. The dove has perched on one of the very curved ends of the boat, holding a bough in its beak. Eight human figures appear in busts above the side of the boat. One of them, wearing a crown and holding a bough, is

meant for Noah. But we are here very far from the stylised and patterned picture of MSS G. 2–3. An English illustrated bible is likely to have supplied most of the elements of the picture, and it looks as if, at this point, representative scenes in Irish manuscripts get closer in style to foreign models or to imitations such as the illustrations of the Waterford charter roll and the Red Book of the Exchequer.

On the whole, both for contents and presentation, the book is not very different from the Yellow Book of Lecan. They both give a fair idea of the type of family-scrap-book-cum-genealogical-record that was becoming the fashion among Irish princelings of the early fifteenth century, and of the elaborate decoration that they expected for them.

Another book, that of the O'Kellys (Leabhar Uí Mháine; R.I.A., MS D. ii. 1),[1] is of the same type. It was written at two different periods. The older part, written before 1372 by Seoán Mór Ó Dubhagáin, has already been dealt with. It has little decoration. But ff 103–12 were written by Fáelán Mac a' Ghabhann for Muircheartach Ó Ceallaigh, bishop of Clonfert, probably before he became archbishop of Tuam in 1393. This has quite spectacular initials boldly drawn and filled in by red and yellow. The book has again about the same contents as the Book of Ballymote and the surviving part of the Yellow Book of Lecan.

The Book of Lismore, another large patron's book, should be mentioned here, though it has only one decorated initial. It was copied at the end of the fifteenth century in County Cork, for Fínghin Mac Carthaigh Riabhach (d. 1505).[2] With the fifteenth century, the patronage of the scribes and historiographers extends clearly to the gaelicised families of Anglo-Norman origin. Thus the Book of Fermoy, a miscellaneous collection of manuscripts with practically no decoration, is connected with the Roche family. MS Rawlinson B. 512 was written by various scribes—Maolsheachlainn, Giolla Brighde Mac Maoltuile, one of the Duigenans, Dubhthach, etc. for John Plunkett, third Baron Dunsany. It contains, among other things, the 'Tripartite life of St Patrick', the 'Martyrology of Óengus' and some Irish penitentials. It has some interesting animal initials which remain of fairly consistent style through the changes of hands in the script and may, as a consequence, be due to a painter different from the scribes.

The Butlers also showed a taste for books in the native script containing well-known Irish texts. James, fourth earl of Ormond, the 'White Earl', has always been known to have been strongly gaelicised; he spoke Irish, and, as Mr Kenneth Nicholls has shown, he was probably the first of the Anglo-Irish lords to appoint a brehon to his service, Domhnall Mac Flannchadha, to whom he granted lands in Tipperary.[3] So his patronage of Irish scribes falls

[1] A facsimile was published by the I.M.C. (Dublin, 1942) with introduction by R. A. S. Macalister. See R. A. Breathnach in *Great books of Ireland* (Dublin, 1967), pp 77–89.

[2] A facsimile was published by the I.M.C. (Dublin, 1950) with introduction by R. A. S. Macalister.

[3] See above, pp 552–3.

into an expected pattern. But he was certainly fortunate in the quality of the scribes who worked for him. What can be described as 'the Book of the White Earl' has been studied by Myles Dillon and by Anne and William O'Sullivan. It consists of twelve folios which were inserted into a slightly later manuscript written for his nephew, Edmund mac Richard.[1] We are very far here from the timid attempts of the Ó Cianáins and even from the best of the Book of Bally-mote. The sumptuous initials of this book are not a more or less servile repeti-tion of twelfth-century work. They are, on the old data, new creations merging foliage patterns into the traditional 'wire initial' with 'mosaic' background. The foliage pattern is probably inspired by foreign models, but it is so completely integrated that the borrowing is only realised on second thoughts. The initials are large, bold, and drawn in firm lines and bright colours. The work of the scribe also is dazzling. He plays like a virtuoso with various sizes of script, the larger size having a majestic decorative quality. The contents are no less remarkable: the 'Martyrology of Óengus', the 'Acallam na Senórach' and a *dindsenchus*.

28b

If the head of the family was so gaelicised in his tastes, junior branches went even further. The White Earl's nephew, Edmund mac Richard Butler, had a Gaelic Irish mother and married one of the O'Carrolls. He was frequently in charge of the earldom when the earl was abroad, and he seems to have travelled incessantly, staying in his own castles and in those of the earl. Through him we glimpse a relationship between patron and scribes very different from the purely mercenary one that we can assume from most of our manuscripts. His scribes lived with Edmund; they shared in his family life and his various pre-occupations. He drove them to the point of making them write on Sundays or on Good Friday and had them writing by candlelight. They stood all this good-humouredly, obviously because they liked him. But they aired their feelings in inscriptions all over the books they were writing for him. We can follow their wanderings: occasionally they were in Pottlerath, Edmund's seat near Callan. Edmund had built a castle there which was razed about 1800, but a church which was obviously the castle chapel remains and gives the idea that it may have been a fairly important building. At other times they were in Edmund's court at Kilkenny, or in the castles of the earl in Carrick-on-Suir or Gowran; but there were also, as the scribes complain, 'desolate places'. There were several scribes, the chief ones being Seaán Buidhe Ó Cléirigh and Giolla na Náemh Mac Aodhagáin, so that we are still in the orbit of the Mac Egans. The manuscript which they wrote for Edmund (Laud MS 610) can be described, from one of the inscriptions, as the Book of Pottlerath (Leabhar na Rátha) and can be dated to 1454. It is amongst its pages that the Book of the White Earl was inserted—twelve folios squeezed among the 110 of the later book. It is well

---

[1] Bodl., Laud Misc. MS 610; one bifolium in T.C.D., MS 1436 (E. 4. 1). See Myles Dillon, 'Laud Misc. 610' in *Celtica*, v (1960), pp 64–76; vi (1963), pp 135–55; Anne and William O'Sullivan, 'Three notes on Laud Misc. 610' in *Celtica*, ix (1971), pp 135–51, Byrne, *1000 years of Ir. script*, pp 25–7.

written, and abundantly decorated with a variety of not always very skilfully drawn initials. It falls short of the standard of the work done about half a century earlier for the White Earl. But it has its interest also for the deliberate acceptance of forms of initials or ornaments current in non-Irish manuscripts of the time, such as fine scrolls or patterns of flowers and the flippant mixing of them with the most traditional Irish patterns. It is not complete integration, as in the Book of the White Earl; it remains juxtaposition. The scribes are obviously well-read and perfectly aware of the methods of decoration of their contemporaries, and perhaps want us to realise that if they are using mostly Irish patterns it is not out of ignorance of other fashions but from deliberate choice. The library of the earl in Kilkenny or Carrick, and Edmund's own library,[1] were probably well stocked with foreign books, and from this inspiration come the squiggles on f. 37ᵛ or the flowers on f. 43ᵛ.

The book was given in ransom by Edmund mac Richard to Thomas Fitz-Gerald of Desmond, in 1462 (inscription on f. 110ᵛ).[2] He gave at the same time another book described as the Book of Carrick (Leabhar na Carraigi), which Robin Flower identified with B.L. Add. MS 30512 because they have roughly the same later history.[3] This may have been kept in the earl's library at Carrick, though we are told that the book was written for Edmund. Its use as ransom by Edmund is nothing very surprising, considering that he had already appropriated the Book of the White Earl. He certainly does not seem to have drawn a sharp line between his own books and those belonging to the head of the family, whose place he was so often occupying, and whose duties he was fulfilling.

The Book of Carrick introduces us to a very original scribe, who was probably an author at the same time, Uilliam Mac an Leagha, who has signed the book in several places. An aura of confusion surrounds him, as his name has been mixed with that of an Iollann Mac an Leagha, father of several other scribes, Maoleachloinn, Connla, and Eóghan Mac an Leagha. Perhaps the solution of the difficulty is that Iollann liked to call himself Uilliam, playing on the similarity of the two names. There are at least two signatures of Iollann in texts which seem to be written by Uilliam, and Uilliam liked to disguise his name through the worst tricks of abbreviation and decorative calligraphy, so that in a few cases the confusion is easily possible. The whole problem would need to be reexamined from a palaeographical point of view.

Several manuscripts are signed by Uilliam: in addition to the Book of Carrick there are B.L., Add. MS 11809, R.I.A., MS 23. P. 3 (ff 1–17), and part of Bibl. Nat., MS Celtique 1, and to him can be ascribed, from the similarity of

---

[1] The catalogue of the books in the library of Gerald, earl of Kildare, drawn up in 1526, gives an idea of the mixture of foreign and Irish books that composed such collections; see *Facs. nat. MSS Ire.*, III, ii, pl. LXIII, and above, p. 736.

[2] See above, p. 599.

[3] *B.M. cat. Ir. MSS*, ii, 470. The O'Sullivans (op. cit.) disagree with Flower's identification of the Book of Carrick with B.L. Add. MS 30512.

hand, T.C.D., MS 1298, N.L.I., MS G. 9, and B.L., Egerton MS 91. From inscriptions in R.I.A., MS 23. P. 3, it was written in 1467 at Melaigh Móir, a short distance south of Windgap, on the Kilkenny–Tipperary border, for Aodh Mág Raith who, according to the *A.U.*, died in 1491;[1] B.L., Add. MS 11809 is supposed to come from Cashel. This fits in, both in time and place, with the writing of a book before 1462 for Edmund Butler who lived in the same neighbourhood.

In spite of his name—'the son of the physician'—Uilliam Mac an Leagha does not seem to have written medical treatises. His books contain lives of saints, homilies, prayers, with an excursion into mythology represented by a 'Life of Hercules' translated from a contemporary printed book.

His style of decoration is in no way hackneyed, though it is based on the time-honoured wire-and-ribbon initials. But he handles them in his own monumental way and can make them very impressive. He is at his best in the book written for Aodh Mág Raith. The first twelve pages are an incomplete copy of the 'Martyrology of Óengus', each of the months starting with a large initial. Some are made of very large ribbon animals on a background of loose interlacing outlined on red. Others are of the 'wire' type, with ferocious claws. Altogether, these few pages are perhaps the most lavishly decorated and most strictly planned of all the books we have examined so far.

The other patron's book due to him was unfortunately not finished, and most of the squares prepared for initials have remained blank. It is MS Celtique 1 in the Bibliothèque Nationale.[2] It was started in 1473 (f. 7^r) and was written for Donnchadh, son of Brian Dubh Ó Briain. The beginning of the manuscript is due to Uilliam Mac an Leagha and various other scribes. Uilliam has signed it in several places (ff 7^r, 28^r, 29^v). Among the scribes who worked with him, there is one called Flaithrí, an Ó Maolchonaire name. The end is partly written by Maoleachloinn (or, as he signed himself here, Mailechlainn Mac Illainn), in 1497 (f. 95^r). One may assume that William was dead by then and that Maoleachloinn finished the book begun twenty years earlier. It starts with the 'History of the children of Israel', which is found also in others of the great 'bibliothecae', and which William boasts of having written in two summer days (f. 7^r), and goes on with various other religious texts, 'Dialogue of the body and soul', 'History of the monks of Egypt', 'Lives of Irish saints', etc.

In others of the manuscripts ascribed to Uilliam, the characteristic very large ribbon-animal on a background of interlace appears generally. It is so constant

---

[1] According to William Carrigan, *The history and antiquities of the diocese of Ossory* (4 vols., Dublin, 1905), iv, 322, the castle of Melaigh Moir belonged to the earl of Ormond. Aodh may simply have been in charge of it. This, up to a point, links a second manuscript of Uilliam Mac an Leagha with the Butlers. According to a rental of the earl of Ormond, 'les rymours' (the Magrath poets) occupied Mellagh and other lands free of rent (*Ormond deeds, 1413—1509*, no. 234; N.L.I., MS D. 1807).

[2] The best account of the manuscript is that by Henri d'Arbois de Jubainville in *Rev. Celt.*, xi (1890), pp 389–405. It has been included in Henri Omont, *Catalogue des manuscrits celtiques et basques de la Bibliotheque nationale* (Paris, 1890). See also Flower in *B.M. cat. Ir. MSS*, ii, 470 and Walsh, *Ir. men of learning*, pp 206–14, both extremely confusing.

that there can be very little doubt that he was responsible for the decoration of his own manuscripts.

The sons of Iollann, in addition to living in widely different parts of the country, seem to have been prone, like most scribes, to a wandering life. One of them, Maoleachloinn, who wrote the medical MS no. 15 in the King's Inn library, was *ollamh* of medicine to the two MacDonaghs whose seats were at Ballymote and Tír Ailealla. This brings us back to the background of the Book of Ballymote. In a mournful note where the rain seems to add to the natural propensity of scribes for loneliness, he complains that, as he was staying at Herbertstown 'in the Eustace country' (County Kildare), he was separated from his father and favourite brother, Eóghan, who were in Munster and from his other brother, Connla, who lived at Mag Luirg. He did not write only medical texts, as we find him writing the lives of saints in MS Celtique 1 and copying psalms and prayers in Gaelic MS IV of the Advocates' library in Edinburgh. Connla wrote the R.I.A., MSS 24. B. 3 and 23 N. 29, both medical manuscripts, and—sign of the new times—he wrote on paper; while T.C.D., MS 423 is a family affair involving Connla, Maoleachloinn and some other relatives. The dates are, of course, slightly later than those of the manuscripts of Uilliam-Iollann, and they bring us right into the sixteenth century (1496, 1509, 1512).

So the production of the Mac an Leagha family is largely made up of religious texts of all descriptions. But to them also are due copies of medical texts of a type which became common in the sixteenth century. Fr Francis Shaw has defined their purely artificial character.[1] They derived from school texts copied probably by Irish students in some of the continental universities renowned for their medical courses, such as Montpellier, Padua, Salerno. They were probably as divorced from practical Irish medicine as some of the legal texts were from the actual law practice. But copying them was a normal occupation for an *ollamh* of medicine, and their possession enhanced his status. Among the religious texts, it is interesting to find beside lives of Irish saints and Irish homilies a near-contemporary continental text like the 'Meditations of the Pseudo-Bonaventura'. The borrowing of the 'Life of Hercules' from a recently printed volume is also a token of change. All this is part of new trends of which one could find many other instances.

These trends are manifest also in some aspects of the decoration. In a few manuscripts of the time, the interest shifts from the initials to little figures which are probably inspired by the 'bas-de-page' of foreign manuscripts. One of them, however, MS 17 in the King's Inn library, has a very eclectic approach to various sources of inspiration. It gives us what no other post-invasion manuscript had shown so far: an introductory page whose ornaments cover the whole *31a* surface of the vellum. There is an elaborate frame made of various kinds of interlacings and a fret-pattern enclosing an enlarged, ornamental initial, some

[1] Francis Shaw, 'Irish medical men and philosophers' in Ó Cuív, *Seven centuries*, pp 87–101. Cf. above, pp 705–6.

rubricated letters and the beginning of the text. Unfortunately, the page is slightly marred by an incoherent interlacing. It is in poor condition and it is difficult to ascertain what colours were used, but it remains an ambitious scheme nearly successfully carried out. The animal which introduces the text is strangely similar to those drawn by the scribes of the Book of Pottlerath. Coincidence perhaps, or common inspiration, unless it is an indication that the manuscript belongs again to the same neighbourhood which had seen the work of the Butler scribes and of the Mac an Leagha family. The initials which are found further in the text are of indifferent quality, but some of the lower margins have vivid, if extremely uncouth, sketches of little figures at work, one *31b* of them using a triangular spade, another beating a sheaf of corn with a flail.[1]

These figures are not completely isolated. They have a close kinship with slightly more skilful ones found in Adv. MS 72. 1. 2 in the National Library of *31c* Scotland. This tract is bound with a medical treatise of unknown provenance, though nearly certainly Irish. The text starts with a capital made of an animal of the same type as that on the first page of King's Inns MS 17. Then come, with appropriate texts, the signs of the zodiac depicted by little uncoloured drawings, most expressive and amusing. This again derives certainly from the calendar of a foreign-type manuscript. A palaeographical study of these pages might well reveal that they are the work of one of the scribes of the Mac an Leagha group.

Another book, which in the presentation of the illustrations as 'bas-de-page' drawings is not very different from King's Inns MS 17, has to be mentioned here, though it does not, properly speaking, belong to the series of manuscripts in Irish script and an Irish style of decoration. It is that Cistercian ordinal *27* mentioned earlier,[2] which was written at Mellifont by Donnchadh Ó Ceallaigh for the abbot of Rosglas (Monasterevin) in 1501. It is a most disconcerting, diverting, and erratic book, as far as decoration goes. The initials are gauche and unobtrusive. The decoration is entirely in the margins, and a good deal in the lower margins as in King's Inns MS 17. But for weirdness, sense of movement, and unexpectedness it leaves the other manuscript far behind. The pictures are a constant, if sometimes elusive, commentary on the text. They are all painted in pale yellow, red, and green. On one page, two figures pass in the swing of a dancing rhythm, blowing enormous horns; elsewhere a stag is caught in a net; a piper blows his bagpipes; extraordinary monsters roll their eyes; crowned heads, like playing-card figures, appear from the edge of the page; an abbot kneels, crosier in hand; a lamb passes, sometimes with a long scroll of foliage in its mouth. Many old habits of Irish scribes are still followed: a hole in the vellum is made acceptable by a bright painted border and some spirals, a correction in the margin is emphasised by an ornament or a pointing hand, a word under the lower line of text is an excuse for exuberant decoration, and as

[1] Rough as these figures are, they can be compared with the hunting scene fresco in the Cistercian abbey of Holy Cross; cf. above, p. 771.   [2] Above, p. 789.

in King's Inns MS 17 the shoes worn by the two dancers are of the type found in pre-1169 manuscripts. But on the whole, the style is un-Irish in inspiration. In many of its aspects it recalls, though on a much lower artistic level, another very unusual manuscript also in the Bodleian library, the 'Kennicott Bible', a Hebrew manuscript written at Corunna in 1476. The way in which the lamb and a good many other figures are stamped with a monogram is found through most of the illuminated parts of the bible, and the mixture of sacred and grotesque is about the same. This remains a mysterious connection, though Corunna is in fact the harbour for Compostela, and it is just possible that on a journey to the famous shrine the scribe of our manuscript had seen some of the works of the famous illuminators of the Ibn Hayyim family, one of whom decorated the bible.[1]

In any case, this manuscript, like the two preceding ones, shows an interest in figure illustration which will become even more strongly marked in the later part of the sixteenth century. The whole century, as would be expected, is a chaotic period as far as writing and decoration of manuscripts is concerned. From the early years, there are still some ordinary books, mostly serviceable and unspectacular. But after the first two decades the effects of the political situation are strongly felt. The number of patrons who are settled and secure enough to have a group of scribes and *ollamain* as part of their retinue becomes smaller and smaller. However, they are still to be found in the north and the west, and when the ruling families of Gaelic or 'old foreigner' stock felt themselves threatened in their prestige and their landed possessions, they were able to find scribes to issue their claim or their protest in handsome form, perhaps more handsome than anything that had been made so far in medieval Ireland.

Such a claim, in a disguised way, was no doubt the new 'Life of St Columba' compiled at Lifford castle (County Donegal) around 1532 to the order and under the direction of Maghnus Ó Domhnaill. St Columba was the unassailable pride of the O'Donnell family, the tutelary figure which justified the unique importance they attributed to themselves. In the introduction to the 'Life' he is said to have refused the kingship of Ireland 'and the presidency of the Irish clergy'. The 'Life' was compiled chiefly by translating into Irish the few fragments of Adomnan's 'Vita Columbae' that could be found, with additions from various sources and the use of poems attributed to St Columba. The work of compilation and copying was done in the castle of Lifford, County Donegal, which Maghnus had built in 1527, and where the 'Life' was completed in 1532. Two sixteenth-century versions have survived. One of them, which is now MS A. 8 in the library of the Franciscan House of Studies

[1] It is a strange coincidence that for the very year 1501, when the manuscript was written, the *A.F.M.* mention two people who obviously had just come back from the 'voyage to Spain': Edmund, son of Richard Burke (of the Mayo Burkes), and probably the poet who had accompanied him, Domhnall Ó hUiginn, 'chief preceptor of the schools of Ireland'. (The O'Higginses were poets to the Mac William Burkes.)

in Killiney, was copied by Eóghan Carrach Ó Siaghail for Niall Connallach Ó Néill (colophon on p. 66d infra). It has a very handsome binding in repoussé leather with a pattern of interlacings. Its decoration is limited to a large animal initial in the beginning of the text, whose interlacings are outlined on a green background. Niall Ó Néill was a brother-in-law of Maghnus Ó Domhnaill, having married one of his sisters. The other copy is a manuscript written in a most beautiful fluid script (Bodl., Rawlinson MS B. 514).[1] It is also a luxury book produced for an important patron. Like the copy in the Franciscan library, it has an old binding, in sealskin, now rather moth-eaten, with bronze corners.[2] The very even appearance of its script and the tendency to slightly isolated paragraphs may not be without influence from printing. It was meant to have an elaborate decoration, and there is a large space reserved for a miniature in the beginning of the text which was never filled. Fortunately the portrait of the saint on the opposite page has been painted, and it is the most arresting figure illustration met so far in the Irish books of the medieval and renaissance periods.

32a

It shows the saint nearly in a full-face position under a curved frame of scrolls of foliage. He wears an elaborate mitre with crockets and fleur-de-lys terminations. His vestments are carefully described: the blue chausuble, probably of round shape, over a red dalmatic slit on the sides, the fringed ends of the stole appearing below, over an ample alb of soft material. He is wearing black shoes. He is shown blessing with his right hand; his left hand, which wears a maniple, holds a crosier with crook turned inward, so an abbot's crosier. There are parallels for such a figure in carvings of the late fifteenth and sixteenth century in Ireland: for example, two nearly identical carvings of archbishops, one on the tomb of an unknown woman in St Canice's, Kilkenny[3] and the other on a font at Rathmore, County Meath.[4] In both cases the mitre has the same edging of crockets as on the illumination. They are both undated, but ecclesiastics with similar mitres are found on the surround of the 'altar tomb' at Rathmore which is probably that of Sir Thomas Plunkett, who died in 1471. Except for the shape of the mitre, other carved figures come very close to the portrait of St Columba. The little figure of an archbishop inserted in the wall of St Mary's parish church in Kilkenny is one, but more striking even is the effigy of Walter Wellesley,[5] who, after having been bishop of Kildare, became prior of the abbey of Great Connell. He is shown as prior, with the in-turned crosier, and his vestments correspond fairly closely to those given to St Columba; he died in 1539. The red roses of simple shape, shown on both

[1] *Betha Colaim Chille: life of Columcille*, ed. Andrew O'Kelleher and Gertrude Schoepperle (Urbana, Ill., 1918). See also Byrne, *1000 years of Ir. script*, p. 31.

[2] Strickland Gibson, *Some notable Bodleian bindings* (2 vols, Oxford, 1901–4), pl. 21.

[3] For this carving and those quoted in the following pages, see Hunt, *Figure sculpture*.

[4] Helen M. Roe, *Medieval fonts of Meath* ([Navan], 1968), pl. XXXVII.

[5] Moved recently from Great Connell to Kildare cathedral.

sides of the figure of the saint, have parallels on some of the Kilkenny carved tombs, where they are less surprising than in an O'Donnell book.[1]

All analogies, however, are not with carvings. The patterned background may be an imitation of that of so many fifteenth-century illuminations derived from Franco-Flemish miniatures, but it could also embody a memory of stained glass, and the presentation of the figure in its rounded frame of foliage could well be a simplification of that of a window. As the painted glass decoration of Kilkenny cathedral has disappeared, it is impossible to know what influence it may have had on carvings and on miniature painting.

These manuscripts of the 'Life of St Columba' come rather as a surprise from a milieu which has not left much earlier proof of scribal activity. A manuscript in the British Library, Egerton MS 1781, was partly written in Donegal in the second half of the fifteenth century. It is practically devoid of ornament. The Book of the MacSweeneys, 'Leabhar Chlainne Suibhne' (R.I.A., MS 24. P. 25), is probably nearer to the 'Life', being a family book, partly history of the clan and partly collection of poetry connected with it, but it dates from 1513–14 and 1532–44, and is consequently contemporary with Maghnus's work of compilation. It has only a few, not very skilful, initials.

That the O'Donnells, like all other Irish chiefs, had their historians and poets, the O'Clerys among them, is obvious. And they had built up a taste for collecting manuscripts over a long time. In the fourteenth century they had acquired the Lebor na hUidre. It was taken from them by the Connachtmen in 1340 and only retrieved in 1470 by Aodh Ruadh Ó Domhnaill. Then Aodh Dubh, his son, got the Book of Ballymote in 1522 from Mac Donchadha of Ballymote, paying for it the high price of 140 milch cows. The close contacts, by war, diplomacy, and marriage alliances, which the O'Donnells had at that time with the north of Connacht would doubtless make it easy for them to buy or borrow books there, to attract western scribes and learned men when they needed them, or get scribes trained there. Nevertheless, the close connections with carvings in the centre of Ireland make it possible that the painter, if not the scribe, had come from that neighbourhood.[2]

The other lavishly illuminated book of the sixteenth century, the Book of the Burkes, is slightly later. It is a slim volume of 75 folios, 22 of which have remained blank.[3] It is, as far as we know, the last of the great family books

---

[1] There is a striking example of this dog-rose type on a slab from the tomb of the tenth earl of Ormond (d. 1614), inserted artificially in the tomb of the eighth earl, Piers Butler, in St Canice's; James Graves and J. G. A. Prim, *The history, architecture and antiquities of the cathedral church of St Canice, Kilkenny* (Dublin, 1867), p. 182.

[2] The presence of an O'Clery amongst the scribes working for Edmund Butler may indicate a connection.

[3] T.C.D., MS 1440 (F. 4. 13). For list of contents of the manuscript, see *T.C.D. cat. Ir. MSS*, no. 1440. For text and translation, see Tomás Ó Raghallaigh in *Galway Arch. Soc. Jn.*, xiii (1927), pp 50–60, 101–37; xiv (1928–9), pp 30–51, 142–67. Various articles on topics connected with the book and photographs of its illustrations appear also in the first volumes of the journal. The only

written in Irish, but its text has remained rather bleak, the poems that were probably intended to fill the blank pages never having been copied.

It was made for one of the MacWilliam Burkes of Mayo, Sir Seaán, son of Oliver, whose name is the last mentioned in the genealogical list of the book. He was chosen as head of the MacWilliam Burkes in 1571 and died in 1580. His mother was a daughter of Aodh Dubh Ó Domhnaill and so a sister to Maghnus Ó Domhnaill for whom the 'Life of St Columba' was compiled, and to the wife of Niall Connallach Ó Néill for whom the copy of the 'Life of St Columba' now in the Franciscan library was made. The author of the poem in praise of Sir Seaán copied in the Burke volume is greatly impressed by this O'Donnell ancestry, and has a rather amusing remark about the tonic effect it had on 'the soft blood of the Burkes', as if, after four centuries of marrying O'Brien and O'Kelly, O'Flaherty and O'Malley wives, there could have been much of the original 'softness' of the Burke blood left! In fact it would have been hard to be more gaelicised than they were. Sidney, in a letter to the council, informs them that 'I found McWilliam very sensible; though wantinge the English tongue, yet understandinge the lattin; a lover of quiett and cyvilitie'. In fact a true kinsman of that Edmund Burke (d. 1514) whom the Four Masters define as 'a man whose domestics were the orders and the ollavs'.

The core of the text consists in two symmetrical documents written, the first in Irish, the second in Latin, in two different scripts. They are rather fantastic, connecting the Burkes with Charlemagne, Baldwin, king of Jerusalem, and the kings of France and England, claims of which only the last can probably be sustained. The genealogical sequence, when checked on the Irish annals and on the English documents, appear just as fanciful.

As far as the script and initials go, this text is very unremarkable. But six blank pages after the genealogy, the book's great display of pictures comes as a *32b* surprise. There are four scenes of the Passion, followed by nine portraits of the Burkes mentioned in the genealogies and one page devoted to their coat of arms. They are large pictures, extremely crude and brutal in colour, but arresting by their originality and their vehemence. Movements are awkward but convincing; there is practically no feeling for space, but all sorts of linear rhythms organise the compositions. Verisimilitude does not exist: skies are red or yellow, dogs are green, there is a constant disproportion of the figures, but a sort of brutal integrity emanates from these images.

They start with pictures of the Passion quite obviously inspired by German sixteenth-century coloured woodcuts which were in great demand in all the west of Europe at the time. Like them, they are gaudy and violently realistic.[1]

point that has hardly been dealt with is the date of the manuscript. This explains why it has been thought useful to give a note on the subject in an appendix (pp 814–15).

[1] See, for example, a woodcut in the Chicago Art Institute, where the whole body of Christ is covered with red drops and the crown of thorns is similar to that in the Book of the Burkes. Also the *Boek van der Bedroffenisse* [sorrows] *Marien*, published in Magdeburg in 1486; it is a Low German

First comes Christ before Pilate, a claustrophobic scene of violence where the repetition of two nearly identical profiles has an obsessive quality. Christ is dressed in a bright red garment, his hands tied by a rope. Pilate sits with his legs crossed on a throne decorated with what the artist obviously intends to be a pagan carving. The sky is bright yellow.

In the 'Flagellation', the dramatic effect comes not only from the vehemence of gestures but also from the gory portrayal of the body and face of Christ, totally covered with red drops of blood. The background is of a purple tone with black stars. Little rectangles of gold are imperfectly affixed on Christ's loincloth and on the background.

The third picture is extremely strange, as it is a combination of an 'Ecce Homo' with a 'Christ of Pity'. Christ, spattered with blood and draped in a purple cloak, sits on some sort of wooden throne with steps. He wears the crown of thorns and holds the reed. But all five wounds are clearly indicated, so that the popular devotional image of the 'Christ of Pity' is combined with the historical representation of the mocking of Christ. On both sides, figures with enormous hands point at this central figure; the red background is patterned with scrolls of wispy white foliage.

The 'Carrying of the cross' has all the nearly unbearable intensity found in renderings of the scene by German artists of the fifteenth and sixteenth centuries. But it is constructed on a few simple rhythms by means of the vertical lances of the soldiers and the formalised zigzag patterns of the women's draperies. Our Lady, her head surrounded by a red halo, dominates the centre of the scene.   32b

These Passion pictures have one parallel in Irish art of the medieval period: the series of carvings coming probably from the tomb erected around 1470 by Mór Ní Bhriain, wife of Terence MacMahon (Toirdhealbhach Mac Mathghamhna) in the Franciscan friary at Ennis.[1] There, the scenes of the Passion are obviously inspired by English alabasters of the fifteenth century. The style is less crude than in the Burke book, but the relation to the models and the resultant awkward eagerness in the rendering of the scenes is about the same.[2]

The last of the Passion scenes pairs off rather ludicrously with the first of the genealogical figures holding the shield of the Burkes. But the confrontation has the useful effect of giving a convincing demonstration that both series are by the same hand. The range of colours, the treatment of the backgrounds, the application of little rectangles of gold are the same. The helmets are identical and so is the portrayal of the horses, and the same idiosyncrasies govern the drawings of hands and faces.

devotional tract cast in the form of a dialogue between Christ and the Virgin. In the engraving of the 'Carrying of the cross', Christ has only a partly hidden halo, while the Virgin has a very emphatic one with double edge. See *Early printed books: major acquisitions of the Pierpont-Morgan library, 1924–1974* (New York, 1974).

[1] See Hunt, *Figure sculpture*, pp 120–24.
[2] Above, p. 772.

It is more difficult to suggest a model that inspired these figures than it is in the case of the Passion scenes.[1] But some of their costumes, based on contemporary fashions, give an interesting confirmation of the dates already proposed for the various parts of the text. From that point of view, the two key figures are the first one, Richard Mór (lord of Connacht 1227–43), and the second, his son William (d. 1270). Richard wears a high-crowned felt hat with a large flat brim, of a type that was common with slight variants in the Low Countries for centuries but came into fashion in England, as contemporary dated portraits show, around 1570–75, and remained in favour until about 1610–12.[2] The costume of William, however, is more narrowly datable because of the small ruff, which was replaced at the turn of the century by either a linen collar or a thick, wide ruff. Associated as it is here with a small round cap and skirt-like baggy trousers, it is exactly the costume worn by Leicester in a portrait of 1565 and in the drawing and painting of him made by Federico Zuccaro in 1575. So this would come as a confirmation of the dates 1578 and 1584 suggested by the texts. Most of the other figures—William son of William, Thomas son of Edmund Albanach, Ricard son of Edmund na Féasóige (the bearded), Seaán son of Ricard, and Seaán son of Oliver—wear armour of mail, some of them with helmets. These figures fit in fairly well with some carved ones, especially with the galloglass of the panels incorporated in the tomb of Fedlimid Ó Conchobhair in Roscommon Abbey, the effigy on the Ó Catháin tomb in Dungiven, County Londonderry, and the effigy of a Burke knight at Ballynakill church, Glinsk, County Galway. These figures are all armed either in a padded aketon or a coat of mail over an aketon, with a pisane (large collar) pointed in front, but like the figures in the de Burgh volume they do not have metal discs protecting either shoulders or elbows. Their armour may be archaic like many of those represented on Irish tombs, whether, as John Hunt suggests, it was taken from the reserves of the armoury, or whether a certain conventional version of an armour had been adopted once for all by a sculptor, regardless of whether it had become out of fashion. A strange legend clings to the Burke effigy at Glinsk, which may have given it a tremendous imitation value; it was supposed to have been the effigy of the Burke who had founded Athassel, and to have been sent at the dissolution of the monastery for safe keeping to the Burke who was considered as the head of the family. But if it did influence the portraits, it was only as a free imitation. Except for Seaán, who rides a horse, the aketon is not shown in the paintings, as the sleeves of the coat of mail are full length and the coat seems to end in a kind of frill; it is also somewhat

---

[1] A late English manuscript on paper, dated 1564, containing romances transcribed from printed texts (Bodl., Douce MS 261) shows some of the heroes in contemporary costume, outlined on blank backgrounds. Though the presentation is less skilful than in the Book of the Burkes, the process is similar; see Otto Pächt and J. J. G. Alexander, *Illuminated manuscripts in the Bodleian Library*, vol. iii *(British, Irish and Icelandic schools)* (Oxford, 1973).

[2] See Eric Mercer, *English art, 1553—1625* (Oxford, 1962), and Roy Strong, *The English icon* (London and New York, 1969), *passim*.

shorter than that of the Glinsk knight, so that the legs have to be protected by armour.

These figures, each isolated on its page, have a much more natural appearance than those on the overcrowded pages of the Passion scenes. The drawing is crude, but the effect is excellent, the figures encroaching on the frame and combined with it with a great sense of balance. They have very much the same qualities as the carvings done in the sixteenth century by Irish sculptors. Perhaps these two illustrated manuscripts, the Bodleian 'Life of St Columba' and the Book of the Burkes, show what Irish painting, based on representation but keeping some elements of stylisation, could have been if it had had the chance to develop.

But the times were hardly conducive to mural or easel painting, and as far as illumination is concerned these books are already anachronic, as they date from a time when everywhere the manuscript was giving way to the printed book. It is the paradox of book-production in Irish that during the following centuries this anachronism will live on. The early attempts at printing in Irish characters were purely of a propagandist nature, while all the efforts at preserving the texts of the past made in the seventeenth century were first and foremost done by hand, even if they eventually took their final shape in print at Louvain or elsewhere. However, the scribes of that period did not usually waste their efforts on such futile embellishments as illuminated initials. It is with some of the eighteenth-century scribes that occasionally an attempt is shown at emulating the ornaments of the manuscripts they were copying, or even at inventing, with varying success, a new system of decoration, and thus the old animal-initial lived on, in a sort of mummified fashion, until well into the second decade of the nineteenth century.[1]

---

[1] Since this chapter was written, a valuable study of Irish manuscripts, with special emphasis on calligraphy, has been published: Timothy O'Neill, *The Irish hand: scribes and their manuscripts from the earliest times to the seventeenth century, with an exemplar of Irish scripts*, with introduction by F. J. Byrne (Mountrath, 1984). It includes twenty-six black-and-white reproductions from major manuscripts to 1636, and fifty-three examples of calligraphy from *c.*600 to 1983.

The dating of the Book of the Burkes

THE dating of the Book of the Burkes rests on some data contained in the text. It seems obvious that it was made for Sir Seaán Burke, son of Oliver, whose name appears last in the lists. He became head of the MacWilliam Burkes in 1571 after a long struggle both with the English and with other Burke competitors (he was beaten by the queen's forces at the battle of Shrule). His portrait is accompanied in the Book by a long notice saying that 'he suffered greater hardship than any of his ancestors, defending his own patrimony, i.e., he and his kindred fought seven battles in his time before he secured sovereignty'. He died in 1580. He appears in the documents in Irish echoing contestations about territorial rights in the beginning of the book, in one of which he is said to have brought his complaint (apparently about the encroachments of another Burke) to 'the captain and council, viz., the archbishop of Tuam, and Master Bacon, and Justice Dillon, and Edward White' who made an order in his favour. 'And Mac William has this order, written in English, from the hand of the council.'

One sentence in the body of the book would be of utmost importance in giving the date of the composition: 'And of the descendants of Elizabeth, daughter of the Brown Earl [who married Lionel, duke of Clarence], is the queen of England, i.e. Elizabeth that now is, 1578 [Elizabeth *so ann* 1578], so that it is through the blood of the children of William Burk she came to the crown.' Unfortunately this part of the text, both in the Irish and the Latin documents, has been inserted over an erasure. It is possible that the scribe was using documents older than the time of Elizabeth and that the suitability of the insertion only appeared later. Not very much later, though, as the insertion seems to be in the same hand as the bulk of the text. In any case this shows that the last revision of that part of the book was made in 1578 and that the text itself was not copied much earlier. 1578 is two years before the death of Sir Seaán, and the poems inserted at the end of the book are probably contemporary with this. They were written in praise of Seaán by Tadhg Dall Ó hUiginn and Ruaidhrí, son of Domhnall Ó hUiginn. They deal with very much the same matter as the genealogies. The second ends:

> Four score and five hundred,
> A thousand from the birth of Christ—
> The profound sorrow was destined
> To the notable death of John.

But this again is an addition, written in black ink in a different hand from that of the brown ink text of the rest of the poem.

The book ends with two legal deeds in Latin between Walter Ciotach Burke, son of Seaán, and the Barretts who laid claim to the possession of Belleek castle. They are both dated 1584. Walter had a son, Theobald, who was the head of the MacWilliam Burkes from 1593 to 1600, and who subsequently died in Spain. The book, however, probably stayed in Ireland, as a later hand, which has added comments in English on the first pages, has noted: 'Olyverus Bourke mac Sheamus[1] died the last daye of December Anno Dom. 1619 in his house at Inisquoe.' The same hand has inserted in the margin of one of the enumerations of Burke possessions 'The lands now in question'. The book was probably used as a document in some of the land transactions of the seventeenth century.

Altogether, the main part of the text seems to date from the time when Sir Seaán Burke was alive and in possession of the title (1571–80), to have been corrected in his lifetime (1578) and shortly after his death (addition to the poem), and to have received additions in 1584.

[1] Oliver has been identified as a younger son of Seaán and brother of Walter Ciotach.

CHAPTER XXIX

Coinage to 1534: the sign of the times

MICHAEL DOLLEY

THE isolation of pre-Christian Ireland from the classical world is reflected in the absence of coinage from her economy. There is no certain record of a Greek or even Hellenistic coin having been found in Ireland, and the same is true for the Ancient British series. There are more than ninety recorded findings of Roman coins, but in all but a dozen cases the import of the coins in question can be shown to have occurred in modern times. The authentic tally consists of two second-century hoards of silver coins from north Antrim, fourth-century hoards of copper and gold coins from Ireland's Eye and Newgrange respectively, and an early fifth-century hoard of silver coins and ornaments from near Coleraine, together with a few single finds falling within the same chronological bracket as the hoards and ranging from Kerry to Donegal but avoiding Connacht. The finds in no case suggest that the coins were thought of as anything more than a reserve of precious metal, and the essential coinlessness of the Irish economy was to persist until the sixteenth century. Stock served the function of money, and the fact that the *cumal* or female slave was never categorised in the same way as the cow where the Irish law texts are concerned is good evidence that the *cumal* was a purely nominal money of account, a notional multiple of the cow.

Early Christian Ireland remained singularly coinless. There are two nineteenth-century findings in Leinster of single tremisses from Merovingian France, but no record of the discovery of a single Anglo-Saxon coin earlier than the last decade of the eighth century. In the ninth century contact with the vikings did result in the import into Ireland of a number of Carolingian and English silver coins, but the trickle became a relative flood only after the first quarter of the tenth century. There are sixty-four coin-hoards that can be dated between c. 825 and c. 1175, none of them from west of the Shannon, and an appreciable number of single-finds. In the first half of the tenth century a small number of Kufic silver dirhems appear to have arrived by way of Scandinavia, and after the millennium the dwindling number of continental silver deniers comes to an abrupt end. After the 980s, too, there is a marked falling off in the

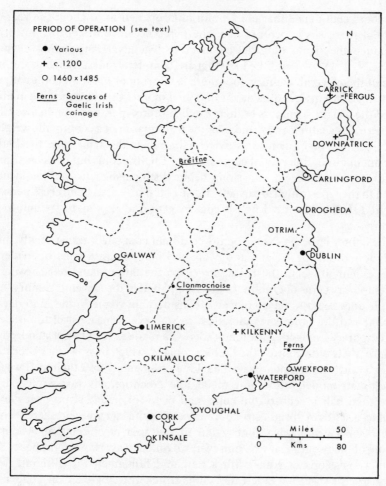

PERIOD OF OPERATION (see text)

● Various
+ c. 1200
○ 1460×1485

Ferns Sources of
Gaelic Irish
coinage

N

CARRICK
+ -FERGUS

DOWNPATRICK
+

CARLINGFORD

○ DROGHEDA

O TRIM

GALWAY

● DUBLIN

● Clonmacnoise

● LIMERICK

+ KILKENNY

Ferns

○ KILMALLOCK

WEXFORD

WATERFORD

Bréifne

CORK

○ YOUGHAL

○ KINSALE

0   Miles   50
0   Kms   80

Map 17 MINTS, 997–1505, by K. M. Davies

number of English silver pennies, and about the middle of the eleventh century they finally disappear from the hoards, which are now composed exclusively of the issues of a mint that had been established by Sitric Silkbeard at Dublin in the late 990s. Some of the later issues of Edward the Confessor and those of Harold, the two Williams, and Henry I must have reached Ireland, for the types are imitated on the Dublin coinage, but it remains a curious fact that the only Anglo-Norman coin found to date in Ireland is a fragmentary penny of Stephen from the recent excavations in Dublin.

The earliest issues of the Hiberno-Norse mint at Dublin imitate slavishly contemporary pennies of Ethelred II of England. A few are even struck from dies that had seen service in the English mints, and these enable us to say with some confidence that the Dublin mint opened in or about the year 997. Many of these silver pennies bear the name of Sitric Silkbeard, but others reproduce the name of Ethelred or have legends incorporating elements (OGSEN, THYMN, and the like) that are completely mysterious. In the early years of the eleventh century, too, there is copying of the Irish copies at more than one centre in Scandinavia. At first the Dublin imitations more than maintained the weight standards of their English prototypes, but even before Clontarf there was a falling away, and over the next quarter of a century the weight of the Hiberno-Norse penny was twice reduced. At the same time the Dublin mint put out imitations not of contemporary English coins but of its own earlier imitations, the different emissions being distinguished by various symbols added to the types which are usually those of the so-called 'long cross penny' of Ethelred II, the heaviest English coin ever to find its way to Ireland in any quantity.

The lighter Hiberno-Norse penny could not compete internationally, and is rarely found outside Ireland and Man, and here mention must be made of a series essentially from the 1030s, struck on the latter island but copying the contemporary coins of Dublin. In the second half of the eleventh century, however, it does seem to have enjoyed a considerable vogue in the hinterland of Dublin, and the prototypes included, as we have seen, most of the issues of contemporary England. An attempt was even made to restore the standard, but by the early twelfth century the Dublin coinage, which by now can be reckoned an Irish one, was in a poor way. The 'long cross penny' of Ethelred II was still the ultimate model, but weight, metal, and execution alike are wretched. For more than half a century the coins had been for practical purposes anepigraphic, a series of upright strokes representing the legends, and there seems to have been a progressive contraction in the area of circulation. About the middle of the twelfth century, however, we find at least two and probably three parallel emissions of coins with a new and fundamentally different fabric. These are the so-called bracteates, coins struck by a single die on a paper-thin flan so that the design is embossed from behind. The model appears to have been German, and there are two distinct series. One is struck in relatively good silver with novel types, and there is much to commend the association of these pieces with Toirrdelbach Ua Conchobair and a mint at Clonmacnoise. A subsidiary issue could even be slightly later in date and emanate from Ferns. The second series is notably base and modelled on mid-twelfth-century English pence, and here the mint is certainly Dublin. Together the two series constitute a coinage that is properly described as Irish and not Hiberno-Norse, but any chance that either might have had of becoming nationally viable was utterly cast down with the coming of the Anglo-Normans.

The earliest coins of the Anglo-Normans seem to have been struck at Dublin *c.* 1185. They are silver halfpence with a profile portrait and the simple obverse legend IOHANNES. In the early 1190s they were superseded by an extensive series of silver halfpence and farthings, struck originally at Dublin but after 1195 or 1196 at Waterford and Limerick as well. Halfpence only, too, are known from Carrickfergus and an apparently adulterine mint at Kilkenny. The penny was eschewed, perhaps because of the inferior status of the lordship, and the halfpence and farthings appear not to have circulated outside Ireland. By 1199 the series would seem to have come to an end where the lordship proper was concerned, but in Ulster John de Courcy appears to have followed up an earlier emission of irregular halfpence by a fairly extensive series predominantly of farthings emanating from Downpatrick and Carrickfergus. On almost all these issues the name of Patrick appears in the place where one would have expected to find that of de Courcy's secular overlord. In 1204, however, King John resolved on a major reform of the Anglo-Irish coinage. Not only was striking concentrated at Dublin, but it was no longer left even partially in the control of private individuals. Robert of Bedford, a clerk in the royal service and a future bishop of Lismore (1218–23), was given sole charge, and a very large number of silver pence was struck to the same standard as the English, albeit with distinctive types. Significantly these are found more often outside Ireland than inside the colony, which had to make do with relatively small numbers of half-pence and farthings. It is estimated that the quantity of silver struck may have been of the order of some £50,000, and the bulk of the new pence seems to have been shipped over to England and used by John to further his continental ambitions. A whole generation later they were to be the subject of imitation in west Germany, perhaps the highest tribute that could be paid to their quality, and good evidence, too, that they had reached Europe in considerable quantity. By 1210 or thereabouts supplies of silver once more appear to have been running low, and Robert of Bedford withdrew from the oversight of the coinage without first obtaining the king's permission. Two men by the name of William, one with the surname Wace and likewise presumably a clerk in the king's service, took over the coinage, and for a few months the output of Dublin was supplemented at mints reopened at Limerick and Waterford. Wace's name appears on coins of the former city, and in due course he was to be rewarded with the bishopric of the latter. For the last years of John's reign, however, the Irish mints stood idle, with the royal revenues made up increasingly of English money brought privately into Ireland by Anglo-Norman lords bent on the capital development of their new domains.

The coins of John remained current for more than forty years, but a major recoinage in England in 1249 could not be ignored indefinitely where the king's land of Ireland was concerned. Circulating in Ireland by this time were large quantities of obsolete English pence, so that an Irish recoinage was clearly indicated. A clerk in the king's service, one Roger of Haverhill, was given an overall surveillance of its production, but the coins bear the names of two men, Davi[d] and Ric[h]ard, who have been identified with the London moneyers David of Enfield and Richard Bonaventure. Striking was confined to Dublin, and the only denomination struck was the penny, the voided long cross of the reverse type sufficiently facilitating division where necessary into halves and quarters. This reverse type, incidentally, was common to both the Anglo-Irish and the English coinages, which again were struck to one and the same standard, and the only obvious difference between the two series was that on the Dublin coins the king's portrait was surrounded by a triangular frame, whereas on those from English mints it appeared in a roundel. Many of the accounts for the coinage have survived. Exchanges (*cambia*) were set up at Limerick and Carrickfergus, at which obsolete coins and bullion could be brought in and exchanged for the new pence, and at Dublin a total of more than £43,000 was struck between October 1251, when the mint opened, and its closure in 1254. Nearly 3,000 of the pence have survived, and this is perhaps the only medieval coinage where we are able to state exactly how many dies were used, and in what combinations, to produce a known volume of coin. Some 1,500 of the coins extant today derive from a vast treasure unearthed in Brussels in 1908, a hoard critical not just for what it tells us about Anglo-Irish coins reaching the continent, but also for its inclusion of several hundred Low Countries imitations. These last are invaluable testimony to the extent to which Anglo-Irish coins were included by Henry III and by Richard of Cornwall in their continental subsidies, and to the parity of esteem which the Dublin penny shared with its English counterpart.

When the Dublin mint closed in 1254 it was because all available silver had been called in and coined, and a study of the actual pieces makes it clear that output had dwindled for some time before the closure. Also avoided by this cessation of production was the ambiguity that would have resulted later in 1254 when Edward was created lord of Ireland and so would have been entitled to an Irish coinage of his own. On the death of Henry in 1272, Edward became king of England as well, but continued to coin there in the name of his dead father. In the mid-1270s there is some documentary evidence for the existence of a Dublin moneyer by the name of Richard Olaf, and it has been suggested with some plausibility that there should be given to this period a handful of rare Dublin pennies by a moneyer, Ric[h]ard, of the same type as earlier but from dies unrepresented in hoards from the 1250s and 1260s and of a style analogous with that of the English pence of Edward in Henry's name. In 1279 the young king decided on a major recoinage, at least where England was concerned. Production was concentrated in a relatively small number of mints, and especially London and Canterbury, while as well as pence, halfpence and farthings were struck in considerable quantity. By 1281 Dublin was following suit, and soon afterwards Waterford opened, hardly a coincidence when Stephen de Fulbourn occupied the see and also headed the royal administration. In 1282, though, the Waterford mint closed, apparently because of a dearth of silver, and by 1283 Dublin too had ceased production. It has been estimated that the sum struck at the two mints was of the order of £40,000, and it was doubtless his success in finding money for his royal master that explains why the smoothly efficient de Fulbourn survived apparently well-founded charges of peculation. As before, the coins were shipped overseas in quantity, their assimilation into the English series being facilitated by identity of reverse type. Again, too, the principal difference where the obverse was concerned was the framing of the royal portrait by a triangle instead of a circle. Most of the coins struck were pence, but some halfpence and farthings were produced to meet local needs.

By the 1290s Edward was seriously pressed for coined silver, and in 1294 the Dublin and Waterford mints came back into production; Stephen de Fulbourn had been translated to Tuam in 1286 but had been succeeded as bishop of Waterford by his brother Walter, another treasurer of Ireland well versed in the finances of the lordship. Silver, however, was hard to come by, and it is doubtful if output over this period exceeded a few hundred pounds. In 1295 one of the Anglo-Irish, Thomas fitz Maurice FitzGerald, became head of the Irish administration. His estates were concentrated in Desmond, and it cannot well be coincidence that the Waterford mint should have ceased to strike at precisely this juncture while a mint is found for the first time at Cork. Both here and at Dublin, however, production of coin continued to be exiguous. The arrival of Wogan as justiciar at the end of 1295 predictably put paid to the operation of the provincial mints, and striking was once more confined to Dublin. By 1302 all available silver had been coined, and it has been estimated that the total output over the years 1294–1302 was of the order of only £10,000. Within a decade the damage done to the Irish economy by the export of so much coin was plain for all to see, and Wogan had even been driven to promise that any money raised by taxation would be spent in the colony and not shipped overseas.

One consequence of the Bruce invasion does seem to have been an increase in the volume of English money circulating in Ireland, though it has still to be established how much of this was due to deliberate subsidy and how much a consequence of a reduction in royal interference with silver used by private individuals to finance the capital development of their estates or to make purchases of the colony's staple exports of corn and hides. By the 1330s, however, the want of an Irish mint was once more a major grievance where the Anglo-Irish were concerned, and the extreme shortage of coin was positively stimulating the import of inferior money from France. Accordingly Edward III authorised in 1339 a coinage at Dublin of pence, halfpence, and farthings, but only two halfpence have come down to us, and it is possible that the penny and even the farthing were never struck. Except for the triangle on the obverse the halfpence conformed closely to the English model, and they were appreciably lighter than their precursors of a generation earlier. The English coinage likewise was having to face up to international movements in the price of silver, and in the 1340s and 1350s there were sensational developments which included the introduction of new denominations in the silver, the groat (subject of unsuccessful experimentation in 1279) and half-groat, and of gold, again the subject of premature introduction in 1257. All these developments passed Ireland by, and no Anglo-Irish coins of any description appear to have been struck between the end of the 1330s and the mid-1420s.

In the second half of the fourteenth century the Anglo-Irish coinage consisted essentially of the English penny of Edward I and Edward II, supplemented by meagre imports of the groat and half-groat of Edward III and the penny of Richard II. The condition of the coins worsened steadily, and the loss by wear and clipping became so pronounced that it has even been possible to suggest an approximate chronology for hoards of the period on the basis of the average weight of the individual pieces. During the last quarter of the century there was a further complication where the north-east of the island was concerned. Here there was import in quantity of the contemporary Scottish groat, an inferior piece which in theory was valued at no more than threepence but seems often to have passed for an English groat when all coin was acquiring a scarcity value. There could be no better commentary, though, on the dearth of silver in the colony than the failure of the Dublin mint to reopen on the two occasions in the last decade of the century when the English king was actually in Ireland on protracted visits. A new problem, too, was raising its head, the production among the Gaelic Irish in the area immediately inland from Meath and Louth of forgeries of English and Scottish pieces made by soldering together impressions on foil of the obverses and reverses of genuine coins.

In the first half of the fifteenth century what had been a nuisance became a major abuse. The striking at Dublin in 1425 of what appears to have been a nominal issue of English-type pence (two specimens only have survived) proved to be a drop in the ocean where the island's coinage needs were concerned, and soon the ever dwindling band of worn pennies from the two preceding centuries gave place to what was, in practice, an independent Anglo-Irish coinage, even if it was one that seems to have been totally without lawful authority. Considerable quantities of English groats of Edward III and of Henry IV in particular were sheared down to about half their proper size, two denominations being created according as to whether the clipping removed both or only one of the concentric legends of the reverse type. A further supply of coins of the smaller denomination was obtained by shearing down English half-groats as far as the tressure framing the portrait, and these three classes of mutilated pieces appear to have dominated the colony's currency for a generation and more. They had one merit; they were at once immediately recognisable and totally unacceptable outside Ireland, so that their general export was out of the question. On the other hand, it was of the essence of the malpractice that such sheared coins were peculiarly vulnerable to imitation among the Gaelic Irish, who produced plated versions of the kind just described in very great numbers. Bréifne seems to have been the centre of distribution if not of production of these counterfeits, which passed by the name of 'O'Reilly's money', and in 1447 and again in 1456 they were the subject of parliamentary denunciation in the most vigorous terms.

At the heart of the problem was the preponderant flow of precious metal out of Ireland. In 1460 the Anglo-Irish were able at last to exploit the political scene in England to their own advantage, and the celebrated parliament that met first at Drogheda and later at Dublin to further the cause of Richard of York proceeded at once to mount a full-dress assault upon the official assumption that the coinage of Ireland had necessarily to be of the same weight and fineness as that of England. The outcome was a surprisingly large and varied Anglo-Irish coinage where the different denominations weighed only three-quarters as much as their English counterparts. A consequence, of course, was that English coins were worth more when brought in and spent in Ireland, and the result was a stimulation of trade which brought English silver flooding into the colony. At first groats only were struck, and these only at Dublin. Curiously, too, the obverse type was a simple crown within a tressure, and there was no legend. Soon, however, the number of denominations and of mints was increased, and the name of Edward IV began to appear on the coins even if normally accompanied only by his Irish title. Waterford was soon established as Ireland's second mint, and Limerick, Galway, and Trim followed suit in quick succession, though production at Galway was almost at once curtailed, perhaps because of a disastrous fire. Groats, half-groats, and pennies were struck, and the portrait was restored, so that the coins were much more 'English-looking' and thus when brought to England easily confused with the heavier models and so unpopular. The early 1460s, too, witnessed the introduction of halfpence both in silver and in billon, a silver-copper alloy, and of farthings and half-farthings in billon or overt copper on an apparently Scottish model. Nowhere else in these islands was there such diversity and experimentation, though the English king was clearly unhappy about the degree of freedom enjoyed by mints over which he could not exercise any real degree of control. In 1467 rights of coinage were formally extended to Drogheda and Carlingford, though coins of the latter mint have still to be found, and by the 1470s there was in addition a flourishing if technically adulterine mint at Cork. At other places the absence of a strong central authority meant that unofficial coinage was rife. Coins have come down to us with the mint-signature of Wexford, and there is contemporary evidence for striking at Kilmallock, Kinsale, and Youghal, though here the culprits appear not to have incorporated the names of the places in the legends of the coins that they were alleged to be producing in considerable quantity. Only in 1468 does there appear to have been any serious attempt from the English side to terminate a state of affairs that threatened to become subversive of all authority, Anglo-Irish as well as English. In 1467 there had been ordained a second devaluation of the Irish groat which would have reduced its weight to no more than half that of its English counterpart. Dublin, Trim, and Drogheda actually struck the new 'doubles', but in the following year the new pieces were cried down and given a new value approximating to their silver content. There were limits to the English king's patience, and until his recall Tiptoft showed himself as resolute as ruthless.[1]

The brief Lancastrian restoration in 1470 seems not to have affected Yorkist control of the Irish mints, and its only consequence where the coins were concerned was that the victorious Edward IV now made a largely unsuccessful attempt to have his English title included in the legends of his Irish coins. Intermittently, too, moves were made to reduce the number of mints in operation, and by the end of the reign Dublin, Waterford, and Drogheda alone remained, the last seeming to owe its survival to the fact that the master-mind behind the Anglo-Irish coinage at this juncture was one Germyn Lynch, a native of the place, and a man of the most dubious probity. Between 1470 and 1483, too, production of coin does appear generally to have slackened, with increasing emphasis laid upon the production of pence instead of groats. The thinking may have been that the groat was the standard coin of international trade, the penny being liable to export only in relatively trivial amounts, so that this development neatly avoided offending English commercial interests. Only at the very end of the reign do groats appear to have been struck on any scale, and then only at Dublin and Drogheda but not Waterford, the coins being once more distinguished from their English counterparts by a large rose in the centre of the reverse. By now relations between Kildare and the English crown were more than strained, and the Yorkist badge was perhaps a reminder to Edward IV of the debt his father had owed the Geraldines.

The accession of Richard III was almost immediately followed by the issue of coins from Dublin of a novel type. The royal portrait was again discarded, and its place taken by a shield with the English and French arms quarterly. The reverse type was no less distinctive, the three crowns of the badge of Ireland disposed one above the other. A coinage with approximately the same types had been contemplated a year or two earlier, but it was to have been a coinage of pence and halfpence, whereas the pieces now struck were groats. They survived in circulation for more than a century, and were later to be known as 'cross-keel' (*cros chaol*) groats because of the wire-line crosses that quartered obverse and reverse alike. Lip-service was paid to the English king by the inclusion in the legend of his name and his English, French, and Irish titles, but from the first there was a carelessness about the interpretation of the instructions from England that perhaps is best described as revealing. A second mint was eventually set up at Waterford, but while Richard lived production here seems to have been exiguous. His death may well have brought no tear to the Great Earl's eye, but the accession of the Tudor Henry VII was a potential death-blow to Geraldine ambitions, even though for

---

[1] Cf. above, pp 600–01.

several years an eventual Yorkist restoration seemed very much on the cards. Butler Waterford was quick to set Henry's name and initial upon its coins, but from Dublin the coins now went out with the king's name omitted. At the same time Dublin began to strike half-groats and pence alike regally anonymous. In 1487 Lambert Simnel was crowned as Edward VI in Christ Church, and after a period of initial resistance the Waterford mint does appear to have passed into Geraldine control. It is not only Dublin groats that were briefly distinguished by the name and/or initial of Edward, and there was a large if short-lived anonymous coinage of groats and half-groats of Waterford make that sport miniature shields with the Geraldine (and FitzEustace?) saltires on either side of the English armorial. Almost immediately, though, striking was once more concentrated at Dublin where a series of groats, half-groats, and pence is marked with Henry's name or initial. Too late, in the event, the Great Earl thought it prudent to face up to the reality that the Tudors had come to stay. The coins were of uneven workmanship but still generally competent, old dies being used up in combination with new ones for the sake of economy. One curious variant of reverse legend substitutes the reiterated vocative KERIE (= kyrie) DOMINE for the normal DOMINUS HYBERNIAE. How long striking continued is far from clear, but it was probably at least as late as 1490.

The restoration of Kildare in 1496 is no less mirrored in the last phase of the coinage of Dublin in the name of Henry VII. The new coins were virtually all groats with only a very few half-groats. The types were purely English, and the execution generally execrable. Little care appears to have been taken to maintain the fineness of the silver, and many if not all the pieces fell appreciably short of sterling standard. The legends were equally aberrant, ADIUTORIUM being substituted for ADIUTOREM MEUM and even in one case PRO-VIDEBO for POSUI. The dies were engraved locally, and with so little competence that it seems to have been realised that any attempt to follow the English model in 1502 and substitute a naturalistic profile bust for the traditional facing portrait would have been to court disaster. Accordingly the latest coins in the series are the groats, which genuflect towards the change in England by omitting the tressure that had been a feature of the facing-bust groat since its inception a century and a half before, but which retain the full-face bust. By 1505 the Dublin mint had closed its doors, and for the whole of the next generation the colony's need for coin was to be met by the import in surprising quantity of English groats and half-groats with the distinctive profile portraits of Henry VII and Henry VIII. These might often be clipped, but when later in the sixteenth century the Gaelic Irish began to go over for the first time to the use of coin their excellence was generally recognised, with the result that it was occasionally stipulated in documents that particular payments were to be made in *salfás* (half-face, i.e. profile) money. It is important to realise, though, that the old Anglo-Irish issues were not demonetised, and continued to circulate beside the imported English pieces in some cases until well into the seventeenth century. Not the least of the problems confronting the Tudors in their attempts to solve the problem of an acceptable coinage for Ireland was the farrago of obsolete and obsolescent coinages that was the legacy of three-and-a-half centuries of alternation between systematic exploitation and cynical neglect.

POSTSCRIPT

SINCE the above was written there have been four hoards with coins, three from Ireland and one from the Isle of Man, which throw considerable light both on the ordering of the Hiberno-Norse series and on the chronology of coin-use in Ireland. Earliest in point of date of deposit is one recovered in 1981 at Lough Ennel in County Westmeath, which must be assigned to the critical quinquennium *c.* 910–*c.* 915, when Dublin was in Irish hands. The oriental hacksilver apart, it is dominated by Kufic dirhems and sheared fragments thereof, a class of material not thrown up by the Dublin excavations, while the very few occidental coins have a pronounced East Anglian flavour. In 1980 a group of eight coins was found in a souterrain on the southern outskirts of Dundalk. One is Hiberno-Norse and seven English, with a preponderance of pennies of the Winchester mint. Taken in conjunction with the 1848 find from Bradda mountain on the Isle of Man, it leaves little room for doubt that coinage at Dublin did not begin until the summer of 997. In 1978 a major discovery from the termon of Clonmacnoise seems to have been composed entirely of Dublin coins of Dolley Phases II, III, and V, and to have been concealed no earlier than the 1070s. This 'skipping' of Dolley Phase IV is also found in the cases of a major hoard of roughly the same date which began to come to light on the Isle of Man in 1972 and is now firmly associated with the churchyard at Kirk Michael, and of a long run of coin-finds from the continuing excavations at different sites in Dublin. The same phenomenon can be observed in the case of the Scandinavian coin-hoards, and between them the two new hoards must clinch the attribution to Man of a distinctive insular coinage of Irish type and given the name of Hiberno-Manx. The explanation of the failure of coins of Dolley Phase IV to occur in so many contexts may well be geographical, and it seems likely that the coins in question represent an ephemeral coinage at Waterford *c.* 1065 under the aegis of Diarmait mac Máel na mBó.

The coins from the three Irish finds have been or will shortly be published by Michael Kenny of the National Museum of Ireland, to whom I am indebted for details of the coins and for much stimulating and worthwhile discussion of the problems they pose.

BIBLIOGRAPHY

P. W. ASPLIN

INTRODUCTION

WE are fortunate in having—in the works of Giraldus Cambrensis—a detailed, if biased, description of Ireland at the time of the coming of the Anglo-Normans. For the next three centuries we have nothing comparable—only brief accounts by such as Creton. However, much can be inferred from the descriptions of sixteenth-century travellers, whose works are listed in volume III. Events are reported tersely in the Gaelic and Anglo-Irish Annals, but they lack the vivid detail to be found in chronicles of other countries. Apart from the semi-legendary 'Book of Howth', the Anglo-Irish (as Campion was to complain in the sixteenth century) did not compose any sustained narrative history. The Gaelic Irish, however, did compose two such works: the 'Caithréim Thoirdhealbhaigh', a lively but unreliable account of the wars in Thomond from *c.* 1276 to 1318, and the chronicle of thirteenth-century Connacht that has been disguised by its incorporation into the Annals of Loch Cé and Annals of Connacht. This tradition was taken up at the very end of the period of autonomous Gaelic lordship, in the 'Life of Hugh Roe O'Donnell' by Lughaidh O'Clery. Information can be gleaned from passing references to Ireland in chronicles of English abbeys—essential reading, in any case, for the English background to Irish affairs.

The church also recorded much else. Papal letters and lists of annates are among the documents preserved in the Vatican, while the magnificent series of Armagh registers heads an important group of episcopal records surviving in Ireland. The distribution of church or cross lands is recorded in cartularies of Irish monasteries and cathedrals, complemented by those of English and Scottish houses with lands or daughter-houses in Ireland. This picture is rounded off by the extents taken at the dissolution.

Land holdings also feature prominently in the mass of detail contained in family archives, of which those of the Butlers of Ormond hold pride of place. These are augmented by English inquisitions *post mortem*. Further records have been preserved in the muniments of Dublin and other cities, and evidences of trade with Ireland can be found in the records of English and continental ports such as Bristol and Bruges.

Some chancery rolls were destroyed in a fire in St Mary's abbey as early as 1304, but most records of Irish central government perished in an explosion and fire at the Irish record office in 1922. However, several had already been published in transcript or calendar, while others have survived in the manuscript transcripts and calendars prepared by the record commissioners and by antiquaries such as Sir James Ware. Many individual documents have been printed in local histories and other works researched before 1922. Of great importance now is the material preserved, largely as a result of medieval administrative practices, in the Public Record Office in London. A project to reconstruct some at least of the lost Irish chancery rolls, from copies and transcripts there and elsewhere, was initiated by A. J. Otway-Ruthven and is continuing under the direction of J. F. Lydon. In the case of the exchequer, complete copies of Irish issue and receipt rolls were transmitted to the English exchequer. Furthermore, many magnates had lands on both sides of the Irish Sea, with the result that legal disputes were frequently referred to English courts whose records have survived.

Section II A of the following bibliography lists the archives where surviving original material and transcripts may be found. An attempt has been made in section III to include as much as possible as has appeared in print, except for short extracts of purely local significance, and some very general collections which will be listed in volume X. Much of this has been officially sponsored—the publications of the record commissions and record offices in both England and Ireland, the Rolls Series, and since 1928 the Irish Manuscripts Commission—but a significant role has been played by the Irish Archaeological Society, the Royal Society of Antiquaries of Ireland, and local societies as well as individual editors. Other transcripts will be found in some secondary works listed in section IV.

The historian can also learn much from unwritten sources. Sculpture, coins, and other artefacts have been collected by museums and individuals for centuries, although the scholarly assessment of their significance in the study of their creators is a comparatively recent development. Field monuments have been noted by travellers and surveyors, especially in a fine series of letters by John O'Donovan for the nineteenth-century ordnance survey. The possibilities of combining archival and field work were ably demonstrated by G. H. Orpen in a series of masterly papers, culminating in the four volumes of his *Ireland under the Normans* (Oxford, 1911–20). For the next four decades most Irish archaeologists concentrated on the rich megalithic heritage, but recent years have seen a growing interest in the distribution of medieval sites by the Group for the Study of Irish Historical Settlement, major excavations in the medieval city of Dublin, and at sites such as Mellifont abbey and Trim castle. Not all of this work has yet been published, but the bulk of what has is recorded in section IV D of this bibliography, with more specialised items on the visual arts and coinage in sections IV B 15 and IV B 8 respectively.

For secondary works the intention has been to list everything of significance relating specifically to medieval Ireland published before 1985; very few later publications were available in time for inclusion. For works on the British and continental backgrounds and on more general topics such as visual arts, limitations of space have dictated a more selective approach. The aim has been to include everything specifically mentioned or implied by the contributors to this volume and such other material as is appropriate to balance the coverage. However, in accordance with editorial policy, but excepting a few items of particular importance for the middle ages, works relevant to the periods of more than two volumes of *A new history of Ireland* have been omitted; they will be listed in the general bibliography in volume X.

The entries have been grouped according to the scheme for other volumes of the series, and the user should approach by way of the table of contents on pp 829–30. An item has normally been listed only once—in the section in which it is most significant and, it is hoped, most readily found—with limited cross-referencing. The general references at the beginning of some sections should help the reader to locate most material relevant to his enquiry. In section III, on published sources, the general arrangement is by the origin of the manuscript material; in section IV (secondary works), by subject. Within each section the entries are listed alphabetically, usually by author or body responsible for the work's intellectual content, occasionally, where this approach is inappropriate, under title. However, in some sections, notably on local and family history and archaeology, subheadings in small capitals have been used to group related works.

In individual entries an author with only one forename has this given in full where known, regardless of title-page usage. Where an author has more than one forename these are represented only by initials, unless more information is required to distinguish between people with the same initials. Most titles are given in full, but some of the longer ones have been shortened. Places and year of publication are given for monographs, followed where appropriate by series title in parenthesis. For articles in periodicals, the title of the periodical is given, abbreviated where possible in accordance with *Rules for contributors to Irish Historical Studies* (ed. T. W. Moody, revised ed., Dublin, 1968), followed by volume number, date, and pagination. Part numbers are normally omitted unless a volume contains more than one part with independent pagination or the part also constitutes a separate monograph. Similar information has been given for articles in *Festschriften* and other composite works, but in these cases the place and date of publication and series title of the volume are given in parenthesis after its title. All abbreviations are explained on pp xxxi–xlviii.

The compiler acknowledges with gratitude the assistance of contributors who supplied lists of works relevant to their chapters and comments on the first draft of this bibliography. In addition, Mr Francis Heaney suggested items for inclusion in the section on numismatics. Every effort has been made to verify the bibliographical details of each entry, either at source or in standard reference works such as the *National union catalog*. The resources and staffs of the libraries of the Royal Irish Academy, Trinity College, Dublin, and the University of Glasgow have been invaluable. So also have been the many bibliographies and published catalogues consulted; some of these are listed in section I, others will appear in the general bibliography in volume X.

CONTENTS

I BIBLIOGRAPHIES

In addition to printed works, this section contains general guides to manuscripts. Works on the manuscript contents of a single repository are listed under the repository in sect. II A.

Asplin, P. W. A. *Medieval Ireland, c.1170—1495: a bibliography of secondary works*. Dublin, 1971. (A New History of Ireland. Ancillary Publications, i.)

—— The writings of Professor A. J. Otway-Ruthven to 1980. In Lydon, *Eng. & Ire.* (1981), pp 255–63.

Baxter, J. H., Johnson, Charles, and Willard, J. F. An index of British and Irish Latin writers, 400–1520. In *Archivum Latinitatis Medii Aevi (Bulletin du Cange)*, vii (1932), pp 110–219; reprint, Hildesheim, 1972.

Bautier, R. H., and Sornay, Janine. *Les sources de l'histoire économique et sociale du moyen âge.* 2 vols. Paris, 1968.

A bibliography of the history of Wales. Prepared by the History and Law Committee of the Board of Celtic Studies of the University of Wales. 2nd ed. Cardiff, 1962; Supplement 1– . In *Bulletin of the Board of Celtic Studies*, xx (1963)– .

Boyce, G. C. *Literature of medieval history, 1930–1975: a supplement to Louis John Paetow's 'A guide to the study of medieval history'.* 5 vols. Millwood, 1981.

Bromwich, Rachel. Medieval Celtic literature: a select bibliography. Toronto, 1974. (Toronto Medieval Bibliographies, v.)

Brooks, E. St J. The sources for medieval Anglo-Irish history. In *Hist. Studies*, i (1958), pp 86–92.

Brown, I. D., and Dolley, Michael. A bibliography of coin hoards of Great Britain and Ireland, 1500–1967. Royal Numismatic Society, London, 1971. (Special Publications, vi.)

Caenegem, R. C. van. *Guide to the sources of medieval history.* With the collaboration of F. L. Ganshof. Amsterdam, New York, Oxford, 1978. (Europe in the Middle Ages, ii.)

Chevalier, Ulysse. *Répertoire des sources historiques du moyen âge.*
Bio-bibliographie. 2 vols. Paris, 1903–5. *Topo-bibliographie.* 2 vols. Montbéliard, Paris, 1894–1904.

Conway, Colmcille. Sources for the history of the Irish Cistercians, 1142–1540. In *Ir. Cath. Hist. Comm. Proc.*, 1958, pp 16–23.

Cosgrove, Art. Medieval Ireland, 1169–1534. In Lee, *Ir. histor. 1970–79* (1981), pp 13–33.

Crosby, E. U., Bishko, C. J., and Kellogg, R. L. *Medieval studies: a bibliographical guide.* New York and London, 1983.

Dunning, P. J. The letters of Innocent III as a source for Irish history. In *Ir. Cath. Hist. Comm. Proc.*, 1958, pp 1–10.

Ferguson, M. A. H. *Bibliography of English translations from medieval sources, 1943–1967.* New York, 1974. (Records of Civilization: Sources and Studies, lxxxviii.)

Flanagan, U. G. The church in Ireland in the mid-fifteenth century. In *I.C.H.S. Bull.*, new ser., i, no. 62 (1952), pp 6–7.

Gilbert, J. T. *Account of facsimiles of national manuscripts of Ireland.* London, 1884.

Graves, E. B. (ed.). *A bibliography of English history to 1485.* Oxford, 1975.

Guth, D. J. *Late-medieval England, 1377–1485.* Cambridge, 1976. (Conference of British Studies Bibliographical Handbooks.)

Gwynn, Aubrey. Bibliographical note on medieval Anglo-Irish history. In *Hist. Studies*, i (1958), pp 93–9.

Hardy, Sir T. D. *Descriptive catalogue of materials relating to the history of Great Britain and Ireland to the end of the reign of Henry VII.* 3 vols in 4. London, 1862–71 (Rolls Series, xxvi); reprint, [Nendeln], New York, 1964.

Hawkes, William. The liturgy in Dublin, 1200–1500: manuscript sources. In *Reportorium Novum*, ii (1958–60), pp 33–67.

International Bibliography of Historical Sciences. Vols i–xliv, Paris, 1926–79. Vols xlv– , Munich, New York, London, Paris, 1980– .

International medieval bibliography. 1968– . Leeds, 1968– .

Kenney, J. F. *The sources for the early history of Ireland: an introduction and guide*. Vol. i: *Ecclesiastical*. New York, 1929. (Records of Civilization, xi); 2nd ed., New York, Shannon, 1966; reprint, Dublin, 1979.

Lapidge, Michael, and Sharpe, Richard. *A bibliography of Celtic-Latin literature, 400– 1200*. R.I.A., Dublin, 1985.

Levine, Mortimore. *Tudor England, 1485–1603*. Cambridge, 1968. (Conference on British Studies Bibliographical Handbooks.)

Mac Niocaill, Gearóid. Gaelic Ireland to 1603. In Lee, *Ir. histor.*, *1970–79* (1981), pp 1–12.

Otway-Ruthven, A. J. Medieval Ireland, 1169–1485. In *I.H.S.*, xv, no. 60 (Sept. 1967), pp 359–65. (Thirty Years' Work in Irish History); revised ed. in Moody, *Ir. histor.*, *1936–70* (1973), pp 16–22.

Paetow, L. J. *A guide to the study of medieval history*. Berkeley, 1917; rev. ed., New York, 1931; revised and corrected ed., with errata compiled by Gray C. Boyce and an addendum by Lynn Thorndike. Millwood, 1980.

Pierpont-Morgan Library. *Early printed books: major acquisitions of the Pierpont-Morgan Library, 1924–1974*. New York, [1974].

Potthast, August. *Bibliotheca historica medii aevi: Wegweiser durch die Geschichtswerke des europäischen Mittelalters von 375–1500*. Berlin, 1862; Supplement. Berlin, 1868; 2. verbesserte und vermehrte Aufl. 2 vols. Berlin, 1896.

Quinn, A. M., and Hair, P. E. H. The writings of D. B. Quinn: a bibliography of publications to mid-1976. In K. R. Andrews, Nicholas P. Canny, and P. E. H. Hair (ed.), *The westward enterprise* (Liverpool, 1979), pp 303–9.

Repertorium Fontium historiae medii aevi, primum ab Augusto Potthast digestum, nunc cura collegii historicorum e pluribus nationibus emendatum et auctum. 1– . Istituto Storico Italiano per il Medio Evo, Rome, 1962– .

Ross, Noel. The historical writings of Diarmuid Mac Iomhair. In *Louth Arch. Soc. Jn.*, xx (1981–5), pp 175–9.

Royal Historical Society. *Writings on British history, 1901–1933*. Vol. ii: *The middle ages*. London, 1968.

Schneyer, J. B. *Repertorium der lateinischen Sermones des Mittelalters für die Zeit von 1150– 1350*. 9 vols. Münster, 1969–80. (Beiträge zur Geschichte der Philosophie und Theologie des Mittelalters, xliii.)

    2. Aufl., Bde 1–4, 1973–4.

Shaw, Francis. Medieval medico-philosophical treatises in the Irish language. In *Féilsgríbhinn Eóin Mhic Néill* (1940), pp 144–57.

Wilkinson, Bertie. *The high middle ages in England, 1154–1377*. Cambridge, 1978. (Conference on British Studies Bibliographical Handbooks.)

Williams, E. A. A bibliography of Giraldus Cambrensis, *c.* 1147–*c.* 1223. In *Nat. Lib. Wales Jn.*, xii (1961–2), pp 97–140.

Williams, H. F. *An index of medieval studies published in Festschriften, 1865–1946, with special reference to Romanic material*. Berkeley, Los Angeles, 1951.

II MANUSCRIPT SOURCES

A ARCHIVES AND GUIDES

This section lists manuscript repositories with catalogues, guides, indexes, and reports relating to them. Published transcripts, translations, and calendars of the manuscripts themselves are recorded in sect. III and are referred to here only when they serve as the only published guide to the archive concerned. Reports incorporating calendars may be found in both sections. Most repositories contain unpublished catalogues of their contents; these are not recorded here.

The listing of a repository does not imply ready access to its contents. In particular, admission to private archives is usually at the discretion of their owners.

See R. H. Bautier, *Annuaire international des archives, à jour en janvier 1975. International directory of archives, as of January 1975* (Paris, 1975). (Archivum, xxii–xxiii.)

R. J. Hayes (ed.), *The manuscript sources for the history of Irish civilisation* (11 vols, Boston, Mass., 1965); *First supplement, 1965–75* (3 vols, Boston, Mass., 1979).

P. O. Kristeller, 'Latin manuscript books before 1600: a list of the printed catalogues and unpublished inventories of extant collections' in *Traditio*, vi (1948), pp 227–317; ix (1953), pp 393–418; new ed., rev., New York, 1960; reprint, 1965.

1 IRELAND

See 'Manuscript collections in private keeping: reports in National Library' in *Anal. Hib.*, no. 23 (1966), pp 371–87.

Supersedes list in *Anal. Hib.*, no. 20 (1958), pp 311–18. Some collections have since been deposited in N.L.I.

Ó Fiannachta, Pádraig, *Clár lámhscríbhinní Gaeilge: leabharlanna na cleire agus mionchnuasaigh* (2 vols, Dublin, 1978–80).

Ahascragh, Co. Galway

Clonbrock

See J. F. Ainsworth and Edward MacLysaght, 'Dillon papers' in *Anal. Hib.*, no. 20 (1958), pp 17–55.

Ardee, Co. Louth

Rathbrist

See unpublished report by J. F. Ainsworth in N.L.I. on the papers of Mrs H. Kieran Verdon.

Armagh

Public Library

See Franz Blatt, 'Studia Hibernica' in *Classica et Mediaevalia*, xiv (1953), pp 226–32.

James Dean, *Catalogue of manuscripts in the Public Library of Armagh, 1928* (Dundalk, [1928]).

H. W. Love, *The records of the archbishops of Armagh, being an indexed catalogue of manuscripts, documents and books in the Archiepiscopal Registry of Armagh* (Dundalk, 1965).

Belfast

Public Record Office of Northern Ireland

See Kenneth Darwin, 'The Public Record Office of Northern Ireland' in *Archives*, vi (1963–4), pp 108–16.

Report of the deputy keeper of the records, 1924— (Belfast, 1925–).

Bray, Co. Wicklow

Estate Office, Newtown Vevay

See unpublished report by J. F. Ainsworth in N.L.I. on the papers of the earl of Meath.

Bridgetown, Co. Wexford

Rathronan Castle

See unpublished report by J. F. Ainsworth in N.L.I. on the papers of Miss Kathleen Browne.

Claremorris, Co. Mayo

Castlemacgarrett

See unpublished report by J. F. Ainsworth in N.L.I. on the papers of Lord Oranmore and Browne.

Clonmel, Co. Tipperary

Town Hall

See unpublished report by J. F. Ainsworth in N.L.I. on the muniments of the corporation of Clonmel.

Cork

University College Library

See Pádraig de Brún, *Clár lámhscríbhinní Gaeilge Ollscoile Chorcaí* (2 vols in 1, Dublin, 1967).

Dublin

Archbishop Marsh's Library

See J. R. Scott, *Catalogue of the manuscripts remaining in Marsh's Library, Dublin*, ed. Newport J. D. White (Dublin, [1913]).

Christ Church Cathedral

The original Christ Church deeds were deposited in P.R.O.I. *c.* 1870 and destroyed in 1922; transcripts of the more important survive in Novum Registrum. Also contains Liber Albus and Liber Niger.

Corporation archives, City Hall

See J. T. Gilbert, 'Archives of the Municipal Corporation of the City of Dublin' in *H.M.C. rep. 1* (1874), app., p. 129.

Diocesan Registry (Church of Ireland)

See Registry of the United Dioceses of Dublin and Glendalough and Kildare.

Genealogical Office, Dublin Castle.

See John Barry, 'Guide to records of the Genealogical Office, Dublin, with a commentary on heraldry in Ireland and on the history of the Office' in *Anal. Hib.*, no. 26 (1971), pp 1–43; reprint, Shannon, 1971.

King's Inns Library

See Pádraig de Brún, *Catalogue of Irish manuscripts in King's Inns Library, Dublin* (Dublin, 1972).

Marsh's Library

See Archbishop Marsh's Library.

National Library of Ireland

See C. A. Empey, 'Ormond deeds in National Library of Ireland' in *Butler Soc. Jn.*, i, no. 7 (1977), pp 519–21.

Robin Flower, 'The Phillips collection of Irish MSS at Cheltenham' in *Anal. Hib.*, no. 3 (1931), pp 225–8.
MSS deposited in N.L.I.

Charles McNeill, 'Harris: Collectanea de rebus Hibernicis' in *Anal. Hib.*, no. 6 (1934), pp 248–450.

Nessa Ní Sheaghdha, *Catalogue of Irish manuscripts in the National Library of Ireland* (Dublin, 1961–).

Kenneth Nicholls, 'Further notes on Ormond material in National Library' in *Butler Soc. Jn.*, i, no. 7 (1977), pp 522–6.

Reports of the Council of Trustees, National Library of Ireland, 1949/50– (Dublin, 1950–).

Pembroke Estates Management Ltd

See *Calendar of ancient deeds and muniments preserved in the Pembroke Estate Office, Dublin* (Dublin, 1891).

Public Library, Pearse Street

See Douglas Hyde and D. J. O'Donoghue, *Catalogue of the books and manuscripts comprising the library of the late Sir John Gilbert* (Dublin, 1918).

Public Record Office of Ireland

See M. C. Griffith, 'A short guide to the Public Record Office of Ireland' in *I.H.S.*, viii, no. 29 (Mar. 1952), pp 45–58; reprint, Dublin, 1952; 2nd ed., 1964.
Most of the medieval records described in Herbert Wood, *A guide to the records deposited in the Public Record Office of Ireland* (Dublin, 1919), were destroyed in 1922.

Philomena Connolly, 'The Irish memoranda rolls: some unexplored aspects' in *Ir. Econ. & Soc. Hist.*, iii (1976), pp 66–74.

Early rolls and original inquisitions salved. In *P.R.I. rep. D.K. 55* (1922–3), pp 97–8.

Index to 'Liber munerum publicorum Hiberniae' in *P.R.I. rep. D.K. 9* (1877), pp 21–58.

List of some records not salved, duplicates or copies of which are preserved in the Public Record Office, in other repositories, or in private custody, or which have been printed, or of which there are printed or manuscript calendars or repertories. In *P.R.I. rep. D.K. 55* (1922–3), pp 133–44.

J. F. Lydon, 'Survey of the memoranda rolls of the Irish exchequer, 1294–1509' in *Anal. Hib.*, no. 23 (1966), pp 49–134.

Memorandum on the destruction and reconstruction of the records. In *P.R.I. rep. D.K. 55* (1922–3), pp 17–24.

Report of the deputy keeper of the public records in Ireland (Dublin, 1869–).

Herbert Wood, 'The public records of Ireland before and after 1922' in *R. Hist. Soc. Trans.*, 4th ser., xiii (1930), pp 17–49.

Registry of the United Dioceses of Dublin and Glendalough and Kildare
Contains Crede Mihi and Archbishop Alen's Register.

See J. T. Gilbert, 'Archives of the see of Dublin' in *H.M.C. rep. 10*, app. v (1885), pp 204–19.

Representative Church Body Library

See Geraldine Fitzgerald, 'Manuscripts in the Representative Church Body Library' in *Anal. Hib.*, no. 23 (1966), pp 307–09.

J. B. Leslie, *Catalogue of manuscripts in possession of the Representative Church Body, . . . Dublin* ([Dublin], 1938).

Royal Irish Academy

See T. F. O'Rahilly and others, *Catalogue of Irish manuscripts in the Royal Irish Academy* (Dublin, 1926–).

St Patrick's Cathedral
Contains Dignitas Decani.

St Werburgh's Church

See unpublished report by J. F. Ainsworth in N.L.I. on the parochial records of the parish of St Werburgh.

Trinity College Library

See T. K. Abbott, *Catalogue of the manuscripts in the Library of Trinity College, Dublin* (Dublin, 1900; reprint, Hildesheim, 1980).

—— and E. J. Gwynn, *Catalogue of the Irish manuscripts in the Library of Trinity College, Dublin* (Dublin, 1921).

J. L. Robinson, 'On the ancient deeds of the parish of St John, Dublin, preserved in the Library of Trinity College' in *R.I.A. Proc.*, xxxiii (1916–17), sect. C, no. 7, pp 175–224.

Galway

James Hardiman Library, University College
See J. T. Gilbert, 'Archives of Galway', in *H.M.C. rep. 10*, app. v (1885), pp 380–520.

Kilkenny

City Hall

See J. T. Gilbert, 'Report to the Historical MSS Commission on the records of the Corporation of Kilkenny' in *H.M.C. rep. 1* (1874), app., pp 129–30.

St Canice's Library

See J. T. Gilbert, 'Archives of the see of Ossory: Right Rev. W. Pakenham Walsh, D.D., bishop of Ossory, Ferns, and Leighlin' in *H.M.C. rep. 10*, app. v (1885; reprint, 1895), pp 219–65.

Killavullen, Co. Cork

Carrigacunna Castle

See unpublished report by J. F. Ainsworth in N.L.I. on the papers of Major R. H. Humphreys.

Killiney, Co. Dublin

Franciscan Library, Dún Mhuire

See Myles Dillon, Canice Mooney, and Pádraig de Brún, *Catalogue of Irish manuscripts in the Franciscan Library, Killiney* (Dublin, 1969).

Canice Mooney, 'Franciscan Library, Killiney: a short guide for the student of Irish church history' in *Archiv. Hib.*, xviii (1955), pp 150–56.

Maynooth, Co. Kildare

St Patrick's College Library

See Pádraig Ó Fiannachta, *Lámhscríbhinní Gaeilge Choláiste Phádraig, Má Nuad*, pts ii–vii (Maynooth, 1965–73).

C. W. Russell, 'The Black Book of Limerick' in *H.M.C. rep. 3* (1872), app., pp 434–5.

Paul Walsh, *Catalogue of Irish manuscripts in Maynooth College Library*, pt i (Maynooth, 1943).

Mountnugent, Co. Cavan

Farrenconnell

See J. F. Ainsworth and Edward MacLysaght, 'Nugent papers' in *Anal. Hib.*, no. 20 (1958), pp 126–215.

New Ross

Tholsel

See unpublished report by J. F. Ainsworth in N.L.I. on the muniments of the Corporation of New Ross.

Oughterard, Co. Galway

Clonriff

See unpublished report by J. F. Ainsworth in N.L.I. on the papers of Lieut. Gen. J. C. d'Arcy.

Portarlington, Co. Leix

Woodbrook

See unpublished report by J. F. Ainsworth in N.L.I. on the papers of Major H. F. Chetwode-Aiken.

Waterford

City Hall

See J. T. Gilbert, 'Archives of the municipal corporation of Waterford' in *H.M.C. rep. 10*, app. 5 (1885; reprint, 1895), pp 265–39.

—— 'Report from J. T. Gilbert on the records of the Corporation of Waterford' in *H.M.C. rep. 1* (1874), app., pp 131–2.

Wexford

St Peter's College

Hore papers.

2 GREAT BRITAIN

See Edward Bernard, *Catalogi librorum manuscriptorum Angliae et Hiberniae in unum collecti cum indice alphabetico* (Oxford, 1967; reprint, Hildesheim, [1980?]).

Bulletin of the National Register of Archives (H.M.C., London, 1948–67).

A companion to the reprint of Reports i—ix of the Historical Manuscripts Commission (Nendeln, 1977).
Contains updating notes and corrections.

Historical Manuscripts Commission, *Guide to the location of collections described in the Reports and Calendars series, 1870—1980* (London, 1982. Guide to Sources for British History, iii.)

—— *Record repositories in Great Britain* (London, 1964; 7th ed., 1982).

N. R. Ker, *Medieval libraries of Great Britain: a list of surviving books* (London, 1941. Royal Historical Society Guides and Handbooks, iii; 2nd ed., 1964).

—— *Medieval manuscripts in British libraries* (Oxford, 1969–).

National inventory of documentary sources in the United Kingdom (microfiche, Cambridge, 1984–).

National Register of Archives, *List of accessions to repositories*, 1956– (London, 1957–).
1954–5 published in its *Bulletin*, vi (1955) and viii (1956); *Index, 1954–8* (London, 1967).

Aberystwyth

National Library of Wales

See J. H. Davies, *Catalogue of manuscripts. Vol. i: Additional manuscripts in the collections of Sir John Williams, Bart., G.C.V.O.* (Aberystwyth, 1921).

Handlist of manuscripts in the National Library of Wales (Aberystwyth, 1943–).

'The National Library of Wales' in *Anal. Hib.*, no. 1 (1930), pp 223–5.
List of MSS of Irish interest.

Bristol

Bristol Record Office

See Elizabeth Ralph, *Guide to the Bristol Archives Office* (Bristol, 1971).

——and Betty Masters, 'The City of Bristol Record Office' in *Archives*, iii, no. 18 (1957), pp 88–96. (Local Archives of Great Britain, xiv.)

Cambridge

University Library

See *A catalogue of the manuscripts preserved in the Library of the University of Cambridge* (6 vols, Cambridge, 1856–67).

'MSS relating to Ireland (uncatalogued)' in *Anal. Hib.*, no. 1 (1930), pp 225–8.

Canterbury

Canterbury Cathedral Archives and Library and Diocesan Record Office

See J. B. Sheppard, 'Report of an examination of the historical MSS belonging to the dean and chapter of Canterbury' in *H.M.C. rep. 5*, app. (1876), pp 427–62; *8*, app. 1 (1881), pp 315–55; *9*, app. 1 (1883), pp 72–129.

C. E. Woodruff, *Catalogue of the manuscript books … in the library of Christ Church, Canterbury* (Canterbury, 1911).

Carlisle

Carlisle Dean and Chapter Library

See Joseph Stevenson, 'The Carlisle cathedral MSS' in *H.M.C. rep. 2*, app. (1874), pp 123–5.

Chester

Chester City Record Office

See J. C. Jeaffreson, 'The manuscripts of the corporation of the city of Chester' in *H.M.C. rep. 8*, app. 1 (1881), pp 355–403.

Durham

Durham Dean and Chapter Library

See R. A. B. Mynors, *Durham Cathedral manuscripts to the end of the twelfth century* (Oxford, 1939).

Thomas Rud, *Codicum manuscriptorum ecclesiae cathedralis Dunelmensis catalogus classicus*, ed. James Raine (Durham, 1825).

Department of Palaeography and Diplomatic, The Prior's Kitchen, The College

See J. C. Davies, 'The muniments of the dean and chapter of Durham' in *Durham University Journal*, xliv (1952), pp 77–87.

—— 'Ecclesiastical and palatinate archives at Prior's Kitchen, Durham' in *Journal of the Society of Archivists*, i (1955–9), pp 185–91.

—— 'Official and private record and manuscript collections in the Prior's Kitchen, Durham' in *Journal of the Society of Archivists*, i (1955–9), pp 261–70.

W. A. Pantin, *Report on the muniments of the dean and chapter of Durham* (Frome, London, 1939).

See also Aubrey Gwynn in *Archiv. Hib.*, xi (1944), pp 37–8.

Edinburgh

National Library of Scotland

See *Catalogue of manuscripts acquired since 1925* (4 vols, Edinburgh, 1938–82).

H. W. Meikle, 'Catalogues of MSS in National Library of Scotland' in *Scot. Hist. Rev.*, xxv (1928), pp 221–3.

Summary catalogue of the Advocates' manuscripts (Edinburgh, 1971).

Scottish Record Office

See William Angŭs, 'Accessions of public records to the Register House since 1905' in *Scot. Hist. Rev.*, xxvi (1947), pp 26–46.

Annual Report of the Keeper of the Records of Scotland (Edinburgh, 1950–).

Sir James Fergusson, 'The public records of Scotland' in *Archives*, i (1949–52), no. 8 (1952), pp 30–38; ii (1953–6), no. 9 (1953), pp 4–10.

John Imrie, 'The modern Scottish Record Office' in *Scot. Hist. Rev.*, liii (1974), pp 194–210.

Matthew Livingstone, *A guide to the public records of Scotland deposited in H.M. General Register House, Edinburgh* (Edinburgh, 1905).

Exeter

Devon Record office

See *Brief guide. Pt i: Official and ecclesiastical* (Exeter, 1969).

London

British Library

See M. A. E. Nickson, *The British Library: guide to the catalogues and indexes of the Department of Manuscripts* (2nd rev. ed., London, 1982).

Supersedes T. C Skeat, 'The catalogues of the British Museum. 2: Manuscripts' in *Journal of Documentation*, vii (1951), pp 18–60, reprinted as *The catalogues of the manuscript collections in the British Museum* (London, 1953, rev. ed., 1962).

Samuel Ayscough, *A catalogue of the manuscripts preserved in the British Museum* (2 vols, London, 1782).

Sir Edward Bond, *Index to the additional manuscripts . . . preserved in the British Museum and acquired in the years 1783–1835* (London, 1849).

List of additions to the manuscripts in the British Museum in the years MDCCCXXXVI–MDCCCXL (London, 1843).

Catalogue of additions to the manuscripts, 1841/1845– (London, 1850–).

'Rough register' of acquisitions of the Department of Manuscripts, British Library, 1961/1965– (London, 1974– . List & Index Society, Special series, vii–).

A catalogue of the Harleian manuscripts in the British Museum (4 vols, London, 1808–12).

A catalogue of the Lansdowne manuscripts in the British Museum (London, 1819).

A catalogue of the manuscripts in the Cottonian Library deposited in the British Museum (London, 1802).

H. J. Ellis and F. B. Bickley, *Index to the charters and rolls in the Department of Manuscripts, British Museum* (2 vols, London, 1900–12).

Robin Flower, 'Manuscripts of Irish interest in the British Museum' in *Anal Hib.*, no. 2 (1931), pp 292–340.

S. H. O'Grady, *Catalogue of Irish manuscripts in the British Museum* (3 vols, London, 1926–53).

Vol. ii by Robin Flower; vol. iii by Robin Flower, revised by Myles Dillon.

E. J. L. Scott, *Index to the Sloane manuscripts in the British Museum* (London, 1904).

Sir G. F. Warner and J. P. Gilson, *Catalogue of western manuscripts in the Old Royal and King's collections* (4 vols, London, 1921).

A. G. Watson, *Catalogue of dated and datable manuscripts, c.700—1600, in the Department of Manuscripts, the British Library* (2 vols, London, 1979).

C. E. Wright, *Fontes Harleiani: a study of the sources of the Harleian collection of manuscripts in the British Museum* (London, 1972).

British Museum

See British Library.

House of Lords Record Office

See M. F. Bond, *Guide to the records of parliament* (London, 1971).

List of main classes of records (London, 1957).

Lambeth Palace Library

See E. G. W. Bill, *A catalogue of manuscripts of Lambeth Palace Library* (2 vols, Oxford, 1972–6).

M. R. James and Claude Jenkins, *A descriptive catalogue of the manuscripts in the Library of Lambeth Palace* (Cambridge, 1930–32).

Issued in 5 parts.

Lincoln's Inn Library

See Joseph Hunter 'Report . . . on the manuscripts in the library of the Honourable Society of Lincoln's Inn' in *General report to the king in council from the honourable board of commissioners on the public records* (London, 1837), pp 351–91; reprinted in his *Three catalogues* (London, 1838) and separately as *A catalogue of the manuscripts in the library of the Honourable Society of Lincoln's Inn* (London, 1838).

Public Record Office

See *Guide to the contents of the Public Record Office* (3 vols, London, 1963–8).

Most medieval records are described in vol. i.

G. J. Hand, 'Material used in "Calendar of documents relating to Ireland" ' in *I.H.S.*, xii, no. 46 (Oct. 1960), pp 99–104.

Catalogue of microfilm ([London], 1976).

Chancery common law pleadings (C43, C44) (London, 1971. List & Index Society, lxvii).

Chancery files, etc.: class list (C236—265; C267—269; C271) (London, 1976. List & Index Society, cxxx).

Chancery miscellanea (8 vols, London, 1966–74. List & Index Society, vii, xv, xxvi, xxxviii, xlix, lxxxi, lxxxviii, cv).

Pt viii (1974): *Yorkshire, Wales, Ireland, Channel Islands, divers counties, transcripts of records*; Ireland (pp 193–7).

Class list of records of the exchequer, king's remembrancer (2 vols, London, 1973–4. List & Index Society, xci, cviii).

Class list of records of the exchequer, lord treasurer's remembrancer (London, 1972. List & Index Society, lxxxii).

Class list of records of the treasury of receipt (London, 1968. List & Index Society, xxiii).

A descriptive catalogue of ancient deeds in the Public Record Office (6 vols, P.R.O., London, 1890–1915).

Exchequer K.R. & L.T.R. memoranda rolls (London, 1965. List & Index Society, iv).

Exchequer K.R. customs accounts (E. 122) (2 vols, London, 1969–70. List & Index Society, xliii, lx).

Exchequer K.R. ecclesiastical documents (London, 1965. List & Index Society, ii).

Exchequer (K.R.) sheriffs' accounts (E. 199): class list (London, 1976. List & Index Society, cxxvii).

Exchequer of receipt: receipt and issue rolls (London, 1966. List & Index Society, xvii).

Index of persons and places, memoranda roll[s], Queen's remembrancer, Exchequer, 1272/1273–[1287/88] [(P.R.O., London, 1968)].
Duplicated typescript to accompany microfilm of original rolls, see sect. III A1.

List and index of warrants for issues, 1399–1485. With an appendix: Indentures of war, 1297–1527 (New York, 1964. P.R.O., Lists and Indexes. Supplementary Series, no. ix, vol. 2).

List of foreign accounts enrolled on the great rolls of the exchequer: [Henry III to Richard III] (P.R.O., London, 1900. P.R.O., Lists and Indexes, xi; reprint, New York, 1963).

List of the records of parliament and council, etc. (London, 1968. List & Index Society, xxxiv).

List of various accounts and documents connected therewith, formerly preserved in the exchequer and now in the Public Record Office (P.R.O., London, 1912. P.R.O., Lists and Indexes, xxxv; reprint, New York, 1963).

E. W. Safford, *Itinerary of Edward I* (2 vols, London, 1974–6. List & Index Society, ciii, cxxxii).

Supplementary list of accounts, various of the exchequer (New York, 1969. P.R.O., Lists and Indexes. Supplementary Series, no. ix, vol. 1).

Wellcome Institute for the History of Medicine

See S. A. J. Moorat, *Catalogue of western manuscripts on medicine and science in the Wellcome Historical Medical Library. 1: MSS written before 1650 A.D.* (London, 1962. Publications of the Wellcome Historical Medical Library. Catalogue Series).

Maidstone

Kent Archives Office

See A. J. Horwood, 'The manuscripts of the Right Honourable Lord de l'Isle and Dudley at Penshurst Place, Co. Kent' in *H.M.C. rep. 3* app. (1872), pp 227–33.
MSS deposited in Kent Archives Office, 1969.

Felix Hull, *Guide to the Kent County Archives Office* (Maidstone, 1958). *First supplement*, 1971; *second supplement*, 1981.

Manchester

John Rylands University Library

Robert Fawtier, 'Hand-list of additions to the collection of Latin manuscripts in the John Rylands Library, 1908–1920' in *John Rylands Lib. Bull.*, vi (1921–2), pp 186–206.

—— 'Hand-lists of charters and deeds in the possession of the John Rylands Library' in *John Rylands Lib. Bull.*, vii (1922–3), pp 526–44; viii (1924), pp 276–97, 456–508; ix (1925), pp 248–85.

M. R. James, *A descriptive catalogue of the Latin manuscripts in the John Rylands Library at Manchester* (2 vols, Manchester, 1921).

Moses Tyson, 'Hand-list of charters, deeds and similar documents in the possession of the John Rylands Library, ii' in *John Rylands Lib. Bull.*, xvii (1933), pp 130–77; xviii (1934), pp 393–454.

Hand-list of charters, deeds and similar documents in the possession of the John Rylands Library (4 vols, Manchester, 1925–75).

By Robert Fawtier, Moses Tyson, and Frank Taylor. Vols i–ii originally published in *John Rylands Lib. Bull.*, vii–xviii.

Oxford

See Paul Morgan, *Oxford libraries outside the Bodleian* (Oxford, 1973; 2nd ed., 1980).

Bodleian Library

See R. W. Hunt [and others], *A summary catalogue of western manuscripts in the Bodleian Library at Oxford* (7 vols in 8, Oxford, 1895–1953).

Otto Pächt and J. J. G. Alexander, *Illuminated manuscripts in the Bodleian Library, Oxford* (3 vols, Oxford, 1966–73).

Concordance of Bodleian shelf marks and addenda. By B. C. Barker-Benfield (Oxford, 1974). Vol. iii: *British, Irish and Icelandic schools*.

H. O. Coxe, *Laudian manuscripts* (Oxford, 1973. Quarto Catalogues, ii).

J. T. Gilbert, 'Manuscripts of the right honourable Lord Talbot de Malahide, Malahide Castle, Co. Dublin', in *H.M.C. rep. 8*, app. i, (1883), pp 493–9.

Most MSS deposited in Bodleian Library, 1977.

Charles McNeill, 'Report on recent acquisitions in the Bodleian Library, Oxford' in *Anal. Hib.*, no. 1 (1930), pp 1–178; no. 2 (1931), pp 1–291.

University College Library

See Paul Morgan, *Oxford libraries outside the Bodleian* (1973), pp 140–45.

3 THE CONTINENT

AUSTRIA

See Kaiserliche Akademie der Wissenschaften in Wien, *Mittelalterliche Bibliothekskataloge Österreichs* (6 vols, Vienna, 1915–71).

Bde 3–5 and *Nachtrag zu Bd 1* by Österreichische Akademie der Wissenschaften.

Vienna

Österreichische Nationalbibliothek

See *Catalogus codicum manuscriptorum Bibliothecae Palatinae Vindobonensis* (Vienna, 1836–).

Österreichisches Staatsarchiv

See Ludwig Bittner, *Gesamtinventar des Wiener Haus-, Hof- und Staatsarchivs* (5 vols, Vienna, 1936–40. Inventare Österreichischer Staatlicher Archive, v: Inventare des Wiener Haus-, Hof- und Staatsarchivs, 4–8).

Constantin von Böhm, *Die Handschriften des Kaiserlichen und Königlichen Haus-, Hof- und Staatsarchivs* (Vienna, 1873); *Supplement* (1874); reprint in 1 vol. (Wiesbaden, 1968).

BELGIUM

See Albert Brounts and others, *Manuscrits datés conservés en Belgique* (Brussels, 1968–   ).

Jacques Nicodème, *Répertoire des inventaires d'archives conservées en Belgique, parus avant le 1er janvier 1969. Repertorium van inventarissen van archieven in België bewaard, verschenen vóór 1 januari 1969* (Brussels, 1970. Bibliographia Belgica, cvii; Archives et Bibliothèques de Belgique. Numéro Spécial, ii).

Brussels

Algemeen Rijksarchief
   See Archives générales du Royaume

Archives générales du Royaume
   See Maurits van Haegendoren, *Les Archives générales du Royaume . . . Het Algemeen Rijksarchief* (Brussels, 1955).

Bibliothèque royale Albert Ier
   See Joseph van den Gheyn, and others, *Catalogue des manuscrits de la Bibliothèque royale de Belgique* (13 vols, Brussels, 1901–48).

Bibliothèque royale de Belgique
   See Bibliothèque royale Albert Ier.

FRANCE

See *Catalogue général des manuscrits des bibliothèques publiques des départements* (7 vols, Paris, 1849–85).

Catalogue général des manuscrits des bibliothèques publiques de France. Départements (Paris, 1886–   ).

Direction des archives de France, *Catalogue des inventaires, répertoires, guides de recherche et autres instruments de travail des archives départementales, communales et hospitalières en vente dans les services départementaux d'archives à la date du 31 décembre 1961* (Paris, 1962).

—— *État des inventaires des archives nationales, départementales, communales et hospitalières au 1er janvier, 1937* [by H. Courteault] (Paris, 1938).
   Supplément, 1937–54 [by R. H. Bautier] (Paris, 1955).

Michel Duchein, 'Access to archives in France' in *Archives*, xv (1981–2), pp 26–9.

Charles Samaran and Robert Marichal, *Catalogue des manuscrits en écriture latine, portant les indications de date, de lieu ou de copiste* (Paris, 1959–   ).

Bordeaux

Archives départementales de la Gironde
   See André Betge-Brezetz, *Guide des archives de la Gironde* (Bordeaux, 1973).

   G. Chauvet and J. Barennes, *Répertoire numérique des minutes notariales et terriers de la Garde-Note (3E)* (Bordeaux, 1913).

   Inventaire-sommaire des archives départementales antérieures à 1790. Gironde (Bordeaux, 1877–   ).

      Archives civiles. Serie E. Supplément, by Gaston Ducaunes-Duval (4 vols, Bordeaux, 1898–1908).

Archives municipales de Bordeaux

See Xavier Védère, *Archives municipales* (Bordeaux, 1946).

—— *Catalogue des manuscrits* (Bordeaux, 1938).

Évreux

Archives départementales de l'Eure

See Marcel Baudot, *État sommaire des documents conservés aux Archives du département de l'Eure* (Évreux, 1939).

Inventaire-sommaire des Archives départementales antérieures à 1790. Eure (Évreux, 1862–).

Archives ecclésiastiques. Sér. G—H (2 vols, Évreux, 1886–93).

Répertoire numérique de la série (Évreux, 1909–).

Paris

Archives nationales

See Jean Favier, *Les Archives nationales: état général des fonds* (Paris, 1978–).

Supersedes *État sommaire par séries des documents conservés aux Archives nationales* (Paris, 1891).

Guide du lecteur (Paris, 1966).

Werner Paravicini, *Das Nationalarchiv in Paris: ein Führer zu den Beständen aus Mittelalter und der Frühen Neuzeit* (Munich, [etc.], 1980. Dokumentation Westeuropa, iv).

Bibliothèque nationale

See *Les catalogues imprimés de la Bibliothèque nationale: liste établie en 1943, suivi d'un supplément (1944—1952)* (Paris, 1953).

Léopold Delisle, *Inventaire des manuscrits latins conservés à la Bibliothèque nationale sous les numéros 8823—18613* (Paris, 1871; reprint, Hildesheim, 1974).

Originally published as 'Inventaire des manuscrits conservés à la Bibliothèque impériale sous les nos 8823–11503 du Fonds latin' in *Bibliothèque de l'École des Chartes*, xxiii, 5e sér., t. 3 (1862), pp 277–308, 469–512; xxiv, 5e ser., t. 4 (1863), pp 185–236. — 'Inventaire des manuscrits latins de Saint-Germain-des-Prés, [nos 11504–14231]' in *Bibliothèque de l'École des Chartes*, xxvi, 6e sér., t. 1 (1865), pp 185–214, 343–76, 528–56; xxix, 6e sér., t. 4 (1868), pp 220–60. — 'Inventaire des manuscrits latins de Saint-Victor conservés à la Bibliothèque impériale sous les numéros 14232–15175' in *Bibliothèque de l'École des Chartes*, xxx, 6e sér., t. 5 (1869), pp 1–79. — 'Inventaire des manuscrits latins de la Sorbonne conservés à la Bibliothèque impériale sous les numéros 15176–16718 du Fonds latin' in *Bibliothèque de l'École des Chartes*, xxxi (1870), pp 1–50, 135–61. — 'Inventaire des manuscrits latins de Notre-Dame et d'autres fonds conservés à la Bibliothèque nationale sous les numéros 16719–18613' in *Bibliothèque de l'École des Chartes*, xxxi (1870), pp 463–565. Each part also published separately, Paris, 1863–71.

—— *Manuscrits latins et français ajoutés aux fonds des nouvelles acquisitions pendant les années 1875—1891: inventaire alphabétique* (2 vols, Paris, 1891).

Philippe Lauer, *Catalogue général des manuscrits latins* (5 vols, Paris, 1939–66).

Fonds latin, nos 1–3535; *Table des tomes i et ii* [nos 1–2692], by Pierre Gasnault and Jean Vezin (Paris, 1968).

Anicet Melot, *Catalogus codicum manuscriptorum Bibliothecae Regiae* (4 vols, Paris, 1739–44).

T. iii–iv: *Codices Latini* [nos 1–8822].

'Nouvelles acquisitions du Département des manuscrits de la Bibliothèque nationale', 1891/1892– . In *Bibliothèque de l'École des Chartes*, liii– (1892–).

Title varies. Separate cumulations published at irregular intervals.

Henri Omont, 'Catalogue des manuscrits celtiques et basques de la Bibliothèque nationale' in *Rev. Celt.*, xi (1890), pp 389–432; reprint, Paris, 1890.

—— *Nouvelle acquisitions du Département des manuscrits pendant les années 1891–1910: répertoire alphabétique des manuscrits latins et français* (Paris, 1912).

Bibliothèque Saint-Geneviève

See C. A. Kohler, *Catalogue des manuscrits de la Bibliothèque Saint-Geneviève* (2 vols, Paris, 1893–6 [i.e. 1893–8]).

'Supplément' in *Catalogue général des manuscrits des bibliothèques publiques de France. Départements*, xlv (1915), pp 57–126.

Troyes

Archives départementales de l'Aube

See Bernard Gildas, *Guide des Archives départementales de l'Aube* (Troyes, 1967).

Inventaire-sommaire des Archives départementales antérieures à 1790 (Troyes, 1864–).

Répertoire numérique de la série (Troyes, 1933–).

Répertoire sommaire des documents antérieurs à 1800 conservés dans les archives communales (Troyes, 1911).

Henri d'Arbois de Jubainville, 'Les archives du département de l'Aube et le tableau général numérique par fonds des archives départementales antérieures à 1790' in *Bibliothèque de l'École des Chartes*, xxiv, 5e sér., t. 4 (1863), pp 449–70; reprint, Paris, 1863.

Bibliothèque municipale

Les plus beaux manuscrits et les plus belles reliures de la Bibliothèque de Troyes (Troyes, 1935).

GERMANY

See Königlich Bayerischen Akademie der Wissenschaften in München, *Mittelalterliche Bibliothekskataloge: Deutschlands und der Schweiz* (3 vols, Munich, 1918–32).

ITALY

See Piero d'Angiolini and Claudio Pavone (ed.), *Guida generale degli archivi di stato italiani* (Ufficio centrale per i bene archivistici, Rome, 1981–).

Giuseppe Mazzatinti and others, *Inventari dei manoscritti delle biblioteche d'Italia* (Florence, 1890–).

Luigi Schiaparelli, Pietro Fedele, and Alfonso Gallo, *Guida storico e bibliografica degli archivi e delle biblioteche d'Italia* (6 vols in 8, Rome, 1932–40).

Not completed.

Florence

Biblioteca Mediceo Laurenziana

See A. M. Bandini, *Catalogus codicum latinorum Bibliothecae Mediceae Laurentianae* (4 vols, 1774–7).

Rome

Archivum Generale Augustinianorum, Collegio Internazionale Agostiniano

See F. X. Martin and Alberic de Meijer, 'Irish material in the Augustinian Archives, Rome, 1354–1624' in *Archiv. Hib.*, xix (1956), pp 61–134.

Archivum Generale Ordinis Fratrum Minorum Capuccinorum

Collegio di San Clemente

See L. E. Boyle, 'Manuscripts and incunabula in the library of San Clemente' in L. E. Boyle, E. M. C. Kane, and Federico Guidobaldi, *San Clemente miscellany*, ii: *Art and archaeology*, ed. Luke Dempsey (Rome, 1978), pp 152–78.

Conleth Kearns, 'Archives of the Irish Dominican College, San Clemente, Rome: a summary report. Compiled in October 1952' in *Archiv. Hib.*, xviii (1955), pp 145–9.

Collegio di Sant' Isidoro

See Benignus Millet, 'The archives of St Isidore's College, Rome' in *Archiv. Hib.*, xl (1985), pp 1–13.

Santa Sabina

See Hugh Fenning, 'Irish material in the registers of the Dominican masters general, 1390–1649' in *Archivum Fratrum Praedicatorum*, xxxix (1969), pp 249–336.

Turin

Biblioteca nazionale

See Giuseppe Luca Pasini, Antonia Rivautella, and Francesco Berta, *Codices manuscripti Bibliothecae Regii Taurinensis athenaei* (Turin, 1749).

Vatican City

Archivio Segreto Vaticano

See L. E. Boyle, *A survey of the Vatican Archives and of its medieval holdings* (Pontifical Institute of Mediaeval Studies, Toronto, 1972. Subsidia Mediaevalia, i).

P. J. Corish, 'Irish history and the papal archives' in *Ir. Theol. Quart.*, xxi (1954), pp 375–81.

K. A. Fink, *Das Vatikanische Archiv: Einführung in die Bestände und ihre Erforschung* (2. vermehrte Aufl., Rome, 1951. Bibliothek des Deutschen Historischen Instituts in Rom, xx).

Martino Giusti, *L'Archivio Segreto Vaticano* (Vatican City, 1978).

M. J. Haren, 'Vatican Archives as a historical source to *c.* 1530' in *Archiv. Hib.*, xxxix (1984), pp 3–12.

Leslie Macfarlane, 'The Vatican Archives: with special reference to sources for British medieval history' in *Archives*, iv (1959–60), pp 29–44, 84–101.

C. S. Burns, 'Sources for British and Irish history in the Instrumenta Miscellanea of the Vatican Archives' in *Archivum Historiae Pontificiae*, ix (1971), pp 7–141.

R. J. Dodd, 'Vatican Archives. Instrumenta Miscellanea: documents of Irish interest' in *Archiv. Hib.*, xix (1956), pp 135–40.

U. G. Flanagan, 'Papal letters of the fifteenth century as a source for Irish history' in *Ir. Cath. Hist. Comm. Proc.*, 1958, pp 11–15.

Martino Giusti, *Inventario dei Registri Vaticani* (Vatican City, 1981). (Collectanea Archivi Vaticani, viii.)

Biblioteca Apostolica Vaticana

See Jean Bignami-Odier, 'Guide au département des manuscrits de la Bibliothèque du Vatican' in *Mélanges d'Archéologie et d'Histoire de l'École Française de Rome*, li (1934), pp 205–39; reprint, Paris, 1934.

Cathaldus Giblin, 'Vatican Library: MSS Barberini Latini: a guide to the material of Irish interest on microfilm in the National Library, Dublin' in *Archiv. Hib.*, xviii (1955), pp 67–144.

4 THE U.S.A.

See Seymour de Ricci, *Census of medieval and renaissance manuscripts in the United States and Canada* (3 vols, New York, 1935–40).

Vols i–ii reprinted New York, 1961; *Supplement*, originated by C. U. Faye, continued and edited by W. H. Bond, New York, 1962.

National Historical Publications Commission, *A guide to archives and manuscripts in the United States*, ed. P. M. Hamer (New Haven, 1961).

National inventory of documentary sources in the United States (microfiche, Cambridge, Mass., 1983–).

B SOURCES CITED

1 IRELAND

Belfast

Public Record Office of Northern Ireland
Registers of the archbishops of Armagh.

Dublin

Corporation archives, City Hall
Dublin city records MS 36/2, Recorder's book.

National Library of Ireland

D	Ormond deeds.
1–4	Collectanea de rebus Hibernicis, compiled by Walter Harris, vols i–iv.
761	Excerpts from the Irish pipe rolls, Hen. III–Edw. III.
2066–8	Cartulary relating to the Shee family, 13th–16th centuries.
2506–7	Ormond papers.
2551	Ormond papers.
2689	Canon Leslie collection: typescript copy of Bishop Reeves's calendar of Primate Prene's register, 1430–76.
4140	Pedigrees, genealogical notes, and transcripts of charters pertaining to the Blake family.
	Wicklow MSS (unsorted collection).

Public Record Office of Ireland

EX 2/1	Calendar of memoranda rolls.
KB 1	Justiciary rolls.
PRO 7/1	Transcript of statute roll 2–3 Rich. III.
RC 8	Record commission calendar of memoranda rolls.
RC 9	Record commission repertories to inquisitions (exchequer).

RC 11	Record commission calendar of pipe rolls.
RC 13	Record commission transcript of statutes.
	Ferguson collection, vols iii–iv.
	Chancery pleadings.

Royal Irish Academy

D. i. 3	Lebor Gabála: genealogical.
D. iv. 1	Lebor Gabála: Life of St Cuimin.
D. v. 1	Lebor Gabála.
12. D. 10	Extracts from pipe rolls, 1264–1543.
12. D. 12	Calendar of memoranda rolls, Edw. I–Edw. II.
23. E. 26	Genealogies.
23. O. 48	Liber Flavus Fergusiorum.
24. D. 10	Miscellaneous: O'Gorman papers.
24. H. 17	Extracts from memoranda rolls, 1383–1643.

Trinity College Library

79 (formerly B. 1. 4)	Breviarium cum psalterio, 15th century.
82 (B. 3. 1)	Missal from the priory of Kilcormac, 15th century.
86 (B. 3. 10)	Breviarium cum psalterio, 15th century.
97 (B. 3. 5)	Varia de vita monastica, 14th century.
123 (A. 5. 8)	S. Augustini in Genesin ad literam, 15th century.
543/2 (E. 2. 19)	List of mayors and bailiffs of Dublin, 1 Hen. V–26 Hen. VIII.
557 (K. 6. 1–13)	Registers of the archbishops of Armagh (copies), 13 volumes.
578 (E. 3. 10)	Miscellanea de rebus Hibernicis ab Usserio collecta.
584 (E. 3. 22)	Chronica Hiberniae, by Philip Flattisbury.
591 (E. 3. 28)	Collectanea de rebus Hibernicis (including the Dublin Chronicle).
594 (E. 3. 33)	Collections concerning Ireland and especially Meath, 16th century.
656 (F. 4. 25)	Extracts from the inquisitions of the properties of suppressed monasteries, 17th century.
664 (F. 4. 30)	Collectanea de rebus Hibernicis, 17th century.
671 (F. 3. 13)	Notes from records in Bermingham Tower, 17th century.
842 (F. 3. 16)	Collections relating to Ireland, 17th century.
1282 (H. 1. 8)	Annals of Ulster.
1298 (H. 2. 7)	Genealogical and historical collections, 15th century.
1316–17 (H. 2. 15)	Legal texts, glossaries, and miscellanea.
1318 (H. 2. 16)	Yellow Book of Lecan.
1346 (H. 4. 4)	Miscellaneous verse and prose, 18th century.
1429 (I. 6. 12)	Collection of Irish deeds, 15th–17th centuries.
1436 (E. 4. 1)	Medical and physical treatises, 15th–16th centuries.
1440 (F. 4. 13)	Historia et genealogia familiae de Burgo, 16th century.
3397 (N. 5. 12)	Poems, tales, and history of families in County Cavan.

Wexford

St Peter's College

Hore MSS 1	Transcripts of memoranda rolls.

2 GREAT BRITAIN

Cambridge

University Library

Miscellaneous MSS Additional 3392C, (i) Giraldus 'Expugnatio'.
                                                      (ii) 'De rebus gestis in Hibernia', 1314–18.
                                                      (iii) List of abbots of St Mary's, Dublin.

London

British Library

Additional MS 4791	Extracts from memoranda rolls.
Additional MS 4797	Fragment of the Register of St John the Baptist without the New Gate, Dublin; obits of earls of Desmond to 1560.
Additional MS 7965	Wardrobe Book, 25 Edw. I.
Additional MS 15524	Original book of the customs paid for wines exported from Bordeaux, 1444–5.
Additional MS 30512	'Leabhar Uí Maolconaire', a fifteenth-century collection of legends, lives of saints, and other pieces in prose and verse in Irish.
Additional MS 59899	Day-book of treasurer of chamber, 1503–6.
Cotton MS Tiberius A XI	Register of St Mary's Abbey, Dublin.
Cotton MS Vespasian E IX, ff 86–109	'Noumbre of weyghtes', a discourse of weights and measures and of several sorts of merchandise in England and Ireland.
Egerton MS 90	Law tracts and miscellaneous verse in Irish, 15th–16th centuries.
Egerton MS 1782	A collection of tales, etc., in prose and verse in Irish compiled by the scribes of the family of Ó Maoilchonaire, probably for Art Buidhe Mac Murchadha Caomhánach (d. 1517).
Egerton MS 3323	Fragments of schoolbook from Glendalough, 1106.
Harleian MS 3756	The rental of Gerald FitzGerald, earl of Kildare.
Lansdowne MS 159	Various papers concerning the state and government of Ireland, Hen. VIII–James I.
Royal MS 18 C. XIV	Accounts of William Hatteclyffe, under-treasurer of Ireland, 1495–6.

Lambeth Palace Library

MS 46	Collection of 'Clementinae' written by Roderic Ó Lachtnáin.
MSS 614, 625, 635	Part of the collection, relating to Irish affairs, of Sir George Carew.

Public Record Office
Chancery

C 1	Early chancery proceedings.
C 47	Chancery miscellanea.
C 54	Close rolls.
C 66	Patent rolls.
C 76	Treaty (formerly French) rolls.
C 132–6	Inquisitions post mortem.

Exchequer

E 28	Council and privy seal records.
E 40	Ancient deeds.
E 101	King's remembrancer, accounts various.
E 122	Customs accounts.
E 159	Memoranda rolls (K.R.)
E 163	Miscellanea.
E 368	Memoranda rolls (L.T.R.)
E 372	Pipe rolls.
E 401	Receipt rolls.

Privy Seal office

P.S.O. 1	Warrants for privy seal.

Special collections

SC 1	Ancient correspondence.
SC 6	Ministers' accounts.
SC 11	Rentals and surveys.

State papers

S.P. 1	State papers, Henry VIII.
S.P. 60–63	State papers, Ireland, Henry VIII–Elizabeth.

Transcripts

PRO 31/8	Record Commission transcripts from foreign archives.

Oxford

Bodleian Library

Auct. F. 3. 15	Glosses in Irish on treatises in Latin on calendar, philosophy, etc.
Carte 55–7	Correspondence, political papers, and other collections of Sir William Fitzwilliam, chiefly relating to public affairs in Ireland, where he was lord deputy.
Laud Misc. 460	Copy of a Latin commentary on the Book of Job, containing glosses in Irish, 11th–12th centuries.
Laud Misc. 610	A 15th-century miscellany of texts.
Laud Misc. 614	Chronicles and other materials relating to Ireland, vol. iv of Carew's collections.
Rawlinson A 237	Miscellaneous papers relating to Ireland.
B 179	Ranulf Higden, 'Polychronicon'.

Rawlinson B 485	Latin saints' lives, 14th century.
B 488	Annals of Tigernach and other annals.
B 495	Register of St Mary's Abbey, Dublin.
B 498	Cartulary of the Hospital of St John the Baptist without the New Gate, Dublin.
B 500	Register of the Abbey of St Thomas.
B 501	Register of the proceedings of the Chapters of the Hospital of St John of Jerusalem, 1325–39.
B 502	Book of Leinster.
B 505	Saints' lives, late 14th century; copy of B 485.
B 506	Legal, genealogical, and topographical collections, late 14th century.
C 32	Ordinal, Cistercian use.
C 185	Christ Church psalter.
C 892	Gradual, 12th century.

3 THE CONTINENT

Brussels

Bibliothèque royale Albert Ier

| MSS 7672–4 | Lives of Irish saints, 14th century. |

Florence

Biblioteca Laurenziana

| MS Plut. LXXVIII 19 | Boethius, 'De consolatione philosophiae', prefaced by a short Life of Boethius attributed to Johannes Scottus Eriugena, 12th century. |

Vatican City

Archivio Segreto Vaticano

Registrum Lateranum 1097.

III PRINTED SOURCES

A RECORDS

1 RECORDS OF CENTRAL ADMINISTRATION

Anglo-Norman letters and petitions from All Souls MS 182. Ed. M. D. Legge. Anglo-Norman Text Soc., Oxford, 1941. (Anglo-Norman Texts, iii.)

The background to the arrest of Sir Christopher Preston in 1418. Ed. A. J. Otway-Ruthven. In *Anal. Hib.*, no. 29 (1980), pp 71–94.
P.R.O., E. 163/7/12.

British Library Harleian manuscript 433. Ed. Rosemary Horrox and P. W. Hammond. 4 vols. Richard III Society, Upminster, 1979–83.

Calendar of inquisitions miscellaneous (Chancery), [1219—1422]. 7 vols. P.R.O., London, 1916–69; reprint, vols i–iii, Nendeln, 1973.

CHANCERY ROLLS. *Calendar of various chancery rolls: supplementary close rolls, Welsh rolls, scutage rolls . . . 1277—1326.* P.R.O., London, 1912; reprint, Nendeln, 1976.

CHANCERY WARRANTS. *Calendar of chancery warrants . . . 1244—1326.* P.R.O., London, 1927.

Chartae, privilegia et immunitates: being transcripts of charters and privileges to cities, towns, abbeys and other bodies corporate . . . 1171 to 1395. Rec. Comm. Ire., Dublin, 1889.

A charter of John, lord of Ireland, in favour of Matthew Ua Hénni, archbishop of Cashel. Ed. K. W. Nicholls. In *Peritia*, ii (1983), pp 267–76.

CHARTER ROLLS. *Calendar of charter rolls . . . 1226—[1516].* 6 vols. P.R.O., London, 1903–27; reprint, Nendeln, 1972.
'Appendix, A.D. 1215–1288' in vol. vi.

—— *Calendarium rotulorum chartarum et inquisitionum ad quod damnum.* [Ed. John Caley and Robert Lemon. Rec. Comm., London], 1803.

—— *Rotuli chartarum . . . [1199—1216].* Ed. T. D. Hardy. Rec. Comm., London, 1837.

Chester customs accounts, 1301—1566. Ed. K. P. Wilson. Liverpool, 1969. (Record Society of Lancashire and Cheshire, cxi.)

CLOSE ROLLS. *Calendar of the close rolls . . . 1272—[1509].* 47 vols. P.R.O., London, 1892–1963; reprint, *1272—1461*, 42 vols, Nendeln, 1970–72.

—— *Close rolls of the reign of Henry III . . . 1227—[1272].* 14 vols. P.R.O., London, 1902–38; reprint, Nendeln, 1970.

—— *Rotuli litterarum clausarum . . . [1204—27].* Ed. T. D. Hardy. 2 vols. Rec. Comm., London, 1833–44.

—— See also Patent rolls, below.

COUNCIL. *A roll of the proceedings of the king's council in Ireland . . . 1392—93.* Ed. James Graves. London, 1877 (Rolls Series, lxix); reprint, Nendeln, 1965.
See also *Documents on the affairs of Ireland*, sect. III C below.

Curia regis rolls . . . Richard I—[21 Henry III]. 15 vols. P.R.O., London, 1922–72; reprint, vols i–xi, Nendeln, 1971.

CURIA REGIS ROLLS. *Rotuli curiae regis . . . 6 Richard I—[1 John].* Ed. Sir Francis Palgrave. 2 vols. Rec. Comm., London, 1835.

Diplomatic documents preserved in the Public Record Office. Vol. i: *1101—1272.* Ed. Pierre Chaplais. P.R.O., London, 1964.

Documents illustrative of English history in the thirteenth and fourteenth centuries, selected from the records of the queen's remembrancer of the exchequer. Ed. Henry Cole. [Rec. Comm.], London, 1844.

Edward II and the revenues of Ireland in 1311–12. Ed. J. F. Lydon. In *I.H.S.*, xiv, no. 53 (Mar. 1964), pp 39–57.

EXCHEQUER. *Calendar of ancient deeds, series B.* 4 vols. London, 1973–6. (List & Index Society, xcv, ci, cxiii, cxxiv.)

—— Extracts from certain rolls forming part of Pope Nicholas's taxation, A.D. 1291, found among the records in the exchequer at Westminster . . . containing the dioceses of Limerick, Emly, Cashell, Cork, and Waterford. In *Rec. Comm. Ire. rep. 1816–20*, pp 61–70.

—— Extracts from the great roll of the Irish exchequer relating to Waterford and Ross, A.D. 1273–1483. Ed. P. H. Hore. In *Cork Hist. Soc. Jn.*, 2nd ser., xxiv (1918), pp 16–28.

—— Guide to English financial records for Irish history, 1461–1558, with illustrative extracts, 1461–1509. Ed. D. B. Quinn. In *Anal. Hib.*, no. 10 (1941), pp 1–69.

—— Irish exchequer memoranda of the reign of Edward I. Ed. Mary Bateson. In *E.H.R.*, xviii (1903), pp 497–513; correction by J. H. Round, ibid., p. 709.

—— *Liber niger scaccarii nec non Wilhelmi Worcestrii annales*. Ed. Thomas Hearne. 2 vols, Oxford, 1728; 2nd ed., 2 vols, London, 1771; reprint, 1774.

—— *The Red Book of the exchequer*. Ed. Hubert Hall. 3 vols. London, 1896. (Rolls Series, [xcix]); reprint, Nendeln, 1965.

—— Three exchequer documents from the reign of Henry the Third. Ed. J. F. Lydon. In *R.I.A. Proc.*, lxv (1966–7), sect. C, no. 1, pp 1–27.

The exchequer rolls of Scotland, A.D. 1264–[1600]. Ed. John Stuart [and others]. 23 vols. Edinburgh, 1878–1908.

FIANTS. Calendar to fiants of King Henry VIII. In *P.R.I. rep. D.K. 7* (1875), app. x, pp 27–110; *18* (1886), app. vi, pp 147–8.

FINE ROLLS. *Calendar of the fine rolls . . . 1272–[1509]*. 22 vols. P.R.O., London, 1911–62; reprint, vols i–xiii, Nendeln, 1971.

FITZROY. Henry Fitzroy, duke of Richmond, and his connexion with Ireland, 1529–30. Ed. D. B. Quinn. In *I.H.R. Bull.*, xii (1935), pp 175–7.

GASCON ROLLS. *Rôles gascons, 1242–[1317]*. Ed. Francisque-Michel [and others]. 5 vols. Paris, 1885–1962. (Collection de Documents Inédits sur l'Histoire de France, [xxix]. Série 1: Histoire Politique.)
   T. 4 also published as *Gascon rolls . . . 1307–1317*, ed. Yves Renouard (P.R.O., London, 1962).

Grants, etc. from the crown during the reign of Edward the Fifth: from the original docket-book, MS Harl. 433 . . . Ed. J. G. Nichols. London, 1854. (Camden Soc., [O.S.], lx.)

Inquisitions of 1224 from the miscellanea of the exchequer. Ed. K. W. Nicholls. In *Anal. Hib.*, no. 27 (1972), pp 103–12.

INQUISITIONS POST MORTEM. *Calendar of inquisitions post mortem and other analogous documents . . . Henry III–[15 Richard II]*. 16 vols. P.R.O., London, 1904–74; reprint, vols i–xiv, Nendeln, [c. 1965–.]

—— *Calendar of inquisitions post mortem and other analogous documents . . .* [Series 2]: *Henry VII*. 3 vols. P.R.O., London, 1898–1955; reprint, Nendeln, [c. 1965].

—— *Calendarium inquisitionum post mortem sive excaetarum*. Ed. John Caley and John Bayley. 4 vols. London, 1806–28.

The justiciar and the murder of the MacMurroughs in 1282. Ed. Robin Frame. In *I.H.S.*, xviii, no. 70 (Sept. 1972), pp 223–30.

Letters and papers, foreign and domestic, of the reign of Henry VIII . . . Ed. J. S. Brewer, [James Gairdner and R. H. Brodie]. 23 vols in 28. P.R.O., London, 1862–1932; 2nd ed., vol. i, 1920; reprint, 21 vols in 37, Vaduz, 1965.

LIBERATE ROLLS. *Calendar of the liberate rolls ... 1226–[1272].* 6 vols. P.R.O., London, 1916–64.

—— *Rotuli de liberate ac de misis et praestitis regnante Johanne.* Ed. T. D. Hardy. Rec. Comm., London, 1844.

MEMORANDA ROLLS. *Calendar of memoranda rolls (exchequer) ... 1326–1327.* P.R.O., London, 1968.

See also *Exchequer K.R. & L.T.R. memoranda rolls.* London, 1965. (List & Index Society, iv.)

—— An indenture concerning the king's munitions in Ireland, 1532. Ed. S. G. Ellis. In *Ir. Sword*, xiv (1980), pp 100–03.

From Irish memoranda roll. 24 Hen. VIII, m. 15 (St Peter's College, Wexford, Hore MSS I).

—— Memoranda rolls; king's remembrancer, [1217–1307]. [P.R.O., London, 1968?]. 18 reels of microfilm.

Includes lord treasurer's remembrancer's roll of 1276/7, for which period no K.R. roll has survived. See also *Index of persons and places, memoranda roll[s], Queen's remembrancer, Exchequer, 1271/1273–[1287/88].* [P.R.O., London, 1968], duplicated typescript to accompany microfilm of original rolls.

MISAE ROLLS. See LIBERATE ROLLS.

The parliamentary writs and writs of military summons. Ed. Francis Palgrave. 2 vols in 4. Rec. Comm., London, 1827–34.

PATENT ROLLS. *Calendar of the patent and close rolls of chancery in Ireland of the reigns of Henry VIII, Edward VI, Mary, and Elizabeth.* Ed. James Morrin. Vol. i. Dublin, 1861.

—— *Calendar of patent rolls of Ireland, 5 & 6 Henry VII to 34 Henry VIII.* Rec. Comm. Ire., Dublin, [1830?].

—— *Calendar of the patent rolls ... 1232–[1509].* 53 vols. P.R.O., London, 1891–1971; reprint, Nendeln, 1971–2.

—— *Calendarium rotulorum patentium.* Ed. Thomas Astle and John Caley. Rec. Comm., London, 1802.

—— *Patent rolls of the reign of Henry III ... 1216–[1232].* 2 vols. P.R.O., London, 1901–3; reprint, Nendeln, 1971.

—— *Rotuli litterarum patentium ...* Ed. T. D. Hardy. Vol. i, pars 1: *1201–16.* Rec. Comm., London, 1835.

—— *Rotulorum patentium et clausorum cancellariae Hiberniae calendarium.* Ed. Edward Tresham. Vol. i, pars 1: *Hen. II–Hen. VII.* Rec. Comm. Ire., Dublin, 1828.

PIPE ROLLS. An account of military expenditure in Leinster, 1308. Ed. Philomena Connolly. In *Anal. Hib.*, no. 30 (1982), pp 1–5.

Account of Philip de Staunton, P.R.O.I., Co. 590, copied from pipe roll of 3 Edw. II.

—— Accounts of the great rolls of the pipe of the Irish exchequer for the reign of Edward I. In *P.R.I. rep. D.K. 36* (1904), pp 22–77; *37* (1905), pp 24–55; *38* (1906), pp 29–104.

—— Accounts of the great rolls of the pipe of the Irish exchequer for the reign of Edward II. In *P.R.I. rep. D.K. 39* (1907), pp 21–74; *42* (1911), pp 11–78.

—— Accounts on the great rolls of the pipe of the Irish exchequer for the reign of Henry III. In *P.R.I. rep. D.K. 35* (1903), pp 29–50.

PIPE ROLLS. Catalogue of accounts on the great rolls of the pipe of the Irish exchequer
for the reign of Edward III. In *P.R.I. rep. D.K. 43* (1912), pp 15–67; *44* (1912),
pp 18–61; *45* (1913), pp 24–56; *47* (1915), pp 19–77; *53* (1926), pp 17–54; *54* (1927),
pp 21–64.

—— The enrolled account of Alexander Bicknor, treasurer of Ireland, 1308–14. Ed.
J. F. Lydon. In *Anal. Hib.*, no. 30 (1982), pp 7–46.

—— *The great roll of the pipe . . . 1158/1159*— London, 1884–. (Publications of the Pipe
Roll Society, i– .)

—— *The Irish pipe roll of 14 John, 1211–1212*. Ed. Oliver Davies and D. B. Quinn. Belfast, 1941. (*U.J.A.*, 3rd ser., iv, supplement.)

—— [On the account of Thomas de Chaddisworth, custodee of the temporalities of
the archbishop of Dublin from 1221 to 1256 from the great roll of the pipe.]
Trans. Sir William Betham. In *R.I.A. Proc.*, v (1850–53), pp 145–62.

PRAESTITA ROLL. See LIBERATE ROLLS.

PRIVY COUNCIL. *Proceedings and ordinances of the privy council of England, [1386–1542]*. Ed.
Sir Harris Nicolas. 7 vols. Rec. Comm., London, 1834–7.

Register of Edward, the Black Prince . . . 1346–[1365]. 4 vols. P.R.O., London, 1930–33.

RICHARD II. Unpublished letters from Richard II in Ireland, 1394–5. Ed. Edmund
Curtis. In *R.I.A. Proc.*, xxvii (1924–7), sect. C, no. 14, pp 276–303.

Rotuli de oblatis et finibus . . . tempore regis Johannis. Ed. T. D. Hardy. Rec. Comm.,
London, 1835.

Rotuli Scotiae in turri Londinensi et in domo capitulari Westmonasteriensi asservati. [Ed. D. Macpherson, J. Caley, and W. Illingworth.] 2 vols. Rec. Comm., London, 1814–19.

*Rotuli selecti ad res Anglicas et Hibernicas ex archivis in domo capitulari West-monasteriensi
deprompti*. Ed. Joseph Hunter. Rec. Comm., London, 1834.

STATE PAPERS. *Calendar of the state papers relating to Ireland of the reigns of Henry VIII,
Edward VI, Mary, and Elizabeth, 1509–[1603]*. Ed. H. C. Hamilton, [E. G. Atkinson
and R. P. Mahaffy]. 11 vols. P.R.O., London, 1860–1912; reprint, Nendeln, 1974;
microfilm, Washington, *c.* 1979– .

—— *State papers . . . Henry VIII*. 11 vols. Rec. Comm., London, 1830–52.

TESTA DE NEVILL. *Liber feodorum: the book of fees, commonly called Testa de Nevill, A.D. 1198–
[1293]*. 3 vols. P.R.O., London, 1920–31.

Treaty rolls . . . 1234–1339. 2 vols. P.R.O., London, 1955–72.

The visitation of the archbishop of Cashel to Waterford and Limerick, 1374–5. Ed.
F. Donald Logan. In *Archiv. Hib.*, xxiv (1976–7), pp 50–54.

3 English chancery documents: P.R.O., C.54/216/m.717, C.85/214/45–46.

2 RECORDS RELATING TO LOCAL ADMINISTRATION

The 'bonnacht' of Ulster. Ed. Edmund Curtis. In *Hermathena*, xlvi (1931), pp 87–105.

BORDEAUX. Registre de la comptablie de Bordeaux, 1482–3. Ed. M. G. Ducaunnes-
Duval. In *Archives Historiques du Département de la Gironde*, l (1915).

Bristol charters, 1378–1499. Ed. H. A. Cronne. [Bristol], 1946. (Bristol Record Society's
Publications, xi.)

Bristol town duties . . . Ed. Henry Bush. Bristol, 1828.

BRISTOL. *The Little Red Book of Bristol*. Ed. Francis B. Bickley. 2 vols. Bristol, 1900.

—— *Notes or abstracts of the wills contained in the volume entitled The Great Orphan Book and Book of Wills in the Council House at Bristol*. Ed. T. P. Wadley. Bristol and Gloucestershire Archaeological Society, Bristol, 1886 [i.e. 1882–6].

—— *The overseas trade of Bristol in the later middle ages*. Ed. E. M. Carus-Wilson. [Bristol], 1937. (Bristol Record Society's Publications, vii.)

Chester customs accounts. See sect. III A 1 above.

CORK. A landgable roll of Cork City. Ed. E. Bolster. In *Collect. Hib.*, xiii (1970), pp 7–20. B.L. Add. Roll 8671, dated 1377/1413.

DESMOND. Rental of Connello, [c. 1452]. In John Begley, *Diocese of Limerick* (Dublin, 1927), pp 323–33.

DUBLIN. *Calendar of ancient records of Dublin*. Ed. J. T. Gilbert. 18 vols. Dublin, 1889–1922. Vols viii–xviii ed. Rosa Mulholland Gilbert, Lady Gilbert.

GALWAY. Gilbert, J. T. Archives of the town of Galway: Queen's College, Galway. In *H.M.C. rep. 10*, app. v (1885), pp 380–520.

—— *Report on documents relating to the wardenship of Galway*. Ed. Edward MacLysaght. I.M.C., Dublin, 1944. (*Anal. Hib.*, no. 14.)

KILKENNY. *Liber primus Kilkenniensis: the earliest of the books of the corporation of Kilkenny now extant*. Ed. Charles McNeill. I.M.C., Dublin, 1931. Corrigenda by A. J. Otway-Ruthven in *Anal. Hib.*, no. 26 (1970), pp 71–87.

—— *Liber primus Kilkenniensis*. Ed. and trans. A. J. Otway-Ruthven. Kilkenny, 1961.

LIXNAW. An early rental of the lord of Lixnaw. Ed. the marquess of Lansdowne. In *R.I.A. Proc.*, xl (1931–2), sect. C, no. 1, pp 1–18.

Mac Niocaill, Gearóid. *Na buirgéisí, XII—XV aois*. 2 vols. Dublin, 1964.

MUINTÍR EOLAIS. Meabhrán dlí ó Mhuintír Eolais, 1497–1513. Ed. Gearóid Mac Niocaill. In *Galvia*, iv (1957), pp 25–6. N.L.I., MS 3, f. 17ʳ.

PEMBROKESHIRE. *A calendar of the public records relating to Pembrokeshire*. Ed. Henry Owen. 3 vols. London, 1911–18. (Cymmrodorion Record Series, vii.)

ROSS. Charters of Earl Richard Marshall of the forests of Ross and Taghmon. Ed. G. H. Orpen and E. St J. Brooks. In *R.S.A.I. Jn.*, lxiv (1934), pp 54–63.

ST SEPULCHRE. Notices of the manor of St Sepulchre, Dublin, in the fourteenth century. Ed. James Mills. In *R.S.A.I. Jn.*, xix (1889), pp 31–41, 119–26. Extent of 1326 (pp 37–41) and rental of 1382 (pp 119–26).

Sheriff's accounts of the honour of Dungarvan, of Tweskard in Ulster, and of County Waterford, 1261–63. Ed. Edmund Curtis. In *R.I.A. Proc.*, xxxix (1929–31), sect. C, no. 1, pp 1–17.

TIPPERARY. Sheriff's accounts for County Tipperary, 1275–6. Ed. Edmund Curtis. In *R.I.A. Proc.*, xlii (1934–5), sect. C, no. 5, pp 65–95.

URIEL. The county of Uriel account, 1281–3. Ed. J. F. Lydon. In *Louth Arch. Soc. Jn.*, xix (1977–80), pp 197–205.

WATERFORD. Gilbert, J. T. Archives of the municipal corporation of Waterford. In *H.M.C. rep. 10*, app. v (1885), pp 265–39.

YOUGHAL. Early charters relating to Youghal. Ed. Richard Caulfield. In *Gentleman's Magazine*, ii (1864), pp 191–4.

3 STATUTES

See D. B. Quinn, 'Government printing and the publication of the Irish statutes in the sixteenth century' in *R.I.A. Proc.*, xlix (1943–4), sect. C, no. 2, pp 45–129.
Table of printed acts, to 1586, in editions of the Irish statutes, 1572–1786, with their numeration on the statute rolls (pp 82–127).

The acts of the parliament of Scotland. [Ed. Thomas Thomson and Cosmo Innes.] 12 vols. Edinburgh, 1814–44.

The bills and statutes of the Irish parliaments of Henry VII and Henry VIII. Ed. D. B. Quinn. In *Anal. Hib.*, no. 10 (1941), pp 71–169.

Parliaments and councils of medieval Ireland. Vol. i: Ed. H. G. Richardson and G. O. Sayles. I.M.C., Dublin, 1947.

Recueil des actes de Henry II. Ed. Léopold Delisle and Élie Berger. 5 vols. Paris, 1906–27. (Chartes et diplômes relatifs à l'histoire de France.)

Rotuli parliamentorum . . . [1278–1503]. 7 vols. [London, 1783–1832].

Rotuli parliamentorum Anglie hactenus inediti, MCCLXXIX–MCCCLXXIII. Ed. H. G. Richardson and G. O. Sayles. R. Hist. Soc., London, 1935. (Camden Third Series, li.)

A statute of the fortieth year of King Edward III, enacted in a parliament held in Kilkenny, A.D. 1367, before Lionel, duke of Clarence, lord lieutenant of Ireland. Ed. James Hardiman. Ir. Arch. Soc., Dublin, 1843. (In *Tracts relating to Ireland*, ii.)

Statute rolls of the parliament of Ireland: . . . reign of King Edward the Fourth. Ed. H. F. Berry and J. F. Morrissey. 2 vols. Dublin, 1914–39. (Irish Record Office Series of Early Statutes, iii–iv.)

Statute rolls of the parliament of Ireland: reign of King Henry the Sixth. Ed. H. F. Berry. Dublin, 1910. (Irish Record Office Series of Early Statutes, ii.)

Statutes and ordinances and acts of the parliament of Ireland: King John to Henry V. Ed. H. F. Berry. Dublin, 1907. (Irish Record Office Series of Early Statutes, i.)

The statutes at large passed in the parliaments held in Ireland, . . . 1310 to 1761. 8 vols. Dublin, 1765; . . . *1310–1800*. Ed. J. G. Butler. 20 vols. Dublin, 1786–1801.

The statutes of the realm. 11 vols in 12. Rec. Comm., London, 1810–28.

Two hitherto unpublished membranes of Irish petitions presented at the midsummer parliament of 1302 and the Lent parliament of 1305. Ed. G. J. Hand. In *R.I.A. Proc.*, lxxi (1971), sect. C, no. 1, pp 1–18.

4 LEGAL RECORDS

An ancient record relating to the families into which were married the co-heiresses of Thomas fitz Anthony, seneschal of Leinster. Ed. J. P. Prendergast. In *Kilkenny & S.E. Ire. Arch. Soc. Proc.*, new ser., iv [*R.S.A.I. Jn.*, viii] (1864–6), pp 139–53.

Calendar of the justiciary rolls . . . of Ireland . . . : Edward I [1295–1307]. Ed. James Mills. 2 vols. P.R.O.I., Dublin, 1905–14.

Calendar of the justiciary rolls . . . of Ireland: I to VII years of Edward II [1308–14]. Ed. Herbert Wood and A. E. Langman; revised by M. C. Griffith. P.R.O.I., Dublin, [1956].

Cúis dlí idir ab agus rí. Ed. Colmcille [Conway]. In *Seanchas Ardmhacha*, iv (1960–62), pp 92–102.

P.R.O., Chancery Misc., Bundle 87, file 2, 7 Edw. III, Placita apud Limerick, 6 Edw. III, Rex v. Ab. na Mainistreach Móire.

English law in medieval Ireland: two illustrative documents. Ed. M. P. Sheehy. In *Archiv. Hib.*, xxiii (1960), pp 167–75.

Haas, Elsa de and Hall, G. D. H. (ed.). *Early registers of writs*. London, 1970. (Publications of the Selden Society, lxxxix.)

Includes 'The Irish register "Hib.", British Museum [now British Library] Cottonian MSS, Julius D II, folios 143b–147b, 150a'. Text and translation (pp 1–17); commentary by G. D. H. Hall (pp xxxiii–xl). Register sent to Ireland by Henry III, 10 Nov. 1227.

The legal proceedings against the first earl of Desmond. Ed. G. O. Sayles. In *Anal. Hib.*, no. 23 (1966), pp 1–47.

The partition of the de Verdon lands in Ireland in 1332. Ed. A. J. Otway-Ruthven. In *R.I.A. Proc.*, lxvi (1967–8), sect. C, no. 5, pp 401–55.

Les reports des cases... 10 vols. London, 1678–80.

Vols [ii–viii]: *Les reports del cases in ley...*

Les reports des cases in les ans des roys Edward V, Richard III, Henrie VII & Henrie VIII.... London, 1679.

Select cases concerning the law merchant. Ed. Charles Gross [and Hubert Hall]. 3 vols. London, 1908–32. (Publications of the Selden Society, xxiii, xlvi, xlix.)

Select cases in the council of Henry VII. Ed. C. G. Bayne and W. H. Dunham. London, 1958. (Publications of the Selden Society, lxxv.)

The social state of the southern and eastern counties of Ireland in the sixteenth century: being the presentments of the gentlemen, commonalty and citizens of Carlow, Cork, Kilkenny, Tipperary, Waterford, and Wexford, made in the reigns of Henry VIII and Elizabeth. Ed. H. F. Hore and James Graves. Historical and Archaeological Association of Ireland, Dublin, 1870. (The Annuary of the Royal Historical and Archaeological Association of Ireland, 1868–1869.)

The year book series. 47 vols. London, 1903–69. (Publications of the Selden Society, xvii, xix, xx, xxii, xxiv, xxvi, xxvii, xxix, xxxi, xxxiii, xxxiv, xxxvi–xxxix, xli–xliii, xlv, xlvii, l, lii, liv, lxi, lxiii, lxv, lxx, lxxxi, lxxxv, lxxxvi.)

1307–21.

5 ECCLESIASTICAL RECORDS

This section includes official communications and correspondence. Other writings by medieval churchmen are listed in sect. III B, below.

ACHONRY. Dhá athchuinge as Achadh Chonaire [1504]. Ed. Eric Mac Fhinn. In *Galvia*, viii (1961), pp 27–30.

ALEXANDER III. *Opera omnia, id est epistolae et privilegia ...* Ed. J.-P. Migne. Paris, 1855. (Patrologia Latina, cc); reprint, Turnhout, *c.* 1967; microcard, Washington, 1960; microfiche, Tumba, 196–?; Zug, 1975?

'Epistolae et privilegia', mii–miv, of 1172. Columns 883–6 refer to Ireland.

ALL HALLOWS, DUBLIN. *Registrum prioratus omnium sanctorum juxta Dublin.* Ed. Richard Butler. Ir. Arch. Soc., Dublin, 1845.

ARDFERT. Obligationes pro annatis diocesis Ardfertensis, [1421–1517]. Ed. J. O'Connell. In *Archiv. Hib.*, xxi (1958), pp 1–51.

ARMAGH. Archbishop Cromer's register. Ed. L. P. Murray [and Aubrey Gwynn]. In *Louth Arch. Soc. Jn.*, vii (1929–32), pp 516–24; viii (1933–6), pp 38–49, 169–88, 257–74, 322–51; ix (1937–40), pp 36–41, 124–30; x (1941–4), pp 116–27, 165–79.

—— A calendar of the register of Archbishop Fleming. Ed. H. J. Lawlor. In *R.I.A. Proc.*, xxx (1912–13), sect. C, no. 5, pp 94–190.

—— A calendar of the register of Archbishop Sweteman. Ed. H. J. Lawlor. In *R.I.A. Proc.*, xxix (1910–11), sect. C, no. 8, pp 213–310.

—— Documents relating to the medieval diocese of Armagh. Ed. Aubrey Gwynn. In *Archiv. Hib.*, xiii (1947), pp 1–26.

—— An edition, with introduction and notes, of the register of Archbishop Mey, and a calendar of the register of Archbishop Prene. By W. G. H. Quigley and E. F. D. Roberts. (Ph.D. thesis, Q.U.B., 1955.)

—— *The register of John Swayne, archbishop of Armagh and primate of Ireland, 1418–1439.* Ed. D. A. Chart. Belfast, 1935.

—— *Registrum Iohannis Mey: the register of John Mey, archbishop of Armagh, 1443–1456.* Ed. W. G. H. Quigley and E. F. D. Roberts. Belfast, 1972.

—— The vindication of the earl of Kildare from treason, 1496. Ed. G. O. Sayles. In *I.H.S.*, vii, no. 25 (Mar. 1950), pp 39–47 (Select Documents, viii); reprint in G. O. Sayles, *Scripta diversa* (London, 1982), pp 89–97.
Notarial instrument, Octavian's register, f. 30.

ATHENRY. Regestum monasterii fratrum praedicatorum de Athenry. Ed. Ambrose Coleman. In *Archiv. Hib.*, i (1912), pp 201–21.

AUGUSTINIANS. Irish material in the Augustinian general archives, Rome, 1354–1624. Ed. F. X. Martin and Albericus de Meijer. In *Archiv. Hib.*, xix (1956), pp 61–134, 141–6.

BATH. *Two chartularies of the priory of St Peter at Bath...* Ed. William Hunt. [London], 1893. [Somerset Rec. Soc., vii.]

BERNARD. Deux épitres de Saint Bernard et de son secrétaire. Ed. Jean Leclercq. In *Studien und Mitteilungen zur Geschichte des Benediktiner-Ordens*, lxix (1957), 227–31; reprint in Jean Leclercq, *Recueil d'études sur Saint Bernard et ses écrits* (3 vols, Rome, 1962–9), ii (1966), pp 313–18.

Canterbury professions. Ed. Michael Richter. Torquay, 1974. (Canterbury and York Society, lxvii.)

CASHEL. Obligationes pro annatis diocesis Cassellensis, [1433–1534]. Ed. L. Ryan and W. Skehan, from transcript by M. A. Costello. In *Archiv. Hib.*, xxviii (1966), pp 1–32.

CHRIST CHURCH, CANTERBURY. *Christ Church letters...* Ed. J. B. Sheppard. London, 1877. [Camden Soc., new ser., xix.]

CHRIST CHURCH, DUBLIN. Calendar to Christ Church deeds [1174–1684]. [Ed. M. J. McEnery.] In *P.R.I. rep. D.K. 20* (1888), app. 7, pp 36–122; *23* (1891), app. 3, pp 75–152; *24* (1892), app. 8, pp 100–94.

—— A calendar of the Liber Niger and Liber Albus of Christ Church, Dublin. Ed. H. J. Lawlor. In *R.I.A. Proc.*, xxvii (1908–09), sect. C, no. 1, pp 1–93.

—— Some unpublished texts from the Black Book of Christ Church, Dublin. Ed. Aubrey Gwynn. In *Anal. Hib.*, no. 16 (1946), pp 281–337.

See also HOLY TRINITY, below.

CISTERCIANS. *Letters from the English abbots to the chapter at Cîteaux, 1442–1521*. Ed. C. H. Talbot. R. Hist. Soc., London, 1967. (Camden Fourth Series, iv.)

—— Some Irish Cistercian documents. Ed. G. H. Orpen. In *E.H.R.*, xxviii (1913), pp 303–13.

—— Three unpublished Cistercian documents. Ed. Fr Colmcille [Conway]. In *Louth Arch. Soc. Jn.*, xiii (1953–6), pp 252–78.

CLEMENT VII. Papal letters of Clement VII of Avignon (1378–94) relating to Ireland and England. Ed. Charles Burns. In *Collect. Hib.*, xxiv (1982), pp 7–44.

CLOGHER. Fragments of a lost register of the diocese of Clogher. Ed. H. J. Lawlor. In *Louth Arch. Soc. Jn.*, iv (1916–20), pp 226–57.

—— Medieval sources: Registrum Clogherense. Ed. M. P. Sheehy. In *Clogher Rec.*, iv (1961–2), pp 1–5.

—— The register of Clogher. Ed. K. W. Nicholls. In *Clogher Rec.*, vii (1969–72), pp 361–431.

CLONFERT. Obligationes pro annatis diocesis Clonfertensis, [1420–1531]. Ed. P. K. Egan. In *Archiv. Hib.*, xxi (1958), pp 52–74.

CLOYNE. Obligationes pro annatis diocesis Cloynensis, [1413–1526]. Ed. Denis Buckley, from transcript by M. A. Costello. In *Archiv. Hib.*, xxiv (1961), pp 1–30.

—— *Rotulus pipae Clonensis*. Ed. Richard Caulfield. Cork, 1859; reprint with translation by John O'Riordain as: The pipe roll of Cloyne. In *Cork Hist. Soc. Jn.*, xix (1913), pp 53–61, 116–25, 157–67; xx (1914), pp 42–50, 83–96, 124–39, 183–90; xxi (1915), pp 29–37, 91–100, 136–45, 190–95; xxii (1916), pp 135–41; xxiii (1917), pp 161–9, 212–25.

The concordat between Primate John Mey and Henry O'Neill (1455). Ed. and trans. Katharine Simms. In *Archiv. Hib.*, xxxiv (1976–7), pp 71–82.

Text from Register of John Prene.

CONNACHT. A list of the monasteries in Connacht, 1577. Ed. K. W. Nicholls. In *Galway Arch. Soc. Jn.*, xxxiii (1972–3), pp 28–43.

Part 2 of 'A rentall of Mounster and Connaugh', 4 Feb. 1576/7, P.R.O., S.P.63/57, no. 13, I.

CORK. Obligationes pro annatis diocesis Corcagiensis, [1421–1526]. Ed. Angela Bolster, from transcripts by M. A. Costello. In *Archiv. Hib.*, xxix (1970), pp 1–32.

DERRY. *Acts of Archbishop Colton in his metropolitan visitation of the diocese of Derry, A.D. MCCCXCVII, with a rental of the see estates at that time*. Ed. William Reeves. Ir. Arch. Soc., Dublin, 1850.

DOWN. *Ecclesiastical antiquities of Down, Connor and Dromore: consisting of a taxation of those dioceses compiled in the year MCCCVI*. Ed. William Reeves. Dublin, 1847.

DUBLIN. *Calendar of Archbishop Alen's register, c.1172–1534*. Ed. Charles McNeill. R.S.A.I., Dublin, 1950.

See also H. J. Lawlor, 'Note on the Register of Archbishop Alen' in *Hermathena*, xiv, no. 33 (1907), pp 296–306.

—— The charters of John, lord of Ireland, to the see of Dublin. Ed. Gearóid Mac Niocaill. In *Reportorium Novum*, iii (1961–4), pp 282–306.

—— *Crede Mihi: the most ancient register book of the archbishop of Dublin before the reformation*. Ed. J. T. Gilbert. Dublin, 1897.

—— Obligationes pro annatis diocesis Dublinensis, 1421–1520. Ed. Ambrose Coleman. In *Archiv. Hib.*, ii (1913), app., pp 1–37.

—— Provincial and diocesan decrees of the diocese of Dublin during the Anglo-Norman period. Ed. Aubrey Gwynn. In *Archiv. Hib.*, xi (1944), pp 31–117.

—— *Register of wills and inventories of the diocese of Dublin ... 1457–1483*. Ed. H. F. Berry. R.S.A.I., Dublin, 1898.

—— *Registrum diocesis Dublinensis: a sixteenth century Dublin precedent book*. Ed. N. B. White. I.M.C., Dublin, 1959.

—— The Reportorium Viride of John Alen, archbishop of Dublin, 1533. Ed. N. B. White. In *Anal. Hib.*, no. 10 (1941), pp 173–222.

Dugdale, William. *Monasticon Anglicanum*. Ed. John Caley. 6 vols in 8. London, 1817–30; reprint, 6 vols, 1846; Amersham, 1970.

DUISKE. See GRAIGUENAMANAGH.

ELPHIN. Obligationes pro annatis diocesis Elphinensis, [1426–1548]. Ed. Gearóid Mac Niocaill. In *Archiv. Hib.*, xxii (1959), pp 1–27.

EMLY. Obligationes pro annatis diocesis Imelacesis, [1429–1532]. Ed. Liam Ryan and Walter Skehan from transcript by M. A. Costello. In *Archiv. Hib.*, xxviii (1966), pp 33–44.

The episcopal rentals of Clonfert and Kilmacduagh [*c.* 1565–7]. Ed. K. W. Nicholls. In *Anal. Hib.*, no. 26 (1971), pp 130–43.

EXETER. *Monasticon diocesis Exoniensis: records illustrating the ancient foundations in Cornwall and Devon*. Ed. George Oliver. Exeter, 1846; *Additional supplement*, 1854.

Extents of Irish monastic possessions, 1540–1541. Ed. N. B. White. I.M.C., Dublin, 1943.

FERNS. Letter from the archbishops of Tuam and Dublin to William Marshall, earl of Pembroke, requiring him to restore the possessions of the bishopric of Ferns ... 1216. Ed. Albert Way. In *Kilkenny Arch. Soc. Proc.*, new ser., iv [i.e. *R.S.A.I. Jn.*, viii] (1864–6), pp 137–9.

—— Obligationes pro annatis diocesis Fernensis, 1413–1524. Ed. Joseph Ranson. In *Archiv. Hib.*, xviii (1955), pp 1–15.

FORE. Cairteacha meán-aoiseacha do mhainistir Fhobhair, xii–xiii céad. Ed. M. P. Sheehy. In *Seanchas Ardmhacha*, iv (1961), pp 171–5.

FURNESS. *The coucher book of Furness abbey*. Ed. J. C. Atkinson [and John Brownbill]. 2 vols in 6. Chetham Soc., Manchester, 1886–1919. (Remains Historical and Literary connected with the Palatine Counties of Lancaster and Chester, new ser., ix, xi, xiv, lxxiv, lxxvi, lxxviii); microfiche, Bishops Stortford and Teaneck, 1974.

GLASTONBURY. *A feodary of Glastonbury abbey, 1342*. Ed. F. W. Weaver. London, 1910. (Somerset Rec. Soc., xxvi.) Microfilm, Washington, [196?].

—— *The great chartulary of Glastonbury*. Ed. Aelred Watkin. 1 vol. in 3. Frome, 1947–56. (Somerset Rec. Soc., lix, lxiii, lxiv.)

GRAIGUENAMANAGH. The charters of the Cistercian abbey of Duiske ... Ed. C. M. Butler and J. H. Bernard. In *R.I.A. Proc.*, xxxv (1918), sect. C, no. 1, pp 1–188.

HOLM CULTRAM. *The register and records of Holm Cultram, [c.1236]*. Ed. Francis Grainger and W. G. Collingwood. Cumberland & Westmoreland Antiq. Soc., Kendal, 1929. (Record Ser., vii.)

—— *Some records of a Cistercian abbey: Holm Cultram, Cumberland*. Ed. G. E. Gilbanks. London, [1899].

HOLY TRINITY, DUBLIN. *Account roll of the priory of the Holy Trinity, Dublin, 1337–1346*. Ed. James Mills. R.S.A.I., Dublin, 1891.

—— The registrum novum: a manuscript of Holy Trinity cathedral: the medieval charters. Ed. M. P. Sheehy. In *Reportorium Novum*, iii (1961–4), pp 249–81.

INNOCENT III. The letters of Innocent III to Ireland. Ed. P. J. Dunning. In *Traditio*, xviii (1962), pp 229–53.

—— Letters of Pope Innocent III to Ireland: a calendar ... Ed. P. J. Dunning. In *Archiv. Hib.*, xiii (1947), pp 27–44.

See also P. J. Dunning, 'The letters of Innocent III as a source for Irish history' in *Ir. Cath. Hist. Comm. Proc.*, 1958, pp 1–10.

INNOCENT IV. Letters of Pope Innocent IV relating to Ireland. Ed. Canice Mooney. In *Collect. Hib.*, ii (1959), pp 7–12.

Irish possessions of St Thomas of Acre. Ed. E. St J. Brooks. In *R.I.A. Proc.*, lviii (1956–7), sect. C, no. 2, pp 21–44.

KELLS. The register of Kells. [Ed. N. B. White.] In *Ir. mon. deeds, 1200–1600* (1936), pp 300–13.

KILDARE. Obligationes pro annatis diocesis Darensis, 1413–1521. Ed. Ambrose Coleman. In *Archiv. Hib.*, ii (1913), app., pp 39–72.

KILKENNY. See OSSORY.

KILLALOE. Obligationes pro annatis diocesis Laoniensis, 1421–1535. Ed. D. F. Gleeson. In *Archiv. Hib.*, x (1943), pp 1–103.

KILMAINHAM. *Registrum de Kilmainham: register of chapter acts of the hospital of St John of Jerusalem in Ireland, 1326–1339*... Ed. Charles McNeill. I.M.C., Dublin, [1932].

LEXINGTON, STEPHEN OF. *Letters from Ireland, 1228–1229*. Trans. Barry W. O'Dwyer. Kalamazoo, 1982. (Cistercian Fathers Series, xxviii.)

—— Registrum epistolarum Stephani de Lexinton abbatis de Stanlegia et de Savigniaco. Ed. Bruno B. Griesser. In *Analecta Sacri Ordinis Cisterciensis*, ii (1946), pp 1–118; viii (1952), pp 181–378.

LIMERICK. *The Black Book of Limerick*. Ed. James MacCaffrey. Dublin, 1907.

See also C. W. Russell, 'The Black Book of Limerick' in *H.M.C. rep. 3* (1872), app. pp 434–5. Description and history of the cartulary of Limerick cathedral.

—— Obligationes pro annatis diocesis Limiricensis, 1421–1519. Ed. Michael Moloney. In *Archiv. Hib.*, x (1943), pp 104–62.

LISMORE. Obligationes pro annatis diocesis Lismorensis, 1426–1529. Ed. Patrick Power. In *Archiv. Hib.*, xii (1946), pp 15–61.

LLANTHONY. *The Irish cartularies of Llanthony Prima & Secunda*. Ed. E. St J. Brooks. I.M.C., Dublin, 1953.

MELLIFONT. An important Mellifont document. [Ed. Colmcille Conway.] In *Louth Arch. Soc. Jn.*, xiv (1957–60), pp 1–13.
Inspeximus, 1348.

—— Original charter granted by John, lord of Ireland, to the abbey of Mellifont. Ed. Aquilla Smith. In *Ir. Arch. Soc. Misc.*, i (1846), pp 158–60.

—— Seven documents from the old abbey of Mellifont. Ed. Fr Colmcille [Conway]. In *Louth Arch. Soc. Jn.*, xiii (1953–6), pp 35–67.

NAVAN. A charter of John de Courcy to the abbey of Navan. Ed. E. St J. Brooks. In *R.S.A.I. Jn.*, lxiii (1933), pp 38–45.

ORMOND DEEDS. *Irish monastic and episcopal deeds, A.D. 1200—1600* . . . Ed. N. B. White. I.M.C., Dublin, 1936.

OSENEY. *Cartulary of Oseney abbey*. Ed. H. E. Salter. 6 vols. Oxford, 1929–36. (Oxford Hist. Soc., lxxxix–xci, xcvii, xcviii, ci.)

OSSORY. Ancient charters in the Liber Albus Ossoriensis. Ed. H. F. Berry. In *R.I.A. Proc.*, xxvii (1908–9), sect. C, no. 3, pp 115–25.

—— Calendar of the Liber Ruber of the diocese of Ossory. Ed. H. J. Lawlor. In *R.I.A. Proc.*, xxvii (1908–9), sect. C, no. 5, pp 159–208.

—— Obligationes pro annatis diocesis Ossoriensis, 1413–1531. Ed. T. J. Clohosey from transcript by M. A. Costello. In *Archiv. Hib.*, xx (1957), pp 1–37.

O'TOOLE. Goblet of St Lorcán Ua Tuathail, archbishop of Dublin, 1161–1180. Ed. M. V. Ronan. In *R.S.A.I. Jn.*, lxiii (1933), pp 122–4.
Bibl. Ste Geneviève, Paris, MS 1833, p. 317.

PAPAL BULLS. The popes and the ecclesiastical history of medieval Ireland: critical texts of the papal bulls, 1070–1254, with historical annotations. By M. P. Sheehy. (Ph.D. thesis, N.U.I. (U.C.D.), 1960.)

PAPAL REGISTERS. *Calendar of entries in the papal registers relating to Great Britain and Ireland: papal letters*. Ed. W. H. Bliss [and others]. P.R.O., London, 1893– .
Vol. xv– published I.M.C., Dublin. Vol. xv: *Innocent VIII: Lateran registers, 1484—1492* (1978) contains important introductory matter by M. J. Haren and Leonard Boyle.

Pontificia Hibernica: medieval papal chancery documents concerning Ireland, 640—1261. Ed. M. P. Sheehy. 2 vols. Dublin, 1962–5.

RENEHAN. *Collections on Irish church history from the MSS of . . . Laurence F. Renehan . . .* Ed. Daniel McCarthy. 2 vols. Dublin, 1861–74.

ROSS. Obligationes pro annatis diocesis Rossensis, [1432–1533]. Ed. James Coombes, from transcript by M. A. Costello. In *Archiv. Hib.*, xxix (1970), pp 33–48.

ST ALBANS. *Registrum abbatiae Johannis Whethamstede*. Ed. H. T. Riley. London, 1872. (Rolls Series, [xxviii]. Chronica monasterii S. Albani, [vi]. Registra quorundam Abbatum Monasterii S. Albani, i); reprint, [New York], 1965.

—— *Registra Johannis Whethamstede, Willelmi Albon, et Willelmi Walingforde*. Ed. H. T. Riley. London, 1873. (Rolls Series, [xxviii]. Chronica Monasterii S. Albani, [vi]. Registra quorundam Abbatum Monasterii S. Albani, ii); reprint, [New York], 1965.

ST ANDREWS. *Liber cartarum prioratus Sancti Andree in Scotia*. Bannatyne Club, Edinburgh, 1841.

ST CATHERINE'S, DUBLIN. Some ancient deeds of the parishes of St Catherine and

St James, Dublin, 1296–1743. Ed. H. F. Twiss [afterwards Berry]. In *R.I.A. Proc.*, xxxv (1918–20), sect. C, no. 7, pp 265–81.

ST JOHN'S, DUBLIN. A fifteenth-century building account from Dublin. Ed. James Lydon. In *Ir. Econ. & Soc. Hist.*, ix (1982), pp 73–5.

T.C.D., MS 1477, no. 131.

ST JOHN THE BAPTIST'S, DUBLIN. *Registrum chartarum hospitalis Sancti Johannis Baptistae extra novam portam civitatis Dublin: register of the hospital of S. John the Baptist without the New Gate, Dublin*. Ed. E. St J. Brooks. I.M.C., Dublin, 1936.

The folio missing from this edition has been printed from B.L. Add. MS 4797, no. 3 as E. St J. Brooks, 'Hospital of St John the Baptist, Dublin' in *Anal. Hib.*, no. 8 (1938), pp 443–4.

ST JOHN THE BAPTIST'S, DUBLIN. An unpublished fragment of the register of the hospital of St John the Baptist, Dublin. Ed. Gearóid Mac Niocaill. In *R.S.A.I. Jn.*, xcii (1962), pp 67–9.

ST MARY'S, DUBLIN. *Chartularies of St Mary's abbey, Dublin; with the register of its house at Dunbrody, and annals of Ireland*. Ed. J. T. Gilbert. 2 vols. London, 1884. (Rolls Series, [lxxx]); reprint, [Nendeln], 1965.

ST MARY'S HOSPITAL, DROGHEDA. A medieval foundation in the borough of Drogheda in Oirghialla. Ed. M. P. Sheehy. In *Louth Arch. Soc. Jn.*, xiv (1957–60), pp 154–9.

ST NICHOLAS, EXETER. Unpublished charters relating to Ireland, 1177–82, from the archives of the city of Exeter. Ed. E. St J. Brooks. In *R.I.A. Proc.*, xliii (1935–7), sect. C, no. 11, pp 313–66.

ST PATRICK'S DUBLIN. Calendar of documents contained in the chartulary commonly called 'Dignitas Decani' of St Patrick's cathedral. Ed. J. H. Bernard. In *R.I.A. Proc.*, xxv (1904–5), sect. C, no. 9, pp 481–507.

—— Cambridge University Additional MS 710. Ed. G. J. Hand. In *Reportorium Novum*, ii (1958–60), pp 17–32.

—— *The 'Dignitas Decani' of St Patrick's cathedral, Dublin*. Ed. N. B. White. I.M.C., Dublin, 1957.

ST SAVIOUR'S CHANTRY, WATERFORD. Registrum cantariae S. Salvatoris Waterfordensis: (B.M. Harl. 3765). Ed. Gearóid Mac Niocaill. In *Anal. Hib.*, no. 23 (1966), pp 135–222.

ST THOMAS'S, DUBLIN. *Register of the abbey of St Thomas, Dublin*. Ed. J. T. Gilbert. London, 1889. (Rolls Series, [xciv]); reprint, [Wiesbaden], 1965.

ST WERBURGH'S, DUBLIN. Some ancient deeds of the parish of St Werburgh, Dublin, 1243–1676. Ed. H. F. Twiss [afterwards Berry]. In *R.I.A. Proc.*, xxxv (1918–20), sect. C, no. 8, pp 282–315.

Sheehy, M. P. (ed.). Unpublished medieval notitiae and epistolae [1217–36]. In *Collect. Hib.*, vi (1964), pp 7–17.

Sliocht do 'Riaghail na sacart'. Ed. 'Connla'. In *Irisleabhar Muighe Nuadhad*, 1919, pp 73–9.

.STANLEY. Collections towards the history of the Cistercian abbey of Stanley. Ed. W. de G. Birch. In *Wiltshire Archaeological Society Magazine*, xv (1875), pp 239–307.

TEMPLARS. Documents relating to the suppression of the Templars in Ireland. Ed. Gearóid Mac Niocaill. In *Anal. Hib.*, no. 24 (1967), pp 181–226.

TRISTERNAGH. *Registrum cartarum monasterii B.V. Mariae de Tristernagh . . .: register of the priory of . . . Tristernagh*. Ed. M. V. Clarke. I.M.C., Dublin, 1941.

TUAM. Obligationes pro annatis provinciae Tuamensis, [1413–1548]. Ed. J. F. O'Doherty, from transcript by M. A. Costello. In *Archiv. Hib.*, xxvi (1963), pp 56–117.

ULSTER. *De annatis Hiberniae: a calendar of the first fruits' fees levied on papal appointments to benefices in Ireland, A.D. 1400 to 1535, extracted from the Vatican and other Roman archives* ... Ed. M. A. Costello. With an introduction by Ambrose Coleman and supplementary notes by W. H. Grattan Flood. Vol. i: *Ulster*. Dundalk, 1909.

VATICAN ARCHIVES. Miscellanea Vaticano-Hibernica. Ed. John Hagan. In *Archiv. Hib.*, vi (1917), pp 94–155.
Includes Avignon correspondence with the English crown, 1330–36, from Barberini Lat. 2126 (pp 129–50).

—— Sources of British and Irish history in the Instrumenta Miscellanea. In *Archivum Historiae Pontificiae*, ix (1971), pp 7–141.

—— Vatican Archives: Instrumenta miscellanea: documents of Irish interest, [1260–1805]. Ed. R. J. Dodd. In *Archiv. Hib.*, xix (1956), pp 135–40.

Visitations of the dioceses of Clonfert, Tuam, and Kilmacduagh, c. 1565–7. Ed. K. W. Nicholls. In *Anal. Hib.*, no. 26 (1970), pp 144–58.
Roland de Burgo, from T.C.D., MS 568 (E. 3. 16), and Christopher Bodkin, from a copy in T.C.D., MS 582 (E. 3. 13).

WATERFORD. Obligationes pro annatis diocesis Waterfordensis, 1421–1507. Ed. Patrick Power. In *Archiv. Hib.*, xii (1946), pp 1–14.

Wilkins, David (ed.). *Concilia magnae Britanniae et Hiberniae [446–1717]*. 4 vols. London, 1737.

6 INSTITUTIONAL AND BUSINESS RECORDS

The merchant tailors' guild: that of St John the Baptist, Dublin, 1418–1841. Ed. H. F. Berry. In *R.S.A.I. Jn.*, xlviii (1918), pp 19–64.

The register of the Guild of the Holy Trinity: St Mary, St John the Baptist, and St Katherine of Coventry. Ed. M. D. Harris. 2 vols. London, 1935–44. (Publications of the Dugdale Society, xiii, xix.)
Vol. ii: *Records of the Guild of the Holy Trinity* ... Ed. Geoffrey Templeman.

7 FAMILY AND PERSONAL RECORDS

BARRY. Some unpublished Barry charters. Ed. K. W. Nicholls. In *Anal. Hib.*, no. 27 (1972), pp 113–19.

Blake family records. Ser. i: 1300–1600. Ed. M. J. Blake. London, 1902.

BURKE. A charter of William de Burgo. Ed. K. W. Nicholls. In *Anal. Hib.*, no. 27 (1972), pp 120–22.

—— Feudal charters of the de Burgo lordship of Connacht, 1237–1325 (B.M. Add. MSS 6041). Ed. Edmund Curtis. In *Féil-sgríbhinn Eóin Mhic Néill* (1940), pp 286–95.

—— Seanchas na mBúrcach: réamh-rádh. Ed. and trans. Tomás Ó Raghallaigh. In *Galway Arch. Soc. Jn.*, xiii (1927–8), pp 50–60, 101–37; xiv (1928–9), pp 30–51, 142–67.

BUTLER. Curtis, Edmund (ed.). Original documents relating to the Butler lordship of Achill, Burrishoole and Aughrim, 1236–1640. In *Galway Arch. Soc. Jn.*, xv (1931–3), pp 121–8.

CAREW. *Calendar of the Carew manuscripts preserved in the archiepiscopal library at Lambeth*. Ed. J. S. Brewer and W. Bullen. 6 vols. P.R.O., London 1867–73.

Corpus genealogiarum Hiberniae. Ed. M. A. O'Brien. Dublin, 1962.

DE COURCY. Dower charter of John de Courcy's wife. Ed. A. J. Otway-Ruthven. In *U.J.A.*, 3rd ser., xii (1949), pp 77–81.

DOWDALL, GEORGE. Documents concerning primate Dowdall. Ed. Thomas Gogarty. In *Archiv. Hib.*, i (1912), pp 248–76; ii (1913), pp 242–55.

Dowdall deeds. Ed. Charles McNeill and A. J. Otway-Ruthven. I.M.C., Dublin, 1960.

FITZGERALD. The Geraldines of Desmond. Ed. S. Hayman. In *R.S.A.I. Jn.*, 4th ser., v (1879–82), pp 211–35, 411–40; vii (1885–6), pp 66–92.

—— The rental book of Gerald Fitzgerald, ninth earl of Kildare, begun in the year 1518. Ed. H. F. Hore. In *R.S.A.I. Jn.*, 2nd ser., ii (1858–9), pp 266–80, 301–10; iv (1862–3), pp 110–37; v (1864–6), pp 501–18, 525–46.

—— Gilbert, J. T. Historical memoirs of the Geraldine earls of Desmond. In *H.M.C. rep. 3* (1872), app., pp 431–2.

See also '"Red Book" of the earls of Kildare: contents.' in *H.M.C. rep. 9*, app. 2, pp 265–93.

—— *The red book of the earls of Kildare*. Ed. Gearóid Mac Niocaill. I.M.C., Dublin, 1964. Original MS now in T.C.D.

—— Unpublished Geraldine documents. Ed. S. Hayman. J. Graves, H. Fitzgibbon. In *R.S.A.I. Jn.*, 3rd ser., i (1868), pp 356–416; 459–559; 4th ser., i (1870), pp 591–616; iv (1876–8), pp 14–52, 157–66, 246–64; reprint, 4 vols. Dublin, 1870–81.

FITZRALPH, RICHARD. Two sermons of Primate Richard FitzRalph, preached before the provincial councils of Armagh on 7 February 1352 and 5 February 1355. Ed. Aubrey Gwynn. In *Archiv. Hib.*, xiv (1949), pp 50–65.

Geinealaigh Clainne Aodhagáin, A.D. 1400–1500: ollamhain i bhféineachus is i bhfilidheacht. Ed. Cáitilin Ní Maol-Chróin. In *Measgra i gCuimhne Mhichíl Uí Chléirigh* (Dublin, 1944), pp 132–9.

GORMANSTON. *Calendar of the Gormanston register, [c.1175–1397]*. Ed. James Mills and M. J. McEnery. R.S.A.I., Dublin, 1916.

—— The Gormanston register—Viscount Gormanston, Gormanston Castle, Ireland. In *H.M.C. rep. 4* (1874), app., pp 573–84.

Hackett, Sir John. *Letters, 1526–1534*. Ed. E. F. Rogers. Morgantown, W. Va., 1971. (Archives of British History and Culture, i–ii.)

LISRONAGH. Rental of the manor of Lisronagh, 1333, and notes on 'betagh' tenure in medieval Ireland. Ed. Edmund Curtis. In *R.I.A. Proc.*, xliii (1935–7), sect. C, no. 3, pp 41–76.

MACMAHON. Cíos Mhic Mhathghamhna. Ed. and trans. Seosamh Ó Dufaigh. In *Clogher Rec.*, iv (1961–2), pp 125–34.

Text formerly published by Paul Walsh in *Irisleabhar Muighe Nuadhad*, 1930, pp 17–19, and by Séamus Pender in *Études Celt.*, i (1936), pp 248–60.

MAGAURAN. *The book of Magauran. Leabhar Méig Shamhradháin*. Ed. Lambert McKenna. Institute for Advanced Studies, Dublin, 1947.

Maguire, Maghnus. *Me Guidhir Fearmanach. The Maguires of Fermanagh*. Ed. Patrick Dineen. Society for the Preservation of the Irish Language, Dublin, 1917.

MORTIMER. The muniments of Edmund de Mortimer, third earl of March, concerning his liberty of Trim. Ed. Herbert Wood. In *R.I.A. Proc.*, xl (1931–2), sect. C, no. 7, pp 312–55.

O'BRIEN. *The Inchiquin manuscripts*. Ed. John Ainsworth. I.M.C., Dublin, 1961.

The O'Clery book of genealogies. Ed. Séamus Pender. I.M.C., Dublin, 1951. (*Anal. Hib.*, no. 18.)

O'Donnell genealogies. Ed. Paul Walsh. In *Anal. Hib.*, no. 8 (1938), pp 373–418.

The O Doyne (Ó Duinn) manuscript: documents relating to the family of O Doyne (Ó Duinn) from Archbishop Marsh's Library, Dublin, MS Z.4.2.19. Ed. K. W. Nicholls, I.M.C., Dublin, 1983. (Survey of Irish Lordships. Special vol.)

O'NEILL. Letter from Domnal O'Neill to Fineen Mac Carthy, 1317. Ed. Herbert Wood. In *R.I.A. Proc.*, xxxvii (1924–7), sect. C, no. 7, pp 141–8.

See also Diarmuid Ó Murchadha, 'Is the O'Neill–MacCarthy letter of 1317 a forgery?' in *I.H.S.*, xxiii, no. 89 (May 1982), pp 61–7 (Select Documents, xxxvi), which includes text from B.L. Add. MS 34727, ff 268–9.

Ó Raithbheartaigh, Toirdhealbhach (ed.). *Genealogical tracts, 1*. I.M.C., Dublin, 1932.

ORMOND. *Calendar of Ormond deeds, 1172–1603*. Ed. Edmund Curtis. 6 vols. I.M.C., Dublin, 1932–43.

See also C. A. Empey, 'Ormond deeds in National Library of Ireland' in *Butler Soc. Jn.*, i, no. 7 (1977), pp 519–21, and K. W. Nicholls, 'Further notes on Ormond material in National Library' in *Butler Soc. Jn.*, i, no. 7 (1977), pp 522–6.

—— *The Red Book of Ormond*. Ed. N. B. White. I.M.C., Dublin, 1932.

PEMBROKE. *Calendar of ancient deeds and muniments preserved in the Pembroke Estate Office, Dublin*. Dublin, 1891.

PIPPARD. Estate of Benedict Pippard of Pippardeston, A.D. 1316. Ed. Dermot MacIvor. In *Louth Arch. Soc. Jn.*, xiv (1957–60), pp 165–9.

RAYMOND LE GROS. An unpublished charter of Raymond le Gros. Ed. E. St J. Brooks. In *R.S.A.I. Jn.*, lxix (1939), pp 167–9.

ROCHE. Liosta de thailte Róisteacha, 1461. Ed. Éamonn de hÓir. In *Dinnseanchas*, ii (1966–7), pp 106–12.

List of Roche lands in Fermoy.

SYDNEY. *Letters and memorials of state... written and collected by Sir Henry Sydney..., Sir Philip Sydney and... Sir Robert Sydney*. Ed. Arthur Collins. 2 vols. London, 1746.

—— Horwood, A. J. The manuscripts of the right honourable Lord de l'Isle and Dudley at Penshurst, Co. Kent. In *H.M.C. rep. 3* (1872), app., pp 227–33.

—— *Report on the manuscripts of Lord De l'Isle and Dudley, preserved at Penshurst Place*. 6 vols. H.M.C., London, 1925–66. (H.M.C., lxxvii.)

TALBOT. Gilbert, J. T. Manuscripts of the right honourable Lord Talbot de Malahide, Malahide Castle, Co. Dublin. In *H.M.C. rep. 8*, app. i, pp 493–9.

Exemplification of act of parliament at Trim, A.D. 1447 (p. 499).

DE VERDON. Otway-Ruthven, A. J. (ed.). The partition of the de Verdon lands in Ireland in 1332. In *R.I.A. Proc.*, lxvi (1967–8), sect. C, no. 5, pp 401–55.

WYNCHEDON. The testament of John de Wynchedon of Cork, anno 1306. Ed. Denis O'Sullivan. In *Cork Hist. Soc. Jn.*, lxi (1956), pp 75–88.

8 OTHER RECORDS

Cáipéisi ón gceathrú céad déag. Ed. Gearóid Mac Niocaill. In *Galvia*, v (1959), pp 33–42.

The request of the Irish for English law, 1277–80. Ed. A. J. Otway-Ruthven. In *I.H.S.*, vi, no. 24 (Sept. 1949), pp 261–70. (Select Documents, vi.)

B CONTEMPORARY WORKS

1 CONTEMPORARY HISTORIES

Adam of Usk. *Chronicon . . . 1377–1404*. Ed. E. M. Thompson. 2nd ed. Royal Society of Literature, London, 1904.

Andreas, Bernard. *Historia regis Henrici septimi*. Ed. James Gairdner. London, 1858. (Rolls Series, [x]); reprint, New York, 1966; microfiche, Washington, [1967?].

Annala as Breifne. Ed. Éamonn de hÓir. In *Breifne*, iv (1970–75), pp 59–86.

Annála Connacht: the Annals of Connacht, A.D. 1224–1544. Ed. A. M. Freeman. Dublin, 1944; reprint, 1970.

> Introduction and Irish text, 1224–1412, originally published in *Rev. Celt.*, l (1933), pp 1–23, 117–41, 272–88, 339–56; li (1934), pp 46–111, 199–300.

Annala rioghachta Eireann: Annals of the kingdom of Ireland by the Four Masters, from the earliest period to the year 1616. Ed. John O'Donovan. 7 vols. Dublin, 1851; reprints, 1854, New York, 1966; 2nd ed., Dublin, 1856; reprint, Birmingham, Ala., 1966.

Annala Uladh: Annals of Ulster . . .: a chronicle of Irish affairs . . . 431 to 1541. Ed. W. M. Hennessy [and Bartholomew MacCarthy]. 4 vols. Dublin, 1887–1901.

Annála Uladh. *The Annals of Ulster (to A.D. 1131)*. Ed. Seán Mac Airt and Gearóid Mac Niocaill. Pt 1: Text and translation. Dublin Institute for Advanced Studies, Dublin, 1983.

Annála Uladh agus Annála Locha Cé, 1014–1220. Ed. Gearóid Mac Niocaill. In *Galvia*, vi (1959), pp 18–25.

Annales de Monte Fernandi (Annals of Multifernan). Ed. Aquilla Smith. Ir. Arch. Soc., Dublin, 1842. (In *Tracts relating to Ireland*, ii.)

Annales monastici. Ed. H. R. Luard. 5 vols. London, 1864–9. (Rolls Series, xxxvi); reprint, [Nendeln], 1965.

Annals from the Book of Leinster, [475–1189. Ed. Whitley Stokes.] In *Tripartite life of Patrick*, ii (1887), pp 512–29.

Annals of Boyle. *Annales Buelliani*. Ed. Charles O'Conor. Buckingham, 1825. (Rerum Hibernicarum Scriptores, ii.)

—— The annals in Cotton MS Titus A xxv. Ed. A. M. Freeman. In *Rev. Celt.*, xli (1924), pp 301–30; xlii (1925), pp 283–305; xliii (1926), pp 358–84; xliv (1927), pp 336–61.

Annals of Christ Church. Ed. Aubrey Gwynn. In *Anal. Hib.*, no. 16 (1946), pp 324–9.

The annals of Clonmacnoise, being annals of Ireland from the earliest period to A.D. 1408. Trans. Conall Mageoghagan. Ed. Denis Murphy. R.S.A.I., Dublin, 1896.

Annals of Duisk. See 'Late medieval Irish annals', below.

The annals of Inisfallen, reproduced in facsimile from the original manuscript (Rawlinson B 503) in the Bodleian Library. Ed. R. I. Best and Eoin Mac Neill. R.I.A., Dublin, 1933.

The annals of Inisfallen (MS Rawlinson B 503). Ed. Seán Mac Airt. Dublin, 1951.

Annals of Ireland, A.D. 1162–1370. Ed. J. T. Gilbert. In *Chartul. St Mary's, Dublin*, ii (1886, reprint, 1965), pp 303–98; English translation in William Camden, *Britannia* (ed. Richard Gough, London, 1789), iii, 670–90.
Bodleian Library MS Laud 526.

Annals of Ireland: fragment: A.D. 1308–1310 and 1316–1317. Ed. J. T. Gilbert, in *Chartul. St Mary's, Dublin*, ii (1886, reprint, 1965), pp 293–302.

Annals of Ireland from . . . 1443 to 1468. Trans. Dudley Firbisse. Ed. John O'Donovan. In *Ir. Arch. Soc. Misc.*, i (1846), pp 198–302.

The annals of Loch Cé: a chronicle of Irish affairs, 1014–1590. Ed. W. M. Hennessy. 2 vols. London, 1871. (Rolls Series, [liv]); reprints, I.M.C., Dublin, 1939; [Vaduz, 1965].
See also 'Annála Uladh agus Annála Locha Cé', above.

The annals of Nenagh. Ed. D. F. Gleeson. In *Anal. Hib.*, no. 12 (1943), pp 155–64.

Annals of Ross. See Clyn.

Annals of Senat. See Annala Uladh.

The annals of Tigernach. Ed. Whitley Stokes. In *Rev. Celt.*, xvi (1895), pp 374–419; xvii (1896), pp 6–33, 119–263, 337–420; xviii (1897), pp 9–59, 150–97, 267–303.

Annals of Ulster. See Annala Uladh.

The battle of Faughart. Ed. Henry Morris. In *Louth Arch. Soc. Jn.*, i (1903–7), no. 2, pp 77–91.

Benedict of Peterborough. See *Gesta regis Henrici secundi*.

Benet. John Benet's chronicle for the years 1400 to 1462. Ed. G. L. Harriss and M. A. Harriss. In *Camden Miscellany*, xxiv (R. Hist. Soc., London, 1972; Camden Fourth Series, ix), pp 151–233.

The book of Howth. In *Cal. Carew MSS*, [v] (1871, reprint, 1974), pp 1–260.

The book of Fenagh. Ed. W. M. Hennessy and D. H. Kelly. Dublin, 1875; reprint, I.M.C., Dublin, 1939.
Supplementary volume. Ed. R. A. S. Macalister. I.M.C., Dublin, 1939.

Bray, Thomas. The conquest of Ireland. In *Cal. Carew MSS*, [v] (1871, reprint, 1974), pp 261–318.

The Brut, or the chronicles of England. Ed. F. W. D. Brie. 2 vols. London, 1906–8. (Early English Text Society, Original Series, cxxxi, cxxxvi); reprint, vol. i, London, 1960; vol. ii, New York, [1969?].

Brut y Tywsogyon, or, The chronicle of the princes: Red Book of Hergest version. Ed. Thomas Jones. Board of Celtic Studies, University of Wales, Cardiff, 1955. (History and Law Series, xvi.)

Campion, Edmund. *Two bokes of the histories of Ireland.* Ed. A. F. Vossen. Assen, 1963.

Case, Thomas. Annales monasterii Beata Marie Virginis, juxta Dublin. Ed. J. T. Gilbert. In *Chartul. St Mary's, Dublin*, ii (1886, reprint, 1965), pp 241–92.

Chronicque de la traison et mort de Richart Deux, roi Dengleterre. Ed. Benjamin Williams. English Historical Society, London, 1846.

Chronicum Scotorum: a chronicle of Irish affairs . . . to A.D. 1135, with a supplement . . . 1141 to 1150. Ed. W. M. Hennessy. London, 1866. (Rolls Series, xlvi); reprint, [Vaduz], 1964.

Clyn. *The annals of Ireland by Friar John Clyn and Thady Dowling, together with the Annals of Ross*. Ed. Richard Butler. Ir. Arch. Soc., Dublin, 1849.

Diceto, Ralph de. *Opera historica: the historical works*. Ed. William Stubbs. 2 vols. London, 1876. (Rolls Series, [lxviii]); reprint, [New York], 1965.

Dowling. See Clyn.

Eadmer. *Historia novorum in Anglia*. Ed. Martin Rule. London, 1884. (Rolls Series, [lxxxi]); reprint, [Nendeln?], 1965.

An English chronicle of the reigns of Richard II, Henry IV, Henry V, and Henry VI, written before... 1471. Ed. J. S. Davies. London, 1856. (Camden Society, [Old Series], lxiv.)

The English conquest of Ireland, A.D. *1166—1185, mainly from the 'Expugnatio Hibernica' of Giraldus Cambrensis*. Ed. F. J. Furnivall. Pt i. London, 1896. (Early English Text Society, Original Series, cvii); reprint, New York, [1969].
See also Giraldus Cambrensis, below.

Fordun, Johannis de. *Scotichronicon . . . cum . . . continuatione* [by Walter Bower]. Ed. Thomas Hearne. 5 vols. Oxford, 1722; ed. Walter Goodall. 2 vols. Edinburgh, 1747–59.

A fragment of Irish annals. Ed. and trans. Brian Ó Cuív. In *Celtica*, xiv (1981), pp 83–104. 1467–8.

Fragmentary annals from the west of Ireland. Ed. E. J. Gwynn. In *R.I.A. Proc.*, xxxvii (1925–7), sect. C, no. 8, pp 149–57.

Froissart, Jean. *Chronicles*. Ed. and trans. John Jolliffe. London, [1967].

—— *Oeuvres*. Ed. J. M. B. C. Kervyn de Lettenhove. 25 vols. Bruxelles, 1867–77; reprint, Osnabrück, 1967.

Gervase of Canterbury. *Historical works*. Ed. William Stubbs. 2 vols. London, 1879–80. (Rolls Series, [lxxiii]); reprint, [Nendeln], 1965.
Vol. i: *Chronicle of the reigns of Stephen, Henry II, and Richard I.*

Gesta Henrici quinti: the deeds of Henry the fifth. Ed. Frank Taylor and J. S. Roskell. Oxford, 1975. (Oxford Medieval Texts.)

—— *Henrici Quinti Angliae regis gesta . . . ab anno* MCCCCXIV *ad* MCCCCXXII. Ed. Benjamin Williams. English Historical Society, London, 1850; reprint, [Nendeln?, 1964?].

Gesta regis Henrici secundi Benedicti abbatis: the chronicle of the reigns of Henry II and Richard I, A.D. 1169—1192, known commonly under the name of Benedict of Peterborough. Ed. William Stubbs. 2 vols. London, 1867. (Rolls Series, xlix); reprint, [Nendeln?, 1965?].

Giraldus Cambrensis. *Expugnatio Hibernica: the conquest of Ireland*. Ed. A. B. Scott and F. X. Martin. Dublin, 1978. (A New History of Ireland. Ancillary Publications, iii.)
See also *The English conquest of Ireland*, above, and sect. III B 2, below.

—— *Historical works . . .* Trans. Sir R. C. Hoare. Ed. Thomas Wright. London, 1863. (Bohn's Antiquarian Library); reprint, New York, [1968].

Grace, Jacobus. *Annales Hiberniae*. Ed. and trans. Richard Butler. Ir. Arch. Soc., Dublin, 1842.

Hanmer. *The chronicle of Ireland*. Collected by Meredith Hanmer, 1571. Dublin, 1633; reprinted in *Anc. Ir. hist.* (ed. James Ware, Dublin, 1809; reprint, Port Washington, London, 1970), ii.
To 1284. Continued by Henry of Marlborough, see below.

Henry of Marlborough. Chronicle of Ireland. Trans. James Ware. In *Historie of Ireland* (ed. James Ware, Dublin, 1633), iii, 207–23; reprinted in *Anc. Ir. hist.* (ed. James Ware, Dublin, 1809, reprint, Port Washington, London, 1970), ii, 1–32.
1285–1421.

Histoire des ducs de Normandie et des rois d'Angleterre. Ed. Francisque-Michel. Paris, 1840. (Société de l'Histoire de France, [xviii]); reprint, 1965.

Incerti scriptoris chronicon angliae de regnis trium regum Lancastrensium: Henrici IV, Henrici V et Henrici VI, [1399—1455]. Ed. J. A. Giles. London, 1848.

John of Glastonbury. *Chronica sive historia de rebus Glastoniensibus*. Ed. Thomas Hearne. 2 vols. Oxford, 1726.

The Kilkenny chronicle in Cotton MS. Vespasian B XI. Ed. Robin Flower. In *Anal. Hib.*, no. 2 (1931), pp 330–40.

Late medieval Irish annals: two fragments. Ed. K. W. Nicholls. In *Peritia*, ii (1983), pp 87–102.
Includes 'The annals of Duisk' [1167–1533] (pp 92–102).

Limerick, Killaloe, and Kells, 1194–1250. Ed. and trans. Anne O'Sullivan. In *Éigse*, xvii (1977–9), pp 451–5.
Annalistic entries from T.C.D., MS 1309.

Loftus. The annals of Dudley Loftus. By N. B. White. In *Anal. Hib.*, no. 10 (1941), pp 223–38.
1100–1643. Extracts, pp 231–8.

MacCraith, Seán Mac Ruaidhrí. *Caithréim Thoirdhealbhaigh*. Ed. and trans. S. H. O'Grady. 2 vols. London, 1929. (Ir. Texts Soc., xxvi–xxvii.)

Major, John. *Historia majoris Britanniae*. Paris, 1521.

Marlborough, Marleburrough. See Henry of Marlborough.

Miscellaneous Irish annals (A.D. 1114—1437). Ed. Séamus Ó hInnse. Institute for Advanced Studies, Dublin, 1947.

Monstrelet, Enguerrand de. *Chronicles*. Trans. Thomas Johnes. 5 vols and 4 vols. Hafod, 1809; reprints, 13 vols, London, 1810; 2 vols, London, 1840; 1867.

Murimuth, Adam. *Adae Murimuth continuatio chronicarum*. Ed. E. M. Thompson. London, 1889. (Rolls Series, xciii); reprint, Nendeln, 1965.

Paris, Matthew. *Chronica majora*. Ed. H. R. Luard. 7 vols. London, 1872–83. (Rolls Series, [lvii]); reprint, [Nendeln?], 1964.

—— *Chronicles of Matthew Paris: monastic life in the thirteenth century*. Ed. and trans. Richard Vaughan. Gloucester, New York, 1984.

Ricart, Robert. *The maire of Bristowe is Kalendar*. Ed. Lucy Toulmin Smith. London, 1872. (Camden Society, New Series, v.)

Roger of Howden. *Chronica*. Ed. William Stubbs. 4 vols. London, 1868–71. (Rolls Series, [li]); reprint, [Nendeln], 1964.

Roger of Wendover. *Chronica, sive, Flores historiarum*. Ed. H. O. Coxe. 4 vols. English Historical Society, London, 1841–2; reprint, [Nendeln, 1964].

—— *Liber qui dicitur Flores historiarum: The flowers of history*. Ed. G. Hewlett. 3 vols. London, 1886–9. (Rolls Series, [lxxxiv]); reprint, [Nendeln?], 1965.

Sigeberti Gemblacensis Chronographia. Ed. L. C. Bethmann. In *Monumenta Germaniae Historica, Scriptores*, vi (Hannover, 1844; reprint, Stuttgart, 1980), pp 268–535.

Includes 'Auctarium Aquicinense, [651–1167]' (pp 392–8), 'Auctarium Affligemense, [597, 1005–1163]' (pp 398–405).

Stanihurst, Richard. *De rebus in Hibernia gestis*. Antwerp, 1584; reprint in Raphael Holinshed, *Chronicles* (ed. John Hooker and others, London, 1587), ii, pp 9–45, 82–106; part trans. as 'On Ireland's past' in Colm Lennon, *Richard Stanihurst the Dubliner, 1547–1618: a biography* (Blackrock, 1981), pp 131–60.

Torigni, Robert de. *Chronique, A.D. 94—1186*. Ed. Léopold Delisle. 2 vols. Société de l'histoire de Normandie, Rouen, 1872–3. Ed. Richard Howlett. London, 1889 (Rolls Series, [lxxxii]: Chronicles of the reigns of Stephen, Henry II, and Richard I, iv); reprint, [Nendeln], 1964.

Twelfth- and thirteenth-century Irish annals in Vienna. Ed. Dagmar Ó Riain-Raedel. In *Peritia*, ii (1983), pp 127–36.

Two old Drogheda chronicles. Ed. Diarmuid Mac Iomhair. In *Louth Arch. Soc. Jn.*, xv (1961–4), pp 88–95.

Vergil, Polydore. *The Anglica historia . . . A.D. 1485—1537*. Ed. and trans. Denys Hay. London, 1950. (Camden 3rd Ser., lxxiv.)

Walsingham, Thomas. *Historia Anglicana, 1272—[1422]*. Ed. H. T. Riley. 2 vols. London, 1863–4. (Rolls Series, [xxviii]: Chronica Monasterii S. Albani, i–ii); reprint, [Nendeln?], 1965.

Walter of Coventry. *Memoriale...: the historical collections of Walter of Coventry*. Ed. William Stubbs. London, 1872–3. (Rolls Series, [lviii]); reprint, [Wiesbaden, 1965?]).

Includes annals of Barnewell priory, 1202–25 (vol. ii, 196–279).

Whethamstede, John. *Registrum abbatiae Johannis Whethamstede*. Ed. H. T. Riley. London, 1872. (Rolls Series, [xxviii]: Chronica Monasterii S. Albani, [x]: Registra quorundam Abbatum Monasterii S. Albani qui Saeculo XVmo Floruere, i); reprint, Nendeln, 1965.

William of Malmesbury. *De gestis regum Anglorum libri quinque. Historiae novellae libri tres*. Ed. William Stubbs. 2 vols. London, 1887–9. (Rolls Series, [xc]); reprint, [Nendeln], 1964.

William of Newburgh. *Historia rerum Anglicarum*. Ed. Richard Howlett. In *Chronicles of the reigns of Stephen, Henry II and Richard I* (London, 1884–5, Rolls Series, [lxxxii]; reprint, [Nendeln], 1964), i–ii, pp 1–500.

2 OTHER CONTEMPORARY WRITING

Official communications and correspondence of churchmen are listed in sect. III A 5.

Agallamh na Seanórach. Ed. Nessa Ní Shéaghdha. 3 vols. Dublin, 1942–5. (Leabhair ó Láimhsgríbhnibh, vii, x, xv.)

An ancient Norman-French poem on the erection of the walls of New Ross in Ireland, A.D. 1265. Ed. Frederic Madden. In *Archaeologia*, xxii (1829), pp 307–22.

Armed forces of the Irish chiefs in the early 16th century. Ed. Liam Price. In *R.S.A.I. Jn.*, lxii (1932), pp 201–7.

Dated 1480s by K. W. Nicholls in *N.H.I.*, iii, 32.

Barbour, John. *The Bruce*. Ed. W. M. Mackenzie. London, 1909. Ed. W. W. Skeat. 2 vols in 4. London, 1870–89. (Publications of the Early English Text Society, Extra Series, xi, xxi, xxix, lv); reprints, 2 vols, Edinburgh, 1894. (Publications of the Scottish Text Society, xxxi–xxxii); Edinburgh, 1904; London, 1968.

Bernard of Clairvaux. *Vita S. Malachiae*. Ed. Aubrey Gwynn. In *Sancti Bernardi Opera* (ed. Jean Leclercq, C. H. Talbot, H. M. Rochais, Rome, 1957–), iii (1963), pp 295–378; trans. as *Life of St Malachy of Armagh*. Ed. H. J. Lawlor. London, 1920.

Betha Mhuire Eigiptacdha. Ed. and trans. A. M. Freeman. In *Études Celt.*, i (1936), pp 78–113.

Boek van der Bedroffenisse Marien. Magdeburg, 1486.

The Book of Ballymote. Ed. Robert Atkinson. R.I.A., Dublin, 1887.

The Book of Lecan. Leabhar Mór Mhic Fhir Bhisigh Leacain. Ed. Kathleen Mulchrone. I.M.C., Dublin, 1937. (Facsimiles in collotype of Irish Manuscripts, ii.)

The Book of Leinster, formerly Lebar na Núachongbála. Ed. R. I. Best, Osborn Bergin, and M. A. O'Brien. 5 vols. Dublin, 1954–67.

The Book of Mac Carthaigh Riabhach; otherwise, The Book of Lismore. Ed. R. A. S. Macalister. I.M.C., Dublin, 1950. (Facsimiles in collotype of Irish Manuscripts, v.)

BOOK OF THE DEAN OF LISMORE. *Poems from the Book of the Dean of Lismore, with a catalogue of the book and indexes*. Ed. E. C. Quiggin. Ed. James Fraser. Cambridge, 1937.

The Book of Uí Maine; otherwise called 'The Book of the O'Kellys'. Ed. R. A. S. Macalister. I.M.C., Dublin, 1942. (Facsimiles in collotype of Irish Manuscripts, iv.)

Bracton, Henry de. *De legibus et consuetudinibus Angliae*. Ed. Sir Travers Twiss. 6 vols. London, 1878–83. (Rolls Series, [lxx]); reprint, [Nendeln?], 1964. Ed. G. E. Woodbine. 4 vols. New Haven, 1915–42. (Yale Historical Publications, Manuscripts and Edited Texts, iii.) Ed. and trans. S. E. Thorne. Cambridge, Mass., 1968–76.

Cairt ó Mhaolmhordha Ó Raighilligh, 1558. Ed. Gearóid Mac Niocaill. In *Breifne*, i (1959), pp 134–6.

Carn Fraoich soitheach na saorchlann. Ed. and trans. James Carney. In *Celtica*, ii (1954), pp 154–94.

Ceart Uí Néill. In *Leabhar Cloinne Aodha Buidhe* (ed. Tadhg Ó Donnchadha. I.M.C., Dublin, 1931), pp 41–7. Trans. Myles Dillon. In *Studia Celt.*, i (1966), pp 1–18.

Ceart Uí Néill: a discussion and translation of the document. By Éamon Ó Doibhlin. In *Seanchas Ardmhacha*, v (1969–70), pp 324–58.

Chiericati, Francesco. Francesco Chiericati a Isabella d'Este Gonzaga, 1517. In *Portiola Quattro Documenti d'Inghilterra* (Mantua, 1868); reprint, ed. B. Marsalia. In *Atti del Accademia Olimpica di Vicenza* (1873), pp 80–92.
   Translated in J. P. Mahaffy, 'Two early tours in Ireland' in *Hermathena*, xviii, no. 40 (1914), pp 10–15.

Crichad an Chaoilli: being the topography of ancient Fermoy. Ed. Patrick Power. Cork and London, 1932. (Irish Historical Documents, ii.)

A contemporary narrative of the proceedings against Dame Alice Kyteler, prosecuted for sorcery in 1324 by Richard de Ledrede, bishop of Ossory. Ed. Thomas Wright. London, 1843. (Camden Society, xxiv.)

[Creton, Jean.] Poème sur la déposition de Richard II. In *Chroniques de Froissart*, ed. J. A.

Buchon, xiv (Paris, 1826, Collection des Chroniques Nationales Francaises, xxiv), pp 321–466. Translation of a French metrical history of the deposition of King Richard II. Ed. and trans. John Webb. In *Archaeologia*, xx (1824), pp 1–423.

Croker, T. C. (ed.). *The popular songs of Ireland*. London, 1839.

Dán do Chormac Mág Shamhradháin, easpag Ardachaidh 1444–?1476. Ed. Gearóid Mac Niocaill. In *Seanchas Ardmhacha*, iv (1960–61), pp 141–6.

Durmart le Gallois. *Li romans de Durmart le Galois*. Ed. Edmund Stengel. Tübingen, 1873; *Durmart le Galois: roman arthurien du treizième siècle*. Ed. Joseph Gildea. 2 vols. Villanova, 1965–6.

FITZGERALD. Duanaire Ghearóid Iarla. Ed. Gearóid Mac Niocaill. In *Studia Hib.*, iii (1963), pp 7–59.

Flannacán mac Cellaich rí Breg hoc carmen. Ed. and trans. Kathleen Mulchrone. In *Jn. Celtic Studies*, i (1949–50), pp 80–93.

FORTIBRAS. The Irish version of *Fierabras*. Ed. Whitley Stokes. In *Rev. Celt.*, xix (1898), pp 14–57, 118–67, 252–91, 364–93; xx (1899), p. 212.

Fragments of two mediaeval treatises on horses. Ed. and trans. Brian Ó Cuív. In *Celtica*, ii (1954), pp 30–63.

The genealogies, tribes, and customs of Hy Fiachrach, commonly called O'Dowda's country. Ed. and trans. John O'Donovan. Ir. Arch. Soc., Dublin, 1844.

Giraldus Cambrensis. *Autobiography*. Ed. and trans. H. E. Butler. London, 1937.

—— *Topographia hibernica et Expugnatio hibernica*. Ed. J. F. Dimock. London, 1867. (Rolls Series, [xxi]. Giraldi Cambrensis Opera, v); reprint, [Nendeln?, 1964].

—— Giraldus Cambrensis in Topographia Hibernie: text of the first recension. Ed. J. J. O'Meara. In *R.I.A. Proc.*, lii (1948–50), sect. C, no. 4, pp 113–78. *The first version of the Topography of Ireland*. Trans. J. J. O'Meara. Dundalk, 1951; rev. ed. as *The history and topography of Ireland*. Mountrath, 1982; paperback, Harmondsworth, 1982. (Penguin Classics.)

Heuser, Wilhelm (ed.). *Die Kildare-Gedichte: die ältesten mittelenglischen Denkmäler in Anglo-Irischer Überlieferung*. Bonn, 1904. (Bonner Beiträge zur Anglistik, xiv.)

Histoire de Guillaume le Maréchal. Ed. Paul Meyer. 3 vols. Paris, 1891–1901. (Société de l'Histoire de France, cclv, cclxviii, ccciv.)

The inauguration of O'Conor. Ed. and trans. Myles Dillon. In *Med. Studies presented to A. Gwynn* (1961), pp 186–202.

Innocent III. *An Irish version of Innocent III's De contemptu mundi*. Ed. J. A. Geary. Washington, 1931.

Instructio pie vivendi et superna meditandi. Ed. and trans. John McKechnie. 2 vols. London, 1933–46. (Ir. Texts Soc., xxix.)

An Irish astronomical tract. Ed. and trans. Maura Power. London, 1914. (Ir. Texts Soc., xiv.)

Irish bardic poetry: texts and translations, together with an introductory lecture by Osborn Bergin. Ed. David Greene and Fergus Kelly. Institute for Advanced Studies, Dublin, 1970.

The Irish lives of Guy of Warwick and Bevis of Hampton. Ed. and trans. F. N. Robinson. In *Z.C.P.*, vi (1908), pp 9–180, 273–338, 556.

The Irish versions of the letter of Prester John. Ed. David Greene. In *Celtica*, ii (1954), pp 117–45.

John of Gaddesdon. *Rosa Anglica, seu Rosa medicinae Johannis Anglici: an early modern Irish translation of part of John of Gaddesden's text-book of mediaeval medicine*. Ed. and trans. Winifred Wulff. London, 1929. (Ir. Texts Soc., xxv.)

John of Salisbury. Metalogicus. In his *Opera omnia* (ed. J. A. Giles, 5 vols, Oxford, 1848. Patres Ecclesiae Anglicanae), v, pp 1–207. In *Patrologia Latina* (ed. J. P. Migne, Paris, 1855; reprinted, 1900; Turnhout, *c.* 1967; microcard, Washington, 1960; microfiche, Tumba, 196–?; Zug, 1975?), cxcix, columns 823–946; as *Metalogicon*. Ed. C. C. J. Webb. Oxford, 1929. *Metalogicon*. Trans. Donal D. McGarry. Berkeley, Los Angeles, 1955; reprint, 1962.

'Lacnunga': a magico-medical commonplace book. Ed. J. H. G. Grattan. In John H. G. Grattan and Charles Singer, *Anglo-Saxon magic and medicine* ... (Oxford, 1952), pp 95–205.

Lanfranc. *Opera*. Ed. J. A. Giles. 2 vols. Oxford, 1844. (Patres Ecclesiae Anglicanae.) Opera omnia. In *Patrologia Latina* (ed. J. P. Migne, Paris, 1854; reprint, 1880; Turnhout, *c.* 1967; microcard, Washington, 1960; microfiche, Tumba, 196–?; Zug, 1975?), cl, columns 1–782.

Lapidaries in Irish. Ed. David Greene. In *Celtica*, ii (1954), pp 67–95.

Leabhar Breac, the Speckled Book, otherwise styled Leabhar Mór Dúna Doighre, the Great Book of Dún Doighre. R.I.A., Dublin, 1876.

Le Bouvier, Gilles [*dit* Berry]. *Le livre de la description des pays*. Ed. E. T. Hamy. Paris, 1908. (Recueil de Voyages et de Documents pour servir à l'Histoire de la Géographie depuis le XIIIe Siècle jusqu'à la Fin du XVIe Siècle, xxii.)

Ledrede, Richard. *The Latin hymns of Richard Ledrede*. Ed. Theo Stemmler. Mannheim, 1975. (Poetria Mediaevalis, i.)

—— *The Latin poems of Richard Ledrede*. Ed. Eric Colledge. Pontifical Institute of Medieval Studies, Toronto, 1974. (Studies and Texts, xxx.) From the Red Book of Ossory. See below, Red Book of Ossory, and Rigg, A. G., below, sect. IV B 9.

The libelle of Englyshe polycye: a poem on the use of sea-power, 1436. Ed. Sir George Warner. Oxford, 1926.

Lorgaireacht an tSoidhigh Naomhtha. Ed. and trans. Sheila Falconer. Dublin, 1953.

Mac Con Midhe, Giolla Brighde. [Poem on the battle of Dun (1260). Ed. John O'Donovan.] In *Celtic Soc. Misc.* (1849), pp 145–83.

—— A thirteenth-century poem on Armagh cathedral. Ed. Seán Mac Airt and Tomás Ó Fiaich. In *Seanchas Ardmhacha*, ii (1956–7), pp 145–62.

—— *The poems of Giolla Brighde Mac Con Midhe*. Ed. N. J. A. Williams. [London], 1980. (Ir. Texts Soc., li.)

Mac Craith, Seán Mac Ruaidhrí. *Caithréim Thoirdhealbhaigh*. Ed. S. H. O'Grady. 2 vols. London, 1929. (Ir. Texts Soc., xxvi, xxvii.)

McKenna, Lambert (ed.). *Aithdioghluim dána: a miscellany of Irish bardic poetry*. 2 vols. Dublin, 1939–40. (Ir. Texts Soc., xxxvii, xl.)

McKenna, Lambert (ed.). *Dioghluim dána*. Dublin, 1938.

Magninus of Milan. *Regimen na sláinte: regimen sanitatis*. Ed. Séumas Ó Ceithearnaigh. 3 vols. Dublin, 1942–4. (Leabhair ó Láimhsgríbhnibh, ix, xi, xiii.)

Mahaffy, J. P. (ed.). Two early tours in Ireland. In *Hermathena*, xviii (1914–19), no. 40 (1914), pp 1–16.

Marco Polo. The Gaelic abridgement of the book of Ser Marco Polo. Ed. and trans. Whitley Stokes. In *Z.C.P.*, i (1897), pp 245–73, 362–438.

Maundeville, John. The Gaelic Maundeville. Ed. and trans. Whitley Stokes. In *Z.C.P.*, ii (1899), pp 1–63, 225–312.

A mediaeval handbook of gynaecology and midwifery. Ed. Winifred Wulff. London, 1934. (*Ir. texts*, v.)
    From R.I.A. 23. F. 19, with variants from R.I.A. 24. M. 36 and T.C.D., MS 1436 (E. 4. 1).

A Middle English fragment from the First Book of Kilkenny. Ed. Francis E. Richardson. In *N. & Q.*, ccvii (1962), pp 47–8.
    Religious verse.

The Ó Cianáin miscellany. Ed. James Carney. In *Ériu*, xxi (1969), pp 122–47.

Ó Dálaigh, Áongus Rúadh. O'Conor's house at Cloonfree. Ed. and trans. E. C. Quiggin. In E. C. Quiggin (ed.), *Essays and studies presented to W. Ridgeway* (Cambridge, 1913), pp 333–52.

Ó Dálaigh, Gofraidh Fionn. Filidh Éireann go haointeach: William Ó Ceallaigh's Christmas feast to the poets of Ireland, A.D. 1351. Ed. and trans. Eleanor Knott. In *Ériu*, v (1911), pp 50–69.

—— Historical poems. Ed. Lambert McKenna. In *Ir. Monthly*, xlvii (1919), pp 1–5, 102–7, 166–70, 224–8, 283–6, 341–4, 397–403, 455–9, 509–14, 563–9, 622–6.

—— A poem. Ed. Osborn Bergin. In E. C. Quiggin (ed.), *Essays and studies presented to W. Ridgeway* (Cambridge, 1913), pp 323–32.

Ó Dálaigh, Mathghamhain. A poem for Fínghin Mac Carthaigh Riabhach. Ed. Brian Ó Cuív. In *Celtica*, xv (1983), pp 96–110.

Ó Dálaigh, Muiredhach. A religious poem ascribed to Muiredhach Ó Dálaigh. Ed. William Gillies. In *Studia Celt.*, xiv–xv (1979–80), pp 81–6.

Ó Domhnaill, Maghnus. *Betha Colaim Chille*. Ed. Andrew O'Kelleher and Gertrude Schoepperle. Urbana, 1918. (Univ. of Illinois Bulletin, xv, no. 48.)

Ó hUiginn, Philip. *Philip Bocht Ó hUiginn*. Ed. Lambert McKenna. Dublin, 1931.

Ó hUiginn, Tadhg Dall. *A bhfuil aguinn*. Ed. Eleanor Knott. 2 vols. London, 1920–21 [i.e. 1922–6]. (Ir. Texts Soc., xxii–xxiii.)
    Half-title: Bardic poems.

Peter of Cornwall's account of St Patrick's Purgatory. Ed. Robert Easting. In *Anal. Bolland.*, xcvii (1979), pp 397–416.

A poem composed for Cathal Croibhdhearg Ó Conchubhair. Ed. and trans. Brian Ó Cuív. In *Ériu*, xxxiv (1983), pp 157–74.

Political poems and songs relating to English history, composed during the period from the accession of Edw. III to that of Ric. III. Ed. Thomas Wright. 2 vols. London, 1859–61. (Rolls Series, [xiv]); reprint, [Nendeln?], 1965.

Raymond de Perelhos. *Voyage au purgatoire de St Patrice: visions de Tindal et de St Paul: textes languedociens du quinzième siècle*. Ed. Alfred Jeanroy and Alphonse Vignaux. Toulouse, 1903. (Bibliothèque Méridionale, sér. 1, t. viii.)

Pt i has running title: Voyage de Raimon de Perelhos au purgatoire de Saint Patrice. Trans. in part in J. P. Mahaffy, 'Two early tours in Ireland' in *Hermathena*, xviii, no. 40 (1914), pp 3–9.

Red Book of Ossory. *The lyrics of the Red Book of Ossory*. Ed. R. L. Greene. Oxford, 1974. (Medium Aevum Monographs, new ser., v.)

See also Ledrede, Richard, above, and Rigg, A. G., in sect. IV B 9, below.

Sailing directions for the circumnavigation of England, and for a voyage to the straits of Gibraltar, from a 15th century MS. Ed. James Gairdner. London, 1889. (In Works issued by the Hakluyt Society, lxxix); reprint, New York, [1963?].

Bound with *Tractatus de globis et eorum usu*, but separately paged.

Senchas Fer n-Alban. Ed. and trans. John Bannerman. In *Celtica*, vii (1966), pp 142–62; viii (1968), pp 90–111; ix (1971), pp 217–65.

Senchas Már. *The oldest fragments of the Senchas Már*. Ed. R. I. Best and Rudolf Thurneysen. I.M.C., Dublin, 1931. (Facsimiles in collotype of Irish Manuscripts, i.)

—— *A text on the forms of distraint*. Ed. D. A. Binchy. In *Celtica*, x (1973), pp 72–86.

Extracts from Senchas Már from T.C.D., MS 1337 (H. 3. 18).

The siege of Carrickfergus castle, 1315–16. Ed. G. O. Sayles. In *I.H.S.*, x, no. 37 (Mar. 1956), pp 94–100. (Select Documents, xvii.) Reprint in G. O. Sayles, *Scripta diversa* (London, 1982), pp 212–18.

Smaointe Beatha Chríost.i. innsint Ghaelge a chuir Tomás Gruamdha Ó Bruacháin (fl. c.1450) ar an Meditationes vitae Christi. Ed. Cainneach Ó Maonaigh. Dublin, 1944.

Song of Dermot. *Anglo-Norman poem on the conquest of Ireland by Henry the Second*. Ed. Francisque-Michel, London, 1837. *The song of Dermot and the earl: an Old French poem from the Carew manuscript no. 596 in the archiepiscopal library at Lambeth Palace*. Ed. G. H. Orpen. Oxford, 1892.

Spenser, Edmund. A vewe of the present state of Ireland. In his *Prose works*, ed. Rudolf Gottfried (Baltimore, 1949), pp 39–231. *A view of the present state of Ireland*. Ed. W. L. Renwick. London, 1934; reprint, Oxford, 1970.

Written in 1596 and originally published in *Ancient Irish histories* (1633); see below, p. 879. Also reprinted in *Ireland under Elizabeth and James I*, ed. Henry Morley (London, 1890), pp 35–212.

Stair Ercuil ocus a bás. The life and death of Hercules. Ed. and trans. Gordon Quin. Dublin, 1939. (Ir. Texts Soc., xxxviii.)

The Stowe version of Táin Bó Cuailnge. Ed. Cecile O'Rahilly. Dublin, 1961.

Symon Simeonis. *Itineraria Symonis Simeonis et Willelmi de Worcestre*. Ed. James Nasmith. Cambridge, 1778. *Itinerarium Symonis Semeonis ab Hybernia ad Terram Sanctam*. Ed. Mario Esposito. Institute for Advanced Studies, Dublin, 1960 (Scriptores Latini Hiberniae, iv). Trans. in Eugene Hoade (ed.), *Western pilgrims: the itineraries of Fr Simon Fitzsimons (1322–23) [and others]* (Jerusalem, 1952: Publications of the Studium Biblicum Franciscanum, xviii; reprint, 1970).

Thomas, William. *The pilgrim: a dialogue on the life and actions of King Henry the Eighth*. Ed. Abraham d'Aubant. In his *Works* (London, 1774). Ed. J. A. Froude. London, 1861.

Three medieval poems from Kilkenny. Ed. St J. D. Seymour. In *R.I.A. Proc.*, xli (1932–4), sect. C, no. 8, pp 205–9.

The topographical poems of John O'Dubhagain and Giolla na naomh Ó Huidhrin. Ed. John O'Donovan. Ir. Arch. and Celtic. Soc., Dublin, 1862.

Topographical poems by Seaán Mór Ó Dubhagáin and Giolla-na-naomh Ó'hUidhrín. Ed. James Carney. Dublin, 1943.

The tribes and customs of Hy-Many, commonly called O'Kelly's country. Ed. and trans. John O'Donovan. Ir. Arch. Soc., Dublin, 1843; reprint, Cork, 1976.

Two Irish poems written from the Mediterranean in the thirteenth century. Ed. Gerard Murphy. In *Éigse*, vii (1953–5), pp 71–9.

Two medieval Arabic accounts of Ireland. Ed. David James. In *R.S.A.I. Jn.*, cviii (1978), pp 5–9.

Uí Dhálaigh, Mac Cearbhaill Bhuidhe. A vision concerning Hugh O'Connor (d. 1309). Ed. Peter O'Dwyer. In *Éigse*, v (1945–7), pp 79–91.

Vallancey, Charles. Memoir of the language, manners, and customs of an Anglo-Saxon colony settled in the baronies of Forth and Bargie in the county of Wexford, Ireland, in 1167, 1168, and 1169. In *R.I.A. Trans.*, ii (1787–8), Antiquities, pp 19–41.
Includes text of medieval song with parallel modern translation (pp 36–41).

Vie et miracles de S. Laurent, archevêque de Dublin. Ed. Charles Plummer. In *Anal. Bolland.*, xxxiii (1914), pp 121–86.

The virtues of herbs in the Loscombe manuscript: a contribution to Anglo-Irish language and literature. Ed. Arne Zettersten. Lund, 1967. (Acta Universitatis Lundensis. Sectio i: Theologica, Juridica, Humaniora, v.)
Text of 14th century Anglo-Irish poem by 'John Gardener' from Wellcome Historical Medical Library MS 406.

Vitae sanctorum Hiberniae ex codice olim Salmanticensi nunc Bruxellensi. Ed. W. W. Heist. Brussels, 1965. (Subsidia Hagiographica, xxviii.)

The walling of New Ross: a thirteenth century poem in French. Ed. Hugh Shields. In *Long Room*, xii–xiii (1975–6), pp 24–33.

The Yellow Book of Lecan. Ed. Robert Atkinson. R.I.A., Dublin, 1896.

C SOURCE COMPILATIONS

Ancient Irish histories. [Ed. James Ware.] 2 vols. Dublin, 1633; reprint, 1809; 4 vols in 2. Port Washington, London, 1970. (Kennikat Press Scholarly Reprints. Series in Irish History and Culture.)
Works of Spenser, Campion, Hanmer, and Marlborough. Each work paged separately.

Calendar of documents preserved in France, illustrative of the history of Great Britain and Ireland. Ed. J. H. Round. Vol. i: A.D. 918–1206. P.R.O., London, 1899.
No more published.

Calendar of documents relating to Gaultier from 1250 to 1350 (approx.), from the notebooks of Feardorcha Funnell. In *Decies*, no. 14 (May 1980), pp 61–6. (Medieval Waterford, vi.)

Calendar of documents relating to Ireland . . ., 1171—[1307]. Ed. H. S. Sweetman and G. F. Handcock. 5 vols. P.R.O., London, 1875–86; reprint, Nendeln, 1974.

See also G. J. Hand, 'Material used in "Calendar of documents relating to Ireland"' in *I.H.S.*, xii, no. 46 (Oct. 1960), pp 99–104.

Calendar of documents relating to Scotland preserved in her majesty's public record office, London, 1108—[1509]. Ed. Joseph Bain. 4 vols. Edinburgh, 1881–8.

Cartulaire de l'ancienne estaple de Bruges: recueil de documents concernant le commerce intérieur et maritime, les relations internationales et l'histoire économique de cette ville. Ed. L. Gilliodts-van Severen. 4 vols. Société d'Émulation de Bruges, Bruges, 1904–6. (Recueil de Chroniques, Chartes et Autres Documents concernant l'Histoire et les Antiquités de la Flandre. Format grand in-8°.)

Cartulaire de l'ancien grand Tonlieu de Bruges faisant suite au Cartulaire de l'ancienne Estaple: recueil de documents concernant le commerce intérieur et maritime, les relations internationales et l'histoire économique de cette ville. Ed. L. Gilliodts-van Severen. 2 vols. Société d'Émulation de Bruges, Bruges, 1908–9. (Recueil de Chroniques, Chartes et Autres Documents concernant l'Histoire et les Antiquités de la Flandre. Format grand in-8°.)

Curtis, Edmund. *Richard II in Ireland, 1394—5, and submissions of the Irish chiefs*. Oxford, 1927.

—— and McDowell, R. B. (ed.). *Irish historical documents, 1172—1922*. London, 1943; reprint, 1968.

Dickinson, W. C., Donaldson, Gordon, and Milne, I. A. (ed.). *A source book of Scottish history*. Vol. i: *From the earliest times to 1424*. London, 1952; 2nd ed., 1958.

Diplomatica: unpublished medieval charters and letters relating to Ireland. Ed. M. P. Sheehy. In *Archiv. Hib.*, xxv (1962), pp 123–35.

Documents illustrative of the history of Scotland . . . 1286—1306. Ed. Joseph Stephenson. 2 vols. Scottish Record Office, Edinburgh, 1870.

Documents on the affairs of Ireland before the king's council. Ed. G. O. Sayles. I.M.C., Dublin, 1979.

Documents on the early stages of the Bruce invasion of Ireland, 1315–1316. Ed. J. R. S. Phillips. In *R.I.A. Proc.*, lxxix (1979), sect. C, no. 11, pp 247–70.

Ellis, Sir Henry (ed.). *Original letters illustrative of English history . . .* 11 vols. London, 1824–46.

[1st ser.], 3 vols., 1824; 2nd ser., 4 vols, 1827; 3rd ser., 4 vols, 1846.

Facsimiles of national manuscripts of Ireland. Ed. J. T. Gilbert. 4 vols. Dublin, 1874–84.

Hansisches Urkundenbuch. Ed. Konstantin Höhlbaum and others. 10 vols. Verein für Hansische Geschichte, Halle, Leipzig, 1876–1938.

Bd vii, Halbbd 2 not published.

Harris, Walter (ed.). *Hibernica, or, some antient pieces relating to Ireland . . .* 2 vols. Dublin, 1747–50; reprint, 1770.

Historic and municipal documents of Ireland, A.D. 1172—1320, from the archives of the city of Dublin, etc. Ed. J. T. Gilbert. London, 1870. (Rolls Series, [liii]); reprint, [Nendeln?], 1964.

Lascelles, Rowley. *Liber munerum publicorum Hiberniae, ab an. 1152 usque ad an. 1827; or, the establishments of Ireland . . . Report*. 7 vols. Rec. Comm. Ire., London, 1824.

See also 'Index to "Liber munerum publicorum Hiberniae"' in *P.R.I. rep. D.K.* 9 (1877), app. 3, pp 21–58.

Letters and papers illustrative of the reigns of Richard III and Henry VII. Ed. James Gairdner. 2 vols. London, 1861–3. (Rolls Series, [xxiv]); reprint, [Nendeln], 1965.

Materials for a history of the reign of Henry VII from original documents preserved in the Public Record Office. Ed. William Campbell. 2 vols. London, 1873–7. (Rolls Series, [lx]); reprint, [Nendeln], 1965.

Materials for the history of the Franciscan province of Ireland, A.D. 1230–1450. Ed. E. B. Fitzmaurice and A. G. Little. Manchester, 1920. (British Society of Franciscan Studies, ix); reprint, Farnborough, 1966.

Materials for the history of Thomas à Becket. Ed. J. C. Robertson and J. B. Sheppard. 7 vols. London, 1875–85. (Rolls Series, [lxvii]); reprint, [Nendeln?], 1965.

Maxwell, Constantia (ed.). *Irish history from contemporary sources, 1509–1610*. London, 1923.

Meyer, Kuno (ed.). Mitteilungen aus irischen Handschriften. In *Z.C.P.*, viii (1912), pp 559–65.
 Includes Forfess Fer Fálgae, from B.M. (now B.L.) MS Egerton 1782, f. 19a (pp 564–5).

Nicholls, K. W. (ed.). Inquisitions of 1224 from the miscellanea of the exchequer. Some unpublished Barry charters; a charter of William de Burgo. In *Anal. Hib.*, no. 27 (1972), pp 101–22.

O'Rahilly, T. F. (ed.). *Dánta Grádha: an anthology of Irish love poetry, A.D. 1350–1750*. Pt 1: Text. Dublin, 1916; 2nd ed., Cork, 1926.

Parliamentary texts of the later middle ages. Ed. and trans. Nicholas Pronay and John Taylor. Oxford, 1980.

Pollard, A. F. (ed.). *The reign of Henry VII from contemporary sources*. 3 vols. London, 1913–14. (University of London Historical Series, i.)

Recueil des actes de Henry II, roi d'Angleterre. Ed. Léopold Delisle and Élie Berger. 4 vols. Paris, 1906–27. (Chartes et Diplômes relatifs à l'Histoire de France, [vii].)

Ronan, M. V. (ed.). Some medieval documents. In *R.S.A.I. Jn.*, lxvii (1937), pp 229–41.

Royal and historical letters during the reign of Henry the Fourth... Ed. F. C. Hingeston. 2 vols. London, 1860–1965. (Rolls Series, [xviii]; vol. i reprint, [Nendeln?, 1964].

Royal and other historical letters illustrative of the reign of Henry III, from the originals in the public record office. Ed. W. W. Shirley. 2 vols. London, 1862–6. (Rolls Series, [xxvii]); reprint, [Nendeln?], 1965.

Rymer, Thomas. *Foedera, conventiones, litterae, et cujuscunque generis acta publica, inter reges Angliae et alios quosvis imperatores, reges, pontifices, principes, vel communitates, ab ineunte saeculo duodecimo*. 20 vols. London, 1704–32.

—— *Foedera, conventiones, litterae, et cujuscunque generis acta publica inter reges angliae et alios quosvis imperatores, reges, pontifices, principes, vel communitates ab... 1066 ad nostra usque tempora habita ut tractata*. Ed. Adam Clarke and Frederick Holbrooke. 4 vols in 7. Rec. Comm., London, 1816–69.

—— *Syllabus (in English) of the documents relating to England and other kingdoms contained in the collection known as 'Rymer's Foedera', 1066–[1654]*. By T. D. Hardy. 3 vols. London, 1869–85; reprint, New York, 1974.

Smit, H. J. (ed.). *Bronnen tot de geschiedenis van den handel met Engeland, Schotland en Ierland, 1150—1585*. 2 vols in 4. 's-Gravenhage, 1928–50. (Rijks Geschiedkundige Publicatien, lxv, lxvi, lxxxvi, xci.)

Strongbow's conquest of Ireland. Translations from the works of Gerald de Barri, Roger of Howden [and others] by F. P. Barnard. London, 1888. (English History by Contemporary Writers.)

Smyly, J. C. (ed.). Old deeds in the library of Trinity College, 1246–1538. In *Hermathena*, lxvi (1945), pp 25–39; lxvii (1946), pp 1–30; lxix (1947), pp 31–48; lxx (1947), pp 1–21; lxxi (1948), pp 36–51; lxxii (1948), pp 115–20; lxxiv (1949), pp 60–67.

Theiner, August (ed.). *Vetera monumenta Hibernorum et Scotorum historiam illustrantia*. Rome, 1864; reprint, Osnabrück, 1969.
1216–1547.

University of Oxford. *Munimenta academica; or, documents illustrative of academical life and studies at Oxford*. Ed. Henry Anstey. 2 vols. London, 1868. (Rolls Series, [i]); reprint, [Nendeln], 1964.

Ussher, James (ed.). *Veterum epistolarum Hibernicarum sylloge*. Dublin, 1632; reprints, Paris, 1665; Herborn, 1696; in his *Whole works* (ed. C. R. Elrington, Dublin, 1847), iv, 383–572.

IV SECONDARY WORKS

A GENERAL HISTORY

Bagwell, Richard. *Ireland under the Tudors*. 3 vols. London, 1885–90; reprint, 1963.

Barrow, G. W. S. *The kingdom of the Scots: government, church and society from the eleventh to the fourteenth century*. London, 1973.

Barry, J. G. The Norman invasion of Ireland: a new approach. In *Cork Hist. Soc. Jn.*, lxxv (1970), pp 105–24.

Byrne, F. J. *Irish kings and high-kings*. London, 1973.

Cahill, Edward. Ireland in the Anglo-Norman period, 1170–1540. In *I.E.R.*, 5th ser., xlviii (1936), pp 142–60.

Clanchy, M. T. *England and its rulers, 1066—1272: foreign lordship and national identity*. [Glasgow], 1983. (The Fontana History of England.)

Conway, Agnes. *Henry VII's relations with Scotland and Ireland, 1485—1498. With a chapter on the acts of the Poynings' parliament, 1494—95, by Edmund Curtis*. Cambridge, 1932.

Cosgrove, Art. The Gaelic resurgence and the Geraldine supremacy, c. 1400–1534. In Moody & Martin, *Ir. hist.* (1967; 2nd ed., 1984), pp 158–73.

—— *Late medieval Ireland, 1370–1541*. Dublin, 1981. (Helicon History of Ireland.)

Curtis, Edmund. *A history of mediaeval Ireland from 1110 to 1513*. Dublin, 1923; 2nd ed. as *A history of medieval Ireland from 1086 to 1513*. London, 1938; reprint, 1968.

—— Richard, duke of York, as viceroy of Ireland, 1447–1460. With unpublished materials for his relations with native chiefs. In *R.S.A.I. Jn.*, lxii (1932), pp 158–86.

Davies, Sir John. *A discoverie of the true causes why Ireland was never entirely subdued . . . untill . . . his maiesties happie raigne*. [London], 1612; reprint, Shannon, 1969; and in Henry Morley (ed.), *Ireland under Elizabeth and James I* (London, 1890), pp 213–342.

Davies, R. R. *Historical perception: Celts and Saxons*. Cardiff, 1979. (Inaugural Lectures, University of Wales.)

Davis, H. W. C. *England under the Normans and Angevins*. London, 1905.

Dillon, Myles, and Chadwick, N. K. *The Celtic realms*. London, 1967; 2nd ed., 1972.

Dolley, Michael. *Anglo-Norman Ireland, c.1100—1318*. Dublin, 1972. (Gill History of Ireland, [iii].)

Donaldson, Gordon. *Scottish kings*. London, 1967.

Duncan, A. A. M. *Scotland: the making of the kingdom*. Edinburgh, 1975. (The Edinburgh History of Scotland, i.)

Edwards, Robin Dudley. *Ireland in the age of the Tudors*. London and New York, 1977.

Frame, Robin. *Colonial Ireland, 1169—1369*. Dublin, 1981. (Helicon History of Ireland.)

—— War and peace in the medieval lordship of Ireland. In Lydon, *English in med. Ire.* (1984), pp 118–41.

Gaibrois Riaño de Ballesteros, Mercedes. *Historia del reinado de Sancho IV de Castille*. 3 vols. Madrid, 1922–8.

Gilbert, Sir J. T. *A history of the viceroys of Ireland. With notices of the castle of Dublin and its chief occupants in former times*. Dublin and London, 1865.

Green, V. H. H. *The later Plantagenets: a survey of English history between 1307 and 1485*. London, 1955.

Hennig, John. Medieval Ireland in Cistercian records. In *I.E.R.*, 5th ser., lxxiii (1950), pp 226–42.

Jacob, E. R. *The fifteenth century, 1399—1485*. Oxford, 1961. (The Oxford History of England, vi.)

Keating, Geoffrey. *Foras feasa ar Eirinn. The history of Ireland*. Ed. and trans. David Comyn and P. S. Dinneen. 4 vols. London, 1902–14. (Ir. Texts Soc., iv, viii, ix, xv.)

Kerr, D. A. The Gaelic revival: its origins and development. (M.A. thesis, N.U.I. (U.C.D.), 1949.)

Leland, Thomas. *The history of Ireland from the invasion of Henry II*. 3 vols. Dublin, 1773; 3rd ed., 1774; reprint, 1814.

Lloyd, Sir J. E. *A history of Wales from the earliest times to the Edwardian conquest*. 2 vols. London, 1911; 3rd ed., 1939.

Lydon, J. F. *Ireland in the later middle ages*. Dublin, 1973. (Gill History of Ireland, vi.)

—— *The lordship of Ireland in the middle ages*. Dublin and London, 1972.

—— The medieval English colony, c. 1300–c. 1400. In Moody & Martin, *Ir. hist.* (1967), pp 144–57; revised version as 'The medieval English colony (13th and 14th centuries)' in *Ir. hist.* (2nd ed., 1984), pp 144–57.

McKisack, May. *The fourteenth century, 1307—1399*. Oxford, 1959. (The Oxford History of England, v.)

MacNeill, Eoin. *Phases of Irish history*. Dublin, 1919; reprint, 1968.

Martin, F. X. The Anglo-Norman invasion, 1169–c. 1300. In Moody & Martin, *Ir. hist.* (1967), pp 123–43; revised version as 'The Normans: arrival and settlement, 1169–c. 1300' in *Ir. hist.* (2nd ed., 1984), pp 123–43.

Martin, F. X. *No hero in the house: Diarmait Mac Murchada and the coming of the Normans to Ireland*. Dublin, [1976]. (O'Donnell Lecture, xix, 1975.)

Neville, Grace. Franco-Irish relations in the later middle ages. In *Études Irlandaises*, v (1980), pp 55–61.

Nicholls, K. W. Anglo-French Ireland and after. In *Peritia*, i (1982), pp 370–403.

Nicholson, R. G. *Scotland: the later middle ages*. Edinburgh, 1974. (Edinburgh History of Scotland, ii.)

Ó Corráin, Donncha. *Ireland before the Normans*. Dublin and London, 1972. (Gill History of Ireland, ii.)

O'Doherty, J. F. The Anglo-Norman invasion, 1167–71. In *I.H.S.*, i, no. 2 (Sept. 1938), pp 154–7. (Historical Revision, iii.)

O'Rahilly, Cecile. *Ireland and Wales: their historical and literary relations*. London, 1924.

Orpen, G. H. The effects of Norman rule in Ireland, 1169–1333. In *A.H.R.*, xix (1913–14), pp 245–56.

—— Ireland, 1315–c. 1485. In *Camb. med. hist.*, viii (1936), pp 450–65.

—— Ireland to 1315. In *Camb. med. hist.*, vii (1932), pp 527–47.

—— *Ireland under the Normans, 1169–1333*. 4 vols. Oxford, 1911–20; reprint, 1968.

Otway-Ruthven, A. J. *A history of medieval Ireland. With an introduction by Kathleen Hughes*. London, 1968; 2nd ed., London and New York, 1980.
Reviewed by F. X. Martin in *Studia Hib.*, xiv (1974), pp 143–60.

Poole, A. L. *From Domesday Book to Magna Carta, 1087–1216*. Oxford, 1951. (The Oxford History of England, iii); 2nd ed., 1955.

Powicke, Sir F. M. *The thirteenth century, 1216–1307*. Oxford, 1953. (The Oxford History of England, iv); 2nd ed., 1962.

Quinn, D. B. Henry VIII and Ireland, 1509–34. In *I.H.S.*, xii, no. 48 (Sept. 1961), pp 318–44. (Historical Revision, xiii.)

Ramsay, Sir J. H. *The genesis of Lancaster . . . 1307–99*. 2 vols. Oxford, 1913. (Scholar's History of England, v–vi.)

Richardson, H. G. Norman Ireland in 1212. In *I.H.S.*, iii, no. 10 (Sept. 1942), pp 144–58.

Richey, A. G. *A short history of the Irish people down to the date of the plantation of Ulster*. Ed. R. R. Kane. Dublin and London, 1887.

Richter, Michael. *Irland im Mittelalter: Kultur und Geschichte*. Stuttgart, 1983.

Roche, Richard. *The Norman invasion of Ireland*. Tralee, 1970.

Sheehy, M. P. *When the Normans came to Ireland*. Cork, 1975.

Tuck, Anthony. *Richard II and the English nobility*. London, 1973.

Warren, W. L. *Henry II*. London, 1973.

—— The interpretation of twelfth-century Irish history. In *Hist. Studies*, vii (1969), pp 1–19.

—— *King John*. London, 1961; 2nd ed., 1966.
See also sect. B 1 below.

Williams, A. H. *An introduction to the history of Wales*. Vol. ii, pt i: *The middle ages, 1063–1284*. Cardiff, 1948.

Young, J. I. A note on the Norse occupation of Ireland. In *History*, new ser., xxxv (1950), pp 11-33.

B SPECIAL FIELDS AND TOPICS

I POLITICAL HISTORY

Balfour-Melville, E. W. M. *James I, king of Scots, 1406–37*. London, 1936.

Barrow, G. W. S. *Robert Bruce and the community of the realm in Scotland*. London, 1965; 2nd ed., Edinburgh, 1976.

Bradshaw, Brendan. Cromwellian reform and the origins of the Kildare rebellion, 1533–34. In *R. Hist. Soc. Trans.*, 5th ser., xxvii (1977), pp 69–93.

Duncan, A. A. M. *The nation of Scots and the Declaration of Arbroath*. London, 1970. (Historical Association Pamphlets. General Series, no. 75.)

Ellis, S. G. Henry VII and Ireland, 1491–1496. In Lydon, *Eng. & Ire.* (1981), pp 237–54.

—— The Kildare rebellion and the early Henrician reformation. In *Hist. Jn.*, xix (1976), pp 807–30.

—— Thomas Cromwell and Ireland, 1532–40. In *Hist. Jn.*, xxiii (1980), pp 497–519.

—— *Tudor Ireland: crown, community and the conflict of cultures, 1470–1603*. London and New York, 1985.

—— Tudor policy and the Kildare ascendancy in the lordship of Ireland, 1496–1534. In *I.H.S.*, xx, no. 79 (Mar. 1977), pp 235–71.

Fergusson, Sir James. *The Declaration of Arbroath*. Edinburgh, 1970.

Flanagan, Marie-Thérèse. Strongbow, Henry II and Anglo-Norman intervention in Ireland. In John C. Holt and John Gillingham (ed.), *War and government in the middle ages: essays in honour of J. O. Prestwich* (Woodbridge, New York, 1984), pp 62–77.

Frame, Robin. The Dublin government and Gaelic Ireland in the late thirteenth and fourteenth centuries. (Ph.D. thesis, University of Dublin, 1971.)

—— *English lordship in Ireland, 1318–1361*. Oxford, 1982.

—— English officials and Irish chiefs in the fourteenth century. In *E.H.R.*, xc (1975), pp 748–77.

—— English policies and Anglo-Irish attitudes in the crisis of 1341–1342. In Lydon, *Eng. & Ire.* (1981), pp 86–103.

—— The justiciarship of Ralph Ufford: warfare and politics in fourteenth-century Ireland. In *Studia Hib.*, xiii (1973), pp 7–47.

—— Power and society in the lordship of Ireland, 1272–1377. In *Past & Present*, no. 76 (Aug. 1977), pp 3–33.

Griffith, M. C. The Talbot–Ormond struggle for control of the Anglo-Irish government, 1414–47. In *I.H.S.*, no. 8 (Sept. 1941), pp 376–97.

Griffiths, R. A. *The reign of King Henry VI: the exercise of royal authority, 1422–1461*. London, 1981.

—— Duke Richard of York's intentions in 1450 and the origins of the Wars of the Roses. In *Journal of Medieval History*, i (1975), pp 187–209.

Harbison, Sheila. William of Windsor, the court party and the administration of Ireland. In Lydon, *Eng. & Ire.* (1981), pp 153–74.

Johnston, Dorothy. The interim years: Richard II and Ireland, 1395–1399. In Lydon, *Eng. & Ire.* (1981), pp 175–95.

—— Richard II and the submissions of Gaelic Ireland. In *I.H.S.*, xxii, no. 85 (Mar. 1980), pp 1–20.

—— Richard II's departure from Ireland, July 1399. In *E.H.R.*, xcviii (1983), pp 785–805.

Norgate, Kate. The bull *Laudabiliter*. In *E.H.R.*, vii (1893), pp 18–52.

O'Doherty, J. F. Rome and the Anglo-Norman invasion of Ireland. In *I.E.R.*, 5th ser., xlii (1933), pp 131–45.

O'Toole, Edward. Art Mac Murrough and Richard II. In *Kildare Arch. Soc. Jn.*, xi (1930–33), pp 10–23.

Otway-Ruthven, A. J. Ireland in the 1350s: Sir Thomas de Rokeby and his successors. In *R.S.A.I. Jn.*, xcvii (1967), pp 47–59.

Phillips, J. R. S. The mission of John de Hothum to Ireland, 1315–1316. In Lydon, *Eng. & Ire.* (1981), pp 62–85.

Piveronus, P. J. The Desmond imperial alliance of 1529: its effect on Henry VIII's policy toward Ireland. In *Eire-Ireland*, x (1975), no. 2, pp 19–31.

Prestwich, Michael. *War, politics and finance under Edward I*. London, 1972.

Quinn, D. B. *The Elizabethans and the Irish*. Ithaca, 1966. (Folger Monographs on Tudor and Stuart Civilization.)

Richter, Michael. The first century of Anglo-Irish relations. In *History*, lix (1974), pp 195–210.

Roberts, Glyn. Wales and England: antipathy and sympathy, 1282–1485. In *Welsh Hist. Rev.*, i (1963), pp 375–96.

Sheehy, M. P. The bull *Laudabiliter*: a problem in medieval diplomatique and history. In *Galway Arch. Soc. Jn.*, xxix (1960–61), pp 45–70.

Tuck, Anthony. *Anglo-Irish relations, 1382–1393*. In *R.I.A. Proc.*, lxix (1970), sect. C, no. 2, pp 15–31.

Warren, W. L. John in Ireland, 1185. In *Essays presented to M. Roberts* (1976), pp 11–23.

—— King John and Ireland. In Lydon, *Eng. & Ire.* (1981), pp 26–42.

Watt, J. A. Laudabiliter in medieval diplomacy and propaganda. In *I.E.R.*, 5th ser., lxxxvii (1957), pp 420–32.

2 CONSTITUTIONAL AND ADMINISTRATIVE HISTORY

Baldwin, J. F. *The king's council in England during the middle ages*. Oxford, 1913.

Ball, F. E. *The judges in Ireland, 1221–1921*. 2 vols. London, 1926; New York, 1927.

Bateson, Mary. The laws of Breteuil. In *E.H.R.*, xv (1900), pp 73–8, 302–18, 496–523, 754–7; xvi (1901), pp 92–110, 332–45.

Betham, Sir William. *Dignities, feudal and parliamentary, and the constitutional legislature of the United Kingdom: the nature and functions of the aula regis, the magna concilia, and the communia concilia of England, and the history of the parliaments of France, England, Scotland, and Ireland, investigated and considered with a view to ascertain the origin, progress and final establishment of legislative parliaments and of the history of a peer or lord of parliament*. Vol. i. Dublin and London, 1830.

No more published. Chapters x–xiii (pp 225–379) deal with Ireland to 1485. Revised ed. as *The origin and history of the constitution of England and of the early parliaments of Ireland* (Dublin, London, and Edinburgh, 1834).

Binchy, D. A. Ancient Irish law. In *Ir. Jurist*, new ser., i (1966), pp 84–92.

—— *Celtic and Anglo-Saxon kingship*. Oxford, 1970. (O'Donnell Lecture, 1967–8.)

—— Distraint in Irish law. In *Celtica*, x (1973), pp 22–71.

—— The linguistic and historical value of the Irish law tracts. In *Brit. Acad. Proc.*, xxix (1943), pp 195–227. (The Sir John Rhŷs Memorial Lecture, 1943.)

—— MacNeill's study of the ancient Irish laws. In F. X. Martin and F. J. Byrne (ed.), *The scholar revolutionary: Eoin MacNeill, 1867–1945, and the making of the new Ireland* (Shannon, 1973), pp 37–48.

Bradshaw, Brendan. The beginnings of modern Ireland. In Brian Farrell (ed.), *The Irish parliamentary tradition* (Dublin, 1973), pp 68–87.

—— *The Irish constitutional revolution of the sixteenth century*. Cambridge, 1979.

Brand, Paul. Ireland and the literature of the early common law. In *Ir. Jurist*, new ser., xvi (1981), pp 95–113.

Brynmor-Jones, Sir David. The Brehon laws and their relation to the ancient Welsh institutes. In *Cymmrod. Soc. Trans.*, 1904–5, pp 7–36.

—— Foreign elements in Welsh medieval law. In *Cymmrod. Soc. Trans.*, 1916–17, pp 1–51.
Pt 1 only. No more published.

Cam, H. M. The evolution of the medieval English franchise. In *Speculum*, xxxii (1957), pp 427–42; reprint in her *Law-finders and law-makers* (London, 1962), pp 22–43.

Chrimes, S. B. *An introduction to the administrative history of mediaeval England*. Oxford, 1959. (Studies in Mediaeval History, vii.)

Clarke, M. V. *Medieval representation and consent: a study of early parliaments in England and Ireland*. London, 1936.

Cosgrove, Art. A century of decline. In Brian Farrell (ed.), *The Irish parliamentary tradition* (Dublin, 1973), pp 57–67.

—— Parliament and the Anglo-Irish community: the declaration of 1460. In *Hist. Stud.*, xiv (1983), pp 25–41.

Curtis, Edmund. The acts of the Drogheda parliament, 1494–5, or 'Poynings' laws'. In Agnes Conway, *Henry VII's relations with Scotland and Ireland* (Cambridge, 1932), pp 118–43.
Appendices contain a list of chapters and selected transcripts (pp 201–19).

Davies, R. R. Lordship or colony? In Lydon, *English in med. Ire.* (1984), pp 142–60.

Edwards, Sir J. G. The Normans and the Welsh March. In *Brit. Acad. Proc.*, xlii (1956), pp 155–77.

Edwards, Robin Dudley. 'Magna Carta Hiberniae.' In *Féil-sgríbhinn Eóin Mhic Néill* (1940), pp 307–18.

—— and Moody, T. W. The history of Poynings' law. Pt 1: 1494–1615. In *I.H.S.*, ii, no. 8 (Sept. 1941), pp 415–24. (Historical Revision, iv.)

Ellis, A. G. The destruction of the liberties: some further evidence. In *I.H.R. Bull.*, liv (1981), pp 150–61.

Ellis, S. G. Parliament and community in Yorkist and Tudor Ireland. In *Hist. Studies*, xiv (1983), pp 43–68.

—— Parliaments and great councils, 1483–99: addenda et corrigenda. In *Anal. Hib.*, no. 29 (1980), pp 96–111.

—— Privy seals of chief governors in Ireland, 1392–1560. In *I.H.R. Bull.*, li (1978), pp 187–94.

—— The struggle for control of the Irish mint, 1460–*c.*1506. In *R.I.A. Proc.*, lxxviii (1978), sect. C, no. 2, pp 17–36.

Eyton, R. W. *Court, household and itinerary of King Henry II*. London, 1878.

Frame, Robin. The immediate effect and interpretation of the 1331 ordinance 'Una et eadem lex': some new evidence. In *Ir. Jurist*, new ser., vii (1972), pp 109–14.

—— The judicial powers of the medieval Irish keepers of the peace. In *Ir. Jurist.*, new ser., ii (1967), pp 308–26.

Galbraith, V. H. The Modus tenendi parliamentum. In *Journal of the Warburg and Courtauld Institutes*, xvi (1953), pp 81–99; reprint in his *Kings and chroniclers: essays in English medieval history* (London, 1982).

Gale, Peter. *An inquiry into the ancient corporate system of Ireland and suggestions for its immediate restoration and general extension. With an appendix containing numerous original documents*. London and Dublin, 1834.

Griffiths, R. A. Richard, duke of York, and the royal household in Wales, 1449–50. In *Welsh Hist. Rev.*, viii (1976–7), pp 14–25.

Gwynn, Aubrey. Edward I and the proposed purchase of English law for the Irish, *c.*1276–80. In *R. Hist. Soc. Trans.*, 5th ser., x (1960), pp 111–27.

Hand, G. J. Aspects of alien status in medieval English law, with special reference to Ireland. In Dafydd Jenkins (ed.), *Legal History Studies, 1972: papers presented to the Legal History Conference, Aberystwyth, 18–21 July 1972* (Cardiff, 1975), pp 129–35.

—— The common law in Ireland in the thirteenth and fourteenth centuries: two cases involving Christ Church, Dublin. In *R.S.A.I. Jn.*, xcvii (1967), pp 97–111.

—— English law in Ireland, 1172–1351. In *N.I. Legal Quart.*, xiii (1972), pp 393–422.

—— *English law in Ireland, 1290–1324*. Cambridge, 1967. (Cambridge Studies in English Legal History.)

—— The forgotten statutes of Kilkenny: a brief survey. In *Ir. Jurist*, new ser., i (1966), pp 299–312.

—— Procedure without writ in the court of the justiciar of Ireland. In *R.I.A. Proc.*, lxii (1961–3), sect. C, no. 2, pp 9–20.

—— The status of the native Irish in the lordship of Ireland, 1272–1331. In *Ir. Jurist*, new ser., i (1966), pp 93–115.

Hayes-McCoy, G. A. The making of an O'Neill: a view of the ceremony at Tullaghoge, Co. Tyrone. In *U.J.A.*, 3rd ser., xxxiii (1970), pp 89–94.

Helmholz, R. H. *Marriage litigation in medieval England*. Cambridge, 1974. (Cambridge Studies in English Legal History.)

Holdsworth, W. S. *A history of English law*. Vol. i: *The judicial system*. 7th ed. Ed. A. L. Goodhart and H. G. Hanbury. London, 1956.

Hollister, C. W. *The military organization of Norman England*. Oxford, 1965.

Hooker, John. *Parliaments in Elizabethan England: John Hooker's 'Order and usage'*. Ed. Vernon F. Snow. London, New Haven, 1977.

Hunnisett, R. F. *The medieval English coroner*. Cambridge, 1961. (Cambridge Studies in English Legal History.)

Hurnard, Naomi. The Anglo-Norman franchises. In *E.H.R.*, lxiv (1949), pp 289–327, 433–60.

Johnston, W. J. The first adventure of the common law. In *Law Quart. Rev.*, xxxvi (1920), pp 9–30.

Jolliffe, J. E. A. *Angevin kingship*. London, 1955; 2nd ed., 1963.

—— *The constitutional history of medieval England from the English settlement to 1485*. London, 1937; 3rd ed., 1954.

Lydon, J. F. The Irish church and taxation in the fourteenth century. In *I.E.R.*, 5th ser., ciii (1965), pp 158–65; reprint in *Ir. Cath. Hist. Comm. Proc.*, *1964* (1967), pp 3–10.

—— William of Windsor and the Irish parliament. In *E.H.R.*, lxxx (1965), pp 252–67.

Lynch, William. *The law of election in the ancient cities and towns of Ireland traced from original records. With fac-simile engravings and an appendix of documents*. London, 1831.

—— *A view of the legal institutions, honorary hereditary offices, and feudal baronies established in Ireland during the reign of Henry the Second*. London, 1830.

Mac Niocaill, Gearóid. Aspects of Irish law in the late thirteenth century. In *Hist. Studies*, x (1976), pp 25–42.

—— The contact of Irish and common law. In *N.I. Legal Quart.*, xxiii (1972), pp 16–23.

—— The 'heir designate' in early medieval Ireland. In *Ir. Jurist*, iii (1968), pp 326–9.

—— The interaction of laws. In Lydon, *English in med. Ire.* (1984), pp 105–17.

—— Irish law and the Armagh constitutions of 1297. In *Ir. Jurist*, new ser., vi (1971), pp 339–44.

—— Jetsam, treasure trove, and the lord's share in medieval Ireland. In *Ir. Jurist*, new ser., vi (1971), pp 103–10.

—— Land-tenure in sixteenth-century Thomond: the case of Domhnall Óg Ó Cearnaigh. In *N. Munster Antiq. Jn.*, xvii (1977), pp 43–50.

—— Litigation in later Irish law. In *Ir. Jurist*, new ser., ii (1967), pp 299–307.

—— The origins of the betagh. In *Ir. Jurist*, new ser., i (1966), pp 292–8.

Maitland, F W. The introduction of English law into Ireland. In *E.H.R.*, iv (1889), pp 516–17; reprint in his *Collected papers* (ed. H. A. L. Fisher, Cambridge, 1911), ii, 81–3.
See also Pollock, Frederick, and Maitland, F. W., below.

Martin, F. X. The coming of parliament. In Brian Farrell (ed.), *The Irish parliamentary tradition* (Dublin, 1973), pp 37–56.

Milsom, S. F. C. *The legal framework of English feudalism*. Cambridge, 1976. (Maitland Lectures, 1972.)

Mitchell, James. A reputed decree of Galway corporation, 1518. In *Galway Arch. Soc. Jn.*, xxxiii (1972–3), pp 78–9.

Morris, W. A. *The mediaeval English sheriff to 1300*. Manchester, 1927. (Publications of the University of Manchester, Historical Series, xlvi); reprint, 1969.

Muldoon, James. The remonstrance of the Irish princes and the canon law tradition of the just war. In *Amer. Jn. Legal. Hist.*, xx (1978), pp 309–25.

Murphy, Bryan. The status of the native Irish after 1331. In *Ir. Jurist*, new ser., ii (1967), pp 116–38.

Ó Corráin, Donnchadh. Irish regnal succession: a reappraisal. In *Studia Hib.*, xi (1971), pp 7–39.

—— Nationality and kingship in pre-Norman Ireland. In *Hist. Studies*, xi (1978), pp 1–35.

Otway-Ruthven, A. J. Anglo-Irish shire government in the thirteenth century. In *I.H.S.*, v, no. 17 (Mar. 1946), pp 1–28.

—— The chief governors of mediaeval Ireland. In *R.S.A.I. Jn.*, xcv (1965), pp 227–36.

—— The constitutional position of the great lordships of south Wales. In *R. Hist. Soc. Trans.*, 5th ser., viii (1958), pp 1–20.

—— The mediaeval Irish chancery. In *Album Helen Maud Cam*, ii (1960), pp 119–38.

—— The native Irish and English law in medieval Ireland. In *I.H.S.*, vii (1950–51), pp 1–16.

Owen, Henry. *The administration of English law in Wales and the marches*. London, 1900; reprint with appendices as 'English law in Wales and the marches' in *Y Cymmrodor*, xiv (1901), pp 1–41.

Plucknett, T. F. T. *The legislation of Edward I*. Oxford, 1949; reprint, 1962.

Pollock, Frederick, and Maitland, F. W. *The history of English law before the time of Edward I*. 2 vols. Cambridge, 1895; 2nd ed., 1898; reprint with introduction and bibliography by S. C. F. Milsom, 1968.

Post, Gaines. *Studies in medieval legal thought*. Princeton, 1964.

Powicke, Sir F. M. *King Henry III and the Lord Edward*. 2 vols. Oxford, 1947.

Prestwich, Michael. The Modus tenendi parliamentum. In *Parliamentary History: a yearbook*, i (1982), pp 221–5.

Price, Liam. The origin of the word *betagius*. In *Ériu*, xx (1966), pp 185–90.

Quinn, D. B. Anglo-Irish local government, 1485–1534. In *I.H.S.*, i, no. 4 (Sept. 1939), pp 354–81.

—— The early interpretation of Poynings' law, 1494–1534. In *I.H.S.*, ii, no. 7 (Mar. 1941), pp 241–54. Corrections. In *I.H.S.*, iii, no. 9 (Mar. 1942), pp 106–7.

—— Parliaments and great councils in Ireland, 1461–1568. In *I.H.S.*, iii, no. 9 (Mar. 1942), pp 60–77.

—— Tudor rule in Ireland in the reigns of Henry VII and Henry VIII, with special reference to the Anglo-Irish financial administration. (Ph.D. thesis, University of London, 1934.)

Richardson, H. G. The Irish parliament rolls of the fifteenth century. In *E.H.R.*, lviii (1943), pp 448–61.

—— Magna Carta Hiberniae. In *I.H.S.*, iii, no. 9 (Mar. 1942), pp 31–3. (Historical Revision, v.)

—— Norman Ireland in 1212. In *I.H.S.*, iii, no. 10 (Sept. 1942), pp 144–58.

Richardson, H. G. The Preston exemplification of the Modus tenendi parliamentum. In *I.H.S.*, iii, no. 10 (Sept. 1942), pp 187–92. (Historical Revision, vii.)

—— and Sayles, G. O. *The administration of Ireland, 1172–1377*. I.M.C., Dublin, 1963. 'Introduction' reprinted in *Anal. Hib.*, no. 29 (1980), pp i–x, 1–69.

—— and —— *The governance of medieval England from the Conquest to Magna Carta*. Edinburgh, 1963; reprint, 1974.

—— and —— *The Irish parliament in the middle ages*. Philadelphia and London, 1952. (Études présentées à la Commission Internationale pour l'Histoire des Assemblées d'Etats, x); 2nd ed., 1964.

—— and —— The Irish parliaments of Edward I. In *R.I.A. Proc.*, xxxviii (1928–9), sect. C, no. 6, pp 128–47; reprint in their *The English parliament in the middle ages* (London, 1981), ch. xv.

—— and —— *Parliament in medieval Ireland*. Dublin Historical Association, Dundalk, 1964. (Medieval Irish History Series, i.)

Roderick, A. J. The feudal relation between the English crown and the Welsh princes. In *History*, new ser., xxxvii (1952), pp 201–12.

Sayles, G. O. Modus tenendi parliamentum: Irish or English? In Lydon, *Eng. & Ire.* (1981), pp 122–52; reprint in his *Scripta diversa* (London, 1982), pp 331–60. See also Richardson, H. G., and Sayles, G. O., above.

Simms, Katharine. The legal position of Irishwomen in the later middle ages. In *Ir. Jurist*, new ser., x (1975), pp 96–111.

Stenton, Sir F. M. *The first century of English feudalism, 1066–1166*. Oxford, 1932; 2nd ed., 1961.

Stewart-Brown, Ronald. *The serjeants of the peace in medieval England and Wales*. Manchester, 1936. (Publications of the University of Manchester, ccxlvii. Historical Series, lxxi.)

Studd, J. R. The Lord Edward and King Henry III. In *I.H.R. Bull.*, l (1977), pp 4–19.

de Varebeke, H. J. Abbots in Anglo-Norman parliaments. In *N. Munster Antiq. Jn.*, xv (1972), pp 17–21.

Webb, J. J. *Municipal government in Ireland: mediaeval and modern*. Dublin, 1918.

West, F. J. *The justiciarship in England, 1066–1232*. Cambridge, 1966. (Cambridge Studies in Medieval Life and Thought, new ser., xii.)

Wood, Herbert. The office of chief governor of Ireland, 1172–1509. In *R.I.A. Proc.*, xxxvi (1921–4), sect. C, no. 12, pp 206–38.

—— The titles of the chief governors of Ireland. In *I.H.R. Bull.*, xiii (1935–6), pp 1–8.

—— Two chief governors of Ireland at the same time. In *R.S.A.I. Jn.*, lviii (1928), pp 156–7.

3 *ECCLESIASTICAL HISTORY*

For works on specific localities, including ecclesiastical jurisdictions, see sect. IV B 13 below. For works on individual churchmen, see sect. IV B 16 below.

Archdall, Mervyn. *Monasticon Hibernicum*. Dublin and London, 1786; incomplete revised ed. by P. F. Moran. 2 vols. Dublin, 1873–6.

Backmund, Norbert. *Monasticon Praemonstratense*. 3 vols. Straubing, 1949–56 [i.e. 1949–60].

Barraclough, Geoffrey. *Papal provisions*. Oxford, 1935; reprint, London, 1971.

Barry, J. G. The appointment of coarb and erenach. In *I.E.R.*, 5th ser., xciii (1960), pp 361–5.

—— The coarb and the twelfth-century reform. In *I.E.R.*, 5th ser., lxxxviii (1957), pp 17–25.

—— The coarb in medieval times. In *I.E.R.*, 5th ser., lxxxix (1958), pp 24–35.

—— The distinction between coarb and erenagh. In *I.E.R.*, 5th ser., xciv (1960), pp 90–95.

—— The duties of coarbs and erenaghs. In *I.E.R.*, 5th ser., xciv (1960), pp 211–18.

—— The erenagh in the monastic Irish church. In *I.E.R.*, 5th ser., lxxxix (1958), pp 424–32.

—— The extent of coarb and erenagh in Gaelic Ulster. In *I.E.R.*, 5th ser., xciv (1960), pp 12–16.

—— The lay coarb in medieval times. In *I.E.R.*, 5th ser., xci (1959), pp 27–39.

—— The office and function of coarb and erenagh in the Irish church. (Ph.D. thesis, N.U.I. (U.C.C.), 1952.)

—— Survivals of organisation of the early Irish church in late medieval and early modern Irish society. (M.A. thesis, N.U.I. (U.C.C.), 1949.)

—— The status of coarbs and erenaghs. In *I.E.R.*, 5th ser., xciv (1960), pp 147–53.

Bennett, R. F. *The early Dominicans*. New York, 1937.

Bethell, Denis. English monks and Irish reform in the eleventh and twelfth centuries. In *Hist. Studies*, viii (1971), pp 111–35.

Bradshaw, Brendan. *The dissolution of the religious orders in Ireland under Henry VIII*. Cambridge, 1974.

Brady, W. M. *The episcopal succession in England, Scotland, and Ireland, A.D. 1400 to 1875*. 3 vols. Rome, 1876–7; reprint, with a new introduction by A. F. Allison, Farnborough, 1971.
Vol. ii: *Ireland*.

Breatnach, Pádraig A. *Die Regensburger Schottenlegende, Libellus de fundacione ecclesie Consecrati Petri: Untersuchung und Textausgabe*. München, 1978. (Münchener Beiträge zur Mediävistik und Renaissance-Forschung, xxvii.)

Brooke, Z. N. *The English church and the papacy, from the Conquest to the reign of John*. Cambridge, 1931; reprint, 1969.

Brooks, Eric St John. Irish daughter houses of Glastonbury. In *R.I.A. Proc.*, lvi (1953–4), sect. C, no. 4, pp 287–95.

Buckley, Denis. The church in Ireland in the fifteenth century. iii: Diocesan organization, Cloyne. In *Ir. Cath. Hist. Comm. Proc.*, 1956, pp 8–11.

Burke, Thomas. *Hibernia Dominicana*. Cologne, 1762. *Supplementum*, 1772.

Carville, Geraldine. The Cistercian settlement of Ireland. In *Studia Monastica*, xv (1973), pp 23–41.

Cheney, C. R. A group of related synodal statutes of the thirteenth century. In *Med. studies presented to A. Gwynn* (1961), pp 114–32.

Collins, J. T. Church government in the south of Ireland, A.D. 1471 to 1484. In *Cork Hist. Soc. Jn.*, lxii (1957), pp 14–21.

Colmcille, Fr, see Conway, Colmcille.

Conway, Colmcille. Decline and attempted reform of the Irish Cistercians, 1445–1531. In *Collectanea Ordinis Cisterciensium Reformatorum* (Abbaye des Trappistes, West-malle, Belgium), xviii (1956), pp 290–305; xix (1957), pp 146–62, 371–84.

Cook, G. H. *English monasteries in the middle ages*. London, 1961.

Corish, P. J. The church in Ireland in the fifteenth century. v: Summing up. In *Ir. Cath. Hist. Comm. Proc.*, 1956, pp 14–16.

Cosgrove, Art. Irish episcopal temporalities in the thirteenth century. In *Archiv. Hib.*, xxxii (1974), pp 63–71.

Coulton, G. C. *Scottish abbeys & social life*. Cambridge, 1933. (Cambridge Studies in Medieval Life and Thought.)

Curtis, Edmund. Notes on episcopal succession in Ireland under Richard II. In *R.S.A.I. Jn.*, lvi (1926), pp 82–7.

Dickinson, J. C. *Monastic life in medieval England*. London, 1961.

Dunning, P. J. The Arroasian Order in medieval Ireland. In *I.H.S.*, iv, no. 16 (Sept. 1945), pp 297–315.

—— Irish representatives and Irish ecclesiastical affairs at the Fourth Lateran Council. In *Med. studies presented to A. Gwynn* (1961), pp 90–113.

—— Pope Innocent III and Ireland. (Ph.D. thesis, N.U.I. (U.C.D.), 1960.)

—— Pope Innocent III and the Irish kings. In *Jn. Ecc. Hist.*, viii (1957), pp 17–32.

Edwards, Robin Dudley. The kings of England and papal provisions in fifteenth-century Ireland. In *Med. studies presented to A. Gwynn* (1961), pp 265–80.

Edwards, Ruth Dudley. Ecclesiastical appointments in the province of Tuam. In *Archiv. Hib.*, xxxiii (1975), pp 91–100.

Egan, P. K. The church in Ireland in the fifteenth century. ii: Diocesan organization, Clonfert. In *Ir. Cath. Hist. Comm. Proc.*, 1956, pp 4–8.

Falkiner, C. L. The hospital of St John of Jerusalem in Ireland. In *R.I.A. Proc.*, xxvi (1906–7), sect. C, no. 12, pp 275–317.

Flanagan, J. G. The formative development of the Dominican and Franciscan orders in Ireland, with special reference to the Observant reform. (M.A. thesis, N.U.I. (U.C.C.), 1947.)

Flanagan, Marie-Thérèse. Hiberno-papal relations in the late twelfth century. In *Archiv. Hib.*, xxxiv (1976–7), pp 55–70.

—— Irish monastic charters, 1142–1230. (M.A. thesis, N.U.I. (U.C.D.), 1973.)

Flanagan, U. G. Papal provisions in Ireland, 1305–78. In *Hist. Studies*, iii (1961), pp 92–103.

Flood, W. H. G. The Premonstratensians in Ireland. In *I.E.R.*, 5th ser., ii (1913), pp 624–31.

Gwynn, Aubrey. *Anglo-Irish church life: fourteenth and fifteenth centuries*. Dublin and Sydney, 1968. (Corish, *Ir. catholicism*, ii, fasc. 4.)

—— The centenary of the synod of Kells. In *I.E.R.*, 5th ser., lxxvii (1952), pp 161–76, 250–64.

—— The first bishops of Dublin. In *Reportorium Novum*, i (1955–6), pp 1–26.

—— The first synod of Cashel. In *I.E.R.*, 5th ser., lxvi (1945), pp 81–92; lxvii (1946), pp 109–22.

—— Ireland and the English nation at the Council of Constance. In *R.I.A. Proc.*, xlv (1938–40), sect. C, no. 8, pp 183–233.

—— Lanfranc and the Irish Church. In *I.E.R.*, 5th ser., lviii (1941), pp 1–15.

—— Papal legates in Ireland during the twelfth century. In *I.E.R.*, 5th ser., lxiii (1944), pp 361–70.

—— *The twelfth century reform*. Dublin and Sydney, 1968. (Corish, *Ir. catholicism*, ii, fasc. 1.)

—— and Hadcock, R. N. *Medieval religious houses: Ireland*. London, 1970.

Hadcock, R. N. The order of the Holy Cross in Ireland. In *Med. studies presented to A. Gwynn* (1961), pp 44–53.

Hand, G. J. The church and English law in medieval Ireland. In *Ir. Cath. Hist. Comm. Proc.*, 1959, pp 10–18.

—— *The church in the English lordship, 1216–1307*. Dublin and Sydney, 1968. (Corish, *Ir. catholicism*, ii, fasc. 3.)

—— Medieval cathedral chapters. In *Ir. Cath. Hist. Comm. Proc.*, 1956, pp 11–14.

Hughes, Kathleen. Additional note on the office of St Finnian of Clonard. In *Anal. Bolland.*, lxxv (1957), pp 337–9.

—— *The church in early Irish society*. London, 1966.

—— The offices of S. Finnian of Clonard and S. Cíanán of Duleek. In *Anal. Bolland.*, lxxiii (1955), pp 342–72.

Janauschek, Leopold. *Originum Cisterciensium*. Tomus i. Vienna, 1877. No more published.

King, Robert. *A primer of the history of the holy catholic church in Ireland*. 3rd ed. 2 vols. Dublin, 1845–6; *Supplementary volume*. Dublin, 1851.

Knowles, David. *The monastic order in England: a history of its development . . ., 940–1216*. 2nd ed. Cambridge, 1966.

—— *The religious orders in England*. 3 vols. Cambridge, 1950–59.

Lee, G. A. The leper hospitals of the Upper Shannon area. In *Old Athlone Soc. Jn.*, i (1969–75), pp 222–9.

Lucas, A. T. The plundering and burning of churches in Ireland, 7th to 16th century. In Etienne Rynne (ed.) *North Munster Studies* (Limerick, 1967), pp 172–229.

Lynch, Anthony. Religion in late medieval Ireland. In *Archiv. Hib.*, xxxvi (1981), pp 3–15.

McNeill, T. E. The Premonstratensian houses of Carrickfergus, White Abbey, and Woodburn. In *Peritia*, ii (1983), pp 265–6.

Mac Niocaill, Gearóid. *Na manaigh liatha in Éirinn, 1142–c.1600*. Dublin, 1959.

Martin, F. X. The Augustinian friaries in pre-reformation Ireland. In *Augustiniana*, vi (1956), pp 346–84.

—— The Irish Augustinian reform movement in the fifteenth century. In *Med. studies presented to A. Gwynn* (1961), pp 230–64.

—— The Irish friars and the observant movement in the fifteenth century. In *Ir. Cath. Hist. Comm. Proc.*, 1960, pp 10–16.

Meehan, C. P. *The rise and fall of the Irish Franciscan monasteries*. Dublin and London, 1869; 5th ed., [1877].

Mooney, Canice. *The church in Gaelic Ireland: thirteenth to fifteenth centuries*. Dublin, 1969. (Corish, *Ir. catholicism*, ii, fasc. 5.)

—— Ciníochas agus náisiúnachas san eaglais in Éirinn, 1169–1534. In *Galvia*, x (1964–5), pp 4–17.

—— *The first impact of the reformation*. Dublin and Melbourne, 1967. (Corish, *Ir. catholicism*, iii, fasc. 2.)

—— The Franciscans in Ireland. In *Terminus*, viii (1954), pp 66–9, 84–7, 105–8, 126–8, 150–53, 180–82; ix (1954), pp 193–5; x (1954), pp 226–8, 245–50; xi (1955), pp 5–9, 39–41, 85–9, 128–32; xii (1956), pp 14–17, 40–44; xiii (1956), pp 58–62, 88–92, 105–10, 139–44; xiv (1957), pp 13–17, 24, 28–40, 62–6, 87–9, 112–14.

Mould, D. D. C. P. *The Irish Dominicans*. Dublin, 1957.

Neary, Anne. The origins and character of the Kilkenny witchcraft case of 1324. In *R.I.A. Proc.*, lxxxiii (1983), sect. C, no. 13, pp 333–50.

Ní Catháin, Próinséas. The liturgical background of the Derrynavlan altar service. In *R.S.A.I. Jn.*, cx (1980), pp 127–48.

Nicholls, K. W. Medieval Irish cathedral chapters. In *Archiv. Hib.*, xxxi (1973), pp 102–11.

—— Rectory, vicarage, and parish in the western Irish dioceses. In *R.S.A.I. Jn.*, ci (1971), pp 53–84.

O'Brien, A. F. Episcopal appointments and ecclesiastical gravamina during Prince Edward's lordship of Ireland. (M.A. thesis, N.U.I. (U.C.D.), 1961.)

—— Episcopal elections in Ireland, *c.*1254–72. In *R.I.A. Proc.*, lxxiii (1973), sect. C, no. 5, pp 129–76.

O'Connell, J. The church in Ireland in the fifteenth century. i: Diocesan organization: Kerry. In *Ir. Cath. Hist. Comm. Proc.*, 1956, pp 1–4.

O'Dwyer, B. W. The crisis in the Cistercian monasteries in Ireland in the early thirteenth century. In *Analecta Cisterciensis*, xxxi (1975), pp 267–304; xxxii (1975), pp 3–112.

—— Gaelic monasticism and the Irish Cistercians, *c.*1228. In *I.E.R.*, 5th ser., cviii (1967), pp 19–28; reprint in *Ir. Cath. Hist. Comm. Proc.*, 1965–7 (1968), pp 25–34.

—— The impact of the native Irish on the Cistercians in the thirteenth century. In *Jn. Relig. Hist.*, iv (1967), pp 287–301.

—— The problem of reform in the Irish Cistercian monasteries and the attempted solution of Stephen of Lexington in 1228. In *Jn. Ecc. Hist.*, xv (1964), pp 186–91.

O'Dwyer, Peter. The Carmelite order in pre-Reformation Ireland. In *I.E.R.*, 5th ser., cx (1968), pp 350–63; reprint in *Ir. Cath. Hist. Comm. Proc.*, 1968 (1969), pp 49–62.

O'Sullivan, Benedict. The coming of the friars. In *Ir. Rosary*, lii (1948), pp 165–70, 211–17, 283–8.

—— Medieval Irish Dominican studies. In *Ir. Rosary*, lii (1948), pp 351–6; liii (1949), pp 39–44, 91–7, 154–9, 242–7, 304–9; liv (1950), pp 49–54, 86–92, 169–75, 224–30, 375–81; lv (1951), pp 37–44, 93–9, 167–75, 221–6, 281–6, 373–8; lvi (1952), pp 43–9, 107–12, 163–9, 219–25, 288–93, 356–63; lvii (1953), pp 21–8.

Perroy, Édouard. *L'Angleterre et le grand schisme d'occident*. i: *Étude sur la politique religieuse de l'Angleterre sous Richard II, 1378–1399*. Paris, 1933.

Phillips, W. A. (ed.). *History of the Church of Ireland from the earliest times to the present day*. 3 vols. London, 1933.

Richardson, H. G. Some Norman monastic foundations in Ireland. In *Med. studies presented to A. Gwynn* (1961), pp 29–43.

Seymour, St John D. The coarb in the medieval Irish church, *circa* 1200–1550. In *R.I.A. Proc.*, xli (1932–4), sect. C, no. 10, pp 219–31.

Simms, Katharine. The archbishopric of Armagh and the O'Neills, 1347–1471. In *I.H.S.*, xix, no. 73 (Mar. 1974), pp 38–55.

Stokes, G. T. *Ireland and the Anglo-Norman church*. London, 1889.

Thomson, W. R. *Friars in the cathedral: the first Franciscan bishops, 1226–1261*. Pontifical Institute of Mediaeval Studies, Toronto, 1975. (Studies and Texts, xxxiii.) 'Ireland: the king, the pope, and the friars' (pp 137–48).

Tipton, C. L. The Irish Hospitallers during the great schism. In *R.I.A. Proc.*, lxix (1970), sect. C, no. 3, pp 33–43.

Walsh, Katherine. Archbishop FitzRalph and the friars at the papal court in Avignon, 1357–60. In *Traditio*, xxxi (1975), pp 223–45.

Watt, J. A. *The church and the two nations in medieval Ireland*. Cambridge, 1970. (Cambridge Studies in Medieval Life and Thought, 3rd ser., iii.)

—— *The church in medieval Ireland*. Dublin, 1972. (The Gill History of Ireland, [v].)

—— English law and the Irish church: the reign of Edward I. In *Med. studies presented to A. Gwynn* (1961), pp 133–67.

—— Negotiations between Edward II and John XXII concerning Ireland. In *I.H.S.*, x, no. 37 (Mar. 1956), pp 1–20.

—— The papacy and episcopal appointments in thirteenth-century Ireland. In *Ir. Cath. Hist. Comm. Proc.*, 1959, pp 1–9.

—— The papacy and Ireland in the fifteenth century. In R. B. Dobson (ed.), *The church, politics, and patronage in the fifteenth century* (Gloucester, 1984), pp 133–45.

Williams, Patrick. The papacy and episcopal appointments in Ireland, 1305–34. (M.A. thesis, N.U.I. (U.C.D.), 1961.)

Wood, Herbert. The Templars in Ireland. In *R.I.A. Proc.*, xxvi (1906–7), sect. C, no. 14, pp 327–77.

4 *MILITARY HISTORY*

Armstrong, Olive. *Edward Bruce's invasion of Ireland*. London, 1923.

Butler, George. The battle of Piltown, 1462. In *Ir. Sword*, vi (1963–4), pp 196–212.

Connolly, Philomena. The financing of English expeditions to Ireland, 1361–1376. In Lydon, *Eng. & Ire.* (1981), pp 104–21.

De hÓir, Siobhán. Guns in medieval and Tudor Ireland. In *Ir. Sword*, xv (1982–3), pp 76–88.

Frame, Robin. The Bruces in Ireland, 1315–18. In *I.H.S.*, xix, no. 73 (Mar. 1974), pp 3–37.

Harbison, Peter. Native Irish arms and armour in medieval Gaelic literature, 1170–1600. In *Ir. Sword*, xii (1976), pp 173–99, 270–84.

Hayes-McCoy, G.A. The early history of guns in Ireland. In *Galway Arch. Soc. Jn.*, xviii (1938–9), pp 43–65.

—— The gallóglach axe. In *Galway Arch. Soc. Jn.*, xvii (1936–7), pp 101–21.

—— *Irish battles*. London, 1969.

—— Strategy and tactics in later medieval Ireland: a general survey. In *I.C.H.S. Bull.*, no. 20 (1942), pp 1–3.

Lydon, J. F. The Bruce invasion of Ireland. In *Hist. Studies*, iv (1963), pp 111–25.

—— Edward I, Ireland, and the war in Scotland, 1303–1304. In Lydon, *Eng. & Ire.* (1981), pp 43–61.

—— The hobelar: an Irish contribution to mediaeval warfare. In *Ir. Sword*, ii (1954–6), pp 12–16.

—— Ireland's participation in the military activities of English kings in the thirteenth and early fourteenth century. (Ph.D. thesis, University of London, 1955.)

—— An Irish army in Scotland, 1296. In *Ir. Sword*, v (1961–2), pp 184–90.

—— Irish levies in the Scottish wars, 1296–1302. In *Ir. Sword*, v (1961–2), pp 207–17.

—— Richard II's expeditions to Ireland. In *R.S.A.I. Jn.*, xciii (1963), pp 135–49.

Mac Íomhair, Diarmuid. The battle of Fochart, 1318. In *Ir. Sword*, viii (1967–8), pp 192–209.

—— Bruce's invasion of Ireland and first campaign in County Louth. In *Ir. Sword*, x (1971–2), pp 188–212.

McKerral, Andrew. West Highland mercenaries in Ireland. In *Scot. Hist. Rev.*, xxx (1951), pp 1–14.

MacNeill, Eoin. Military service in medieval Ireland. In *Cork Hist. Soc. Jn.*, xlvi (1941), pp 6–15.

Morris, John E. *The Welsh wars of Edward I*. Oxford, 1901.

Nicholson, R. G. Ireland and the Scottish wars of independence. In *I.C.H.S. Bull.*, new ser., ix (1962–3), nos 96–7, p. 1.

—— An Irish expedition to Scotland in 1335. In *I.H.S.*, xiii, no. 51 (Mar. 1963), pp 197–211.

—— A sequel to Edward Bruce's invasion of Ireland. In *Scot. Hist. Rev.*, xlii, no. 133 (Apr. 1963), pp 30–40.

Ó Domhnaill, Seán. Warfare in sixteenth-century Ireland. In *I.H.S.*, v, no. 17 (Mar. 1946), pp 29–54.

Ó Murchadha, Diarmuid. The battle of Callann, A.D. 1261. In *Cork Hist. Soc. Jn.*, lxvi (1961), pp 105–15.

Orpen, G. H. The battle of Dundonell (Baginbun), A.D. 1170. In *R.S.A.I. Jn.*, xxxiv (1904), pp 354–60.

Otway-Ruthven, A. J. Knight service in Ireland. In *R.S.A.I. Jn.*, lxxxix (1959), pp 1–15.

—— Royal service in Ireland. In *R.S.A.I. Jn.*, xcviii (1968), pp 37–46.

Prince, A. E. The army and navy. In *The English government at work, 1327–36*, i (Cambridge, Mass., 1940), pp 332–93.

—— The strength of English armies in the reign of Edward III. In *E.H.R.*, xlvi (1931), pp 353–71.

Sayles, G. O. The battle of Faughart. In G. A. Hayes-McCoy (ed.), *The Irish at war* (Cork, 1964), pp 23–34; reprint in his *Scripta diversa* (London, 1982), pp 267–75.

Sherborne, J. W. Indentured retinues and English expeditions to France, 1369–1380. In *E.H.R.*, lxxix (1964), pp 718–46.

Simms, Katharine. The battle of Dysart O'Dea and the Gaelic resurgence in Thomond. In *Dal gCais*, v (1979), pp 59–66.

—— Warfare in the medieval Gaelic lordships. In *Ir. Sword*, xii (1975–6), pp 98–108.

Westropp, T. J. The battle of Dysert O'Dea, May 10, 1318. In *Ir. Monthly*, xlvi (1918), pp 365–75.

5 HISTORICAL GEOGRAPHY

Andrews, J. H. A geographer's view of Irish history. In Moody & Martin, *Ir. hist.* (1967; 2nd ed., 1984), pp 17–29.

Beresford, M. W., and Hurst, J. G. (ed.). *Deserted medieval villages*. London, 1971; New York, 1972.
   R. E. Glasscock, 'Ireland' (pp 279–301).

Buchanan, R. H. Field systems of Ireland. In Alan R. H. Baker and Robin A. Butlin (ed.), *Studies of field systems in the British Isles* (Cambridge, 1973), pp 580–618.

Butlin, R. A. Some observations on the field systems of medieval Ireland. In *Geographia Polonia*, xxxviii (1978), pp 31–6.

Darby, H. C. *Domesday England*. Cambridge, 1977.

—— (ed.). *A new historical geography of England*. Cambridge, 1973.
   R. A. Donkin, 'Changes in the early middle ages' (pp 75–135); R. E. Glasscock, 'England *circa* 1334' (pp 136–85); A. R. H. Baker, 'Changes in the later middle ages' (pp 186–247).

Douglas, G. R. See Prior, D. B., Stephens, Nicholas, and Douglas, G. R., below.

Evans, E. E. *The personality of Ireland: habitat, heritage and history*. Cambridge, 1973. (Wiles Lectures.)

Falkiner, C. L. The counties of Ireland: an historical sketch of their origin, constitution, and gradual delimitation. In *R.I.A. Proc.*, xxiv (1902–4), sect. C, no. 11, pp 169–94.

Glasscock, R. E. Moated sites and deserted boroughs and villages: two neglected aspects of Anglo-Norman settlement in Ireland. In Stephens & Glasscock, *Ir. geog. studies* (1970), pp 162–77.

Godwin, Harry. *The history of the British flora: a factual basis for phytogeography*. Cambridge, 1956.
'The special case of Ireland' (pp 345–9).

Graham, B. J. Anglo-Norman settlement in County Meath. In *R.I.A. Proc.*, lxxv (1975), sect. C, no. 11, pp 223–48.

—— The evolution of the settlement pattern of Anglo-Norman Eastmeath. In R. H. Buchanan, R. A. Butlin, Desmond McCourt (ed.), *Fields, farms, and settlement in Europe* (Holywood, 1976), pp 38–47.

—— The evolution of urbanization in medieval Ireland. In *Journal of Historical Geography*, v (1979), pp 111–25.

—— *Medieval Irish settlement: a review*. Lancaster, 1980. (Historical Geography Research Series, iii.)

—— Medieval settlements in County Meath. In *Ríocht na Mídhe*, v, no. 4 (1974), pp 40–59.

—— The settlement pattern of Anglo-Norman Eastmeath, 1170–1660. (Ph.D. thesis, Queen's University, Belfast, 1972.)

—— The towns of medieval Ireland. In R. A. Butlin (ed.), *The development of the Irish town* (London and Totowa, 1977), pp 28–60.

Hadcock, R. N. *[Map of] monastic Ireland*. Ordnance Survey, Dublin, 1960; 2nd ed., 1965.

Hayes-McCoy, G. A. (ed.). *Ulster and other Irish maps, c.1600*. I.M.C., Dublin, 1964.

Hogan, James. The tricha cét and related land-measures. In *R.I.A. Proc.*, xxxviii (1928–9), sect. C, no. 7, pp 148–235.

Hurst, J. G. See Beresford, M. W., and Hurst, J. G., above.

Jäger, Helmut. Land- und Forstwirtschaftliche Bodennutzung im mittelalterlichen Irland. In *Wirtschaftsgeographische Studien*, v (1979), pp 87–107; revised version, trans. Niall Burgess as 'Land use in medieval Ireland: a review of the documentary evidence' in *Ir. Econ. & Soc. Hist.*, x (1983), pp 51–65.

Ladurie, E. le Roy, see Le Roy Ladurie, Emmanuel.

Lamb, H. H. The early medieval warm epoch and its sequel. In *Palaeogeography, Palaeoclimatology, Palaeoecology*, i (1965), pp 13–37.

Leister, Ingeborg. *Peasant openfield farming and its territorial organisation in Co. Tipperary*. Marburg/Lahn, 1976.

Le Roy Ladurie, Emmanuel. *Histoire du climat depuis l'an mil*. Paris, 1967; revised version, translated by Barbara Bray as *Times of feast, times of famine: a history of climate since the year 1000*. New York, 1971; London, 1972.

McCracken, Eileen. *Irish woods since Tudor times: distribution and exploitation*. Newton Abbot, 1971.

Mac Íomhair, Diarmuid. The boundaries of Fir Rois. In *Louth Arch. Soc. Jn.*, xv (1961–4), pp 144–79.

Martin, Geoffrey. Plantation boroughs in medieval Ireland. With a handlist of boroughs to c.1500. In *Hist. Studies*, xiii (1981), pp 23–53.

Mason, W. S. *A statistical account or parochial survey of Ireland*. 3 vols. Dublin, 1814–19.

Ordnance Survey of Ireland. *Dublin c.840–c.1540: the medieval town in the modern city (1:2,500)*. With an introduction by H. B. Clarke. Dublin, 1978.

Orme, A. R. *Ireland*. London, 1970. (The World's Landscape, iv.)

Orpen, G. H. Ptolemy's map of Ireland. In *R.S.A.I. Jn.*, xxiv (1894), pp 115–28.

Prior, D. B., Stephens, Nicholas, and Douglas, G. R. Some examples of mudflow and rockfall activity in north-east Ireland. In *Slopes: form and process* (Institute of British Geographers, London, 1971. Special Publication, no. 3), pp 129–40.

Proudfoot, V. B. Economy and settlement in rural Ireland. In Lloyd Laing (ed.) *Studies in Celtic survival* (Oxford, 1977. British Archaeological Reports, xxxvii), pp 83–106.

Quinn, D. B. *England and the discovery of America, 1481–1620*. London and New York, 1974.

Robinson, Brian. A geography of contradictions: Ireland in Giraldus Cambrensis' 'Topography of Ireland'. In *Ir. Geography*, vii (1974), pp 81–7.

Simms, Anngret. Irland: Überformung eines keltischen Siedlungsraumes am Rande Europas durch externe Kolonisationsbewegungen. In *Gefügemuster der Erdoberfläche: Festschrift zum 42. deutschen Geographentag* (Göttingen, 1979), pp 261–308.

—— Settlement patterns and medieval colonisation in Ireland: an example of Duleek in County Meath. In Pierre Flatrès (ed.) *Paysages ruraux européens* (Rennes, 1979), pp 159–77.

—— Rural settlement in medieval Ireland: the example of the royal manors of Newcastle Lyons and Esker in south County Dublin. In B. K. Roberts and Robin E. Glasscock (ed.) *Villages, fields and frontiers: studies in European rural settlement in the medieval and early modern periods: papers presented at the meeting of the Permanent European Conference for the Study of the Rural Landscape, held at Durham and Cambridge, England, 10–17 September 1981* (Oxford, 1983. BAR. International Series, clxxxv), pp 133–53.

Stephens, Nicholas. See Prior, D. B., Stephens, Nicholas, and Douglas, G. R., above.

Westropp, T. J. Brazil and the legendary islands of the North Atlantic: their history and fable: a contribution to the 'Atlantis' problem. In *R.I.A. Proc.*, xxx (1912–13), sect. C, no. 8, pp 223–60.

—— Early Italian maps of Ireland. In *R.I.A. Proc.*, xxx (1912–13), sect. C, no. 16, pp 361–428.

Williams, P. W. Limestone morphology in Ireland. In Stephens & Glasscock, *Ir. geog. studies* (1970), pp 105–24.

6 TOPOGRAPHY

Camden, William. *Britannia, sive, florentissimorum regnorum Angliae, Scotiae, Hiberniae et insularum adiacentium ex intima antiquitate choreographica descripto*. London, 1586. [2nd ed.], London, 1607; reprint, Hildesheim, New York, 1970. (Anglistica & Americana, lvii); trans. Philemon Holland. 2 vols. London, 1610; rev. ed., 1637; trans. Edmund Gibson. London, 1695; reprint with introduction by Stuart Piggott. Newton Abbot and New York, 1971; 2nd ed., rev. with large additions. 2 vols. London, 1722; 3rd ed., 1753; 4th ed., 1772; trans. and enlarged Richard Gough. 3 vols. London, 1789; 2nd ed. 4 vols, 1806; reprint, Hildesheim, New York, 1974. (Anglistica & Americana, lxxiii.)
Title varies.

Conway, Colmcille. The lands of St Mary's Abbey, Dublin. In *R.I.A. Proc.*, lxii (1961–3), sect. C, no. 3, pp 21–84.

—— The lands of St Mary's Abbey, Dublin, at the dissolution of the abbey: the demesne lands and the grange of Clonliffe. In *Reportorium Novum*, iii (1961–4), pp 94–107.

Hughes, T. J. Town and baile in Irish place-names. In Stephens & Glasscock, *Ir. geog. studies* (1970), pp 244–58.

Hurley, Vincent. The distribution, origins, and development of Temple as a church name in the south-west of Ireland. In *Cork Hist. Soc. Jn.*, lxxxiv (1979), pp 74–94.

Mac Iomhair, Diarmuid. Townlands of County Louth in A.D. 1301. In *Louth Arch. Soc. Jn.*, xvi (1965–8), pp 42–9.

Nicholls, K. W. Some place-names from 'The Red Book of the earls of Kildare'. In *Dinnseanchas*, iii (1968–9), pp 25–37.

Ó Muráile, Nollaig. The barony names of Fermanagh and Monaghan. In *Clogher Rec.*, xi (1982–5), pp 387–402.

Otway-Ruthven, A. J. Two obsolete place-names in Co. Meath. In *Dinnseanchas*, iv (1970–71), p. 7.

Price, Liam. *The place-names of Co. Wicklow.* 7 fascs. Institute for Advanced Studies, Dublin, 1945–67.

Simms, Anngret. Medieval Dublin: a topographical analysis. In *Ir. Geography*, xii (1979), pp 25–41.

Walsh, Paul. *The placenames of Westmeath.* Institute for Advanced Studies, Dublin, 1957.

7 ECONOMIC AND SOCIAL HISTORY

Aalen, F. H. A. Transhumance in the Wicklow mountains. In *Ulster Folklife*, x (1964), pp 65–72.

Azevedo, Pedro de. Comercio anglo-portugûes no meado do sec. XV. In *Boletim de Segunda Classe, Academia das Sciencias de Lisboa*, viii (1913–14).

Bannerman, J. W. M. The lordship of the Isles. In Jennifer M. Brown (ed.), *Scottish society in the fifteenth century* (London, 1977), pp 209–40.

See also J. W. M. Bannerman, 'The lordship of the Isles: historical background' in K. A. Steer and J. W. M. Bannerman, *Late medieval monumental sculpture in the West Highlands* (Royal Commission on the Ancient and Historical Monuments of Scotland, Edinburgh, 1977), pp 201–13; Ronald Williams, *Lords of the Isles: the clan Donald and the early kingdom of the Scots* (London, 1984).

Berardis, Vincenzo. *Italy and Ireland in the middle ages.* Dublin, 1950.

Beresford, M. W. *New towns of the middle ages.* London, 1967.

Bernard, Jacques. The maritime intercourse between Bordeaux and Ireland, *c.* 1450–*c.* 1520. In *Ir. Econ. & Soc. Hist.*, vii (1980), pp 7–21.

—— *Navires et gens de mer à Bordeaux (vers 1400—vers 1550).* 3 vols. Paris, 1968.

Berry, H. F. Proceedings in the matter of the custom called tolboll, 1308 and 1385: St Thomas' abbey v. some early Dublin brewers, &c. In *R.I.A. Proc.*, xxviii (1909–10), sect. C, no. 10, pp 169–73.

—— The records of the Dublin gild of merchants, known as the Gild of the Holy Trinity, 1438–1671. In *R.S.A.I. Jn.*, xxx (1900), pp 44–68.

Bridbury, A. R. *England and the salt trade in the later middle ages*. Oxford, 1955.

Broome, D. M. See Tout, T. F., and Broome, D. M., below.

Burwash, Dorothy. *English merchant shipping, 1460–1540*. Toronto, 1947; reprint, 1969.

Carus-Wilson, E. M. *Medieval merchant venturers*. London, 1954; reprint, 1967.

—— The overseas trade of Bristol. In Eileen Power and M. M. Postan (ed.), *Studies in English trade in the fifteenth century* (London, 1933), pp 183–246.

Childs, W. R. *Anglo-Castilian trade in the later middle ages*. Manchester, 1978.

—— Ireland's trade with England in the later middle ages. In *Ir. Econ. & Soc. Hist.*, ix (1982), pp 5–33.

Clarke, H. B., and Simms, Anngret. Ireland and the comparative study of urban origins in medieval Europe. In *Celtic Cultures Newsletter* (Unesco Project for the Study and Promotion of Celtic Cultures, Dublin), i (1983), pp 32–5.

—— and —— (ed.). *The comparative history of urban origins in non-Roman Europe: Ireland, Wales, Denmark, Germany, Poland, and Russia from the ninth to the thirteenth century*. 2 vols. Oxford, 1985. (BAR, International Series, cclv.)

Conway, Colmcille. Taxation of the Irish Cistercian houses, *c.* 1329–1479. In *Cîteaux*, xv (1964), pp 144–60.

Cosgrove, Art. Marriage in medieval Ireland. In Art Cosgrove (ed.), *Marriage in Ireland* (Dublin, 1985), pp 25–50.

Creston, R. Y. *Coracles et Currachs*. Brest, 1956. (Ar Falz, v, suppl. Tud ha Bro: Cahiers du Groupe d'Études d'Ethnographie Bretonne, vi.)

Cullen, L. M. *Life in Ireland*. London and New York, 1968.

Curtis, Edmund. The clan system among English settlers in Ireland. In *E.H.R.*, xxv (1910), pp 116–20.

Ekvall, R. B. Demographic aspects of Tibetan nomadic pastoralism. In Brian Spooner (ed.), *Population growth: anthropological implications* (Cambridge, Mass., 1972), pp 269–85.

Ellis, S. G. The Irish customs administration under the early Tudors. In *I.H.S.*, xxii, no. 87 (Mar. 1981), pp 271–7. (Historical Revision, xix.)

—— Taxation and defence in late medieval Ireland: the survival of scutage. In *R.S.A.I. Jn.*, cvii (1977), pp 5–28.

Empey, C. A., and Simms, Katharine. The ordinances of the White Earl and the problem of coign in the later middle ages. In *R.I.A. Proc.*, lxxv (1975), sect. C, no. 8, pp 161–87.

Evans, E. E. *Irish folk ways*. London, 1957.

Fenton, Alexander. Net-drying, pot-drying, and graddaning: small-scale grain drying and processing techniques. In *Saga och Sed* (Uppsala, 1982), pp 92–101.

Finot, Jules. *Étude historique sur les relations commerciales entre la Flandre & l'Espagne au moyen âge*. Paris, 1899.

de Fréville de Lorme, C. E. *Mémoire sur le commerce de Rouen*. 2 vols. Rouen, 1857.

Gailey, Alan. Spade tillage in south-west Ulster and north Connacht. In *Tools and Tillage*, i (1968–71), pp 225–36.

Graham, B. J. The towns of medieval Ireland. In R. A. Butlin (ed.), *The development of the Irish town* (London and Totowa, 1977), pp 28–60.

Graham, J. M. Transhumance in Ireland. In *Advancement of Science*, x (1953), pp 74–9.

Green, A. S. *The making of Ireland and its undoing, 1200–1600*. London, 1908; 2nd ed., 1909; reprint, Dublin, 1920.

Gross, Charles. *The gild merchant: a contribution to British municipal history*. 2 vols. Oxford, 1890.

Guinness, H. S. Dublin trade gilds. In *R.S.A.I. Jn.*, lii (1922), pp 143–63.

Gwynn, Aubrey. The Black Death in Ireland. In *Studies*, xxiv (1935), pp 25–42.

—— Irish society in the fifteenth century. In *Iris Hibernia*, iii (1953–7), no. 5, pp 33–42.

—— Medieval Bristol and Dublin. In *I.H.S.*, v, no. 20 (Sept. 1947), pp 275–86.

Hand, G. J. The dating of the early fourteenth-century ecclesiastical valuations of Ireland. In *Ir. Theol. Quart.*, xxiv (1957), pp 271–4.

Harvey, P. D. A. The English inflation of 1180–1220. In *Past & Present*, no. 61 (Nov. 1973), pp 3–30.

Hatcher, John. *Plague, population, and the English economy, 1348–1530*. London, 1977.

—— See also Miller, Edward, and Hatcher, John, below.

Henchy, James (Ó hInnse, Séamus). Fosterage in early and medieval Ireland. (Ph.D. thesis, N.U.I. (U.C.D.), 1943.)

—— Fosterage in medieval Ireland. In *I.C.H.S. Bull.*, no. 44 (Mar. 1946), pp 1–2.

Henry, P. L. The land of Cokaygne: cultures in contact in medieval Ireland. In *Studia Hib.*, xii (1972), pp 120–41.

Hilton, R. H. *A medieval society: the West Midlands at the end of the thirteenth century*. London, 1966.

James, M. K. *Studies in the medieval wine trade*. Ed. E. M. Veale. Oxford, 1971.

Jensen, Merrill, and Reynolds, R. L. European colonial experience: a plea for comparative studies. In A. Giuffré (ed.), *Studi in onore di Gino Luzzato* (Milan, 1949–50), iv, 75–90.

Jones, W. R. England against the Celtic fringe: a study in cultural stereotypes. In *Journal of World History*, xiii (1971), pp 155–71.

Kaeuper, R. W. *Bankers to the crown: the Riccardi of Lucca and Edward I*. Princeton, 1973.

Leask, A. K. See Longfield, A. K.

Lewis, E. A. A contribution to the commercial history of mediaeval Wales. In *Y Cymmrodor*, xxiv (1913), pp 86–188.

Longfield, A. K. *Anglo-Irish trade in the sixteenth century*. London, 1929.

—— Anglo-Irish trade in the sixteenth century, as illustrated by the English customs accounts and port books. In *R.I.A. Proc.*, xxxvi (1921–2), sect. C, no. 17, pp 317–32.

de Lorme, C. E. de Fréville. See de Fréville de Lorme, C. E., above.

Lucas, A. T. Cattle in ancient and medieval Irish society. In Vincent Grogan (ed.), *The O'Connell School Union record, 1937–58* (Dublin, [1958]), pp 75–85, 87.

—— Irish ploughing practices. In *Tools and Tillage*, ii, no. 1 (1972), pp 52–62; no. 2 (1973), pp 67–83; no. 3 (1974), pp 149–60; no. 4 (1975), pp 195–210.

Lucas, A. T. Notes on the history of turf as fuel in Ireland to 1700 A.D. In *Ulster Folklife*, xv–xvi (1970), pp 172–202.

Lucas, H. S. The great European famine of 1315, 1316, and 1317. In *Speculum*, v (1930), pp 343–77.

Lydon, J. F. The middle nation. In Lydon, *English in med. Ire.* (1984), pp 1–26.

—— The problem of the frontier in medieval Ireland. In *Topic*, 13 (1967), pp 5–22.

McClintock, H. F. *Old Irish and Highland dress*. Dundalk, 1943; 2nd ed., 2 vols or 2 vols in 1, 1950.

McEneaney, Eamonn. Waterford and New Ross trade competition, *c.* 1300. In *Decies*, xii (1979), pp 16–24. (Medieval Waterford, ii.)

McEnery, M. J. Address on the state of agriculture and the standard of living in Ireland in the years 1240–1350. In *R.S.A.I. Jn.*, l (1920), pp 1–18.

Maclean, Loraine (ed.). *The middle ages in the Highlands*. Inverness Field Club, Inverness, 1981.

MacLeod, Catriona. Fifteenth century vestments in Waterford. In *R.S.A.I. Jn.*, lxxxii (1952), pp 85–98.

Mac Niocaill, Gearóid. Socio-economic problems of the late medieval Irish town. In *Hist. Studies*, xiii (1981), pp 7–21.

Mallett, M. E. Anglo-Florentine commercial relations, 1465–1491. In *Econ. Hist. Rev.*, 2nd ser., xv (1962–3), pp 250–65.

Matthew, Elizabeth. The financing of the lordship of Ireland under Henry V and Henry VI. In A. J. Pollard (ed.), *Property and politics: essays in later medieval English history* (Gloucester, 1984), pp 97–115.

Michel, Francisque. *Histoire du commerce et de la navigation à Bordeaux, principalement sous l'administration anglaise*. 2 vols. Bordeaux, 1867–70.

Miller, Edward, and Hatcher, John. *Medieval England: rural society and economic change, 1086–1348*. London and New York, 1978. (Social and Economic History of England.)

Mills, James. Tenants and agriculture near Dublin in the fourteenth century. In *R.S.A.I. Jn.*, xxi (1890–91), pp 54–63.

Mitchell, G. F. Littleton Bog, Tipperary: an Irish agricultural record. In *R.S.A.I. Jn.*, xcv (1965), pp 121–32.

Mollat, Michel. *Le commerce maritime normand à la fin du moyen âge*. Paris, [1952].

—— *Comptabilité du port de Dieppe au XVe siècle*. Paris, 1951.

Munro, J. H. A. *Wool, cloth and gold: the struggle for bullion in Anglo-Burgundian trade, 1340–1478*. Brussels and Toronto, 1972.

Murray, Athol. The customs accounts of Kirkcudbright, Wigtown, and Dumfries, 1434–1560. In *Transactions of the Dumfriesshire and Galloway Natural History and Antiquarian Society*, 3rd ser., xl (1961–2), pp 136–62.

Nicholls, K. W. *Gaelic and gaelicised Ireland in the middle ages*. Dublin, 1972. (The Gill History of Ireland, [iv].)

—— *Land, law, and society in sixteenth-century Ireland*. [Dublin, 1978]. (O'Donnell Lectures, xx.)

Ó hInnse, Séamus. See Henchy, James, above.

O'Kelly, Maria. The Black Death in Ireland, 1348. (M.A. thesis, N.U.I. (U.C.C.), 1973.)

O'Loan, J. J. The history of agriculture in early Ireland. (Ph.D. thesis, N.U.I. (U.C.D.), 1965.)

—— A history of early Irish farming. In *Dept Agric. Jn.*, lx (1963), pp 178–219; lxi (1964), pp 242–84; lxii (1965), pp 131–97.

O'Neill, Timothy. Irish trade in the later middle ages: a survey. (M.A. thesis, N.U.I. (U.C.D.), 1979.)

—— Piracy off the southern and western coasts of Ireland in the later middle ages. In *Annual Observer* (Newcastle West Historical Society), 1980, pp 39–41.

O'Sullivan, M. D. *Italian merchant bankers in Ireland in the thirteenth century*. Dublin, 1962.

Otway-Ruthven, A. J. The character of Norman settlement in Ireland. In *Hist. Studies*, v (1965), pp 75–84.

—— Enclosures in the medieval period. In *Ir. Geography*, v (1964–8), no. 2, pp 35–6.

—— The organization of Anglo-Irish agriculture in the middle ages. In *R.S.A.I. Jn.*, lxxxi (1951), pp 1–13.

—— Royal service in Ireland. In *R.S.A.I. Jn.*, xcviii (1968), pp 37–46.

Phillips, J. R. S. The Anglo-Norman nobility. In Lydon, *English in med. Ire.* (1984), pp 87–104.

Platt, Colin. *Medieval Southampton: the port and trading community, A.D. 1000—1600*. London and Boston, 1973.

Postan, M. M. (ed.). *The agrarian life in the middle ages*. 2nd ed. Cambridge, 1966. (The Cambridge Economic History of Europe, i.)
1st ed., ed. J. H. Clapham and Eileen Power. Cambridge, 1941.

—— *The medieval economy and society: an economic history of Britain in the middle ages*. London, 1972; reprint, Harmondsworth, 1975. (The Pelican Economic History of Britain, i.)

Proudfoot, V. B. Clachans in Ireland. In *Gwerin*, ii (1958–9), pp 110–22.

—— The economy of the Irish rath. In *Medieval Archaeology*, v (1961), pp 94–122.

Quinn, D. B. *England and the discovery of America, 1481—1620*. London, 1974.

—— Ireland and sixteenth century European expansion. In *Hist. Studies*, i (1958), pp 20–32.

—— The Irish parliamentary subsidy in the fifteenth and sixteenth centuries. In *R.I.A. Proc.*, xlii (1934–5), sect. C, no. 11, pp 219–46.

Reynolds, R. L. See Jensen, Merrill, and Reynolds, R. L., above.

Richards, A. I. African kings and their royal relations. In *Journal of the Royal Anthropological Institute of Great Britain and Ireland*, xci (1961), pp 135–50.

Richardson, H. G., and Sayles, G. O. Irish revenue, 1278–1384. In *R.I.A. Proc.*, lxii (1961–2), sect. C, no. 4, pp 87–100.

Round, J. H. Early Irish trade with Chester and Rouen. In his *Feudal England* (London, 1895; reprints, 1909, 1964), pp 465–7.

Rudisill, George. See Strayer, J. R., and Rudisill, George, below.

Russell, J. C. Late-thirteenth-century Ireland as a region. In *Demography*, iii (1966), pp 500–12.

Sayles, G. O. See Richardson, H. G., and Sayles, G. O., above.

Simms, Anngret. See Clark, H. B., and Simms, Anngret, above.

Simms, Katharine. Guesting and feasting in Gaelic Ireland. In *R.S.A.I. Jn.*, cviii (1978), pp 67–100.

—— Women in Norman Ireland. In Margaret MacCurtain and Donncha[dh] Ó Corráin (ed.), *Women in Irish society* (Dublin, 1978), pp 14–25.

—— See also Empey, C. A., and Simms, Katharine, above.

Strayer, J. R., and Rudisill, George. Taxation and community in Wales and Ireland, 1272–1327. In *Speculum*, xxix (1954), pp 410–16.

Stubbs, W. C. The weavers' guild: the Guild of the Blessed Virgin Mary, Dublin, 1446–1840. In *R.S.A.I. Jn.*, xlix (1919), pp 60–88.

Thrupp, S. L. A survey of the alien population of England in 1440. In *Speculum*, xxxii (1957), pp 262–73.

—— Aliens in and around London in the fifteenth century. In A. E. J. Hollaender and William Kellaway (ed.), *Studies in London history presented to Philip Edmund Jones* (London, 1969), pp 249–72.

Titow, J. Z. *English rural society, 1200–1350*. London and New York, 1969. (Historical Problems: Studies and Documents, iv.)

Touchard, Henri. *Le commerce maritime breton à la fin du moyen âge*. Paris, 1967. (Annales Littéraires de l'Université de Nantes, i.)

Tout, T. F., and Broome, D. M. A national balance sheet for 1362–3, with documents subsidiary thereto. In *E.H.R.*, xxxix (1924), pp 404–19.

Treadwell, Victor. The Irish customs administration in the sixteenth century. In *I.H.S.*, xx, no. 80 (Sept. 1977), pp 384–417.

Vendryes, Joseph. Les moulins en Irlande et l'aventure de Ciarnot. In *Revue Archéologique*, xiv (1921), pp 263–372.

Verlinden, Charles. Les influences médiévales dans la colonisation de l'Amérique. In *Revista de Historia de América*, xxx (1950), pp 440–50.

—— *Précédents médiévaux de la colonie en Amérique*. Comisión de Historia, Instituto Panamericano de Geografía e Historia, Mexico City, 1954. (Programme d'Histoire de l'Amérique. 2: Période Coloniale, v.)

—— La problème de la continuité en histoire coloniale. In *Revista de Indias* (Madrid), xii (1951), pp 219–30.

—— Sentido de la historia colonial americana. In *Estudios Americanos* (Seville), iv (1952), pp 551–64.

Webb, J. J. *The guilds of Dublin*. Dublin, 1929.

Went, A. E. J. Fisheries of the river Liffey. In *R.S.A.I. Jn.*, lxxxiii (1953), pp 163–73; lxxxiv (1954), pp 41–58.

—— Foreign fishing fleets along the Irish coast. In *Cork Arch. Soc. Jn.*, liv (1949), pp 17–24.

—— The Galway fishery. In *R.I.A. Proc.*, xlviii (1942–3), sect. C, no. 5, pp 233–53; xlix (1943–4), sect. C, no. 5, pp 187–219.

Went, A. E. J. Irish monastic fisheries. In *Cork Hist. Soc. Jn.*, lx (1955), pp 47–56.

Wilson, K. P. The port of Chester in the later middle ages. (Ph.D. thesis, University of Liverpool, 1965.)

8 HISTORY OF COINAGE

Several of the excavation reports listed in sect. IV D below include reports on associated finds of coins.

Allen, Derek. The Boyton find of coins of Edward I and II. In *Numismatic Chronicle*, 5th ser., xvi (1936), pp 115–54.

—— The supposed halfpence of King John. In *Numismatic Chronicle*, 5th ser., xviii (1938), pp 282–92. (Two notes on English coins, i.)

Bateson, J. D. A medieval coin hoard from Newtownards, County Down. In *U.J.A.*, 3rd ser., xli (1978), pp 102–3.

Beauford, William. An account of antient coins found at Ballylinam in the Queen's County, Ireland, with conjectures thereon. In a letter to Joseph Cooper Walker. In *R.I.A. Trans.*, i (1787), pp 139–60.

Blackburn, Mark, and Dolley, Michael. The Hiberno-Norse element of the list hoard from Sylt. In *Brit. Numis. Jn.*, xlix (1979), pp 17–25.

Blunt, C. E. Coin hoards in the National Museum of Ireland, Dublin. In *Brit. Numis. Jn.*, xxvii (1952–4), pp 213–15.

Briggs, C. S., and Dolley, Michael. An unpublished hoard from north County Dublin with pennies of Eadgar. In *Seaby's Coin and Medal Bulletin*, no. 654 (Feb. 1973), pp 47–50.

Carlyon-Britton, Raymond. On the Irish coinage of Lambert Simnel as Edward VI. In *Numismatic Chronicle*, 6th ser., i (1941), pp 133–5.

—— On the proposed attribution of certain Irish coins to Edward V. In *Numismatic Chronicle*, 6th ser., i (1941), pp 128–32.

—— Two unpublished Irish coins. In *Brit. Numis. Jn.*, xxvi (3rd ser., vi, 1951), pp 350–51. Pennies of Edward III, Dublin, and Richard III, Waterford.

Dolley, Michael. Anglo-Irish monetary policies, 1172–1637. In *Hist. Studies*, vii (1969), pp 45–64.

—— The coins from Beal Boru. In *Cork Hist. Soc. Jn.*, lxvii (1962), pp 18–27.

—— The continental hoard-evidence for the chronology of the Anglo-Irish pence of John. In *Numismatic Circular*, lxxiv (1966), pp 30–32.

Découverte en France d'un groat anglo-irlandais du XVe siècle. In *Club Français de Médaille* (Paris), no 51/52 (1976), pp 144–50.

—— The Dover hoard: the first English hoard with groats of Edward I. In *Brit. Numis. Jn.*, xxviii (1955–7), pp 147–68. Includes P. E. Lasko, 'The container' (pp 166–8).

—— Dr George Petrie's hoard of Anglo-Irish coins of King John. In *Numismatic Circular*, lxxiv (1966), pp 127–9.

—— The Dublin pennies in the name of Sihtric Silkbeard in the Hermitage Museum in Leningrad. In *R.S.A.I. Jn.*, xciii (1963), pp 1–8.

Dolley, Michael. The earliest German imitations of Anglo-Irish coins. In Peter Berghaus and Gert Hatz (ed.), *Dona Numismatica: Walter Hävernick zum 23. Januar dargebracht* (Hamburg, 1965), pp 213–18.

—— An 'ex voto' of eleventh-century silver coins from Co. Westmeath. In *Ríocht na Mídhe*, vi, no. 3 (1977), pp 19–22.

—— Four neglected Irish finds of Anglo-Irish coins of John. In *U.J.A.*, 3rd ser., xxix (1966), pp 130–37.

—— A fourth find of ninth-century coins from Ireland? In *Brit. Numis. Jn.*, xxxvi (1967), pp 32–5.
6 coins in Nat. Mus. Ire.

—— George Petrie and a century of Irish numismatics. In *R.I.A. Proc.*, lxxii (1972), sect. C, no. 8, pp 165–93. (Aspects of George Petrie, iii.)

—— A Hiberno-Manx coinage of the eleventh century. In *Numismatic Chronicle*, cxxxvi (7th ser., xvi, 1976), pp 75–84.

—— Hiberno-Norse coins from the Lockett Collection. In *British Museum Quarterly*, xxiii (1960–61), pp 45–8.

—— *The Hiberno-Norse coins in the British Museum*. London, 1966. (Sylloge of Coins of the British Isles, B, i [Consecutive series, viii].)
Includes comprehensive bibliography.

—— The Hiberno-Norse coins in Gotlands Fornsal, Visby. In *Brit. Numis. Jn.*, xlviii (1978), pp 20–34.

—— The Hiberno-Norse coins in the University Coin-Cabinet at Uppsala. In *Numismatic Chronicle*, cxxxix (7th ser., xix, 1979), pp 225–9.

—— A Hiberno-Norse penny of Dublin found in Wigtownshire. In *Transactions of the Dumfriesshire and Galloway Natural History and Antiquarian Society*, 3rd ser., xliv (1967), pp 122–5.

—— The 'Ireland' find (*c.* 1842) of profile halfpence of John. In *Numismatic Circular*, lxxiv (1966), pp 66–7.

—— Irish hoards with thirteenth- and fourteenth-century Scottish coins. In *Seaby's Coin and Medal Bulletin*, no. 617 (Jan. 1970), pp 4–10.

—— The Irish mints of Edward I in the light of the coin-hoards from Ireland and Great Britain. In *R.I.A. Proc.*, lxvi (1967–8), sect. C, no. 3, pp 235–97.

—— *Medieval Anglo-Irish coins*. London, 1972.

—— Medieval British and Irish coins as dating evidence for the archaeologist. In *World Archaeology*, i (1969–70), pp 200–07.

—— The myth of a coinage of the Ostmen of Dublin in the name of Tymme Sjaellands-far. In *Brit. Numis. Jn.*, xxix (1958–9), pp 275–88.

—— A note on the Anglo-Saxon mint at Berkeley. In *Transactions of the Bristol and Gloucestershire Archaeological Society*, lxxx (1961), pp 80–89.
Concerned mainly with the Dunroby hoard.

—— A note on the attribution of the regally anonymous 'three-crown' coinage given by Smith and Coffey to Edward IV. In *Numismatic Circular*, lxxvi (1968), p. 118.

—— A small find of 14th century coins from West Limerick. In *N. Munster Antiq. Jn.*, viii (1961), pp 157–67.

—— A small find of twelfth- and thirteenth-century pennies from Tullintowell. In *Brit. Numis. Jn.*, xxxv (1966), pp 113–15.

—— The sequence and chronology of the 'portrait' Anglo-Irish groats of Henry VII. In *Numismatic Circular*, lxxvii (1969), pp 370–74.

—— Some Hiberno-Norse coins of Dublin recently discovered on the Baltic island of Gotland. In *R.S.A.I. Jn.*, xcviii (1968), pp 57–62. (Two numismatic notes, i.)

—— Tre kroner—tri choróin: a note on the date of the 'three crown' coinage of Ireland. In *Numismatiska Meddelanden*, xxx (1965), pp 103–12.

—— *Viking coins of the Danelaw and of Dublin*. British Museum, London, 1965.
    See also Blackburn, Mark, Briggs, C. S., above, and Galster, Georg, below.

—— and Hackman, W. D. The coinages for Ireland of Henry VIII. In *Brit. Numis. Jn.*, xxxviii (1969), pp 84–108.

—— and Lane, S. N. A find of fifteenth century groats from Co. Dublin. In *R.S.I.A. Jn.*, cii (1972), pp 143–50.

—— and —— A parcel of late eleventh-century Hiberno-Norse coins found in northern Italy. In *Brit. Numis. Jn.*, xxxvii (1968), pp 25–8.

—— and Mac Niocaill, Gearóid. Some coin names in *Ceart Uí Néill*. In *Studia Celt.*, ii (1967), pp 119–24.

—— and O'Sullivan, William. The chronology of the first Anglo-Irish coinage. In Etienne Rynne (ed.), *North Munster Studies* (Limerick, 1967), pp 437–78.

—— and—— The Corofin (Co. Clare) hoard: late twelfth–early thirteenth centuries. In *Brit. Numis. Jn.*, xxxiv (1965), pp 98–103.

—— and Seaby, W. A. *Anglo-Irish coins: John—Edward III, Ulster Museum, Belfast*. London, 1968. (Sylloge of Coins of the British Isles, C [i], pt 1 [Consecutive series, x].)

—— and —— The anomalous long-cross coins in the Anglo-Irish portion of the Brussels hoard. In R. A. G. Carson (ed.), *Mints, dies and currency: essays in honour of Albert Baldwin* (London, 1971), pp 291–317.

—— and —— A find of thirteenth-century pewter tokens from the National Museum excavations at Winetavern Street, Dublin. In *Numismatic circular*, lxxix (1971), pp 446–8.

—— and —— Le money del Oraylly (O'Reilly's money). In *Brit. Numis. Jn.*, xxxvi (1967), pp 114–17.

—— and —— A parcel of Edwardian sterlings in the Ulster Museum. In *Seaby's Coin and Medal Bulletin*, no. 597 (May 1968), pp 161–6.

Dolley, R. H. M. See Dolley, Michael.

Dowle, Anthony, and Finn, Patrick. *The guide book to the coinage of Ireland from 995 A.D. to the present day*. London, 1969.

Dykes, D. W. The coinage of Richard Olof. In *Brit. Numis. Jn.*, xxxiii (1964), pp 73–9.

—— The Irish coinage of Henry III. In *Brit. Numis. Jn.*, xxxii (1963), pp 99–116.

Finn, Patrick. See Dowle, Anthony, and Finn, Patrick, above.

Frazer, William. On two finds of coins of Edward 1st and 2nd, obtained in Ireland, and also some foreign sterlings. In *R.I.A. Proc.*, 2nd ser., i: Polite literature and antiquities (1879), pp 70–72.

Gallagher, Colm. Neglected documentary evidence for the currency of the 14th-century Scottish coins in N.E. Ireland. In *Brit. Numis. Jn.*, xxxvi (1967), pp 93–5.

Galster, Georg, Dolley, Michael, and Jensen, J. S. *Royal collection of coins and medals, National Museum, Copenhagen. Pt v: Hiberno-Norse and Anglo-Irish coins*. London, 1975. (Sylloge of Coins of the British Isles, xxii.)

Hackman, W. D. See Dolley, Michael, and Hackman, W. D., above.

Harris, E. J. Inner circle diameter as a criterion to distinguish between the heavy and light groats of the Irish issues of Edward IV. In *Seaby's Coin and Medal Bulletin*, no. 627 (Nov. 1970), p. 403.

—— Notes on the Irish hammered coinage. In *Seaby's Coin and Medal Bulletin*, no. 569 (Dec. 1965), pp 366–9.

Jensen, J. S. See Galster, Georg, above.

Lane, S. N. The medieval coinage of Ireland. (M.Litt. thesis, University of Dublin, 1966.)

—— See also Dolley, Michael, and Lane, S. N., above.

Leask, H. G. The mint, Carlingford. In *Louth Arch. Soc. Jn.*, xi (1946–8), pp 305–8.

Lindsay, John. *Notices of remarkable medieval coins*. Cork, 1849.

MacIlwaine, J. B. S. Notes on some Irish coins found at Trim. In *Brit. Numis. Jn.*, 1st ser., x (1913), pp 309–12.

Mac Niocaill, Gearóid. See Dolley, Michael, and Mac Niocaill, Gearóid, above.

Nolan, Patrick. *A monetary history of Ireland*. 2 vols. London, 1926–8.

North. J. J. *The coinages of Edward I & II*. London, 1968.

O'Sullivan, William. *The earliest Anglo-Irish coinage*. Nat. Mus. Ire., Dublin, 1964.

—— The earliest Irish coinage. In *R.S.A.I. Jn.*, lxxix (1949), pp 190–235; reprint, Nat. Mus. Ire., Dublin, 1961.

—— See also Dolley, Michael, and O'Sullivan, William, above.

Parsons, H. A. The mint at Galway. In *Numismatic Chronicle*, 6th ser., viii (1948), pp 97–100.

—— Remarks on a Trim groat marked B on the obverse. In *Numismatic Chronicle*, 6th ser., v (1945), pp 142–7.

Rice, Gerard. The coins and tokens of Drogheda. In *Journal of the Old Drogheda Society*, iv (1983), pp 9–12.

Sainthill, Richard. Two unpublished letters of a distinguished Cork antiquary. Ed. Michael Dolley. In *Cork Hist. Soc. Jn.*, lxviii (1963), pp 55–65.
To Jonathan Rashleigh.

—— A further unpublished letter of a distinguished Cork antiquary. Ed. Michael Dolley. In *Cork Hist. Soc. Jn.*, lxxiii (1968), pp 31–9.

Seaby, Peter (ed.). *Coins and tokens of Ireland*. 9th ed., London, 1970. (Standard Catalogue of British Coins, iii.)

Seaby, W. A. A bronze weight box from Grey Abbey, Co. Down. In *U.J.A.*, 3rd ser., xxi (1958), pp 91–100.
Appendix: 'The Montgomery collection of coins' (pp 97–100).

Seaby, W. A. *Hiberno-Norse coins, Ulster Museum, Belfast*. London, 1984. (Sylloge of Coins of the British Isles, xxxii: Ulster Museum, Belfast, pt ii.)

—— Medieval coin hoards in north-east Ireland. In *Numismatic Chronicle*, 6th ser., xv (1955), pp 161–71.

—— A St Patrick halfpenny of John de Courci. In *Brit. Numis. Jn.*, xxix (1958–9), pp 87–90.

—— See also Dolley, Michael, and Seaby, W. A., above.

—— and Stewart, B. H. I. H. A fourteenth-century hoard of Scottish groats from Balleny townland, Co. Down. In *Brit. Numis. Jn.*, xxxiii (1964), pp 94–106.

Simon, James. *Simon's essay on Irish coins and of the currency of foreign monies in Ireland*. 2nd ed. *With Mr* [Thomas] *Snelling's supplement*. Dublin, 1810.

Smith, Aquilla. The human hand on Hiberno-Danish coins. In *Numismatic Chronicle*, 3rd ser., iii (1883), pp 32–9.

—— Irish silver coins of Henry VIII. In *Numismatic Chronicle*, new ser., xix (1879), pp 157–84.

—— On inedited silver farthings coined in Ireland. In *Numismatic Chronicle*, new ser., iii (1863), pp 149–61.

—— On the Irish coins of Edward IV. In *R.I.A. Trans.*, xix (1838–43), Antiquities, no. 1, pp 3–49.

—— On the Irish coins of Henry the Seventh. In *R.I.A. Trans.*, xix (1838–43), Antiquities, no. 2, pp 50–83.

—— On the Irish coins of Richard III. In *Numismatic Chronicle*, 3rd ser., i (1881), pp 310–33.

Stewart, B. H. I. H. See Seaby, W. A., and Stewart, B. H. I. H., above.

Symonds, Henry. The Irish silver coinages of Edward IV. In *Numismatic Chronicle*, 5th ser., i (1921), pp 108–25.

Talvio, Tuukka. *The National Museum, Helsinki, and other public collections in Finland: Anglo-Saxon, Anglo-Norman, and Hiberno-Norse coins*. London, 1978. (Sylloge of Coins of the British Isles, xxv.)

Thompson, J. D. A. *Inventory of British coin hoards, A.D. 600–1500*. London, 1956.

Warhurst, Margaret. *Merseyside county museums: ancient British issues and later coins from English, Irish and Scottish mints to 1279, with associated foreign coins*. London, 1982. (Sylloge of Coins of the British Isles, xxix.)

9 HISTORY OF LANGUAGE AND LITERATURE

Bennett, J. A. W., and Smithers, G. V. *Early Middle English verse and prose*. Oxford, 1966.

Best, R. I. Bodleian MS Laud 610. In *Celtica*, iii (1956), pp 338–9.

—— The Yellow Book of Lecan. In *Jn. Celt. Studies*, i (1950), pp 190–92.

De Bhaldraithe, Tomás. Roisín/ruisín. In *Ériu*, xxxi (1980), pp 169–71.

Binchy, D. A. Lawyers and chroniclers. In Ó Cuív, *Seven centuries* (1961), pp 58–71.

Bliss, A. J. The inscribed slates at Smarmore. In *R.I.A. Proc.*, lxiv (1964–6), sect. C, no. 2, pp 33–60.

Bliss, A. J. Language and literature. In Lydon, *English in med. Ire.* (1984), pp 27–45.

Bruford, Alan. *Gaelic folktales and mediaeval romances: a study of the Early Modern Irish 'romantic tales' and their oral derivatives*. Folklore of Ireland Society, Dublin, 1966 [i.e. 1969]. (Béaloideas, xxxiv.)

Cahill, Edward. Norman French and English languages in Ireland, 1170–1540. In *I.E.R.*, 5th ser., li (1938), pp 159–73.

Carney, James. *The Irish bardic poet*. Dublin, 1967. (New Dolmen Chapbooks, iv.)

Clanchy, M. T. *From memory to written record: England, 1066–1307*. London, 1979.

Curtis, Edmund. The spoken languages of medieval Ireland. In *Studies*, viii (1919), pp 234–54.

Dillon, Myles. Laud. Misc. 610. In *Celtica*, v (1960), pp 64–76; vi (1963), pp 135–55.

—— (ed.). *Irish sagas*. Dublin, 1959. (Thomas Davis Lectures, 1955.)

Easting, Robert. The date and dedication of the Tractatus de Purgatorio Sancti Patricii. In *Speculum*, liii (1978), pp 778–83.
Henry of Sawtrey.

Flower (Robin). *The Irish tradition*. Oxford, 1947.

Gwynn, Aubrey. Some notes on the history of the Book of Leinster. In *Celtica*, v (1960), pp 8–12.

Hackett, Michael. William Fleta's treatise, 'De remediis contra temptaciones': manuscript tradition, text, and historical significance. (Ph.D. thesis, N.U.I. (U.C.D.), 1955.)

Henry, P. L. A linguistic survey of Ireland: preliminary report. In *Lochlann*, i (1958), pp 49–208.

Hickes, George. *Linguarum vett. septentrionalium thesaurus grammatico-criticus et archaeologicus*. 7 pts in 2 vols. Oxford, 1705.

Hogan, J. J. *The English language in Ireland*. Dublin, 1927.

Mac Cana, Próinsias. *The learned tales of medieval Ireland*. Institute for Advanced Studies, Dublin, 1980.

—— The rise of the later schools of filidheacht. In *Ériu*, xxv (1974), pp 126–46.

McIntosh, Angus, and Samuels, M. L. Prolegomena to a study of mediaeval Anglo-Irish. In *Medium Aevum*, xxxvii (1968), pp 1–11.

Mac Niocaill, Gearóid. À propos du vocabulaire social irlandais au bas moyen âge. In *Études Celt.*, xii (1968–71), pp 512–46.

Minnis, A. J. 'Authorial intention' and 'literal sense' in the exegetical theories of Richard FitzRalph and John Wyclif: an essay in the medieval history of biblical hermeneutics. In *R.I.A. Proc.*, lxxv (1975), sect. C, no. 1, pp 1–31.

Murphy, Gerard. Irish storytelling after the coming of the Normans. In Ó Cuív, *Seven centuries* (1961), pp 72–86.

—— *The Ossianic lore and romantic tales of medieval Ireland*. Dublin, 1955. (Irish Life and Culture, xi.)

Ó Concheanainn, Tomás. The reviser of Leabhor na nUidre. In *Éigse*, xv (1973–4), pp 277–88.

Ó Cuív, Brian. Literary creation and Irish historical tradition. In *Brit. Acad. Proc.*, xlix (1965), pp 233–62.

Oskamp, Hans P. A. The Yellow Book of Lecan proper. In *Ériu*, xxvi (1975), pp 102–21.

O'Sullivan, Anne, and O'Sullivan, William. Three notes on Laud Misc. 610 (or the Book of Pottlerath). In *Celtica*, ix (1971), pp 135–51.

Pickering, O. S. An unrecognized extract from the 'South English Legendary'. In *N. & Q.*, ccxvii (1972), p. 407.

Quiggin, E. C. Prolegomena to the study of the later Irish bards, 1200–1500. In *Brit. Acad. Proc.*, v (1911–12), pp 89–143; reprint, American Committee for Irish Studies, New York, 1967. [Reprints in Irish Studies, ii.]

Richardson, F. E. A Middle English fragment from the First Book of Kilkenny. In *N. & Q.*, ccvii (1962), pp 47–8.

Rigg, A. G. The Red Book of Ossory. In *Medium Aevum*, xlvi (1977), pp 269–78.

Samuels, M. L. See McIntosh, Angus, and Samuels, M. L., above.

Seymour, St J. D. *Anglo-Irish literature, 1200–1582*. Cambridge, 1929; reprint, Philadelphia, 1978.

Simms, Katharine. Propaganda use of the *Táin* in the later middle ages. In *Celtica*, xv (1983), pp 142–9.

Smithers, G. V. See Bennett, J. A. W., and Smithers, G. V., above.

Sommerfelt, Alf. The English forms of the names of the main provinces of Ireland. In *Lochlann*, i (1958), pp 223–7.

Stanford, W. B. Towards a history of classical influences in Ireland. In *R.I.A. Proc.*, lxx (1970), sect. C, no. 3, pp 13–91.

—— *Ireland and the classical tradition*. Dublin, 1976.

Stemmler, Theo. The vernacular snatches in the Red Book of Ossory: a textual case-history. In *Anglia*, xcv (1977), pp 122–9.

Todd, J. H. *A descriptive catalogue of the contents of the Irish manuscript commonly called 'The Book of Fermoy'*. Dublin, 1868; reprint, R.I.A., Dublin, 1889. (Irish Manuscripts Series, i.)

Vising, Johan. *Anglo-Norman language and literature*. London, 1923. (Language and Literature Series.)

Wagner, Heinrich. A linguistic atlas and survey of Irish dialects. In *Lochlann*, i (1958), pp 9–48.

Walsh, Paul. *Irish men of learning*. Ed. Colm Ó Lochlainn. Dublin, 1947.

Williams, Glanmor. Language, literacy and nationality in Wales. In *History*, lvi (1971), pp 1–16.

Williams, J. E. Caerwyn. The court poet in medieval Ireland. In *Brit. Acad. Proc.*, lvii (1971), pp 85–135. (Sir John Rhŷs Memorial Lecture, 1971.)

10 HISTORIOGRAPHY

Brooks, Eric St John. Two charters of Prince John, lord of Ireland. In *R.S.A.I. Jn.*, lxxxv (1955), pp 226–7.

Byrne, F. J. Senchas: the nature of Gaelic historical tradition. In *Hist. Studies*, ix (1974), pp 137–59.

Clanchy, M. T. Remembering the past and the good old law. In *History*, lv (1970), pp 165–76.

Cosgrove, Art. Hiberniores ipsis Hibernis. In Art Cosgrove and Donal Macartney (ed.), *Studies in Irish history presented to R. Dudley Edwards* (Dublin, 1979), pp 1–14.

Elton, G. R. *England, 1200–1640*. London, 1969. (Sources of History.)

Gransden, Antonia. *Historical writing in England*. 2 vols. London, 1974–82.

—— Propaganda in English medieval historiography. In *Journal of Medieval History*, i (1975), pp 363–81.

Gwynn, Aubrey. The Annals of Connacht and the abbey of Cong. In *Galway Arch. Soc. Jn.*, xxvii (1956–7), pp 1–9.

—— Cathal Mac Maghnusa and the Annals of Ulster. In *Clogher Rec.*, ii (1957–9), pp 230–43, 370–84.

—— Were the 'Annals of Innisfallen' written at Killaloe? In *N. Munster Antiq. Jn.*, viii (1958–61), pp 20–33.

Hand, G. J. The date of the 'Crede Mihi'. In *Reportorium Novum*, iii (1963–4), pp 368–70.

Harriss, G. L. A fifteenth-century chronicle at Trinity College, Dublin. In *I.H.R. Bull.*, xxxviii (1965), pp 212–18.

Hughes, Kathleen. *Early Christian Ireland: introduction to the sources*. London, 1972. (Sources of History.)

Jack, R. I. *Medieval Wales*. London, 1972. (Sources of History.)

Jourdan, G. V. *Sir James Ware, historian and antiquary, 1594–1666*. [Dublin], 1953.

Long, Joseph. Dermot and the Earl: who wrote 'the Song'? In *R.I.A. Proc.*, lxxv (1975), sect. C, no. 13, pp 263–72.

Lynch, John. *Cambrensis eversus ... 1662*. Ed. Matthew Kelly. Celtic Soc., Dublin, 1848–52.

McKinlay, Robert. Barbour's Bruce. In *Records of the Glasgow Bibliographical Society*, vi (1916–18), pp 20–38.

McNamara, L. F. An examination of the medieval Irish text 'Caithréim Thoirdhealbhaigh': the historical value. In *N. Munster Antiq. Jn.*, viii (1958–61), pp 182–92.

Mac Niocaill, Gearóid. *The medieval Irish annals*. [Dublin, 1975.] (Medieval Irish History Series, iii.)

Moran, T. W. The medieval Gaelic genealogies. In *Ir. Geneal.*, iv (1968–73), pp 267–74, 417–28; v (1974–9), pp 5–20, 269.

Nic Ghiollamhaith, Aoife. Dynastic warfare and historical writing in North Munster, 1276–1350. In *Cambridge Medieval Celtic Studies*, ii (1981), pp 73–89.

Nicholls, K. W. The Irish genealogies: their value and defects. In *Ir. Geneal.*, v (1974–9), pp 256–61.

O'Curry, Eugene. *Lectures on the manuscript materials of ancient Irish history*. Dublin, 1861.

O'Doherty, J. F. Historical criticism of the 'Song of Dermot and the Earl'. In *I.H.S.*, i, no. 1 (Mar. 1938), pp 4–20; Correspondence, pp 294–6.

O'Dwyer, B. W. The annals of Connacht and Loch Cé and the monasteries of Boyle and Holy Trinity. In *R.I.A. Proc.*, lxxii (1972), sect. C, no. 4, pp 83–101.

O'Dwyer, B. W. St Bernard as an historian: the 'Life of St Malachy of Armagh'. In *Jn. Relig. Hist.*, x (1978–9), pp 128–41.

O'Farrelly, J. J. The annals of Innisfallen. In *Ivernian Soc. Jn.*, i (1908–9), pp 110–18.

O'Sullivan, Helen. Irish annals of the eleventh and twelfth centuries. (M.A. thesis, N.U.I. (U.C.D.), 1970.)

Plummer, Charles. On two collections of Latin lives of Irish saints in the Bodleian Library: Rawl. B. 485 and Rawl. B. 505. In *Z.C.P.*, v (1905), pp 429–54.

Richter, Michael. Gerald of Wales: a reassessment on the 750th anniversary of his death. In *Traditio*, xxix (1973), pp 379–90.

—— Giraldiana. In *I.H.S.*, xxi, no. 84 (Sept. 1979), pp 422–37.
See also sect. IV B 16 below.

Ryan, M. T. The historical value of the Expugnatio Hibernica of Giraldus Cambrensis as an account of the Anglo-Norman invasion. (M.A. thesis, N.U.I. (U.C.D.), 1967.)

Smalley, Beryl. *Historians in the middle ages*. London, 1974.

Stokes, Whitley. The Annals of Ulster. In *Rev. Celt.*, xviii (1897), pp 74–86.

Walsh, Paul. *The Four Masters and their work*. Dublin, 1944.

Warren, W. L. The historian as 'private eye'. In *Hist. Studies*, ix (1974), pp 1–18.

Westropp, T. J. On the external evidences bearing on the historic character of the 'Wars of Torlough' by John, son of Rory MacGrath. In *R.I.A. Trans.*, xxxii (1902–4), sect. C, pt 2, pp 133–98.

11 HISTORY OF EDUCATION

Gwynn, Aubrey. The medieval university of St Patrick's, Dublin. In *Studies*, xxvii (1938), pp 199–212, 437–54.

McGrath, Fergal. *Education in ancient and medieval Ireland*. Dublin, 1979.

Maxwell-Lyte, Sir H. C. *A history of the University of Oxford to 1530*. London, 1886.

Mulchrone, Kathleen. The rights and duties of women with regard to the education of their children. In *Studies in Ir. law* (1936), pp 187–205.

Rashdall, Hastings. *The universities of Europe in the middle ages*. 3 vols. Oxford, 1895; new ed. Ed. F. M. Powicke and A. B. Emden. Oxford, 1936; reprint, 1958.

12 SCIENTIFIC AND MEDICAL HISTORY

Grattan, J. H. G., and Singer, C. J. *Anglo-Saxon magic and medicine*. Oxford, 1952. (Publications of the Wellcome Historical Medical Museum, new ser., iii.)

Hilton, R. H., and Sawyer, P. H. Technical determinism: the stirrup and the plough. In *Past & Present*, no. 24 (Apr. 1963), pp 90–100.

Logan, Patrick. Medieval hospital system in Breifne. In *Breifne*, iv (1970–75), pp 52–8.

Sawyer, P. H. See Hilton, R. H., and Sawyer, P. H., above.

Shaw, Francis. Irish medical men and philosophers. In Ó Cuív, *Seven centuries* (1961), pp 87–101.

—— Medicine in Ireland in medieval times. In William Doolin and Oliver Fitzgerald (ed.), *What's past is prologue* (Dublin, 1952), pp 10–14.

Shrewsbury, J. F. D. *A history of bubonic plague in the British Isles*. Cambridge, 1970.

Singer, C. J. See Grattan, J. H. G., and Singer, C. J., above.

White, Lynn. *Medieval technology and social change*. [London], 1962.

13 LOCAL AND FAMILY HISTORY

For archaeological works, see sect. IV D; for military engagements, see sect. IV B 4.

ABBEYLARAGH. Kearney, Patrick. The Cistercian abbey at Abbeylaragh, A.D. 1205–1540. In *Teathbha*, i (1969–73), pp 202–5.

ADARE. Wyndham-Quin, Caroline, countess of Dunraven. *Memorials of Adare manor. With historical notices of Adare*, by [E. R. Wyndham Quinn], earl of Dunraven. Oxford, 1865.

ARDEE. Mac Íomhair, Diarmuid. Ardee manor in A.D. 1336. In *Louth Arch. Soc. Jn.*, xiv (1957–60), pp 160–64.

—— —— Fasti of Saint John's Priory, Ardee. In *Seanchas Ardmhacha*, vii (1973–4), pp 176–8.

ARDGLASS. *A guide to Jordan's castle, Ardglass, Co. Down*. Belfast, 1963.

ARMAGH. Gwynn, Aubrey. Armagh and Louth in the 12th and 13th centuries. In *Seanchas Ardmhacha*, i (1954–5), no. 1, pp 1–11; no. 2, pp 17–37.

—— —— Canterbury and Armagh, 1414–1443. In *Studies*, xxxii (1943), pp 495–509.

—— —— *The medieval province of Armagh, 1470–1545*. Dundalk, 1946.

—— Lynch, Anthony. The province and diocese of Armagh, 1417–71. (M.A. thesis, N.U.I. (U.C.D.), 1979.)

—— Simms, Katharine. The O'Hanlons, the O'Neills, and the Anglo-Normans in thirteenth-century Armagh. In *Seanchas Ardmhacha*, ix (1978–9), pp 70–94.

—— Stuart, James. *Historical memoirs of the city of Armagh*. Newry, 1819; rev. ed. by A. Coleman. Dublin, 1900.

—— Watt, J. A. Ecclesia inter Anglicos et inter Hibernicos: confrontation and co-existence in the medieval diocese and province of Armagh. In Lydon, *English in med. Ire.* (1984), pp 46–64.

ATHENRY. Blake, Martin. The abbey of Athenry. In *Galway Arch. Soc. Jn.*, ii (1902), pp 65–90.

—— MacAlister, R. A. S. The Dominican church at Athenry. In *R.S.A.I. Jn.*, xliii (1913), pp 197–222.

ATHLONE. Conlan, Patrick. The medieval priory of Saints Peter and Paul in Athlone. In Harman Murtagh (ed.), *Irish midland studies: essays in commemoration of N.W. English* (Old Athlone Society, Athlone, 1980), pp 73–83.

—— Orpen, G. H. Athlone Castle: its early history, with notes on some neighbouring castles. In *R.S.A.I. Jn.*, xxxvii (1907), pp 257–76.

BALLINASLOE. Egan, P. K. The parish of Ballinasloe, Co. Galway. (Ph.D. thesis, N.U.I. (U.C.G.), 1960.)

BALLINTOBER. Claffey, J. A. Ballintubber castle, Co. Roscommon. Pt 1. In *Old Athlone Soc. Jn.*, i (1969–75), pp 143–6.
No more published.

BALLINTOBER, CO. MAYO. Egan, T. A. *Ballintubber abbey*. Ballintober, 1963.

BECTIVE. Leask, H. G. Bective abbey, Co. Meath. In *R.S.A.I. Jn.*, xlvi (1916), pp 46–57.

BLACK ABBEY. Hamilton, G. E. Black Abbey, County Down. In *R.S.A.I. Jn.*, ii (1921), pp 166–78.

BLACKROCK. O'Reilly, P. J. Tobernea holy well, Blackrock, County Dublin. In *R.S.A.I. Jn.*, xxxii (1902), pp 178–86.

BLUND. Brooks, E. St John. Archbishop Henry of London and his Irish connections. In *R.S.A.I. Jn.*, lx (1930), pp 1–22.

BRAGANSTOWN. Lydon, J. F. The Braganstown massacre, 1329. In *Louth Arch. Soc. Jn.*, xix (1977–80), pp 5–16.

BRÉIFNE. Simms, Katharine. The O'Reillys and the kingdom of East Breifne. In *Breifne*, v, no. 19 (1979), pp 305–19.

BRISTOL. Seyer, Samuel. *Memoirs, historical and topographical, of Bristol and its neighbourhood*. 2 vols. Bristol, 1821.

—— Sherborne, J. W. *The port of Bristol in the middle ages*. Bristol Branch of the Historical Association, Bristol, 1965. (Local History Pamphlets, xiii. Port of Bristol Series.)

BUTLER. Byrne, A. T. An córus féodach i gcriochaibh na mBuitléireach ó'n XII go dtí an XV aois. (M.A. thesis, N.U.I. (U.C.C.), 1941.)

—— Empey, C. A. The Butler lordship in Ireland to 1509. (Ph.D. thesis, University of Dublin, 1970.)

—— —— The Butler lordship. In *Butler Soc. Jn.*, i (1968–71), pp 174–87.

—— —— and Simms, Katharine. The ordinances of the White Earl and the problem of coign in the later middle ages. In *R.I.A. Proc.*, lxxv (1975), sect. C, no. 8, pp 161–87.

—— Round, J. H. The earldoms of Ormond in Ireland. In Joseph Foster, *Collectanea Genealogica* (4 vols, London, 1882–7), iii (1887), pp 84–93.

CARLINGFORD. Leask, H. G. *King John's castle, Carlingford, Co. Louth*. Dublin, [1941].

CARLOW. Mills, James. Accounts of the earl of Norfolk's estates in Ireland, 1279–1294. In *R.S.A.I. Jn.*, xxii (1892), pp 50–62.

—— Nugent, W. F. Carlow in the middle ages. In *R.S.A.I. Jn.*, lxxxv (1955), pp 62–76.

CARRICK-ON-SUIR. Empey, C. A. The manor of Carrick-on-Suir in the middle ages. In *Butler Soc. Jn.*, ii, no. 2 (1982), pp 206–14.

CARRICKFERGUS. Jope, E. M. *A guide to Carrickfergus castle*. Belfast, 1957.

—— M'Skimin, Samuel. *The history and antiquities of the county of the town of Carrickfergus*. Belfast, 1811; 2nd ed., Belfast, 1823; 3rd ed., 1829; reprint, 1832; new [i.e. 4th] ed. Ed. E. J. McCrum. Belfast, 1909.

CASHEL. Leask, H. G. *St Patrick's Rock, Cashel, Co. Tipperary*. Dublin, [1940].

CASTLEKEVIN. Orpen, G. H. Castrum Keyvini: Castlekevin. In *R.S.A.I. Jn.*, xxxviii (1908), pp 17–27.

CASTLEKNOCK. Brooks, E. St J. The grant of Castleknock to Hugh Tyrel. In *R.S.A.I. Jn.*, lxiii (1933), pp 206–20.

CASTLEMORE. Orpen, G. H. The castle of Raymond le Gros at Fodredunolan. In *R.S.A.I. Jn.*, xxxvi (1906), pp 368–82.

CLARE. Altschul, Michael. *A baronial family in medieval England: the Clares, 1217–1314*. Baltimore, 1965. (The Johns Hopkins University Studies in Historical and Political Science, ser. 83, no. 2.)

—— Gleeson, D. F. A fourteenth-century Clare heresy trial. In *I.E.R.*, 5th ser., lxxxix (1958), pp 36–42.

CLONCURRY. O'Loan, J. J. The manor of Cloncurry, Co. Kildare, and the feudal system of land tenure in Ireland. In *Dept. Agric. Jn.*, lviii (1961), pp 14–36.

CONNACHT. Edwards, Robin Dudley. Anglo-Norman relations with Connacht, 1169–1224. In *I.H.S.*, i, no. 2 (Sept. 1938), pp 135–53.

—— Knox, H. T. Occupation of Connaught by the Anglo-Normans after A.D. 1237. In *R.S.A.I. Jn.*, xxxii (1902), pp 132–8, 393–406; xxxiii (1903), pp 58–74, 179–89, 284–94.

—— O'Flaherty, Roderic. *A chorographical description of West or h-Iar Connaught, written A.D. 1684*. Ed. James Hardiman. Ir. Arch. Soc., Dublin, 1846.
Appendix includes several medieval documents.

—— Orpen, G. H. Richard de Burgh and the conquest of Connaught. In *Galway Arch. Soc. Jn.*, vii (1911–12), pp 129–47.

—— Walton, Helen. The English in Connacht. (Ph.D. thesis, University of Dublin, 1980.)

CORK. Bolster, Evelyn. *A history of the diocese of Cork from the earliest times to the reformation*. Shannon, 1972.

—— Gibson, C. B. *The history of the county and city of Cork*. 2 vols. London, 1861; reprint, Cork, 1974.

—— O'Sullivan, Denis. The monastic establishments of medieval Cork. In *Cork Hist. Soc. Jn.*, xlviii (1943), pp 9–18.

—— —— Three little-known monastic establishments in mediaeval Cork. In Séamus Pender (ed.), *Féilscríbhinn Torna* (Cork, 1947), pp 203–8.

—— O'Sullivan, William. *The economic history of Cork city from the earliest times to the Act of Union*. Dublin, 1937.

—— Smith, Charles. *The antient and present state of the county and city of Cork*. 2 vols. Dublin, 1750; new ed., Cork, 1815; reprint, Cork, 1893–4. (*Cork Hist. Soc. Jn.*, suppl.)

Curtis, Edmund. Murchertach O'Brien, high king of Ireland, and his Norman son-in-law, Arnulf de Montgomery, *circa* 1100. In *R.S.A.I. Jn.*, li (1921), pp 116–24.

DERRYNAVLAN. Byrne, F. J. Derrynavlan: the historical context. In *R.S.A.I. Jn.*, cx (1980), pp 116–26.

DESMOND. Jefferies, Henry. Gaelic Desmond and Anglo-Norman Cork in the reign of Diarmaid McCarthy, 1151–1185. (B.A. dissertation, N.U.I. (U.C.C.), 1982.)

DROGHEDA. Bradley, John. The topography and layout of medieval Drogheda. In *Louth Arch. Soc. Jn.*, xix (1977–80), pp 98–127.

—— Gwynn, Aubrey. A forgotten abbey of St Mary's, Drogheda. In *Louth Arch. Soc. Jn.*, xiii (1953–6), pp 190–99.

DUBLIN. Bernard, J. H. *The cathedral church of St Patrick*. Dublin, 1903; 3rd ed., revised by J. E. L. Oulton, 1940.

DUBLIN. Berry, H. F. Catalogue of the mayors, provosts, and bailiffs of Dublin city, A.D. 1229 to 1447. In *R.I.A. Proc.*, xxviii (1909–10), sect. C, no. 2, pp 47–61.

—— —— History of the religious gild of S. Anne in S. Audoen's Church, Dublin, 1430–1740, taken from its records in the Haliday Collection, R.I.A. In *R.I.A. Proc.*, xxv (1904–5), sect. C, no. 3, pp 21–106.

—— —— Some ancient deeds of the parish of St Werburgh, Dublin, 1243–1676. In *R.S.A.I. Jn.*, xlv (1915), pp 32–44.

—— Burke, Nuala. Dublin's north-eastern city wall: early reclamation and development at the Poddle–Liffey confluence. In *R.I.A. Proc.*, lxxiv (1974), sect. C, no. 3, pp 113–32.

—— Chart, D. A. *The story of Dublin*. London, 1932. (Medieval Town Series [xxxii]); reprint, Nendeln, 1971.

—— Crawford, M. V. *The pictorial history of the cathedral church of the Holy Trinity: Christ Church cathedral, Dublin*. [Dublin, 1967.]

—— Edwards, Robin Dudley. The beginnings of municipal government in Dublin. In *Dublin Hist. Rec.*, i (1938–9), pp 2–10.

—— *Focus on medieval Dublin*. Ed. Howard Clarke. In *Dublin Arts Festival, 21–30 April, 1978* (Dublin, 1978).
Separately paged centre supplement.

—— Gilbert, J. T. *A history of the city of Dublin*. 3 vols. Dublin, 1854–9; reprint with index, 1861; abridged ed., by R. M. Gilbert. Dublin, 1903.

—— Gwynn, Aubrey. The origins of St Mary's abbey, Dublin. In *R.S.A.I. Jn.*, lxxix (1949), pp 110–25.

—— Hand, G. J. The medieval chapter of St Patrick's cathedral, Dublin. 1. The early period, *c.* 1219–*c.* 1279. In *Reportorium Novum*, iii (1961–4), pp 229–48.

—— —— The rivalry of the cathedral chapters in medieval Dublin. In *R.S.A.I. Jn.*, xcii (1962), pp 193–206.

—— Harris, Walter. *The history and antiquities of the city of Dublin*. Dublin, 1766.

—— Jackson, Victor. The palace of St Sepulchre. In *Dublin Hist. Rec.*, xxviii (1974–5), pp 82–92.

—— Lewis-Crosby, E. H. *Christ Church cathedral, Dublin: a short history*. Dublin, [1949?]; 3rd ed., 1961.

—— McNeill, Charles. New Gate, Dublin. In *R.S.A.I. Jn.*, li (1921), pp 152–65.

—— Mason, W. M. *The history and antiquities of the collegiate and cathedral church of St Patrick near Dublin, from its foundation in 1190 to the year 1819*. Dublin, 1820.

—— Otway-Ruthven, A. J. The medieval church lands of Co. Dublin. In *Med. studies presented to A. Gwynn* (1961), pp 54–73.

—— Robinson, J. L. Churchwarden's accounts, 1484–1600, St Werburgh's church, Dublin. In *R.S.A.I. Jn.*, xliv (1914), pp 132–42.

—— Ronan, M. V. Anglo-Norman Dublin and diocese. In *I.E.R.*, 5th ser., xlv (1935), pp 148–64, 274–91, 485–504, 576–95; xlvi (1935), pp 11–30, 154–71, 257–75, 377–93, 490–510, 577–96; xlvii (1936), pp 28–44, 144–63, 459–68; xlviii (1936), pp 170–93, 378–96; xlix (1937), pp 155–64.

DUBLIN. Smyth, A. P. *Scandinavian York and Dublin: the history and archaeology of two related viking kingdoms*. 2 vols. Dublin, 1975–9.

—— Walsh, T. P. Dublin in the eleventh and twelfth centuries. (M.Phil. thesis, N.U.I. (U.C.D.), 1972.)

DUISKE. See GRAIGUENAMANAGH.

DUNBOYNE. Butler, T. B. The barony of Dunboyne. In *Ir. Geneal.*, ii (1943–55), pp 66–81, 107–21, 130–36, 162–4.

DUNBRODY. Morrin, James. Historical notes of the abbey of Dunbrody. In *Transactions of the Ossory Archaeological Society*, i (1874–9), pp 407–31.

DUNDRUM. Orpen, G. H. Dundrum Castle, County Down, identified with the 'Castrum de Rath'. In *R.S.A.I. Jn.*, xxxix (1909), pp 23–9.

DUNLUCE. *A guide to Dunluce castle, Co. Antrim*. Belfast, 1966.

EMLY. Seymour, St J. D. *The diocese of Emly*. Dublin, 1913.

FARNEY. Shirley, E. P. *Some account of the territory or dominion of Farney in the province and earldom of Ulster*. London, 1845.

FORE. Leask, H. G. *Fore, Co. Westmeath: national monuments in the charge of the Commissioners of Public Works: St Fechin's church, the town gateways, and the Benedictine priory*. Dublin, [1938].

Gallwey, Hubert. Some early Norman families in Co. Wexford. In *Old Wexford Soc. Jn.*, iii (1970–71), pp 56–61; iv (1972), pp 53–6.

GALWAY. Hardiman, James. *The history of the town and county of the town of Galway*. Dublin, 1820; reprint, Galway, 1958.

—— Knox, H. T. Occupation of the county of Galway by the Anglo-Normans after 1237. In *R.S.A.I. Jn.*, xxxi (1901), pp 365–70.

—— O'Sullivan, M. D. *Old Galway: the history of a Norman colony in Ireland*. Cambridge, 1942; reprint, with introduction by W. J. Hogan, Galway, 1983.

Gamurrini, Eugenio. *Istoria-genealogica delle famiglie nobili Toscane et Umbre*. 5 vols. Florence, 1668–85.

GERALDINES. Fitzgerald, Brian. *The Geraldines: an experiment in Irish government, 1169–1601*. London and New York, 1951.

—— Fitzgerald, C. W., marquis of Kildare. *The earls of Kildare and their ancestors, from 1057 to 1773*. 3rd ed., Dublin, 1858. *Addenda*, Dublin, 1862; *2nd addenda*, Dublin, 1866.

—— Nicholls, K. W. The Geraldines of Allen. In *Ir. Geneal.*, iv (1968–73), pp 93–108, 194–200.

—— Orpen, G. H. The Fitz Geralds, barons of Offaly. In *R.S.A.I. Jn.*, xliv (1914), pp 99–113.

GLENDALOUGH. Ronan, M. V. Union of the dioceses of Glendaloch and Dublin in 1216. In *R.S.A.I. Jn.*, lx (1930), pp 56–72.

GRAIGUENAMANAGH. Carville, Geraldine. *Norman splendour: Duiske abbey, Graignamanagh*. Belfast, 1979.

—— Hughes, E. W. Duiske abbey, Graignamanagh: abbey triumphant. In *Old Kilkenny Rev.*, n.s., i (1974–8), pp 254–60.

Grey Abbey, County Down. H.M.S.O., Belfast, 1964.

HOLM CULTRAM. Gilbanks, G. E. *Some records of a Cistercian abbey: Holm Cultram, Cumberland*. London, [1900?].
Mother house of Grey abbey: account of its foundation (pp 37–9).

HOLY CROSS. Carville, Geraldine. *The heritage of Holy Cross*. Belfast, 1973.

—— Hartry, Malachy. *Triumphalia chronologica monasterii Sanctae Crucis in Hibernia. De Cisterciensium Hibernorum viris illustribus*. Ed. and trans. Denis Murphy. Dublin, 1891; reprint, 1895.
Author known as Father John, *fl.* 1640.

—— Hayes, W. J. *Holy Cross abbey*. Dublin, 1973.

INCHIQUIN. O'Brien, A. F. The settlement of Imokilly and the formation and descent of the manor of Inchiquin, Co. Cork. In *Cork Hist. Soc. Jn.*, lxxxvii (1982), pp 21–6.

—— —— The territorial ambitions of Maurice Fitz Thomas, first earl of Desmond, with particular reference to the barony and manor of Inchiquin, Co. Cork. In *R.I.A. Proc.*, lxxxii (1982), sect. C, no. 3, pp 59–88.

INISLOUNAGHT. Conway, Colmcille. The Cistercian abbey of Inislounaght. In *Clonmel Hist. Soc. Jn.*, i, no. 4 (1956), pp 3–52.

JERPOINT. Conway, Colmcille. The origins of Jerpoint abbey, Co. Kilkenny. In *Cîteaux*, xiv (1963), pp 293–306.

—— Hegarty, Maureen. Jerpoint. In *Old Kilkenny Rev.*, xxiii (1971), pp 4–14.

—— Leask, H. G. *Jerpoint Abbey, Co. Kilkenny*. Office of Public Works, Dublin, [1939].

KAVANAGH. Nicholls, K. W. The Kavanaghs, 1400–1700. In *Ir. Geneal.*, v (1974–9), pp 435–47.

KELLS, KILKENNY. Empey, C. A. A case study of the primary phase of Anglo-Norman settlement: the lordship of Kells. In *Old Kilkenny Rev.*, iii (1984–), pp 32–40.

—— —— The sacred and the secular: the Augustinian priory of Kells in Ossory, 1193–1541. In *I.H.S.*, xxiv, no. 94 (Nov. 1984), pp 131–51.

KELLS, MEATH. O'Connell, Philip. Kells: early and medieval. In *Ríocht na Midhe*, ii, no. 1 (1959), pp 18–36; no. 2 (1960), pp 8–22.

KERRY. Butler, W. F. T. Two Kerry baronies in the sixteenth century. In *Cork Hist. Soc. Jn.*, 2nd ser., xxxiii (1928), pp 1–10; xxxiv (1929), pp 15–21.
Magunihy and Iveragh.

—— Smith, Charles. *The antient and present state of the county of Kerry*. Dublin, 1756; reprint, Cork, 1980.

—— Walsh, Katherine. Franciscan friaries in pre-reformation Kerry. In *Kerry Arch. Soc. Jn.*, ix (1976), pp 16–31.

KILDARE. Otway-Ruthven, A. J. Knights' fees in Kildare, Leix, and Offaly. In *R.S.A.I. Jn.*, xci (1961), pp 163–81.

—— —— The medieval county of Kildare. In *I.H.S.*, xi, no. 43 (Mar. 1959), pp 181–99.

KILKENNY. Empey, C. A. The cantreds of the medieval county of Kilkenny. In *R.S.A.I. Jn.*, ci (1971), pp 128–34.

—— —— (ed.). *A worthy foundation: the cathedral church of St Canice, Kilkenny, 1285–1985*. Mountrath, 1985.

—— Graves, James, and Prim, J. G. A. *The history, architecture and antiquities of the cathedral church of St Canice, Kilkenny*. Dublin, 1857.

KILKENNY. Healy, William. *History and antiquities of Kilkenny county and city*. Vol. i. Kilkenny, [1893].
No more published.

—— Leask, H. G. St Canice's cathedral, Kilkenny. In *R.S.A.I. Jn.*, lxxix (1949), pp 1–9.

—— Morrin, J. L. The Kilkenny witchcraft case, 1325. In *Ossory Arch. Soc. Trans.*, i (1874–9), pp 213–39.
See also Neary, Anne, above, sect. IV B 3.

KILLALOE. Gleeson, D. F. The coarbs of Killaloe diocese. In *R.S.A.I. Jn.*, lxxix (1949), pp 160–69.

—— —— The episcopal succession of Killaloe, A.D. 1317–1626. In *N. Munster Antiq. Jn.*, ii (1940–41), pp 51–62.

—— Gwynn, Aubrey, and Gleeson, D. F. *A history of the diocese of Killaloe*. [Vol. i]. Dublin, [1962].
No more published.

KILMORE. Gwynn, Aubrey. Origins of the diocese of Kilmore. In *Breifne*, i (1958–61), pp 293–306.

KINALECHIN. Gray, Andrew. Kinaleghin: a forgotten Irish Charterhouse of the thirteenth century. In *R.S.A.I. Jn.*, lxxxix (1959), pp 35–58.

KNOCKTOPHER. Empey, C. A. Medieval Knocktopher: a study in manorial settlement. In *Old Kilkenny Rev.*, new ser., ii (1979–83), pp 329–42, 441–52.

DE LACY. Morris, J. E. Ludlow: a study in local history. In *History*, new ser., i (1916–17), pp 159–73.

—— Synott, N. J. Notes on the family of de Lacy in Ireland. In *R.S.A.I. Jn.*, xlix (1919), pp 113–31.

—— Wightman, W. E. *The Lacy family in England and Normandy, 1066–1194*. Oxford, 1966.

LEINSTER. Mills, James. The Norman settlement in Leinster: the cantreds near Dublin. In *R.S.A.I. Jn.*, xxiv (1894), pp 160–75.

—— Smyth, A. P. *Celtic Leinster: towards a historical geography of early Irish civilisation, A.D. 500–1600*. Dublin, 1982.

LIMERICK. Empey, C. A. The settlement of the kingdom of Limerick. In Lydon, *Eng. & Ire.* (1981), pp 1–25.

—— Gwynn, Aubrey. The diocese of Limerick in the twelfth century. In *N. Munster Antiq. Jn.*, v (1946–8), pp 35–48.

—— Hand, G. J. The medieval chapter of St Mary's cathedral, Limerick. In *Med. studies presented to A. Gwynn* (1961), pp 74–89.

—— Hewson, R. F. St Mary's cathedral, Limerick: its development and growth. In *N. Munster Antiq. Jn.*, iv (1944–5), no. 2, pp 55–67.

—— Lenihan, Maurice. *Limerick: its history and antiquities*. Dublin, 1866.

LISMORE. Sanderlin, S. L. The monastery of Lismore. (M.Litt. thesis, University of Dublin, 1974.)

LONDONDERRY. *Ordnance survey of the county of Londonderry. Vol. i: Memoir of the city and north-western liberties of Londonderry. Parish of Templemore*. Dublin, 1837.

LOUGH ERNE. Simms, Katharine. The medieval kingdom of Lough Erne. In *Clogher Rec.*, ix (1977), pp 126–41.

LOUTH. Flanagan, Marie-Thérèse. St Mary's abbey, Louth, and the introduction of the Arroasian observance into Ireland. In *Clogher Rec.*, x (1978–81), pp 233–4.

MACCARTHY. Butler, W. F. T. The pedigree and succession of the house of Mac Carthy Mór, with a map. In *R.S.A.I. Jn.*, li (1921), pp 32–48.

MACSWEENEY. Walsh, Paul (ed.). *Leabhar Chlainne Suibhne: an account of the Mac Sweeney families in Ireland, with pedigrees*. Dublin, 1920.

MALLOW. Berry, H. F. The manor of Mallow in the thirteenth century. In *R.S.A.I. Jn.*, xxiv (1894), pp 14–24.

MANDEVILLE. Curtis, Edmund. The MacQuillan or Mandeville lords of the Route. In *R.I.A. Proc.*, xliv (1937–8), sect. C, no. 4, pp 99–113.

—— Greeves, J. R. H. Robert I and the de Mandevilles of Ulster. In *Transactions of the Dumfriesshire and Galloway Natural History and Antiquarian Society*, 3rd ser., xxxiv (1955–6), pp 59–73.

MARISCO. Brooks, E. St J. The family of Marisco. In *R.S.A.I. Jn.*, lxi (1931), pp 22–38, 89–112; lxii (1932), pp 50–74.

MARSHALL. Griffith, L., and others. The alleged descent of the Marshalls from Dermot Mac Murrough. In *Genealogist's Magazine*, vi (1932–4), pp 311–13, 362–6, 410, 460.

—— Hall, Hamilton. The Marshall pedigree. In *R.S.A.I. Jn.*, xliii (1913), pp 1–29.

MAYO. Knox, H. T. *A history of the county of Mayo to the close of the sixteenth century*. Dublin, 1908.

MEATH. Brady, John. Anglo-Norman Meath. In *Ríocht na Midhe*, ii, no. 3 (1961), pp 38–45.

—— Brooks, E. St J. 14th century monastic estates in Meath: the Llanthony cells of Duleek and Colp. In *R.S.A.I. Jn.*, lxxxiii (1953), pp 140–49; reprint in *Annala Dhamhliag*, vi (1977), pp 12–24.

—— Cogan, Anthony. *The diocese of Meath: ancient and modern*. 3 vols. Dublin, 1862–70.
Vol. i reprinted with title: *The ecclesiastical history of the diocese of Meath* (Dublin, 1874).

—— Hadcock, R. N. The origin of the Augustinian order in Meath. In *Ríocht na Midhe*, iii (1963–6), pp 124–31.

—— Lynch, Anthony. Some metropolitan visitations of Meath in the fifteenth century. In *Ríocht na Midhe*, vii, no. 2 (1982–3), pp 3–11.

—— Walsh, Paul. The Ua Maelechlainn kings of Meath. In *I.E.R.*, 5th ser., lvii (1941), pp 165–83.

MELLIFONT. Conway, Colmcille. The abbatial succession at Mellifont, 1142–1539. In *Louth Arch. Soc. Jn.*, xv (1961–4), pp 23–38.

—— —— *Comhcheilg na Mainistreach Móire*. Dublin, 1968.

—— —— *The story of Mellifont*. Dublin, 1958.

—— Murray, L. P. The last abbot of Mellifont. In *Louth Arch. Soc. Jn.*, viii (1933–6), pp 223–33.

MELLIFONT. O'Dwyer, B. W. The conspiracy in the Mellifont filiation of Cistercian monasteries in Ireland, 1216–31. (Ph.D. thesis, N.U.I. (U.C.D.), 1968.)

—— —— *The conspiracy of Mellifont, 1216—1231: an episode in the history of the Cistercian order in medieval Ireland*. Dublin Historical Association, Dublin, 1970. (Medieval Irish History Series, ii.)

DE MONTGOMERY. Mason, J. F. A. Roger de Montgomery and his sons, 1067–1102. In *R. Hist. Soc. Trans.*, 5th ser., xiii (1963), pp 1–28.

MUCKROSS. Leask, H. G. *The friary of Muckross*. Office of Public Works, Dublin, [1941].

MULLINGAR. Fenning, Hugh. The Dominicans of Mullingar, 1237–1610. In *Ríocht na Midhe*, iii (1963–6), pp 105–13.

MUNSTER. Butler, W. F. T. The divisions of south Munster under the Tudors. In *Cork Hist. Soc. Jn.*, 2nd ser., iii (1897), pp 121–36, 233–46.

—— Lee, G. A. The leper hospitals of Munster. In *N. Munster Antiq. Jn.*, x (1966–7), pp 12–26.

—— Martin, F. X. The first Normans in Munster. In *Cork Hist. Soc. Jn.*, [2nd ser.], lxxvi (1971), pp 48–71.

—— Power, Patrick. The Cistercian abbeys of Munster. In *Cork Hist. Soc. Jn.*, 2nd ser., xxxiii (1928), pp 75–82; xxxiv (1929), pp 22–9, 91–7; xxxv (1930), pp 43–6.
No more published.

MURRISK. Leask, H. G. Murrisk abbey, Co. Mayo. In *R.S.A.I. Jn.*, lxxiii (1943), pp 137–41.

NEWCASTLE. Orpen, G. H. Novum Castrum McKynegan, Newcastle, County Wicklow. In *R.S.A.I. Jn.*, xxxviii (1908), pp 126–40.

NEW ROSS. Glasscock, R. E. Some parallels to New Ross. In *Old Wexford Soc. Jn.*, vii (1978–9), pp 31–4.

—— Orpen, G. H. *New Ross in the thirteenth century*. Dublin, 1911.

Nicholas, Thomas. *Annals and antiquities of the counties and county families of Wales*. 2 vols. London, 1872; reprint, 1875.

NORRAGH. Curtis, Edmund. The barons of Norragh, Co. Kildare, 1171–1660. In *R.S.A.I. Jn.*, lxv (1935), pp 84–101.

O'DONNELL. Walsh, Paul. Scots Clan Domhnaill in Ireland. In *I.E.R.*, 5th ser., xlviii (1936), pp 23–42.

O'BRIEN. O'Donoghue, John. *Historical memoir of the O'Briens*. Dublin, 1860.

O'NEILL. Mathews, Thomas. *The O'Neills of Ulster: their history and genealogy*. 3 vols. Dublin, 1907.

—— Simms, Katharine. The archbishops of Armagh and the O'Neills, 1347–1471. In *I.H.S.*, xix, no. 73 (Mar. 1974), pp 38–55.

O'REILLY. *A genealogical history of the O'Reillys. Written in the eighteenth century by Eóghan Ó Raghallaigh and incorporating portion of the earlier work of Dr Thomas Fitzsimons, vicar-general of the diocese of Kilmore*. Ed. James Carney. Cumann Sheanchais Bhreifne, [Cavan], 1959.

ORMOND. Gleeson, John. *History of the Ely O'Carroll territory, or ancient Ormond, situated in north Tipperary and north-western King's County, Ireland*. Dublin, 1915.

OSSORY. Carrigan, William. *The history and antiquities of the diocese of Ossory*. 4 vols. Dublin, 1905; reprint, Kilkenny, 1981.

—— Orpen, G. H. Motes and Norman castles in Ossory. In *R.S.A.I. Jn.*, xxxix (1909), pp 314–42.

Power, Patrick. *Waterford and Lismore: a compendious history of the united dioceses*. Cork, 1937.

POWERSCOURT. Price, Liam. Powerscourt and the territory of Fercullen. In *R.S.A.I. Jn.*, lxxxiii (1953), pp 117–32.

DE RIDELISFORD. Brooks, E. St J. The de Ridelisfords. In *R.S.A.I. Jn.*, lxxxi (1951), pp 115–38; lxxxii (1952), pp 45–61.

ROSCREA. Gleeson, D. F. *Roscrea: a history of the Catholic parish of Roscrea from the earliest times to the present day, with some account of the territories of Uí Cairin and Éile Uí Cearbhaill*. Dublin, 1947.

ROSS. Dunning, P. J. Pope Innocent III and the Ross election controversy. In *Ir. Theol. Quart.*, xxvi (1959), pp 346–59.

—— Kiely, M. A. Episcopal succession of Ross in the fifteenth century. In *I.E.R.*, 5th ser., xlvii (1936), pp 158–65.

—— Lyons, M. C. An account of the manor of Old Ross, September 1284 to September 1285. In *Decies*, xviii (1981), pp 33–40; xix (1981), pp 18–31. (Medieval Series, viii.)
Pt ii: Textual appendix: 'The account of David Trillec, reeve of Old Ross, from 29th of September 1284 to 29th of September 1285', P.R.O., S.C. 6 1238/48.

SAVAGE. Savage-Armstrong, G. F. *The ancient and noble family of the Savages of the Ards*. London, 1888; some chapters revised and enlarged as *A genealogical history of the Savage family in Ulster*. London, 1906.

SKREEN. Otway-Ruthven, A. J. Parochial development in the rural deanery of Skreen. In *R.S.A.I. Jn.*, xciv (1964), pp 111–22.

SLANE. Westropp, T. J. 'Slane in Bregia', County Meath: its friary and hermitage. In *R.S.A.I. Jn.*, xxxi (1901), pp 405–30; xxxii (1902), p. 192.

STABANNON. Sayles, G. O. Ecclesiastical process and the parsonage of Stabannon in 1351. In *R.I.A. Proc.*, lv (1952–3), sect. C, no. 1, pp 1–23; reprint in his *Scripta diversa* (London, 1982), pp 99–122.

TALBOT. Pollard, A. J. The family of Talbot, lords Talbot and earls of Shrewsbury, in the fifteenth century. (Ph.D. thesis, University of Bristol, 1968.)

TEMPLEYBRICK. Mulholland, John. The vanished medieval settlements of Templeybrick. In *Decies*, no. 2 (May 1976), pp 5–8.

TERRYGLASS. Leask, H. G. Terryglass castle, Co. Tipperary. In *R.S.A.I. Jn.*, lxxiii (1943), pp 141–4.

THOMOND. Curtis, Edmund. The wars of Turlogh: an historical document. In *The Irish Review*, ii (1912–13), pp 577–86, 644–7; iii (1913–14), pp 34–41.

—— Gwynn, Aubrey. Richard II and the chieftains of Thomond. In *N. Munster Antiq. Jn.*, vii (1954–7), no. 3, pp 1–8.

—— Westropp, T. J. The Normans in Thomond. In *R.S.A.I. Jn.*, xxi (1890–91), pp 284–93, 381–7, 462–72.

TINTERN. Bernard, J. H. The foundation of Tintern Abbey, Co. Wexford. In *R.I.A. Proc.*, xxxiii (1916–17), sect. C, no. 17, pp 527–9.

TIPPERARY. Empey, C. A. The cantreds of medieval Tipperary. In *N. Munster Antiq. Jn.*, xiii (1970), pp 22–9.

See also his 'The Norman period, 1185–1500' in William Nolan (ed.), *Tipperary: history and society* (Dublin, 1985), pp 71–91.

TÍR EOGHAIN. Orpen, G. H. The Normans in Tirowen and Tirconnell. In *R.S.A.I. Jn.*, xlv (1915), pp 275–88.

TRIM. Butler, Richard. *Some notices of the castle and of the abbies and other religious houses at Trim.* Trim, 1835; 2nd ed., as *Some notices of the castle of Trim*, 1840; 3rd ed., as *Some notices of the castle and of the ecclesiastical remains of Trim*, 1854; 4th ed., as *Some notices of the castle and of the ecclesiastical buildings of Trim*, Dublin, 1861.

3rd ed., reprinted, with a short life of Richard Butler by C. C. Ellison (Meath Archaeological and Historical Society, Tara, 1978).

TUAM. Edwards, Ruth Dudley. Ecclesiastical appointments in the province of Tuam, 1399–1477. In *Archiv. Hib.*, xxxiii (1975), pp 91–100.

TYREL. Brooks, E. St J. The Tyrels of Castleknock. In *R.S.A.I. Jn.*, lxxvi (1946), pp 151–4.

UÍ MAINE. Kelleher, J. V. Uí Maine in the annals and genealogies to 1225. [Pt 1]. In *Celtica*, ix (1971), pp 61–112. [No more published.]

ULAID. Byrne, F. J. The history of the kingdom of Ulaid. (M.A. thesis, N.U.I. (U.C.D.), 1959.)

ULSTER. Curtis, Edmund. The medieval earldom of Ulster, 1333–1603. In *Belfast Natur. Hist. Soc. Proc.*, 1930/31, pp 67–80.

—— McNeill, T. E. *Anglo-Norman Ulster: the history and archaeology of an Irish barony, 1177–1400.* Edinburgh, 1980.

—— Orpen, G. H. The earldom of Ulster. In *R.S.A.I. Jn.*, xliii (1913), pp 30–46, 133–43; xliv (1914), pp 51–66; xlv (1915), pp 123–42; l (1920), pp 167–77; li (1921), pp 68–76.

—— Quinn, D. B. Anglo-Irish Ulster in the early sixteenth century. In *Belfast Natur. Hist. Soc. Proc.*, 1933/4 (1935), pp 56–78.

—— Sayles, G. O. Medieval [Ulster]. In *Belfast in its regional setting: a scientific survey* (British Association, Belfast, 1952), pp 98–103; reprint in his *Scripta diversa* (1982), pp 123–8.

—— Sheane, Michael. *Ulster in the middle ages.* Stockport, [1982].

—— Simms, Katharine. 'The king's friend': O'Neill, the crown, and the earldom of Ulster. In Lydon, *Eng. & Ire.* (1981), pp 214–36.

WALL. Gallwey, Hubert. *The Wall family in Ireland, 1170–1970.* Naas, 1970.

Walsh, Paul. Origins of King's County: the King's County and Uí Failghe. In *I.B.L.*, xxvi (1938), pp 50–56.

WATERFORD. Dunning, P. J. Pope Innocent III and the Waterford–Lismore controversy, 1198–1216. In *Ir. Theol. Quart.*, xxviii (1961), pp 215–32.

—— Empey, C. A. County Waterford in the thirteenth century. In *Decies*, no. 13 (Jan. 1980), pp 6–16. (Medieval Waterford, iii.)

WATERFORD. Lydon, J. F. The city of Waterford in the later middle ages. In *Decies*, no. 12 (Sept. 1979), pp 5–15. (Medieval Waterford, i.)

—— McEneaney, Eamonn. The government of the municipality of Waterford in the thirteenth century. In *Decies*, no. 13 (Jan. 1980), pp 17–27. (Medieval Waterford, iv.) See also sect. IV B 7, above.

—— Medieval Waterford. 1–8. In *Decies*, nos 12–19 (1979–81).

—— Nolan, Tom. The order of Knights Templar in the Waterford area. In *Decies*, no. 14 (May 1980), pp 52–60. (Medieval Waterford, v.)

—— O'Neill, M. A. The diocese of Waterford, 1096–1363. (M.A. thesis, N.U.I. (U.C.C.), 1969.)

—— Power, Patrick. The town wall of Waterford. In *R.S.A.I. Jn.*, lxxiii (1943), pp 118–36.

—— Ryland, R. H. *The history, topography and antiquities of the county and city of Waterford*. London, 1824.

—— Smith, Charles. *Antient and present state of the county and city of Waterford*. Dublin, 1746; 2nd ed., 1774; reprint, Cork, 1969.
2nd ed.: *Ancient* . . . .

WEXFORD. Brooks, E. St J. *Knights' fees in counties Wexford, Carlow and Kilkenny, 13th—15th century*. I.M.C., Dublin, 1950.

—— Hore, H. F. *History of the town and county of Wexford*. Ed. P. H. Hore. 6 vols. London, 1900–11.

WICKLOW. Millett, Benignus. The Friars Minor in County Wicklow, Ireland (1260–1982). In *Archivum Franciscanum Historicum*, lxxvii (1984), pp 110–36.

—— Price, Liam. The Byrnes' country in County Wicklow in the sixteenth century. In *R.S.A.I. Jn.*, lxiii (1933), pp 224–42; lxvi (1936), pp 41–66.

14 HISTORY OF THE IRISH ABROAD

Binchy, D. A. The Irish Benedictine congregation in medieval Germany. In *Studies*, xviii (1929), pp 194–210.

Breatnach, P. A. The origins of the Irish monastic tradition at Ratisbon (Regensburg). In *Celtica*, xiii (1980), pp 58–77.

Gwynn, Aubrey. The continuity of the Irish tradition at Würzburg. In *Herbipolis jubilans: 1200 Jahre Bistum Würzburg: Festschrift zur Säkularfeier der Erhebung der Kiliansreliquien* (Würzburg, 1952), pp 57–81.

—— Some notes on the history of the Irish and Scottish Benedictine monasteries in Germany. In *Innes Review*, v (1954), pp 5–27.

Hammermayer, Ludwig. Die irischen Benediktiner 'Schottenklöster' in Deutschland und ihr institutioneller Zusammenschluss vom 12. bis 16. Jahrhundert. In *Studien und Mitteilungen zur Geschichte des Benediktiner-Ordens und seiner Zweige*, lxxxvii, Heft 3–4 (1976), pp 249–337.

McCabe, Herbert. An Irishman in China in the fourteenth century. In *Assisi*, xiii (1941), pp 34–5.

15 HISTORY OF ARCHITECTURE, SCULPTURE, AND DECORATIVE ARTS

Aalen, F. H. A. The evolution of the traditional house in western Ireland. In *R.S.A.I. Jn.*, xcvi (1966), pp 47–58.

Anderson, Jorgen. Temptation in Kilkea. In *Kildare Arch. Soc. Jn.*, xv (1971–6), pp 243–50.
See also Harbison, Peter, below.

Armitage, E. S. *The early Norman castles of the British Isles*. London, 1912.
'Motte-castles in Ireland' (pp 323–50).

Armstrong, E. C. R. Processional cross, pricket-candlestick, and bell, found together at Sheephouse, near Oldbridge, Co. Meath. In *R.S.A.I. Jn.*, xlv (1915), pp 27–31.

Aubert, Marcel. *L'architecture cistercienne en France*. 2 vols. Paris, 1943; 2nd ed., 1947.

—— *La sculpture française au moyen âge*. Paris, 1946.

Bilson, John. The architecture of the Cistercians, with special reference to some of their earlier churches in England. In *Archaeological Journal*, lxvi (1909), pp 185–280.

Bond, Francis. *An introduction to English church architecture from the eleventh to the sixteenth century*. 2 vols. London, 1913.

Bradley, John. A medieval figure at Calliaghstown, County Meath. In *R.S.A.I. Jn.*, cx (1980), pp 149–52.

—— Medieval floor tiles from the Franciscan friary, Waterford. In *Decies*, xxiv (1983), pp 40–41. (The Archaeology of Waterford, vii.)

Brannon, N. F. A late medieval carved stone from Drumeil townland, County Londonderry. In *U.J.A.*, 3rd ser., xliv–xlv (1981–2), pp 204–5.

—— A medieval carved stone from Errigal Keerogue church, County Tyrone. In *U.J.A.*, 3rd ser., xliv–xlv (1981–2), pp 200–03.

de Breffny, Brian, and Mott, George. *The churches and abbeys of Ireland*. London, 1976.

Campbell, Åke. Notes on the Irish house. In *Folk-liv*, i (1937), pp 207–34.

Carter, Jack. Undescribed medieval heads of County Laois. In *Éile*, i (1982), pp 53–8.

Champneys, A. C. *Irish ecclesiastical architecture*. London and Dublin, 1910; reprint, Shannon, 1970.

Crawford, H. S. A descriptive list of Irish shrines and reliquaries. In *R.S.A.I. Jn.*, liii (1923), pp 74–93, 151–76.

—— The mural paintings and inscriptions at Knockmoy abbey. In *R.S.A.I. Jn.*, xlix (1919), pp 25–34.

Curtis, Edmund. Some medieval seals out of the Ormond archives. In *R.S.A.I. Jn.*, lxvi (1936), pp 1–8; Some further medieval seals out of the Ormond archives, including that of Donal Reagh MacMurrough Kavanagh, king of Leinster. In ibid., lxvii (1937), pp 72–6.

Duport, Marie. La sculpture irlandaise à la fin du moyen-âge. In *La Revue de l'Art*, xxx (1934), pp 49–62.

Eames, E. S. *Catalogue of medieval lead-glazed earthenware tiles in the Department of Medieval and Later Antiquities, British Museum*. 2 vols. London, 1980.
See also Thomas Fanning, 'The British Museum catalogue of medieval tiles: a review, incorporating the Irish evidence' in *N. Munster Antiq. Jn.*, xxiii (1981), pp 9–16.

Evans, E. E. Sod and turf houses in Ireland. In Geraint Jenkins (ed.), *Studies in folk life* (London, 1969), pp 79–90.

Fergusson, Peter. Early Cistercian churches in Yorkshire and the problem of the Cistercian crossing tower. In *Society of Architectural Historians Jn.*, xxix (1970), pp 211–21.

Fitzgerald, Lord Walter. Kentstown churchyard. In *Ir. Mem. Assoc. Jn.*, viii (1910–12), pp 608–10.

Frankl, Paul. *Gothic architecture*. Harmondsworth and Baltimore, 1962. (Pelican History of Art, xix.)

Gardner, Arthur. See Prior, E. S., below.

Gibson, Strickland. *Some notable Bodleian bindings, 12th to 18th cents.* Oxford, 1901–4.

Gillet, Louis. *Histoire artistique des ordres mendiants*. Paris, 1912.

Glasscock, R. E. Mottes in Ireland. In *Château Gaillard*, vii (1975), pp 95–110.

Gwynn, Edward. The manuscript known as the Liber Flavus Fergusiorum. In *R.I.A. Proc.*, xxvi (1906–7), sect. C, no. 2, pp 15–41.

Harbison, Peter. Some further sculpture in Ennis priory. In *N. Munster Antiq. Jn.*, xix (1977), pp 39–42.
Continues article by John Hunt, below.

—— Some medieval sculpture in Kerry. In *Kerry Arch. Soc. Jn.*, vi (1973), pp 9–25.

—— Some medieval Thomond tomb-sculpture: lost, found, and imaginary. In *N. Munster Antiq. Jn.*, xiv (1971), pp 29–36.

—— Temptation in Kilkea again: 15th century representation of St Anthony. In *Kildare Arch. Soc. Jn.*, xvi (1979–80), pp 68–72.
See also Anderson, Jorgen, above.

—— Three decorated wooden beams of the thirteenth century in Rothe House Museum, Kilkenny. In *Old Kilkenny Rev.*, xxv (1973), pp 34–41.

—— Twelfth and thirteenth century Irish stonemasons in Regensburg (Bavaria) and the end of the 'school of the west' in Connacht. In *Studies*, lxiv (1975), pp 333–46.

Henry, Françoise. Irish Cistercian monasteries and their carved decoration. In *Apollo*, lxxxiv (1966), pp 260–67.

—— *The book of Kells*. London, 1974.

—— and Marsh-Micheli, G. L. A century of Irish illumination (1070–1170). In *R.I.A. Proc.*, lxii (1962), sect. C, no. 5, pp 101–64.

Hunt, John. The influence of alabaster carvings on medieval sculpture in Ennis friary. Ed. Peter Harbison. In *N. Munster Antiq. Jn.*, xvii (1975), pp 35–41.

—— *Irish medieval figure sculpture, 1200–1600: a study of Irish tombs, with notes on costume and armour*. 2 vols. Dublin and London, 1974.

—— Rory O'Tunney and the Ossory tomb sculptures. In *R.S.A.I. Jn.*, lxxx (1950), pp 22–8.

—— See also Ó Ríordáin, S. P., below.

King, H. A. Late medieval crosses in County Meath, *c.* 1470–1635. In *R.I.A. Proc.*, lxxxiv (1984), sect. C, no. 2, pp 79–115.

—— A medieval tile from Greenoge, Co. Meath. In *Ríocht na Midhe*, vii, no. 3 (1984), pp 63–6.

Lasteyrie, Robert de. *L'architecture religieuse en France à l'époque gothique*. 2 vols. Paris, 1926–7.

—— *L'architecture religieuse en France à l'époque romane: ses origines, son développement*. Paris, 1912; 2e éd., 1929.

Lawlor, H. C. Mote and mote-and-bailey castles in de Courcy's principality of Ulster. In *U.J.A.*, 3rd ser., i (1938), pp 155–64; ii (1939), pp 46–54.

Lawlor, H. J. The monuments of the pre-reformation archbishops of Dublin. In *R.S.A.I. Jn.*, xlvii (1917), pp 109–38.

Leask, H. G. Castles and their place in Irish history. In *Ir. Sword*, x (1971–2), pp 235–43.

—— *Irish castles and castellated houses*. Dundalk, 1941; 2nd ed., 1944.

—— *Irish churches and monastic buildings*. 3 vols. Dundalk, 1955–60.

Lumley, I. W. J. The Holy Ghost friary, Waterford: an architectural account. In *Decies*, xx (1982), pp 4–21.

Mâle, Émile. *L'art religieux du XIII* siècle en France*. Paris, 1898; 8th ed., 1948.

Manning, Conleth. The Inistioge priory cloister arcade. In *Old Kilkenny Rev.*, n.s., i (1974–8), pp 190–200.

Marsh-Micheli, G. L. See Henry, Françoise, and Marsh-Micheli, G. L., above.

Martin, A. R. *Franciscan architecture in England*. Manchester, 1937. (British Society of Franciscan Studies, xviii); reprint, Farnborough, 1966.

Mercer, Eric. *English art, 1553–1625*. Oxford, 1962. (Oxford History of English Art, vii.)

Mooney, Canice. Franciscan architecture in pre-reformation Ireland. In *R.S.A.I. Jn.*, lxxxv (1955), pp 133–73; lxxxvi (1956), pp 125–69; lxxxvii (1957), pp 1–38, 103–24.

Mott, George. See de Breffny, Brian, above.

Muhlhausen, Ludwig. Contributions to the study of the tangible material culture of the Gaoltacht. In *Cork Hist. Soc. Jn.*, 2nd ser., xxxviii (1933), pp 67–71; xxxix (1934), pp 41–51.
No more published.

Murray, Hilary. Documentary evidence for domestic buildings in Ireland, *c.* 400–1200, in the light of archaeology. In *Medieval Archaeology*, xxiii (1979), pp 81–97.

Ó Concheanainn, Tomás. Gilla Ísa Mac Fir Bhisigh and a scribe of his school. In *Ériu*, xxv (1974), pp 157–71.

—— The scribe of the Leabhar Breac. In *Ériu*, xxiv (1973), pp 64–79.

Ó Danachair, Caoimhín. The bothán scóir. In Etienne Rynne (ed.), *North Munster studies* (Limerick, 1967), pp 489–98.

—— The combined byre-and-dwelling in Ireland. In *Folk Life*, ii (1964), pp 58–75.

—— Irish tower houses and their regional distribution. In *Béaloideas*, xlv–xlvii (1977–9), pp 158–63.

—— Traditional forms of the dwelling-house in Ireland. In *R.S.A.I. Jn.*, cii (1972), pp 77–96.

O'Neill, Timothy. *The Irish hand*. With an introduction by F. J. Byrne. Mountrath, 1984.

Ó Ríordáin, S. P., and Hunt, John. Medieval dwellings at Caherguillamore, Co. Limerick. In *R.S.A.I. Jn.*, lxxii (1942), pp 37–63.

O'Sullivan, William. Notes on the scripts and make-up of the Book of Leinster. In *Celtica*, vii (1966), pp 1–31.

Power, Patrick. The Cistercian abbeys of Munster. In *Cork Hist. Soc. Jn.*, xliii (1938), pp 1–11, 96–100.

Prior, E. S., and Gardner, Arthur. *An account of medieval figure-sculpture in England*. Cambridge, 1912.

Rae, E. C. Irish sepulchral monuments of the later middle ages. In *R.S.A.I. Jn.*, c (1970), pp 1–38; ci (1971), pp 1–39.

—— The medieval fabric of the cathedral church of St Patrick in Dublin. In *R.S.A.I. Jn.*, cix (1979), pp 29–73.

—— The Rice monument in Waterford cathedral. In *R.I.A. Proc.*, lxix (1970), sect. C, no. 1, pp 1–15.

—— The sculpture of the cloister of Jerpoint abbey. In *R.S.A.I. Jn.*, xcvi (1966), pp 59–91.

Richardson, Hilary. Derrynavlan and other early church treasures. In *R.S.A.I. Jn.*, cx (1980), pp 92–115.

Ritter, Raymond. *Châteaux donjons et places-fortes: l'architecture militaire française*. Paris, 1953.

Roe, H. M. Illustrations of the Holy Trinity in Ireland: 13th to 17th centuries. In *R.S.A.I. Jn.*, cix (1979), pp 101–50.

—— *Medieval fonts of Meath*. [Navan], 1968.

Ryan, Gerrard. Medieval tower houses in the barony of Bunratty Lower. In *The Other Clare*, vii (Mar. 1983), pp 17–21.

Sauerländer, Willibald. *Gotische Skulptur in Frankreich, 1140–1270*. Munich, 1970; trans. by Janet Sondheimer as *Gothic sculpture in France, 1140–1270*. London, 1972; New York, [1973].

Stalley, R. A. *Architecture and sculpture in Ireland, 1150–1350*. Dublin, 1971.

—— *Christ Church, Dublin: the late romanesque building campaign*. Ballycotton, Co. Cork, 1973. (Gatherum Series, ii.)

—— Corcomroe abbey: some observations on its architectural history. In *R.S.A.I. Jn.*, cv (1975), pp 21–46.

—— Irish Gothic and English fashion. In Lydon, *English in med. Ire.* (1984), pp 65–86.

—— The long middle ages: from the twelfth century to the reformation. In Brian de Breffny (ed.), *The Irish world* (London and New York, 1977), pp 71–98.

—— The medieval sculpture of Christ Church cathedral, Dublin. In *Archaeologia*, cvi (1979), pp 107–22.

—— Mellifont abbey: some observations on its architectural history. In *Studies*, lxiv (1975), pp 347–67.

Steer, K. A., and Bannerman, J. W. M. *Late medieval monumental sculpture in the West Highlands*. Edinbugh, 1977.

Stone, Lawrence. *Sculpture in Britain: the middle ages*. Harmondsworth, 1955. (The Pelican History of Art, ix.)

Strong, Roy. *The English icon: Elizabethan & Jacobean portraiture*. London and New York, 1969. (Studies in British Art.)

Thompson, A. H. *Military architecture in England during the middle ages*. London, 1912.

Treasures of early Irish art, 1500 B.C. to 1500 A.D.: from the collections of the National Museum of Ireland, Royal Irish Academy, Trinity College, Dublin. Ed. Polly Cone. [New York], 1977.
Exhibition catalogue.

Viollet le Duc, Eugène. *Dictionnaire raisonné de l'architecture française du XIe au XVIe siècle*. 10 vols. Paris, 1854–68.
Table analytique et synthétique. Paris, 1889.

Westropp, T. J. The churches of County Clare and the origin of the ecclesiastical divisions in that county. In *R.I.A. Proc.*, 3rd ser., vi (1900–2), no. 1, pp 100–80.

—— Ennis abbey and the O'Brien tombs. In *R.S.A.I. Jn.*, xxv (1895), pp 135–54.

—— Paintings at Adare 'abbey', County Limerick. In *R.S.A.I. Jn.*, xlv (1915), pp 151–2.

—— A survey of the ancient churches in the county of Limerick. In *R.I.A. Proc.*, xxv (1904–5), sect. C, no. 8, pp 327–480.

Wright, E. P. On the bell of Kilmainham. In *R.S.A.I. Jn.*, xxx (1900), pp 40–43.

16 BIOGRAPHY

BLAKE. Curtis, Edmund. The pardon of Henry Blake of Galway in 1395. In *Galway Arch. Soc. Jn.*, xvi (1934–5), pp 186–9.

DE BRANA. McRoberts, David. The Greek bishop of Dromore. In *Innes Review*, xxviii (1977), pp 22–38.
George de Brana.

DE BURGH. Blake, M J. William de Burgh: progenitor of the Burkes in Ireland. In *Galway Arch. Soc. Jn.*, vii (1911–12), pp 83–101; reprint with revisions, Galway, 1911.

—— Claffey, J. A. Richard de Burgo, earl of Ulster, 1280–1326. (Ph.D. thesis, N.U.I., (U.C.G.), 1970.)

BUTLER. Empey, C. A. From rags to riches: Piers Butler, earl of Ormond, 1515–39. In *Butler Soc. Jn.*, ii, no. 3 (1984), pp 299–314.

CLARENCE. Curtis, Edmund. The viceroyalty of Lionel, duke of Clarence, in Ireland, 1361–1367. In *R.S.A.I. Jn.*, xlvii (1917), pp 165–81; xlviii (1918), pp 65–73.

COLTON. Watt, J. A. John Colton, justiciar of Ireland (1382) and archbishop of Armagh (1383–1404). In Lydon, *Eng. & Ire.* (1981), pp 196–213.

DE COURCY. Hall, Hamilton. A third John de Courcy. In *Proceedings of the Somersetshire Archaeological and Natural History Society*, lviii (1912), pt 2: Papers, etc., pp 18–28.

CUMIN. Gwynn, Aubrey. Archbishop John Cumin. In *Reportorium Novum*, i (1955–6), pp 285–310.

D'Arcy, R. F. *The life of John, first baron Darcy of Knayth*. London, 1933.

DARTAS. Curtis, Edmund. Janico Dartas, Richard the Second's 'Gascon squire': his career in Ireland, 1394–1426. In *R.S.A.I. Jn.*, lxiii (1933), pp 182–205.

DESMOND. Cosgrove, Art. The execution of the earl of Desmond, 1468. In *Kerry Arch. Soc. Jn.*, viii (1975), pp 11–27.

DESMOND. Sayles, G. O. The rebellious first earl of Desmond. In *Med. studies presented to A. Gwynn* (1961), pp 203–29; reprint in his *Scripta diversa* (London, 1982), pp 239–66.

FITZGERALD. Fitzgerald, R. T. D. Discovery of the burial place of Gerald, son of Maurice Fitzgerald, justiciar of Ireland, 1232–1245. In *Ir. Geneal.*, v (1974–9), pp 166–8.

—— See also KILDARE, below.

FITZRALPH. Gwynn, Aubrey. Richard FitzRalph, archbishop of Armagh. In *Studies*, xxii (1933), pp 389–405, 591–607; xxiii (1934), pp 395–411; xxiv (1935), pp 25–42, 558–72; xxv (1936), pp 81–96.

—— —— The sermon-diary of Richard FitzRalph, archbishop of Armagh. In *R.I.A. Proc.*, xliv (1937–8), sect. C, no. 1, pp 1–57.

—— Leff, Gordon. *Richard FitzRalph, commentator of the Sentences: a study in theological orthodoxy*. Manchester, 1963.

—— Walsh, Katherine. *A fourteenth-century scholar and primate: Richard FitzRalph in Oxford, Avignon, and Armagh*. Oxford, 1981.

FITZROY. Quinn, D. B. Henry Fitzroy, duke of Richmond, and his connexion with Ireland, 1529–30. In *I.H.R. Bull.*, xii (1934–5), pp 175–7.

FLEMING. Johnson, R. L. How Nicholas Fleming became archbishop of Armagh. In *Louth Arch. Soc. Jn.*, xiii (1953–6), pp 279–87.

GILLA MEIC LIAC. Gogarty, Thomas. Gilla Mic Liag Mac Ruaidhri, primate of Armagh, 1137–1174. In *I.E.R.*, 5th ser., xi (1918), pp 113–49; xii (1918), pp 121–39.

GIRALDUS CAMBRENSIS. Davies, J. C. Giraldus Cambrensis, 1146–1946. In *Archaeologia Cambrensis*, xcix (1947), pp 85–108, 256–80.

—— Martin, F. X. Gerald of Wales, Norman reporter on Ireland. In *Studies*, lviii (1969), pp 279–92.

—— Powicke, Sir F. M. Gerald of Wales. In *John Rylands Lib. Bull.*, xii (1928), pp 389–410; reprint in his *The Christian life in the middle ages, and other essays* (Oxford, 1935; reprint, 1966), pp 107–29.

—— Bartlett, Robert. *Gerald of Wales, 1146–1223*. Oxford, 1982. (Oxford Historical Monographs.)

—— See also sect. IV B 10, above.

HENRY OF LONDON. Gwynn, Aubrey. Henry of London, archbishop of Dublin: a study in Anglo-Norman statecraft. In *Studies*, xxxviii (1949), pp 297–306, 389–402.

KILDARE. Bryan, Donough. *Gerald Fitzgerald, the Great Earl of Kildare, 1456–1513*. Dublin and Cork, 1933.

DE LACY. Lloyd, Sir J. E. Who was Gwenllian de Lacy? In *Archaeologia Cambrensis*, 6th ser., xix [i.e. lxxiv] (1919), pp 292–8.

LEDREDE. Lanigan, K. M. Richard de Ledrede, bishop of Ossory. In *Old Kilkenny Rev.*, xv (1963), pp 23–9.

—— Neary, Anne. Richard Ledrede: English Franciscan and bishop of Ossory, 1317–c. 1360. In *Butler Soc. Jn.*, ii, no. 3 (1984), pp 273–82.

MAC DALBAIG. Flanagan, Marie-Thérèse. Mac Dalbaig: a Leinster chieftain. In *R.S.A.I. Jn.*, cxi (1981), pp 5–13.

MACHTALEWI. Brooks, E. St John. Machtalewi, a Leinster chieftain. In *R.S.A.I. Jn.*, lxxi (1941), pp 53–5.

MAC MAOL ÍOSA. Gwynn, Aubrey. Nicholas Mac Maol Íosa, archbishop of Armagh, 1272–1303. In *Féil-sgríbhinn Eóin Mhic Néill* (1940), pp 394–405.

—— Mac Íomhair, Diarmuid. Primate Mac Maoilíosa and County Louth. In *Seanchas Ardmhacha*, vi (1971), pp 70–93.

MAC MURCHADA. Curran, D. J. Diarmaid Mac Murchadha, king of Leinster. (M.A. thesis, N.U.I. (U.C.C.), 1966.)

—— Ó Corráin, Donnchadh. The education of Diarmait Mac Murchada. In *Ériu*, xxviii (1977), pp 71–81.

MALACHY. Gwynn, Aubrey. St Malachy of Armagh. In *I.E.R.*, 5th ser., lxx (1948), pp 961–78; lxxi (1949), pp 134–48, 317–31.

—— Scott, Brian. *Malachy*. Dublin, 1976.

MARSHALL. Painter, Sidney. *William Marshall*. Baltimore, 1933. (Johns Hopkins Historical Publications.)

Ó DOMHNAILL. Simms, Katharine. Niall Garbh II O Donnell, king of Tír Conaill, 1422–39. In *Donegal Annual*, xii, no. 1 (1977), pp 7–21.

O'GIBELLAN. Berry, H. F. Some remarks on a notice in *Revue Celtique* of Maurice O'Gibellan, a fourteenth century canonist, in connexion with his knowledge of Ogham. In *R.S.A.I. Jn.*, xxxii (1902), pp 158–62.
Comment on Rudolf Thurneysen, 'Du langage secret dit *Ogham*' in *Rev. Celt.*, vii (1886), pp 369–74.

O'TOOLE. Gwynn, Aubrey. Saint Lawrence O'Toole as legate in Ireland, 1179–1180. In *Anal. Bolland.*, lxviii (1950), pp 223–40; and as *Extraits des Anal. Bolland.*, dccccxvii.

—— Legris, Albert. *Life of St Laurence O'Toole, archbishop of Dublin, 1128–1180*. Dublin, 1914.

—— —— *Saint Laurent O'Toole, archevêque de Dublin*. Eu, 1908.

—— O'Doherty, J. F. *Laurentius von Dublin und das irische Normannentum*. Munich, 1933. (Inaugural-Dissertation zur Erlangung der Doktorwürde der Philosophischen Fakultät, I. Sektion, der Ludwig-Maximilians-Universität zu München.)

—— —— St Lawrence O'Toole and the Anglo-Norman invasion. In *I.E.R.*, 5th ser., l (1937), pp 449–77, 600–25; li (1938), pp 131–46.

—— Roche, M. F. The Latin lives of St Laurence of Dublin. (Ph.D. thesis, N.U.I. (U.C.D.), 1981.)

OTTO. Williamson, D. M. The legate Otto in Scotland and Ireland, 1237–1240. In *Scot. Hist. Rev.*, xxviii (1949), pp 12–30.

PAYN. Martin, F. X. An Irish Augustinian disputes at Oxford: Adam Payn, 1402. In C. P. Mayer and W. Eckermann (ed.), *Scientia Augustiniana: Studien über Augustinus, den Augustinismus und den Augustinorden: Festschrift für Adolar Zumkeller* (Würzburg, 1975), pp 289–322.

PRENE. Stalley, R. A. William of Prene and the royal works in Ireland. In *British Archaeological Association Journal*, cxxxi (1978), pp 30–49.

SIMNEL. Hayden, Mary. Lambert Simnel in Ireland. In *Studies*, iv (1915), pp 622–38.

TALBOT. Bernard, J. H. Richard Talbot, archbishop and chancellor, 1418–1449. In *R.I.A. Proc.*, xxxv (1918–20), sect. C, no. 5, pp 218–29.

TIPTOFT. Mitchell, R. J. *John Tiptoft, 1427—1470*. London, 1938.

UA CONCHOBAIR. Gwynn, Aubrey. Tomaltach Ua Conchobair, coarb of Patrick, 1181–1201. In *Seanchas Ardmhacha*, viii (1977), pp 231–74.

VALENCE. Phillips, J. R. S. *Aymer de Valence, earl of Pembroke, 1307—24: baronial politics in the reign of Edward II*. Oxford, 1972.

WINDSOR. Clarke, M. V. William of Windsor in Ireland, 1369–1376. In *R.I.A. Proc.*, xli (1932–3), sect. C, no. 2, pp 55–130; reprint in her *Fourteenth century studies* (Oxford, 1937; reprint, 1969), pp 146–241.

C BIOGRAPHICAL AND OTHER WORKS OF REFERENCE

Berry, H. F. Sheriffs of the County Cork: Henry III to 1660. In *R.S.A.I. Jn.*, xxxv (1905), pp 39–52.

Contemporaries of Erasmus: a biographical register of the renaissance and reformation. Ed. P. G. Bietenholz. Toronto, 1985– .

Dictionary of the middle ages. Ed. J. R. Strayer. i– . New York, 1982– .

Emden, A. B. *A biographical register of the University of Cambridge to 1500*. Cambridge, 1963.

—— *A biographical register of the University of Oxford to A.D. 1500*. 3 vols. Oxford, 1957–9.

Hughes, J. L. J. (ed.). *Patentee officers in Ireland, 1173—1826*. I.M.C., Dublin, 1960.

Lexikon des Mittel Alters. i– . Munich and Zurich, 1977– .

Mooney, Canice. Irish Franciscan provincials. In *Archivum Franciscanum Historicum*, lvi (1963), pp 3–11.

Richardson, H. G., and Sayles, G. O. *The administration of Ireland, 1172—1377*. I.M.C., Dublin, 1963.

Zupko, Ronald Edward. *A dictionary of English weights and measures from Anglo-Saxon times to the nineteenth century*. Madison (Wis.), and London, 1968.

D ARCHAEOLOGY

For works covering both archaeology and local history, see sect. IV B 12; for works treating artefacts and structures from an artistic or architectural viewpoint, see sect. IV B 14; for works on numismatics, see sect. IV B 8.

Annual report of the Commissioners of Public Works in Ireland. 1st– . Dublin, 1833– .

ARMAGH. Lynn, C. J. Excavation in the Franciscan friary church, Armagh. In *U.J.A.*, 3rd ser., xxxviii (1975), pp 61–80.

BALLINDERRY. Hencken, H. O. Ballinderry crannog no. 1. In *R.I.A. Proc.*, xliii (1935–7), sect. C, no. 5, pp 103–39.

Barrett, G. F. The ring-fort: a study in settlement geography, with special reference to southern Donegal and the Dingle area, Co. Kerry. (Ph.D. thesis, Queen's University, Belfast, 1972.)

Barrett, G. F. Aerial photography and the study of early settlement structures in Ireland. In *Aerial Archaeology*, vi (1980), pp 27–38.

Barry, T. B. Anglo-Norman ringwork castles: some evidence. In Terence Reeves-Smyth and Fred Hammond (ed.), *Landscape archaeology in Ireland* (Oxford, 1983. BAR, British Series, cxvi), pp 295–314.

—— *The medieval moated sites of south-eastern Ireland: Counties Carlow, Kilkenny, Tipperary and Wexford*. Oxford, 1977. (British Archaeological Reports, xxxv.)

—— Moated sites in Ireland. In F. A. Aberg (ed.), *Medieval moated sites* (Council for British Archaeology, London, 1978; Research Report, xvii), pp 56–9.

—— The shifting frontier: medieval moated sites in Counties Cork and Limerick. In F. A. Aberg and A. E. Brown (ed.), *Medieval moated sites in north-west Europe* (Oxford, 1981; BAR, International Series, cxxi), pp 71–85.
See also WATERFORD and WEXFORD, below.

CARRICKFERGUS. McNeill, T. E. *Carrickfergus Castle, County Antrim*. Belfast, 1981. (Northern Ireland Archaeological Monographs, i.)

CASHEN. O'Kelly, M. J. A wooden bridge on the Cashen river, Co. Kerry. In *R.S.A.I. Jn.*, xci (1961), pp 135–52.

CASTLEINCH. Prendergast, Ellen. Medieval jug from Castleinch. In *Old Kilkenny Rev.*, new ser., i (1974–8), pp 238–44.

CASTLETOWNROCHE. Gwynn, A. M., Mitchell, G. F., and Stelfox, A. W. The exploration of some caves near Castletownroche, Co. Cork. In *R.I.A. Proc.*, xlvii (1941–2), sect. B, no. 14, pp 371–90. (Studies in Irish Quaternary Deposits, iv.)

CLONARD. Sweetman, P. D. Excavation of medieval 'field boundaries' at Clonard, County Meath. In *R.S.A.I. Jn.*, cviii (1978), pp 10–22.

CLONTUSKERT. Fanning, Thomas. Excavations at Clontuskert priory, Co. Galway. In *R.I.A. Proc.*, lxxvi (1976), sect. C, no. 5, pp 97–169.

CLOUGH CASTLE. Waterman, D. M. Excavations at Clough Castle, Co. Down. In *U.J.A.*, 3rd ser., xvii (1954), pp 103–63.

CORK. Hurley, Maurice, and Dower, Denis. The medieval town wall of Cork. In *Cork Hist. Soc. Jn.*, lxxxvi (1981), pp 1–20.

Delaney, T. G. The archaeology of the Irish town. In M. W. Barley (ed.), *European towns: their archaeology and early history* (London, 1977), pp 47–64.

DERRYNAVLAN. Ryan, Michael (ed.). *The Derrynaflan hoard.* i: *A preliminary account*. Nat. Mus. Ire., Dublin, 1983.

DEVENISH. Waterman, D. M. St Mary's priory, Devenish: excavation of the east range, 1972–4. In *U.J.A.*, 3rd ser., xlii (1979), pp 34–50.

DONEGAL. Lacy, Brian. *Archaeological survey of County Donegal*. Lifford, 1983.

DOWN. Archaeological Survey of Northern Ireland. *An archaeological survey of County Down*. Belfast, 1966.

DROGHEDA. Sweetman, P. D. Archaeological excavations at Shop Street, Drogheda, Co. Louth. In *R.I.A. Proc.*, lxxxiv (1984), sect. C, no. 5, pp 171–224.
Part of 13th-century wooden quayside.

DROMORE. Waterman, D. M. Excavations at Dromore motte, Co. Down. In *U.J.A.*, 3rd ser., xvii (1954), pp 164–8.

DUBLIN. Bradley, John (ed.). *Viking Dublin exposed: the Wood Quay saga*. Dublin, 1984.

—— Burke, Nuala. *Dublin's Wood Quay*. Navan, 1977.

—— Clarke, H. B. The topographical development of early medieval Dublin. In *R.S.A.I. Jn.*, cvii (1977), pp 29–51.

—— McAuley, Eileen. The significance of Wood Quay. In *Dublin Hist. Rec.*, xxxii (1978–9), pp 122–8.

—— Maxwell, Nicholas (ed.). *Digging up Dublin*. Dublin, 1980.

—— Murray, Hilary. *Viking and early medieval buildings in Dublin: a study of the buildings excavated under the direction of A. B. Ó Ríordáin in High Street, Winetavern Street and Christchurch Place, Dublin, 1962–63, 1967–76*. Oxford, 1983. (BAR. British Series, cxix.)

—— National Museum of Ireland. *Viking and medieval Dublin: National Museum excavations, 1962–1973: catalogue of exhibition*. Dublin, 1973.

—— Ó Ríordáin, Breandán. Excavations at High Street and Winetavern Street, Dublin. In *Medieval Archaeology*, xv (1971), pp 73–85, plates v–x.

—— —— The High Street excavations. In *Proceedings of the seventh viking congress* (Dublin, 1976), pp 135–40.

—— Wallace, P. F. Anglo-Norman Dublin: continuity and change. In Donnchadh Ó Corráin (ed.), *Irish antiquity: essays and studies presented to Professor M. J. O'Kelly* (Cork, 1981), pp 147–67.

—— —— The archaeological significance of Wood Quay, Dublin. In *An Cosantóir*, xxxix (1979), pp 141–7.

—— —— *Viking and Norman Dublin: the Wood Quay excavations*. Dublin, 1985.

—— —— Wood Quay, Dublin. In *Popular Archaeology*, ii, no. 9 (Mar. 1981), pp 24–7.

—— —— Carpentry in Ireland. A.D. 900–1300: the Wood Quay evidence. In S. McGrail (ed.), *Woodworking techniques before A.D. 1500* (Oxford, 1982. BAR. International Series, cxxix; Archaeological Series, National Maritime Museum, Greenwich, vii), pp 263–99.

—— See also Clarke & Simms, *Comparative history of urban origins*, above, sect. IV B 7, and below, sect. IV E.

DUNSHAUGHLIN. Mitchell, G. F. Some lacustrine deposits near Dunshaughlin, County Meath. In *R.I.A. Proc.*, xlvi (1940–41), sect. B, no. 2, pp 13–37. (Studies in Irish Quaternary Deposits, [i].)

FERNS. Sweetman, P. D. Archaeological excavations at Ferns castle, County Wexford. In *R.I.A. Proc.*, lxxix (1979), sect. C, no. 10, pp 217–45.

Glasscock, R. E., and McNeill, T. E. Mottes in Ireland: a draft list. In *Bulletin of the Group for the Study of Irish Historic Settlement*, iii (1972), pp 27–51.

Graham, B. J. Clachan continuity and distribution in medieval Ireland. In Pierre Flatrès (ed.), *Paysages ruraux européens* (Rennes, 1979), pp 147–57.

GRAIGUENAMANAGH. Bradley, John, and Manning, Conleth. Excavations at Duiske abbey, Graiguenamanagh, Co. Kilkenny. In *R.I.A. Proc.*, lxxxi (1981), sect. C, no. 16, pp 397–426.

GREENCASTLE, DOWN. Gaskell-Brown, Cynthia. Excavations at Greencastle, Co. Down, 1966–1970. In *U.J.A.*, 3rd ser., xlii (1979), pp 51–65.

——, DONEGAL. Waterman, D. M. Greencastle, County Donegal. In *U.J.A.*, 3rd ser., xxi (1958), pp 74–88.

Harbison, Peter. *The archaeology of Ireland*. London, 1976.

—— *Guide to the national monuments in the Republic of Ireland*. Dublin, 1970; rev. ed., 1975.

IKERRIN. Stout, G. T. *Archaeological survey of the barony of Ikerrin*. Roscrea Heritage Society, [Roscrea], 1984.

Jessen, Knud. Studies in Late Quaternary deposits and flora-history of Ireland. In *R.I.A. Proc.*, lii (1948–50), sect. B, no. 6 (1949), pp 85–290.

KELLS. Barry, T. B., Culleton, Edward, and Empey, C. A. Kells motte, County Kilkenny. In *R.I.A. Proc.*, lxxxiv (1984), sect. C, no. 4, pp 157–70.

—— Fanning, Thomas. Excavations at Kells priory, Co. Kilkenny. In *Old Kilkenny Rev.*, xxv (1973), pp 61–4.

See also his 'Interim report on the excavations at Kells priory, Co. Kilkenny, 1980' in *Old Kilkenny Rev.*, new ser., ii (1979–82), pp 245–8, and short reports in *Excavations* (Belfast), 1973, pp 15–16; 1974, pp 19–20; 1975/6, p. 13.

KERRY. O'Donovan, John. *The antiquities of the county of Kerry*. Ed. J. B. Keane. Cork, 1983.

KILKENNY. Bradley, John. The town wall of Kilkenny. In *Old Kilkenny Rev.*, new ser., i (1974–8), pp 85–103, 209–18.

KILMACLENINE. Olden, Thomas. On some ancient remains at Kilmaclenine, with illustrations from the Pipa Colmani. In *R.I.A. Proc.*, xvi (1879–88), pp 119–28.

Laing, Lloyd. *The archaeology of late Celtic Britain and Ireland, c.400–1200*. London, 1975.

LIMERICK. Lynch, Ann. Excavations of the medieval town defences at Charlotte's Quay, Limerick. In *R.I.A. Proc.*, lxxxiv (1984), sect. C, no. 9, pp 281–331.

LISMAHON. Waterman, D. M. Excavations at Lismahon, Co. Down. In *Medieval Archaeology*, iii (1959), pp 139–76.

LORRHA. Talbot, E. J. Lorrha motte, County Tipperary. In *N. Munster Antiq. Jn.*, xv (1972), pp 8–12.

LOUGH GUR. Mitchell, G. F. A pollen diagram from Lough Gur, County Limerick. In *R.I.A. Proc.*, lvi (1953–4), sect. C, no. 7 (1954), pp 481–8. (Studies in Irish Quaternary Deposits, ix.)

Lynn, C. J. The medieval ringfort: an archaeological chimera? In *Irish Archaeological Research Forum*, ii (1975), no. 1, pp 29–36.

McNeill, T. E. Anglo-Norman Ireland and the dating of English pottery. In *U.J.A.*, 3rd ser., xliv–xlv (1981–2), pp 198–200.

—— Mediaeval raths?: an Anglo-Norman comment. In *Irish Archaeological Research Forum*, ii (1975), no. 1, pp 37–9.

MAPASTOWN. Mitchell, G. F. Further identifications of macroscopic plant fossils from Irish Quaternary deposits, especially from a late-glacial deposit at Mapastown, Co. Louth. In *R.I.A. Proc.*, lv (1952–3), sect. B, no. 12 (1953), pp 225–82. (Studies in Irish Quaternary Deposits, viii.)

MEATH. Graham, B. J. The mottes of the Norman liberty of Meath. In Harman Murtagh (ed.), *Irish Midland Studies* (Athlone, 1980), pp 39–56.

MELLIFONT. De Paor, Liam. Excavations at Mellifont abbey, Co. Louth. In *R.I.A. Proc.*, lxviii (1969), sect. C, no. 2, pp 109–64.

Mitchell, G. F. The giant deer in Ireland. In *R.I.A. Proc.*, lii (1948–50), sect. B, no. 7 (1949), pp 291–314. (Studies in Irish Quaternary Deposits, vi.)

—— The pleistocene period in Ireland. In *Meddelelser Dansk Geologisk Forening*, xii (1951), pp 111–14.

—— Post-boreal pollen diagrams from Irish raised bogs. In *R.I.A. Proc.*, lvii (1954–6), sect. B, no. 14 (1956), pp 185–251. (Studies in Irish Quaternary Deposits, xi.)

—— The reindeer of Ireland. In *R.I.A. Proc.*, xlvi (1940–41), sect. B, no. 14 (1941), pp 183–8. (Studies in Irish Quaternary Deposits, iii.)

—— Studies in Irish Quaternary deposits, vii. In *R.I.A. Proc.*, liii (1950–51), sect. B, no. 11 (1951), pp 111–206.

—— Two inter-glacial deposits in south-east Ireland. In *R.I.A. Proc.*, lii (1948–50), sect. B, no. 1 (1948), pp 1–14. (Studies in Irish Quaternary Deposits, v.)

NEWCASTLE LYONS. Edwards, K. J., Hamond, F. W., and Simms, Anngret. The medieval settlement of Newcastle Lyons, County Dublin: an interdisciplinary approach. In *R.I.A. Proc.*, lxxxiii (1983), sect. C, no. 14, pp 351–76.

NEWTOWNSTEWART. Jope, E. M., Jope, H. M., and Johnson, E. A. Harry Avery's castle, Newtownstewart, Co. Tyrone: excavations, 1950. In *U.J.A.*, 3rd ser., xiii (1950), pp 81–92.

Proudfoot, V. B. Irish raths and cashels: some notes on chronology, origins, and survivals. In *U.J.A.*, 3rd ser., xxxiii (1970), pp 37–48.

RATHMULLEN. Lynn, C. J. The excavation of Rathmullen, a raised rath and motte in County Down. In *U.J.A.*, 3rd ser., xliv–xlv (1981–2), pp 65–171.

RATOATH. Mitchell, G. F. Some lacustrine deposits near Ratoath, Co. Meath. In *R.I.A. Proc.*, xlvi (1940–41), sect. B, no. 13 (1941), pp 173–82. (Studies in Irish Quaternary Deposits, ii.)

RIGSDALE. Sweetman, P. D. Excavations of a medieval moated site at Rigsdale, County Cork, 1977–78. In *R.I.A. Proc.*, lxxxi (1981), sect. C, no. 5, pp 193–205.

ROSS. Culleton, Edward, and Colfer, William. The Norman motte at Old Ross: method of construction. In *Old Wexford Soc. Jn.*, v (1974–5), pp 22–5.

SHANNON. Rynne, Etienne. Some destroyed sites at Shannon airport, County Clare. In *R.I.A. Proc.*, lxiii (1962–4), sect. C, no. 7 (1964), pp 245–77.

SWORDS. Fanning, Thomas. An Irish medieval tile pavement: recent excavations at Swords castle, County Dublin. In *R.S.A.I. Jn.*, cv (1975), pp 47–82.

—— —— A medieval tile pavement from Swords castle, Co. Dublin. In *Medieval Archaeology*, xix (1975), pp 205–9 + plate xvi.

TRALEE. Mitchell, G. F. The Quaternary deposits between Fenit and Spa on the north shore of Tralee Bay, Co. Kerry. In *R.I.A. Proc.*, lxx (1970), sect. B, no. 6, pp 141–62.

TRIM. Sweetman, P. D. Archaeological excavations at Trim castle, Co. Meath, 1971–74. In *R.I.A. Proc.*, lxxviii (1978), sect. C, no. 6, pp 127–98.

—— —— Trim castle archaeological excavations. In *Ríocht na Midhe*, v, no. 4 (1974), pp 68–77.

Twohig, D. C. Norman ringwork castles. In *Bulletin of the Group for the Study of Irish Historical Settlement*, v (1978), pp 7–9.

ULSTER. McNeill, T. E. Ulster mottes: a checklist. In *U.J.A.*, 3rd ser., xxxviii (1975), pp 49–56.

WATERFORD. Barry, T. B. The moated sites of County Waterford. In *Decies*, x (Jan. 1979), pp 32–6.

WATERFORD. Carroll, J. S. The walls and defences of Waterford. In *Decies*, iv (Feb. 1977), pp 16–18; v (May 1977), pp 6–10.

—— Moore, Michael. City walls and gateway at site of St Martin's Castle. In *Decies*, xxiii (1983), pp 50–61. [The Archaeology of Waterford, iii.]

Waterman, D. M. Somersetshire and other foreign building stone in medieval Ireland, *c.* 1175–1400. In *U.J.A.*, 3rd ser., xxxiii (1970), pp 63–75.

WEXFORD. Barry, T. B. The medieval moated sites of County Wexford. In *Old Wexford Soc. Jn.*, vi (1976–7), pp 5–17.

—— Cahill, Mary, and Ryan, Michael. An investigation of the town wall at Abbey Street, Wexford. In *Old Wexford Soc. Jn.*, viii (1980–81), pp 56–64.

—— Hadden, George. Some earthworks in Co. Wexford. In *Cork Hist. Soc. Jn.*, [2nd ser.], lxix (1964), pp 118–22.

—— Wallace, P. F. Wexford town: Oyster Lane. In T. G. Delany (ed.), *Excavations* (Belfast), 1974, p. 28.

WYTHEMAIL. Hurst, D. G., and Hurst, J. G. Excavations at the medieval villages of Wythemail, Northamptonshire. In *Medieval Archaeology*, xii (1969), pp 167–203.

E COMPOSITE WORKS

Almqvist, Bo., and Greene, David (ed.). *Proceedings of the seventh viking congress, Dublin, 15—21 August 1973*. [Dublin], 1976.

Buchanan, R. H., Jones, Emrys, and McCourt, Desmond (ed.). *Man and his habitat: essays presented to Emyr Estyn Evans*. London, 1971.

——, Butlin, R. A., and McCourt, Desmond (ed.). *Fields, farms and settlement in Europe: papers presented at a symposium, Belfast, July 12—15, 1971*. Ulster Folk and Transport Museum, Holywood, 1976.

Butler, W. F. T. *Gleanings from Irish history*. London, 1925.

Clarke, H. B., and Simms, Anngret (ed.). *The comparative history of urban origins in non-Roman Europe: Ireland, Wales, Denmark, Germany, Poland, and Russia from the ninth to the thirteenth century*. 2 vols, Oxford, 1985. (BAR International Series, cclv.)

Corish, P. J. (ed.). *A history of Irish catholicism*. 28 fascs in 16. Dublin, etc., 1967–72. No more published.

Falkiner, C. L. *Illustrations of Irish history and topography, mainly of the seventeenth century*. London, 1904.

Lydon, James (ed.). *England and Ireland in the later middle ages: essays in honour of Jocelyn Otway-Ruthven*. Dublin, 1981.

—— (ed.). *The English in medieval Ireland: proceedings of the first joint meeting of the Royal Irish Academy and the British Academy, Dublin, 1982*. R.I.A., Dublin, 1984.

Murtagh, Harman (ed.). *Irish midland studies: essays in commemoration of N.W. English*. Old Athlone Society, Athlone, 1980.

O'Brien, Sylvester (ed.). *Measgra i gcuimhne Mhichíl Uí Chléirigh. i. Miscellany of historical and linguistic studies in honour of Brother Michael Ó Cléirigh, O.F.M., chief of the Four Masters, 1643–1943*. Dublin, 1944.

Ó Corráin, Donnchadh (ed.). *Irish antiquity: essays and studies presented to Professor M. J. O'Kelly*. Cork, 1981.

Ó Cuív, Brian (ed.). *Seven centuries of Irish learning, 1000–1700*, [Dublin], 1961. (Thomas Davis Lectures, 1958.) Reprint, Cork, 1971.

Round, J. H. *The commune of London and other studies*. London, 1899.

Rynne, Etienne (ed.). *North Munster studies: essays in commemoration of Monsignor Michael Moloney*. Thomond Archaeological Society, Limerick, 1967.

Sayles, G. O. *Scripta diversa*. London, 1982.

Ware, James. *The whole works of Sir James Ware concerning Ireland*. Ed. Walter Harris. 2 vols. Dublin, 1764.

Watt, J. A., Morrall, J. B., and Mártin, F. X. (ed.). *Medieval studies presented to Aubrey Gwynn, S.J.* Dublin, 1961.

INDEX

Persons of rank are indexed primarily under the family name, cross references being given from the title. In the cases of a few individuals, belonging to the English royal family, the main entry appears under the title, by which they would be most widely known; thus Lionel, duke of Clarence, appears under Clarence.

Surnames of Irish dynastic families are entered, first in their Middle Irish form (as used in the text to 1333), then in the Modern Irish form (as used in the text from 1334), and then, in brackets, in their anglicised form; for example, Mac Diarmata, Mac Diarmada (MacDermot).

Surnames in Ua are indexed under Ua if they do not occur after 1216; otherwise they are indexed under Ó. Thus Ua Briain, Ua Conchobair will be found under Ó, but Ua Sechnussaig under Ua.

Mac and Mág are treated as identical.

In names of Norman origin beginning with 'Fitz', the distinction between patronymic and surname is indicated by spacing. Thus 'Fitz Gerald' is a patronymic, 'FitzGerald' a surname.

A name such as 'de Valence' is entered in that form but under 'V'.

Members of dynastic families, such as de Burgh (Burke), FitzGerald, Mac Carthaig(h), Ó Néill, are entered in alphabetical order. References to the family are indexed first, followed by named individuals.

Place names are identified, where possible, by their modern location.

The following abbreviations are used:

abp	archbishop	dau.	daughter
bp	bishop	J.	justiciar
bro.	brother	K.	keeper of great seal
C.	chancellor	kg	king
D.	deputy	L.	lieutenant

In the cases of a few kings and officeholders, the details of status and periods of tenure have been simplified for the purpose of this index, and the saltire (×) has been used with the terminal dates of their activities. Thus Thomas FitzGerald, seventh earl of Kildare, appears as 'chief governor (1454 × 1478)', and Domnall Ó Néill as 'king of Tír Eógain (1283 × 1325)'. Full details are given in the succession lists in volume IX.

Abbot, Nicholas, merchant, 494, 520
absentee acts, 526–7
absenteeism, 169, 385, 450; effects on defence, 269, 271–2, 374; effects on estate manage-
ment, 462–3, 466–7; efforts to control, 379, 449, 526–7, 680; absentee bishops, 587
'Acallam na Senórach', 692, 700, 802
acre, size of, 460n
Adam of Usk, chronicler, 525
Adare, Co. Limerick, 760, 766
administration, see central administration; local administration
Adrian IV, pope (1154–9), 1, 50, 57, 59, 360; see also *Laudabiliter*
Adurnus, James, of Genoa, 494
Áes Cluana (Esclon), fief, 130
áes dána, 39
Affreca, dau. of Godred, kg of Man, 18, 135, 746, 747
Aghaboe, Co. Kilkenny, 24, 27

Aghade, Co. Carlow, convent at, 49
Aghadoe, Co. Kerry, 31
Aghalurcher, Co. Fermanagh, 434
agriculture, 411–13, 474; Anglo-Norman influ-
ence on, 151–2, 169, 211, 480–81; arable land, 459–62, 467–8; field systems, 468–72, 477; labour services, 211, 382, 386, 449, 456–7, 463–5; see also demesne cultivation; pas-
toralism
Ailech, 13–14, 15
Airgialla (Oirghialla, Oriel, Uriel), 104, 127, 147, 788; MacMahon influence, 632, 768, 793; status of, 13–14, 151–7; Riot of Uriel, 280
Airthir (Orior), 16–17
Albany, duke of, see Stewart, Murdoch
Albert, Cardinal, papal legate, 81, 87, 95, 98
Alderseye, Jenkin, merchant, 520
Alen, John, abp of Dublin (1529–34), 456, 676, 678, 682–6
——, John, clerk of council, 676, 683–4